Compaq ASE Certification Study Guide

(Exam 010-397, Exam 010-078, Exam 010-067)

Syngress Media, Inc.

Osborne McGraw-Hill

Berkeley New York St. Louis San Francisco Auckland Bogotá Hamburg London Madrid Mexico City
Milan Montreal New Delhi Panama City Paris São Paulo Singapore Sydney Tokyo Toronto

Osborne McGraw-Hill
2600 Tenth Street
Berkeley, California 94710
U.S.A.

For information on translations or book distributors outside the U.S.A., or to arrange bulk purchase discounts for sales promotions, premiums, or fund-raisers, please contact Osborne/**McGraw-Hill** at the above address.

Compaq ASE Certification Study Guide (Exam 010-397, Exam 010-078, Exam 010-067)

1234567890 DOC DOC 90198765432109

ISBN 0-07-212095-9

Publisher
Brandon A. Nordin

Associate Publisher and Editor-in-Chief
Scott Rogers

Senior Acquisitions Editor
Gareth Hancock

Associate Acquistions Editor
Timothy Green

Editorial Management
Syngress Media, Inc.

Senior Project Editor
Mark Karmendy

Acquisitions Coordinator
Tara Davis

Series Editor
Thomas E. Eck

Technical Editor
Derrick Rountree

Copy Editor
Kathleen Faughnan

Proofreader
Carol Burbo

Indexer
Richard Shrout

Computer Designers
Mickey Galicia and Dick Schwartz

Illustrators
Beth Young and Brian Wells

Series Design
Roberta Steele

Cover Design
Regan Honda

This book was composed with Corel VENTURA 8.

FOREWORD

From Global Knowledge

At Global Knowledge we strive to support the multiplicity of learning styles required by our students to achieve success as technical professionals. In this series of books, it is our intention to offer the reader a valuable tool for successful completion of the Compaq ASE Certification Exams.

As the world's largest IT training company, Global Knowledge is uniquely positioned to offer these books. The expertise gained each year from providing instructor-led training to hundreds of thousands of students worldwide has been captured in book form to enhance your learning experience. We hope that the quality of these books demonstrates our commitment to your lifelong learning success. Whether you choose to learn through the written word, computer-based training, Web delivery, or instructor-led training, Global Knowledge is committed to providing you the very best in each of those categories. For those of you who know Global Knowledge, or those of you who have just found us for the first time, our goal is to be your lifelong competency partner.

Thank you for the opportunity to serve you. We look forward to serving your needs again in the future.

Warmest regards,

Duncan Anderson
President and Chief Executive Officer, Global Knowledge

The Global Knowledge Advantage

Global Knowledge has a global delivery system for its products and services. The company has 28 subsidiaries, and offers its programs through a total of 60+ locations. No other vendor can provide consistent services across a geographic area this large. Global Knowledge is the largest independent information technology education provider, offering programs on a variety of platforms. This enables our multi-platform and multi-national customers to obtain all of their programs from a single vendor. The company has developed the unique CompetusTM Framework software tool and methodology which can quickly reconfigure courseware to the proficiency level of a student on an interactive basis. Combined with self-paced and on-line programs, this technology can reduce the time required for training by prescribing content in only the deficient skills areas. The company has fully automated every aspect of the education process, from registration and follow-up, to "just-in-time" production of courseware. Global Knowledge, through its Enterprise Services Consultancy, can customize programs and products to suit the needs of an individual customer.

Global Knowledge Classroom Education Programs

The backbone of our delivery options is classroom-based education. Our modern, well-equipped facilities staffed with the finest instructors offer programs in a wide variety of information technology topics, many of which lead to professional certifications.

Custom Learning Solutions

This delivery option has been created for companies and governments that value customized learning solutions. For them, our consultancy-based approach of developing targeted education solutions is most effective at helping them meet specific objectives.

Self-Paced and Multimedia Products

This delivery option offers self-paced program titles in interactive CD-ROM, videotape and audio tape programs. In addition, we offer custom development of interactive multimedia courseware to customers and partners. Call us at 1 (888) 427-4228.

Electronic Delivery of Training

Our network-based training service delivers efficient competency-based, interactive training via the World Wide Web and organizational intranets. This leading-edge delivery option provides a custom learning path and "just-in-time" training for maximum convenience to students.

ARG

American Research Group (ARG), a wholly-owned subsidiary of Global Knowledge, one of the largest worldwide training partners of Cisco Systems, offers a wide range of internetworking, LAN/WAN, Nortel Networks, FORE Systems, IBM, and UNIX courses. ARG offers hands on network training in both instructor-led classes and self-paced PC-based training.

Global Knowledge Courses Available

Network Fundamentals

- Understanding Computer Networks
- Telecommunications Fundamentals I
- Telecommunications Fundamentals II
- Understanding Networking Fundamentals
- Implementing Computer Telephony Integration
- Introduction to Voice Over IP
- Introduction to Wide Area Networking
- Cabling Voice and Data Networks
- Introduction to LAN/WAN protocols
- Virtual Private Networks
- ATM Essentials

Network Security & Management

- Troubleshooting TCP/IP Networks
- Network Management
- Network Troubleshooting
- IP Address Management
- Network Security Administration
- Web Security
- Implementing UNIX Security
- Managing Cisco Network Security
- Windows NT 4.0 Security

IT Professional Skills

- Project Management for IT Professionals
- Advanced Project Management for IT Professionals
- Survival Skills for the New IT Manager
- Making IT Teams Work

LAN/WAN Internetworking

- Frame Relay Internetworking
- Implementing T1/T3 Services
- Understanding Digital Subscriber Line (xDSL)
- Internetworking with Routers and Switches
- Advanced Routing and Switching
- Multi-Layer Switching and Wire-Speed Routing
- Internetworking with TCP/IP
- ATM Internetworking
- OSPF Design and Configuration
- Border Gateway Protocol (BGP) Configuration

Authorized Vendor Training

Cisco Systems

- Introduction to Cisco Router Configuration
- Advanced Cisco Router Configuration
- Installation and Maintenance of Cisco Routers
- Cisco Internetwork Troubleshooting
- Cisco Internetwork Design
- Cisco Routers and LAN Switches
- Catalyst 5000 Series Configuration
- Cisco LAN Switch Configuration
- Managing Cisco Switched Internetworks
- Configuring, Monitoring, and Troubleshooting Dial-Up Services
- Cisco AS5200 Installation and Configuration
- Cisco Campus ATM Solutions

Bay Networks

- Bay Networks Accelerated Router Configuration
- Bay Networks Advanced IP Routing
- Bay Networks Hub Connectivity
- Bay Networks Accelar 1xxx Installation and Basic Configuration
- Bay Networks Centillion Switching

FORE Systems

- FORE ATM Enterprise Core Products
- FORE ATM Enterprise Edge Products
- FORE ATM Theory
- FORE LAN Certification

Operating Systems & Programming

Microsoft

- Introduction to Windows NT
- Microsoft Networking Essentials
- Windows NT 4.0 Workstation
- Windows NT 4.0 Server
- Advanced Windows NT 4.0 Server
- Windows NT Networking with TCP/IP
- Introduction to Microsoft Web Tools
- Windows NT Troubleshooting
- Windows Registry Configuration

UNIX

- UNIX Level I
- UNIX Level II
- Essentials of UNIX and NT Integration

Programming

- Introduction to JavaScript
- Java Programming
- PERL Programming
- Advanced PERL with CGI for the Web

Web Site Management & Development

- Building a Web Site
- Web Site Management and Performance
- Web Development Fundamentals

High Speed Networking

- Essentials of Wide Area Networking
- Integrating ISDN
- Fiber Optic Network Design
- Fiber Optic Network Installation
- Migrating to High Performance Ethernet

DIGITAL UNIX

- UNIX Utilities and Commands
- DIGITAL UNIX v4.0 System Administration
- DIGITAL UNIX v4.0 (TCP/IP) Network Management
- AdvFS, LSM, and RAID Configuration and Management
- DIGITAL UNIX TruCluster Software Configuration and Management
- UNIX Shell Programming Featuring Kornshell
- DIGITAL UNIX v4.0 Security Management
- DIGITAL UNIX v4.0 Performance Management
- DIGITAL UNIX v4.0 Intervals Overview

DIGITAL OpenVMS

- OpenVMS Skills for Users
- OpenVMS System and Network Node Management I
- OpenVMS System and Network Node Management II
- OpenVMS System and Network Node Management III
- OpenVMS System and Network Node Operations
- OpenVMS for Programmers
- OpenVMS System Troubleshooting for Systems Managers
- Configuring and Managing Complex VMScluster Systems
- Utilizing OpenVMS Features from C
- OpenVMS Performance Management
- Managing DEC TCP/IP Services for OpenVMS
- Programming in C

Hardware Courses

- AlphaServer 1000/1000A Installation, Configuration and Maintenance
- AlphaServer 2100 Server Maintenance
- AlphaServer 4100, Troubleshooting Techniques and Problem Solving

ABOUT THE CONTRIBUTORS

About Syngress Media

Syngress Media creates books and software for Information Technology professionals seeking skill enhancement and career advancement. Its products are designed to comply with vendor and industry standard course curricula, and are optimized for certification exam preparation. Visit the Syngress Web site at www.syngress.com.

Contributors

Roneil Icatar (MCSE, ASE) works as a Senior Systems Engineer for GE Capital IT Solutions. He designs and builds Microsoft BackOffice solutions on Compaq servers for customers ranging from government and educational institutions to large corporations. When he's not working, he's sharing his knowledge by contributing to magazine articles and other publications, teaching computer related classes, and participating in Internet newsgroups. Roneil has been working in the computer industry for nearly a decade since he graduated from Rensselaer Polytechnic Institute. He currently lives in Hartford, Connecticut with his wife Julianne, where they are expecting their first child in May.

Louis Gary (ASE, MCNE) is the Network Manager at Hamilton Beach/Proctor-Silex, Inc., the leading manufacturer of small kitchen electric appliances. Louis has been installing network servers for over six years and has installed close to 50 Compaq servers. He is currently working on four new networks, an AS/400 Domino server, and an international wide area network expansion project. Louis holds a Bachelor of Science degree in Mechanical Engineering from the University of Virginia, and a Masters degree in Business Administration from the Darden School at UVA.

Andy Stewart (Master ASE in Enterprise Storage, MCSE+I, CNE, CCNA, PSE, NTP/NCP, CCA) is a Senior Systems Engineer with Inacom. Inacom is a global technology services company supplying an integrated set of services to design, procure, build, install, and manage their distributed environment. Andy would like to thank his family and friends for their love and support, but especially his wife Stephanie, son Nicolas, and daughter Taylor… without them, nothing is important.

Steve Hendrie (MCP, ASE, CNA) currently works as a Senior Information Technology Analyst at Hershey Foods Corporation supporting a large Microsoft NT network. Prior to working at Hershey, he worked as a project manager at DuPont during their NetWare to NT conversion. Steve started his career at Cardinal Technologies, Inc. where he worked as a Systems Administrator.

Glenn N. Wuenstel (MCSE, Master ASE) is a Senior Distributed Systems Analyst for South Carolina Electric & Gas. He holds a Bachelor of Science degree in Computer Science. Industry certifications include Microsoft Certified Systems Engineer and Compaq Master ASE in High Availability and Clustering. His latest project is architecting a Storage Area Network solution for SCE&G. Hobbies include Ryu Te Karate, SCUBA diving, and reading.

Ken Brumfield (MCSE, ASE, CNE) is an independent consultant specializing in managing, design, and implementation of technical solutions.

David Allonby (MCSE, ASE) is a Network Engineer with Lanway Corporate Business Systems, a leading UK Microsoft Certified Solution Provider. He is currently involved in the configuration, installation, and support of networked systems for a diverse client base. He specializes in Microsoft BackOffice on Compaq products.

Brian Sheaffer (MCSE) works as a specialist for Perot Systems Corporation. He is currently on assignment as a Web/Internet engineer at a major European investment bank where he works on the global standards for various intranet and extranet Web applications. For over five years, he has been heavily involved with Compaq server products as a Microsoft Windows NT administrator at two large distribution and manufacturing companies.

Brian Mayo (MCSE) is the Manager of Network Administration for Primetech. Primetech, with subsidiaries Taylor Newcomb Industries and Pacific Fluid Systems, is a regional distributor of hydraulic and pneumatic products serving the industrial, mobile, and aerospace markets. Brian has been a contributing writer for several books, including the *CCNA Cisco Certified Network Associate Study Guide* and the *MCSE Windows 98 Study Guide*, both for Osborne/McGraw-Hill. You can also frequently find articles written by Brian in the *Microsoft Certified Professional Journal.* He can be reached via e-mail at bmayo@primetechinc.com.

Terry Knaul (ASE, MCSD, MCSE) presently works for a national IT consulting firm. He has worked in the IT field for more than nine years with such companies as Procter & Gamble, Fidelity Investments, and Ernst & Young LLP. He is currently on assignment as regional IT manager with a global insurance company. He is a Microsoft Certified System Engineer (MCSE) as well as a Microsoft Certified Solution Developer (MCSD). Terry also freelances as an application developer and Web designer. In his free time he is an avid runner (having finished a marathon) and cycling wanna-be who competes in triathlons.

Brian Frederick (MCSE, ASE, MCNE, Network+) is a Systems Engineer with over seven years of technical background. Brian started working with computers with an Apple II+. Brian attended the University of Northern Iowa and is married with two adorable children. Brian's hobbies include his kids, family, and golfing. Brian is a Systems Engineer for Entre Information Systems, a leading Midwest Novell Platinum Partner and Microsoft Certified Solution Provider. Entre is a sister company to New Horizons Computer Learning Company, a premier Microsoft ATEC and Novell Authorized Training Partner. Brian owes his success to his parents and brother for their support and backing during his Apple days and in college, and to his wife and children for their support and understanding when dad spends many hours in front of their computer.

Ed Schlichtenmyer (CTT, CNI, ACI, CNP) is president of Wyne Island Consulting, an educational consulting firm based in Houston, Texas. He has 14 years of experience in the network computing industry and eight years of technical training experience.

Series Editor and From the Field Sidebars

Thomas Eck (MCSE+I, MCSD, MCDBA, ASE, CCA, GCA, CNA) is a specialist with Perot Systems Corporation in the Global Financial Services industry division. Currently, he is working as a Systems Architect and project manager on contract with a major European investment bank. His unique role at the bank allows him to define the global implementation standards employed for the bank's intranet and extranet Web infrastructure and also lead a group to research and develop new and innovative ways to solve workflow and interoperability issues using Web and thin-client technology. Additionally, Thomas provides support and consultancy to the various global development, engineering, and deployment teams within the bank environment.

Outside the office, Thomas has served as a contributing author and editor of several titles for Osborne/McGraw-Hill and also contributes regularly to *MCP Magazine*.

Technical Editor

Derrick Rountree (ASE, CNE, MCSE, CCNA) has a degree in Electrical Engineering from Florida State University. Derrick has worked for Alltel Information Systems, Prudential Health Care, and is currently working for an integrator in South Florida. Derrick has also worked for Boson.com Testing Software. Derrick would like to thank his mother, Claudine, and his wife, Michelle, who he credits for his success.

ACKNOWLEDGMENTS

We would like to thank the following people:

- Richard Kristof of Global Knowledge for championing the series and providing access to some great people and information.
- All the incredibly hard-working folks at Osborne/McGraw-Hill: Brandon Nordin, Scott Rogers, and Gareth Hancock for their help in launching a great series and being solid team players. In addition, Tara Davis, Tim Green, and Mark Karmendy for their help in fine-tuning the book.
- A special thank you to Marge Noak at Compaq Corporation for lending us a Remote Insight Board to complete the work on the RIB chapter.

CONTENTS AT A GLANCE

Part I

Compaq Systems Technologies (Exam 010-397)

1 Bus Subsystem 3

2 Microprocessor Architecture 15

3 Memory Subsystem 27

4 Cache Subsystems 53

5 Expansion Bus 67

6 Multiprocessing Architectures 81

7 Support Software 97

8 Disk Technologies 115

9 Drive Array Technology 131

10 Fibre Channel 149

11 Software 173

12 Networking 197

13 Compaq Servers 209

14 Options 245

15 Diagnostics and Utilities 261

16 Recovery Server 287

Part II
Compaq Systems Management (Exam 010-078)

17 Systems Management Overview 305

18 Industry Vocabulary 321

19 Compaq Server Management Technology 343

20 Desktop and Portable Management Technology 361

21 Management PC Configuration 377

22 Compaq Insight Manager 391

23 Compaq Intelligent Manageability 427

24 Compaq Remote Insight Board 453

25 Version Control 477

26 Integration Server 493

27 Web-Based Management 511

Part III
Compaq/Windows NT Integration and Performance (Exam 010-067)

28 Microsoft Windows NT Product Theory 545

29 Compaq SmartStart for Windows NT 575

30 Compaq and Windows NT Support 603

31 Enhancing NT Reliability Using Compaq Products 657

32 Windows NT Performance Tuning 695

A Self Test Answers 761

B About the CD 861

C About the Web Site 867

D Inspect Report 869

Glossary 883

Index 899

CONTENTS

Foreword iii
About the Contributors vii
Acknowledgments xi
Preface xxxvii
Introduction xli

Part I
Compaq Systems Technologies (Exam 010-397) **1**

1 Bus Subsystem **3**
Buses 4
Address Bus 4
Data Bus 6
Control Bus 6
Bus Performance 7
Wait State 8
Maximum Data Throughput Between Two Devices 8
Burst Transfer 10
Certification Summary 10
Two-Minute Drill 11
Self Test 13

2 Microprocessor Architecture **15**
Features of Pentium and Pentium Pro Microprocessors 16
Sizes of the Address and Data Buses 17
Sizes of the Caches 18
The Memory a Microprocessor Can Address 19
First-Level Cache on a Pentium Microprocessor 20

Instruction Pipelining 21
Certification Summary 22
Two-Minute Drill 23
Self Test 25

3 Memory Subsystem 27

Implementing Memory Devices in the Various Subsystems of a Server 28
DRAM and SRAM 29
DRAM Features 29
SRAM Features 32
Types of DRAM 33
Conventional DRAM 34
FPM 34
EDO 35
BEDO 35
Synchronous DRAM (SDRAM) 36
SIMMs and DIMMs 38
SIMM 38
DIMM 39
Types of Error Detection and Correction in Compaq Servers . . 41
Features of Error Detecting and Correcting Techniques 43
Reporting Memory Errors on Compaq Servers 44
Troubleshooting Memory Errors on a Compaq Server 46
Certification Summary 46
Two-Minute Drill 47
Self Test 51

4 Cache Subsystems 53

Cache Memory Subsystem 54
Cache Hits 55
Cache Misses 55
Components of a Cache Memory Subsystem 55
SRAM 56
Cache Directory 56
Cache Management Logic 56

Types of Cache Architecture 57
Look-Through and Look-Aside Cache Architecture 58
Write-Through and Write-Back Architecture 59
Performance of a Cache Subsystem 61
Operating System 61
Cache Size 62
Application 63
Certification Summary 63
Two-Minute Drill 63
Self Test 65

5 Expansion Bus 67
ISA Buses 68
EISA Buses 69
Burst Transfer Rate of an EISA Bus Master Device 69
PCI Buses 69
Architecture 70
PCI Hot Plug 70
Shared Slots 73
Dual Peer and Bridged PCI Buses 73
Certification Summary 77
Two-Minute Drill 77
Self Test 79

6 Multiprocessing Architectures 81
Symmetric and Asymmetric Multiprocessing 82
Asymmetric Multiprocessing 84
Symmetric Multiprocessing 85
Shared Cache 88
Upgrading a Processor 88
Major Differences Between Dual and Quad Multiprocessing . . 90
Certification Summary 92
Two-Minute Drill 93
Self Test 94

7 Support Software 97

Compaq SmartStart and Support Software CD 98
Systems Configuration Utility 100
    Add Remove Hardware 102
    View or Edit Details 103
    Diagnostics and Utilities 103
    Save Settings and Exit 104
Configuring a PCI Board 105
Configuring ISA Boards 106
Advanced Features of System Configuration 107
Certification Summary 108
Two-Minute Drill 109
Self Test 111

8 Disk Technologies 115

SCSI 116
    SCSI-2 117
    Fast SCSI-2 117
    Fast-Wide SCSI-2 117
    Ultra SCSI 118
SCSI Transfer Rates and Data Widths 119
    SCSI and Overall Data Transfer Performance 119
SCSI ID Settings 120
Types of SCSI Cabling Requirements 122
    Passive Termination 123
    Active Termination 123
    Termination Notes 123
Certification Summary 125
Two-Minute Drill 126
Self Test 128

9 Drive Array Technology 131

Compaq SMART Array Controller and Compaq
  SMART-2 Array Controller 132
Fault Prevention and Fault Tolerance Features 134

RAID Levels of Fault Tolerance 135
RAID Level 0—Data Striping without Parity 135
RAID Level 1—Mirrored 136
RAID Level 4—Data Striping with Dedicated Parity . . 138
RAID Level 5—Data Striping with Distributed Parity . . 139
Operation and Configuration Issues of Hot-Pluggable Hard Disks 140
Hardware Data Striping 141
Logical Volumes Supported by the SMART Array Controller . . 141
Protecting Write Data in the SMART Array Controller and SMART-2 Array Controller 141
Online Spares 142
Drive Array Advanced Diagnostics (DAAD) 143
Converting a SMART Array Controller to a SMART-2 Array Controller 143
Certification Summary 144
Two-Minute Drill 145
Self Test 147

10 Fibre Channel 149

Overview of Fibre Channel Architecture 150
Benefits 151
Technical Features and Limitations of Channels and Networks 151
Fibre Channel Topologies 155
Point-to-Point 156
Fibre Channel Arbitrated Loop 156
Fibre Channel Switched Fabric 158
Using RAID with Fibre Channel on Compaq Hardware 159
Compaq Fibre Channel Storage System 159
Compaq RAID Array 4000 160
Compaq RAID Array 8000 and Enterprise Storage Array 12000 162
How Fibre Channel Differs from SCSI 163

Building High Availability File Servers Using Compaq Fibre Channel Products 164
Certification Summary 168
Two-Minute Drill 169
Self Test 171

11 Software 173
Compaq SmartStart 174
Compaq Insight Manager 176
Problem Alerting 182
Remote Monitoring 184
Management Agents 185
Using Compaq Insight Manager with Other Management Systems 186
Using Compaq Rack Builder Software 186
Types of Reports from Rack Builder Software 189
Certification Summary 192
Two-Minute Drill 193
Self Test 194

12 Networking 197
Compaq NetFlex-2 and NetFlex-3 Networking Boards 198
NetFlex-2 ENET-TR 200
NetFlex-2 Dual Port ENET 200
NetFlex-2 TR 201
NetFlex-2 Dual Port TR(142132-001) 201
NetFlex-3/E 201
NetFlex-3/P 201
Upgrading from 10 Mbps to 100 Mbps with NetFlex-3 202
Compaq Netelligent Network Controllers 202
Netelligent 10/100 TX PCI UTP Controller 202
Netelligent 4/16 TR PCI UTP/STP Controller 203
100 Base-TX and 100 VG-AnyLAN 203
Certification Summary 205
Two-Minute Drill 205
Self Test 207

13 Compaq Servers 209
ProSignia Servers 211
ProLiant Servers 213
Upgrading Memory 217
Processors Available 221
Level-2 Cache 223
Processor Speed 223
Processor Power Module 224
Compaq Pre-Failure Warranty 225
Hard Drives 225
Memory 229
Processors 231
Dual Peer PCI Buses 232
Fault Tolerant Features 236
PCI Hot Plug 236
Redundant Processor Power Modules 236
Hot-Pluggable Redundant Power Supplies 236
ProLiant Cluster Ready 237
Redundant System Fans 237
Redundant Network Interface Cards (NICs) 237
ECC Memory 237
Pre-Failure Alerting 237
Certification Summary 239
Two-Minute Drill 240
Self Test 243

14 Options 245
Compaq Storage Expansion Systems 246
Compaq ProLiant Storage System 246
Compaq ProLiant Storage System/F 247
Differences Between ProLiant Storage System and ProLiant Storage System/F 247
Compaq Racks and Rack Options 248
Compaq Racks 249
Compaq Rack Options 249
Compaq's Rack Builder Software 250

Choosing a Compaq Digital Linear Tape (DLT) over a DAT Solution 252
Differences between DAT and DLT Devices 252
Compaq Auto-Loaders and Tape Libraries 253
Remote Insight Option 254
Redundant Power Supply 255
Certification Summary 255
Two-Minute Drill 256
Self Test 258

15 Diagnostics and Utilities 261

Compaq Diagnostics 262
Launching the Diagnostics 263
Running the Diagnostics and Utilities 264
Obtaining Compaq Support Tools and Utilities 269
Power-On Self-Test Operation and Error Reporting 270
POST Steps and Messages 271
Error Reporting 273
ROMPaq 273
Server Health Logs 277
Drive Array Advanced Diagnostics 278
Inspect 279
Certification Summary 282
Two-Minute Drill 283
Self Test 285

16 Recovery Server 287

Standby and Online Recovery Servers 288
Installation 289
Requirements of the Primary and Secondary Server 291
Disk Storage Location 291
Recovery Server Switch Location 294
Recovery Server Interconnect 294
Disconnected Interconnect 294

Failure of the Primary Server 295
Insight Manager 295
Standby Recovery Server 296
Online Recovery Server 296
Advantages and Disadvantages 297
Certification Summary 299
Two-Minute Drill 299
Self Test 301

Part II

Compaq Systems Management (Exam 010-078) 303

17 Systems Management Overview 305

Network Management 306
Systems Management 307
Management Platforms 310
HP OpenView 310
IBM NetView 312
Novell ManageWise 313
Management Applications 315
Compaq Insight Manager 315
Certification Summary 316
Two-Minute Drill 317
Self Test 319

18 Industry Vocabulary 321

SNMP 322
SET 325
GET 326
Traps 327
Community Names 329
Requirements for SNMP Usage 331
Management Agents 332
MIB 332

Internet Assigned Numbers Authority and MIB Creation 333
Managed Elements 334
Object Definitions 334
MIB Browsers 336
Certification Summary 338
Two-Minute Drill 339
Self Test 340

19 Compaq Server Management Technology 343

Compaq Full-Spectrum Fault Management 344
Compaq Fault Prevention 344
Fault Tolerance 347
Compaq Recovery Server 349
Compaq Rapid Recovery Engine 351
Server Health Logs 351
Automatic Server Recovery 352
Remote Maintenance 354
Certification Summary 355
Two-Minute Drill 356
Self Test 358

20 Desktop and Portable Management Technology 361

Desktop Management Task Force 362
Desktop Management Interface 362
Management Information File 363
The Features of Intelligent Manageability 363
Configuration Management 363
Asset Management 365
Security Management 368
Fault Management 368
Integration Management 370
Desktop Agents 370
Requirements for Windows NT and Windows 9x 371

Polling of the Desktop Agents 372
Certification Summary 372
Two-Minute Drill 372
Self Test 375

21 Management PC Configuration 377

Management PC Requirements 378
Operating System Support 378
Hardware Requirements 379
Other Requirements 379
Installing Insight Manager on the Management PC 381
Obtaining Insight Manager 381
Preinstallation Considerations 381
Installing Insight Manager 381
Certification Summary 387
Two-Minute Drill 387
Self Test 389

22 Compaq Insight Manager 391

Automatic Data Collection 392
Enabling Data Collection 393
Configuring Data Collection 394
Reporting on Collected Data 394
Server Reboot Feature 398
Enabling Remote Server Reboot 399
Rebooting a Server 399
Alarm Logs 400
Viewing Alarms 400
Viewing Alarm Details 401
Printing Alarms 402
SNMP Community Names 403
Setting Community Name in OS 404
Setting Default Community Name in CIM 406
Configure the Device Community Name 406
Hiding Community Names 407

In-Band Management 408
Out-of-Band Management 409
Alarm Forwarding 409
Enabling Alarm Forwarding 410
Configuring E-Mail Destinations 411
Configuring Pager Destinations 413
Server Filtering 415
Single Filter Mode vs. Multiple Filter Mode 415
Using Built-In Server Filters 415
Creating Custom Server Filters 418
Color Coded Status 419
Certification Summary 421
Two-Minute Drill 421
Self Test 423

23 Compaq Intelligent Manageability 427

Compaq Insight Manager LC 428
Product Procurement and Installation 428
Operation of Insight Manager LC 433
Compaq Insight Manager XE 436
How XE Differs from LC 437
Production Procurement and Installation 437
Operation of Insight Manager XE 439
Additional Management Products Available 441
Compaq Intelligent Cluster Administrator 441
Compaq Power Management 442
Certification Summary 448
Two-Minute Drill 449
Self Test 451

24 Compaq Remote Insight Board 453

Hardware Components of Remote Insight Board 454
The PCI Bus 455
Integrated NIC 456
PC Card Modem/Serial Port 456
Video Adapter 457
8MB of On-Board Memory 458

Installing and Configuring the Remote Insight Board 458
Remote Insight Board Features and Benefits 463
In-band and Out-Of-Band Management 464
Web Interface 465
Remote Console 466
Remote Insight Playback Capabilities 468
Remote Reboot 468
Alert Notification 469
Certification Summary 472
Two-Minute Drill 472
Self Test 474

25 Version Control 477
Version Control Color Codes 479
Green, Yellow, and Red Version Control Status Flags .. 480
Reasons to Upgrade 480
Downloading Current Databases 483
Database Update from CD 484
Database Update from the Internet 485
Update Interval for the Version Control Database 487
Certification Summary 488
Two-Minute Drill 488
Self Test 490

26 Integration Server 493
Integration Server 494
Operating Systems Supported by the Compaq Integration Server 495
Compaq Integration Maintenance Utility and Windows NT 495
Compaq Integration Maintenance Utility and NetWare 496
Push and Pull Architecture 497
Access Methods 497
Access via the Internet or Dial-Up 497
Update via CD 498

Compaq PEZ Files 500
PEZ Files on the SmartStart CDs 501
PEZ Files on the Integration Server 502
Creating an Integration Server 502
Requirements for Setting Up the Integration Server ... 502
NetWare Volume Name for IS and Required Usernames 503
Windows NT Share Name for IS and Required Usernames 504
Certification Summary 505
Two-Minute Drill 505
Self Test 508

27 Web-Based Management 511

Web-Based Enterprise Management (WBEM) 512
Advantages of Systems Management Using the Web ... 514
Overview of Current Web Management Offerings in Compaq Products 515
Installing the Web Agents 516
Disabling the Web Agents 517
Using the Web Management Functions of Insight Agents 4.01 and Up 517
Browser Requirements 518
Managing a Server Using a Browser 518
Managed Components 523
Security 530
Changing Passwords 533
The Future of Compaq Systems Management: Insight Manager XE 537
Limitations of Insight Manager XE 538
Certification Summary 539
Two-Minute Drill 539
Self Test 541

Part III

Compaq/Windows NT Integration and Performance (Exam 010-067) 543

28 Microsoft Windows NT Product Theory 545

Windows NT Versions 546
Windows NT Workstation 547
Windows NT Server 548
Windows NT Server, Enterprise Edition 549
Windows NT Server, Terminal Server 550
Windows 2000 553
Windows NT Architecture 553
Architectural Modules 556
User Mode Versus Kernel Mode 556
Hardware Abstraction Layer 557
Microkernel 559
Components of the Windows NT Executive 559
I/O Manager 560
Object Manager 561
Security Reference Monitor 561
Process Manager 562
Local Procedure Call Facility 563
Virtual Memory Manager 563
Window Manager 564
Graphics Device Interface 564
Graphics Device Drivers 565
Windows NT Environment Subsystems 565
MS-DOS Environment 566
Windows 16-Bit Environment 567
OS/2 Subsystem 567
POSIX Subsystem 568
Windows 32-Bit Subsystem 569
Certification Summary 569
Two-Minute Drill 570
Self Test 573

29 Compaq SmartStart for Windows NT 575

SmartStart 576
SmartStart Requirements 577
Booting from the SmartStart CD 578
Choosing the SmartStart Path 578
Server Profile Diskette 581
Choose Operating System 581
System Configuration and Disk Configuration 581
Compaq Products and Windows NT Configuration ... 582
Windows NT Setup (Graphical) 587
Manual Configuration Versus Assisted Integration 589
SmartStart Installation (Manual Configuration) 590
Using an Integration Server 591
Installing with SmartStart 592
Software Maintenance on Existing Installations 593
SmartStart Installation Versus Installing from Microsoft Media 596
Hardware Configuration 596
Manual Windows NT Installation and Configuration .. 598
SmartStart Subscription 598
Certification Summary 599
Two-Minute Drill 599
Self Test 601

30 Compaq and Windows NT Support 603

Compaq Server Support Diskettes for Windows NT 604
Obtaining the SSD 605
Running the SSD 605
HALs Provided by Compaq 607
The Hardware Abstraction Layer 608
Windows NT 3.x 608
Windows NT 4.0 and Later 610
Upgrading from a Single Processor to a Multiprocessor .. 610
HAL Recovery Option 611

Compaq Systems Management Driver for Windows NT 612
Loading the Driver 612
BOOT.INI File 613
Shutdown Script 616
Compaq Devices Supported in Windows NT 617
Compaq Devices Supported with Windows NT Base Product 617
Compaq Tape Drives Supported by Windows NT 618
Compaq Devices Supported with the SSD 619
Compaq Devices Supported Only with the SSD 622
Compaq Device Drivers 622
Supporting Compaq Insight Management Agents for Windows NT 622
Supporting the Compaq SMART and SMART-2 Array Controller 623
Supporting the Compaq UPS with Windows NT 625
Compaq Power Management Software 625
Compaq ProLiant Storage System 627
Compaq SCSI Controller Driver Support 628
Loading a Compaq SCSI Controller Driver from the Windows NT SSD 628
Updating the SCSI Driver 629
Upgrading a SmartStart Windows NT 3.51 and Windows NT 4.0 Installation 630
Preparing for the Upgrade 630
Upgrading to NT 4.0 632
Post Upgrade Tasks 632
Configuring the Insight Agents Control Panel 633
Compaq Utilities 635
Compaq On-Line Array Configuration Utility 636
Compaq Advanced Network Control Utility 636
Compaq Integrated Management Display Utility 638
Compaq Enhanced Integrated Management Display Service 638
Compaq PCI Hot Plug Utility 640
Compaq Power Down Manager 641

Compaq Power Supply Viewer 644
Determining the Current Windows NT Build Revision and Service Pack Level 645
Determining the Current Version of a Compaq Device Driver 648
Using Version Control to Determine Driver Versions .. 650
Certification Summary 651
Two-Minute Drill 651
Self Test 654

31 Enhancing NT Reliability Using Compaq Products 657

RAID Fault Tolerance Levels 658
RAID 0 659
RAID 1 659
RAID 4 659
RAID 5 660
Configuring a Boot Partition for Windows NT Software Fault Tolerance 663
Creating the Recovery Disk 663
Windows NT Software RAID 5 667
Compaq Hardware-Based Fault Tolerance 667
Compaq Hardware Mirroring 668
Hardware RAID 4 670
Hardware RAID 5 670
Differences Between the SMART and the SMART-2 Controllers 672
Compaq ProLiant Storage System 675
Standby Recovery Server 676
Primary Server Hardware Failure 677
Primary Server Operating System Failure 677
Recovery Server Interconnect Cable Is Disconnected ... 677
Restoring After a Failover 678
Requirements 678
Continuity of Service 679
Setting Up a Standby Server 679

Online Recovery Server 680
Continuity of Service 682
Compaq Advanced Network Fault Detection and Correction .. 684
Installation of the Advanced Network Utilities 684
Adding Bridged PCI Devices to a ProLiant 5000, 6000, 6500, and 7000 685
Certification Summary 687
Two-Minute Drill 687
Self Test 690

32 Windows NT Performance Tuning 695

Windows NT Performance Monitor 696
Using Performance Monitor 698
Display Modes 698
Uses for Each Mode 707
Saving Your Settings 710
Windows NT Memory Subsystem 712
Paged Pool and Nonpaged Pool Memory 712
Determining System Cache Size 713
The Paging File 714
Windows NT Virtual Memory Manager 718
Memory Subsystem and Disk Subsystem Interaction ... 719
Memory Usage by Process 721
Calculating the Optimum Amount of Memory for a System 722
Configuring the Server Component in the Network Control Panel 723
Disk Performance Factors 725
DISKPERF Parameter 725
Setting a Process's Base Priority 726
Subsystem Load by Server Role 729
Highest Load Subsystems in a Client-Server Environment 730
Highest Load Subsystems in a Resource-Sharing Environment 731

Performance Monitor Counters 732
Processor 732
Memory 738
Disk 743
Network 748
Identifying a Bottleneck 752
Certification Summary 752
Two-Minute Drill 753
Self Test 756

A Self Test Answers 761

Chapter 1 Answers 762
Chapter 2 Answers 764
Chapter 3 Answers 767
Chapter 4 Answers 769
Chapter 5 Answers 772
Chapter 6 Answers 775
Chapter 7 Answers 777
Chapter 8 Answers 782
Chapter 9 Answers 785
Chapter 10 Answers 787
Chapter 11 Answers 790
Chapter 12 Answers 793
Chapter 13 Answers 796
Chapter 14 Answers 800
Chapter 15 Answers 802
Chapter 16 Answers 805
Chapter 17 Answers 808
Chapter 18 Answers 811
Chapter 19 Answers 815
Chapter 20 Answers 817
Chapter 21 Answers 820
Chapter 22 Answers 822

Chapter 23 Answers 825
Chapter 24 Answers 828
Chapter 25 Answers 831
Chapter 26 Answers 833
Chapter 27 Answers 835
Chapter 28 Answers 838
Chapter 29 Answers 841
Chapter 30 Answers 845
Chapter 31 Answers 849
Chapter 32 Answers 855

B About the CD 861

Installing the Personal Testing Center 862
Test Type Choices 862
Live 863
Managing Windows 863
Saving Scores as Cookies 863
Using the Browser Buttons 864
JavaScript Errors 864
Practice 864
Review 864
Scoring 865

C About the Web Site 867

Access Global Knowledge 868
What You'll Find There. 868

D Inspect Report 869

Glossary 883

Index 899

PREFACE

This book's primary objective is to help you prepare for and pass the required Compaq ASE exams so you can begin to reap the career benefits of certification. We believe that the only way to do this is to help you increase your knowledge and build your skills. After completing this book, you should feel confident that you have thoroughly reviewed all of the objectives that Compaq has established for the exams.

In This Book

This book is organized around the actual structure of the Compaq ASE exams administered at Sylvan Testing Centers. Compaq has let us know all the topics we need to cover for the exams. We've followed their list carefully, so you can be assured you're not missing anything.

In Every Chapter

We've created a set of chapter components that call your attention to important items, reinforce important points, and provide helpful exam-taking hints. Take a look at what you'll find in every chapter:

- Every chapter begins with the **Certification Objectives**—what you need to know in order to pass the section on the exam dealing with the chapter topic. The Certification Objectives headings identify the objectives within the chapter, so you'll always know an objective when you see it!
- **On the Job** notes point out procedures and techniques important for coding actual applications for employers or contract jobs.
- **Certification Exercises** are interspersed throughout the chapters. These are step-by-step exercises that mirror vendor-recommended labs. They help you master skills that are likely to be an area of focus on the exam. Don't just read through the exercises; they are hands-on practice that you should be comfortable completing. Learning by doing is an effective way to increase your competency with a product.

- **From the Field** sidebars describe the issues that come up most often in the training classroom setting. These sidebars give you a valuable perspective into certification- and product-related topics. They point out common mistakes and address questions from actual classroom discussions.
- **Q & A** sections lay out problems and solutions in a quick-read format. For example:

QUESTIONS AND ANSWERS	
How would you manage a heterogeneous network consisting of many different brands of servers, network hardware, and DMI-compliant desktop PCs?	Use Insight Manager XE. This product allows you to manage any networked device that supports SNMP and DMI.
What if you need to perform automatic data collection for historical data purposes?	Use Insight Manager. Insight Manager allows you to perform ADC, whereas XE does not allow you to perform ADC.

- The **Certification Summary** is a succinct review of the chapter and a restatement of salient points regarding the exam.
- The **Two-Minute Drill** at the end of every chapter is a checklist of the main points of the chapter. It can be used for last-minute review.
- The **Self Test** offers questions similar to the multiple choice questions found on the certification exams. The answers to these questions, as well as explanations of the answers, can be found in Appendix A. By taking the Self Test after completing each chapter, you'll reinforce what you've learned from that chapter, while becoming familiar with the structure of the exam questions.

Some Pointers

Once you've finished reading this book, set aside some time to do a thorough review. You might want to return to the book several times and make use of all the methods it offers for reviewing the material:

1. *Re-read all the Two-Minute Drills,* or have someone quiz you. You also can use the drills as a way to do a quick cram before the exam.
2. *Review all the Q & A scenarios* for quick problem solving.
3. *Re-take the Self Tests.* Taking the tests right after you've read the chapter is a good idea, because it helps reinforce what you've just learned. However, it's an even better idea to go back later and do all the questions in the book in one sitting. Pretend you're taking the exam. (For this reason, you should mark your answers on a separate piece of paper when you answer the questions the first time.)
4. *Complete the exercises.* Did you do the exercises when you read through each chapter? If not, do them! These exercises are designed to cover exam topics, and there's no better way to get to know this material than by practicing.
5. *Check out the Web site.* Global Knowledge Network invites you to become an active member of the Access Global Web site. This site is an online mall and information repository that you'll find invaluable. You can access many types of products to assist you in your preparation for the exams, and you'll be able to participate in forums, online discussions, and threaded discussions. No other book brings you unlimited access to such a resource. You'll find more information about this site in Appendix C.

INTRODUCTION

CERTIFICATION OBJECTIVE 1.01

How to Take a Compaq ASE Certification Examination

Shout Above the Noise with the ASE Credential

With the tremendous number of IT professionals using operating system vendor certifications as a means to stand apart from their peers, savvy system administrators who have already obtained these certifications are augmenting these credentials with complimentary titles in order to demonstrate proficiency in multiple areas.

For those administrators and engineers that regularly work with Compaq hardware, there is no better choice to demonstrate proficiency with both network and systems hardware technology than the Compaq ASE certification track. By creating a certification that requires a complimentary credential from Microsoft or Novell, Compaq assures that IT professionals holding the ASE credential are well versed, not only in hardware technology, but also system integration.

At the highest level, there are three categories of ASE certification: Associate ASE, ASE, and Master ASE. Within each category, a candidate can choose from several specialty tracks as follows:

- Associate ASE
    - Intel/NetWare Specialist
    - Intel/Windows NT Specialist
    - Intel+StorageWorks Specialist

- ASE [Requires matching vendor certification using Microsoft (MCSE/MCSE+I) or Novell premium operating system certifications (CNE/MCNE)]
  - Alpha/OVMS Specialist
  - Alpha/Tru64UNIX Specialist
  - Critical Problem Resolution Specialist
  - Intel/NetWare Specialist
  - Intel/Windows NT Specialist
  - Intel+StorageWorks Specialist
- Master ASE [Requires Full ASE Status]
  - Baan Specialist
  - Enterprise Management Specialist
  - Enterprise Storage Specialist
  - High Availability and Clustering Specialist
  - Internet/Intranet Specialist
  - Messaging and Collaboration Specialist
  - Oracle Specialist
  - SAP Specialist
  - SQL Server Specialist

Due to the wide spectrum of specialty tracks offered by Compaq for the ASE credential, this book will only focus on obtaining the Intel/Windows NT Specialist title within the Associate ASE/ASE categories.

To successfully obtain the ASE credential in the Intel/Windows NT Specialist track, you must successfully complete the following requirements:

- Obtain a Microsoft MCSE/MCSE+I title (ASE only)
- Pass the Compaq Systems Technologies exam
- Pass the Windows NT Integration and Performance exam
- Pass the Compaq Systems Management exam
- Submit the ASE application within six months of the first exam attempt

Unlike most vendor certifications, after passing all three exams you will not be considered a valid recipient of the ASE credential until an application is completed and sent to Compaq for processing. In essence, this application is a nondisclosure agreement made between you and Compaq, which covers all ASE exam material and any future proprietary information you might obtain as part of your ASE benefits package.

Why Choose the Compaq ASE Certification Track?

In addition to a nifty looking framed certificate for your wall, Compaq offers the following benefits to all ASEs in good standing:

Benefit	Description
ActiveAnswers	Access to an extranet Web site that provides structured information and tools for deploying enterprise solutions.
ASE TidBytes Newsletter	Quarterly publication covering subjects about engineering and sales support, ASE success stories, and upcoming events.
Compaq ASE Connection	Access to an ASE-only Web site with product purchase information, ASE logo merchandise, and access to technical information. E-mail access to Compaq technical support and access to databases containing product information, software utilities, and more.
Compaq ASE Product Purchase Plan	Compaq products at a discounted rate.
Compaq QuickFind Subscription	Compaq sales, service, and support information.
Compaq SmartStart Subscription	Compaq deployment utilities, product information, server management tools (Compaq Insight Manager), and drivers.
Compaq Software Support CDs	Updates of OS software for Compaq Servers and all standard Compaq utilities.
Day-of-Announcement Product Kits	Sales and technical information and tools for Systems Engineers.
New Product Training	Product training in a self-paced computer based training format.
NT ResourcePaq	Resource kit that increases the value of Compaq server, workstation, and desktop products within Windows NT environments.

In addition, ASEs and Master ASEs (i.e. **not** Associate ASEs) also receive the following benefits:

Benefit	Description
Compaq Engineering Conferences	Early registration for Compaq conferences with significant discounts (historically, these have been free to all ASEs).
Compaq Technical Support Hotline	Free priority access to Compaq Technical Support.

Exam Information

All three one-hour exams in the Intel/Windows NT Specialist track are comprised of 50 multiple choice questions for which you must answer at least 42 correct to achieve a final score or 84 or above.

To prepare for the exams, you should download the Compaq ASE Test Self Assessment Study Guides from http://www.compaq.com/training/ase-tsas.html. In addition to providing a full listing of the current objectives for each exam, these guides provide invaluable information regarding current test series ID numbers and course identification numbers. Unlike Microsoft exams, Compaq changes test objectives, test series, and course identification numbers frequently, so be sure to check this Web link before registering or studying for an exam.

Ready for the Journey?

If you are ready to start the process of becoming an ASE, you must first register with Compaq to obtain a student ID number. This can be done by simply calling 1-800-732-5741 (United States candidates only) or 800-392-7024 (Canadian candidates only) and giving the operator some basic personal information.

With a student number in hand, you are ready to register for the exams by calling Sylvan Prometric at 800-366-EXAM. The cost for each exam is $100.00 and can be taken any number of times without restriction if you should fail to complete a test successfully.

Due to the volatility of today's hardware market, Compaq requires all candidates to complete all three tests successfully within a six-month interval. After obtaining the ASE credential, you will also be subject to continuing education requirements to help assure your knowledge remains up-to-date. As a result, your ASE credential is valid only for one year from the date of issuance, at which point you will be required to submit an application for continuance. Please note, this does not mean that you will be required to retake all three exams, you simply must reaffirm your willingness to participate in the ASE program.

On the day of the exam, be sure to bring two forms of identification to the test center along with your student identification number. This number (rather than your Social Security number) is used to track your progress through the certification process and assure that you have completed all objectives within the allotted time interval.

After completing all three exams, simply send your test scores and proof of your MCSE credential (a copy of your transcript or MCSE/MCSE+I certificate is adequate) to Compaq for processing. Within 6-8 weeks, you will receive an ASE Welcome Kit that will commence a small onslaught of monthly benefits mailings from Compaq.

By combining the knowledge derived through attendance at the Compaq courses, hands-on experience with Compaq products, and the expert guidance brought to you by the authors of this book, you will soon be well on your way to augmenting your Microsoft certification with the Compaq ASE credential.

Part I

Compaq Systems Technologies (Exam 010-397)

ASE

ACCREDITED SYSTEMS ENGINEER

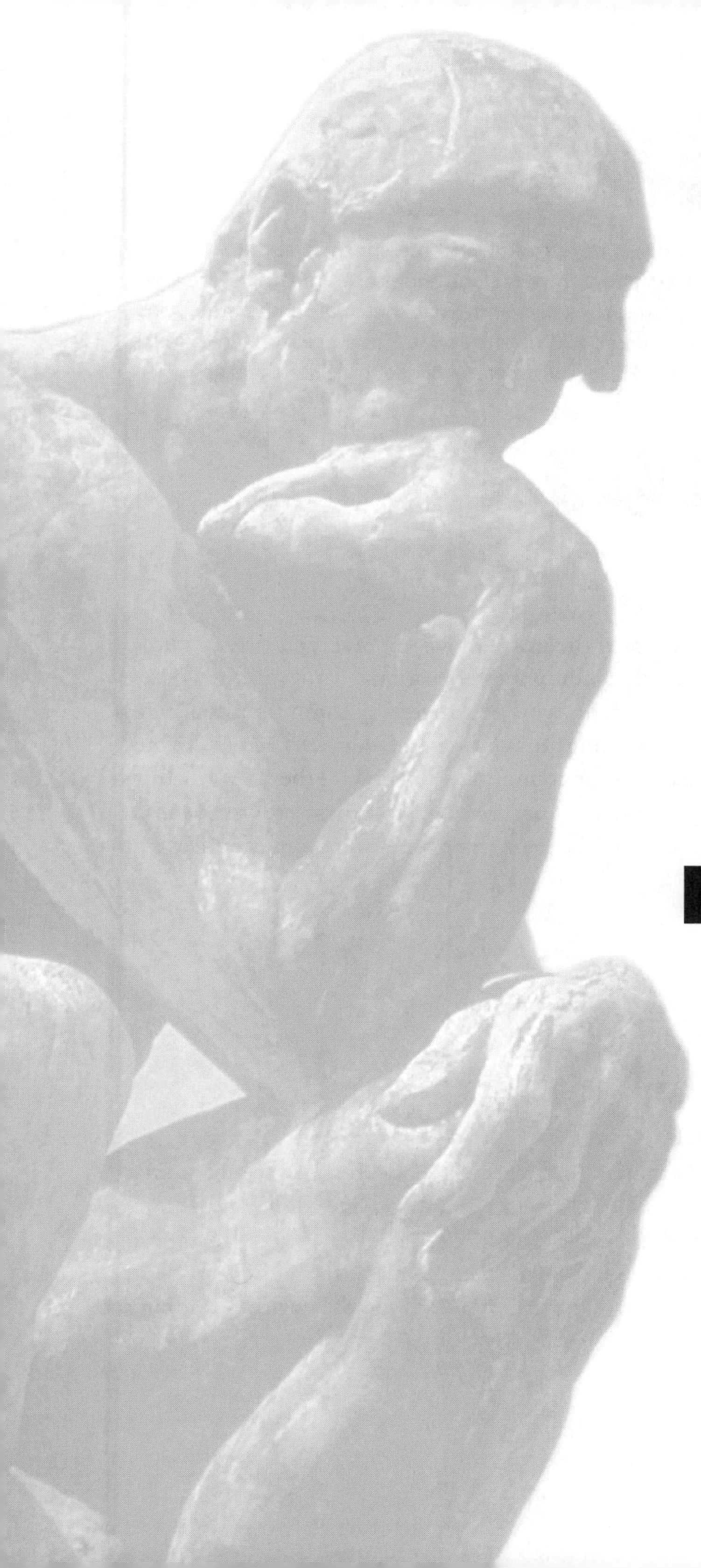

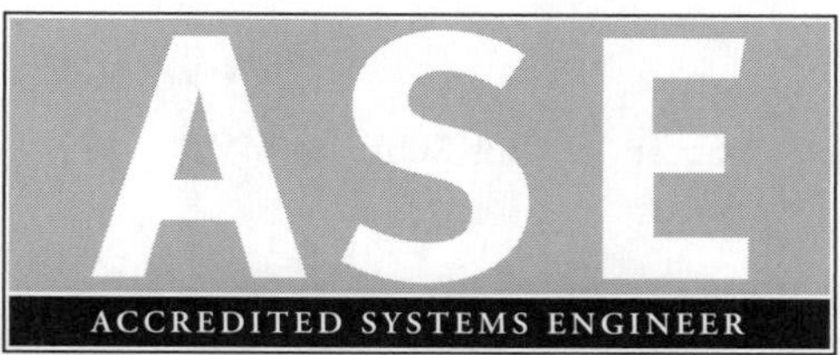

1

Bus Subsystem

CERTIFICATION OBJECTIVES

1.01 Buses

1.02 Wait State

1.03 Maximum Data Throughput Between Two Devices

1.04 Burst Transfer

To achieve the ASE certification, you will have to know some specifics about what makes the components inside a Compaq computer communicate. In this chapter, we will look at the computer buses—what they are, and what their respective functions are. We will also look at the different transfer rates and methods used to increase or maximize transfer throughput. This chapter will be the basis for what you will see in other chapters.

CERTIFICATION OBJECTIVE 1.01

Buses

Assuming that you have seen the inside of a computer, you already know that there are many different components that must work together. The way these different components work together is by communicating across the system or host bus. Reading and writing of data occurs across the bus. The bus architecture allows for communication among the CPU, memory, and I/O subsystems. Physical connections between these subsystems make the system work as a whole. There are three buses to become familiar with for the exam:

- Address bus
- Data bus
- Control bus

Address Bus

When it comes to computers, and especially networks, you see the term "address" a lot. Within an Intel-based system, you have different memory or I/O addresses, where data resides. In order for a device to access data from another device, the address information has to be on the address bus. The address tells the device where the data resides when the device is reading and where the data can be written. The address is unique to that device. Two devices cannot have the same I/O address or memory address, or they would conflict.

The main thing to remember about the address bus is that it transports the source and destination address for the data that is travelling on the data bus. It tells the device subsystems the address where the data will be stored or where the data can be read. We see analogies to this process every day in our mailboxes. Our home address lets the post office know how to get information to us, and we know who has sent us mail by the return addresses on the mail we receive.

Bus Width

The amount of data that processors can handle in a timely manner varies. The width of the address bus determines how much data can be handled on the address bus, which determines the addressable memory size for the CPU. The addressable memory size is 2^x, where x equals the number of bits in the address bus. The higher the value of x, the bigger the theoretical addressable memory size. There are then limitations to each type of processor. Table 1-1 shows common Intel processor types, along with the number of address lines (width) and the maximum memory.

TABLE 1-1 Processor Types Address Lines

Processor Type	Number of Address Lines	Theoretical Maximum Memory
80486	32	4 Gigabytes
Pentium	32	4 Gigabytes
Pentium Pro	64	64 Gigabytes
Pentium II	64	64 Gigabytes

Data Bus

Inside your computer, data is transferred between the different components. These components include memory, processor, and other I/O subsystems. The data bus is what is used to transport data between devices, as well as to determine how much data can be sent at one time. The data bus is made up of lines that each carry a bit of information at a time. A data bus is made up of multiples of eight bits, because eight bits make up a byte. So the bus width is naturally divisible by bytes.

The speed and the width of the data bus affect the performance of the system. The wider the data bus, the higher the throughput, because more information can be passed in a single operation. The faster processors use the widest possible data bus to assure maximum throughput, and thus, maximum performance. Table 1-2 shows common Intel processors and the width of the data bus for each one.

Control Bus

The control bus is used to identify the type of bus cycle and to determine when the cycle is complete. The control bus carries control signals that determine whether data will be read or written. It also determines if the operation is being performed to memory or to I/O. There are four basic types of bus cycles:

- Memory Write
- I/O Write
- Memory Read
- I/O Read

TABLE 1-1

Processors and Data Bus Width

Processor	Width of Data Bus
80386	32 Bits
80486	32 Bits
Pentium / Pentium Pro / Pentium II	64 Bits

QUESTIONS AND ANSWERS	
What transports the source and destination address for the data that is travelling on the data bus?	Address bus
What is used to transport data between devices as well as determine how much data can be sent at one time?	Data bus
What is used to identify the type of bus cycle and determine when the cycle is complete?	Control bus
What would be the result of decreasing the clock speed?	Performance deteriorates
What would be the result of increasing the width of the bus?	Performance improves
What would be the result of implementing burst cycles?	Performance improves

When data is transferred, a bus cycle must occur. A bus cycle involves sending out address information and then transferring the data to that address. Be sure to know what each bus does within a given configuration. You will see questions on this topic.

Bus Performance

When processes require two or more bus cycles, they can hurt system performance. To increase performance, certain steps can be taken. The first of these is to increase the clock speed of the processor. This in turn makes bus cycles faster. Another step would be to increase the width of the bus, which will increase the amount of data per bus cycle.

If you can increase the speed of devices that communicate with the processor, you also increase system performance. Installing high-speed memory or extra cache helps the speed of the system. Lastly, you can use a modified bus cycle, such as a burst cycle.

To review, the methods to help increase system performance are

- Increase the clock speed of the processor
- Increase the width of the bus so more data travels per bus cycle
- Increase the speed of devices communicating with the processor
- Implement burst cycles or modified bus cycles

CERTIFICATION OBJECTIVE 1.02

Wait State

A wait state is the period of time in which a CPU or a bus must sit idle due to the differing clock speeds of components in the system. For example, the most common wait state encountered is between memory components and the CPU. In a zero wait state system, the CPU is allowed to run at full speed and does not require any time-outs to compensate for slower memory. Due to the difference in speed between main memory and the CPU, typically some other form of technology must be introduced to allow the CPU to run at full speed, such as a caching subsystem. The relatively small, but extremely fast, L2 cache is used to match the CPU's insatiable appetite for memory resources and allows the system to run at its maximum potential.

CERTIFICATION OBJECTIVE 1.03

Maximum Data Throughput Between Two Devices

The maximum data throughput is equivalent to the amount of data that can flow across a bus during a given amount of time. This is how you can measure a computer's performance against others. The data throughput is determined by a formula, which you will probably see or use on the exam. To calculate the maximum data transfer rate, multiply the bus speed by the bus width. The bus speed is in MHz. The bus width is in bytes. Once you have this value, you can divide the value by the cycles per transfer to get the maximum transfer rate (MTR).

$$\text{Maximum Data Transfer Rate} = \frac{(\text{Bus Speed} \times \text{Bus Width})}{\text{Cycles per second}}$$

A shortened version of the formula would read (F x W) / N = MTR. The frequency times the width, divided by the number of clock cycles, equals the maximum transfer rate. Here is a sample calculation:

$$\frac{(10{,}000{,}000 \text{ cycles per second} \times 4 \text{ bytes per transfer}) = 22{,}000{,}000 \text{ bytes per second}}{2 \text{ cycles per transfer}}$$

The maximum transfer rate comes down to the amount of data that can travel across the bus in a given period of time. This is one of the ways to measure a computer's performance. Increasing the maximum transfer rate increases the overall performance of the computer. The maximum transfer rate is given in bytes transferred per second. With today's computers, you will usually see the maximum transfer rate expressed as megabytes per second (MB/s).

FROM THE FIELD

Bus Mastering

To help improve performance across the bus, manufacturers have introduced the bus mastering architecture for system buses. Bus mastering allows a controller to communicate directly with other devices on the bus without requiring CPU resources. Intel's Peripheral Component Interconnect bus (PCI) is just one example of a bus architecture that takes full advantage of this technology.

Most discussion of bus-mastering technology tends to be centered on IDE controllers. Bus master IDE technology improves performance significantly on multitasking operating systems.

If you are using a non-Compaq IDE controller in your system, make sure that all hardware and the system driver support bus mastering to achieve the best possible performance. In addition to the IDE controller, bus-mastering-compatible IDE drives must be used as well. To identify a bus-mastering-compatible IDE drive, look in the specifications to see if it supports DMA multiword modes.

—Thomas E. Eck, MCSE+I, MCSD, ASE, CCA, CNA

CERTIFICATION OBJECTIVE 1.04

Burst Transfer

A burst mode transfer is a data transmission in which data is temporarily sent significantly faster than usual. Depending on the type of bus, this can be accomplished in different ways. In the data bus, for example, a burst mode transfer is achieved by allowing a single device exclusive access to the bus. Obviously, if this one device were allowed to monopolize the bus in a sustained fashion, no other device could communicate, thus lowering the overall performance of the bus.

Like the marathon runner who can only sprint near the finish line, burst mode transfers allow greater performance, but they are unsustainable and potentially detrimental to overall performance if used too frequently.

CERTIFICATION SUMMARY

The basic communication components of a computer are the various buses. The three different kinds of buses in any system are the address bus, the data bus, and the control bus. The bus architecture allows for communication among the processor, memory, and I/O subsystems.

The address bus handles the I/O addresses and memory locations of the various devices. It tells devices where the data resides when reading and where data can be written. Two devices cannot have the same I/O address or memory address, or they would conflict. The address bus transports the source and destination address for the data that is travelling on the data bus.

The control bus is used to identify the bus cycle. It also determines when the cycle is complete. As the name implies, the control bus is in complete control of the bus cycle. The four types of cycles are Memory Write, Memory Read, I/O Read, and I/O Write.

There are various ways to increase the system performance. One method is to increase the clock speed of the processor. Increasing the width of the data bus will also increase the performance. You can also increase the speed of devices that communicate with the processor. Lastly, we can improve performance by implementing burst cycles. Burst cycles ensure that data is transferred every clock cycle by temporarily seizing control over the bus.

Wait states are introduced when devices cannot respond within one cycle. A zero wait state is more prevalent today, since processors and devices are much faster and technologies have evolved to overcome previous limitations that caused wait states. The formula to calculate the maximum data throughput is the frequency times the width of the data bus, divided by the clock cycles. This can be written $(F \times W) / N = \text{MTR}$.

✓ TWO-MINUTE DRILL

- ❑ The bus architecture allows for communication among the CPU, memory, and I/O subsystems.
- ❑ There are three buses to become familiar with for the exam:
  - ❑ Address bus
  - ❑ Data bus
  - ❑ Control bus
- ❑ The main thing to remember about the address bus is that it transports the source and destination address for the data that is travelling on the data bus.
- ❑ The width of the address bus determines how much data can be handled on the address bus, which determines the addressable memory size for the CPU.
- ❑ The data bus is what is used to transport data between devices, as well as to determine how much data can be sent at one time.
- ❑ The wider the data bus, the higher the throughput, because more information can be passed in a single operation.
- ❑ The control bus is used to identify the type of bus cycle and to determine when the cycle is complete.
- ❑ There are four basic types of bus cycles:
  - ❑ Memory Write
  - ❑ I/O Write
  - ❑ Memory Read
  - ❑ I/O Read

- When processes require two or more bus cycles, they can hurt system performance.
- A wait state is the period of time in which a CPU or a bus must sit idle due to the differing clock speeds of components in the system.
- The maximum data throughput is equivalent to the amount of data that can flow across a bus during a given amount of time.
- A burst mode transfer is a data transmission in which data is temporarily sent significantly faster than usual.
- Burst mode transfers allow greater performance, but they are unsustainable and potentially detrimental to overall performance if used too frequently.

SELF TEST

The following Self Test questions will help you measure your understanding of the material presented in this chapter. Read all the choices carefully, as there may be more than one correct answer. Choose all correct answers for each question.

1. What bus handles the various I/O ranges that devices use?
   A. Data
   B. Address
   C. Control
   D. None of the above
2. What is one factor that determines how much data can be handled on a bus in a computer?
   A. Width of the bus
   B. Length of the bus
   C. Number of connectors on the bus
   D. All of the above
3. What is the maximum addressable memory size of a Pentium processor?
   A. 4MB
   B. 64MB
   C. 4GB
   D. 64GB
4. What is used to determine how much data can be sent between devices at one time?
   A. Address bus
   B. Data bus
   C. Control bus
   D. Memory bus
5. How many bits make up a byte?
   A. 6
   B. 7
   C. 8
   D. 12
6. What are two factors that affect the performance of the data bus?
   A. Speed
   B. Length
   C. Width
   D. Number of connectors
7. What is the width of the data bus on a computer with an 80486 processor?
   A. 32 bits
   B. 64 bits
   C. 32 bytes
   D. 64 bytes
8. What is used to determine the type of bus cycle?
   A. Address bus
   B. Data bus
   C. Control bus
   D. Processor bus
9. What is used to determine when the bus cycle is complete?
   A. Address bus

B. Control bus
C. Data bus
D. Memory bus

10. Which of the following is not one of the basic types of bus cycle?
    A. Memory Write
    B. Memory Read
    C. I/O Read
    D. Memory Burst

11. Which of the following will not increase bus performance?
    A. Increasing the clock speed of the processor
    B. Widening the bus
    C. Making sure all of your devices are ISA devices and not PCI devices
    D. Installing high-speed memory

12. What is known as an extra bus cycle and is used if a device cannot respond in one cycle?
    A. Slow machine
    B. Wait state
    C. Burst cycle
    D. Double cycle

13. What is the term equivalent to the amount of data that can flow across a bus during a given amount of time?
    A. Maximum data throughput
    B. Minimum data throughput
    C. Wait state
    D. Clock cycle

14. What is the formula for calculating the maximum data throughput?
    A. $(F \text{ x } W) / R =$ MTN
    B. $(W \text{ x } N) / F =$ MTR
    C. $(W \text{ x } R) / N =$ MTR
    D. $(F \text{ x } W) / N =$ MTR

15. What happens in a burst cycle?
    A. Data is transferred every other clock cycle.
    B. Data is transferred every clock cycle.
    C. Double the data is transferred every clock cycle.
    D. Double the data is transferred every other clock cycle.

ASE
ACCREDITED SYSTEMS ENGINEER

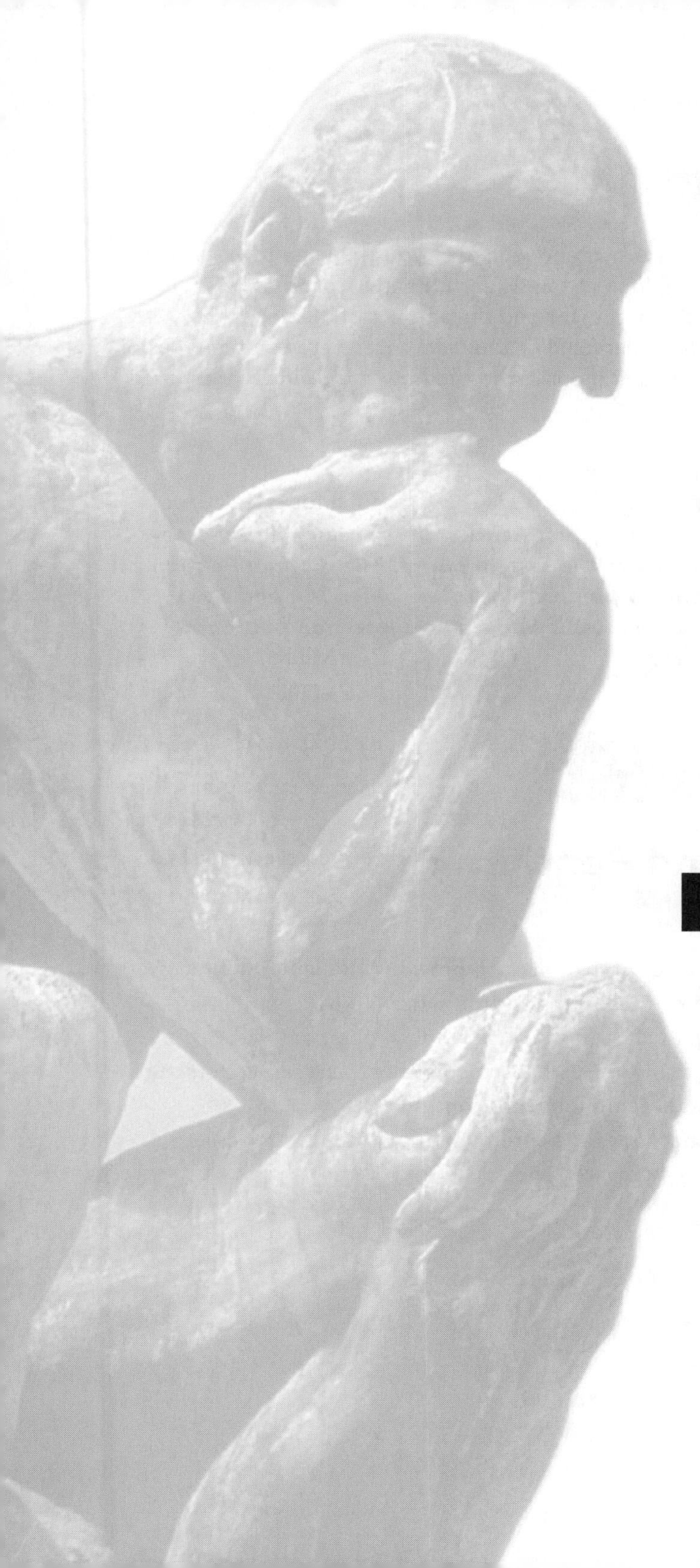

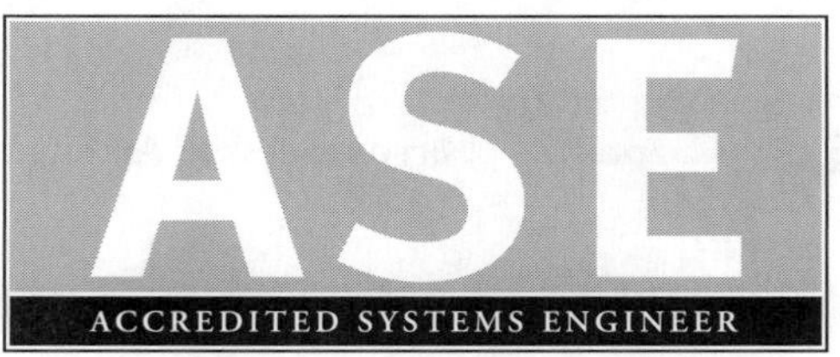

2

Microprocessor Architecture

CERTIFICATION OBJECTIVES

2.01	Features of Pentium and Pentium Pro Microprocessors
2.02	The Memory a Microprocessor Can Address
2.03	First-Level Cache on a Pentium Microprocessor
2.04	Instruction Pipelining

Today's processors have many different components that you will need to know for your exam. In this chapter, we will look at the different Pentium processors. We will look at the architecture of the processor and the amount of memory that a processor can address. This is important to understanding the differences between the types of Pentium processors. We will also get into details about cache and how it is used. The last area we will look at is instruction pipelining.

I remember when I saw my first Pentium II processor and the new method for connecting to the system board. The original Pentiums were attached by many pins, similar to the older 386 and 486 processors. The new processor had a single insertion point and was more like a card.

CERTIFICATION OBJECTIVE 2.01

Features of Pentium and Pentium Pro Microprocessors

Pentium processors are compatible with previous 486 and 386 processors but offer advanced features. The Pentium series (75 MHz and faster) provides the same basic features that the 486DX does, but with enhancements. Some of these enhancements are superscalar architecture, 64-bit data bus, and on-chip interrupt controller.

The enhancements with the Pentium and Pentium Pro processors include:

- Superscalar architecture
- Branch prediction
- 3.3v microprocessor
- 64-bit data bus

- .6 micron technology
- On-chip interrupt controller
- Pipelined floating-point unit
- Dual processor mode

One of the biggest advantages of the Pentium processor is its capacity to handle more than one process at a time. That is because of the superscalar architecture, which has two Arithmetic Logic Units (ALUs) and dual instruction pipelines.

Pentium processors also have a pre-fetch queue. While the processor is handling one instruction, it can be decoding the next instruction in the pre-fetch queue. The Pentium processor also features two different types of cache. There is an 8KB data cache and an 8KB instruction cache. Two caches are needed to support two pipelines. With this configuration, you can support two processes in one clock cycle.

Branch prediction is what allows the processor to remember the path taken for a particular process. This in turn will speed up future processes that utilize the same path. Also, the Pentium processor supports 256-bit internal bursting to the instruction cache. This means that data can be transmitted in larger blocks, resulting in higher transfer rates.

Another feature that is new to the Pentium and newer processors is the capacity to have multiple processors on board. The Advanced Programmable Interrupt Controller allows up to 60 microprocessors. (You will never see a board with so many processors.) Another term to be familiar with is dual processor mode. What this means is that two processors can use the second-level cache simultaneously.

Sizes of the Address and Data Buses

Most processors other than the Pentium processors have a processor bus equal to the size of their data bus. Pentium processors have an address bus that is 32 bits in size. To process 64-bit instructions, they use two ALUs.

Both 386 and 486 processors used a 32-bit data bus. Think of Pentium processors as using a 64-bit data bus. Figure 2-1 shows this in graphic form.

FIGURE 2-1

Data bus size comparison

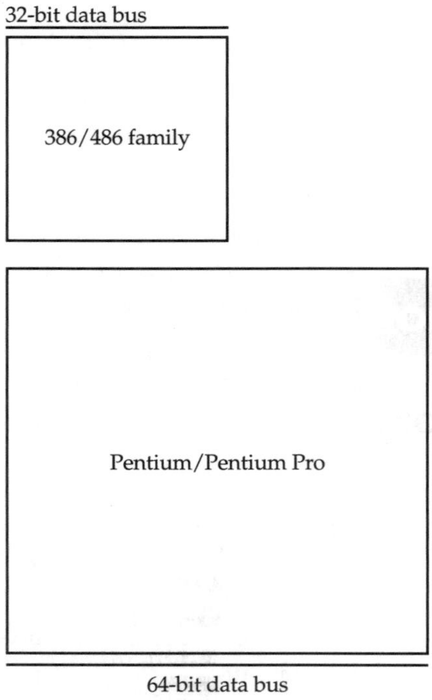

Sizes of the Caches

After the 386/20 processor came about, the need for cache was also evident to prevent wait states when memory couldn't keep up with the processor. There are two types of cache: first-level cache (L1) and second-level cache (L2). First-level is the quicker of the two and usually resides internally to the processor. It can be implemented externally and still be first-level cache. Second-level cache takes the information when there is a cache miss in the first level. Second-level cache is larger than first-level cache. This still ensures zero wait states. Second-level cache often gets to be as big as 512KB.

Compaq offers Pentium Pro processors with up to 1024KB of L2 cache. Compaq Alpha processors can go as high as 4096KB per processor.

It is common, when upgrading workstations to a higher level of onboard cache, to see a noticeable difference in performance. Be sure to take into account the amount of cache when considering types of processors.

CERTIFICATION OBJECTIVE 2.02

The Memory a Microprocessor Can Address

To understand the amount of memory that a Pentium processor can handle, we need to know what the different kinds of memory are. The first and probably the most important for this section is called Dynamic Random Access Memory (DRAM). DRAM is the main memory or RAM. Today, DRAM speeds are around 60 to 70 nanoseconds. There are three common types of DRAM: Fast Page Mode, Extended Data Out, and Burst Extended Data Out.

Other types of memory include:

- **SDRAM** Synchronous DRAM. In SDRAM, memory is divided into two banks, which can be accessed independently.
- **SRAM** Static Random Access Memory. This memory type is extremely fast—usually 5–25 nanoseconds. This memory is used exclusively in cache memory.
- **EPROM** Erasable Programmable Read-Only Memory. This is a subset of the ROMs on the system board, which are erasable by ultraviolet light or electronically.
- **EEPROM** Electronically Erasable Programmable Read-Only Memory. This is the same as EPROM.

- **CMOS** Complementary Metal Oxide Semiconductor. This is a volatile memory, which uses very low power. The main system configuration is kept here.
- **ROM** Read-Only Memory. ROM is used to store boot code and POST processes. It resides in I/O boards.

Be sure to match speeds with memory, or you can run into conflicts and problems with the system in which you have installed it. Some systems will still boot but you will see serious errors. Other systems do not even boot up when the memory is an issue. There are also systems that will sound a post beep sequence to alert the user to an error.

CERTIFICATION OBJECTIVE 2.03

First-Level Cache on a Pentium Microprocessor

To get the best performance, the memory reads must take place in the first-level cache most of the time. Table 2-1 shows the different sizes of first-level cache.

TABLE 2-1

First-Level Cache Sizes

Processor Type	First-Level Cache
Pentium	32KB
Pentium II	32KB
Pentium II Xeon	32KB
Pentium III	64KB
Pentium III Xeon	64KB

FROM THE FIELD

Processor Termination Cards

When installing Pentium II and Pentium III processors in a multiprocessor machine, each end of the AGLT+ bus must be terminated. The installation of a processor obviously terminates one end, but if you have only installed one processor in a machine that can hold two, you are required to insert a termination card into the unused slot.

While this requirement is obvious when a new machine is shipped, if you remove a Pentium II or Pentium III processor from a machine running two processors, you also will be required to reinstall the termination card.

When a new machine is shipped, these termination cards are usually installed. Before placing the machine into production, it is a good idea to label this card and set it aside for future use if you should need to revert temporarily to a single-processor configuration.

—*Thomas E. Eck,*
MCSE+I, MCSD, ASE, CCA, CNA

CERTIFICATION OBJECTIVE 2.04

Instruction Pipelining

Pipelining is a process in which multiple instructions are overlapped so many processes can be handled at once. There is a five-stage pipeline used by the Pentium processor. The five stages are as follows:

1. Pre-fetch.
2. Decoding of the instruction.

3. Generation of memory address, if instruction includes a memory reference.
4. Execution of the instruction.
5. Results are stored or "written back."

Under normal and ideal conditions, each of these would only require one cycle. Pipelining allows more than one instruction to be handled simultaneously.

CERTIFICATION SUMMARY

The Pentium line of microprocessors offers enhancements over the 486 and 386 processors, including superscalar architecture, 64-bit data bus, and on-chip interrupt controller. One of the biggest advantages of the Pentium processor is that it handles more than one process at a time.

Pentium processors have a pre-fetch queue. Branch prediction allows the processor to remember the path taken for a particular process. Another new feature of the Pentium is the capacity to have more than one processor on board.

Pentium processors access a 64-bit data bus. 386 and 486 processors use a 32-bit data bus. Pentium processors have an address bus that is only 32 bits in size, so they use two ALUs. The first- and second-level cache improve performance by keeping wait states near zero.

Instruction pipelining overlaps many instructions, to allow more instructions to be handled at once. There are five stages to the pipeline: pre-fetch, decoding of the instruction, generation of memory address (if instruction includes a memory reference), execution of the instruction, and storing or "writing back" the result.

TWO-MINUTE DRILL

- The enhancements with the Pentium and Pentium Pro processors include:
  - Superscalar architecture
  - Branch prediction
  - 3.3v microprocessor
  - 64-bit data bus
  - .6 micron technology
  - On-chip interrupt controller
  - Pipelined floating-point unit
  - Dual processor mode
- The superscalar architecture of the Pentium processor, which has two Arithmetic Logic Units (ALUs) and dual instruction pipelines provides the capacity to handle more than one process at a time.
- Pentium processors also have a pre-fetch queue.
- The Advanced Programmable Interrupt Controller allows up to 60 microprocessors.
- Dual processor mode means that two processors can use the second-level cache simultaneously.
- Pentium processors have an address bus that is 32 bits in size.
- Compaq offers Pentium Pro processors with up to 1024KB of L2 cache. Compaq Alpha processors can go as high as 4096KB per processor.
- Be sure to take into account the amount of cache when considering types of processors.
- There are three common types of DRAM: Fast Page Mode, Extended Data Out, and Burst Extended Data Out.

- Other types of memory include:
  - SDRAM
  - SRAM
  - EPROM
  - EEPROM
  - CMOS
  - ROM
- Be sure to match speeds with memory, or you can run into conflicts and problems with the system in which you have installed it.
- To get the best performance, the memory reads must take place in the first-level cache most of the time.
- Pipelining is a process in which multiple instructions are overlapped so many processes can be handled at once.
- The five-stage pipeline used by the Pentium processor is:
  1. Pre-fetch.
  2. Decoding of the instruction.
  3. Generation of memory address, if instruction includes a memory reference.
  4. Execution of the instruction.
  5. Results are stored or "written back."

SELF TEST

The following Self Test questions will help you measure your understanding of the material presented in this chapter. Read all the choices carefully, as there may be more than one correct answer. Choose all correct answers for each question.

1. Which of the following is not an enhancement with the Pentium line of processors?
   - A. Superscalar architecture
   - B. Branch prediction
   - C. 3.4v microprocessor
   - D. 64-bit data bus
2. How many Arithemetic Logic Units does a Pentium processor have?
   - A. One
   - B. Two
   - C. Three
   - D. Four
3. When the Pentium processor is decoding one instruction, where does it decode the next instruction?
   - A. RAM
   - B. On the hard disk
   - C. In the pre-fetch queue
   - D. In the post-fetch queue
4. What are the three common types of memory?
   - A. Fast Page Mode
   - B. Extended Data Out
   - C. Extra Data Out
   - D. Burst Extended Data Out
5. How many stages are there to a pipeline with a Pentium processor?
   - A. Four
   - B. Three
   - C. Five
   - D. Six
6. Which of the following is not one of the five stages in pipelining?
   - A. Pre-fetch
   - B. Decoding the instruction
   - C. Execution of the instruction
   - D. Generation of data address
7. What helps the processor remember the path taken for a particular process?
   - A. Pre-fetch queue
   - B. RAM
   - C. Branch prediction
   - D. Write-back cache
8. What does CMOS stand for?
   - A. Complementary Metal Oxide Conductor
   - B. Company Middle Oxidation Centralization
   - C. Complementary Metal Oxide Semiconductor
   - D. Coprocessor Metal Oxide Semiconductor

9. What does EPROM stand for?
   - A. Erasable Programmable Read-Only Memory
   - B. Electronic Programmable Read-Only Memory
   - C. Erasable Primary Read-Only Memory
   - D. Erasable Programmable Right-Only Memory

10. Which of the following is an enhancement of the Pentium series of processor?
    - A. Superscalar architecture
    - B. 32-bit data bus; no 64-bit compatibility
    - C. Off-chip interrupt controller
    - D. Branch prediction

11. What are the two different types of cache on a Pentium processor?
    - A. A 16KB data cache and a 16KB instruction cache
    - B. An 8KB data cache and an 8KB instruction cache
    - C. A 1MB data cache and a 1MB instruction cache
    - D. A 4MB data cache and a 4MB instruction cache

12. What allows for the capacity to have two or more processors? (Select two.)
    - A. Advanced Programmable Interrupt Controller
    - B. Single processor mode
    - C. Dual processor mode
    - D. Advanced Programmable Integer Counter

13. What does DRAM stand for?
    - A. Dual Rail Access Memory
    - B. Double Random Access Memory
    - C. Dynamic Random Access Memory
    - D. Dynamic Role Access Memory

14. What is the most common memory speed in today's computers?
    - A. 50 nanoseconds
    - B. 75 nanoseconds
    - C. 60 nanoseconds
    - D. 120 nanoseconds

15. How many instructions can be handled per clock cycle?
    - A. Seven
    - B. Two
    - C. One
    - D. Zero

3

Memory Subsystem

CERTIFICATION OBJECTIVES

3.01 Implementing Memory Devices in the Various Subsystems of a Server

3.02 DRAM and SRAM

3.03 Types of DRAM

3.04 SIMMs and DIMMs

3.05 Types of Error Detection and Correction in Compaq Servers

3.06 Features of Error Detecting and Correcting Techniques

3.07 Reporting Memory Errors on Compaq Servers

3.08 Troubleshooting Memory Errors on a Compaq Server

Memory is a computer system's primary workspace, working in tandem with the caching subsystem to store data, programs, and processed information that can be made directly accessible to the cache, and subsequently, the CPU. On a high level, memory is key to a server's operation because it forms one of the endpoints of the critical link between an application, the caching subsystem, and the CPU itself. A server's memory also determines the size and number of applications and services that can be run simultaneously, and helps to optimize the capabilities of the increasingly powerful microprocessors being introduced.

Internally, computer memory is arranged as a matrix of *memory cells* (bit cells) laid out in rows and columns, like squares on a checkerboard. Each memory cell is used to store a single bit of data, which can be instantaneously retrieved by indicating the row and column location (or address) of the data. Because these bits of data can be individually accessed, retrieved, and modified at random, the type of main memory used in computers is called Random Access Memory (RAM).

RAM is a volatile form of memory, which means that it must have power in order to retain data. When the power is turned off, data held in RAM is lost. Contrast this to physical storage media such as magnetic media (hard disks, floppy disks, and tapes) that can retain data even without power. Despite the advantage of persistent data storage, magnetic and optical media have significantly slower access times and are not well suited to acting as part of a system's memory subsystem.

CERTIFICATION OBJECTIVE 3.01

Implementing Memory Devices in the Various Subsystems of a Server

The memory subsystem on Compaq servers is organized into banks. The size of the bank is dependent upon the width in bits of the memory subsystem known as the memory bus. This should not be confused with the width in bits of the microprocessor that is controlling the system. Usually they are equal, but there are a few situations when this may not be the case. To use a simple example, imagine you had an eight-bit processor with an eight-bit memory subsystem containing eight one-megabyte chips. When the processor needs to read any data, the address it generates isn't going to be a single bit. Rather, it will be eight bits (one byte), read one bit at a time from each of the eight chips in the bank.

This concept can be carried over into to a more modern example of a 64-bit Pentium processor. A bank of memory in the memory subsystem must equal the number of data lines from the CPU—in other words, 64 bits. This way, when the 64-bit wide bank of memory is addressed, eight bytes will be delivered or received. From this concept, we can see why there are differences in the number of memory modules required for each class of processor.

CERTIFICATION OBJECTIVE 3.02

DRAM and SRAM

There are two main types of RAM, Dynamic RAM (DRAM) and Static RAM (SRAM). DRAM must be continually rewritten in order for it to maintain its data. This is done by placing the memory on a refresh circuit that rewrites the data several hundred times per second. DRAM is used for most system memory because it is cheap and small.

Static RAM, on the other hand, will maintain its data as long as power is provided to the memory chips, and does not need to be rewritten periodically. SRAM is very fast but much more expensive than DRAM, and is often used as cache memory due to its speed.

DRAM Features

Dynamic RAM is a type of memory that can only hold its data if it is continuously accessed by a refresh circuit. Hundreds of times each second, the contents of each memory cell is read by the refresh circuit, regardless of whether the memory cell is being used by the computer at that time. Because of the design and construction of the cells, it is the reading action itself that refreshes the contents of the memory. In DRAM memory, if this does not happen regularly, the memory loses its contents, even if power is continuously supplied to it. This refreshing action is the very reason the memory is called dynamic. DRAM is what is typically found in personal computers for the system's main memory.

The other theoretical option is SRAM. At first glance, it might seem like a logical choice to use SRAM as the main memory subsystem, since DRAM chips are actually slower than SRAM ones, and they require the overhead of the refresh circuit. If you were to design a system, it would make sense not to want the computer's memory to be made out of something that can only hold a value for a small fraction of a second. Furthermore, if you really dig into the design of DRAM, the DRAM architecture is more complicated and slower than the SRAM architecture.

Despite all of these factors, there are very simple reasons why DRAM chips are the preferred choice—they are quite a bit cheaper and are physically smaller. In fact, DRAM chips typically take up only about 1/4 the silicon area of SRAM. If you were to build a 64MB chip of base memory from SRAM, it would be very expensive, large, and would add complexity to the thermal characteristics of the system design.

Hardware engineers at Compaq choose to withstand the overhead of the refresh circuit in order to allow the use of larger amounts of the more inexpensive and smaller form factor memory. While the refresh circuit would at first seem to be problematic, the many years of DRAM development have improved the design.

The reason DRAM is smaller and cheaper than SRAM is that DRAM uses only one transistor and one capacitor. This capacitor, when supplied current, will hold an electrical charge if the bit being stored contains a 1, or it will hold no charge if the bit being stored contains a 0. The transistor is then used to read the charge of the capacitor. One drawback to using capacitors is the refresh cycle. Capacitors only hold a charge for a short period of time. The capacitors used in memory are very small and are designed so that their charges will disappear fairly quickly. The refreshing of the chip is performed by reading every row in the chip, one at a time. When the read is performed, it is destructive by nature, thus yielding the term *destructive read.* Just by reading the data bit, the original bit value is destroyed at the intersection of the row and column. The process of reading the contents of each capacitor reestablishes the charge, and thus the original value.

DRAM chips are manufactured using a method that is very similar to how processors are created. First, a silicon substrate is etched with the patterns that make up the transistors, capacitors, and support structures for each bit. You may now be thinking, "If they are so similarly made, why do processors cost so much more than memory?" The reason DRAM is so much less expensive than a processor is because it is simply the repetition of these simple structures. There isn't the same complexity involved in memory manufacturing as there is in making a single chip with several million individually located transistors.

As stated earlier, all types of memory are arranged in an XY grid pattern of rows and columns. First, the *row address* is sent to the memory chip and latched, then the *column address* is sent in a similar fashion. This row-and-column addressing scheme (called *multiplexing*) allows a large memory address to use fewer pins. If the CPU requests information from cell 1023, the memory controller would go to row 10 and then over to column 23. Multiplexing slows access time, but it saves on pin count. To access 1MB (1,048,576) memory locations using a multiplexing scheme, where each address line is used twice, requires only 10 lines (plus one extra control signal). Without multiplexing, 20 address lines would be required.

To read a memory cell, we place a row address on the *address bus* lines (all the address lines together are called an address bus) and activate the Row Access Select (RAS) line. Upon completion of this task, the subsystem waits for 15ns while the holding circuitry latches the row address. We then place a column address on the address bus and activate the Column Access Select (CAS) line. Now, we have to wait for the level-checking circuitry to determine if the location contains a 0 or a 1. This information appears as a high or low voltage on the data output pin.

You will often see DRAM memory listed as running at specific speed, such as 70ns. This is somewhat misleading. A specific memory location can be found within the promised 70ns, but it must then wait for 70ns, so the total access cycle is 140ns. This allows the internal circuitry to refresh the memory in all locations addressed by the row address and to do other internal housekeeping.

When you access memory with a read or write (or just to refresh), all column locations within the row address are refreshed. This is very important to remember because during refresh, a lot of power is consumed in a very short time. This power can be measured as the voltage multiplied by the current. Peak power demands for the refresh cycle are often extreme. A poorly designed or failing power supply can cause the voltage to sag and memory locations will not refresh completely.

SRAM Features

Static RAM is a type of RAM that holds its contents without the need for the additional refresh circuit. In fact, SRAM will hold its data for as long as there is power running to the circuit. SRAM chips are used where speed is more important than cost and size, such as in the caching subsystem. Unfortunately, to design a ProLiant 6000 with 512MB of SRAM would be prohibitively expensive in terms of monetary, thermal, and physical size. Instead, a more suitable application for SRAM is in Level 1 (L1) and Level 2 (L2) cache memory. It is used here because the cache memory needs to be extremely fast to service the memory subsystem effectively. In such small amounts, it will not be physically large or prohibitively costly.

SRAM is composed of transistors—up to four per bit cell. This is the primary reason they consume so much power and why they run so much hotter. The bit (0 or 1) is stored by a sort of latch in the transistor that will flip-flop to represent a 0 or 1. Another item to remember about SRAM is that reads are nondestructive by nature, unlike DRAM. See Chapter 4 on Caching Subsystems to learn more about the implementation of SRAM in Compaq hardware.

CERTIFICATION OBJECTIVE 3.03

Types of DRAM

Architecturally speaking, there are several different types of DRAM. However, when you investigate the underlying functionality, you will find that all these memory types are actually quite similar. They differ mostly in the ways that they are organized and in the methods in which they are accessed. As newer and faster processors are released, memory needs to run increasingly faster and more efficiently. Hardware designers have been continuously introducing faster memory architectures, resulting in a significant overall increase in the speed of the memory subsystem found in current hardware designs. When it comes right down to it, the differences between the various DRAM technologies are really not that great. The reason is that many requests for data by the processor are actually satisfied from either the primary or secondary cache, which results in the masking of many of the improvements in DRAM efficiency. Also, memory is just one piece of the puzzle in overall server performance. Depending upon the amount of memory you are comparing, *more* system memory is often more important to bolstering overall system performance than *better* system memory.

While several varieties of DRAM exist on the market today, the real differences between the various DRAM technologies are primarily a result of how the DRAM inside the module is connected, configured, and addressed. There may also be some differences resulting from special enhancement circuits that may have been added to the module. For example, some of the more cutting-edge memory modules actually include a mini SRAM cache implemented directly in the DRAM module to improve performance.

Typical DRAM—the kind that has been used in PCs for quite some time—is said to be *asynchronous.* This means that the memory is not synchronized to the system clock. When a memory access is made, a certain period of time elapses before the memory value appears on the bus. The speed of the signal is not coordinated with the system clock at all. The asynchronous approach to memory access works well in lower-speed memory bus systems, but it is definitely not acceptable for use in high-speed (greater than 66 MHz) memory systems.

There is another type of DRAM called Synchronous DRAM (SDRAM). SDRAM's timing is synchronized to the system clock. By tying all signals to the system clock, the timing itself is much tighter and better controlled. SDRAM is much faster than asynchronous DRAM and can be used to improve the performance of the system.

Conventional DRAM

Conventional DRAM refers to the original implementation of DRAM memory, and it is the slowest of the DRAM methods. It uses a memory addressing method in which the first row address is sent to the memory followed by the column address. It is the most basic type of memory available and doesn't require anything special for compatibility. This type of DRAM, especially for servers, is now obsolete and is being replaced by fast page mode memory and other newer, faster memory technologies.

FPM

Fast Page Mode (FPM) memory is not significantly faster than conventional DRAM. While standard DRAM requires that a row and column be sent for each individual access, FPM works by only sending the row address once for multiple accesses to memory locations that are near each other. This results in an improvement in access time. FPM memory is an improved version of its predecessor, Page Mode memory, which is rarely found in modern system configurations. Despite its name, Fast Page Mode is actually the slowest memory technology still in use today. Most machines made in the last several years that have been designed to use conventional asynchronous RAM will support FPM. As with conventional DRAM, FPM doesn't require anything special for compatibility or support. The result, however, offers slower performance than most other memory technologies. It is also not suitable for high-speed memory buses over 66 MHz, because excessive numbers of wait states would have to be added. FPM DRAM typically allows burst system timings as fast as 5-3-3-3 at 66 MHz.

EDO

Of all the asynchronous DRAM technologies used, Extended Data Out (EDO) is the most common. EDO memory is often referred to as *hyper page mode* DRAM. EDO is faster than FPM memory because of the memory access design. Unlike conventional RAM, which performs memory accesses in succession, EDO memory has its timing circuits modified such that one access to memory can begin before the last one has finished. Therefore, EDO memory is slightly faster than FPM memory, resulting in a performance boost of 3–5 percent over FPM in most systems. Both vendors and the trade magazines have hyped EDO memory, but in real-world performance measurements, it offers a minimal increase in speed over FPM memory.

EDO is now being replaced by SDRAM as the technology of choice for both high-speed servers and desktop platforms. EDO memory is still not usually suitable for high-speed (75 MHz and higher) memory buses, since the architectural differences between EDO and FPM memory is negligible. EDO typically will have burst timings as fast as 5-2-2-2 at 66 MHz, but only when using a chipset optimized for use with EDO memory. EDO can possibly run on faster buses, but the memory timing may have to be reduced, potentially reducing the overall performance of the memory subsystem.

BEDO

Burst EDO memory (BEDO) is yet another improvement to emerge from conventional asynchronous RAM. With BEDO memory, pipelining technology and special latches are used to allow much quicker access times over standard EDO. BEDO memory will operate with much higher memory bus speeds compared to EDO. In fact, when used with a supporting chipset, BEDO will support system timings of 5-1-1-1.

From a manufacturing perspective, BEDO is desirable because it allows for a significant improvement in DRAM performance with minimal increases in production costs. To put the speed increase in perspective with the topics covered earlier, BEDO provides a greater improvement over EDO than EDO does over FPM. Despite this fact, BEDO has never really caught on and remains a standard with very little support from the manufacturing community. In terms of performance, BEDO competes with SDRAM, but SDRAM is the dominant leader in the marketplace. The most significant reason that BEDO has lost out to SDRAM is that BEDO is not supported by the Intel chipset, while SDRAM is. Obviously, chipset support is crucial for memory technologies to gain acceptance. Considering Intel's significant market share, it is really no wonder BEDO has not gained greater acceptance in the marketplace.

Synchronous DRAM (SDRAM)

Synchronous DRAM is a relatively new technology that differs from earlier types of memory architectures in that it does not run asynchronously to the system clock. SDRAM memory is tied directly to the system clock and is designed to be able to read or write from memory in burst mode. With zero wait states, burst mode occurs, after the initial read or write latency, at one clock cycle per access. This can occur with memory bus speeds of 100 MHz and higher. When used alongside a supporting chipset, SDRAM can run at a 5-1-1-1 system timing. SDRAM achieves this faster access time because of a number of design improvements, including *internal interleaving.* Just as in EDO, half the module is allowed to begin an access, while the other half is finishing an access.

SDRAM is quickly becoming the memory standard for both servers and desktop PCs. The reason for this is its synchronized design, which will support the higher bus speeds being introduced for the faster processors. SDRAM doesn't offer that much of an observable performance increase over EDO in many systems, because the system cache masks much of the difference. Another factor that disguises the speed increase is the fact that many systems are running on relatively slow 66-MHz system buses. Now that most Pentium II and Pentium III systems use a 100-MHz bus, SDRAM will quickly replace older technologies, since it is one of the few architectures designed to work at these higher operating speeds.

When you see descriptions of SDRAM modules, you usually see its speed rated in two ways. First, there is a nanosecond rating, just like conventional asynchronous DRAM. Second, there is a MHz rating such as 83 MHz or 100 MHz. Because SDRAM modules are synchronous, it is essential that they be fast enough for the system in which they are being used. With asynchronous DRAM memory such as EDO or FPM, it is a common practice to add extra wait states to the access timing in order to compensate for the slower memory. One of the benefits of SDRAM, however, is that because of its high speed, you are able to run with zero wait states. One frequent misconception regarding the nanosecond/MHz rating ratio is to assume that the reciprocal of the nanosecond rating can run at that speed. For instance, it would be natural to think that if the module is rated for 10ns, it would be able to run at 100 MHz. While this may work in theory, in practice this is not a desirable configuration; such small tolerances would leave the system with little room for comfort. In the real world, you actually want memory that is rated slightly higher than the speed that is absolutely required. This being the case, the 10ns modules should really only be used for systems of up to 83-MHz bus speed operation.

Systems that are built at 100 MHz require faster memory, which is why the *PC100* specification was developed. Intel created a formal specification for SDRAM capable of being used in these higher-speed systems, dubbed PC100. PC100 modules are generally rated at 8ns, and there are several internal timing pieces that have to be included in order to have a module certified as PC100 compliant.

One thing to remember is that SDRAM is still a DRAM-based technology, and therefore will continue to have some form of latency. When you see a reference to a module running at eight nanoseconds, remember that is only referring to the second, third, and fourth accesses in a four-access burst. The first access is still relatively slow at five cycles, which is exactly like conventional EDO and FPM memory.

You will find two basic variations in the composition of SDRAM modules: *2-clock* and *4-clock*. They use the same DRAM chips, but differ in access method and layout. The 2-clock variation is structured so that each clock signal controls two different DRAM chips on the module, whereas a 4-clock SDRAM has clock signals such that each has the capability to control four different DRAM chips. The more common variation is the 4-clock type.

One of the most common Compaq ProLiant models you will encounter is the 3000 series. The ProLiant 3000 comes standard with one 128MB DIMM that occupies one of the eight DIMM sockets on the memory board. The memory can be expanded to a maximum of 4GB.

CERTIFICATION OBJECTIVE 3.04

SIMMs and DIMMs

The majority of memory modules you will run across will come in one of two formats, SIMMs and DIMMs. The Single Inline Memory Module (SIMM) is the most common memory module format around. SIMMs are available in two varieties, 30-pin and 72-pin. 30-pin SIMMs were one of the first types manufactured and were popular during the time of the third- and fourth-generation motherboards. 72-pin SIMMs can be found in fourth-, fifth- and sixth-generation PC designs.

The Dual Inline Memory Module (DIMM) is a larger module with 168 pins, and is 64 bits in width. DIMMS are of a different form factor and are the de facto standard for modern day servers. Since DIMMs are a newer form factor than SIMMs, you will not find them in smaller sizes such as 1MB or 4MB, simply because newer machines are never configured with such a small amount of system RAM.

SIMM

SIMMs are mounted on motherboards in specially designed sockets, engineered in such a way so as to ensure that once the memory module is inserted, it will be held in place tightly. SIMMs are typically inserted into their sockets at a 60 degree angle and are then tilted upward until they are perpendicular to the motherboard. There are small, metal clips on each side of the socket that will help snap the SIMM in place, and the SIMM is also keyed with a notch on one side to prevent someone from inserting it backwards.

Most 30-pin SIMMs you will find will range in size from 1 to 16MB. Each 30-pin module has 30 pins and provides one byte of data (eight bits). In parity modules there is one additional bit. 72-pin SIMMs provide four bytes of data at a time (32 bits) plus an optional four bits for parity/ECC in parity/ECC versions.

Apart from the pin differences, SIMMs are available in two different styles: *single-sided* and *double-sided.* These terms are a reference to whether or not DRAM chips are found on both sides of the SIMM. All 30-pin SIMMs are single-sided. 72-pin SIMMs can be either single-sided or double-sided. Some double-sided SIMMs are constructed as *composite SIMMs.* What this means is that internally, they are wired as if they were actually two single-sided SIMMs back to back. This doesn't change how many bits of data the module can address, nor how many you are required to use. There are some motherboards that cannot handle composite SIMMs, because they are different in terms of their electrical requirements.

72-pin SIMMs that are 1MB, 4MB, and 16MB in size are normally single-sided, while those 2MB, 8MB, and 32MB in size are generally double-sided. This is why there are so many motherboards that will only work with 1MB, 4MB, and 16MB SIMMs. You should always check your motherboard to see what sizes of SIMMs it supports. Composite SIMMs will not work in a motherboard that does not support them. SIMMs that are constructed with 32 chips are almost always composite.

DIMM

If you have ever installed DIMMs, you know they are a little sensitive in terms of the way they need to be inserted. SIMMs have contacts on both sides of the circuit board. A 72-pin SIMM has 72 contacts on each side of the circuit board, but each pair is connected. This yields some fault tolerance and allows for more forgiving connections, given that each pin has two sides. A DIMM, on the other hand, has different connections on each side of the circuit board. This means that a 168-pin DIMM has 83 pads on each side, and they are therefore not redundant. This allows the DIMM to be constructed in a smaller footprint than a SIMM of the same width would be, but makes DIMMs a bit more sensitive to correct insertion and good contact.

DIMMs are inserted into special sockets on the motherboard, which are very similar to those used for SIMMs. The DIMM design is the memory format of choice for the newest memory technologies such as SDRAM, and is found in almost all servers and workstations produced by Compaq today.

You will find DIMMs offered in several different varieties, and you need to make sure you know the differences when it comes time to add memory. They are available in two different voltages, 3.3V and 5.0V, and they can be either buffered or unbuffered. These varieties produce a total of four different combinations, but the most common type today in low-end Compaq servers is the 3.3-volt, unbuffered DIMM

FROM THE CLASSROOM

Proper Memory Modules

With the myriad of options for upgrading memory in Compaq servers and workstations, it is very easy to reduce the availability of system resources by selecting an improper memory module. To find the correct module for any current production Compaq server product, navigate to http://www.compaq.com/products/servers/options/memory/selector.html.

From this site, you can find the proper memory modules for each model of current production Compaq servers, find the Compaq model number for each module, and even purchase the memory from Compaq Direct.

If you need to upgrade the memory in a Compaq desktop, you can navigate to http://www.compaq.com/products/desktops/deskpro_opt_memory.html to view model numbers and compatibility charts for various Compaq desktops.

If your enterprise elects to use non-Compaq memory modules, or needs to find the part numbers to upgrade legacy hardware, you can navigate to http://www.vikingcomponents.com to find the equivalent memory product for any Compaq server, workstation, desktop, or laptop. This site also features a cross-reference database to find the Viking Components memory module based on the entry of a Compaq part number.

—Thomas E. Eck, MCSE+I, MCSD, ASE, CCA, CNA

CERTIFICATION OBJECTIVE 3.05

Types of Error Detection and Correction in Compaq Servers

Because memory is an electronic storage device, it has the potential to return information that is different from what was originally stored. Certain technologies are more likely to do this than others. Because of how it is made, DRAM is likely to return errors occasionally. DRAM chips store information as a charge in small capacitors that must be continually refreshed to ensure that the data is not lost. This method of data storage is much less reliable than the static, flip-flop storage method used by SRAM.

Since every bit of memory is either a 1 or a 0, this helps to eliminate many errors, because slightly distorted values are usually recoverable. To best illustrate this scenario, consider that in a 5-volt system, a 1 is +5V and a 0 is 0V. If the memory that is read in is found to be +4.3V, the system can decipher that this is most likely a 1, even though the value doesn't quite hit +5V. The reason for this is that the only other choice would be a 0 and 4.3 is much closer to 5 than to 0. There is the possibility that occasionally a +5V might be read as +1.9V, and it would then be considered a 0 instead of a 1. When a situation such as this happens, a memory error has occurred.

There are two types of errors that can occur in a memory subsystem. The first kind is called a *repeatable* or *hard* error. In a hard error, a physical piece of hardware is broken and will continually return incorrect information. For instance, a bit may be stuck in a capacitor so that it always returns a 0, no matter what is written to it. Hard errors are often the result of loose memory modules, damaged chips, or other physical problems. Although memory errors are never good, a hard error is preferable to a soft error, as it is relatively easy to diagnose and correct. Hard errors are usually consistent and repeatable.

The second type of error is called a *transient* or *soft* error. This type of memory error occurs when a bit is read back with the wrong value once, but subsequent reads function correctly. Obviously, this type of problem is much more difficult to diagnose. Unfortunately, it is also the more common type. A soft error will usually repeat itself, but it can take anywhere from seconds to years for this to happen. Soft errors are sometimes caused by memory that is physically bad, but more often than not, they are the result of bad motherboards, memory system timings that are set too fast, static shocks, or other problems that are not necessarily directly related to the memory subsystem. In addition, stray radioactivity that is naturally present in materials used in PC systems can cause the occasional soft error. Often, what are called operating system bugs or random glitches are transient errors that occur on systems not implementing any type of error correction.

DRAM chips that are used today are far more reliable than those of five to ten years ago. Unfortunately, because of this, many server vendors have dropped error-detection support from their entry-level systems. Even with the reliability of today's memory, the problems stemming from the lack of error detection in system hardware have intensified. One reason is that more memory is being used. Many years ago, the typical server had 16MB; it is not uncommon to find 1GB of memory in application servers today. Add to this the fact that servers today have much higher clock speeds than they used to, with typical memory buses running three to ten times the speed of their predecessors, and the need for error detection and correction becomes even more pronounced.

As IT professionals, we have to accept the fact that memory errors are going to occur. How much damage results depends on when the errors happen and what they are. If a server experiences an error in the video memory, such that the color of a pixel on the screen is inverted from a one to a zero, it obviously won't cause a major system outage. However, if the server is running a CHKDSK on its hard disk, and the memory location containing information to be written to the hard disk is corrupted, it's obviously a different story.

The only true protection from memory errors is to use some sort of memory detection or correction protocol. Some protocols can only detect errors in one bit of an eight-bit data byte; others can detect errors in more than one bit automatically. Others can both detect and seamlessly correct memory problems.

CERTIFICATION OBJECTIVE 3.06

Features of Error Detecting and Correcting Techniques

Most memory modules encountered in practice are going to be either nonparity or parity. There are some, however, that are available as dedicated, ECC-only modules. Nonparity is also called *regular* memory; it has one bit of storage for each bit of data. Parity memory has not only the one bit of storage for each bit of data; it also has an extra bit of storage for every eight bits of data. This extra bit is used to store information about the data that the system can later use for error detection or correction. This method can be used in parity or ECC mode. A newer type of technology, ECC modules, also include extra bits of information, but they can only be used in ECC mode.

Parity memory will typically work in a nonparity system, only because the extra parity bits can be ignored. However, nonparity memory will not work in a parity system unless the BIOS can support disabling parity-checking functionality. If you attempt to use nonparity memory in a parity system without such support, a parity error will be generated as soon as the system boots up.

Parity checking provides single-bit error detection for the system memory, but does not handle multiple-bit errors, and it provides no method to correct the errors. For this reason, an advanced error detection and correction protocol was developed, which takes error detection a step beyond simple parity checking. The method is called Error Correcting Circuit (ECC). This method not only detects both a single-bit and a multiple-bit error; it will actually correct single-bit errors transparently. Just like parity checking, ECC requires a setting in the BIOS program to be enabled.

ECC memory uses a special algorithm to encode information into a block of bits containing enough information to permit the recovery of a single bit error in the protected data. Unlike parity memory, which uses a single bit to provide protection to eight bits, ECC uses a larger grouping of seven bits to protect 64 bits. It would seem that special ECC memory modules must be designed specifically for use in ECC mode, but most modern machines that support ECC will also function in ECC mode using standard parity memory modules. Since parity memory includes one extra bit for every eight bits of data, 64 bits worth of parity memory is 72 bits wide, yielding the required overhead to allow ECC. In fact, parity SIMMs are 36 bits wide (two are used in a fifth- or sixth-generation system) and parity DIMMs are 72 bits, as opposed to the 32 bits and 64 bits found in the respective nonparity versions. In order to use ECC, the system requires a chipset supporting ECC. When this chipset is present and ECC mode is enabled in the BIOS, ECC will function using ordinary parity memory modules; and in fact this is the standard way that most motherboards that support ECC operate. The chipset basically "groups" the parity bits together into the seven-bit block needed for ECC.

CERTIFICATION OBJECTIVE 3.07

Reporting Memory Errors on Compaq Servers

There is no doubt that the subsystem implemented in Compaq servers is extremely reliable and well designed. The memory modules in Compaq workstations and servers undergo a very thorough and extensive qualification process to ensure each module's compliance to the specifications mandated by Compaq engineers. Compaq also includes a Pre-Failure warranty on all servers, which will allow customers the option to replace a SIMM that encounters even one soft error.

No matter how well a memory subsystem is designed, memory errors are still going to occur. This is why the aforementioned technologies have been developed—to help decrease error occurrences.

One of the technologies already discussed, ECC memory, has the capability to correct a detected single-bit error within a 64-bit block of memory. When this happens, the system will continue seamlessly as if nothing had ever happened. When an error is detected and corrected, it would be useful to know this; a pattern of errors can indicate a hardware problem that needs to be addressed

ECC will detect, but not correct errors of two, three, or even four bits, in addition to detecting and correcting single-bit errors. ECC memory deals with these multi-bit errors in a similar fashion to how parity handles single-bit errors: a non-maskable interrupt (NMI) that instructs the system to shut down in order to prevent data corruption. While multi-bit errors are extremely rare in memory, they do occur. Compaq implemented this basic ECC method in their ProSignia line, as well as some of the earlier ProLiant models such as the 1500.

Compaq then developed and patented something known as Advanced ECC memory, and introduced it in the high-end ProLiant models. Advanced ECC uses a proprietary distribution logic, which uses single-bit and adjacent-bit correcting code. It utilizes something known as TriFlex architecture on a 128-bit data path with 16 check bits. This still requires nothing beyond industry standard SIMMs, yet it allows for the correction of not only any single bit error, but also any single four-bit-wide soft or hard DRAM error. Advanced ECC memory allows for the complete failure of an entire DRAM device without causing any kind of server crash or failure.

on the job

Compaq memory is extremely reliable because of the rigorous testing that takes place, and should be the only type of memory used in your servers. Compaq's manufacturing facility is ISO 9002-certified, and they only purchase memory from suppliers who meet their very stringent qualifications. This, coupled with the pre-failure warranty, Is more than enough reason to use only Compaq memory in your Compaq servers.

CERTIFICATION OBJECTIVE 3.08

Troubleshooting Memory Errors on a Compaq Server

Advanced ECC errors are logged into the Server Health Logs. The Server Health Logs store environment information in nonvolatile RAM, which can be viewed later to determine why a server crashed, and what would be the next best step to prevention or recovery. You can view the information stored in the Server Health Logs via Compaq's Insight Manager, which comes standard with all ProSignia and ProLiant servers.

Insight Manager is a utility you will learn more about later in this book, but in brief, it is a server management tool that allows in-depth monitoring and configuration management from a single application. You can view the events as they occur or look through historical data to see what fault events occurred on a given server and decide from that information what action should be taken.

Insight Manager is an invaluable tool on Compaq-specific networks. Besides the capability to manage ProSignia and ProLiant servers, Insight Manager agents are available for Compaq Professional Workstations, Deskpros, and Armada and LTE notebooks. Agents are available for a wide variety of operating systems, including NetWare, IntranetWare, Windows NT, Windows 9x, OS/2, SCO Openserver, and UnixWare.

CERTIFICATION SUMMARY

Memory is arranged as a matrix of memory cells laid out in rows and columns, like squares on a checkerboard. Each memory cell is used to store a bit of data, which can be instantaneously retrieved by indicating the row and column location (or address) of the data.

The majority of memory modules are implemented in one of two form factors: SIMMs and DIMMs. SIMMs are available in two varieties, 30-pin and 72-pin. A DIMM is larger than a SIMM and has 168 pins.

There are two main types of RAM, Dynamic RAM (DRAM) and Static RAM (SRAM). DRAM must be continually rewritten in order for it to maintain its data. This is done by placing the memory on a refresh circuit that rewrites the data several hundred times per second. DRAM is used for most system memory because it is cheaper to manufacture and physically smaller. Static RAM maintains its data as long as power is provided to the memory chips, thus eliminating the refresh cycle and destructive reads found in DRAM. While SRAM is very fast, it is much more expensive and runs hotter than DRAM. SRAM is typically used as cache memory due to its speed.

There are two types of errors that can occur in a memory subsystem. The first kind is called a repeatable or hard error. In a hard error, a physical piece of hardware (such as a memory chip) is damaged and continually returns incorrect information. The second type of error is called a transient or soft error. This type of error occurs when a bit is read back with the wrong value on a sporadic basis, making this type of error difficult to diagnose and remedy.

The two most common types of error checking in memory are parity checking and ECC. Parity checking provides single-bit error detection for the system memory, but does not handle multiple-bit errors, and provides no method to correct the errors. ECC not only detects both single-bit and a multiple-bit errors; it actually corrects single-bit errors transparently.

TWO-MINUTE DRILL

- ❑ The memory subsystem on Compaq servers is organized into banks.
- ❑ The size of the bank is dependent upon the width in bits of the memory subsystem known as the memory bus.

- ❑ There are two main types of RAM, Dynamic RAM (DRAM) and Static RAM (SRAM).
- ❑ DRAM must be continually rewritten in order for it to maintain its data.
- ❑ SRAM will maintain its data as long as power is provided to the memory chips, and does not need to be rewritten periodically.
- ❑ The refreshing action is the very reason that DRAM is called dynamic.
- ❑ DRAM chips are the preferred choice—they are quite a bit cheaper and are physically smaller.
- ❑ The reason DRAM is smaller and cheaper than SRAM is that DRAM uses only one transistor and one capacitor.
- ❑ SRAM chips are used where speed is more important than cost and size, such as in the caching subsystem.
- ❑ A more suitable application for SRAM is in Level 1 (L1) and Level 2 (L2) cache memory.
- ❑ SRAM is composed of transistors—up to four per bit cell.
- ❑ While several varieties of DRAM exist on the market today, the real differences between the various DRAM technologies are primarily a result of how the DRAM inside the module is connected, configured, and addressed.
- ❑ Typical DRAM is said to be *asynchronous*. The memory is not synchronized to the system clock.
- ❑ Conventional DRAM uses a memory addressing method in which the first row address is sent to the memory followed by the column address.
- ❑ Fast Page Mode (FPM) works by only sending the row address once for multiple accesses to memory locations that are near each other.
- ❑ Extended Data Out (EDO) memory is often referred to as *hyper page mode* DRAM. EDO is faster than FPM memory because of the memory access design.

- ❑ Burst EDO memory (BEDO) memory, pipelining technology, and special latches are used to allow much quicker access times over standard EDO.
- ❑ Synchronous DRAM memory is tied directly to the system clock and is designed to read or write from memory in burst mode.
- ❑ The Single Inline Memory Module (SIMM) is the most common memory module format around.
- ❑ The Dual Inline Memory Module (DIMM) is a larger module with 168 pins, and is 64 bits in width.
- ❑ SIMMs are mounted on motherboards in specially designed sockets, engineered in such a way so as to ensure that once the memory module is inserted, it will be held in place tightly.
- ❑ DIMMs have different connections on each side of the circuit board. This means that a 168-pin DIMM has 83 pads on each side, and they are therefore not redundant.
- ❑ DRAM is likely to return errors occasionally.
- ❑ There are two types of errors that can occur in a memory subsystem. The first kind is called a *repeatable* or *hard* error. The second type of error is called a *transient* or *soft* error.
- ❑ The only true protection from memory errors is to use some sort of memory detection or correction protocol.
- ❑ Most memory modules encountered in practice are going to be either nonparity or parity.
- ❑ Parity checking provides single-bit error detection for the system memory, but does not handle multiple-bit errors, and it provides no method to correct the errors.
- ❑ Error Correcting Circuit (ECC) not only detects both a single-bit and a multiple-bit error; it will actually correct single-bit errors transparently.
- ❑ Compaq developed and patented something known as Advanced ECC memory.
- ❑ Advanced ECC uses a proprietary distribution logic, which uses single-bit and adjacent-bit correcting code.

- The Server Health Logs store environment information in nonvolatile RAM, which can be viewed later to determine why a server crashed, and what would be the next best step to prevention or recovery.
- Insight Manager is a server management tool that allows in-depth monitoring and configuration management from a single application.

SELF TEST

The following Self Test questions will help you measure your understanding of the material presented in this chapter. Read all the choices carefully, as there may be more than one correct answer. Choose all correct answers for each question.

1. The technology behind memory storage would best be described as
   A. Individual cylinders, eight bits deep, arranged in 32 rows
   B. A three-dimensional cube
   C. A matrix of rows and columns
   D. All of the above
2. Which type of memory requires constant refreshing in order to keep its contents?
   A. DRAM
   B. SRAM
   C. Both A and B
   D. Neither A nor B
3. A DRAM chip is composed of
   A. Multiple transistors and no capacitors
   B. Eight capacitors and one transistor
   C. Multiple concurrent capacitors
   D. One transistor and one capacitor
4. Which type of memory is transistor based and does not multiplex (and reads are not destructive)?
   A. DRAM
   B. SRAM
   C. Both A and B
   D. Neither A nor B
5. When memory is not "in step" with the system clock, what is it called?
   A. Defective memory
   B. Congruous
   C. Synchronous
   D. Asynchronous
6. What is the correct order of memory technologies in terms of performance, going from the slowest type to the fastest?
   A. EDO, BEDO, FPM
   B. SDRAM, FPM, EDO
   C. FPM, EDO, SDRAM
   D. EDO, FPM, SDRAM
7. The speed of SDRAM is measured by what two criteria?
   A. MHz and nanoseconds
   B. Nanoseconds and KHz
   C. MHz and KHz
   D. MHz and milliseconds
8. A DIMM is how many pins wide?
   A. 30
   B. 72
   C. 144
   D. 168

9. A parity SIMM will have how many extra bits over conventional memory?
   A. Four
   B. One
   C. Two
   D. Nine
10. If part of a SIMM has been damaged, what kind of error would this be?
   A. Transient
   B. Hard
   C. Dormant
   D. Soft
11. ECC memory uses how many extra bits to protect how many regular bits?
   A. Seven extra for 64 regular
   B. One extra for eight regular
   C. Four extra for 32 regular
   D. Nine extra for eight regular
12. What utility is provided with Compaq ProSignia and ProLiant servers for monitoring a server's health and for viewing historical hardware faults (such as memory errors)?
   A. SmartStart
   B. Event Manager
   C. Insight Manager
   D. Baseline Diagnostics
13. The arrangement of memory addressing in rows and columns is called:
   A. Muxing
   B. Spreadsheet Addressing
   C. Tabular Access
   D. Multiplexing
14. The composition of SDRAM modules can be found in which of the following two formats?
   A. 2-clock and 4-clock
   B. 1-clock and 8-clock
   C. 2-bit and 4-clock
   D. 1-bit and 8-clock
15. Which of the following statements could you assume was true if you had a 72-pin 16MB SIMM?
   A. It is single-sided.
   B. It is double-sided.
   C. It really only has 30 pins.
   D. It really only has 36 pins.

ASE

ACCREDITED SYSTEMS ENGINEER

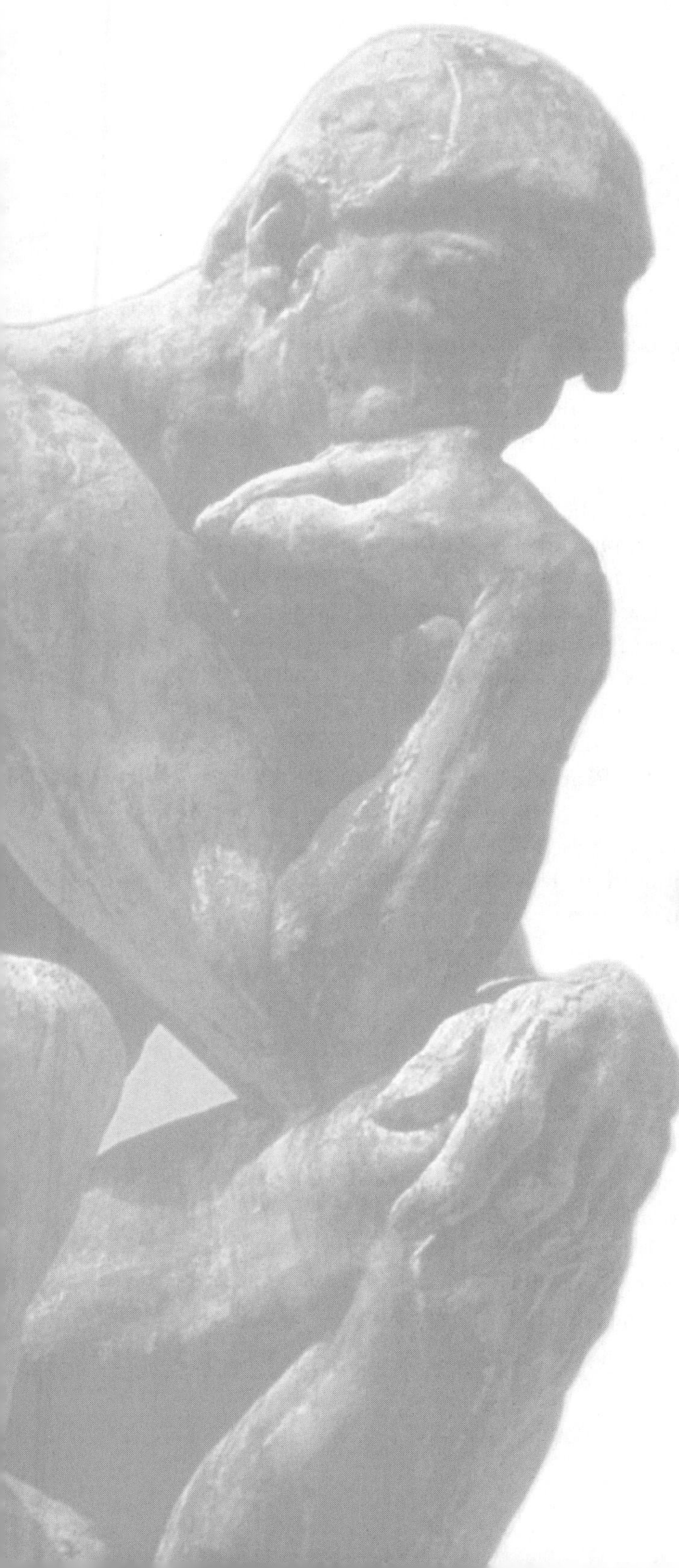

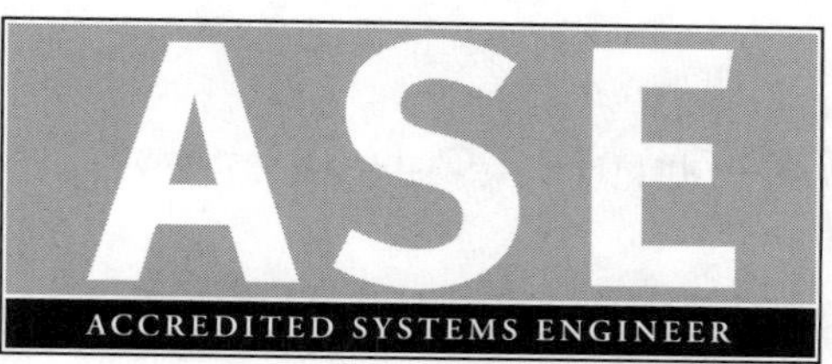

4

Cache Subsystems

CERTIFICATION OBJECTIVES

4.01	Cache Memory Subsystem
4.02	Components of a Cache Memory Subsystem
4.03	Types Of Cache Architecture
4.04	Performance of a Cache Subsystem

The evolution of high-performance processors continues to tax memory bandwidth. Main memory speeds are too slow to service processor requests. Wait states occur, reducing the impact of upgrading to faster processors. The solution is to introduce a faster memory device (cache) between the processor and main memory.

Cache is a relatively small amount of fast memory used to store recently used information. With respect to the CPU, there are two levels of cache: Level 1 (L1) and Level 2 (L2).

L1 cache, beginning with the Intel 486 processor, is integrated with the CPU. L1 cache is the first place for the microprocessor to obtain data. The most common implementation is internal to the microprocessor, because performance of the first-level cache is imperative to overall performance. In Pentium and Pentium Pro processors, Level 1 cache consists of two dedicated 8KB banks, one for data and the one for instructions. Pentium II and Pentium III processors increase the L1 cache size to two 16KB banks.

L2 cache is implemented on the system board (486DX and Pentium) or in the CPU (Pentium Pro, Pentium II, and Pentium III). By integrating Level 2 cache into the processor, the processor can communicate with cache by way of a dedicated cache bus. The result is improved performance and reduced system bus utilization. This chapter will discuss characteristics and performance aspects of L2 cache.

CERTIFICATION OBJECTIVE 4.01

Cache Memory Subsystem

In systems that incorporate cache, the processor will look first to cache for its memory request. If the information is in cache, a cache hit occurs. The processor receives the data in zero wait states. If the data is not in cache, a cache miss occurs. The processor then suffers wait states while slower main memory responds with the requested information.

Cache Hits

Cache is populated as the processor makes requests of information. Cache is designed to store the most recently used (MRU) data and thereby improve CPU to memory speed. A cache hit occurs when the processor requests data that is stored in cache.

Cache hit rates are expressed as a percentage. To calculate the cache hit rate, divide the number of cache hits by the total number of requests and multiply by 100. Ideal hit rates are near 90 percent. It is important to note that, while cache subsystems strive for the high cache hit rates, 100 percent cache hit rates are not possible.

Cache Misses

Cache misses occur when the processor requests data not found in cache. A cache miss causes the processor to obtain the data it is requesting from slower main memory. Though we implement cache subsystems to reduce the processor's requests to main memory, we cannot eliminate those requests. There will always be new or updated information.

We can mitigate the effect of accessing slower main memory by choosing the most effective cache subsystem components.

CERTIFICATION OBJECTIVE 4.02

Components of a Cache Memory Subsystem

While we think of cache as simply a transistor-based, high-speed memory device, it consists of three main components: SRAM, cache directory, and cache management logic. These components can be described using a branch library as an analogy.

A branch library is full of books (*data*), but it doesn't contain every book in the system. It can't, because there is only so much shelf space (*SRAM*) available. To help locate books, the branch uses a card catalogue (*cache directory*), which contains information on the location of those books, and the dates they were acquired. Managing the branch is the librarian (*cache management logic*). The librarian is responsible for maintaining the bookshelves and the card catalogue, and requesting from the central library any books not found in the branch.

SRAM

SRAM, like the library shelves in our analogy, is the actual storage device. It stores information at the intersection of rows and columns. Because SRAM is transistor-based, it does not suffer from any refresh requirements and can respond to processor requests at up to 5ns. Cache sizes vary from 8KB through 2MB.

Cache Directory

The cache directory is simply an index of data locations. Much like a card catalogue, the cache directory provides the cache management logic with information on where to find data requested by the processor.

Cache Management Logic

In our library analogy, the librarian represents cache management logic. Just as the librarian's experience and expertise determines the efficiency of operations at the library, so the cache management logic programming determines the performance characteristics of the cache. Its job is to respond to cache misses based on its policy programming. This programming can be very simple or very complex. As the complexity grows, so does the potential for coherency problems, increased cost, and performance enhancements.

CERTIFICATION OBJECTIVE 4.03

Types of Cache Architecture

A common question among purchasers of network computing systems is, "Why do I have to buy a server, when I can just as easily install the network operating system on this desktop?" One of the answers is the system architecture. Figure 4-1 shows the traditional system architecture model.

Cache architectures comprise a critical component of the system architecture. Cache architectures vary based on their handling of hits and misses. Some architectures are designed for stand-alone computers, while others are designed with the multiuser system in mind. These different architectures have different impacts, both on how expensive the cache memory is to build and on how effective it is in operation. These architectures are called policies.

Policies identify what to do when a cache hit or miss occurs. Specifically, policies can be broken into read policies (Look-Aside and Look-Through) and write policies (Write-Through and Write-Back).

FIGURE 4-1

System architecture model

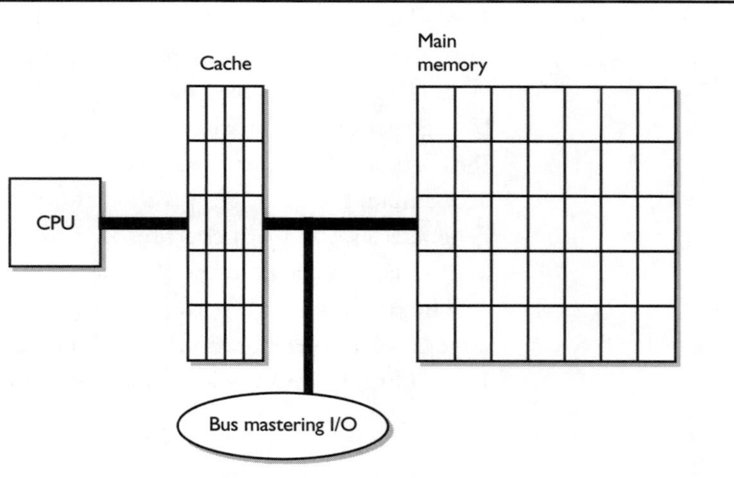

Look-Through and Look-Aside Cache Architecture

Look-Aside and Look-Through cache policies relate to the handling of cache read activity. Issues to consider when choosing between these policies include bus utilization, performance, and cost.

Look-Aside

Look-Aside cache is a simple architecture. Used primarily in stand-alone 486 and Pentium class computers, it provided reasonably high performance and relatively small cost.

When the processor makes a request in systems using Look-Aside cache, the request is generated across the entire system bus. Every device on the bus—cache, expansion cards, and main memory—sees the request. If the requested data is in cache, cache responds. If the data is not in cache, main memory is already processing the request without the need for the processor to generate a second request.

The result is a cost-effective solution with good performance. Unfortunately, Look-Aside cache drives up system bus utilization.

Look-Through

Look-Through cache is more complex. It is designed to lower bus utilization in network servers, while maintaining high performance.

Look-Through cache policies supports concurrent system bus operations by segregating the initial processor read request from the system bus. While the request is being serviced by cache, bus mastering I/O devices are free to access main memory. However, in the event of a cache miss, the processor generates a second request. This is called the lookup penalty, because it uses additional bus cycles to transfer the data.

The result is a high-performance system architecture that benefits from large cache implementations. The following table shows a comparison of Look-Through and Look- Aside characteristics.

Feature	Look-Aside	Look-Through
Bus utilization	High	Reduced
Performance	One request	Lookup penalty on cache misses
Cost	Low	High
Complexity	Low	High

Write-Through and Write-Back Architecture

Write-Through and Write-Back cache policies relate to the handling of cache write activity. Like read policies, bus utilization, performance, and cost are the primary considerations when choosing between these two policies.

The process of cache writes follows a series of steps. The processor retrieves information from main memory. That information is changed and written to cache. That new data in cache is now considered *dirty* and the corresponding data in main memory is considered *stale*. The activity of updating the stale data is addressed by either the Write-Through or Write-Back policy.

Write-Through

Of the write policies, Write-Through is the simpler. After each cache write, the processor also issues a write to main memory. Consequently, data is consistent. However, system bus utilization is increased. Write-Through is a cost-effective solution for most stand-alone systems.

A small real estate office supporting only five users asked me to recommend a system to serve as their network server. The majority of the applications used would be word processing. I advised the customer that, while an entry-level server class system is the best choice, a standard desktop PC using Write-Through cache would be acceptable.

Write-Back

The Write-Back policy is far more complex. It presents a potential for data coherency problems, because it allows data to remain dirty in cache and stale in main memory until it is requested by a bus master device. The result is decreased bus utilization. Figure 4-2 shows the coherency issues for Write-Back cache policy.

The Write-Back cache process supports reduced system bus utilization through the cache management logic's capability to monitor the system bus for requests to main memory. Until a request is registered for stale data in main memory, no update occurs. When a bus master device requests stale information, the cache management logic stops the bus, flushes the dirty cache to main memory, and restarts the bus to allow access to newly updated data.

The result is a high-performance solution for multiuser systems that benefits greatly from larger cache sizes. The following table compares the characteristics of Write-Through and Write-Back cache.

Feature	Write-Through	Write-Back
Bus utilization	High	Reduced
Performance	Two requests	High
Cost	Low	High
Complexity	Low	High

on the job

As a consultant, new customers asked me to recommend a system to serve as their network server. They were looking at using a desktop PC to save money. I discovered, after assessing the needs of the customer, that the server would be highly utilized by many users. The primary function of the server was to be a database application. My recommendation was to acquire a server class system that employs Write-Back cache to reduce system bus utilization.

FIGURE 4-2

Write-Back cache

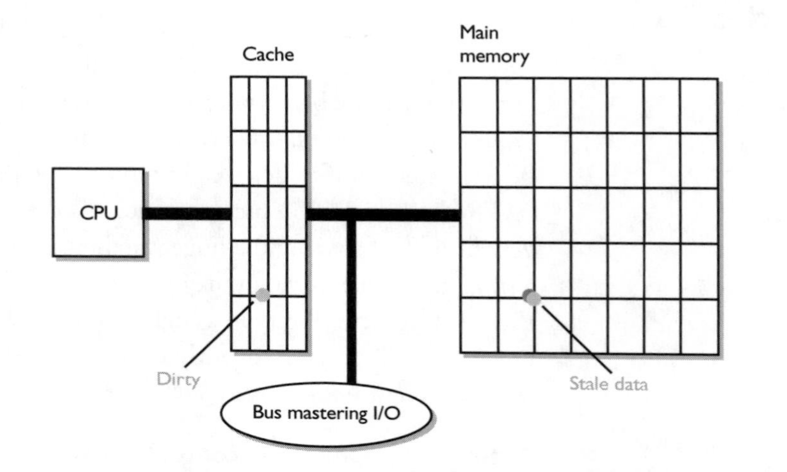

CERTIFICATION OBJECTIVE 4.04

Performance of a Cache Subsystem

Cache subsystem performance has many variables. In addition to the cache policy (read and write policies described in the preceding section), operating system, cache size, and application are all factors that affect performance.

Operating System

An operating system (OS) will affect the overall cache subsystem performance. Depending on the efficiency of the operating system, the OS may compete with applications for cache storage and recall. As operating systems become more complex, so grows the processor/cache activity to support OS services. The more efficient the OS, the more cache is available for application work.

Cache Size

Cache size affects performance, depending on the work being done. When large data files are being processed or large numbers of users are making requests of the server, small cache sizes are overwhelmed. Cache can also be overwhelmed if undersized in multiple processor environments.

Think of the library metaphor described earlier. Imagine a library with very little shelf space and a huge warehouse full of books. If this library is in a small town, the librarian may have little trouble keeping up with books on shelves. Place this library in a highly populated college town and you can imagine the librarian frequently running between the warehouse and shelves to retrieve new books. More shelf space would definitely be necessary.

A start-up graphics arts company asked me to recommend a desktop standard for their staff of 200. Because of the high volume of PCs, the customer was looking at the relatively inexpensive systems that do not have cache. My recommendation was to make the investment in systems that implement cache because of the performance gain.

QUESTIONS AND ANSWERS	
I am concerned about system bus utilization on my network server.	Make certain that the server write policy is Write-Back. Write-Back cache will reduce overall system bus performance, because it updates main memory only when a bus master device requests that data.
I have a stand-alone desktop PC. Bus utilization is not as big an issue as price.	Write-Through cache is less costly to implement because it will update main memory on every cache write.
My Dad wants to surf the Internet and send e-mails to us kids. Is it okay for him to buy a PC that does not have (or has a very small) Level 2 cache?	Yes, provided that he understands that graphics and database programs will suffer performance degradation because of the additional time it takes for the processor to retrieve data from main memory.
My server is supporting a read-intensive database that receives requests from many users.	The Look-Through cache policy is the correct choice in this situation. The processor makes its first request for information to cache, thereby reducing system bus utilization.

Application

Different types of applications place different demands on the cache subsystem. Typically, multiuser database applications take advantage of large cache sizes using Write-Back cache policies. Similarly, graphics and computer-aided design (CAD) applications will benefit from large cache and Write-Back cache implementations.

CERTIFICATION SUMMARY

The use of cache in systems is one of the four main methods of improving bus performance through the increase of CPU-to-memory speed. Of its three main components—SRAM, cache directory, and cache management logic—the latter is the location architecture implementation.

Cache architecture deals with read and write activity. For reads, the two main architectures (policies) are Look-Aside (easy to implement, high bus utilization) and Look-Through (complex to implement, low bus utilization). Write policies are primarily either Write-Through (easy to implement, high bus utilization) and Write-Back (complex to implement, low bus utilization).

Cache's capability to improve system performance depends on policy implementation, operating system, application, and cache size.

TWO-MINUTE DRILL

- ❑ Cache is a relatively small amount of fast memory used to store recently used information.
- ❑ There are two levels of cache: Level 1 (L1) and Level 2 (L2).
- ❑ In systems that incorporate cache, the processor will look first to cache for its memory request.
- ❑ Cache is designed to store the most recently used (MRU) data and thereby improve CPU-to-memory speed.
- ❑ A cache hit occurs when the processor requests data that is stored in cache.

- ❑ Cache misses occur when the processor requests data not found in cache.
- ❑ A Cache Memory Subsystem consists of three main components: SRAM, cache directory, and cache management logic.
- ❑ SRAM is the actual storage device.
- ❑ The cache directory is simply an index of data locations.
- ❑ Cache management logic programming determines the performance characteristics of the cache.
- ❑ Cache architectures vary based on their handling of hits and misses.
- ❑ Architectures are called policies.
- ❑ Policies can be broken into read policies (Look-Aside and Look-Through) and write policies (Write-Through and Write-Back).
- ❑ Look-Aside cache is a simple architecture providing reasonably high performance and relatively small cost.
- ❑ When the processor makes a request in systems using Look-Aside cache, the request is generated across the entire system bus.
- ❑ Look-Through cache policies supports concurrent system bus operations by segregating the initial processor read request from the system bus.
- ❑ In Write-Through, after each cache write, the processor also issues a write to main memory.
- ❑ The Write-Back policy allows data to remain dirty in cache and stale in main memory until it is requested by a bus master device.
- ❑ In addition to the cache policy, operating system, cache size, and application are all factors that affect performance.
- ❑ The OS may compete with applications for cache storage and recall.
- ❑ Cache size affects performance, depending on the work being done.
- ❑ Different types of applications place different demands on the cache subsystem.

SELF TEST

The following Self Test questions will help you measure your understanding of the material presented in this chapter. Read all the choices carefully, as there may be more than one correct answer. Choose all correct answers for each question.

1. Implementation of cache provides
   A. Reduced cost of ownership
   B. Zero wait-state data transfers
   C. Proprietary system architecture
   D. Standardized system architecture
2. Components of the cache subsystem include cache management logic, cache directory, and _____ ?
   A. SRAM
   B. DRAM
   C. SDRAM
   D. EDO
3. SRAM stores information:
   A. On disk
   B. At rows and columns
   C. In the cache directory
   D. None of the above
4. What is the cache directory?
   A. High-level file system
   B. Storage for most recently used data
   C. Index of cache data locations
   D. Distributed database
5. What is the cache subsystem component responsible for policy implementation?
   A. SRAM
   B. Cache directory
   C. Cache management logic
   D. Distributed database
6. What are the two types of cache policies?
   A. Most recently and least recently used
   B. Look-Aside and Look-Through
   C. Write-Back and Write-Through
   D. Read and write activity
7. Which cache policy allows the address request to be seen by the entire system bus?
   A. Look-Aside
   B. Look-Through
   C. Write-Through
   D. Write Back
8. What is a disadvantage to Look-Through cache?
   A. High bus utilization
   B. Lookup penalty
   C. Data inconsistency
   D. None of the above

9. Information that has been updated in cache and is waiting to be updated in main memory is called:
   A. Stale
   B. Invalid
   C. Dirty
   D. Unnecessary
10. What is the write policy that updates main memory on every cache write?
   A. Look-Aside
   B. Look-Through
   C. Write-Through
   D. Write-Back
11. What is the write policy that provides reduced bus utilization?
   A. Look-Aside
   B. Look-Through
   C. Write-Through
   D. Write-Back
12. Which write policy updates when a bus master device requests stale information in main memory?
   A. Look-Aside
   B. Look-Through
   C. Write-Through
   D. Write-Back
13. Which of the following can affect cache performance?
   A. Cache policy
   B. Cache size
   C. Operating system
   D. All the above
14. What should be the cache size implementations for systems supporting a large number of users?
   A. Relatively large
   B. Relatively small
   C. Cache is unnecessary with a large numbers of users.
   D. Cache is not affected by a large numbers of users.
15. Database application performance improves with cache sizes that are
   A. Relatively large
   B. Relatively small
   C. Cache is unnecessary with a large numbers of users.
   D. Cache is not affected by a large numbers of users.

ASE
ACCREDITED SYSTEMS ENGINEER

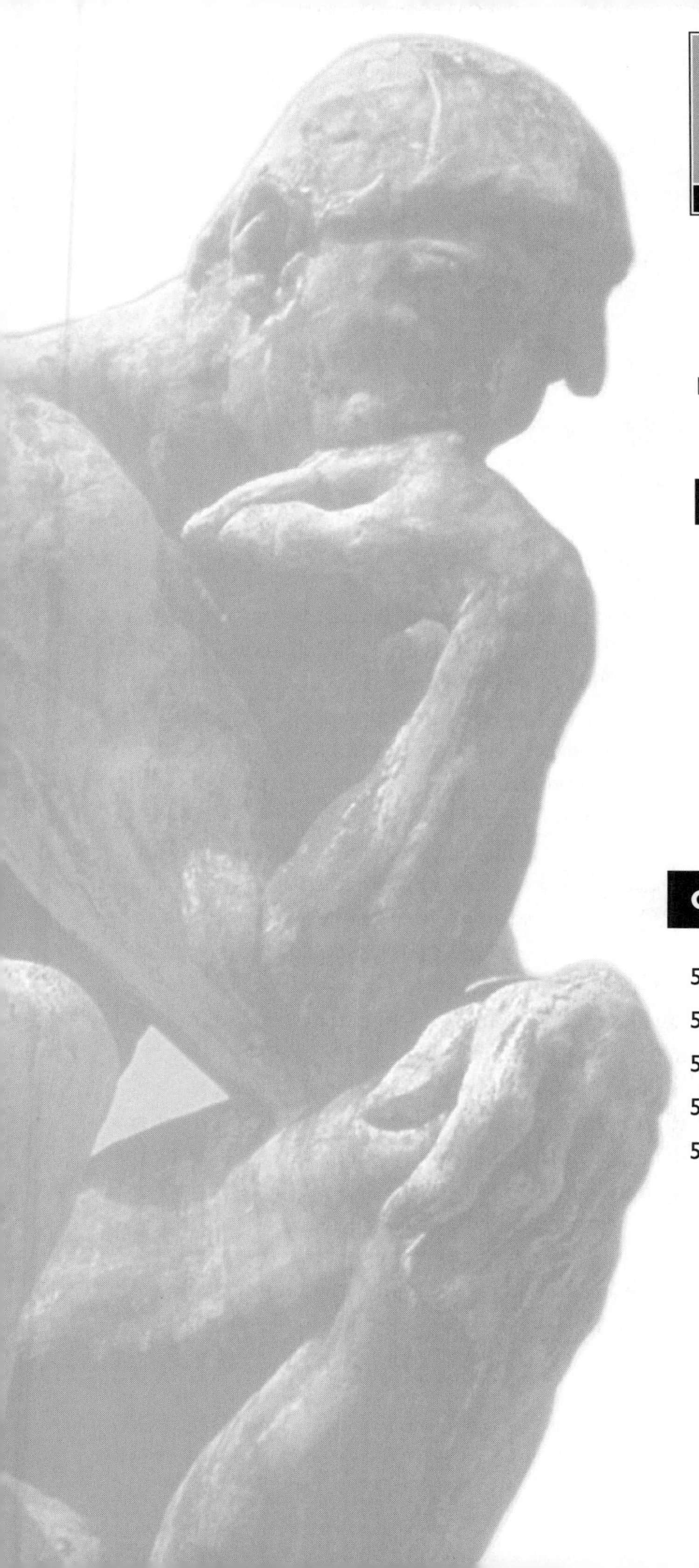

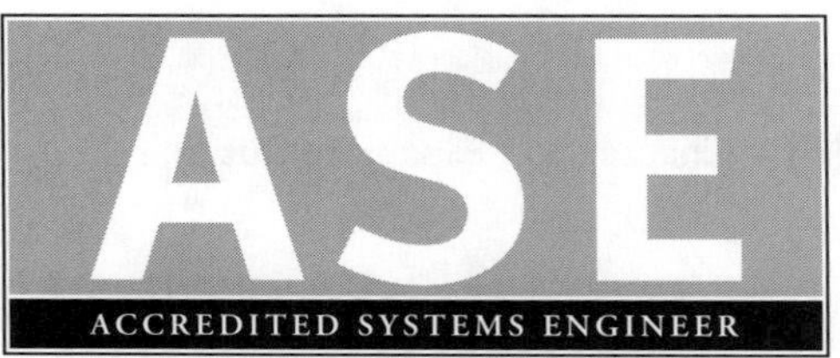

5

Expansion Bus

CERTIFICATION OBJECTIVES

5.01 ISA Buses

5.02 EISA Buses

5.03 PCI Buses

5.04 Shared Slots

5.05 Dual Peer and Bridged PCI Buses

This chapter will assist you in understanding the bus speeds/transfer rates, bus widths, architecture, and other characteristics of ISA, EISA, and PCI buses, as well as shared slots.

CERTIFICATION OBJECTIVE 5.01

ISA Buses

ISA (Industry Standard Architecture) adapters are divided into two groups, 8-bit ISA and 16-bit ISA. Eight-bit ISA was originally defined in the IBM PC and was expanded to 16-bit ISA in the definition of the IBM PC/AT. The main difference between the two definitions was that the original data bus was doubled from 8-bits to 16-bits and the address bus was expanded from a 20-bit address to a 24-bit address. The typical bus speed of both 8-bit and 16-bit ISA adapters is 8.33 MHz.

The original method of configuring ISA adapters entailed keeping written lists of all resources being used in the system, such as I/O and interrupt requests (IRQs). When adding a new adapter, you first had to check your list to locate available settings, then manually configure the adapter using DIP switches and jumpers. If the new adapter was inadvertently set to a value that was already being used, the system would hang or crash, or other problems would occur.

The development that probably saved the ISA standard was the plug and play (PnP) specification. This specification defined an application program interface (API) for dynamic allocation of a PnP adapter's resources by the BIOS or operation system. The process would select IRQs, I/O, and memory settings for the adapter, and configure the adapter accordingly, thus avoiding conflicts with other adapters in the system. In order for this to work, the adapter, the BIOS, and the operating system must be specified as plug and play compliant.

CERTIFICATION OBJECTIVE 5.02

EISA Buses

The EISA (Extended Industry Standard Architecture) specification is an extension of the ISA specification. It provides additional functionality, such as 32-bit memory addressing and 33-Mbps bus bandwidth, while maintaining ISA compatibility. A new configuration process was introduced with EISA, which required the use of a configuration utility, the EISA Configuration utility (ECU). Sparing the administrator the task of keeping a list of all used settings, this utility assigned resources for the system and adapters (a precursor to plug and play). In order to use the utility, each adapter required a .CFG file that described the adapter and any required resources. If an adapter does not have a .CFG file, the utility allows you to create one. Once the configuration process is complete, you have to set the DIP switches and jumpers to the correct settings (as with legacy ISA adapters).

Burst Transfer Rate of an EISA Bus Master Device

EISA bus master devices use burst mode to transfer data at a faster rate than normal, giving EISA a 33-Mbps data transfer rate.

Bus mastering is a feature that allows a controller connected to the bus to communicate directly with other devices on the bus without going through the CPU, thus increasing performance.

Burst mode is a data transmission mode in which data is sent faster than normal. Burst mode is implemented by allowing a device to seize control of the bus while not allowing other devices to interrupt.

CERTIFICATION OBJECTIVE 5.03

PCI Buses

The Peripheral Component Interconnect (PCI) bus is a local-bus design produced by Compaq, DEC, IBM, Intel, and NCR in 1991. The PCI standard provides substantial improvements over ISA and EISA buses.

PCI has become the adapter architecture of choice. It is very flexible, can be used in multiple system architectures (including IBM compatibles and Apple). PCI can be logically expanded to hundreds of slots or vertical slots with hierarchical designs using PCI-to-PCI bridges.

For a comparison between ISA, PCI, and EISA bus types, see Table 5-1.

Architecture

PCI's design includes a buffered local bus. The bus always uses a PCI bridge, thus removing the PCI bus from the host bus. This method keeps the PCI bus processor independent. PCI bridging allows buffering and bursting to occur, yielding better utilization in multitasking environments. PCI also provides 32-bit and 64-bit support, making it quite appropriate for Pentium and higher systems. It has 33/66-MHz bus speeds, with accesses as fast as 60 ns, and a transfer rate of 133 Mbps. PCI provides jumperless support, using registers that contain information required for device detection and configuration, essentially making PCI plug and play.

When clients are looking to get the maximum performance from their servers, one of the first things I look at are the expansion slots. Frequently in older servers that haven't been upgraded lately, you'll find ISA adapters. Replacing all the ISA and EISA adapters possible with PCI adapters will greatly improve the performance of the server. The most common things you will run across are ISA network adapters and EISA array controllers. Replace these with PCI versions if at all possible.

PCI Hot Plug

The latest development in PCI technology is PCI hot plug capabilities. There are three major capabilities:

- Hot replacement allows the removal of a failed PCI adapter and insertion of an identical adapter into the same slot while the server is online.
- Hot upgrade allows the replacement of an existing adapter with an upgraded adapter, or replacing the adapter's driver with an upgraded driver while the server is online.

- Hot expansion allows the installation of an additional adapter into a previously empty slot while the server is online.

To properly hot-plug an adapter, you use a software utility to tell the server to "shut off" a PCI slot. Thus you remove power and access to the slot so you may safely add or remove adapters without causing damage to the server and/or adapter.

FROM THE FIELD

Hot-Plug PCI and Windows 2000

While Windows NT 4.0 supports hot-replacement of PCI adapters on hot-plug PCI equipped server products, the architecture and process remains rather complex. However, under Windows 2000, Hot-Plug PCI allows new devices to be added or upgraded while the machine is powered up.

As part of the Plug-and-Play strategy implemented in Windows 2000, all independent hardware vendors are required to support the Plug-and-Play standard for Windows 2000 drivers. This mandate assures that all drivers Compaq develops for hot-plug PCI in Microsoft's new OS will support hot replacement, hot upgrade, and hot expansion.

Unlike the 4-component architecture found under Windows NT 4.0 (PCI Hot Plug Utility, Remote Monitor Service, System Management Driver, and a hot-plug-aware PCI device driver), the architecture supporting Windows 2000 is fully supported without the need for additional utilities and applications.

To replace or install a PCI card in a hot-swap machine running Windows 2000, simply:

1. Open the machine and insert the card
2. Press the PCI Hot Plug Button to notify the server to power up the slot
3. When the Add New Hardware dialogue appears (if doing a hot-upgrade/expansion), simply follow the wizard to install the driver.

Without a doubt, Hot-Swap PCI technology on Windows 2000 machines will change the computing environment by allowing upgrades to be performed at almost any time with little concern for downtime.

—Thomas E. Eck, MCSE+I, MCSD, ASE, CCA, CNA

TABLE 5-1 Quick Comparison of Bus Technologies

Bus Type	ISA	EISA	PCI
Data Path	8/16 bits	32 bits	32/64 bits
Bus Speed	8.33 MHz	8.33 MHz	33/66 MHz
Maximum Bandwidth	8 Mbps	33 Mbps	133/524 Mbps
IRQ Sharing	No	Yes	Yes
Bus Master Capable	1 per bus	Yes	Yes
Plug and Play	PnP adapters only	No	Yes
Configuration	Dip switches and jumpers, .CFG files, PnP configuration program	.CFG file and ECU or SCU	PnP (if OS enabled), BIOS configured, or ECU/SCU

Not long ago, I received an emergency call because a client's server had a failed network adapter. I arrived on site and was told by the network manager that they could tolerate no downtime. (The network was down anyway, because the server had only one network adapter and it was dead.) I slid the server out of the rack, opened the top, and saw white riser cards between the PCI slots. Yes, they were hot-swap PCI slots! (The riser cards isolate the PCI slots so you cannot accidentally bump another card with the one you are adding or removing, causing a short.) Well, you have to keep the client happy, so I went into the server, told it to disable the slot with the failed adapter, removed the adapter, inserted the new one, and re-enabled the slot. The server was off and running again. The entire procedure took about seven minutes, and the client was impressed.

CERTIFICATION OBJECTIVE 5.04

Shared Slots

You may run across a system with EISA/ISA and PCI shared slots. This term means that at any time, only one of the slots may be populated. If you have the ISA slot populated, you cannot also install the PCI slot. Sharing imposes a physical limitation, as the slots on the motherboard are placed too closely together to install both adapters at once. Shared slots provide flexibility, giving you a choice of adapter architecture to install.

A friend bought a PCI Ethernet adapter to replace the ISA NIC he was using. He complained that all of his PCI slots were populated, so he wouldn't have room for the PCI adapter, even if he removed the ISA adapter. I asked him when he bought the motherboard. "About four months ago," he replied. When I looked in his case, I saw a shared slot with the ISA slot populated by a modem. I removed the ISA NIC, moved the ISA modem to the slot the NIC was in, installed the PCI NIC in the shared slot, and turned it on. Windows 98 saw the network card (I had to kill the ISA card in the OS) and all was well. As I was leaving, he asked me where I found the PCI slot. "I had one in my pocket," I replied.

CERTIFICATION OBJECTIVE 5.05

Dual Peer and Bridged PCI Buses

The dual-peer PCI bus provides two PCI buses, independently connected to the host processor bus with two host-to-PCI bridges. Figure 5-1

FIGURE 5-1 Dual peer PCI

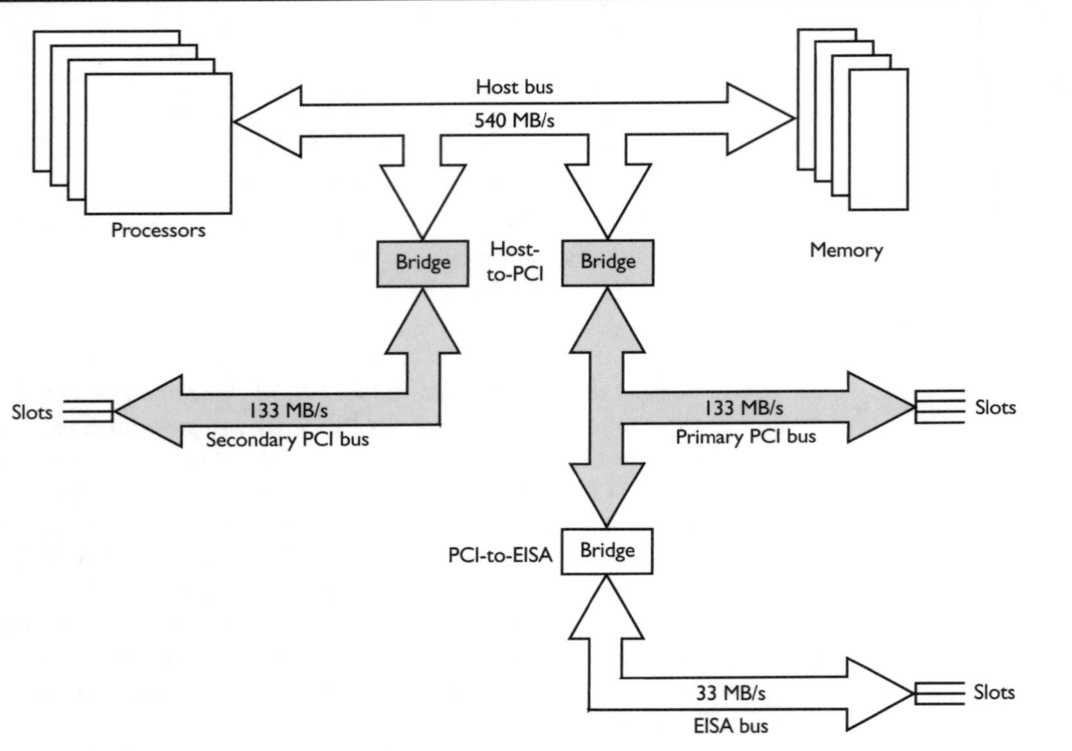

illustrates this arrangement. Since each PCI bus runs independently, it is possible to have two PCI bus masters transferring data at the same time, producing better overall performance.

It is important to remember to balance the PCI buses. For example, if you are installing two PCI network adapters, for best performance place one network adapter on each PCI bus, giving each network adapter maximum bus bandwidth.

The bridged PCI architecture, shown in Figure 5-2, requires all processed transactions on the bridged PCI bus (the secondary bus) to go through the PCI-to-PCI bridge to reach the primary bus, then through the host-to-PCI bridge. (See Table 5-2.) This arrangement provides only one path to the host bus, so no load balancing is required on systems using this architecture.

FIGURE 5-2 Bridged PCI

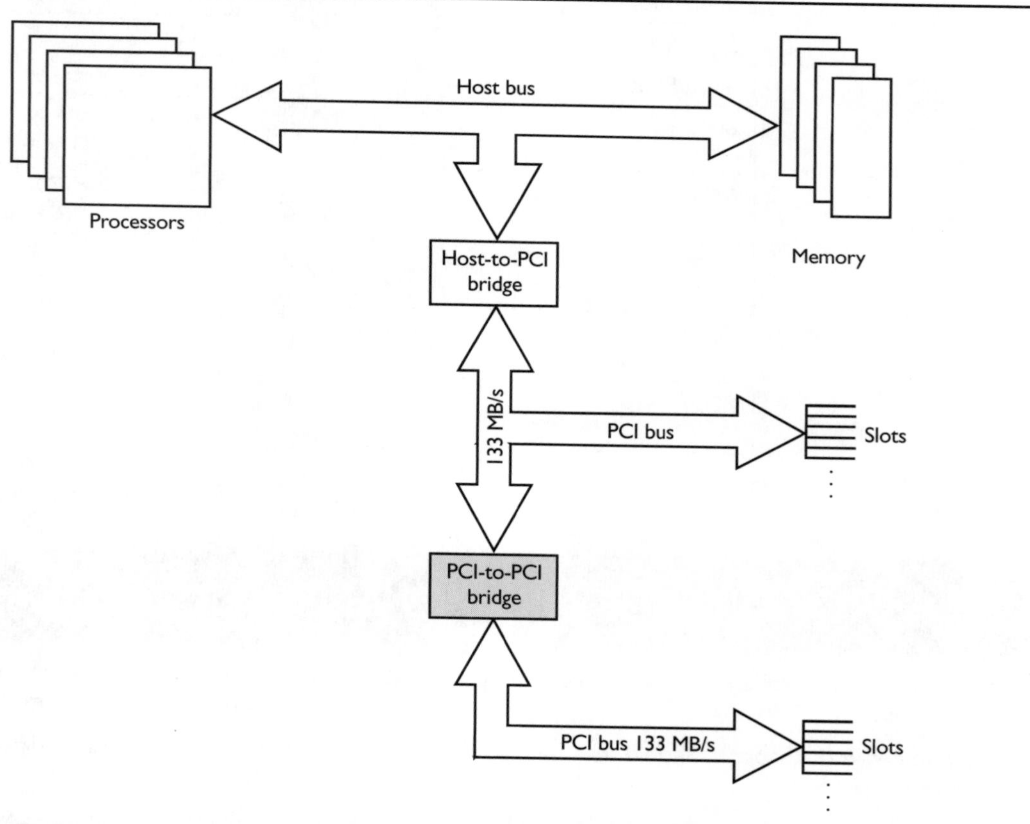

TABLE 5-2

Bus Architectures

PCI Architecture	Bridged	Dual Peer (or better)
400	X	
800	X	
1600/1600R	X	
1850R	X	
3000/3000R		X
5000/5000R		X
5500/5500R		X
6000		X (Three-Peer)
6400R		X (64-bit)
6500		X (64-bit)
7000		X (Three-Peer)
8000		X (Multi-Peer 64-bit)
8500		X (Multi-Peer 64-bit)

QUESTIONS AND ANSWERS

I have two array controllers. Should I place them on the same bus?	No. You should place each array controller on a different bus to provide the best transfer rate.
I have two network adapters. Should they be placed on different buses?	Yes. Placing network adapters on different buses yields a better transfer rate.
I have one array controller and one network adapter. Do I need to place these on different buses?	Yes. Putting them on different buses will provide each with the maximum bandwidth.
I have two array controllers and two network adapters. How should they be arranged?	Put one network adapter and one array controller on each bus.
I have three array controllers. How can I balance them?	Since there are only two PCI buses in a dual peer arrangement, you will have to install two array controllers on one of the buses.

CERTIFICATION SUMMARY

In this chapter, you learned the characteristics of the three most commonly used bus architectures: ISA, EISA, and PCI. While EISA is quickly dropping out of sight, you will still see it in older models of servers.

The chapter described the PCI architecture. PCI's design includes a buffered local bus. The bus always uses a PCI bridge, thus removing the PCI bus from the host bus. This method keeps the PCI bus processor independent. You also learned about PCI's hot plug capabilities: hot replacement, hot upgrade, and hot expansion.

The chapter explained the benefits and drawbacks of shared slots. Shared slots provide flexibility but impose a physical limitation: the slots on the motherboard are placed too closely together to install two adapters at once.

You learned how the dual-peer PCI bus improves overall performance by having two PCI bus masters transferring data at the same time. In a dual-peer bus, two PCI buses are independently connected to the host processor bus with two host-to-PCI bridges.

TWO-MINUTE DRILL

- ISA (Industry Standard Architecture) adapters are divided into two groups, 8-bit ISA and 16-bit ISA.
- The development that probably saved the ISA standard was the plug and play (PnP) specification.
- The EISA (Extended Industry Standard Architecture) provides additional functionality, such as 32-bit memory addressing and 33-Mbps bus bandwidth, while maintaining ISA compatibility.
- EISA bus master devices use burst mode to transfer data at a faster rate than normal, giving EISA a 33-Mbps data transfer rate.
- Burst mode is implemented by allowing a device to seize control of the bus while not allowing other devices to interrupt.
- The Peripheral Component Interconnect (PCI) standard is very flexible, can be used in multiple system architectures (including IBM compatibles and Apple), and can be logically expanded to hundred of slots or vertical slots with hierarchical designs using PCI-to-PCI bridges.

- PCI bridging allows buffering and bursting to occur, yielding better utilization in multitasking environments.
- The latest development in PCI technology is PCI hot plug capabilities.
- EISA/ISA and PCI shared slots provide flexibility, giving you a choice of adapter architecture to install.
- The dual-peer PCI bus provides two PCI buses, independently connected to the host processor bus with two host-to-PCI bridges.

SELF TEST

The following Self Test questions will help you measure your understanding of the material presented in this chapter. Read all the choices carefully, as there may be more than one correct answer. Choose all correct answers for each question.

1. What data widths does ISA support?
   A. 8-bit
   B. 16-bit
   C. 32-bit
   D. 64-bit
2. What are the two methods of configuring ISA adapters?
   A. .CFG file
   B. Plug and play
   C. Jumpers
   D. ECU
3. What is the bus bandwidth of EISA adapters?
   A. 8 Mbps
   B. 33 Mbps
   C. 133 Mbps
   D. 524 Mbps
4. If no .CFG file is available for a given EISA adapter, how do you configure the adapter?
   A. Download a .CFG file from Compaq's Web site.
   B. Create a .CFG file.
   C. Install the adapter without a .CFG file.
   D. You cannot continue.
5. What data paths does PCI support?
   A. 8-bit
   B. 16-bit
   C. 32-bit
   D. 64-bit
6. PCI adapters use a technology closely resembling:
   A. Plug and play
   B. Manual configuration
   C. Osmosis
   D. Configuration files
7. What are the three capabilities of PCI hot plug?
   A. Hot replacement
   B. Hot upgrade
   C. Hot downgrade
   D. Hot expansion
8. Which of the following statements is true of PCI hot plug adapters?
   A. They allow you to remove and install adapters while the server is online.
   B. They do not allow you to remove and install adapters while the server is online.

C. They are no different from any other PCI adapter.

D. They are installed in a different type of slot that other PCI adapters.

9. What do white riser cards between the PCI slots indicate?

A. The slot is not PCI hot plug compatible.

B. The slot is disabled.

C. The slot is a reserve.

D. The slot is PCI hot plug compatible.

10. What does a shared slot enable you to do?

A. Install two PCI adapters into the same slot.

B. Install an EISA/ISA adapter or a PCI adapter into the slot.

C. Install an EISA or an ISA adapter into the slot.

D. Install an EISA and an ISA adapter into the slot.

11. How many buses does a dual-peer PCI bus provide?

A. One

B. Two

C. Three

D. Four

12. How many PCI bus masters can be on a dual-peer PCI bus?

A. None

B. One

C. Two

D. Four

13. How must you install adapters in a dual-peer PCI bus?

A. Load balance.

B. Place like adapters on the same bus.

C. Populate the first bus before adding adapters to the second bus.

D. It doesn't matter.

14. How many paths to the bus host are on a bridged PCI bus?

A. One

B. Two

C. Three

D. Four

15. When should bridged PCI buses be load balanced?

A. Always

B. Never

C. Only when using like adapters

D. Only when performance declines

ASE
ACCREDITED SYSTEMS ENGINEER

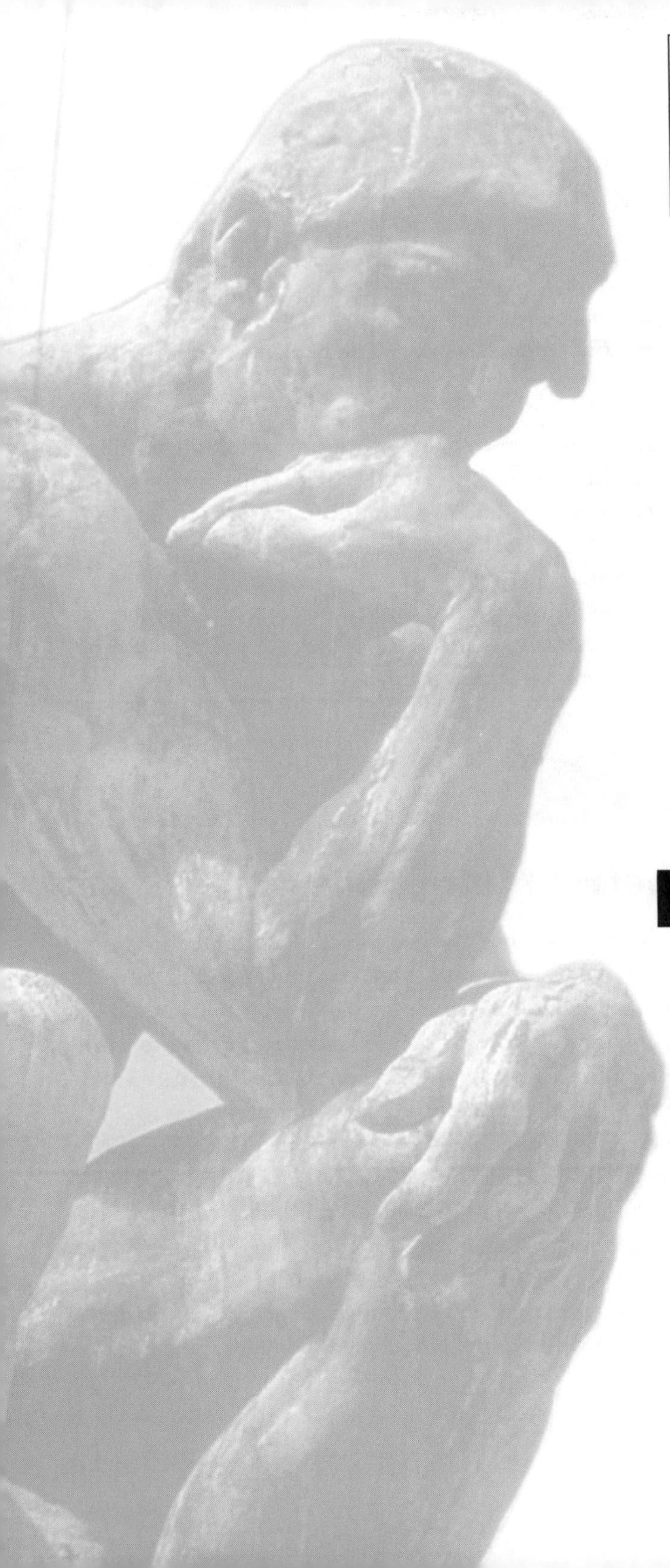

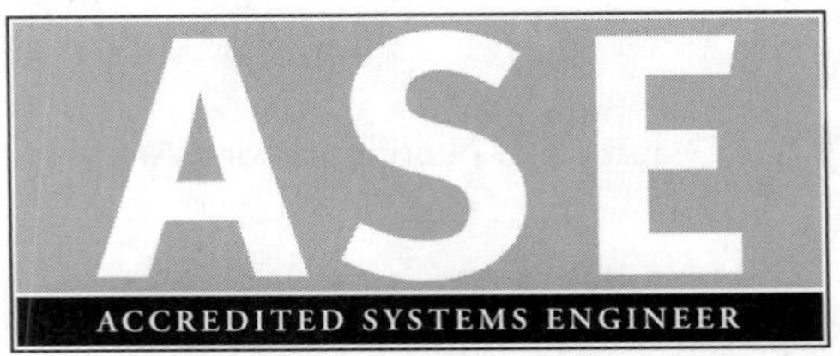

6

Multiprocessing Architectures

CERTIFICATION OBJECTIVES

6.01	Symmetric and Asymmetric Multiprocessing
6.02	Shared Cache
6.03	Major Differences Between Dual and Quad Multiprocessing

This chapter introduces you to the world of multiprocessing. Though relatively new on the technology scene, the symmetric multiprocessing (SMP) and asymmetric multiprocessing (ASMP) models are vital cogs in the machinery of heavy-duty processing. You will see a description of how these models work and be presented with examples of how these models are used.

The chapter will also familiarize you with processing systems that utilize second-level cache to assist in more efficient processing. These two systems are shared-cache, dual processing systems and multi-cache, multiprocessing systems. You will be exposed to the advantages and limitations of each of these two processing systems

Multiprocessing systems were developed to alleviate processing bottlenecks. By allowing multiple processors to share the workload, the processes can be executed in a quicker and more efficient manner.

CERTIFICATION OBJECTIVE 6.01

Symmetric and Asymmetric Multiprocessing

The evolution of multiprocessing began when someone attempted to work on one task while having a computer work on another task in the background. At first, operating systems were unable to accommodate this demand. Gradually, applications were written that allowed the user to work on two items at the same time, although the first ones were extremely slow. This began what is known as multitasking. In short, multitasking is a CPU executing several processes by alternating the time devoted to each process instead of running them both concurrently.

First, let's look at multitasking. Multitasking is available in two flavors. *Cooperative multitasking* occurs when the process currently occupying the CPU offers the resources of the CPU to other processes. The name is descriptive of its function in that the processes must cooperate in order for this type of multitasking to work. If one process does not cooperate, it is monopolizing the CPU and preventing other processes from running. Operating systems that employ this type of multitasking are Macintosh operating systems and Windows 3.*x* operating systems.

One way to think of cooperative multitasking is to imagine that you are stuck in traffic and the traffic lights aren't functioning. The flow of traffic depends on the drivers. If everyone is polite and takes turns going through the intersection, things can go rather smoothly. However, should one stream of traffic continuously go through the intersection and not allow others to pass, things can get clogged up quite rapidly (not to mention causing more than car radiators to overheat). The procedure for deciding which traffic goes through the intersection needs some improvement.

In contrast, *preemptive multitasking* does not leave the decision to share CPU resources with the process. These decisions are made by the operating system. The processing capabilities of the CPU are shared among processes in spite of a process's desire to be selfish. Operating systems that employ preemptive multitasking are UNIX, Windows 95, Windows 98, Windows NT, and OS/2.

To return to our traffic analogy, imagine that you are stuck in traffic but this time there is a police officer directing traffic. This cop has the discretion to choose which traffic to let through and which traffic to hold up. If traffic is heavier in one direction, the cop can allow more congested streets to empty while those less-congested streets wait a little longer. Although some drivers are still waiting longer than others, this method of directing traffic makes traffic move more efficiently for the greatest number of people possible. This is roughly how preemptive multitasking works. Though not necessarily the most efficient method of handling processes, preemptive multitasking at least allows the operating system to manage traffic. The real limitation of preemptive multitasking is the operating system.

These two methods of multitasking are for operating systems that support multitasking. Operating systems that support multiprocessing distribute the workload among the processors. The responsibility for managing this workload is the job of the scheduler, which arranges for the execution of processes in such a way as to make the greatest use of the available processing power. The arrangement consists of distributing the waiting processes among the existing processors. This is called multiprocessing. The difference between multitasking and multiprocessing is that multiprocessing involves the simultaneous execution of more than one process, rather than the processor alternating time to processes.

Now, let's move on to multiprocessing. As was the case for multitasking, there are two different modes of multiprocessing. However, multiprocessing by definition requires more than one processor, whereas multitasking can be performed with only one processor. The two different models for multiprocessing are asymmetric multiprocessing and symmetric multiprocessing. Asymmetric multiprocessing delegates certain functions to each processor, while symmetric multiprocessing allows the system to make the best possible use of the processor power.

Asymmetric Multiprocessing

Asymmetric multiprocessing operating systems generally dedicate one processor to run the operating system and utilize the other processor for performing other tasks. The processors may or may not be identical, but the main characteristic is that each processor does not have equal access to the system resources, as shown in Figure 6-1.

As the figure illustrates, each processor is responsible for specific tasks, which are determined by the operating system.

FIGURE 6-1

Asymmetric multiprocessing

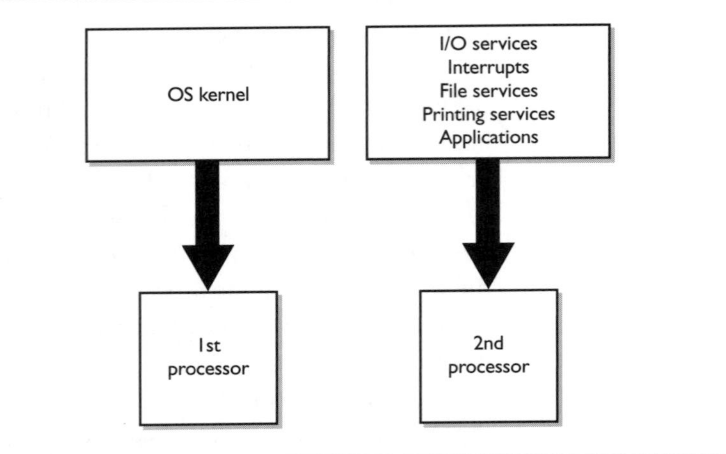

An analogy to asymmetric multiprocessing can be seen in the world of medicine. Imagine a medical clinic with many doctors, whose specialties enable them to treat only certain kinds of patients. A cardiologist would be able to treat someone with a heart condition, but not someone with a skin condition. If more people come to the clinic with skin problems than with heart problems, dermatology patients may have to wait longer than cardiology patients do. Indeed, the cardiologist may have no patients in the waiting room, while the dermatologist has several. This arrangement may not seem like the most efficient use of the available doctors' time, but the limitations of the doctors' specialties make it necessary.

Compaq Systempro systems use AMP. These systems used two processors, but only one processor, the boot processor, could process interrupts. The second processor could run applications, but could not process interrupts from system components.

Symmetric Multiprocessing

Simply put, symmetric multiprocessing allows each processor equal access to system resources. Operating systems that employ symmetric multiprocessing include Linux, Sun's Solaris, and Windows NT. Each of these operating systems affords each processor the capability to run the operating system and to share memory. The symmetric multiprocessing model allows for the multiple threads of a single process to be spread equally across multiple processors, as shown in Figure 6-2.

As Figure 6-2 illustrates, all tasks are balanced equally among the available processing power. This model ensures that the processors are utilized in the most efficient manner. The scheduler is responsible for managing the presentation of processes to be executed by the processors.

on the job

Implement symmetric multiprocessing if you want the processor utilization to be somewhat balanced. This will allow you to take full advantage of the processor's capabilities. If one processor's utilization is dramatically higher than another processor's, you are not receiving the full benefits of multiprocessing. Symmetric multiprocessing makes better use of the total processing power than asymmetric multiprocessing.

FIGURE 6-2

Symmetric multiprocessing

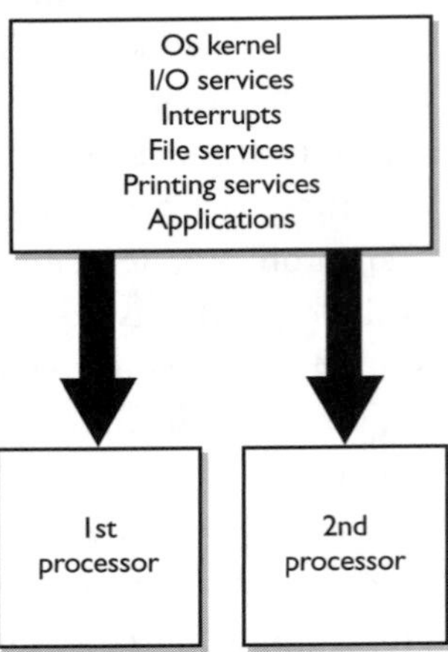

An analogy to symmetric multiprocessing can be seen in a veterinary clinic. Unlike the doctors in the medical clinic, a veterinarian may treat virtually any type of animal for any type of illness. If there are several vets in a clinic, then each patient waiting for treatment can be placed in the same queue and treated, without having to wait for a specialist. The receptionist performs the tasks of the scheduler, and doctors handle the patients assigned to them.

You might think that adding more processors increases the processing power in a direct ratio to the number of processors. However, this is simply not true. The reason for this is that there is a certain amount of overhead associated with each processor. This is similar to the concept of using RAID 5 when configuring drive arrays. Configuring four drives in a RAID 5 configuration does not result in the actual storage space of the four drives combined, because of the overhead associated with RAID 5 configurations. After four processors, adding more processors results in less efficiency. The

Pentium II processor will not support more than two processors in an SMP system. However, with the new Xeon line of processors, you are now able to place four processors in a server. There is even a new eight-way architecture that will allow you to install eight processors in a server.

One last word about multiprocessing. Compaq is the first to implement the new Highly Parallel System Architecture in their servers. This architecture uses dual memory controllers, which increases memory bandwidth (providing two to four times as much memory bandwidth as other systems) as well as a dual peer-PCI bus, which provides greater I/O bandwidth, which allows the system to balance resources (twice the I/O bandwidth of other systems). Enhancing the memory and I/O subsystems will drastically reduce bottlenecks caused by the increased traffic from multiple CPUs.

QUESTIONS AND ANSWERS

Which of the two multiprocessing models allows for the most efficient balancing of processes?	Symmetric processing allows each processor equal access to the system resources and can execute any task presented to it.
Looking at the processor utilization of my system, one processor is busy most of the time, while the other processor is idle. Why is that?	This would be a characteristic of asymmetric processing, in which specific tasks are carried out by specific processors.
Will adding more processors allow my server to process tasks more efficiently?	Yes, although four processors offer the optimal level of performance.
When planning the installation of a new network, how should these multiprocessing models affect the decision-making process?	The multiprocessing model you wish to employ can affect which operating system you choose.
What is the difference between multiprocessing and multitasking?	Multiprocessing by definition means that you have more than one process being executed at the same time.

FROM THE FIELD

Upgrading a Processor

Windows NT actually uses two different Hardware Abstraction Layers (HALs) for single and multiprocessor machines. Simply upgrading the processor will not cause Windows NT to load the proper HAL, and instead you must manually update the HAL using the Compaq SSD (Compaq systems only), the NT Resource Kit UPTOMP.EXE utility, or, if you are really brave, copying the proper files into the SYSTEM32 directory.

If you wish to update a multiprocessor server or workstation from a uniprocessor configuration to the multiprocessor HAL, you can use the Support Software Diskette (SSD) to quickly and safely update Windows NT to the proper HAL after installing the additional processor(s).

On Compaq systems, employment of the SSD method to update the HAL is preferable to the UPTOMP.EXE found in the NT Resource Kit.

Although this process can also be performed manually by simply copying the proper files to the SYSTEM32 directory, it is advisable to let the SSD determine which HAL is best suited to your Compaq machine. For more information on how to upgrade from the uniprocessor HAL to the multiprocessor HAL manually, see MS KB article Q156358.

—Thomas E. Eck, MCSE+I, MCSD, ASE, CCA, CNA

CERTIFICATION OBJECTIVE 6.02

Shared Cache

Before we discuss shared cache, let's first take a quick refresher course on cache.

- Cache provides a computer system with a high-speed storage mechanism. It minimizes the number of times the system has to access system memory.
- Cache can be either a reserved section of main memory or an independent, high-speed device.
- Memory caching uses static RAM (SRAM); system memory uses dynamic RAM (DRAM). The larger the size of the cache, the less often the computer needs to access DRAM.

- Processors contain memory caches, which are built into their architecture. These are called first-level (L1) caches. Generally, these caches are relatively small, which necessitated the implementation of a larger, external cache, called second-level (L2) caches. These caches sit between the CPU and the DRAM. Both L1 and L2 caches are composed of SRAM, but L2 caches are typically much larger.

Shared cache, also known as dual processing, means that a system contains multiple processors but accesses a single second-level cache. These systems check the first-level cache, and if the data does not appear in the first-level cache, they check the second-level cache. This model is further enhanced by a cache controller, which reduces the access time to the second-level cache. Shared cache is a low-cost method of making the machine capable of executing processes faster. Figure 6-3 illustrates what a shared cache system may look like.

FIGURE 6-3

A shared cache, dual processor system

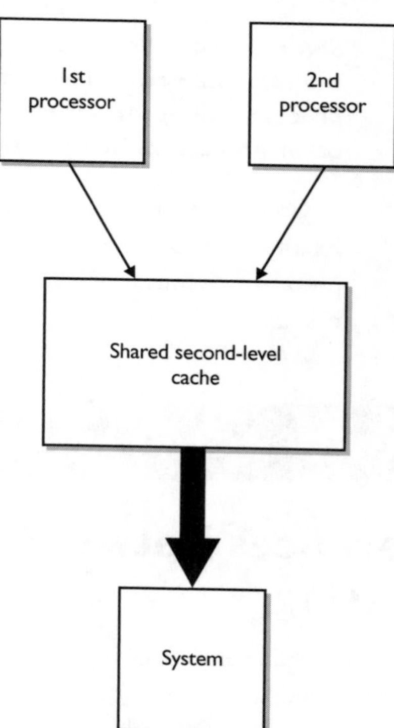

QUESTIONS AND ANSWERS

What is second-level cache?	Second-level cache is an external cache that processors can use when their first-level cache space is exhausted.
How does having a second-level cache assist in speeding up the execution of processes?	Second-level cache allows for the storage of more information into faster SRAM, which reduces the frequency with which the system memory needs to be accessed.
When should I choose to implement a dual processing model?	A dual processing model boosts the processing power of your server as well as being very economical.
Does Compaq have any servers that offer this technology?	Yes, Compaq has several models that employ the dual processor technology. These include the 800, 1200, 1600, 2500, and 3000.

Shared cache allows each processor to store and retrieve data from the same L2 cache. This may be beneficial because it can allow a processor to access information that may have been stored by the other processor. This greatly decreases the access time to that data.

Compaq offers several systems that employ the dual processor architecture. Examples include the 800, 1200, 1600, 2500, and 3000. This dual processor architecture is a good choice for an entry-level server, balancing cost and performance.

CERTIFICATION OBJECTIVE 6.03

Major Differences Between Dual and Quad Multiprocessing

Quad multiprocessing is another multiprocessing architecture utilized by Compaq servers. Quad multiprocessing, like shared cache dual processing, uses a second-level cache. However, in quad multiprocessing, each processor has its own second-level cache. With the larger number of external second-level caches, there is a larger total available space for data, which further reduces the frequency with which the main memory is accessed. Figure 6-4 gives a rudimentary representation of what a quad processing system might look like.

on the Job

You should employ quad processing technology when you want to have a larger amount of L2 cache than is employed in the dual processing model. Even if using the same size of L2 cache, by dedicating a separate L2 cache to each processor, you can increase your total L2 cache by four times over the dual processing model.

Compaq offers several servers that can employ quad processing architecture. The 5500, 6000, 6400, and 7000 all offer the capability to upgrade to four processors. Each of these systems also gives you the option

FIGURE 6-4

A multi-cache, quad processing system

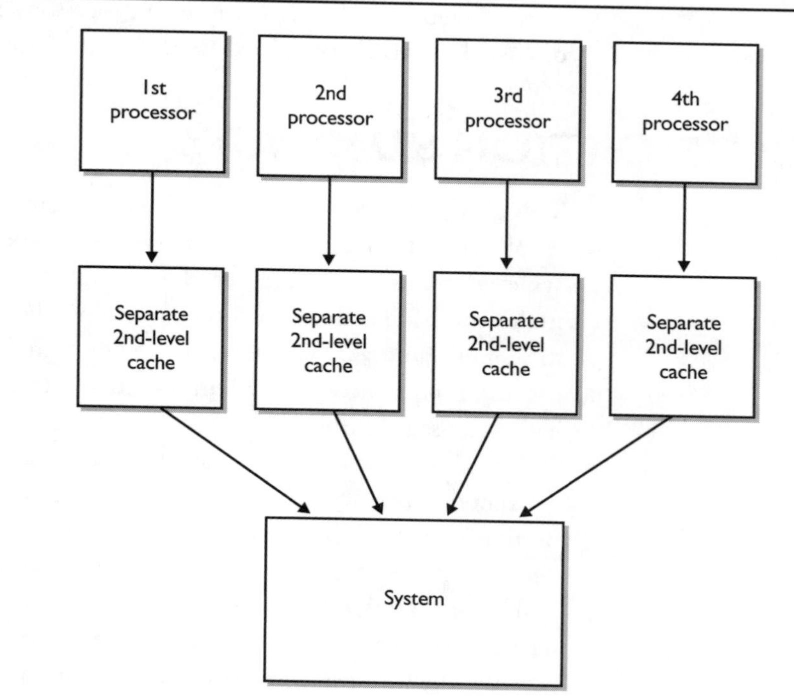

QUESTIONS AND ANSWERS	
What is the advantage of quad processing over dual processing?	Quad processing uses four processors and has a separate, external second-level cache for each processor. The larger amount of second-level cache reduces the frequency with which the system has to access system memory.
When should I consider using quad processing?	Quad processing may be deemed beneficial when processor speed is more important than the cost of implementing a quad processing system, or when setting up an application server that will experience heavy utilization.
Does Compaq have any servers that take advantage of this technology?	Yes. Compaq has several models that can utilize quad processing. These include the 5500, 6000, 6400, and 7000.

of upgrading to a 2MB L2 cache per processor. Although quad processing provides you with the highest level of processor performance of the models discussed in this chapter, it is also the most costly.

CERTIFICATION SUMMARY

This chapter has presented the various multiprocessing architectures employed in Compaq servers. The first section dealt with asymmetric and symmetric multiprocessing, which uses multiple processors. Asymmetric multiprocessing is that which does not allow the processors equal access to system resources. Symmetric processing is that which does allow the processors equal access to system resources, thereby providing a more balanced usage of the processors.

The second section dealt with a shared cache, dual processor architecture. This model employs a shared second-level cache among the processors to minimize the frequency with which the system accesses the system memory. This is a model that provides a good balance between cost and performance.

The final section handled quad processing architecture, which uses a separate, external second-level cache for each processor. This model provides the best available performance, although it incurs a greater cost than dual processing.

TWO-MINUTE DRILL

- Multiprocessing systems were developed to alleviate processing bottlenecks.
- Multitasking is a CPU executing several processes by alternating the time devoted to each process instead of running them both concurrently.
- *Cooperative multitasking* occurs when the process currently occupying the CPU offers the resources of the CPU to other processes.
- *Preemptive multitasking* does not leave the decision to share CPU resources with the process. These decisions are made by the operating system.
- Asymmetric multiprocessing operating systems generally dedicate one processor to run the operating system and utilize the other processor for performing other tasks.
- Symmetric multiprocessing allows each processor equal access to system resources.
- Compaq is the first to implement the new Highly Parallel System Architecture in their servers.
- Cache provides a computer system with a high-speed storage mechanism.
- Shared cache, also known as dual processing, means that a system contains multiple processors but accesses a single second-level cache.
- Compaq offers several systems that employ the dual processor architecture. Examples include the 800, 1200, 1600, 2500, and 3000.
- Quad multiprocessing, like shared cache dual processing, uses a second-level cache. However, in quad multiprocessing, each processor has its own second-level cache.
- Compaq offers several servers that can employ quad processing architecture: the 5500, 6000, 6400, and 7000.

SELF TEST

The following Self Test questions will help you measure your understanding of the material presented in this chapter. Read all the choices carefully, as there may be more than one correct answer. Choose all correct answers for each question.

1. Dual processing systems are characterized by:

   A. Shared, external second-level cache
   B. Separate, external second-level cache for each processor
   C. Two processors
   D. Four processors

2. Which is the multiprocessing model in which a processor may not be allowed to offer the same services as another processor?

   A. Asymmetric multiprocessing
   B. Symmetric multiprocessing
   C. Dual processing
   D. Quad processing

3. Which of the following are characteristics of symmetric multiprocessing?

   A. Equal access to system resources
   B. Handling of certain system functions restricted to one processor
   C. Balanced processing
   D. Use by Windows NT

4. Which of the following models offer quad processing?

   A. Model 3000
   B. Model 5500
   C. Model 800
   D. Model 6000

5. Which is the multiprocessing model in which the workload is balanced among the available processors?

   A. Asymmetric multiprocessing
   B. Symmetric multiprocessing
   C. Dual processing
   D. Quad processing

6. You would like to build a system with multiprocessors that will provide you with the largest amount of L2 cache to the processors. Which of the following would you choose?

   A. Dual processing
   B. Quad processing
   C. Asymmetric multiprocessing
   D. Symmetric multiprocessing

7. Which of the following is a characteristic of asymmetric multiprocessing?

   A. Equal access to system resources
   B. Unequal access to system resources
   C. Balanced processing
   D. Use by a majority of Compaq technologies

8. You would like to build a system with multiprocessors that will provide you the most efficient use of all the processing power. Which of the following would you choose?

   A. Dual processing
   B. Quad processing
   C. Asymmetric multiprocessing
   D. Symmetric multiprocessing

9. Quad processing systems are characterized by:

   A. Shared, external second-level cache
   B. Separate, external second-level cache for each processor
   C. Two processors
   D. Four processors

10. You are installing a server with multiprocessors. You decide that you want to dedicate processors to certain functions, to ensure that the operating system always has a processor dedicated to itself. Which of the following would you employ?

    A. Dual processing
    B. Quad processing
    C. Asymmetric multiprocessing
    D. Symmetric multiprocessing

11. A processor can use an independent, high-speed storage device that can speed up processing. Which of the following would you associate with this technology?

    A. L1 cache
    B. L2 cache
    C. Dual processing
    D. Quad processing

12. You are installing a server and with two processors and you would like them to share the same L2 cache. Which of the following would you choose?

    A. Dual processing
    B. Quad processing
    C. Asymmetric multiprocessing
    D. Symmetric multiprocessing

13. How many Xeon processors can you put into one system?

    A. Two
    B. Four
    C. Eight
    D. Ten

14. Which of the following models offer dual processing?

    A. Model 6400
    B. Model 1200
    C. Model 6000
    D. Model 1600

15. Which multiprocessing architecture is characterized by each processor having a separate second-level cache?

    A. Asymmetric multiprocessing
    B. Symmetric multiprocessing
    C. Shared cache, dual processing
    D. Multi-cache, multiprocessing

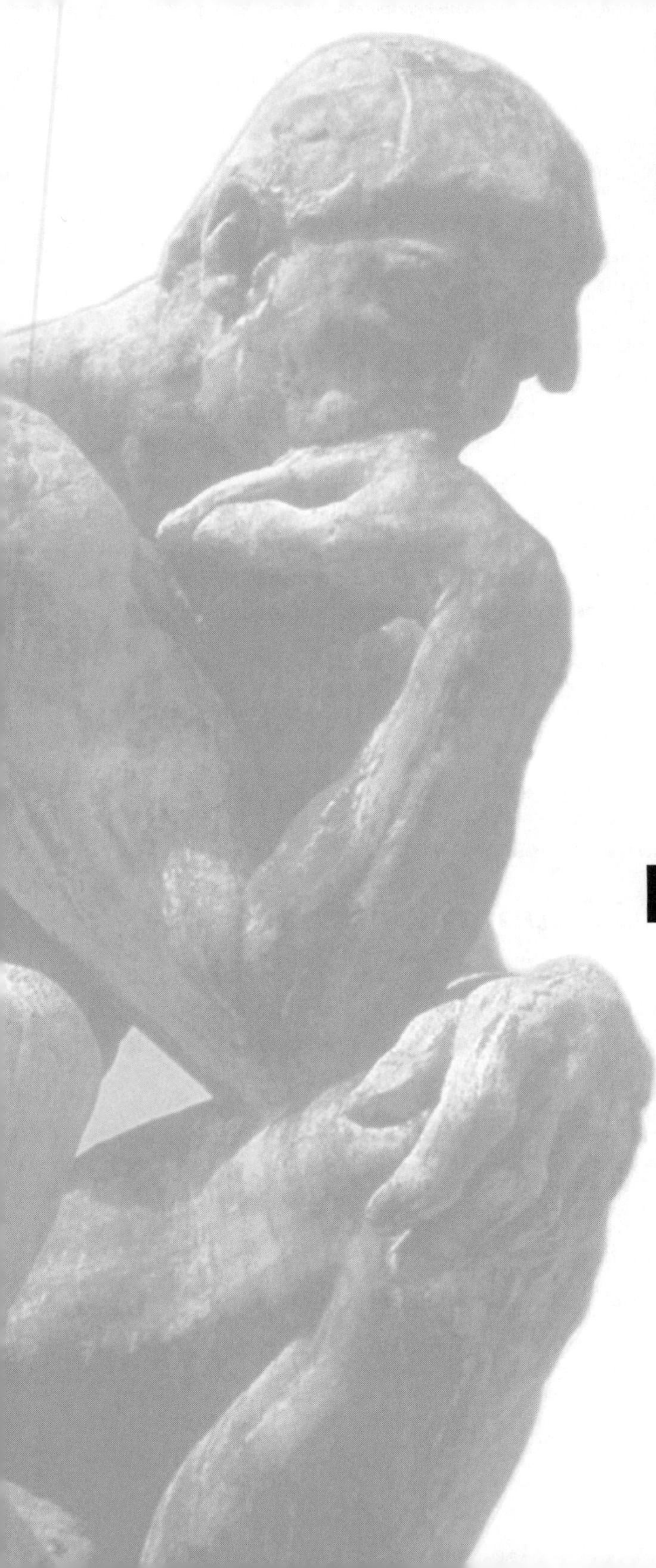

7

Support Software

CERTIFICATION OBJECTIVES

7.01	Compaq SmartStart and Support Software CD
7.02	Systems Configuration Utility
7.03	Configuring a PCI Board
7.04	Configuring ISA Boards
7.05	Advanced Features of System Configuration

This chapter will provide you with an introduction to the support software that Compaq makes available to help you properly set up, configure, and maintain the configuration of your Compaq server. We will look briefly at the SmartStart and Support Software CD that provides the tools necessary to perform this task.

You will also be provided with an overview of the Compaq Systems Configuration Utility. This utility is Compaq's tool for configuring a wide range of Compaq Server parameters that are vital to getting the most out of the features that Compaq has made available.

In addition to the task of defining your Compaq hardware settings, we will also be looking at some of the more advanced features available to you, such as viewing the server's health logs, and configuring your remote access parameters.

Together, this information will get you on your way to being able to properly configure and maintain the Compaq servers in your enterprise.

CERTIFICATION OBJECTIVE 7.01

Compaq SmartStart and Support Software CD

The Compaq SmartStart and Support Software CD is an indispensable tool for installing and configuring a Compaq server. Assuming that you are using a SmartStart-supported operating system, it is likely to be the first thing you will use when booting up your Compaq Server. Using SmartStart, you will be able to:

- Configure the hardware settings for your Compaq server
- Choose the operating system you wish to install
- Set the date and time on the server
- Load Compaq device drivers and management agents
- Create a disk to replicate the configuration of this server to other servers

The Compaq SmartStart and Support Software CD is supplied with all Compaq servers. It comes as part of the SmartStart package that contains a variety of Compaq software to help you quickly configure a Compaq server with all the features that makes Compaq servers so popular for enterprise server configurations. The SmartStart and Support Software CD is made up of the following three components:

- The Systems Configuration Utility
- Compaq Support Software such as the Compaq System Support Diskette (SSD)
- Compaq utilities such as the Array Configuration Utility, DiskBuilder (Compaq's tool for creating software diskettes), and ROM and OptionPAQs (Compaq's firmware and BIOS files)

This CD is part of software distribution called Compaq SmartStart, which contains a wide range of software packages, user guides, and manuals. The details of this complete software kit, along with an in-depth look at the SmartStart server installation process, will be discussed in a later chapter. In this chapter, we will focus primarily on the support software component.

During the setup process of a Compaq server, the SmartStart installation process creates a small partition on the server's hard disk. This partition is called the system configuration partition. It is approximately 32MB in size and will always be located at the very beginning of the drive.

The setup process will use this space to store the following programs:

- The Compaq Systems Configuration Utility
- Compaq ROMPaqs
- Compaq Inspect
- Compaq Array Configuration

Additionally, the system configuration parameters are saved to configuration files that are also saved in this partition. Though all of these features can be run from either the CD or floppy disks, having them locally on the server provides for much quicker access along with the convenience of accessing these utilities without having the SmartStart CD handy.

When all is said and done, the system partition houses the System Configuration Utility that provides the support software necessary to configure, maintain, and even troubleshoot your server's configuration.

CERTIFICATION OBJECTIVE 7.02

Systems Configuration Utility

The Systems Configuration Utility is used to perform a variety of server configuration and maintenance tasks. It can be run from floppy disks or

FROM THE FIELD

SmartStart Revisions

Compaq releases a new version of the SmartStart utilities approximately every two months to accommodate the latest additions to the product line. As an ASE, you will receive a free subscription to SmartStart that will allow you to keep your hardware up-to-date and to ensure that all peripheral firmware is compatible with your system.

Following the old adage, "If it ain't broke, don't fix it," it is probably best to avoid updating the system partition unless there is a specific requirement to do so. Usually, the requirement to update firmware comes from a failed attempt to perform an upgrade (such as installing a Service Pack) or when installing new hardware in the system.

While Compaq does perform extensive regression testing, before attempting to update all servers in the data center to the newest ROMPaq or SmartStart revision, you may wish to verify compatibility in a test/non- production environment. This can significantly reduce the risk of a system outage due to an unforeseen compatibility issue.

—Thomas E. Eck,
MCSE+I, MCSD, ASE, CCA, CNA

SmartStart CD, or it can be accessed on the system partition during the server bootup process. You may also be prompted to enter the Systems Configuration Utility upon any configuration errors during the server's POST (Power-On Self Test). It is also run during a SmartStart server installation. The Systems Configuration Utility is the backbone of Compaq's support software package.

The preferred method of accessing the Systems Configuration Utility is by pressing the F10 key when prompted during the bootup process. This option is presented to you immediately after the system POST by the message "Press F10 for system partition utilities" appearing in the top left of the screen. (On older servers, this message is replaced by a block cursor appearing in the top right corner of the screen.) This option is convenient because it can be accessed without the SmartStart media, but it is important to make sure that this information is kept up-to-date.

Booting from the SmartStart CD after the server is configured is still an option. The utility will scan the system to determine whether the server has already been configured. Providing it has, the process will simply load the system configuration utility with the same options you would have available had you chosen the F10 option.

As mentioned earlier, the System Configuration Utility provides a great deal of system options. The initial menu screen of the System Configuration Utility will present you with the following choices:

- **System Configuration Utility** This option is the primary focus of this chapter and will be discussed in more detail in the next section. This option will take you to another menu where you will be able to set up and configure hardware, run server diagnostics or perform ROMPaq updates.
- **Array Configuration Utility** Providing that your server is equipped with a SMART SCSI controller, you will be able to select this option from the menu as well. This option allows you to configure the hard disk array connected to the SMART controller.
- **Create/Update System Partition** As mentioned earlier, it is a good practice to keep your system partition up to date. This option will allow

you to update the system partition on a server. You simply need a newer version of the SmartStart software to perform the upgrade.

- **System Erase Utility** This option will do exactly what it says: erase your computer. Selecting this option will erase all data from all drives in an array or connected to the SCSI controller. Due to the destructive nature of this operation, you should only use this option when you want to perform a complete reinstall of your Compaq Server.
- **Create Support Software** Selecting this menu option will allow you to build (or *punch-out* in Compaq terms) Support Software Diskettes that you can then use on your servers. This software consists of everything from driver software to diagnostics and configuration tools.
- **Exit SmartStart** Quits the SmartStart program

The System Configuration Utility option contains the majority of the options that you will be using to maintain the server itself. Upon selecting this option you will be presented with another menu, which offers the following choices:

- Add/Remove Hardware
- View or Edit Details
- Diagnostics and Utilities
- Save Settings and Exit

Though each of these items seem rather self-explanatory, let's take a more in-depth look at the functions available under each menu choice.

Add Remove Hardware

This option will allow you to add or remove hardware devices from your system configuration. By selecting this menu option, your server will verify that all hardware has been identified and configured. You will then have the ability to add or remove devices that may not automatically be detected, such as many ISA devices. More information on configuring ISA devices can be found later in this chapter.

View or Edit Details

From here you will be able to view or edit all of the details available on your server's configuration. There is a large range of settings available to you from this option.

First, you can view the settings of your Compaq hardware devices. You can enable/disable any of the built-in devices such as SCSI controllers or network adapters. You also have the ability to change the system resources that some of these devices use. You may also enable or disable the onboard serial and parallel ports if desired.

Second, you can configure some of the basic system-specific options. These items include items such as the boot drive sequences and keyboard preferences.

Third, you can configure Compaq-specific features of the servers. For example, you can enable your server's Automatic Server Recovery (ASR) features. You can also specify the network settings required if you plan to use Compaq's capability to access the System Configuration Utility from a remote computer.

Diagnostics and Utilities

Choosing this menu option will present you with another menu from which you can perform a variety of system diagnostic and maintenance tasks. These menu options consist of:

- **Test Computer** This option will run a variety of diagnostics on the system hardware of your computer. The hardware tested includes the system processor, memory, keyboard, parallel/printer port, disk drive, serial ports, modems, fixed disks, tape drives, video cards, network cards, SCSI disks, CD-ROMs, and mouse or other pointing devices.

- **Inspect Computer** This menu will utilize the Compaq Inspect Utility. This utility queries your server to obtain a variety of system environment and configuration information. This information consists of memory configurations, system board information, and other general configuration information.
- **Upgrade Firmware** This option will upgrade the system firmware of your Compaq server. You can upgrade the system BIOS and firmware, but you cannot upgrade Option ROMs from this menu option.
- **Diagnose Drive Array** If your server is equipped with a SMART drive controller, this option will allow you to perform a set of diagnostics on the drive array and the controller. These diagnostics can provide valuable information on the health of your drive array and it's configuration.

on the job

Firmware and BIOS upgrades are part of the ever-changing world of server administration. However, caution should be applied whenever an upgrade is made available. It is never a good idea to go into a firmware upgrade blindly. You should make sure that you have researched the upgrade thoroughly before applying it to your computer. Find out what issues the upgrade addresses and determine whether it applies to you. Also, make sure that there aren't any other device or software upgrades that have to be performed in conjunction with the firmware upgrade. Failure to follow these steps can result in your system failing to function correctly. Also, remember that if you are going to perform the upgrade from the system partition, you may have to upgrade the system partition before performing the upgrade to ensure that you have the latest file versions available.

Save Settings and Exit

This option simply does what it says. It saves any changes that you have made to the configuration files and exits the System Configuration Utility. This option results in the computer rebooting and running with the new system configuration.

QUESTIONS AND ANSWERS	
What is the best way to run the System Configuration Utility?	The easiest and fastest way would be simply to boot your server with the SmartStart Support Software CD in the CD-ROM. This will provide the fastest means of running the utilities.
If it isn't necessary to have the System Configuration Utility on a system partition, why use the disk space for it?	Though it isn't necessary, it is definitely convenient. Having the system partition allows you access to the System Configuration Utility without needing to have a CD or floppy disks handy. With the size of today's hard disks, the 32MB of space needed is minimal when compared to the convenience.
How important is it to keep the System Configuration up-to-date?	This depends on the reason for each upgrade. Compaq always makes complete release notes available on their software updates. The best advice is to review these notes and decide if they apply to you and if they are worth the time you will spend to upgrade the partition.
I need to make a change to my Compaq server, but do not want to make it unavailable. Is it possible to run the System Configuration Utility without taking the server down?	There is no way to run the System Configuration Utility once the OS has been loaded. The System Configuration Utility can only be accessed during the boot process.

CERTIFICATION OBJECTIVE 7.03

Configuring a PCI Board

PCI devices can be configured by the computer system without jumpers or the worry of hardware conflicts. This capability makes setting up your Compaq server a breeze.

You can actually install all of your PCI devices, such as network adapters and SMART Array Controllers, into the computer without having to specify a single address or IRQ setting. While the System Configuration

Utility is running, it will identify all of your PCI hardware and automatically assign it the appropriate hardware settings, avoiding conflicts.

As mentioned in the preceding "View or Edit Details" section, you can still change these settings manually, if you desire. However, in most cases there really should be no reason to do this.

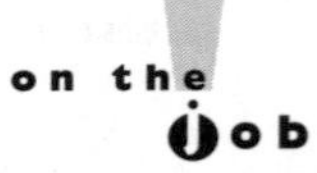

The Compaq Inspect utility provides you with a good means of documenting your server's hardware configuration. For support reasons, it is often very helpful to know the hardware and to know how it is configured in your server. For example, if a device in your system fails and renders the system unusable, having your hardware documented will provide you with a great point of reference to the information you need to obtain a replacement part. These reports also provide an easy means for you to help keep inventory records accurate and up-to-date. Another common use of this information is to identify the hardware resources being used in your machine. Having this information available allows you to identify available resources for a device you may wish to add to your computer.

CERTIFICATION OBJECTIVE 7.04

Configuring ISA Boards

Unlike PCI devices, most ISA boards require that you specify their settings via jumpers or switches located on the board. They also lack the onboard software that makes them detectable to the same system that configures the PCI devices. Because of this, the system configuration may not be able to see them and add them to the configured device list of your server. This may also lead to the system configuration setting a PCI device to the same hardware settings as your ISA device, causing a hardware conflict.

To get around this potential problem, Compaq recommends taking the following steps to help ensure that all devices are discovered and configured properly.

1. Place your ISA devices into the computer first, keeping the PCI devices out for now. This will allow you to configure the devices in the System Configuration Utility manually. By doing this, you are making the system aware of the ISA devices and the system resources that they are using.
2. Add your PCI devices. Because the system has already been made aware of the ISA cards and their resources, it is able to configure the PCI devices with settings that will not result in a hardware conflict.

Using this process is much easier than manually trying to set the settings for all of your devices at once. It allows the system configuration to automatically maintain the settings for your PCI devices that will make the addition of future hardware much easier.

These days, most of the devices can be configured automatically. However, from time to time it will be necessary to add an ISA device, such as an internal modem, to your computer. If this requirement is known at the time that the server is being set up, then the steps just described will work fine. However, sometimes the requirement comes after the server has already been configured and put online. In this case, you may not want to remove all of your PCI devices and follow these steps. The Compaq Inspect Utility could identify the resources currently in use. Once you have this information, it should be relatively easy to configure the new device with settings that will not result in a conflict.

CERTIFICATION OBJECTIVE 7.05

Advanced Features of System Configuration

You can enter the Advanced Mode of the system configuration at any time by pressing CTRL-A on your keyboard. Upon pressing this key combination, you should receive a pop-up window that states that Advanced Mode has been enabled.

By entering into this mode of operation, you can view and modify the server's health and error logs. This information can be found under the System Diagnostics and Utilities option from the System Configuration Utility main menu.

If your server has experienced and logged any errors, you will be able to view them, clear them, or mark them corrected. It should be noted that although the errors can be viewed from many locations, such as Compaq Insight Manager, this is the only way that these errors can be cleared from the system's integrated log.

CERTIFICATION SUMMARY

This chapter covered a component of the SmartStart software that is critical to configuring and maintaining your server. The SmartStart and Support Software CD is comprised of the Systems Configuration Utility, Compaq Support Software, and Compaq utilities.

The System Configuration Utility is Compaq's primary means of configuring your Compaq Server. It is used to install and configure hardware, set system-specific settings, and run a variety of diagnostics and utilities. You learned how to configure ISA and PCI hardware devices using this tool.

Compaq diagnostic utilities are a vital aspect of supporting and maintaining your Compaq servers. They allow you to test the hardware of your system, query your server to obtain system environment and configuration information, upgrade your system firmware, and perform diagnostics on the drive array and the controller.

Advanced features of the System Configuration Utility allow you to view and modify the server's health and error logs.

TWO-MINUTE DRILL

- ❑ The Compaq SmartStart and Support Software CD is an indispensable tool for installing and configuring a Compaq server.
- ❑ Compaq releases a new version of the SmartStart utilities approximately every two months to accommodate the latest additions to the product line.
- ❑ The system partition houses the System Configuration Utility that provides the support software necessary to configure, maintain, and even troubleshoot your server's configuration.
- ❑ The Systems Configuration Utility is used to perform a variety of server configuration and maintenance tasks. It also contains the majority of the options that you will be using to maintain the server itself.
- ❑ The Add Remove Hardware option will allow you to add or remove hardware devices from your system configuration.
- ❑ From the View or Edit Details option you will be able to view or edit all of the details available on your server's configuration.
- ❑ Choosing the Diagnostics and Utilities menu option allows you to perform a variety of system diagnostic and maintenance tasks including:
    - ❑ Test Computer
    - ❑ Inspect Computer
    - ❑ Upgrade Firmware
    - ❑ Diagnose Drive Array
- ❑ The Save Settings and Exit option saves any changes that you have made to the configuration files and exits the System Configuration Utility.

- PCI devices can be configured by the computer system without jumpers or the worry of hardware conflicts.
- While the System Configuration Utility is running, it will identify all of your PCI hardware and automatically assign it the appropriate hardware settings, avoiding conflicts.
- Most ISA boards require that you specify their settings via jumpers or switches located on the board, so Compaq recommends a step-by-step process to help ensure that all devices are discovered and configured properly.
- You can enter the Advanced Mode of the system configuration at any time by pressing CTRL-A on your keyboard. By entering into this mode of operation, you can view and modify the server's health and error logs.

SELF TEST

The following Self Test questions will help you measure your understanding of the material presented in this chapter. Read all the choices carefully, as there may be more than one correct answer. Choose all correct answers for each question.

1. Which of the following is not a component of the SmartStart and Support Software CD?

   A. The Systems Configuration Utility

   B. Compaq Insight Management software

   C. Compaq utility software

   D. Compaq support software

2. Which of the following options can be performed using the software on the SmartStart and Support Software CD?

   A. Create Support Software Diskettes.

   B. Run server diagnostics.

   C. Run the Array Configuration Utility.

   D. All of the above

3. Which of the following is not a menu option available when running the SmartStart?

   A. System Configuration Utility

   B. Array Configuration Utility

   C. Create/Update the System Partition

   D. None of the above

4. When is the System Configuration Partition created?

   A. Upon running the System Configuration Utility by pressing F10

   B. Upon the installation of the server's operating system

   C. Upon running the System Configuration Utility from the Smart-Start CD during the initial server setup

   D. Upon running the System Configuration Partition Creation Utility from the Utilities folder of the SmartStart Support Software CD

5. Which of the following would not normally be found on the System Configuration Partition?

   A. The Array Diagnostic Utility

   B. The System Configuration Utility

   C. Hardware device drivers, such as NIC drivers, for your installed operating system

   D. System ROM Upgrade files

6. Which of the following is not a means of accessing the System Configuration Utility?

   A. Choosing the option for the System Configuration Utilities in the Compaq Utilities and Software program group in Windows NT

   B. Selecting the appropriate option during a POST error

C. Booting the server with a set of floppy disks containing the System Configuration Utility

D. Booting the server with the Smart-Start CD

7. Which of the following tasks would warrant running the System Configuration Utility?

A. You receive a hardware configuration error during POST at bootup.

B. You need to install the driver for a new controller card that you just installed.

C. You have added memory to your server.

D. All of the above

8. Which task could not be performed from the System Configuration Utility?

A. Running the Array Configuration Utility

B. Adding a network adapter

C. Removing a SCSI controller

D. Configuring the parameters of your UPS

9. Which of the following scenarios would warrant the use of the System Erase option?

A. You need to undo the configuration options you just selected in the System Configuration Utility.

B. You have to correct an incorrect hardware configuration and start over.

C. You no longer require any of the information stored on the server and wish to perform a completely new installation, including the operating system.

D. You wish to reset all server parameters with the exception of the hard disk contents.

10. Which System Configuration Utility menu option would you choose if you wanted to erase the critical error log of your Compaq Server?

A. View or Edit Details

B. Diagnostics and Utilities

C. Add/Remove Hardware

D. You can't erase the critical error log of a Compaq Server.

11. Which System Configuration Utility menu option would you choose if you wanted to change the network configuration for your remote access to the System Configuration Utility?

A. View or Edit Details

B. Diagnostics and Utilities

C. Add/Remove Hardware

D. You cannot configure this option from within the System Configuration Utility.

12. If installing an ISA board during the initial setup, what steps should be taken to assure the proper configuration of all devices in the server?

A. Add the ISA device along with all PCI devices and allow the System Configuration Utility to configure all devices.

B. Add the PCI devices first, determine which settings they have been assigned, and then configure the ISA device so that it doesn't conflict.

C. Add the ISA device first and manually add it via the Add/Remove Hardware menu option. Then add the remaining PCI devices and allow the System Configuration Utility to configure them.

D. ISA devices are not supported by the System Configuration Utility.

13. If installing an ISA board after the initial server setup, what steps should be taken to assure the proper configuration of all devices in the server?

A. Add the ISA device along with all PCI devices and allow the System Configuration Utility to configure the new device.

B. Determine which settings have been assigned to the PCI devices and then configure the ISA device so that it doesn't conflict.

C. Remove the PCI devices, then add the ISA device first and manually add it via the Add/Remove Hardware menu option. Then add the remaining PCI devices and allow the System Configuration Utility to configure them.

D. ISA devices cannot be added after the server has been configured.

14. You would like to see a detailed summary of your Compaq server's configuration. Which System Configuration Utility menu option would allow you to obtain this information?

A. Add/Remove Hardware

B. View or Edit Details

C. Diagnostics and Utilities

D. None of the above

15. How do you enable the Advanced Mode of the System Configuration Utility?

A. This mode is enabled by default.

B. By selecting the Advanced Mode option from the System Configuration Utility Main menu

C. By pressing the CTRL-A key combination from within the System Configuration Utility menu

D. Advanced mode cannot be enabled from within the System Configuration Utility.

ASE

ACCREDITED SYSTEMS ENGINEER

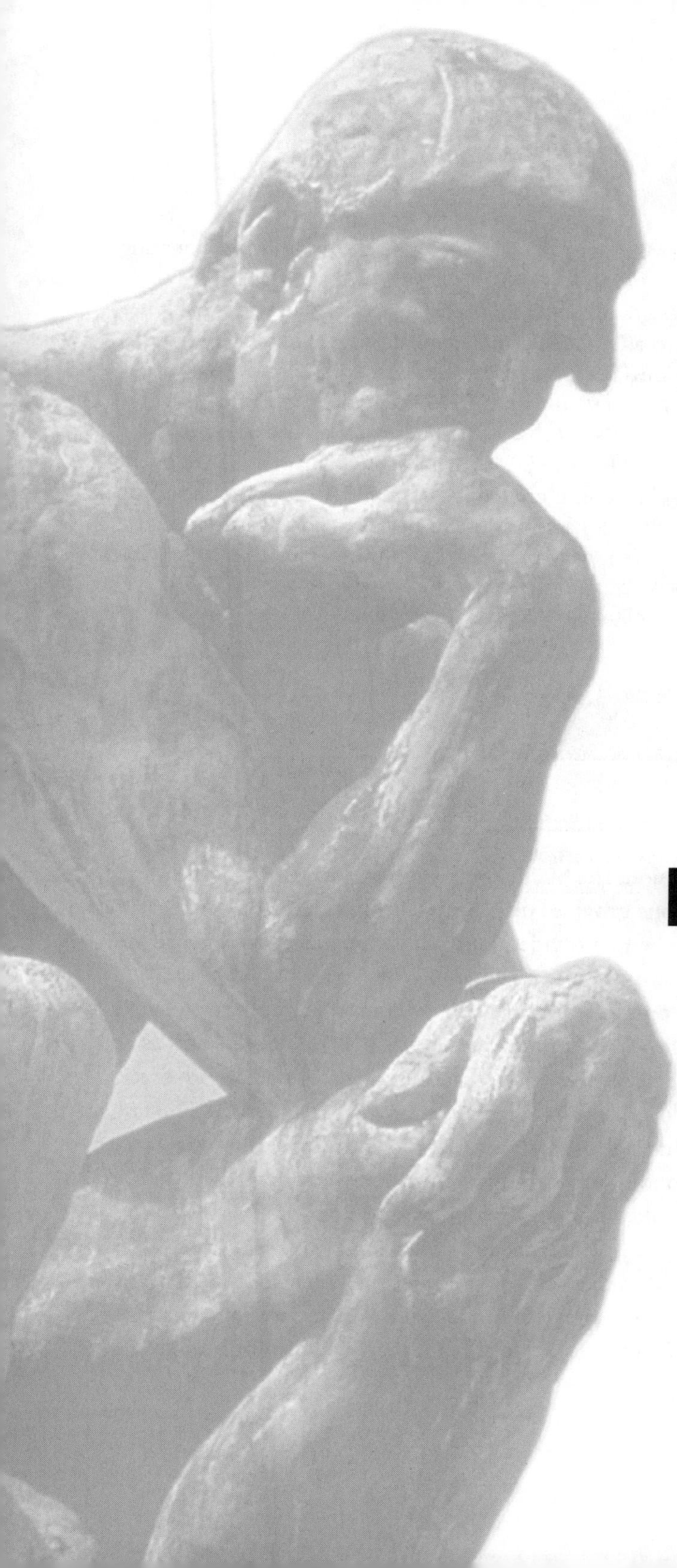

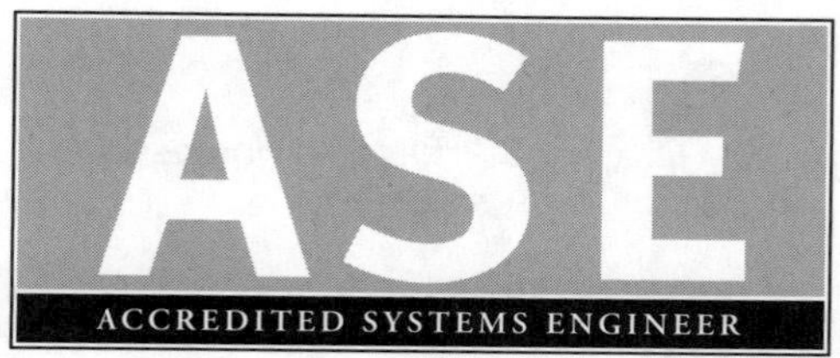

8

Disk Technologies

CERTIFICATION OBJECTIVES

8.01	SCSI
8.02	SCSI Transfer Rates and Data Widths
8.03	SCSI ID Settings
8.04	Types of SCSI Cabling Requirements

SCSI (small computer system interface) is a system-level I/O bus designed for connecting peripheral devices such as hard disks, tape and DAT drives, CD-ROM drives, and scanners. The SCSI standard was designed to attach intelligent controllers to a cable, allowing signals and data to flow in parallel to all attached intelligent devices. The advantage of SCSI is the capability to control up to eight devices (16 on later versions of SCSI) or logical units (LUN). However, one SCSI ID is always assigned to the SCSI controller, reducing the maximum of available IDs by one. One of the LUNs is the SCSI adapter card, also known as a host bus adapter (HBA), which is the controller for the SCSI chain. A SCSI chain consists of the controller, cables, and all attached devices. Unlike IDE controllers, the HBA doesn't need to be told the number of cylinders, heads, or sectors on each drive; the device is intelligent enough to manage the functions as well as any errors that may occur. Due to the flexibility of the SCSI standard, compatibility issues arose, thus prompting updates to the standard such as SCSI-2, which provided tighter definitions and all but eliminated these compatibility issues.

CERTIFICATION OBJECTIVE 8.01

SCSI

Regardless of the version, the SCSI standard includes a number of unique characteristics. The bus provides distributed arbitration or bus-contention logic. The priority scheme provides control to the highest-priority device that is contending for use of the eight-bit bus.

Communication on the SCSI bus is allowed between only two devices at a time. When two devices communicate on the bus, one device acts as an *initiator*, while the other is the *target*. The initiator originates an operation, selects the target devices, and handles communication and data. The target receives, manages, and performs these operations. Information transfers on the bus are asynchronous and conform to a request/acknowledge (REQ/ACK) handshake, followed by one byte of data.

Synchronous transfer means that the signal is dependent on the occurrences of specific events such as timing signals. Asynchronous transfer is the exact opposite—the signal may start and stop at any time regardless of timing signals. Asynchronous mode is faster than synchronous mode.

SCSI-2

SCSI-2 is the second eight-bit implementation of the SCSI standard, consisting of the SCSI standard with many improvements. There are two implementations of SCSI-2, *single-ended interface* and *differential interface.*

Single-ended interfaces are more common. They are used for internal cabling, whereas differential interfaces are used for external cabling. Differential interfaces use a twisted-pair cabling scheme for signals. The signal integrity is verified at the cable end before the data is passed to the devices.

Single-ended and differential cabling and electrical characteristics are very different and should not be used on the same bus. Differential cabling can be up to 25 meters; single-ended cabling supports a maximum of six meters.

Fast SCSI-2

The Fast SCSI-2 standard improved over SCSI-2 by doubling the transfer rate on the data bus to 10MB/second. As with SCSI-2, the bus is eight-bit and utilizes 50-pin internal and external cables. Other than these differences, SCSI-2 and Fast SCSI-2 are essentially the same.

Fast-Wide SCSI-2

The wide version of the SCSI-2 standard is the most widely used version of SCSI today. It does away with many of the limitations of eight-bit devices and is most commonly implemented as 16-bit, using a 68-pin cable and a transfer rate of 20MB/second. Because Fast-Wide SCSI-2 is a 16-bit implementation, there are 16 legal device IDs available (0–15).

Throughput is increased by widening the bus on which the data travels. While Fast SCSI-2 is limited to a transfer rate of 10MB/second, Fast-Wide SCSI-2 offers a transfer rate of 20MB/second by moving more data per transfer.

Fast-Wide mode is chosen on a drive-by-drive basis, through negotiation between the controller and the drive during the Command Setup phase.

What this means is that a Fast SCSI-2 controller can be used with both Fast SCSI-2 and Fast-Wide SCSI-2 drives. The reverse is also true, Fast-Wide SCSI-2 controllers can communicate with both types of drives.

In my preconsulting days, I learned the hard way that Compaq only supports eight IDs per bus. I was configuring a server for a client with nine external hard disks and a tape drive. I proceeded to set the IDs 0 through 6, 8, and 9, and set the tape drive to 15. When I booted the machine, nothing happened. I rechecked all IDs and termination, but the machine still wouldn't boot. After approximately an hour of fighting with the situation, I decided to consult the book. After maybe three minutes of searching the manual, I found, plain as day, the statement: Compaq supports only eight SCSI IDs per bus. Needless to say, I haven't forgotten that fact since. When in doubt, read the manual!

Ultra SCSI

Ultra SCSI is fast becoming the de facto standard in many corporate servers. Ultra SCSI comes in two flavors: Wide-Ultra SCSI-3, a 16-bit implementation, and Ultra-Wide SCSI, a 32-bit implementation. Both versions of Ultra SCSI have transfer rates of 40MB/second.

The newest version of SCSI is Ultra2-SCSI. Ultra2-SCSI comes in two flavors, single channel and dual channel. Single channel achieved a transfer rate of 80MB/second, while dual channel boasts a transfer rate of 160MB/second. The maximum cable length of Ultra2-SCSI is 12 meters. Ultra2-SCSI is an excellent choice for systems running high-end, cutting-edge software solutions such as multimedia production, digital video editing, and viewing.

Ultra2-SCSI drives are low voltage differential (LVD) devices. LVD increases the maximum burst transfer rate to 80MB/second, provides data integrity, extends the bus cable lengths to 25 meters (12 meters with 16 devices), and provides easy system configuration for up to 16 devices. LVD is compatible with the existing installed SCSI bus. A DiffSens circuit determines the type of SCSI bus the device is being used on (LVD or single-ended), and configures the drive to the appropriate bus capability.

CERTIFICATION OBJECTIVE 8.02

SCSI Transfer Rates and Data Widths

Table 8-1 details the SCSI versions and their corresponding rates and widths. It is important to know this information by heart.

SCSI and Overall Data Transfer Performance

The completion of an I/O request to or from a SCSI device requires three stages:

- **Command Setup** To set up a request, the controller initiates a SCSI command to an individual device by addressing the device using its SCSI ID.
- **Data Transfer** Once the device receives a command, it transfers or receives data from the controller.
- **Command Complete** After the requested data has been transferred, the drive transmits a completion status back to the controller and transitions the bus back to a free state so it may receive the next request.

TABLE 8-1 Transfer Rates and Data Widths of SCSI Standards

Version	Transfer Rate	Data Width
SCSI-1	5MB/second	8-bit
SCSI-2	5MB/second	8-bit
Fast SCSI-2	10MB/second	8-bit
Fast-Wide SCSI-2	20MB/second	16-bit
Wide-Ultra SCSI-3	40MB/second	16-bit
Ultra-Wide SCSI	40MB/second	32-bit
Ultra2-SCSI	80MB/second	32-bit and 64-bit

Drive performance depends on various operations. Two of the most common specifications used to measure performance are seek time and latency. Since the SCSI-1 standard was created, these operations have improved by more than 60 percent. Random and sequential data throughputs have increased by approximately 600 percent. While advances in hardware technologies have achieved these gains, a major factor in these advances is Tagged Command Queuing (TCQ).

Tagged Command Queuing

Implementing queuing is optional for SCSI-2 using two methods, tagged and untagged. Tagged queuing allows a device to accept multiple commands until its command queue is full. These commands are queued for execution at a later time. The device that sent the command may specify a fixed order of execution, specify that the command sent be executed immediately, or add and delete commands.

Queuing achieves its goal by allowing a drive a number of commands and performing those commands while off the SCSI bus, thus freeing up the bus so other devices may use it. The device will indicate that is has completed the commands, or its buffer is full and is ready to transfer data.

Untagged queuing is supported by SCSI and SCSI-2 devices. It allows a device to accept one command at a time. It is, however, able to accept a second command while processing the original command—the devices are still able to remove themselves from the SCSI bus while performing the command, thus freeing up the bus. This method is obviously slower than tagged queuing.

CERTIFICATION OBJECTIVE 8.03

SCSI ID Settings

SCSI IDs are normally set on devices via jumpers or dip switches (jumpers are the more common selectors). IDs are automatically assigned on hot-pluggable hard disks. There are eight (0–7) legal IDs on SCSI and

SCSI-2 buses, and 16 (0-15) on Wide buses. However, as stated earlier, Compaq only supports eight IDs per bus. ID jumpers/dip switches are in blocks of three (or four for Wide devices) with each jumper being assigned a value of 1, 2, 4, or 8. SCSI IDs are determined by calculating the values of the shorted jumpers (or dip-switches in the On position). No jumpers shorted indicates SCSI ID 0.

Table 8-2 shows how jumper values correspond to SCSI IDs.

Lower SCSI IDs have priority on the bus, so the system's boot hard disk should be set to ID 0. Normally, hard disks come factory-set to ID 0, CD-ROM drives to 3, tape drives to 6, and SCSI adapters to 7. In most

TABLE 8-2 SCSI IDs and Corresponding Jumper Values

SCSI ID	Jumper Value 1	Jumper Value 2	Jumper Value 4	Jumper Value 8
0				
1	X			
2		X		
3	X	X		
4			X	
5	X		X	
6		X	X	
7	X	X	X	
8				X
9	X			X
10		X		X
11	X	X		X
12			X	X
13	X		X	X
14		X	X	X
15	X	X	X	X

situations this ID assignment will work, but if more than three hard drives are to be installed, the ID of the CD-ROM must be increased, as all hard disk IDs should be lower than all other devices. Tape drives must always be the highest ID, with the adapter being the exception.

As a consultant, one of the most common problems I run into is clients who have configured their own server, but cannot get it to boot. The first thing I always do is remove all SCSI devices and check the IDs. Ninety-five percent of the time, the IDs are the problem. Either the hard disks were installed all set to default (hard disks come factory-set at ID 0) or one of the hard disks is set to the same ID as either the CD-ROM drive (if it's not an IDE drive) or the tape drive. Always begin the hard disk ID at 0, set the CD-ROM and/or tape drive to the highest IDs available (5 and 6). If you are using hot-pluggable hard disks, make sure that you are not manually setting the drives' IDs, as the hot-pluggable backplane takes care of this for you. Double-checking your SCSI IDs will save you time and a few headaches.

CERTIFICATION OBJECTIVE 8.04

Types of SCSI Cabling Requirements

There are three types of SCSI cabling, Centronics, 50-pin, and 68-pin (internal and external). Centronics cables are used mainly for SCSI-1 connections and are only available as external cables. Use 50-pin cables for SCSI-1, SCSI-2, and Fast SCSI-2 drives, and are available as both internal and external. Use 68-pin cables for Wide and Ultra devices, also as internal and external.

All SCSI chains require termination in one form or another. While there are four methods of termination, only two are widely used and approved as a standard: passive and active. Both ends of the SCSI bus must be terminated, which means that if there are only internal devices, the adapter itself must be terminated, as well as the last device on the chain (or the cable itself).

Passive Termination

Passive termination has been used since SCSI-1. It isn't the cleanest way to terminate a SCSI bus. Passive termination is achieved by placing a terminating resistor on either end of the SCSI chain. The problem with this method is that the SCSI cable is usually over-terminated, meaning there is a mismatched impedance causing reflections of the signal as it bounces off the ends of the SCSI chain. This may result in data errors. This problem is multiplied when using multiple drives and higher speeds.

Active Termination

Active termination was added with the SCSI-2 standard and is the most widely used and preferred method of SCSI bus termination. By using a regulated voltage, the required terminated resistance is achieved, and each signal is completed via the terminating circuit, thus nearly eliminating all data errors. Active termination is achieved by a jumper or dip-switch on the last device on the SCSI chain, or as a small, block-like piece attached to the last connection on the cable itself. The controller is usually either self-terminating or set via the controller's BIOS software.

Termination Notes

There are a few important facts regarding termination that you must know in order to configure a SCSI bus properly. Keeping these items in mind will help you avoid problems and greatly reduce your stress level.

- Hot-pluggable drives should not be terminated, as the hot-plug backplane handles the termination of the SCSI bus.

- When mixing both internal and external SCSI devices on the same chain, the controller must not be terminated, but the last external device and last internal device on the chain must be terminated.
- To enable termination, some hard disks require both a termination jumper and a termination power jumper to be set.

A problem I frequently run into at client sites is termination errors. They range from having too many devices terminated, to having the wrong devices terminated, or having no termination at all. Always double-check your termination.

Another issue is active termination blocks on the SCSI cable that have gone bad. If your server will not boot, and everything seems to be set correctly after you have checked all drives for ID and termination errors, try replacing the active terminator on the end of the cable. I have revived many "dead" servers this way.

FROM THE FIELD

Cable Check

When ordering Compaq SCSI hardware, be sure you have all appropriate cabling for the server. Compaq is very good about providing almost all necessary cabling for basic configurations, but you may need termination devices or extra internal ribbon cables for advanced options, such as an optional drive cage.

After becoming an ASE, Compaq will send you a subscription to QuickFind which provides you with part numbers and a searchable database of their products. This CD is very handy for ordering spare parts and additional cables or simply learning more about the internals of a machine.

—Thomas E. Eck,
MCSE+I, MCSD, ASE, CCA, CNA

QUESTIONS AND ANSWERS	
I installed a Fast SCSI-2 hard disk, but my system has a Fast-Wide SCSI-2 adapter. Will this work?	Yes. Fast-Wide SCSI-2 adapters can control Fast SCSI-2 drives. However, you will need a 50-pin-to-68-pin adapter to attach the drive to the cable.
I installed a Fast-Wide SCSI-2 adapter and eight external hard disks with IDs set from 0 to 8. I made sure none of the IDs was set to 7, to avoid a conflict with the adapter. However, the system will not boot.	While there are 16 legal device IDs available with Fast-Wide SCSI-2, Compaq supports only eight IDs per channel. Move one of the drives to another channel or another adapter.
The system I am configuring will be used for digital video editing. What SCSI version should I use?	Definitely use Ultra2-SCSI. The 80MB/second transfer rate is a must for this sort of application.
I must install six Fast SCSI-2 hard disks, a CD-ROM drive, and a tape drive into the system. I only have room for one SCSI adapter. What should I do?	Install an IDE CD-ROM drive, thus freeing up a needed SCSI ID. A second option is to install a multichannel SCSI adapter and place a SCSI CD-ROM on the second SCSI channel.
The SCSI chain in my server is using a passive terminator. I seem to be getting a large amount of data errors. How can I resolve this issue?	Replace the passive terminator with an active one. Active terminators eliminate the signal bounce that you may experience with passive termination.

CERTIFICATION SUMMARY

In this chapter, we learned about the six versions of the SCSI standard: SCSI-1, SCS1-2, Fast SCSI-2, Fast-Wide SCSI-2, Wide-Ultra SCSI-3, and Ultra-Wide SCSI. First, we learned that SCSI is a system-level channel bus designed for interconnecting peripheral devices such as hard disks, CD-ROMS, and tape drives. Each version of SCSI has been a major improvement over the preceding version. We discovered that SCSI controllers do not need to be instructed as to the physical specifications of devices. The local devices are intelligent enough to manage these functions.

We covered the transfer rates and data widths of all SCSI versions and the three stages of SCSI I/O requests: Command Setup, Data Transfer and Command Complete. We learned how to determine the SCSI ID of a device, what it should be set to, how to terminate the SCSI chain, and the difference between passive and active termination. We also learned that you should never set SCSI IDs or termination on hot-pluggable drives.

TWO-MINUTE DRILL

- Communication on the SCSI bus is allowed between only two devices at a time.
- There are two implementations of SCSI-2, *single-ended interface* and *differential interface*.
- The Fast SCSI-2 standard improved over SCSI-2 by doubling the transfer rate on the data bus to 10MB/second.
- Because Fast-Wide SCSI-2 is a 16-bit implementation, there are 16 legal device IDs available (0–15).
- Ultra SCSI comes in two flavors: Wide-Ultra SCSI-3, a 16-bit implementation, and Ultra-Wide SCSI, a 32-bit implementation.
- Table 8-1 details the SCSI versions and their corresponding rates and widths.
- The completion of an I/O request to or from a SCSI device requires three stages:
  - Command Setup
  - Data Transfer
  - Command Complete
- SCSI IDs are normally set on devices via jumpers or dip-switches (jumpers are the more common selectors).
- Compaq only supports eight IDs per bus.
- There are three types of SCSI cabling, Centronics, 50-pin, and 68-pin (internal and external).

- ❑ All SCSI chains require termination in one form or another.
- ❑ Passive termination is achieved by placing a terminating resistor on either end of the SCSI chain.
- ❑ Active termination is achieved by a jumper or dip-switch on the last device on the SCSI chain, or as a small, block-like piece attached to the last connection on the cable itself.
- ❑ There are a few important facts regarding termination that you must know in order to configure a SCSI bus properly.

SELF TEST

The following Self Test questions will help you measure your understanding of the material presented in this chapter. Read all the choices carefully, as there may be more than one correct answer. Choose all correct answers for each question.

1. Communication is allowed between how many devices on the bus at one time?

   A. One

   B. Two

   C. Three

   D. All

2. What are the two implementations of SCSI-2?

   A. Single-ended interface

   B. Dual-ended interface

   C. Differential interface

   D. Asynchronous interface

3. What is the maximum length supported using single-ended interface cabling?

   A. 3 meters

   B. 6 meters

   C. 9 meters

   D. 12 meters

4. What is the maximum length supported using differential interface cabling?

   A. 25 meters

   B. 30 meters

   C. 35 meters

   D. 40 meters

5. Fast SCSI-2 utilizes 68-pin cables.

   A. True

   B. False

6. Choose the two true statements regarding Fast-Wide SCSI-2.

   A. There are eight legal IDs available

   B. There are 16 legal IDs available

   C. Compaq supports 16 IDs per bus

   D. Compaq supports eight IDs per bus

7. How is Fast-Wide mode chosen?

   A. By the jumpers on the drives

   B. By the settings on the adapter

   C. The cable determines it

   D. On a drive-by-drive basis

8. What is the maximum cable length of Ultra2-SCSI?

   A. 8 meters

   B. 12 meters

   C. 16 meters

   D. 25 meters

9. What is the transfer rate of Fast-Wide SCSI-2?

   A. 5MB/second

   B. 10MB/second

   C. 20MB/second

   D. 40MB/second

10. What is the data width of SCSI-2?

    A. 8-bit

    B. 16-bit

C. 32-bit
D. 64-bit

11. What is the data width of Ultra2-SCSI?
A. 8-bit
B. 16-bit
C. 32-bit
D. 64-bit

12. Which is not a SCSI I/O request stage?
A. Command Setup
B. Command Transfer
C. Data Transfer
D. Command Complete

13. Tagged command queuing allows a device to accept multiple commands.
A. True
B. False

14. To what ID are most SCSI controllers set?
A. 0
B. 3
C. 6
D. 7

15. Which is not a common type of SCSI cable?
A. Centronics
B. 25-pin
C. 50-pin
D. 68-pin

16. Which type of termination uses a regulated voltage?
A. Passive
B. Active

17. Hot-pluggable drives should be manually terminated.
A. True
B. False

18. Some hard disks require a termination power jumper.
A. True
B. False

ASE

ACCREDITED SYSTEMS ENGINEER

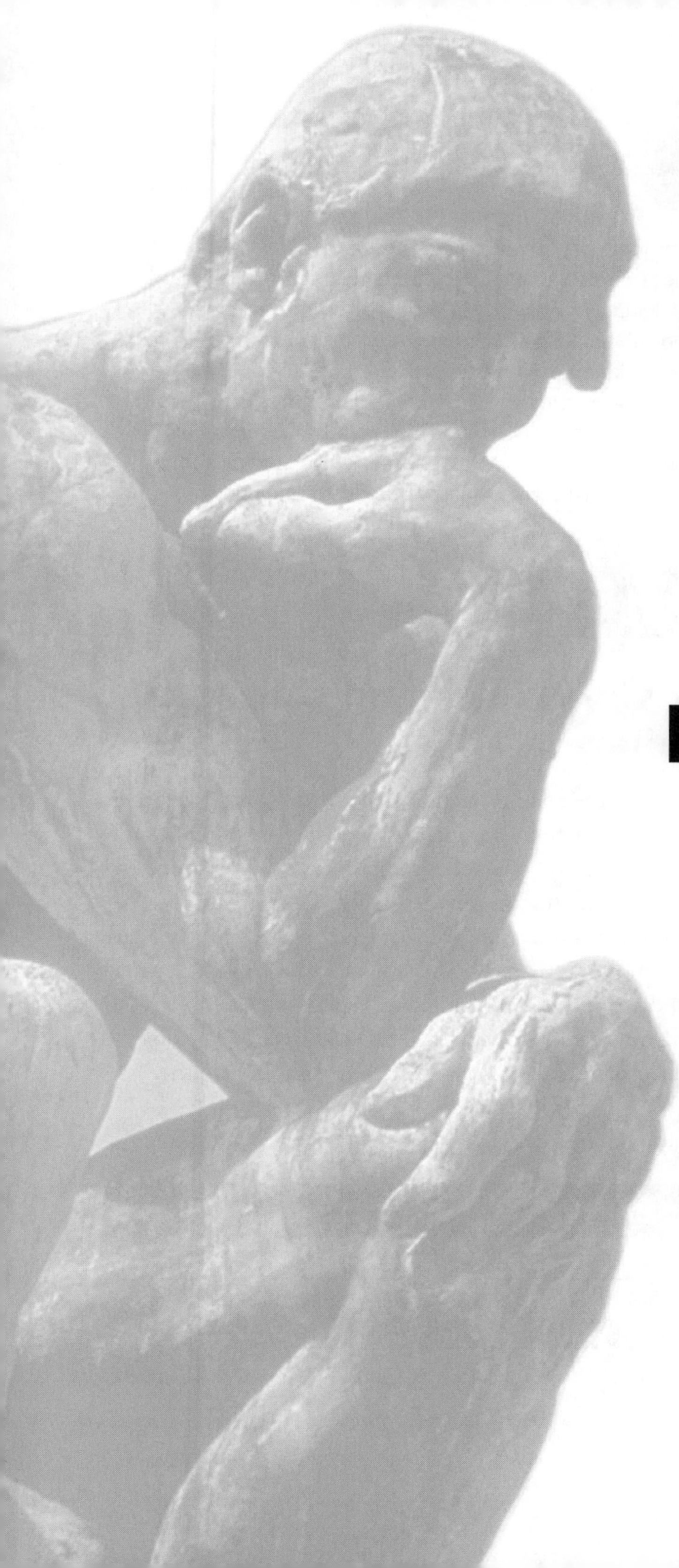

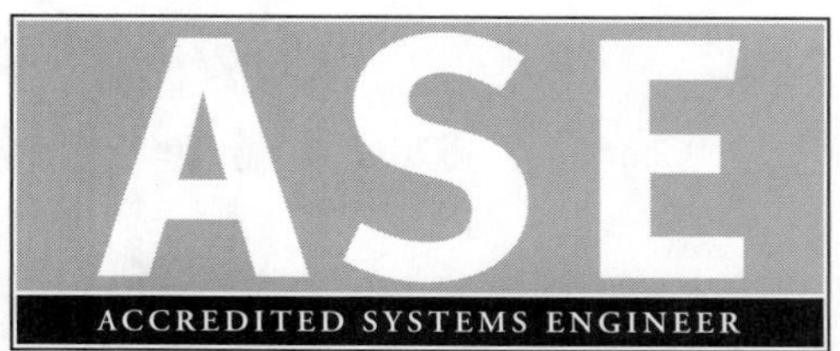

9

Drive Array Technology

CERTIFICATION OBJECTIVES

9.01	Compaq SMART Array Controller and Compaq SMART-2 Array Controller
9.02	Fault Prevention and Fault Tolerance Features
9.03	RAID Levels of Fault Tolerance
9.04	Operation and Configuration Issues of Hot-Pluggable Hard Disks
9.05	Hardware Data Striping
9.06	Logical Volumes Supported by the SMART Array Controller
9.07	Protecting Write Data in the SMART Array Controller and SMART-2 Array Controller
9.08	Online Spares
9.09	Drive Array Advanced Diagnostics (DAAD)
9.10	Converting a SMART Array Controller to a SMART-2 Array Controller

This chapter will cover array technologies. We will cover the Compaq SMART array controllers and their characteristics, fault prevention, and tolerance. Array technology is probably the most significant advance in storage to date. Before arrays, administrators were forced to rely on multiple single drives, with the only form of fault tolerance being a tape backup. If a drive failed, data would be unavailable until it could be restored from tape. Now, with array technologies, barring a major catastrophe, data loss should never occur. We will cover the RAID levels in detail, specifying the advantages and disadvantages of each, as well as hot-pluggable drives, data striping, on-line hot spares and DAAD. Pay close attention to this chapter, as it is an intricate part of system engineering.

CERTIFICATION OBJECTIVE 9.01

Compaq SMART Array Controller and Compaq SMART-2 Array Controller

A drive array is simply a collection of hard disks that are logically addressed as a single larger drive. Arrays bring many advantages to today's servers, including high-speed data rates, the capacity to handle simultaneous multiple requests, flexible configuration, increased storage capacity, and high reliability.

For high-performance data protection, the Compaq SMART family of array controllers are ideal for most critical tasks. SMART array controllers provide the data availability and peace of mind required to increase business productivity and lower a company's total cost of ownership (TCO). Tables 9-1 and 9-2 detail the characteristics of Compaq's SMART array controllers.

TABLE 9-1 Compaq SMART Family of Array Controllers Comparison

	SMART	SMART-2	SMART-2SL	SMART-2DH
SCSI Channels	2	2	1	2
Cache Capacity	4MB (Read/Write)	4MB (Read/Write)	8MB (Read Only)	16MB (Read/Write)

TABLE 9-1 Compaq SMART Family of Array Controllers Comparison *(continued)*

	SMART	SMART-2	SMART-2SL	SMART-2DH
Write Cache	Yes	Yes	No	Yes
Battery Backed Cache	Yes	Yes	No	Yes
Online Capacity Expansion	No	Yes	No	Yes
Online Spare	Yes	Yes	Yes	Yes
Array Accelerator	Yes	Yes	No	Yes
RAID Levels Supported	0,1,4,5	0,1,4,5	0,1,5	0,1,4,5
Maximum Capacity	14 drives	14 drives	7 drives	14 drives

on the job

When designing servers for clients, I recommend array controllers in this order: SMART-2DH, SMART-2, SMART, SMART-2SL. The reasoning behind this is that the SMART-2DH is the most feature-rich controller. It offers 16MB of read/write cache, battery backup, online capacity expansion, 14 drives on two channels, and an array accelerator, and it supports RAID levels 0, 1, 4, and 5.

If money is an obstacle, I then recommend the SMART-2 controller. The SMART-2 controller offers most of the same features of the SMART-2DH, but is lower in price due to it having just 4MB of read/write cache.

For smaller servers, where it is not likely drives will be added to the system after the initial install, I recommend the SMART controller.

I very rarely recommend the SMART-2SL controller, because it has only read cache and no array accelerator and battery-backed cache. SMART-2SL is normally used for very small end servers, where housing less important data and downtime will not be a major issue.

CERTIFICATION OBJECTIVE 9.02

Fault Prevention and Fault Tolerance Features

Compaq incorporates many fault prevention and fault tolerant features into its array controllers. Some of the features are RAID levels of 0, 1, 4, and 5, the capability to hot-swap drives (which are indicated by a burgundy color for quick identification), and automatic data reconstruction of an online spare drive. These features will be covered in detail in sections to follow.

TABLE 9-2 Compaq SMART Family of Array Controllers Comparison

	SMART 221	SMART 230 Plus	SMART 3100ES	SMART 3200
SCSI Channels	1	1,3	3	2
Cache Capacity	6MB (Read Only)	4, 8MB (Read/Write)	64MB (Read/Write)	64MB (Read/Write)
Write Cache	No	Yes	Yes	Yes
Battery Backed Cache	No	Optional	Yes	Yes
Online Capacity Expansion	No	Yes	Yes	Yes
Online Spare	Yes	Yes	Yes	Yes
Array Accelerator	No	Yes	Yes	Yes
RAID Levels Supported	0,1,5	0,1,5	0,1,4,5	0,1,4,5
Maximum Capacity	15 drives	7, 21 drives	21 drives	15 drives

CERTIFICATION OBJECTIVE 9.03

RAID Levels of Fault Tolerance

RAID is an acronym for Redundant Array of Inexpensive Drives. In the single-user environment, a single drive with a tape backup is usually all that is needed. However, in the multiple-user server environment, a more robust solution is warranted. This is where RAID comes in. The RAID standard defines six levels, of which the Compaq array controllers support four. Table 9-3 describes the type of protection provided by each RAID level. (Note: A tape drive should still be utilized to back up the data.)

We will now look at RAID levels 0, 1, 4 and 5 in more detail.

RAID Level 0—Data Striping without Parity

RAID 0, data striping without parity, takes data and distributes it throughout all the drives in the array. However, it does not calculate parity information. This method is used mainly when drive read/write speed is preferred over fault tolerance.

Advantages

The following chart illustrates how a file is broken down into stripes and written across multiple disks. This greatly reduces the amount of time a drive head must wait for the target sector to be positioned under the head (latency). Using this RAID level, all of the disk space is used for data.

Disk 0	Disk 1	Disk 2
Stripe 1	Stripe 2	Stripe 3

Disadvantages

Data striping is a faster write procedure than writing to a single drive, because all three drives are writing at the same time. Thus, in the preceding chart, the write is three times faster than the same amount of data written on a single disk.

TABLE 9-3 Types of Protection Provided by Each RAID Level

Level	Type of Protection
RAID 0	Data Striping without Parity
RAID 1	Mirrored
RAID 2	Complex Error Correction (no longer used)
RAID 3	Parallel-Transfer, Dedicated Parity (no longer used)
RAID 4	Data Striping with Dedicated Parity
RAID 5	Data Striping with Distributed Parity

However, using this RAID level provides no fault tolerance; if one drive should fail, all data is lost due to its being striped across all the drives.

The more drives added to the array, the more likely it is that there will be a disk failure. While the Meantime Between Failure (MTBF) of a single drive may be 250,000 hours, with an array of five of the same type of drive, you get a MTBF of 50,000 hours (divide the 250,000 by five). The lower MTBF is because, when you have multiple drives, you have multiple hardware components that can fail. Therefore, if your situation calls for fault tolerance, RAID 0 will not be the appropriate solution.

The Striping Factor

Striping configures multiple, single disks into one large, logical drive. The logical drive is arranged so that data is written across all physical disks in the array. The number of sectors per block is called the striping factor. Depending on the controller in use, the striping factor can be modified. Remember, any change to the logical drive's striping factor, volume size, or RAID level is data-destructive! The default striping factor for all operating systems is 8KB; however, UNIX is 4KB. The smaller the striping factor is, the better the disks' storage is utilized.

RAID Level 1—Mirrored

RAID 1, mirroring, writes identical data to an even number of drives. Therefore, if one of the drives in the mirror set fails, an identical copy of the

FROM THE FIELD

Increasing Page File Performance

Microsoft has incorporated a rather complex memory management model in the Windows platform to help overcome the insatiable demand Windows' applications make upon memory resources. When an NT machine runs out of physical memory, it begins moving data to disk, which has a significantly slower access time than memory. With this architecture in place, lacking memory can detriment not only the memory subsystem performance, but also the disk and processor performance.

If you have two 2.1GB drives laying about the shop, you can create a hardware RAID-0 array for the swap file. RAID-0 provides the best performance of all disk array technologies but is often ignored since it actually increases the risk of catastrophic data loss by a factor of 100 percent. Since the swap partition data is not important, we can easily recover from a loss of one or both of these drives.

For best performance, however, we should avoid the use of the swap file altogether. In systems with large amounts of memory, you can disable the ability for Windows NT to use the page file for pageable drivers and system code by modifying the registry. Using a registry editor, navigate to the following key:

HKEY_LOCAL_MACHINE\SYSTEM\CurrentControlSet\Control\Session Manager\Memory Management

Change the DisablePagingExecutive value to 1. This will force drivers and the kernel to remain in memory, thus improving performance on systems with large amounts of memory.

—*Thomas E. Eck,*
MCSE+I, MCSD, ASE, CCA, CNA

data is available on the second drive. The most common implementation of this is an operating system installation.

Advantages

The following chart illustrates how data is written to two separate drives. All data on Disk 0 has an exact copy on Disk 1. If the first drive should fail, the mirrored drive has an exact copy; nothing is lost and everyone is happy.

RAID 1 requires an even number of identical disks (minimum of two) and allows for *split seeks* (the drive with the requested data nearest to the head will be read, thus slightly improving the read performance).

Disk 0	Disk 1
Stripe 1	Stripe 1
Stripe 2	Stripe 2
Stripe 3	Stripe 3

Disadvantages

Although mirroring is a good, fault-tolerant technique, it is rather expensive because it requires double the storage space. Only half of the total disk space is used for data storage, while the other half is used for mirroring the same data.

RAID Level 4—Data Striping with Dedicated Parity

RAID 4, data striping with dedicated parity, builds on the technology of RAID 0 by adding parity calculations on a dedicated disk. The parity allows any drive in the array to fail and still have all data available. Once the failed drive is replaced, data on the new drive is rebuilt and life is back to normal.

Advantages

The following chart illustrates how data is striped to multiple drives as in RAID 0, but with the parity sum calculated and written to a dedicated drive. If a drive were to fail while using this fault tolerance solution, the data on the failed drive could be calculated and retrieved from the parity drive when needed. RAID level 4 requires a minimum of three disks, with a maximum of 14. This is a very cost-effective, fault-tolerant solution, as only one disk is used for data storage (known as the N+1 formula: number of drives required for storage, plus one for parity).

Disk 0	Disk 1	Disk 2	Disk 3
Stripe 1	Stripe 2	Stripe 3	Parity

Disadvantages

The biggest disadvantage is the time taken to calculate the parity information and write it to a single disk drive.

RAID Level 5—Data Striping with Distributed Parity

RAID 5, data striping with distributed parity, improves upon RAID 4 by distributing the parity information through all disks in the array. This method quickens the read/write capability and greatly improves the performance, thus making RAID 5 the most popular array configuration for most situations.

Advantages

The following chart illustrates how data is striped to multiple drives as in RAID 4, but with the parity sum calculated and also striped across the array. If a drive were to fail while using this fault tolerance solution, the data on the failed drive could be calculated and retrieved from the parity stripes when needed. With parity striped across the entire array, performance is increased, since all disks do not need to access a single disk for parity information. RAID level 5 also requires a minimum of three disks, with a maximum of 14. This is a very cost-effective, fault-tolerant solution, as only one disk is used for data storage (the N+1 formula). RAID 5 is considered the best solution for fault tolerance and I/O-intensive applications, making it the ideal configuration for high-performance business servers.

Disk 0	Disk 1	Disk 2	Disk 3
Stripe 1	Stripe 2	Stripe 3	Parity
Stripe 4	Stripe 5	Parity	Stripe 6
Stripe 7	Parity	Stripe 8	Stripe 9
Parity	Stripe 10	Stripe 11	Stripe 12

Disadvantages

There are no significant disadvantages to hardware RAID 5.

The level of RAID used depends largely on the type of data being written to the drives. The normal configuration I recommend is RAID 1 (mirroring) for the operating system (Windows NT, NetWare), and RAID 5 (data striping with distributed parity) for the data drives (applications, user directories).

The only scenario where I would recommend RAID 0 (data striping without parity) is when money is tight and the company requires that all drives be used for data storage. I can't say that I've ever recommended RAID 4 (data striping with dedicated parity). It is very popular and many of the engineers I work with recommend this configuration. However, this isn't always the best solution. When installing applications (such as SAP or Oracle), you should consult the software manuals, knowledge bases, and technical support.

CERTIFICATION OBJECTIVE 9.04

Operation and Configuration Issues of Hot-Pluggable Hard Disks

Hot-pluggable hard disks allow a failed physical drive in a fault-tolerant volume to be replaced without bringing the server down. Hot-pluggable drives enhance the use of an online spare drive by allowing the failed drive to be replaced while the system is still up, thus freeing up the online spare for recovery of future drive failures. Remember that replacement hard disks must be equal to, or larger than, the hard disk being replaced, and can be shared between an internal and external array.

An array controller supporting both hot-pluggable drives and hot-pluggable bus/drive cages is required for this function. The drives are configured by using the Compaq ARRAY CONFIGURATION utility. In this utility, you may set the drives up as single units (RAID 0, 1, 4, or 5) and specify an online spare.

CERTIFICATION OBJECTIVE 9.05

Hardware Data Striping

Hardware data striping takes data that is to be written to the logical disk and stripes it across all disks in the array. Data sent to the array controller for submission to the disks in the array is split into blocks. The controller then writes the blocks to each disk in the array, beginning with the disk with the next available full block. Hardware striping is preferred over software striping, because the array controller's processor handles all data splitting, I/O activity, and parity calculations, thus freeing up the system's processor for other functions.

CERTIFICATION OBJECTIVE 9.06

Logical Volumes Supported by the SMART Array Controller

The SMART array controller supports up to eight logical volumes. A logical volume consists of one drive or multiple drives configured in an array. Each logical volume is presented to the operating system as a single physical disk. The array controller handles all reads and writes to the array.

CERTIFICATION OBJECTIVE 9.07

Protecting Write Data in the SMART Array Controller and SMART-2 Array Controller

An array accelerator with onboard cache (4MB on a SMART controller, 16MB on a SMART-2 controller) reads ahead and caches upcoming data.

This read-ahead caching, along with write posting (data written to disk is first written to the accelerator cache) and battery backup, improves performance and preserves disk write in the case of a system failure. In the event of a system failure, the battery backup preserves data written to the accelerator cache. Once the system comes back online, a message is displayed at POST and data in the accelerator cache is written to disk. If the array controller fails, the accelerator may be transferred to another array controller, thus allowing the data in the cache to be written to disk.

CERTIFICATION OBJECTIVE 9.08

Online Spares

An online spare is a backup disk that replaces the role of any drive that may fail in an array. An array controller that supports online spares can both detect drive failures and rebuild data to the online spare in the background. An online spare must be equal to, or larger than, the drive it will be replacing. Once the failed drive has been replaced, data is reconstructed onto the new drive and the online spare becomes available again to replace the next failed drive. Compaq SMART array controllers support up to four online spare drives. The online spare may be either internal or external, but is always powered-on and spun-up.

I received an emergency page one night around 2:00 a.m. from a client. The message read "Help! Failed drive on Exchange box! Must be up and functional by 8:00 a.m.! Call me!" Naturally, I called the client, who was in a panic. Knowing that the system was configured with RAID 5 and an online spare, I told him that the online spare would take care of the failed drive and everything would be fine until I could get in there in the morning. Nevertheless, the administrator insisted that I come in and repair the situation. I sleepily got up and dressed, stopped by the office and picked up another 18.2GB hot-swappable drive, and drove to the client's site. When the panicked administrator

let me in, I calmly walked to the server room, pulled the failed drive out of the ProLiant 6000, and slid in the replacement drive. I handed the administrator two invoices (one for the drive and one for my time), told him the drive would be rebuilt by the time the first person arrived in the morning, then turned around and went home. With Compaq's hot-swappable drives configured as RAID 5 with an online spare, there's no need to panic.

CERTIFICATION OBJECTIVE 9.09

Drive Array Advanced Diagnostics (DAAD)

Drive Array Advanced Diagnostics is a utility that determines if problems exist with the array controller(s) by issuing multiple commands to the controller(s). This data can be saved to a file for archival purposes or forwarded to Compaq Technical Support. However, DAAD normally will provide enough information to correct the situation almost immediately. DAAD does not write any information to the controller or drive and therefore is safe to use on systems with data written to the arrays.

CERTIFICATION OBJECTIVE 9.10

Converting a SMART Array Controller to a SMART-2 Array Controller

Essentially, the SMART array controller and the SMART-2 are the same, with the only differences being the battery-backed cache and the online capacity expansion capability. The SMART array controller has 4MB of battery-backed cache, while the SMART-2 controller has 16MB. To upgrade from SMART to SMART-2 array controller, you need only upgrade the array accelerator/battery pack.

QUESTIONS AND ANSWERS

Our servers will hold data that must be available 24/7, with no downtime due to drive failure. What would you recommend?	Hot-swappable drive with an on-line spare.
We require an array controller, but have a very limited budget. What array controller do you recommend?	SMART array controller. If money if very tight, SMART-2SL.
What's the difference between read cache and read/write cache on an array controller?	On an array controller with read/write cache, data is read ahead and loaded to the controller's onboard cache, thus increasing performance. In the write mode, data is first written to the controller's cache, then written to disk. If the server should go down, or the controller should fail, once the situation is corrected, the data in the battery-backed cache will be written to disk, thus saving the data.
What is the benefit of hot-pluggable drives?	Hot-pluggable drives allow a failed physical drive to be replaced while the system is still up and running.
How much storage may we have on a single channel with a SMART-2DH controller?	254GB (14 x 18.2GB).
What is the most fault-tolerant configuration of hot-swappable drives that provides the best performance?	RAID 5 with an online spare.
What is a logical drive?	A number of physical drives grouped together as a single drive. To the operating system, it appears as a single physical drive.

CERTIFICATION SUMMARY

This chapter explained the differences among the Compaq SMART array controllers and the conversion of a SMART controller to a SMART-2 controller by upgrading the array accelerator/battery pack. We covered logical drives and the six RAID levels (0–5). However, levels 2 and 3 are no longer used in the industry; thus Compaq does not support them. RAID 0 is data striping without parity, RAID 1 is mirroring, RAID 4 is data striping with dedicated parity, and RAID 5 is data striping with distributed parity. The best overall RAID level is RAID 5. We learned that hot-swappable hard disks combined with online spares could be the difference between total fault tolerance and standing in the unemployment line.

TWO-MINUTE DRILL

- ❑ Array technology is probably the most significant advance in storage to date.
- ❑ A drive array is simply a collection of hard disks that are logically addressed as a single larger drive.
- ❑ Advantages of arrays are high-speed data rates, the capacity to handle simultaneous multiple requests, flexible configuration, increased storage capacity, and high reliability.
- ❑ Compaq's SMART array controllers provide the data availability and peace of mind required to increase business productivity and lower a company's total cost of ownership (TCO).
- ❑ Compaq incorporates many fault prevention and fault-tolerant features into their array controllers such as:
  - ❑ RAID levels of 0, 1, 4, and 5
  - ❑ The capability to hot-swap drives
  - ❑ Automatic data reconstruction of an online spare drive
- ❑ The RAID standard defines six levels, of which the Compaq array controllers support four.
- ❑ RAID 0, data striping without parity, takes data and distributes it throughout all the drives in the array. It does not calculate parity information.
- ❑ Striping configures multiple, single disks into one large, logical drive.
- ❑ RAID 1, mirroring, writes identical data to an even number of drives.
- ❑ RAID 4, data striping with dedicated parity, builds on the technology of RAID 0 by adding parity calculations on a dedicated disk.
- ❑ RAID 5, data striping with distributed parity, improves upon RAID 4 by distributing the parity information through all disks in the array.

- Hot-pluggable hard disks allow a failed physical drive in a fault-tolerant volume to be replaced without bringing the server down.
- The Compaq ARRAY CONFIGURATION utility allows you to set the drives up as single units (RAID 0, 1, 4, or 5) and specify an online spare.
- Hardware data striping takes data that is to be written to the logical disk and stripes it across all disks in the array.
- Hardware striping is preferred over software striping, because the array controller's processor handles all data splitting, I/O activity, and parity calculations, thus freeing up the system's processor for other functions.
- The SMART array controller supports up to eight logical volumes.
- An array accelerator with onboard cache (4MB on a SMART controller, 16MB on a SMART-2 controller) reads ahead and caches upcoming data.
- An online spare is a backup disk that replaces the role of any drive that may fail in an array.
- Drive Array Advanced Diagnostics (DAAD) is a utility that determines if problems exist with the array controller(s) by issuing multiple commands to the controller(s).
- To upgrade from SMART to SMART-2 array controller, you need only upgrade the array accelerator/battery pack.

SELF TEST

The following Self Test questions will help you measure your understanding of the material presented in this chapter. Read all the choices carefully, as there may be more than one correct answer. Choose all correct answers for each question.

1. How many drives does the SMART-2 array controller support?
   A. Seven
   B. Eight
   C. Fourteen
   D. Fifteen
2. What is the cache capacity of the SMART-2DH array controller?
   A. 4MB (read)
   B. 4MB (read/write)
   C. 8MB (read)
   D. 16MB (read/write)
3. Which array controllers do not support online capacity expansion?
   A. SMART
   B. SMART-2
   C. SMART-2SL
   D. SMART-2DH
4. What RAID level uses drive mirroring?
   A. RAID 0
   B. RAID 1
   C. RAID 4
   D. RAID 5
5. RAID level 4 uses distributed parity.
   A. True
   B. False
6. Which RAID level is not fault tolerant?
   A. RAID 0
   B. RAID 1
   C. RAID 4
   D. RAID 5
7. What is the default striping factor?
   A. 4KB for all operating systems
   B. 8KB for UNIX, 4KB for all other operating systems
   C. 8KB for all operating systems
   D. 4KB for UNIX, 8KB for all other operating systems
8. RAID level 1 is a cost-effective solution.
   A. True
   B. False
9. What is the maximum number of disks supported by RAID 4?
   A. 3
   B. 7
   C. 14
   D. 21

10. Parity is distributed across the entire array using RAID 5.

    A. True

    B. False

11. The server must be brought down before inserting a hot-swappable drive.

    A. True

    B. False

12. Hardware data striping is preferred over software data striping.

    A. True

    B. False

13. How many logical volumes does Compaq's SMART array controller support?

    A. Four

    B. Six

    C. Eight

    D. Ten

14. How is write data protected in SMART and SMART-2 array controllers?

    A. Online expansion

    B. Battery backup

    C. Array accelerator

    D. Online spares

15. What is the maximum number of online spares supported by the SMART array controller?

    A. One

    B. Two

    C. Three

    D. Four

16. The Drive Array Advanced Diagnostics is data destructive.

    A. True

    B. False

17. What allows a SMART array controller to be upgraded to a SMART-2 array controller?

    A. Processor

    B. Memory

    C. Accelerator/battery pack

    D. It cannot be upgraded.

ASE

ACCREDITED SYSTEMS ENGINEER

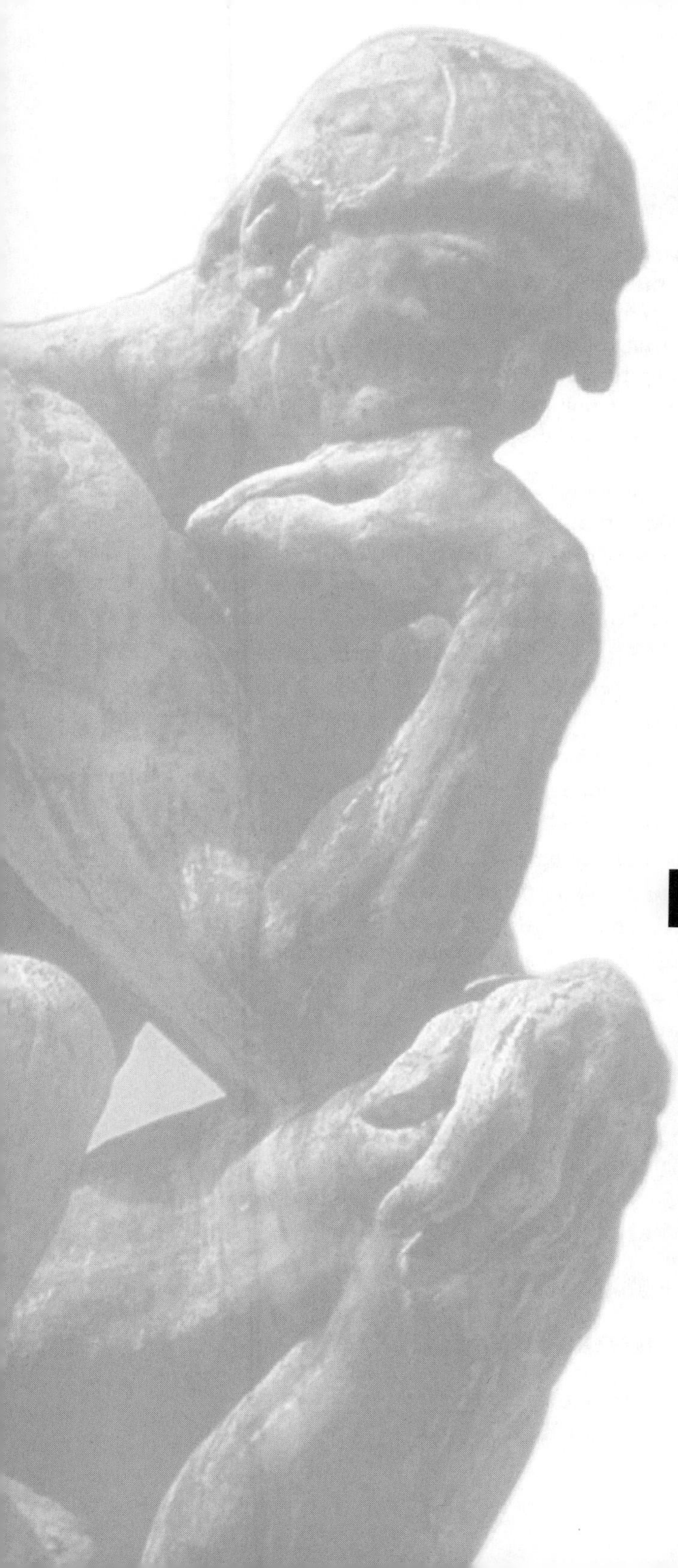

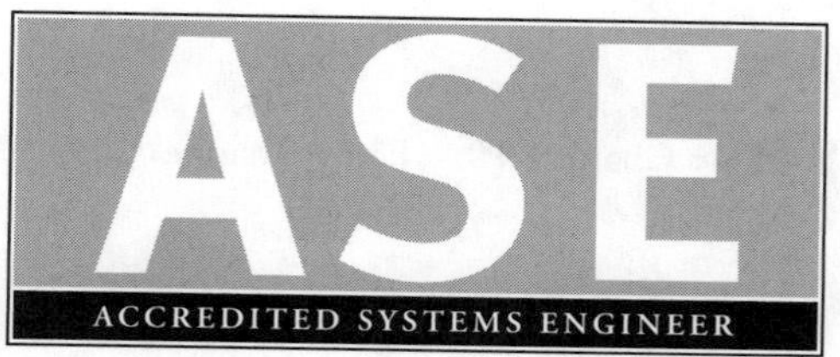

10

Fibre Channel

CERTIFICATION OBJECTIVES

10.01 Overview of Fibre Channel Architecture

10.02 Fibre Channel Topologies

10.03 Using RAID with Fibre Channel on Compaq Hardware

10.04 How Fibre Channel Differs from SCSI

10.05 Building High Availability File Servers Using Compaq Fibre Channel Products

Fibre Channel is a set of ANSI standard protocols (X3.230-1994). The distinctive spelling was chosen to differentiate the standards from the fiber media. Fibre Channel can run over various media including copper, multimode fiber, and single-mode fiber. *Multimode fiber* is a media capable of transmitting optical signals of up to 500m (1600ft). *Single-mode fiber* can transmit optical signals up to 10km (6.2mi). The most commonly used medium to implement Fibre Channel is currently multimode fiber. This is primarily due to the cost of the single-mode fiber and the lasers that drive the optical signal.

Most current implementations utilize a *Fibre Channel Arbitrated Loop* (FC-AL) design. You can think of an FC-AL as being similar to Token Ring in that bandwidth is shared among all nodes and only one pair of nodes can communicate at a time. Compaq offers a 7-port or 12-port hub in support of FC-AL. This allows a single server, utilizing one PCI slot, to connect to approximately 2.2TB of storage. Such a configuration would consist of a server connected to a 12-port hub with 11 Compaq Fibre Channel Arrays populated with 12 x 18GB 1" drives (11 drives x 18GB x 11 Fibre Channel Arrays = 2.2 TB of RAID 5 storage).

Compaq currently supports Microsoft Cluster Server (MSCS) on both the 7-port and 12-port hubs. However, the 12-port hub is only allowed to utilize seven ports when being used in an MSCS environment. This is a technical limitation to the 12-port hub. Each server in the cluster requires one port, leaving five ports for Fibre Arrays; therefore, an MSCS configuration can support up to approximately 1TB.

Throughout this chapter, we will be discussing the terminology, theory, and practice associated with Fibre Channel. We will also touch on the latest releases from Compaq concerning FC. These include 16-port Fibre Channel Switches and how these advances bring us closer to a true *Storage Area Network* (SAN). A SAN is a configuration in which storage is on a separate network than normal network communications.

CERTIFICATION OBJECTIVE 10.01

Overview of Fibre Channel Architecture

Fibre Channel uses a fast and efficient serial communication method. Fibre Channel currently supports 100 MBps speeds. To ensure that the data arrives without corruption, a strong CRC (cyclic redundancy check) is used in conjunction with an encoding scheme. The Fibre Channel standard supports full duplex. At this time, Compaq supports only half duplex. Originally, Compaq supported Fibre Channel over copper media. This was an inexpensive way to start into the Fibre Channel arena. However, there are drawbacks to using copper. The distance is limited to 25m (82ft), the cables are thick and hard to work with, and copper is subject to electrical interference. For purposes of our discussion, we will stick to fiber media throughout the rest of the chapter.

Benefits

For today's data-intensive applications, a high-speed, flexible solution such as Fibre Channel is a must. Fibre Channel, with a bandwidth of 100 MBps instead of SCSI at 40 MBps (80 MBps ultra 2), offers performance to support ever increasing data demands. With so much data being stored, backup strategies are becoming more and more important. Being able to separate your servers and storage offers many benefits. Compaq currently offers a backup solution that can back up your data directly from the storage unit to tape. This benefit makes Fibre Channel more appealing.

The FC-AL supports up to 127 devices in a single arbitrated loop. *Fibre Channel Switched Fabric*, where a Fibre Channel Switch replaces the hub, can support up to 16 million devices! These features make Fibre Channel well suited as a building block for the emerging Storage Area Network concept.

Technical Features and Limitations of Channels and Networks

It is important to understand the role that Fibre Channel plays in the entire network. A basic concept is that of channels and networks. A *channel* is the connection between a computer and peripheral devices such as disk drives, tape drives, printers, and modems. The computer knows that these devices are attached and has a dedicated path to the devices. The channel connection relies on the high speeds derived from a known path and pays the price for speed with a decrease in flexibility. A *network* on the other hand, is the connection between computers, such as client workstations, servers, midrange systems, and mainframes. The nature of a network is such that flexibility is the key requirement and the trade-off is speed. To put it in familiar terms, channels run protocols like SCSI and IDE, while networks run protocols like Ethernet and Token Ring.

Fibre Channel, therefore, fits into the channel definition, right? Well, yes, but it also fits into the network definition. It combines features of both channels and networks. A Fibre Channel network can run many protocols at the same time. SCSI and IDE run as well as TCP and other protocols. This is a major strength and benefit of the Fibre Channel technology.

Attenuation is the loss of power. Here are a few of the things that can cause attenuation.

- **Scattering** Takes place when a light ray strikes an impurity in the fiber and is shot off in different directions
- **Absorption** Caused by impurities
- **Chromatic dispersion** Caused by different wavelengths of light traveling down the fiber at different speeds
- **Modal dispersion** Means that the light rays travel different paths down the fiber
- **Macro bends** Caused when the fiber has a bend radius of less than 1.5 inches. Some of the light rays can't follow the bend and are lost. Micro bends occur when the fiber doesn't follow a linear path.
- **Micro bends** Most often occur during cable management when the fiber is either pulled too tightly against something or a tie-wrap is cinched down into the fiber

So far we've talked about Fibre Channel, copper media, and fiber media, and gone over some fiber media features. Now let's go over what the actual fiber medium looks like and some of its basic physical characteristics. First, fiber has layers. The innermost layer is called the *core.* The core consists of highly purified glass and actually carries the light. The *cladding* is the next layer that encompasses the core and is also made of highly purified glass. The cladding functions as reflector to keep the light waves within the core. There is a substance called *dopant* that is actually added to the core fiber during manufacture. The dopant causes the core and cladding to have different properties; it is this difference that keeps the light in the core. The final layer is called the *buffer.* It serves as a protective coating for the core and cladding. Figure 10-1 illustrates fiber media. The most outwardly

FIGURE 10-1

Fiber media construction

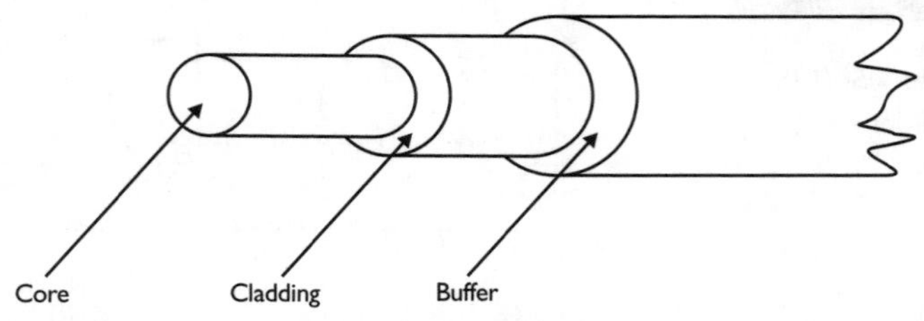

noticeable feature of the buffer is the bright orange color that is commonly used, although it is available in other colors. This makes it very easy to spot fiber amongst any other cables.

There are a couple of differences between single-mode and multimode fiber. Single-mode fiber has a core that is so small that only a single wavelength of light can travel down it at a time. Compaq uses single-mode fiber with a core of 9 micrometers (μm) and a cladding of 125 μm. Figure 10-2 illustrates single-mode fiber. These types of measurements are usually expressed as 9/125.

Multimode fiber has a larger core and can support multiple wavelengths at the same time, hence the name. Fiber media is commonly used in the telecommunications industry. The most common multimode fiber existing in the U.S. is 50/125. Europe commonly uses a multimode fiber 62.5/125. The 62.5/125 fiber requires a stronger laser to drive the light than 50/125. The reason for the difference in formats was that there were issues in the U.S. concerning the higher-output laser devices. Compaq has chosen to use a 50/125 multimode fiber, as shown in Figure 10-3.

Fiber can also have either a *step-index* or a *graded-index*. Graded-index fiber uses a dopant to vary the properties of the core. Light that travels straight down the axis of the fiber actually goes less distance than light that

FIGURE 10-2

Compaq uses a 9/125 single-mode fiber

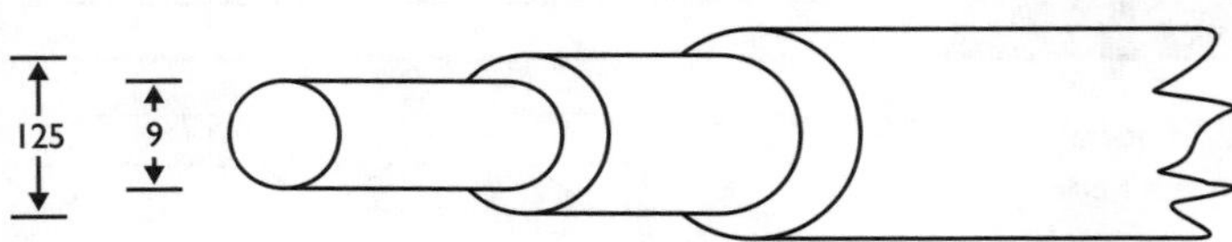

FIGURE 10-3

Compaq uses a 50/125 multimode fiber

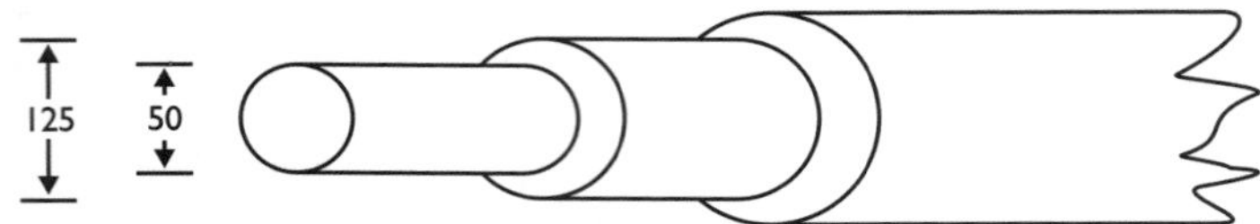

bounces off the cladding. Figure 10-4 illustrates the different paths that light can travel in a fiber. The dopant variation allows light that travels the longest path through the fiber to go faster. This greatly reduces dispersion.

Fibre Channel Hubs are devices that are used in Fibre Channel Arbitrated Loops. We will discuss FC-AL in a later section. The physical connections to the hub are in a star topology, with the hub at the center. The logical layout is actually a loop. The function of the hub is to change the connections from the star layout into a loop. The word arbitrated should set off a bell. What this means is that the access of devices to an FC-AL is shared with all devices in the loop. Only one pair of devices can communicate at a time in an FC-AL. Those devices own the loop for a period of time and communicate at the full 100-MBps rate. This is an important fact that bears restating: the FC-AL is shared access, but when access is granted, it is at full speed. *Fibre Channel Switches* are the devices used to create a Fibre Channel Switched Fabric (FC-SW). The switch allows multiple pairs of devices to use the fabric at the same time. There are correlations that can be drawn between traditional networks and FC-SW. Networks have migrated from loops to hubs to switches as need for speed and capacity increased. Similarly, as the need for speed and capacity increases in the Fibre Channel world, the migration from hubs to switches will occur.

The *host bus adapter* (HBA) is the card that goes in the server. The HBA is then connected to a hub or switch port. Compaq currently offers an EISA

FIGURE 10-4

Light travels different paths down the fiber. This is an example of modal dispersion.

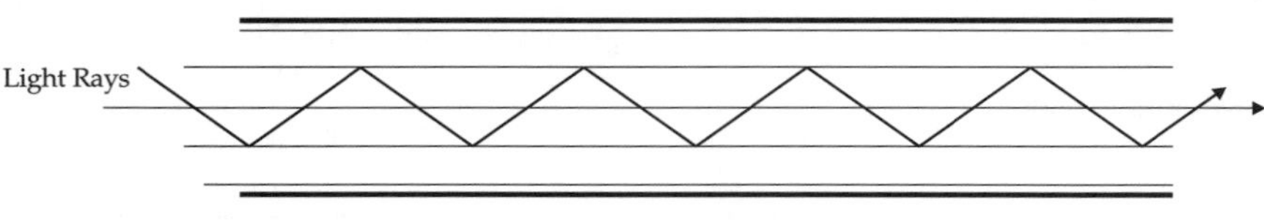

or PCI version of the HBA. The HBA replaces the SCSI adapter or RAID controller for external storage devices.

Gigabit Interface Converter (GBIC, pronounced G-bik) is the device that converts the electrical signal to an optical signal. There are two types of GBIC used in Fibre Channel: GBIC *short wave* (GBIC-SW) and GBIC *long wave* (GBIC-LW). The GBIC-SW is used with multimode fiber and the GBIC-LW is used with single-mode fiber.

CERTIFICATION OBJECTIVE 10.02

Fibre Channel Topologies

A *topology* is the name for a set of items that connect two or more ports. These items may include GBIC, media, hubs, and switches. There are some terms common to the three topologies.

- **Node** A node is a Fibre Channel device. A disk array is an example of a node.
- **Link** A link is a pair of fiber cables. One cable is used for transmitting and one cable is used for receiving. Together the two cables make up a link. There are five types of Fibre Channel Ports.
- **Port** A port varies with the device. An *N_Port* is a port on a node. There are ports for FC-AL and FC-SW. Table 10-1 illustrates the various types of ports.

TABLE 10-1

The Five Port Types

Port Type	Connection
N_Port	Node port
NL_Port	Node connected to an FC-AL
L_Port	Hub port
F_Port	FC-SW port
FL_Port	FC-SW port attached to an FC-AL

Point-to-Point

Point-to-Point is a topology in which an N_Port is connected directly to another N_Port. A server with an HBA connected to a disk array with a Fibre Channel Controller is a practical example of a point-to-point connection. This is the most basic of all the FC topologies. The next step up is the Fibre Channel Arbitrated Loop.

Fibre Channel Arbitrated Loop

The FC-AL uses a hub to create the arbitrated loop. Changing N_Ports into NL_Ports creates the loop. The arbitrated loop works much like Token Ring. The information flows in one direction around the loop and only one pair of ports can communicate at any one time. Again, it is very important to remember that the loop is shared access, but that once a pair of ports has access to the loop, they communicate at the full 100 MBps.

The storage hub functions as the center of the physical star in the FC-AL. Figure 10-5 illustrates the role of the storage hub. All of the ports in the figure are NL_Ports. Also note that each transmit connects to a receive. What the figure doesn't show is that the hub routes each port to the next port.

The data flows around the loop in only one direction. The hub also has intelligence built in that will detect when a node is inserted into the loop. The hub detects faults in ports and will bypass ports that have malfunctioned or lost power. The FC-AL works well with Microsoft Cluster Server to provide the shared storage required.

There are two types of arbitrated loops. The *private* loop is the type we have just discussed. The hub is connected with various nodes and all ports are NL_Ports. In a *public* loop, one port on the hub is changed to an FL_Port. This port connects the hub to a Fibre Channel Switch. This allows the use of the less expensive hubs, where appropriate, and provides the growth and flexibility of the switches. A private loop supports up to 127 devices. When the private loop becomes a public loop, one of the available connections becomes an FL_Port and thus public loops support 126 nodes.

FIGURE 10-5

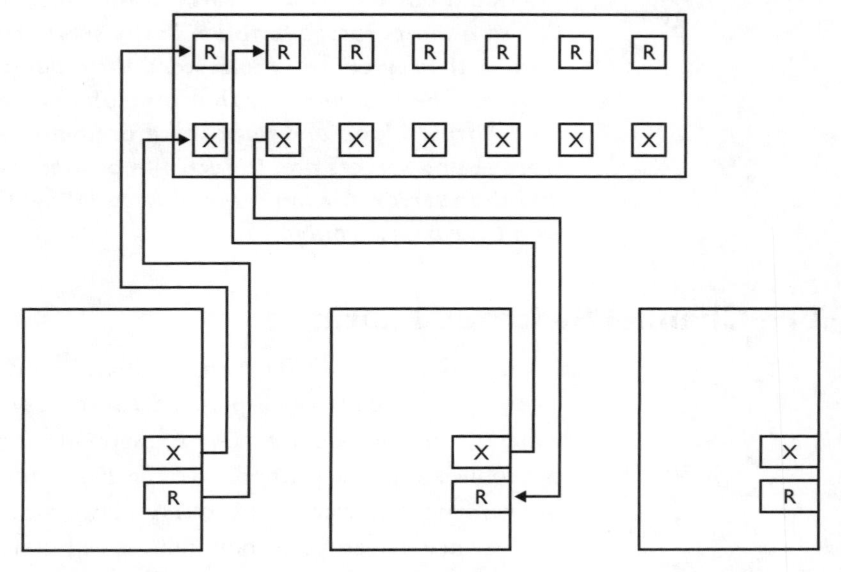

Seven-port hub with three nodes connected in an arbitrated loop

QUESTIONS AND ANSWERS

Why is there no power switch on the hub?	The hub should always be powered on first, so there is no power switch.
How do I know which fiber is transmit and which is receive in the pair?	The fiber cables are keyed so that they only go in one way. You can't get into any trouble this way.
I need to add another node to the hub. Do I need to power it off?	No, you can insert and remove GBICs and fiber from the hub under power. That is what the bypass protection is for.
What is LRF support and why do I need it?	LRF (Little Rubber Feet) support is provided with the Compaq Storage Hub for those times when you don't rack mount the hub.

We had a power loss to our Microsoft Cluster Server configuration due to a temperature problem in the server room. When things cooled off and the servers tried to restart, they didn't see the Fibre Channel storage. The problem was that the hub acts as the controlling party in an arbitrated loop and must therefore be powered up before the storage and servers are. In fact, the proper sequence is hub, storage, and then server. Always remember to follow this sequence and you won't have any trouble.

Fibre Channel Switched Fabric

In order to have an FC-SW, you must have an FC switch. Compaq is currently offering both an 8-port and a 16-port switch. Both of these switches run in full-duplex mode and support speeds up to 1 Gbps. A switch can connect multiple pairs of nodes together at the same time. For example, in a configuration where two servers and two storage arrays are connected to a single switch, server A can communicate with storage node B, while server B communicates with storage node A. These communications take place at the same time at the full 100-MBps bandwidth. This can be extended to the maximum connections for the switch standard. Thus, eight million nodes can communicate at the same time, at least in theory. The switch overcomes the limitations in bandwidth that are found in the hub and arbitrated loop solutions. In illustrations, you will usually see the fabric drawn in a cloud shape. This is done to simplify the drawing, because the fabric may consist of many switches and hubs that allow any two nodes to communicate. Figure 10-6 shows a basic FC-SW.

The FC_SW is the topology that will enable a complex SAN environment to exist. The current compelling reason to combine hubs and switches is the same as that for your current network: cost. A 16-port switch costs $28,000. That works out to $1,750 per port. In comparison, the current price of a 7-port hub is about $800—about $115 per port. It is obvious that by combining hubs and switches, cost can be significantly reduced. So far, we have been discussing terminology and basic building blocks. Now let's discuss some of the Compaq-specific hardware features.

FIGURE 10-6

Common representation of Fibre Channel Switched Fabric

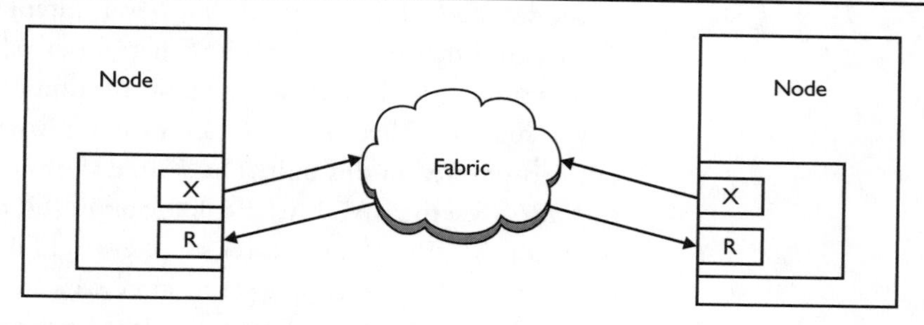

CERTIFICATION OBJECTIVE 10.03

Using RAID with Fibre Channel on Compaq Hardware

There are currently one base, and two high-end Fibre Channel Array offerings from Compaq. The base offering was originally the Fibre Channel Storage System and has become the new RA4000. The major difference between the two is that the RA4000 offers a dual path to the array to have *no single point of failure* (NSPOF). All of these offerings are external storage systems, which means that they have one or two array controllers located in the storage units. The different models offer varying levels of RAID protection and will be addressed separately. Let's begin by looking at the original system.

Compaq Fibre Channel Storage System

The Compaq Fibre Channel Storage System comes in either a tower or rack mount model. The tower model is a 4U design. RAID 0, 1, 4, and 5 are supported. The unit supports up to eight 1.6" drives or 12 1" drives. Redundant power supplies are supported and the fan assembly is hot-pluggable. Fibre Channel is used to connect the array to a device such as another node, hub, or switch. However, internally, the unit uses SCSI connections that run at 40 MBps. There are two buses in this unit. Hot plug is supported throughout the unit, including hot-plug drives, fans, and power supplies. There are two slots for Fibre Array Controllers, but only one is supported in this unit. The second slot was provided for future upgrades (See the RAID Array 4000 later in this chapter). There are status lights for the drives, fans, power supplies, and Fibre Array Controller. The drive, fan, and power supply status indicators are standard; green is operational and amber indicates a fault. The status indicator on the front of the Fibre Channel Storage System will be green for normal operation and amber to indicate a fault in one or more of the subsystems. The Fibre Array Controller has an LED for each drive and one for transmit and receive.

The Fibre Array Controller has 16MB of read cache on the board and accommodates another 16MB (48MB option) on a daughtercard. The daughtercard cache is battery-backed and is user-configurable for any combination of read or write caching. If a failure occurs in the Fibre Array Controller, the daughtercard can be moved to another Fibre Array Controller, maintaining the cache information via the battery. Online capacity expansion is also supported. Compaq Insight Manager supports the Fibre Array Controller for performance monitoring and Compaq's pre-failure warranty. As stated earlier, there are two buses in the unit, but the Fibre Array Controller supports 80 MBps via an inter-controller link.

Compaq RAID Array 4000

The Compaq RAID Array 4000 (RA4000) comes in either a tower or rack mount model. The tower model is a 4U design. The unit supports up to eight 1.6" drives or 12 1" drives. The RA4000 also supports redundant power supplies and a hot-pluggable fan assembly. Rather than repeat all the feature of the Fibre Channel Storage System, only the differences between the two units will be highlighted.

RAID 0, 0 +1, 1, 4, and 5 are supported. Redundant Fibre Array Controllers are supported in the RA4000 to ensure NSPOF. When redundant Fibre Array Controllers are present, they function in an active/passive role. Only one Fibre Array Controller can be used at a time. The RA4000 also requires a different HBA than the old system. The Fibre Channel Storage System can be upgraded to an RA4000. You must purchase another Fibre Array Controller and new HBAs. The existing Fibre Array Controller firmware can be upgraded to support the redundant option. Figure 10-7 shows the RA4000 in a redundant mode.

Many analysts believe that the RA4000 will be the cornerstone for most Fibre Channel installations in the near future. It offers excellent performance for the price. It is also easy to configure and maintain, while offering flexibility and expandability. Let's take a brief look at the Compaq RAID Array 8000 and Enterprise Storage Array 12000.

on the job

I planned for what I expected normal growth to be on the users home directory storage unit and left enough space to store some miscellaneous directories. I filled the RA4000 with 18GB drives and connected it to my Windows NT 4.0 SP5 server. Of course, I ran out of storage shortly after migrating all of the users data to the drives and I couldn't afford any more downtime. Using Fibre Channel, I was able to add another RA4000 on the fly. If you have a test system with an HBA, you can hook up an RA4000 and format the system and even populate it with data. Then simply power down the system and move the RA4000 to the production environment. When everything is physically in place, the last thing you do is power up the RA4000, without doing anything to the production system! When the RA4000 is fully powered up and has completed the self-tests, run Windows NT Disk Administrator on the production server. It will immediately recognize the new unit and assign a drive letter. You are ready to use the new space.

FIGURE 10-7

An RA4000 connected to a 7-port hub with redundant controllers

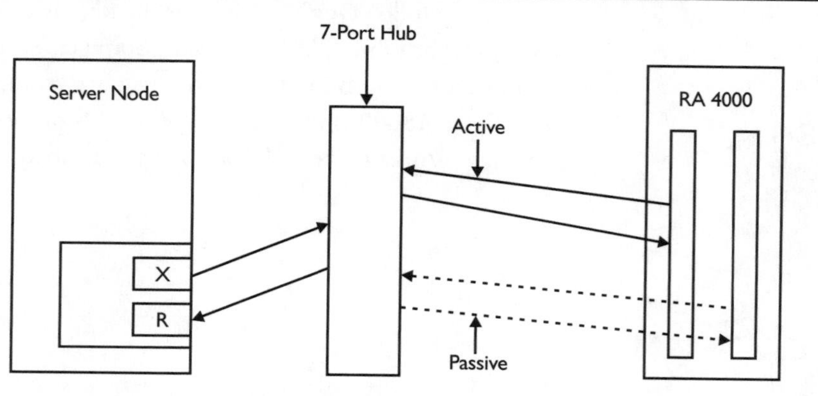

Compaq RAID Array 8000 and Enterprise Storage Array 12000

The RAID Array 8000 (RA8000) and the Enterprise Storage Array 12000 (ESA12000) are the high-end products in the Compaq Fibre Channel Storage line.

The ESA12000 is a packaged offering of two RA8000s in one cabinet. There is a separate part number to order the ESA12000, but the individual pieces are the same parts, and part numbers, as the RA8000. The ESA12000 is offered to simplify the order process for the consumer.

The RA8000 is available in a desktop-high pedestal cabinet or a rack mount. Each RA8000 cabinet supports up to 24 1.6" drives. The RA8000 has support for dual controllers in an active/active mode. Each controller also has support for up to two FC connections. This gives each controller an aggregate of 200 MBps and offers redundancy with a single controller in case of a path failure. Up to three RA8000 cabinets can be combined with a controller/controller pair, for a total 72 drives. That's approximately 1.3TB with 18GB drives. The RA8000 supports RAID levels 0, 0+1, 1, and 3/5. Each controller also supports up to 512MB of cache, for a total of 1GB of cache for a controller pair.

The RA8000, when combined with switches, allows up to four Microsoft Clusters to be connected to the same unit. That is eight servers connected to one storage unit. Now you can see the beginning of the SAN.

There is a firmware upgrade that can be applied to the controllers to allow for hardware data replication between separate RA8000 units over the Fibre Channel. Combined with single-mode fiber, this allows site-independent mirroring of data. This is great news for the Disaster Recovery folks. Don't forget that the data is being mirrored across the Fibre Channel at Fibre Channel speeds. Some enterprises have achieved data transfers of 56GB in 10 minutes over a 10km link.

The RA8000 is the result of years of StorageWorks experience. StorageWorks is the technology that Compaq acquired along with the purchase of Digital Equipment Corporation. The technology is already very robust and when combined with Fibre Channel, the possibilities are wide open. This is serious storage for high availability data demands.

We recently placed a new, mission-critical system into production. Because it is mission-critical, we used some High Availability (HA) solutions to mirror the data between two physical sites. This would allow us to continue to run in case of a disaster that took down an entire site. A few months after the system went live, we started to have problems with a particular function. It seems we had to store millions of very small files and add to them tens of thousands more each night. This situation soon began causing problems with the amount of time it took the HA solutions to mirror the data. It began to take more than 24 hours to do a complete mirror of the data. This is unacceptable for a mission-critical system. The RA8000 with the upgraded firmware known as Data Replication Manager seems to be a solution. It mirrors the data at the hardware level and thus doesn't care about the size or number of files.

CERTIFICATION OBJECTIVE 10.04

How Fibre Channel Differs from SCSI

Now that we have looked in depth at Fibre Channel, let's step back and compare it with SCSI. You will see that SCSI currently plays a very important role in the total Fibre Channel solution.

- Fibre Channel and SCSI perform many of the same functions
- SCSI runs at 40 MBps (80 MBps ultra 2), while Fibre Channel runs at 100 MBps

- SCSI storage must be located near the server; Fibre Channel can be located up to 10km away. Compaq is currently working on supporting distances greater than 150km via Fibre Channel.
- SCSI uses relatively inflexible cable that is subject to electromagnetic interference (EMI). Fibre Channel uses a fiber medium, which is flexible and not subject to EMI—a great advantage.
- SCSI supports one to four arrays per slot. Fibre Channel supports up to 11 with a 12-port hub and many, many more with switches.

As different as SCSI and Fibre Channel are, Compaq currently uses Fibre Channel to their storage arrays and SCSI within the array. Furthermore, Compaq recommends that you still use SCSI in the server for the system drives. This brings us to the point where it makes sense to discuss how all of these parts fit together in the real world to create a Fibre Channel solution.

CERTIFICATION OBJECTIVE 10.05

Building High Availability File Servers Using Compaq Fibre Channel Products

Compaq has a complete Fibre Channel solution for creating high availability servers. A basic system, consisting of one server, a 7-port hub, and one RA4000 with redundant controllers was pictured in Figure 10-7. This configuration would support up to 252GB of space with RAID 5. The use of the hub instead of a point-to-point topology allows for future expansion. Up to five more RA4000 storage systems could be added to the system, resulting in approximately 1.5TB of available RAID 5 storage. To take this system to NSPOF, simply add another HBA in the server and a second 7-port hub. Figure 10-8

FIGURE 10-8 A "no single point of failure" configuration of a server and an RA4000

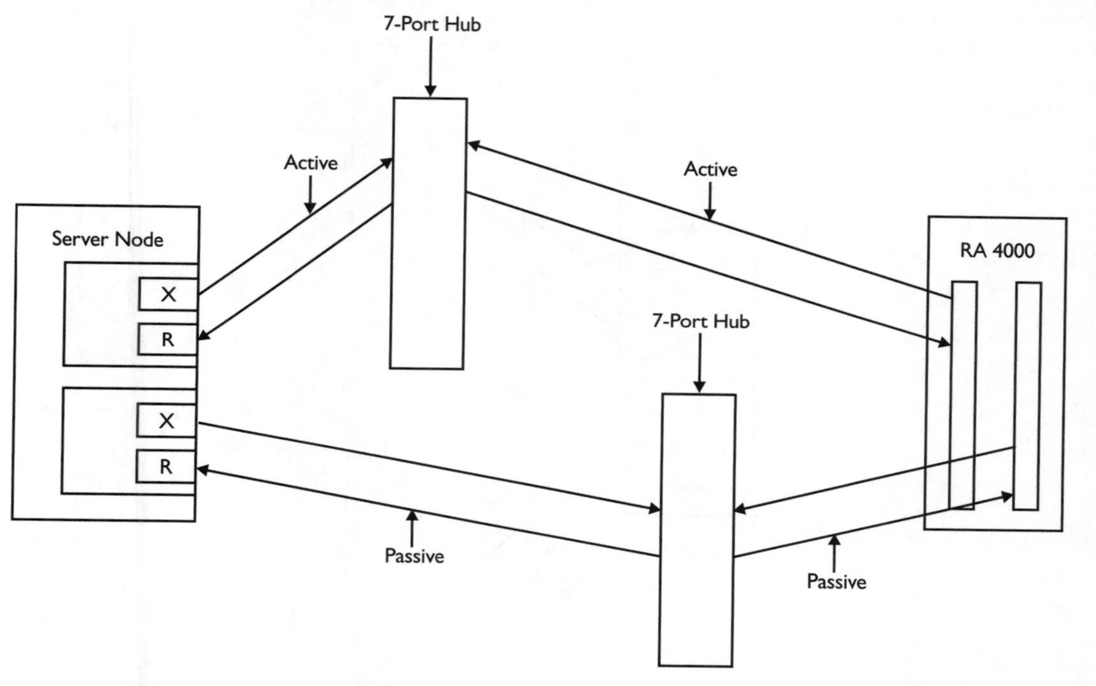

illustrates NSPOF with a single server and a single RA4000. Notice that there are two HBAs in the server and two Fibre Array Controllers in the RA4000.

The HBAs can run in active/active mode, while the RA4000 Array Controllers only run in active/passive mode. Figure 10-9 illustrates a configuration in which another RA4000 is added to the picture. By adding the second storage device, the HBAs in the server can both be active at the same time. This is quite a performance increase.

FIGURE 10-9

A server with two active HBAs connected NSPOF to two Fibre Channel Storage Arrays

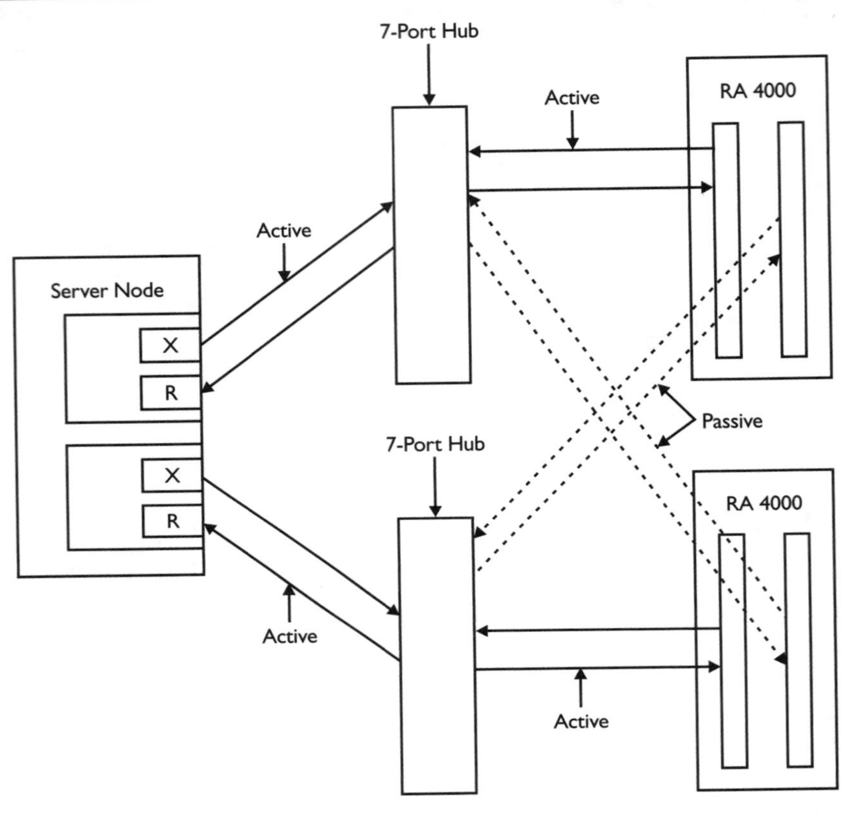

There are a few things to keep in mind when designing and building a Fibre Channel solution. Determine what level of protection you require. If the system is mission critical, then you may need to go with a clustered solution to ensure that there is NSPOF. A Microsoft Cluster Server solution with NSPOF consists of:

- Two ProLiant servers
- Four Host Bus Adapters
- Two hubs, either 7-port or 12-port
- One RA4000 with redundant Fibre Array Controllers

Figure 10-10 illustrates a basic NSPOF system using Fibre Channel technology.

These are just a few simple configurations that implement Fibre Channel technology. All of these solutions use FC-AL. You can see how introducing a switch would greatly expand the possibilities. Now that you have seen how easy and flexible Fibre Channel is, let's review what you have learned so that you will be ready to implement your own solution.

FIGURE 10-10 A cluster configured with NSPOF

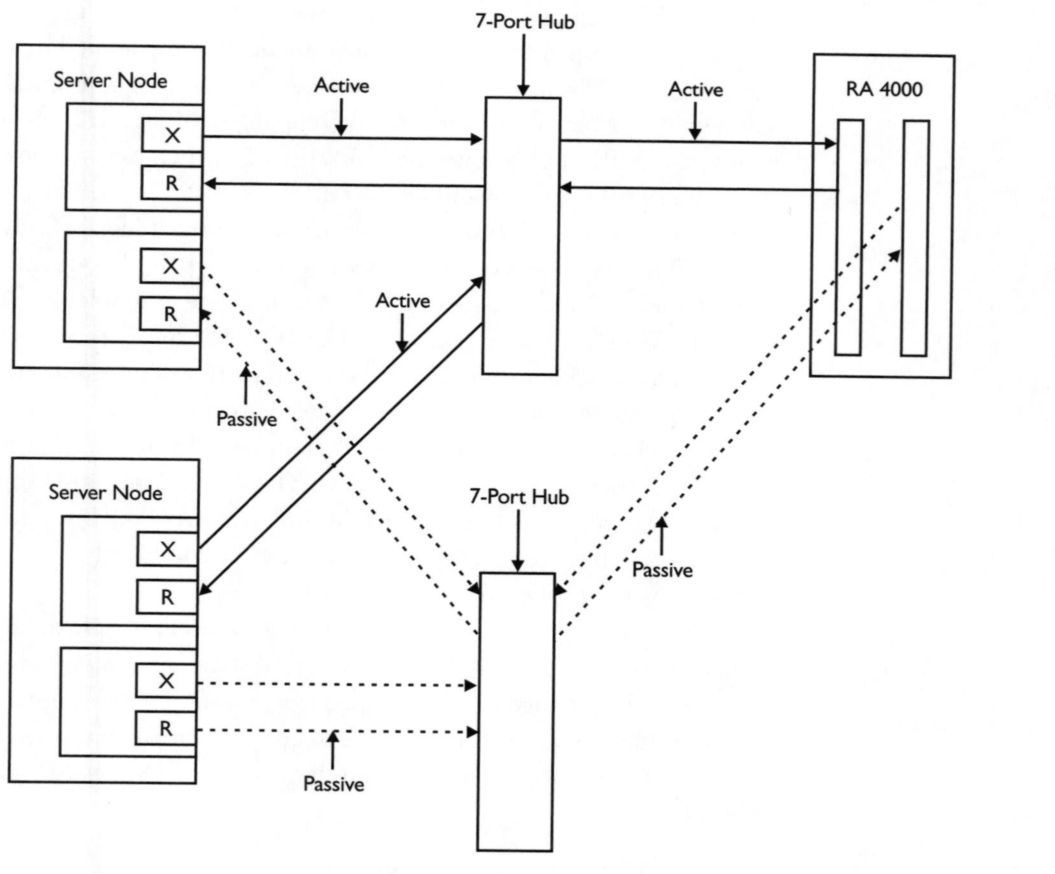

CERTIFICATION SUMMARY

Fibre Channel is an open set of standards. It can run over copper as well as fiber media. Current implementations from Compaq run at 100 MBps bandwidth in half duplex, although the standard supports full duplex. There is a strong CRC and encoding scheme used to ensure data integrity. Physically, the fiber is made up of three parts: the core, cladding, and buffer. The core is the glass medium that actually carries the signal, while the cladding is used to keep the signal within the core. The buffer is to protect the other two elements. Compaq has implemented two types of fiber for different applications. A 50/125 multimode fiber is used for distances between two meters and 500 meters. For distances up to 10 kilometers, Compaq uses a 9/125 single-mode fiber medium. The Host Bus Adapter from Compaq is available in either EISA or PCI and functions to connect the server to the Fibre Channel topology. A Gigabit Interface Converter (GBIC) plugs into the HBA, hub, or switch port to convert the electrical signal to optical and vice versa.

A Fibre Channel Hub is used to create an arbitrated loop (FC-AL), in which all nodes share access to the loop. Only one pair of nodes can communicate at a time on an FC-AL. Another type of topology is the Fibre Channel Switched Fabric (FC-SW). The FC-SW requires the use of Fibre Channel Switches and can accommodate up to 16 million connections. Compaq offers include a 7-port or 12-port hub as well as an 8-port or 16-port switch. These hubs and switches support the full range of Fibre Channel Storage options from Compaq. The RAID Array 4000 supports eight 1.6" drives or 12 1" drives, while an RAID Array 8000 supports 24 1.6" drives. Up to three RA8000 cabinets can be combined with a pair of Fibre Array Controllers to provide 72 1.6" drives.

Fibre Channel provides a fast and flexible means to handle today's demands for storage. Fibre Channel's layered standard also provides a path for tomorrow's storage needs. Compaq has chosen to use this open standard as the building block for their storage offerings. Compaq has recently received recognition in the industry as have a true vision regarding Storage Area Networks.

TWO-MINUTE DRILL

- ❑ Fibre Channel provides a fast and flexible means to handle today's demands for storage.
- ❑ Fibre Channel is a set of ANSI standard protocols (X3.230-1994).
- ❑ *Multimode fiber* is a media capable of transmitting optical signals of up to 500m (1600ft).
- ❑ *Single-mode fiber* can transmit optical signals up to 10km (6.2mi).
- ❑ The most commonly used medium to implement Fibre Channel is currently multimode fiber.
- ❑ Most current implementations utilize a *Fibre Channel Arbitrated Loop* (FC-AL) design.
- ❑ Compaq currently supports Microsoft Cluster Server (MSCS) on both the 7-port and 12-port hubs.
- ❑ Fibre Channel uses a fast and efficient serial communication method.
- ❑ The Fibre Channel standard supports full duplex, however, at this time, Compaq supports only half duplex.
- ❑ Compaq currently offers a backup solution that can back up your data directly from the storage unit to tape.
- ❑ A *channel* is the connection between a computer and peripheral devices such as disk drives, tape drives, printers, and modems.
- ❑ A *network* is the connection between computers, such as client workstations, servers, midrange systems, and mainframes.
- ❑ A Fibre Channel network can run many protocols at the same time.
- ❑ *Attenuation* is the loss of power.
- ❑ *Fibre Channel Hubs* are devices that are used in Fibre Channel Arbitrated Loops.
- ❑ *Fibre Channel Switches* are the devices used to create a Fibre Channel Switched Fabric (FC-SW).
- ❑ Compaq currently offers an EISA or PCI version of the HBA.

- A *topology* is the name for a set of items that connect two or more ports and may include GBIC, media, hubs, and switches.
- *Point-to-Point* is a topology in which an N_Port is connected directly to another N_Port.
- The FC-AL uses a hub to create the arbitrated loop.
- In order to have an FC-SW, you must have an FC switch. Compaq is currently offering both an 8-port and a 16-port switch.
- There are currently one base and two high-end Fibre Channel Array offerings from Compaq.
- The Compaq Fibre Channel Storage System comes in either a tower or rack mount model.
- The Fibre Array Controller has 16MB of read cache on the board and accommodates another 16MB (48MB option) on a daughtercard.
- Compaq Insight Manager supports the Fibre Array Controller for performance monitoring and Compaq's pre-failure warranty.
- The Compaq RAID Array 4000 (RA4000) comes in either a tower or rack mount model.
- Many analysts believe that the RA4000 will be the cornerstone for most Fibre Channel installations in the near future.
- The RAID Array 8000 (RA8000) and the Enterprise Storage Array 12000 (ESA12000) are the high-end products in the Compaq Fibre Channel Storage line.
- StorageWorks is the technology that Compaq acquired along with the purchase of Digital Equipment Corporation.
- SCSI currently plays a very important role in the total Fibre Channel solution.
- As different as SCSI and Fibre Channel are, Compaq currently uses Fibre Channel to their storage arrays and SCSI within the array.
- Compaq has a complete Fibre Channel solution for creating high-availability servers.

SELF TEST

The following Self Test questions will help you measure your understanding of the material presented in this chapter. Read all the choices carefully, as there may be more than one correct answer. Choose all correct answers for each question.

1. What is the current bandwidth of Fibre Channel?

   A. 10 Mbps
   B. 10 MBps
   C. 100 Mbps
   D. 100 MBps

2. Which media types are supported by Fibre Channel?

   A. Single-mode fiber and multimode fiber
   B. Single-mode fiber and copper
   C. Multimode fiber and copper
   D. Single-mode fiber, multimode fiber, and copper

3. A channel is best described as:

   A. Hardware-intensive
   B. Software-intensive
   C. The sales avenue for purchasing the equipment
   D. Cables that connect two computers

4. Which best describes attenuation?

   A. Loss of the signal
   B. Negotiation during boot of FC-AL devices
   C. Loss of power
   D. Signal loss at break in the fiber

5. When do you use a short-wave GBIC?

   A. With single-mode fiber
   B. With multimode fiber
   C. With hubs, but not switches
   D. With switches, but not hubs

6. Why is graded-index multimode fiber used?

   A. It produces less dispersion.
   B. It is the only type of multimode fiber available.
   C. It decreases the bandwidth of multimode fiber.
   D. It increases the amount of attenuation.

7. How many devices can communicate simultaneously in a Fibre Channel Arbitrated Loop?

   A. Up to eight million pairs of nodes
   B. Up to 126 devices
   C. Up to 127 devices
   D. Two

8. What are the minimum requirements for a Fibre Channel solution?

   A. Host bus adapter, multimode fiber with GBICs, and a hub
   B. Host bus adapter, multimode fiber with GBICs, hub, and storage array
   C. Host bus adapter, multimode fiber with GBICs, and storage array
   D. Host bus adapter, two multimode fibers with GBICs, hub, and storage array

9. What type of port must be present to have a public loop?

   A. NL_port
   B. FL_port
   C. F_port
   D. N_port

10. A private loop supports how many devices?

    A. Two
    B. 126
    C. 127
    D. Eight million

11. What redundant parts are available for an RA4000?

    A. Fans and power supplies
    B. Fans, power supplies, and controllers
    C. Power supplies and controllers
    D. Fans and controllers

12. What is one of the major advantages of fiber over copper?

    A. Common bright orange color
    B. Flexibility allowing a smaller bend radius
    C. Resistance to pinching
    D. Resistance to electromagnetic interference

13. A link consists of how many fibers?

    A. One
    B. Two
    C. 126
    D. 127

14. A Fibre Channel Fabric is commonly represented by which symbol?

    A. Cloud
    B. Square
    C. Rectangle
    D. Circle

15. How many devices are supported with Microsoft Cluster Server and a Compaq 12-port storage hub?

    A. 11
    B. 12
    C. Seven
    D. Three

ASE

ACCREDITED SYSTEMS ENGINEER

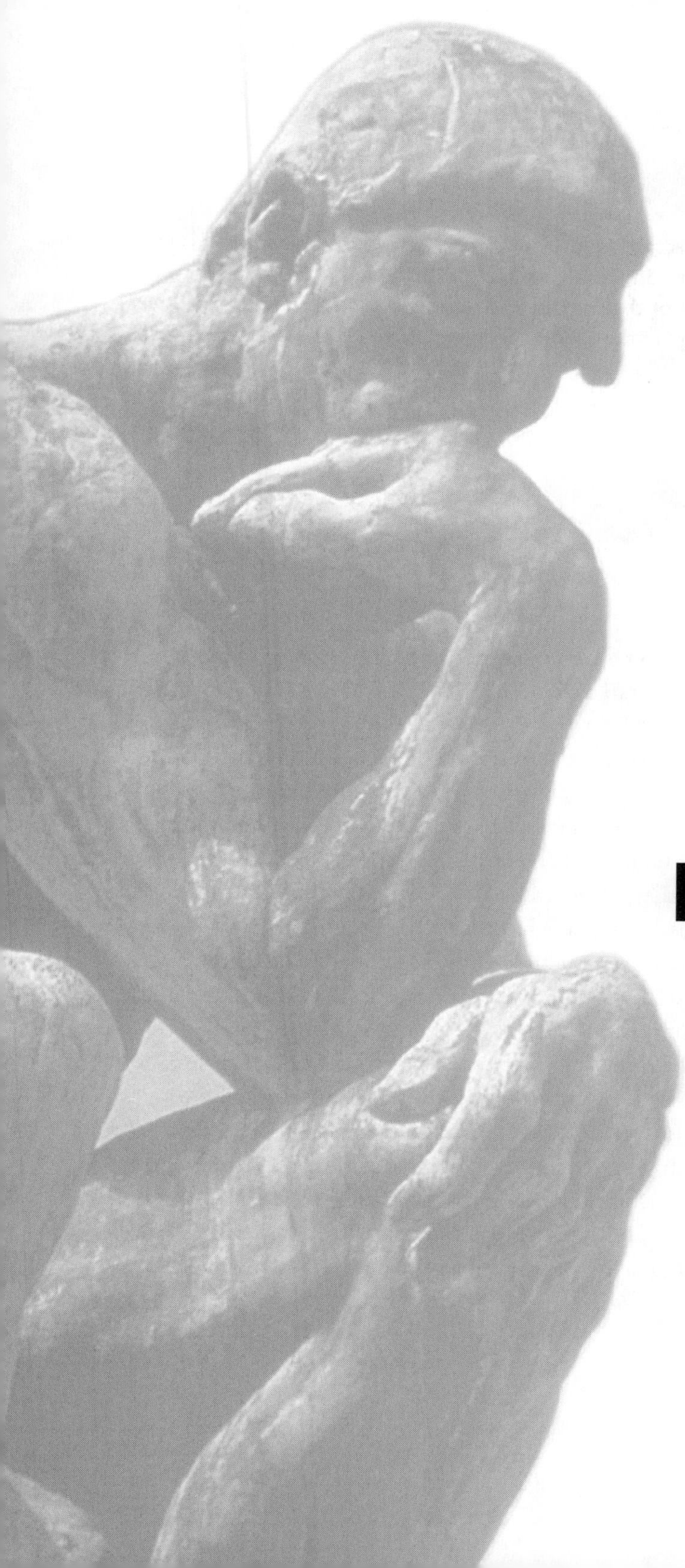

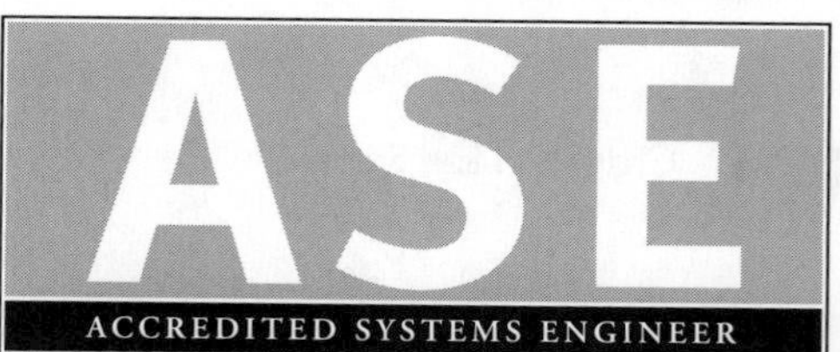

11

Software

CERTIFICATION OBJECTIVES

11.01 Compaq SmartStart

11.02 Compaq Insight Manager

11.03 Problem Alerting

11.04 Remote Monitoring

11.05 Management Agents

11.06 Using Compaq Insight Manager with Other Management Systems

11.07 Using Compaq Rack Builder software

Compaq supplies administrators with a multitude of tools to make their jobs easier. These tools help with the installation, configuration, and management of servers. In this chapter, we will cover a few of the more important tools. We will discuss Rack Builder, which helps in preinstallation design and ordering. We will cover Compaq SmartStart, which aids in installation and configuration. We will also cover Insight Manager, which helps manage servers.

CERTIFICATION OBJECTIVE 11.01

Compaq SmartStart

Compaq SmartStart is a collection of software and utilities. If you insert the Compaq SmartStart CD in a Windows 95 or Windows NT machine with auto-run enabled, it will bring up the Disk Builder utility, shown in Figure 11-1. This is a good place to start. The Disk Builder utility can be used to create floppy disks for all the utilities contained on the CD.

You can use the Disk Builder utility to create ROMPaq firmware upgrades for various Compaq Servers. This is especially useful if you plan to do a SmartStart installation on a Compaq SystemPro/XL. SystemPro/XL systems need a firmware upgrade in order to be able to boot to the SmartStart CD. This is because the firmware shipped with these servers does not support the El Torito boot specification. El Torito is a standard designed to allow computers to boot from a CD-ROM.

You can also make diskettes for the Compaq System Erase utility. The System Erase utility will erase your hard drives and any configuration information stored in system ROM or on the array controller. It is recommended you do a system erase before performing an installation.

You can also use Disk Builder to make diskettes for the Compaq System Configuration utility. This utility is used to configure a new server. First, it will create the system partition. After installation, the system partition can

FIGURE 11-1

The Compaq Disk Builder utility

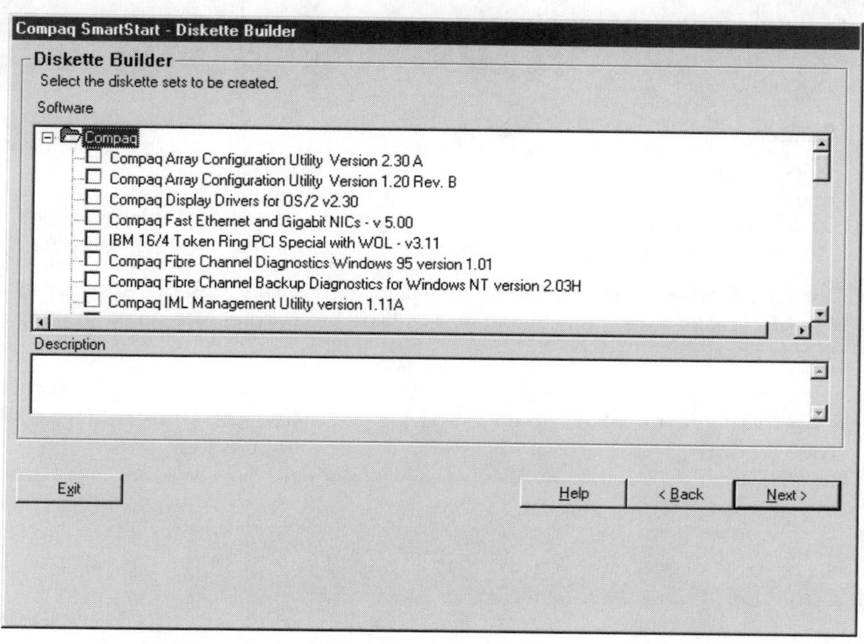

be accessed by pressing F10 as the server is booting up. Next, the configuration utility walks you through configuring your system hardware. The setup program configures most of your hardware for you. You can view or modify the suggestions made by the setup program.

You also get the Array Configuration utility. The Array Configuration utility is used to configure your array controller. You can use this utility to configure your hard drives and set up hardware-based fault tolerance (RAID).

Finally, you can make Compaq System Diagnostics diskettes. The Compaq System Diagnostics utility can be used to determine hardware problems, such as conflicting IRQ settings. This can save you hours in problem resolution time.

QUESTIONS AND ANSWERS

I want to redo my Compaq server completely, adding new drives and loading Windows NT 4.0. What should I do first?	Run the System Erase utility to completely erase previous configuration information.
I have a SystemPro/XL system. How can I get it to do a SmartStart install of NT 4.0?	Use Disk Builder to make a ROMPaq diskette and update the BIOS on your system.
One of the drives in my stripe set has failed. How do I make sure the rebuild takes as little time as possible?	Use the Array Configuration utility to increase the rebuild rate on your array controller.
I have recently added a new EISA NIC card to my system. What should I do if I am having trouble booting?	Use the Compaq Diagnostics utility to check the IRQ and DMA settings of all the expansion boards in your system.

CERTIFICATION OBJECTIVE 11.02

Compaq Insight Manager

Compaq Insight Manager is a remote Simple Network Management Protocol (SNMP) monitoring application that lets you monitor the status of your server hardware. Imagine having to visit your server every hour or so to check on it. This would be very bothersome, especially if you had to go to a different floor, or inside a locked server room. Insight Manager eliminates this bother.

Insight Manager can save you a lot of headaches. I suggest checking your servers every morning when you get into work and every afternoon when you return from lunch. This way you can detect a downed server before a majority of the users are trying to access it. It's much easier to troubleshoot a problem with 50 users waiting than with 5000 users waiting.

Insight Manager is located on the management CD. Let's go over the steps to install Insight Manager. The Insight Manager setup program is located under INSIGHT\WIN32\ENG\SETUP. The setup program starts off with a few warnings. The first screen contains the general copyright warning. It also suggests that you close all Windows programs before proceeding.

The second screen lets you know that the program will install the Borland database engine. It tells you that you must close all applications that use this engine before continuing.

Next comes the usual name and company name screen. You must enter something in both boxes in order for the setup program to allow you to continue.

After the confirmation, you see the window in Figure 11-2, which asks which components you want to install. There are two options: Compaq Insight Manager and Microsoft Systems Management Server Launch Support. Choosing the second option allows you to launch Insight Manager from within Microsoft SMS.

Next you are asked where you want to install the application. The default is usually fine. However, some people like to install applications on a partition other than the boot partition.

Now we get to the important stuff. This is where you can set some of your Insight Manager configuration options, such as enabling auto-discovery of IPX devices. When that is enabled, Insight Manager

FIGURE 11-2

Insight Manager installation options screen

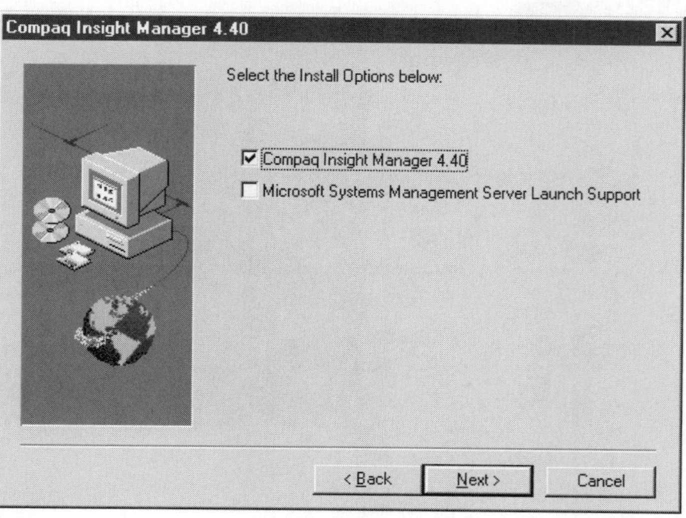

searches the network for devices running IPX, which are usually NetWare servers. You can also enable auto-discovery of NetWare Virtual Terminal (NVT) devices, as shown in Figure 11-3.

In the same window, you can set the version control delay period. Insight Manager's Version Control utility will notify you when the device drivers loaded on a particular machine are out of date. This delay period will determine how old your version database can be before it is considered out of date. When your version database becomes out of date, you will receive a warning whenever you try to use Insight Manager's Version Control feature.

Finally, in this same window, you can configure the Borland database engine so that it will still support any Windows 3.1 applications you may have on your machine.

Next, a dialog will be presented asking where you want to place the Insight Manager icons.

At the Review Settings page, if you don't have any changes to make, click Next, and the files will be copied to your hard drive. After the files have been copied, you select whether you want to view the README file. Installation is now complete.

FIGURE 11-3

Insight Manager configuration options screen

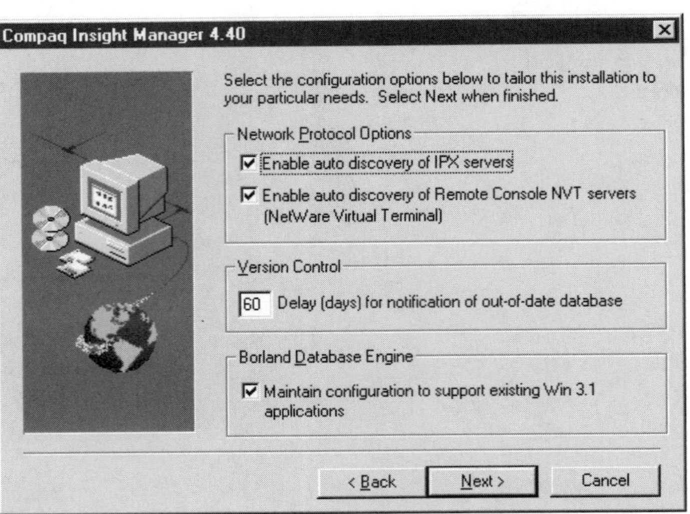

When you first open Insight Manager, you see the window shown in Figure 11-4. This is the Insight Manager Startup Checklist. After verifying that you have completed the necessary tasks, you can disable this screen. When you go into Insight Manager for the first time, the device list screen will be blank, unless during setup you configured Insight Manager to auto-find devices. If you did, any devices it found will appear in the device list.

We will now go through the steps of adding servers to our device list. To begin, you can either select Setup | Device List or select the Device List icon from the toolbar. This brings you to the Device List Setup window, shown in Figure 11-5, where you can select the IP device list or the IPX device list. Your IP devices can be sorted by name or IP address.

To add a new IP device, click the IP Device List command button in the Device List Window and then select New. You can then enter the IP address and the device name, or just enter the device name and select WINS/DNS Address Resolution. The newly added devices are placed immediately in your Responsible Device List. The responsible devices are

FIGURE 11-4

Insight Manager Startup Checklist

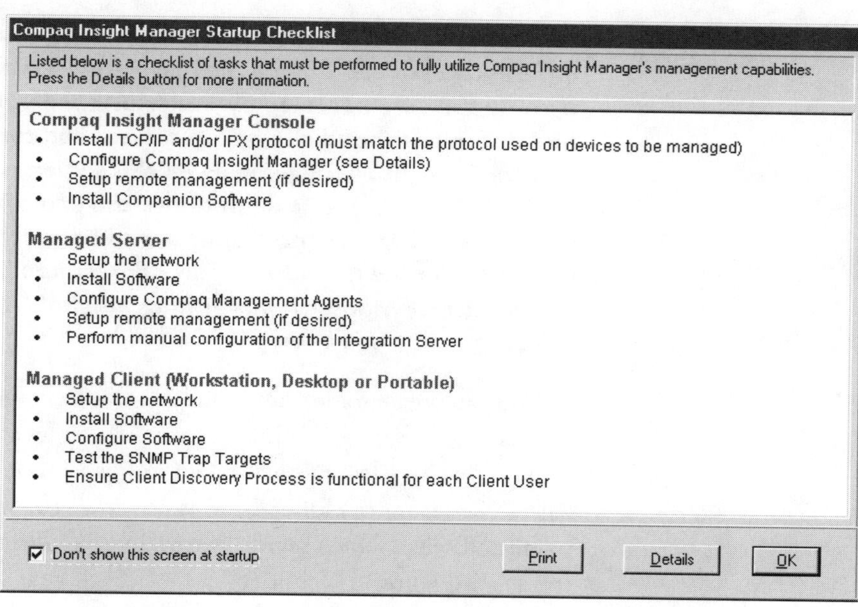

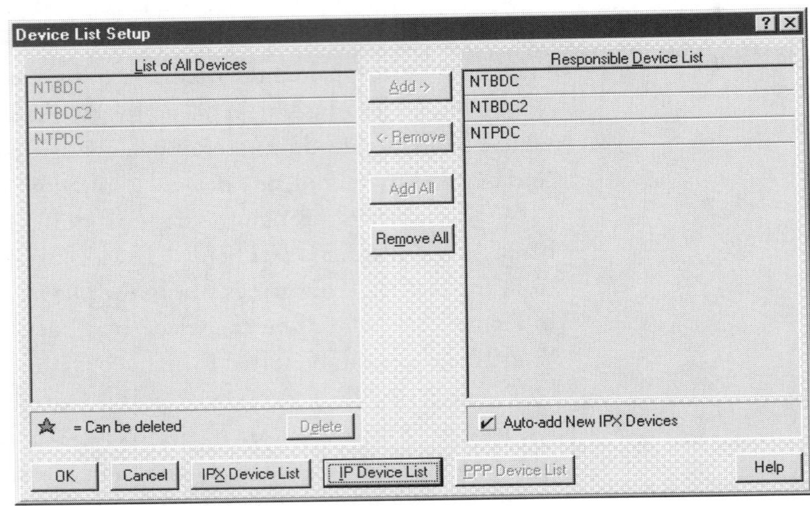

FIGURE 11-5

Insight Manager Device List window

the ones that will show up in the Insight Manager Device List window, as shown in Figure 11-6.

It is important to note that Insight Manager doesn't know the difference between servers. You give your servers a name, and you set up how they are accessed by Insight Manager. I remember once we had decommissioned one of our servers and turned it off. The problem was that Insight Manager showed this server as still being online. I couldn't figure it out. It wasn't until the end of the day that I realized what was wrong. Insight Manager had been set up to access the server with a dedicated IP address. This address had been given to a new server. Insight Manager was getting a signal from the new server, not the server that had been powered off.

You can create folders to group your servers together. This is useful if you have servers serving different purposes or located in different places. You do this by selecting the Setup Groups icon on the Device List toolbar. Select New from the Filter Groups window. You can give the group a new name and select which servers you want to add to the group. Now, as you can see in Figure 11-7, under All Devices there is your newly created group with the servers you added.

FIGURE 11-6

Insight Manager Device List screen

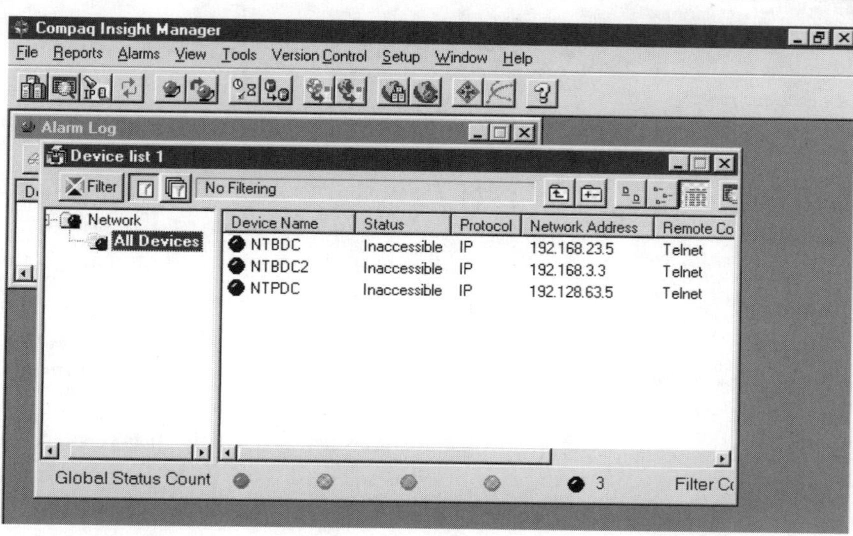

FIGURE 11-7

Device list with the newly created group

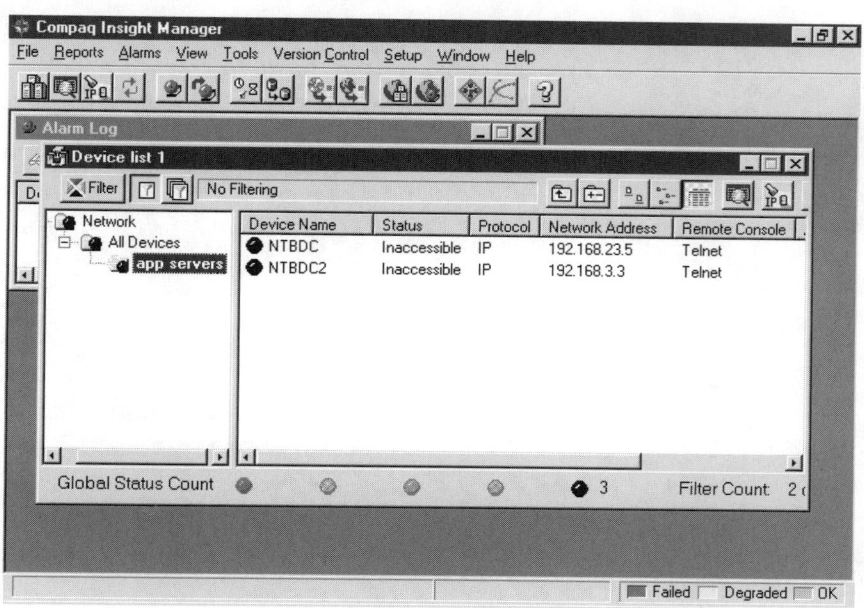

CERTIFICATION OBJECTIVE 11.03

Problem Alerting

Compaq Insight Manager allows for alerts to be triggered by certain events. These events can range from a hard disk failure to a total server failure. This feature will keep you from constantly having to monitor your servers. You can set up how these alerts will be sent.

To configure alerts, select Alarms from the Insight Manager menu. From this menu you can set up visual alarms, audible alarms, pager forwarding, and e-mail forwarding. If you select Visual Alarms, a pop-up message will appear on your screen when an alarm is triggered. When the Audible Alarms option is selected, Insight Manager will beep when an alarm is triggered. Selecting Pager Forwarding will cause a message to be sent to a numeric or an alphanumeric pager when an alarm is triggered. Selecting E-mail Forwarding will cause an e-mail message to be sent to a predetermined address when an alarm is triggered. The e-mail addresses and pager numbers can be configured under Alarms | Destinations. The Alarm Destinations screen is shown in Figure 11-8.

FIGURE 11-8

Compaq Insight Manager Alarm Destinations screen

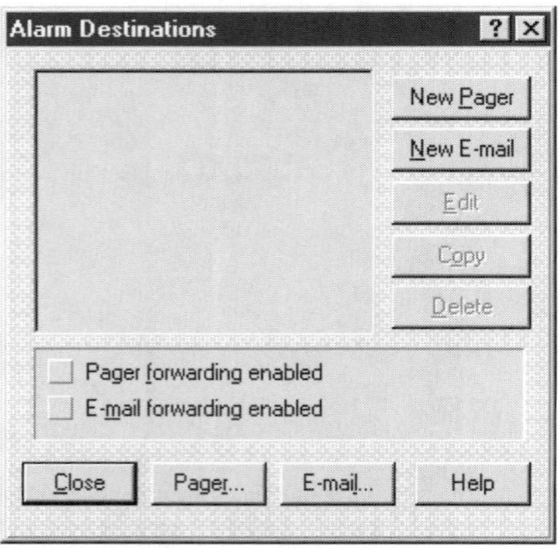

Device accessibility alarms can set off an alarm when an accessible device becomes inaccessible, or when a previously inaccessible device becomes accessible.

Alarms can be set off by individual server components for which thresholds have been set. You can receive an alarm for specific criteria that you set, such as a server being low on disk space.

EXERCISE 11-1

Setting a Threshold for Bytes Transmitted

1. From the Device View window, choose the NIC information button.

2. Choose Network Interface Statistics.
3. Under Transmit Statistics, select Bytes Transmitted.
4. When you move your cursor over the Bytes Transmitted statistic, it will display the Quick Menu Display icon.

5. You can either click the icon or press F6. The quick menu will display.

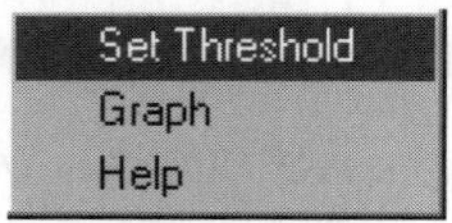

6. Select Set Threshold. The Threshold List window will appear.
7. Set the Polling Interval. This will determine how often Insight Manager will check the status of the device.
8. Next, set the Threshold Top, which is the maximum value for the threshold, and the Threshold Bottom, which is the minimum value.
9. Your threshold is activated after you press Set.

CERTIFICATION OBJECTIVE 11.04

Remote Monitoring

After you have added your servers, set up your groups, and configured your thresholds, you are ready to begin monitoring. If you double-click one of your servers, you will bring up the Device Data window. From this window, you can choose one of the options shown in Figure 11-9: Configuration, Recovery, System Board, Expansion Boards, Utilization, NIC, or Mass Storage.

- **Configuration button** Gives system configuration information, including processor, memory, disk controller, security, recovery, and I/O information.
- **Recovery button** Gives information about Automatic Server Recovery, server logs, power supplies, and Remote Insight.
- **System Board button** Gives information about processors, memory, ROM version, and serial number.
- **Expansion Boards button** Gives a list of expansion boards installed in your system, along with their slot numbers and the resources used by each one.
- **Utilization button** Gives information on processor and system bus utilization.
- **NIC button** Allows you to access NIC model, slot, and interface statistics.
- **Mass Storage button** Gives information on logical and physical drives, including size, status, controller, and driver information.

FIGURE 11-9

Device View selection options

CERTIFICATION OBJECTIVE 11.05

Management Agents

At the center of Compaq Insight Manager are the management agents. The management agents are what allow Insight Manager to monitor Compaq systems. If the management agents are not loaded, then Insight Manager will give you a "device inaccessible" message.

The Insight Manager agents can be obtained from the Management CD. You run [CD drive]\AGENTS\WIN-NT\ENG\CPQMGMT\INSTALL to begin the server agent installation. Note that you must have already run the SSD and installed the systems management driver in order to install the server management agents. During the installation, you are given several choices as to which agents you want to install. You can install agents for only the particular server components you are interested in. It is not an "all or nothing" decision.

In order to install the desktop management agents, run [CD Drive Letter]\AGENTS\DESKTOP\DM435\ENG\FILES\SETUP. You are asked if you want to run a typical or a custom setup. You then choose which components you would like to install. The choices are the base component, the DMI component, the SNMP component, and the DMI Web component. After you confirm your settings, the installation proceeds. You are then asked to reboot your computer.

CERTIFICATION OBJECTIVE 11.06

Using Compaq Insight Manager with Other Management Systems

Compaq Insight Manager is considered a management application. A management application is designed to manage one specific type of component. For example, Insight Manager is designed to manage your Compaq servers. Many management applications can be integrated into *management platforms.* Management platforms are designed to manage your entire environment. You can integrate Insight Manager with a management platform, which would mean you need only select the Insight Manager icon or button to manage your Compaq servers. Each management platform is different, so when you are selecting a management platform, you might want to check with either Compaq or the software manufacturer to verify Insight Manager compatibility.

CERTIFICATION OBJECTIVE 11.07

Using Compaq Rack Builder Software

Compaq has developed a tool to aid in the configuration of their racks. The Compaq Rack Builder software can be used to predesign your Compaq rack.

This allows you to develop the configuration that will best fit your environment. The Rack Builder software will give you valuable information to help you determine what components you can put into a rack. Rack Builder can be downloaded from the Web or installed from the Rack Builder CD. Compaq racks and servers also come with a copy of Rack Builder.

To install Rack Builder from the Rack Builder CD, run Setup from the directory containing the language you would like to use to install Rack Builder. For example: to install Rack Builder in English, run [CD drive]\US\SETUP. You must then agree to the terms of the license agreement. Next you are asked for a destination folder. If the directory does not exist, it will be created. After the files are copied, you are asked which parts database you would like to use. The choices are North American and International. The installation completes, giving you a chance to view the README file, if you desire.

After starting Rack Builder, you should configure the options for your rack, using the Options menu shown in Figure 11-10. You select the rack

FIGURE 11-10

Rack Builder options menu

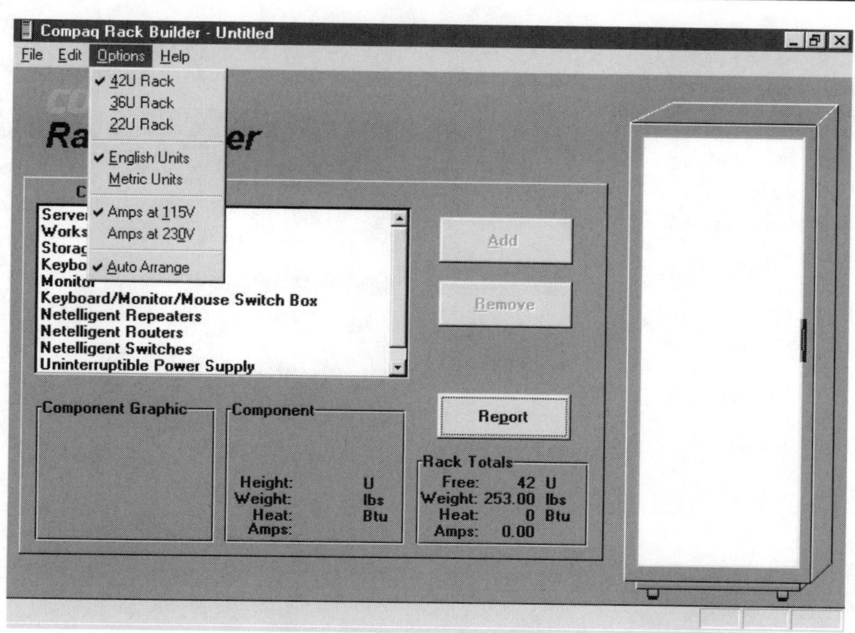

size: 22U, 36U, or 42U. Next, you select whether you want to use English or metric units. Then, you choose amperage at 115 or 230 volts. Finally, you select whether you want Rack Builder to auto-arrange the components you add to the rack.

You can now begin to configure your rack. Select all of the components you would like to add to your rack. You can choose servers, workstations, network components, and other equipment. As you select each component, Rack Builder gives you a graphic of that component, statistics for it, and total rack statistics. After you have selected a component, choose Add to add it to the rack. You can also add unlisted components to the rack. When you select this option, the dialog box in Figure 11-11 asks you for the necessary information about the component and gives it a generic picture so that it can be placed in the diagram.

Once you have added everything you would like to the rack, you can run the report. When you run the report, a little dialog box will pop up, letting you know whether warnings have been generated for your rack configuration.

FIGURE 11-11

Rack Builder Unlisted Component configuration screen

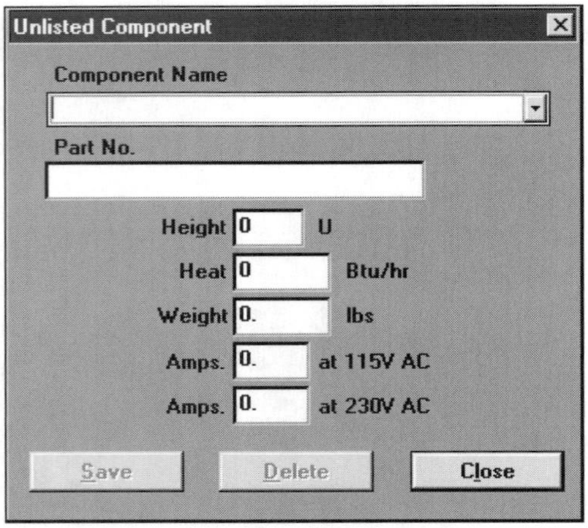

Types of Reports from Rack Builder Software

The Compaq Rack Builder software will develop a three-page, printable report. The first page of the report is site-planning information. The second is order information. The third is a rack graphic.

The Site Planning report, shown in Figure 11-12, includes component information and warnings. The report will also give you part name, height, weight, heat, and current consumption for each component. This information will be very useful in deciding where you physically locate your rack. You need to place your rack where you can get the necessary power. The report will let you know if your electrical consumption or heat discharge will produce a dangerous environment. You will also be given suggestions for optimizing your configuration, if you have turned off the auto-arrange feature.

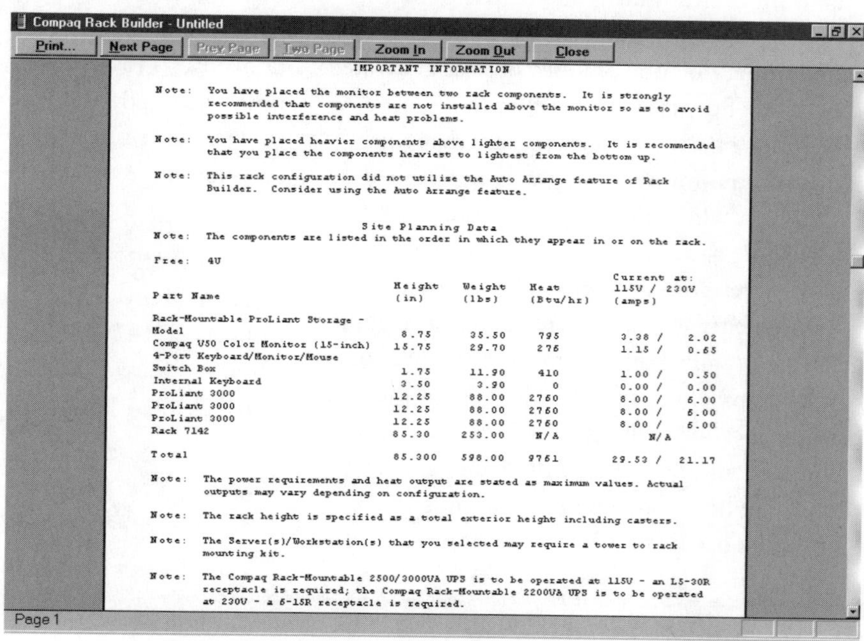

IMPORTANT INFORMATION

Note: You have placed the monitor between two rack components. It is strongly recommended that components are not installed above the monitor so as to avoid possible interference and heat problems.

Note: You have placed heavier components above lighter components. It is recommended that you place the components heaviest to lightest from the bottom up.

Note: This rack configuration did not utilise the Auto Arrange feature of Rack Builder. Consider using the Auto Arrange feature.

Site Planning Data

Note: The components are listed in the order in which they appear in or on the rack.

Free: 4U

Part Name	Height (in)	Weight (lbs)	Heat (Btu/hr)	Current at: 115V / 230V (amps)
Rack-Mountable ProLiant Storage - Model	8.75	35.50	795	3.38 / 2.02
Compaq V50 Color Monitor (15-inch)	15.75	29.70	276	1.15 / 0.65
4-Port Keyboard/Monitor/Mouse Switch Box	1.75	11.90	410	1.00 / 0.50
Internal Keyboard	3.50	3.90	0	0.00 / 0.00
ProLiant 3000	12.25	88.00	2760	8.00 / 6.00
ProLiant 3000	12.25	88.00	2760	8.00 / 6.00
ProLiant 3000	12.25	88.00	2760	8.00 / 6.00
Rack 7142	85.30	253.00	N/A	N/A
Total	85.300	598.00	9761	29.53 / 21.17

Note: The power requirements and heat output are stated as maximum values. Actual outputs may vary depending on configuration.

Note: The rack height is specified as a total exterior height including casters.

Note: The Server(s)/Workstation(s) that you selected may require a tower to rack mounting kit.

Note: The Compaq Rack-Mountable 2500/3000VA UPS is to be operated at 115V - an L5-30R receptacle is required; the Compaq Rack-Mountable 2200VA UPS is to be operated at 230V - a 6-15R receptacle is required.

FIGURE 11-12

Rack Builder report site configuration page

on the job

Be careful how you arrange components in your rack. If your rack is seven feet tall and you are five feet tall, you don't want to place the monitor on the top of the rack! I was at one site where everyone who had to access the servers had to stand on a phone book in order to type. Apparently, the person who designed the racks was very tall. He placed the keyboards too high for the other administrators to use. Note also that Rack Builder will display a warning if a component is located on top of the monitor.

FROM THE FIELD

Consider Heat Dispersion in Site Planning

Compaq servers generate a tremendous amount of heat during the course of daily operation. Using Rack Builder, you can determine the total amount of heat generated by a set of components so that the facilities/HVAC team can assure that the proper amount of cooling will be supplied to the room where the rack is located.

Failure to account for heat when planning a site can result in damage to the server components and unexpected loss of availability. Before installing any equipment, be sure you are fully aware of the HVAC schedule for the site. Many locations raise and lower the set points for ventilation systems in the evening/early morning hours and also on weekends when structure occupation is at a minimum.

Also, when installing machines with Pentium III Xeon processors in a 7000-series rack, you must order the new high airflow door inserts to accommodate the additional heat generated by these processors.

The part numbers for these rack retrofits are as follows:

High Air Flow Rack Door Insert for the 7122 Rack:	157847-B21
High Air Flow Rack Door Insert for the 7142 Rack:	327281-B21
High Air Flow Rack Door Insert for the 7142 Rack (6-pack):	327281-B22

—Thomas E. Eck, MCSE+I, MCSD,ASE, CCA, CNA

The Order Information page, shown in Figure 11-13, gives you valuable information that you can use when ordering your rack, server, and components. This information includes part number, part name, and quantity. Not only does the Order Information page include the components you added to the rack, it also includes all the necessary equipment that you will need to set up your rack (mounting kits, for example). The information on this page is what you will need to supply to your vendor when ordering your equipment.

Finally, the graphic page will give you a printout of what your rack will look like. This graphic is similar to the graphic on the original screen, where you added the components. The only difference is that the components on the graphic page are labeled, as you can see in Figure 11-14.

FIGURE 11-13

Rack Builder report Order Information page

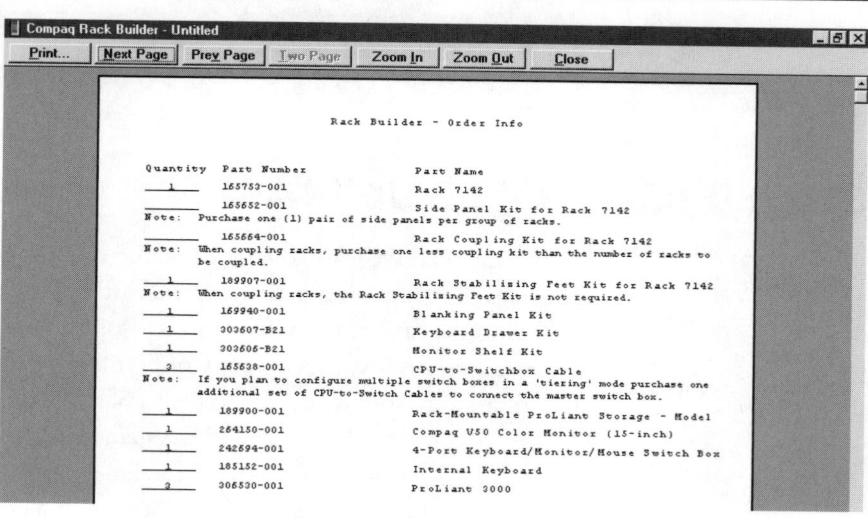

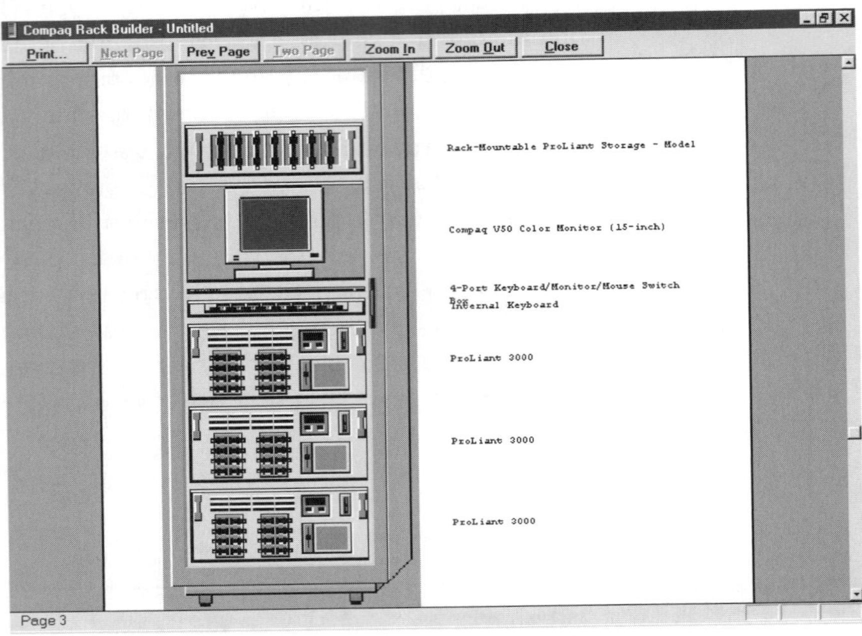

FIGURE 11-14 Rack Builder report graphic page

CERTIFICATION SUMMARY

In this chapter, we learned about the different tools and utilities Compaq provides to make using their products easier. We covered the Disk Builder utility on the SmartStart CD (to make floppy disks for ROMPaqs), the System Erase utility, the System Configuration utility, the Array Configuration utility, and the System Diagnostics utility.

Compaq Insight Manager and the management agents are used to monitor activity on your servers. This can save you valuable time in problem diagnosis. We covered the forms that alarms could take: visual, audible, pager forwarding, and e-mail forwarding. We went through the steps of setting a threshold to trigger an alarm.

Compaq also supplies you with the Rack Builder utility. Rack Builder is used to pre-configure your Compaq rack. The report generated by Rack Builder will help you optimize your configuration and aid in the ordering process.

TWO-MINUTE DRILL

- Compaq SmartStart is a collection of software and utilities.
- You can use the Disk Builder utility to create ROMPaq firmware upgrades for various Compaq Servers.
- Compaq Insight Manager is a remote Simple Network Management Protocol (SNMP) monitoring application that lets you monitor the status of your server hardware.
- The Insight Manager setup program is located on the management CD under INSIGHT\WIN32\ENG\SETUP.
- When you first open Insight Manager, you see the Insight Manager Startup Checklist window.
- To add servers to your device list, begin by selecting either Setup | Device List or the Device List icon from the toolbar.
- You can create folders to group your servers together, which is useful if you have servers serving different purposes or located in different places.
- Compaq Insight Manager allows for alerts to be triggered by certain events.
- After you have added your servers, set up your groups, and configured your thresholds, you are ready to begin monitoring.
- From the Device Data window, you can choose one of these options: Configuration, Recovery, System Board, Expansion Boards, Utilization, NIC, or Mass Storage.
- Management agents are what allow Insight Manager to monitor Compaq systems and can be obtained from the Management CD.
- Many management applications can be integrated into *management platforms*.
- Management platforms are designed to manage your entire environment.
- The Compaq Rack Builder software can be used to predesign your Compaq rack.
- Rack Builder can be downloaded from the Web or installed from the Rack Builder CD. Compaq racks and servers also come with a copy of Rack Builder.
- The Compaq Rack Builder software will develop a three-page, printable report: Page one of the report is site-planning information. Page two is order information. Page three is a rack graphic.

SELF TEST

The following Self Test questions will help you measure your understanding of the material presented in this chapter. Read all the choices carefully, as there may be more than one correct answer. Choose all correct answers for each question.

1. If you wanted to make ROMPaq diskettes, what utility would you use?
   A. Rack Builder
   B. Disk Builder
   C. Insight Manager
   D. Disk Activator
2. Which cannot be done by the Array Configuration utility?
   A. Configure array controller.
   B. Set up RAID.
   C. Configure hard drives.
   D. All of the above can be done with the Array Configuration utility.
3. Where in Insight Manager would you go to check if both of your redundant power supplies are functioning?
   A. View Device Data | Recovery
   B. View Device Data | Configuration
   C. View Device Data | Utilization
   D. View Device Data | Mass Storage
4. What Compaq servers need a firmware upgrade in order to boot to the SmartStart CD?
   A. ProLiant 6500
   B. ProLiant 3000
   C. ProLinea/XL
   D. SystemPro/XL
5. Before doing a SmartStart system install, what Compaq utility would you use to erase all system Configuration information?
   A. Array Configuration
   B. ROMPaq
   C. System Erase
   D. None of the above
6. If you need to access the System Configuration utility on the system partition, what key would you press when the server is booting?
   A. ESC
   B. F10
   C. ALT-C
   D. SPACE
7. You believe your system has an IRQ conflict. What should you do to verify the current configuration?
   A. Run the System Erase utility.
   B. Run the Compaq System Diagnostics utility.
   C. Load a new ROMPaq.
   D. Run the Array Configuration utility.
8. What is the name of the management protocol used by Insight Manager?
   A. IP
   B. IPX
   C. SSD
   D. SNMP

9. You want to load Insight Manager. On what Compaq CD can it be found?
   A. The Management CD
   B. The SmartStart CD
   C. The Rack Builder CD
   D. The Insight CD
10. Servers running what protocol can be configured for auto-discovery during Insight Manager installation?
    A. IP
    B. SNMP
    C. DLC
    D. IPX
11. How can you tell if the driver you have installed for your network cards is up to date?
    A. Use the Compaq Diagnostics utility.
    B. Use Version Control in Insight Manager.
    C. Use the System Configuration utility.
    D. Using the version info report from Rack Builder.
12. How can Insight Manager monitor your servers if you don't know the IP addresses?
    A. Using WINS/DNS
    B. Using a LMHOSTS file
    C. Using a HOSTS file
    D. You must know the IP address of your servers in order to use Insight Manager.
13. Which of the following cannot be accessed from the Device Data window in Insight Manager?
    A. System configuration
    B. System board information
    C. NIC information
    D. All can be accessed from the Device Data window.
14. You are using Rack Builder to configure your Compaq rack. Where would you go find the height and weight for all the components you added to your rack?
    A. The Site Planning page
    B. The Order Information page
    C. The graphic page
    D. None of the above
15. You are using Rack Builder to configure your Compaq rack. Where would you go to find the part number for all the components you added to your rack?
    A. The Site Planning page
    B. The Order Information page
    C. The graphic page
    D. None of the above

ASE

ACCREDITED SYSTEMS ENGINEER

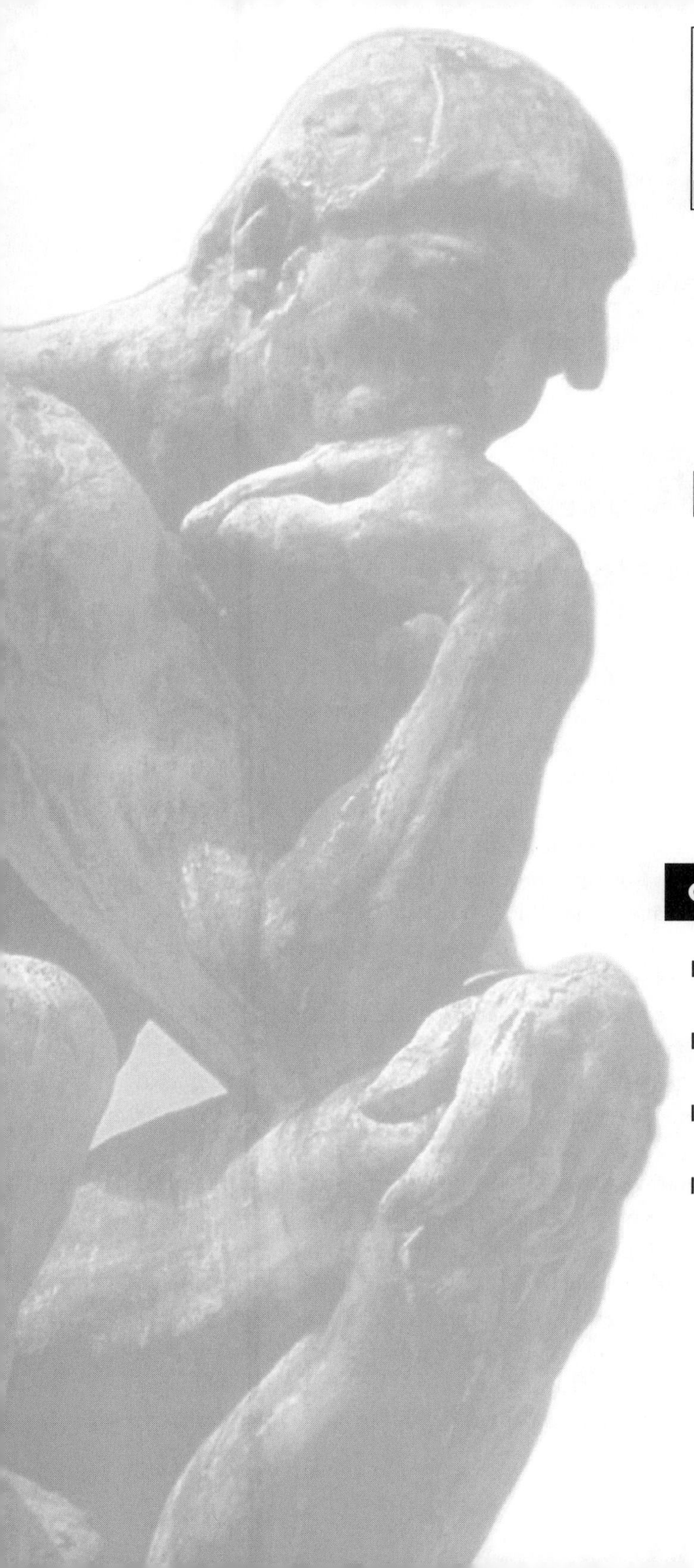

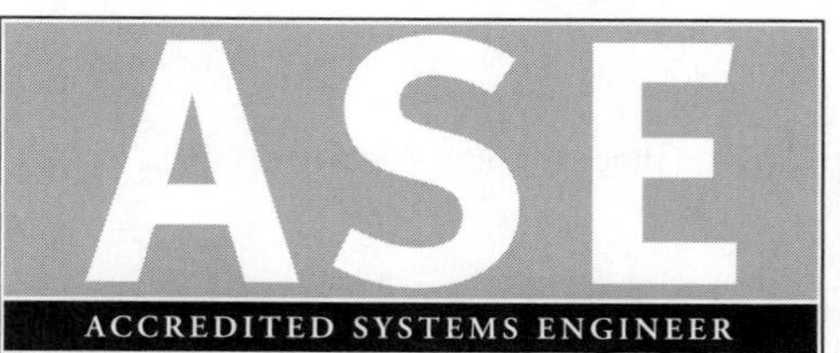

12

Networking

CERTIFICATION OBJECTIVES

12.01 Compaq NetFlex-2 and NetFlex-3 Networking Boards

12.02 Upgrading from 10 Mbps to 100 Mbps with NetFlex-3

12.03 Compaq Netelligent Network Controllers

12.04 100 Base-TX and 100 VG-AnyLAN

This chapter discusses three kinds of network controllers offered by Compaq: the NetFlex-2, NetFlex-3, and Netelligent controller cards. Compaq didn't take a "one size fits all" approach to networking. Different cards fit different needs. These cards provide high quality and high performance. In this chapter, we will discuss some of the basic characteristics of these cards.

CERTIFICATION OBJECTIVE 12.01

Compaq NetFlex-2 and NetFlex-3 Networking Boards

Compaq NetFlex-2 network controllers use Packet Blaster technology. Packet Blaster technology development was a collective effort by Texas Instruments and Compaq. A Packet Blaster is a LAN accelerator that increases throughput while decreasing CPU usage.

Compaq NetFlex-3 network controllers use ThunderLAN technology. ThunderLAN was also jointly developed by Compaq and Texas Instruments. It allows for support of both 10 Mbps and 100 Mbps on a single device. This makes it possible for a 10-Mbps Ethernet card to be upgraded to 100 Mbps. ThunderLAN provides support for 100BaseT and 100VG-AnyLAN architectures.

Compaq network controllers offer support for a wide range of operating systems. They can be run on Windows NT, Novell NetWare, SCO UnixWare, SCO OpenServer, and OS/2 platforms. The NetFlex-2 cards come with a different driver for each operating system. The NetFlex-3 cards come with one universal driver. This driver can interpret commands for each of the different operating systems. This is due in part to the ThunderLAN technology used by the NetFlex-3 cards. The drivers for the various cards can be loaded from the disk provided with the cards or from the Compaq SSDs. Using the SSDs for driver installation is recommended. That way you will have more up-to-date drivers for all of your server components.

Compaq network controllers are fully integrated with Compaq Insight Manager. After you load the Insight agents for a card, Insight Manager will give you numerous stats on the adapter, including lost frames, transmission errors, and other valuable data. Insight Manager can also issue an alert when the card has failed.

Compaq NetFlex-3 controllers allow for the configuration of a *network controller pair*, which provides fault tolerance. Network controller pairs are two NICs that are configured to act as one. One card is the primary and one is the secondary. When the primary fails to receive a response from the network, the secondary controller takes over. The MAC address and the IP address from the primary controller are copied to the secondary controller. The secondary controller then takes over all network communications. The switchover is virtually instantaneous. This can be very advantageous in environments where downtime is intolerable. Network controller pairs can be configured through the SSD or the Advanced Network Configuration Utility in the Control Panel.

on the job

Care must be taken when using a network controller pair. One card will be disabled and not communicate with the network. If, for some reason, you have to test your connections, you will not get a response from the disabled card. I once ran across a case where the network cabling was not very well labeled and there were many connections that weren't being used. In order to find out which connections weren't being used, a monitor was set up to measure traffic on the lines. All the lines that had a secondary NIC on them were marked as inactive and disconnected. Luckily, there were no network failures before we realized what had happened.

QUESTIONS AND ANSWERS

Where can I find the drivers for my NetFlex-3 controller?	On the disks that came with the card or the Compaq SSDs
I am running SCO OpenServer. Can I still use a NetFlex-2 network card?	Yes. SCO OpenServer is supported by all Compaq network cards.
My network controller says it has a Packet Blaster. What is its purpose?	Packet Blasters help to increase throughput
How can I check to see if my NetFlex-2 network card is functioning properly?	Network card status can be checked through Insight Manager
I have a 10-Mbps NetFlex-2 Ethernet card. Can it be upgraded to 100 Mbps?	No. Only NetFlex-3 cards can be upgraded.

NetFlex-2 ENET-TR

The NetFlex-2 ENET-TR adapter is Compaq part number 142213-001. This is a high-speed, bus-mastering, EISA network controller. NetFlex-2 ENET-TR controllers offer support for both Token Ring and Ethernet networks. The NetFlex-2 ENET-TR uses Packet Blaster technology to increase throughput. It offers transfer rates of 10 Mbps on Ethernet networks in half-duplex mode or 20 Mbps in full-duplex mode on 10BaseT wiring. The card comes with an RJ-45 connector for 10BaseT networks. It also can be ordered with a DB-15 connector that can support an AUI connection. There is an optional AUI-to-BNC transceiver that can be ordered for the card (Compaq part number 142108-001) to allow BNC connections.

The NetFlex-2 ENET-TR adapter also offers transfer rates of 4 Mbps or 16 Mbps on Token Ring networks. The card comes with a DB-9 or an RJ-45 connector for Token Ring. The DB-9 connector is for use with STP cabling, and the RJ-45 connector is for use with UTP cabling.

NetFlex-2 Dual Port ENET

The Compaq NetFlex-2 Dual Port ENET is Compaq part number 142131-001. It is a 32-bit EISA controller. This card has two Ethernet interfaces integrated onto one board. The Dual Port ENET card offers several advantages. It is like having two network cards taking up only one slot on the motherboard. It is also cheaper than buying two separate NetFlex-2 cards.

The Compaq Dual Port ENET card offers premium performance. It has two Packet Blasters (one for each channel) for increased throughput. It is capable of 10 Mbps in half-duplex mode and 20 Mbps in full-duplex mode. The card can be bought with connectors for both 10BaseT and AUI. You can also purchase the optional AUI-to-BNC transceiver (142108-001) for this card. This card is also fully integrated with Insight Manager.

on the job

Be careful when using dual-port network cards. If you are not going to use both ports, you should disable one of them. This is where confusion can occur. Make sure you note which port you have actually disabled. Nothing can be more frustrating than spending hours troubleshooting a network connectivity problem only to find out that you simply plugged the network cable into the wrong port.

NetFlex-2 TR

The NetFlex-2 TR controller is Compaq part number 199520-001. It is a 32-bit, EISA Token Ring network card. The card supports a DB-9 or an RJ-45 connection. The NetFlex-2 TR controller uses Packet Blasters to increase throughput. It can support transfer rates of 4 Mbps or 16 Mbps. It is fully integrated with Insight Manager.

NetFlex-2 Dual Port TR(142132-001)

The Compaq NetFlex-2 Dual Port TR controller is Compaq part number 142132-001. It is a 32-bit EISA bus-mastering network controller card. The NetFlex-2 Dual Port TR controller contains two Token Ring interfaces on one EISA controller. Having two Token Ring controllers integrated on one card offers the same advantages as the Dual ENET card. The Dual Port TR card is also priced lower than two single-port NetFlex-2 Token Ring cards. The Dual Port TR card uses Packet Blaster technology. It supports transfer rates of 4 Mbps or 16 Mbps. The card comes with two RJ-45 connectors for UTP cabling, or two 9-pin D-shells through a DB-26 interface for STP.

NetFlex-3/E

The NetFlex-3/E network card is Compaq part number 169800-001. The NetFlex-3/E is a high-performance EISA Ethernet network card. It uses ThunderLAN technology for increased performance. Natively, it can support 20 Mbps in full-duplex mode. However, it can be upgraded to support 100-Mbps Ethernet connections. The NetFlex-3/E is available with RJ-45 and BNC connections.

NetFlex-3/P

The NetFlex-3/P is Compaq part number 169810-001. It offers the same features as the NetFlex3/E. It is just a PCI version of the same card. Like the NetFlex3/E, the NetFlex-3/P can be upgraded to support 100-Mbps Ethernet.

CERTIFICATION OBJECTIVE 12.02

Upgrading from 10 Mbps to 100 Mbps with NetFlex-3

NetFlex-3 Ethernet controllers can be upgraded from 10 Mbps to 100 Mbps. This is made possible by the ThunderLAN technology developed by Compaq and Texas Instruments. The upgrade can be performed by purchasing the optional upgrade modules from Compaq. The 100Base-TX UTP module is Compaq part number 169804-001. The 100VG-AnyLAN UTP module is part number 169802-001. Thanks to the ThunderLAN technology, little else is needed to upgrade these cards.

CERTIFICATION OBJECTIVE 12.03

Compaq Netelligent Network Controllers

Compaq also offers the Netelligent generation of network controllers. As is the case with the NetFlex-2 and NetFlex-3 families, there are several Netelligent controllers. The two we will be discussing here are the Netelligent 10/100 TX PCI UTP Controller and the Netelligent 4/16 TR PCI UTP/STP Controller. These two controllers are by far the most popular.

Netelligent 10/100 TX PCI UTP Controller

The Netelligent 10/100 TX UTP Controller is Compaq part number 317600-B21. It is an Intel-based Ethernet network controller. In fact, it is often referred to as the Netelligent 10/100 TX PCI Intel UTP controller. It uses an Intel 82558 chipset. The drivers for this card are compatible with the Intel Fast Ethernet NICs, and vice versa.

The Netelligent 10/100 is auto-sensing. It can sense what speed the network is capable of and adjust itself accordingly. It also supports both full and half duplex, which means that it is capable of speeds of up to 200 Mbps. It has an RJ-45 connector and can be used on category 3, 4, or 5 networks.

The Netelligent 10/100 is fully integrated with Compaq Insight Manager. Insight Manager can be used to collect statistics and monitor activity. All that is needed are the management agents for the controller. The Netelligent 10/100 supports the SNMP protocol. This allows it to be managed by any SNMP management application. It also can be used in a Compaq NIC controller pair to provide fault tolerance.

Netelligent 4/16 TR PCI UTP/STP Controller

The Netelligent 4/16 TR PCI UTP/STP Controller is Compaq part number 268009-001. It can operate on Token Ring networks running at 4 Mbps or 16 Mbps. This controller has an RJ-45 and a DB-9 connector. It will support UTP Cat. 3, Cat. 4, and Cat. 5, and STP types 1, 1A, 2, and 6.

The Netelligent 4/16 was designed for top performance. It supports 32-bit bus mastering. It also has a scalable clock architecture. The onboard clock can adjust itself to either 4 MHz or 6 MHz. This allows for an increased processing rate in systems that can handle it.

The Netelligent 4/16 network controller, like other Compaq controllers, is fully integrated with Compaq Insight Manger. It also supports Compaq's NICStart software. NICStart is a DOS-based tool that Compaq designed for use with some of its Netelligent network adapters. NICStart comes on a bootable floppy disk. It can be used to set configuration parameters on Netelligent cards. It can also be used to run diagnostics on Netelligent network adapters. NICStart is another one of the many tools Compaq has developed to make administration easier.

CERTIFICATION OBJECTIVE 12.04

100 Base-TX and 100 VG-AnyLAN

100Base-TX is based on the 10BaseT standard. It uses a Carrier Sense Multiple Access/Collision Detection (CSMA/CD) media access method. 100Base-TX supports half- and full-duplex networking, allowing for a maximum throughput of 200 Mbps. 100Base-TX networks are constructed with category 5 cabling. They can support cable lengths of up to 100 meters from the hub to the workstation. A 100Base-TX network is very inexpensive to implement, which is why it is the common choice for 100-Mbps networks.

100VG-AnyLAN networking is based on a *demand priority* access method. In a demand priority network, the hub controls who has access to the network. Demand priority allows setting of network priorities, which allows one network device to be given priority over another. 100VG-AnyLAN networks also support Token Ring formats, which provide an easier migration from Token Ring networks to Ethernet.

Care must be taken when adding network controllers to Compaq servers. Some Compaq servers are very touchy when it comes to adding expansion boards. Depending on what type of server you have, SCSI controllers and network controllers must be added to certain slots. Consult your documentation for the best configuration for your server.

FROM THE FIELD

NC3131 Modular NIC

While network technology does not appear to be progressing at quite the same pace as the technology that enables faster processor clock speeds, clearly we have seen some shifts in the industry over the last few years. To address this issue, Compaq has always offered a modular approach to NIC card design in certain products in their network card product line, and today, the choice is the NC3131 NIC.

Without additional modules, this card supports two 10/100 auto-sensing ports on a 32/64-bit PCI card. If you should wish to move to a bonded Fast-Ethernet configuration or Gigabit configuration, you can easily do so by snapping on an expansion module.

Should you wish to have four ports on a single card, you simply snap on the NC3132 Dual-port upgrade card. For those moving to Gigabit Ethernet, you can add the NC6132 1000SX upgrade module.

By taking this modular approach to server configuration, you can reduce some of the financial and compatibility burdens associated with upgrading to newer technologies as they become available.

—Thomas E. Eck, MCSE+I, MCSD, ASE, CCA, CNA

CERTIFICATION SUMMARY

Compaq offers several network cards. Network cards can be monitored through integration with Insight Manager. Compaq also allows for fault tolerance through the establishment of controller pairs. Compaq NICs can support both Token Ring and Ethernet on the same card, or two Token Ring connections on one card, or two Ethernet connections on one card. The NetFlex-3 cards allow for easy migration from 10 Mbps Ethernet to 100 Mbps Ethernet. Compaq NICs can take advantage of the 10BaseT, 100Base-TX, and 100VG-AnyLAN technologies.

TWO-MINUTE DRILL

- ❑ There are three kinds of network controllers offered by Compaq: the NetFlex-2, NetFlex-3, and Netelligent controller cards.
- ❑ Compaq NetFlex-2 network controllers use Packet Blaster technology.
- ❑ A Packet Blaster is a LAN accelerator that increases throughput while decreasing CPU usage.
- ❑ Compaq NetFlex-3 network controllers use ThunderLAN technology.
- ❑ Compaq network controllers are fully integrated with Compaq Insight Manager.
- ❑ Network controller pairs can be configured through the SSD or the Advanced Network Configuration Utility in the Control Panel.
- ❑ The NetFlex-2 ENET-TR adapter is a high-speed, bus-mastering, EISA network controller, which offers support for both Token Ring and Ethernet networks.
- ❑ The Compaq NetFlex-2 Dual Port ENET card has two Ethernet interfaces integrated onto one board and offers premium performance.
- ❑ The NetFlex-2 TR controller card supports a DB-9 or an RJ-45 connection.
- ❑ The Compaq NetFlex-2 Dual Port TR controller contains two Token Ring interfaces on one EISA controller.

- The NetFlex-3/E network card is a high-performance EISA Ethernet network card.
- The NetFlex-3/P offers the same features as the NetFlex3/E. It is just a PCI version of the same card.
- NetFlex-3 Ethernet controllers can be upgraded from 10 Mbps to 100 Mbps, which is made possible by the ThunderLAN technology.
- Compaq also offers the Netelligent generation of network controllers.
- The Netelligent 10/100 TX UTP Controller is an Ethernet network controller and an Intel-based network controller.
- The Netelligent 10/100 is auto-sensing and is fully integrated with Compaq Insight Manager.
- The Netelligent 4/16 TR PCI UTP/STP Controller was designed for top performance and can operate on Token Ring networks running at 4 Mbps or 16 Mbps.
- 100Base-TX is based on the 10BaseT standard and uses a Carrier Sense Multiple Access/Collision Detection (CSMA/CD) media access method.
- 100VG-AnyLAN networking is based on a *demand priority* access method.

SELF TEST

The following Self Test questions will help you measure your understanding of the material presented in this chapter. Read all the choices carefully, as there may be more than one correct answer. Choose all correct answers for each question.

1. What technology is used on NetFlex-2 network cards to increase throughput?
   A. Packet Blaster
   B. ThunderLAN
   C. LAN Blaster
   D. None of the above
2. NetFlex-3 Ethernet controllers can be upgraded from 10 Mbps to 100 Mbps. What makes this possible?
   A. Packet Blaster technology
   B. ThunderLAN technology
   C. LAN Blaster technology
   D. Packet Sync technology
3. Which operating systems are compatible with Compaq NetFlex-2 controllers?
   A. Windows NT
   B. Novell NetWare
   C. OS/2
   D. All of the above
4. If you believe your NetFlex-3 controller is dropping frames, how can you check?
   A. By using the SSDs
   B. By instituting a controller pair
   C. By using Insight Manager
   D. By using a Packet Blaster
5. Compaq NetFlex-3 controllers have a universal driver for all operating systems. What makes this possible?
   A. Packet Blaster technology
   B. ThunderLAN technology
   C. LAN Blaster technology
   D. Packet Sync technology
6. You want to use a PCI network controller in order to maximize the performance of your server. Which of the following should you use?
   A. NetFlex-3/E
   B. NetFlex-2 ENET/TR
   C. NetFlex-2 Dual Port ENET
   D. NetFlex-3/P
7. What connectors are available for NetFlex-2 ENET TR controllers?
   A. DB-15
   B. AUI
   C. RJ-45
   D. All of the above
8. What access method do 100Base-TX networks use?
   A. Token passing
   B. CSMA/CD
   C. Demand priority
   D. CSMA/CA

9. What access method do 100VG-AnyLAN networks use?

   A. Token passing
   B. CSMA/CD
   C. Demand priority
   D. CSMA/CA

10. Your Ethernet network is currently running at 10 Mbps. You plan to upgrade to 100 Mbps in the near future. What network controllers should you buy for your new servers?

    A. NetFlex-3/E
    B. NetFlex-2 Dual ENET
    C. NetFlex-2 ENET TR
    D. NetFlex-2 Dual TR

11. You bought a NetFlex-2 controller card and are ready to configure it. Where should you run NICStart from?

    A. The floppy disk that came with the NIC
    B. The SmartStart CD
    C. The Management CD
    D. None of the above

12. You have lost the drivers for your Netelligent 10/100 TX PCI UTP controller. What drivers can be substituted for these until you can get the proper drivers?

    A. Intel Fast Ethernet controller drivers
    B. Proteon Fast Ethernet controller drivers
    C. SMC Fast Ethernet controller drivers
    D. IBM Fast Ethernet controller drivers

13. You have just installed a Netelligent 10/100 TX controller in your system, but it cannot be monitored through Insight Manager. What is most likely the cause?

    A. The drivers for the card are missing.
    B. The management agents for the card are missing.
    C. The card is not installed properly.
    D. The Netelligent 10/100 card is not supported by Insight Manager.

14. You believe your Netelligent NIC is having an internal hardware failure. What can you do to determine if this is indeed the case?

    A. Run Windows NT Performance Monitor.
    B. Run SmartStart.
    C. Run NICStart.
    D. None of the above

15. You currently have a 10BaseT network running on category 3 cabling. You have NetFlex-2 network cards. What must be done in order for you to upgrade your network to 100 Mbps?

    A. Purchase new network cards.
    B. Purchase new cabling.
    C. Reload your network drivers.
    D. All of the above

ASE

ACCREDITED SYSTEMS ENGINEER

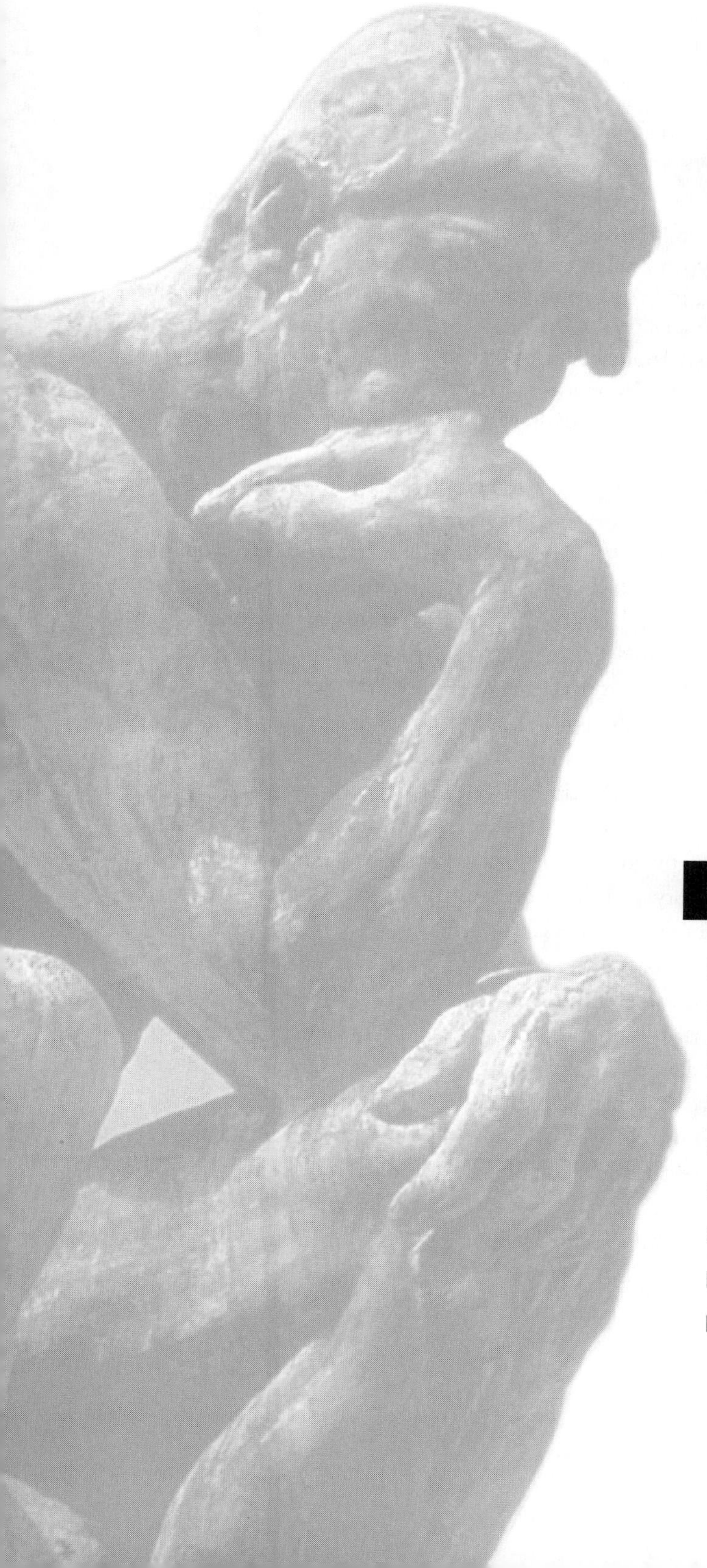

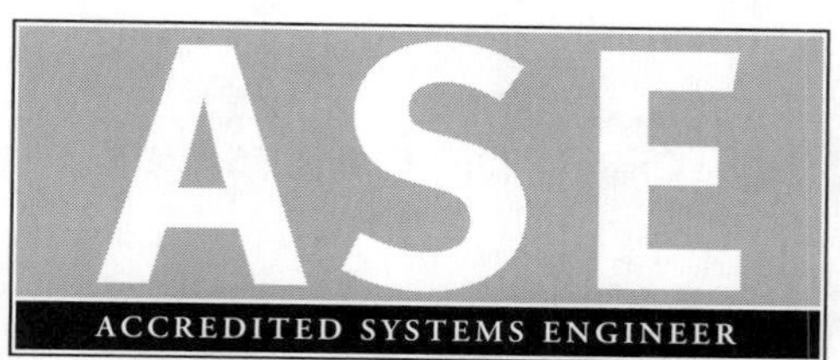

13

Compaq Servers

CERTIFICATION OBJECTIVES

13.01 ProSignia Servers

13.02 ProLiant Servers

13.03 Upgrading Memory

13.04 Processors Available

13.05 Level-2 Cache

13.06 Processor Power Module

13.07 Compaq Pre-Failure Warranty

13.08 Dual Peer PCI Buses

13.09 Fault Tolerant Features

Compaq has designed its servers to include the best technologies offering high performance, quality, availability, and maintainability with a lower total cost of ownership. Both the ProSignia and ProLiant server product lines provide significant features and technologies that make Compaq servers the preferred choice of many systems engineers and IT managers. This chapter will look at a brief history of these servers and the evolution of their key components. From the 486 processor to the Pentium III Xeon, Compaq has delivered state-of-the-art servers that meet the needs of a variety of end users.

Compaq server technology has been enhanced through Compaq's engineering efforts in memory specifications and system design that ultimately help maximize memory subsystem performance. This chapter will review the processor-to-memory bus specifications of the recent server products, explore issues related to upgrading memory on these servers, and touch on the steps Compaq takes to assure the server owner that memory will not be a cause of system performance problems.

Compaq has consistently worked with Intel as the primary supplier of server processors. Designing systems that can maximize the Intel Pentium, Pentium Pro, Pentium II, Pentium II Xeon, and Pentium III Xeon processors, Compaq has servers that can grow and scale to any business need. This chapter will explore the processors in use on Compaq servers, issues of cache memory and the processor installed, and processor power requirements delivered with special modules.

Performance of a server is defined in different ways, but the ability to keep a server running at almost nonstop levels will be discussed in this chapter. Compaq's high availability design requirements include pre-failure component awareness and a warranty that will provide component replacements before that part actually fails. Performance of add-on PCI devices is critical to overall system performance, and Compaq's dual peer PCI bus architecture and balancing I/O board requirements will be discussed in this chapter. Finally, several fault tolerant design features will be identified that are integral to Compaq's server architectures.

CERTIFICATION OBJECTIVE 13.01

ProSignia Servers

Based upon the success and strengths of the SystemPro family of servers, the ProSignia servers originally provided more compact form factors than other servers in Compaq's product line. The original ProSignia systems incorporated the EISA standard for the expansion bus, but integrated many components into the system board to leave open the slots for other devices. Up to eight hard drives could be integrated into this system with the Fast-Wide SCSI controller. An IDE CD-ROM drive was standard on this system, and it was the first server to offer the Compaq Insight Manager. This product has since been discontinued.

In early 1994, the ProSignia VS was announced. Utilizing the 486 processor family, this server also incorporated a 32-bit Fast-SCSI-2 controller into the system board along with a 32-bit NetFlex-L Ethernet controller. There were five internal drive slots and up to 128MB of system memory capability. Five EISA expansion slots rounded out this now discontinued system.

The ProSignia 500 was announced in 1994 and offered 256KB of shared secondary write-back cache in the FlexSMP architecture. Integrated into the system board was a 32-bit Fast-SCSI-2 controller, a 32-bit NetFlex-L Ethernet controller and a 1024x768 video graphics controller. This system contained six expansion slots supporting PCI/EISA/ISA devices and was expandable to 298MB using industry-standard SIMMs. Eight internal storage bays allowed over 30GB of storage capacity. A CD-ROM drive was also standard on this now discontinued system.

In 1995, Compaq announced the ProSignia 300 with an integrated 32-bit Fast-SCSI-2 controller. This system was optimized for running network operating systems rather than desktop applications and supported Standby

Recovery Server and Online Recovery Server features. This server could be converted to a rack-mountable form factor with an optional kit. The ProSignia 300 has been discontinued.

Announced in 1997, the ProSignia 200 was designed as a workgroup server. It included 512KB second-level (L2) Cache memory and the 32-bit Wide-Ultra SCSI-3 controller in a single Pentium II processor system. The ProSignia 200 system could only support 128MB of memory with industry standard SIMMS, but was upgradeable to ECC memory. The ProSignia 200 Small Business (SBS) model could handle 192MB of industry standard EDO SIMMs, but could be upgraded to 384MB using fast page mode (FPM) ECC memory kits from Compaq. PCI expansion architecture and a 16X CD-ROM (8X on the original 200 model) make this a strong choice for small businesses. This tower form factor system is still available from Compaq.

In late 1998, Compaq announced the ProSignia 720 and 740 Servers. The 720 provided model choices that utilized the Pentium II processor at 350, 400, or 450 MHz, whereas the 740 incorporates the Pentium III processor running at 500 MHz. Both are equipped with 100-MHz front-side bus and 512KB of Level 2 Cache. Both systems have six expansion slots supporting PCI and ISA devices. The 720 also can support one AGP device. The 720 can support up to 384MB of SDRAM DIMMs, but the 740 comes equipped with ECC RAM that can be upgraded to 1GB. Both have integrated Netelligent 10/100 TX network interface adapters, Wide Ultra2 SCSI controllers, and 1024x768 video graphics controllers. Three-year warranties come standard with these systems, which are still available from Compaq.

The newest ProSignia is the NeoServer, announced in March 1999. This server comes with a preinstalled operating system that supports all shared server requirements for file/print, backup, e-mail, and Internet. Each server comes standard with 6GB EIDE hard drives, 10/100 TX network controller, eight-port hub, 56K modem, and a ProSignia NeoServer Control Center. An expansion drive of 6GB is available, as is an 8GB backup drive, all of which utilize EIDE.

CERTIFICATION OBJECTIVE 13.02

ProLiant Servers

There have been over 15 ProLiant Servers released by Compaq since the first ones in 1993. The ProLiant 1000, 2000, and 4000 were announced in September 1993 and provided for EISA bus architecture, an integrated Fast-SCSI-2 controller and an SVGA video controller in the system board, standard CD-ROM drives, and Error Correcting Code (ECC) memory modules. The ProLiant 1000 came standard with 16MB of RAM and one processor (486 or Pentium). The 2000 came with 32MB of ECC RAM as standard and offered the option of running one to four processors. The 4000 also allowed the use of four processors using the FlexSMP system architecture and came standard with 64MB of ECC RAM. The 1000 provided seven expansion slots, whereas the 2000 and 4000 provided eight expansion slots supporting 8/16/32-bit EISA and ISA modules. Maximum memory capacity in the 4000 was 512MB. All three of these systems incorporated hot-pluggable drive architecture, with six bays available on the 1000 and five bays available on both the 2000 and 4000 models. The 2000 and 4000 allowed for redundant power supply options, as well. All three models came standard with Compaq's NetFlex-2 ENET-TR controller. All three of these early models were groundbreaking in many of the features introduced onto servers that are still minimum requirements in today's servers. All have been discontinued.

After these early ProLiant servers, Compaq announced the ProLiant 1500 in February 1995 and the ProLiant 4500 in February 1996. Incorporating the FlexSMP System Architecture, the 1500 allowed for an upgrade to dual processing. This was a good workgroup server with maximum memory capacity of 256MB of ECC RAM, five hot-pluggable SCSI drive bays and eight expansion slots supporting EISA and PCI expansion cards. The 4500 provided up to four processors, including an offline backup processor with automatic recovery. Similar to the 1500 in expansion capabilities, the 4500 could expand to 1GB of ECC RAM. Only four hot-pluggable SCSI drive bays were available on this model, however. Both systems incorporated 512KB secondary write-back cache for enhanced system performance and also featured an integrated 32-bit Fast-Wide SCSI-2 controller on the system board. Quad speed CD-ROM drives were the standard and a redundant power supply option was available on both of these systems, which have been discontinued.

Later in 1996, Compaq introduced the ProLiant 5000 and 2500. Both systems provided multiprocessor capabilities, with optional redundant processor power modules for maximized system availability. Offline backup processors also provided for increased system availability. Wide-Ultra SCSI controllers, 10/100-Mbps auto-sensing Ethernet modules, and Pentium Pro processors were standard. The 2500 could support up to 1GB of ECC RAM, whereas the 5000 handled 4GB with industry standard DIMMs. Both systems included Level-2 Cache and improved serviceability features in the chassis designs. CD-ROM drives were now coming with 8X performance. Both models have been discontinued.

In 1997, Compaq introduced the ProLiant 800, 850R, 1200, 1600, 3000, 5500, 6000, 6500 and 7000. The 800, 1200, and 1600 were strong workgroup servers with Pentium II processors. Because the 1200 relied on the early Pentium II processor, it could only support up to 512MB of memory, whereas the 800 and 1600 had 100-MHz Pentium II Deschutes processors and handled up to 1GB of memory. Integrated 10/100 Ethernet, hot-pluggable drives, and Level-2 ECC cache memory were standard on these models. The earliest model released of the ProLiant 850R did not include hot-plug drives, but subsequent models did. All of these systems were the first servers to move completely off the EISA standard and provide PCI- and ISA-compatible expansion slots. All (except the initial 850R) incorporated the integrated Wide-Ultra SCSI-3 controller. The 850R model, a rack-mountable form factor, supported up to two Pentium Pro 200 MHz. The ProLiant 800 and 1600 supported dual Pentium II processors; however, the 1200 supported a single Pentium II processor. In August 1999, Compaq announced a new dual processor-configured

ProLiant 800 and 1600 featuring the new Intel Pentium III processor, as well as a new ProLiant 1850R (rack mountable) model.

The 3000, 5500, 6000, 6500, and 7000 servers are still in production and provide complete systems with room to grow. Available in both tower and rack mount versions, the 3000 features up to two Pentium II 400-MHz or 450-MHz processors with 512KB of Level-2 Cache memory. The Highly Parallel System Architecture is utilized on this system and includes dual memory controller and dual peer PCI buses. Dual Channel Wide-Ultra SCSI-3 controller supports up to eight hot-plug SCSI drives. CD-ROM performance is now 24X standard. Shipping with 128MB of memory, the 3000 is expandable to 4GB using 100MHz SDRAM. Eight expansion slots include PCI/EISA/ISA compatibility. This system includes an Integrated Management Display and Integrated Remote Console for improved manageability.

At its introduction, the ProLiant 6000 provided the highest level of system expansion to date in the Compaq line. Up to four 500MHz Pentium III Xeon processors, 8GB of ECC EDO DIMM memory, nine PCI slots, one ISA modem slot, and two redundant power supplies are available, depending upon the model selected. Integrated into the system board is a Dual Channel Wide-Ultra SCSI-3 controller with two SCSI channels. Data rates up to 40MBps per channel are double the transfer rate of the earlier Fast-Wide SCSI-2 Controllers. Dual 10/100 Ethernet modules and conversion to rack-mountable form factors round out the features of this model. This system includes an Integrated Management Display and Integrated Remote Console for improved manageability.

The 6500 is a rack-mounted server designed for 24x7 multiserver environments. Pentium III Xeon processors combined with five PCI hot-pluggable expansion slots and a slim form factor make this model attractive to space hungry, high-performance shops. Up to four processors can be configured into this model, and the 256MB of standard EDO Buffered DIMM Memory can be expanded to 4GB. Up to seven 1" hot-pluggable SCSI drives can be installed, with maximum capacity of 127.4GB. There are two 750-watt redundant power supplies, also hot-pluggable, and the same Dual Channel Wide-Ultra SCSI-3 controller for fast data throughput.

The 7000 takes this system to the next level with memory expansion limited to only 8GB. Room for up to 21 1" hot-pluggable SCSI drives limits the internal storage to 327.6GB! The SMART Array 3100ES controller provides three-channel RAID support, and there are five hot-plug 64-bit PCI slots in addition to four 32-bit PCI and one ISA slots. Release levers on all slots combine with many other design features to make this server one of the easiest to service, with minimal tools. This rack-mounted system is still in production. This system includes an Integrated Management Display and Integrated Remote Console for improved manageability.

The ProLiant 5500 is available in both tower or rack-mount form factors and utilizes the Highly Parallel System Architecture for better usage of bandwidth. Dual memory controllers and dual peer PCI buses improve the throughput as well, providing increased system performance. The 5500 Pentium III Xeon supports up to four processors, with 100-MHz front-side bus and cache access at full processor speed. There are seven expansion slots supporting PCI and/or ISA devices. This system supports up to 10 1" hot-pluggable SCSI drives, and utilizes the 64-bit Dual Channel Wide Ultra2 SCSI controller. The power supply is hot-pluggable, but this feature is most useful when the optional redundant power supply option is installed. Redundancy in fans, network controllers, and SMART Array 3200 controllers can provide a high degree of fault tolerance. This system includes an Integrated Management Display and Integrated Remote Console for improved manageability.

To answer the demand for higher and higher performance capabilities, Compaq announced its new ProLiant models in 1999. The ProLiant 8000 and 8500 servers are eight-way system architectures based upon the Pentium III Xeon processors. These systems' capabilities are based upon the Profusion chipset co-developed by Compaq, Intel, and Corollary. They include the standard Compaq features of PCI hot plug technology, redundant hot plug power supplies, drives, fans, redundant processor power supplies, and auto processor bus recovery. These high-end servers include dual 100-MHz processor buses, dual 100-MHz memory buses (each with its own memory controller), and dedicated 100-MHz I/O buses. They support up to 16GB of two-way, cache line interleaved SDRAM and three Compaq designed host-to-PCI bridges supporting up to 11 expansion slots. The Pentium III 550-MHz processors include full-speed cache on the processor module as well as options for 512KB, 1MB, or 2MB of L2 cache. The ProLiant 8500 incorporates an integrated SMART Array Controller that supports two channels—one internal and one external. The ProLiant 8000 comes with the Compaq SMART Array 4250ES controller, and can support a second redundant controller. Each 4250ES controller has three channels, and can support all 21 drives that can be installed into the 8000 as a single array. The ProLiant 8000 is a rack-mountable or stand-alone form factor. In a rack, it uses 14U, whereas when set up as a stand-alone, it provides its own casters for maneuverability. The ProLiant 8500 is a rack-mountable form factor comprising only 7U, and can house up to four hot-plug SCSI hard drives.

Compaq announced the ProLiant 6400R, a rack-mountable server very similar to the 8500 except that the 6400R supports only four processors (not eight) and has only six I/O expansion slots (not 11). This server also reduced the rack space required to 4U. The 6400R, 8000, and 8500 provide the easy-access design features for serviceability of hardware components. Toolless retaining features, slide-in processor drawers, accessible hot-plug PCI bays, and the time-tested hot-plug drive features make these models some of the easiest servers in the industry to work on. These features translate to reduced downtime and fewer bandages when upgrades are required.

CERTIFICATION OBJECTIVE 13.03

Upgrading Memory

It is very important to know what type of memory is in your server. Compaq has changed the memory types from model to model, and sometimes within a model, as is the case with the ProLiant 1600. Basically, there are two types of memory used by Compaq servers: EDO or ECC. You cannot mix them up. The server must have all of the correct type and only that type. ECC memory can be in 60ns SDRAM DIMMs or 70ns SIMMs. DIMMs (Dual Inline Memory Modules) have 64-bit modules, whereas SIMMs (Single Inline Memory Modules) have 32-bit bus widths. The server can contain only SIMMs or only DIMMs, not both.

The ProLiant 400 comes with ECC memory and has a maximum of 384MB total. These are DIMMs and can be added or removed in single modules. ECC memory utilizes an additional eight bits of address bus to write parity information about each memory location in the module. If a memory location fails due to electrical or environmental causes, the parity information stored in the module will be used to correct the value of that memory location. Therefore, the memory module can correct single-bit errors within that module.

The ProLiant 800 uses 60ns EDO DIMMs on the 200MHz/66MHz systems. These are replaced singly with a maximum capacity of 512MB on the system. The 350-, 400-, and 500/100-MHz systems used 100-MHz SDRAM and could be upgraded in single modules up to a maximum of 1GB.

Table 13-1 summarizes ProLiant servers and the memory modules required by each. It is important to be aware that each server may also have specific installation guidelines, depending upon how many modules you are adding. For example, information such as which memory location bank must be filled before another, and whether the modules are inserted in pairs or singly is very important to know about your specific server. Compaq publishes memory upgrade charts on its Web site at ftp://ftp.compaq.com/pub/supportinformation/techpubs/qrg/. From this page, select the server you wish to upgrade, and you will be provided with all upgrade information, including the memory upgrade charts for that server. Wherever different module speed ratings are shown as being useable, all memory installed in that server must have identical speeds. When pairs or quads are required, each set must be identical in memory amount, access speed, and type (EDO, FPM, ECC).

TABLE 13-1 Memory Modules Required by ProLiant Servers

Server	Max. Memory	Memory Type	Notes
ProLiant 400	384MB	DIMMs	Install single: 32MB, 64MB, 128MB 100MHz ECC SDRAM DIMMs
ProLiant 800	1024MB	DIMMs	Install single: 32MB, 64MB, 128MB, 256MB 100MHz ECC SDRAM DIMMs
ProLiant 850R	512MB	DIMMs	Install single: 32MB, 64MB, 128MB 60ns EDO DIMMs
ProLiant 1200	512MB	DIMMs	Install pairs: 32MB, 64MB, 128MB, 256MB 60ns EDO DIMMs
ProLiant 1500	256MB	DIMMs	Install pairs: 32MB, 64MB, 128MB DIMMs
ProLiant 1500R	208MB	DIMMs	Install pairs: 8MB, 16MB, 32MB, 64MB 70ns DIMMs
ProLiant 1500R	256MB	DIMMs	Install pairs: 8MB, 16MB, 32MB, 64MB 60ns DIMMs
ProLiant 1600	512MB	DIMMs	Install pairs: 32MB, 64MB, 128MB, 256MB 60ns EDO DIMMs
ProLiant 1850R	1024MB	DIMMs	Install single: 32MB, 64MB, 128MB, 256MB 100-MHz ECC SDRAM DIMMs
ProLiant 2000	512MB	SIMMs	Install four each: 16MB, 32MB, 64MB, 128MB 60ns 70/80ns ECC SIMMs
ProLiant 2500	1024MB	DIMMs	Install single: 32MB, 64MB, 128MB, 256MB 60ns DIMMs
ProLiant 2500R	1024MB	DIMMs	Install single: 32MB, 64MB, 128MB, 256MB 60ns DIMMs
ProLiant 3000	512MB	DIMMs	Install pairs: 16MB, 32MB, 64MB, 128MB, 256MB 60ns DIMMs
ProLiant 3000	4096MB	DIMMs	Install single: 32MB, 64MB, 128MB, 256MB, 512MB 100MHz DIMMs
ProLiant 3000R	512MB	DIMMs	Install pairs: 16MB, 32MB, 64MB, 128MB, 256MB 60ns DIMMs

TABLE 13-1 Memory Modules Required by ProLiant Servers *(continued)*

Server	Max. Memory	Memory Type	Notes
ProLiant 4000	4096MB	SIMMs	Install four each: 16MB, 32MB, 64MB, 128MB 70/80ns ECC SIMMs
ProLiant 4500	512MB	SIMMs	Install four each: 16MB, 32MB, 64MB, 128MB, 256MB 70/80ns ECC SIMMs
ProLiant 4500R	1024MB	SIMMs	Install four each: 16MB, 32MB, 64MB, 128MB, 256 MB 70/80ns ECC SIMMs
ProLiant 5000	2048MB	DIMMs	Install four each: 64MB, 128MB, 256MB, 512MB 60ns ECC DIMMs
ProLiant 5000R	2048MB	DIMMs	Install four each: 64MB, 128MB, 256MB, 512MB 60ns ECC DIMMs
ProLiant 5500	512MB	DIMMs	Install pairs: 16MB, 32MB, 64MB, 128MB, 256MB 60ns DIMMs
ProLiant 5500	4096MB	DIMMs	Install four each: 32MB, 64MB, 128MB, 256MB, 512MB, 1024MB 60ns EDO DIMMs
ProLiant 5500R	4096MB	DIMMs	Install four each: 32MB, 64MB, 128MB, 256MB, 512MB, 1024MB 60ns EDO DIMMs
ProLiant 6000	4096MB	DIMMs	Install four each: 64MB, 128MB, 256MB, 512MB, 1024MB 60ns EDO DIMMs
ProLiant 6400R	4096MB	DIMMs	Install four each: 128MB, 256MB, 512MB, 1024MB 50/60ns EDO DIMMs
ProLiant 6500	4096MB	DIMMs	Install four each: 64MB, 128MB, 256MB, 512MB, 1024MB 60ns FPM/EDO DIMMs
ProLiant 7000	4096MB	DIMMs	Install four each: 64MB, 128MB, 256MB, 512MB, 1024MB 60ns FPM/EDO DIMMs
ProLiant 8000	16386MB	DIMMs	Install pairs: 256MB, 512MB, 1024MB 100-MHz SDRAM DIMMs
ProLiant 8500	16386MB	DIMMs	Install pairs: 256MB, 512MB, 1024MB 100-MHz SDRAM DIMMs

When installing memory, the SIMMs and the DIMMS usually have different installation methods as well. The older SIMMs required the installation of the module at a 45° angle, and then you rocked the module into place, locking it into its socket. The newer DIMMS were designed with installation guides in the sockets that permitted the installation of the module directly downward into the socket. Two rocker arms at either end are used both to lock the DIMM into place and to push the DIMM out of the socket when removing it with a simple motion.

Although several memory manufacturers sell memory that is designed to replace Compaq memory, Compaq will not support warranty claims on systems that have third-party memory. For desktop systems, this may be a low risk, but for servers, it is probably worth the few extra dollars to buy Compaq memory. Not only is it tested more rigorously, but Compaq service support will assist you and express-ship replacement memory in the event of a problem.

CERTIFICATION OBJECTIVE 13.04

Processors Available

Compaq servers have allowed for different processors and processor quantities. From the beginning, Compaq servers have been designed to meet the requirements of all types of environments—from the workgroup to the small business to large database operations. Table 13-2 lists the servers and the processors and processor quantities available at the end of 1999.

TABLE 13-2 Processor Configurations Available on Compaq Servers

Server	Model	Processor	Quantity
ProSignia	PII	Pentium II (350/400/450)	1
	700	Pentium III (500)	1
	NeoServer	Pentium III	1
ProLiant	400 Not available in North America	Pentium II (450) Pentium III (500/550/600)	1
	800	Pentium II (350/450) Pentium III (500/550/600)	1 or 2
	1600	Pentium III (500/550/600)	1 or 2
	3000	Pentium III (500/550/600)	1 or 2
	5500	Pentium II (450) Pentium III (500/550)	1 to 4
	6000	Pentium II (400/450) Pentium III (500)	1 to 4
	6500	Pentium II (400/450) Pentium III (500)	1 to 4
	7000	Pentium II (400/450) Pentium III (500)	1 to 4
	8000	Pentium III (550)	1 to 8
	1600R	Pentium II (400/450) Pentium III (500/550/600)	1 or 2
	1850R	Pentium II (400/450) Pentium III (500/550/600)	1 or 2
	3000R/5500R	Pentium II (300/400/450) Pentium III (500/550/600)	1 or 2
	6400R	Pentium III (550)	1 to 4
	8000	Pentium III (550)	1 to 8
	8500	Pentium III (550)	1 to 8

CERTIFICATION OBJECTIVE 13.05

Level-2 Cache

Whether the processor is Pentium Pro or Pentium II, there are two levels of cache memory designed into the processor to provide faster system performance. Through the use of cache, the processor can have the data it needs available within faster memory devices and closer to the CPU. Cache memory is accessed much faster than system memory, enhancing the CPU's ability to process instructions and move data at an optimal rate. In symmetric multiprocessing (SMP) systems, cache memory is critical to scaleable performance improvements.

In the Pentium Pro Architecture, the primary cache is Level 1 (L1) which is divided into two equal sized caches of 8KB, one for instructions and one for data. The secondary cache is Level 2 (L2) and is connected to the CPU through a 64-bit bus, which can handle up to four concurrent accesses. These caches and the processor operate at the same speed. The L1 cache is located on the processor die, whereas the L2 cache is located on a different die, allowing for more room for this secondary cache store.

In the Pentium II Architecture, there are also primary (L1) and secondary (L2) cache stores. In the Pentium II, the L1 cache is larger, and the L2 cache bus is slower than in the Pentium Pro. The L1 cache is now 32KB, or twice that of the Pentium Pro, and allows more data to be available to the processor at the optimal location. L2 cache is now moved off the processor die onto a module card within the Pentium II processor module and is composed of standard SRAM memory components.

Processor Speed

Because of the physical separation, L2 cache in the Pentium II cannot run at the processor frequency (speed) and performs at 50 percent of the processor speed. Table 13-3 shows the processor/cache combinations defined by Intel.

TABLE 13-3 Pentium Pro and Pentium II Processor/Cache Combinations

Processor	Core Frequency L1 Frequency (MHz)	L2 Cache Frequency (MHz)	L2 Cache Size (KB)
Pentium Pro 16KB L1 cache size	166	166	512
Pentium Pro 16KB L1 cache size	200	200	256, 512, 1024
Pentium II 32KB L1 cache size	233	116.5	512
Pentium II 32KB L1 cache size	266	133.3	512

CERTIFICATION OBJECTIVE 13.06

Processor Power Module

Compaq ProLiant servers with Pentium Pro, Pentium II, and Pentium III processors provide individual processor power modules to supply regulated power to each system CPU. The ProLiant 6400, 6500, and 7000 provide redundant options for these processors, such that an online spare can be installed to avoid system downtime due to power module failure. If the system has two processors, three processor power modules may be installed, with the third providing redundancy for the two dedicated ones. The ProLiant 8000, 8500, and ProLiant 6400/6500/7000 models with 2MB of L2 cache provide redundant processor power modules for each processor.

Processor power modules are designed to support today's and future Xeon processors and are programmable. Each module also contains redundant circuitry to provide the highest level of fault protection.

CERTIFICATION OBJECTIVE 13.07

Compaq Pre-Failure Warranty

Compaq servers have had pre-failure warranty coverage since 1993. With the introduction of Compaq Insight Manager version 2.0, Compaq began to include with each ProSignia and ProLiant server a pre-failure warranty based upon the diagnosis and notification of impending system component failure that is provided from this management tool. As a result, scheduled replacements for system components can be made to minimize unexpected critical system errors that would disrupt business operations.

Originally, this coverage applied to components with the functionality to provide pre-failure alerts. These included ECC memory and server hard drives, SMART array controllers, and IDA and IDA-2 drives. Currently, Compaq has extended this coverage to processors in the Pentium Pro and Pentium II/III systems. Since the components that most likely could bring a server down because of a failure are the processor, memory, and hard drives, Compaq has all of these covered under pre-failure warranty with the use of Insight Manager.

Insight Manager is discussed in detail in Chapter 22. It is through Insight Manager and its agents that the server can be monitored regardless of operating system. Agents exist for NetWare, Windows NT, UNIX, and OS/2. These agents provide information to the management application and can generate alarms if the changing conditions indicate that a failure scenario is approaching. These alarms are stored in the Insight Manager Alarm Log and can be made to display graphical or audible messages, including the forwarding of a message to a digital pager. If during configuration the software detects a Compaq hard drive with no monitor and performance support, the systems engineer receives a warning that the pre-failure warranty is not enabled unless a newer version of the software is installed.

Hard Drives

In order to detect problems before they occur, Compaq drives are monitored for specific operating statistics. Should these indicators fall below factory-preset thresholds, the drive may be replaced under the Compaq Pre-Failure

Warranty program. For servers, this warranty covers any drive attached to array controllers, including SCSI hard drives (except for the 535MB Fast-SCSI-2 hard drive) attached to IDA, IDA-2, or SMART SCSI array controllers, and S.M.A.R.T. (Self Monitoring and Reporting Technology) hard drives using Wide-Ultra SCSI. If the preestablished threshold is exceeded, the monitored component may be replaced prior to actual failure.

Compaq hard drive array controllers monitor over 15 critical indicators as well as functional tests such as seek times (short, average, long) and recoverable/unrecoverable data error rates. If the controller detects that any of these parameters has been exceeded during a period test, a background task notifies the Insight Manager. After receiving an alert, the system administrator can follow on-screen instructions to obtain a description of the error and recommended actions to resolve the problem.

S.M.A.R.T. drives were introduced in 1997 with the Wide-Ultra SCSI technology. S.M.A.R.T. drives are designed to notify the host system when a drive is experiencing abnormal operational conditions. By taking internal measurements of certain leading indicators, S.M.A.R.T. hard drives can identify that they are going to fail. Drive failures can be predictable or unpredictable, depending upon how gradual the degradation of performance indicators is. Because some unpredictable failures can occur quite rapidly, Compaq recommends that all drives should be replaced within 24 hours if they have been identified through a S.M.A.R.T. report to be failing.

Third-party drives are not covered under Pre-Failure Warranty because they have not undergone Compaq's stringent qualification tests. Some hot-pluggable hard drives that are advertised to be 100 percent Compaq-compatible have been known to provide false pre-failure indications.

If a drive error occurs, it will be recorded in the Alarm Log. Within Insight Manager, the systems engineer can identify the degraded server by either a yellow or red indication (yellow for degraded; red for failed). Identify the server object from within the Responsible Server List Window, and double-click it to open the device. A window will open as shown in Figure 13-1.

Click the Mass Storage button once. Note that in the event of a failure, the icon border will change from green to yellow if the system is considered degraded, and from green or yellow to red if the system is considered failed.

The Mass Storage Overview will display the controllers that are included in your system, as shown in Figure 13-2. Click the + sign beside the

FIGURE 13-1

Insight Manager device information

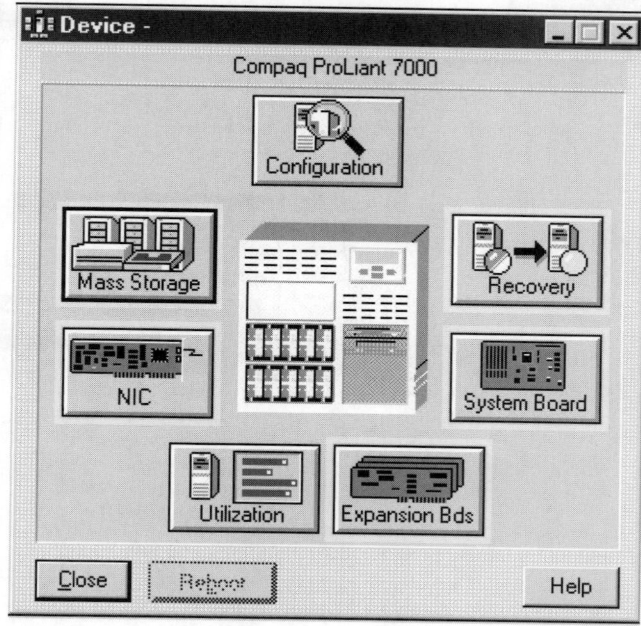

controller with the drives attached, and it will expand to show the physical drives. Double-click any of the drive objects shown, and the Physical Drives screen (also shown in Figure 13-2) will open. On the right-hand side of the window, you can see a quick view of the status of the drive highlighted on the left side. The Action field is where there would be an indication to replace the drive, if necessary.

Now you can see the Indicators button at the bottom of the screen. Click this button to get more information about the drive and its performance and you will be presented with a screen similar to that shown in Figure 13-3. This dialog shows the administrator all Predictive, Problem, and Failure indicators. If you have a drive that is experiencing problems or has exceeded a preset threshold for failure indication, you would see that information in this view. In order to process a warranty replacement with Compaq Service, you would need to note the cause of the drive failure where the action requirement is to Replace Drive.

FIGURE 13-2

Mass Storage Overview and Physical Drives as shown in Insight Manager

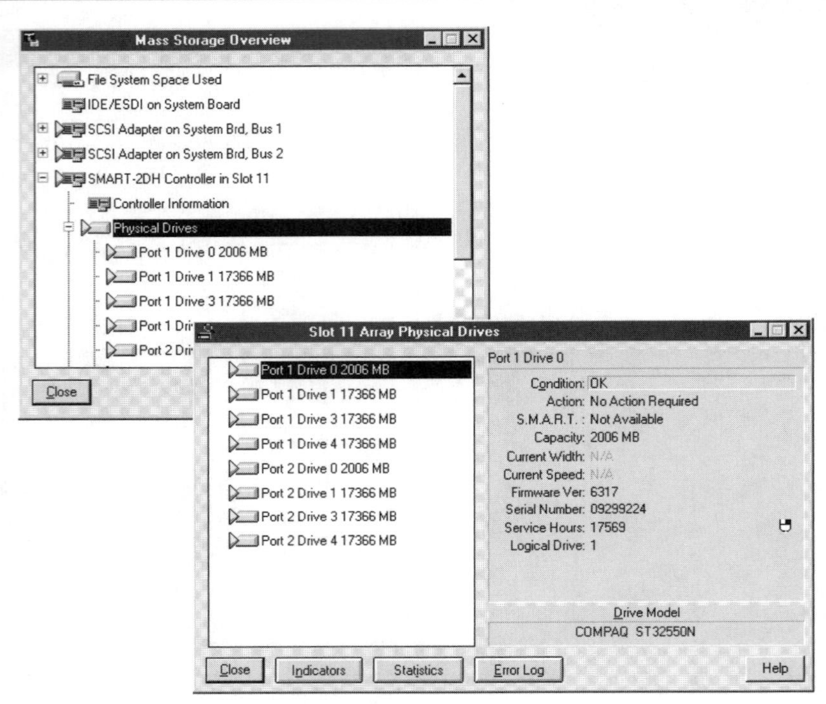

FIGURE 13-3

Drive indicators for Pre-Failure Warranty advice in Insight Manager

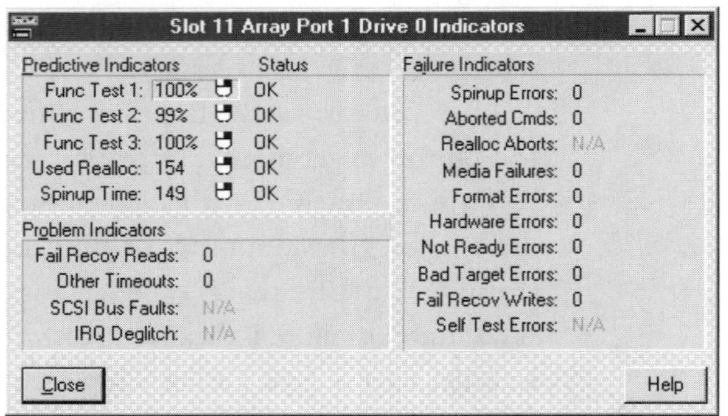

Memory

System integrity and the productivity a company experiences through uninterrupted system operation are critical to today's environment. Failure of a memory subsystem can lead to system downtime or performance degradation that can affect performance of all related systems. To avoid this impact on server operations, ECC memory and Pre-Failure Warranty systems provide basic fault avoidance.

Two types of errors can occur within memory subsystems. A *hard error* occurs when a cell in a Dynamic Random Access Memory (DRAM) module fails such that it prevents data from being stored reliably in one or more locations. A hard error can abend a system. A *soft error* results when a temporary loss of charge affects the data stored in a memory location, but subsequent accesses correctly store data in that location. Although routinely observed in DRAM cells, soft errors should not occur very often. In fact they should occur months or years apart. To protect the system from data loss, parity non-maskable interrupt (NMI) and ECC hardware technologies are built into Compaq servers, depending upon the architecture. ECC memory-based servers are supported under the Pre-Failure Warranty. Both SIMMs and DIMMs are covered when the predefined thresholds for correctable errors have been exceeded. Nonrepeatable correctable soft errors are not covered, but all soft errors are recorded and verifiable through Insight Manager.

Third-party memory is not covered under Pre-Failure Warranty, as these modules are not tested and qualified to Compaq specifications. Damage resulting from third-party memory modules that fail would not be covered under Pre-Failure Warranty.

Memory errors are recorded in the Integrated Management Log of Insight Manager. After selecting the server object, choose the Recovery button from the screen shown in Figure 13-1. This opens the Server Recovery window, as shown in the upper left view in Figure 13-4. Select the Integrated Log button to reveal the Integrated Management Log, as shown in the lower right view of Figure 13-4.

FIGURE 13-4

Finding memory error information for Pre-Failure Warranty

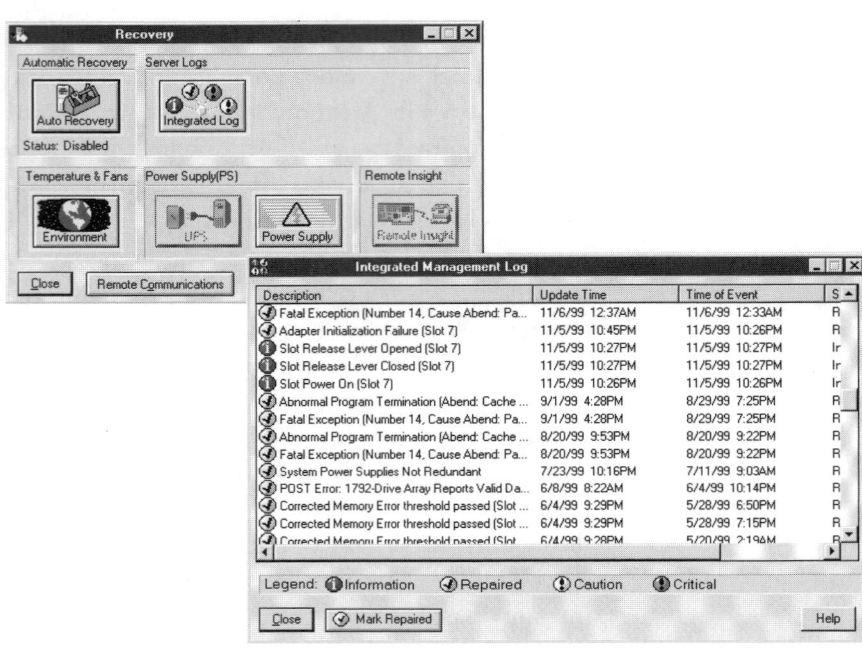

If the error was noted with the following yellow symbol, then the item is considered degraded, and corrective action is required.

If the error was noted with the following red symbol, then the item is considered failed. This failed condition usually will be associated with a failure of the server in the case of memory errors.

If the error is within the correctable memory function of the ECC memory, the server could be correcting the error repeatedly and replacement is warranted immediately. In Figure 13-4, the Integrated Management Log shows entries for Corrected Memory Errors.

Always make a note of the error message and provide that information to Compaq Service when obtaining the Pre-Failure Warranty replacement of the memory component.

Processors

Intel's Pentium Pro processor introduced Machine Check Architecture (MCA), which enabled the Pentium Pro processor to provide enhanced reliability for the server. Pentium Pro and later processors contain ECC functionality, allowing Compaq to include all Pentium Pro, Pentium II, and Pentium II/III Xeon processors under the Pre-Failure Warranty. As is the case with the other components covered, when a monitored error threshold is exceeded, an event occurs which is logged to the Critical Event Log and reported to Insight Manager. Pre-failure alerting is provided based upon detected degradation of the processor, and Insight Manager notifies the system administrator through established methods of visual or audible alarms or paging.

Identifying processor errors that are predictive of a failure is also easy to do with Insight Manager. From the window shown in Figure 13-1, choose the System Board button to display the window shown in Figure 13-5. The processor will be identified and if any proactive steps are required, the recommendation will appear under the Action column. For healthy systems,

FIGURE 13-5

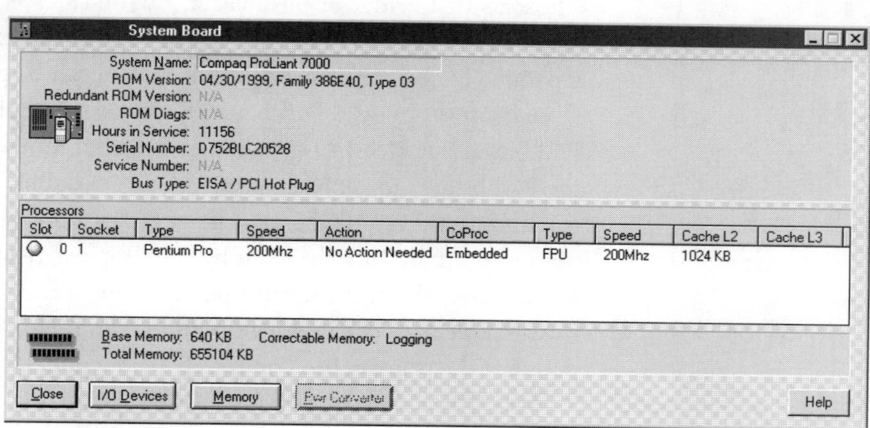

System Board information from Insight Manager shows processor and memory status

as shown in Figure 13-5, the notation is No Action Needed. Additionally, you may locate information about the system memory, and you can see that correctable memory errors are being logged. Clicking the Memory button brings up a screen with the actual physical memory devices (DIMMs or SIMMS) and another way to get to the Integrated Management Log for error messages. When communicating with Compaq Service, provide the information shown on this screen for Pre-Failure Warranty processor replacement.

CERTIFICATION OBJECTIVE 13.08

Dual Peer PCI Buses

Introduced on the ProLiant 5000 server models, the dual peer PCI bus architecture provides for two PCI buses supported by independent PCI bridges to the host bus. With this system configuration, each PCI bus runs without impacting the other, so each bus master can be transferring data simultaneously. If the server system is configured correctly, various high-bandwidth devices may be installed to the different buses to balance the load, increasing overall throughput and performance.

Figure 13-6 depicts this dual peer PCI architecture. Note how the main host bus is connected in parallel to the secondary PCI buses through a host-to-PCI bridge or bus master. As you can see, if attached devices are installed in a balanced manner across the I/O slots supported by these separated buses, performance of the system can be greatly enhanced.

In contrast, bridged PCI bus architecture can support multiple secondary PCI buses, but each I/O device must communicate sequentially through the PCI bridges to get back to the primary host bus. Because of this design, throughput is fixed by the capacity of the first bridge in the chain. There is no need to try to balance the loads by choosing where to install peripherals, as all traffic moves through the same path. See Figure 13-7 for a representation of this architecture. The installation rule of thumb for this architecture is to populate the primary bus completely before populating the secondary bus.

FIGURE 13-6

Dual peer PCI architecture provides faster access to I/O devices

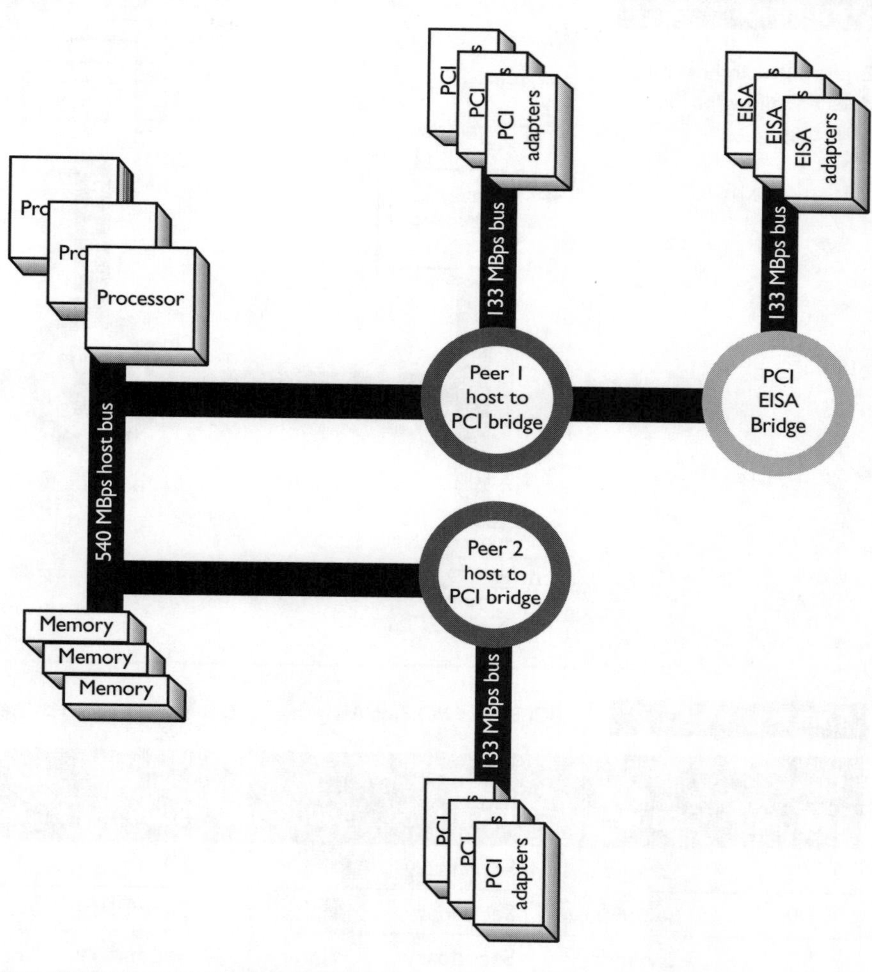

ProLiant 2500 servers provide the bridged PCI architecture, and by design each expansion slot is assigned to a primary or secondary PCI bus location. ProLiant 1200, 1600, 3000, 5000, 5500, 6000, 7000, and 6500 include the dual peer PCI bus architecture. Table 13-4 shows how each system spreads the I/O slots to the primary and secondary PCI buses. Remember that only in the dual peer systems can you obtain load

FIGURE 13-7

Bridged PCI architecture does not allow for load balancing

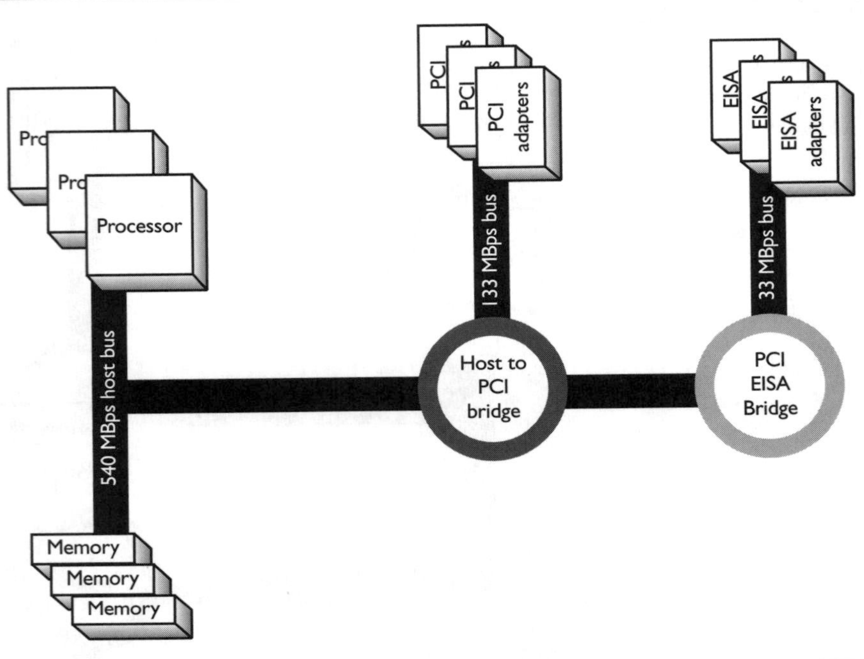

TABLE 13-4 PCI Bus-to-I/O Slot Assignments Defined for Each ProLiant

Slot Number	2500	1200/1600	3000/5500	5000	6000/7000	6500
1	Secondary	Secondary	Primary			Primary
2	Secondary	Secondary	Primary	Secondary		Primary
3	Secondary	Secondary	Primary	Secondary	Primary	Secondary
4	Primary	Primary	Primary	Secondary	Primary	Secondary
5	Primary	Primary	Secondary	Primary	Primary	Secondary
6	Primary	Primary	Secondary	Primary	Primary	Secondary
7			Secondary	Primary	Secondary	Secondary
8			Secondary	Primary	Secondary	Secondary
9					Secondary	
10					Secondary	
11					Secondary	

balancing performance improvements by carefully choosing the slot to connect your high bandwidth peripherals.

When installing peripherals to the dual peer PCI bus-based systems, care should be taken to balance these devices across each bus so as to obtain optimal system performance. For example, when installing multiple controllers, split the controllers among the buses. Some guidelines on splitting controllers would include:

- Separating network controllers onto each bus when there is more than one NIC
- Separating array controllers onto different buses
- Putting all NICs on one bus and a single high-speed array controller on the other

on the job

Don't forget where your PCI boards are installed as you add to your server, especially when adding network controllers. You may need to move an existing board to a different slot to balance the load created by a new board. Drive array controllers and network controllers are typically added as system demands grow.

When configuring a server for redundancy and in order to achieve high availability, install both active and standby boards to the primary bus. Since your backup network controller or backup array controller is not active, it does not generate much traffic on the bus. If it becomes active, you will want the same performance levels as the primary device. If the only PCI boards are a network controller and an array controller, it is acceptable to place both on the same bus, even if no devices are subsequently installed on the secondary bus, since the traffic generated by these devices will not saturate the bus. The trade-off in this configuration is for hot plug replacement of both the primary and secondary device, should either fail. Alternatively, splitting these primary and secondary devices across the hot-plug (primary bus) slots and non-hot-plug (secondary bus) slots might provide slightly higher performance, but at the risk of requiring a server shutdown to replace the secondary device on the non-hot-plug slot.

PCI bus performance analysis and management is available in a number of tools. Insight Manager monitors the PCI bus utilization on servers with SCO UNIX and Novell NetWare operating systems. Bus use measurements are available in Insight Manager for each bus, whether PCI or EISA. For Windows NT, Compaq offers a Performance Monitor Add-On Enhancement Tool for simplified management of objects and their counters in the Compaq EISA and PCI buses, power supply, and NetFlex-3 controllers. Compaq provides this tool for Windows NT at the following URL: http://www.compaq.com/solutions/frontline.

CERTIFICATION OBJECTIVE 13.09

Fault Tolerant Features

Compaq servers have industry-leading, standards-based fault tolerant features that provide for minimal downtime requirements—both planned and unplanned. This section will briefly discuss each feature that is available on Compaq servers.

PCI Hot Plug

Removal and replacement of failed PCI boards is now possible without shutting down the server. Systems engineers may replace identical boards in real time without excessive downtime.

Be careful to note what the operating system requirements are for replacing a board without shutting down. Windows NT, NetWare, OS/2, and UNIX will each have their own methods to recognize the new hardware and may or may not actually allow the board to function without a power cycle or operating system restart.

Redundant Processor Power Modules

Protection against power fluctuations that can cause a CPU to fail is improved by this redundant technology, which also protects against the failure of a power circuit supporting a server's main processor.

Hot-Pluggable Redundant Power Supplies

By providing load balancing, health and status reporting via Insight Manager, and auto-sensing of power properties, these features greatly maximize system uptime. Hot-pluggable capabilities allow component replacement within normal business hours.

ProLiant Cluster Ready

This class of server is designed to take advantage of ProLiant Cluster technology, which provides fail-over to backup server systems under Microsoft, Novell, and SCO applications.

Redundant System Fans

Early systems that required subordinate cooling fans were at the mercy of overheating if a fan failed. Redundant fans eliminate this mechanical failure mode, and hot-pluggable fans allow replacement without bringing down the server.

Redundant Network Interface Cards (NICs)

Configuration of a second network card as a spare that is online in case of a failure of the primary card can eliminate common network outages of servers that are otherwise functioning properly.

ECC Memory

ECC memory allows the system to avoid a system failure due to soft memory errors that can arise due to electrical fluctuations in memory circuits. Single-bit memory errors may be corrected on the fly without causing corruption in data or a system halt.

Pre-Failure Alerting

Compaq Insight Manager works with agents on servers to monitor and report on conditions that indicate imminent failure of a processor, memory module, or SCSI hard drive. When there is a degraded component covered by the Pre-Failure Warranty, notification messages from Insight Manager may be used to request advance replacement of the component from Compaq. This pre-failure alerting allows the system administrator to plan system downtime at opportune times.

QUESTIONS AND ANSWERS

Which servers are best for workgroups?	ProSignia servers are designed for small, high-performance requirements, at an entry-level price. Most workgroup requirements are for few clients and restricted budgets. ProSignia servers have performance capabilities that are well suited for workgroups. Their entry-level pricing is made possible by fewer hot-swap features, limited expansion, and fewer processor options.
Which servers are best for departmental and small business needs?	ProSignia and the ProLiant 800 and 1600. The ProSignia servers can deliver the performance needed, and the ProLiant servers are scaleable as business needs grow.
Which servers are best for medium-to-large business needs?	ProLiant. Depending upon actual requirements, ProLiant servers can scale from the smallest company to the largest business.
Which servers are best for space-constrained rack installations?	ProLiant servers with the "R" in the model number and the ProLiant 8500. Rack-mounted server models can be installed into Compaq rack enclosures or third-party racks with proper installation methods.
Which servers are best for high availability and heavy-duty database support?	ProLiant 5500, 6000, 6500, 7000, 8000, 8500. Multiprocessor and significant redundant and fault tolerant features in these models make them ideal for heavily loaded servers.
Can I use any kind of memory in Compaq servers?	Memory must be matched to the system and cannot be mixed. For demanding server duties, use Compaq memory. Different systems use ECC, EDO, DIMMs, or SIMMs. Compaq memory is tested more thoroughly than generic brands.
What is the I/O bus on Compaq servers?	Depends upon the model. The older models had shared PCI buses; the newer ones have dual peer PCI buses. For load balancing, dual peer PCI buses allow for better overall system performance.
Can server components be replaced prior to failure, under warranty?	Pre-Failure Warranty coverage includes processors, memory, and SCSI hard drives. Use of Compaq Insight Manager to identify failure conditions in devices will minimize system downtime.

CERTIFICATION SUMMARY

This chapter may seem like nothing more than speeds and feeds, marketing fluff, or rehashed sales literature. Ultimately, the systems engineer or technical manager must be able to compare server technology within a manufacturer's product line and against other manufacturers' product lines. The Compaq server product line provides choices that meet the needs of any application requirement. Compaq servers have continued to advance and evolve to incorporate the latest technologies, with the needs of the server environment always paramount.

With the introduction of the ProSignia server line, Compaq introduced Insight Manager and the concept of pre-failure warnings of server components. A warranty to match soon evolved. ProSignia and ProLiant servers kept pace with the introductions of newer and faster processor technologies from Intel, and eight-way multiprocessor systems are available today to support the most demanding, computing-intensive applications. High-speed bus architectures in both I/O device buses and memory buses have allowed Compaq servers to maintain performance edges over other brands.

High Availability Architecture, Highly Parallel System Architecture, and FlexSMP Architecture have all been developed by Compaq to let ProLiant and ProSignia servers perform at the highest levels. System uptime has been maximized by hot-plug, hot-swap, dual components, such as fans, drives, PCI adapters, processor power supplies, system power supplies, and processors. The newest server designs allow almost complete disassembly without the need for special tools, or in some cases, any tools. The Compaq server product lines can suit any situation: workgroup, small business, department, or enterprise.

TWO-MINUTE DRILL

- Both the ProSignia and ProLiant server product lines provide significant features and technologies that make Compaq servers the preferred choice of many systems engineers and IT managers.
- Based upon the success and strengths of the SystemPro family of servers, the ProSignia servers originally provided more compact form factors than other servers in Compaq's product line.
- The original ProSignia systems incorporated the EISA standard for the expansion bus, but integrated many components into the system board to leave open the slots for other devices.
- The newest ProSignia is the NeoServer, announced in March 1999.
- There have been over 15 ProLiant Servers released by Compaq since the first ones in 1993.
- To answer the demand for higher and higher performance capabilities, Compaq announced its new ProLiant models in 1999. The ProLiant 8000 and 8500 servers are eight-way system architectures based upon the Pentium III Xeon processors.
- The new servers include the standard Compaq features of PCI hot plug technology, redundant hot plug power supplies, drives, fans, redundant processor power supplies, and auto processor bus recovery.
- Basically, there are two types of memory used by Compaq servers: EDO or ECC.
- The server can contain only SIMMs or only DIMMs, not both.
- Table 13-1 summarizes ProLiant servers and the memory modules required by each.
- Compaq publishes memory upgrade charts on its Web site at ftp://ftp.compaq.com/pub/supportinformation/techpubs/qrg/.
- Table 13-2 lists the servers and the processors and processor quantities available at the end of 1999.
- Whether the processor is Pentium Pro or Pentium II, there are two levels of cache memory designed into the processor to provide faster system performance.

- ❑ In the Pentium Pro Architecture, the primary cache is Level 1 (L1) which is divided into two equal sized caches of 8KB, one for instructions and one for data.
- ❑ In the Pentium II Architecture, there are also primary (L1) and secondary (L2) cache stores.
- ❑ Table 13-3 shows the processor/cache combinations defined by Intel.
- ❑ Compaq ProLiant servers with Pentium Pro, Pentium II, and Pentium III processors provide individual processor power modules to supply regulated power to each system CPU.
- ❑ Processor power modules are designed to support today's and future Xeon processors and are programmable. Each module also contains redundant circuitry to provide the highest level of fault protection.
- ❑ Compaq servers have had Pre-Failure Warranty coverage since 1993.
- ❑ It is through Insight Manager and its agents that the server can be monitored regardless of operating system.
- ❑ In order to detect problems before they occur, Compaq drives are monitored for specific operating statistics.
- ❑ Compaq hard drive array controllers monitor over 15 critical indicators as well as functional tests such as seek times (short, average, long) and recoverable/unrecoverable data error rates.
- ❑ S.M.A.R.T. drives are designed to notify the host system when a drive is experiencing abnormal operational conditions.
- ❑ Third-party drives are not covered under Pre-Failure Warranty because they have not undergone Compaq's stringent qualification tests.
- ❑ ECC memory and Pre-Failure Warranty systems provide basic fault avoidance.
- ❑ Memory errors are recorded in the Integrated Management Log of Insight Manager.
- ❑ Intel's Pentium Pro processor introduced Machine Check Architecture (MCA), which enabled the Pentium Pro processor to provide enhanced reliability for the server.

- Identifying processor errors that are predictive of a failure is easy to do with Insight Manager.
- Introduced on the ProLiant 5000 server models, the dual peer PCI bus architecture provides for two PCI buses supported by independent PCI bridges to the host bus.
- Compaq servers have industry-leading, standards-based fault tolerant features that provide for minimal downtime requirements. These include:
    - PCI Hot Plug
    - Redundant Processor Power Modules
    - Hot-Pluggable Redundant Power Supplies
    - ProLiant Cluster Ready
    - Redundant System Fans
    - Redundant Network Interface Cards (NICs)
    - ECC Memory
    - Pre-Failure Alerting

SELF TEST

The following Self Test questions will help you measure your understanding of the material presented in this chapter. Read all the choices carefully, as there may be more than one correct answer. Choose all correct answers for each question.

1. Which of the following servers has a preinstalled operating system?

   A. ProLiant 400

   B. ProSignia VS

   C. ProSignia Neoserver

   D. ProLiant 8000

2. Which servers were the first to eliminate the EISA bus and support only PCI and ISA devices?

   A. ProSignia Neoserver

   B. ProLiant 4000

   C. ProLiant 6400R

   D. ProLiant 800, 1200, 1600

3. What is the data transfer rate of Wide-Ultra SCSI-3?

   A. 20 Mbps

   B. 40 Mbps

   C. 40 MBps

   D. 80 MBps

4. Which of the following are features of Highly Parallel System Architecture?

   A. Redundant Network Interface Cards

   B. Dual-memory controller

   C. ECC memory

   D. Dual peer PCI buses

5. Which memory types can be found in Compaq servers?

   A. EDO

   B. ECC

   C. DIMMs

   D. SIMMs

   E. All of the above

6. Which of the following statements are true?

   A. SIMMs may be installed only singly; DIMMs may be installed only in pairs in Compaq servers.

   B. SIMMs and DIMMs may only be installed singly or in pairs in Compaq servers.

   C. SIMMs are installed only in groups of four modules; DIMMs may be installed singly, in pairs, or in groups of four, depending upon the Compaq server.

   D. SIMMs are installed only singly; DIMMs are installed only in pairs or groups of four, depending upon the Compaq server.

7. Which servers support multiprocessor configurations?

   A. ProLiant 400

   B. All current ProLiant servers available in the USA

   C. ProSignia servers

   D. SystemPro servers

8. Which processor has an L1 cache of 16KB?
   A. 80486
   B. Pentium
   C. Pentium Pro
   D. Pentium II Xeon

9. The Pentium II processor has how much L1 cache memory?
   A. 16KB
   B. 24KB
   C. 32KB
   D. 64KB

10. Why is it not possible for the Pentium II to access L2 cache at 100 percent of the processor speed?
    A. L2 cache is on an external module, not on the processor die.
    B. The address bus is only half as wide.
    C. The memory bus is longer.
    D. Pentium II does not have L2 cache.

11. When did Compaq begin to offer Pre-Failure Warranties?
    A. With the introduction of Insight Manager v2.0
    B. When SCSI drives were available with hot-pluggable capability
    C. After the introduction of ECC memory
    D. After the release of Windows NT Server v3.51

12. Which component is not covered under Pre-Failure Warranty from Compaq?
    A. PCI bridges
    B. SCSI hard drives
    C. Compaq ECC memory
    D. Pentium Pro, Pentium II, and Pentium III Xeon processors

13. What will be the Compaq Service response if the Insight Manager Physical Drive Parameters screen shows the required action "Replace Drive" and the SCSI drive is still running?
    A. Compaq will sell you a hard drive.
    B. Compaq will replace the drive after you send the bad drive to them.
    C. Compaq will open a case and wait for the drive to fail.
    D. Compaq will ship a replacement drive before failure upon verification of system warranty validity.

14. Dual peer PCI bridges address which performance bottleneck in a server?
    A. Memory access
    B. I/O device access
    C. Hard drive access
    D. None of the above

15. Which of the following is not a fault tolerant feature of Compaq ProLiant servers?
    A. PCI hot plug
    B. Hot-pluggable redundant power supplies
    C. Dual peer PCI bridge
    D. Redundant system fans

ASE

ACCREDITED SYSTEMS ENGINEER

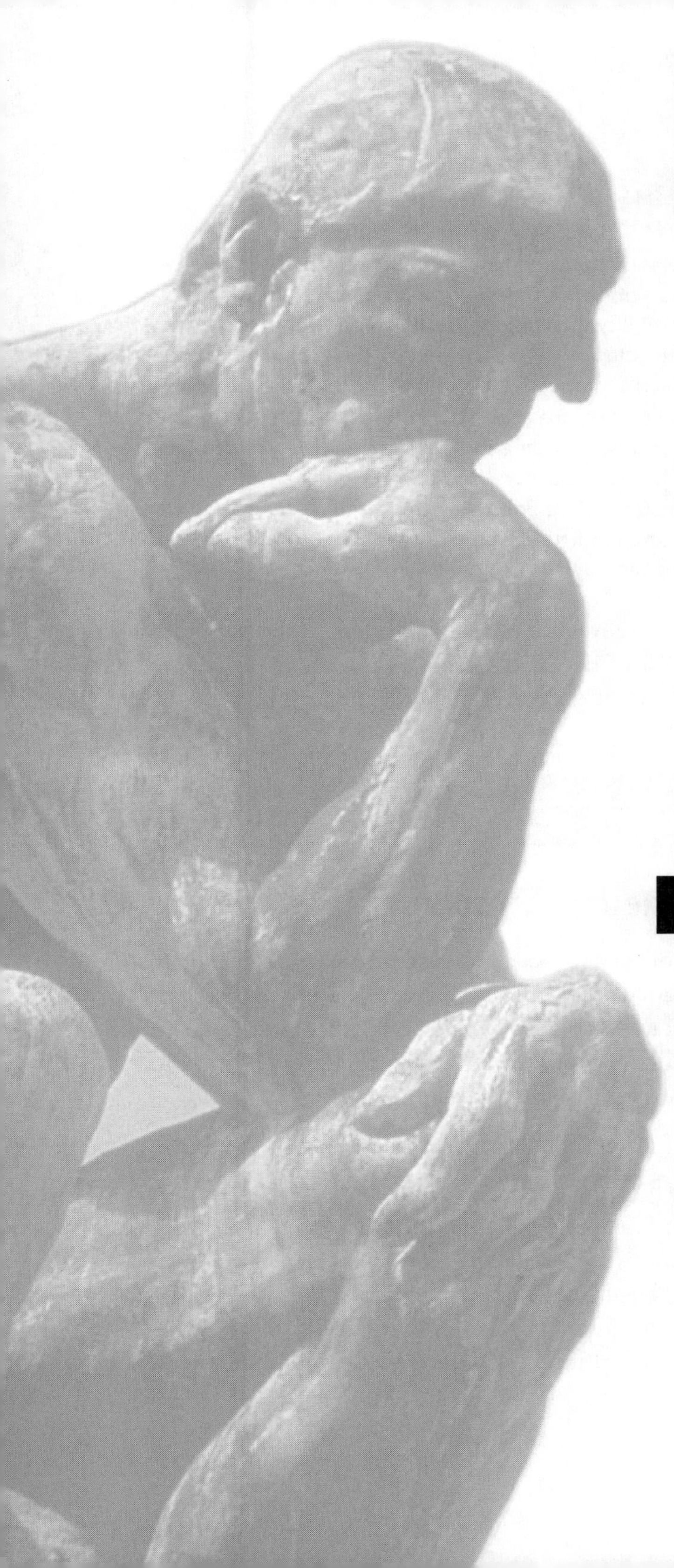

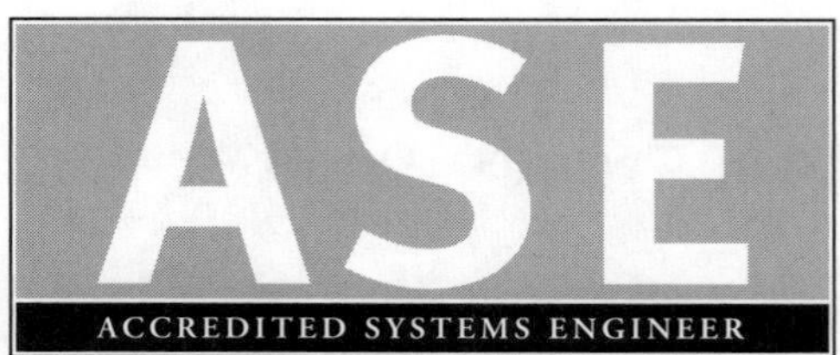

14

Options

CERTIFICATION OBJECTIVES

14.01 Compaq Storage Expansion Systems

14.02 Compaq Racks and Rack Options

14.03 Choosing a Compaq Digital Linear Tape (DLT) over a DAT Solution

14.04 Remote Insight Option

14.05 Redundant Power Supply

In this chapter, we will discuss the various options that can enhance the functionality of a Compaq server solution. Compaq offers various options to improve remote manageability, increase resource availability, provide physical security for a server solution, and provide data recovery. These solutions are provided by the Compaq Storage Expansion Systems, Compaq Racks and Rack Options, DLT and DAT tape solutions, Remote Insight Board, and Redundant Power Supplies that are used with most Compaq server class hardware. Compaq has several storage systems, including the ProLiant Storage System and the ProLiant Storage system/F, the ProLiant U1 and U2 arrays, and fiber-channel storage. We will talk about the capabilities of each in the next section. Following this discussion, we will cover the tools provided by Compaq to lay out and configure Compaq rack units. Additionally, the various options that can be added to these rack units will be discussed..

To help provide a recoverable, manageable, and reliable server platform, we will discuss the use of DAT/DLT tape storage subsystems, the Remote Insight Board, and redundant power supplies.

CERTIFICATION OBJECTIVE 14.01

Compaq Storage Expansion Systems

To help improve both system scalability and reliability, Compaq offers several types of external SCSI storage expansion systems for use with Compaq servers. In this section, we will examine the storage systems in the current product line, as well as the retired storage systems you may encounter when entering a client data center.

Compaq ProLiant Storage System

Compaq's ProLiant Storage System is an external storage cabinet that can hold up to seven 1.6" or 1" drives. The Storage System can use any Compaq hot-pluggable drive that meets the Fast-Wide or Fast-SCSI-2 specification. The maximum capacity of the Storage System is 127GB with the use of seven 18.2GB drives. LEDs on the system indicate whether each drive is being accessed or whether a drive is down. The ProLiant Storage System has an optional duplexing option kit that allows two RAID controllers to access the same storage system. This option enables you to duplex two RAID arrays to eliminate any single points of failure in the array. If one controller card were to fail, a second will still meet the needs of the server. This option can be very useful when you are trying to maximize the fault tolerance on mission-critical enterprise data.

For systems that must maintain the highest uptime statistics, you can duplex the controllers in a system to eliminate the array controller as a single point of failure in the system. When combined with a system that supports hot-plug PCI, you can even swap the failed card while the server is running.

Compaq ProLiant Storage System/F

The ProLiant Storage System/F is also an external storage cabinet that can hold up to seven 1.6" or 1" drives using a single bus. The ProLiant Storage System/F can hold more drives by taking advantage of the dual bus architecture of this model. In the dual bus configuration, the ProLiant Storage System/F can hold eight 1.6" drives or twelve 1" drives. The maximum capacity of the ProLiant Storage System/F is 145.6GB with the use of 18.2GB drives in the dual bus model. The ProLiant Storage System/F supports Fast-Wide SCSI-2 drives. You can use Wide-Ultra drives, but the storage system does not support the data transfer rate and the drives will only run at Fast-Wide SCSI-2 speeds.

Differences Between ProLiant Storage System and ProLiant Storage System/F

There are several differences between the ProLiant Storage System and the ProLiant Storage System/F.

- The ProLiant Storage System/F can hold a maximum of twelve 1" or eight 1.6" drives compared to the ProLiant Storage System, which holds seven 1" or 1.6" drives

- The ProLiant Storage System/F takes up 4U instead of the 5U taken by the ProLiant Storage System. This allows two more units to be included in a Compaq 7142 rack.
- Both systems have optional redundant power supplies. The ProLiant Storage System/F has redundant fans, hot-pluggable power supplies, and hot-pluggable fans.
- Each of the ProLiant Storage Systems is offered in a stand-alone or rack mount configuration.
- The ProLiant Storage System has the look of the ProLiant 4500 and the ProLiant Storage System/F has the look of the ProLiant 2500.

In conclusion, the ProLiant Storage System is a versatile storage option, but the ProLiant Storage System/F is the system to choose when you need more of the high-availability features.

With the recent acquisition of Digital's product line, many of the storage features from that company's line now sport the Compaq brand on their front bezels. The F1 and F2 arrays are no longer part of the product line, but are important for the exam. To view the entire new selection of Compaq storage products, visit Compaq's Web site at http://www.compaq.com/products/storageworks/raidstoragesystems.html

CERTIFICATION OBJECTIVE 14.02

Compaq Racks and Rack Options

You can mount Compaq servers and other hardware into Compaq Racks. The racks follow the industry standard 19" width, so any 19" rack-mountable hardware should fit into your Compaq Racks. Compaq has several models of racks and a multitude of rack options that we will discuss in this section. They also have rack-building software that assists you in the planning and ordering stages of your installation. Compaq rack-building software comes with every rack-mountable server that Compaq sells.

If you have not yet purchased a Compaq server, you can plan for your server configuration by downloading either Rack Builder or Compaq's new Web-based tool, Rack Builder Pro, at:

http://www.compaq.com/products/servers/options/rackacces/rackbuilder.html

Compaq Racks

The three different types of racks available from Compaq are the Compaq Rack 7142, Compaq Rack 7122, and the Compaq Rack 4136. All of the Compaq Racks are 19" industry standard racks and include front and back doors. The difference among the racks is the amount of equipment, measured in units (Us), that they hold.

Rack Model	Rack Units
7142U	42U
7122U	22U
4136	36U

All Compaq racks are made by Rittal, which can provide additional configurations if none of those in the chart suits the needs of your data center.

Compaq Rack Options

You can add many options to Compaq Racks. Two models of switch boxes are available, allowing you to have one keyboard mouse and monitor for several servers. One switch box controls up to four servers; the other model can control up to eight servers. Another available option is a monitor shelf to mount your monitor in the rack; or for those that prefer a really slick solution, an LCD monitor that slides out of the rack is also available. A keyboard drawer is yet another available option you can add. There is a keyboard that fits into the 19" industry standard rack and that includes a trackball so no external mouse is needed, thus providing the best solution for servers requiring physical security. You can also add cable management arms to the server shelves to keep cables neatly confined. Compaq also offers power strips that mount on the sides of the rack so you do not have to run as many power cords outside the rack and rack-mountable UPS units.

To get an idea of the wide range of Compaq Rack options available today, please visit http://www.compaq.com/products/servers/options/rackacces/cpqrakopt1.html for a more comprehensive list of today's options.

Compaq's Rack Builder Software

Compaq's Rack Builder software is an application that runs in Windows. The Rack Builder software contains information on the different rack-mountable hardware from Compaq. It assists you in configuring your rack and lists the Us required by each piece of equipment. The Rack Builder software will also add in hardware needed to mount your components, and it will print a three-page summary of what you have added and the associated part numbers, to aid in the ordering process.

To help prepare your data center for the arrival of the server, Rack Builder also allows you to calculate the thermal and electrical requirements for servers currently in the database. You can also add non-Compaq hardware to the Rack Builder software by entering the dimensions of the components, so you can make sure all of your equipment will fit in the space you have available in your racks. The rack building software is available with the purchase of Compaq Rack Mount Servers or by download from Compaq's Web site.

Upon completion of the rack configuration, three reports are generated:

- **Site planning report** The site planning report includes information such as height, weight, heat, and current. This is very valuable information to ensure that the chosen rack will fit in the data center, will not overtax the cooling system, and will allow the electricians to make the proper preparations prior to the arrival of the rack.

- **Order info** The order information page is ideal for checking that you have all parts required to install the server successfully. It also will aid procurement of the hardware once the engineering effort has been completed.
- **Rack graphic** To aid the persons tasked with the physical installation of each server in the rack, the graphic shows the precise placement within the rack that allows optimal weight distribution and use of the keyboard drawer/monitor.

FROM THE FIELD

Using Visio to Document the Rack Configuration

For those organizations that wish to use a more robust drawing program to permanently document the rack configuration, Visio offers a collection of network equipment stencils for use with their products. Among the 16,000 stencils currently available in the Visio Network Equipment add-on for Visio 5.0b and above, there is a huge list of Compaq equipment. To see which Compaq stencils are available, navigate to:

http://www.visio.com/ solutions/networkequipment/catalog/shapes.asp?company=Compaq

After completing your masterpiece, you can use the EXPORT functions of Visio to export your work into DXF format (for AutoCAD) or into a variety of image formats (.BMP or PCX, for example). While the Compaq Rack Builder software does an excellent job of preparing the reports and a rough sketch of the final configuration, most enterprises will wish to maintain this information on a Web site, database, or AutoCAD drawing. Developers familiar with VBA can even customize these drawings to become front ends to launch the Web-based management agents.

While the Compaq Rack Builder and Rack Builder Pro utilities are excellent applications, Visio or a more robust CAD application will most likely provide better documentation of the established environment.

—Thomas E. Eck, MCSE+I, MCSD, ASE, CCA, CNA

CERTIFICATION OBJECTIVE 14.03

Choosing a Compaq Digital Linear Tape (DLT) over a DAT Solution

Compaq offers Digital Audio Tape (DAT) and Digital Linear Tape (DLT) devices. Both the DAT and DLT use SCSI-2 interfaces. The DAT devices can have up to 2.8GB/hour throughput. The DLT devices' throughput is up to 9GB/hour. There are several reasons to choose a DLT device over a DAT device, and we will discuss those reasons in the following section.

I have been using Compaq DLT drives for several years now and I have found them extremely reliable and fast. The DLT technology has proven its worth in large environments that require massive amounts of data to be backed up in a small amount of time.

Differences between DAT and DLT Devices

One of the main reasons to choose a DLT device over a DAT device is the speed. A DLT drive can back up 9GB an hour compressed or 4.5GB an hour native. The DAT drive can back up a maximum of 2.8GB an hour. Another reason DLT is a more effective solution is the amount of data each tape can hold. DAT drives are available in 2/4GB, 4/8GB, and 12/24GB models. The 2/4GB can back up 2GB native or 4GB compressed. The DLT models include 15/30GB and 35/70GB. The DAT tape is considerably smaller than the DLT, but the DLT enables you to back up more data to a single tape at a much faster rate.

The reason DLT is so much faster than DAT is because of the technology behind the design of each. DAT tapes use the Helical Scan technology. Helical Scan devices wrap the tape around the read/write heads in a circular motion. The DLT technology uses an affixed read/write head that the tape passes in a parallel motion. Helical Scan also writes the data in a vertical motion as opposed to the DLT technology, which writes the data in a horizontal motion. Since the DLT technology does not wrap the tape around the head and it writes in a horizontal motion, it allows the tape to pass more freely with less stress on the tape. The DLT technology also permits reading and writing at the same time. Table 14-1 lists key features of DLT.

Compaq Auto-Loaders and Tape Libraries

Compaq offers auto-loaders for DAT tape devices and tape libraries for DLT tape devices. An auto-loader is a DAT tape device that will automatically load another tape when the first one either becomes full or has completed the backup job it was configured to perform. Tape libraries have slots available for multiple tapes and allow you to schedule a backup job per slot or choose to write the backup job across multiple tapes with parity in a RAID 5 configuration. A common application for both auto-loaders and tape libraries is to have them on one server, backing up many servers, so you only have to replace tapes at one location. The tape libraries used with DLT tapes offer the added functionality of assigning jobs to specific slots; an example would be slot 1 assigned to Monday, slot 2 assigned to Tuesday, and so on.

TABLE 14-1 DLT Features

Feature	Description
Tape longevity	DLT tapes last up to 10X longer than DAT.
Speed	DLT tapes back up at a maximum of 9GB an hour. DAT tapes back up at a maximum of 2.8GB an hour.
Tape libraries	DLT tape libraries can use RAID 5 technology to speed up backup process.
Technology	The DLT technology uses a stationary read/write head instead of the Helical Scan technology's rotational head.

CERTIFICATION OBJECTIVE 14.04

Remote Insight Option

The Compaq Remote Insight Board is a remote control option board that you can add to Compaq servers. It enables full remote control of a server before the operating system loads. This helps the administrator remotely troubleshoot a server that has gone down or is having problems booting. The Remote Insight Board has a microprocessor, modem, serial port, keyboard port, video controller, memory, and battery. The Remote Insight Board operates independently of the server. When configured, the Remote Insight Board allows dial-up connectivity with the Point-to-Point Protocol (PPP) and ANSI-compliant terminal emulation packages. The administrator can access a server that has locked up in the operating system and send a RESTART command to either warm or cold reboot the server. It can be configured with up to twelve different user accounts with varying levels of security. The Remote Insight Board stores logs of the server to aid in troubleshooting. The onboard battery offers up to 30 minutes of battery life in the event of a power failure. The Remote Insight Board is fully compatible with Compaq Insight Manager for SNMP management. Table 14-2 lists key features of the Remote Insight Board.

TABLE 14-2 Remote Insight Board Features

Feature	Description
Remote console	The Remote Insight Board allows the administrator to view the entire boot process of the server.
Dependability	The Remote Insight Board is independent of the operating system, and its battery backup it makes it available even when the server has lost power.
Access	The Remote Insight Board can be accessed by PPP or by an ANSI-compliant terminal emulation package.
Troubleshooting	The Remote Insight Board stores critical event logs for viewing, regardless of the server's state.
Security	The Remote Insight Board supports up to 12 different user accounts with varying levels of security.

CERTIFICATION OBJECTIVE 14.05

Redundant Power Supply

The Compaq redundant power supply is an optional, hot-pluggable power supply that can be added to ProLiant servers. It allows for redundancy of the power supplies used to convert high-voltage AC to the low-voltage DC current expected by the server. If one power supply goes bad or loses power, the redundant power supply will take over. The hot-pluggable technology allows you to replace a bad power supply with a new one without ever having to down the server. This is essential for any mission-critical server.

Using Insight Manager, it is even possible to monitor the status of a power supply and acknowledge events related to a failed power supply in a redundant configuration.

Many enterprises have established server standards that include the use of a redundant power supply configuration in servers that support this feature. When you consider the level of redundancy built into almost every other subsystem in a server, it makes sense simply to carry this through to the power supplies as well.
The relatively small cost of a redundant power supply configuration can save the enterprise a huge expense if a failure is averted.

CERTIFICATION SUMMARY

The ProLiant Storage System and ProLiant Storage System/F are the two storage expansion systems available from Compaq that are currently covered on the exam. The ProLiant Storage System/F allows you to add more drives and has some high-availability features that are not offered by the ProLiant Storage System. Both of the storage systems can be configured in a dual bus mode, allowing multiple arrays to be housed in one cabinet.

We also covered Compaq Racks and Rack Options. Compaq offers three different rack models: Compaq Rack 7142, Compaq Rack 7122, and Compaq Rack 4136. Each of the racks complies with the industry-standard 19" width. You can order different accessories for your racks, such as switch boxes, shelving, and cable management. Compaq also has rack building software available to help in the ordering and design process of your rack building.

Compaq offers DAT and DLT tape devices in a single-tape configuration, or in a multiple-tape configuration with the use of auto-loaders and tape libraries. We covered the differences in the architecture of Helical Scan compared to the DLT technology and saw that DLT is a much faster technology.

The chapter covered the Remote Insight Board. This option board allows remote server management, independent of the operating system. The Remote Insight Board comes with a microprocessor, modem, serial port, memory, video controller, keyboard port, and battery. You can access the Remote Insight Board through PPP or an ANSI-compliant terminal emulation package.

The last section of this chapter covered the redundant power supplies offered by Compaq. The redundant power supply is an important feature in high-availability servers, because it enables power redundancy to the server. With hot-pluggable power supplies, you can replace an existing bad power supply without having to take the server down.

TWO-MINUTE DRILL

- To help improve both system scalability and reliability, Compaq offers several types of external SCSI storage expansion systems for use with Compaq servers.
- Compaq's ProLiant Storage System is an external storage cabinet that can hold up to seven 1.6" or 1" drives.
- The ProLiant Storage System/F can hold more drives by taking advantage of the dual bus architecture of this model.
- There are several differences between the ProLiant Storage System and the ProLiant Storage System/F.
- The ProLiant Storage System is a versatile storage option, but the ProLiant Storage System/F is the system to choose when you need more of the high-availability features.

- ❑ Compaq rack-building software comes with every rack-mountable server that Compaq sells.
- ❑ The three different types of racks available from Compaq are the Compaq Rack 7142, Compaq Rack 7122, and the Compaq Rack 4136.
- ❑ You can add many options to Compaq Racks.
- ❑ To get an idea of the wide range of Compaq Rack options available today, please visit http://www.compaq.com/products/servers/options/rackacces/cpqrakopt1.html.
- ❑ The Rack Builder software contains information on the different rack-mountable hardware from Compaq. It assists you in configuring your rack and lists the Us required by each piece of equipment.
- ❑ Compaq offers Digital Audio Tape (DAT) and Digital Linear Tape (DLT) devices.
- ❑ A DLT drive can back up 9GB an hour compressed or 4.5GB an hour native.
- ❑ The DAT drive can back up a maximum of 2.8GB an hour.
- ❑ Review Table 14-1 for a listing of key features of DLT.
- ❑ Compaq offers auto-loaders for DAT tape devices and tape libraries for DLT tape devices.
- ❑ An auto-loader is a DAT tape device that will automatically load another tape when the first one either becomes full or has completed the backup job it was configured to perform.
- ❑ Tape libraries have slots available for multiple tapes and allow you to schedule a backup job per slot or choose to write the backup job across multiple tapes with parity in a RAID 5 configuration.
- ❑ The Compaq Remote Insight Board is a remote control option board that you can add to Compaq servers. It enables full remote control of a server before the operating system loads.
- ❑ The Compaq redundant power supply is an optional, hot-pluggable power supply that can be added to ProLiant servers. It allows for redundancy of the power supplies used to convert high-voltage AC to the low-voltage DC current expected by the server.

SELF TEST

The following Self Test questions will help you measure your understanding of the material presented in this chapter. Read all the choices carefully, as there may be more than one correct answer. Choose all correct answers for each question.

1. What are the two types of storage systems offered by Compaq?
   A. Compaq ProLiant Storage System/C
   B. Compaq ProLiant Storage System
   C. Compaq ProLiant Storage System/F
   D. Compaq ProLiant Storage System/Q
2. How many drives can the ProLiant Storage System support?
   A. Fourteen 1.6" and fourteen 1"
   B. Seven 1.6" and seven 1"
   C. Eight 1.6" and ten 1"
   D. Seven 1.6" and eight 1"
3. How many drives can the ProLiant Storage System/F support in the dual bus mode?
   A. Seven 1.6" and seven 1"
   B. Seven 1.6" and ten 1"
   C. Eight 1.6" and eight 1"
   D. Eight 1.6" and twelve 1"
4. What type of drives are supported in the ProLiant Storage System? (Select two.)
   A. SCSI-1
   B. SCSI-2
   C. Fast SCSI-2
   D. Fast-Wide SCSI-2
   E. Wide-Ultra SCSI-3
   F. Ultra-Wide SCSI
5. How many ProLiant Storage System/F rack mount devices can fit in a 42U rack?
   A. 12
   B. 8
   C. 10
   D. 4
6. How many different racks are offered by Compaq?
   A. Eight
   B. Four
   C. Five
   D. Three
7. How many Us can a Compaq Rack 4136 hold?
   A. 4136
   B. 41
   C. 36
   D. 136
8. What devices are controlled by a Compaq switch box? (Choose all that apply.)
   A. Keyboard
   B. Modem
   C. Mouse

D. Video controller

E. Tape device

9. How many servers can a Compaq switch box support? (Select two.)

A. 12

B. 10

C. 8

D. 4

10. Select two characteristics of DLT technology.

A. Uses Helical Scan technology

B. Backs up a maximum of 2.8GB an hour

C. Backs up a maximum of 9GB an hour

D. Passes the tape past the head in a horizontal motion

11. Select three components of the Remote Insight Board.

A. Microprocessor

B. Mouse

C. Keyboard

D. Memory

E. Serial Port

12. How can you access the Remote Insight Board? (Select two.)

A. PPP

B. SLIP

C. ANSI-compliant terminal emulation package

D. Infrared

13. How many user accounts can be configured on the Remote Insight Board?

A. 16

B. 10

C. 12

D. 8

14. How long is the battery life on the Remote Insight Board?

A. 10 minutes

B. 20 minutes

C. 30 minutes

D. 60 minutes

15. What is the purpose of a redundant power supply?

A. To supply more power so processing can take place faster

B. To charge up the batteries of the server in case of a power failure

C. To provide a backup power supply if the primary supply goes bad

D. To share the load of the server power

ASE
ACCREDITED SYSTEMS ENGINEER

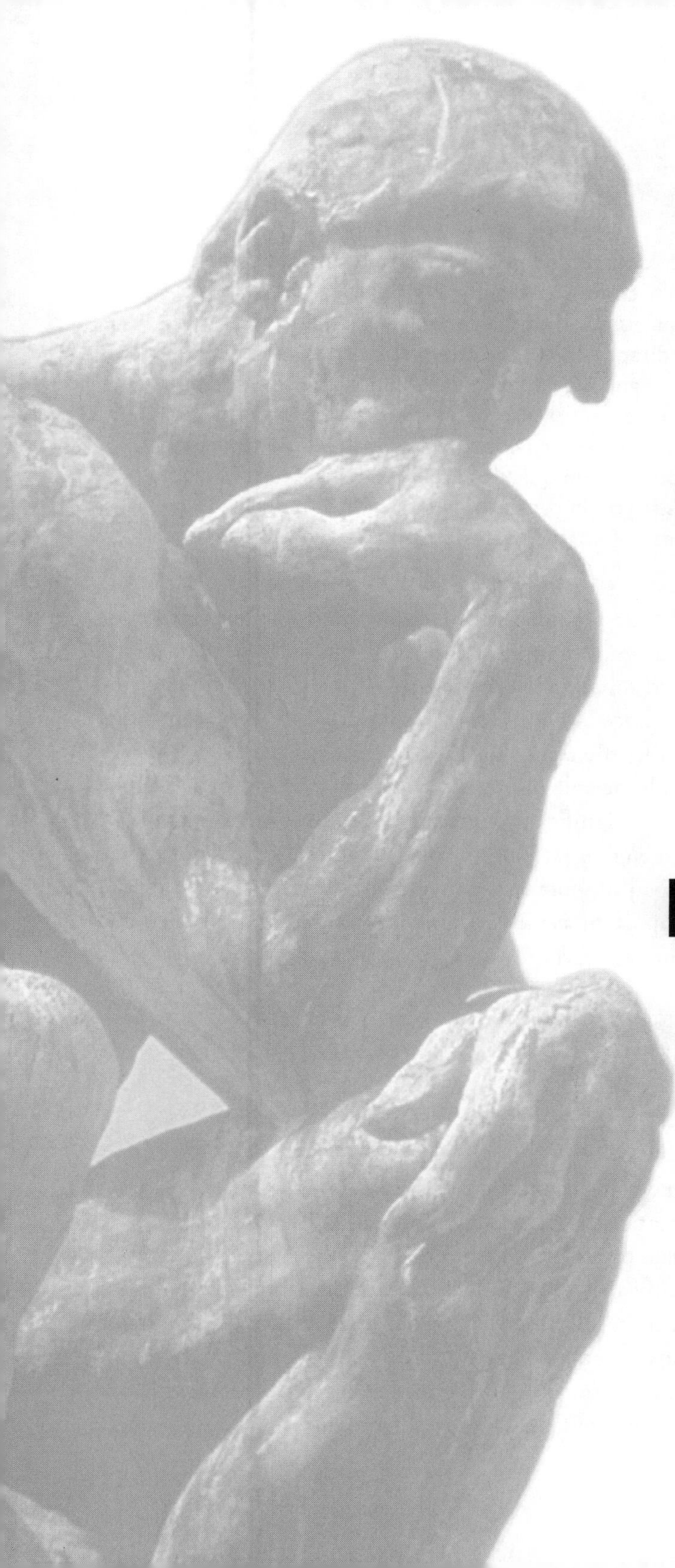

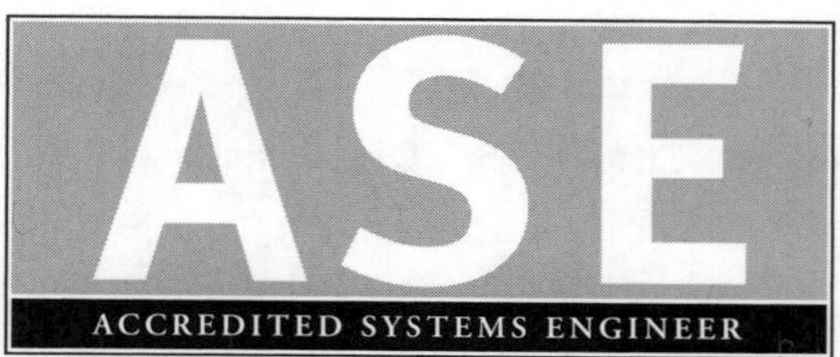

15

Diagnostics and Utilities

CERTIFICATION OBJECTIVES

- 15.01 Compaq Diagnostics
- 15.02 Obtaining Compaq Support Tools and Utilities
- 15.03 Power-On Self-Test Operation and Error Repxorting
- 15.04 ROMPaq
- 15.05 Server Health Logs
- 15.06 Drive Array Advanced Diagnostics
- 15.07 Inspect

This chapter covers several robust tools provided by Compaq to maintain and support the server hardware itself. When it comes to maintaining a server, the systems engineer must understand the configuration of the server, add-on adapters and peripheral devices such as SCSI adapters and tape drives, and the system software or BIOS that drives that system or device. The ability to diagnose problems based upon the server's boot process, before any operating system is launched, must also be in the systems engineer's tool kit. You will learn about the Diagnostics and Utilities provided by Compaq—how to install them, and how to use them to configure your system quickly and identify its setup. Power-On Self-Test processes will be presented to assist you in recognizing server health during this critical stage of server operation. The process of upgrading system and device BIOS levels will be thoroughly reviewed.

Many of these tools are provided with each server, in the box. However, the latest versions of diagnostic utilities and BIOS upgrades are available from Compaq through subscription services or off the Internet. The systems engineer also needs to know where to find the logs that the server maintains so that he or she can identify trends in system performance. Finally, the systems engineer should be able to produce a complete report of the server's configuration, including significant operating system information, and provide it to Compaq engineers, should troubleshooting steps require the involvement of Compaq support organizations. In short, documenting the configuration is important as viewing and changing it, and this chapter will discuss these Compaq server features.

CERTIFICATION OBJECTIVE 15.01

Compaq Diagnostics

Compaq Servers come with diagnostic tools that allow the systems engineer to identify system components and analyze functionality. Older servers may require these diagnostics be run from bootable diskettes. On servers delivered since the early 1990s, and on all ProLiants, Compaq has allowed the systems engineer to install these diagnostics in what is called the System Partition on the primary bootable fixed disk drive. It does not matter which method you choose to run the diagnostics, they are presented in an easy-to-follow, graphical interface. Figure 15-1 provides a look at the menu

FIGURE 15-1

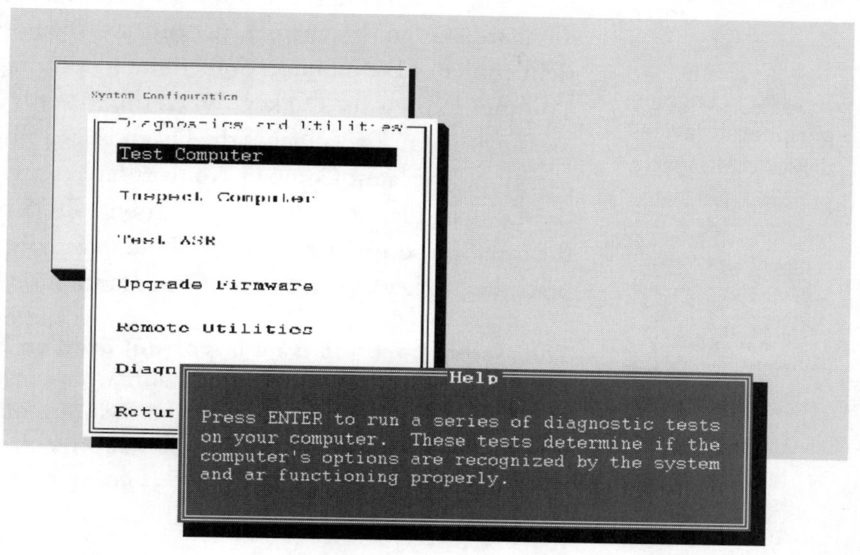

The Diagnostics and Utilities Menu provides several options

options in the Compaq Server Diagnostics. The rest of this section will discuss how to launch these diagnostics using either of two methods, and then an explanation of the diagnostic utility will be presented.

Launching the Diagnostics

For older servers, such as early ProSignia models, the systems engineer received a set of diskettes with the server, which provided the Compaq diagnostics and utilities. In order to run the diagnostics, the server had to be shut down and then turned back on with the diagnostic diskette in the floppy disk drive so that the system would boot from this diskette. Many of these systems are still in use, so it is important to maintain these support diskettes in good condition, as well as maintain the operating condition of the floppy disk drive itself.

All ProLiant servers, and all servers built by Compaq in the past several years, allow the engineer to install the diagnostics and utilities to a system partition that is created when the server is set up for the first time. Using Compaq's SmartStart or the Diagnostic and Utilities Diskettes, the systems engineer creates a nonbootable partition on the primary boot drive and installs the Diagnostics and Utilities there. During the boot process, discussed later in this chapter, the cursor is then presented to the upper right corner of the monitor. Sometimes (depending upon model) there is a prompt to press the F10 key. When the cursor is in the upper right corner, pressing the F10 key launches the Diagnostics and Utilities from the system partition. The latest Compaq ProLiant servers present a splash screen with the Compaq logo instead of the traditional DOS type display. When this is the case, the bottom right corner of the screen displays text advising you to press the F10 key to run System Configuration.

on the job

The system partition is an important area on the server to create and save critical system support software, in addition to diagnostics and utilities. Using the system partition location eliminates the risk of losing utility diskettes or failing to keep track of the version that is right for the server and the BIOS running on that server.

Running the Diagnostics and Utilities

After pressing F10, when running the system partition-based utilities, the systems engineer will be presented with a Compaq identification screen that pauses the application launch. Pressing any key gets beyond this screen and presents the system engineer with the menu shown in Figure 15-2.

All of the utilities discussed in this chapter can be run from the Diagnostic and Utilities menu option shown earlier. The other options are covered elsewhere in this book. They include the utilities to configure the hardware and disk array systems (System Configuration menu) and to prepare and install the operating system (Operating System Installation).

When running the Diagnostics and Utilities from the bootable diskette, you will be presented directly into the menu shown in Figure 15-3. This same screen will appear after you select the option for Diagnostics and Utilities from the Main Menu shown in Figure 15-2.

Test Computer

Select Test Computer to run diagnostic tests on the computer, if you want to verify that the system is recognizing all of the devices that are installed. You will be presented with the screen shown in Figure 15-4.

FIGURE 15-2

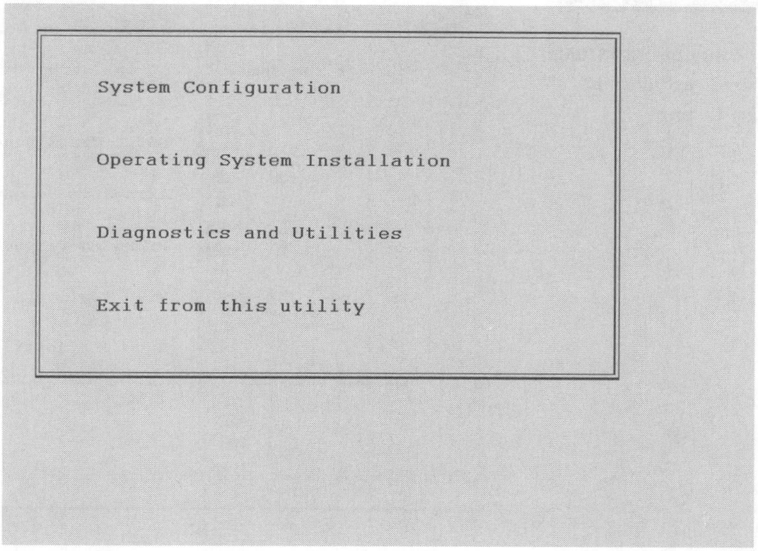

The main menu of Compaq's system partition-based utilities

```
System Configuration

Operating System Installation

Diagnostics and Utilities

Exit from this utility
```

FIGURE 15-3

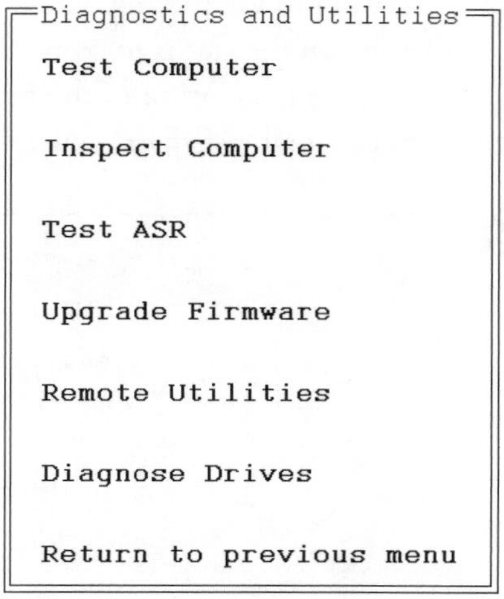

Diagnostics and Utilities menu provides six utilities for troubleshooting

```
Diagnostics and Utilities
Test Computer

Inspect Computer

Test ASR

Upgrade Firmware

Remote Utilities

Diagnose Drives

Return to previous menu
```

FIGURE 15-4

Diagnostics options include automated testing and selective testing

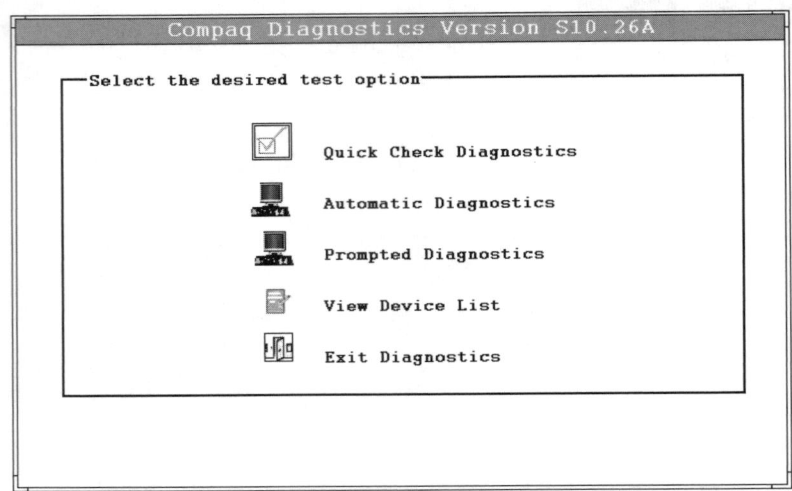

The Quick Check Diagnostics anticipates testing all Input/Output (I/O) devices. To do so, you will need to have blank diskettes, tape cartridges, and CD-ROMs to place in these devices during the testing. Disconnect any modem or phone lines from all serial ports. As shown in Figure 15-5, you will be provided with progress indicators throughout the testing. In addition to identifying which series of tests are being conducted, you will be shown the status to completion of each step.

At the conclusion of the testing, summary results are presented on the screen. If all tests pass, you will see an acknowledgment notice. Otherwise,

FIGURE 15-5

Quick Check Diagnostics provides indicators that show progress of testing

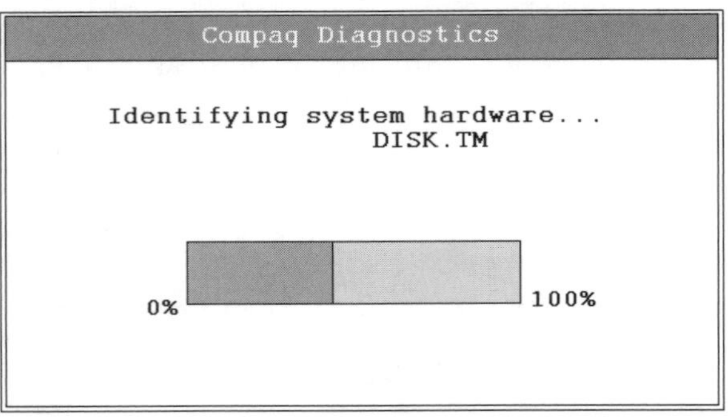

you will be provided with a list of diagnostic error codes, which will direct you more closely to the components or subsystems that are problematic. The Maintenance and Service Guide for your server should provide you with a list of these codes and their meanings. In this guide, Compaq has also provide a recommended action(s) to correct the problem.

on the job

Quick Check Diagnostics is thorough, but if you have focused your analysis of a problem on one subsystem of the computer, you could waste a lot of time by just letting these diagnostics run. If your system has a lot of memory and you know the problem is not memory related, for example, choose the Automated Diagnostics. You can select just the subcomponents you wish to test, but these tests still run automatically.

Automatic Diagnostics will allow you to automate testing of just those system components you want to examine. You can select the devices to test and the number of times to go through the testing sequences. Prompted Diagnostics allows you to be very specific in how a device is tested. You may also simply view the devices visible to the system by choosing View Device List. This information is displayed as in Figure 15-6.

FIGURE 15-6

You can print a list of installed devices within the Diagnostic Utility

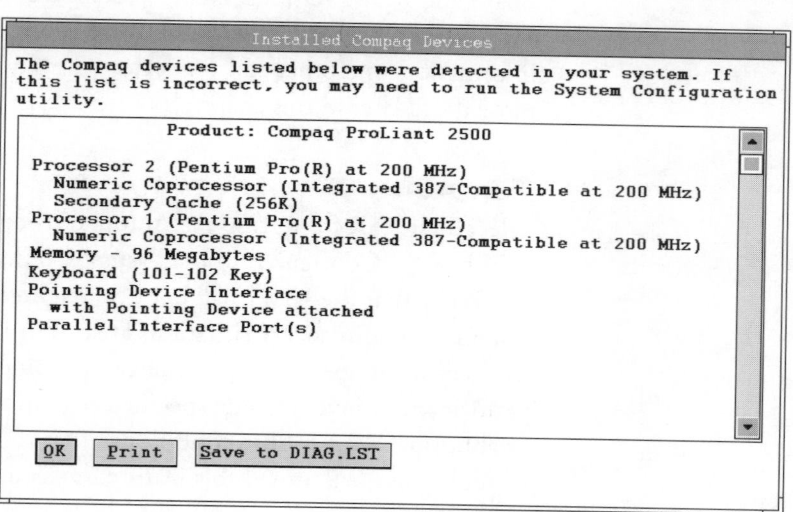

FROM THE FIELD

Using Diagnostics to Burn-In Hardware

Generally, you run diagnostics when you suspect that there is a hardware fault in your server. However, another good time to run diagnostics is when you first receive and build your server. Statistics show that if a component is going to fail, it will fail within the first few dozen hours of running. It is better to discover a failed or failing part before you place the server into your production environment.

When you first build your server, set up the diagnostics program to run in automated mode in a continuous loop. You can have the diagnostics run for several hours or several days to make sure that your hardware is functioning properly. After the diagnostics run for a couple of days, you can at least feel comfortable putting the server into production knowing that you will not have a hardware failure.

—Roneil Icatar, MCSE, MCP+I, ASE

Inspect Computer

Select Inspect Computer to collect and display the configuration information for your system. Information can be obtained on the System Board and ROM versions, memory, resources such as interrupts and I/O addresses, serial and parallel ports, drive configurations and drive history information, and other add-on devices. This utility will be discussed in more detail later in this chapter.

Test ASR

Select Test ASR for testing the Automatic Server Recovery settings on your system. Configured in the System Configuration application, testing will verify that the server will boot to diagnostics or boot the operating system, should recovery situations arise. The system can be set for recovery from operating system lock ups, blue screens, or when hardware performance moves outside specified parameters, such as fan operation or abnormal temperature conditions. This test will actually restart your server if you have turned this feature on. You may choose to have the server restart into these diagnostics if you have installed them on the system partition. Otherwise, you may choose to have the server restart the operating system. Using the Test ASR selection, you can simulate this restart to assure yourself that it is working.

Upgrade Firmware

Select Upgrade Firmware to run the ROMPaq upgrade utility. This utility is discussed in more detail later in this chapter and is used to replace ROMs in the various devices and system boards with newer versions.

Remote Utilities

Select Remote Utilities if you have installed remote options for managing the server. If you have installed remote management capabilities, you have the option, through modem or network access, of using all system partition utilities. You can view Health Logs, run disk-based diagnoses, restart the server while the operating system is running, run the configuration utilities, and update the server's firmware. All software must be installed on the system partition. To run disk diagnostics, the server recovery option should be set to boot the system utilities.

Diagnose Drives

Select Diagnose Drives to run the Drive Array Advanced Diagnostics (DAAD) utility. This utility is designed for use with the SMART Array technology of Compaq Servers. It is important to match the version of DAAD with the BIOS running on the drives, and upgrading the BIOS on the drives should accompany upgrading the version of this utility. This utility will discussed in more detail later in this chapter.

CERTIFICATION OBJECTIVE 15.02

Obtaining Compaq Support Tools and Utilities

There are several ways to obtain the Compaq Support Tools and Utilities. Each server comes with a CD-ROM containing these programs. They are contained in the SmartStart and Support Software CD. This CD is bootable by Compaq Servers and is used to run system configuration or to create diskettes with the various utilities and ROMPaqs. The latest software from Compaq for servers may be obtained off the Compaq support Web site. For servers, the URL to use is http://www.compaq.com/support/servers/index.html. One of the benefits of becoming a Compaq Accredited Systems Engineer (ASE) is that you will have a subscription to the SmartStart program and you will receive updates as they are released to the public.

Downloading software involves the download of what Compaq calls SoftPaqs. These files allow the creation of bootable or utility diskettes that can be used to run software or upgrade the system partition. If you obtain a CD version of the Diagnostics and Utilities, you may either boot the server from the CD or create the diskettes from the CD.

CERTIFICATION OBJECTIVE 15.03

Power-On Self-Test Operation and Error Reporting

Upon bootup of any PC system, the system BIOS runs through several diagnostics to determine if the system devices are working. This process is called the Power-on Self-Test (POST) operation. The results of these tests are presented to the observer through messages on the monitor and/or through beeps from the system speaker. Figure 15-7 shows the screen display after the POST has completed and is ready for the operating system to load.

FIGURE 15-7

POST displays status messages

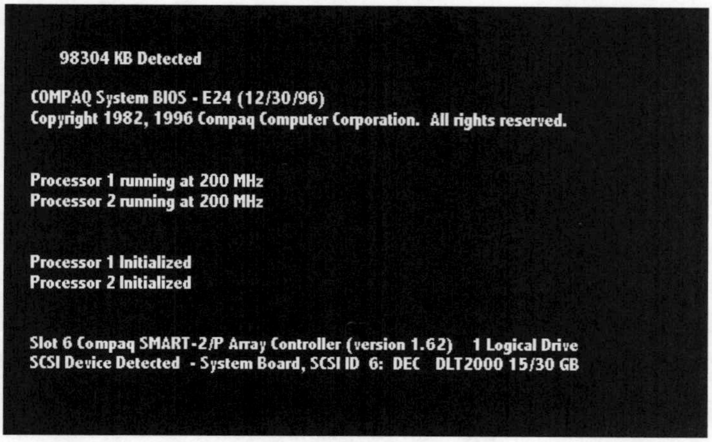

```
    98304 KB Detected

COMPAQ System BIOS - E24 (12/30/96)
Copyright 1982, 1996 Compaq Computer Corporation.  All rights reserved.

Processor 1 running at 200 MHz
Processor 2 running at 200 MHz

Processor 1 Initialized
Processor 2 Initialized

Slot 6 Compaq SMART-2/P Array Controller (version 1.62)   1 Logical Drive
SCSI Device Detected  - System Board, SCSI ID  6:  DEC   DLT2000 15/30 GB
```

POST Steps and Messages

The first test is on system I/O devices. You can watch the devices and see the system test (in this order) the keyboard, power supply, system board, memory and memory expansion boards, controllers, disk drives, CD-ROM drive, hard drives, other drives, and then the monitor. During these steps, the keyboard lights flash, indicating that the system is able to access and control the keyboard subsystem. Then the floppy disk drive is accessed to query whether a disk has been inserted, thus lighting its access light. Similarly, the CD-ROM drive and bootable hard drive are accessed, also lighting their indicator lights. Finally, the monitor is tested and an image appears, first with the Compaq logo, then with the POST operations results messages.

BIOS Version Notification

The first message displayed on your screen after the Compaq logo is the Basic Input Output System (BIOS) version. It is important to note the

BIOS family and version date that your system is running. Compaq updates the BIOS on all systems periodically to add enhancements and the ability to use newer technologies that may not have existed when the system was originally designed, such as fiber channel adapters or gigabit Ethernet adapters. You will learn how to upgrade the BIOS on your server later in this chapter.

Memory Test

The second test to generate a message is the memory test. The system will access every bank of memory and register the amount it finds, increasing the count until it reaches the last bank. This memory counting process is actually displayed above the BIOS information on the top line of the monitor display area. The total memory is displayed on the screen in kilobytes (KB), except in the case of the ProLiant 8000/8500, which displays the count in megabytes. If this memory count is not the same as what the system was last configured for, you will receive a memory error message. On some older systems, this memory error message would lead to a prompt to run the system configuration utility by pressing F10. On newer systems, you have the option of continuing with the current memory being updated into the configuration registers. This allows you to proceed when you know you have added or deleted memory and the count by the system is correct.

Keep in mind that 1KB equals 1024 bytes and 1MB is 1024KB, so if you are expecting to see a number like 64,000 for 64MB, you will actually see 65,536

Processor Initialization

In the next step, the system BIOS initializes all processors in the system. Until this time, only the main processor was operating. Now, if more than one processor is present on the system, they all will be initialized. The POST messages appear identifying what processors are found and what their configuration is. These processors are then initialized into their normal running mode and the status of this step is displayed.

Additional Processor Boards and Peripherals

Next, the system identifies any additional processor boards, such as SMART Array controllers. The BIOS that exists on these processor boards is identified and any attached devices, such as hard drives, tape drives, and CD-ROM drives are identified. In the case of hard drives, the latest Compaq BIOS displays icons that represent each drive as the system spins it up. This is another section for the system engineer to observe for BIOS revision dates. BIOS upgrades for these devices will also be discussed later in this chapter.

Error Reporting

Throughout these tests, the results are processed and communicated through the display and/or a series of beeps of the system. Common error messages include those of memory quantities changing, keyboard errors, and drive failures. If the error is nonfatal, you will be presented with options to press F1 to continue or F10 to run system configuration utilities. Those that are fatal to system operation will be identified on the screen or through beeps, especially if the display system is affected. Compaq provides a listing of the meanings of the various diagnostic beeps on their Web site at http://www.compaq.com/support/techpubs/customer_advisories/post.html and in the Server Maintenance and Service Guide, which comes with each server.

CERTIFICATION OBJECTIVE 15.04

ROMPaq

Compaq servers are designed for easy maintenance and upgrade of the BIOS. Compaq server BIOSs may be upgraded through flash upgrade programs that you run by booting the system off a bootable diskette created for this process. These programs are called ROMPaqs. Obtain the correct BIOS upgrade software from either your SmartStart subscription CD or the Compaq Web site. When you run the Diskette Builder utility, you have the opportunity to select the ROMPaq for the system and add-on devices you need.

You will need to create a diskette with the ROMPaq for the server you intend to upgrade. You will also need to select the Options ROMPaq to create diskettes with BIOS upgrades for peripheral and add-on devices, such as SCSI adapters, array controllers, hard drives, DAT drives, and DLT drives. Be sure you have plenty of diskettes handy as the Options ROMPaq can take at least 10 diskettes for a complete set.

When you use the SmartStart CD to create your software, you will run the Diskette Builder utility. This utility is shown in Figure 15-8. Select the diskette sets you want, and you will be told how many diskettes are required to make up your request. Diskette Builder will then prompt you for diskettes, notify you what to place on each label, and create the diskettes. If you are reusing diskettes from an older set (a great practice!) Diskette Builder will allow you to overwrite each diskette.

If you download your software from the Internet, you will be identifying and downloading what Compaq calls a SoftPaq. You may search for your

FIGURE 15-8

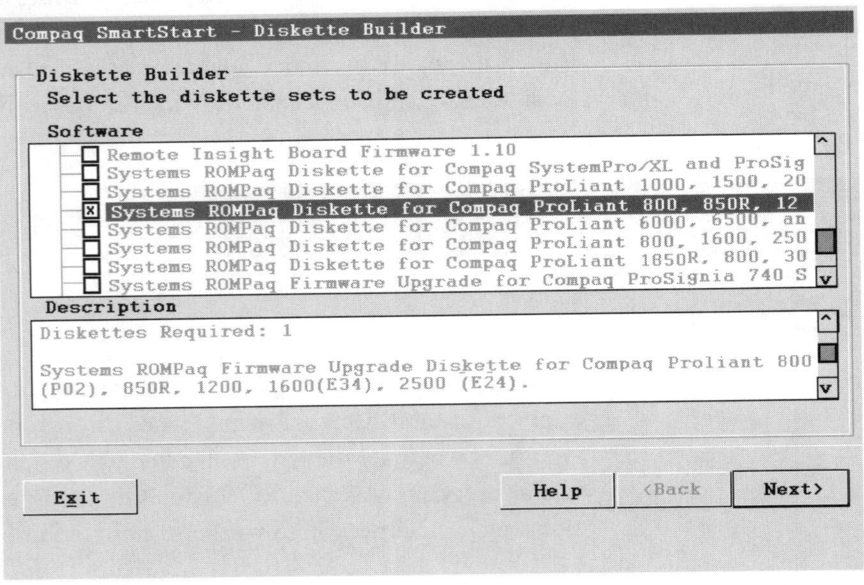

Compaq Diskette Builder allows the creation of many different diskette sets for ROMPaq and other software

ROMPaq software at http://www.compaq.com/support/files/server/index.html, which is shown in Figure 15-9. Notice that these ROMPaqs are located on the Web page for all server-related software, including operating system support files and other system utilities.

The file you download will be a file entitled SP*nnnnn*.EXE, where *nnnnn* represents a sequential number (for example, SP8437.EXE). Be sure to download this file to a folder on your local system where no other files are located. After downloading the file, double-click the filename from within your Windows Explorer, or type the name of the file to run the extraction process within a DOS window. You will see a screen similar to the one in Figure 15-10.

Follow directions to install the software to a 3 1/2" floppy diskette. Repeat this process for all other SoftPaqs you require to create the BIOS upgrade diskettes you will need for your system.

FIGURE 15-9

Compaq Web site for server support software downloads

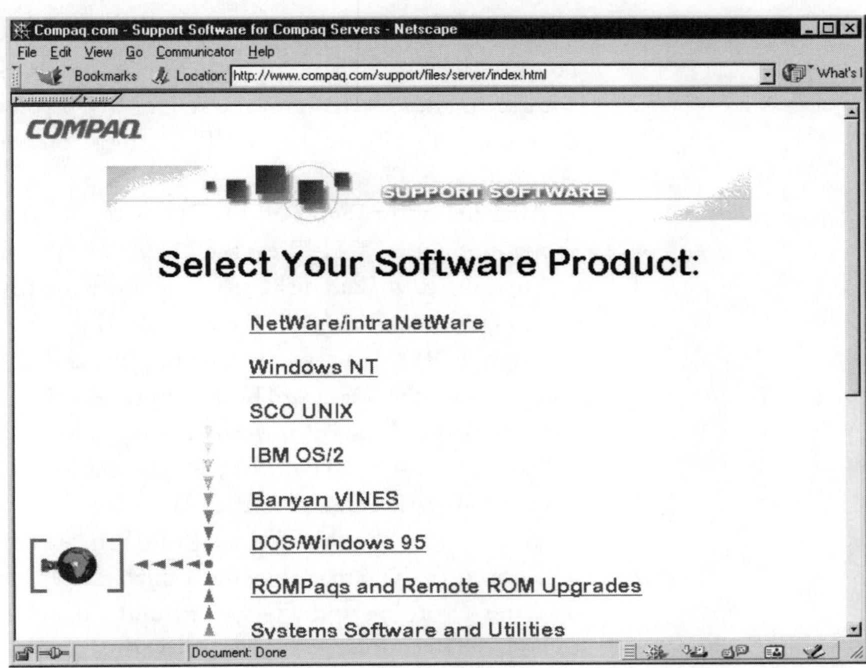

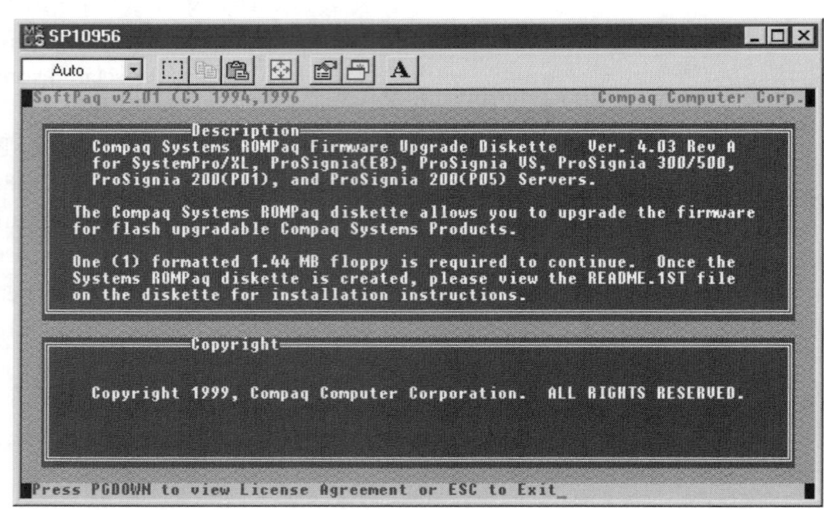

FIGURE 15-10

The SoftPaq diskette creation process is easy to follow

With all your diskettes created, you now proceed through a series of cold boots of the system. You cannot upgrade the BIOS with a warm boot. Start with the main ROMPaq for the system BIOS you are upgrading. Turn the computer on and note the POST diagnostic messages that come up. These were shown in Figure 15-7.

After the system boots off the ROMPaq diskette, you will see the screen shown in Figure 15-11. Press the ENTER key to continue.

First, the ROMPaq diskette will identify the BIOS on your system and match it with the one(s) on the diskette. If you have a diskette with no appropriate ROMPaq, you will be notified and allowed to skip that diskette and go to another. You will be able to review the current BIOS version on the machine and the BIOS version that the ROMPaq will install. ROMPaq will also save a backup copy of your current ROM on the ROMPaq diskette in case you want to revert to the older BIOS.

When upgrading the Options ROMPaq, at times more than one BIOS will appear in the screen showing available ROM versions. If you label the diskettes according to the Diskette Builder instructions, you won't have to boot all 10 Options ROMPaq diskettes. If you know what is on your system, you can select the diskettes you need. Boot each diskette as

FIGURE 15-11

ROMPaq Firmware Upgrade Utility initial screen

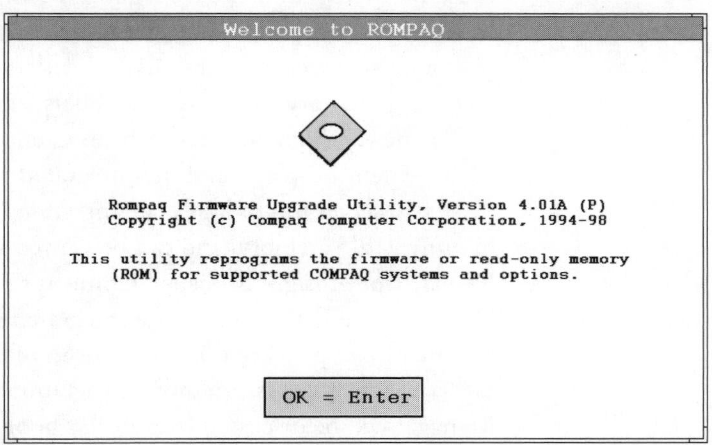

appropriate, and select the BIOS to upgrade from each one. When there is more than one disk possibility Options ROMPaq will direct you to the appropriate one. For example, if you have different SCSI controllers or hard drive sizes, you will probably need to run ROMPaq for those different BIOS requirements. Options ROMPaq will identify your requirements and direct you to the one diskette of the 10 that has the BIOS your system needs. When this occurs, insert the appropriate disk and choose Refresh/Change Disk. ROMPaq then identifies the devices in your system that match what is on that diskette.

CERTIFICATION OBJECTIVE 15.05

Server Health Logs

Compaq servers that have Automatic Server Recovery-2 (ASR-2) have the capability to log hardware incidents and configuration changes. This information is captured in the Critical Error Log and the Revision History Table, which are stored in nonvolatile RAM memory. The Critical Error Log captures errors in memory as well as hardware or software errors that cause the system to fail. This log may be viewed through several methods, including the Inspect Utility and the Diagnostics Utility. The Revision History Table records additions and deletions of system components including memory, adapters, controllers, and so on.

The newer, high-end servers from Compaq support Integrated Management Displays, and the Integrated Management Log (IML) replaces these two server health logs. The Integrated Management Log is also stored in nonvolatile memory, and can be viewed with the Integrated Management Display from Insight Manager, Compaq's management utility, the Survey Utility, or the IML Utility. The Integrated Management Display is an optional LCD panel that is on the front of the server and displays status messages, error codes, and other programmable information. Insight Manager will be discussed later in this book. Compaq's Survey Utility is a tool available for Windows NT or Novell NetWare servers that can periodically record server configuration information and provide notations recognizing changing system components or devices.

CERTIFICATION OBJECTIVE 15.06

Drive Array Advanced Diagnostics

Drive Array Advanced Diagnostics (DAAD) is required to troubleshoot Compaq Drive Array Controllers. It is a DOS-based utility that collects information from the array controllers in the system. DAAD will provide a list of what was found defective after sending commands to test the controller's ability to function. DAAD will not affect data or configurations of the array and its drives.

DAAD can be run from the system partition or the CD or utility diskettes. It is possible to generate a report from the DAAD utility. The result of running this utility will be a status message. The Maintenance and Service Guide for your server should include a list of possible messages and the recommended action to take for each message. Figure 15-12 shows how DAAD analyzes the configuration and provides error codes if tests generate such information. If a problem is detected, you can diagnose the problem by the error code. From the System View screen shown in Figure 15-12,

FIGURE 15-12

DAAD physical drive analysis screen

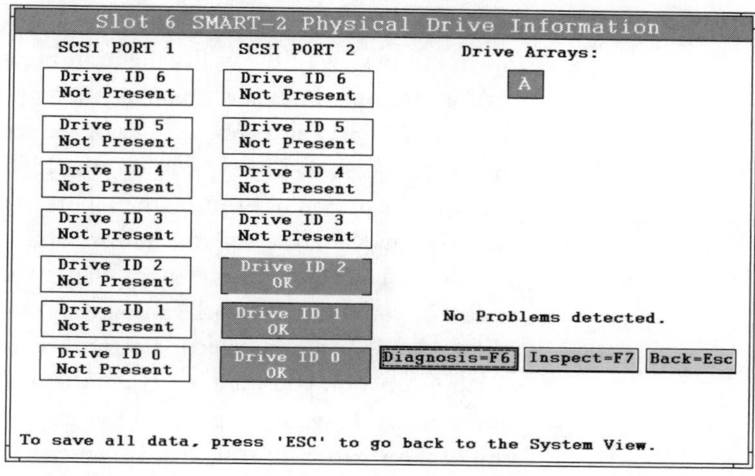

you can quickly determine whether the system is seeing all the drives and whether the diagnostic has identified any problems.

In this example, there is one array, A, comprised of three drives with IDs 0, 1, and 2. This system can support up to 14 drives, and those bays appear with the notation Not Present reflecting the absence of drives. You can proceed with a diagnosis if any error messages are identified, or you may proceed to the Inspect Utility and focus on the status of each drive.

The latest Compaq Array Controllers use a new Array Diagnostic Utility (ADU), which is installed and is required to run from the system partition. This new utility provides the same basic information as the DAAD, but it cannot be run from boot diskettes.

CERTIFICATION OBJECTIVE 15.07

Inspect

The Inspect option will collect your operating system startup files, your memory configuration, and information about the ROM version on your system. This is important information that Compaq support may want to see to help diagnose problems. Your choices as to what to report on are shown in the view of the utility menu in Figure 15-13.

After running the Inspect report, you may view it on the display monitor. You may also choose to print the report. If you have a printer directly attached, you may print it to the LPT1 printer port. Otherwise, you have the option of printing the report to a file. The report does not have to include all the available information; you may select what you want to include. The report can be more than 10 pages long, depending on the devices in your system and the amount of memory your system contains. Figure 15-14 shows the selection screen where you can identify exactly what information you want to save in the report. A copy of a typical output file is shown in Appendix D. It is very detailed and can provide a lot of information to you or to a Compaq support engineer when you are researching a configuration problem.

FIGURE 15-13

The Inspect utility options

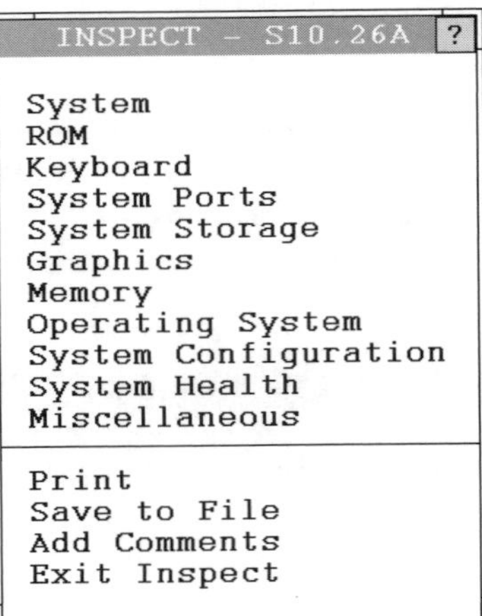

FIGURE 15-14

Inspect provides selectable reporting capability to a text file

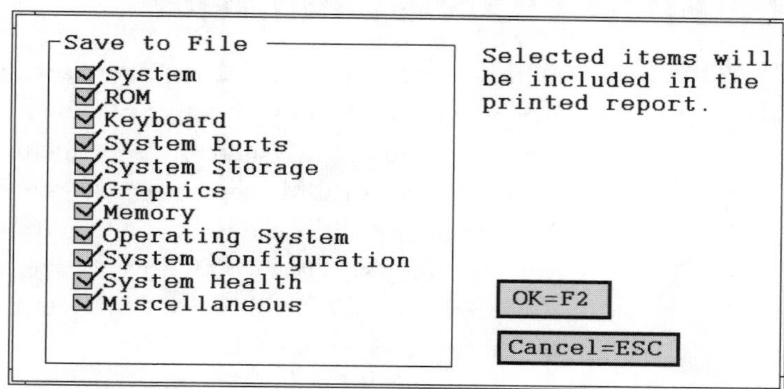

QUESTIONS AND ANSWERS

How do I know if the server is booting properly?	Observe POST error messages. A series of beeps of varying lengths indicates subsystem faults that should be explored.
How do I know if I have the latest BIOS?	Compare the POST information with the Compaq Web site for that server's BIOS family. When the server boots, one of the first informational lines is the BIOS family and date.
How do I identify what hardware is recognized by the system?	Run the Test Computer utility. If you don't see a device you expect, then it is not being recognized by the system.
How do I identify how my system is configured?	Run the Inspect utility. This utility incorporates the boot files for the operating system running on the server as well as significant support files.
What files do I need to upgrade the BIOS?	ROMPaqs from Compaq's Web site or quarterly CDs. ROMPaq is a type of file located within Compaq's SoftPaq libraries.
What do I run to analyze the performance of my drive array?	DAAD. On newer servers, run the utility called ADU.
How can I review how the server has performed over time?	Look at the server health logs. The server will maintain detailed logs of the error messages that occurred at boot as well as abend messages from the operating system.
How can I verify what the server will do in the event of an abend or system failure?	Run the Test ASR utility. This utility simulates and forces the server to run the recovery method you have selected.

CERTIFICATION SUMMARY

In this chapter, you have learned about several Compaq utilities and tools to diagnose the health of your server system. These applications are available from Compaq through more than one method of delivery: Internet downloads, CD-ROM subscriptions, and with the server on CD-ROM. Most of these utilities can be stored in and run from the system partition you create on the server's boot drive, or they can be run from floppy diskettes. The CD-ROMs created by Compaq are designed to be bootable on the latest server models.

The diagnostic utilities are menu driven and cover all of the systems and subsystems on your server. The POST process provides information on the server's health, and delivers visual and auditory feedback to direct you to the problem. BIOS upgrades are provided through Compaq's ROMPaq diskettes. These diskettes are easily created from CD-ROM or downloaded as SoftPaq programs from Compaq's support Web site. Booting the server from one of these ROMPaq diskettes leads the system engineer through an easy upgrade process, with the option to revert to the older version of the BIOS, if desired.

All servers maintain records of component changes, memory changes, and physical errors in server health logs kept in nonvolatile RAM. These records and logs are viewable through Compaq's Insight Manager system, Integrated Display, or from the reports created from the Survey and Inspect utilities. Compaq provides more focused diagnostics for drive arrays through the DAAD utility, which is provided with all array controllers. The Inspect utility allows for the testing of individual components or the entire system in automated or manual processes. The output from the Inspect utility can be viewed, printed, or saved to a file.

Through these several utilities and diagnostic tools, the systems engineer should be able to install and support any Compaq server.

TWO-MINUTE DRILL

- The latest versions of diagnostic utilities and BIOS upgrades are available from Compaq through subscription services or off the Internet.
- Compaq Servers come with diagnostic tools that allow the systems engineer to identify system components and analyze functionality.
- For older servers, such as early ProSignia models, the systems engineer received a set of diskettes with the server, which provided the Compaq diagnostics and utilities.
- All ProLiant servers, and all servers built by Compaq in the past several years, allow the engineer to install the diagnostics and utilities to a system partition that is created when the server is set up for the first time.
- Using Compaq's SmartStart or the Diagnostic and Utilities Diskettes, the systems engineer creates a nonbootable partition on the primary boot drive and installs the Diagnostics and Utilities there.
- Each server comes with a CD-ROM containing the Compaq Support Tools and Utilities.
- The latest software from Compaq for servers may be obtained off the Compaq support Web site at http://www.compaq.com/support/servers/index.html.
- SoftPaqs are downloaded software, which allow the creation of bootable or utility diskettes that can be used to run software or upgrade the system partition
- One of the benefits of becoming a Compaq Accredited Systems Engineer (ASE) is that you will have a subscription to the SmartStart program and you will receive updates as they are released to the public.

- ❑ Upon bootup of any PC system, the system BIOS runs through several diagnostics to determine if the system devices are working, which is called the Power-on Self-Test (POST) operation.
- ❑ Compaq provides a listing of the meanings of the various diagnostic beeps on their Web site at http://www.compaq.com/support/techpubs/customer_advisories/post.html and in the Server Maintenance and Service Guide.
- ❑ Compaq server BIOSs may be upgraded through flash upgrade programs called ROMPaqs that you run by booting the system off a bootable diskette created for this process.
- ❑ Compaq servers that have Automatic Server Recovery-2 (ASR-2) have the capability to log hardware incidents and configuration changes.
- ❑ Drive Array Advanced Diagnostics (DAAD) is required to troubleshoot Compaq Drive Array Controllers.
- ❑ The Inspect option will collect your operating system startup files, your memory configuration, and information about the ROM version on your system.

SELF TEST

The following Self Test questions will help you measure your understanding of the material presented in this chapter. Read all the choices carefully, as there may be more than one correct answer. Choose all correct answers for each question.

1. Which is the best method for launching Compaq utilities or diagnostics?
   A. From the Internet
   B. From a floppy diskette
   C. From the system partition
   D. From within the operating system
2. Which key sequence is pressed to access the utilities in the system partition?
   A. F1
   B. DEL
   C. CTRL-X
   D. F10
3. Under which conditions should the systems engineer press the key sequence to access the utilities in the system partition?
   A. When the cursor begins blinking in the upper right corner of the screen
   B. When the computer system beeps two times
   C. When the monitor blanks out
   D. When the screen displays the message "Press F10 for Setup"
4. When booting the server from diagnostic diskettes, which is not an option you may select?
   A. Test Computer
   B. Test ASR
   C. Diagnostics and Utilities
   D. Diagnose Drives
5. When running the Test Computer option from the Diagnostics and Utilities menu, what are you prompted to have available and/or installed?
   A. ASE handbook
   B. Floppy diskettes, CD-ROMs, and tape cartridges
   C. System serial number
   D. Loopback plug
6. What reference is important for resolving error messages generated from the Test Computer process?
   A. Compaq Quality Statement
   B. http://www.compaq.com/support/index.html
   C. Server Maintenance and Service Guide for a specific server
   D. Peripheral Component Installation Guide for servers
7. What is ASR?
   A. Attempted System Reboot
   B. Accredited Systems Resource
   C. American Society of Researchers
   D. Automatic Server Recovery
8. What is a SoftPaq?
   A. Compaq's name for driver and software update download files

B. Compaq's utility for creating software on diskettes

C. Compaq's quarterly software subscription update

D. Compaq's name for nonserver utilities

9. Where can the systems engineer find the meaning of POST error beeps?

A. On Compaq's Web site

B. In the Server Maintenance and Service Guide

C. On the inside of the server access cover

D. In the server's ROMPaq

10. Which of the following is not updated by ROMPaqs?

A. System BIOS

B. SCSI Drive BIOS

C. Array Controller BIOS

D. Network Adapter BIOS

11. Upgrading the BIOS requires which of the following?

A. Cold boot

B. Warm boot

C. CTRL-ALT-DEL boot

D. Changing jumper settings on the system board

12. How many BIOS upgrades can be done at one time?

A. One

B. Two

C. Three

D. One or more

13. What are the two logs maintained in nonvolatile RAM, commonly called the server health logs?

A. Critical Error Log

B. POST Message Log

C. Updated System Log

D. Revision History Table

14. Which is not a way to view the server health logs?

A. Integrated Management display

B. POST message display

C. Insight Manager

D. Survey utility

15. DAAD collects information from which subsystems?

A. Diagnostics

B. CD-ROM drives

C. Drive arrays

D. Tape drives

16. The Inspect utility allows the engineer to test which of these subsystems automatically?

A. System, ROM, and keyboard

B. System ports, storage, and graphic devices

C. Memory, operating system, and system configuration

D. All of the above

ASE
ACCREDITED SYSTEMS ENGINEER

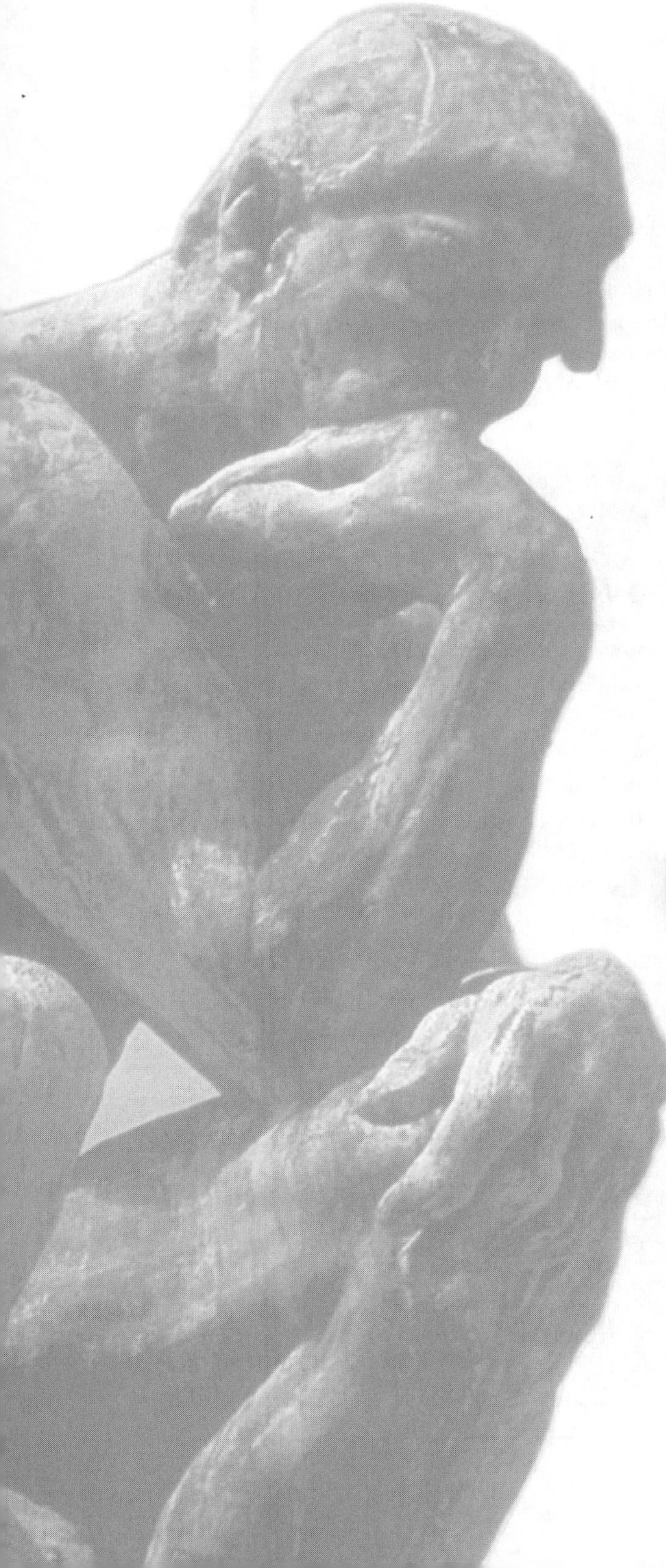

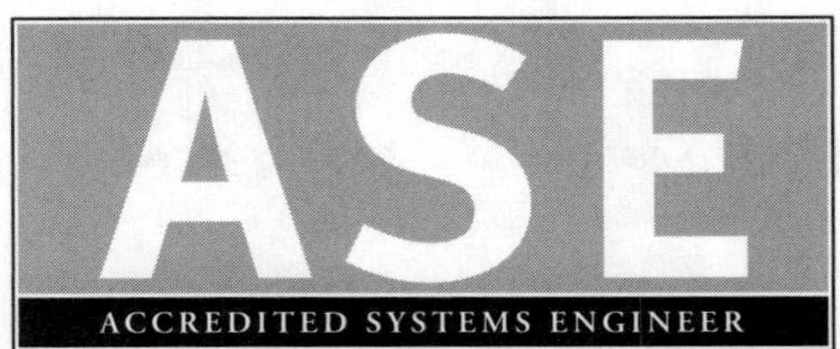

16

Recovery Server

CERTIFICATION OBJECTIVES

16.01	Standby and Online Recovery Servers
16.02	Requirements of the Primary and Secondary Server
16.03	Disk Storage Location
16.04	Recovery Server Interconnect
16.05	Failure of the Primary Server
16.06	Advantages and Disadvantages

The Compaq Recovery Server Option is one of the more popular features offered by Compaq. Recovery Server provides fault tolerance in the case of a hardware failure. Recovery Server goes far beyond RAID or network controller pairs—Recovery Server provides redundant servers. The secondary server takes over in the event of a failure of the primary server. There are two recovery server methodologies: Standby Recovery Server and Online Recovery Server. We will discuss both of these in this chapter.

CERTIFICATION OBJECTIVE 16.01

Standby and Online Recovery Servers

Table 16-1 describes some of the basic differences between Standby and Online Recovery Servers. These differences and others will be discussed in detail later in the chapter.

Standby Recovery Server is supported for Windows NT 3.5*x* and 4.0, Novell NetWare 3.12 and 4.*x*, SCO OpenServer 5, and SCO UnixWare 2.1.*x* and 7.*x*. Online Recovery Server is a little less robust, only supporting Windows NT 3.5*x* and 4.0. Although it is limited in the operating systems it supports, it is still a very useful tool for Windows NT administrators.

Standby Recovery Server is supported by many Compaq server platforms. Compatibility, however, is dependent upon the operating system being used.

TABLE 16-1 Differences between Standby and Online Recovery Servers

	Online Recovery Server	Standby Recovery Server
Placement of Drives	Drives in individual servers and the external array	All drives in external array
Server Models	Don't have to be the same	Must be the same
Placement of Operating System	Internal to each server	In the common array
Operating Systems Supported	Windows NT	Windows NT, Novell NetWare, SCO OpenServer, SCO UnixWare

At the time of this writing, all of the following are supported for the Windows NT platform: ProSignia 200, ProSignia 300, ProSignia 500, ProLiant 850R, ProLiant 1500, ProLiant 1600, ProLiant 1850R, ProLiant 2000, ProLiant 2500, ProLiant 3000, ProLiant 4000, ProLiant 4500, ProLiant 5000, ProLiant 5500, ProLiant 6000, ProLiant 6500, and ProLiant 7000. One key factor to remember is that under Windows NT, the primary server and the secondary server must be identical right down to slot usage.

To help you determine which machines support online and standby configuration, consider the chart at http://www.compaq.com/solutions/enterprise/highavailability-rso-pid.html.

The following servers are supported by Standby Recovery Server on the Novell NetWare platform: ProSignia 300, ProSignia 500, ProLiant 1500, ProLiant 1600, ProLiant 1850R, ProLiant 2000, ProLiant 2500, ProLiant 3000, ProLiant 4000, ProLiant 4600, ProLiant 4500, ProLiant 5000, ProLiant 5500, ProLiant 6000, ProLiant 6500, and ProLiant 7000.

With SCO the following Compaq servers are supported in a Standby Recovery Server model: ProSignia 300, ProSignia 500, ProLiant 800, ProLiant 850, ProLiant 1500, ProLiant 2000, ProLiant 2500, ProLiant 4000, ProLiant 4500, ProLiant 5000, ProLiant 6000, and ProLiant 7000. Compaq also provides a chart showing which servers can be used together. This chart can be accessed at http://www.compaq.com/solutions/enterprise/RSO-unixware21.html

Unlike the standby configuration, Online Recovery Server does not require that the primary server and the secondary server be identical. Online recovery server for Windows NT supports the following Compaq server platforms: ProSignia 300, ProSignia 500, ProLiant 850R, ProLiant 1500, ProLiant 1600, ProLiant 2000, ProLiant 2500, ProLiant 3000, ProLiant 4000, ProLiant 4500, ProLiant 5000, ProLiant 5500, ProLiant 6000, ProLiant 6500, ProLiant 7000. Since each server will carry its copy of the operating system, any two of these servers can be paired together successfully.

Installation

Both Standby and Online Recovery Servers are simple to install. Let's look at the prerequisites, then we'll go through the procedure for setting up each option.

QUESTIONS AND ANSWERS

Can I use Compaq Recovery Server with my Linux machine?	No. Linux is not supported under the Compaq Recovery Server Option.
Can I use two Compaq ProLiant 6000s with Online Recovery Server?	Yes. ProLiant 6000s are supported under Online Recovery Server.
Can I use two ProLiant 5000s with Standby Recovery Server and SCO UnixWare?	Yes. ProLiant 5000s are supported.
Can I use one ProLiant 6500 and one ProLiant 5500 with Standby Recovery Server and Windows NT?	No. The servers must have identical configurations in Standby Recovery Server.

We already know which operating systems and server platforms are supported. So let's start with the Recovery Server Option (RSO) Kit. There are three different Recovery Server Option Kits. The one you order will be dependent on which type of external array you have.

- If you have a ProLiant Storage System Model 1, you need RSO kit 213817.
- If you have a ProLiant Storage System/F1, you need RSO kit 272829.
- If you have a ProLiant Storage System/U1, you need RSO kit 304117.

You will need to order one RSO kit for each ProLiant storage system used. The Recovery Server Option Kit will include Recovery Server software, a Recovery Server switch, a Recovery Server interconnect, a 12-foot standard-to-wide external SCSI-2 cable, and a 12-foot Fast Wide SCSI-2 adapter cable.

It should be noted that in order for you to install the Recovery Server Option, you may need to update your system firmware and your controller firmware. As a matter of practice, I would recommend you do this whether it is required or not. You may also need to update your version of Insight Manager to support Recovery Server. Versions 2.60 and above support the Recovery Server Option.

CERTIFICATION OBJECTIVE 16.02

Requirements of the Primary and Secondary Server

We have already discussed the server models and operating systems required for each configuration. Now let's look at some of the other requirements. For Standby Recovery Server, you must have one switchable ProLiant storage system with a recovery server switch installed and a SMART, SMART-2, SMART-2SL, SMART-2P, SMART-2E, or SMART-2DH controller in each server attached to the storage system. The array controllers in both servers must also be the same and in the same slot. The network cards in both servers must also be the same and should be in the same slot.

For Online Recovery Server, you must have at least one local storage disk in each server for the operating system. You must have at least one switchable ProLiant storage system with a recovery server switch installed. Each server must also have one disk controller for its local disks and one controller attached to the switchable ProLiant storage system. The controller for the local disks must be a Fast SCSI-2, Fast-Wide SCSI-2, SMART, SMART-2, SMART-2SL, SMART-2P, SMART-2E, or SMART-2DH controller. The controller for the storage system must be a SMART, SMART-2, SMART-2SL, SMART-2P, SMART-2E, or a SMART-2DH controller.

CERTIFICATION OBJECTIVE 16.03

Disk Storage Location

One of the differences between Standby and Online Recovery Servers is the location of the disks. In Standby Recovery Server, all disks are common to both servers, as shown in Figure 16-1. Hard disks are only located in the

ProLiant storage systems. This is the main reason why servers in the Standby Recovery model must have similar hardware configurations—there is only one copy of the operating system. Different hardware configurations would cause problems when the secondary server took over. When the primary server fails and the secondary server takes over, the secondary server assumes the full identity of the primary server.

This disk arrangement for Online Recovery Server is a bit different. Not only are there hard disks in the ProLiant storage systems, there are also disks

FIGURE 16-1

Disk storage location for Compaq Standby Recovery Server

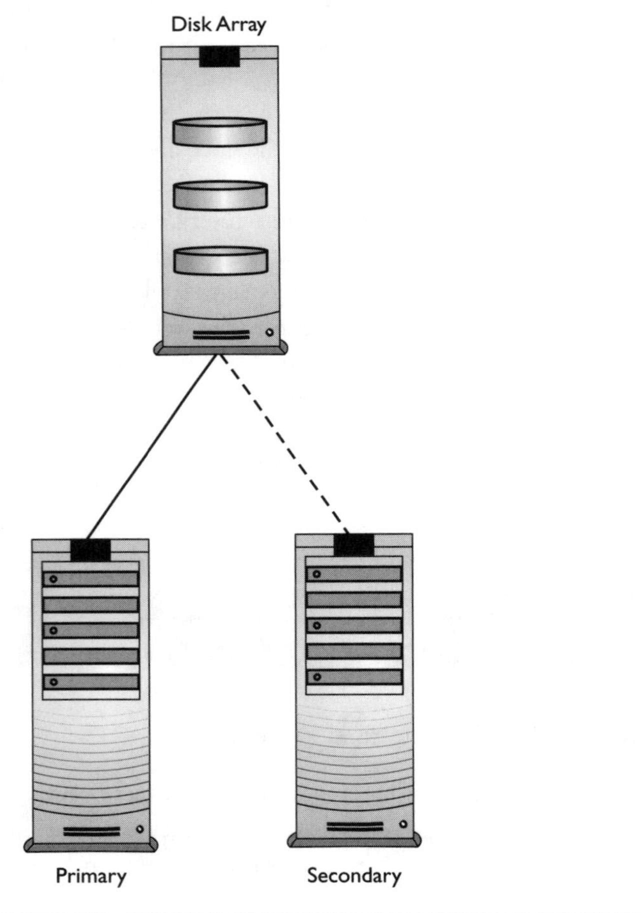

internal to each server, as shown in Figure 16-2. This arrangement allows for a separate copy of the operating system to be installed for each server, giving you a lot more flexibility. You can also have external drive arrays connected to each server that are not connected to the recovery server switch. You can install separate applications on the internal disks or the separately connected arrays. This is good for applications that you do not want shared. Because there are separate operating systems for each server,

FIGURE 16-2

Disk storage location for Compaq Online Recovery Server

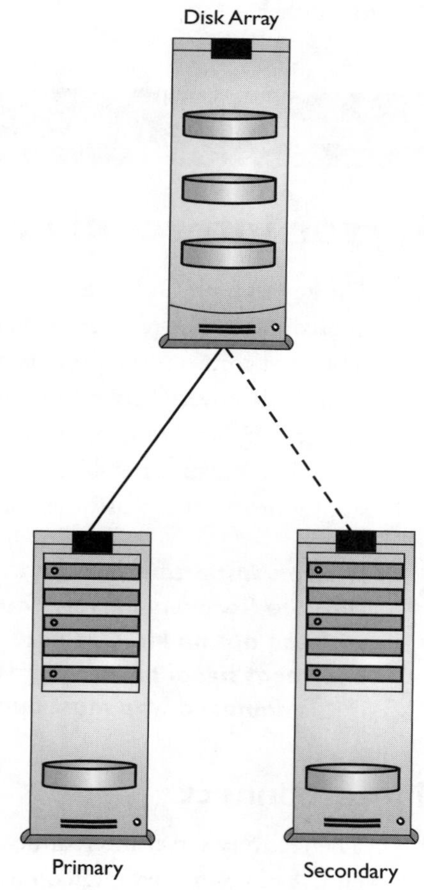

each server has its own identity. When the primary server fails, only the applications installed on the common array are switched over.

Recovery Server Switch Location

The recovery server switch is also included in the recovery server option. You must have one recovery server switch for each ProLiant storage system in your recovery server configuration. The recovery server switch is a SCSI switch that is installed in the back of each ProLiant storage system. The switch is capable of switching the control of the SCSI bus from one server to another.

CERTIFICATION OBJECTIVE 16.04

Recovery Server Interconnect

The key to both Online and Standby Recovery is the recovery server interconnect. The recovery server interconnect is a specially designed serial cable that connects the primary and the recovery server. This cable comes with the Recovery Server Option Kit. The *heartbeat* signal travels through the recovery server interconnect. The heartbeat is a signal that lets each server know that it is still connected to the other server. Once the heartbeat stops, one server will assume that the other server has failed.

It is very important to note that standard serial cables will not work with the Recovery Server. You must use the serial cable that comes with the option kit. Ordinary serial cables will not transmit the heartbeat signal properly. If you lose your interconnect cable, or if it is damaged, you must purchase a new one from Compaq.

Disconnected Interconnect

The recovery server interconnect could become disconnected from either end. A disconnected interconnect will stop the transmission of the heart beat signal. This will trigger a failure, because it will be assumed that the other server is down and cannot respond. The heartbeat cable is the only means of transmission between the two servers. Without it, one server has no way of knowing that the other server is functioning.

It is recommended that you routinely check your interconnect cable to make sure it is secure. If you are moving components or moving racks, you should check the cable after you finish. You don't want your servers failing over unnecessarily, especially if the primary server is still up and functioning.

CERTIFICATION OBJECTIVE 16.05

Failure of the Primary Server

A disconnected interconnect cable and a down server are not the only things that can trigger a failover. Any event that keeps the primary server from sending the heartbeat signal would trigger a failover. There may be an operating system failure on the primary server. The primary server may not be down, but may be unable to transmit the signal. A damaged cable can also cause the heartbeat signal not to transmit. It is important to note that a failover does not always signify a down server.

Insight Manager

Compaq designed its Recovery Server Option to be integrated with Insight Manager. When the primary server fails, you will receive alerts through Insight Manager. First, you will receive an alert informing you that one of your servers is inaccessible. You will also receive an alert informing you that a failover has occurred. If the interconnect cable becomes disconnected from the primary server, Insight Manger will send you an alert letting you know that the primary server is being shut down because of a cable failure. This happens just before the failover takes place.

Standby Recovery Server

During normal operation, in a standby server configuration, the primary server is processing all of the requests. The secondary server does a POST test and then executes its Compaq Recovery Agent (CRA). The CRA is stored in the server's ROM BIOS. The CRA is what actually monitors the heartbeat signal from the primary server. Every time the recovery server receives a heartbeat message, it will send an acknowledgment message back to the primary server.

If the recovery server does not receive a heartbeat from the primary server within a given period of time, then the failover process is initiated. First, the CRA in the secondary server will send instructions to the recovery server switch installed in the drive array to tell it to transfer control of the drives over to the recovery server. Next, the recovery server will boot from the drives in the drive array. After the recovery server boots up, it will assume the network identity of the primary server. The old primary server then assumes the role of the secondary server.

on the job

You cannot test your Standby Recovery Server process by simply shutting down the primary server. When the primary server goes through a normal shutdown, the CRA in the recovery server is sent a notification, so it knows not to initialize a failover. In order to test your recovery server configuration, you would have to simulate an abnormal shutdown of the primary. You might try powering off the primary server while it is running. However, I wouldn't suggest doing this on a production server.

Online Recovery Server

During normal operation in an Online Recovery Server configuration, both servers are online. Each server has its own identity. They are both capable of servicing requests from clients. Each server runs a Compaq Recovery Agent. The two CRAs will monitor the heartbeat signal coming from the other server. If the heartbeat signal is not received within the set time period, a failover will occur.

During the failover, the CRA will tell the recovery server switch to switch control of the common array to the server that is still functional. Only the disks in the common array attached to the recovery server switch will be switched over. The internal disks and the separately connected arrays will not be switched over. Therefore, only the operating system on the live server and the applications on the switched disk will continue to function.

CERTIFICATION OBJECTIVE 16.06

Advantages and Disadvantages

When deciding which configuration to institute in your environment, you must consider the advantages and disadvantages of each. Cost is usually a consideration, as is the need for uninterrupted service. You have to determine what is acceptable for your environment.

Standby Recovery Server does not require that each server have its own copy of the operating system, which will save you money on hard drives. Since both servers will have the same identity, you don't have to worry about reconfiguring any workstations in the event of a failover. All applications are protected in the event of a failover. Standby Recovery Server also supports a wider range of operating systems. Because only one server will be active at a time, one server is doing nothing productive, which can be costly. If the external array fails, then both servers will be down.

With Online Recovery Server, both servers will be online and can service client requests, keeping you from having an idle server. Since the operating system is not stored in the switched array, failure of the switched array does not necessarily mean failure of the two servers. Because both servers are already online, no reboot is required during a failover. Some client reconfiguration may be necessary after a failover. You may have to redirect your clients to request information only from the functioning server. Because each server has its own operating system, more disks are needed than in the Standby Recovery Server model.

FROM THE FIELD

Performance Considerations for Standby and Online Recovery Server Configurations

Before implementing a recovery server in your enterprise, it is essential to understand that overall disk subsystem performance may be dramatically affected by the recovery server installation. To provide data integrity for the array, you must disable the write-cache for all SMART controllers servicing shared storage. If disk subsystem performance is critical, it may be beneficial to look into an alternative increased availability offering from Compaq.

When evaluating the decision to utilize a standby or recovery server implementation, you may also want to consider failover time as part of the equation. In the standby configuration, the standby server is idling in a POST mode, thus forcing you to wait a predictable, but rather significant amount of time for the system to come back online.

To calculate the amount of time that will elapse before the server becomes available again, use the following guidelines:

- **Loss of Heartbeat** Depending on the type of failure, this can be a matter of seconds (catastrophic hardware failure) to several minutes in the case of a software failure.
- **Heartbeat Timeout** After the loss of the heartbeat signal, the server will wait a predetermined amount of time (1, 2, 3, 4, 5 or 10 minutes).
- **Array Initialization** The standby server must exit the looping POST routine and begin initialization of the array controller and drives.
- **Operating System Initialization** The time required to boot the operating system.
- **Application Initialization** The standby server becomes fully active only after all services and applications have been started.

In online configurations, the switchover time is less than that of the standby server because the drives are already initialized and the server is already booted to the operating system.

Whichever solution you choose for your enterprise, there is little doubt that a recovery server solution can provide a more proactive approach to maintaining customer expectations for system availability.

—Thomas Eck,
MCSE+I, MCSD, ASE, CCA, CNA

CERTIFICATION SUMMARY

In this chapter, we talked about the Compaq Recovery Server Option. There are two configurations for Compaq Recovery Server: Standby Recovery Server and Online Recovery Server. We talked about the requirements for each configuration. Standby Recovery Server is supported for Windows NT, Novell NetWare, SCO OpenServer, and SCO UnixWare. Online Recovery Server is only supported for Windows NT. Standby Recovery Server also requires that the two servers be identical; Online Recovery Server does not. We went through what happens during normal operation and when a failover occurs. We also discussed the advantages and the disadvantages of each configuration, to help you decide which configuration would be best for your organization.

TWO-MINUTE DRILL

- ❑ Recovery Server provides fault tolerance in the case of a hardware failure.
- ❑ There are two recovery server methodologies: Standby Recovery Server and Online Recovery Server.
- ❑ To help you determine which machines support online and standby configuration, consider the chart at http://www.compaq.com/solutions/enterprise/highavailability-rso-pid.html.
- ❑ Both Standby and Online Recovery Servers are simple to install.
- ❑ There are three different Recovery Server Option Kits.
- ❑ You will need to order one RSO kit for each ProLiant storage system used.
- ❑ For Standby Recovery Server, you must have one switchable ProLiant storage system with a recovery server switch installed and some type of SMART controller in each server attached to the storage system as well as other important requirements.
- ❑ For Online Recovery Server, you must have at least one local storage disk in each server for the operating system as well as other important requirements.

- In Standby Recovery Server, all disks are common to both servers.
- The disk arrangement for Online Recovery Server is a bit different. Not only are there hard disks in the ProLiant storage systems, there are also disks internal to each server.
- You must have one recovery server switch for each ProLiant storage system in your recovery server configuration.
- The key to both Online and Standby Recovery is the recovery server interconnect.
- The recovery server interconnect is a specially designed serial cable that connects the primary and the recovery server. This cable comes with the Recovery Server Option Kit.
- The heartbeat is a signal that lets each server know that it is still connected to the other server.
- A disconnected interconnect will stop the transmission of the heartbeat signal.
- Any event that keeps the primary server from sending the heartbeat signal would trigger a failover.
- Compaq designed its Recovery Server Option to be integrated with Insight Manager.
- When the primary server fails, you will receive alerts through Insight Manager.
- The Compaq Recovery Agent (CRA) is what actually monitors the heartbeat signal from the primary server.
- During normal operation in an Online Recovery Server configuration, both servers are online. Each server has its own identity.
- When deciding which configuration to institute in your environment, you must consider the advantages and disadvantages of each.

SELF TEST

The following Self Test questions will help you measure your understanding of the material presented in this chapter. Read all the choices carefully, as there may be more than one correct answer. Choose all correct answers for each question.

1. If you plan to build an OS/2 server, which recovery server configuration would be most beneficial?
   A. Online Recovery Server
   B. Standby Recovery Server
   C. Either of these
   D. None of these
2. What server can be used for the secondary server when the primary server is a ProLiant 5000 and you want to use Standby Recovery Server?
   A. ProLiant 5000
   B. ProLiant 6000
   C. ProLiant 1500
   D. All of these
3. You want to use Compaq Online Recovery Server. What operating systems can you use?
   A. Windows NT 4.0
   B. Novell NetWare 4.11
   C. SCO UnixWare
   D. SCO OpenServer
4. What events can trigger a failover in Compaq Standby Recovery Server?
   A. A disconnected interconnect
   B. A Windows NT trap (blue screen)
   C. A Novell NetWare abend
   D. All of these
5. You want to use Compaq Standby Recovery Server. What server platforms can you use to load Windows NT?
   A. ProLiant 7500
   B. ProLiant 6000
   C. ProLiant 3500
   D. All of these
6. In Standby Recovery Server, what is the secondary server doing while the primary server is running?
   A. Running a POST test
   B. Servicing user requests
   C. Running Windows NT diagnostics
   D. It is powered off.
7. Which of the following is not included in the Recovery Server Option Kit?
   A. A Fast-Wide SCSI-2 adapter cable
   B. Proliant Switchable array
   C. Two SCSI-2 hard drives
   D. All of these are included.

8. If your recovery server interconnect cable becomes damaged, which of the following can be used a replacement?
   A. A null modem cable
   B. A printer cable
   C. A straight through cable
   D. None of these
9. You want to use Compaq Standby Recovery Server. What operating system can you use?
   A. Windows NT 3.1
   B. Windows NT 3.51
   C. Novell NetWare 3.11
   D. All of the above
10. Which of the following controllers can be used to connect to the switchable ProLiant array?
    A. Fast SCSI-2
    B. Fast-Wide SCSI-2
    C. SMART-2DH
    D. All of these
11. You want to use Compaq Standby Recovery Server. What server platforms can you use to load Novell NetWare?
    A. ProLinea 566
    B. ProLiant 5000
    C. ProSignia 200
    D. None of these
12. What device is used to monitor the heartbeat signal and institute a failover?
    A. The SCSI array controller
    B. The recovery server interconnect
    C. The CRA
    D. The switchable array controller
13. Which of the following controllers can be used for the local disks in Compaq Online Recovery Server?
    A. SMART-2
    B. Fast-Wide SCSI-2
    C. SMART-2DH
    D. All of the above
14. If you are using Compaq Standby Recovery Server and have a NetFlex-3 controller in the primary server, what network controller can you use in the secondary server?
    A. NetFlex-2
    B. Netelligent
    C. NetFlex-3
    D. Any controller is fine.
15. You want to use Compaq Online Recovery Server. What server platforms can you use to load Novell NetWare?
    A. ProLiant 1500
    B. ProLiant 5000
    C. ProLiant 6000
    D. None of the above

Part II

Compaq Systems Management (Exam 010-078)

ASE
ACCREDITED SYSTEMS ENGINEER

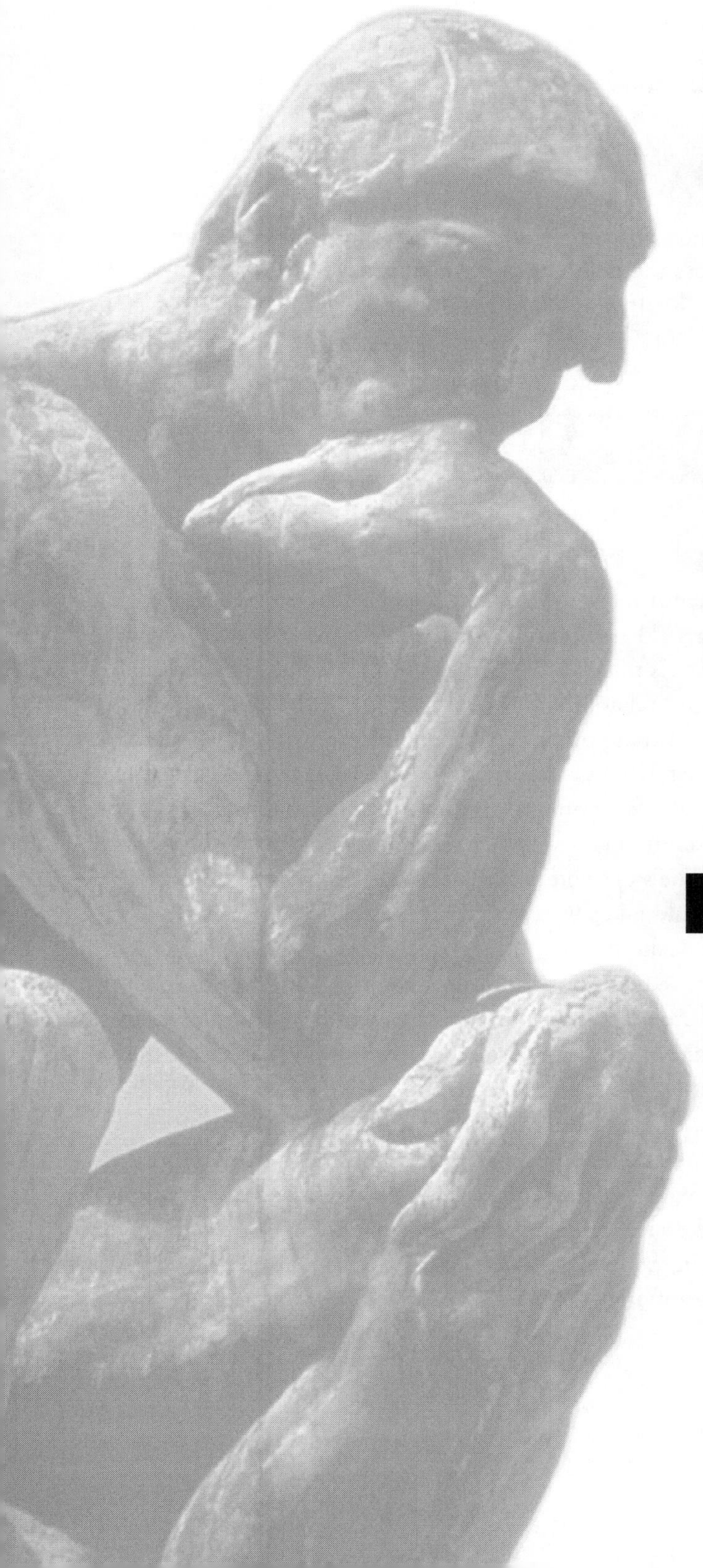

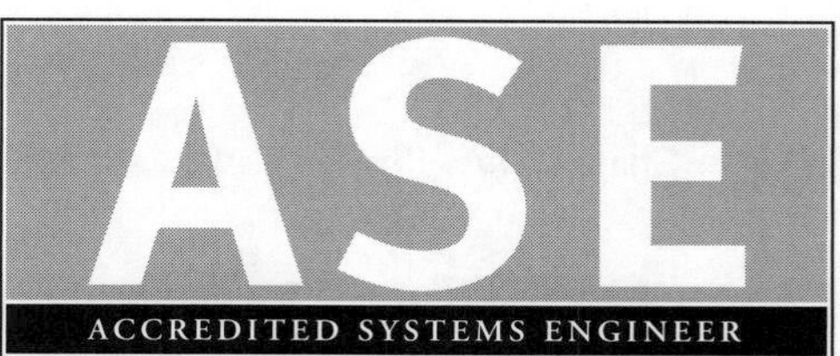

17

Systems Management Overview

CERTIFICATION OBJECTIVES

17.01 Network Management

17.02 Management Platforms

17.03 Management Applications

This chapter covers both network management and systems management, and the purposes of each. We will discuss the difference between management platforms and management applications. A rundown of some of the more popular management platforms and applications will also be presented.

CERTIFICATION OBJECTIVE 17.01

Network Management

Network management involves the management of the physical and logical network components. These components include hubs, routers, and the information that travels through the network. There are three main goals of network management: reliability, low overhead, and efficiency.

It is very important that you have a dependable network. If you can't rely on your network, then what good is it? You don't want users constantly wondering if the network is going to go down, or if their data is being lost or corrupted. You should take every step, within reason, that you can to reduce downtime. The steps you take may be limited because of your budget, but you should take all steps that are feasible. You will save yourself a lot of headaches.

You should try to reduce your administrative overhead. A well-developed network will eliminate the need for an excessive number of administrators. This will not only aid in reducing costs, but it can save you a lot of trouble. Too many administrators can lead to confusion. If one administrator makes a change and doesn't notify the others about the change and why it was made, you could end up with one administrator undoing what another just did. If your organization is such that you must have multiple administrators, make sure changes are well documented. There's no greater frustration than trying to manage a network that someone else keeps changing without notifying you.

on the job

I had a friend who worked for a company that had many remote clients. This company had several engineers who serviced these clients remotely. The problem was that the engineers did not communicate with each other. They were always undoing each other's work. When one engineer made a change, he or she wouldn't let the others know. So, when the next engineer came along to troubleshoot a problem, he would reconfigure the system to the way he was most comfortable with, not knowing that settings were different for a reason. Needless to say, there were always a bunch of angry techs. This could have all been avoided if they just communicated with each other.

An efficient network is a cost-effective network. It is the network administrator's job to make sure that network components are running efficiently. Inefficiently configured network components can lead to a drop in overall network performance. A slow network can be almost as bad a down network. You should make sure that you do not have unnecessary nodes attached to the network. This will reduce both costs and network traffic. You should also make sure that your equipment is upgraded when necessary. Upgrading too soon may be a waste of money. Not upgrading soon enough may cause a drop in performance.

on the job

Remember newer is not always better. If there is no real reason to do an upgrade, then you probably shouldn't. Upgrades almost always introduce new problems. Why take the chance if it isn't necessary? I'm not saying you should keep equipment for twenty or thirty years. Just upgrade cautiously.

Systems Management

Systems management covers a wide range of topics. It involves the entire working environment. Systems management can be broken down into five categories: desktop management, configuration management, performance management, fault management, and security management.

First, we'll discuss desktop management. This involves the management of the user desktops. Desktop management incorporates the installation and maintenance of client hardware and software. It is your responsibility to ensure that users' desktops appear the way you want them to. One way to achieve this is with system and user policies. You can use the Policy Editor for Windows NT (shown in Figure 17-1) or Novell's ZENworks.

Configuration management involves making sure that workstations and servers are configured the way you want them to be. This, too, can be accomplished with the use of policies. If you have control over system configurations, you can ensure that all systems are running as efficiently as possible.

Performance management is used to ensure efficiency. You can start by instituting a configuration that will maximize your system performance. Then baselines can be established. When a system falls below the established baseline, you know it is time to do some performance tuning. The

FIGURE 17-1

Windows NT Policy Editor

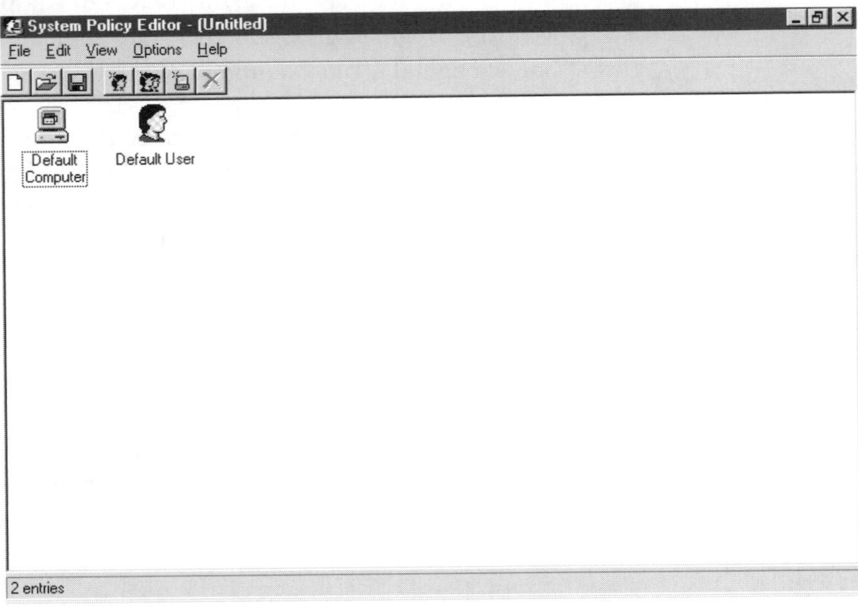

Windows NT Performance Monitor, shown in Figure 17-2, can be of great use to you. You can use it to monitor performance of various systems components. Performance Monitor can monitor, log, and report on everything from available memory to disk utilization.

Fault management is another name for disaster recovery and disaster prevention. Fault management can be accomplished with the institution of a reliable RAID or backup system. An uninterruptible power source (UPS) is also a good device to use when considering fault management.

Security management is very important. You must protect your data. Inadequate security can lead to corruption or even loss of data. Security management doesn't just mean protecting your systems from outside users or users with malicious intent. The average user within your organization can be a security risk. You wouldn't want employees to be able to access sensitive information that is not intended for them; such as payroll information. You also wouldn't want to put a user in a position where he or she could accidentally delete important data. Properly securing your

FIGURE 17-2

Windows NT Performance Monitor, chart view

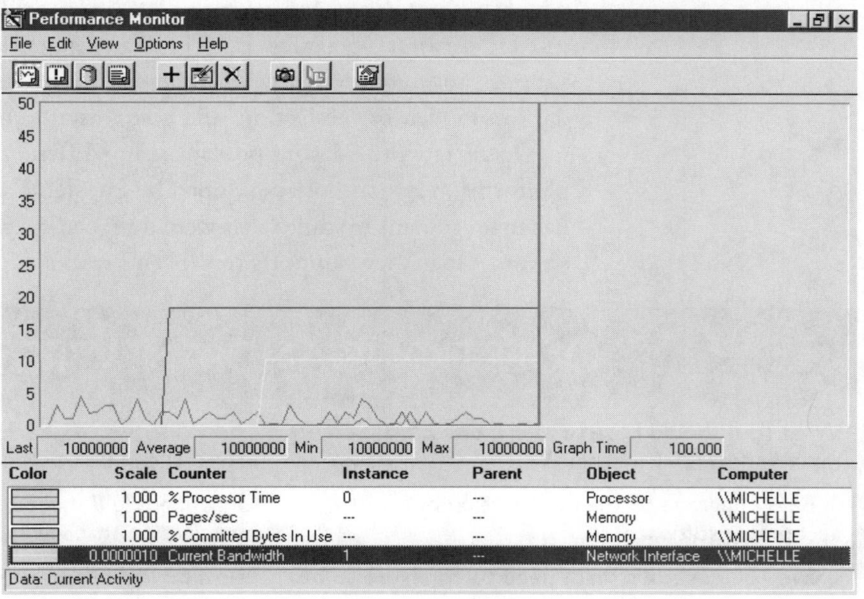

environment might mean instituting passwords and password policies and setting file permissions.

CERTIFICATION OBJECTIVE 17.02

Management Platforms

Management platforms are intended to provide a total network or systems management solution. Management platforms are often comprised of smaller, more specialized units. These units piece together to form the total solution. There are several management platforms on the market today, including HP OpenView, IBM NetView, Novell ManageWise, and SunNet Manager. We will concern ourselves with the first three.

HP OpenView

The HP OpenView Management platform provides support for more than just HP servers. OpenView is a true management platform, meaning it supports several different environments. It offers installation management, data and inventory collection, and configuration management.

OpenView provides support for many different hardware and software platforms, not just those developed by Hewlett Packard. In fact, OpenView has management modules that were designed specifically for other types of servers. OpenView supports servers and workstations running Windows,

QUESTIONS AND ANSWERS	
What tool should I use to check disk utilization on my Windows NT machine?	The Windows NT Performance Monitor can be use to check disk utilization
Should I upgrade to the new version of my accounting software?	Only upgrade if there are enhancements in the new version that will be of use to you
I have 100 desktops that I need to configure to be exactly the same. What is the best way to do this?	Use a policy creation application and apply the policy to all of the desktops

FROM THE FIELD

HP OpenView

As Internet related technologies proliferate at breakneck speeds, there is little doubt that customer's uptime expectations are also substantially increased. While IT support is all too often a reactive process, there are several tools that will help you take a more proactive approach to managing your enterprise.

HP OpenView is often considered the de facto standard for a wide variety of management tasks. Although the base product is a fairly robust SNMP console (with the ability to compile MIBs, etc.), HP offers additional components that will allow management of everything from Application Management through Web Transaction Observation.

Even though it is not the ultimate panacea for dissolving a highly reactive environment, HP OpenView is clearly a step in the right direction. The list of components offered to extend this management platform is impressive in and of itself. Check out http://www.openview.hp.com/products to learn more.

In addition to HP developed modules, numerous third parties take advantage of the extensible nature of OpenView and produce highly customized components to manage their processes, hardware, and software. If you have a large development team in your enterprise, you too can customize OpenView to create views that will allow your IT personnel to identify problems before a call hits first-line support.

—Thomas E. Eck, MCSE+I, MCSD, ASE, CCA, CNA

NetWare, and UNIX. This is due to the fact that OpenView is based on the Simple Network Management Protocol (SNMP). SNMP is platform independent; it allows OpenView to manage any of these operating systems, provided the system is running the SNMP protocol.

OpenView allows you to perform mass installations. You can install software on multiple computers across the network without visiting the desktops one-by-one. Just configure the setup options you want and OpenView will handle the rest. OpenView also provides an easy way to install its software to all the machines on your network.

HP OvenView can be used to collect data from the machines on your network. It allows you to do a network inventory of all the nodes on your network. This lets you know what you have and where it is. Inventories can be of great benefit when the time comes to consider upgrades and plan for the future.

OpenView also can do configuration management. You can apply configuration policies to the nodes on your network. This will ensure that all servers and workstations are configured efficiently. The best part is that you don't have to configure each machine separately; OpenView does it for you.

IBM NetView

NetView is an SNMP network management platform. It supports a multitude of network environments and allows you to centralize management of your diverse network. NetView is an open environment platform, which means that third-party applications can be integrated into the NetView platform.

At the root of NetView are object collections. You can organize your collections around certain criteria. This allows you to collect information only on network components that you are concerned about. NetView will provide real-time information about your network components.

NetView also allows for the creation of policies. With the NetView Policy Manager, you can issue a policy to one or multiple network devices. This can be a great advantage to you when you have multiple network devices that need to be configured.

NetView also allows you to save information about your components. This will aid in the development of baselines. Baselines can be very important in problem diagnosis. A well-developed and definitive baseline can help point out where your network may be having problems. You will be able to tell which components are not performing up to their usual levels.

Using NetView, you can capture network packets, which can be deciphered and analyzed. Packet analysis can provide answers to some of your more complex network problems. You can determine which devices are sending out broadcast messages that may be flooding the network. You can also find out which devices are sending out "garbage" packets.

Protocol analyzers can provide simple answers to what seem like very complex problems. I was at one client site that had both Windows NT and NetWare servers. The client was preparing for a coming hurricane, so they downed all of their servers. Thankfully, the hurricane never came. But, after they turned their servers back on, their network was extremely slow. No one could figure out why. Finally, we used a network monitor. The monitor showed that all IPX traffic bound for the NetWare servers was routing through one of the Windows NT servers. Apparently, the Windows NT server came up first, and assumed the role of the primary IPX router.

NetView can be configured to alert you in response to network problems. Alerts can be sent through paging e-mail and voice mail. You can configure network thresholds, and when these thresholds are met, a report is generated alerting you to the problem. Say you have a network segment that you suspect is being overloaded. You can set an event to alert you when a predefined threshold is met. According to the frequency of the alerts, you can decide if that segment needs to be further divided in order to reduce traffic.

Novell ManageWise

ManageWise is the network management platform developed by Novell. ManageWise is based on SNMP, the industry standard for network management. SNMP can be used to control everything from workstations to routers. ManageWise allows you to monitor servers, Novell Directory Services, and network traffic.

With the SNMP protocol, ManageWise allows you to control all of your network resources from one location. A workstation running SNMP and the management console together can monitor and control almost any SNMP-enabled device. A ManageWise monitoring station can analyze network traffic, do file transfers, modify device configurations, and gather inventory and performance information.

ManageWise provides an alarm monitoring system. This can be very helpful in notifying you of a device failure. ManageWise can also alert you to pending problems through the use of built-in thresholds. You can minimize downtime by taking care of potential problems before they occur. There are close to a thousand alarms available in Novell ManageWise. ManageWise includes a large number of alarms available for Novell's Directory Services.

ManageWise is not just limited to Novell servers; it can be used to monitor both Novell NetWare and Windows NT servers. All that is necessary is to load the management agent on the desired servers. You can monitor disk space, volume sizes, available memory, and much more. You can establish performance baselines that will aid in problem detection.

ManageWise also comes with a remote-control feature. ManageWise can be used to remotely manage Windows 3.*x*, Windows 95/98, Windows NT, DOS, and OS/2 workstations. You can manipulate files through editing or file transfers. You can remotely control applications on a user's desktop. You can also set up a process to notify you when a user's config files change.

ManageWise provides network inventory functionality. You can inventory workstations, servers, routers, and most other network devices. This will give you a complete listing of what is on your network. You can get a listing of all the hardware and software on your client workstations. ManageWise comes with several built-in reports that can be customized to display only the network information that is of interest to you. Network inventories can assist in planning and troubleshooting.

ManageWise also provides network analysis with Novell's LANalyzer. The LANalyzer can monitor traffic on Ethernet, Fast Ethernet, Token Ring, and FDDI networks. It can display real-time network statistics, which will help in identifying bottlenecks and other network problems. The Novell LANalyzer can also be used to develop baseline and trend information.

ManageWise includes InocuLAN antivirus software. InocuLAN is a product of Computer Associates. InocuLAN can provide virus protection on both servers and workstations. A ManageWise license allows you complete access to all of the InocuLAN virus updates that are available on the Computer Associates Web site.

ManageWise also provides support for various management applications. It currently supports management applications from Compaq and Seagate, among other companies.

CERTIFICATION OBJECTIVE 17.03

Management Applications

Management applications are usually written by hardware or software companies in order to allow management of their products. Some examples of management applications are HP NetServer Assistant, Cabletron Spectrum, and Network General Sniffer. The management application we will be concerned with is Compaq's Insight Manager.

Compaq Insight Manager

Insight Manager is the management application supplied by Compaq to manage Compaq servers and desktops. Insight Manager is a robust management application that allows data collection, reporting, and alerting.

The Compaq management agents are the key to Insight Manager. The management agents can be obtained from the SmartStart Management CD. There are different sets of agents for servers and for desktops. The agents use the SNMP protocol, which must be loaded before the management agents can be loaded.

The next step is to set up a management workstation. First, SNMP must be loaded onto the management station. Next, you must load the Insight Manager application. After configuring the management console (shown in Figure 17-3), you are ready for data collection.

You can start with just the basic system configuration data. This includes processors, memory, and disk space. You can also collect more advanced statistics. For instance, you can gather network adapter and disk controller information and much more.

The information you collect can be prepared into comprehensive reports. You can organize these reports according to machines, groups of machines, or like characteristics. For instance, you can develop a report on all machines with 200 MHz Pentium processors. Insight Manager comes with dozens of built-in reports, but you can also create your own.

FIGURE 17-3

Insight Manager management console

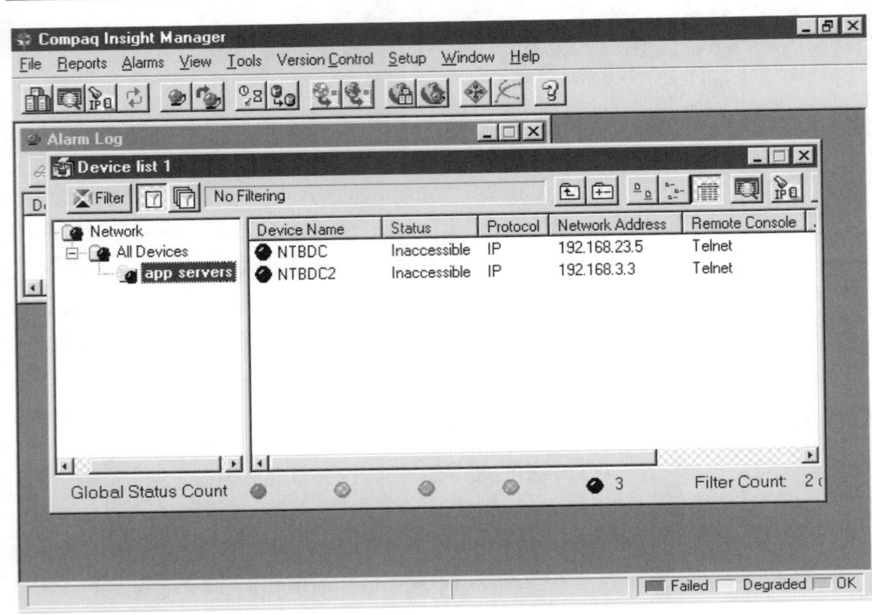

Insight Manager also provides alerts. You can be alerted when a preconfigured event occurs. Alerts can be visible, audible, or sent through e-mail or alphanumeric pager. You can configure an alert to be sent on one of the events predefined by Compaq, or when a user-defined threshold is exceeded.

CERTIFICATION SUMMARY

Management can be divided into systems management and network management. Management products can be classified as management platforms or management applications. Three of the more common management platforms are Novell ManageWise, IBM NetView, and HP OpenView. Some of the more common management applications are HP NetServer Assistant, Cabletron Spectrum, Network General Sniffer, and

Compaq Insight Manager. Management platforms are robust products that offer integration with several different environments. Management applications are more specialized programs that offer support usually for just one type of environment.

✓ TWO-MINUTE DRILL

- ❑ Network management involves the management of the physical and logical network components and include hubs, routers, and the information that travels through the network.
- ❑ The three main goals of network management are reliability, low overhead, and efficiency.
- ❑ Systems management can be broken down into five categories:
  - ❑ Desktop management
  - ❑ Configuration management
  - ❑ Performance management
  - ❑ Fault management
  - ❑ Security management
- ❑ Desktop management incorporates the installation and maintenance of client hardware and software.
- ❑ Configuration management involves making sure that workstations and servers are configured the way you want them to be.
- ❑ Performance management is used to ensure efficiency.
- ❑ Fault management is another name for disaster recovery and disaster prevention.
- ❑ Security management is very important and is used to protect your data. Inadequate security can lead to corruption or even loss of data.
- ❑ Management platforms are intended to provide a total network or systems management solution.

- HP OpenView supports several different environments. It offers installation management, data and inventory collection, and configuration management.
- IBM NetView is an SNMP network management platform, which supports a multitude of network environments and allows you to centralize management of your diverse network.
- Novell ManageWise is based on SNMP and allows you to monitor servers, Novell Directory Services, and network traffic.
- Management applications are usually written by hardware or software companies in order to allow management of their products.
- Insight Manager is the management application supplied by Compaq to manage Compaq servers and desktops.
- Insight Manager is a robust management application that allows data collection, reporting, and alerting.

SELF TEST

The following Self Test questions will help you measure your understanding of the material presented in this chapter. Read all the choices carefully, as there may be more than one correct answer. Choose all correct answers for each question.

1. Which of the following is not a management application?
   A. Insight Manager
   B. Network General Sniffer
   C. HP NetServer Assistant
   D. HP OpenView
2. Which of the following is not a management platform?
   A. IBM NetView
   B. Novell ManageWise
   C. Insight Manager
   D. All are platforms
3. Which is not a part of systems management?
   A. Security management
   B. Performance management
   C. Configuration management
   D. All are a part of systems management.
4. Which is not a goal of network management?
   A. Reliability
   B. Low overhead
   C. Efficiency
   D. All are goals of network management.
5. What application would you use to monitor your hard disk performance?
   A. Performance Monitor
   B. Policy Editor
   C. Profile Monitor
   D. ZENworks
6. You are getting slow performance from your network. What should you use to check your network statistics?
   A. Policy Editor
   B. Performance Monitor
   C. LANalyzer
   D. NetShow
7. You want all of your Windows NT Server users to have the same desktop. What should you use?
   A. Windows NT Policy Editor
   B. LANalyzer
   C. Performance Monitor
   D. ZENworks
8. You want all of your NetWare Server users to have the same desktop. What should you use?
   A. ZENworks
   B. Windows NT Policy Editor
   C. Performance Monitor
   D. None of the above

9. Under which management category does RAID fall?

   A. Security management
   B. Desktop management
   C. Fault management
   D. Configuration management

10. Under which management category do equipment upgrades fall?

   A. Desktop management
   B. Security management
   C. Configuration management
   D. Network management

11. Which of the following can be the result of a lack of data security?

   A. Data corruption
   B. Data loss
   C. Compromised confidentiality
   D. All of the above

12. Which of the following is not a function of Novell ManageWise?

   A. Software distribution
   B. Remote control
   C. File transfers
   D. All are functions of ManageWise.

13. What can be done to protect your data from harm?

   A. Password implementation
   B. Set file permissions
   C. Physically secure your equipment
   D. All of the above

14. What is the management protocol used by IBM NetView?

   A. SMTP
   B. SNMP
   C. TCP
   D. UDP

15. Which of the following is not a feature of Insight Manager?

   A. Reporting
   B. Alerts
   C. Software distribution
   D. Data collection

ASE
ACCREDITED SYSTEMS ENGINEER

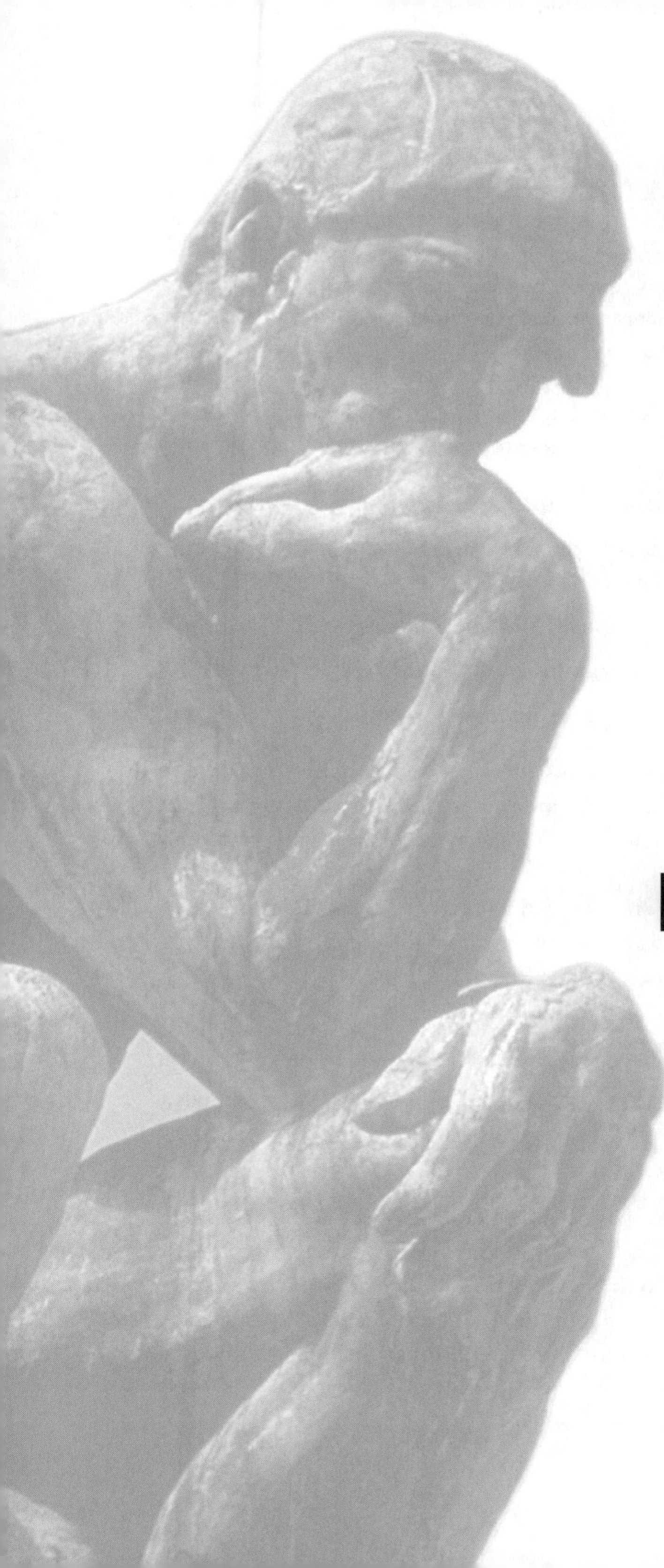

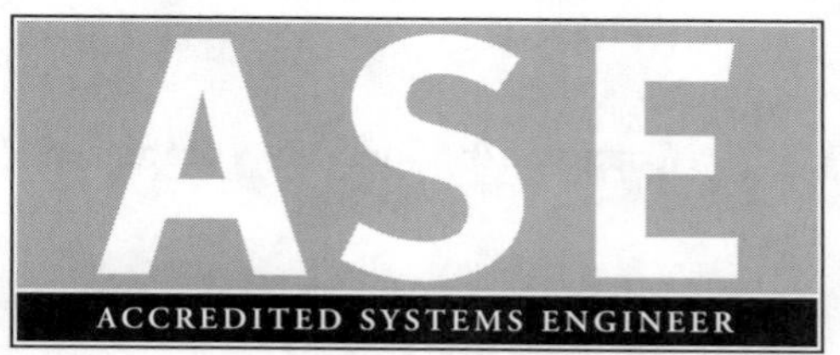

18

Industry Vocabulary

CERTIFICATION OBJECTIVES

18.01 SNMP
18.02 SET
18.03 GET
18.04 Traps
18.05 Community Names
18.06 Requirements for SNMP Usage
18.07 Management Agents
18.08 MIB

In this chapter, we will cover the technology surrounding SNMP (Simple Network Management Protocol). This protocol is one of the main components behind Compaq Insight Manager and therefore, it is imperative that you understand how SNMP fits into the management architecture.

To provide an understanding of the protocol's architecture, we will be covering a variety of topics. These topics will include such items as:

- Defining the components that make up network management
- The differences between a management application and a management agent
- What devices are usually managed on a network
- How SNMP applications communicate across a network
- The requirements for using SNMP successfully in your environment

All of these topics will be instrumental in providing you with the information you will need to understand SNMP, configure and use Compaq's management suite (Compaq Insight Manager), and prepare for your Compaq exam.

By the end of this chapter, you will have a thorough knowledge of how SNMP functions and will be able to apply the concepts to what you will be learning in the Compaq Insight Manager chapters.

CERTIFICATION OBJECTIVE 18.01

SNMP

Network management has become a crucial aspect of the network administrator's job. The need to monitor, view, and configure devices on the network has led to the introduction of many management systems that make an administrator's day-to-day work much easier to manage. At the same time, administrators get better control of their environments and provide better uptime of network services.

When looking at the framework of any good management system, we will see a system built on five components:

- Platform
- Application
- Agent
- Element
- Protocol

In this chapter, we will focus primarily on the protocol portion of this architecture, but to get the most out of the discussion, we need to define each of these components individually.

At the highest level, we have the management platform. This can be defined simply as the system on which the management application and agent will function.

The next two components are the agent and the application. A management application is a program that provides us with the interface to communicate with an agent. Compaq Insight Manager is a perfect example of a management application. A management agent is a software application that resides on the managed device. This component defines the information made available to the management application.

Compaq Insight Agents are an example of a management agent. Understanding the difference between these two components is a very important aspect of the SNMP architecture. It is also important to note that the management agent is not always installed on a computer. Many network devices, such as routers and switches, run a form of an SNMP-configurable agent.

The objects that a management application makes available are called elements. The most common elements on a network are servers, workstations, printers, and network devices such as routers, bridges, and switches. Vendors can also define elements that are subsystems of these devices. For example, not only can a server be defined as an element, but devices such as the processor, hard disks, network adapters, and drive controllers can also be defined as elements.

The protocol provides the means for the agent and application to communicate with one another. As its name implies, SNMP is an example of a management protocol. SNMP has emerged as the industry standard and is used as the protocol of most standards-based management platforms.

SNMP, as explained by Compaq, defines a set of commands that a management application uses to retrieve or change the values made available by a management agent. In simpler terms, it provides a means of communication between a device that we wish to manage, and the system we wish to use to manage it.

To perform its function as defined above, SNMP uses a set of commands (called SET and GET) to communicate with information made available to it by the management agent. The management agent contains all of the parameters that are available to the SNMP client. The information made available can consist of performance thresholds, error conditions, or even device configurations. It is limited only by what information has been defined in the management agent. Another way SNMP communicates is by using a trap. A trap is SNMP's means of notifying or alerting us of a specific condition.

SNMP communicates over the TCP/IP network protocol. This allows for SNMP's use across many network systems and devices. SNMP is used in the industry for everything from configuring and monitoring routers, to the performance of a hard disk array on a Windows NT server. Because of its simplicity and capabilities, SNMP has also been selected as the protocol on which many vendors have based their management solutions.

on the job

The ability to take a proactive approach to managing your network is vital to your success on the job. The use of a management application allows you to monitor your network, even a very large network, with great ease and flexibility. In many cases, it even allows you to become aware of a problem before it becomes a big problem. For example, finding out that your processor is consistently exceeding a threshold, your hard disk is about to fail, or your network switch is encountering a significant number of dropped packets is especially useful to providing a reliable network to your end users. Implementing a network management solution is well worth the cost, if only because of the improved confidence it will bring to the staff supporting it.

CERTIFICATION OBJECTIVE 18.02

SET

The SET command is the first of two commands used by the management application. This command is used to perform the write function of the SNMP protocol. It is used to change, or set, the parameters available in the management agent.

As shown in Figure 18-1, the SET command is actually a two-way communication. The first is the actual SET command itself. This portion contains the information to be set on the management agent. The second portion is in the form of a response trap. This trap simply provides the management application with an acknowledgment that the SET was completed successfully.

Let's say we wanted to define a threshold on our processor utilization. From our management application, we could define a processor utilization of 80 percent. The management application would then send a SET to the management agent configuring the threshold on the managed device.

We will use this processor utilization example throughout this chapter. This will provide us with a common example for many of the different features and functions of SNMP.

FIGURE 18-1 Two-way communication of a SET command

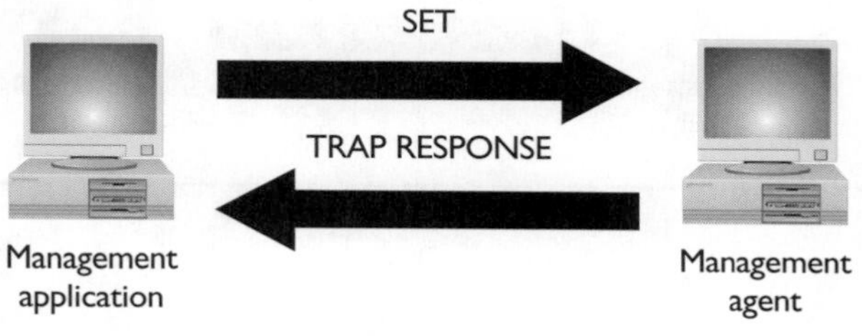

CERTIFICATION OBJECTIVE 18.03

GET

The GET command should be considered the read function of SNMP. When a management application needs to retrieve information from the agent, it uses the GET command to do so.

As with the SET command, the GET command is obviously a two-way process, as shown in Figure 18-2. This time, instead of simply an acknowledgment, the response trap contains the information requested by the GET.

Keeping with our earlier example, let's say we wished to retrieve a managed device's current processor utilization. From our management application, we could query the current processor utilization on the managed device. The application would then send a GET to the managed device. The managed device's agent would process this command and return the information to your application interface, where you would then see the results.

FIGURE 18-2 Two-way communication of the GET command

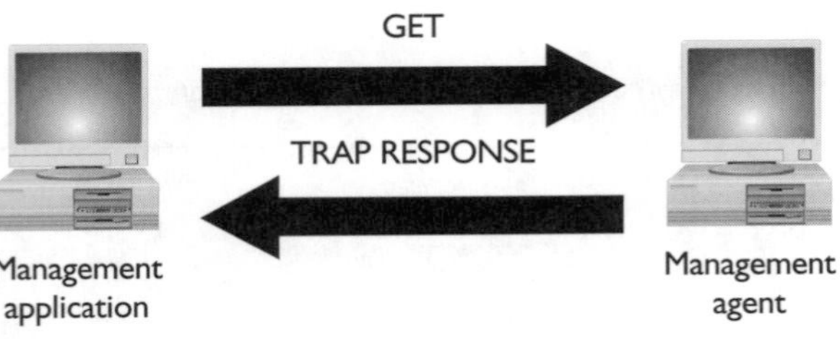

CERTIFICATION OBJECTIVE 18.04

Traps

You have already seen two situations that rely on the use of a trap. Both the SET and GET commands use traps to function. There is one more use of the trap that we have not yet discussed. SNMP agents also have the capability to send an unsolicited trap to a management application based on defined, event-driven criteria.

To understand this aspect of SNMP, let's first discuss the concept of event-driven criteria. A simple way of looking at it is that when a specific event occurs, a specific action should take place. On the job as a Compaq-certified professional, this event could be anything from a software application error to the failure of a managed hardware device, such as a hard disk. In the world of SNMP, the course of action taken is usually to send a message, or trap.

Let's take another look at our CPU utilization threshold, which we discussed earlier. We have seen how we can set this threshold using our management application and the SET command. We have also seen how using the GET command allows us to retrieve the managed object's current CPU utilization. Both of these are nice features to have, but they require us to take action to use any of the information available. We are only made aware of a potential problem if we happen to check the status at the exact moment the problem exists. The trap provides us with a means of being alerted at the moment our threshold is exceeded. When the CPU utilization exceeds 80 percent, the threshold is crossed. The management agent sends the trap to the predetermined location(s). Most management applications are capable of making us aware of the trap by a variety of methods. They support methods as basic as simply logging the trap, to more complex e-mail notifications.

Unlike the SET/GET commands, a trap is only a one-way communication process, as shown in Figure 18-3. This means that when the agent sends the trap, it has no way of knowing whether it was received or not. Providing that the trap destinations are defined correctly and the network is correctly configured and operating, this should not pose too many problems for you.

The destination to which the trap is sent is determined by the SNMP configuration. In Windows NT, the trap destinations are configured within the SNMP Service configuration under Network Properties. Trap destinations are the IP address or network name of the machine to receive the traps. Management agents, such as Compaq Insight Agents, will then use this configuration to determine the trap recipients. Most often, the traps will be sent to the management application. From here, the traps will be recorded and processed accordingly.

on the job

The use of SNMP traps is perhaps one of the most important aspects of an SNMP-based management platform. Often a trap will alert you to a problem and allow you to fix it before you get that panicked call, or that line of angry end users begins to form outside your office. Many management platforms, including Compaq Insight Manager, allow you to configure trap forwarding. This allows you to configure your management application to notify you of a potential problem via e-mail or a page.

FIGURE 18-3 One-way communication of a trap

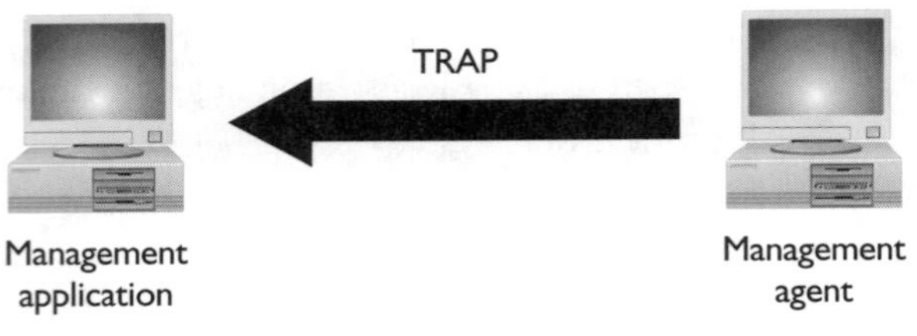

CERTIFICATION OBJECTIVE 18.05

Community Names

By now, you are starting to see some of the power that SNMP brings to you for managing resources on your network. However, you are also probably starting to see that you don't want just anybody to have access to the managed objects that you use SNMP to control. Community names are SNMP's security solution.

A good way to look at a community name is as a password. When configuring SNMP, you provide a list of community names that will have access to the managed objects on the system. Then, the same community name must be supplied in the management application. If the community names match, the application will be permitted to communicate with the management agent. If the names do not match, then access will be denied and no exchange of information will take place. An important detail to note here is that community names are case-sensitive. This is often the cause of many communication problems between the management agent and the management application, for those new to the process.

By default, many applications and systems use the community name of "public." It is recommended that you not only use a different name for your systems, but also remove the "public" community name from the configuration. Because the community name is like a password, the community name you select should be something that would be difficult for outsiders to guess. If users were able to determine your community name, they would have access to whatever capabilities that the management agent provided. The rebooting of a remote computer is an example of a feature available to a server running Compaq Insight Agents that you would probably not want to make available to your general user base. (Note: The Remote Reboot option is not enabled by default, but provides an example of a feature available to SNMP that would require some security measure to be in place.)

Care should be taken when choosing the community name. Because there are many different types of devices that can utilize SNMP, each with its own set of management capabilities, you may want to use more than one community name. For example, you probably don't want to use the same community name for your network switches or routers as you do for your Windows NT servers. This will provide an additional layer of security between the different devices in your enterprise, while also allowing more separation in the management tools that you use.

The SNMP configuration offers one additional layer of security. For each community name provided, two potential security settings exist. The first option is READ while the second is READ/CREATE (read/write). This configuration option allows you to use separate levels of security for your environment. For example, if you wanted a group of individuals only to be able to view the elements in your network, you could create one community string that was only set up with READ permission. You would then want to configure the management application to use this restricted community name. Then you could use a second community string for those users whom you wish to allow to modify the elements provided by the management agent.

on the Job

In many larger network enterprises, the roles and responsibilities of support are spread across many different groups. These groups are often of varying experience and expertise and their responsibilities are often different. For example, many organizations use a tiered-support approach, with responsibility and expertise increasing with each tier. Because of this, it is often necessary to provide one group a more restricted level of control than the one above it. Using two community names allows you the flexibility you need to accomplish this. For example, if your organization has a network operations group responsible for frontline support, you may need them to have read control to your network management solution, but you don't want them to be able to change a configuration. You also may have a network administration group that needs to have the ability to configure the management platform. With the use of two community names, along with the appropriate security settings, you can be sure that everyone has the resources they need to perform their jobs, without the fear that someone has too much control.

CERTIFICATION OBJECTIVE 18.06

Requirements for SNMP Usage

SNMP requirements are rather simple. To function, it only needs a network to communicate across, an application that utilizes SNMP, and an agent that defines the objects (elements) to be managed.

With Windows NT, the SNMP service can be installed through the Network Properties interface on the Services tab. Once installed, there are only a few configuration requirements you have to meet before SNMP will be ready for use.

First, upon installing the service, you will be asked to provide the community names that you wish to use. Because you may be using multiple applications, each with its own community string, you are able to enter more than one. As noted, community names are case-sensitive, so be sure to enter each one correctly. An incorrectly entered community name will result in the failure of SNMP application communication.

The second configuration option you will need to enter is the SNMP trap destination. This option tells the SNMP service where to send traps that the management agent wishes to send. This way, when the CPU threshold that we have configured is crossed, the trap will know where to go so that we are made aware of the situation and can look into the problem.

It is important to note that both the SNMP service and the TCP/IP protocol must be installed for Compaq Insight Manager to function. In fact, besides the hardware requirements required by Compaq Insight Manager, these are the only two common requirements that need to be present for this management platform to function.

CERTIFICATION OBJECTIVE 18.07

Management Agents

So far, we have referred to an agent primarily as a software application that has been installed on a managed device. However, because these devices are not always capable of running applications (such as in the case of a network bridge), agents can also reside in the device's firmware. Any device that is going to be managed must be defined as an element within the management agent.

The agent code defines all of the parameters available to the management system. They can either be written into a device's software driver or incorporated as a separate application. This separate application will communicate with the device either through its driver or firmware to provide these parameters to the management system. Compaq has chosen to use the separate-application approach in their management agent software.

The easiest way to look at the role the management agent plays in your management system is as a middleman. Basically, the agent provides the interface between your management application and the element you are managing.

CERTIFICATION OBJECTIVE 18.08

MIB

So far in this chapter, we have looked at the role the management agent plays. We have discussed the fact that the agent provides the definition of a managed element to the application. What we haven't discussed is how these definitions are formatted. Before we do, let's spell out exactly what information these definitions contain. Basically, the definition contains the properties of the object defined, the functions that are supported against the object, and the information that can be retrieved on the object. We refer to these definitions as the Management Information Base (MIB).

Now let's take this information and look at it in a way we can understand. To do this, we will return to our CPU utilization example. In this example, the CPU represents our element. The CPU's utilization would represent an example of a property, as would the CPU utilization threshold that we have been working with. Using the SET command to define the threshold would be an example of a function that can be performed against the object. The CPU's utilization or trap are examples of information that can be obtained or retrieved from the object.

The CPU utilization model is an easy way to look at a MIB; it is very simple in its structure. Many managed elements actually contain hundreds or even thousands of pieces of information. In order to handle this amount of information, a structured format is needed to make the MIB manageable. It is equally important, if not more so, to ensure that the definitions used by one organization will never interfere or conflict with that of another. To accomplish this, the collection of information is organized in a hierarchical structure, where it is made available to the network management protocol (SNMP). This structure is in a complex, tree format that is a based on an equally complex numbering system. Each MIB is represented by a numeric object identifier. This tree is actually a global entity with each vendor (or on a larger scale, each organization) being given its own branch and numbering range to use. This is done very much the same way IP addressing is structured.

Internet Assigned Numbers Authority and MIB Creation

As mentioned, the MIB format is tree based on a numeric value system. At the top of this tree are the branches assigned to the various standards organizations. The Internet Assigned Numbers Authority is one of these standards organizations. It is the responsibility of this standards organization to delegate the administration of the numeric identifier and range that each vendor or organization can use.

Once a vendor has been supplied with its own range of MIB identifiers, it can then define the objects it wishes those MIBs to contain. Each number the vendor is given can be assigned to a different element that the vendor wishes to make available to its management platform.

This process assures that each vendor has a unique identifier and thereby eliminates the possibility of two vendors creating MIBs that can conflict with one another.

Managed Elements

At the beginning of the chapter, you were given a simple description of an element. It was defined as an object that a management agent makes available to the management application. Now that you have been introduced to the term MIB, it is safe to tell you that these elements are sometimes called MIB objects.

In the simplest form, a managed element, is a server, workstation, or network device (router, switch, bridge, hub) that you wish to manage. Many vendors break these elements into the various subsystems. For example, let's say that we have a managed element that is a Windows NT server on our network. The vendor can then define the hard disk on this server as another element. To go another step, the various drive parameters such as read/write buffers and I/O errors can be defined as yet another set of managed elements.

Each of these elements is identified using one of the numeric identifiers provided to the vendor by the Internet Assigned Numbers Authority. Each of these subsystems falls on a branch further down the MIB tree, as Figure 18-4 illustrates. (This figure does not represent the MIB tree in its entirety; there are many sections of the tree that are not represented in this figure. However, it should provide you with a basic overview of how the tree is structured in the MIB definition process. This tree will also aid in obtaining an understanding on the next section, "Object Definitions.")

Object Definitions

Each object definition or MIB is uniquely identified in the MIB hierarchy by a numeric identifier called an object ID. These numbers are assigned by the Internet Assigned Numbers Authority. The next thing we're going to look at is just how these numeric values correspond to the objects defined on the MIB tree.

To best explain this, we will use Compaq's MIB as our example. This example will not only work to demonstrate how the MIB numbering

FIGURE 18-4 Representation of the MIB hierarchy

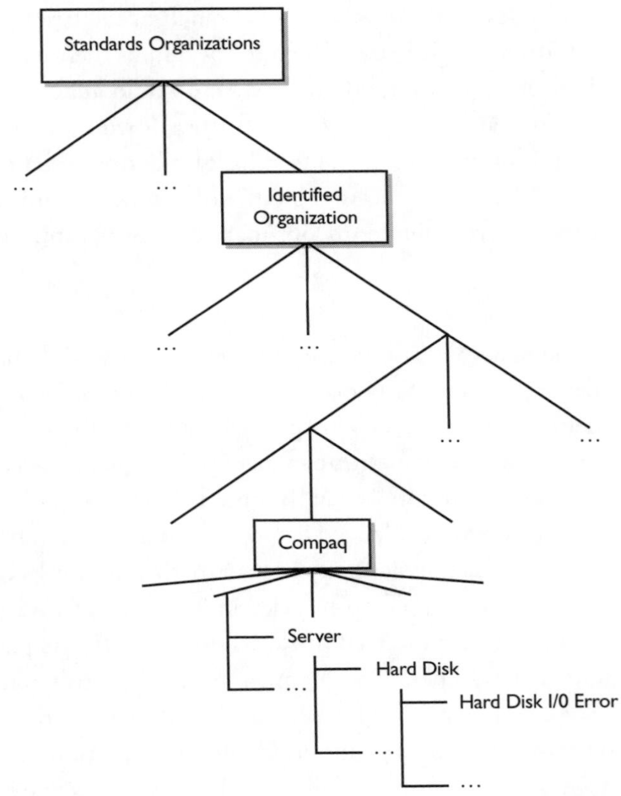

system integrates with the hierarchy, but will provide you with information important to your certification process.

First, let's look at the Compaq root MIB number. Compaq has been given the MIB ID of 1.3.6.1.4.1.232 by the Internet Assigned Numbers Authority. This is the point from which all elements that Compaq defines will start. Keep in mind that, although the Internet Assigned Numbers Authority is responsible for assigning Compaq the initial root level ID, it is Compaq's responsibility to assign the appropriate numeric IDs at the lower levels.

Now, let's return to the hard disk example and the tree shown in Figure 18-4. As you drill down to each subsystem, the numeric identifier is extended by one value. Each branch of the tree is represented by an additional digit being placed to the end of the root MIB. Table 18-1 is a look at how this numbering scheme would appear.

You can see that, as you go further down in the tree, the numeric identifier increases in value. This numbering system is the backbone of the MIB hierarchy and provides us with a unique numbering system to prevent conflicts from rendering our management platform unusable.

MIB Browsers

Because SNMP is a standard management protocol, many vendors have developed third-party management applications that are capable of accessing defined objects. A software package that is capable of reading, monitoring, or modifying the properties of a managed element is called a MIB browser.

Another purpose of a MIB browser is to display all of the definitions contained within a MIB. Developers can use these applications to obtain the MIB information necessary to manage their network. Understanding what is available to an application is vital in the design of your management solution.

Some common MIB browsers include software packages such as HP OpenView, Tivoli, and many other third-party applications. Compaq Insight Manager itself is a form of a MIB browser, as it is capable of viewing, monitoring, and modifying information in the Compaq MIB.

What makes some of these packages so attractive is their versatility with other vendors' MIBs. Packages like HP OpenView allow a central management solution to many different aspects of your network. They can

TABLE 18-1 MIB Numbering Conventions (Using Compaq's ID as an Example)

Object Name	Object Identifier
Compaq Enterprise Root ID	1.3.6.1.4.1.232
Server	1.3.6.1.4.1.232.x
Hard Disk	1.3.6.1.4.1.232.x.x
Hard Disk I/O Error	1.3.6.1.4.1.232.x.x.x

interface with various components and provide a central repository of information, rather then requiring a multivendor solution.

Many management applications, such as HP OpenView, have the capability to compile MIBs on their own. This allows administrators to take an even more hands-on approach to managing their network environments. You should note, however, that even though Compaq makes MIBs available to many third-party management applications, Compaq Insight Manager is not capable of compiling MIB information.

QUESTIONS AND ANSWERS

I have a large TCP/IP network that consists of a variety of equipment supplied by many different vendors. How can I possibly manage this?	Large networks pose more of a challenge than a small, single-vendor environment. A standards-based management platform utilizing SNMP would be your best bet.
My network is supported by a multitiered support environment. I want the bottom level to be able to view management statistics, but I don't feel comfortable with them being able to change the configuration. How can I restrict these users without locking out the top-level support personnel?	Separate community strings will solve this problem. Simply use a READ ONLY community string for restricted access. Then use a READ/WRITE string for the higher-level support staff.
I need to see what elements are defined in the MIB of my management application. How can I do this?	A MIB browser allows you to view this type of information. There is a huge variety of MIB browsers available, in a wide price range.
Are there any pitfalls to using the default community name of "public" for my community string?	Because "public" is the default community string, you are not offering any type of security by using it. Anybody with a PC could install an SNMP-based management application and access any information available to it. This is not a desirable situation in most environments.
My various vendors all supply their own management software. I know there are also many single-vendor solutions available. Which should I use?	There is no easy answer here. The best thing to do is weigh the ease of management, the cost of deployment and ownership, and the features that each package offers. Each corporation takes a different approach. The best you can do is research what best fits your organization.

CERTIFICATION SUMMARY

In this chapter, we have covered many topics that will be important to you in your pursuit of Compaq certification. What's more, understanding how network management works will make you a much more efficient network administrator.

Key points of this chapter included the five building blocks of the network management system. These were the management platform, application, agent, element, and protocol. Understanding these five components is necessary to understanding not only SNMP, but network management on a whole.

Next, you were introduced to the SET and GET commands. These commands are the backbone of the SNMP communication process. They are the primary communications functions of SNMP, the network management protocol, providing the communication required between the management application and the agent. Equally important is the SNMP trap. The trap provides the SET and GET with the appropriate responses they require. It also provides administrators with the alerting capabilities of SNMP.

We also covered SNMP security via a community name, noting the importance of appropriate naming conventions and security applications. Remember that community names are case-sensitive. The most common SNMP community name is "public" and it is the default of many SNMP installations and applications.

SNMP requirements were discussed. You were shown that SNMP requirements are very few: a network to communicate across, an application that uses SNMP, and an object or element that can be managed. Along with this information, you learned that TCP/IP and SNMP were also required in order to use Compaq Insight Manager.

The last portion of the chapter focused primarily on the architecture of the MIB information. We learned that a MIB is essentially the definition of an element. It defines the properties of the elements, the information available, and the functions supported. We saw the hierarchical structure of the MIB and how it uses a numeric tree hierarchy that is overseen by the Internet Assigned Numbers Authority. Another important detail that was introduced was the Compaq Enterprise MIB identifier. Being able to identify 1.3.6.1.4.1.232 as the Compaq Enterprise ID will be of some importance in your certification process.

Together, these items should provide you with the fundamentals of network management. This understanding of network management will prove invaluable when you cover the chapter on Compaq Insight Manager.

✓ TWO-MINUTE DRILL

- ❑ The framework of any good management system should be built on five components: platform, application, agent, element, and protocol.
- ❑ SNMP has emerged as the industry standard and is used as the protocol of most standards-based management platforms.
- ❑ A trap is SNMP's means of notifying or alerting us of a specific condition.
- ❑ SNMP communicates over the TCP/IP network protocol.
- ❑ The GET command should be considered the read function of SNMP.
- ❑ For each community name provided, two potential security settings exist: READ and READ/CREATE (read/write).
- ❑ It is important to note that both the SNMP service and the TCP/IP protocol must be installed for Compaq Insight Manager to function.
- ❑ Each MIB is represented by a numeric object identifier.
- ❑ A managed element is any server, workstation, or network device (router, switch, bridge, hub) that you wish to manage.
- ❑ Compaq has been given the MIB ID of 1.3.6.1.4.1.232 by the Internet Assigned Numbers Authority.
- ❑ Some common MIB browsers include software packages such as HP OpenView, and Tivoli. Compaq Insight Manager is a form of a MIB browser, as it is capable of viewing, monitoring, and modifying information in the Compaq MIB.

SELF TEST

The following Self Test questions will help you measure your understanding of the material presented in this chapter. Read all the choices carefully, as there may be more than one correct answer. Choose all correct answers for each question.

1. Which of the following is not a command used by SNMP?
   A. SET
   B. READ
   C. GET
   D. Trap
2. Which of the following scenarios would require the use of SET?
   A. A defined threshold on a system running a management agent has been broken.
   B. A defined threshold on a system running a management application has been broken.
   C. A threshold is being defined by the management application on a management agent.
   D. The status of a threshold on a management agent is being queried by the management application.
3. Which of the following scenarios would call for the use of an SNMP GET?
   A. The current definition of a CPU threshold is requested on a machine running the management application only.
   B. The current definition of a CPU threshold is requested on a machine running the management agent only.
   C. A threshold has been exceeded on a machine that is running the management application only.
   D. A threshold has been exceeded on a machine that is running the management agent only.
4. Which of the following is not a function of an SNMP trap?
   A. To provide a response to a SET command
   B. To provide notification of an event in the management application
   C. To return the information requested from a GET command
   D. To provide notification of an event in the management agent
5. Let's assume that you have just configured an SNMP-based management application and agent on the Windows NT servers on your network. You are in the process of defining a CPU utilization threshold of 80 percent on your Windows NT servers

when you come across a server that will not allow you to configure the threshold. You are, however, able to view the information that the agent has made available. Which of the following is the most likely cause of this problem?

A. The machine with the management application is using a different community string than the machine with the agent installed.

B. The community string on the box that you cannot configure is in the wrong case.

C. The community string has only been given READ permissions on the Windows NT server where the management agent has been installed.

D. SNMP has not been installed on the management agent server.

6. Which of the following is not a requirement of SNMP?

A. A management server

B. An element to be managed

C. A network to communicate across

D. A management application that utilizes SNMP to communicate with an agent

7. A MIB contains which of the following pieces of information?

A. The properties of a managed element

B. The functions that can be performed against an element

C. The information that is available on a defined element

D. All of the above

8. The numeric ranges assigned as MIB identifiers are overseen by which standards organization?

A. International Standards Numbering Organization

B. Internet Number and Standards Organization

C. Internet Assigned Numbers Authority

D. Internet Assigned Numbers Organization

9. Which of the following could not be an element?

A. A Compaq server

B. A managed Ethernet HUB

C. An hard disk array controller

D. Computer Memory

E. None of the above

10. Which of the following object IDs could belong to a Compaq element?

A. 1.3.6.1.4.3.134.2.3

B. 1.3.6.1.3.4.122.1

C. 1.3.6.1.4.1.232.1.2

D. 1.3.6.1.4.4.276.2.3

11. Which of the following is a function of a MIB browser?

A. Send a trap in response to an event occurring on a managed element.

B. Identify the MIB information of a particular management agent.
C. Identify management applications on the network.
D. Browse a non-SNMP network.

12. Configuring a threshold parameter would be a function of which of the following management components?
    A. The management agent
    B. The management protocol
    C. The management processor
    D. The management application

13. Which of the following is not a component of a management system?
    A. Platform
    B. Element
    C. Processor
    D. Protocol

14. Which of the following can be found at the top of the MIB tree?
    A. The Department of Defense
    B. A network device vendor
    C. A standards organization
    D. There is no such thing as a MIB tree

15. When would you use a trap to configure a managed element?
    A. When you need to configure the element from the management application
    B. When you need to configure the element from a machine that is not part of the management platform
    C. When a management application is not available
    D. A trap cannot be used to configure an element.

ASE

ACCREDITED SYSTEMS ENGINEER

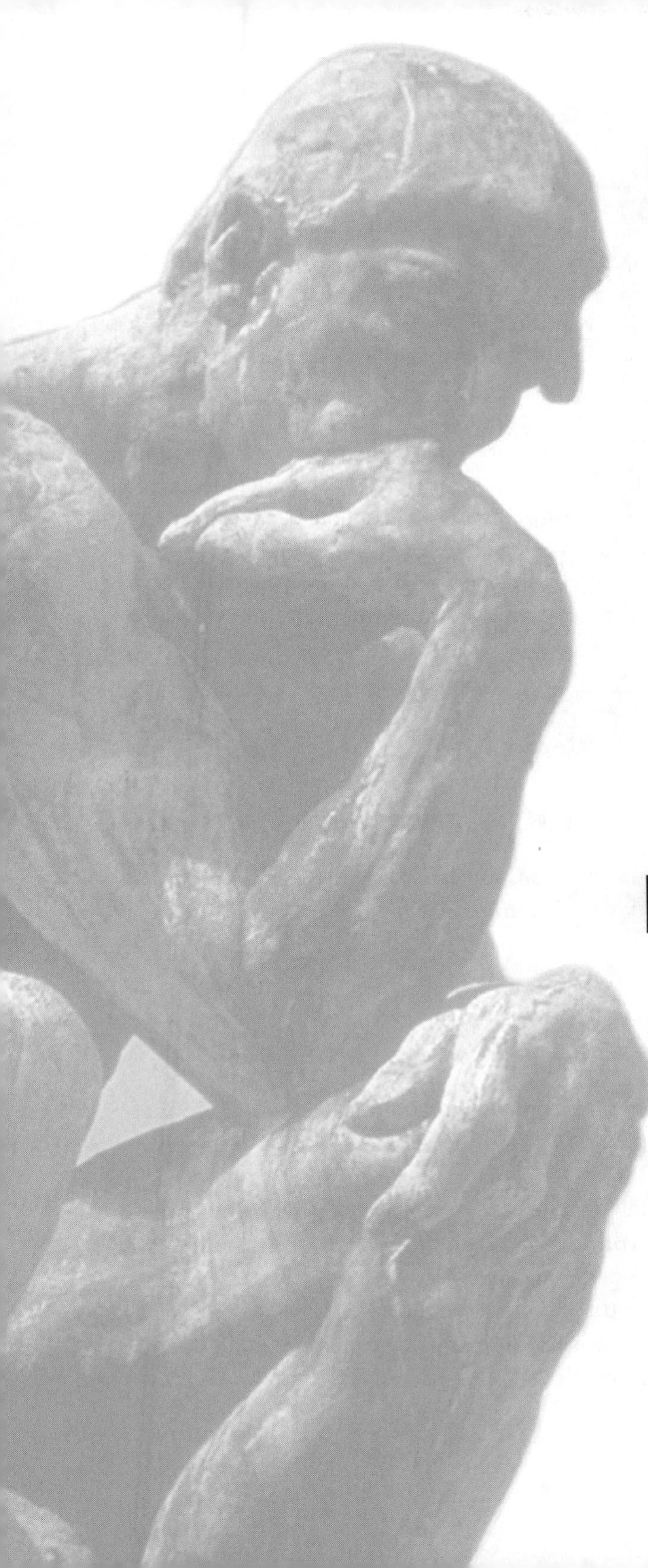

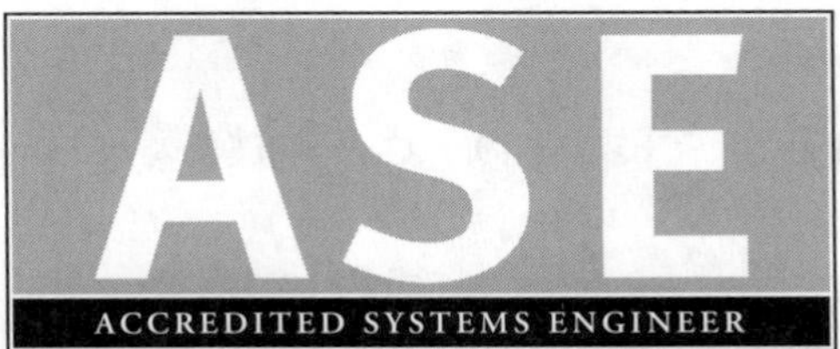

19

Compaq Server Management Technology

CERTIFICATION OBJECTIVES

19.01	Compaq Full-Spectrum Fault Management
19.02	Compaq Recovery Server
19.03	Compaq Rapid Recovery Engine

Compaq Server Management Technology is composed of features that allow maximum utilization and availability of Compaq servers. The attributes that make up Compaq Server Management Technology are based on the concept of Full-Spectrum Fault Management, which is made up of three main pieces: Fault Prevention, Fault Tolerance, and Rapid Recovery.

The Fault Prevention capabilities are integrated with the server monitor components for predictable failures. Compaq's Fault Tolerance capabilities are designed to reduce the impact of an unavoidable hardware or software failure. Finally, Rapid Recovery is designed to assist in bringing the system back into production as quickly as possible when the other two Fault Management features are incapable of preventing the failure of a subsystem.

CERTIFICATION OBJECTIVE 19.01

Compaq Full-Spectrum Fault Management

Compaq Full-Spectrum Fault Management is a blend of utilities and innovations that are designed to minimize the downtime of the server. Together these features attempt to address all of the issues that could cause unplanned server downtime.

Compaq Fault Prevention

Fault prevention is tightly integrated with Compaq's Pre-Failure Warranty initiative. To prevent faults, Compaq server and Deskpro desktop products perform tracking and trend analysis of critical subsystems in order to anticipate failures. The parts that are monitored include memory, hard disks, processors, network interfaces, and the environment status (temperature and fan operational states).

Memory is monitored for two types of errors that would indicate the degradation in the performance of the installed memory modules: correctable and uncorrectable.

Correctable memory errors are also known as soft errors. These are memory errors that do not cause the system to fail and force a reboot. When soft errors occur, it becomes necessary for the memory to use an error recovery algorithm in order to salvage the lost data. An example of this process can be found in ECC memory, which detects both single-bit and multiple-bit errors, and can recover from single-bit errors. (The process is further described in Chapter 3.) Soft errors are logged in the Correctable Error Log (described later in the section on Rapid Recovery).

Uncorrectable memory errors are also known as hard errors. Hard errors cause a situation in which the OS is unable to retrieve data from RAM. Often this will cause the OS to crash, requiring a reboot. However, there is a positive side to this situation; the block of memory that failed is now marked as "bad" and that information is stored in nonvolatile RAM (NVRAM) by the Compaq server. The error is also logged into the Critical Error Log (described later in the section on Rapid Recovery). Marking the bad memory means the server can still be used. When the server comes back online after rebooting, the information contained in NVRAM prevents the defined memory region from being used again, thereby preventing the failure that would occur if data were stored in the failed location.

In a correctable error, when the OS attempts to access a given memory address, the information stored in that location cannot be retrieved. Due to the error-checking algorithm that defines ECC memory, the hardware is able to recover the information contained in the bit of memory that failed. The recovery of the information allows the memory subsystem to provide the information that was requested.

In an uncorrectable error, when the OS attempts to access a given byte, the information contained in more than one of the bits is not accessible. ECC memory cannot recover this information because the error-checking algorithm is not capable of interpolating multiple-bit read failures, thus preventing the information requested from being returned. This triggers a failure that causes the Compaq server to map the memory region as unavailable, storing the condition of that memory region in NVRAM. After the bad area is marked as such in NVRAM, the server can be brought back online. If the OS again tries to write to the location that failed the last time, the information is redirected to an area of memory that has not failed.

on the job

You will notice that an uncorrectable error has occurred on a server during POST, when the memory check does not count up to a standard amount. For example, instead of counting to 65535KB (or 64MB) the system might count up to 65279KB (not quite 64MB).

The storage subsystem, which consists of two main parts, hard disks and controllers, is monitored for a number of potential problems. Several variables on each component of the subsystem are monitored. Self Monitoring Analysis and Reporting Technology (SMART) is designed to detect possible hard disk failures, allowing the replacement of the part prior to failure. Drive Parameter Tracking monitors 15 operational parameters, such as variations in spin up and seek times, uncorrectable read and write errors, and mechanical status. Dynamic Sector Repairing continually performs background surface scans on the hard disk drives during inactive periods and automatically remaps the bad sectors, ensuring that data cannot be corrupted if the system tries to write to the failed location. In the case of array controllers, several environment variables are monitored. The battery health is one example. Another is Array Accelerator Tracking, which monitors the integrity of the Array Accelerator Cache, allowing pre-failure preventative maintenance.

The server's environmental systems are also monitored. Three subsystems must be monitored:

- **Power** Power supplies are constantly monitored for any indicators that they will not be able to continue to supply the server with the necessary current. Power monitoring extends to monitoring of Compaq UPSs for AC power failure.
- **Fans** Fans provide the cooling necessary to prevent the server from overheating. Not only is fan power status monitored, but also the fan's speed. In addition to monitoring, Compaq servers also allow you to install and configure additional fans in critical areas such as processors and hard drive cages.
- **Temperature** Overall temperature within the server chassis is monitored. If the temperature exceeds a predefined threshold, a warning is sent out to provide enough time to adjust the external or internal variables that are preventing the server from maintaining a safe state.

Fault Tolerance

The Fault Tolerance facet of Compaq's Full-Spectrum Fault Management is designed with the assumption that something is going to fail. The technologies utilized minimize the damage from a component failure. Fault Tolerance features include storage, processor, power supply, and NIC.

Storage Subsystem

The storage subsystem is the system most prone to failure due to the high number of moving parts within the mechanical components involved (the hard drives). In order to provide more information regarding the storage subsystem, an important piece of industry information must be understood: RAID. Compaq provides the following RAID levels with the SMART line of Array controllers: 0, 0+1, 1, 4, 5. Controller redundancy options are also available in the newer SMART ES models on the ProLiant 6000s, 6500s, 7000s, and 8000s, to further increase data availability.

RAID level 0 is also known as disk striping, where data is distributed across multiple hard drives. It is important to be aware of the fact that in RAID 0, all data is lost if one drive fails.

RAID level 1 (disk mirroring) ensures that both disks contain the same data, so that if either disk fails, all of the necessary data is still available on the surviving hard disk.

RAID 0+1 is a combination of RAID levels 0 and 1 (striping and mirroring). A RAID 0+1 array consists of two identically sized striped sets (RAID 0) that are mirrored (RAID 1) allowing performance and redundancy to be achieved in the array.

RAID 4 (data guarding) and RAID 5 (distributed data guarding) use the equivalent of one disk's worth of space to store parity information. The difference between RAID 4 and 5 is that a RAID 5 distributes the parity information across all disks in the array, allowing for increased read performance.

If the storage subsystem is configured utilizing RAID technology, the failure of a single hard drive will not cause a loss of data nor cause the system to crash due to an inability to access the hard drive.

A fault tolerant feature of the storage subsystem is the ability to swap hard drives while the system is online (hot plug). When a hard disk fails, the server does not have to be brought down in order to replace the hard disk, allowing for repair without interruption of services.

Another Fault Tolerance feature is the online spare. The online spare is an extra hard drive that is installed in the server but not configured as part of the array. The array controller is aware of this drive and in the event that a hard drive fails, the array controller spins up the spare and allows the array to rebuild, using the spare to replace the failed drive. This provides additional fault tolerance because it allows two drives to fail within a short time without causing loss of data.

Processor

Two processor features allow for fault tolerance: off-line backup processor and pre-failure warranty (Pentium Pro processor). The off-line processor is a spare processor that is already installed in the server in case the primary processor fails. If there is a processor failure, the server will experience downtime. However, if there is an off-line processor, the server will automatically reboot and configure the old off-line processor as the new primary processor.

Compaq's concept of a pre-failure warranty is reflected in Compaq Insight Manager (CIM), which monitors the processor for erratic or out-of-order behaviors. As in the case of hard drives and environmental systems, the pre-failure warranty allows for a proactive approach to processor replacement, thus preventing unplanned downtime of a server.

Network Interface Cards

Compaq's Netelligent line of NICs provides for the ability to form *controller pairs*, which are groupings of ports. For fault tolerance of a network connection, two ports on the same network adapter (dual port models only) or on two different adapters are grouped together by the driver to form a single logical network connection. The driver is constantly monitoring the link state of the primary connection. If the primary fails, the driver activates the port that is configured as the secondary, and all communication now travels over this port. Once the link is restored to the primary port, the driver reconfigures the network adapters so that the primary port is now the active port.

It is important that both connections to the controller pair are on the same network segment. Since the controller pair is presented to the OS as a single network adapter, the OS assigns protocol information to the controller pair and the NIC driver determines which port to send the information to.

CERTIFICATION OBJECTIVE 19.02

Compaq Recovery Server

Another feature included in the list of fault management technologies is the Compaq Recovery Server. There are two versions of the recovery server available: online and standby. The Online Recovery Server option is a Fault Prevention feature, which allows automatic transfer of operations from a failed server to a backup server. The Standby Recovery Server option, a Fault Tolerant feature, allows transfer of operations to an identically configured backup server.

The initial setup of each recovery server option is very similar. Both configurations require a single external storage unit connected to two Compaq servers with SMART array controllers. One server is configured as a primary, with the other server relegated to the role of secondary. The two servers are then connected via a heartbeat cable, which is monitored by the secondary server to ensure that the primary server is online. If the secondary server fails to receive a heartbeat signal from the primary, the secondary server takes control of the storage unit and begins to provide the services that were interrupted.

A couple of differences in configuration and functionality distinguish the Online Recovery Server from a Standby Recovery Server. In the Online Recovery Server configuration, both the primary and secondary servers are online, meaning that the OS is loaded and initialized. Because of this design requirement, the only OSs that currently support such a configuration are Windows NT 3.5*x* and 4.0. The primary difference in the configuration of the two servers is the storage arrangement. The Online Recovery Server must have additional storage mounted internally, containing the OS and all applications that will be running on the server. The reason that the system requires internal storage is that only one server can use the storage unit at a time. Since both servers are online at the same time, each needs its own storage space for the system software.

In the Standby Recovery Server configuration, all of the storage must be external, allowing the OS, application software, and data to be stored in the same location. This permits the identical configuration of both servers as far as the software components are concerned, so almost any OS can be used, including NetWare, Windows NT, and SCO UnixWare. In this configuration the primary server must boot, come online, and start sending out a heartbeat signal before the secondary server can be turned on. When the secondary server is powered up, it pauses after POST, going into a standby mode. In this state, the server monitors the heartbeat signal that the primary server is now emitting. Similar to the Online Recovery Server, as soon as the standby server fails to receive a heartbeat signal, the secondary server takes control of the storage unit and continues the boot process.

Recovery from a failover happens similarly on each of the recovery server options. In both cases, the entire system will experience downtime. Both servers need to be powered down. The system reinitializes by powering up the primary server first, allowing the system to come online before powering up the second server.

on the Job

There are certain limitations to both of the recovery server options. In the case of the online server, the failover is nearly instantaneous, but since these are two servers on the same network, each need its own identification. What this means is that each server needs a separate name and IP or IPX address. The client no longer knows how to communicate with the server unless a solution for redirecting the client is designed.

The Standby Recovery Server is limited in two ways. If the primary crashes due to a software failure stemming from the configuration of the server, the same configuration errors will exist on the other server, since the two servers share the same storage subsystem. The other issue is a downtime issue, referring to the amount of time it takes the secondary server to boot into the operating system. In this writer's opinion, the Standby Recovery Server is a viable option only if you are concerned about mitigating the risks associated with single points of failure in hardware that is not protected by redundant systems.

CERTIFICATION OBJECTIVE 19.03

Compaq Rapid Recovery Engine

The Compaq Rapid Recovery Engine is a system that performs a series of tasks designed to return the server to a functional state in the event of a failure. The Rapid Recovery Engine is a three-step process: Server Health Logging, Automatic Server Recovery (ASR) and ASR-2 (ProLiant servers), and Remote Maintenance. These functions are designed to minimize the need for user intervention.

Server Health Logging stores critical information pertaining to the configuration of the server. Then, ASR reboots the system, scans the logs, and corrects errors that have been identified. These errors include errors in the processor, memory, environment, and errors that do not cause system failure (soft errors). ASR-2 provides the additional functionality of paging a network administrator (assuming a modem is installed in the server) when the server crashes and restores itself to an operational state. Finally, for issues that ASR cannot resolve, Remote Maintenance allows a system administrator to remotely access the server to investigate its state. Remote maintenance also allows the administrator to run System Diagnostics and the System Configuration Utility, if they are stored in the system partition.

on the job

When configuring a Compaq server, it is always an excellent idea to make sure the system partition is installed and up-to-date. This allows for additional functionality and ease of use. Some of the capabilities provided by installing the system partition include the Remote Maintenance feature and the ability to upgrade the system BIOS remotely. With the system partition, the tools and utilities are always available when working on the server, and it's significantly faster than booting off of floppy-disk versions of the utilities.

Server Health Logs

Server Health Logs store information pertinent to the identification and resolution of server failures, and allow changes to be made in the hardware configuration to adjust for failure of subsystems. There are two parts to the Server Health Logs, the Correctable Error Log and the Critical Error Log. All information contained in these logs is stored in NVRAM and as such, is maintained even in a powerless state. The Correctable Error Log keeps track of errors that occurred in memory, which were correctable. The Critical Error Log records catastrophic errors that occurred in any of the subsystems. In addition, it keeps track of OS crashes (Windows NT blue screen or NetWare Abend).

Critical Error Logs

The Critical Error Log plays a very important role in the recovery of the server, when in the next step ASR uses the information stored in this log to make adjustments in the hardware configuration of the server. Since the Critical Error Log stores information regarding the failure of server subsystems, you can get a list of events that have occurred by viewing the error log through either the Inspect utility, the Diagnostics utility, or Insight Manager. The Diagnostics utility, if unable to resolve the error, will suggest corrective action.

Automatic Server Recovery

An important feature of the Rapid Recovery Engine is Automatic Server Recovery. ASR is supported by the following Compaq systems: SystemPro/XL, ProSignia, ProSignia VS, ProSignia 300 and 500, and ProLiant line of servers. ASR is supported by the following OSs: NetWare 3.*x*, 4.*x*, 5.*x*, Windows NT, SCO UNIX or UnixWare, and OS/2. If a catastrophic error occurs in either the hardware or software, ASR allows the server to reboot automatically and reconfigure itself to resolve any the errors that occurred. When the server has recovered, it will boot into the Compaq Utilities (if installed on the system partition) or perform a normal reboot and allow the OS to load, depending on the option selected in the System Configuration Utility.

Three parts constitute ASR: hardware timer, server failure notification, and remote maintenance. The hardware timer is integrated into the system board. Unless it is reset by the OS driver it will assume that the OS is no longer responding and will reboot the server. Server failure notification is a system that allows you to configure ASR to page an administrator with a notification of the server failure. In order to enable Server Failure Notification, a Hayes-compatible modem must be installed and configured through Compaq Diagnostics with a number to dial out to.

When ASR is activated, it follows a five-step process to resolve the issues.

1. When the hardware timer is not reset, ASR reboots the server.
2. After the reboot occurs, the error is logged to the Critical Error Log for use in reconfiguration of the server at a later stage and resetting the server when the information has been successfully logged.
3. When the server is again functional, a page is sent to the administrator as specified via the System Configuration Utility.
4. After the page is completed, the server begins to resolve the errors logged to the Critical Error Log, such as memory errors, by reconfiguring the server (deallocating bad memory blocks).
5. The server is rebooted to either the OS (unattended recovery) or Compaq Utilities (attended recovery).

Another version of ASR, known as ASR-2, is only available on the ProLiant line of servers. Although it does not provide administrator paging on system failure, ASR-2 provides some additional functionality that is lacking in the original version of ASR, such as the ability to recover from processor board failure and excessive internal temperature. After the OS comes back online, the Insight Agents send an alert to a management PC running Compaq Insight Manager or another piece of monitoring software, which then notifies an administrator that the server is back online. Finally, if the server is running on a Compaq Uninterruptible Power Supply (UPS), ASR-2 can page the administrator if there is an AC power failure.

In order to configure ASR, several options need to be set. ASR is installed and configured through either SmartStart or the Compaq System Configuration Utility. After ASR is enabled through either of these methods, the appropriate device driver must be installed in the OS. The device drivers correspond to the operating systems as follows:

- **NetWare** CPQHLTH.NLM
- **SCO UNIX or UnixWare** cpqasrd
- **Microsoft Windows NT** SYSMGMT.SYS
- **OS/2** CPQHLTH.SYS and CPQHLTH.EXE

After ASR is enabled, several security issues and features should be noted. For example, if a power-on password is configured, this feature is bypassed when the server reboots, thereby allowing ASR to boot to the Compaq Utilities or the OS. If it has been determined that additional security is needed on the server, two configuration options are helpful. The first is to enable network server mode through the Compaq Utilities, which ensures that the server keyboard is locked until a password is entered. The second method is to set an administrator password, thus preventing modifications to the system through the System Configuration Utility until the administrator password is entered.

Remote Maintenance

When the server reboots, if it is configured to boot to the Compaq Utilities, Remote Maintenance capabilities allow the system administrator to call in to the server through a communications program or Insight Manager. These remote capabilities can be utilized through either a direct serial connection or an autoanswer-capable, Hayes-compatible modem. Once the system administrator has connected to the server, several capabilities become available: reconfiguring the server via System Configuration Utilities, running diagnostics, and gathering information on the server via Inspect.

QUESTIONS AND ANSWERS	
If I didn't use SmartStart to install and configure the server, how would I enable ASR?	You need to do two things to enable ASR. First, load the Compaq System Configuration Utility and enable ASR. Second, load the appropriate driver for the OS.
If I enable ASR through the System Configuration Utility and I don't load the OS driver, what will happen?	The process by which ASR determines if the OS is still functioning requires the OS driver to reset a timer on the system board. In other words, if the driver is not installed, it will seem to the system board as if the OS has failed, and it will reset the server even though no errors have occurred.
What fault tolerant options can be used to prevent the loss of data?	Any of the following RAID levels provide for data protection: 0+1, 1, 4, or 5.
What is the difference between the Correctable Error Log and the Critical Error Log?	The Correctable Error Log stores only information pertaining to memory errors from which the hardware was able to recover. The Critical Error Log stores information regarding a failed component or OS failure.

CERTIFICATION SUMMARY

The three parts of Full-Spectrum Fault Management define Compaq Server Management Technology. Full-Spectrum Fault Management technologies cover the following areas: Fault Prevention, Fault Tolerance, and Rapid Recovery. Fault Prevention monitors operation parameters of key subsystems in an attempt to predict the failure of a component. Fault Prevention monitoring permits use of Compaq's Pre-Failure Warranty, meaning that when an alert is registered that an operational threshold has been exceeded, the part in question can be replaced under warranty even if it has not actually failed. To enhance the Fault Prevention efforts, the second piece of Full-Spectrum Fault Management, Fault Tolerance, assists in bolstering the resiliency of the system. In the event that all efforts at Fault

Prevention fail, Fault Tolerance features prevent the failure of a component by providing redundancy of subsystems, such as redundant power supplies. If both the Fault Prevention and Fault Tolerance features are not adequate, the features of Rapid Recovery assist in bringing the servers back online as quickly as possible.

In order to minimize downtime, Rapid Recovery has three features that restore functionality to the system: Server Health Logs, Automatic Server Recovery, and Remote Maintenance. Server Health Logs consist of the Correctable Error Log and the Critical Error Log, which store information pertaining to events that have occurred within subsystems on the server. ASR then utilizes the Critical Error Log in order to reconfigure the server to adjust for the error and reboot the system to an operational state. ASR can be configured to reboot to either the Compaq Utilities or the OS. If ASR reboots the system into the Compaq Utilities, Remote Maintenance features allow remote access to the utilities through either a serial connection or a dial-up connection.

TWO-MINUTE DRILL

- The attributes that make up Compaq Server Management Technology are based on the concept of Full-Spectrum Fault Management, which is made up of three main pieces: Fault Prevention, Fault Tolerance, and Rapid Recovery.
- Compaq Full-Spectrum Fault Management is a blend of utilities and innovations that are designed to minimize the downtime of the server.
- To prevent faults, Compaq server and Deskpro desktop products perform tracking and trend analysis of critical subsystems in order to anticipate failures.
- The technologies utilized in Fault Tolerance minimize the damage from a component failure. Fault Tolerance features include storage, processor, power supply, and NIC.
- Compaq Recovery Server consists of two versions: online and standby.

- ❑ The Online Recovery Server option is a Fault Prevention feature, which allows automatic transfer of operations from a failed server to a backup server.
- ❑ The Standby Recovery Server option, a Fault Tolerant feature, allows transfer of operations to an identically configured backup server.
- ❑ The Rapid Recovery Engine is a three-step process: Server Health Logging, Automatic Server Recovery (ASR) and ASR-2 (ProLiant servers), and Remote Maintenance.
- ❑ Server Health Logs store information pertinent to the identification and resolution of server failures, and allow changes to be made in the hardware configuration to adjust for failure of subsystems.
- ❑ ASR reboots the system, scans the logs, and corrects errors that have been identified.
- ❑ Remote Maintenance allows a system administrator to remotely access the server to investigate its state.
- ❑ Remote maintenance also allows the administrator to run System Diagnostics and the System Configuration Utility, if they are stored in the system partition.

SELF TEST

The following Self Test questions will help you measure your understanding of the material presented in this chapter. Read all the choices carefully, as there may be more than one correct answer. Choose all correct answers for each question.

1. What are the three parts that make up Compaq Full-Spectrum Fault Management?
   A. Fault Prevention, Fault Tolerance, Remote Maintenance
   B. Fault Tolerance, Fault Recovery, Fault Prevention
   C. Fault Prevention, Fault Tolerance, Rapid Recovery
   D. Fault Monitoring, Fault Recovery, Fault Prevention
2. Which of the following is not a feature of Fault Prevention?
   A. Pre-Failure Warranty
   B. Temperature sensing
   C. Network Performance monitoring
   D. Hard Disk Available Space monitoring
3. Which is not a fault tolerant system?
   A. System board
   B. Network Interface Card
   C. Power supply
   D. Storage system
4. What fault tolerant features are not provided with ECC memory?
   A. Detect single bit errors
   B. Correct adjacent bit errors
   C. Detect adjacent bit errors
   D. Correct single bit errors
5. If you wanted to have an identically configured redundant server, which option would you use?
   A. Online Recovery Server
   B. External storage plugged into a different server
   C. Off-Line backup processor
   D. Standby Recovery Server
6. What are the three components of Rapid Recovery?
   A. Critical Error Logs, Automatic Server Recovery, Remote Maintenance
   B. Server Health Logging, Automatic Reboot, Remote Maintenance
   C. Server Health Logging, Automatic Server Recovery, Remote Maintenance
   D. Server Health Logging, Automatic Server Recovery, Failure Notification
7. What information is not stored in the Critical Error Logs?
   A. Correctable memory errors
   B. Hard drive failures
   C. Network link failures
   D. Internal fan failure

8. What methods are available for viewing the Critical Error Logs?
   A. Compaq Insight Manger
   B. Inspect utility
   C. Compaq Diagnostics
   D. Event Viewer
9. Which is a feature that is available in ASR but not ASR-2?
   A. Recovery from excessive internal temperature
   B. Administrator paging on system failure
   C. Administrator paging when system comes back online
   D. Recovery from processor board failure
10. Which of the following ASR drivers does Windows NT use?
   A. CPQHLTH.NLM
   B. cpqasrd
   C. SYSMGMT.SYS
   D. CPQHLTH.SYS
11. Which of the following is not a tool that can be used to install and configure ASR?
   A. System Configuration Utility
   B. SmartStart installation program
   C. Compaq Insight Manager
   D. Compaq SSD
12. What are the options that can be configured on reboot from ASR?
   A. Boot to the operating system
   B. Scan the hard drive
   C. Boot to Compaq Utilities
   D. Remap bad memory locations
13. What no longer works when a server is recovering via ASR?
   A. Network password
   B. Keyboard password
   C. Power-on password
   D. Administrator password
14. Which security feature can be used to protect against unauthorized access to the Compaq Utilities?
   A. Network password
   B. Keyboard password
   C. Power-on password
   D. Administrator password
15. Which are the connection methods allowed to utilize Remote Maintenance?
   A. Remote console
   B. Modem
   C. Serial connection
   D. Systems Management software

ASE

ACCREDITED SYSTEMS ENGINEER

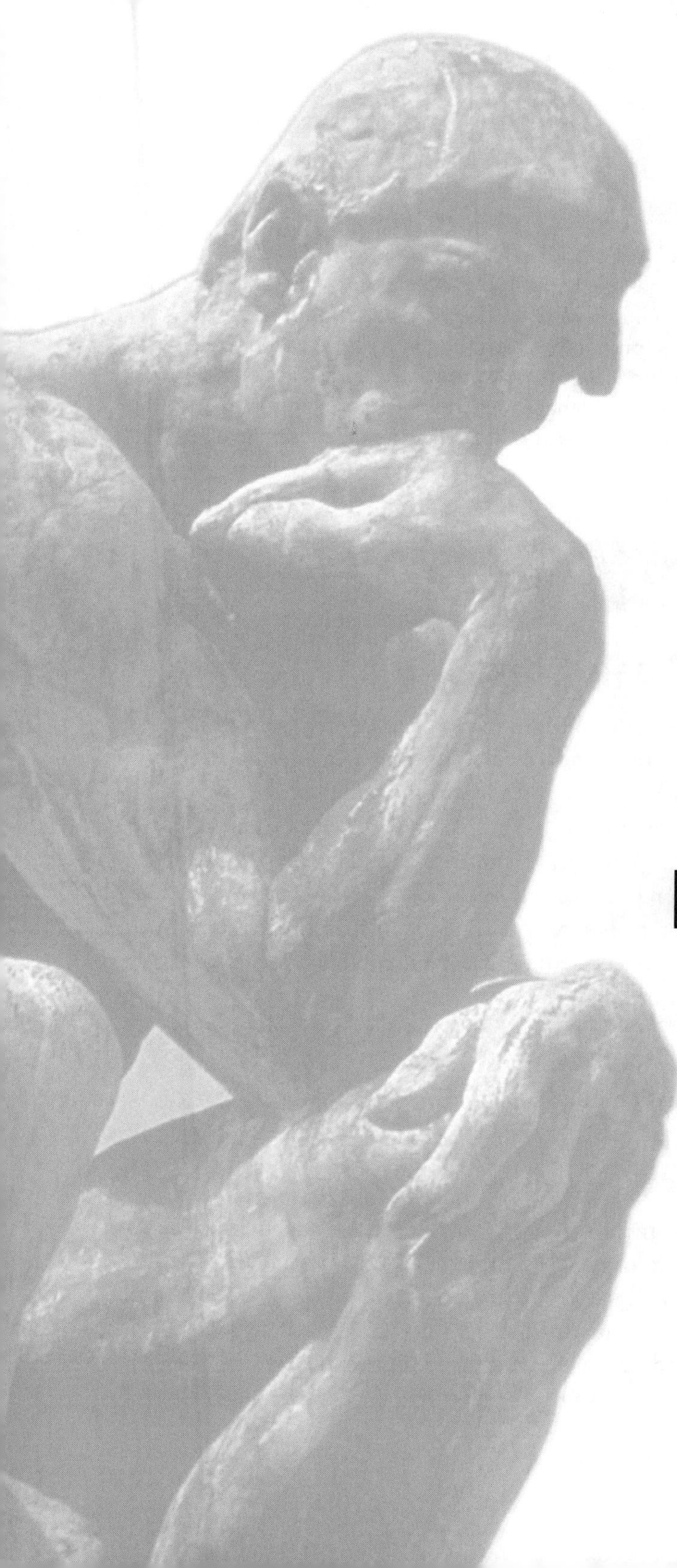

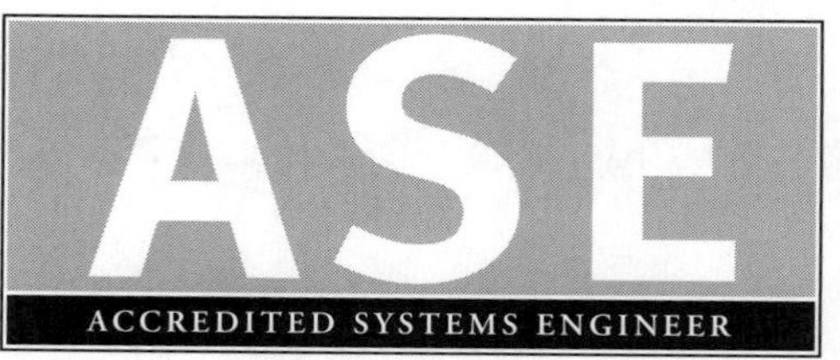

20

Desktop and Portable Management Technology

CERTIFICATION OBJECTIVES

20.01 Desktop Management Task Force

20.02 The Features of Intelligent Manageability

20.03 Desktop Agents

20.04 Polling of the Desktop Agents

Compaq has been an integral part of the Desktop Management Task Force, helping to develop a standard for system management. The Desktop Management Task Force has laid out a system by which different vendors can all come together to provide a universal system for management. Compaq has developed a system called Intelligent Manageability. Intelligent Manageability is a collection of applications and standards that allow for a robust management environment. Intelligent Manageability allows Compaq systems to be managed and maintained easily by Compaq applications, as well as applications developed by other vendors, such as HP OpenView.

CERTIFICATION OBJECTIVE 20.01

Desktop Management Task Force

Formed in 1992, the Desktop Management Task Force (DMTF) is the group that defines the standards used for managing desktops. It is a committee composed of various leaders in the computer industry. Members include Compaq, IBM, Microsoft, Novell, Intel, and several other computer giants. The DMTF's main goal is to establish standards that can be agreed upon by a majority of computer and software manufacturers, making it easier for companies to write applications that can be used to manage various computer components without having to modify the software for each individual vendor platform.

The Desktop Management Task Force has developed two standards for desktop management: the Desktop Management Interface and the Management Information File.

Desktop Management Interface

The Desktop Management Interface (DMI) serves as the interface between the components being managed and the management software. The DMI is composed of two interfaces. The first is the component interface, which allows the desktop components to send information to management programs. The second part is the management interface, which allows the management programs to read and write management information.

Management Information File

The Management Information File (MIF) is analogous to the Management Information Base (MIB) used with SNMP. The MIF, however, is a little more robust than an MIB. The MIF can be a text file or collection of management agents used to gather information. It defines the components to be measured and the way in which they will be measured.

There are two types of MIFs: standard MIFs and vendor MIFs. Standard MIFs are those developed by the Desktop Management Task Force. These MIFs are used on standard PCs, network adapters, and printers. Vendor MIFs define characteristics unique to specific vendors.

Management Information Files have their own language that is used to describe components and report information. The DMTF developed the MIF grammar so there would be a standard for reporting. The MIF grammar describes the syntax and descriptions to be used. The MIF grammar outlines what details of a component will be given and how these details will be reported.

CERTIFICATION OBJECTIVE 20.02

The Features of Intelligent Manageability

Compaq Intelligent Manageability is divided into five categories: Configuration Management, Asset Management, Security Management, Fault Management, and Integration Management. Aggregating these functions into a single platform, Compaq Intelligent Manageability makes it easier for you to deploy, configure, and manage your servers.

Configuration Management

Configuration Management involves loading drivers, doing system updates, and managing configuration files. Configuration Management allows you to ensure that your desktops and portables are running as efficiently as possible. The tools Compaq has developed for Configuration Management include:

- System Software Manager (SSM)
- Remote Security Management
- Remote ROM Flash
- Remote wake-up and shutdown
- Support Software CD
- Compaq Info Messenger
- Compaq Restore CD
- ACPI-ready hardware

We will briefly discuss the Compaq Restore CD, Remote ROM Flash, and the Support Software CD.

Compaq Restore CD

The Compaq Restore CD allows you to recover from a catastrophic hard drive failure. Restore CDs are available for both Compaq desktops and portables. Restore CDs should come with your computer, but you can also order these CDs from Compaq. The Restore CD provides all the drivers and Compaq OEM files you need to restore your system functionality. The restore CD also comes with a boot disk that can be used for installation. After booting to the boot disk, you will be asked if you want to perform a restore. You will then be asked to insert your Windows 95 or 98 CD. You must supply this CD yourself. The installation will then continue. Any drivers you need can be installed from the Compaq Restore CD.

Many people assume that the Windows installation files are on the Restore CD, but they are not. Make sure you realize that your Windows CD will be required when using the Compaq Restore CD. If you do not have the Windows CD, this restore process cannot be completed. If you going off site to restore a machine, make sure you take your Windows CD with you.

Remote ROM Flash

Compaq desktops and laptops also support Remote ROM Flash. Periodically, Compaq develops updated BIOS revisions for its products. Manually updating the BIOS on your servers can be a tedious task, especially if you have a large number of servers. Updating the BIOS on all desktops is almost impossible when you consider the number of workstations most large organizations have. Remote ROM Flash makes it easier. With Remote ROM Flash, you don't have to visit each machine in order to update the BIOS. There are many applications that can remotely update the BIOS on machines that support Remote ROM Flash. This can save time compared to going to each machine and updating BIOSs manually.

Support Software CD

The Support Software CD is an HTML-based application. It can be used to view information and load drivers for Compaq desktops and portables. The Support Software CD pack includes separate CDs for desktops, portables, and workstations. The CDs also offer support for five languages (English, German, French, Dutch, and Japanese). All you need to do is insert the CD for your model and language, and choose the appropriate option from the home page, shown in Figure 20-1. If the requested file or information is not on the CD, you will be hyperlinked to the Compaq Web site.

Asset Management

Asset Management involves inventory data collection and tracking. Asset Management is important from both an accounting standpoint and from a systems management standpoint. It allows your accounting department to keep track of which divisions are responsible for which assets. Assets management also allows an administrator to know what machines have been upgraded or need to be upgraded. The tools Compaq has developed for Asset Management include:

- Fingerprint Identification Technology
- DMI 2.0 support
- DMI BIOS
- DIMM Serial Presence Detect

FIGURE 20-1

The Compaq Support Software CD home page

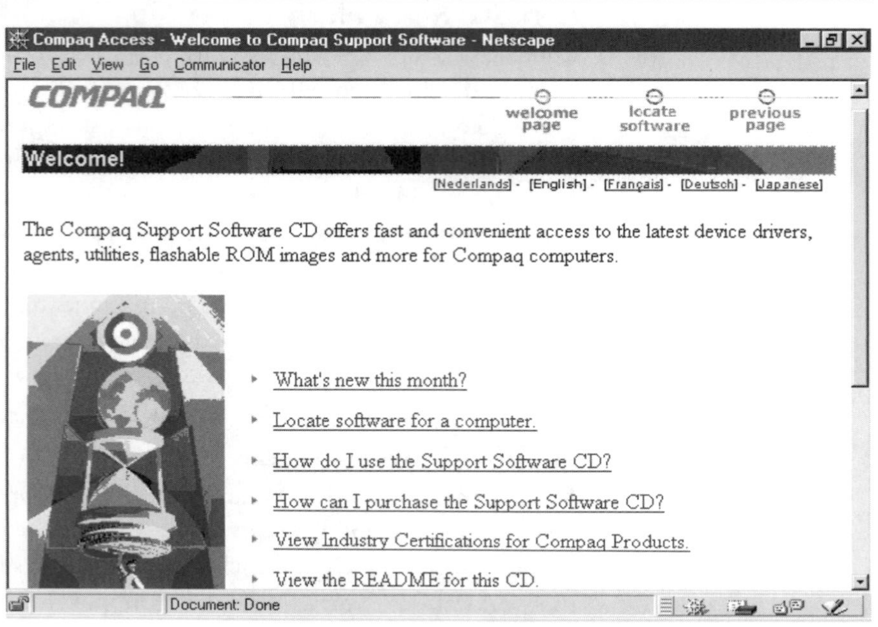

QUESTIONS AND ANSWERS

Does the Compaq Support Software CD support French?	Yes. The Support Software CD supports English, German, French, Dutch, and Japanese.
Can I get information on Compaq Workstation Products Certification through the Support Software CD?	Yes. The Support Software CD can provide information on the ASE program and Compaq product certifications.
What happens if a driver I need is not located on the Support CD?	The Support CD will direct you to the Compaq Web site location where you can download the needed driver.
Can I get BIOS upgrades from the Support CD?	Yes. BIOS upgrades can be located through the Support CD.

We will discuss DIMM Serial Presence Detect and the DMI support that Compaq has developed.

DIMM Serial Presence Detect

Compaq systems detect and record the serial number of the memory DIMMs installed in the system. When the memory is changed, causing a change in serial numbers, the system notifies you. The system lets you know the serial numbers of the DIMMs that were previously installed in the system and the serial numbers of the DIMMs that are currently installed in the system. This feature protects against someone secretly swapping out the memory in a Compaq system.

on the job

Note that the system cannot tell the difference between memory that has been replaced by an administrator and memory replaced by some unauthorized person. If you upgrade the memory in a system, the user will receive the memory warning the next time the system boots up. So after replacing memory, allow the system to boot up completely so you can clear the message. If you don't, you will undoubtedly receive a call from the user about the message.

DMI 2.0 Support

Compaq is a front-runner in DMI support and helped to develop the original DMI specification. Compaq desktops and portables are fully DMI 2.0 compatible. This means that they can be managed by any DMI 2.0-compliant application. These applications include: Unicenter TNG by Computer Associates, OpenView Desktop Administrator by Hewlett-Packard, LANDesk Management Suite by Intel, LANDesk Client Manager by Intel, Zero Administration Client Suite by Network Associates, WinLAND by Seagate, and NetCensus by Tally Systems. DMI support is provided through the Compaq Insight Manager Agents version 4.20 and later. These agents provide MIF conformance and allow for alerting and Web administration.

Security Management

Compaq realizes that physical system security is very important. Therefore, Compaq has developed several methods to protect your systems. The tools Compaq uses for Security Management include:

- Smart Cover Lock
- Memory change alert (discussed earlier in this chapter)
- Configuration control hardware
- Ownership tag
- Smart Cover Sensor

We will discuss the Smart Cover Lock and the Smart Cover Sensor in the next two sections.

Smart Cover Lock

The Smart Cover Lock protects the internal components of your system from physical access by intruders. This will keep someone from removing or swapping out components. The Smart Cover Lock is a device attached to the back of system. It prevents the cover from being removed. With the Smart Cover Lock, your system cannot be opened by anyone whom you have not authorized.

Smart Cover Sensor

The Smart Cover Sensor is internal to your system and is activated once your system is opened. After the cover is reattached and your system is powered on, you will be alerted that your cover has been removed previously. The alert will continue to be given until the sensor is reset. This keeps someone from opening your machine and powering it up, hoping that the alert will only be given once.

Fault Management

One component of particular interest to administrators is Compaq's Fault Management. Fault Management can save a lot of time, and in some cases a lot of money. Fault Management can greatly reduce downtime, which is the nemesis of most administrators. Compaq Fault Management features include:

- ECC Memory
- ECC Fault Prediction and pre-failure warranty
- SMART hard drives
- Hard drive pre-failure warranty
- Ultra ATA Integrity Monitoring
- Thermal sensor

We will discuss the Hard Drive Pre-failure Warranty and the Thermal Sensor.

Hard Drive Pre-failure Warranty

Compaq hard drives come with what is called a pre-failure warranty. This can reduce downtime due to hard drive failures. The Compaq desktop and portable agents monitor hard drive status. When the agents detect an imminent hard drive failure, they notify you. You can order a replacement from Compaq, and the hard drive can then be swapped out after hours. This way, you can avoid the problems caused by a failed hard drive.

Don't rely on the Compaq agents to predict all hard drive failures. There are problems that cannot be predicted, such as power surges. Either advise your users to store all critical data on a server that is backed up on a regular basis, or install some form of backup software on the user's machine. This will guard against the loss of critical data.

Thermal Sensor

Most Compaq desktops come equipped with a thermal sensor. This is like an internal thermometer that monitors the temperature of your system. When the temperature reaches unacceptable levels, the system notifies you. This allows you to shut down your system and check for a problem before permanent damage can be done. Some systems automatically shut your system down once the temperature reaches a certain level. This is helpful if your system overheats when you are not there to receive the alert.

Integration Management

Integration Management allows your system to be integrated easily into an existing network. This can sometimes present a problem if the new system is different from the existing systems. Compaq has taken steps to ease this transition. Compaq Integration Management includes:

- Web-enabled agents
- Compaq Insight Manager
- Compaq Management Solution Partners Program
- Wired for Management support
- Net PC Technologies support

We will discuss the Compaq Management Solution Partners Program.

Management Solution Partners Program

Compaq developed the Management Solution Partners Program in an attempt to standardize PC management. The Management Solution Partners Program was developed before the DMI standard. Because of this, vendors that adhere to the Management Solution Partners Program standards can allow for centralized management even if they do not support DMI. This allows Compaq products to be managed by an even greater range of management products.

CERTIFICATION OBJECTIVE 20.03

Desktop Agents

The Compaq Insight Management Desktop Agents allow support for Intelligent Manageability on Compaq desktops. The desktop agents allow DMI support, DMI and SNMP Web agents, and alerting. The desktop agents come preinstalled on all new Compaq desktops and portables, allowing for manageability right out of the box. You can also install the

Compaq agents from the Compaq Management CD. As Figure 20-2 shows, you can install the base components, DMI support, and SNMP support.

Requirements for Windows NT and Windows 9x

The Compaq desktop agents support Windows 95, Windows 98, Windows NT Workstation 3.51, and Windows NT Workstation 4.0. There are a few requirements that must be met in order to install the desktop agents. For Windows 95, it is recommended that you install the Microsoft Windows Sockets update. TCP/IP and SNMP must be installed on any platform in order for the desktops to be remotely managed. Microsoft Internet Explorer, version 4.01 or later, is required for Web management.

On Windows NT machines, if you install SNMP after having applied a service pack, you will have to reinstall the service pack. SNMP will not function properly without the service pack being reinstalled.

FIGURE 20-2

Desktop agent installation screen

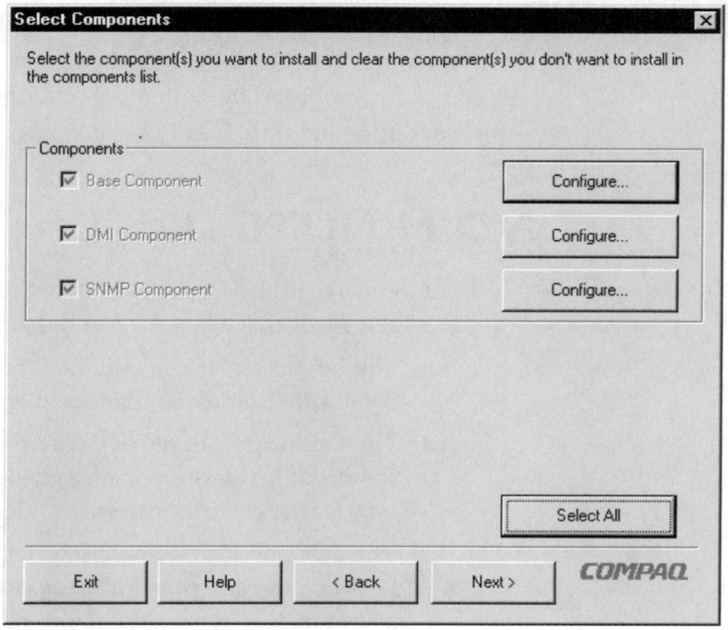

CERTIFICATION OBJECTIVE 20.04

Polling of the Desktop Agents

After the agents are installed on the systems to be managed, you need to install a management application. The ones Compaq offers are Insight Manager, Insight Manager XE, and Insight Manager LC. These applications work by polling the desktop agents. At regular intervals, the agents will be polled and information will be gathered. The usage of Insight Manager products is covered in detail in Chapters 11, 17, 22, and 27.

CERTIFICATION SUMMARY

Compaq has developed a robust management system called Intelligent Manageability, making Compaq systems easier to manage and configure. Compaq has been an integral part of the Desktop Management Task Force and the development of the Desktop Management Interface. Compaq products can be managed by systems that adhere to the DMI 2.0 specification and even those that don't. Compaq has made it possible for their desktops and portables to be integrated into almost any environment.

TWO-MINUTE DRILL

- ❑ Intelligent Manageability is a collection of applications and standards that allow for a robust management environment.
- ❑ The Desktop Management Task Force (DMTF) is the group that defines the standards used for managing desktops.
- ❑ The Desktop Management Task Force has developed two standards for desktop management: the Desktop Management Interface and the Management Information File.
- ❑ The Desktop Management Interface (DMI) serves as the interface between the components being managed and the management software; it is composed of two interfaces.

- ❑ The first interface is the component interface, which allows the desktop components to send information to management programs.
- ❑ The second interface is the management interface, which allows the management programs to read and write management information.

❑ The Management Information File (MIF) is analogous to the Management Information Base (MIB) used with SNMP.

❑ There are two types of MIFs: standard MIFs and vendor MIFs.

❑ Compaq Intelligent Manageability is divided into five categories:

- ❑ Configuration Management
- ❑ Asset Management
- ❑ Security Management
- ❑ Fault Management
- ❑ Integration Management

❑ Configuration Management involves loading drivers, doing system updates, and managing configuration files.

❑ Asset Management involves inventory data collection and tracking.

❑ The tools Compaq uses for Security Management include:

- ❑ Smart Cover Lock
- ❑ Memory change alert
- ❑ Configuration control hardware
- ❑ Ownership tag
- ❑ Smart Cover Sensor

❑ Compaq Fault Management features include:

- ❑ ECC Memory
- ❑ ECC Fault Prediction and pre-failure warranty
- ❑ SMART hard drives
- ❑ Hard drive pre-failure warranty
- ❑ Ultra ATA Integrity Monitoring
- ❑ Thermal sensor

- Integration Management allows your system to be integrated easily into an existing network.
- The Compaq Insight Management Desktop Agents allow support for Intelligent Manageability on Compaq desktops.
- The Compaq desktop agents support Windows 95, Windows 98, Windows NT Workstation 3.51, and Windows NT Workstation 4.0.
- Management applications, such as Insight Manager, Insight Manager XE, and Insight Manager LC work by polling the desktop agents. At regular intervals, the agents will be polled and information will be gathered.

SELF TEST

The following Self Test questions will help you measure your understanding of the material presented in this chapter. Read all the choices carefully, as there may be more than one correct answer. Choose all correct answers for each question.

1. What entity designed the DMI 2.0 standard?

   A. Desktop Management Task Force
   B. Desktop Management Institute
   C. Desktop Compliance Organization
   D. Desktop Compliance Task Force

2. Which of the following companies is not a member of the Desktop Management Task Force?

   A. Intel
   B. Microsoft
   C. Novell
   D. Veritas

3. Which of the following is not a part of the Desktop Management Interface?

   A. Component Interface
   B. Management Interface
   C. Desktop Interface
   D. All are parts of the Desktop Management Interface.

4. Which component of the DMI allows the desktop components to send information to management programs?

   A. Component Interface
   B. Management Interface
   C. Desktop Interface
   D. Agent Interface

5. Which component of the DMI allows the management programs to read and write management information?

   A. Component Interface
   B. Management Interface
   C. Desktop Interface
   D. Agent Interface

6. Which of the following is analogous to the Management Information File?

   A. Management Information Base
   B. Management Agent
   C. The Registry
   D. None of the above

7. Which of the following cannot be included in a Management Information File?

   A. Text files
   B. Management agents
   C. Executable files
   D. All of these can be a part of a Management Information File.

8. Which of the following is not a type of Management Information File?

   A. Standard MIFs
   B. Vendor MIFs
   C. Agent MIFs
   D. All of these are types of MIFs.

9. Which of the following is not a category of Intelligent Manageability?
   A. Configuration Management
   B. Fault Management
   C. Installation Management
   D. Integration Management
10. Which of the following are not components of Compaq Asset Management?
    A. DMI BIOS
    B. DMI 2.0 support
    C. DIMM Serial Presence Detect
    D. SMART hard drives
11. Which is not a component of Compaq Configuration Management?
    A. Remote ROM Flash
    B. Remote wake-up and shutdown
    C. Thermal sensor
    D. Support Software CD
12. Which of the following is not a part of Compaq Security Management?
    A. Smart Cover Lock
    B. Ownership tag
    C. Smart Cover Sensor
    D. All of the above are components of Compaq Security Management.
13. Which of the following is not a part Compaq Fault Management?
    A. ECC Memory
    B. SMART hard drives
    C. Thermal sensor
    D. Memory Change Alert
14. Which of the following is not a part of Compaq Integration Management?
    A. Insight Manager
    B. Management Solutions Partners Program
    C. Support Software CD
    D. Net PC Technologies Support
15. Which of the following operating systems support Compaq desktop agents?
    A. Windows NT 3.51
    B. Windows NT 4.0
    C. Windows 95
    D. All of the above

21

Management PC Configuration

CERTIFICATION OBJECTIVES

21.01 Management PC Requirements

21.02 Installing Insight Manager on the Management PC

In the previous few chapters, you learned several basic concepts of server management. You read about some management tools that you can use to see how your network is running. One of the tools introduced briefly was Compaq's Insight Manager. Insight Manager is Compaq's tool to manage and monitor their servers. Insight Manager runs on a management PC from which you can manage all of the servers in your environment. You will learn more about using Insight Manager in Chapter 22, but first we will go over the configuration of the management PC. This chapter will introduce you to the minimum requirements for running Insight Manager. We will also cover the installation of Insight Manager on the management PC.

CERTIFICATION OBJECTIVE 21.01

Management PC Requirements

This section will discuss the requirements to run Compaq Insight Manager (CIM) on a management PC. From this management PC, you will be able to manage and control all of the Compaq servers in your environment. The factors that you will need to consider include the operating system running on your management PC, the hardware installed on the management PC, and other considerations that we will discuss.

Operating System Support

Since Insight Manager is a 32-bit application, you will need to install it on a 32-bit operating system. You cannot install Insight Manager on Windows for Workgroups 3.*x*. The following operating systems are supported:

- Windows 95
- Windows 98
- Windows NT 3.51
- Windows NT 4.0
- Windows 2000

Hardware Requirements

This section describes the minimum hardware requirements necessary to run Insight Manager on your management PC. Keep in mind that these are the recommended minimums specified by Compaq. You will want to increase these requirements in most cases to increase performance, especially if you will be running other applications on your PC.

- 24MB of RAM on Windows 9*x* PCs (32MB recommended)
- 32MB of RAM on Windows NT PCs (48MB recommended)
- 35MB of free disk space (20MB for program files, 15MB for database)
- VGA or better video adapter
- Network Interface Card supported by Windows 9*x*, Windows 2000, or Windows NT
- Hayes-compatible modem (for Insight Asynchronous Management, Remote Console, Remote Insight, or Alarm Forwarding)

Other Requirements

Besides a 32-bit OS and a minimum set of hardware, you will also need the following to install Insight Manager:

- TCP/IP
- SNMP or WinSNMP
- IPX/SPX (to manage Novell servers via IPX protocol)
- Remote Access Service (RAS) or Dial-Up Networking (for Insight Asynchronous Management, Remote Console, Remote Insight, or Alarm Forwarding)
- If you will be running Insight Manager on a Windows 95 PC, you will also have to install the Kernel32 Update from http://www.microsoft.com/windows95/downloads/contents/WUAdminTools/S_WUNetworkingTools/W95Kernel32/Default.asp Warning! This update should not be installed on PCs with

Windows 95 OEM Service Release (OSR) 2 or later. You can view the Windows version in the System applet of Control Panel. If the Windows version is 4.00.950 B or later, you do not need to install the Kernel32 Update.

In most cases, you will probably install Insight Manager on the PC that you use for general day-to-day tasks. You may want to consider installing Insight Manager on a dedicated PC that only runs Insight Manager and is configured to alert you in the event of server failures and emergencies. You can then leave this PC in a locked closet with limited access. One major advantage of this approach is that since this PC will only be running Insight Manager, you can probably get away with installing the minimum hardware requirements specified. Another advantage is that you don't have to worry about leaving your own PC logged onto the network at all times to continuously monitor the servers.

QUESTIONS AND ANSWERS

Can I install Insight Manager if I have Windows 95 installed with 24MB of RAM?	Although this configuration meets the minimum requirements for Insight Manager, you should still upgrade the memory to at least 32MB for increased performance.
Can I install Insight Manager if I have Windows for Workgroups 3.11 with 32MB of RAM?	You cannot install Insight Manager on a 16-bit operating system such as Windows for Workgroups. You will need to upgrade to either Windows 95/98 or Windows NT.
Can I install Insight Manager to manage servers at a remote office via modem?	You will need to install a Hayes-compatible modem and either Dial Up Networking or Remote Access Service.
I have Windows NT installed with 32MB of RAM, but only 20MB of free disk space. Can I install Insight Manager?	First, you should upgrade the memory to at least the recommended minimum of 48MB. Second, you will need to free up disk space. You could delete .TMP files in the TEMP directory or .DMP files in the WINNT directory. You could also remove any unnecessary applications such as games or Window accessories. If you have Windows NT Service Pack 3 or later, you could remove the UNINSTALL directory in the WINNT directory.

CERTIFICATION OBJECTIVE 21.02

Installing Insight Manager on the Management PC

This section will discuss the process of installing Insight Manager on the Management PC. We will first go over the sources from which you can obtain Insight Manager, then we will go over the installation itself.

Obtaining Insight Manager

Compaq provides Insight Manager with every ProSignia and ProLiant server that they sell. The actual Insight Manager application is located on the red Management CD that ships with the server, not on the green SmartStart CD.

Usually, the version of Insight Manager that ships with the server is a couple of versions older than the current version. Compaq makes the latest version of Insight Manager available for download from their Web site: http://www.compaq.com/support/files/server/softpaqs/mgmtsol/cimcmplt.html

Once you download the latest version from the Web site, you must extract the source files to a temporary directory on your hard disk. You can then run the setup program to update the current version of Insight Manager.

You can also load Insight Manager from an Integration Server on your network. For more information on Integration Server, refer to Chapter 26.

Preinstallation Considerations

Before you install Insight Manager on your management PC, make sure you have enough free disk space available (about 35MB). Also, make sure that you close any Windows applications, including any version of Insight Manager that you have running, before you start the installation.

Installing Insight Manager

Installing Insight Manager is a fairly simple process. You can usually perform a successful install by choosing all the default settings that the setup program presents to you. The following exercise outlines the steps necessary to install Insight Manager, highlighting points to which you should pay particular attention.

EXERCISE 21-1

Installing Insight Manager on the Management PC

The steps for installing CIM version 4.23 are as follows:

1. On the management PC, insert the Compaq Management CD and go to the \INSIGHT\WIN32\ENG directory. Or if you downloaded Insight Manager, go to the directory where you extracted the files.
2. Run SETUP.EXE. The Welcome screen appears. Click Next.
3. A window appears stating that the Borland Database Engine will be installed, as shown in Figure 21-1.
4. Close any applications that use the Borland Database Engine, then click Next.

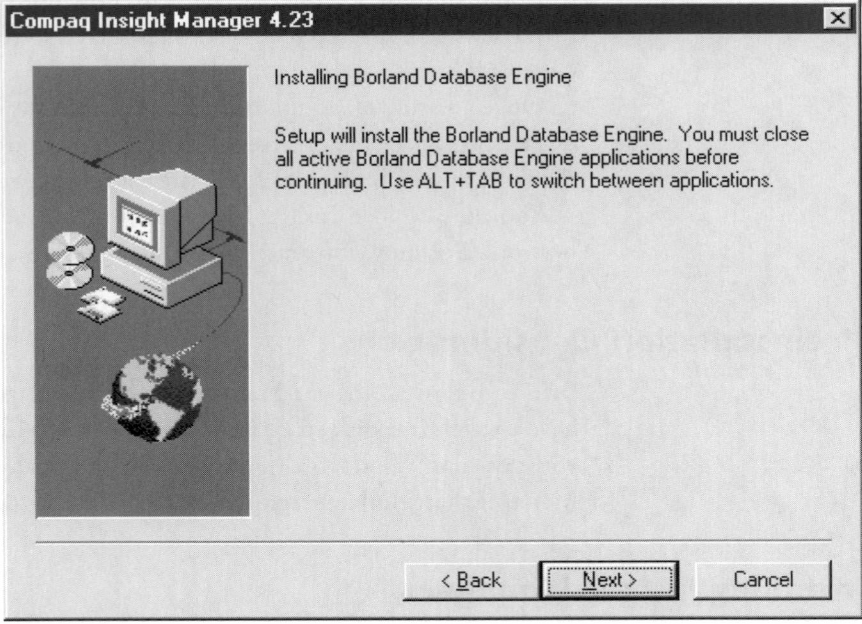

FIGURE 21-1

All Borland Database Engine Applications should be closed before installing Insight Manager

5. Enter your Name and Company information and click Next.
6. The screen asks you to confirm the information that you just entered. Click Back to change the information or click Yes to continue.
7. (This step applies only if you are installing Insight Manager on a Windows NT server. If you are installing onto Windows 95, skip to the next step.) The Install Options screen appears as in Figure 21-2. Make sure that Compaq Insight Manager is selected. If you are installing Insight Manager on a Microsoft Systems Management Server Management Station, select Microsoft Systems Management Server Launch Support. Click Next to continue.
8. Type in the path where you want to install the Insight Manager application. By default, Insight Manager will be installed in C:\PROGRAM FILES\COMPAQ\INSIGHT MANAGER. Click Next to continue.

FIGURE 21-2

The Install Options allow you to specify SMS support

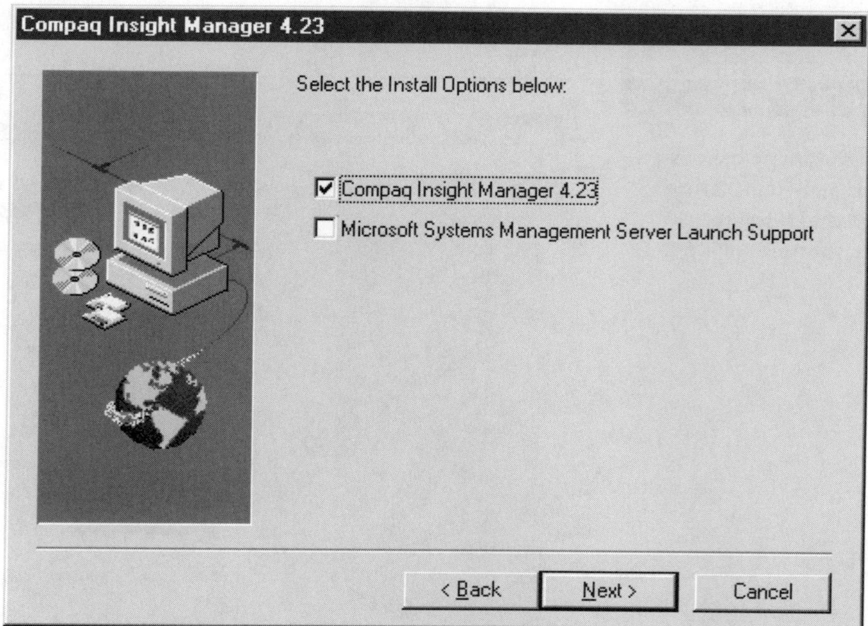

9. The configuration screen shown in Figure 21-3 appears. Here you can set the following options.
   Enable auto discovery of IPX servers Select this option to automatically add servers running IPX to the list of Responsible Devices. If you do not have any servers running IPX, deselect this option to improve performance.
   Enable auto discovery of Remote Console NVT servers Select this option to discover servers using the NetWare Virtual Terminal discovery. Disable this option to improve performance if you will not be auto discovering servers using NVT.
   Version Control Enter the number of days after which the Version Control database is considered out of date. After the number of days passes, Insight Manager will inform you that the database is out of date and allow you to update the database.
   Borland Database Engine Enable Maintain configuration to support existing Win 3.1 applications if you are using 16-bit applications that use the Borland Database Engine. Deselect this option if you are not using applications that use the 16-bit version of the engine.
   Click Next to continue.

FIGURE 21-3

Setting these options properly can enhance Insight Manager performance

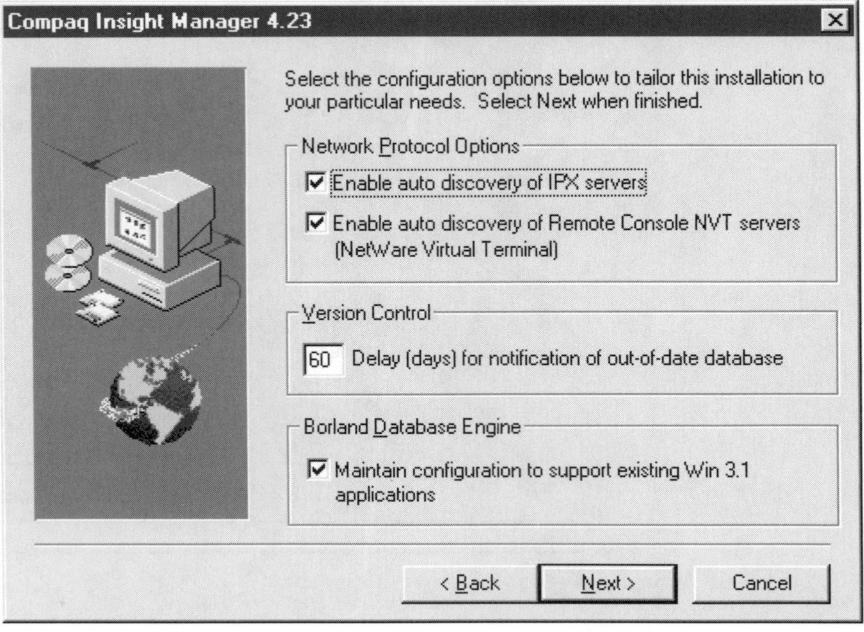

10. (If you selected to install support for Systems Management Server in step 7, complete this step, otherwise skip to the next step.) Enter the path to the SMS executable file (SMS.EXE) then click Next. Enter the name of the SMS database, the SQL administrative account (usually **sa**), and the administrative account's password. Select OK to continue.
11. Select the Program Folder where you'd like to place the Insight Manager icons. By default, the program icons will be created in the COMPAQ INSIGHT MANAGER folder.
12. The screen shows the current settings, which you can review. To change any of the settings, click Back. To continue, click Next. The setup program will begin to copy files to your hard disk and you will see an installation progress bar, as shown in Figure 21-4.

FIGURE 21-4 You can learn about new features while files are being copied

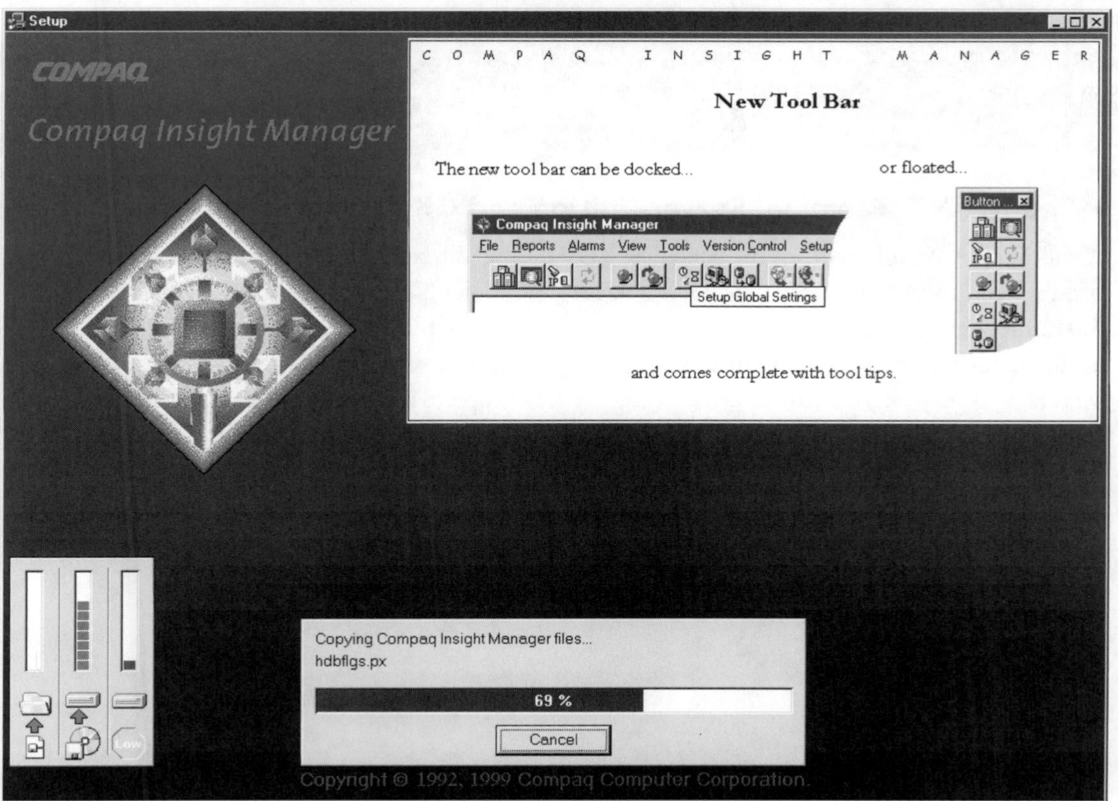

13. Once the setup program has finished copying the files, a final window appears informing you that the installation is complete. You have the option of viewing the README file. Click Finish to complete the installation.

Insight Manager is a great tool to monitor your servers, but what if you want to take a quick look at your server and your management PC is on the other side of the building? With Insight Manager 4.01 and later, you can use a Web browser to monitor your servers. Although the browser does not have the alert features of the full product, you can quickly use a Web browser to see if there are any failures on your servers. For more information on the Web-enabled agents, refer to Chapter 27.

FROM THE FIELD

Windows NT Terminal Server Edition and CIM Management Console

Although the Web-based Insight Manager XE product and the Web-enabled agents in release 4.01 and later provide the thinnest client available for remote management of Compaq servers, you may want to consider implementing a Windows NT Server, Terminal Server Edition machine for remote management of your environment.

Terminal Server is a thin-client solution that yields reasonable performance even over a slow WAN link or asynchronous connection. Using Citrix MetaFrame, you can even run a Windows NT desktop from an HTML browser.

By establishing a single Terminal Server for use by support personnel, you can have a complete remote management solution that includes user management, domain infrastructure management, and even management of all servers running the Compaq Insight Management Agents.

—Thomas E. Eck, MCSE+I, MCSD, ASE, CCA, CNA

CERTIFICATION SUMMARY

In this chapter, you learned about the requirements for installing Insight Manager on a management PC. You learned about the minimum hardware requirements, OS requirements, and in the case of Windows 95, a software patch. You also went through a detailed walk-through of installing Insight Manager on a PC. Although the installation is fairly straightforward, there are a couple of areas that you need to pay special attention to in order to optimize Insight Manager performance, such as disabling auto discovery of IPX servers or Remote Console NVT servers.

TWO-MINUTE DRILL

- ❑ Insight Manager is Compaq's tool to manage and monitor their servers.
- ❑ The factors that you will need to consider to run Compaq Insight Manager (CIM) on a management PC include the operating system running on your management PC and the hardware installed on the management PC, as well as a few other considerations.
- ❑ Since Insight Manager is a 32-bit application, you will need to install it on a 32-bit operating system.
- ❑ You cannot install Insight Manager on Windows for Workgroups 3.*x*.
- ❑ There are recommended minimum hardware requirements necessary to run Insight Manager on your management PC, specified by Compaq.
- ❑ You will want to increase the minimum hardware requirements in most cases to increase performance.
- ❑ You will also need the following to install Insight Manager:
  - ❑ TCP/IP
  - ❑ SNMP or WinSNMP
  - ❑ IPX/SPX (to manage Novell servers via IPX protocol)
  - ❑ Remote Access Service (RAS) or Dial-Up Networking (for Insight Asynchronous Management, Remote Console, Remote Insight, or Alarm Forwarding)

- ❑ If you will be running Insight Manager on a Windows 95 PC, you will also have to install the Kernel32 Update from http://www.microsoft.com/windows95/downloads/contents/WUAdminTools/S_WUNetworkingTools/W95Kernel32/Default.asp.

❑ You may want to consider installing Insight Manager on a dedicated PC that only runs Insight Manager and is configured to alert you in the event of server failures and emergencies.

❑ Compaq provides Insight Manager with every ProSignia and ProLiant server that they sell.

❑ Before you install Insight Manager on your management PC, make sure you have enough free disk space available (about 35MB).

❑ You can usually perform a successful install by choosing all the default settings that the setup program presents to you.

❑ Review the chapter exercise to install Insight Manager prior to the exam.

SELF TEST

The following Self Test questions will help you measure your understanding of the material presented in this chapter. Read all the choices carefully, as there may be more than one correct answer. Choose all correct answers for each question.

1. Which of the following operating systems is not supported by Insight Manager?
   A. Windows NT
   B. Windows for Workgroups
   C. Windows 95
   D. Windows 98
2. What is the minimum amount of memory you should have in order to install Insight Manager under Windows NT?
   A. 16MB
   B. 24MB
   C. 32MB
   D. 64MB
3. Which of the following do you need to support Insight Asynchronous Management?
   A. Hayes-compatible modem
   B. Super VGA video card
   C. Compaq Survey Utility
   D. Null modem cable
4. Which of the following is not an additional requirement for Insight Manager?
   A. TCP/IP
   B. SNMP
   C. IPX/SPX
   D. NetBEUI
5. Which of the following is not a valid source to obtain Insight Manager?
   A. SmartStart CD
   B. Management CD
   C. Compaq Web site
   D. Integration Server
6. How much free disk space should you have before installing Insight Manager?
   A. 5MB
   B. 15MB
   C. 35MB
   D. 50MB
7. What is the default installation directory where Insight Manager is installed?
   A. C:\PROGRAM FILES\COMPAQ\INSIGHT MANAGER
   B. C:\COMPAQ\INSIGHT MANAGER
   C. C:\PROGRAM FILES\INSIGHT MANAGER
   D. C:\INSIGHT MANAGER

8. You have 100 NetWare servers running IPX/SPX. You want to be able to manage the servers using Insight Manager, but you do not look forward to adding them all to the database. What feature of Insight Manager allows you to add the servers automatically?
   A. Import a text file containing the names of all your servers
   B. Enable auto discovery of IPX servers
   C. Enable auto discovery of NetWare servers
   D. There is no such feature.
9. You are running a pure TCP/IP network. What is one method of improving performance for Insight Manager?
   A. Enable auto discovery for TCP/IP devices
   B. Disable auto discovery of NetWare servers
   C. Disable auto discovery of IPX servers
   D. Enable auto discovery of Remote Console NVT servers
10. After you install Insight Manager, your existing Borland Database applications fail to run. How can you prevent this from happening again?
   A. Select the option to Maintain Configuration to Support Existing Win 3.1 Applications.
   B. Install Insight Manager to a different partition.
   C. Select the option to autodiscover Borland applications.
   D. Make sure you install version 4.20 or later of Insight Manager.

ASE
ACCREDITED SYSTEMS ENGINEER

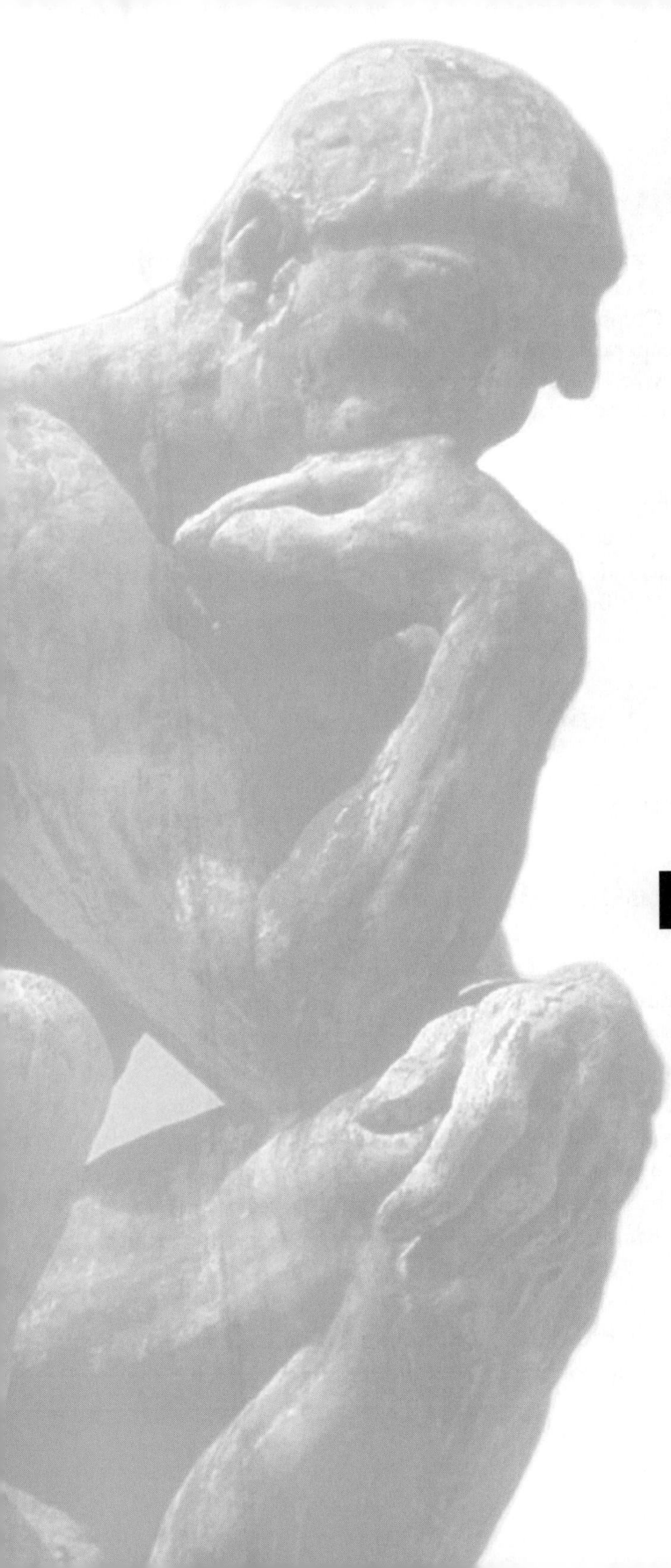

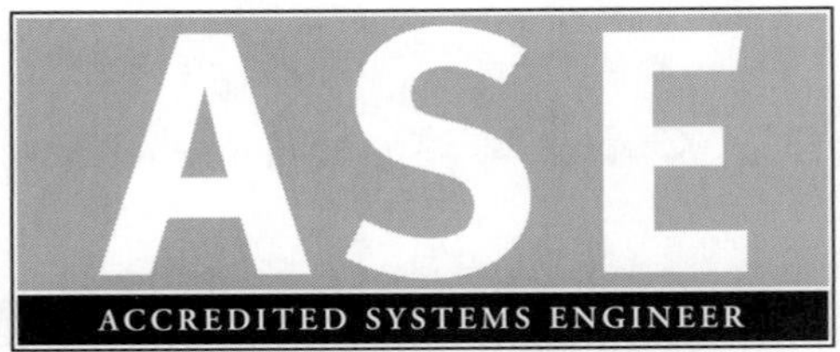

22

Compaq Insight Manager

CERTIFICATION OBJECTIVES

22.01 Automatic Data Collection

22.02 Server Reboot Feature

22.03 Alarm Logs

22.04 SNMP Community Names

22.05 In-Band Management

22.06 Out-of-Band Management

22.07 Alarm Forwarding

22.08 Server Filtering

22.09 Color Coded Status

This chapter will discuss Compaq Insight Manager (CIM), Compaq's utility to manage and monitor their servers and desktops. In particular, we will concentrate on the CIM application when managing Compaq servers. We will focus heavily on collecting data from your servers and automatically generating reports. We'll also look into configuring CIM to alert you when there is something wrong with one of your servers. Compaq developed Insight Manager to make your life as a systems administrator much easier, and this chapter will help you make the most of CIM.

There are some functions of CIM that will not be discussed in this chapter as they are discussed in detail in other chapters. These functions are Version Control, Integration Server, Asynchronous Management, Remote Insight Board, and Web Based Management.

CERTIFICATION OBJECTIVE 22.01

Automatic Data Collection

Insight Manager can display a great wealth of information about your servers. Much of that information is obtained in real time and shows the current state of your servers. However, you may want to know the utilization of your server during certain times of the day for the past week, or track the number of errors received on a particular network card. CIM can collect server information at specified intervals and store that information in a database. You can then create reports and graphs for the information to spot trends or potential trouble areas for your servers.

You should know that you can only collect data for Compaq servers running the Insight Agents. You cannot collect data from third-party servers or Compaq servers that are not running the agents. In addition, you cannot collect data for Compaq desktops or for Compaq Netelligent networking products. From each CIM management console, you can perform data collection on a maximum of 100 servers.

This section will help you get the most from the Automatic Data Collection (ADC) function of CIM. We will discuss how to enable and configure ADC and how to interpret the data in a meaningful way once you have collected it.

Enabling Data Collection

By default, data collection is not enabled for any servers that you are managing in CIM, since the data could potentially grow to large amounts. You can also adversely affect network performance during the collection interval, especially if you are collecting data from a large number of servers. You must enable data collection on a server-by-server basis for servers that you'd like to monitor over time. This also means that you must have added the server you want to monitor to the Device List in CIM.

To enable data collection for a particular server, follow these steps:

1. In the Device List in CIM, select the server for which you'd like to enable data collection.
2. Right-click the server and select Device Setup (see Figure 22-1).
3. Select Automatic Data Collection to enable data collection.

FIGURE 22-1

Enabling Automatic Data Collection in the Device Setup screen

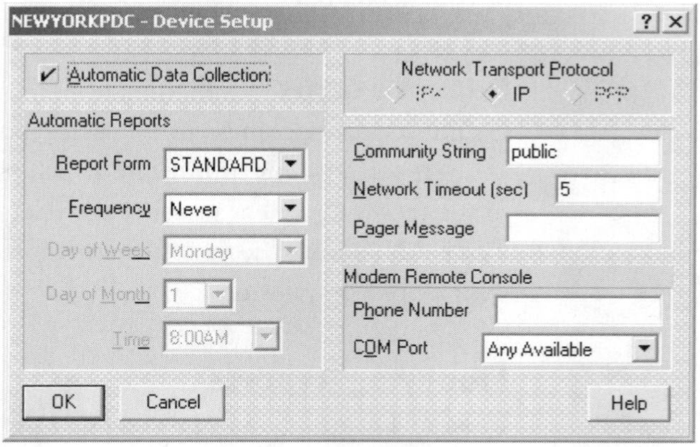

Configuring Data Collection

The only option that you can set for data collection is the interval at which CIM will connect to the servers to collect the data. CIM has different interval settings for servers that are connected via the local network and for servers that are connected via modem (asynchronously). The default interval for locally connected servers is 30 minutes. This is also the minimum value that you can set for local servers. As you add servers from which to collect data, you should also consider increasing the interval, since you may adversely affect network performance. In general, you should increase the interval by 30 minutes for every 20 servers that you add.

The default interval for asynchronous servers is 12 hours, since you must dial into these servers via modem. The minimum interval is one hour, although it is recommended that you not set this to less than 6 hours.

Reporting on Collected Data

Once you have collected data on your servers, you'll want to generate reports to show the status and health of your servers. Insight Manager comes with several report forms that neatly format the collected data into meaningful output, such as a graph. You can customize the reports to fit your environment. You can also run the reports manually or have the report print out automatically at set intervals so that you can have a historical log of your server data.

Report Forms

Insight Manager comes with several report forms that specify the format for your report. The forms indicate which monitored items are to be included in the report as well as whether the data is presented graphically or textually. Table 22-1 shows the various report forms that are built into CIM, along with a brief description.

Modifying Reports

Insight Manager allows you to modify the existing report forms or to create a new one from scratch. You should be aware that CIM allows you to report on a lot of information. In fact, CIM can report on almost 500 different counters

TABLE 22-1 The Default Built-In Report Forms

Report Form	Description
CONFIG	Prints configuration information for the selected device without graphs
DRIVES	Reports on information regarding the disk drives in your servers
ENVIRON	Reports on the environmental status (such as temperature and fan status) for your servers
RAPREC	Reports on the Rapid Recovery subsystem, which monitors Automatic Server Recovery, the Critical Error Log, the Correctable Memory Log, and the Compaq UPS
NOGRAPH	Prints the same information as the STANDARD report but without graphs
SCSI	Reports information on devices attached to your SCSI controllers
SECURITY	Reports on the security settings (such as BIOS password) that are enabled/disabled for your system
STANDARD	Reports on all the monitored systems of your server. The report may graph certain values, such as temperature, over time.

for your servers. Fortunately, CIM also allows you to copy from the existing report forms so that you can simply modify them to suit your needs.

EXERCISE 22-1

Creating a New Form

1. In CIM, click Reports | Forms. The Report Forms window appears.

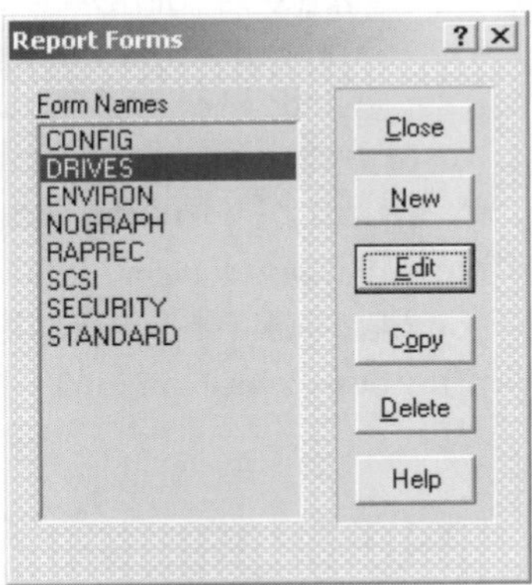

2. Click the New button. The New Form window appears.
3. Type in a name for the new form.

To copy an existing report form, perform the following steps:

1. In the Report Forms window, select the form that you want to copy, then press the Copy button. The Copy Form window appears.
2. Type in a new name for the report.

To modify an existing report form, perform the following steps:

1. In the Report Forms window, select the form that you want to modify, then press the Edit button. The Edit Form window appears.

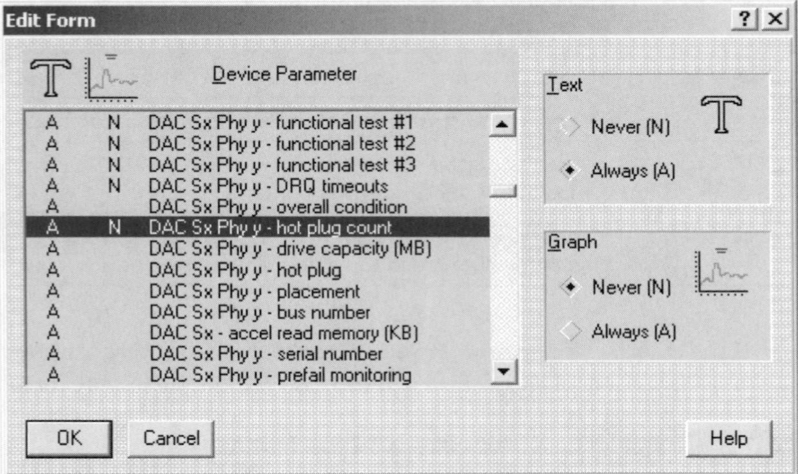

2. In the list of device parameters, select the parameters that you want to enable by selecting the parameter and clicking Always in the Text window or the Graph window.

Manually Printing Reports

Now that you have all your data collected and your forms formatted just as you like, how can you finally show off all of your beautiful data? You can print out a report manually for your device.

EXERCISE 22-2

Printing a Report Manually

1. Make sure that you have a default printer enabled. In CIM, select File | Print Setup and make sure that your default printer is selected.
2. In the Device List window, select the server for which you want to print out a report.
3. Right-click the device and select Print Report. The Print Historical Report window appears as follows.

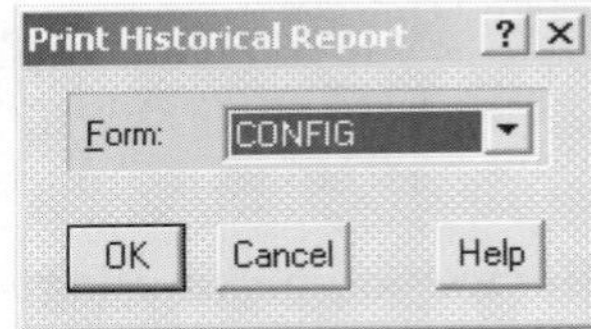

4. Select the form that you want to use for the report and click OK. The Print Report window appears asking for confirmation to print.
5. Click OK.

Note that if you do not have ADC enabled for a device, only the CONFIG form will be available for the report.

Automatically Printing Reports

You can also have CIM automatically print certain reports at a specified interval to give you a historical log of your server data. To use this function, you must have Automatic Data Collection enabled for a device. To configure automatic printing of reports, perform the following steps:

1. In the Device List, select the server for which you want to enable automatic reports.
2. Right-click the server, and select Device Setup (see Figure 22-1).
3. Make sure that the Automatic Data Collection option is selected.

4. In the Automatic Reports section, set the following options:
   a. **Report Form** The form that you want to use to format the report.
   b. **Frequency** The interval that you want to print the report. This can be set to Never, Hourly, Daily, Weekly, or Monthly.
   c. **Day of Week** If the frequency is set to Weekly, allows you to select which day of the week the report is printed.
   d. **Day of Month** If the frequency is set to Monthly, allows you to select the day of the month the report is printed.
   e. **Time** Allows you to specify the time during the day that the report is printed.

Before you begin using Automatic Reports, print out a manual report first so that you can get an idea of how many pages will be printed. You can then plan the time of day when the report will be printed so that you do not tie up a shared network printer. Also, make sure that there is enough paper in the printer. There is nothing worse than coming in the next morning and finding your printer without paper!

CERTIFICATION OBJECTIVE 22.02

Server Reboot Feature

The Server Reboot feature of CIM allows you to reboot a server from your management console. You can either boot to the operating system or boot to the Compaq utilities located on the System Partition. You must allow a server to be rebooted remotely by configuring the Insight Agents on the server. In addition, the SNMP community strings must match on both the management console and the managed server. (See the SNMP Community Names later in this chapter.)

This feature is particularly convenient in several scenarios, such as when a server is in a locked closet, at another building or site, or if the user interface on the server is locked for some reason. Remote reboot allows you to shut down a server gracefully without having to shut it down by pressing the power button.

Enabling Remote Server Reboot

Before you can remotely reboot a server using CIM, you must enable the remote reboot function in the Insight Agents applet in Control Panel using the following steps:

1. Log in to the server as a user with administrator rights.
2. Open Control Panel | Insight Agents. The Insight Agents applet appears.
3. Select the SNMP Settings Tab.

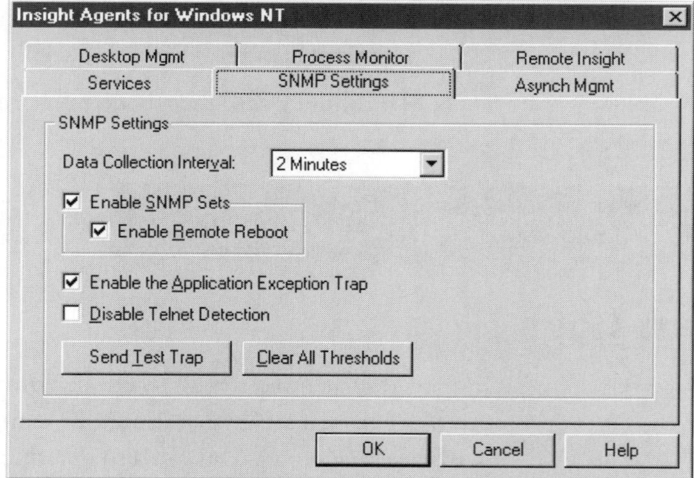

4. Select the Enable SNMP Sets and Enable Remote Reboot options.
5. Restart the Insight Agents service.

Rebooting a Server

You must be very careful when rebooting a server. You must make sure that no one is logged into the server with files open, or else they may lose any changes they make to their files when you reboot the server. Use the Server applet in Control Panel to check if anyone has any open files on the server.

To reboot a server, perform the following steps:

1. In the Device List in CIM, select the server that you would like to reboot.
2. Right-click the server and select View Device Data. The Device View window appears.
3. Press the Reboot button. A Reboot Options window appears.
4. Select whether you want to perform a Normal Reboot (boot to the Operating System) or Reboot to Utilities (boot to the System Partition Utilities), then press Reboot. A confirmation message appears.
5. To continue with the reboot, select Yes. To abort the reboot, select No.

CERTIFICATION OBJECTIVE 22.03

Alarm Logs

Insight Manager displays all received alarms in the Alarm Log. The alarms can range from a server that cannot be contacted to a failed piece of hardware on a server. You can also determine when the alarm was received and whether it has forwarded. Alarm logs are a good starting place for viewing any problems on your servers. This section will discuss how to use the Alarm Log to minimize downtime due to server problems. Later in the chapter, we'll discuss forwarding alarms to your pager or e-mail address.

Viewing Alarms

The Alarm Log is displayed in the Insight Manager application. Although you can minimize the Alarm Log or hide it behind other windows, you cannot close it. CIM will remember the state of the log when you close CIM and will keep that state when you reopen CIM. For example, if the log is minimized when you close CIM, when you reopen CIM, the log will be minimized. The Alarm Log is displayed in Figure 22-2.

By default, the log is sorted in descending order by date and time, then by severity. Therefore, you will always see the most recent and the most severe alerts at the top of the list. To sort by another column, click the column header of the column that you'd like to sort by. To reverse the sort order, click the column again. Table 22-2 gives a description of each of the columns.

If your servers generate many errors, your Alarm Log may grow very large. To keep the list under control, you can delete old alarms by selecting the alarm and clicking the Delete button from the toolbar. You can also right-click the alarm and select Delete Alarm.

Viewing Alarm Details

You can view the details of an alarm by double-clicking the alarm that you are interested in. The Alarm Details window displays the date and time the alarm was received and the device that generated the alarm. A more detailed description of the alarm is given, as well as any alarm-specific details. For

FIGURE 22-2

The Alarm Log gives you a quick glance to error messages

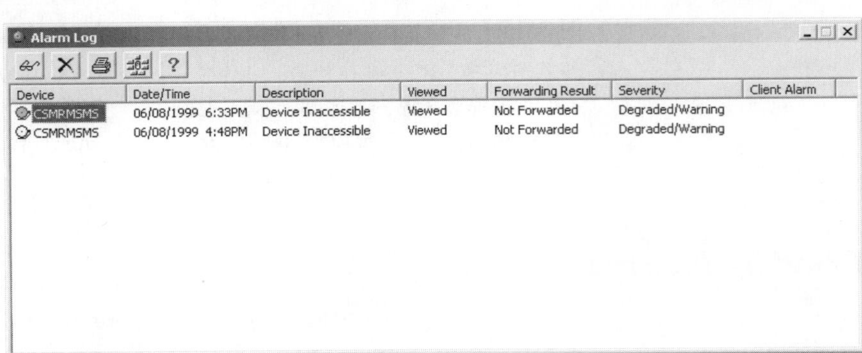

TABLE 22-2 The Sortable Column Headers Available in the Alarm Log

Column	Description
Device	Gives the name of the device that gave the alarm. If you sort by this column, you can view all of the alarms given by a particular device.
Date/Time	The default sort column for the alarms. It displays the date and time that the alarm was received.
Description	Displays a brief description of the alarm. To view the full text of the alarm and a possible resolution, view the Alarm Details.
Viewed	Tells you whether the alarm details have been viewed. You can sort by this column to view all alarms that have not yet been viewed so that you can take action.
Forwarding Result	If alarm forwarding is enabled for a particular server that generates an alarm, this column will inform you whether the alarm was forwarded to your pager or e-mail.
Severity	Displays the severity of the alarm. The color of the icon to the left of the device name corresponds to this severity code.
Client Alarm	Notifies you if the alarm is generated by a managed desktop.

example, if the alarm is a failed disk, the alarm details will show the actual slot where the disk resides. Figure 22-3 shows an example of an Alarm Details window.

From the Alarm Details window, click the Action button to display a possible cause and resolution to the alarm.

Printing Alarms

If you would like a hard copy of all of your alarms, you can print out the list of alarms from the Alarm Log window. You can print the list either by clicking the Printer icon in the toolbar of the Alarm Log or by right-clicking

FIGURE 22-3

The Alarm Details window shows detailed information about the error message

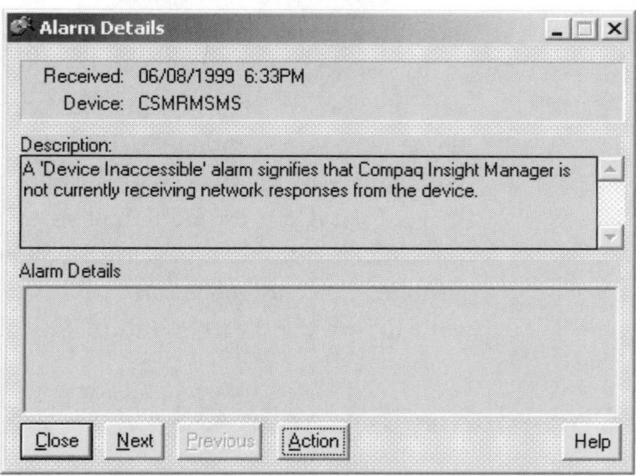

anywhere in the Alarm Log window and selecting Print Log from the Context menu. This will send the Alarm Log to your default printer. Also note that CIM will print the log as you have it sorted in the window, so be sure you have the list sorted the way you'd like before you print it.

CERTIFICATION OBJECTIVE 22.04

SNMP Community Names

SNMP community names (or strings) provide a limited amount of protection for your servers from unauthorized access from rogue Insight Manager consoles. When CIM sends a request for data from a managed server, it sends along with the request an SNMP community string. Before the managed device replies to the request, it checks to make sure that the community string that the console sent matches the community string that is configured locally on the server. If the community strings match, then the request is serviced. If the strings do not match, then the machine will appear as unmanageable. The SNMP community string is case-sensitive.

By default, CIM uses a community string of "public" since many vendors also by default enable the community string "public" on their devices. You can configure a different community string for each device that you manage or use the default string. You can also change the default string that is used if you use a different string on your servers. If you are in an insecure environment, make sure you use a community string other than "public," since someone can easily attach a CIM management console to your network and gather information about your servers.

Setting Community Name in OS

The SNMP community string is configured differently for each operating system. For example, in NetWare you configure the SNMP.NLM, whereas in Windows NT, you configure SNMP through Control Panel. Whichever OS you use, you must be aware that the community string is case-sensitive. This section will discuss setting the community string in Windows NT.

1. In Windows NT, open Control Panel | Network.
2. Select the Services tab.
3. Select SNMP Service and press the Properties button.
4. Select the Security tab.
5. To enter a new Community Name, press the Add button under Accepted Community Names.

on the Job

If you installed your Compaq server using the SmartStart process, then SNMP should have been installed by default. If you didn't use SmartStart, then you'll have to install SNMP separately. If you install SNMP after you have already applied a Windows NT Service Pack, you will receive the error "SNMP Error – Entry Point not found. The procedure entry point SnmpSvcGetEnterpriseOID could not be located in the dynamic link library snmpapi.dll" and Event 7022 in the Event Log. Reapply the latest Service Pack to fix this problem. Refer to Microsoft Knowledge Base Article Q163595 for more information.

FROM THE FIELD

When CIM Is Not an Option

If the security policy for highly secure environments (such as machines in an amber zone or DMZ) does not permit the use of SNMP, you will not be able to include these machines for management using Compaq Insight Manager. However, you may still be able to use some of the little known features of WinMSD to derive information about a machine. While not nearly as comprehensive as the reports generated from CIM, WinMSD can provide valuable information about machines that cannot be reached using SNMP. To use WinMSD to derive information from a remote machine, type the following from a command prompt:

```
winmsd \\computername [options]
```

In this command, \\computername is the NetBIOS name or IP address of the target machine.

By passing a computer name on the command line without any options, WinMSD remains a GUI mode tool, but now derives its information from a remote host. Notice that the Memory tab is removed when examining a remote machine.

To generate a complete report, pass in the /A flag:

```
winmsd \\computername /a
```

This generates a very comprehensive report showing the version, service pack level, BIOS revision date and version, processor, video and disk drive information, memory usage statistics, services, drivers, DMA usage, environment variables, and network information.

For a summary-only report, pass the /S flag as an option. This report is less comprehensive, but often provides enough information for most diagnostic issues.

By default, WinMSD outputs data to a text file named after the NetBIOS name of the target machine in the current directory (for example MYCOMPUTER.TXT). This can also be specified explicitly by passing the /F parameter.

In addition to the creation of a text file, you may wish to send the diagnostic information to the default printer. This can be performed using the /P option flag on the command line.

While WinMSD cannot provide nearly the same amount of data as CIM can, in a pinch (such as when SNMP is not enabled properly on a system), WinMSD can be used for remote troubleshooting.

—Thomas E. Eck,
MCSE+I, MCSD, ASE, CCA, CNA

Setting Default Community Name in CIM

When you add a new managed device to Insight Manager, CIM will configure the default SNMP community name for the device with the name that you have set up for CIM. As mentioned earlier, CIM uses "public" as the default community name. In your environment, however, you may use a standard community string other than "public." You can configure Insight Manager to use your string as the default for new devices rather than using "public."

1. In Insight Manager, select Setup | Global Settings.

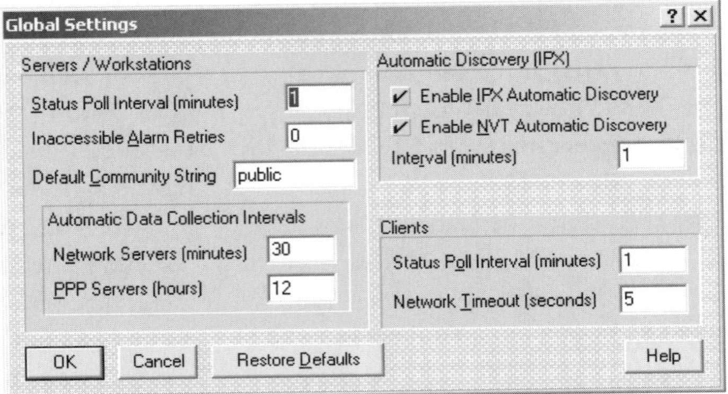

2. In the Default Community String field, enter your community string.

Please note that this string will only take effect for new devices that you add to Insight Manager. It will not affect devices that you are currently managing. To change the community name for those devices, you will have to change their community name manually, as outlined in the next section.

Configure the Device Community Name

You can configure a different community name for each device that you manage. For example, all of your servers in Boston may use a community string of "boston," while all of your servers in New York may use a string of

QUESTIONS AND ANSWERS	
I only have a few administrators and security is not much of a concern.	Use the default "public" string to ease your installation.
I only have a few administrators, but I want to keep the servers secure from rogue SNMP management consoles.	Change the community string to something other than "public" on all of your servers and your management console. To ease the addition of new servers, change the default community string in the Global Settings.
I have several servers that are each managed by a different administrator.	Create a different community string for each server. Set the unique community string at each server and in the Device Setup for each server in CIM.
I have several sites and each site has its own administrator. Each site wants to manage its own servers.	Create a different community string for each site, but don't make it so obvious that it can be easily guessed (such as the city name).

"newyork." To configure the community string for a device, perform the following steps:

1. In the Device List in CIM, select the server on which you'd like to set the community name.
2. Right-click the server and select Device Setup (see Figure 22-1).
3. In the Community String field, type the string that you want to use for this device.

Hiding Community Names

By default, Insight Manager shows the community names that you have set for your devices in the Device Setup windows. If you want to prevent someone from looking over your shoulder and obtaining your community name, you can prevent the string from displaying. If you enable this option, asterisks will appear in place of the community name. To hide community names, select Setup | Application Password in Insight Manager. In the

FIGURE 22-4

The Pager Destination Setup window

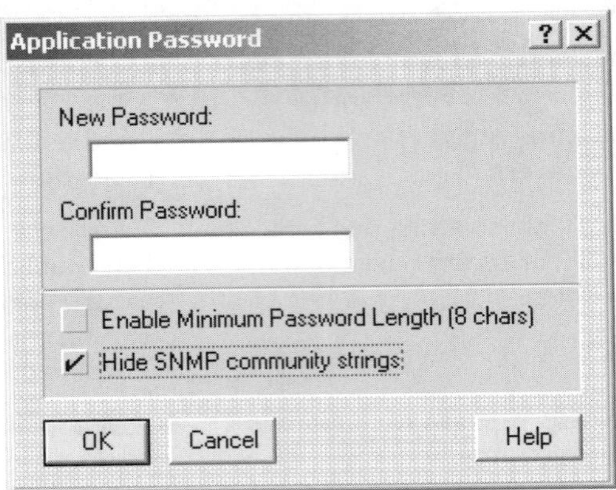

Application Password window (as shown in Figure 22-4), select Hide SNMP Community Strings.

CERTIFICATION OBJECTIVE 22.05

In-Band Management

In-band management refers to the ability to manage a device using the local network and existing network hardware. In-band management requires that the managed device have a network card installed. Insight Manager is an example of an application that can manage devices in-band. This is the preferred method of management if there is a dedicated network between the management console and the managed device.

CERTIFICATION OBJECTIVE 22.06

Out-of-Band Management

Out-of-band management refers to the ability to manage a device via a modem and the Point-to-Point Protocol (PPP). This method of management is particularly useful if there is no dedicated network connection between the management console and the managed device, and the cost of installing a dedicated connection is prohibitive. For more information on configuring out-of-band management, refer to Chapter 23, Asynchronous Management Configuration.

CERTIFICATION OBJECTIVE 22.07

Alarm Forwarding

In a perfect world, you'd be able to sit at your desk, launch CIM, and watch it all day looking for problems on your servers. Unfortunately, you'll probably quickly become bored, or your manager might want you to be more useful elsewhere. Insight Manager can forward any alarms generated by any server to your pager or to an e-mail address. CIM also gives you great flexibility in the forwarding of alarms, including the ability to forward just certain alarms, or to forward alarms from certain servers. You can also tell CIM when to forward alarms, which can be useful so that CIM will not forward alarms to you during normal business hours, when you are probably working near the servers, but will forward alarms after hours when you are away from the office.

Alarm forwarding can be especially useful to determine when a component is about to fail. Compaq offers a pre-failure warranty on several of its components (such as disks and memory) and will replace the part before it actually fails. If Insight Manager warns you that a component is about to fail, you can bring the server down in a controlled environment and replace the component with the replacement that you receive from Compaq. Better yet, if you have hot-swap hard disks attached to a SMART array controller and the disks are configured in a RAID array, you can simply remove the failing hard disk and replace it with the new one!

Enabling Alarm Forwarding

Before you can begin receiving alarms on your pager or in your e-mail, you must enable alarm forwarding for that particular method. You enable alarm forwarding in the Alarm Destinations window in Insight Manager with the following steps:

1. In Insight Manager, select Alarms | Destinations. The Alarm Destinations window appears.

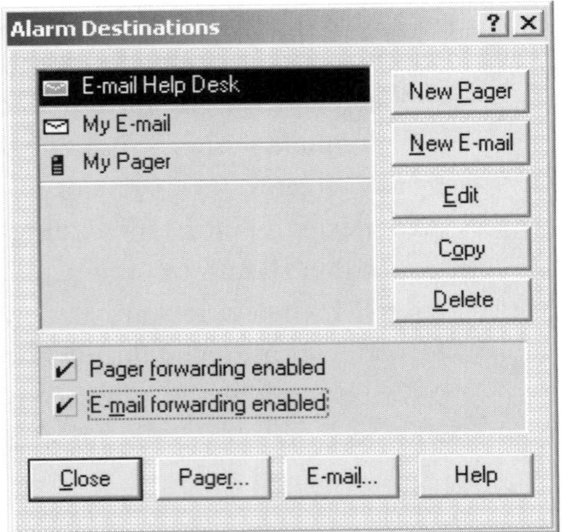

2. Select Pager Forwarding Enabled so that Insight Manager will forward any alarms to your pager. Note that you must have a modem installed and configured on your system to use this feature.

3. Select E-Mail Forwarding Enabled so that Insight Manager will forward any alarms to your e-mail. Note that you must have a MAPI-enabled mail client installed and configured on your system to use this feature.

Configuring E-Mail Destinations

Once you have enabled e-mail forwarding, you must specify e-mail destinations where alarms will be forwarded. You can specify any e-mail address that is accessible from your mail system's directory or global address list. To get to the E-mail Destination Setup window, click on the New E-Mail button in the Alarm Destinations window (see Figure 22-5).

The following bullets describe each section of the E-Mail Destination Setup window.

- **Destination Name** This is the name that will be displayed in the Alarm Destinations window. This should be descriptive, such as "E-mail to Help Desk" or "E-mail Joe."

FIGURE 22-5

Configuring e-mail destinations

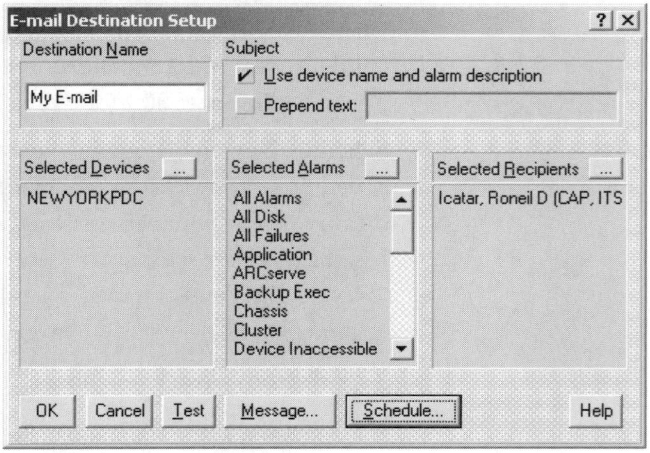

- **Subject** This allows you to select the subject line that will be sent with the e-mail message. By default, the subject line will be the server name and the alarm description. However, you can also specify that some text prepend the server name in the subject line. This allows you to be able to sort your messages based on the subject and the text that you specify.
- **Selected Devices** You can specify that only alarms from certain devices be forwarded to this e-mail destination. This can be used, for example, if different groups are responsible for different servers. Click the Browse button to specify the servers.
- **Selected Alarms** You can also specify that only certain alarms be forwarded to this e-mail destination. For example, you may want all alarms sent to a first-level help desk, but you may want critical failures automatically sent to higher-level technicians. Click the Browse button to select which alarms are forwarded to this e-mail destination.
- **Selected Recipients** This is where you specify the recipients for the set of criteria that you just specified. When you click the Browse button here, your mail clients address book will appear.
- **Message Button** You can select options for the message such as whether to send in normal format or pager format. You can also configure text to be appended to each message, such as "Compaq Technical Support 800-555-1212."
- **Schedule Button** Press the Schedule button to get to the E-Mail Schedule window. From this window, you can specify the times during the day when alarms will be forwarded to this destination. Insight Manager comes with several prebuilt times such as "Always," "Never," "Business Hours," and "Evenings," or you can specify custom hours.
- **Test Button** You can send a test message to verify that your e-mail client is working properly.

Configuring Pager Destinations

Configuring pager destinations is similar to configuring e-mail destinations. In the Alarm Destinations window, click the New Pager button to bring up the window shown in Figure 22-6 and specify a new pager destination. Instead of specifying an e-mail address, you enter the phone number and digits that your modem will dial to forward any alarms.

The sections of the Pager Destination Setup window are as follows:

- **Name** Type in a description for this pager destination. This name will appear in the Alarm Destinations window.
- **Phone Number** This is the number that CIM will dial when an alarm is received. Enter any prefixes (such as 9) and enter any commas to specify pauses in the dialing sequence. For numeric

FIGURE 22-6

The Pager Destination Setup window

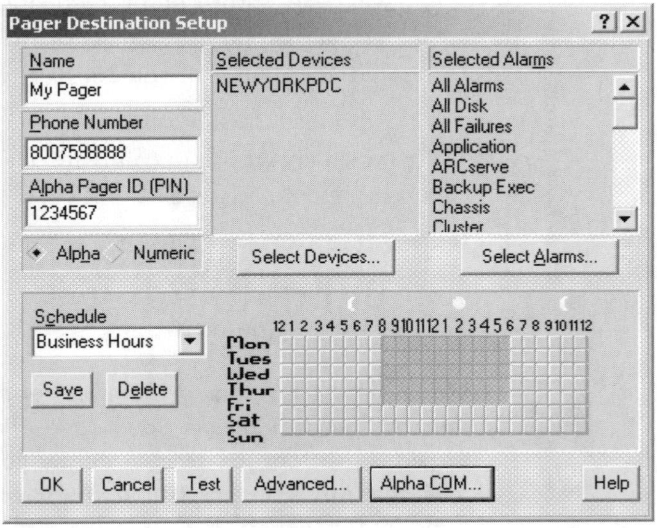

pagers, also enter any necessary pauses after the phone number, after which CIM will append a numeric code for the alarm.

- **Alpha Pager ID (PIN)** For alpha pagers, enter the PIN for this destination. This field is enabled only if the Alpha option is enabled.
- **Selected Devices** You can specify that only alarms from certain devices be forwarded to this pager destination. This option can be used, for example, if different groups are responsible for different servers. Click the Browse button to specify the servers.
- **Selected Alarms** You can also specify that only certain alarms be forwarded to this pager destination. For example, you may want all alarms sent to a first-level help desk, but you may want critical failures automatically sent to higher-level technicians. Click the Browse button to select which alarms are forwarded to this pager destination.
- **Schedule** You can specify the times during the day when alarms will be forwarded to this destination. Insight Manager comes with several prebuilt times such as "Always," "Never," "Business Hours," and "Evenings," or you can specify custom hours.
- **Advanced Button** Brings up the Advanced Alpha Setup window, which allows you to configure options such as additional messages strings and message length.
- **Alpha COM** Allows you to set options for your modem.
- **Test Button** You can send a test message to verify that your paging is working properly.

on the job

Many paging systems now enable sending e-mail messages to your pagers. You should take advantage of this if your paging system provides this feature. First, it allows you to receive descriptive text messages instead of cryptic numeric codes. Second, you won't need a modem attached to your PC to dial the pager.

CERTIFICATION OBJECTIVE 22.08

Server Filtering

In large organizations, you may be managing dozens or even hundreds of servers. This list can quickly become unwieldy and cluttered in the CIM management console. Trying to find servers with certain hardware or with certain settings can be a daunting task. CIM provides the server filtering functionality to allow you to display a subset of your servers that match the criteria that you set. This section will discuss using the built-in filters that ship with Insight Manager and creating your own custom filters.

Single Filter Mode vs. Multiple Filter Mode

Insight Manager allows you to view filters in two modes: single filter and multiple filter. In single filter mode, only a single filter is active. When you select a new filter, the previous filter is deselected. In multiple filter mode, you can select more than one filter by which to sort the list. For example, you can select to view all servers that have Automatic Data Collection enabled as well as CPU utilization greater than 10 percent. The next section lists the built-in filters that you can use to sort the list.

To enable single filter mode or multiple filter mode, click the appropriate button in the Device List window toolbar.

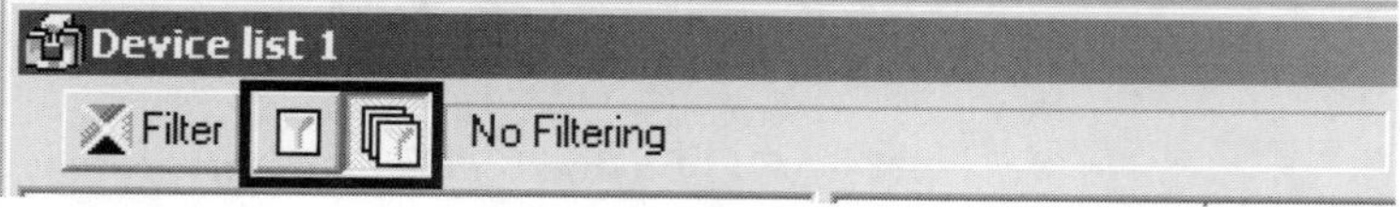

Using Built-In Server Filters

Insight Manager comes with several built-in filters to display a subset of your managed devices. To display the list according to one of the filters, click the Filters button in the Device List (see Figure 22-7).

FIGURE 22-7

Use Server Filters to display servers that match a specified criterion

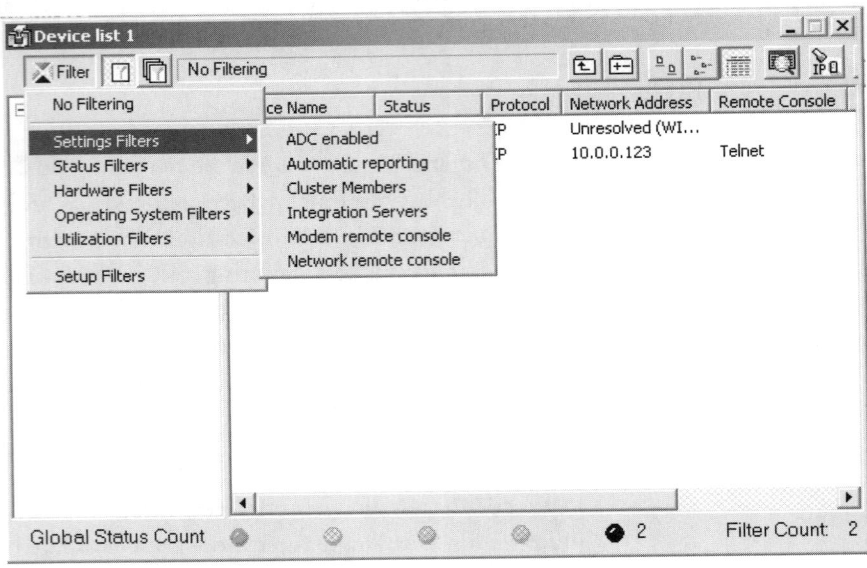

The filters are grouped into five categories: Settings, Status, Hardware, Operating System, and Utilization. Let's take a look at each category.

Settings

The Settings filter allows you to filter a list based on certain configuration settings that you've enabled for your servers.

- **ADC Enabled** Displays servers that have Automatic Data Collection enabled
- **Automatic Reporting** Displays servers that have automatic reporting enabled
- **Cluster Members** Displays servers that are members of clusters. If you have installed Insight Manager over a previous version, this filter will not be available until you create it using the Setup Filters option.

- **Integration Servers** Displays servers that are configured as integration servers
- **Modem Remote Console** Displays devices that are configured to be managed via a modem
- **Network Remote Console** Displays devices that are configured to be managed via the network

Status

This set of filters allows you to display servers based on their current status. This is a dynamic filter; as servers change status, so does their filter membership.

- **Manageable** Displays servers that are manageable—that is, servers that have the Insight Agents running
- **Status Degraded/Failed** Displays servers that have a component that has either degraded or failed
- **Status OK** Displays servers that have a status of OK
- **Status Unmanageable** Displays servers that have a status of unmanageable. These can include servers that do not have the Insight Agents installed or are not accessible by the network.

Hardware

The Hardware filters allow you to display those servers that match your chosen hardware specifications. You can filter based on the amount of memory, processor type, or hard disk space. The built-in filters include the following:

- **Mem >= 24MB** Displays servers that have at least 24MB of memory
- **Pentium Machines** Displays servers that have a Pentium processor installed
- **ProLiant 1500** Displays servers that belong to the ProLiant 1500 family of servers from Compaq

Operating System

These filters allow you to display servers with a specific operating system installed. This is convenient in a large environment where you need to find all servers with, say, NetWare 3.12 installed.

- **NetWare 3.*x*** Displays servers that have NetWare 3.*x* installed
- **NetWare 4.*x*** Displays servers that have NetWare 4.*x* installed
- **Windows NT 3.5, 3.51** Displays servers that have either Windows NT 3.5 or 3.51 installed
- **Windows NT 4.0** Displays servers that have Windows NT 4.0 installed

Utilization

These filters allow you to display servers based on their current utilization. When you select these filters, Insight Manager queries the servers in real time and populates the list with the servers that match your criteria. For this reason, the list may take some time to appear.

- **CPU Util >=10%** Displays servers that have a CPU utilization greater than 10 percent
- **Low CPU Util** Displays servers with low CPU utilization
- **Volumes >= 80% Used** Displays servers that have disks that are greater than 80 percent used

Creating Custom Server Filters

As we have just seen, CIM comes with several convenient built-in filters that you can use immediately to filter your list of servers. However, you may need to create your own custom filters based on the needs of your organization. For example, although there is a filter to display all Pentium servers, you may want to display all servers with a 486 processor. You can create a custom filter to create the list. The following steps show how to display all servers with a 486 processor.

1. In the Device list window, select the Filter button.
2. From the menu that appears, select the Setup Filters option.
3. In the Filter Type field, select Hardware and click New. The Setup Filter window appears.
4. Select Show All System Types and click Next.
5. Select Show Selected to display all processor types, then select all of the 80486 processor types. When you have selected all of the processor types, click Next.

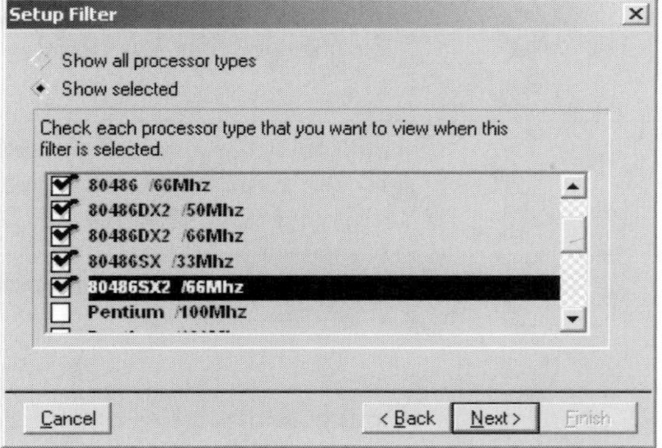

6. Select Show All Memory Configurations and click Next.
7. In the Filter Name field, type a descriptive name for this filter (such as All 486 Servers), then click Finish to create the filter.

CERTIFICATION OBJECTIVE 22.09

Color Coded Status

Insight Manager provides a quick-glance status view of your servers in the Device List window. The color of the icon to the left of the server name indicates the current status of the server. In addition, in the Device Status

Count Bar of the Device List, you can view how many devices are of a given status. Table 22-3 describes the various color codes that a server may display.

TABLE 22-3 Device Status Descriptions

Status	Icon	Description
Failed	(Red)	Indicates that a server or server component has failed and that it is no longer fully functional.
Degraded	(Yellow)	Indicates that a server or server component has degraded. The server is still operational, but should be serviced, such as in the case of a failed disk in a RAID array.
OK	(Green)	Indicates that a server is operating properly.
Not Available	(Grey)	Indicates that a server is responding to SNMP polling, but a status is not available.
Inaccessible	(Black)	Indicates that a server is not responding to SNMP polling.
Undiscovered	(Clear)	Indicates a server that is no longer auto-discovered or in the IP, IPX, or PPP device list.
Unknown		A server will have this status when it is first added to the device list or when Insight Manager is first launched. This should only be a temporary status.
PPP		Indicates a server that is managed via PPP over a modem.

CERTIFICATION SUMMARY

In this chapter, you learned about many of the basic features and some of the more advanced features of Compaq Insight Manager. You learned how to enable automatic data collection for servers and how to print reports based on the data you collected. You learned how to enable a server to be rebooted remotely and how to reboot the server using CIM. You also learned how to use the alarm logs to view any critical messages from your servers.

You discovered that CIM uses SNMP and that the SNMP community string must match on both the servers and the management console. Don't forget that the community string is case-sensitive! You also learned how useful the Alarm Forwarding feature is by forwarding any server messages to your pager or e-mail. The Alarm Forwarding feature is highly flexible and allows you to set many different options when configuring alarms.

Finally, you learned several ways to make the CIM console more usable by using server filters to display only the servers that match certain criteria. You also saw that CIM color-codes the status icons next to the server name so that you can get a quick glimpse of your server's health.

TWO-MINUTE DRILL

- ❑ Compaq Insight Manager (CIM) can display a great wealth of information about your servers.
- ❑ CIM can collect server information at specified intervals and store that information in a database.
- ❑ By default, data collection is not enabled for any servers that you are managing in CIM, since the data could potentially grow to large amounts.
- ❑ The only option that you can set for data collection is the interval at which CIM will connect to the servers to collect the data.
- ❑ Insight Manager comes with several report forms that neatly format the collected data into meaningful output, such as a graph.
- ❑ The Server Reboot feature of CIM allows you to reboot a server from your management console.

- Before you can remotely reboot a server using CIM, you must enable the remote reboot function in the Insight Agents applet in Control Panel.
- When rebooting a server, make sure that no one is logged into the server with files open.
- Insight Manager displays all received alarms in the Alarm Log.
- The Alarm Log is displayed in the Insight Manager application.
- You can view the details of an alarm by double-clicking the alarm that you are interested in.
- You can print out the list of alarms from the Alarm Log window.
- SNMP community names (or strings) provide a limited amount of protection for your servers from unauthorized access from rogue Insight Manager consoles.
- The SNMP community string is configured differently for each operating system.
- When you add a new managed device to Insight Manager, CIM will configure the default SNMP community name for the device with the name that you have set up for CIM.
- You can configure a different community name for each device that you manage.
- In-band management refers to the ability to manage a device using the local network and existing network hardware.
- Out-of-band management refers to the ability to manage a device via a modem and the Point-to-Point Protocol (PPP).
- Insight Manager can forward any alarms generated by any server to your pager or to an e-mail address.
- CIM provides the server filtering functionality to allow you to display a subset of your servers that match the criteria that you set.
- Insight Manager allows you to view filters in two modes: single filter and multiple filter.
- Insight Manager comes with several built-in filters to display a subset of your managed devices. You can also create custom server filters.

SELF TEST

The following Self Test questions will help you measure your understanding of the material presented in this chapter. Read all the choices carefully, as there may be more than one correct answer. Choose all correct answers for each question.

1. What is the default interval for data collection for asynchronous servers?

   A. 30 minutes

   B. One hour

   C. 12 hours

   D. Manual Update

2. What should you set the collection interval to if you are monitoring 60 servers?

   A. 30 minutes

   B. 60 minutes

   C. 90 minutes

   D. 12 hours

3. You want to print a report that lists all error messages that you've received on your server. Which form would you use to format the report?

   A. RAPREC

   B. CONFIG

   C. STANDARD

   D. ERRORS

4. You try to reboot a server using the Remote Reboot function, but the server does not reboot. Which of the following statements is not a valid reason why the server will not reboot?

   A. Remote Reboot is not enabled in the Insight Agents applet in Control Panel.

   B. The Guest account is not enabled on the server.

   C. The SNMP community strings do not match.

   D. The operating system is hung.

5. What is the quickest way to find all failed/critical messages in the Alarm Log?

   A. Right-click the Alarm Log and create a filter for critical messages.

   B. Click the Device column and look for the red (critical) icons.

   C. Click the Severity column.

   D. Click the Critical button on the toolbar.

6. Your company decides to use a standard SNMP community string "corp" instead of using the default "public." You change the default community string to "corp" in Insight Manager and you change the community name to "corp" at each of your servers. After doing so, all currently managed servers' status appears as Unmanageable. Any new servers that you add to the device list appear as OK. What should you do next?

A. Modify the community name for the servers in the Device Setup window.
B. Change the strings back to "public" in both CIM and on the servers.
C. Reinstall SNMP on the server, specifying "corp" as the community string.
D. Click the Refresh button in the Device List window.

7. Which version of management allows you to manage servers using PPP and a modem?

A. In-band management
B. Out-of-band management
C. Synchronous management
D. Upper management

8. Which of the following is an advantage of e-mail forwarding over pager forwarding?

A. You can specify that only alarms from specific servers are sent to an e-mail address.
B. You can specify that only certain alarms are forwarded to an e-mail address.
C. You can send full-text descriptions to e-mail.
D. You can specify multiple recipients per destination.

9. Which of the following is not a built-in category for server filters?

A. Settings
B. Status
C. Utilization
D. Software

10. What does it mean when a server has a status of Not Available?

A. The server is responding to SNMP polling, but no status is available.
B. The server is not responding to SNMP polling.
C. The server is configured for modem but you are not dialed into the server.
D. The server has a duplicate IP address.

11. You try to print a report for a server manually but the only form available is the CONFIG form. You want to be able to print other reports. What should you do?

A. Create a custom report form for the server.
B. Enable Automatic Data Collection.
C. Refresh the status of the server in the Device List.
D. Customize the CONFIG form to include the data you require.

12. In the Device List window, you only want to show servers that have a Pentium Processor and Windows NT 4.0 installed. However, when you select one option, the other option is deselected. What must you do to allow both?

A. Create a custom filter that will display both Pentium machines and Windows NT 4.0 machines.

B. Press the CTRL key when selecting the filters.

C. Enable multiple filter mode.

D. You cannot view both simultaneously.

13. Where do you enable the Hide SNMP Community Strings option?

A. Application Password

B. Global Settings

C. Control Panel | Network | Services | SNMP

D. CIM20.INI

14. What does a black status indicator icon indicate for a server?

A. Inaccessible

B. Undiscovered

C. Degraded

D. Not Available

15. Where do you set the server's SNMP community name in Windows NT?

A. WINNT.INI

B. Control Panel

C. SNMP Manager

D. Insight Manager

ASE

ACCREDITED SYSTEMS ENGINEER

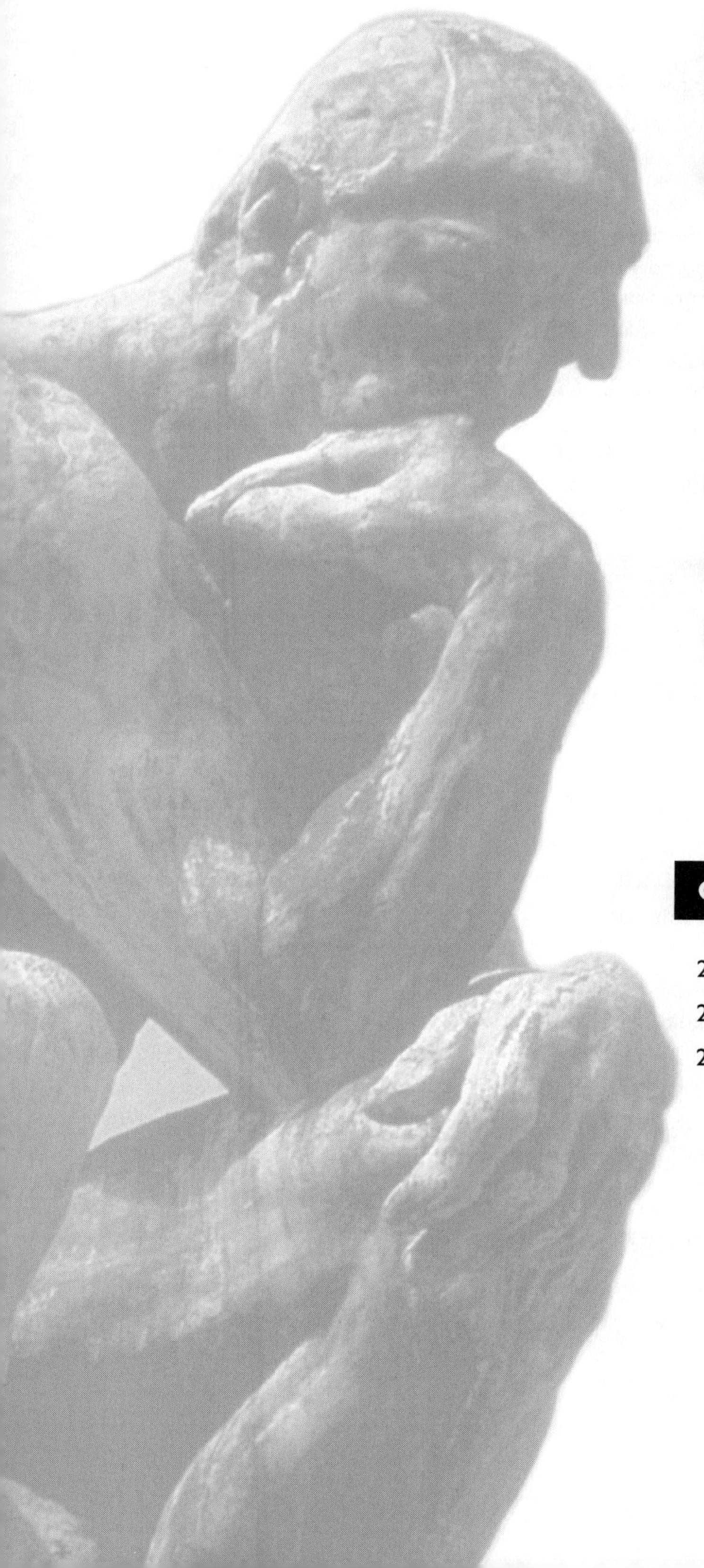

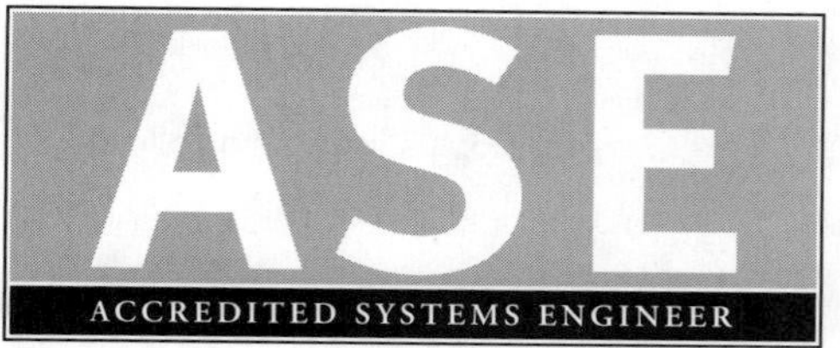

23

Compaq Intelligent Manageability

CERTIFICATION OBJECTIVES

23.01	Compaq Insight Manager LC
23.02	Compaq Insight Manager XE
23.03	Additional Management Products Available

Compaq has continued to increase the functionality of its Intelligent Manageability system by continuing to develop new management applications. These applications allow you to manage all aspects of your system environment, including monitoring devices, performing inventory data collections, and managing system updates. As Compaq does more to increase their Intelligent Manageability offering, the administrator's job will shift from a primarily reactive role to a significantly more proactive one. In this chapter, overviews of the Insight Manager XE, Insight Manager LC, and Compaq Intelligent Cluster Administrator will be presented, along with the Compaq Power Console. These are four tools that you will find very handy in your day-to-day systems management activities.

CERTIFICATION OBJECTIVE 23.01

Compaq Insight Manager LC

Insight Manager LC is one of Compaq's two Web-based tools for managing PCs. Insight Manager LC can be used to monitor not only Compaq PCs, but also PCs from other vendors, due to its compliance with the DMI 2.0 standard. Insight Manager LC can be used to gather system information and do inventories as well as receive alerts when components have failed, or if indicators signal imminent failure of a component. Insight Manager LC can also be used for diagnostics, BIOS upgrades, and updating drivers on Compaq desktops and workstations.

The Insight Manager LC application consists of two parts. On the management station, a combined console is loaded and can be used to monitor both Compaq and non-Compaq hardware via DMI support. There is also the combined client that is loaded on Compaq client stations, which allows Insight Manager LC to provide advanced functionality over Compaq PCs.

Product Procurement and Installation

Insight Manager LC can be obtained in much the same way as the regular Insight Manager software. There are three ways you can get it:

- Server Management Kit shipped with ProLiant servers

- SmartStart Subscription Service
- Download from the Compaq Web site

The combined console can be downloaded as SoftPaq SP12303. The combined client can be downloaded as SoftPpaq SP10945. SP10945 includes the Desktop Management Agents, Remote Management Service, Diagnostics for Windows NT, and Diagnostics for Windows 9*x*.

Prerequisites

The prerequisites for managed PCs without the client are:

- TCP/IP
- Intel DMI 2.0 Service Provider
- Internet Explorer 4.01 Service Pack 1a or higher
- Windows 95 with Windows Sockets 2 update, Windows 98, or Windows NT 4.0

The prerequisites for managed PCs to be run with the managed client are:

- TCP/IP
- Intel DMI Service Provider (included with Compaq Agents)
- Internet Explorer 4.01 Service Pack 1a or higher
- Windows 95 with Windows Sockets 2 update, Windows 98, or Windows NT 4.0
- Compaq Deskpro EN, Deskpro EP, Deskpro EN Series SFF, Deskpro 6000, Deskpro 4000, Deskpro 4000S, Deskpro 4000N, or Deskpro 2000 (exact model requirements can be checked on the Compaq Web site)

The prerequisites for the management PC running the combined console are:

- TCP/IP
- Intel DMI 2.0 Service Provider (included with Compaq agents)

- Internet Explorer 4.01 Service Pack 1a or higher
- Windows 95 with Windows Sockets 2 update, Windows 98, or Windows NT 4.0
- 20MB hard drive space for the Insight Manager LC application and 30MB for the system-level software files to be managed

Installation

Now that we know the prerequisites for the Insight Manager LC combined client and combined console, it's time to install them.

EXERCISE 23-1

Installing the Combined Client

1. Run the SETUP.EXE program. The following screen will appear, letting you know the installation status.

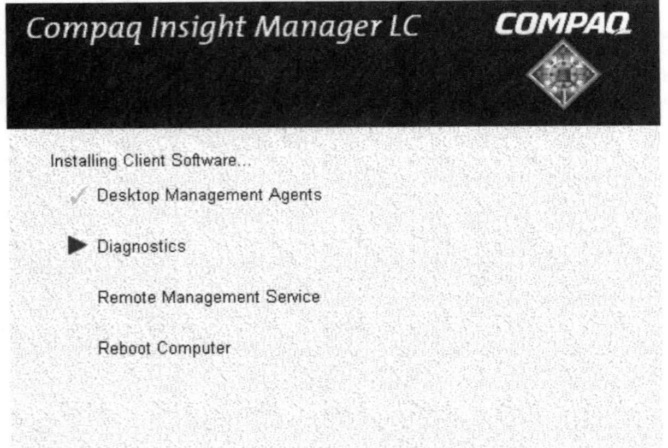

2. As a component loads, there will be a blue arrow next it. After a component finishes installing, a green check mark will appear. First, the Desktop Management agents will load, then the Compaq Diagnostics, and finally the Remote Management Service.

3. After the installation has completed, you will be presented with the following screen, asking you to reboot your machine.

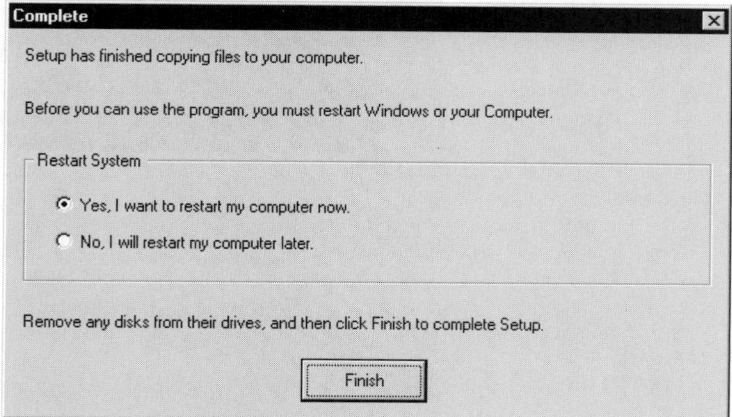

4. After you reboot your machine, you will notice two new items in the Control Panel: The Compaq Diagnostics applet and the Compaq Configuration Record Applet.

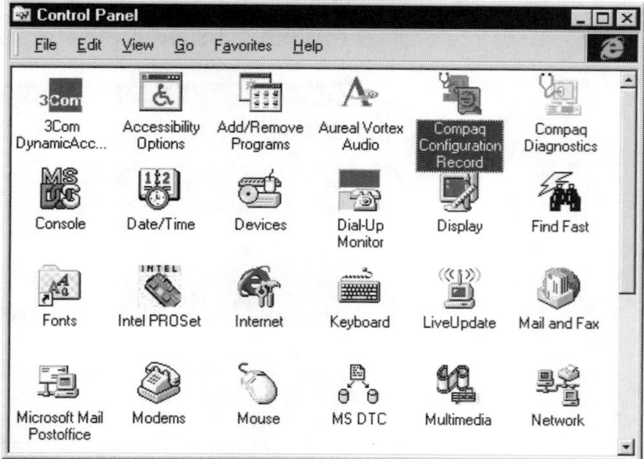

5. After the SETUP.EXE program has run, the following screen appears. This screen enables you to monitor the progress of the installation process.

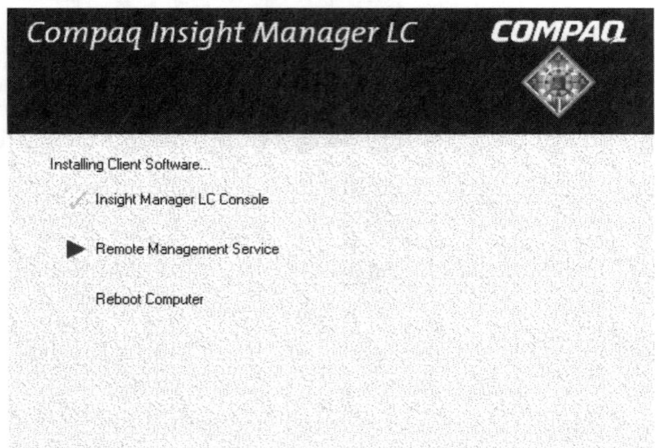

6. This screen is very similar to the screen that appears for the client installation. Again, a blue arrow will note a currently installing component and a green check will note a completed installation.
7. You will then be given the same reboot message.

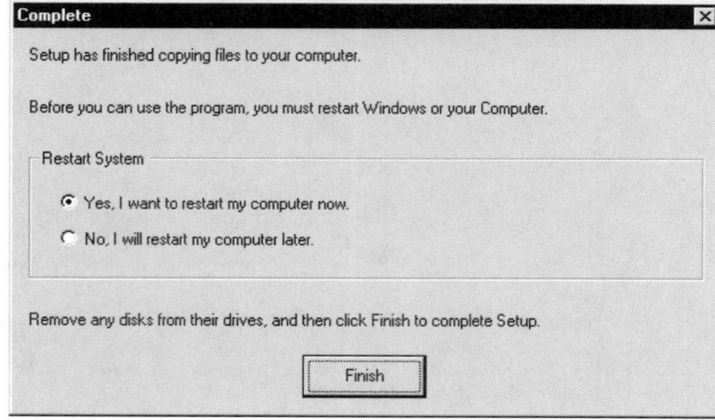

Operation of Insight Manager LC

With the installation process completed, we can now use the management station to start examining the managed devices on the network.

Compaq Diagnostics

When you double-click the Compaq Diagnostics icon in the Control Program, your computer will be scanned and the necessary information will be retrieved. The Compaq Diagnostics utility contains several categories of information to view. The type of information contained in each of the following categories will be described briefly.

- **System** Processor type, co-processor info, ROM information
- **Asset Control** Serial number
- **Input Devices** Keyboard, mouse, and other input device information
- **Communication** Parallel port, COM port, and modem information
- **Storage** Floppy-disk drive, hard-disk drive, and CD-ROM information
- **Video** Video card information
- **Memory** On-board and add-on memory information
- **Multimedia** CD-ROM and sound card information
- **Preferences** User-configurable options like power-save
- **Operating System** Which operating system is loaded and essential OS configuration information
- **Windows** Which version of Windows is loaded and important configuration information such as INI file settings

- **Architecture** Bus information
- **Health** Health logs, POST logs, and ECC memory logs
- **Miscellaneous** CMOS information, BIOS information, and the interrupt vector table

System Configuration Record

The System Configuration Record is essentially a diagnostics utility. In fact, it uses the same files as the Compaq Diagnostics. The only real difference is that the System Configuration Record allows you to save diagnostics information and configuration information, which allows the creation of baselines. It will also allow you to recreate a configuration in case of a machine failure.

When you run the System Configuration Record utility, two files are created: the BASE.LOG file and the NOW.LOG file. The BASE.LOG file contains information retrieved when the utility was run for the first time. The NOW.LOG file contains information from the current configuration. You can compare the two files to find out what configuration changes have been made to your system in order to troubleshoot configuration issues.

Insight Manager LC Console

Insight Manager LC includes five management headings:

- View PCs
- Alerts
- Diagnostics
- Update PC
- Administrator Settings

Briefly, let's discuss what is included under each option.

As Figure 23-1 shows, the View PCs heading allows you to view system and inventory information. This information includes the status and type of

FIGURE 23-1

Insight Manager LC View PC screen

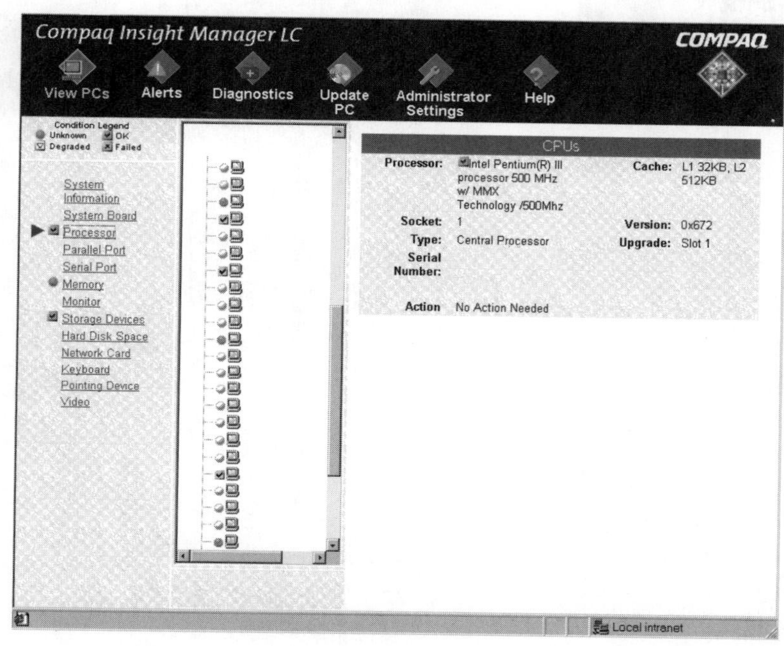

system board, processor(s) installed, parallel port, serial port, memory, and monitor information, storage device types, remaining hard-disk space, network card configuration values, keyboard and pointing device types, and the video adapter configuration.

The Alerts screen shows any alerts that have been received from monitored machines. Using this interface, you can click on any alert to view more information and to clear alerts.

The Diagnostics screen allows you to view diagnostics information for the managed devices and obtain system information and status.

There are three choices on the Update PC screen: Software Update, Update List (or update history) and System Settings

You can use the Administrator Settings screen, shown in Figure 23-2, to set discovery options, such as establishing which discovery methods will be used, and configuring the range of PCs to be pinged.

FIGURE 23-2

PC discovery settings in Insight Manager LC

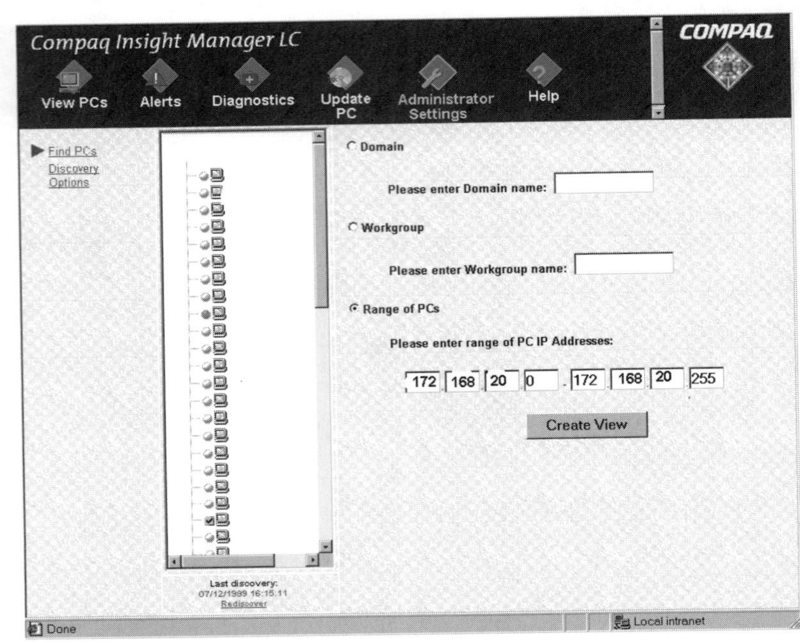

CERTIFICATION OBJECTIVE 23.02

Compaq Insight Manager XE

Compaq Insight Manager is Compaq's flagship Web-based utility for the management of enterprise devices. Insight Manager XE can be used to monitor Compaq servers and workstations, as well as all DMI- and SNMP-compliant devices, providing for an extremely robust management environment. Insight Manager can be used for inventory and data collection, as well as system status reporting, management, and alerting. Insight Manager XE can also be used to provide pre-failure alerts for Compaq devices.

How XE Differs from LC

There are several differences between Insight Manager XE and Insight Manager LC, which may influence your decision to choose one or the other. Insight Manager XE is more robust, allowing management of both servers and workstations, while Insight Manager LC can only be used to manage workstations. Insight Manager XE also provides support for Novell NetWare, while the LC product does not. Insight Manager XE also requires Microsoft SQL server or Microsoft Data Engine for its database, whereas the LC product simply uses a local database for configuration settings. While the startup cost may be a bit higher to implement an XE infrastructure (due to the requirement to run SQL Server), it may be advantageous to do so to allow for increased scalability and future product support.

Production Procurement and Installation

Insight Manager XE can be obtained in much the same way as the regular Insight Manager software and the Insight Manager LC software. There are three ways you can get it:

- Server Management Kit shipped with ProLiant servers
- SmartStart Subscription Service
- Ordered from the Compaq Web Site

The prerequisites for Insight Manager XE are as follows:

- Compaq ProLiant or Prosignia Server
- 128MB RAM if SQL Server is installed on the same server. 96MB RAM if SQL is installed on a different server. 64MB RAM if Microsoft Data Engine is used instead of SQL.
- 35MB for application, 300MB hard disk space for SQL Server database, 55MB for Microsoft Data Engine
- Windows NT Server 4.0 with Service Pack 4
- TCP/IP

- SNMP
- Microsoft Internet Explorer 4.01 with Service Pack 1
- Compaq SSD for Windows version 2.08

Note that the SSD is required for installation. Remember: You should always run the SSD after any Service Pack installation. This will replace any Compaq files that were written over by the Service Pack.

EXERCISE 23-2

Installing Insight Manager XE

1. Start the setup program. The following screen will appear.

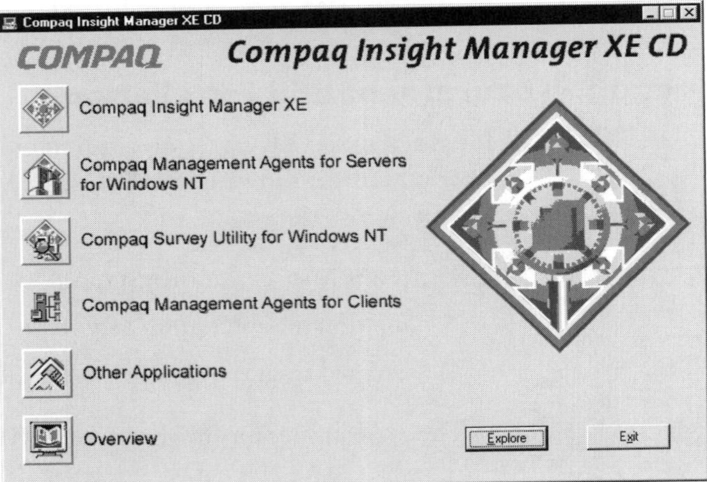

2. Select Insight Manager XE. The following screen will appear.

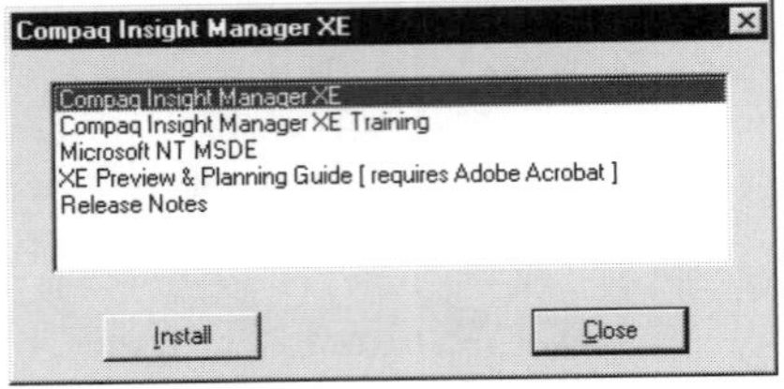

3. Select Insight Manager XE and click Install.
4. You are then given a warning to close all open applications. Select Next.

5. Select Next when shown the Insight Manager XE license agreement.
6. You are asked for a location to install the Insight Manager XE program files. The files will default to the C: drive in a directory called Insight Manager XE.
7. You are prompted for a folder to install the Insight Manager XE icons. The default is usually fine.
8. You are presented with a SQL server login box. Just input the server name, account name, and account password. The datasource name defaults to INSIGHT_DB, and cannot be changed.
9. Click Next for the database install.
10. You are then asked to restart your computer.
11. After your computer restarts, the setup continues and you are brought to the browser login screen. This is how you will log in to Insight Manager XE. The installation is now complete.

on the job

Insight Manager XE will allow you to load SQL Server on any server you wish. However, I would suggest installing the SQL Server on a server that will only be used for that process. SQL can be a very resource-intensive application. If you have a very large environment, it would be beneficial for you not to run SQL on another production box. It could cause a drop in performance.

Operation of Insight Manager XE

Insight Manager XE is fairly simple to use. You start by opening your browser. Type in the following URL: **htpp://*server_name*:280** (where *server name* is the name of the server to be managed). Port 280 is the Insight Manager XE port. You are then given the browser login screen. After logging in, you can begin managing the system. Insight Manager XE retrieves information in three ways:

- **Device discovery** Device discovery is done through *http auto discovery*. In http auto discovery, the management agents send out periodic broadcasts. These broadcasts identify the devices and send a device status to the management station.

- **Polling** Polling is done through range pinging. In range pinging, an IP range is entered under the Insight Manager XE range window. Insight Manager XE pings every address in that range. When a reply is received, Insight Manager XE will then send http, DMI, and SNMP requests to the device in an attempt to receive information back.
- **Querying** A query request is sent to Insight Manager XE from the browser. Then Insight Manager XE sends a request to the Insight Manager XE database. The information is then sent back to Insight Manager XE, which then sends it back to the browser.

on the job

It is important to note that only Compaq systems can respond to http discovery requests. If you want to discover non-Compaq devices, you must configure some other method of discovery.

Insight Manager XE includes three navigation items:

- Manage Devices
- Manage Events
- Administer Insight XE

In the Manage Devices window, there are six choices: Device Overview, Device Queries, Notification Tasks, Control Tasks, Polling Tasks, and Cluster Monitor. Figure 23-3 shows this window with Device Queries selected.

Under Manage Events, there are six choices: Event Overview, Event Queries, Event Tasks, Notification Tasks, Control Tasks, and Polling Tasks.

There are eight choices under the Administer Insight XE heading. These are Discovery, Servers, Accounts, Cluster Configurator, Cluster Settings, Node Settings, Cluster CMX, and Node CMX.

The Servers option allows you to manage the username and password used for SQL Server, SNMP settings, and the e-mail addresses used for notifications.

The Accounts option contains the accounts you created to allow others access to Insight Manager XE.

Discovery controls how devices are discovered. This is where you can change the Insight Manager XE polling range.

FIGURE 23-3

Device Queries screen in Insight Manager XE

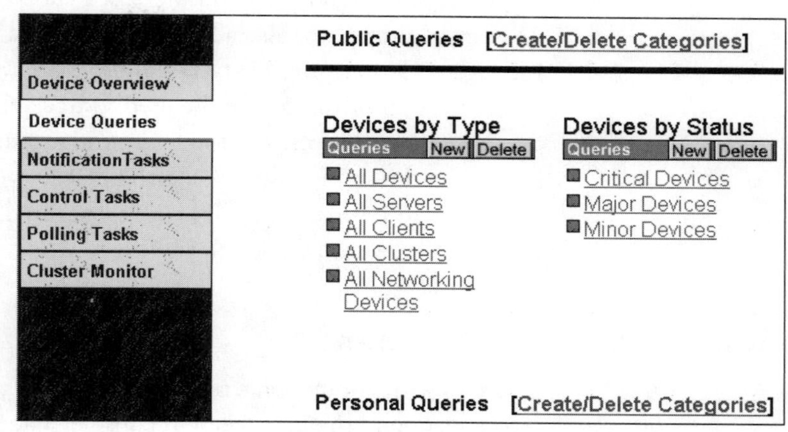

CERTIFICATION OBJECTIVE 23.03

Additional Management Products Available

Compaq developed Insight Manager XE and Insight Manager LC for total system management. Compaq has also developed specialized applications for monitoring just certain components. The two we are going to cover in this section are the Compaq Intelligent Cluster Administrator and the Compaq Power Console.

Compaq Intelligent Cluster Administrator

The Compaq Intelligent Cluster Administrator is a Web-based utility used to monitor Compaq ProLiant Servers running Microsoft Cluster Server. There are two ways to obtain the Compaq Intelligent Cluster Administrator. You can order it as a stand-alone application from Compaq using part number 122284-B22, or you can order it as part of the ProLiant Cluster HA/F500 Enhanced Cluster Kit using part number 379973-B22.

Cluster Administrator cannot be used for initial cluster configuration. It does, however, support up to six preconfigured clusters. The Cluster

Administrator supports all console-based cluster administration functions. Cluster Administrator also adds some advanced features. The Compaq Intelligent Cluster Administrator can be integrated into Insight Manager XE.

Cluster Administrator can be used to track changes to cluster configurations, allowing you to find configuration issues easily. You can back up and restore cluster configurations, as well as replicate configurations from one cluster to another. The Compaq Intelligent Cluster Administrator can also be used to manage cluster log files.

Compaq Power Management

There are two components to the Power Management application: the server agent and the management console. The Power Management software can be obtained from the Compaq Web site or from the Insight Manager XE CD. Prerequisites include the UPS agent.

EXERCISE 23-3

Installing the Management Console from the Insight Manager XE CD

1. The auto-run feature will bring up the installation menu, as in the following illustration.

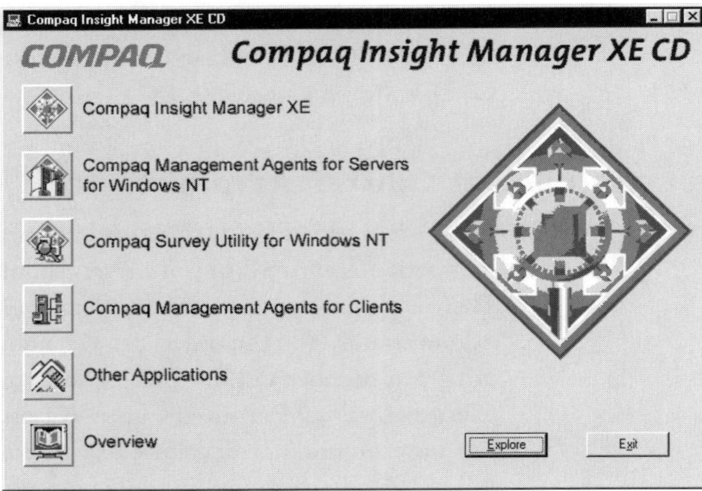

2. Select Other Applications. This will bring up the Other Available Applications Menu.

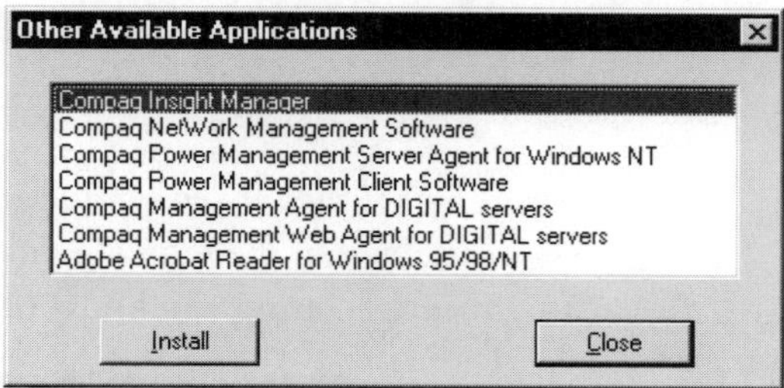

3. Select Compaq Power Management Client Software and press install. You will be presented with the Welcome screen. You are given a copyright warning and the program recommends that you close all other Windows applications before proceeding. Select Next to bring up the Choose Destination Location window.

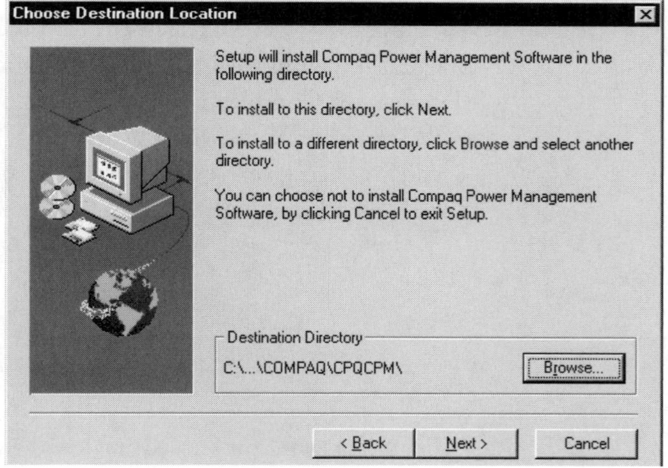

4. You are then given a chance to change the installation directory. The default directory is \PROGRAM FILES\COMPAQ\CPQCPM. After deciding on an installation directory, select Next. The installation program then copies files.

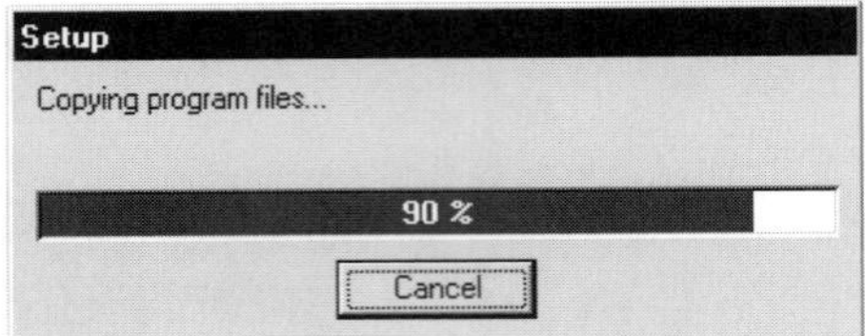

5. You are then given instructions on accessing the online manual, as shown in the following illustration. Select OK. You will see a message letting you know that the installation is complete.

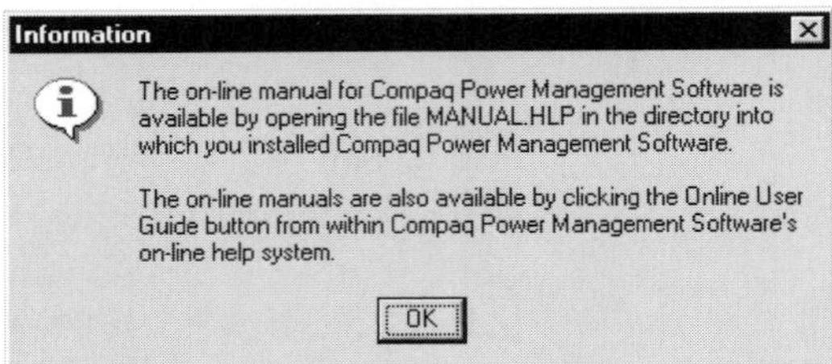

Compaq's Power Management Console is run by double-clicking the CPQCPM icon in the installation directory. When you run the Power Management Console, it will attempt to contact the UPS agent installed on the machine, as shown in Figure 23-4.

You are then given several options as to which screen to display. Let's take a look at what each window allows you to do.

The Status window is used to view the general operational status of your UPS. You can also use this option to determine if your UPS is communicating with the system. The Status window allows you to retrieve the UPS model number, serial number, part number, and revision. You can also get information on the battery status and the power feed status.

The PowerScope window gives information on the actual power features of your UPS. PowerScope shows volts in, volts out, and % load. This window provides information on a Compaq feature called *boost and buck*, which allows the UPS to boost power if it is too low, or buck power if it too high. There is also a Bypass Circuitry option. With this enabled, you can power your equipment straight from the power source, bypassing the UPS. You also get enhanced battery management, filtering, inverter, rectifier/charger, and run-time.

FIGURE 23-4

Compaq Power Console is polling UPS agent

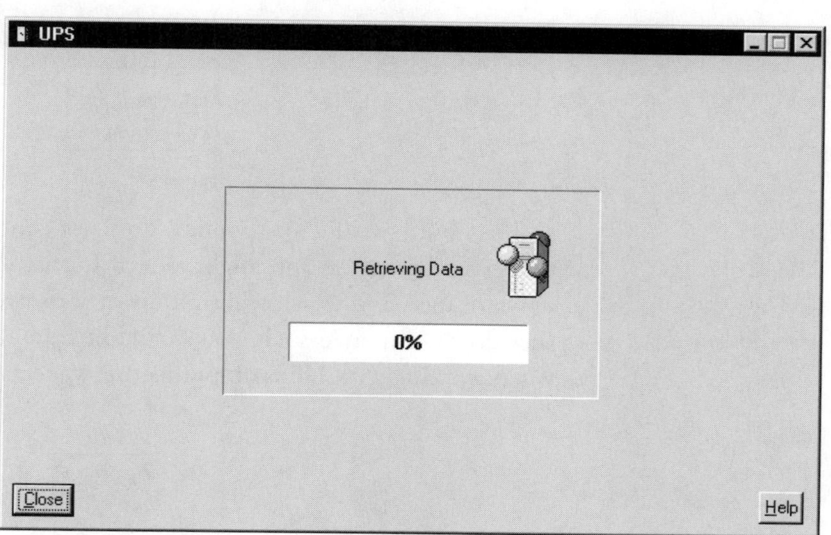

There is a Log selection for the Power Console logs. Here you can review previous events. You can find out when the UPS was powered or shut down, or when there was a fail-over.

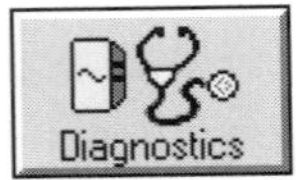

Diagnostics can be helpful in determining if there are problems with your UPS. You can check the communications on the serial port, check the battery status, or simulate a power loss and fail-over to see if your UPS will respond properly.

The Shutdown/Reboot window does not control the shutting down of the server directly, as you might expect. It actually controls the shutting down of the UPS, which will shut down the server whether you want it to shut down or not. As such, you should be careful about selecting this option when working with UPSs on production systems.

Shutdown Timing is what directly controls the shutting down of your server. Under Shutdown Timing, you can configure how long your server will run on the UPS before it shuts down.

Startup Timing is designed for UPSs with more than one load segment. Multiple load segments allow different devices to be powered up at different times. The timing for this can be controlled under Startup Timing using start-up delays.

Alert Handling controls event notifications. You can configure who will be notified in the event of a failure and how they will be notified. You can also configure execute commands that are initiated by a failure.

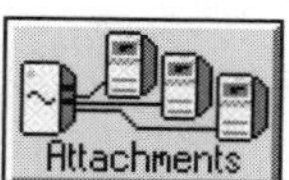

The Attachments window allows you to enable load shedding. Load shedding will keep all of your components from initializing at the same time when power is restored. This could cause an overload of the circuit.

Shutdown Schedule allows you to shut down and restart your system at regular, scheduled intervals. This gives all your components a chance to be reinitialized.

CERTIFICATION SUMMARY

Intelligent Manageability is Compaq's attempt to make administration easier. The Intelligent Manageability applications we discussed in this chapter were Insight Manager LC, Insight Manager XE, Compaq Intelligent Cluster Administrator, and Compaq Power Console. Insight Manager LC is used for workgroup and PC management and can be used to manage any DMI 2.0-compliant system. Insight Manager XE is a more robust enterprise management application, which can be used to monitor both servers and workstations. The Compaq Intelligent Cluster Administrator was designed to monitor ProLiant servers running Microsoft Cluster Server. The Compaq Power Console is used to manage UPSs.

All of these applications are optimized for use with the Compaq Management Agents. Although Insight Manager LC and Insight Manager XE can monitor systems that do not have the agents loaded by using DMI or SNMP support (XE only), you will not get complete management functionality if they are not loaded.

QUESTIONS AND ANSWERS

How can I find out if I had a power failure over the weekend?	Check the Power Console logs.
I want my system to shut down every Friday night. How can I do this?	System shutdowns can be scheduled under Shutdown Schedule.
My boss wants to be alerted whenever there is a power failure. Can I do this?	Alert Handling allows you to configure who will be alerted when a power failure occurs.
How can I check to see if I have set up my UPS correctly?	You can use the Diagnostics feature to test your UPS settings. You can even simulate a power failure.

TWO-MINUTE DRILL

- Compaq has continued to increase the functionality of its Intelligent Manageability system by continuing to develop new management applications to manage all aspects of your system environment including monitoring devices, performing inventory data collections, and managing system updates.
- Insight Manager LC is one of Compaq's two Web-based tools for managing PCs.
- Insight Manager LC can be used to gather system information and do inventories as well as receive alerts when components have failed, or if indicators signal imminent failure of a component.
- Insight Manager LC can also be used for diagnostics, BIOS upgrades, and updating drivers on Compaq desktops and workstations.
- The Compaq Diagnostics utility contains several categories of information to view:
  - **System** Processor type, co-processor info, ROM information
  - **Asset Control** Serial number
  - **Input Devices** Keyboard, mouse, and other input device information
  - **Communication** Parallel port, COM port, and modem information
  - **Storage** Floppy-disk drive, hard-disk drive, and CD-ROM information
  - **Video** Video card information
  - **Memory** On-board and add-on memory information
  - **Multimedia** CD-ROM and sound card information
  - **Preferences** User-configurable options like power-save
  - **Operating System** Which operating system is loaded and essential OS configuration information

    - **Windows** Which version of Windows is loaded and important configuration information such as INI file settings
    - **Architecture** Bus information
    - **Health** Health logs, POST logs, and ECC memory logs
    - **Miscellaneous** CMOS information, BIOS information, and the interrupt vector table
- Insight Manager XE can be used to monitor Compaq servers and workstations, as well as all DMI- and SNMP-compliant devices, providing for an extremely robust management environment.
- Insight Manager XE can be used for inventory and data collection, as well as system status reporting, management, and alerting. Insight Manager XE can also be used to provide pre-failure alerts for Compaq devices.
- There are several differences between Insight Manager XE and Insight Manager LC.
- Insight Manager XE retrieves information in three ways:
    - Device discovery
    - Polling
    - Querying
- Insight Manager XE includes three navigation items:
    - Manage Devices
    - Manage Events
    - Administer Insight XE
- Compaq has also developed specialized applications for monitoring just certain components: the Compaq Intelligent Cluster Administrator and the Compaq Power Console
- The Compaq Intelligent Cluster Administrator is a Web-based utility used to monitor Compaq ProLiant Servers running Microsoft Cluster Server.
- There are two components to the Power Management application: the server agent and the management console.

SELF TEST

The following Self Test questions will help you measure your understanding of the material presented in this chapter. Read all the choices carefully, as there may be more than one correct answer. Choose all correct answers for each question.

1. Which of the following can you use to obtain Insight Manager LC?
   A. Download from Compaq Web site
   B. Smart Start Subscription Service
   C. Server Management Kit
   D. All of the above
2. Which of the following is not a prerequisite of the Insight Manager LC management console?
   A. TCP/IP
   B. IPX
   C. Intel DMI 2.0 Service Provider
   D. Internet Explorer 4.01 Service Pack 1a
3. The Compaq Insight Manager LC client installation adds which of the following applications to the Control Panel?
   A. Compaq Diagnostics
   B. Insight Manager LC
   C. Intelligent Cluster Administrator
   D. Support Source
4. Under what section in the Compaq Diagnostics can you view the system serial number?
   A. Asset Control
   B. System
   C. Input Devices
   D. Communication
5. Under what section in the Compaq Diagnostics can you view the ECC memory logs?
   A. System
   B. Health
   C. Input Devices
   D. Memory
6. In what file does the System Configuration Record store the current diagnostics information?
   A. BASE.LOG
   B. CURRENT.LOG
   C. NOW.LOG
   D. SYSTEM.LOG
7. Under what heading in Insight Manager LC can you view inventory information?
   A. Alerts
   B. Update PC
   C. Administrator Settings
   D. View PC
8. Where in Insight Manager LC would you go to set the ping range?
   A. Administrator Settings
   B. Diagnostics
   C. Alerts
   D. View PC

9. How much RAM is required for Insight Manager XE if you intend to install Microsoft SQL Server on the same server as Insight Manager XE?

    A. 128MB
    B. 96MB
    C. 64MB
    D. 32MB

10. What is the Insight Manager XE administration port?

    A. 25
    B. 64
    C. 128
    D. 280

11. Which of the following is not a method used by Insight Manager XE to gather information?

    A. Device Discovery
    B. Polling
    C. Querying
    D. Sampling

12. Where in Insight Manager XE would you go to configure the name of the SQL server where the Insight Manager database is stored?

    A. SQL
    B. Accounts
    C. Server
    D. Login

13. How many clusters are supported by the Compaq Intelligent Cluster Administrator?

    A. Two
    B. Four
    C. Six
    D. Ten

14. Under what heading in the Compaq Power Console will you find UPS run-time?

    A. Startup Timing
    B. PowerScope
    C. Diagnostics
    D. Shutdown/Reboot

15. Where would you go in the Compaq Power Console to configure a startup delay?

    A. Startup Timing
    B. Diagnostics
    C. PowerScope
    D. Delay Timing

ASE
ACCREDITED SYSTEMS ENGINEER

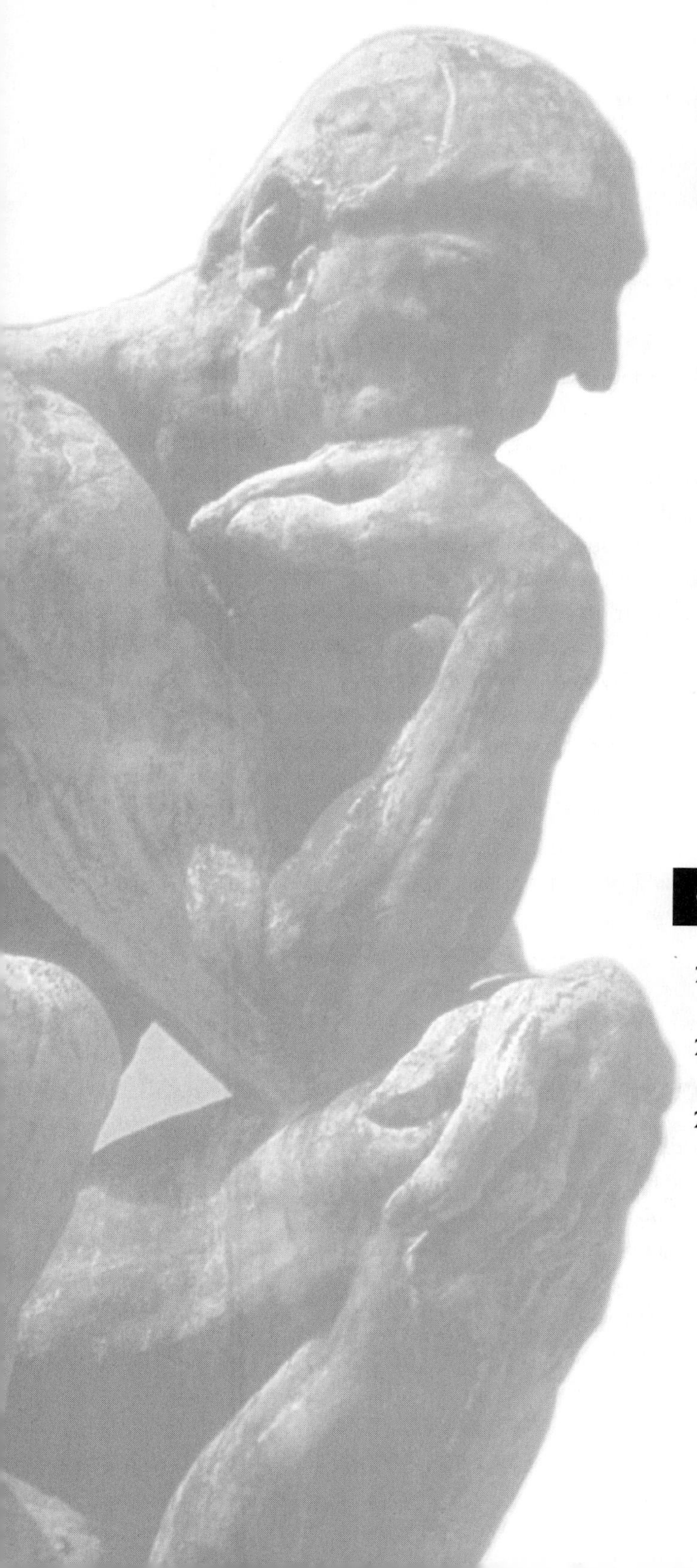

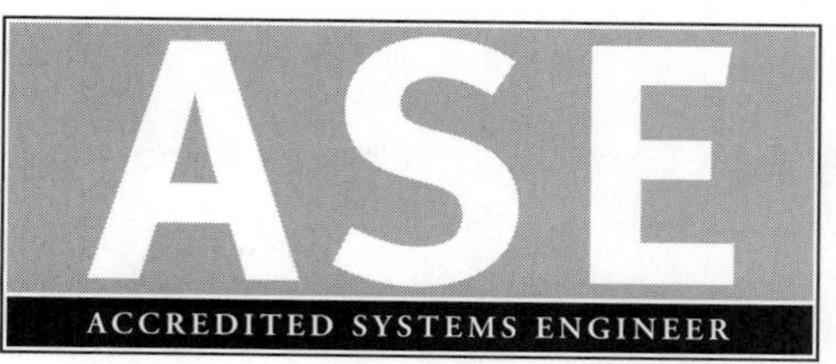

24

Compaq Remote Insight Board

CERTIFICATION OBJECTIVES

24.01 Hardware Components of Remote Insight Board

24.02 Installing and Configuring the Remote Insight Board

24.03 Remote Insight Board Features and Benefits

This chapter presents the Compaq Remote Insight Board (RIB). Compaq provides the RIB as a means of managing and accessing a server from any location, regardless of the server's condition.

We'll start by taking a look at the hardware components of the RIB. The RIB is actually a completely separate computer on one PCI expansion card, serving double duty as both a management piece and the managed server's graphics adapter. It comes standard with an auto-sensing 10/100-Mbps network interface card (NIC), and can have either an internal modem or a serial port for connecting to external devices.

Once we're familiar with the actual hardware, we'll move to the installation and configuration of the RIB for use in a server. While the physical installation is not at all difficult, some preparation is needed before the RIB will be able of function to its full potential.

Finally, we'll discuss the various features of the RIB—what it does and how it benefits you as a server administrator. We'll spotlight the RIB's ability to capture and play back the boot sequence of a server, from memory count through any text-based screens. And we'll finish by taking a look at the RIB's Remote Console feature, which allows remote systems to send keystroke sequences as if they were sent from the actual server keyboard.

CERTIFICATION OBJECTIVE 24.01

Hardware Components of Remote Insight Board

The Compaq RIB, despite its diminutive size, is actually a complete computer on a single PCI card. In its standard configuration, it has a processor (an Intel i960), a video controller, a 10/100 NIC, and 8MB of memory. A modem is optional. It even includes its own rechargeable battery should the server it's in lose power. The RIB also includes a PC Card slot to provide a modem or serial port. Since the modem/serial port is provided as a PC Card, upgrading to newer modem standards is as simple as removing one card and inserting another.

Installation of the RIB is a simple task of opening the server, finding an available PCI slot, inserting the card, and connecting the cables.

The PCI Bus

The RIB is a standard 32-bit Personal Computer Interconnect (PCI) device. The PCI standard was created as a way of improving the expansion capabilities of PC-compatible systems. The original PC allowed peripherals to be added using what came to be known as the Industry Standard Architecture (ISA) bus. To add a graphics adapter, for example, one just needed to open the case and slide a card into a special slot, which was usually attached to the motherboard. But as computers evolved, the limited 16-bit, low-bandwidth ISA bus suffered from poor speed and was often difficult to configure.

Several companies (including Compaq) created extensions to the ISA bus and called it the Extended Industry Standard Architecture (EISA) bus. This new standard doubled ISA's bit rate to 32-bits and its maximum bandwidth to 33 Mbps. EISA also allowed hardware to configure the cards automatically by using standard driver files. These files tell a computer what a card is and how it should be configured (independent of any software driver, however). Moreover, since EISA was only an enhanced ISA, existing ISA cards could still function in an EISA slot. However, ISA cards in EISA slot have none of the EISA benefits; they have no enhanced throughput and no automatic configuration.

Computers continued to evolve, and soon even the EISA bus's performance became slow and haggard compared to other parts of the system. To deal with that issue, Intel created the Peripheral Connect Interface (PCI) bus. PCI, while still 32-bit, increased the bandwidth to 133 Mbps. The higher bandwidth allows more information to be transferred to the RIB in less time. Today's graphical operating systems can require the transfer of large amounts of data just to update the display of the screen. At high resolutions, the higher bandwidth really makes a difference.

PCI also provides another enhancement called bus mastering, which allows an expansion card to function on its own, without the computer's main processor. Compaq's RIB can take advantage of this feature to isolate itself completely from the main system, should the system halt or the OS crash. While the server is functioning, the RIB uses the power and timing supplied from the PCI slot, recharging its onboard battery as needed. If the server loses power, or if the operating system hangs, the RIB can completely isolate itself from the PCI bus and the server, and continue to send alerts or pages, as configured, to warn administrators of issues occurring with the server.

Integrated NIC

Each model of the RIB includes as standard an auto-sensing 10/100-Mbps NIC. This NIC allows connecting the RIB to a local-area network (LAN) for quick and convenient access to the RIB.

The first two generations of management boards provided by Compaq came configured only with modems or serial ports; they did not support any connectivity beyond dial-up phone line connections. Each card in each server required a dedicated phone line or a convoluted modem-sharing device. Each administrator needed a phone line and modem to connect to the RIB. Management of the system was dependent upon a successful modem connection.

The RIB's inclusion of a built-in NIC allows access to the RIB from any machine on the same network, provided that machine uses TCP/IP, whether or not that machine has a modem. (Note: the RIB has several security options, so not everyone has access to its functions.) Also, a centralized RAS/Dial-Up Networking server can provide remote access to the RIB, rather than many separate modems for each RIB.

Having an integrated network connection allows a dedicated connection to a Compaq Insight Manager (CIM) workstation to monitor Simple Network Management Protocol (SNMP) traps. The RIB integrates fully with CIM, sending alerts to it, as well as being fully accessible through it. However, the RIB will forward SNMP traps to any SNMP management program.

PC Card Modem/Serial Port

The original management cards, with integrated modems, were locked into their original modems. As modem speeds increased, the original cards became more and more obsolete. To get around that problem with the RIB, Compaq included an industry-standard PC Card slot in each model. PC Cards are credit card-sized devices that were originally created as a way to provide compatible expandability to laptop computers. By providing the modem/serial port functionality through a PC Card, you can easily upgrade from various models of the RIB by simply upgrading the internal PC Card. As faster modems become available, you can purchase a new PC Card, rather than having to replace the entire RIB.

Having a modem (either a PC Card modem or an external modem connected to a PC Card serial port) enables the RIB to send alphanumeric/numeric pages automatically when problems occur. You must have a modem attached to the RIB for it to send pages. However, if you only have the network connection, the RIB can still send SNMP traps to an Insight Manager workstation, which could then send pages.

It might occur to you that since there is a standard PC Card slot on the RIB, any standard PC Card could be used there. For example, a second network card could be added to create fault tolerance to the network connections. This is not the case, however. While the slot will accept any standard PC Card, only modems are supported.

Video Adapter

The RIB includes its own video adapter and is designed to function as the server's main graphic display, replacing any existing graphics adapter (on some servers, you must remove the card that currently serves as the display adapter). Installation of the RIB is not complete until you connect the monitor to the graphics port on the RIB.

Along with the video adapter, Compaq includes a dedicated video capture chip on the RIB. The video capture chip permits the RIB to send the text displayed on the server to another screen, through either the integrated NIC or the modem. Working from this other screen, known as the Remote Console feature, you can monitor and affect what happens at the server as if you were there, even if you're miles away.

The video capture chip also allows the RIB to capture text screens and save them for redisplay later. This can be used to capture both a server's boot sequence—from the beginning as it counts memory all the way through the OS load—and an OS's crash, such as the infamous Windows NT blue screen of death. At a later point, you can connect to the RIB and replay the screens, at several speeds, to see what happened and when.

By keeping the video capture chip on the same card as the display adapter, Compaq has reduced the path that the screen data must follow from display to capture. If they were on separate cards, the data would have to be transferred across the PCI bus, which, although faster than both the ISA and EISA busses, can still be overtaxed in today's high-performance servers.

8MB of On-Board Memory

Being both a video controller and a video capture device, the RIB requires on-board memory for holding the currently displayed screen as well as any stored screens. To account for this, the RIB has 8MB of video memory. Since the video capture chip can compress the stored screens to take full advantage of that memory, the 8MB is plenty.

CERTIFICATION OBJECTIVE 24.02

Installing and Configuring the Remote Insight Board

While all the ProLiant servers support the RIB, there are a few things that have to be checked before putting the RIB into the chassis. As always, be certain that a recent backup of the server is available. While the installation is pretty simple, there's always a chance something can go wrong!

The most important thing to verify before installing the RIB is what version of the BIOS is installed on the server. BIOS stands for Basic Input/Output System, and it serves as the controller for all data that passes through a computer. Compaq routinely updates the BIOS of their servers through ROMPaqs, downloadable programs that can add functionality or correct problems by reprogramming the BIOS with newer revisions. Before the RIB can be installed, the server must have a recent version of the BIOS or the RIB might not function. If the BIOS doesn't understand the information coming from and going to the RIB, it can't process it. What's worse, if the server's BIOS is too old and does not support the RIB, the server might become inaccessible. ROMPaqs and their documentation are available from Compaq (both on their SmartStart CDs and from their Web site). It is always a good idea to verify that the version of the BIOS on the server is compatible with the RIB.

on the job

The first time I worked with Compaq servers, I was given several rack-mounted ProLiant 4500s to install and configure—all by myself. I'd never seen anything bigger than a desktop, and I had to install these servers with a hardware RAID adapter and external storage arrays. After several hours of trying, I couldn't get a single server to boot. They would count the memory, initialize the processors, and then stop cold. It turned out that the RAID controller required a later version of the BIOS and the server was useless without it. I lost a lot of time and a lot of hair that day. Check the BIOS version!

The second item to verify before physical installation is which slot will accept the RIB. While most Compaq servers allow the RIB to reside in any available PCI slot, certain servers only accept a graphics card in one of the first two or three slots. The documentation provided with the RIB lists which slots are available on which servers. If a compatible slot is not available, other PCI cards will have to be adjusted accordingly. It might sound odd, but there is a good reason. The older specifications for the PCI standard only accounted for three or four PCI slots in a system. Adding more slots required chaining together PCI controllers in such a way that the only way to get to the second set of slots was through the first. Graphics controllers need to be on a primary bus because of all the data it takes to display the images on the screen. Newer specifications allow more than one primary PCI bus—an oxymoron probably, but it works.

Once the BIOS and any slot issues have been dealt with, the physical installation of the RIB consists of sliding it into the appropriate PCI slot and connecting the cables. Pretty simple, once you get around to it.

The first cable to connect is, obviously, the monitor cable. Since the RIB will serve as the server's graphics controller, it will have to be connected to the monitor. Also, any other graphics card will have to be disconnected and removed. (If the graphics controller is integrated into the system board, it will be disabled automatically by the system—a handy feature.) Depending on the operating system and the preexisting graphics controller, the operating system might have to be reconfigured with the graphics driver appropriate to the RIB. Compaq provides with the RIB software support diskettes with all the appropriate drivers, both for the display and for the RIB's NIC and modem. Nongraphical operating systems should not need to be updated.

After connecting the monitor cable, you must next connect the keyboard to the RIB and the server with the keyboard pass-through cable. The pass-through cable has three ends: one for input and two for output. One end attaches to the keyboard, one to the RIB, and the third to the server, as shown in Figure 24-1. While the RIB will function without it, the control part of remote control would be impossible. Once this cable is connected, keystrokes sent from your remote machine will be sent to the server as though they were typed at the local keyboard—literally, since they'll pass through the server's keyboard port!

The final cables to connect are the network and/or phone cables, depending on the capabilities and ultimate configuration of the RIB. Naturally, the other end of the network and phone cables must be connected to the appropriate devices—either hubs or switches for the network cable, and a phone jack for the modem cable. Once these cables

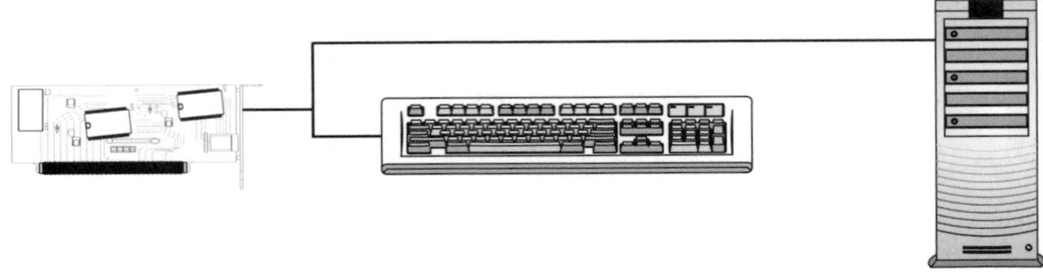

FIGURE 24-1 Connecting the keyboard to both the RIB and the server

are connected, the physical portion of the installation will be complete. Now we're getting to the good stuff.

Once the RIB is physically installed in the server, you must configure the RIB's network adapter and (if so equipped) the modem. These portions of the card are exclusive to the RIB and independent of the rest of the server. Once they are configured, you can access the RIB from a remote location across a network or through a dial-up connection. Luckily, the configuration of these items is a simple matter of assigning IP address information in the Compaq System Configuration Utility (SCU). The SCU is available from Compaq and usually accessible by pressing F10 on the keyboard while a server boots. Alternatively, copies are available on the SmartStart CD as well as from Compaq's Web site. Figure 24-2 shows a portion of the SCU with the NIC information. Naturally, you must make sure that the information entered is valid for your network and setup. Because of the way the RIB performs its remote control functions, only TCP/IP is supported. Other protocols, such as IPX/SPX and NetBEUI are not supported. The later sections of this chapter about the Remote Console and Web View functionality will explain why this is so.

While you're in the Configuration Utility, you also need to set up security by creating users who have access to the various functions of the

FIGURE 24-2

Viewing the RIB's network settings in the System Configuration Utility

```
                         Step 3:  View or edit details                     Help=F1
Slot 2 - Compaq Remote Insight Board/PCI - Bus 2
 Server Identification
  PCI Resources......................... Enabled

 Server Name............................ RIB
 Server ID.............................. 12345678
 Serial Number.......................... P0C6B0GBFHSQSG
 Firmware Version....................... 1.05
 Firmware Date.......................... 6/1/1999

 Network Interface
  Status................................ Enabled
  Transceiver Speed..................... Autoselect
  IP Address............................ 127.  0.  0.  1
  Default Gateway....................... 127.  0.  0.  1
  Subnet Mask........................... 255.255.255.  0
  MAC Address........................... 00 0A D1 D2 C0 E4

 Modem Settings
  Modem Status.......................... Present
  Port Speed............................ 57600
  Data Bits............................. 8
>Edit=ENTER<  <Edit Resources=F6>  <Advanced=F7>  <Done=F10>
```

RIB. The RIB allows up to 10 separate users to be created, each with different passwords and permissions. Users with access to the RIB can be allowed to view previous boot information, add or change other users' security information, or even reboot the server. You might want someone from your Help Desk to have access in order to check the status of a server, but not to reboot that server! In addition, users can be configured to receive pages if the server has problems. Figures 24-3 and 24-4 show some of the user configuration options available.

You can also create users through the RIB's Web interface. Simply point the HTML browser of your choice at the IP address assigned to the RIB. You need to use the SCU to create at least one user with Supervisor rights, who will be able to add users later through a Web browser. We'll look at the Web interface a little later.

Once the network is configured and users are added, the RIB is ready for business.

FIGURE 24-3

Configuring user information in the System Configuration Utility

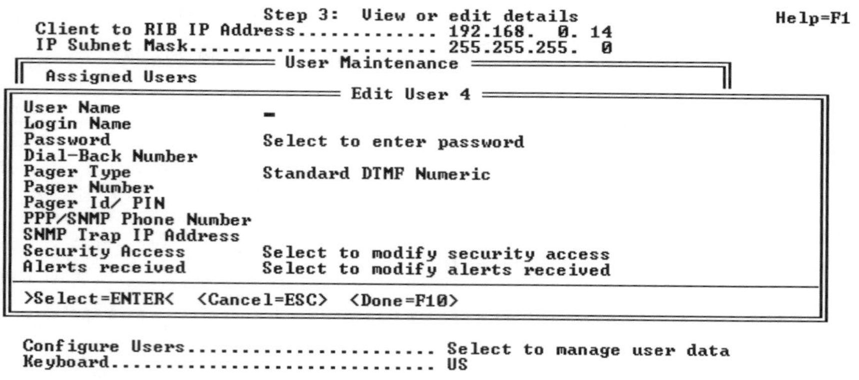

```
                         Step 3:  View or edit details                    Help=F1
  Client to RIB IP Address............. 192.168.  0. 14
  IP Subnet Mask....................... 255.255.255.  0
                         User Maintenance
   Assigned Users
                              Edit User 4
 User Name                -
 Login Name
 Password                 Select to enter password
 Dial-Back Number
 Pager Type               Standard DTMF Numeric
 Pager Number
 Pager Id/ PIN
 PPP/SNMP Phone Number
 SNMP Trap IP Address
 Security Access          Select to modify security access
 Alerts received          Select to modify alerts received

 >Select=ENTER<  <Cancel=ESC>  <Done=F10>

 Configure Users....................... Select to manage user data
 Keyboard.............................. US
```

FIGURE 24-4

Configuring user access with the System Configuration Utility

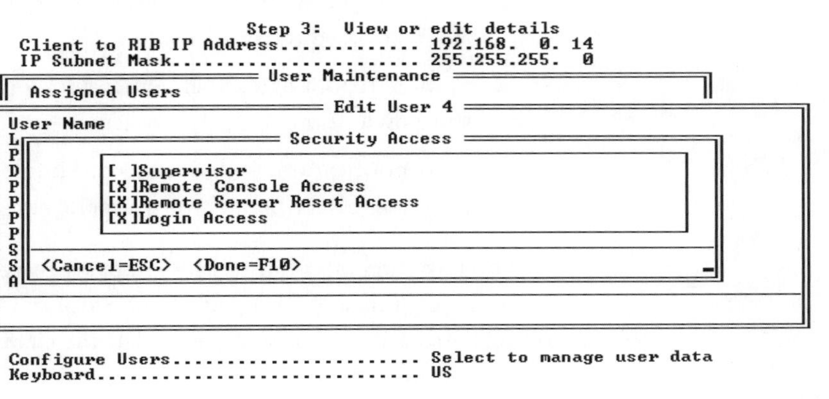

CERTIFICATION OBJECTIVE 24.03

Remote Insight Board Features and Benefits

The Compaq RIB makes available several features and capabilities, including:

- In-band and out-of-band management
- Web integration to provide access to all the management functions from just about anywhere through a standard Web browser (such as Microsoft's Internet Explorer or Netscape's Navigator)
- Remote Console, allowing control of the server in any text-based screens (including some of Compaq's own System Utilities and Setup programs). You can even remotely control a graphical operating system such as Windows NT with a third-party graphical remote control utility.

- Playback of a server's boot process from the memory count through any text-based screens
- Remote reboot of a server, either with a graceful or a forced shutdown of the operating system
- Alert notification, with options of Simple Network Management Protocol (SMNP) and alphanumeric and numeric paging

The RIB integrates fully with Compaq's Insight Manager software and can take advantage of Compaq's Survey utility for providing an inventory of the hardware and software, as well as the change history as hardware or software is modified.

In-band and Out-Of-Band Management

There are usually two ways to manage remote servers, in-band and out-of-band. Basically, in- and out-of-band management simply refers to the type of connectivity that exists between the server and the management console.

In-band management means that the management occurs over existing, permanent channels—for example, when two machines are connected on the same network. With in-band management, the alerts or other management operations occur over the same channels as other, "normal" information would travel.

Out-of-band management requires a separate, dedicated connection, which is usually not permanent. Dial-up connections are examples of out-of-band. When management functions occur, a new connection must be established before information can be transferred. No other information is transferable over an out-of-band connection.

The RIB offers support for both forms of management. Dedicating out-of-band resources can be expensive as all servers and management consoles need access to the dedicated channels to communicate. However, in-band management can be subject to network traffic restrictions, since it shares connectivity.

Since the RIB supports its own network card and modem, it allows easy selection between in-band and out-of-band. If in-band connectivity is unavailable (either temporarily or permanently), out-of-band can be used. As long as the board is configured correctly, the RIB functions the same either way.

Web Interface

The RIB was designed to ease management of Compaq servers, and an important factor is accessibility. Remote management isn't useful if you have to go to a specific location to manage the server. Therefore, all of the RIB's features are accessible from a standard Web browser (including the Remote Console feature). Once the RIB is installed and working, you only need to open a browser and point it at the network address assigned to the RIB. Check the documentation to verify that a specific browser or version is supported. Figure 24-5 shows the opening page of the RIB in Internet Explorer.

FIGURE 24-5

The RIB options as viewed in a Web browser

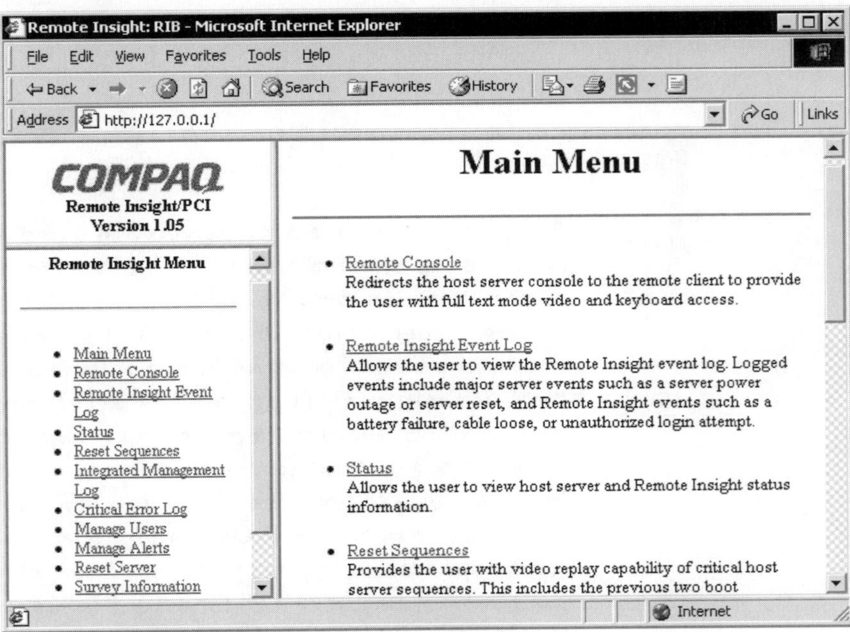

As long as you know the RIB's IP address and have connectivity to it, you can manage that server. Access is available from any machine on your network—from the lowliest laptop to the heartiest high-end workstation—as long as it has a browser.

The Web interface is one of two reasons why the RIB only supports TCP/IP as a network protocol. TCP/IP is integral to the Web standards. There is no such thing as Web over IPX/SPX or NetBEUI, to name two network protocols. (That's not completely true, but it requires additional software to encapsulate the TPC/IP protocol within the other protocol—not very efficient, as it still requires TCP/IP.)

The second reason for TCP/IP-only support is the Remote Console.

Remote Console

One of the most powerful features of the RIB is the ability it gives you to view and control a server as if you were standing at the machine itself. While there are several software applications that allow you to remotely control the server from an operating system perspective, the RIB allows access to software and settings outside and completely independent of the operating system. Whenever a server is off or in the process of rebooting, there is no operating system active. Software that depends on an operating system is completely useless.

At a previous job, one of my servers had a bad memory module hardwired to the motherboard. The server could disable the affected memory location, but at every boot, it would stop to display an error message, requiring someone to press F1 to continue booting the operating system. The server had another issue that caused it to reboot periodically—usually late at night. A replacement motherboard was on order, but was out of stock for several weeks. About once a week, I'd receive a page telling me that the server was down, and I'd have to drive in to the office to press the F1 key. I couldn't automate the process, since it was a boot-time BIOS warning; there was no OS available to run an application to press F1 for me. Being able to dial into a RIB from home would have won me several hours more sleep (a valuable commodity when you work with computers).

From the comfort of your home or desk, you can access a server just about anywhere from bootup to shutdown. With the addition of a third-party graphical remote control software package, you can even access a graphical OS such as Windows NT. Compaq built functionality into the RIB to automatically switch control from the text-based remote console to the third-party application—allowing full control of a Compaq server from anywhere in the world. Third-party applications include Symantec PCAnywhere, Network Associates Remote Desktop, and Compaq's own Carbon Copy. These software packages have the same functions and limitations as if the RIB were not installed—they must be supported by the software and hardware in the server regardless of the RIB. (For example, they must use an existing network card. They cannot use the NIC in the RIB.) Naturally, if the server has been rebooted, you must wait until the third-party software comes online before the RIB can pass control to it.

As mentioned earlier, the Remote Console is one reason why the RIB requires TCP/IP as its network protocol. The Remote Console uses the TCP/IP standard Telnet protocol for communication. Telnet is a simple, text-based program for transferring keystrokes and screen images between two computers, and like the Web protocol, it is not available with any other network protocol.

There are three ways to access the Remote Console.

- The Web interface allows a point-and-click interface to start the Remote Console. Simply select that option from the list and you'll view the text screens in the Web browser.
- Compaq's Insight Manager also allows access to the Remote Console, but you'll have to add the RIB's address manually to the list of managed devices. (See the Insight Manager documentation for information on configuring the device list.)
- You can use a Telnet client, which is a standard part of the TCP/IP suite of protocol tools. As with the Web browser, just use the Telnet client to connect to the IP address of the RIB. You should have configured user access to the RIB as described in the RIB configuration section of this chapter.

Remote Insight Playback Capabilities

Since the RIB serves as the graphics display adapter for the server, capturing the data displayed on the screen is a simple task—the RIB simply saves the data as it sends it to the monitor. Compaq designed the RIB to capture automatically all of the text-based information displayed by the system as it runs through text screens. As it processes text, the RIB compresses the information and saves it through the next three reboots of the server. With each boot, new information is saved and the oldest information is replaced, and compressing the data allows a lot of data to be stored.

Remote playback is a handy feature if a server reboots while no one is available to observe the process. The entire boot process from the memory count, through the computer's self-test, to the start of any graphical application or operating system, is captured and can be replayed later—like a VCR for your server. If any valuable information was displayed too quickly to be seen or was just not observed at all, the RIB is there, ready to play back its screens several times at several different speeds. Popcorn not included.

This feature is exceptionally useful with Windows NT. Windows NT can run into problems that cause the operating system to stop completely, producing the blue screen of death (BSOD). The BSOD screen contains text information as to why the OS had to stop, including the program that caused the problem and what other applications were running at the time. If the BSOD went by unobserved, the RIB's screen capture capability allows it to be displayed later. If you have to copy the information to submit to Microsoft for translation, it's a lot easier to copy the image from the RIB than it is to copy each piece of information by hand!

To access the captured information, open the Web interface and select Reset Sequences from the list of options available. You will be given a list of the last few reboots to view.

Remote Reboot

Another very handy feature of the RIB is the Remote Reboot feature. Remember, the RIB is a completely separate computer inside the server. No matter what state the server is in, the RIB can control it. If for any reason the server itself is unresponsive, the RIB can shut it down, almost as if the server's power button had been pressed. To reboot a server, select Reset Server from the list in the Web interface.

One of my employers had several locations in two states. We chose a major, third-party software package to remote control the Windows NT operating system. After an upgrade to that software, however, we discovered that several of the servers would freeze when the operating system was told to reboot. The problem only affected some servers some of the time, but it always seemed to affect the most distant servers, at the most inconvenient hours. When we finally received the fix for the problem, I came in early to update the servers. Naturally, a couple of the ones in another state froze while I tried to reboot them. I had to wait for the first person to arrive in that office and ask him to push the power button for me. A RIB could have made my arms seem a whole lot longer!

Alert Notification

To be fully useful, the RIB should be able to let you know when there are problems. You wouldn't want your users to notice the trouble first! To meet this requirement, Compaq enabled the RIB to support Simple Network Management Protocol. SNMP is a standard defined in the TCP/IP suite. This protocol allows you to get the status of a device or set the configuration remotely through a common standard.

The RIB supports forwarding SNMP alerts (traps) to an SNMP management console (such as Compaq's own Insight Manager). These traps can then be interpreted by the management software and forwarded through e-mail or an alphanumeric pager to the appropriate people to deal with whatever problem has occurred.

If the RIB is equipped with the PC Card modem, or connected to a serial modem through the optional serial port, it can send pages to an alphanumeric pager directly, without a secondary management console. However, the option of the management console allows for a centralized reporting/paging location and limits the extra hardware required for alert notification (such as extra modems or phone lines).

FROM THE FIELD

The Remote Insight Board Lights-Out Edition (RIB-LOE)

Compaq has recently made available a new version of the Remote Insight Board to complement their remote management offerings under the "Lights-Out Edition" moniker. This new board supports many of the features of the regular Remote Insight Board, but adds a built-in native GUI remote console, a dedicated LAN connection with a built-in DHCP client, and a virtual power button feature.

The standard edition of the RIB requires installation of a third-party software package (like Carbon Copy or similar) to enable a remote console session to a server. The Lights-Out Edition RIB eliminates the need for this by implementing a native remote console on the board.

The Lights-Out edition of the RIB also removes the requirement to enter the IP addresses used for the board manually by implementing a DHCP client and default NetBIOS name for the board.

In addition, the RIB-LOE sports a virtual power button feature, which allows you to perform hard resets and remote power-ups of Compaq ProLiant 1850R and 8000 servers. At the time of this writing, the virtual power button feature is only supported on these two servers in the product line, however, Compaq has committed to supporting additional products in later revisions.

For more information on the Remote Insight Board Lights-Out Edition, check out http://www.compaq.com/manage/remote-lightsout-qs.html.

—Thomas E. Eck,
MCSE+I, MCSD, ASE, CCA, CNA

Alerts can be configured through the Compaq System Configuration Utility and through the RIB's Web interface. Each user configured with access to the RIB can receive alerts specific to that user (hardware technicians alerted to physical problems and software technicians to software problems).

QUESTIONS AND ANSWERS

My network uses IPX/SPX as the network protocol. Can I still use the Remote Insight Board?	You can still use the RIB, but you will have to add and configure the TCP/IP protocol on any machine you want to use to access it
My RIB does not have a modem. Can I configure it to send alerts to my pager?	The RIB will not be able to send you pages unless you add a modem or install an SNMP management console. If you install a management console, it will send the pages once the RIB has been configured to forward the SNMP traps.
My server does not have any free PCI slots. How can I install the RIB?	The RIB requires a PCI slot. If there is none free, you cannot install the RIB. However, if you have a PCI graphics controller in a PCI slot, you should remove it and use the RIB in that slot.
The Remote Console is asking for a password, but won't accept what I'm typing. How can I access it?	The password is defined individually for each user granted access. The password can be reset through the Web interface or through the System Configuration Utility. You will have to have a valid username and password to use the Web interface.
I have two servers in a building across town. It's a pain to go over there if a server goes down, but I don't want to buy a RIB for each. Can one RIB manage both?	No. To manage both servers, each would need its own RIB installed.
When power goes out, I lose connectivity to the server through the network. How could I manage a server then?	The RIB has its own battery to support it for up to two days in the event of a power failure, but that doesn't help network devices or modems stay up without power. An uninterruptible power supply should be used on any device that needs to have power in an outage.
If my server is physically turned off, can I use the RIB to turn it on?	The RIB can't control the physical power switch on a server. It can simulate what happens when the power switch is pressed, but it cannot actually press the switch. Support for a Remote Power On feature might be added in new servers, but currently the RIB is restricted by that physical limitation.

CERTIFICATION SUMMARY

Compaq's Remote Insight Board is a useful management tool for Compaq servers. Basically a separate computer on a PCI card, the RIB allows a server manager to have access to the server as if the machine were right in the room—complete with screen capture, remote control, and remote notification. Formed around the TCP/IP standards that are used on the Internet and most large networks, each RIB function is easily accessible from anywhere on the network, allowing for true remote management.

TWO-MINUTE DRILL

- ❑ Compaq provides the Remote Insight Board (RIB) as a means of managing and accessing a server from any location, regardless of the server's condition.
- ❑ The Compaq RIB is actually a complete computer on a single PCI card.
- ❑ The RIB is a standard 32-bit Personal Computer Interconnect (PCI) device.
- ❑ Each model of the RIB includes as standard an auto-sensing 10/100-Mbps NIC.
- ❑ The RIB's inclusion of a built-in NIC allows access to the RIB from any machine on the same network, provided that machine uses TCP/IP, whether or not that machine has a modem.
- ❑ The RIB integrates fully with CIM, sending alerts to it, as well as being fully accessible through it.
- ❑ Compaq includes an industry-standard PC Card slot in each RIB model.
- ❑ By providing the modem/serial port functionality through a PC Card, you can easily upgrade from various models of the RIB by simply upgrading the internal PC Card.

- The RIB includes its own video adapter and is designed to function as the server's main graphic display, replacing any existing graphics adapter.
- The RIB also has 8MB of video memory.
- The most important thing to verify before installing the RIB is what version of the BIOS is installed on the server.
- Compaq routinely updates the BIOS of their servers through ROMPaqs, downloadable programs that can add functionality or correct problems by reprogramming the BIOS with newer revisions.
- Most Compaq servers allow the RIB to reside in any available PCI slot.
- Once the RIB is physically installed in the server, you must configure the RIB's network adapter and (if so equipped) the modem.
- Using the System Configuration Utility (SCU), assigning IP address information and set up security.
- The Compaq RIB makes available several features and capabilities.
- In- and out-of-band management of remote servers simply refer to the type of connectivity that exists between the server and the management console.
- All of the RIB's features are accessible from a standard Web browser (including the Remote Console feature).
- Remote Console is one of the most powerful features of the RIB. It gives you the ability to view and control a server as if you were standing at the machine itself.
- Using Remote Insight Playback Capabilities, capturing the data displayed on the screen is a simple task—the RIB simply saves the data as it sends it to the monitor.
- Another very handy feature of the RIB is the Remote Reboot feature.
- Compaq enabled the RIB to support Simple Network Management Protocol, which allows you to get the status of a device or set the configuration remotely through a common standard.

SELF TEST

The following Self Test questions will help you measure your understanding of the material presented in this chapter. Read all the choices carefully, as there may be more than one correct answer. Choose all correct answers for each question.

1. The RIB is a PCI card for which of the following reasons?
   - A. The PCI bus has a wider bandwidth than the other busses.
   - B. The ISA bus is too complex to configure easily.
   - C. The EISA bus is slower.
   - D. All of the above
2. In its standard configuration, the RIB includes which of the following?
   - A. 14.4-Mbps modem
   - B. 28.8-Mbps modem
   - C. 10/100-Mbps network interface
   - D. RS-232 serial interface
3. To send alphanumeric pages directly, the RIB must be connected to what?
   - A. The network
   - B. A modem
   - C. A client workstation
   - D. Compaq's Web site
4. What function does the RIB perform for a managed server?
   - A. Graphics adapter
   - B. Network adapter
   - C. Hard drive controller
   - D. Second processor
5. Before installing the RIB, it's important to check the version of what major server component?
   - A. Operating system
   - B. Network driver
   - C. BIOS
   - D. Remote control software
6. The RIB's keyboard cable allows what RIB feature to function?
   - A. Remote control
   - B. Remote reset
   - C. Remote notification
   - D. Remote capture
7. Access to the RIB's features is available through which interfaces?
   - A. A Web browser
   - B. A dedicated, high-end workstation
   - C. A UNIX-based desktop system
   - D. All of the above
8. The RIB's Remote Console feature only allows access to which of the following?
   - A. Text screens
   - B. Graphic screens
   - C. Both text and graphic screens
   - D. Neither text nor graphic screens

9. What will happen if a managed server loses power?
   A. The RIB will stop functioning.
   B. The RIB will continue to operate using its internal battery.
   C. The RIB will display warning messages on the screen.
   D. The RIB will provide power to the server.
10. The RIB uses what protocol for sending alerts across a network?
    A. SMTP
    B. RSH
    C. Telnet
    D. SNMP
11. To install or upgrade a modem in a RIB, which of the following actions must be performed?
    A. Purchase a PC Card modem.
    B. Purchase a USB modem.
    C. Install a software patch.
    D. Upgrade the RIB's firmware.
12. To communicate with a RIB, computers on a network need which protocol?
    A. NetBEUI
    B. IPX/SPX
    C. NWLink
    D. TCP/IP
13. Up to ten users can be configured with what type of access to the RIB?
    A. Access the Remote Console
    B. Receive alerts
    C. Reset the server
    D. All of the above
14. The RIB can capture which of the following screen types?
    A. Boot text
    B. Graphical OS startup screens
    C. Both A and B
    D. Neither A or B
15. For a RIB to reboot a managed server, the server must:
    A. Be reachable across a router
    B. Have a responsive operating system
    C. Have a RIB installed
    D. Have Remote Reboot enabled in the Insight Agents

ASE

ACCREDITED SYSTEMS ENGINEER

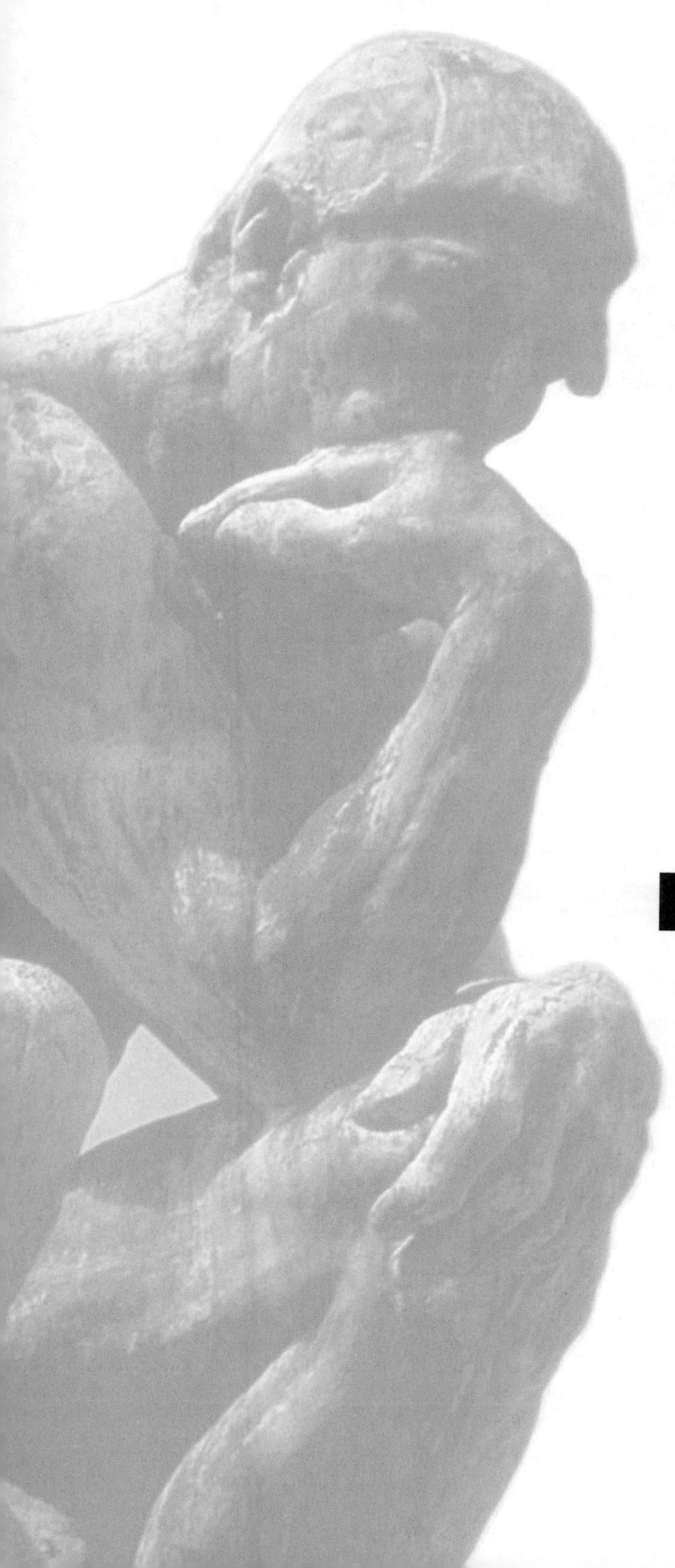

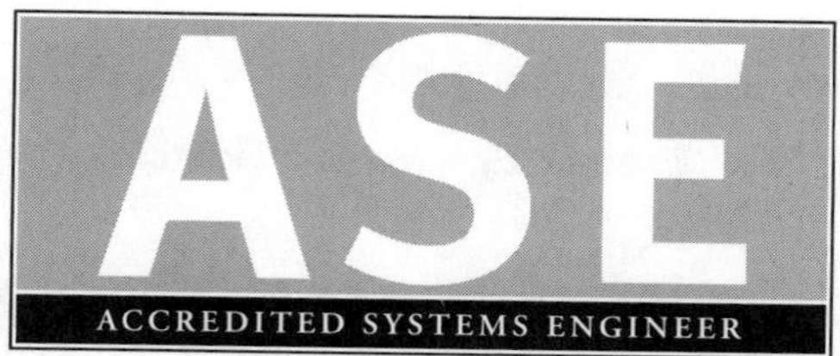

25

Version Control

CERTIFICATION OBJECTIVES

25.01 Version Control Color Codes

25.02 Downloading Current Databases

25.03 Update Interval for the Version Control Database

Version Control is a feature of Compaq's Insight Manager that assists an administrator in tracking driver revisions on the server. When you call technical support, one of the first questions they ask you is, "What version of the drivers are you using?" Then they ask you to install the latest drivers, leaving you to ponder thoughts such as: Just what does the new driver fix? What priority should I place on upgrading the drivers? How could I be proactive in scheduling driver upgrades?

With Version Control, you can answer those three questions. Version Control reports what improvements have been made to various drivers and other Compaq software installed on that server. Version Control, through color-coding, can also indicate the importance of upgrading drivers. And with Version Control, you can review server software versions before placing that call to technical support.

Version Control is a task of the managed server. Right-click the desired server to bring up the task list. Figure 25-1 shows an example of tasks associated with the server, including Version Control.

FIGURE 25-1

Compaq Insight Manager task list

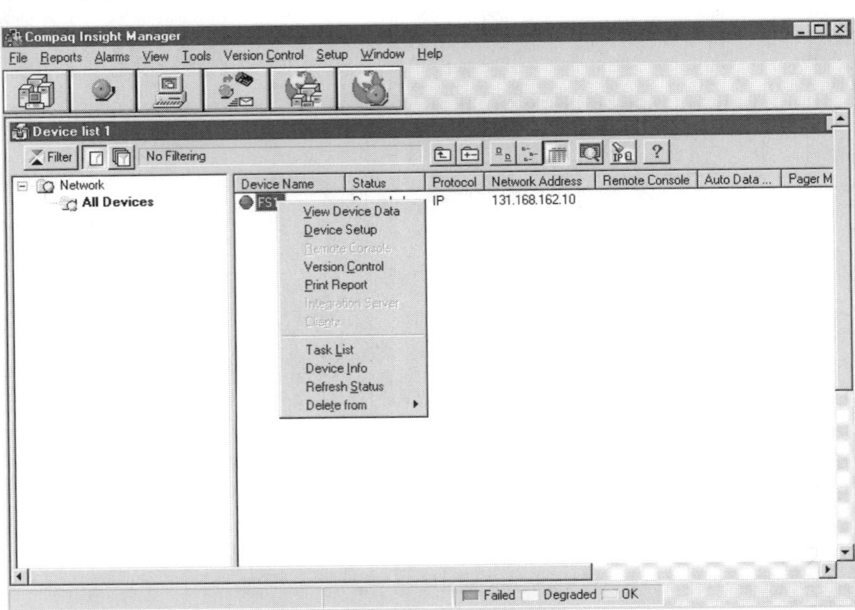

CERTIFICATION OBJECTIVE 25.01

Version Control Color Codes

The Version Control task reports text detail and color codes for each driver in a graphical interface. After you select the Version Control task from the server task list, Version Control interrogates the server for installed software and compares that information with the Compaq Insight Manger version database. The following is an example of the results of this comparison.

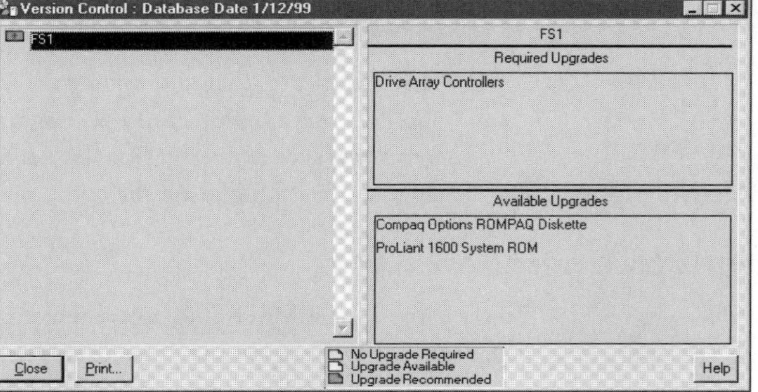

You can see in the illustration that server FS1 has some software that is out of date. To determine specifically which drivers need upgrading, expand the FS1 folder. In the next illustration, you see the expanded view of software installed on server FS1.

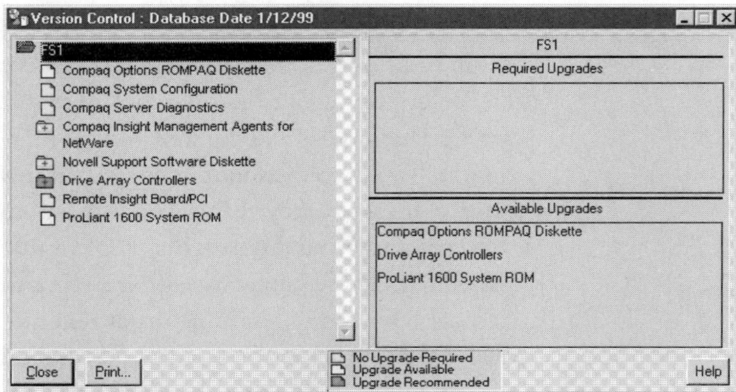

Green, Yellow, and Red Version Control Status Flags

Version control uses a red, yellow, or green flag to designate whether a newer driver is available, is recommended for upgrade, or is current. The flags are used as follows:

- **Green** Indicates that the installed software is current. No further action is required.
- **Yellow** Indicates that an upgrade is available. Though out of date, the software may or may not need to be upgraded. Version Control reports the reason for the upgrade when you highlight the component marked in yellow.
- **Red** Indicates that an upgrade is recommended. Generally, you should place a high priority on upgrading this software. As with items marked in yellow, you can determine the reason for the upgrade by highlighting the component marked in red.

Reasons to Upgrade

In the Upgrade Reasons frame, Version Control provides specific information regarding the reasons you may wish to upgrade the indicated driver. There are two main categories of upgrade reasons: Resolved Problems and New Features. These categories are further subdivided into major and minor.

With information about a driver enhancement, you can determine whether the upgrade affects your environment, aiding in problem resolution. When you know the reason for the upgrade, you can prioritize the upgrade process.

Resolved Problems

Resolved problems are driver enhancements targeting known problems. The description identifies the problem that has been fixed, as well as all appropriate models and combination of models. This information improves your ability to troubleshoot issues related to your own system. Version Control breaks Resolved Problems into subcategories of major and minor.

A major resolved problem is a problem that can cause a server failure or loss of data. These problems exist in common system configurations. Version Control color codes indicating major resolved problems could be red or yellow. Although Version Control may indicate these resolved problems with yellow, they should be addressed as soon as they are discovered.

A minor resolved problem fixes system problems that are rarely seen. They can also resolve inconveniences for which you may have a workaround, but would prefer a resolution. The following is an example of a minor resolved problem.

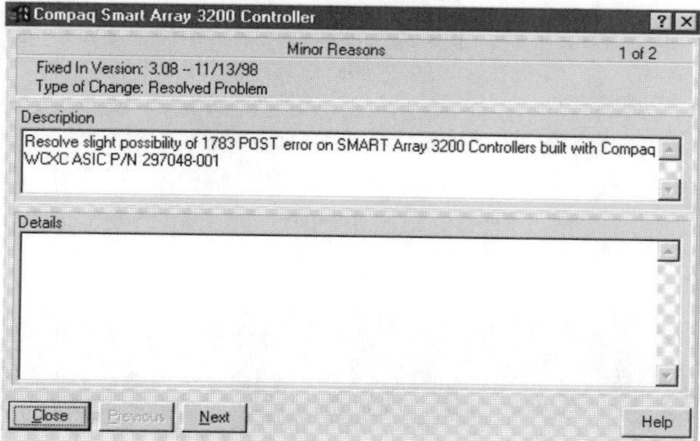

New Feature

The New Feature category of Version Control provides information about what was upgraded in the driver. The description identifies model information necessary for planning hardware upgrades and system performance tuning. As with Resolved Problems, Version Control subdivides New Features into major and minor.

A major new feature reflects upgrades that support new hardware. A common upgrade in this category is the system ROM, as reflected in the next illustration. This upgrade adds support for a new SCSI controller, which did not exist when the ProLiant 1600 was first released.

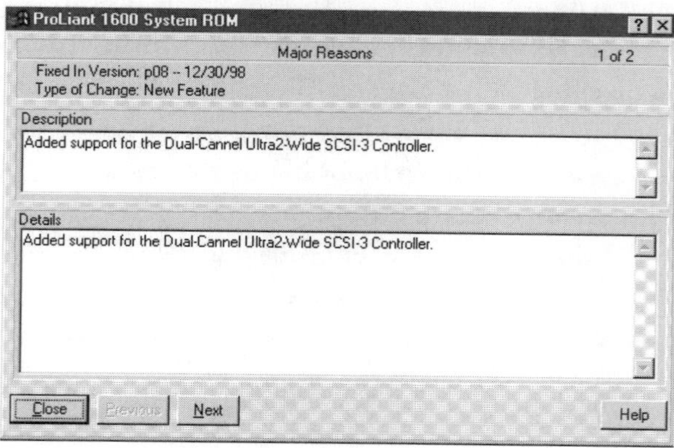

on the job

I received a call from a customer who was having trouble installing a new array controller in the company server. He complained that the system configuration utility would not recognize the new controller. I instructed the customer to use the Version Control utility. We discovered that the server system ROM has been updated to include support for the new controller he was trying to add. After upgrading his system ROM, the system configuration utility was able to recognize and configure the controller.

Minor New Feature upgrades reflect performance enhancements. They generally involve improved software code. The window shown next

FROM THE FIELD

Customer Advisories Can Reduce Upgrade Stress

Even for seemingly trivial tasks like upgrading a service pack, updates to mission-critical enterprise servers should be performed after hours to help mitigate the risk of user data loss and downtime. This is a very real danger when changing drivers without updating the firmware, as in the upgrade to Service Pack 4 when an older SMART-2 array controller is installed. (See customer advisory EM990204 for more information.)

In order to install Windows NT Service Pack 4 on a machine with a SMART-2 array controller, you must first update the array controller firmware to release 3.08 or higher to prevent a blue screen of death during initialization of the operating system. Imagine performing an update to Service Pack 4 and finding that the machine refuses to boot. Armed with the knowledge that this is a known bug, a simple firmware update prior to the installation of NTSP4 avoids the issue altogether.

Before updating a Windows NT machine to a new service pack revision, SSD, or driver, check for any known issues in the Customer Advisories section of the Compaq Web site. This can help you prevent the anxiety associated with seemingly dead machines. The site can be found at: http://www.compaq.com/support/techpubs/customer_advisories

—Thomas E. Eck, MCSE+I, MCSD, ASE, CCA, CNA

identifies a minor new feature that provides more space for PCI options in the ProLiant 1600 ROM. Other upgrades may include more efficient message handling.

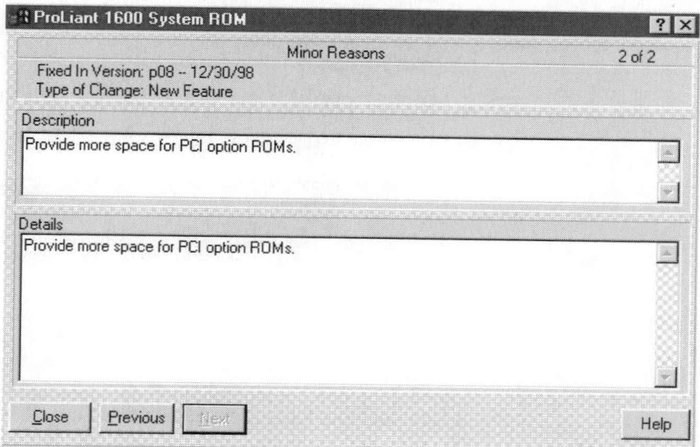

CERTIFICATION OBJECTIVE 25.02

Downloading Current Databases

Think about the dynamic nature of the network computing industry. New systems and peripherals are constantly being introduced. Systems are delivered with ROMs and drivers that contain bugs. Users look for faster and more efficient delivery of services. All of these factors create a need to maintain currency. The Version Control facility supports that need with the capability to download a current database.

From the Compaq Insight Manager menu bar, select Version Control. The drop-down menu lets you update the database from CD or diskette, or from the Internet. Here are the two choices:

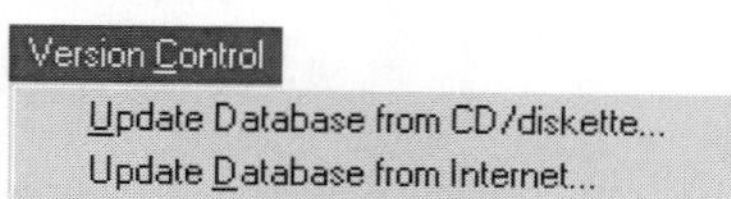

Database Update from CD

Compaq includes the Version Control database on each SmartStart and Management CD. As an ASE, you will receive a subscription to SmartStart that will continue as long as you maintain your ASE status.

When you select to Update Database from CD/diskette, you will see a pop-up window like the one next. By selecting Yes, Compaq Insight Manager will automatically search the CD for the Version Control database.

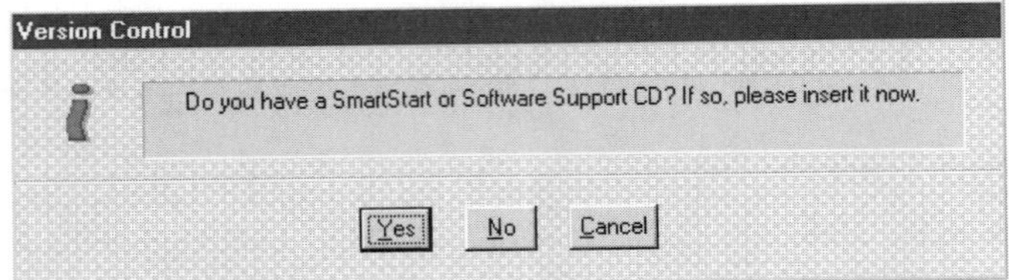

The Version Control database file is DBINFO.DB_, as seen here. Simply select OK.

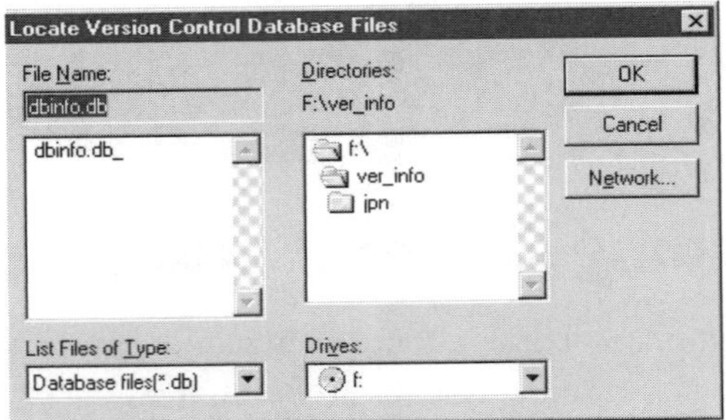

Compaq Insight Manager will copy the database from the CD to your local hard disk. After a few seconds, you will see a pop-up window indicating that the database has been updated, as reflected in the window shown next. You should now use Version Control to check for updated software available for your server.

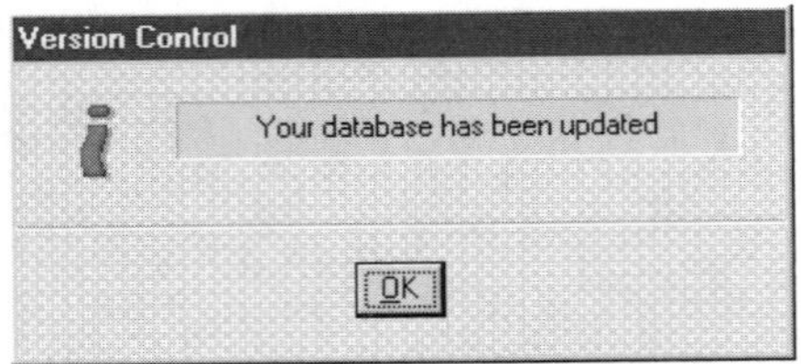

Database Update from the Internet

Another source for the Version Control database is the Internet. Downloading the database from the Internet is quick and easy, and provides a far more current source of the database than the CD.

There is no need to configure Compaq Insight Manager for locating the database. Your only configuration concerns the type of connection you wish to use to download the database. Figure 25-2 describes the three connection options.

Once you have selected your connection type, Compaq Insight Manager will test the Internet Connectivity and begin downloading the Version Control database. Figure 25-3 reflects the beginning of the download process.

While at a customer site reviewing server management procedures, I attempted to update their Version Control database in Compaq Insight Manager. Unfortunately, I had forgotten to bring my copy of the SmartStart CD. Fortunately, the customer had a direct connection to the Internet. We simply selected the Update Database from Internet option. After approximately one minute, the customer's Version Control database was current.

FIGURE 25-2

Version Control database source: Internet

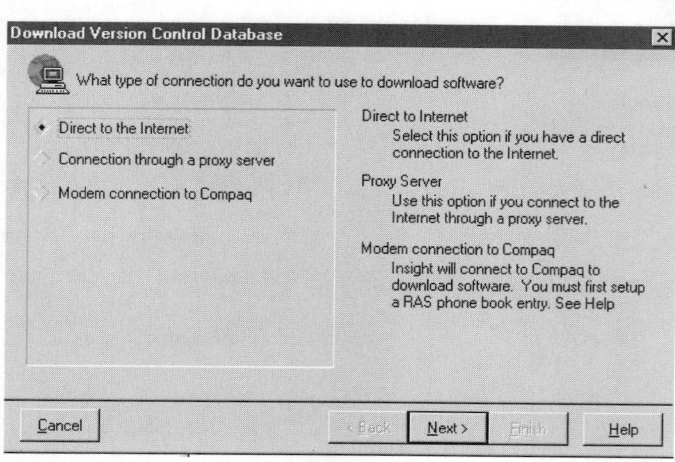

FIGURE 25-3

Testing Internet connectivity

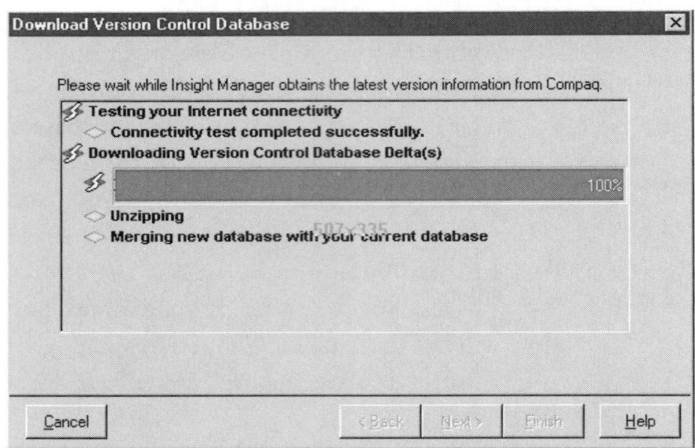

Downloading the Version Control database from the Internet takes approximately one minute, depending on the speed of your connection. The pop-up window reports the progress and ultimate completion of the download, as shown in Figure 25-4. Once the download is finished, you should use Version Control to check for updated software for your server.

FIGURE 25-4

Database download completion

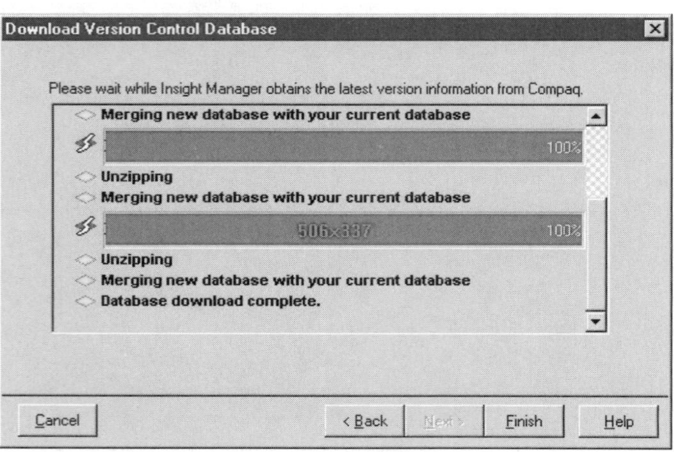

CERTIFICATION OBJECTIVE 25.03

Update Interval for the Version Control Database

Compaq Insight Manager utilizes a reminder feature with Version Control. By default, Version Control will remind you every 60 days that you may wish to download the latest database. As with a tickler file, you can change the default value during the installation of Compaq Insight Manager. Considering the frequency of system changes, it is recommended that the default value be set to 30 days.

A customer was looking to be more proactive in his server management activities. We reviewed his procedures and determined that his environment was relatively dynamic with frequent upgrades and a high premium on performance. Because his goal was to be proactive, rather than reactive, in managing his systems, I recommended that he increase the Version Control database update reminder interval from the default of 60 days to 30 days.

QUESTIONS AND ANSWERS

All my server software is marked green…	No upgrades are available. You are current.
I have mostly green indicators, but a few yellow ones…	The yellow color code indicates that an upgrade is available. Examine the reasons for the upgrade to determine if it affects your system.
One of my drivers is showing up red in Version Control…	The red color code indicates a recommended upgrade. Obtain and upgrade the driver at your earliest convenience.
The Reasons To Upgrade screen indicates a major resolved problem…	The affected driver needs to be upgraded to prevent a potential server crash or data loss.
The Reasons To Upgrade screen indicates a major new feature…	Upgrade this driver if you intend to install the new feature in your system.
How often should I update my Version Control Database?	The default setting is every 60 days. The recommended interval is 30 days.
Where can I find the latest Version Control database?	The database can be found on the Internet and on the SmartStart or Management CDs.

CERTIFICATION SUMMARY

Version Control is a feature of Compaq's Insight Manager that assists an administrator in tracking driver revisions on the server. It reports what improvements have been made to Compaq software installed on that server. Version Control reports the status of your Compaq software using color codes.

The color codes are as follows: Green indicates no upgrade available; Yellow indicates upgrade available; Red indicates upgrade recommended.

Version Control categorizes the available upgrades as resolved problems and new features. These categories are divided into the subcategories of major and minor.

Major resolved problems are those problems that can cause a server failure or loss of data. A minor resolved problem fixes system problems that are rarely seen. Major new features reflect upgrades that support new hardware. Minor new feature upgrades reflect performance enhancements.

Version Control uses a database to compare current software versions with those installed on a server. This database is available from CD (SmartStart and Management) and the Internet. In order to stay current, you should update your Version Control database every 30 days.

TWO-MINUTE DRILL

- ❑ Version Control is a feature of Compaq's Insight Manager that assists an administrator in tracking driver revisions on the server.
- ❑ Version Control reports what improvements have been made to various drivers and other Compaq software installed on that server.
- ❑ Version Control is a task of the managed server.
- ❑ The Version Control task reports text detail and color codes for each driver in a graphical interface.
- ❑ Version control uses a red, yellow, or green flag to designate whether a newer driver is available, is recommended for upgrade, or is current.
- ❑ There are two main categories of upgrade reasons: Resolved Problems and New Features.

- ❑ Resolved problems are driver enhancements targeting known problems.
- ❑ The New Feature category of Version Control provides information about what was upgraded in the driver.
- ❑ The Version Control facility supports that need to maintain currency with the capability to download a current database.
- ❑ Compaq includes the Version Control database on each SmartStart and Management CD.
- ❑ Downloading the database from the Internet is quick and easy, and provides a far more current source of the database than the CD.
- ❑ Version Control will remind you every 60 days that you may wish to download the latest database. You can change the default value during the installation of Compaq Insight Manager. It is recommended that the default value be changed to 30 days.

SELF TEST

The following Self Test questions will help you measure your understanding of the material presented in this chapter. Read all the choices carefully, as there may be more than one correct answer. Choose all correct answers for each question.

1. Version Control is a _____ of the managed server.
   A. Task
   B. Service
   C. Agent
   D. Element

2. Which of the following statements accurately describes Version Control?
   A. It upgrades drivers and agents
   B. It controls driver and agent installation
   C. It checks for current versions of Compaq software
   D. It groups servers in a hierarchical structure

3. Which color indicates that the installed software is current?
   A. Green
   B. Yellow
   C. Red
   D. Black

4. Which color indicates that an upgrade is available?
   A. Green
   B. Yellow
   C. Red
   D. Black

5. Red-coded software indicates that an upgrade is:
   A. Not necessary
   B. Available
   C. Recommended
   D. Unavailable

6. What are the two main categories of upgrade reasons?
   A. Resolved problems and new features
   B. Resolved problems and server health
   C. Asset control and new features
   D. Asset control and server health

7. Which category of upgrade reasons is reserved for those situations that can cause a server failure or loss of data?
   A. Major new feature
   B. Minor new feature
   C. Major resolved problem
   D. Minor resolved problem

8. Which category of upgrade reasons fixes system problems that are rarely seen?
   A. Major new feature
   B. Minor new feature
   C. Major resolved problem
   D. Minor resolved problem

9. Which category of upgrade reasons reflects upgrades that support new hardware?
   A. Major new feature
   B. Minor new feature
   C. Major resolved problem
   D. Minor resolved problem

10. Which category of upgrade reasons reflects performance enhancements?
   A. Major new feature
   B. Minor new feature
   C. Major resolved problem
   D. Minor resolved problem

11. The Version Control menu line option allows you to do which of the following?
   A. Upgrade the Version Control database
   B. Check software versions on a server
   C. Upgrade drivers on a server
   D. Schedule software upgrades

12. Compaq includes the Version Control database on:
   A. Server Profile Disk
   B. SmartStart CD
   C. Server Configuration Disk
   D. Compaq/Windows NT Resource CD

13. Which of the following is the Version Control database file?
   A. SYSMGMT.SYS
   B. CPQRIB.SYS
   C. DBINFO.DB_
   D. TRAPDBH.DB_

14. Besides CD, another source for the Version Control database is:
   A. Info Messenger
   B. Internet
   C. System Partition
   D. Server Support Diskettes

15. What is recommended interval for upgrading the Version Control database?
   A. 15 days
   B. 20 days
   C. 30 days
   D. 45 days

ASE
ACCREDITED SYSTEMS ENGINEER

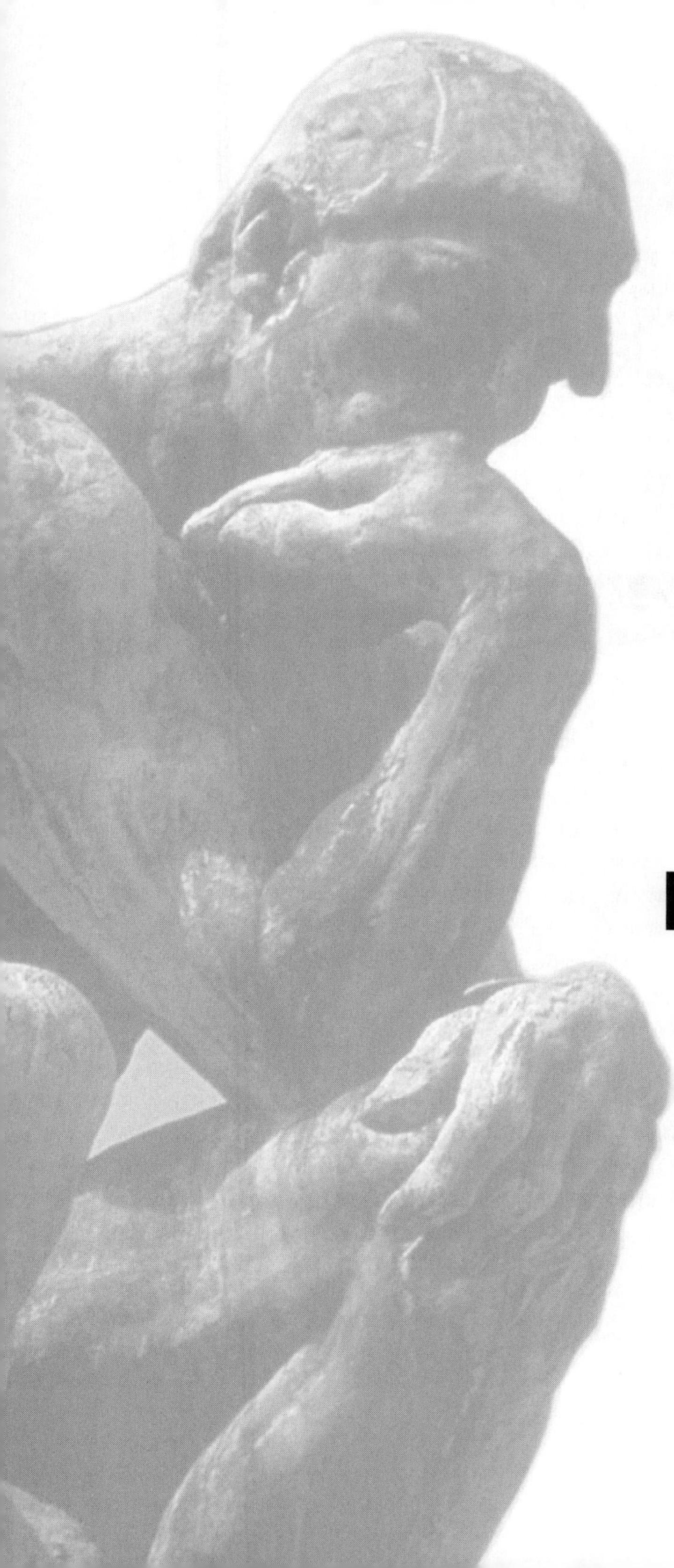

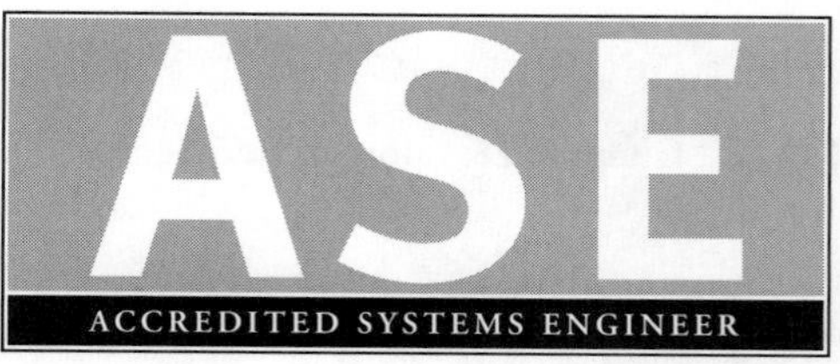

26

Integration Server

CERTIFICATION OBJECTIVES

26.01 Integration Server

26.02 Operating Systems Supported by the Compaq Integration Server

26.03 Push and Pull Architecture

26.04 Compaq PEZ Files

26.05 Creating an Integration Server

This chapter will provide you with an overview of the concept of the Compaq Integration Server, covering five major areas of information. First, we will define the operating systems supported by the Integration Server. Then we will identify the architecture of how the Integration Server is updated, and how it updates the Compaq servers in the environment. This chapter will instruct you in how to create an Integration Server from an existing server, including how PEZ files play an important role in the functioning of the integration server. Finally, the interaction of the Integration Server and the various Compaq utilities will be defined. The information provided will present a comprehensive overview of the Compaq Integration Server (IS).

CERTIFICATION OBJECTIVE 26.01

Integration Server

The IS is a central repository of Compaq system software on the network. It can contain all of the drivers, firmware, and utilities needed by the Compaq servers in an environment. A central location for storage of the software allows for consistency of drivers that have been tested and proved in your enterprise. Existing servers can be updated from the software stored on the IS, and new servers can be configured. Creating the IS also helps to streamline system configuration due to the IS's tight integration with the SmartStart system configuration utility. This integration assists by allowing you to download all of the necessary software from a central location during the SmartStart-assisted install. If you install the correct revision of the drivers during initial system setup, you will not have to count on your version of SmartStart having all of the correct drivers. Nor will you have to install or update the drivers individually after the OS is configured. With a central location for the storage of the system software, the IS provides tighter integration with existing systems and the potential for reduced configuration time, centralized control, and/or standardization of system software.

CERTIFICATION OBJECTIVE 26.02

Operating Systems Supported by the Compaq Integration Server

The IS is supported by two major network operating systems: Windows NT version 3.51 and 4.0 as well as NetWare 3.12, 4.1, and 4.11 (or IntranetWare). What this means is that you can store the system software for these two operating systems on an Integration Server. The IS is accessed using the Compaq Integration Maintenance Utility (CIMU). The CIMU allows you to update all of the software and drivers at one time and reboot once, as opposed to installing each needed driver update individually and rebooting after each install. Administration time is reduced by taking advantage of the tight integration of the IS and CIMU (much easier and quicker than downloading five or six patches and drivers and installing them one at a time).

Compaq Integration Maintenance Utility and Windows NT

In Windows NT, the CIMU is made up of two parts: the Integration Maintenance Utility (IMU) and the System Partition Update Utility (SPUU). The integration Maintenance Utility allows you to update the SSD revision, the version of the Insight Agents, and the CIMU itself as patches and new capabilities are added. The SPUU allows updating of the Compaq System Partition by allowing System Configuration Utility, Drive Array Advanced Diagnostics, and BIOS updates to be copied to the system partition on the selected server.

To install the CIMU, you can connect to the IS or use the SmartStart CD. The CIMU can be installed from the SmartStart CD by going to the \SSNT40\CIMU\ENG directory and executing SETUP.EXE. The other option is to map a drive to the Integration Server, go to the Find Out directory, and fill in the information there. This was installed by default if the Assisted Install option was selected, and if SmartStart was used to configure and install the server. Once installed, the software can be executed by selecting Compaq Products Services from the Start menu.

If you choose to use the CIMU to update the system software, you have the option of picking where to apply the system updates from. You can select either the IS or the SmartStart CD-ROM. When either of the utilities is run, it displays a list of updates available in the location chosen on the IS or on a SmartStart CD. Then all you have to do is put a checkmark next to the software you wish to install and click the button marked Install. The IMU is limited in that it must be run at the console of the server that you wish to update. However, the SPUU can push out the updated software to the chosen server (so you don't have to be at the console).

Compaq Integration Maintenance Utility and NetWare

Under the NetWare operating system, the capabilities of the CIMU are slightly different. First, the SPUU does not exist. Because of the architecture of NetWare, it is impossible to update the information on the system partition while the OS is up and running. In addition, the IMU under NetWare functions slightly differently than under Windows NT. In Windows NT, the IMU calls separate setup utilities (the NTSSD, the Insight Agents install program, and the CIMU install). Under NetWare, everything runs and updates from within the IMU. The management agents, drivers, system software, and CIMU all are updated and installed from the NetWare version of the CIMU. Although the functionality of the Windows NT and NetWare IMU is slightly different, NetWare is still restricted to running the IMU from the console.

In order to execute the maintenance utility on a NetWare server, two NLMs must be loaded:

- **NWSNUT.NLM** Is the NetWare NLM Utility User Interface (version 4.11)
- **CPQMAINT.NLM** Executes the IMU. CPQMAINT.NLM requires NWSNUT.NLM to be loaded and running in order to load. The CPQMAINT.NLM is located on the SmartStart CD

or on the IS in \SSNW\CIMU. This directory can also be copied to one of the volumes on the server so that you don't have to mount a CD in order run it.

CERTIFICATION OBJECTIVE 26.03

Push and Pull Architecture

In order to move the software around, the Integration Server uses Push and Pull architecture. The "pull" refers to downloading the software from Compaq and placing it on the IS. The "push" refers to software being uploaded to the servers in the environment from the IS. Let's look at a few of the Push and Pull techniques for the software transfer.

Access Methods

When downloading the software to the IS, there are three options available: Internet, dial-up, or SmartStart CD. All three options require you to be at a system running Compaq Insight Manager. Figure 26-1 shows the option to select in order to manage the Integration Server.

Access via the Internet or Dial-Up

Using the Internet or dial-up methods, you connect to the Compaq Support Software Server. The Compaq Support Software Server is Compaq's "Integration Server in the Sky." This server is the central repository for all Compaq system software.

In order to update the IS, the PC you are working at must be running CIM. If you want to access it via the Internet from the PC running CIM, you must have access to the Internet via the LAN or a DUN (Dial-Up Networking)/RAS connection to an ISP. Using CIM, you access the Compaq Support Software Server, download the components you need over the Internet, and then place them on the IS.

In the dial-up scenario, CIM can be configured to connect to a Compaq Dial-In Site that has access to the Compaq Support Software Server. Once

FIGURE 26-1

Integration Server management context menu

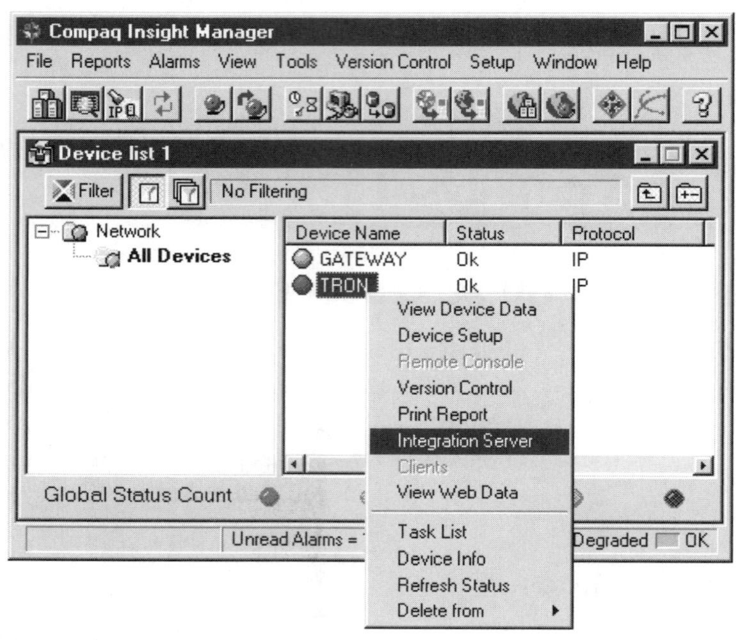

connected, you can select the software you want to download from the Compaq storehouse. In Figure 26-2 we see the menu that displays the various options available for updating the Integration Server.

The download usually takes a while the first time, even over a high-speed link, especially if you are pulling a large selection from the Compaq Support Software Server. You shouldn't be surprised if it takes an hour or more.

Update via CD

As new versions of SmartStart are released, the software can be downloaded from the SmartStart CDs to the IS. The option to use a CD is located in the same dialog box in which the software available for download is listed. Figure 26-3 shows the dialog box in which you are offered the option to select to update the IS from CD by clicking the Add CD button. This dialog box is where you can select the specific pieces of software you would like to download to the IS.

FIGURE 26-2

CIM Integration Server update option selection screen

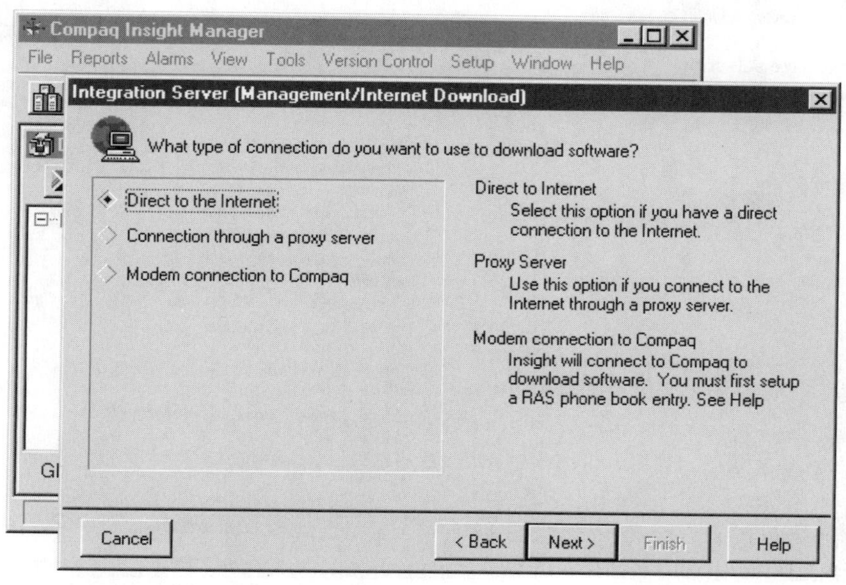

The three options available for pushing or uploading software to the production servers are:

- **Local** Using the CIMU at the server console and selecting the options desired
- **Remote attended** Using a remote control program such as PCAnywhere, Carbon Copy, or NetWare's Rconsole utility to access the server console remotely and run the CIMU
- **Remote unattended** This method is advantageous because it allows you to update multiple servers at once. In order to accomplish a remote install of the software you must use third-party software such as Microsoft Systems Management Server (MS-SMS). According to Compaq, the remote unattended method is not recommended for updating NetWare servers. However, all of the needed files can be copied locally via management software, thereby reducing the overhead of manually placing all the information on each server. Compaq does provide scripting files for use with MS-SMS, which will allow you to update Windows NT servers using the remote unattended method.

FIGURE 26-3

Software selection menu screen

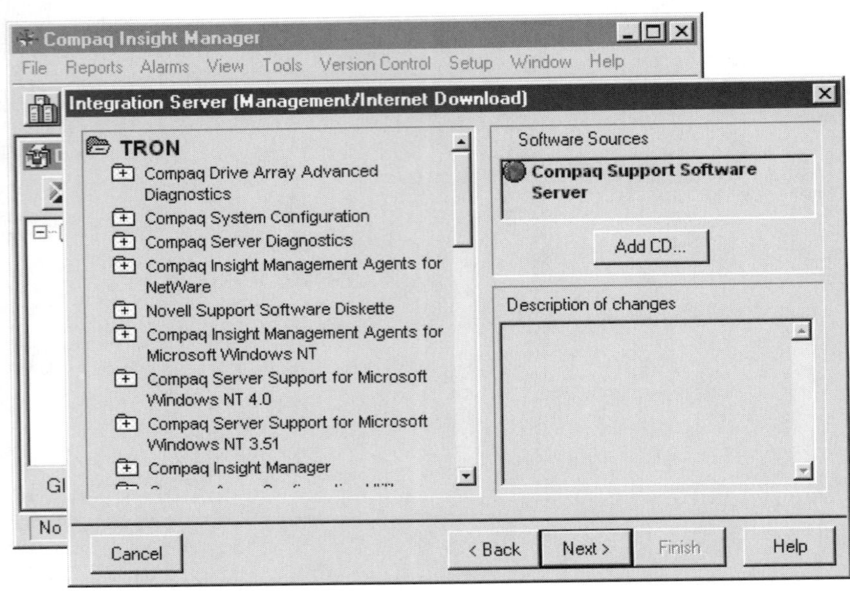

These three methods for updating system software to and from the IS provide the flexibility needed for use in a variety of environments, scaling all the way up to a large enterprise with hundreds of servers.

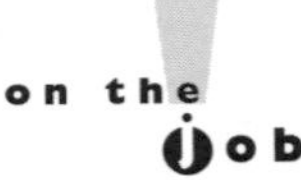

Nothing works perfectly every time. Make sure that you test the update methods before deploying them. When using one of the remote methods for updating the software on a server, it is a good idea to have someone available to go onsite in case something goes wrong.

CERTIFICATION OBJECTIVE 26.04

Compaq PEZ Files

In order to understand how the IS works with all of the other Compaq components, some of the pieces of the Integration Server must be understood. In this section, we'll see how software information is stored on the server. After

FROM THE FIELD

Use Microsoft SMS to Reduce Your Legwork

Although Microsoft SMS does require a significant amount of hardware resources, it can make your life a lot easier when it comes to updating software on a large number of servers. SMS can also save you time updating server software for servers that reside at a remote site since you won't have to travel to the remote site to install the software.

Besides automated software distribution, SMS provides the following tools that help you manage your server and desktop environment:

- Hardware Inventory (Compaq added several extensions that allow you to gather more hardware information for Compaq desktops and servers. For example, you can use SMS to get the serial number for your unit.)
- Software Inventory
- Remote Control Tools and Diagnostics
- Network Diagnostic Tools

For more information on SMS, refer to Microsoft's Web site at http://www.microsoft.com/smsmgmt.

Compaq also included several utilities that you can use to facilitate using SMS with the Integration Server. The utilities are part of the Systems Management Toolkit and can be downloaded from http://www.compaq.com/products/servers/management/dl-cim-toolkit.html.

—Roneil Icatar, MCSE, MCP+I, ASE

the cataloging method is described, we will identify how the following pieces interact with the server: Compaq Insight Manager, SmartStart, and Compaq Integration Maintenance Utilities.

PEZ Files on the SmartStart CDs

There are three files that are critical to proper communication between the pieces of the IS. Two of these files are located on the SmartStart CDs (PEZ is simply the extension that Compaq uses for these files):

- **SSCD.PEZ** Is a database containing a list of all the available items that are found on the SmartStart and Support Software CD (drivers, BIOS updates, and System Partition software).

- **COMPAQ.PEZ** Contains a list of the software that is on the Management CD of the SmartStart package (Insight Agents, CIM, Survey).

PEZ Files on the Integration Server

In order to manage the PEZ files, CIM is needed. In updating the software on the IS, when selecting the CD option you are prompted for the location of the PEZ. Select the drive that has the CD.

After the IS is updated, the information is stored in the third PEZ file, which is found on the Integration Server and is also named COMPAQ.PEZ. It is different than the PEZ of the same name on the Management CD. This one contains a list of all of the software available on the IS, whereas the one on the Management CD contains only the software found on that CD. In Figure 26-4, you see the screens that are used to select the PEZ file.

When one of the CIMU applications is executed, it queries the PEZ files and then displays a list of software available on the server (or CD), allowing you to choose which versions of the software you would like to install. Similarly, when SmartStart is being used in the configuration of a server, once the integration server has been identified in the configuration process, the SmartStart application will also access the PEZ in order to display a list of available options.

CERTIFICATION OBJECTIVE 26.05

Creating an Integration Server

There are two methods for creating the IS. One is to select the appropriate option when configuring the system via SmartStart. The other is to create the proper directory structure on an existing server.

Requirements for Setting up the Integration Server

In order to take advantage of all the IS capabilities, you first need to create the Integration Server itself. The server can be either NetWare 3.12 or 4.1,

FIGURE 26-4

Pick your PEZ

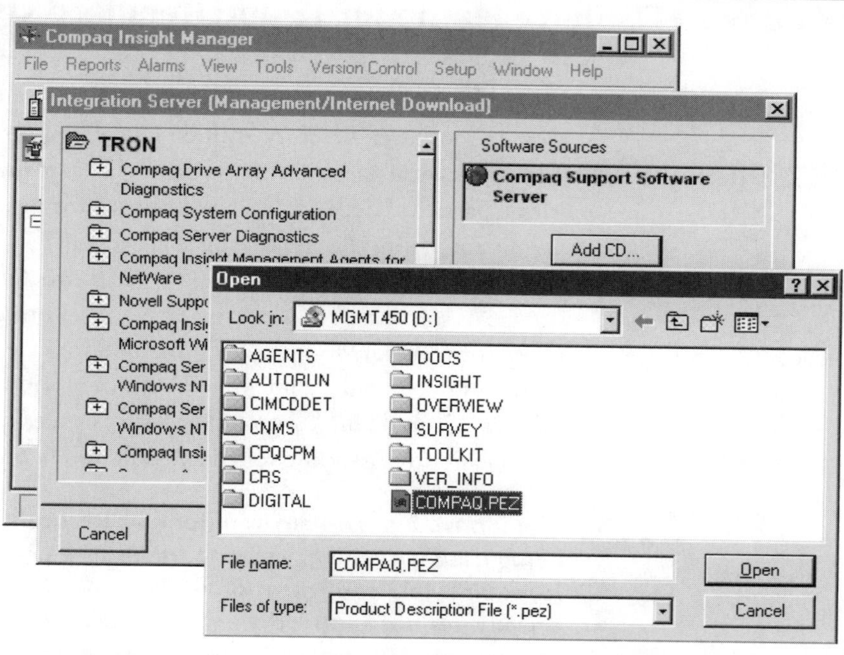

IntranetWare, or a Windows NT 3.51 or 4.0 platform. The server must have the Compaq Insight Management Agents version 3.0 or later installed and running. The server need not be dedicated to the task; it can be a multifunctional system providing other services.

NetWare Volume Name for IS and Required Usernames

To configure a NetWare server using the Install utility, you will need to create and mount a volume named CPQIS1. On the volume just created, make a root level directory labeled CPQIS. Of course, you will need a user ID and password to access this data. In order to allow SmartStart to access the data, create an ID called CPQIS and assign any password that you like to the ID just created (SmartStart will prompt you for one). If the server is in an NDS tree, make sure that it is running in bindery emulation mode with the bindery context pointing to where the user ID is located. The account must have Read and File Scan rights to the entire volume.

Windows NT Share Name for IS and Required Usernames

In order to configure a Windows NT server, a share must be created as CPQIS1 with the Everyone group given Full Control. Within this share, create a root level directory entitled CPQIS, as on a NetWare server. You still need a local account (as opposed to a Domain account) entitled CPQIS with a password defined by you. The account needs Read and Execute permissions from the root of the share down.

The creation of an Integration Server allows for centralized control and storage of software for Compaq Servers. By storing all of the software on Integration Server, you provide a method for ease of access to necessary resources that is tightly integrated with the various Compaq resources and utilities. Centralizing control of software creates an environment where it is much easier to distribute tested software into a production environment.

on the job

If you have a mixed environment where both IPX and TCP/IP are being used, you might want to make sure IPX is installed on the IS. It requires less configuration within SmartStart, since the TCP/IP driver does not support client configuration via DHCP. You will need to know the IP address for the server, as the IP drivers do not support name resolution via WINS or DNS.

QUESTIONS AND ANSWERS	
If you want to update the Integration Server and you don't have Internet connectivity, what method would you use?	Either dial-up or CD-ROM
What utility would you use to update the drivers on the server?	Compaq Integration Maintenance Utility
How do I update the software on the IS?	Using Compaq Insight Manager, right-click the IS and select the option Integration Server from the Context menu
What are PEZ files?	PEZ files are databases that contain a list of the software stored on the SmartStart CDs or the IS

CERTIFICATION SUMMARY

The Compaq Integration server is a central repository of Compaq software, drivers, and BIOS updates on the network. The information is pulled from the Compaq Support Software Server via either the Internet or dial-up method, and placed on the IS using Compaq Insight Manager. CIM also can utilize the SmartStart CDs to update the IS.

The information on the IS is accessed via the Compaq Integration Maintenance Utility. You must use the appropriate version of the CIMU (NetWare or Windows NT). The CIMU provides a list of the software available on the IS and allows you to select the particular versions you would like to install. The CIMU gets the list of software available on the IS from the PEZ files that are stored on the server.

There are three PEZ files that are responsible for keeping track of all the software. COMPAQ.PEZ is located on the Management CD. SSCD.PEZ is on the SmartStart and Support Software CD. COMPAQ.PEZ is located on the IS and contains a list all of the software stored on the IS. (A different file named COMPAQ.PEZ is on the Management CD.)

This information is stored in the directory structure that makes up the Integration Server. The directory structure is as follows: a volume (NetWare) or share (Windows NT) named CPQIS1, with a top-level directory named CPQIS, and an account named CPQIS that has Read and File Scan rights to the entire directory structure in the local account database.

TWO-MINUTE DRILL

- ❑ The IS is a central repository of Compaq system software on the network.
- ❑ With a central location for the storage of the system software, the IS provides tighter integration with existing systems and the potential for reduced configuration time, centralized control, and/or standardization of system software.

- The IS is supported by two major network operating systems: Windows NT version 3.51 and 4.0 as well as NetWare 3.12, 4.1, and 4.11 (or IntranetWare).
- The CIMU allows you to update all of the software and drivers at one time and reboot once.
- In Windows NT, the CIMU is made up of two parts: the Integration Maintenance Utility (IMU) and the System Partition Update Utility (SPUU).
- The SPUU does not exist on NetWare. Under NetWare, everything runs and updates from within the IMU.
- Integration Server uses Push and Pull architecture.
- When downloading the software to the IS, there are three options available: Internet, dial-up, or SmartStart CD.
- The Compaq Support Software Server is the central repository for all Compaq system software.
- As new versions of SmartStart are released, the software can be downloaded from the SmartStart CDs to the IS.
- The three options available for pushing or uploading software to the production servers are:
  - Local
  - Remote attended
  - Remote unattended
- Two of the three files that are critical for proper communication between the pieces of the IS and which are located on the SmartStart CDs are:
  - SSCD.PEZ
  - COMPAQ.PEZ
- After the IS is updated, the information is stored in the third PEZ file, which is found on the Integration Server and is also named COMPAQ.PEZ.

- The two methods for creating the IS are:
  - To select the appropriate option when configuring the system via SmartStart
  - To create the proper directory structure on an existing server
- In order to take advantage of all the IS capabilities, you first need to create the Integration Server itself.
- To configure a NetWare server using the Install utility, you will need to create and mount a volume named CPQIS1.
- In order to configure a Windows NT server, a share must be created as CPQIS1 with the Everyone group given Full Control.
- The creation of an Integration Server allows for centralized control and storage of software for Compaq Servers.

SELF TEST

The following Self Test questions will help you measure your understanding of the material presented in this chapter. Read all the choices carefully, as there may be more than one correct answer. Choose all correct answers for each question.

1. What is the name of Compaq's centralized software store?
   A. Integration Server
   B. SmartStart
   C. Compaq Support Software Server
   D. I386
2. Which is not an OS that is supported by Integration Server?
   A. OS/2
   B. Netware 3.*x*
   C. Windows NT 3.51
   D. IntranetWare
3. What is Compaq's utility for updating the software on a server?
   A. Compaq Insight Manager
   B. Compaq Integration Maintenance Utility
   C. SmartStart
   D. Compaq SSD
4. What file is used to identify the resources available on the Integration Server?
   A. NWSNUT.NLM
   B. COMPAQ.PEZ
   C. CPQMAINT.NLM
   D. SPUU.EXE
5. What utility is used to update and maintain the Integration Server?
   A. Compaq Insight Manager
   B. Compaq Integration Maintenance Utility
   C. SmartStart
   D. Compaq SSD
6. What is the directory structure necessary to create an Integration Server?
   A. \\SERVERNAME\CPQIS\CPQIS1
   B. \\SERVERNAME\IS\COMPAQ
   C. \\SERVERNAME\CPQIS1\CPQIS
   D. \\SERVERNAME\CPQIS\CPQIS
7. What is required to allow access to the Integration Server from SmartStart?
   A. A Windows NT domain account named CPQIS1
   B. An user account with password CPQIS1
   C. Compaq Integration Maintenance Utility
   D. An account local to the server named CPQIS1
8. Which is not a method that can be used to update the software on a server?
   A. Remote attended
   B. Remote unattended

C. Automatic

D. Local

9. Which is not a method that can be used to update the Integration Server?

A. Internet

B. Dial-up

C. File copy

D. CD

10. What is the limitation of the CIMU on NetWare?

A. It does not update Insight Agents

B. It does not update the System Partition

C. It does not update drivers

D. It does not show current driver versions

ASE
ACCREDITED SYSTEMS ENGINEER

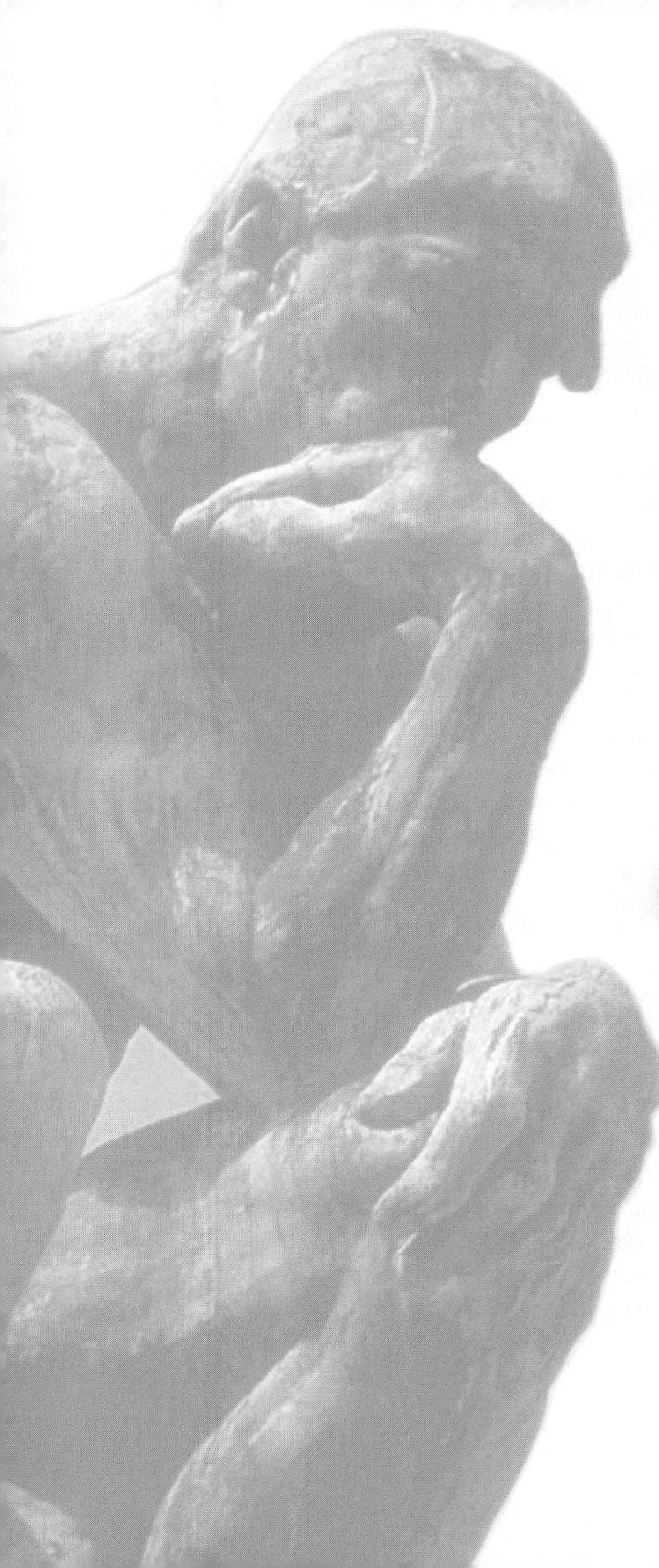

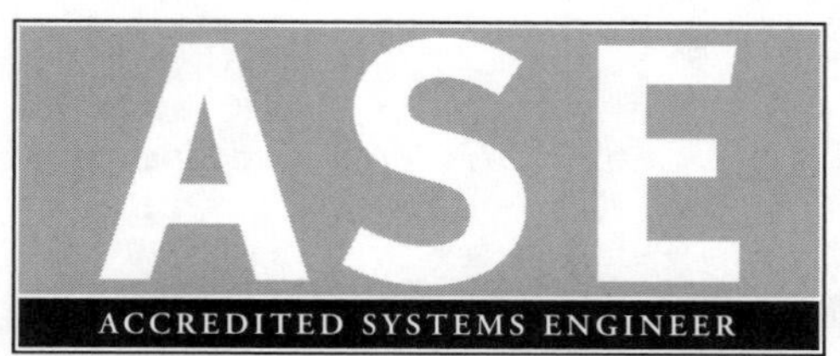

27

Web-Based Management

CERTIFICATION OBJECTIVES

27.01 Web-Based Enterprise Management (WBEM)

27.02 Overview of Current Web Management Offerings in Compaq Products

27.03 Using the Web Management Functions of Insight Agents 4.01 and Up

27.04 The Future of Compaq Systems Management: Insight Manager XE

The Internet and the World Wide Web have certainly changed the way computer professionals work, by giving them a simple, consistent interface to a great deal of information. You can access that information from a variety of platforms, including PCs, Macintosh, and UNIX systems, using a simple Web browser, making it the first truly universal application. The Web has changed from being a useful tool for technical staff to a critical business application for many corporations.

Compaq has recognized the shift in the way corporate networks are evolving and has integrated Web technology into their server products. The previous chapters in this section discussed Compaq's tool for managing their servers with Insight Manager. Insight Manager is run from a management console to monitor Insight Agents that are running on the servers that you want to manage. With the Insight Agents version 4.0 and later, you do not need to use Insight Manager to manage a server, but can instead use a Web browser.

This chapter will introduce you to server management using Web technology for Compaq servers. We will cover the advantages and limitations of using a browser to manage your servers. We will also cover the functionality of the Web agents, including security. Finally, we will discuss Compaq's next generation in server and enterprise management, Insight Manager XE.

CERTIFICATION OBJECTIVE 27.01

Web-Based Enterprise Management (WBEM)

In 1996, five major computer industry vendors (Microsoft, Compaq, Intel, Cisco, and BMC) began an initiative to create a standard method of managing a computer network using Web technology. Previously, network administrators had to rely on different applications and interfaces to manage their hardware. For example, they would use one application (such as Insight Manager) to manage their servers, while using another application (such as HP OpenView) to manage their network equipment. In many networks, you also needed different applications for different brands of servers—Insight Manager for Compaq servers and Netfinity for IBM servers, for example. This was known as the traditional two-tiered architecture, with the two tiers being the management application and the managed device. Using different applications added another level of complexity and an additional instruction set that the administrator needed to learn. Figure 27-1 illustrates this complexity.

The WBEM standard allows a network administrator to use a standard Web browser, with its easy-to-use interface, to manage a diverse network running various platforms. WBEM moves to a three-tiered architecture, adding a management server to the traditional management console/application and managed device (see Figure 27-2). The managed devices continue to run the management agents (Web Agents, SNMP Agents, DMI Agents), while the management server renders the HTML pages generated from information gathered from the agents. An administrator can then use any standard Web browser to read the HTML pages to manage the network devices.

FIGURE 27-1 Separate consoles to manage different systems

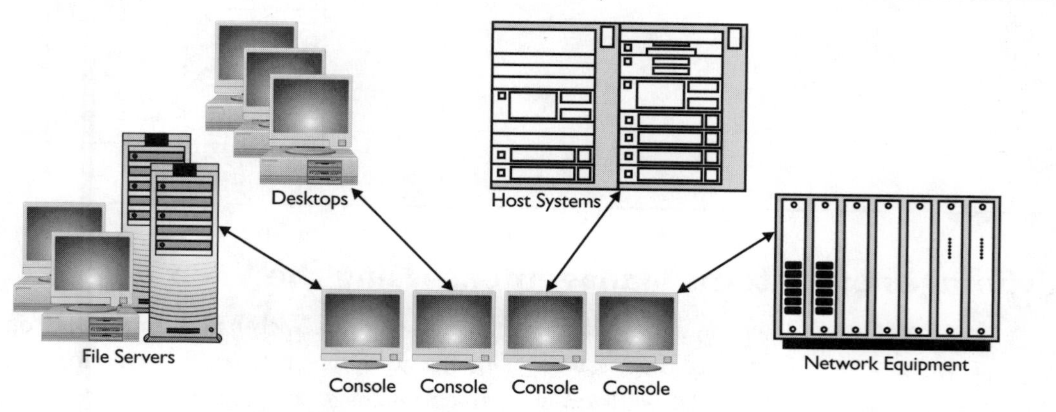

FIGURE 27-2 WBEM allows you to manage your entire network from a single console

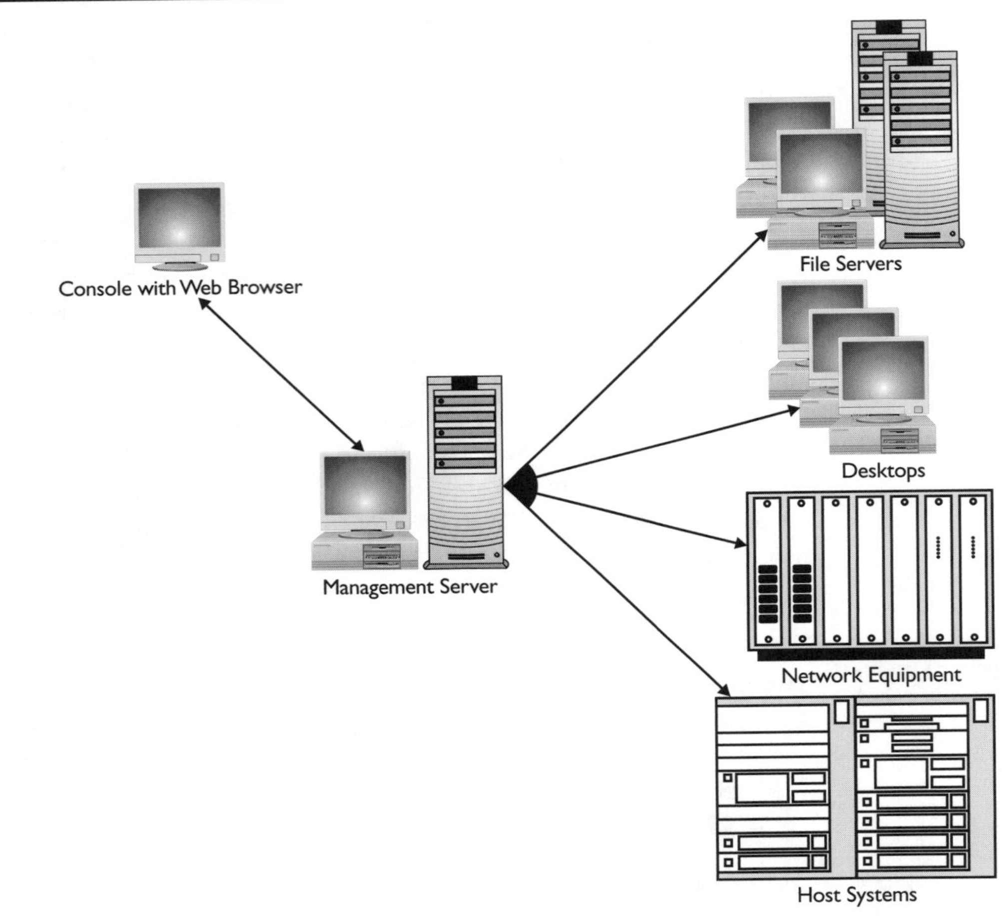

Advantages of Systems Management Using the Web

There are many advantages to moving to a Web-based technology for managing your systems. The first advantage is that you are no longer tied to a particular platform to be able to manage your servers. Insight Manager, for example, will only run on Windows 9*x* or Windows NT platforms. With the Web agents, you can use any standard Web browser to access and manage your servers. These browsers can be running on a Windows 9*x* or Windows NT machine, or even on a UNIX or Macintosh system!

In addition, since the Web agents use the standard HTTP protocol, you can manage your servers over the Internet or over slower WAN links without significant performance degradation. (You will need to open port 2301 in your routers and firewalls first.)

Finally, you no longer need to have the Insight Manager application installed on your management console to manage a server. In addition, you can manage your server from any machine on your network as long as a Web browser is installed on the machine. So if something goes wrong with your server and you are on the other side of the building from your management console, you can fire up a browser on any PC and find out what is wrong with your server.

on the job

Compaq doesn't recommend being able to access the Web agents over an unsecured network such as the Internet for the obvious security risks. You will need to assess your security risks and balance that with your management needs in deciding whether you need access over the Internet. Nonetheless, the possibility is there to manage your servers over the Internet. As long as you take the proper security precautions, with firewalls and/or Virtual Private Networks (VPNs), you should be able to safely manage your servers remotely.

CERTIFICATION OBJECTIVE 27.02

Overview of Current Web Management Offerings in Compaq Products

Prior to the Insight Agents 4.30, Compaq bundled all of the agents into a single package. With Insight Agents 4.30 and later, Compaq split the

Insight Agents into four separate components: Compaq Foundation Agents, Compaq Server Agents, Compaq NIC Agents, and Compaq Storage Agents. Each of these agents runs as a separate service in Windows NT.

The Insight Web Agents is another component provided by Compaq that works in conjunction with the four base components. The Web Agents run as a service under Windows NT. The Web Agents work by reading the information gathered by each of the individual agents and converting the information into HTML pages that can be read by any browser.

Installing the Web Agents

If you perform a Smart Start installation for your server, the Insight Web Agents will be installed as part of the default installation. A new Windows NT service will be installed that you can view in Control Panel | Services. If you need to install the Insight Web Agents or update the agents, you will need to follow these procedures.

You can obtain the Web Agents via two methods: Smart Start subscription or download via the Internet. With a Smart Start subscription, you obtain the latest versions of the Smart Start CD and the Compaq Management CD as soon as they become available. To download the latest agents from the Internet, go to the following link, from which you can download each of the four components:

http://www.compaq.com/products/servers/management/dl-cim-nt.html

One advantage to installing the agents from the CD is that Compaq provides a unified installation for the agents. You can simply run the install program (INSTALL.EXE) from the <CD DRIVE>:\AGENTS\WIN-NT\ENG\CPQMGMT directory.

If you downloaded the agents from the Internet, first you will need to extract each of the agents into separate directories. After you extract the files, you will need to run the install program (INSTALL.EXE) for each of the components separately.

Disabling the Web Agents

In some instances, you may want to disable the Insight Web Agents. For example, if you have a dedicated management console running Insight Manager and you know you will never use a browser to manager a server, you can disable the Web Agents. This will free up memory and resources for the server, and it will plug the security hole the Web Agents potentially provide (see the Security section later in this chapter). You will still be able to use Insight Manager to manage your servers; you just won't be able to use a browser. To disable Insight Web Agents:

1. Open Control Panel | Services.
2. From the list of services, select Insight Web Agents and click Stop. To prevent the Web agents from starting when you boot the server, you must set the service not to start automatically.
3. From the list of services, select Insight Web Agents and click Startup.
4. Select Manual.
5. Click OK.
6. Close the Services applet and then close Control Panel.

CERTIFICATION OBJECTIVE 27.03

Using the Web Management Functions of Insight Agents 4.01 and Up

Now that you are familiar with installing the Web agents, we will discuss how to manage your servers using a Web browser. We will first cover the requirements for your browser, which will be the primary interface you will use to manage the servers. We will then discuss the details of how to gather the information and manage the information from your servers. We will also cover the various components and subsystems that you can manage with the Web Agents. Finally, we will discuss the security implications that are introduced when you install the Web Agents.

Browser Requirements

This section will cover the requirements for your management PC that will be running the Web browser application to manage your servers. Even before we discuss the browser requirements, you should be aware that the TCP/IP protocol must be installed on the management PC. This is the primary protocol used when managing the servers.

The Web browser that you use to manage the server must, at a minimum, support tables, frames, Java, JavaScript, and the Java Development Kit (JDK) 1.1. The two browsers that currently are supported are:

- Microsoft Internet Explorer 4.0 version 4.72.2106.8 or later
- Netscape Navigator 4.04 or later

Note that if you are running Internet Explorer on a Windows NT Workstation PC, you must first install Windows NT Service Pack 3 before installing Internet Explorer.

Managing a Server Using a Browser

To connect to a server running the Web agents using a Web browser, type the following into the URL field for the browser:

http://servername:2301 or http://ip_address:2301

The Web agents use TCP port 2301 to communicate with the Web browser. You must type both the **http://** portion of the address and the **:2301** portion. The device home page will be displayed in the browser (shown in Figure 27-3).

From the device home page, select Compaq Insight Management Agents to take you to the server subsystems status and management information.

FIGURE 27-3

Device Home Page for Insight Web Agents

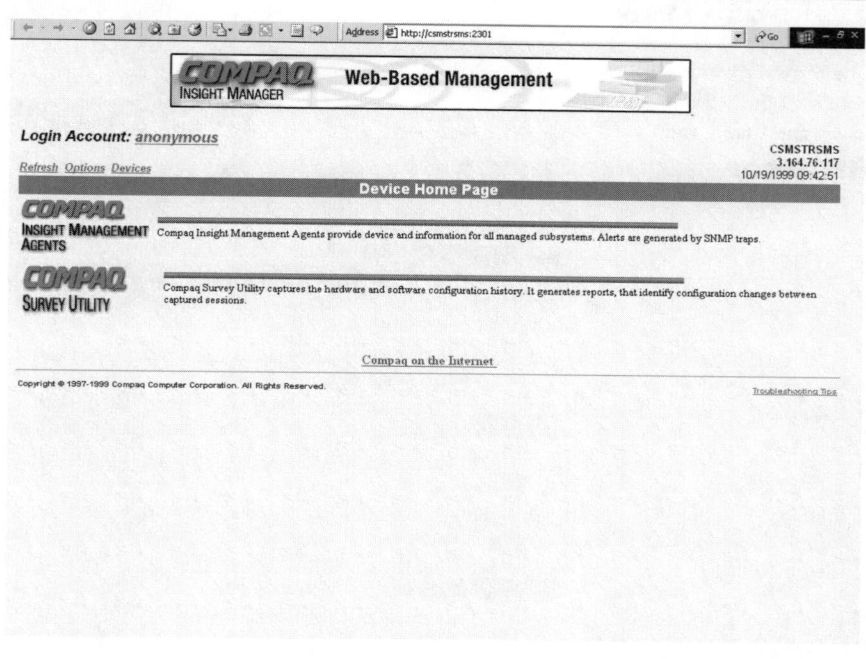

You will first see the device summary status, which gives a quick overview of the status of the major components of the server. The Web page is broken into three frames: title frame, navigation frame, and data frame, as shown in Figure 27-4.

Each of these frames will be discussed shortly. First, we will discuss the options available to the Web Agents.

Agents Options

From the device home page, you can set certain options for the Web Agents for the currently managed server. You first need to log on to the Web Agents with the administrator account. (For details, refer to the Security

FIGURE 27-4

The browser window consists of title frame, navigation frame, and data frame

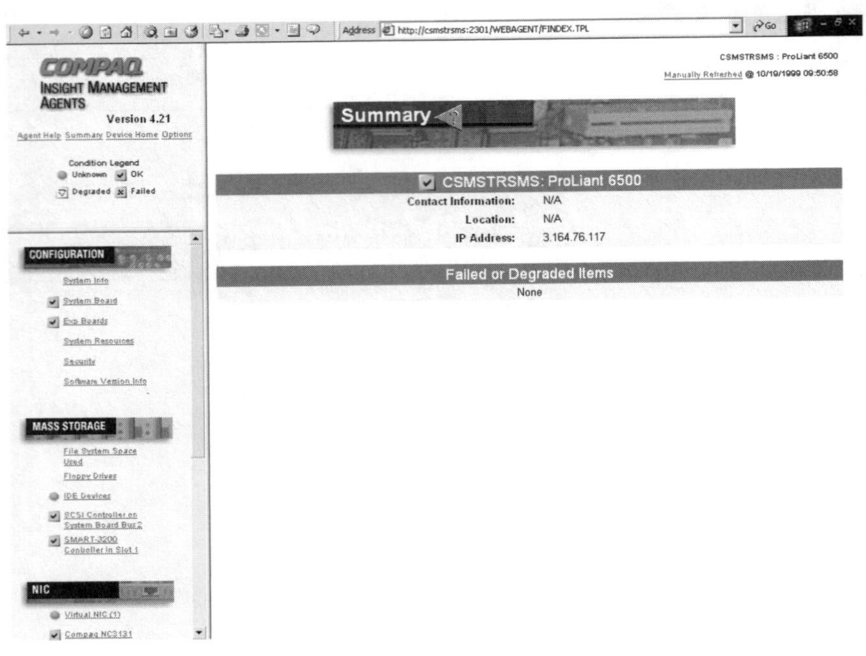

section of this chapter.) Once you are logged on as administrator, click Options from the device home page. Figure 27-5 will appear as shown.

Each of the configuration options is discussed in Table 27-1.

Title Frame

The title frame resides in the upper left corner of the browser window. The frame displays the current version of the Insight Agents running on the server as well as four navigation links:

- **Agent Help** Displays help on using the browser with the Insight Agents
- **Summary** Displays the initial summary screen, which displays device and status information
- **Device Home** Takes you back to the server main page, where you can select Compaq Management Agents or Survey Utility
- **Options** Lets you set certain options for managing this device. These options will be discussed later in the chapter.

FIGURE 27-5

Log on as Administrator to configure the Web Agent options

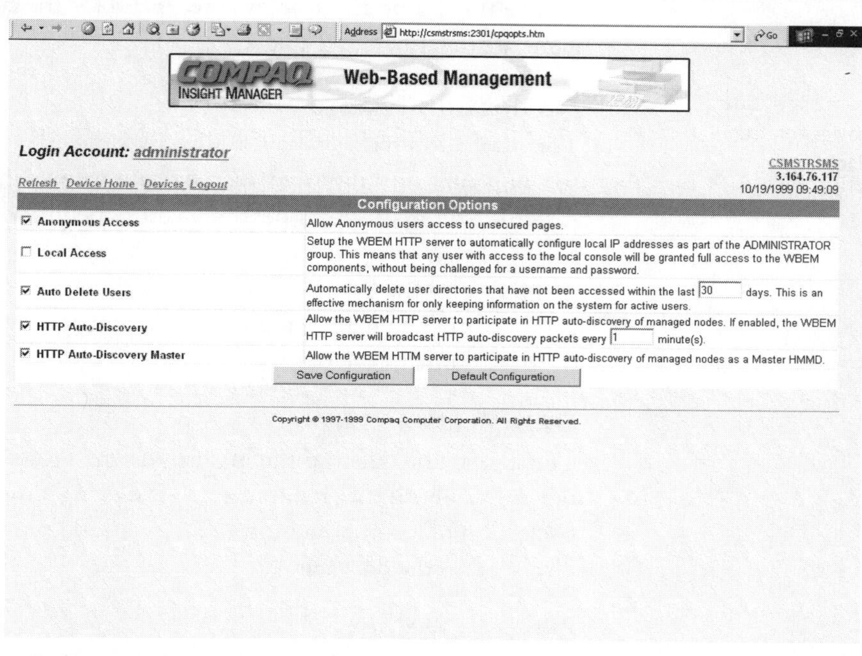

TABLE 27-1

Web Agents Configuration Options

Option	Description
Anonymous Access	Specifies whether the Anonymous account is given access to unsecured pages. By default, this option is enabled. Deselect this option to increase security.
Local Access	Allows the user automatic administration rights to the agents, if the Web Agents are accessed from the local server. By default, this option is disabled.
Auto Delete Users	Deletes user information after a certain number of days of inactivity. By default, this is enabled and set to 30 days of inactivity.
HTTP Auto-Discovery	Specifies whether this server will participate in HTTP auto-discovery of managed nodes. If enabled, the server will send out discovery broadcast packets to generate a list of discovered servers. By default, this option is enabled and configured to send a broadcast packet every minute.

The title frame also displays the legend for the condition icons. These icons are described in Table 27-2.

Navigation Frame

The navigation frame, which is directly below the title frame, displays the components and subsystems of the server for which you can view statistics. A status icon may appear next to a component, indicating the current health of that component. The icons are as described in Table 27-2.

To display the details of a specific component, click the name for that component. The management information and statistics will be displayed in the data frame to the right.

Data Frame

The data frame takes up the majority of the browser space and resides to the right of both the title frame and the navigation frame. When you make a selection of a component in the navigation frame, the desired data is displayed in the data frame.

Device Options

From the navigation frame, click Device Options to bring up the options that you can set for this device in the data frame (shown in Figure 27-6). From here, you can set several options that pertain to your browser, including the use of frames and the refresh rate for the window.

TABLE 27-2

Web Agents Condition Icons

Icon	Description
Unknown	Although the management agents are loaded, the status of a particular component is unknown
OK	The component is functioning properly
Degraded	The component has degraded, but has not yet failed. This can take place in a hard drive that is about to fail, or a tape drive that may need cleaning.
Failed	The component has failed and should be replaced

FIGURE 27-6

Fine-tune browser settings from the Device Options page

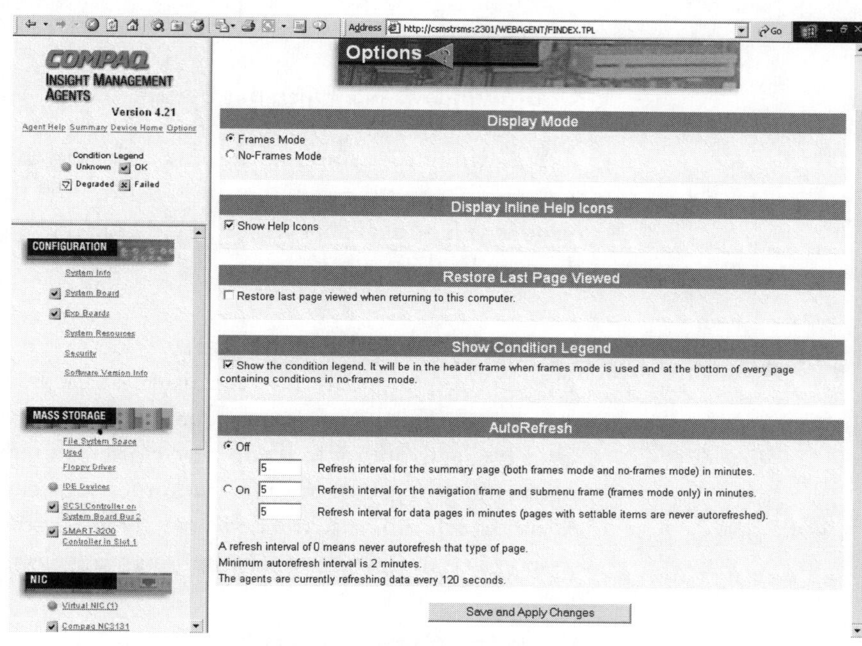

To simplify life, you can add the following URLs to your browser's Favorites list or Bookmarks list. In this way, you won't have to worry about typing in the full path to the server, and you will have a couple of direct links to some of the pages.

Device Home Page *http://servername:2301*

Account Login Page *http://servername:2301/cpqlogin.htm*

Change Password *http://servername:2301/cpqlogin.htm?ChangePassword=yes*

Configuration Options *http://servername:2301/cpqopts.htm*

Devices *http://servername:2301/cpqdev.htm.*

Managed Components

This section will outline the components that can be managed using the Compaq Web Agents. Compaq breaks up the various manageable components into five categories:

- Foundation Agent
- Server Agent

- Storage Agent
- NIC Agent
- Windows NT Operating System

You will not see these categories on the server information page, but you will see the subsystem headings. Also, note that not all of these options will be available. You will only see the options for the hardware that you have installed.

Compaq Foundation Agent

The Compaq Foundation Agent displays basic information on the server subsystems. This information includes software versions and file system space usage. In addition, if you have clusters installed, the Foundation Agent will give you status information for your clusters. The Foundation Agent, which runs as a Windows NT service, also provides threshold support and SNMP alerts. The options available are given in Table 27-3.

Compaq Server Agent

The Compaq Server Agent displays a great deal of information for all the components in the server, ranging from the system board to the server recovery subsystem. The available options are displayed in Table 27-4.

TABLE 27-3 Foundation Agent Subsystem Components

Configuration Subsystem	Description
Software Version Information	Displays the versions of the Compaq system software installed on the server
Cluster Information	Displays information about your clusters, including node status, network status, and cluster software information
Mass Storage Subsystem	
File System Space Used	Displays the disk storage usage for the server. Shows total space available, total space used, and percentage space used.
NIC Subsystem	
ServerNet PCI Adapter	Displays information about the ServerNet PCI adapter, which is used to connect servers in a cluster

TABLE 27-4 Server Agent Subsystem Components

Configuration Subsystem	Description
NIC Subsystem *(continued)*	
System Information	Displays general system information such as server product family, and asset information such as server serial number
System Board	Displays information about the system board, including system ROM versions, and processor and memory information
Expansion Boards	Lists all installed expansion boards, including which slot they are installed in and system resources used
System Resources	Displays which devices are using specific resources. These resources include IRQ, Port Address, DMA Channels, and Memory ranges.
Security	Displays whether certain security features are enabled or disabled. These features include power-on passwords and the ability to boot to a floppy disk.
Mass Storage Subsystem	
Floppy Drives	Displays information on the server's floppy drives
Utilization Subsystem	Displays utilization information for the server's bus subsystem and processor subsystem. The utilization is shown in a bar graph and displays utilization for the preceding 1 minute, 5 minutes, 30 minutes, and 60 minutes. A sample utilization screen is shown in Figure 27-7.
Recovery Subsystem	
Reboot Option	Allows you to reboot the server remotely. You must be logged into the Web Agents as administrator.
Auto Recovery	Displays information regarding the Automatic Server Recovery system. (For more information on the ASR, refer to Chapter 19.)
Critical Errors	Displays any critical errors that have occurred on the server. Also displays what action you should take to correct the problem.
Power On Messages	Displays any error messages that appeared while the server started
Correctable Memory	Indicates when a correctable memory error has occurred. An increasing number of these errors may indicate that a memory module is failing and should be replaced.
Environment	Displays the status of the environment subsystems, which includes the system temperature and the fans. You can also set the action to perform when one of these systems enters a degraded state.

TABLE 27-4 Server Agent Subsystem Components *(continued)*

Configuration Subsystem	Description
Recovery Subsystem *(continued)*	
Power Supply	Displays the condition of the server's power supplies
Power Converter	Displays the status of any installed power converters
Remote Communications	Displays information for the Integrated Remote Console (IRC)
Integrated Management Log	Displays the Integrated Management Log (IML). The IML stores all critical error messages, power-on messages, and other system events. You can mark errors as corrected if you are logged on as administrator.
Remote Insight	If you have a Remote Insight Board installed in your server, this option displays its status information

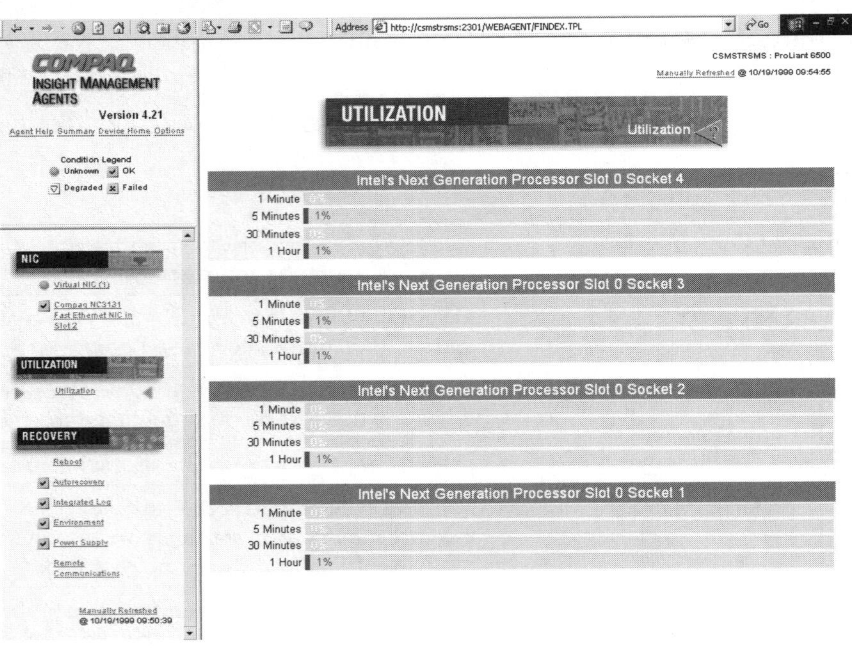

FIGURE 27-7

The Utilization subsystem shows the system usage for the preceding hour

Compaq Storage Agent

The Compaq Storage Agent provides detailed information for the entire storage subsystem for the server, including controllers (IDE, SCSI, and Smart Array) and drives. The available options are displayed in Table 27-5.

Compaq NIC Agent

Table 27-6 displays the options that are made available by the Compaq NIC Agent. This agent displays detailed information on all Compaq NICs installed in your server, as well as network teaming information. You can access all of these options in the NIC Subsystem area of the navigation frame.

Windows NT Operating System

With the Insight Agents 4.23 and later, Compaq uses technology from BMC Software, Inc. to allow you to manage certain aspects of the Windows NT operating system. This new functionality adds two new NT services, Compaq NT Management and PATROL Agent, which you can access

TABLE 27-5

Storage Agent Subsystem Components

Mass Storage Subsystem	Description
IDE Controllers	Displays status information regarding the hard drives and CD-ROMs connected to the server's IDE Controllers
Compaq SCSI Controllers	Displays information on the storage devices connected to the on-board SCSI controllers. This can include hard drives, CD-ROMs, and tape drives. This does not include drives connected to a Smart Array Controller.
Compaq Drive Array Controllers	Displays information for the drives connected to Smart Array Controllers. This option will also display information for the RAID arrays configured for each controller.
Fibre Channel Storage Systems	For servers with a Fibre Channel Storage System installed, this section displays information regarding the components of the storage system, such as the array controllers and physical drives
Fibre Channel Tape Controllers	Displays information for the tape drives connected to fiber tape controllers

TABLE 27-6

NIC Agent Subsystem Components

NIC Subsystem	Description
Virtual NIC	Displays information for the Virtual NIC (present on Windows NT systems only). The Virtual NIC is the interface that allows Windows NT to send packets to itself.
Single NIC	Displays card information and traffic information for each individual NIC installed in the server
Team of NICs	In servers with more than one NIC installed (or NICs with multiple interfaces), this section displays network teaming information
Logical Adapter Information	Each network team appears to the rest of the network as a logical adapter. This section displays information for each logical adapter configured on the server.
NIC Controller Information	Displays physical information about the NIC, such as slot, IRQ, and I/O address
NIC Interface Information	Displays information regarding the various interfaces and protocols for the NIC. This includes IP address (for TCP/IP) and Frame Type (for IPX) and MAC addresses.
Ethernet Statistics	Displays Ethernet packet information for the network card
Token Ring Statistics	Displays Token Ring traffic information for the network card

through Control Panel | Services. The Windows NT Agents allow you to specify thresholds for certain server subsystems and to change the status of the server when those thresholds are met. For example, you can set a threshold to set the server status to Warning after the processor has been measured at 90 percent or greater for 20 minutes. The Windows NT Agents provide management of the following component groups.

- Cache
- Processor
- Logical Disks
- Memory
- NetBEUI

- NetBIOS
- Network Performance
- Physical Disks
- Security
- Server Utilization
- System Health
- TCP

When you first install the NT Management agents, certain defaults are set for a number of the parameters. These defaults are shown in Table 27-7.

TABLE 27-7 Windows NT Operating System Components Preset Thresholds

Section	Parameter	Warning Range Value	Alarm Range Value
Processor	Processor Time in %	90% to 95% for 30 minutes	95% to 100% for 60 minutes
	User Time in %	40% to 50% for 30 minutes	50% to 100% for 60 minutes
	Privileged Time in %	60% to 90% for 30 minutes	90% to 100% for 60 minutes
Memory	Available Bytes in MB	Less than 20MB for 30 minutes	Less than 10MB for 60 minutes
	Page File Usage in %	90% to 95% for 30 minutes	95% to 100% for 60 minutes
	Cache Copy Read/Hits per second	20% to 30% for 30 minutes	0% to 20% for 15 minutes
Disk Utilization	Free Space in %	90% to 95% for 5 minutes	95% to 100% for 5 minutes
	Logical Disk Busy Time in %	60% to 70% for 5 minutes	70% to 100% for 5 minutes
	Physical Disk Busy Time in %	90% to 95% for 5 minutes	95% to 100% for 5 minutes
Network	Network Output Queue Length	Over 250	Over 1000
	TCP Segments Retransmitted per second	Greater than 3%	Greater than 10%

Security

One of the major advantages of the WBEM initiative is that you can use any standard supported browser to manage your servers. However, this also introduces a possible security breach, since any user on the network will be able to access the server using the browser installed on his or her PC. The user would, of course, need to know the server name and the port to connect to, but this is still a possible security hole nonetheless.

Compaq has built some minor security into the Insight Web Agents. By default, when you connect to a device's home page (http://servername:2301), you are connected as the Anonymous user. The anonymous user has read-only access to the server information. If you click the Anonymous name on the device home page, you will be brought to the Account Login page (shown in Figure 27-8).

Use any of the accounts specified in Table 27-8 to log in. Depending on the account that you use, you will have specific rights in certain areas.

FIGURE 27-8

The Account Login screen

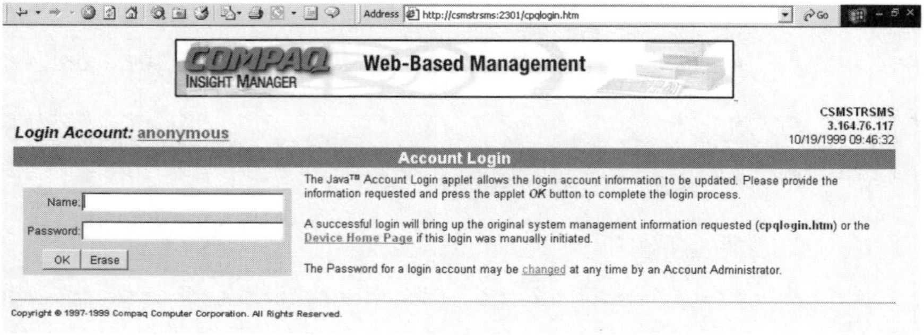

TABLE 27-8

Web Agents Login Accounts

Account	Password
Anonymous	
User	public
Operator	operator
Administrator	administrator

These are the only accounts available for the Web agent. You can change the password for the accounts, but you cannot change the account name or add/delete accounts. Access permission is granted to each account based on the WEBAGENT.INI file (shown in the following code listing). This file resides in %SYSTEMROOT%\SYSTEM32\ CPQMGMT\WEBAGENT.

```
[Default]
read=1
write=0

[Groups]
Sets
Reboot

[Sets]
read=1
write=3
cpqHeThermalDegradedAction
cpqUpsAutoShutdownDelay
cpqHeAsrStatus
cpqHeAsrReboot
cpqHeAsrRebootCount
cpqHeAsrReset
cpqHeAsrPagerStatus
cpqHeAsrPagerNumber
cpqHeAsrPagerMessage
cpqHeAsrCommPort
cpqHeAsrNetworkAccessStatus
cpqHeAsrDialOutStatus
cpqHeAsrDialOutNumber
cpqHeAsrDialInStatus
cpqHeCriticalErrorStatus
cpqHeCorrMemErrCount
cpqHeEventLogEntrySeverity
cpqHePostMsgEv
cpqSm2CntlrAlertStatus
```

```
cpqSm2CntlrSystemId
cpqSm2CntlrBatteryEnabled
cpqSm2EventTotalEntries
cpqMeAlarmStatus

[Reboot]
read=1
write=4
cpqSiRebootFlags
```

The WEBAGENT.INI file consists of four sections: Default, Groups, Sets, and Reboot. The Default section specifies default permissions, while the Groups section specifies the subsections, Sets and Reboot.

In the Sets and Reboot sections, you specify a value for the read= and write= settings, to grant writes to each of the user accounts, where:

- 0=No Access
- 1=Anonymous
- 2=User
- 3=Operator
- 4=Administrator

For example, in the preceding code listing, in the Reboot section, the read parameter is set to 1, which means that any user, Anonymous and higher is able to read the reboot property of a server. In order to reboot the server, you will need write access, and in this case it is set to 4, which means that only the administrator user can reboot the server. If the write= value were set to 3, then Operator or Administrator would be able to reboot the server. (See the next section, Security Sample: Reboot, for an example of security.)

The first thing that you should do after you install the Web agents is change the password for the Administrator account. By default, on all installations, the administrator password is administrator. This could be a security risk. Another drawback to this is that you have to change the passwords on all servers individually, since each server stores its own accounts and passwords. This can take quite some time if you are managing many servers. Procedures on changing the password are given in the next section.

Security Sample: Reboot

This section demonstrates the security available in the Web Agents. Figure 27-9 shows the Anonymous user logged in with the Reboot option selected. In the data frame, you can see that that Reboot option is unavailable.

Figure 27-10 shows an administrator logged into the Web Agents. When the Reboot option is selected, you now have the option to reboot the server.

Changing Passwords

The Insight Web Agents come with four standard user IDs, with their passwords preset according to Table 27-8. To increase security and prevent someone from accessing the Web Agents, you should change the passwords for all of the users, especially the administrator user. In this release of the

FIGURE 27-9

The Anonymous account does not have permission to reboot the server

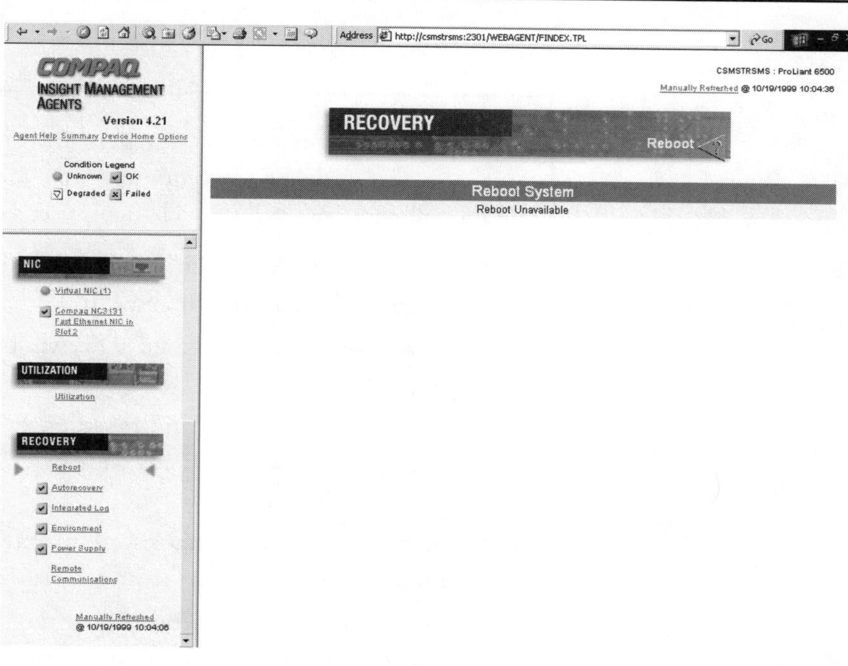

FIGURE 27-10

The Administrator account has the permissions to reboot the server

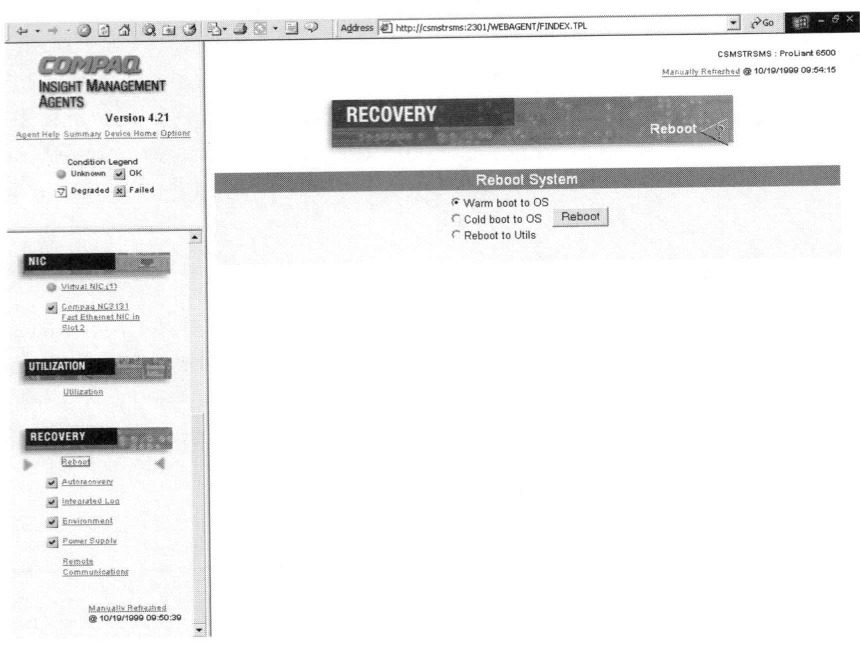

Web Agents, you can only modify the password attribute for a login account. You cannot delete an account or rename an account.

Use the following procedure to change a user's password.

1. In your Web browser, open the server's home page for the Insight Web Agents (http://servername:2301).
2. Click the Login Account name. This will bring you to the Account Login page.
3. Click the word "changed" in the sentence "The password for a login account may be changed at any time by an Account Administrator." Figure 27-11 will appear.
4. In the Account Administrator section, enter **administrator** and the administrator password in the proper fields.
5. In the Change Account section, enter the user ID whose password you want to change, as well as the new password for the user ID. You will have to enter the new password twice to confirm.
6. Press OK when you are done.

FIGURE 27-11

You must know the Account Administrator password to change any password

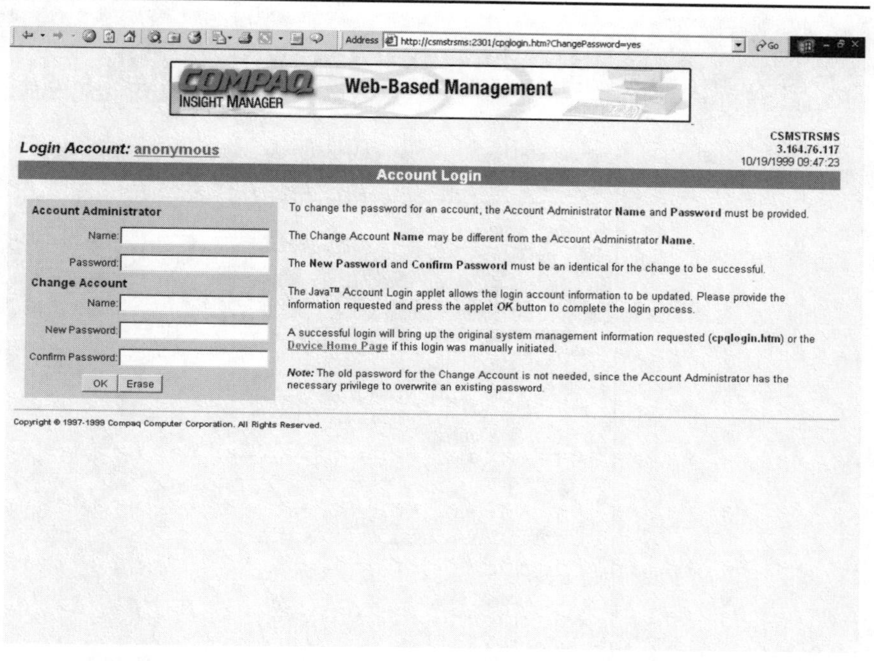

FROM THE FIELD

Using a Port Scanner to Find Web-Manageable Servers

To help further harness the power of the Compaq Web agents, you can easily create an HTML document that displays all manageable servers on a subnet. To help determine what servers are indeed manageable, you can use a network scanner such as Iban Technologies IP Tools 2000.

If you wish to obtain the application shown in the following figure, navigate to http://tucows.erols.com/files5/iptools.zip.

Or visit http://winfiles.cnet.com/apps/98/net-info.html to obtain a listing of other similar utilities.

In Iban's freeware utility, they include a network scanner that allows you to enter an IP subnet and TCP port to find all servers listening on the specified port. By entering TCP port 2301, you can obtain a listing of all servers on a particular class B or class C subnet that can be managed using a Web browser.

FROM THE FIELD *(continued)*

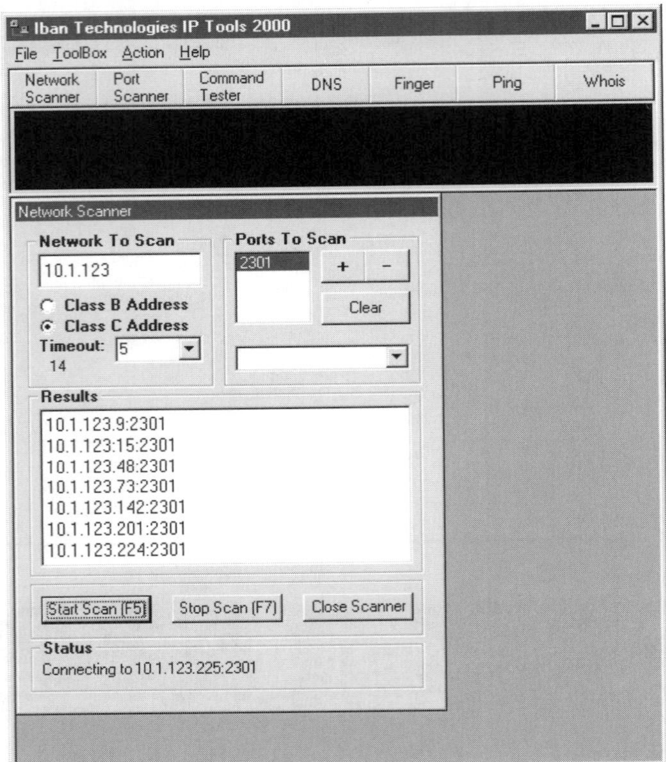

With a list of available servers obtained, you can easily create links to servers and Professional Workstations that can be managed using the Web Agents. If you maintain up-to-date network maps in HTML documents, you can further enhance the usability of these maps by incorporating the ability to click a server to manage it.

—Thomas E. Eck, MCSE+I, MCSD, ASE, CCA, CNA

CERTIFICATION OBJECTIVE 27.04

The Future of Compaq Systems Management: Insight Manager XE

Compaq takes the next step in Web management with Insight Manager XE. Insight Manager XE uses the simple Web-based interface to provide access to all of your network devices. One of the biggest enhancements to Insight Manager XE over the base Insight Manager product is that XE can now manage any device on the network that supports SNMP MIB-2 or DMI V2. This means that you can use Insight Manager XE to not only manage Compaq servers, but also third-party servers, desktops, and network equipment such as routers. This is a tremendous step toward unifying your network management tools into a single utility. In addition, Insight Manager now stores all of its information in a Microsoft SQL Server database.

The following are the new key features for Insight Manager XE.

- Automatic discovery and identification of any device that supports TCP/IP, IPX, and HTTP Web servers
- Data collection of basic inventory data from devices using DMI, SNMP, or HTTP
- Advanced alerting features with a comprehensive event management system
- Advanced management of Compaq clusters and clusters running Microsoft Cluster Service (MSCS)
- Capability to create and delete management accounts
- Better overall management of devices. For example, you can group devices based on status or by device type. Graphical icons give you the ability to see the status of your network equipment at a glance.
- Compaq is providing Insight Manager XE free of charge. You must first register at their Web site and they will ship the CD to you. (Microsoft SQL Server must be purchased separately.)

Limitations of Insight Manager XE

Although Insight Manager greatly improves upon the base Insight Manager software, there are still some features that are not in the XE version. First, there is no automatic data collection capability in XE, so you cannot view historical information for your equipment. Second, XE does not come with a Version Control feature that allows you to compare the software versions installed on a server with a database of current versions. Third, XE does not allow you to perform Integration Server maintenance. With Integration Server maintenance, which is available in Insight Manager, you can update the versions of software stored on the Integration Server by downloading the latest versions from the Internet or from a CD.

QUESTIONS AND ANSWERS	
How would you manage a heterogeneous network consisting of many different brands of servers, network hardware, and DMI-compliant desktop PCs?	Use Insight Manager XE. This product allows you to manage any networked device that supports SNMP and DMI.
What if you need to perform automatic data collection for historical data purposes?	Use Insight Manager. Insight Manager allows you to perform ADC, whereas XE does not allow you to perform ADC.
You have a small network consisting mainly of Compaq servers. You are running older nonmanaged hubs. Do you use Insight Manager or Insight Manager XE?	Insight Manager. In a small network consisting of only Compaq servers, the Insight Manager product is sufficient. The additional cost of Microsoft SQL Server may be prohibitive in installing Insight Manager XE.
You need increased security in managing your servers using WBEM technology. Should you use Insight Manager or Insight Manager XE?	You can use either Insight Manager or Insight Manager XE, although XE is preferred. With the base Insight Manager product, you can change passwords to increase security. However, with XE, you can create and delete management accounts.

CERTIFICATION SUMMARY

The extreme growth of the Internet and the worldwide acceptance of Web technology has changed the way Information Systems personnel manage their networks. Web Based Enterprise Management (WBEM) gives the network manager a simple graphical interface to manage network equipment.

Compaq provides the Insight Web Agents to allow you to manage their servers using any standard Web browser. This allows you to manage your servers from any PC on the network without having to be tied down to any particular management console. The Insight Web Agents allow you to manage virtually every subsystem component for your server. The ubiquitous nature of Web technologies does introduce a security risk, but Compaq added some simple security features with the use of standard login accounts.

The next generation of WBEM is Insight Manager XE, which extends Compaq's management capability to any network device that support SNMP or DMI. This means that Insight Manager is no longer "proprietary" to Compaq servers, but rather, it is now able to manage all devices on the network.

TWO-MINUTE DRILL

- ❑ Compaq has integrated Web technology into their server products.
- ❑ The WBEM standard allows a network administrator to use a standard Web browser, with its easy-to-use interface, to manage a diverse network running various platforms.
- ❑ One of the many advantages to moving to a Web-based technology for managing your systems is that you are no longer tied to a particular platform to be able to manage your servers.
- ❑ Since the Web agents use the standard HTTP protocol, you can manage your servers over the Internet or over slower WAN links without significant performance degradation.
- ❑ You no longer need to have the Insight Manager application installed on your management console to manage a server.
- ❑ You can manage your server from any machine on your network as long as a Web browser is installed on the machine.

- With Insight Agents 4.30 and later, Compaq split the Insight Agents into four separate components: Compaq Foundation Agents, Compaq Server Agents, Compaq NIC Agents, and Compaq Storage Agents.
- Compaq Web Agents work by reading the information gathered by each of the individual agents and converting the information into HTML pages that can be read by any browser.
- You can obtain the Web Agents via two methods: Smart Start subscription or download via the Internet.
- In some instances, you may want to disable the Insight Web Agents.
- TCP/IP protocol is the primary protocol used when managing the servers and must be installed on the management PC.
- The components that can be managed using the Compaq Web Agents are
  - Foundation Agent
  - Server Agent
  - Storage Agent
  - NIC Agent
  - Windows NT Operating System
- Compaq has built some minor security into the Insight Web Agents.
- The Insight Web Agents come with four standard user IDs, with their passwords preset according to Table 27-8.
- Compaq takes the next step in Web management with Insight Manager XE.
- XE can now manage any device on the network that supports SNMP MIB-2 or DMI V2. You can use Insight Manager XE to not only manage Compaq servers, but also third-party servers, desktops, and network equipment such as routers.
- There are still some features that are not in the XE version:
  - No automatic data collection capability
  - No Version Control feature that allows you to compare the software versions installed on a server with a database of current versions
  - No method to perform Integration Server maintenance

SELF TEST

The following Self Test questions will help you measure your understanding of the material presented in this chapter. Read all the choices carefully, as there may be more than one correct answer. Choose all correct answers for each question.

1. What is the difference between the two-tiered architecture and three-tiered architecture with respect to network management?

   A. Management Server
   B. Management Console
   C. Host Systems
   D. Network Equipment

2. What is the role of the Management Server in WBEM's three-tiered architecture?

   A. Runs management agents
   B. Gathers management agents information from managed devices
   C. Generates HTML pages
   D. Both answers B and C

3. Which of the following is not an advantage to using Web technology for systems management?

   A. Can manage from different platforms
   B. Simplified interface
   C. Need Insight Manager installed
   D. Can manage from anywhere on the network

4. Which of the following is not a component of the Insight Agents?

   A. Foundation Agent
   B. Drive Array Agent
   C. Server Agent
   D. NIC Agent

5. What else do you need to install before installing Internet Explorer on a Windows NT Workstation?

   A. Post SP4 Y2K Patch
   B. Compaq Server Support Disk for Windows NT
   C. Service Pack 3 or higher
   D. Internet Explorer 128-bit High Security Patch

6. What TCP port do the Web Agents use?

   A. 21
   B. 80
   C. 1971
   D. 2301

7. Which of the following URLs is a valid address to access the Insight Web Agents?

   A. Servername:2301
   B. http://servername:2301
   C. http://servername
   D. http://servername:1971

8. What are the three frames that compose the browser window when managing a server with the Insight Web Agents?
   A. Title frame
   B. Navigation frame
   C. Options Frame
   D. Data frame
9. You'd like to remove anonymous access to the Web Agents. How would you accomplish this?
   A. Deselect Anonymous Access.
   B. Delete Anonymous account.
   C. Disable Guest Account in NT User Manager.
   D. Change default port.
10. Which agent is responsible for displaying information for the system board?
    A. Foundation Agent
    B. Server Agent
    C. Storage Agent
    D. NIC Agent
11. Which file would you edit to modify the default security permissions for the Web Agents?
    A. WWWAGENT.INI
    B. CIM.INI
    C. CIMWEB.INI
    D. WEBAGENT.INI
12. Which of the following account management tasks can you perform?
    A. Delete an account.
    B. Rename an account.
    C. Change the password.
    D. Disable an account.
13. Which of the following is not an advantage of Insight Manager XE over Insight Manager?
    A. It can manage third-party devices.
    B. It can manage devices using a Web browser.
    C. It automatically discovers devices on the network.
    D. It can create user accounts.
14. Which protocol is not supported by Insight Manager XE for data collection?
    A. HTTP
    B. SNMP
    C. DMI
    D. FTP
15. Which of the following features is not included with Insight Manager XE?
    A. Automatic Data Collection
    B. Version Control
    C. Integration Server Management
    D. All of the above

Part III

Compaq/Windows NT Integration and Performance (Exam 010-067)

ASE
ACCREDITED SYSTEMS ENGINEER

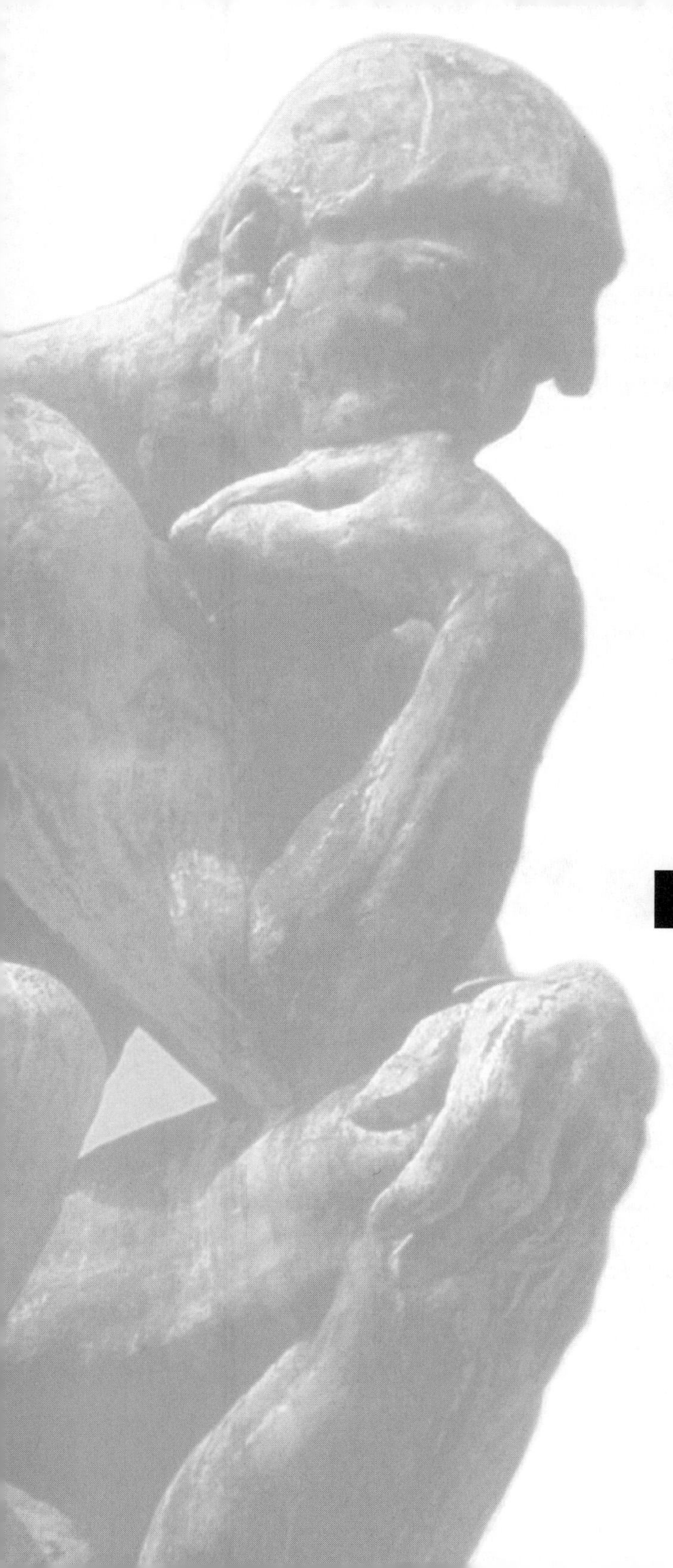

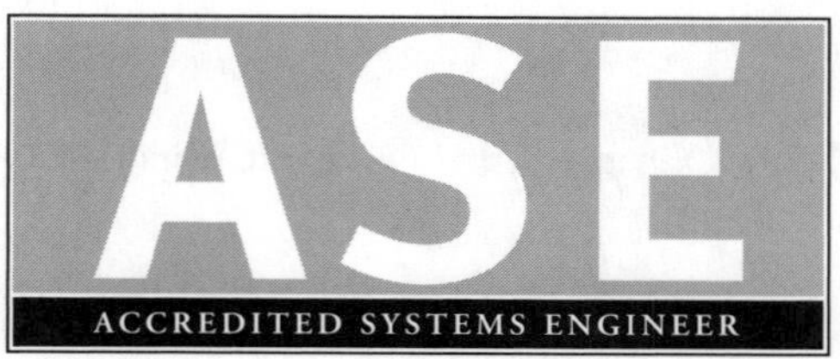

28

Microsoft Windows NT Product Theory

CERTIFICATION OBJECTIVES

28.01 Windows NT Versions

28.02 Windows NT Architecture

28.03 Components of the Windows NT Executive

28.04 Windows NT Environment Subsystems

As you begin Part III on Windows NT integration, it would be a good idea to review the product theory and architecture of the Windows NT operating system. One of the requirements to become a Compaq ASE is to hold a major OS certification, such as the Microsoft Certified Systems Engineer (MCSE) certification. If you are an MCSE or on your way to becoming one, you will certainly need to become familiar with how the OS operates behind the scenes. Becoming familiar with how an OS acts internally is not only essential for designing effective networks, but also for troubleshooting any problems that may arise from day to day.

This chapter will familiarize you with the design goals that Microsoft had when they first created Windows NT. You will also learn the difference between the various "flavors" of Windows NT available on the market, including Windows 2000. Next, we will cover the various components of the Windows NT Executive Services. These executive services provide services to all the different components of the operating system. Finally, you will learn about the different Windows NT environment subsystems, which allow NT to run applications written for different operating systems.

CERTIFICATION OBJECTIVE 28.01

Windows NT Versions

Microsoft designed Windows NT to be a robust operating system that would be portable to all types of systems. As such, Windows NT can run on anything from an older 486 PC (although not too well!) to the latest multiprocessor server with several gigabytes of memory. Using the same code base and architecture, Microsoft has developed different flavors of Windows NT—Workstation, Server, Enterprise Edition, and Terminal Server. This section will briefly describe the purpose of each version and illustrate when to use each version. It will conclude with a discussion of the different versions of Windows 2000.

Windows NT Workstation

Windows NT Workstation was designed to be a secure and scaleable desktop operating system for running business-critical applications or resource-intensive applications (such as engineering programs and CAD). Microsoft targeted NT Workstation to the corporate user, as opposed to Windows 95, which was targeted to the home user. To help the corporate network administrator, Windows NT Workstation has many remote management capabilities that Windows 95 does not have. Since Windows NT is more powerful than Windows 95, it is more resource intensive and requires more hardware to run effectively.

Windows NT Workstation also has enhanced networking capabilities, making it ideal for setting up a small workgroup of ten workstations or fewer. In fact, NT Workstation is programmed to accept only ten simultaneous incoming network connections. With the Dial-Up Networking application, you can allow a single user to dial into the PC via modem. In a workgroup environment, Windows NT Workstation also has greater security than Windows 95, since you can set up user-level access to resources, as opposed to the share-level access used by Windows 95. With user-level access, a user needs a logon ID and password to access network resources. With share-level access, all a user needs to access a resource is the password set for the resource. In a Windows NT domain environment, however, you can set user-level access on both NT Workstation and Windows 95.

NT Workstation has built-in support for the Internet by including a Web server and FTP server, allowing you to set up an Internet Web server or corporate intranet with relative ease and little additional cost. The Web and FTP server do not have the full functionality of the Internet Information Server that ships with Windows NT Server (for example, the Workstation version allows a maximum of ten concurrent connections), but the Workstation version also carries a much smaller footprint in terms of memory and disk usage.

Windows NT Workstation adds support for up to two processors, making it ideal for processor-intensive applications such as computer-aided design (CAD) and 3-D graphics. Windows NT Workstation does not support any software-based fault tolerance for hard disks, meaning that you cannot set up disk mirroring or RAID 5 arrays as you can with Windows NT Server. If you need to set up fault tolerance for your hard disks, you will need to go to a hardware-based solution.

Since Windows NT Workstation was designed for desktop applications, the OS is tuned to increase the foreground application's response time. This ensures that when a user is running many applications at once, the current application receives the maximum processor time.

Windows NT Server

Microsoft designed Windows NT Server to be a secure and robust file/print and application server. Microsoft NT Server is capable of handling a large number of requests from network clients. Windows NT Server accomplishes this by using all available processor and memory resources. For example, in NT Server, the file cache is given the highest priority in memory, while in NT Workstation, the user's foreground application is given the highest priority. There are also no programmed limits for incoming network connections for Windows NT Server, although you are still bound to the number of Client Access Licenses that you purchase from Microsoft. Windows NT Server also supports up to 256 dial-in connections using Remote Access Server, as opposed to NT Workstation, which supports only a single dial-in connection.

Windows NT Server also has drastic improvements in hardware support for higher-end servers. The retail version of NT Server supports up to four processors, but hardware vendors may write a custom HAL so that Windows NT can support up to 32 processors. Windows NT Server also supports fault tolerance for the server disk subsystem by supporting RAID 1 (mirroring/duplexing) and RAID 5 (striping with parity). Although you don't get the same performance and features as a hardware-based fault tolerant solution (such as with the SMART Array Controllers), NT's fault tolerance is a big benefit for companies with limited financial resources. (For more information on Windows NT's fault tolerance, refer to Chapter 31, Enhancing Windows NT Reliability Using Compaq Products.)

Windows NT Server has built-in support for Internet applications with Internet Information Server (IIS). IIS adds many enhancements to the limited version that comes with NT Workstation, such as increased performance and scalability (to run large Web sites) and improved manageability and security.

Windows NT Server, Enterprise Edition

Microsoft released Windows NT Server, Enterprise Edition (NTSEE) in response to larger organizations who needed more scalability, availability, and manageability. Windows NT Server, Enterprise Edition is designed to be used in environments where mission-critical applications need to be available 24 hours a day, seven days a week. The Enterprise Edition builds upon the base NT Server product and adds the following capabilities:

- Microsoft Cluster Server (MSCS)
- Increased processor support
- Increased application memory
- Microsoft Message Queue Server, Enterprise Edition
- Windows NT Load Balancing System (WLBS)

Microsoft Cluster Server (MSCS) enables you to connect two servers to form a cluster for increased performance and availability. If one server fails, the other server in the cluster can be configured to run automatically the services that were running on the failed server. MSCS also performs load balancing between the two servers so that one server is not sitting idle while the other server is heavily stressed. MSCS allows you to perform server upgrades and still keep network applications available.

Windows NT Server, Enterprise Edition now supports up to eight processors out of the box, improving the scalability from the base NT Server product, which only supports up to four processors. As with the base NT Server product, vendors can write a custom HAL that allows Windows NT to support up to 32 processors. Since NTSEE provides an upgrade path from Windows NT Server, a network administrator can install the less expensive NT Server product, and when applications require it, upgrade to NTSEE with minimal effort. This allows network administrators to run the most processor-intensive applications.

Windows NT supports up to 4GB of physical memory in a server. Windows NT allocates up to 2GB to the NT kernel, which actually limits the amount of memory for applications to 2GB. NTSEE includes a feature for 4GB RAM Tuning (4GT), which allows you to allocate 1GB of RAM to the NT kernel and 3GB of RAM for applications. This 50 percent increase in RAM can have a dramatic performance boost for memory-intensive applications.

The Microsoft Message Queue Server (MSMQ) is a form of middleware that provides reliable message delivery for applications between servers. Advanced features of MSMQ include an unlimited number of concurrent users, intelligent routing between servers, and support for connectivity to third party messaging servers.

The Windows NT Load Balancing Service (WLBS) allows you to load balance TCP/IP services among up to 32 servers by "sharing" a common IP address. Clients access the IP services via the common IP address and WLBS routes the request to one of the servers in the group. This allows you to provide load balancing for the applications to improve performance and enhance availability.

Windows NT Server, Terminal Server

Windows NT Server, Terminal Server Edition (TSE) is Microsoft's entry into the growing *thin-client* movement in the network industry. A thin-client runs minimal services locally and runs applications from the Terminal Server. The major advantage of this is that you can run the latest 32-bit applications on older hardware without having to upgrade that hardware. You also centralize the management of your network applications, since you only have to upgrade the single copy on the server. The disadvantage is that you will have an increase in network traffic and the server hardware will have to be considerably increased.

Windows NT Server, TSE supports many different types of clients. The Terminal Server client runs as a window on 32-bit desktop operating systems such Windows 95/98 and Windows NT Workstation. The client also runs as a window on older 16-bit clients such as Windows 3.11. Finally, the client can run on a new type of hardware called Windows-based Terminals.

FROM THE FIELD

Extending the Usability of Windows NT Terminal Server Edition

As a result of a complex licensing agreement between Citrix Systems and Microsoft, many features available in the Citrix WinFrame 1.7 product were not implemented in Windows NT Server 4.0, Terminal Server Edition.

The Citrix ICA protocol allows you to access the equivalent of a Windows NT Workstation desktop from a variety of clients, including many flavors of UNIX, WindowsCE, both major HTML browsers, DOS, and Macintosh, as well as any client capable of hosting a JDK 1.1-compliant application.

In addition to better support for heterogeneous environments, Citrix MetaFrame allows you to shadow user sessions (watch a user session remotely) and provides better support for client port mapping. Using MetaFrame, a client connecting over an ICA protocol connection will be able to access client drives from the Terminal Server session (without manually mapping them) and has access to all printers installed on the local machine in the Terminal Server session.

MetaFrame also allows you to create load-balanced application server farms, on which you can specify a single application to be serviced from any one of the servers in the farm. This not only increases performance for clients, but also allows easier server upgrades and reduces risk of failure. For more information on Citrix MetaFrame, visit http://www.citrix.com.

To support the use of the new ProLiant 8000 and 8500 eight-way servers, Compaq offers a version of Windows NT Server, Terminal Server Edition that supports all eight processors. For more information on the Compaq OEM version of Terminal Server for the ProLiant eight-way servers, check out: http://www.compaq.com/products/servers/technology/8way/8wayterminal.html

—*Thomas E. Eck, MCSE+I, MCSD, ASE, CCA, CNA*

QUESTIONS AND ANSWERS

Which version of Windows NT should I use if I need a highly available system with little or no downtime to run a mission-critical application?	Windows NT Server, Enterprise Edition. NTSEE allows you to cluster two servers together so that if one server fails, the other one will take over. Although this is a relatively expensive solution, it meets your requirement to have a system that is available 24 hours a day, seven days a week.
I have a small office network with five PCs. I need to run 32-bit applications on a stable, secure OS. There is no network administrator on-site. Which version of Windows NT should I use?	Windows NT Workstation. With a network this small, you do not need to install a dedicated server. If you need to share files, you can set up one of the workstations as a "server" to centralize the location of the files.
I have an office full of older PCs (486 and Pentiums) running a mix of Windows for Workgroups and Windows 95. Accounting does not want to spend the money to upgrade all of the PCs to newer models, but a new corporate application has to be deployed to the users. Which version of Windows NT should I use?	Windows NT Server, Terminal Server Edition. TSE allows you to run all of your applications from the Terminal Server, while running a thin-client on your existing machines. This enables you to keep your existing investment in the older PCs, allowing them to run the latest 32-bit applications.
Which version of Windows NT should I use if I need to install a new file server with four processors in a network of 100 users?	Windows NT Server. NT Server is optimized for use in larger networks. Windows NT Workstation is limited to 10 incoming network connections and two processors.
Which version of Windows NT should I use if I have a server with eight processors?	You can use either Windows NT Server or Windows NT Server, Enterprise Edition. NTSEE supports eight processors out of the box. With NT Server, you will have to get a custom HAL from the hardware vendor. In addition, Compaq offers an OEM version of WinNT-TSE to accommodate users wishing to run 150+ concurrent users on a single ProLiant 8*xxx* server.

Windows 2000

Windows 2000 is the next major release for the Windows NT family of operating systems. Ever since the release of Windows 95 and Windows NT, Microsoft had a goal to have a single operating system geared at both the corporate user and the home user. Having multiple operating systems made it difficult for Microsoft because they had to support two drastically different OSs with two different sets of developers. Furthermore, software vendors had a difficult time developing code that was compatible on both Windows 95 and Windows NT.

Windows NT 4.0 was a step closer to the single OS in that it brought the Windows 95 graphical user interface (GUI) to the stable and secure OS of Windows NT. However, Windows NT still had several limitations: it didn't support plug-and-play and did not run well on portable laptop computers.

Windows 2000, or Win2K, represents the culmination of the two operating systems (Win9*x* and Windows NT). Microsoft decided to forego the Windows NT brand name to continue the success of the brand name recognition of Windows.

Just as with Windows NT 4.0, the Win2K family comes with several versions geared to different types of users and organizations. On the desktop side, Win2K combines the stability and security of Windows NT and the ease of use and functionality of Win9*x*. On the server side, Win2K completely overhauls the network domain structure with the Active Directory. Table 28-1 lists the different versions and their major features.

CERTIFICATION OBJECTIVE 28.02

Windows NT Architecture

Windows NT is a completely different OS from the previous operating systems that Microsoft developed. Although the GUI is similar, the NT

TABLE 28-1 Windows 2000 Versions and Features

Version	Corresponds to 4.0 Version	Features
Windows 2000 Professional	NT 4.0 Workstation	"Smart menus" learn your most frequently used menu items Plug-and-play and Power Management Support Improved offline file support with InteliMirror for mobile users Fewer scenarios that require a reboot Improved deployment capabilities
Windows 2000 Server	NT 4.0 Server	Aimed at small or medium size offices Active Directory eases and centralizes the management of all network resources in a standards-based directory Supports up to four processors and up to 4GB of RAM
Windows 2000 Advanced Server	NT 4.0 Server, Enterprise Edition	Aimed at larger corporate environments with greater needs for availability and scalability Supports up to eight processors and up to 8GB of RAM Supports cluster services and load balancing services
Windows 2000 Datacenter	N/A	Aimed at very large environments utilizing Online Transaction Processing (OLTP), data warehousing, or other resource-intensive applications Supports up to 32 processors and 64GB of RAM Supports cluster services and load balancing services

architecture is vastly different from the architecture of DOS and Windows. When Microsoft designed and developed Windows NT, they kept the following design goals in mind:

- **Compatibility** Windows NT had to support existing legacy applications in order to be accepted by the corporate environment. Windows NT also had to run on some older machines that had a limited amount of memory and hard disk space.

- **Scalability and portability** Windows NT is scaleable in that it can run on single processor servers as well as multiprocessor servers. You also do not have to make the initial investment in a multiprocessor server right away, since NT supports being upgraded to multiprocessor capability. Windows NT is also different from previous versions of Windows in that it can run on other platforms besides the Intel *x*86 family of processors. Originally, besides running on the Intel processors, Windows NT also ran on RISC processors, including MIPS, PowerPC, and the Alpha processors. Today, Windows NT only supports the Intel processors and the Alpha.
- **Security** If Windows NT was going to be a viable network server for corporate environments, it had to be secure. Security involves protecting the operating system from malicious outside attack from users and applications.
- **Distributed processing** Distributed processing refers to Windows NT's ability to communicate with other networks. Microsoft accomplished this by making the network products a core component of the OS and including certain protocols (such as TCP/IP and IPX) for connectivity to other networks.
- **Reliability and robustness** In order for an OS to be reliable and robust, it must be able to protect itself from damage from a rogue application. Windows NT accomplishes this by having each application run in its own application space so that if an application crashes, it does not affect the OS or any other running application. In addition, with the Hardware Abstraction Layer (HAL), applications are no longer allowed to access hardware directly, which adds another layer of protection for the OS.
- **Localization** Windows NT is offered in many different languages in many different countries around the world. Windows NT also supports the International Organization for Standardization (ISO) Unicode standard.
- **Extensibility** Microsoft developed Windows NT to be extensible, which means that as technology changes, you can add or remove components to Windows NT without affecting the rest of the

system. For example, if you upgrade your server by adding another processor, you need only run a resource kit utility (or perform the equivalent list of procedures) or Compaq SSD application to upgrade the operating system to support the multiprocessor HAL. You don't have to reinstall the entire OS.

Architectural Modules

Microsoft took a modular approach when they developed Windows NT. They designed NT with different components, each having a different task and responsibility that was independent of other components. In this way, a certain component can be replaced without affecting the rest of the system. For example, if you upgraded a file server from a single processor to a dual processor, you can just replace the component that added multiprocessor capability without having to reinstall the entire operating system.

Briefly, Windows NT is comprised of two modes: user mode and kernel mode (see Figure 28-1). Each of these will be discussed in detail in the next section. Basically, user applications run in a specific environment subsystem that runs in user mode. Processes and applications that run in user mode do not have direct access to hardware. The Windows NT Executive Services run in kernel mode and have direct access to hardware.

User Mode versus Kernel Mode

User mode refers to a less privileged mode of accessing the computer hardware. User applications run in a specific environment subsystem in user mode. In order for user applications to access hardware, they must go through the appropriate layers in kernel mode. For example: to display an OK button on the video screen, an application makes an API call to the Windows Manager, which makes a request to the graphics device interface (GDI), which in turn makes a request to the video card driver. The user application does not need to know how to draw a button, or what video driver is installed, since the intermediate layers take care of translating the request appropriately for the hardware. Again, the advantage of this modular structure is clear, since in order to change the video card in the

FIGURE 28-1

Windows NT architectural model

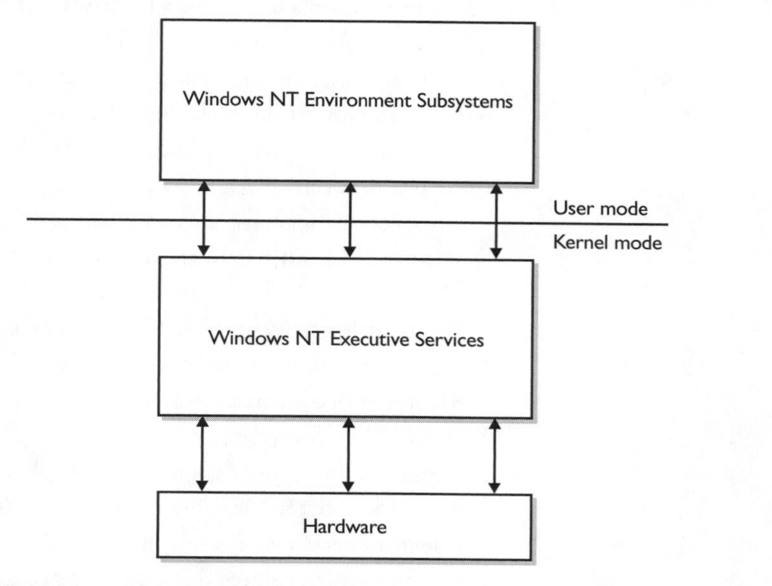

computer, you only have to change the video driver and not the rest of the operating system.

Applications that run in user mode only have access to their own memory address space, which protects them from other applications. However, applications can be granted access to each other's memory space in order to share information.

The code that actually does have access to the hardware runs in kernel mode. Kernel mode is also called privileged mode, protected mode, or Ring 0. The operating system kernel and device drivers run in kernel mode. Code that runs in kernel mode has access to all user mode applications' address spaces. User applications access the kernel mode functions through application program interfaces (APIs).

Hardware Abstraction Layer

The Hardware Abstraction Layer (HAL) is a set of routines and code that directly manipulate the hardware in your system. All user application hardware requests and most OS drivers (including the Windows NT Executive) must go through the HAL in order to be processed. Since the HAL is an independent component of the OS, the HAL can be replaced without having to reinstall the entire OS. Each HAL has specific capabilities optimized for the specific hardware for which it was designed. For example, there is a different HAL used on single-processor servers than on multiprocessor servers. Microsoft ships a standard set of HALs with Windows NT, but hardware manufacturers are free to create their own custom HALs to take advantage of features in their hardware. For example, prior to Windows NT 4.0, Compaq wrote a special HAL for their ProLiant servers that added to the functionality of the original Microsoft HAL (for more information on this custom HAL, refer to Chapter 30, Windows NT Support).

Since the HAL lives between the application and the actual hardware, the HAL "hides" the actual details of the hardware from the application. The application can be written to make general requests to the HAL, which in turn translates those requests to an appropriate format for the specific hardware.

on the job

Having a HAL mismatch is one of the quickest ways to make sure that your server does not boot properly. HAL mismatches can occur for several reasons, including running an incorrect version of the HAL or running a multiprocessor HAL in a single-processor system. If you have a HAL mismatch and Windows NT is not able to boot, you will have to jump through some hoops. If Windows NT is installed on a FAT partition, you can simply copy the proper HAL.DLL to the WINNT\SYSTEM32 directory. If Windows NT is installed on an NTFS partition and the data on the system is not important, then you can simply reinstall NT. If you need access to the data on the downed server, you can reinstall Windows NT to a different directory, then use Explorer to copy the proper HAL.DLL to the original WINNT\SYSTEM32 directory.

Compaq also offers a HAL recovery mode option, which is discussed in Chapter 30. With the HAL recovery mode, Compaq adds an entry to the boot menu for Windows NT that allows you to boot from a known good HAL.

Microkernel

The Microkernel is the traffic cop of the Windows NT architecture. It is responsible for scheduling process threads and handling interrupts and exceptions. The Microkernel schedules threads based on their priority. It will interrupt or preempt a running process if another process with a higher priority requests processing time. The Microkernel is also responsible for coordinating the activity between the different components of the rest of the Windows NT Executive.

In symmetric multiprocessor (SMP) servers, the Microkernel can schedule and assign tasks to any available processor in the server, making sure that no processor sits idle. In addition, the Microkernel uses *soft affinity*, which means that it will try to schedule a process on the processor that it ran on most recently. This can improve performance since there is a greater likelihood that the data from the process may still reside in the processor's cache.

CERTIFICATION OBJECTIVE 28.03

Components of the Windows NT Executive

The Windows NT Executive Services are a set of components that provide a common set of services to the rest of the operating system. Figure 28-2 illustrates this set of services.

The executive services consists of the following components:

- I/O Manager
- Object Manager
- Security Reference Manager
- Process Manager
- Local Procedure Call Facility
- Virtual Memory Manager
- Windows Manager
- Graphics Device Interface
- Graphics Device Drivers

FIGURE 28-2 The Windows NT Executive Services

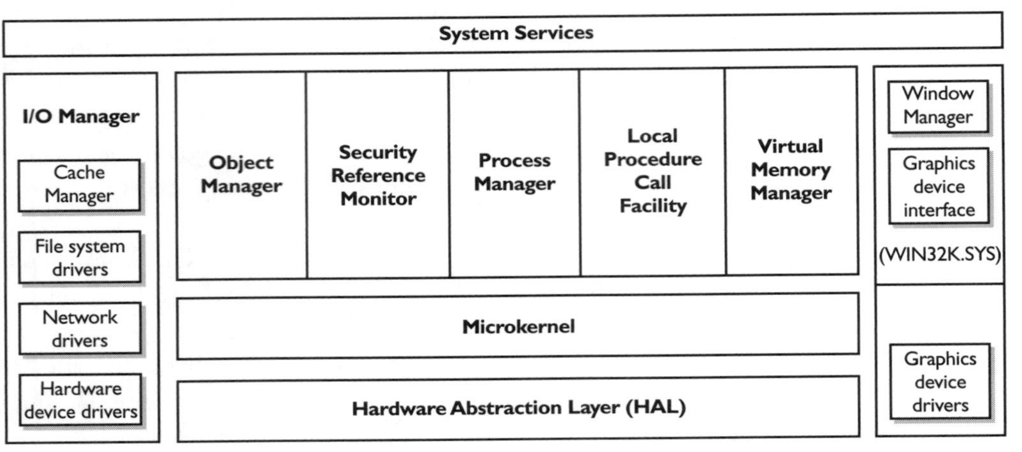

I/O Manager

The I/O Manager handles all input and output for Windows NT by using a layered approach, in which different levels of drivers communicate with each other through the I/O Manager. An example of a low-level device driver is one that would manipulate hardware directly, such as a disk driver or a network card driver. Higher-level drivers (such as file system drivers and network redirectors) simply send I/O requests through the I/O Manager to these lower-level drivers. This modular approach allows you to load or replace device drivers without affecting other drivers.

The I/O Manager uses *asynchronous I/O* whenever possible. With asynchronous I/O, an application submits its request for I/O, then is free to perform other activity. Asynchronous I/O is much more efficient than synchronous I/O. Because the I/O device (such as a hard disk) is much slower than processors, the application can perform other tasks while it waits for the I/O request to be completed.

I/O requests are placed in an I/O queue and the I/O Manager processes these requests in order of priority, not the order in which they are received.

When the I/O Manager processes an I/O request, it simply passes that request to the appropriate device driver, then returns to processing the next request without waiting for the device driver to finish the original request. The device driver notifies the I/O Manager when the I/O request has been completed, and the I/O Manager then notifies the original requesting application.

To improve performance, the I/O architecture caches frequently used files in main memory. Accessing files in memory is much faster than accessing files from a hard disk. The Cache Manager is responsible for managing the cache, which includes keeping track of which files are in the cache and optimizing the size of the cache depending on how much memory is available.

Object Manager

In Windows NT, *objects* are software components that consist of a data type, attributes, and a set of operations. Examples of objects include files, directories, processes, and threads. The Object Manager is responsible for setting the rules for the operating system to access these objects. The Object Manager is responsible for how objects are named, how objects are accessed, and how objects are secured. Since the Object Manager is extensible, new objects can be defined at any time.

Processes and applications access objects through *object handles*. The Object Manager is responsible for creating these object handles, which consist of access control information and a pointer to the object.

Security Reference Monitor

The Security Reference Monitor, illustrated in Figure 28-3, is part of the Windows NT security subsystem. The Security Reference Monitor is responsible for enforcing the security policies of the local system as well as generating security audits. Other components of the NT security subsystem include the following:

- **Logon Process** Handles interactive and remote logon requests from users.

- **Local Security Authority** (LSA) Generates access tokens, manages the local security policy, and provides interactive logon authentication.
- **Security Account Manager** (SAM) This database contains all information about all user accounts and groups for the server. The SAM also provides user authentication services for the LSA.

Process Manager

A *process* is an application or part of an application that consists of a memory address space, a set of objects, and a set of worker threads. A thread is the most basic piece of a process that can be scheduled processor time. The Process Manager is responsible for creating and deleting individual processes and tracking process and thread objects.

FIGURE 28-3 Windows NT security subsystem

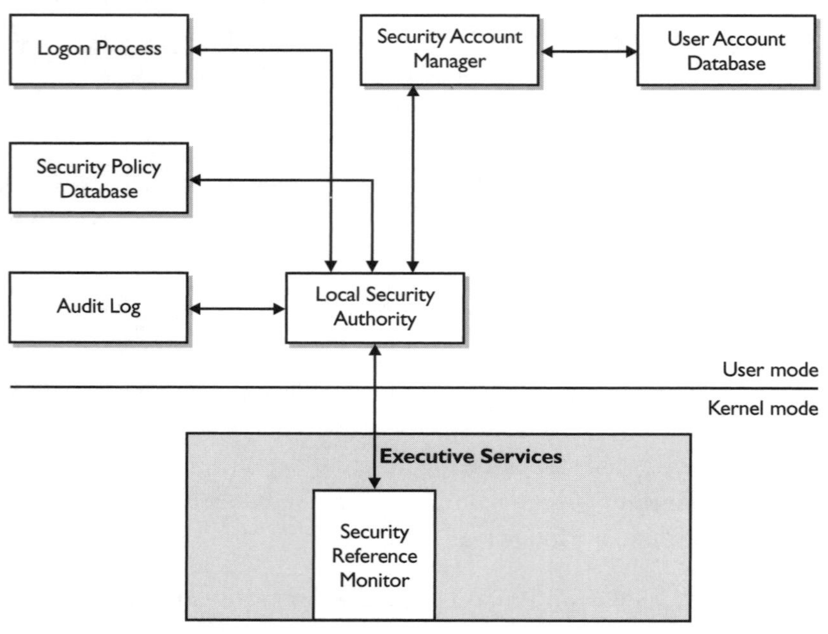

When a process is generated, it is assigned a security access token, which Windows NT uses to determine whether a thread of the process is allowed to access a specific object. The Process Manager works with the Security Reference Monitor and the Virtual Memory Manager to provide this protection.

Local Procedure Call Facility

You read briefly in the introduction that Windows NT provides environment subsystems so that applications written for other operating systems can run on Windows NT. The environment subsystems emulate other subsystems such as MS-DOS and OS/2. You will learn more about environment subsystems later in the chapter. Applications communicate with their respective environment subsystems through Local Procedure Calls (LPCs). The LPC facility provides a mechanism so that the application can send and receive messages from the subsystem.

Virtual Memory Manager

As you learned earlier, Windows NT provides up to 4GB of memory to each process. The 4GB of memory, known as an application's *address space*, will not directly map to an area in physical memory, but rather to virtual memory. Each process has its own address space independent of and protected from other processes' address space. The Virtual Memory Manager (VMM) is responsible for managing NT's memory usage and assigning physical memory to applications and processes.

When an application requests data, it requests it using a virtual address. The VMM is responsible for translating that virtual address to a physical address in RAM. If the information is not in physical RAM, the VMM will swap the information from the pagefile on the hard disk to RAM. Using virtual memory, Windows NT can accommodate several programs with a limited amount of physical memory.

on the job

As you will learn in Chapter 32, Windows NT Performance Tuning, the use of virtual memory can take a heavy toll on system performance and should be avoided. Make sure that there is enough memory in the system to avoid paging. Chapter 32 also has an in-depth discussion on how Windows NT uses the memory subsystem and how to optimize it. In the real world, the most cost-effective method to improve performance on your server is to add memory.

Window Manager

The Window Manager is responsible for the Windows interface that displays windows, buttons, and other screen elements as you work with Windows NT. The Windows Manager works with the graphics device interface to draw any requested screen elements from an application. When there are any changes to the screen elements made by a user (such as resizing a window or clicking a button), the Window Manager relays those changes back to the application for processing.

Along with the GDI, the Window Manager is implemented in a single component, WIN32K.SYS. Prior to Windows NT 4.0, these two components were implemented as a user mode function in the Win32 subsystem. With Windows NT 4.0, these components now run in kernel mode in the Windows NT Executive to improve performance.

Graphics Device Interface

The GDI works with the Window Manager to provide the screen elements of the user interface. In addition to window elements, the GDI is also responsible for displaying other graphics (such as desktop backgrounds) on the user's monitor and to printers. The applications make requests to the GDI, which then translates those requests and send them to the appropriate display driver or printer driver. The GDI does not need to know anything about the hardware (the video card or the printer), since the device driver is what communicates with the actual hardware. This modular approach allows the GDI to remain unchanged if you change video cards or printers (as long as you change the appropriate driver, of course!)

The GDI is implemented along with the Window Manager in WIN32K.SYS. As with the Window Manager, the GDI was implemented in the Win32 subsystem prior to Windows NT 4.0. With Windows NT 4.0 and later, the GDI and the Window Manager are implemented in the Windows NT Executive and run in kernel mode to improve performance.

Graphics Device Drivers

Graphics device drivers are a set of functions that let applications, through the GDI, display graphics and text on a monitor screen or print output to a printer. Graphics device drivers are usually specific to a particular piece of hardware and usually written by the hardware manufacturer. Windows NT comes with common display and printer drivers. The graphics device drivers are responsible for drawing the actual lines and colors for its device.

Prior to Windows NT 4.0, display drivers and printer drivers ran in user mode in the Win32 subsystem. With Windows NT 4.0 and later, the display drivers and printer drivers now run in protected kernel mode to improve performance. This also adds a bit of risk—a vendor could write an unstable video or printer driver that could potentially crash a system, since it is running in kernel mode.

CERTIFICATION OBJECTIVE 28.04

Windows NT Environment Subsystems

Windows NT can run applications written for different operating systems thanks to environment subsystems. These environment subsystems are processes that emulate different operating systems and essentially trick an application into thinking that it is running in its native OS. Each of the subsystems runs in user mode, which means that it does not directly access hardware, but rather it must go through the proper executive services. Also, since each subsystem runs in its own process, a subsystem that crashes cannot affect other subsystems or the Executive itself.

The environment subsystems provided by Windows NT (shown in Figure 28-4) are as follows:

- MS-DOS
- Windows 16-Bit (Win16)

- OS/2
- POSIX
- Windows 32-Bit (Win32)

MS-DOS Environment

MS-DOS applications run on Windows NT in a process known as the NT Virtual DOS Machine (NTVDM) process. The NTVDM is a 32-bit process that emulates an Intel 486 PC running MS-DOS. Each DOS application runs in its own NTVDM process and is allocated its own memory address space, which protects other applications and the operating system from a misbehaving DOS application. An unlimited number of NTVDMs can be run.

FIGURE 28-4

Windows NT environment subsystems

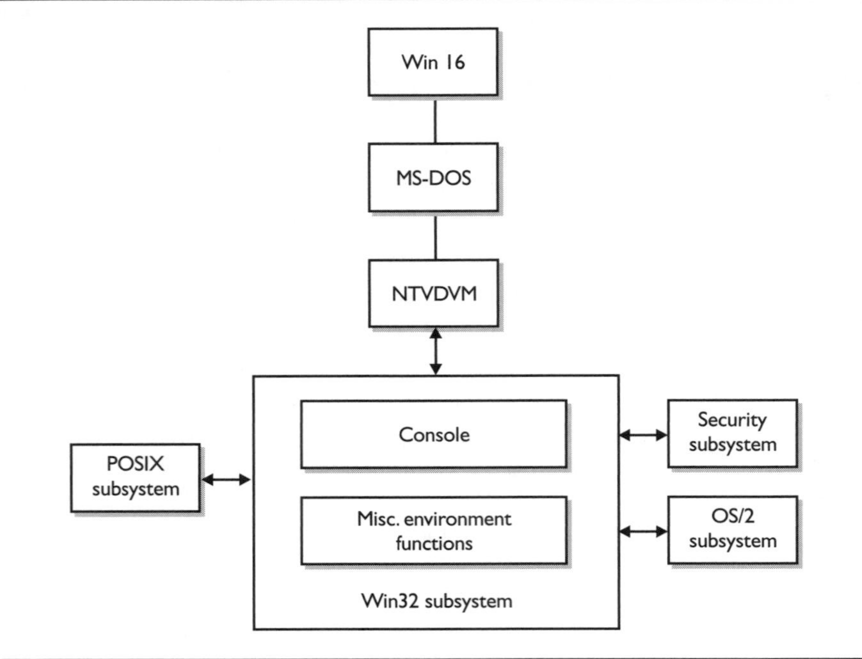

Windows 16-Bit Environment

The Windows 16-bit environment functions slightly differently from the MS-DOS environment. The Win16 environment also runs in an NTVDM, but each 16-bit Windows application runs as a separate thread within the NTVDM. Consequently, all Win16 applications share the same memory address space and a misbehaving Win16 application can crash all other Win16 applications as well as the NTVDM. The Win16 NTVDM is also known as Win16-on-Win32 or WOW.

Another limitation of the Win16 NTVDM is that only one 16-bit application thread can run at a time, even on multiprocessor machines. The Win16 NTVDM, however, can multitask with other processes.

Windows NT 4.0 does permit each 16-bit application to run in its own NTVDM and memory address space. The limitation of this is that separate 16-bit applications aren't able to share information since they are in separate memory spaces. Also, since each application is in its own address space, more memory is consumed. To run a 16-bit application in its own NTVDM and address space, view the application's executable properties and enable the option Run in Separate Memory Space. Alternatively, if you run the application from the Run command line, you can enable the option Run in Separate Memory Space (as in Figure 28-5). From a command line, you can use the command START /SEPARATE *program* (where *program* is the program's executable) to start the application in its own memory space.

OS/2 Subsystem

Windows NT supports OS/2 1.*x* character-based applications through the OS/2 subsystem. The OS/2 subsystem does not support GUI applications or the High Performance File System (HPFS), OS/2's file system.

If you are never going to run OS/2 applications under Windows NT, for added security you should disable the OS/2 subsystem. You can do this by modifying the Registry key,

```
HKEY_LOCAL_MACHINE\System\CurrentControlSet\
Control\SessionManager
```

and changing the value of GlobalFlag to 20100000.

FIGURE 28-5

Win16 applications can run in their own memory space

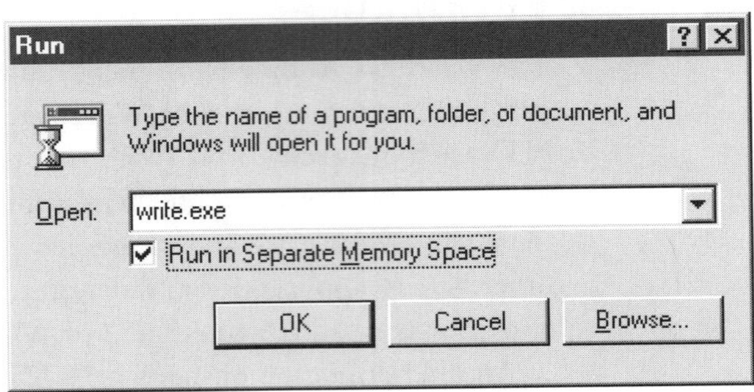

POSIX Subsystem

POSIX stands for Portable Operating System Interface for Computing Environments. It is a set of standards to write applications so that they can run on different operating systems. Although mainly used in UNIX environments, POSIX also can be implemented in non-UNIX environments such as Windows NT.

The Windows NT POSIX subsystem is designed to run each POSIX application in its own protected memory space. In addition, POSIX applications that access the file system have certain requirements, such as case-sensitive file naming. As such, if a POSIX application needs access to the file system, it must be installed on a partition that is formatted NTFS. If the application will not access the file system, then it can be installed on any formatted partition.

Windows NT is being evaluated for a C2-compliant operating system. For an OS to be C2 compliant, it has to pass certain criteria specified by the National Computer Security Center (NCSC). When you first install Windows NT, it is not C2 compliant due to some of the settings of its components, one of which is the presence of the POSIX and OS/2 subsystems. In a high-security environment, you may need to make your server C2 compliant. To do so, you can run the Windows NT Resource Kit utility, C2CONFIG.EXE. This utility will evaluate your system and allow you to perform any necessary tasks, such as removing the POSIX and OS/2 subsystems. This method is much easier than trying to hack the Registry.

Windows 32-Bit Subsystem

The Windows 32-bit (Win32) Subsystem is Windows NT's native subsystem, which runs all 32-bit applications written for NT. As you can see from Figure 28-4, the Win32 subsystem consists of Console Functions and Miscellaneous Environment Functions. Console Functions provide text window support, shutdown, and hard-error handling for applications. Miscellaneous Environment Functions include specialized functions for Win32 applications, such as creating and deleting processes.

Prior to Windows NT 4.0, the Win32 Subsystem also included functions such as graphics (including graphics device drivers), windowing, and messaging support. These functions have been moved into the Windows NT Executive. Although this improves performance, especially video performance, it also adds some instability since an errant video driver can crash the entire server.

CERTIFICATION SUMMARY

This chapter provided an architectural overview of how Windows NT runs under the hood. By understanding how data and processes flow through Windows NT, you can more readily identify and troubleshoot problems that might pop up.

Due to Windows NT's modularity, you can use the same code base with minor modifications to create different versions of NT (such as Workstation and Server). Although each version has a different function in the corporate world, they all use the same architecture. Because of the modularity, you can replace a single component of Windows NT without having to reinstall the entire operating system.

NT is composed of two major modes: user mode and kernel mode. Applications that run in user mode do not have direct access to the hardware and must go through the proper layers in kernel mode. Kernel mode processes have direct access to the hardware.

User applications run in environment systems in user mode. Since each application runs as its own process in its own memory address space, it is protected from other processes in the system. The Windows NT Executive, which provides low-level functions to the rest of the operating system, runs in kernel mode.

TWO-MINUTE DRILL

- One of the requirements to become a Compaq ASE is to hold a major OS certification, such as the Microsoft Certified Systems Engineer (MCSE) certification.
- You will certainly need to become familiar with how the OS operates behind the scenes.
- Microsoft designed Windows NT to be a robust operating system that would be portable to all types of systems.
- Using the same code base and architecture, Microsoft has developed different flavors of Windows NT—Workstation, Server, Enterprise Edition, and Terminal Server.
- Windows NT Workstation was designed to be a secure and scaleable desktop operating system for running business-critical applications or resource-intensive applications.
- Microsoft designed Windows NT Server to be a secure and robust file/print and application server.
- In NT Server, the file cache is given the highest priority in memory, while in NT Workstation, the user's foreground application is given the highest priority.
- Microsoft released Windows NT Server, Enterprise Edition (NTSEE) in response to larger organizations who needed more scalability, availability, and manageability.
- Microsoft Cluster Server (MSCS) enables you to connect two servers to form a cluster for increased performance and availability.
- The Microsoft Message Queue Server (MSMQ) is a form of middleware that provides reliable message delivery for applications between servers.
- The Windows NT Load Balancing Service (WLBS) allows you to load balance TCP/IP services among up to 32 servers by "sharing" a common IP address.
- Windows NT Server, Terminal Server Edition (TSE) is Microsoft's entry into the growing *thin-client* movement in the network industry.
- Windows 2000 is the next major release for the Windows NT family of operating systems.

- ❑ On the desktop side, Win2K combines the stability and security of Windows NT and the ease of use and functionality of Win9*x*.
- ❑ On the server side, Win2K completely overhauls the network domain structure with the Active Directory.
- ❑ Table 28-1 lists the different versions of Win2K and their major features.
- ❑ When Microsoft designed and developed Windows NT, they kept the following design goals in mind:
  - ❑ Compatibility
  - ❑ Scalability and portability
  - ❑ Security
  - ❑ Distributed processing
  - ❑ Reliability and robustness
  - ❑ Localization
  - ❑ Extensibility
- ❑ NT was designed with different components, each having a different task and responsibility that was independent of other components. A certain component can be replaced without affecting the rest of the system.
- ❑ User mode refers to a less privileged mode of accessing the computer hardware.
- ❑ The code that actually does have access to the hardware runs in kernel mode. Kernel mode is also called privileged mode, protected mode, or Ring 0.
- ❑ The Hardware Abstraction Layer (HAL) is a set of routines and code that directly manipulate the hardware in your system.
- ❑ The Microkernel is responsible for scheduling process threads and handling interrupts and exceptions.
- ❑ The Windows NT Executive Services are a set of components that provide a common set of services to the rest of the operating system. Review Figure 28-2.
- ❑ The I/O Manager handles all input and output for Windows NT by using a layered approach, in which different levels of drivers communicate with each other through the I/O Manager.
- ❑ The Object Manager is responsible for setting the rules for the operating system to access objects (software components that consist of a data type, attributes, and a set of operations).

- The Security Reference Monitor is responsible for enforcing the security policies of the local system as well as generating security audits.
- The Process Manager is responsible for creating and deleting individual processes and tracking process and thread objects.
- The Local Procedure Calls (LPCs) facility provides a mechanism so that the application can send and receive messages from the subsystem.
- The Virtual Memory Manager (VMM) is responsible for managing NT's memory usage and assigning physical memory to applications and processes.
- The Window Manager is responsible for the Windows interface that displays windows, buttons, and other screen elements as you work with Windows NT.
- The Graphics Device Interface (GDI) works with the Window Manager to provide the screen elements of the user interface.
- Graphics device drivers are a set of functions that let applications, through the GDI, display graphics and text on a monitor screen or print output to a printer.
- Windows NT can run applications written for different operating systems thanks to environment subsystems.
- Environment subsystems are processes that emulate different operating systems and essentially trick an application into thinking that it is running in its native OS.
- MS-DOS applications run on Windows NT in a process known as the NT Virtual DOS Machine (NTVDM) process.
- The Win16 environment also runs in an NTVDM, but each 16-bit Windows application runs as a separate thread within the NTVDM.
- Windows NT supports OS/2 1.*x* character-based applications through the OS/2 subsystem.
- The Windows NT POSIX subsystem is designed to run each POSIX application in its own protected memory space.
- The Windows 32-bit (Win32) Subsystem is Windows NT's native subsystem, which runs all 32-bit applications written for NT.

SELF TEST

The following Self Test questions will help you measure your understanding of the material presented in this chapter. Read all the choices carefully, as there may be more than one correct answer. Choose all correct answers for each question.

1. How many inbound user connections is Windows NT Workstation limited to?

   A. 5

   B. 10

   C. 100

   D. There is no limit.

2. Which of the following statements is not a reason to use Windows NT Server rather than Windows NT Workstation as a file server in a medium to large networking environment?

   A. Server is optimized for a multiuser environment, while Workstation is optimized for user applications.

   B. Server has fault tolerance capabilities, while Workstation does not.

   C. Server has no limits on the number of inbound connections, while Workstation has a limit of 10.

   D. Server has multiprocessor capabilities, while Workstation does not.

3. You are the network administrator of a large company. You are asked to design a server that must have 24/7 uptime capability. This server will be running a mission-critical application. Which version of Windows NT should you use?

   A. Windows NT Workstation

   B. Windows NT Server

   C. Windows NT Server, Enterprise Edition

   D. Windows NT Server, Terminal Server Edition

4. Which of the following comprise the two modes in which Windows NT runs processes?

   A. User mode and kernel mode

   B. Safe mode and user mode

   C. Privileged mode and protected mode

   D. Environment mode and executive mode

5. Which component of the Windows NT Executive hides the details of the hardware from user applications?

   A. Microkernel

   B. Hardware Abstraction Layer

   C. Process Manager

   D. I/O Manager

6. Which component of the Windows NT Executive is responsible for scheduling process threads?

   A. Microkernel

   B. Hardware Abstraction Layer

   C. I/O Manager

   D. Process Manager

7. Which of the following is not a component of the I/O Manager?

   A. Cache Manager

B. File system driver
C. Network driver
D. Graphics device driver

8. What is asynchronous I/O?
   A. An application must wait for each I/O request to be fulfilled.
   B. An application can perform other functions after submitting an I/O request.
   C. An application submits an I/O request to a serial port.
   D. An application submits an I/O request to the network.

9. Which of the following is not an example of an object in Windows NT?
   A. Files
   B. Directories
   C. Threads
   D. Kernel mode

10. Which component of the Windows NT Security Subsystem runs in kernel mode?
    A. Local Security Authority
    B. Security Account Manager
    C. Security Reference Monitor
    D. Logon Process

11. How are processes and threads related?
    A. A thread is a piece of a process.
    B. A process is a piece of a thread.
    C. A process schedules a thread.
    D. A thread schedules a process.

12. How does the MS-DOS environment differ from the Win16 environment?
    A. Each Win16 application runs in its own NTVDM.
    B. Each DOS application runs in its own NTVDM.
    C. Each DOS application runs as a thread within a single NTVDM.
    D. DOS applications can be configured to run in a separate memory space.

13. Which of the following is a limitation of the POSIX subsystem?
    A. The application must be installed on an NTFS partition.
    B. The application must be installed on a FAT partition.
    C. The application must be installed on a FAT32 partition.
    D. The application must be installed on a UNIX partition.

14. How are environment systems protected from each other?
    A. Each environment system runs in kernel mode.
    B. Each environment system must be installed on a separate partition.
    C. Each environment system runs in its own process.
    D. Each environment system runs as a separate thread.

15. Which components of Windows NT were moved to the NT Executive with Windows NT 4.0?
    A. Win32 Subsystem
    B. Local Security Authority
    C. Console functions
    D. Window Manager

ASE

ACCREDITED SYSTEMS ENGINEER

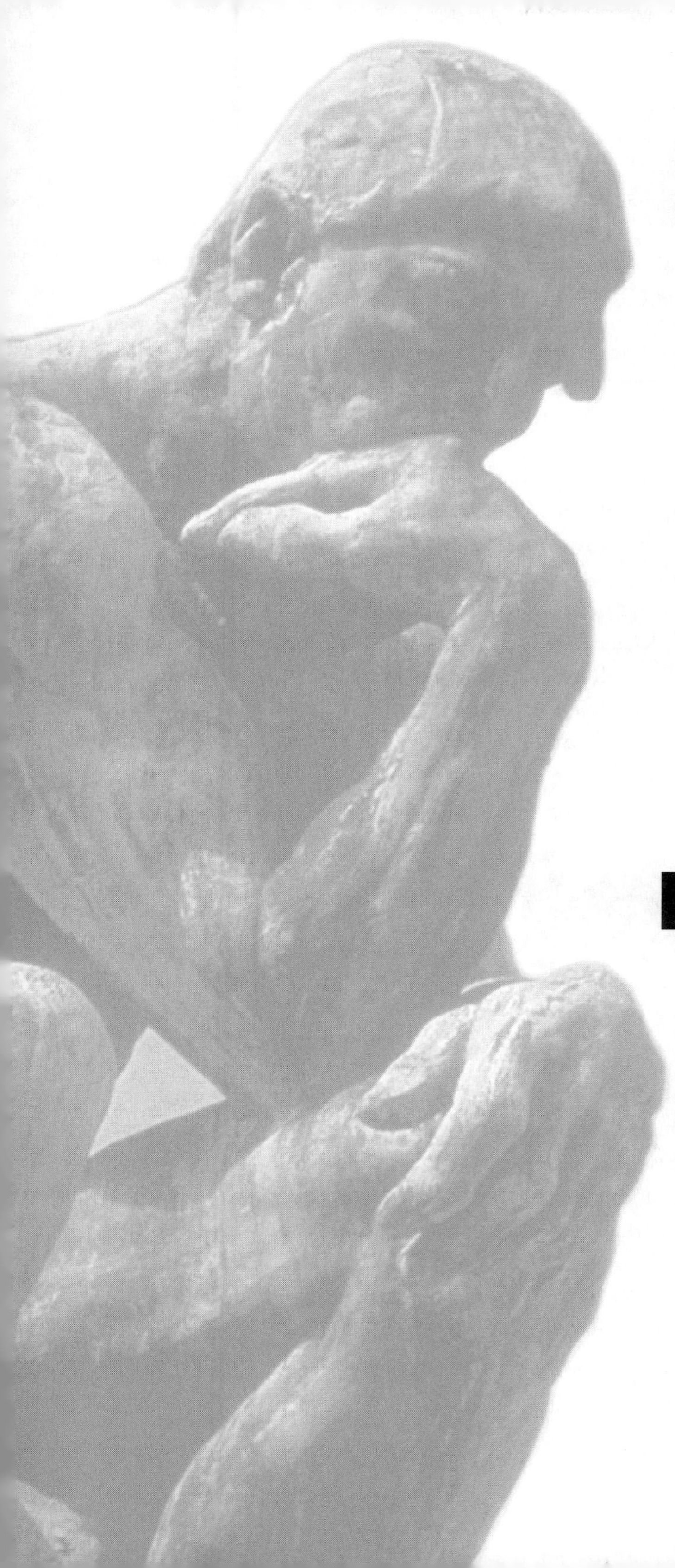

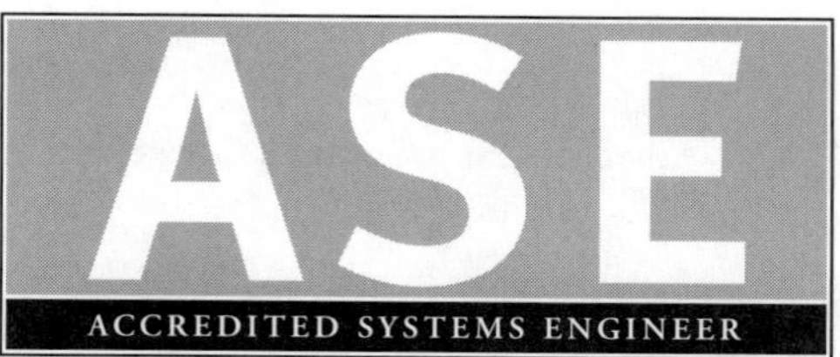

29

Compaq SmartStart for Windows NT

CERTIFICATION OBJECTIVES

29.01 SmartStart

29.02 Manual Configuration Versus Assisted Integration

29.03 Using an Integration Server

29.04 SmartStart Installation Versus Installing from Microsoft Media

29.05 SmartStart Subscription

One of the best ways to ensure that a file server operates optimally in production is to set it up properly from the start. You can set many configuration options when installing a server, which will affect how the server runs on a network. Some options, if not configured properly, can negatively impact performance on the network. Other options cannot be changed without reinstalling the operating system. The system administrator's task, then, is to build a file server consistently and efficiently.

Fortunately, Compaq has developed SmartStart to aid administrators in building Compaq servers. SmartStart simplifies the installation of servers by walking the administrator through several screens for configuring the hardware and operating system. This wizard-like approach ensures that servers are set up in a consistent and streamlined manner.

This chapter will discuss Compaq's SmartStart program for setting up your file server. We will describe in detail what SmartStart is and what it consists of. We will also cover extensively each step of the SmartStart process. Although Compaq provides a SmartStart process for several operating systems, this chapter will only cover the Windows NT path for SmartStart.

CERTIFICATION OBJECTIVE 29.01

SmartStart

SmartStart is a program developed by Compaq to aid the network administrator in building Compaq servers consistently and efficiently. In addition to reducing the amount of time that it takes to build a server, the SmartStart process also creates a more reliable server by giving the administrator a sound set of steps to follow when building a server. This minimizes the chance that the administrator will forget a critical step during the server build. For example, before SmartStart, an administrator would have to install Windows NT on a server manually and then install the Compaq-optimized device drivers afterwards. If the administrator did not install the Compaq drivers, the server would still run, although not necessarily with all of the hardware functionality. With SmartStart, all Compaq drivers are automatically installed at the proper time during the installation.

SmartStart is packaged as a bootable CD that is shipped with every ProLiant and ProSignia server. The SmartStart CD is part of the Server Setup and Management pack of disks, along with the Compaq Management CD, which includes Insight Manager. The Server Setup and Management pack also contains the Server Profile Disk, which is used during the SmartStart setup. The SmartStart CD contains customized programs for different operating systems, including Windows NT, NetWare, and SCO-UNIX. Along with the different operating systems, SmartStart can be run in different languages, including French, Spanish, German, Italian, and Japanese.

The rest of this section will go through the SmartStart process step by step. When you install SmartStart on your server, you may not see all of these steps. For example, if you do not have a Smart Array controller, you will not be prompted to use the Array Configuration Utility.

SmartStart Requirements

To run SmartStart, you will need a Compaq server with the following minimal hardware requirements:

- 32MB of memory
- CD-ROM
- Mouse and keyboard
- VGA monitor
- Supported SCSI controller for hard drives. The SmartStart for Servers booklet that comes with the Server Setup and Management Pack contains a list of supported SCSI controllers.
- System ROM that supports a bootable CD. On older systems, such as Systempro/XLs, you may need to update the system ROM to a newer version.

Booting from the SmartStart CD

The SmartStart CD is a bootable CD. To begin the SmartStart process, simply insert the SmartStart and Support Software CD (it's the green CD in the Server Setup and Management pack) into the CD-ROM drive and reboot the server.

The first screen where you are required to respond prompts you for the language in which you'd like to run SmartStart. You can choose English, French, German, Italian, Spanish, or Japanese.

In the next screen, you enter Regional Settings for the server. Enter the country, keyboard type, and the date and time. Click Next to continue with SmartStart.

Choosing the SmartStart Path

SmartStart provides three paths that you can follow when installing the OS on your server: Assisted Integration, Manual Configuration, and Replicated Install. During this part of the SmartStart process, you select which path you'd like to follow. Each of these paths is described below.

Manual Configuration

Manual Configuration gives you the most flexibility when installing a server and should only be used by more experienced administrators or by those who require a function that the Assisted Integration does not provide. With Manual Configuration, the SmartStart process proceeds much like the Assisted Integration, but it only configures the hardware for the system. Once the hardware configuration is completed, the SmartStart process prompts you to continue with the operating system installation as recommended by the OS manufacturer. In the case of Windows NT, you simply insert the Windows NT Server CD into the CD-ROM and reboot the server. You can then install Windows NT as you normally would. Manual Configuration is covered later in the chapter.

Replicated Install

If you are setting up several servers with identical hardware configurations, you can choose the Replicated Install path. With the Replicated Install path, you first install a server using the Assisted Integration path. The final step during Assisted Integration prompts you to create a replication diskette, which contains all the settings and options that you chose during the SmartStart process. You can then use this disk during the installation of subsequent servers using the Replicated Install path.

Assisted Integration

Assisted Integration provides the simplest installation path by prompting you through the installation of the hardware and the operating system. Assisted Integration will automatically configure the server hardware and load the proper device drivers for Windows NT. This path will also install any custom Compaq applications to support the server hardware. Finally, Assisted Integration also prompts you for information about the OS installation, simplifying the installation of Windows NT. The rest of this section will cover the Assisted Integration path of SmartStart for Windows NT Server 4.0. Table 29-1 shows which paths are available for the various operating systems.

TABLE 29-1 Configuration Paths Available for Each Operating System

Operating System	Assisted Integration	Manual Configuration	Replicated Installation
Windows NT Server 4.0	X	X	X
Windows NT Server, Enterprise Edition 4.0	X	X	X
Windows NT Server 4.0 Terminal Server Edition		X	
BackOffice Small Business Server		X	
Novell NetWare 5	X	X	
Novell NetWare 4.2	X	X	
Novell NetWare 4.11		X	

TABLE 29-1 Configuration Paths Available for Each Operating System *(continued)*

Operating System	Assisted Integration	Manual Configuration	Replicated Installation
NetWare for Small Business 5.0	X	X	
NetWare for Small Business 4.2	X	X	
Netware 3.2		X	
SCO OpenServer 5	X	X	X
SCO UnixWare 7.1. 7.0.1	X	X	X
SCO UnixWare 2.1.3		X	
OS/2 Warp Server 4 and Warp Server Advanced 4	X	X	
Banyan Vines		X	
Citrix Winframe 1.7		X	

QUESTIONS AND ANSWERS

Which path should I use to install Microsoft BackOffice Small Business Server on the server?	Manual. BackOffice SBS only supports being installed using Manual Configuration.
Which path should a new administrator use at a remote site installing SCO UnixWare 7.1 on a ProLiant server? He has little experience in setting up servers.	Assisted Integration. This is an easy path to install any supported operating system. It also provides help during all critical points of the SmartStart installation.
Which path should I use if I have eight ProLiant servers with identical hardware? They will all be running NetWare 5.	Assisted Integration. Unfortunately, NetWare 5 does not support a Replicated Install.
Which path should I use if I have eight ProLiant servers with identical hardware? They will all be running Windows NT Server 4.0.	Assisted Integration for the first server and create a replication disk. Use a Replicated Install for the remaining servers.
I installed Windows NT Server 4.0 on an existing server. How should I install Windows NT on another partition as a recovery option in case the primary installation fails?	Install from Microsoft Media only. Since the system is already configured, you cannot use SmartStart to install the second version of Windows NT. You will have to install from the Windows NT CD and specify the second partition to install NT.

Server Profile Diskette

After you select Assisted Integration, you are prompted to insert the Server Profile Disk. The Server Profile Disk is used by the SmartStart program for temporary storage of information. For example, the SmartStart program must reboot the server several times and uses the Server Profile Disk to track where the program is in the installation process. Therefore, it is very important to leave the Server Profile Disk in the disk drive until you are prompted to remove the disk. Otherwise, the SmartStart installation may fail.

You can find the Server Profile Disk in the back of the Server Setup and Management Pack that ships with the server. You can even use the same Server Profile Disk on different servers since they are not server specific. Unfortunately, you cannot simply use just any blank disk. If you happen to lose your Server Profile Disk, you can download an image from the Compaq Web site to create a profile disk. The URL to the Web site is: http://www.compaq.com/support/files/server/softpaqs/mgmtsol/stprofdsk.html.

Choose Operating System

In the next screen that appears, SmartStart prompts you to choose an operating system to install. All supported operating systems are displayed sorted by manufacturer. To continue with a Windows NT installation, expand the Microsoft folder and place a check mark next to Windows NT Server 4.0 and click Next.

You will be asked to verify your choice of operating system. Click Next to continue.

System Configuration and Disk Configuration

SmartStart will next launch the System Configuration utility and automatically detect and configure your hardware. At one point, you will be able to review the modifications that SmartStart made or continue with the installation.

If you have an array controller installed in the server, SmartStart will automatically launch the Array Configuration Utility so that you can configure your hard disks. Refer to Chapter 9 for more information on drive array technology. The Array Configuration Utility will prompt you through the steps necessary to configure your drive arrays.

Once you have your drives configured, SmartStart will format the first partition and create the System Partition. The System Partition contains the System Configuration Utility, the Server Diagnostics program, as well as other Compaq utilities. After SmartStart formats the partition, it will copy the appropriate program files to the partition.

The server will reboot several times during these procedures. It is important that you keep both the SmartStart CD and the Server Profile Disk in the server during the reboots.

Compaq Products and Windows NT Configuration

After SmartStart copies files to the system partition, it will prompt you through several screens to configure options for the server. These options include settings for Compaq programs (such as Insight Manager) and Windows NT-specific options. Since the process is presented in a wizard-like manner, you can move back and forth between the screens by clicking either Back or Next.

The first screen that you will see prompts you to indicate whether you will be installing software from CD only or from CD and an Integration Server. In brief, an integration server acts as a central storage repository for all Compaq software. (For more information on Integration Servers, refer to Chapter 26.) If you elect to install software from an integration server, you will be prompted for an IP address for your server and for the Integration Server. You will also be prompted for the password for the CPQIS user to connect to the Integration Server. Using SmartStart and an Integration Server is discussed in more depth later in the chapter.

The next screen will display the software that SmartStart automatically selected to install on the server, based on the server hardware. You can select additional software to install or deselect software so that it will not be installed. After you click Next, SmartStart displays a screen showing the software that will be installed on the server. The screen also displays the source location for the software, indicating whether the software will be installed from a CD or an Integration Server (if one was configured).

After you click Next to continue, SmartStart copies files to the disk and may prompt you to insert certain disks, such as the Compaq Management CD.

Replication Disk

After the files are copied to the disk, SmartStart prompts you to create a Replication Disk. Recall that one of the paths that you can take in SmartStart is a Replicated Installation. The Replicated Installation uses a replication disk to store all configuration options when you install a server. You can use this replication disk to build additional servers with identical hardware quickly.

Note that "identical" in this case really means identical. The servers on which you will use the replication disk must be configured exactly as the original server. This includes number of processors and speeds, amount of memory, and number of disks. This also includes expansion cards and the slot in which they are installed.

You can store more than one server configuration (known as a *Replication Profile*) on the same Replication Disk. To use the Replication Disk, choose the Replicated Installation path at the beginning of the SmartStart installation. You can also boot the server with both the replication disk and the SmartStart CD in the server. SmartStart will ask for a minimum set of information (such as the date and time) and the Replication Profile. After SmartStart has the information, it will continue with the rest of the installation without any more intervention from the administrator (aside from swapping CDs when necessary).

After you create the Replication Disk, SmartStart will step you through a series of interviews to configure the Compaq options and Windows NT options.

Automatic Server Recovery

During this portion of SmartStart, you can configure the options for Automatic Server Recovery (ASR). ASR allows the server to detect when a failure has occurred on the server and take the appropriate action. For example, if Windows NT crashes with the blue screen of death, ASR will detect the fault and automatically reboot the server (known as *Software*

FROM THE FIELD

Streamline a Replicated Install Even Further

A replicated installation can greatly reduce the time it takes to build a server and also reduce user interaction with the setup program. However, you may have a need to customize and automate the Windows NT portion of the setup program even further. For example, you may want to install additional services or install to a different directory than the default C:\WINNT. To customize your setup, you must edit the UNATTEND.TXT file on the replication disk. The file is located in the \#intfiles directory, where # is the number corresponding to the replication profile that you want to modify. The UNATTEND.TXT file is a standard text file used in unattended installations for Windows NT. For more information on the options that you can configure in the unattended text file, refer to Microsoft Knowledge Base article Q155197. For more information on automating a Windows NT installation, visit the following Web site: http://www.microsoft.com/ntworkstation/technical/DeploymentDocs/DownGuideAutomate.asp.

(Thanks to Andres Campos for his help on this topic.)

—Roneil Icatar, MCSE, MCP+I, ASE

Recovery). You can select whether the server should boot back into the operating system or into the Compaq diagnostics. Generally, you should select that the server boot into the operating system so that the server services are restored as quickly as possible. However, if you are having frequent crashes, you may want the server to boot automatically into the system utilities, to allow you to diagnose any problems.

You can also set options for thermal shutdown, which automatically shuts down the server when it reaches a certain threshold temperature. Shutting down the server during overheating will prevent damage to the server components caused by the heat.

During my days as a LAN administrator for one company, the air conditioning in the computer room failed over the weekend. We had configured most of the servers to shut down in case of overheating, so they were fine. However, one server was not configured to shut down and was running when we finally came in Monday morning to the blisteringly hot computer room. We manually shut down the server until the air conditioning was restored to the computer room. Over the course of the next several months, we had hard drives and other server components fail at an unusually high rate and eventually had to replace the entire server. Lesson learned: Make sure you have the server configured to shut down before overheating!

Another ASR option that you can set is for an uninterruptible power supply (UPS). If you have a serial cable connecting a UPS to the server, you can have Windows NT shut down automatically if building power is lost and the UPS only has a small amount of power left. Having Windows NT shut down cleanly is much better than having it shut down abruptly if power is lost.

For more information on ASR, refer to Chapter 19, Compaq Server Management Technology.

Windows NT Server Options

SmartStart will prompt you for several options specific to Windows NT. The first screen will ask you for the boot partition information where Windows NT will be installed. You can select the size for the partition to be up to 4096MB. You can also choose the format for your partition to be either NTFS or FAT. You may ask yourself why I am limited to 4GB even though I have a 9GB disk and NTFS? Windows NT actually first starts off installing on a FAT partition, and during the setup converts to NTFS. Since FAT is limited to 4GB, the first Windows NT partition you create will also be limited to 4GB. Any other partitions that you create afterwards can be of any size.

The next screen will prompt you to choose the licensing mode for this server. You can choose either Per Seat or Per Server licensing. If you will be using Per Server licensing, you must also enter the number of licenses for this server.

On this same screen, you can select the role this server will play on your network. You can select to make this server a Primary Domain Controller (PDC), a Backup Domain Controller (BDC), or a member server. The choice you make here is very important because you may not be able to change the machine role after installation without reinstalling Windows NT completely. If you choose to make this server a PDC, you will effectively create a new domain. You'll be prompted for the domain name later in the installation. If you choose to make this server a BDC, you will be prompted for the name of the domain to join later in the installation. Finally, if you choose to make this server a member server, you will be prompted to join either a domain or a workgroup later in the installation.

Insight Agents Options

If you chose to install the Insight Agents, you will next be prompted to configure the agents. You can set three options. First, you can choose to enable or disable the agents. By default, the agents are enabled. Next, you can choose to enable the Enable Remote Reboot option. If you enable this option, which is disabled by default, you will be able to reboot the server remotely using either Insight Manager or a Web browser, if you have the Insight Web Agents installed. Finally, if you will be managing Compaq desktop machines, you can enable the Desktop Management option.

Diskette Builder

After you configure the Insight Agents, you will be prompted to run Diskette Builder to create diskettes with any of the Compaq software. You generally do not need to run Disk Builder at this time since all of the software will be installed from the CDs. You can run Disk Builder later by inserting the SmartStart CD into any PC. The CD is configured to auto-run Disk Builder.

Once you are finished with the SmartStart interviews, the SmartStart program will prompt you for the various CDs that it will need to copy files, including the Windows NT Server CD. After SmartStart finishes copying files to the hard drive, you will be prompted to remove the Windows NT

CD and the Server Profile Disk from the server and reboot. After the server reboots, SmartStart will continue with the graphical portion of the Windows NT setup.

Make sure you remove the Windows NT CD and the Server Profile Disk before rebooting. A coworker of mine accidentally left the Windows NT CD in the drive, then rebooted. Since the Windows NT CD is bootable, it began a whole new installation of Windows NT! My friend wondered why he had to answer questions that he had answered already. He also wondered why none of the Compaq drivers or utilities were installed. Needless to say, he had to restart SmartStart from scratch.

Windows NT Setup (Graphical)

After SmartStart copies the Windows NT files, the server will reboot several times. During this time, Windows NT will convert the primary partition to NTFS if you selected that option earlier. Eventually, you will reach the welcome screen for the graphical portion of the Windows NT setup. After the welcome screen, the license agreement screen appears. Click I Agree to continue with the installation.

The following exercise details the steps necessary to complete the graphical portion of the Windows NT installation.

EXERCISE 29-1

Windows NT Setup (Graphical)

1. Enter your name and organization information in the User Information window and press OK to continue. A screen will appear to verify the information. Press OK to continue, or press Back to modify the information.
2. Enter the CD key. You can obtain the CD key from the Windows NT Server CD or from the CD case. Press OK to continue.
3. Enter the name for the server. Press OK to continue.
4. If you are installing a PDC or a member server, you will be prompted to enter the password for Administrator. Enter the password in both password fields and press OK to continue.

5. Select whether this server will be connected to the network or not. (PDCs must be connected to the network.) You can also specify whether remote access services should be installed. The rest of this exercise assumes that you will connect to a network, but not install any remote services.
6. At the next screen, select whether you would like to install Internet Information Server (IIS) and press OK to continue.
7. Next, you will be prompted to install drivers for the network card(s) installed in your server. Press Detect to have the setup program automatically find the network cards and load the drivers. If the setup program does not detect your network card, click Add to select from a list of available drivers.
8. At the next screen, you can select the protocols to install on the server. By default, TCP/IP is enabled (and cannot be disabled). You can also select IPX/SPX and NetBEUI. Press OK to continue.
9. Next, you can select to install any additional network services. The core set of networking services is enabled by default and cannot be uninstalled. To add services, click the Add button.
10. The setup program then prompts you whether you want to use DHCP to configure an IP address for your server automatically. In general, you will probably want to assign an IP address for your servers statically, so you should select No. You will be prompted for IP address information later in the setup.
11. The SNMP configuration screen appears. Enter the appropriate options for SNMP for your network environment.
12. The TCP/IP properties window appears. Enter the appropriate IP information for your network environment and press OK to continue.
13. A message will appear stating that the network services are starting. Afterwards, you will be prompted to create a new domain (for PDCs) or the name of a domain/workgroup to join (for BDCs and member servers). To join a domain you will have to enter an administrator's name and password.
14. Next, you will be able to set the video controller settings for the server. On newer servers, at this point, the OEM version of

Windows NT does not have the proper drivers for the video cards. You will need to set your video options after SmartStart loads the proper video drivers and reboots.

15. Finally, you will be prompted to reboot the server.

When the server reboots, you will need to finish a couple of tasks that SmartStart did not complete. You will need to create your disk partitions using Disk Administrator since SmartStart only creates and formats the first partition. Second, you will have to perform any optimization (such as tuning the Server service and setting Foreground/Background service priority). These procedures are described in detail in Chapter 32, Windows NT Performance Tuning.

Also, you will need to create an Emergency Repair Disk. Although the SmartStart program updates the repair information (in C:\WINNT\REPAIR), it does not prompt you to create the disk. To create the disk, run the Emergency Repair Disk program (RDISK.EXE /S).

CERTIFICATION OBJECTIVE 29.02

Manual Configuration Versus Assisted Integration

The previous section stepped through an Assisted Integration installation of SmartStart. The Assisted Integration is the simplest method, but it is also the least flexible. For example, SmartStart will always install Windows NT onto the first partition that you create and install to the C:\WINNT directory. In addition, you may wish to install an operating system that does not support the Assisted Integration (see Table 29-1). If you need more flexibility in your installation, you can take the Manual Configuration path instead of the Assisted Integration path. This section will show you the steps to take during a Manual Configuration.

One major disadvantage to this method is that the Compaq-optimized device drivers are not automatically loaded by the Windows NT installation. You will have to install the software manually after you complete the base Windows NT install. (See Chapter 30 for more details on the Compaq software.) For example, Windows NT provides a device driver for the Compaq

Smart Array controller, but Compaq also provides a driver for the controller. Although the Microsoft driver will allow the controller to function properly, the Compaq driver adds several features such as the ability to hot-plug certain models. During the Assisted Integration, the proper Compaq driver is loaded automatically.

SmartStart Installation (Manual Configuration)

Follow these steps when performing a Manual Configuration of SmartStart.

EXERCISE 29-2

SmartStart Manual Configuration

1. The SmartStart process begins, as with the Assisted Integration, by booting to the SmartStart CD.
2. The first screen where you are required to respond prompts you for the language in which you'd like to run SmartStart. You can choose English, French, German, Italian, Spanish, or Japanese.
3. In the next screen, enter Regional Settings for the server. Enter the country, keyboard type, and the date and time. Click Next to continue with SmartStart.
4. On the next screen, select Manual Configuration for the SmartStart path.
5. The SmartStart installation continues, as in the Assisted Integration, by configuring the hardware.
6. If you have a Smart Array Controller installed, the Array Configuration Utility will run.
7. The server then reboots, formats the first partition, creates the System Partition, and copies the Compaq utilities to the System Partition.
8. You are then prompted to run Disk Builder. You can run Disk Builder if you'd like to create disks from the SmartStart CD.
9. Finally, SmartStart prompts you to continue with the operating system installation as specified by the OS manufacturer. In the case of Windows NT, you can simply put the NT CD in the server and reboot.

10. Follow the Windows NT installation as specified in the Windows NT manual.

Once you have completed the Windows NT installation, you will still have to install the Compaq software if you'd like to take advantage of their advanced management capabilities. The following is a list of applications that you will have to install manually if you installed Windows NT using the Manual Configuration path of SmartStart. For more information on each of these applications, refer to Chapter 30, Compaq and Windows NT Support.

- Server Support Disk (SSD) for Windows NT
- Insight Agents
- Survey Utility
- Integration Maintenance Utility (to upgrade software from an Integration Server)
- Array Configuration Utility (if you have a Smart Array Controller installed)
- Power Supply Viewer (if you have hot-plug redundant power supplies installed)
- Updated device drivers (SCSI, NIC, and video)

In addition, you will have to update the Emergency Repair information and create an Emergency Repair Disk (ERD). To update the Emergency Repair information, run RDISK /S from a command prompt. You can also use this program to create or update an Emergency Repair Disk.

CERTIFICATION OBJECTIVE 29.03

Using an Integration Server

During the SmartStart installation, SmartStart asks you whether you would like to install software from just a CD or from an Integration Server and a

CD. In Chapter 26, you learned that an Integration Server is simply a central repository where you can store all Compaq software. You only need to update the software in one location and use this server to load software on all your servers. You can use an Integration Server to load software onto your server at the time of installation using SmartStart. The advantages to using an Integration Server include:

- You only need to update software in one place
- You don't need to carry around multiple CDs (no need to swap CDs during setup)
- Downloading software updates from the Internet is free
- SmartStart that comes with server may not always have latest software versions

The disadvantages include:

- You need network connectivity at the time of installation
- You need more time initially to set up Integration Server
- You need time to keep Integration Server up-to-date

Installing with SmartStart

This section outlines the information that you will need to install software from an Integration Server during the SmartStart process. Recall that during the SmartStart setup, you are asked whether you would like to install software from just the CD-ROM or from an Integration Server and the CD-ROM. If you select the latter option, another screen appears, prompting for information regarding the Integration Server and protocol information. Since you will be installing software over the network, SmartStart must load network card drivers and configure an IP address. Table 29-2 lists the information that you must configure.

After you enter all of the required information, click Next. SmartStart first needs to reboot to start the network card with the configured IP address, then continues with the rest of the server setup.

TABLE 29-2

Integration Server Configuration Options

Option	Description
Integration Server Name	Enter the computer name of the Integration Server
Server IP Address	Enter the IP address for the Integration Server
Local IP Address	Enter the IP address for the server that you are currently building
Subnet Mask	Enter the Subnet Mask that you are using on the network
Default Gateway	If you are accessing an Integration Server on a remote network, you will need to enter a default gateway

When you reach the product selection screen, you will see products that reside on both the SmartStart CD and the Integration Server. Select the appropriate versions of software that you'd like to install.

On the next screen where you verify the software to install, you can see the source location for the products that you will install. Software that will be installed from the Integration Server will be marked as having a source location of the Integration Server.

Software Maintenance on Existing Installations

You can also use an Integration Server once the server is in place to upgrade your server software. Compaq provides the Compaq Integration Maintenance Utility (CIMU) to allow you to download software from an Integration Server. This section will drill down into the steps necessary to update software from an Integration Server on an existing server.

EXERCISE 29-3

Updating Software from an Integration Server

1. Log onto the server using an administrator's account.
2. Click Start | Programs | Compaq Products and Services | Compaq Integration Maintenance Utility.
3. The first time you run the program, you will be prompted to select the language to run CIMU. Select your appropriate language.

FIGURE 29-1

To use an Integration Server, map a drive to the server's CPQIS share

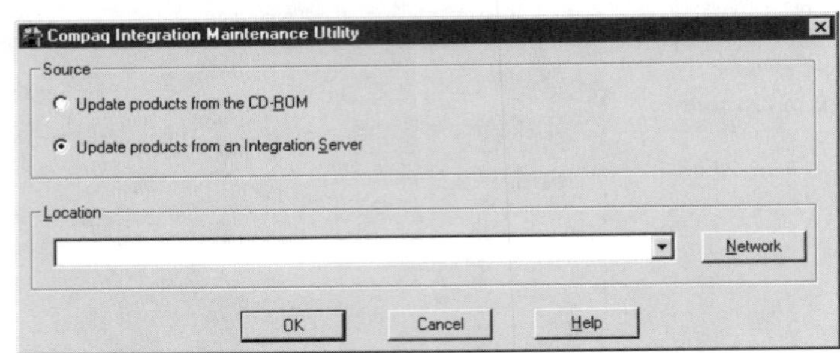

4. The first window you will see is the Compaq Integration Maintenance Utility window, shown in Figure 29-1. It prompts you whether you'd like to install software from the CD-ROM or from an Integration Server. Select Update Products From An Integration Server.
5. To load software from the Integration Server, you will have to first map a drive to that server. Click Network. The Map Network Drive window appears.
6. Select a drive to map and type in the path to the Integration Server (for example, **\\Server\CPQIS1**). You can also browse the network to find the appropriate CPQIS share.
7. Click OK to close the Map Network Drive window and return to the CIMU window.
8. The new mapped drive now appears in the Location field. Click OK. The Compaq Integration Maintenance Utility main window appears (see Figure 29-2).
9. Expand the Compaq tree and select the products that you'd like to install. As you select a product, you can view a description of the product on the right-hand side of the window. To see a list of the products and the order in which they will be installed, select the Products Selected tab.
10. If you select a product that is dependent on another product, you will receive a warning message, as shown in Figure 29-3.

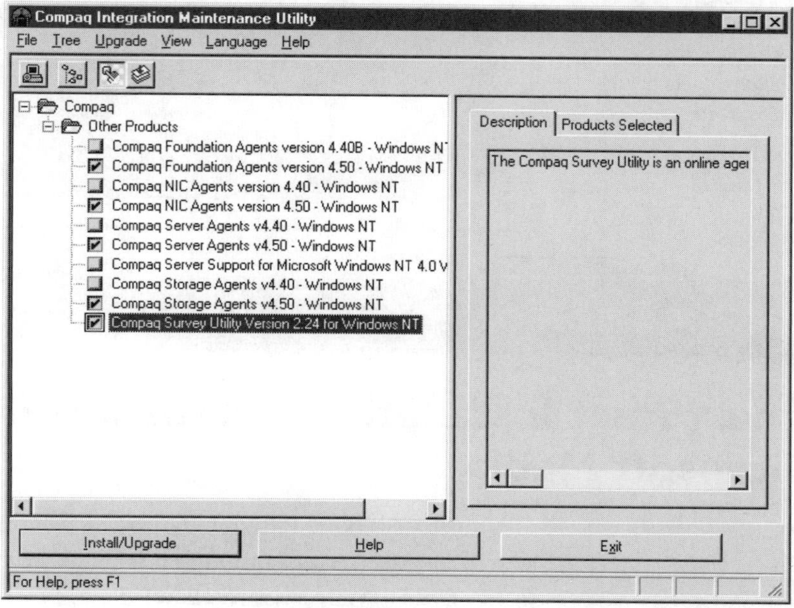

FIGURE 29-2

The CIMU main screen allows you to choose the products to install

11. When you have chosen all the products to upgrade, click Install/Upgrade to begin the upgrade.
12. The warning in Figure 29-4 appears, which states that although a certain product may prompt you to reboot after it installs, you shouldn't reboot until all products have been installed.
13. When all products have been installed, reboot the server.

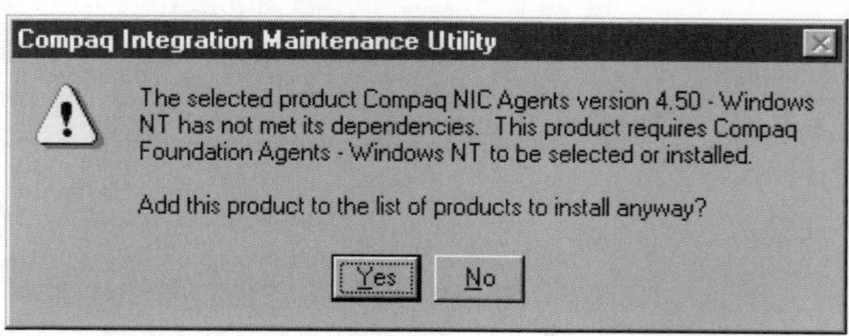

FIGURE 29-3

CIMU will warn you if a selected product requires another product to be installed

FIGURE 29-4

Don't reboot the server until all products have been installed

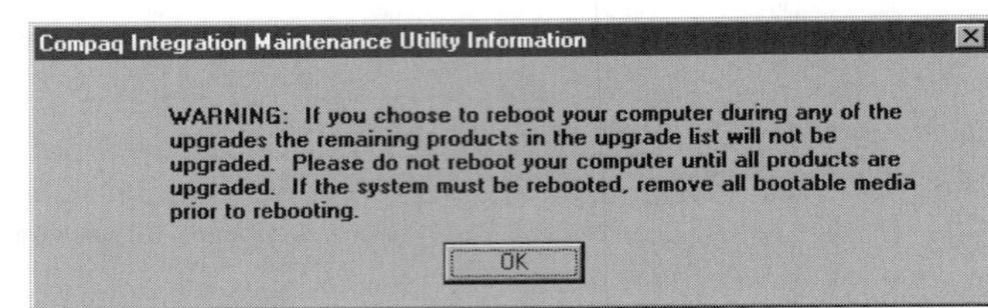

CERTIFICATION OBJECTIVE 29.04

SmartStart Installation Versus Installing from Microsoft Media

Of course, it is not a requirement to use SmartStart to install an operating system on your server (although it is highly recommended). The alternative to using SmartStart is to install Windows NT on the server manually, using traditional methods (such as booting to the Windows NT Server setup disk or booting directly to the Windows NT CD.) This section will outline the steps required to install Windows NT manually directly from the Windows NT CD without using SmartStart.

Hardware Configuration

At a minimum, you must first run the System Configuration Utility to have the server detect and configure all of the hardware installed on the server. To run System Configuration, you must first create the System Configuration disks by using the Disk Builder application. After you create the System Configuration disks, boot to the first disk to start the System Configuration Utility.

Note that you cannot boot to the SmartStart CD to run System Configuration. If you boot to the SmartStart CD on an unconfigured system, SmartStart will assume that you want to perform a SmartStart installation on the server.

Once System Configuration has detected and configured the server hardware, you can continue with the optional steps described here, or continue with the Windows NT installation as outlined in the next section, Manual Windows NT Installation and Configuration.

Configure Drive Arrays

If you have a Smart Array controller installed in the server, you first will have to configure your drive arrays before you copy any files to the hard drives. To configure the arrays, you have to run the Array Configuration Utility using the System Configuration Utility.

Create System Partition

Compaq also strongly suggests that you create a system partition on all servers. The system partition is used to store all Compaq-related programs and files, such as the System Configuration Utility and Server Diagnostics. By having the utilities installed on the system partition, the utilities run more quickly and you do not need to have any CDs or disks on hand to run them. During a SmartStart installation, the system partition is created automatically.

The first time you run the System Configuration Utility on a server, it will prompt you to create the system partition. If you choose not to create the partition, the System Configuration Utility will run from the diskettes. If you do choose to create the partition, the setup program will copy the System Configuration Utility to the system partition and you can choose to either run the program from the system partition or from the diskettes.

If you'd like to create the system partition at a later time, simply run the System Configuration Utility again. From the main menu, select System Configuration. From the submenu, select System Partition | Create.

Install Server Diagnostics

Compaq also suggests that you install the Server Diagnostics program to the system partition so that the program will run more quickly and you do not have to locate the diagnostics disk when you want to perform tests on the server. To copy Server Diagnostics to the system partition, run the System Configuration Utility. From the main menu, select System Configuration. From the submenu, select System Partition | Upgrade. A list of utilities is shown that can be added to the system partition. Select the Server Diagnostics and press OK. Insert the Server Diagnostics disk when prompted.

Manual Windows NT Installation and Configuration

Once you have completed the preliminary setup, you can run the Windows NT setup program as you normally would. You could either boot to the three Windows NT setup disks, or if your server supports a bootable CD-ROM, you can boot directly to the Windows NT Server CD. Refer to the Windows NT User Manual for details on the installation.

Just as with the SmartStart Manual Configuration, you may have to install the following Compaq drivers and applications, depending on the hardware installed on your server.

- Server Support Disk (SSD) for Windows NT
- Insight Agents
- Survey Utility
- Integration Maintenance Utility (to upgrade software from an Integration Server)
- Array Configuration Utility (if you have a Smart Array Controller installed)
- Power Supply Viewer (if you have hot-plug redundant power supplies installed)
- Updated device drivers (SCSI, NIC, and video)

You will also have to update the Emergency Repair information and the Emergency Repair Disk by running RDISK /S.

CERTIFICATION OBJECTIVE 29.05

SmartStart Subscription

Periodically, Compaq releases updated versions of their software. This software is generally available for download from their Web site. Your current version of SmartStart may be outdated by the time you build your next server. In addition, you may not have a fast Internet connection that allows you to download the hundreds of megabytes of information. Compaq allows you to purchase a SmartStart Subscription so that they will send you the latest version of the SmartStart CD and the Management CD when they become available. The subscription lasts for one year.

If you are reading this book, you are probably working to obtain your ASE. Another incentive for earning your ASE is that you receive a free subscription to SmartStart.

CERTIFICATION SUMMARY

In this chapter, you learned that the SmartStart program developed by Compaq allows you quickly and easily to set up a server using a tested and proven set of instructions. SmartStart is a set of interview screens that prompts you for certain information on how you'd like to have your server set up. Since SmartStart follows a given path, you are assured that you do not miss any critical steps during your setup.

For the most thorough and simplest path, you can follow the Assisted Integration path. If you need more flexibility in the installation and need to install the operating system manually, you can run the Manual Configuration Path. Finally, if you have several identical servers, you can run a Replicated Installation.

Finally, you learned that you can purchase a subscription to SmartStart to make sure that you have the latest versions of software available on CD.

TWO-MINUTE DRILL

- ❑ SmartStart is a program developed by Compaq to aid the network administrator in building Compaq servers consistently and efficiently.
- ❑ SmartStart's wizard-like approach simplifies the installation of servers by walking the administrator through several screens for configuring the hardware and operating system.
- ❑ SmartStart is packaged as a bootable CD that is shipped with every ProLiant and ProSignia server.

- SmartStart provides three paths that you can follow when installing the OS on your server: Assisted Integration, Manual Configuration, and Replicated Install.
- The Server Profile Disk is used by the SmartStart program for temporary storage of information.
- SmartStart will launch the System Configuration utility and automatically detect and configure your hardware.
- The Assisted Integration installation of SmartStart is the simplest method, but it is also the least flexible.
- If you need more flexibility in your installation, you can take the Manual Configuration path instead of the Assisted Integration path.
- One major disadvantage to Manual Configuration is that the Compaq-optimized device drivers are not automatically loaded by the Windows NT installation.
- You can use an Integration Server to load software onto your server at the time of installation using SmartStart.
- You can also use an Integration Server once the server is in place to upgrade your server software.
- Compaq provides the Compaq Integration Maintenance Utility (CIMU) to allow you to download software from an Integration Server.
- The alternative to using SmartStart is to install Windows NT on the server manually, using traditional methods.
- Just as with the SmartStart Manual Configuration, using the Manual Windows NT Installation and Configuration method, you may also have to install Compaq drivers and applications, depending on the hardware installed on your server.
- Compaq allows you to purchase a one-year SmartStart Subscription so that they will send you the latest version of the SmartStart CD and the Management CD when they become available.
- Another incentive for earning your ASE is that you receive a free subscription to SmartStart.

SELF TEST

The following Self Test questions will help you measure your understanding of the material presented in this chapter. Read all the choices carefully, as there may be more than one correct answer. Choose all correct answers for each question.

1. Which of the following is not part of the Server Setup and Management Pack?

   A. SmartStart CD

   B. Management CD

   C. Windows NT CD

   D. Server Profile Disk

2. What is the minimum amount of memory required to run a SmartStart installation?

   A. 16MB

   B. 24MB

   C. 32MB

   D. 64MB

3. You boot an older Compaq server with the SmartStart CD in the drive. You receive the error message that the disk is not bootable and to insert a bootable disk. You've tried this same CD in another server and it worked fine. How can you fix the problem?

   A. Update the system ROM.

   B. Replace the CD-ROM.

   C. Create a boot disk.

   D. Boot to the Server Profile Disk.

4. Which SmartStart installation path provides the most flexibility?

   A. Assisted Integration

   B. Manual Configuration

   C. Replicated Installation

5. You have 10 servers to set up for remote offices. Each of the servers is configured identically. Which is the fastest method for deploying these servers?

   A. Assisted Integration

   B. Disk Cloning

   C. Manual Configuration

   D. Replicated Installation

6. Which of the following operating systems does not support the Assisted Integration path for SmartStart?

   A. Windows NT Server 4.0

   B. Windows NT Server 4.0, Enterprise Edition

   C. Windows NT Server 4.0, Terminal Server Edition

   D. Novell NetWare 5

7. What is the purpose of the Server Profile Disk?

   A. Temporary storage for SmartStart

   B. Used for Replicated Install

   C. Storing emergency repair information

   D. Storing copy of server configuration

8. What is stored on the system partition?
   A. Windows NT system files
   B. Compaq system utilities
   C. Emergency repair information
   D. Windows NT boot files
9. Which of the following is not a part of Automatic Server Recovery (ASR)?
   A. Software Recovery
   B. Thermal Shutdown
   C. Emergency Repair Disk (ERD)
   D. UPS Shutdown
10. What is the largest size you can make the primary Windows NT partition during a SmartStart installation?
    A. 250MB
    B. 4GB
    C. 4GB if formatted FAT, unlimited if formatted NTFS
    D. Unlimited
11. What is the best way to create an Emergency Repair Disk?
    A. Copy REPAIR directory to a floppy disk.
    B. Run ERDDISK.EXE.
    C. Run RDISK.EXE.
    D. Run NTBACKUP.EXE.
12. In which of the following cases would you perform a Manual Configuration install of SmartStart?
    A. You need to create a Windows NT partition greater than 4GB.
    B. You need to create a custom Administrator's password.
    C. You need to install Windows NT Server 4.0, Enterprise Edition.
    D. You need to install Windows NT to D:\NTSRV4.
13. One advantage to using an Integration Server is:
    A. You update software in only one place.
    B. You don't need network connectivity at time of installation.
    C. You don't have to keep Integration Server up-to-date.
    D. You don't need much time to set up Integration Server.
14. Which of the following is not necessary to configure if you are installing software from an Integration Server during SmartStart?
    A. Server IP address
    B. Local IP address
    C. Default gateway
    D. Subnet mask
15. You have decided not to use SmartStart to build your server. At a minimum, what do you have to do before installing Windows NT?
    A. Format hard disk.
    B. Run System Configuration Utility.
    C. Create Windows NT setup disks.
    D. Create system partition.

ASE

ACCREDITED SYSTEMS ENGINEER

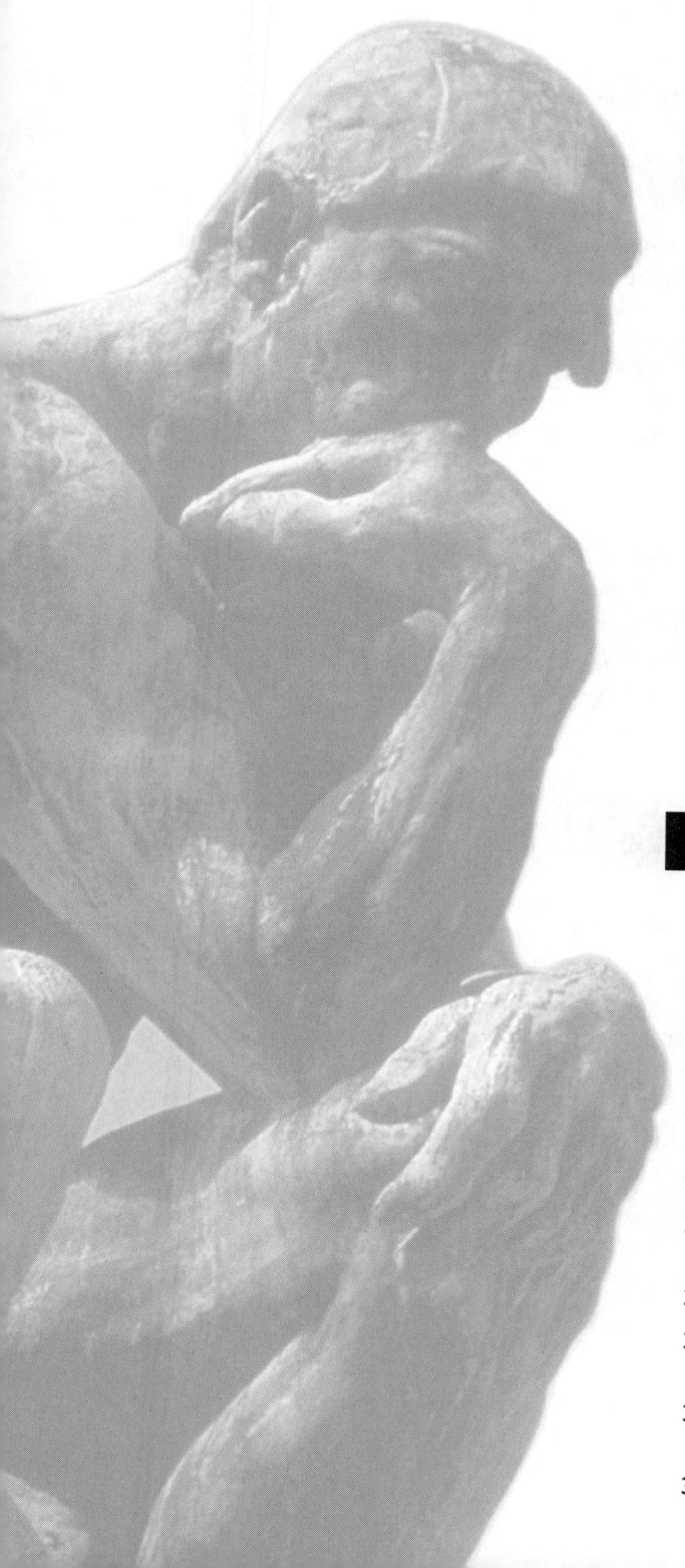

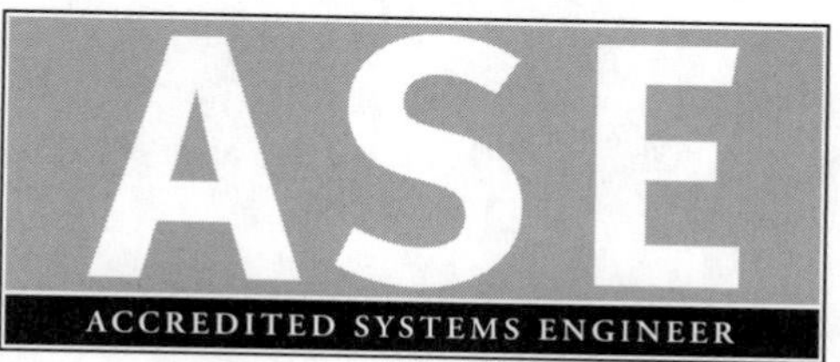

30

Compaq and Windows NT Support

CERTIFICATION OBJECTIVES

30.01	Compaq Server Support Diskettes for Windows NT
30.02	HALs Provided by Compaq
30.03	Compaq Systems Management Driver for Windows NT
30.04	Compaq Devices Supported in Windows NT
30.05	Compaq Device Drivers
30.06	Supporting the Compaq UPS with Windows NT
30.07	Compaq ProLiant Storage System
30.08	Upgrading a SmartStart Windows NT 3.51 and Windows NT 4.0 Installation
30.09	Configuring the Insight Agents Control Panel
30.10	Compaq Utilities

Microsoft's Windows NT and Windows 2000 have become the most popular network operating systems in the world. More and more companies deploy Windows NT-based networks every year and many of them use Compaq servers to deploy the OS. Compaq has worked intimately with Microsoft to make sure that Windows NT will run optimally on the Compaq hardware. Compaq has a working relationship with Microsoft to make sure that all of the Compaq hardware passes the Hardware Compatibility Testing that Microsoft uses to ensure that NT will run on the server. Compaq has also taken a step further by writing custom drivers and applications to maximize NT performance and manageability on their hardware.

This chapter will help you become familiar with the various methods that Compaq uses to provide Windows NT support on their servers. We will cover the drivers that Compaq provides for their various hardware components (network cards and tape drives, for example), as well as the custom applications that Compaq provides to manage their hardware.

CERTIFICATION OBJECTIVE 30.01

Compaq Server Support Diskettes for Windows NT

The Compaq Server Support Diskettes (SSD) for Windows NT contain custom drivers and utilities developed by Compaq to optimize the use of their servers in a Windows NT network environment. The SSD will be your primary tool for installing and updating the Compaq device drivers that will be discussed in this chapter. Therefore, you must first become familiar with the SSD program. This section will introduce you to the SSD program, and explain how to obtain it and how to use it. You can run the SSD program to update the drivers on all the servers in your environment from a single PC.

Obtaining the SSD

By default, when you install a server using SmartStart, all of the custom Compaq drivers and utilities will be loaded automatically. If you have the SmartStart CD, you can create the Server Support Diskettes using the Diskette Builder application. If you did not use SmartStart or if you need to update the drivers and utilities, you can obtain the latest SSD from the Compaq Web site at www.compaq.com. After you download the self-extracting compressed file, you can extract the files to a temporary directory on your server (or the PC from which you want to run the program).

Running the SSD

To install the drivers on the SSD, you run the setup program (SETUP.EXE) from the extracted files. From the SSD main screen (see Figure 30-1), you will see a list of available drivers and utilities. An icon to the left of each driver or utility shows whether it is installed and whether the latest version is installed. A gray icon indicates that the driver is not installed, a yellow icon indicates that the driver is installed but not the latest version, and a green icon indicates that the latest version of the driver is installed. If a driver is not the latest version, you can also view what version is currently installed and what version is available on the SSD.

To install or update a component, select the component in the list, then click the Update or Install button. To remove a driver, select the driver and click Remove.

You can view an activity report of the drivers and utilities that have been modified by clicking Activity Report. This is a convenient method for keeping a change log—a history of all driver updates that have been performed on the server.

In addition, you can update drivers and utilities remotely by selecting Computer | Select from the menu or pressing the Select Computer icon. You then type in the name of the remote server that you want to update or you can browse the network for the server.

FIGURE 30-1

The SSD Main Screen shows all Compaq drivers currently loaded

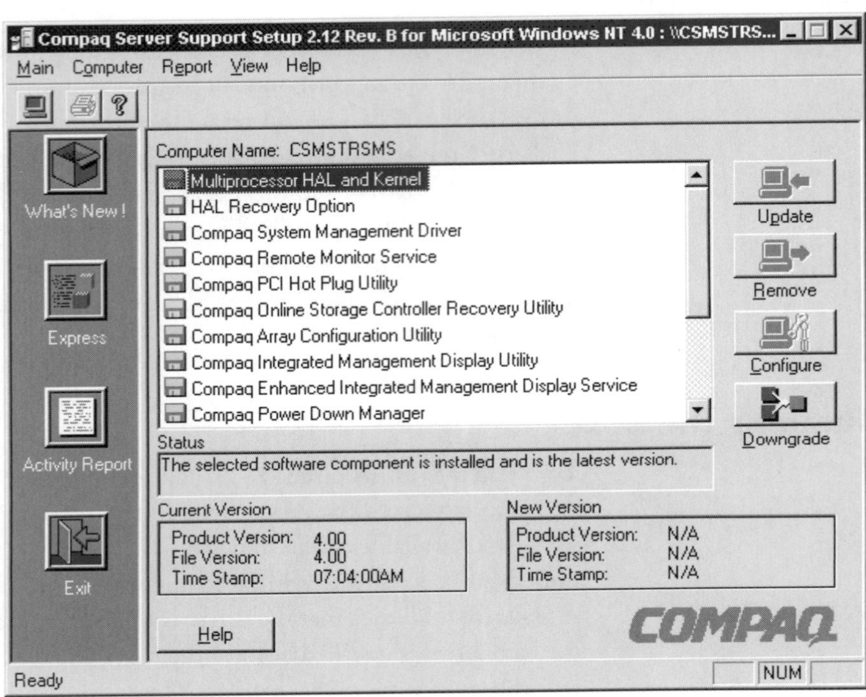

Finally, you can click Express to run an express setup of the SSD. In Express mode (see Figure 30-2), the setup program will automatically determine which components need to be updated (as well as their dependencies) and display them in a list. The program also lists additional components that may be installed if you desire, but will not automatically be installed. You can manually choose to install these components by placing a check box next to the component. Click Update to install all selected components.

With either the custom setup or the express setup, you must reboot the server in order for the changes to take effect.

FIGURE 30-2

The SSD Express Mode automatically selects which software should be installed

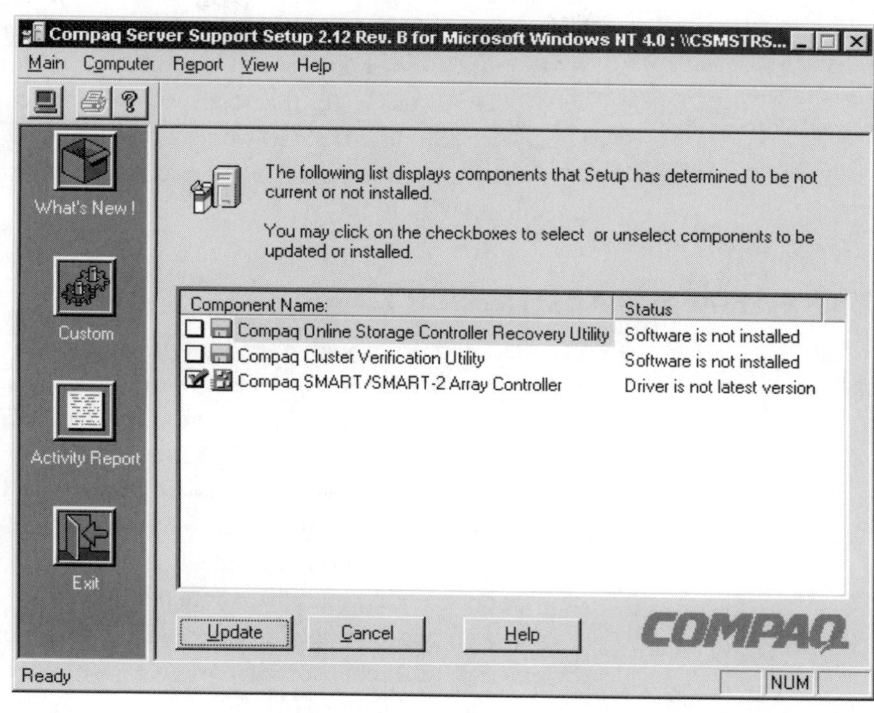

CERTIFICATION OBJECTIVE 30.02

HALs Provided by Compaq

The Hardware Abstraction Layer (HAL), in essence, hides the hardware from the rest of the operating system. The OS accesses the hardware through the HAL, which in turn performs the requested functions on the hardware. This section will discuss the HAL in detail with respect to the Compaq servers. We will look into the advanced features of the custom HALs that Compaq developed for earlier versions of NT. Additionally, we will discuss the HALs that Compaq uses with current versions of NT. Finally, we will discuss a new feature from Compaq called the HAL Recovery Option, which allows you to recover a system that has a corrupted HAL.

The Hardware Abstraction Layer

The HAL is a driver with a set of routines that directly manipulates the hardware in the server. Since all applications must access hardware through the HAL, the applications do not need to have specific information about the hardware. The HAL gives Windows NT a modularity that allows a third-party vendor to write a completely new HAL to take advantage of specific hardware without having to rewrite the end user applications. The HAL also allows hardware manufacturers to write a single device driver that can run on many different hardware platforms.

Microsoft has developed different HALs that allow Windows NT to run on servers with Intel processors, or servers with Compaq's Alpha processor. There is also a different HAL for multiprocessor servers.

Windows NT 3.x

With earlier versions of Windows NT (prior to 4.0), Compaq developed their own custom HAL that replaced the HAL that shipped with Windows NT. The custom HAL included advanced features that supported the Compaq servers. The custom HAL was installed using the Compaq Server Support Diskettes discussed later in the chapter. The Compaq HALs added the following enhancements:

- Support for Insight Manager manageability

- Error logging support through the Systems Management driver
- Built-in mechanisms for Compaq device drivers to dynamically call the HAL and detect which updates were applied to correct potential error conditions
- The Compaq multiprocessor (MP) HAL provides support for distributing interrupts across all processors. With the Microsoft MP HAL, only the first processor would service hardware interrupts.
- Power management for Compaq laptops
- Notification during system boot up that indicates the Compaq HAL version that is installed
- Capability to print to an LPT port during a blue screen of death
- Capability to tune the time slice for all system threads

Table 30-1 lists the custom HALs that Compaq provides for their servers. Although each HAL has a different name, it is renamed to HAL.DLL during installation.

TABLE 30-1 Compaq Custom HALs for NT 3.*x*

HAL	Description
HALISA.DLL	Used for servers with the ISA bus architecture installed
HALUP.DLL	Used for servers with an EISA bus architecture and with a single processor
HALSP.DLL	Used for older servers that were multiprocessor capable. This included the Systempro series and the ProLiant 2000, 4000, and 4500.
HALMPS.DLL	Used for multiprocessor servers that support the Multiprocessor Specifications

Windows NT 4.0 and Later

With Windows NT 4.0 and later, Compaq did not create a custom HAL and instead uses the HALs supplied by Microsoft on the NT CD. This applies to both the single-processor version and the multiprocessor versions. When Windows NT is installed on a Compaq server, the appropriate HAL is installed for the server platform.

Upgrading from a Single Processor to a Multiprocessor

If you upgrade your server by adding more processors, you will have to upgrade the HAL in order for NT to utilize the additional processors. Remember that because the HAL is replaceable, you will not need to reinstall the entire operating system in order for the system to recognize the additional processors. To upgrade the HAL, you will have to use the Compaq Server Support Diskette (SSD) for NT. The process for upgrading the HAL is outlined here, although a more detailed discussion of the SSD is written in a later section. Note that you can use the same steps to downgrade a server from multiprocessor to a single processor.

The following exercise outlines the steps necessary to upgrade a server to use the multiprocessor HAL for Windows NT. This assumes that you are running SSD version 2.12B or later (which is the latest version at the time of this writing).

EXERCISE 30-1

Upgrading to a Multiprocessor HAL

1. Log on to Windows NT with administrative privileges.
2. Run the setup program for the SSD (SETUP.EXE). The Custom Installation screen for the SSD appears as in Figure 30-1.
3. To upgrade the server to support multiple processors, select Upgrade. To downgrade the server from multiprocessor to a single processor, select Downgrade.
4. Insert the Windows NT CD or the Service Pack CD when prompted. You can also specify an alternate location if you have the source files located on a hard disk.
5. Exit the program and reboot the server when prompted.

If you are planning to remove a processor from the server so that it only has one processor, you should downgrade the HAL to the uniprocessor version BEFORE you remove the processor. If you do not, you may experience a HAL mismatch that can prevent Windows NT from booting. If this happens, you can reinstall the second processor and rerun the SSD setup to downgrade the HAL or you can run the HAL Recovery Option as discussed in the next section.

HAL Recovery Option

The Compaq SSD provides the HAL Recovery Option as a method for you to boot your server in the event that the Windows NT HAL becomes corrupted or damaged. The HAL Recovery Option also allows you to recover from a situation where you remove all but one processor from a system but are still running the multiprocessor HAL, which results in a blue screen trap error. You install the HAL Recovery Option using the SSD setup program by selecting it in the Custom Installation screen (as shown in Figure 30-1) and selecting Install. Choosing this option creates a copy of the uniprocessor HAL and kernel files.

The HAL Recovery Option adds a new line to the boot menu when NT starts titled Windows NT Server Version 4.0 [HAL Recovery Mode]. The modified entry in the BOOT.INI file uses the following switches:

- /basevideo
- /HAL=UPHAL.DLL
- /KERNEL=UPKERNEL.EXE
- /CPQRCV=1

(For an explanation of the BOOT.INI and available switches, refer to the later section, "BOOT.INI File.") If you select the Recovery Mode during the system bootup, NT will start using the backup copy of the uniprocessor HAL and kernel files that were created when you installed the Recovery Option.

CERTIFICATION OBJECTIVE 30.03

Compaq Systems Management Driver for Windows NT

Compaq provides a systems management driver that can perform advanced management of your server and Automatic Server Recovery (ASR). The driver, SYSMGMT.SYS, is part of Compaq's Windows NT Server Support Diskettes (SSD). The advanced management features provided by the management driver include:

- Logging critical errors for server components (such as processors and hard disks)
- Automatic Server Recovery
- Automatically shutting down the server in case of extreme heat
- Logging corrected memory errors
- Operating as a Remote Console
- Rebooting the server remotely via Insight Manager
- Executing a script during system shutdown

Loading the Driver

The Systems Management driver is installed by default if you perform a SmartStart installation of your server. If you did not use the SmartStart method for installation, you will have to install the driver manually using the SSD setup program. You will also have to use the SSD setup program if you want to upgrade the management driver.

EXERCISE 30-2

Loading the Compaq Systems Management Driver

1. Run the Setup program from the Compaq SSD.
2. From the list of drivers, select Compaq Systems Management Driver.
3. Select Install or Upgrade.
4. Reboot the server when prompted.

BOOT.INI File

The BOOT.INI file is a special file that Windows NT uses when it boots to generate the startup menu when NT first loads. Windows NT also uses the BOOT.INI file to configure several startup options that we will discuss in this section. These startup options are useful for troubleshooting and debugging.

BOOT.INI Contents

The BOOT.INI file is a simple text file that resides in the root of the boot partition. A sample BOOT.INI file is shown here.

```
[boot loader]
timeout=30
default=multi(0)disk(0)rdisk(0)partition(1)\WINNT
[operating systems]
multi(0)disk(0)rdisk(0)partition(1)\WINNT="Windows NT
Server Ver 4.0"
multi(0)disk(0)rdisk(0)partition(1)\WINNT="Windows NT
Server Ver 4.0 [VGA mode]" /basevideo /sos
```

The file is broken down into two sections: [boot loader] and [operating systems]. The boot loader section specifies which OS is selected by default when the server first boots. The timeout value is the number of seconds the menu will be displayed before the default selection is automatically used. The values for these two settings can be set in the Control Panel | System applet. Open the Startup/Shutdown tab, shown here, and modify the values in the System Startup section.

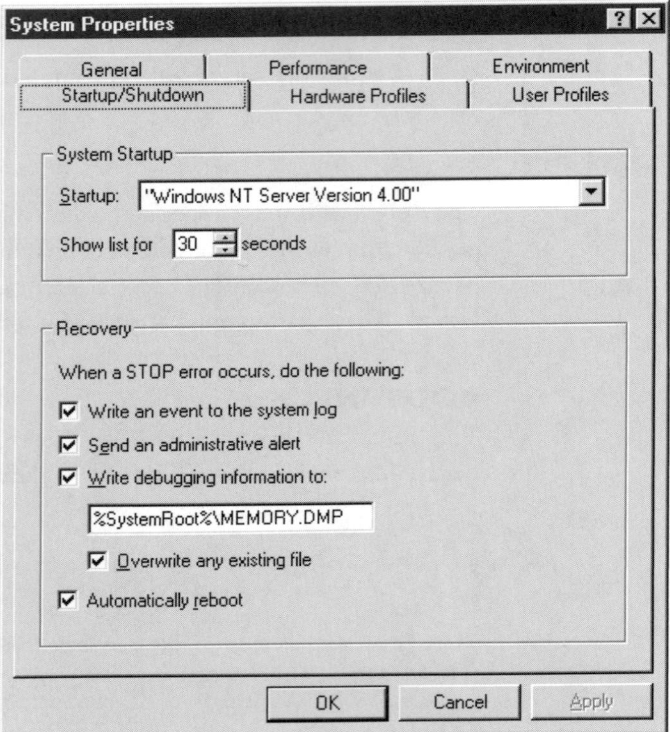

The operating systems section lists the available operating systems on the server as well as the physical disk and partition from which the OS loads. You can also specify the display name for the OS that will be shown in the startup menu.

BOOT.INI Switches

This section will describe the available switches that you can use for loading Windows NT. These switches are seldom used except for troubleshooting purposes. (The next section describes how to modify the BOOT.INI file.) Table 30-2 lists the available switches that you can use in the BOOT.INI file.

TABLE 30-2 BOOT.INI Switches

Switch	Description
/BASEVIDEO	Loads NT with the generic VGA video driver. You can use this switch if you suspect that a newly loaded video driver is preventing Windows NT from loading properly.
/BAUDRATE=nnnn	Sets the baud rate for the COM port when performing debugging
/CRASHDEBUG	Loads the debugger automatically when NT loads, but it remains inactive unless a Kernel error occurs
/DEBUG	Loads the debugger automatically when NT loads and remains running so that a host debugger can connect at any time to diagnose a problem
/DEBUGPORT=COM*x*	Specifies which COM port the host debugger is connected to
/MAXMEM:nn	Specifies the maximum amount of memory that Windows NT will use. This number is in megabytes (MB). This switch is useful if you suspect a faulty memory chip or if you want to test the effects of little memory in your system. This option should not be set to below 8MB or else Windows NT may not boot properly!
/NODEBUG	Does not load the debugger
/NOSERIALMICE=COM*x*	Instructs Windows NT to not look for a mouse on the COM ports. This is useful when a device other than a mouse (such as an Uninterruptible Power Supply) is connected to the COM port.
/SOS	Instructs Windows NT to display each device driver as it loads during the boot process. This is useful if you suspect that a specific driver is preventing NT from booting properly.
/HAL=filename.dll	Specifies an alternate file to use for the NT HAL
/KERNEL=filename.exe	Specifies an alternate file to use for the NT Kernel files

Modifying the BOOT.INI

As was stated earlier, you can specify the Timeout value and the Default OS value for the BOOT.INI using the System applet in Control Panel. To add any of the switches from the previous section, you will have to edit the BOOT.INI file manually. Before you can edit the BOOT.INI file, you will have to change its attributes.

EXERCISE 30-3

Modifying the BOOT.INI file

1. In My Computer or Windows Explorer, click View | Options.
2. On the Options tab, select Show All Files and click OK.
3. Select the BOOT.INI file, which should be in the root of the C: drive.
4. Select File | Properties.
5. On the General tab in the Attributes section, clear the Hidden, System, and Read Only options.
   Note: You can also change the attributes at a command prompt by typing:
   attrib –s –h –r c:\boot.ini
6. Open BOOT.INI file in Notepad.
7. After you make your changes, save the file and close Notepad.
8. Reset the file attributes (Hidden, System, and Read Only) to Enabled either by reversing Step 5 or by typing the following command at a Command Prompt:
   attrib +s +h +r c:\boot.ini

   Example: You want to add an entry to the boot menu that allows you to load Windows NT using only 32MB of RAM (even though you have 128MB installed) and the generic VGA driver. You also want Windows NT to display each device driver as it loads because you suspect that one of the drivers is causing NT to fail on boot. You would add the following line to the BOOT.INI file:

   multi(0)disk(0)rdisk(0)partition(1)\WINNT="Windows NT Server Ver 4.0 [Super Safe Mode]" /basevideo /sos /maxmem:32

Shutdown Script

The Systems Management driver allows you to perform shutdown tasks when the server shuts down through a batch file. The systems management driver calls the file %SYSTEMROOT%\SYSTEM32\CPQSHUT.CMD whenever the system is shut down. The shutdown can be the result of the user clicking Start | Shutdown, an application installation trying to reboot the server, the server overheating, or the user rebooting the server through Insight Manager. The following table lists some of the commands that you can add to the shutdown batch file.

Command	Description
NET STOP *servicename*	Stop a service
NET SEND *destination message*	Send a messenger service message to a particular computer
LOGEVENT.EXE	Resource Kit utility to write an event to the Windows NT Event Log

A special parameter (ABORT) is used if the shutdown is due to overheating. In this case, the script is given two minutes to run before the server will shut down, even if applications are still closing. During other, normal shutdowns, applications are given as much time as needed to close before the server shuts down. Therefore, you should make sure that any programs that you run during a shutdown can complete within two minutes in case the server shutdown is due to overheating.

CERTIFICATION OBJECTIVE 30.04

Compaq Devices Supported in Windows NT

Compaq builds a variety of components for their servers, and each of these components needs a driver to run under Windows NT. For most of these devices, Microsoft has developed a device driver that ships with NT. For maximum performance and manageability, Compaq has developed custom drivers for these devices. This section will discuss each of the Compaq server options and detail where you can find the best driver for each device. We will discuss the major device drivers in a later section.

Compaq Devices Supported with Windows NT Base Product

This section lists the Compaq products that are supported with the Windows NT base product. The drivers for these devices can be found on the Windows NT CD. Updates to these drivers can be found in the

Windows NT Service Packs. Compaq does not make a separate driver for any of these devices.

- SCSI tape devices (see next section)
- IDE CD-ROM drives
- SCSI CD-ROM drives
- Integrated PCI SCSI-2 controller

Compaq Tape Drives Supported by Windows NT

The drivers for most of the Compaq tape drives ship on the Windows NT CD and do not need to be downloaded from a Web site. The following tape drives are supported out of the box with Windows NT.

- Compaq 10/20-GB digital linear tape (DLT) drive
- Compaq 15/30-GB DLT drive
- Compaq 320-/525-MB tape drive
- Compaq 525-MB ACA tape drive
- Compaq 1.2-GB ACA tape drive
- Compaq 1.3-/2.0-GB digital audio tape (DAT) drive
- Compaq 5.0-GB DAT drive
- Compaq 2/8-GB TurboDAT drive
- Compaq 4/16-GB TurboDAT drive
- Compaq 12/24-GB DAT drive

The Compaq 35/70 DLT tape drive is supported, but you will need to download the driver from Compaq's Web site at the following address:

http://www.compaq.com/support/files/server/softpaqs/WINNT/dltdrnt.html

Tape Drives Not Supported

The following tape drives are not supported under Windows NT.

- Compaq 40-/60-MB tape drive

- Compaq 80-/120-MB tape drive
- Compaq 135-MB tape drive
- Compaq 150-/250-MB tape drive

Configuring Tape Drives in Windows NT Setup

Before you install the tape device drivers, you must make sure that you have the proper SCSI controller driver installed and configured. You can check the SCSI driver in Control Panel | SCSI Controllers. The following exercise demonstrates how to install a tape driver.

EXERCISE 30-4

Installing the Tape Device Driver

1. In Control Panel, open the Tape Devices applet.
2. Select the Drivers tab, shown here.

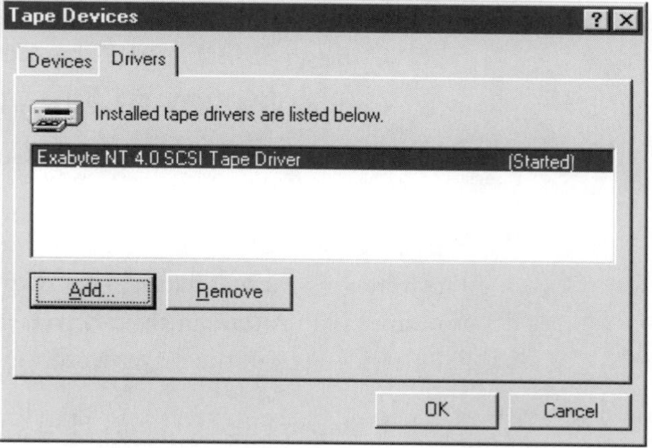

3. Click Add. A list of available tape device drivers appears.
4. Select the appropriate driver from the list and click OK.
5. Close the Tape Devices window.

Compaq Devices Supported with the SSD

This section covers the devices for which Compaq has developed updated drivers at the time of this writing (even though Microsoft has a driver built into the base NT product). The Compaq driver usually adds advanced functionality and manageability for the device. These features will be discussed in the next section, Compaq Device Drivers.

Array Controllers

The following SMART Array controllers are supported under the base Windows NT product. The Compaq drivers for these controllers should be used to take advantage of advanced capabilities of the controllers, including increased manageability.

- Compaq SMART Array 3100ES Controller
- Compaq SMART Array 3200 Controller
- Compaq SMART Array 221 Controller
- Compaq SMART-2DH Array Controller
- Compaq SMART-2/E Array Controller
- Compaq SMART-2/P Array Controller
- Compaq SMART/IDA-2/IDA/IAES Array Controllers
- Compaq SMART-2SL Array Controller

Fibre Channel

The following Fibre Channel Host Controllers are supported under Windows NT. Although these drivers are included with Windows NT Service Pack 4, the driver from the SSD should be loaded.

- Compaq Fibre Channel Host Controller/E
- Compaq Fibre Channel Host Controller/P

SCSI Controllers

The drivers for the following SCSI controllers can be found on the Compaq SSD.

- Compaq 64-Bit Dual Channel Wide-Ultra2 SCSI Controller

- Compaq Dual Channel Integrated Wide-Ultra SCSI-3 Controller
- Compaq Wide-Ultra SCSI-3 Controller
- Compaq 32-Bit Fast-Wide SCSI-2/E Controller
- Fast-SCSI-2 Controller
- Integrated 32-Bit Fast-SCSI-2/P Controller
- Integrated 32-Bit Fast-Wide SCSI-2/P Controller
- Integrated Wide-Ultra SCSI Controller

Network Cards

The drivers for the following network cards can be found on the Compaq SSD. For the advanced capabilities of the Compaq driver, refer to the later section Compaq Advanced Network Control Utility.

- Compaq NC1120 Ethernet NIC
- Compaq NC3120 Fast Ethernet NIC
- Compaq NC3122 Fast Ethernet NIC
- Compaq NC3160 Fast Ethernet NIC
- Compaq NC3161 Fast Ethernet NIC
- Compaq Netelligent 10 T/2 PCI UTP/Coax Controller
- Compaq Netelligent 10 T PCI UTP Controller
- Compaq Netelligent 10/100 TX PCI UTP Controller
- Compaq Netelligent Dual 10/100 TX PCI UTP Controller
- Compaq NetFlex-3/P Controller
- Compaq NetFlex-3/E Controller
- Compaq Netelligent 10/100 TX Embedded UTP/Coax Controller
- Compaq Netelligent 10/100 TX Embedded UTP/AUI Controller
- Compaq Netelligent 10/100 TX Embedded UTP Controller
- Compaq NetFlex-3 Embedded Controller

Video Adapters

The ATI RAGE IIC Video Display Controller video card driver is available on the Compaq SSD. All other video drivers for older video cards can be found in the base Windows NT product.

Compaq Devices Supported Only with the SSD

The following devices are supported only from the Compaq SSD. There is no built-in support in the standard NT product.

- Compaq Remote Insight Board
- Compaq Remote Insight Board/PCI
- Compaq ProLiant Storage Systems
- System Health Logs/Automatic Server Recovery

CERTIFICATION OBJECTIVE 30.05

Compaq Device Drivers

Although Microsoft provides device drivers for most of the Compaq hardware and peripherals, Compaq also provides device drivers that optimize the use of the hardware. Compaq's drivers may also provide extended capabilities and features (such as manageability with Insight Manager) that are not supported with Microsoft's drivers.

This section describes the major device drivers that Compaq provides for their hardware. We will list the basic features provided by the Microsoft driver, and the extended features provided by the Compaq version of the driver.

Supporting Compaq Insight Management Agents for Windows NT

The Compaq Insight Management Agents allow you to manage a server using any SNMP management utility such as Compaq Insight Manager.

The agents run as a service on any Compaq ProLiant or ProSignia server. They monitor and collect information about the different hardware components on the server. The following prerequisites need to be installed before the Insight Agents can be installed on a server.

- A minimum of 25MB free disk space
- Windows NT Server 3.51 with Service Pack 5 or Windows NT Server 4.0 with Service Pack 3 or greater
- TCP/IP
- SNMP Service
- Compaq Server Support Disk (SSD)

If you install TCP/IP or SNMP after a Windows NT Service Pack, you will have to reapply the service pack after you install TCP/IP or SNMP. In addition, if you install TCP/IP or SNMP after installing the Insight Agents, you will have to reinstall the agents after you install TCP/IP or SNMP. For more information on the Insight Agents, refer to Chapter 11, Software.

Supporting the Compaq SMART and SMART-2 Array Controller

The Compaq family of SMART Array controllers provides increased performance and fault tolerance for a server's hard disk subsystem. Although Microsoft develops a driver for the controllers, Compaq also develops a driver with increased functionality. The Compaq driver also allows you to manage the controller using the Insight Agents, and to track statistics and overall component health using Insight Manager. The Compaq driver also supports the PCI Hot Plug function that allows you to replace a controller if it fails while the server remains online.

Manually Installing the SMART Array Driver

If you use Compaq's SmartStart setup to install the server, the Compaq driver is automatically used during the Windows NT portion of the installation. However, if you do not use the SmartStart program, you must install the driver manually using the following steps.

EXERCISE 30-5

Manually Installing the SMART Array Driver

1. Begin the Windows NT Setup by using the three NT setup boot disks. Note that you *cannot* start the setup program by booting the Windows NT CD.
2. During the setup program, you will be prompted to press S to skip the detection of mass storage devices. Press S.
3. Press S again to specify additional devices.
4. From the list of devices that appears, select Other (Requires disk provided by a hardware manufacturer) and press ENTER.
5. Insert the Compaq SSD Disk 2 when prompted and press ENTER.
6. Select Compaq Disk Array and press ENTER.
7. Press ENTER to continue with the NT installation. Insert the SSD Disk 2 again when prompted.

Updating the Driver Using the SSD

This section describes how to update the driver using the SSD program. You may need to update the driver when Compaq releases newer versions of the driver. In addition, if you installed the array manually using the preceding exercise, the hot-plug functionality is not installed. You must first update the driver using the SSD program to obtain hot-plug functionality.

EXERCISE 30-6

Updating the Array Driver

1. Log on to NT with administrative rights.
2. Run the SSD setup program (SETUP.EXE) from the first SSD disk.
3. Select the Compaq SMART/SMART-2 Array Controller, then click Update.
4. Exit the SSD setup program.
5. Reboot the server when prompted.

CERTIFICATION OBJECTIVE 30.06

Supporting the Compaq UPS with Windows NT

A Compaq Uninterruptible Power Supply prevents a server from powering down suddenly due to a loss of power. The UPS has internal batteries that provide power to the server when the normal power supply is interrupted. The batteries only supply a finite amount of power and will eventually discharge, at which point the server will shut down abruptly.

Most UPSs nowadays can communicate with the server through a serial port via a communication cable that is provided with the UPS. The UPS also can come with software that can detect when a power outage has occurred and perform certain tasks such as notifying a management console or performing an orderly shutdown of the server.

This section will discuss the Compaq options for UPSs and how you can use these options to prevent your server from crashing unexpectedly from a loss of power.

Compaq Power Management Software

Every Compaq UPS comes with the Compaq Power Management Software (CPM) that allows you to manage a UPS that is connected to a server. CPM plugs into the Insight Manager console to provide a single seat for administering all functions of your servers. Just as the Insight Agents run on a server and allow you to monitor the hardware components on that server, the Compaq UPS Management Agents must be installed on the server with the UPS in order to manage that UPS. Besides being bundled with the UPS, CPM also comes on the Compaq Management CD that comes with every server. In addition, you can download the CPM from Compaq's Web site.

EXERCISE 30-7

Installing the Compaq UPS Management Agents

1. Make sure that the UPS is connected properly to a serial port on the server.
2. Log on to the server with administrator privileges.
3. From the Compaq Power Management Software CD, run
   <CD Drive Letter>:\Agents\NT\Eng\Setup.exe
   or from the Compaq Management CD, run
   <CD Drive Letter>:\cpqcpm\Agents\NT\Eng\Setup.exe.

EXERCISE 30-8

Installing the Power Management Software

1. From the management PC (the PC with Insight Manager installed), insert the Compaq Power Management Software CD or the Compaq Management CD.
2. From the Power Management Software CD, run
   <CD Drive Letter>:\Insight\Eng\Setup.exe
   or from the Compaq Management CD, run
   <CD Drive Letter>:\cpqcpm\Insight\Eng\Setup.exe.

To access the CPM software, double-click the server in Insight Manager. Click Recovery, then UPS. The following bullets highlight some of the features and functions available through the CPM.

- *Load shedding* allows you to configure nonessential systems to shut down soon after a power interruption. This allows the more essential systems to run longer or to give them more time to shut down gracefully.
- The PowerScope gives a graphical view of power flow through the UPS. The important statistics given in this screen include voltage in, voltage out, current load, and available battery run time.
- You can perform preventive maintenance on the UPS using the diagnostic utility. The diagnostic utility runs the UPS on battery mode for a few seconds and verifies the internal circuitry of the UPS. You can also have CPM remind you to perform the diagnostics every set number of days.

- The three different alert mechanisms for a power failure include: E-mail, Execute Command, and Broadcast Message to Users. You can also specify the message text that will be sent with the alert.
- You can schedule the CPM to automatically shut down and restart the server during certain days of the week.

CERTIFICATION OBJECTIVE 30.07

Compaq ProLiant Storage System

The Compaq ProLiant Storage System is an external storage unit used to house additional hard disks for a ProLiant server. The storage system is connected to a SCSI controller on the server. In general, if you have an array controller (such as SMART or a SMART-2) installed in the server, you should connect the storage system to it in order to take advantage of the fault tolerance that the array controller provides. However, if you do not have an array controller installed, you will have to connect the storage system to one of the SCSI controllers installed. In this case, you can also load the ProLiant Storage System driver, which provides the following benefits.

- Intelligent management of the disk tray online status indicators
- Logging to System Event log for critical conditions of hard disks (such as hot-plug activity or drive failure)
- Capability to manage the drives and storage system using Insight Manager

If you used the SmartStart installation to set up your server, then the ProLiant Storage System driver (PRLNTSS.SYS) should have been loaded automatically. To install the driver manually, run the Compaq SSD setup program (SETUP.EXE), select Compaq ProLiant Storage System, and click Install.

Note that in order to install the ProLiant Storage System driver, you will need a Compaq SCSI controller installed in the server and you will need to load the Compaq version of the SCSI driver from the SSD. This is discussed in the following sections.

Compaq SCSI Controller Driver Support

SCSI controller drivers ship with the standard Windows NT product. These drivers provide basic functionality for the Compaq SCSI controllers. Compaq, however, has developed its own SCSI drivers that provide additional functionality and manageability for the SCSI controllers. The Compaq version of the drivers also supports the Insight Agents, which allow the controllers to be managed via Insight Manager. Additionally, the Compaq version of the driver allows the use of the ProLiant Storage System. The Compaq SCSI Driver (CPQ32FS2.SYS) supports the following models of Compaq SCSI controllers.

- Compaq 64-Bit Dual Channel Wide-Ultra2 SCSI Controller
- Compaq Dual Channel Integrated Wide-Ultra SCSI-3 Controller
- Compaq Wide-Ultra SCSI-3 Controller
- Integrated 32-Bit Fast-Wide SCSI-2/E Controller
- Compaq 32-Bit Fast-SCSI-2 Controller
- Integrated 32-Bit Fast-SCSI-2/P Controller
- Integrated 32-Bit Fast-Wide SCSI-2/P Controller

Loading a Compaq SCSI Controller Driver from the Windows NT SSD

If you perform a SmartStart installation of your server, the proper SCSI drivers are automatically loaded from the SSD. If you perform a manual installation of Windows NT, you will have to specify the location of the Compaq SCSI drivers on the SSD manually.

EXERCISE 30-9

Loading the Compaq SCSI Driver During Setup

1. Begin the Windows NT installation by booting to the NT setup disks. Note that you cannot start the setup by booting to the Windows NT CD.
2. When you are prompted to perform a scan of storage devices, press S to skip the automatic detection of devices.
3. Press S at the next screen to specify additional devices.
4. From the list of devices that appears, select Other (Requires disk provided by a hardware manufacturer) and press ENTER.
5. When prompted, insert the Compaq SSD Disk 2 and press ENTER.
6. From the list of devices that appears, select Compaq 32-Bit SCSI-2 Controllers for Windows NT and press ENTER.
7. Continue with the installation as usual.

Please note that if you do not specify the Compaq version of the SCSI driver manually and instead have Windows NT detect the controller automatically, NT will detect the SCSI controller but load the Windows NT version of the driver. Although your SCSI controller will function, it will not have the advanced features and manageability of the Compaq version of the driver. You will have to install the Compaq version manually from the SSD after the Windows NT installation is complete.

Updating the SCSI Driver

This section will outline the steps necessary to update the SCSI controller driver using the Compaq SSD setup program. You may need to update the driver in the event that Compaq releases an updated version of the driver. You may also need to update the driver if you installed the Windows NT version of the driver during the NT installation.

EXERCISE 30-10

Updating the Compaq SCSI Driver

1. Log on to the server with administrative privileges.
2. Run the Compaq SSD setup program (SETUP.EXE).

3. From the list of components that appears, select Compaq SCSI Controllers and click Install or Update.
4. Install or update any additional components.
5. Exit the program when you are done.
6. Reboot the server when prompted.

CERTIFICATION OBJECTIVE 30.08

Upgrading a SmartStart Windows NT 3.51 and Windows NT 4.0 Installation

Many companies will want to upgrade an existing Windows NT 3.51 network to Windows NT 4.0. The newer version of NT adds many new features that enhance overall network performance and usability. Windows NT 4.0 also includes built-in support for Internet applications with Internet Information Server, a robust Web server.

Although the upgrade process is fairly simple, you must always take the proper precautions to make sure that you do not lose any data. This section will discuss the proper process for upgrading a Windows NT 3.51 server with Compaq software installed to Windows NT 4.0 to achieve minimal downtime.

Preparing for the Upgrade

The most important portion of the upgrade process (as with all major projects) is the planning phase before the actual upgrade. You must have a detailed plan in place to be able to upgrade your server efficiently and safely. You must also have a contingency plan in case not everything goes as smoothly as planned.

Perform a Backup

Before you make any changes to the server, you should always perform a complete backup of the server. You can use Windows NT's built-in backup utility or a third-party backup utility such as Cheyenne ArcServe or Veritas Backup Exec. Whichever program you use, be sure to stop all unnecessary services on the server and disconnect all users to make sure that you get a clean backup. You should also update the emergency repair disk by running RDISK /S from a command prompt.

Determine Disk Requirements

Before you upgrade, you need to make sure that you have enough free disk space available on your server. During the installation, the setup program needs temporary space on the disk to perform the installation. Depending on the installation method, you may need to make more space available. If you are upgrading by booting to the Windows NT CD, you will only need about 10MB of disk space for the upgrade. If you upgrade by running WINNT32.EXE from the CD, or if you perform an over-the-network installation, you will need about 100MB of disk space, since the setup program must copy the NT source file to the local hard disk.

Install Latest SSD and Service Pack for Windows NT 3.51

By installing the latest SSD and service pack for Windows NT 3.51, you ensure that you have the latest available drivers for NT. As of this writing, the latest version of the SSD for Windows NT 3.51 is 1.35A. The latest service pack for NT 3.51 is Service Pack 5.

Disable Unnecessary Services

Although it is not necessary, you should disable any unnecessary services before upgrading the server. Disabling unnecessary services reduces the chance that a legacy application may not be compatible with Windows NT 4.0 and might cause problems. You can disable services in Control

Panel | Services. Compaq suggests that you disable the following services before upgrading to NT 4.0.

- Any virus scanning software
- Compaq Insight Agents
- SNMP Service

Compaq also suggests that you disable the following devices in Control Panel | Devices.

- Compaq ProLiant Storage System
- Compaq Systems Management Service

Upgrading to NT 4.0

You can start the Windows NT upgrade by three methods: running setup directly from the NT 4.0 CD, booting to the NT setup disks, or booting directly to the NT CD.

To start the setup from the Windows NT CD, run WINNT32.EXE /B from the I386 directory on the CD. You can also run the setup program across the network if the NT source files are on a remote server. The /B parameter prevents the setup program from creating the Windows NT boot disks and instead copies the source files to a temporary directory on the hard disk.

To start the setup by booting to the diskettes or the CD, simply insert the first Windows NT setup disk or the NT CD; then reboot the server.

Follow all prompts from the setup program. During the Windows NT 4.0 Installation/Upgrade screen, select to upgrade the existing installation of NT and continue with the rest of the installation.

Post Upgrade Tasks

Once you have completed the upgrade process and you log onto Windows NT for the first time, you may receive several error messages regarding the disabled services. You may also encounter error messages from noncompatible services. Before you start to panic, you should perform the following tasks after the installation.

Reinstall SNMP

After the upgrade, you should remove the SNMP service from Control Panel | Network | Services. After you reboot, reinstall the SNMP service.

Install Latest SSD for Windows NT 4.0

After the server reboots, install the latest SSD for Windows NT 4.0. Note that this is a different version from the SSD for NT 3.51. (As of this writing, the latest version of the SSD for NT 4.0 is 2.12B.) Select the Express setup to update all of the necessary drivers; then reboot the server.

Reinstall Insight Agents

Run the setup program for the Insight Agents from the Compaq Management CD. Choose to update the existing version of the Insight Agents; then reboot the server.

Install Microsoft Service Pack for Windows NT

Once the server reboots, apply the latest service pack for Windows NT 4.0, which as of this writing is version 5. During the installation, the program may prompt you whether you want to overwrite an existing OEM driver. Select No to keep the existing Compaq driver.

CERTIFICATION OBJECTIVE 30.09

Configuring the Insight Agents Control Panel

You have already learned how to use Insight Manager and the Insight Agents to monitor your server's health. The Insight Agents run on the server that you are monitoring, while Insight Manager is the application that runs on a management PC that you use to monitor all of your servers. You can configure the Insight Agents on the server using the Insight Agents applet in Control Panel. In the applet, you can configure whether to enable the Insight Agents and whether to enable rebooting the server remotely, as shown here:

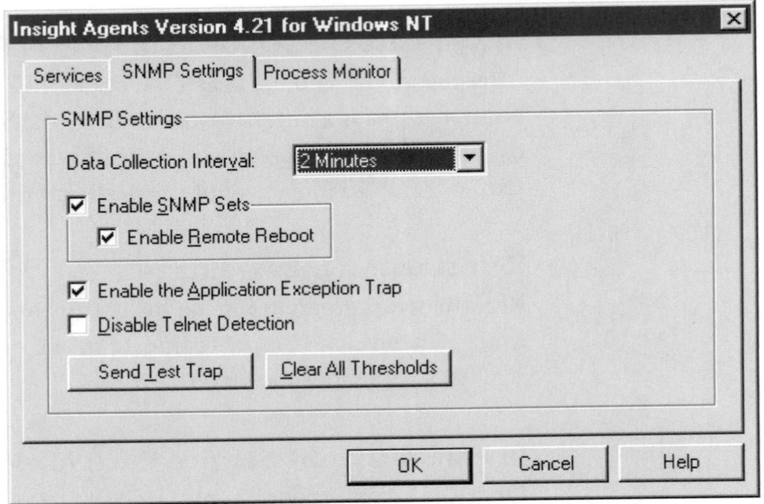

When you first install the Insight Agents, the setup program only activates the services that apply to the hardware installed on your server. For example, the setup program will only activate the Drive Array Information service if you have an array controller installed in the server. However, if you install new hardware or remove hardware from your server, you will have to activate or deactivate the Insight Agents services for that particular hardware component. To add or remove component services, open the Insight Agents applet in Control Panel and switch to the Services tab, shown next. To activate a component, add the service to the Active Agents window. To disable a component, add it to the Inactive Agents window.

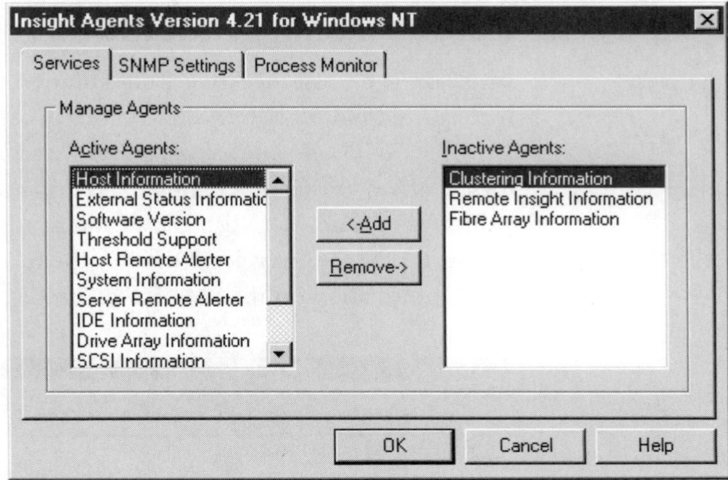

CERTIFICATION OBJECTIVE 30.10

Compaq Utilities

The Compaq SSD installs several utilities that allow you to manage the server hardware with greater efficiency. The utilities that the program installs depend on the hardware that is installed in your server. The utilities that we will cover in this section include the following.

- Compaq On-Line Array Configuration Utility
- Compaq Advanced Network Control Utility
- Compaq Enhanced Integrated Management Display Service
- Compaq Integrated Management Display Utility
- Compaq PCI Hot Plug Utility
- Compaq Power Down Manager
- Compaq Power Supply Viewer

Compaq On-Line Array Configuration Utility

The Compaq On-Line Array Configuration Utility (ACU) allows you to manage and monitor your SMART Array controller from within Windows NT. The ACU, shown next, provides wizards that allow you to create new logical drives or expand existing logical drives when you add new drives to your system. The ACU also allows you to configure controller settings such as settings for the array accelerator or the rebuild and expand priorities. For more information on the SMART controllers, refer to Chapter 31.

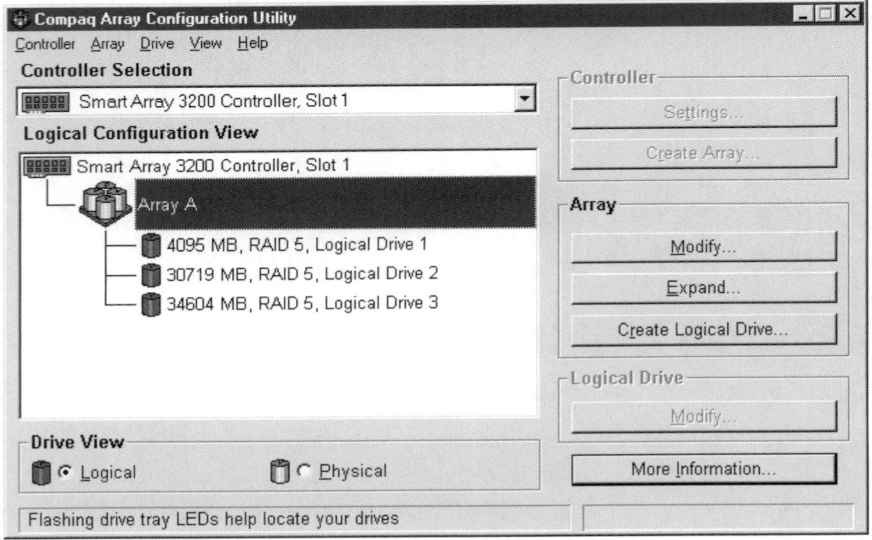

The ACU is installed automatically during a SmartStart installation of the server. To install the ACU manually, you must run the SSD setup program (SETUP.EXE), select Compaq Array Configuration Utility from the Custom Setup screen, then click Install.

Compaq Advanced Network Control Utility

In servers with two Compaq network cards installed, one of the cards can be configured to take over for the other card automatically if it fails or is disconnected from the network. This allows you to remove the NIC as a single point of failure by providing a backup NIC. When the network card driver detects that the primary card has failed, it will automatically switch traffic to the backup card. The Advanced Network Control Utility (shown in Figure 30-3) allows you to configure the options for failover when a NIC fails.

You should pay special attention to the Operating Modes for the network cards, which are: Manual Mode, Switch on Fail Mode, and Smart Switch Mode.

- In Manual Mode, if the primary controller fails, the driver will not switch automatically to the backup NIC. You must manually switch over using the Network Control Utility.
- In Switch on Fail Mode, the driver will automatically reroute traffic to the backup card if the primary NIC fails.
- In Smart Switch Mode, the driver will automatically reroute traffic just as in the Switch on Fail Mode, but if the primary NIC comes back online, the driver will automatically switch back to the primary card.

FIGURE 30-3

Network Teaming allows you to set redundancy for your network cards

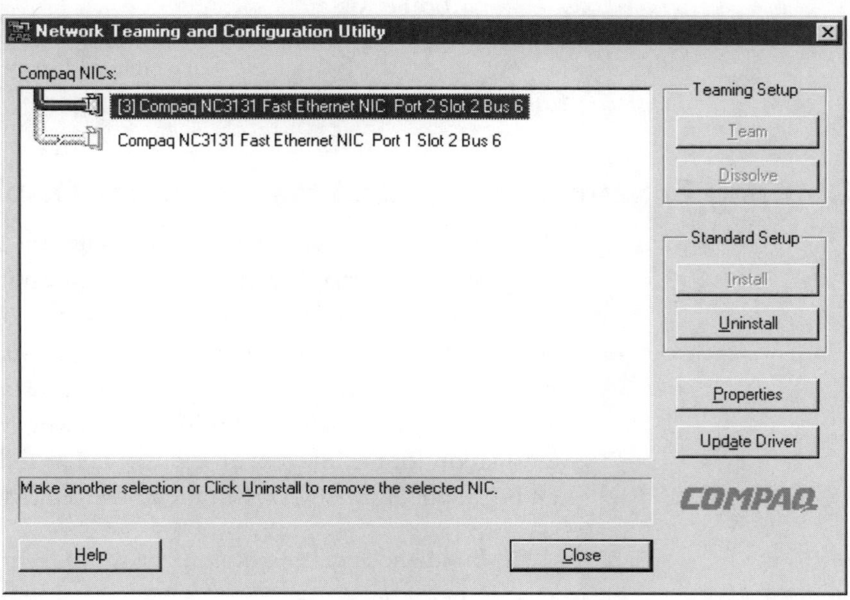

In order to use the Network Control Utility, you must use network cards that are of the same bus type (for example, EISA and EISA, or PCI and PCI). In addition, you must have the Compaq Systems Management driver loaded.

Compaq Integrated Management Display Utility

The Compaq Integrated Management Display (IMD) Utility allows you to set the text that is displayed on the Integrated Management Display on servers that have the IMD hardware installed. The IMD hardware is available on the Compaq ProLiant models 2500, 3000, 5500, 6000, 6500, and 7000. You can also get it as an option on the ProLiant 1200 and 1600. The IMD Utility allows you to display the following information on the IMD.

- Administrator name, phone number, and pager number
- Service contact name, phone number, and pager number
- Server asset tag
- Idle screen text
- Critical errors

You can run the Integrated Management Display Utility from Control Panel.

Compaq Enhanced Integrated Management Display Service

The Compaq Enhanced Integrated Management Display Service enables you to set the text that is displayed on the Integrated Management Display on some servers. The IMD hardware is available on the Compaq ProLiant models 2500, 3000, 5500, 6000, 6500, and 7000. You can also get it as an option on the ProLiant 1200 and 1600. The Enhanced IMD service improves on the regular IMD utility by allowing you to display server information for the idle text on the IMD. The following information can be shown on the IMD with the Enhanced IMD service.

- Build and service pack number
- CPU utilization

- Kernel utilization
- Compaq SSD for Windows NT version
- Memory utilization
- Operating system version
- Processor type
- Processor count
- Server name
- Serial number

To install the Enhanced IMD, run the Compaq SSD and select the Enhanced Integrated Management Display Service and click Install. You can run the Enhanced IMD Utility from Control Panel (see Figure 30-4).

FIGURE 30-4

The Integrated Management Display service allows you to display real-time server information

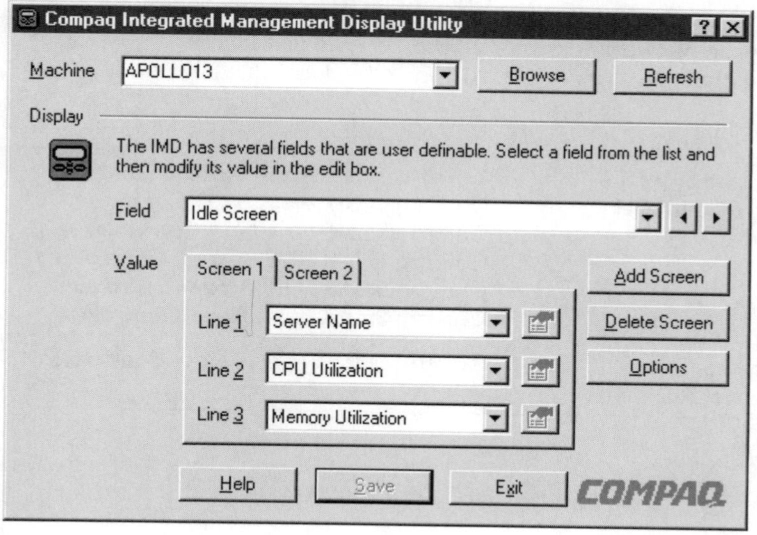

Compaq PCI Hot Plug Utility

Compaq takes advantage of a new industry standard that allows you to remove and replace PCI devices without shutting down your server. To take advantage of the hot-plug capabilities, the device driver must be hot-plug aware. The PCI Hot Plug Utility allows you to monitor the current state of such devices and allows you to turn the power on or turn the power off to the slots where the device is installed. Once you turn the power off to a slot, you can safely remove the card and replace it. Currently, the ProLiant 6400R, 6500, 7000, 8000 and 8500 are capable of hot-plug PCI. The following table lists the current adapters that are hot-plug capable:

Card Family	Card Model
Compaq Network Cards	Compaq NC1120 Ethernet NIC Compaq NC3120 Fast Ethernet NIC Compaq NC3122 Fast Ethernet NIC Compaq Netelligent 10 T PCI UTP Controller Compaq Netelligent 10 T/2 PCI UTP/Coax Controller Compaq Netelligent 10/100 TX PCI UTP Controller Compaq Netelligent Dual 10/100 TX PCI UTP Controller Compaq NetFlex-3/P Controller
Compaq Network Card Modules	10BaseT UTP/BNC Module 10/100TX Module 100 Base-FX Module 100 VG Module
Compaq SMART Array Controllers	Compaq Smart Array 3100ES Controller Compaq Smart Array 3200 Controller Compaq Smart Array 221 Controller Compaq SMART-2DH Array Controller Compaq SMART-2/P Array Controller Compaq SMART-2SL Array Controller
Compaq Fibre Channel Adapters	Compaq Fibre Channel Host Controller/P

Card Family	Card Model
Compaq SCSI Controllers	Compaq 64-Bit Dual Channel Wide-Ultra2 SCSI Controller Compaq Dual Channel Wide-Ultra SCSI-3 Controller Compaq Wide-Ultra SCSI-3 Controller Compaq 32-Bit Fast-Wide SCSI-2/P Controller

The PCI Hot Plug Utility is installed using the Compaq SSD program. You can run the Hot Plug Utility, shown next, from Control Panel. When swapping a card in or out of the server, be sure to first power down the slot in which you will be installing the card by selecting the slot and pressing the Power button.

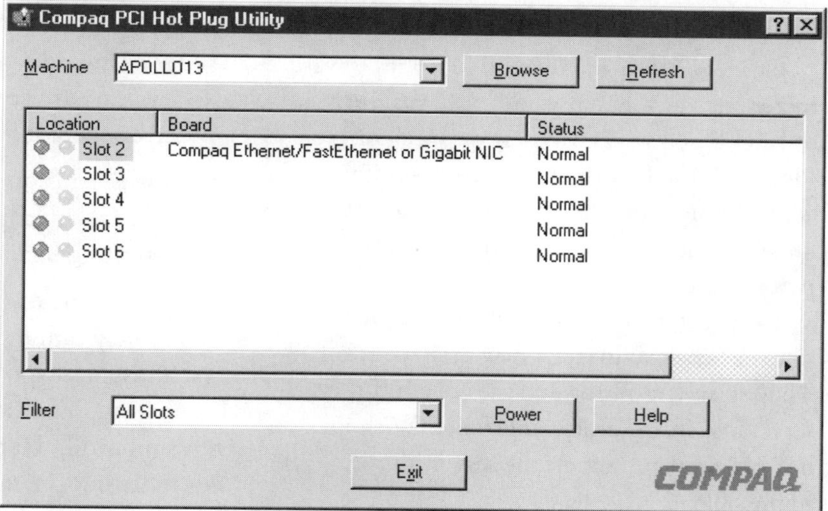

Compaq Power Down Manager

For servers with intelligent power switches installed, you can use the Compaq Power Down Manager, shown next, to specify the server action when you press the server power switch. The servers that currently support the intelligent power switch are the ProLiant 6000, 6500, and 7000. The possible actions when pressing the switch are

- Gracefully shutdown the OS before turning off the power
- Turn the power off to the machine
- Do nothing, disabled

FROM THE CLASSROOM

Hot-Plug Technology Adds Functionality Beyond Failure

Compaq has made incredible strides toward increasing the reliability and manageability of Intel-based servers. When we speak of Hot Plug PCI, the first thing that comes to mind is replacement of a failed PCI component—known as hot-replacement. But how often is that required?

Large enterprises do not want to have to down a server to install a new array controller. They simply want to slide the cover off the server and install a new controller. Without hot-plug capabilities on the server, this is impossible.

Compaq's hot-plug specification allows three types of operations to be performed without downing the server on hot-plug capable servers:

- **Hot-Replacement** Replacing a failed or failing PCI device with an identical model without downing the server
- **Hot-Upgrade** Installing an upgraded device or driver without disrupting server operations
- **Hot-Expansion** Installing a new device in an empty slot without disrupting server operations

If your enterprise is running operations that absolutely cannot be disrupted under any circumstance, you may want to consider a clustered configuration using enterprise-level servers supporting Hot-Plug PCI.

For more information on the Hot Plug PCI initiative at Compaq, check out http://www.compaq.com/support/techpubs/whitepapers/ecg0800698.html.

—Thomas E. Eck, MCSE+I, MCSD, ASE, CCA, CNA

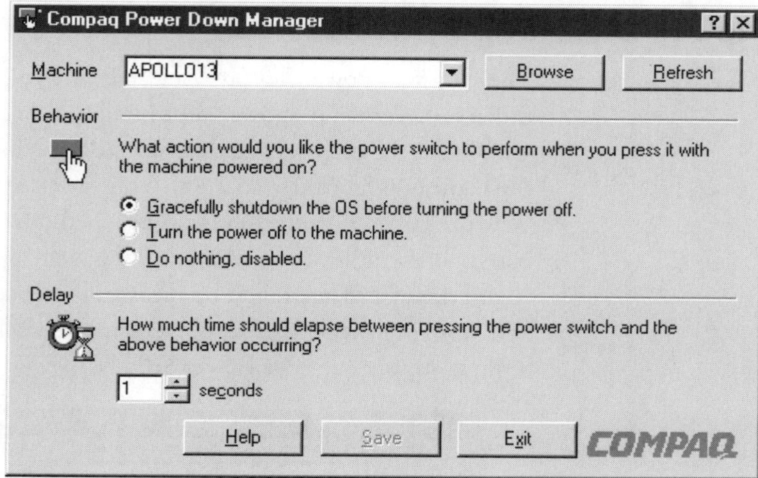

You can also specify a delay for the first two options that determines how many seconds to wait before actually shutting down the server. This can be used as a safety mechanism to prevent accidental shutdowns when the power switch is pressed. If a delay is specified, and the power button is pressed, you can abort the shutdown before the delay time expires.

The Power Down Manager would have been a welcome utility for a co-worker of mine who accidentally pressed the power switch on a live production server during the middle of the day. While in the middle of pressing the button, he realized that he shouldn't have pressed it, but he had to stand there for the rest of the day with the button pressed in until the server could gracefully shut down! If they had had the Power Down Manager installed, they could have set a delay on the switch, or better yet, disabled the switch so that the only way to shut down the server was through a graceful shutdown.

Compaq Power Supply Viewer

The Compaq Power Supply Viewer allows you to view the status and utilization of the IIC power supply subsystem for a particular server. Currently, the only servers that have the IIC power subsystem are the ProLiant 6000, 6500, and 7000. You can use the Power Supply Viewer to view the current utilization of all installed power supplies and determine, based on the utilization, whether the power supplies are redundant. Redundancy is determined by measuring the current load on the supplies and verifying that the other power supplies could handle the load, should a single supply fail. The Power Supply Viewer is displayed here:

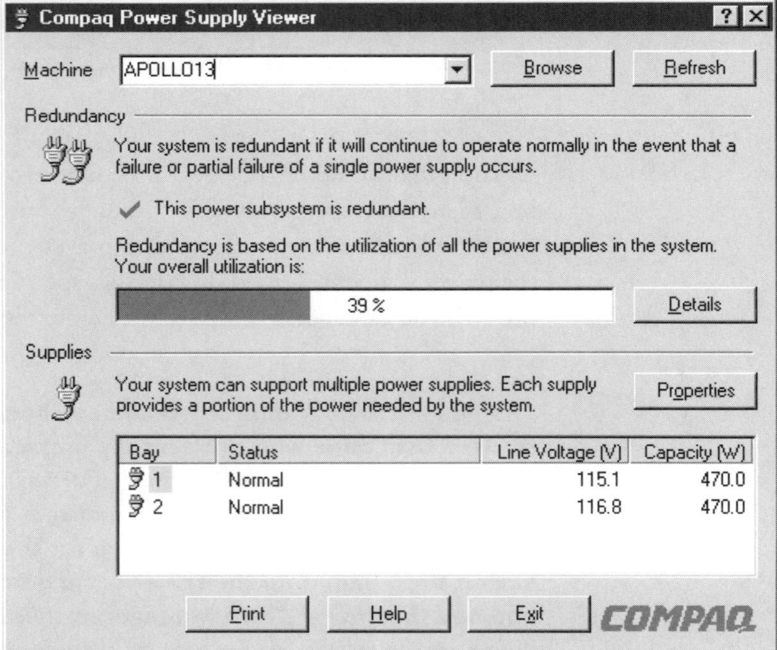

QUESTIONS AND ANSWERS	
I have just added more hard disks to the server. I want to expand the existing array so that the new hard disk space is consolidated with the existing drive space.	Use the Array Configuration Utility, which will allow you to expand an existing array when you add more hard disks. After you expand the array, use NT's Disk Administrator to create a volume set.
I want to add a second NIC to my server to provide fault tolerance. I don't want any downtime at all on the server.	Use a PCI hot-plug capable NIC. After installing the card, use the PCI Hot Plug Utility to power on the slot where you installed the card. Use the Advanced Network Control utility to configure the network teaming.
I want to display the processor utilization on the Integrated Management Display on the server.	Use the Enhanced Integrated Management Display (IMD) Service. You cannot use the regular IMD Service, because it does not allow you to show server utilization statistics.
I want to prevent the server from shutting down if someone accidentally presses the power button.	Use the Power Down Manager to configure the action to take place when the power button is pressed. You can specify that the server performs a graceful shutdown of the OS, or not shut down at all.
I suspect that one of my power supplies is not performing properly.	Use the Power Supply Viewer to view the statistics on your power supplies.

Determining the Current Windows NT Build Revision and Service Pack Level

There are several methods to determine the current version of Windows NT. You may not only need to find the version, but also whether a service pack has been installed or not.

EXERCISE 30-11

Determining Current Version of Windows NT

1. Click Start | Run and type **winver** or open My Computer or Explorer and select Help | About.
2. The About Windows window appears. You can see the version of Windows NT as well as any service pack applied. Windows NT Server 4.0 is installed with Service Pack 4 and is shown here:

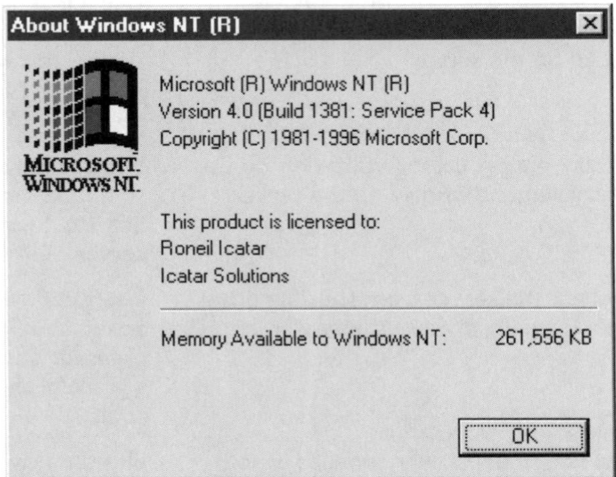

EXERCISE 30-12

Determining Current Version of NT

1. Click Start | Settings | Control Panel | System.
   The System Properties window appears.
2. On the General tab, you can see the version and build number for Windows NT as shown here:

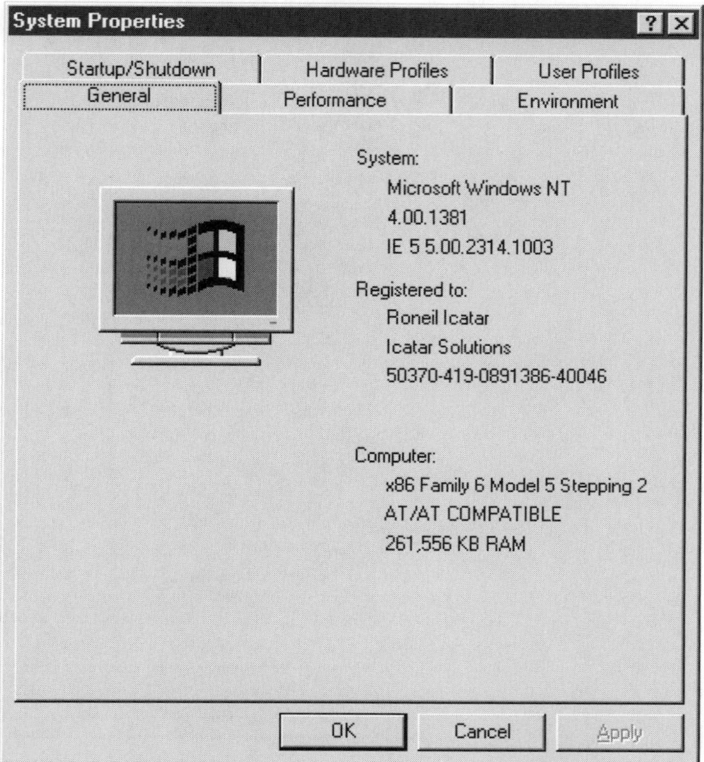

EXERCISE 30-13

Using Windows NT Diagnostics

1. Click Start | Run. The Run dialog box appears.
2. Type **winmsd** and press OK. The Windows NT Diagnostics window appears.
3. Select the Version tab, shown next. You will be able to see the version of Windows NT installed.

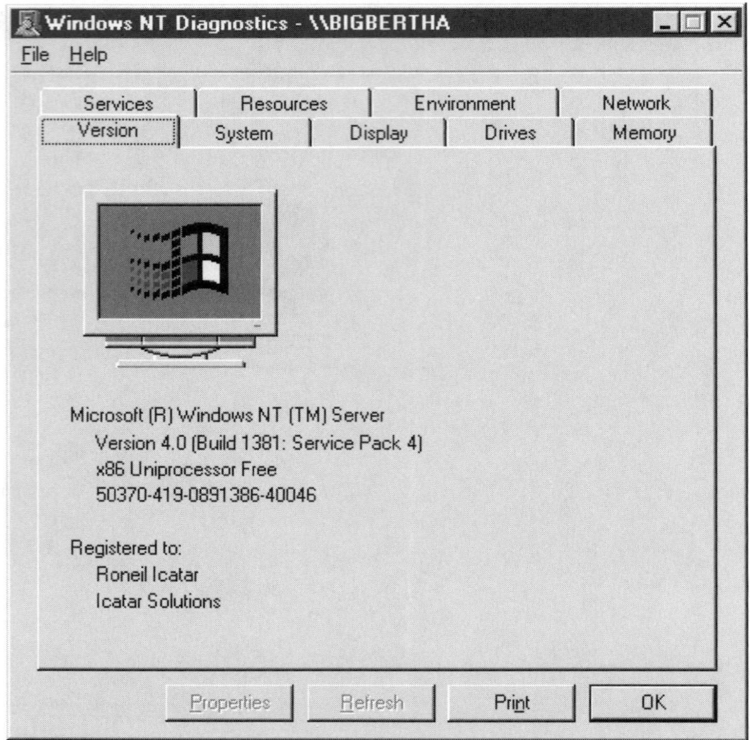

Determining the Current Version of a Compaq Device Driver

Just as you may need to determine the version of Windows NT, you may also need to determine the version number of your Compaq device drivers. There are several methods to determine the revision of the driver so that you can decide whether you need to update the driver. Before you can determine the version, you first have to know the filename for the driver that you are interested in. (This process is detailed in the earlier section, Compaq Device Drivers.) Once you determine the filename, you can look at the file properties to determine the version.

EXERCISE 30-14

Finding Driver Version

1. Determine the filename for the driver whose version you'd like to find.
2. In My Computer or Explorer, open the folder where the file resides.
3. Right-click the file and select Properties. The file Properties window appears as shown here:

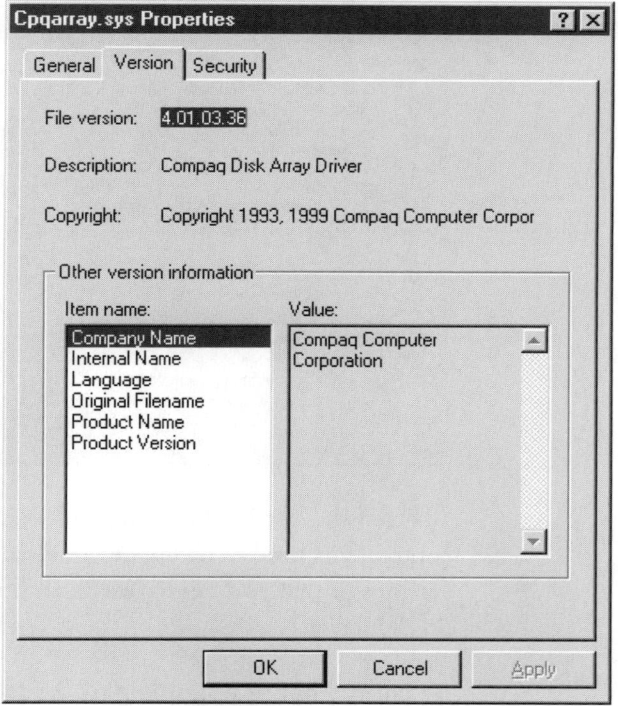

4. Click the Version tab.

You can find the file version from the Version tab of the file Properties window. You can also tell whether the file is from the standard Windows NT CD or from Compaq by checking the Company Name in the Other Version Information window.

Using Version Control to Determine Driver Versions

You can also use Version Control in Insight Manager to determine the versions of the drivers and utilities installed on your server. In Insight Manager, right-click the server that you are interested in and select Version Control. The Version Control window appears, shown next, which displays the version of all Compaq software installed on the server.

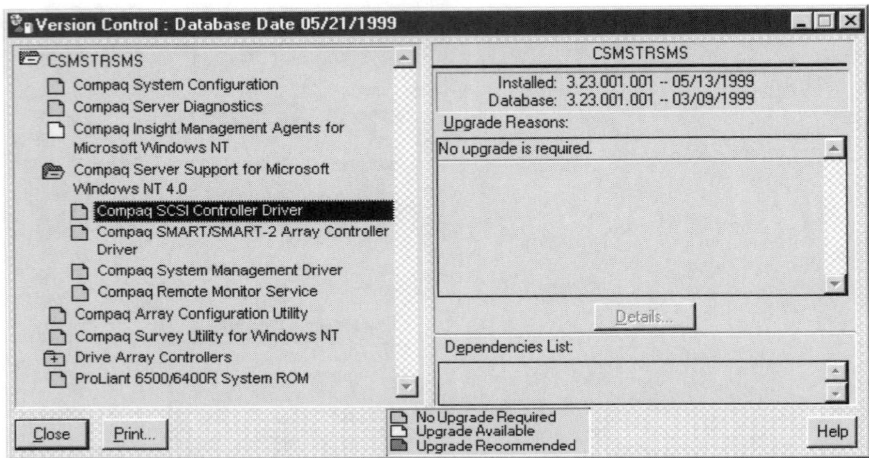

From the Version Control window, you can also determine which components need to be upgraded. Finally, you can print a list of the current versions so that you can have a hard copy of the software revisions installed on the server.

on the Job

Be careful about upgrading to the latest and greatest driver when it is released. Sometimes the newer version may inadvertently introduce a new bug that could cause major problems. Before you install the new version, read the documentation that comes with the driver to see if it fixes any problems that you are currently experiencing. If it doesn't, then you don't need to install the new version. The Version Control application also tells you what the fixes are for the new version. If you do decide to upgrade, make sure that you take the proper precautions before upgrading: perform a complete backup of the system and update the emergency repair disk.

CERTIFICATION SUMMARY

This chapter has shown how Compaq servers support Windows NT. Although Microsoft has developed device drivers for most of the Compaq components, Compaq has developed their own drivers to take advantage of advanced features and manageability of their hardware. You learned how Compaq eased the installation and administration of their custom drivers using the Server Support Diskettes for Windows NT. You also learned how to upgrade an existing NT 3.51 installation to NT 4.0 and how to load the custom Compaq drivers after the upgrade process.

Besides creating custom drivers, Compaq has also developed custom applications and utilities to help manage and configure their hardware. These utilities include the Array Configuration Utility to help configure their drive arrays and the PCI Hot Plug Utility to manage PCI hot-plug devices. Finally, you learned how to determine the currently installed version of Windows NT (including service pack) and Compaq driver.

TWO-MINUTE DRILL

- ❑ The Compaq Server Support Diskettes (SSD) for Windows NT contain custom drivers and utilities developed by Compaq to optimize the use of their servers in a Windows NT network environment.
- ❑ If you have the SmartStart CD, you can create the Server Support Diskettes using the Diskette Builder application.
- ❑ In Express mode the setup program will automatically determine which components need to be updated (as well as their dependencies) and display them in a list.
- ❑ The Hardware Abstraction Layer (HAL) is a driver with a set of routines that directly manipulates the hardware in the server.
- ❑ The HAL gives Windows NT a modularity that allows a third-party vendor to write a completely new HAL to take advantage of specific hardware without having to rewrite the end user applications.
- ❑ Table 30-1 lists the custom HALs that Compaq provides for their servers.

- ❑ With Windows NT 4.0 and later, Compaq did not create a custom HAL and instead uses the HALs supplied by Microsoft on the NT CD.
- ❑ If you upgrade your server by adding more processors, you will have to upgrade the HAL in order for NT to utilize the additional processors.
- ❑ The Compaq SSD provides the HAL Recovery Option as a method for you to boot your server in the event that the Windows NT HAL becomes corrupted or damaged.
- ❑ Compaq provides a systems management driver that can perform advanced management of your server and Automatic Server Recovery (ASR).
- ❑ Windows NT uses the BOOT.INI file to configure several startup options that are useful for troubleshooting and debugging.
- ❑ The Systems Management driver allows you to perform shutdown tasks when the server shuts down through a batch file.
- ❑ Compaq builds a variety of components for their servers, and each of these components needs a driver to run under Windows NT.
- ❑ Drivers for the Compaq products that are supported with the Windows NT base product can be found on the Windows NT CD.
- ❑ Compaq's drivers provide extended capabilities and features (such as manageability with Insight Manager) that are not supported with Microsoft's drivers.
- ❑ The Compaq Insight Management Agents allow you to manage a server using any SNMP management utility such as Compaq Insight Manager.
- ❑ The Compaq family of SMART Array controllers provides increased performance and fault tolerance for a server's hard disk subsystem.
- ❑ Every Compaq UPS comes with the Compaq Power Management Software (CPM) that allows you to manage a UPS that is connected to a server.
- ❑ The Compaq ProLiant Storage System is an external storage unit used to house additional hard disks for a ProLiant server.

- ❑ You can configure the Insight Agents on the server using the Insight Agents applet in Control Panel.
- ❑ The Compaq SSD installs several utilities that allow you to manage the server hardware with greater efficiency.
- ❑ The Compaq On-Line Array Configuration Utility (ACU) allows you to manage and monitor your SMART Array controller from within Windows NT.
- ❑ The Advanced Network Control Utility allows you to configure the options for failover when a NIC fails.
- ❑ The Compaq Integrated Management Display (IMD) Utility allows you to set the text that is displayed on the Integrated Management Display on servers that have the IMD hardware installed.
- ❑ The Compaq Enhanced Integrated Management Display Service enables you to set the text that is displayed on the Integrated Management Display on some servers.
- ❑ The PCI Hot Plug Utility allows you to monitor the current state of such devices and allows you to turn the power on or turn the power off to the slots where the device is installed.
- ❑ For servers with intelligent power switches installed, you can use the Compaq Power Down Manager to specify the server action when you press the server power switch.
- ❑ The Compaq Power Supply Viewer allows you to view the status and utilization of the IIC power supply subsystem for a particular server.
- ❑ You can use Version Control in Insight Manager to determine the versions of the drivers and utilities installed on your server.

SELF TEST

The following Self Test questions will help you measure your understanding of the material presented in this chapter. Read all the choices carefully, as there may be more than one correct answer. Choose all correct answers for each question.

1. Which of the following is not a source where you can obtain the Compaq Server Support Diskettes?
   A. SmartStart CD
   B. Diskette Builder
   C. Management CD
   D. Compaq Web Site
2. What does a gray icon next to a driver name indicate in the SSD Custom Options screen?
   A. The driver is installed properly.
   B. The driver is not installed.
   C. The driver is installed but not the latest version.
   D. The driver is disabled.
3. What does HAL stand for?
   A. Hardware Application Layer
   B. Hardware Abstraction Level
   C. Hardware Application Level
   D. Hardware Abstraction Layer
4. Which of the following best describes Compaq's HAL support for Windows NT 4.0?
   A. You can load the HAL from the SSD.
   B. The Compaq HAL can be found on the SmartStart CD.
   C. The HAL can be found on the Windows NT CD.
   D. The HAL can be found on the Management CD.
5. What should you do after adding a second processor to your server?
   A. Run the Compaq SSD.
   B. Back up your server and reinstall NT.
   C. Nothing, Windows NT will automatically detect the second processor.
   D. Manually copy the multiprocessor HAL to the System32 directory.
6. What is the best method to recover from a HAL mismatch?
   A. Select HAL Recovery Option during Windows NT bootup.
   B. Reinstall Windows NT.
   C. Restore Windows NT from a previous backup.
   D. Reinstall the second processor.
7. Which of the following are characteristics of the Systems Management driver?
   A. Automatic Server Recovery
   B. Allows you to perform a shutdown script
   C. Logs corrected memory errors
   D. All of the above

8. What must you do before modifying the BOOT.INI file?
   A. Enable the Systems Management driver.
   B. Remove the read-only and hidden attributes.
   C. Load Insight Manager.
   D. Specify a Timeout value in Control Panel.
9. Where can you find the drivers for Compaq tape drives?
   A. Windows NT CD
   B. Compaq SSD
   C. Compaq SmartStart CD
   D. Compaq Web site
10. Which of the following is not a requirement for the Insight Management Agents?
    A. TCP/IP protocol
    B. SNMP service
    C. 64MB of RAM
    D. Compaq SSD
11. Which of the following is not an advantage of using the Compaq version of the SMART Array controller driver, as opposed to using the Microsoft version of the driver?
    A. Ability to use Performance Monitor to track statistics of the array controller
    B. Ability to manage using Insight Manager
    C. Ability to hot-plug the array controller card
    D. Increased performance and fault tolerance
12. What is load shedding?
    A. The capacity of the UPS to balance the load among different servers
    B. Shutting down non-essential servers to save power for critical servers in the event of a power loss
    C. The term used for how a server connects to a UPS through the serial port
    D. The term used for power consumption of a server
13. When would you not use the ProLiant Storage System driver?
    A. If you have Windows NT Service Pack 4 installed
    B. If the storage unit is connected to a SCSI controller
    C. If the storage unit is connected to a SMART Array controller
    D. If the server is a ProLiant 2500
14. You manage your server using Insight Manager. You want to check statistics for the server's SCSI controllers, but Insight Manager shows no statistics. The SCSI controllers are working properly, since all devices are functioning properly. What is the probable cause?
    A. Windows NT Service Pack 4 is not installed.
    B. The Microsoft SCSI driver is loaded.

C. You are running Insight Manager earlier than version 4.0.

D. There is a SCSI ID conflict.

15. How would you upgrade an NT 3.51 server over the network?

A. Run WINNT.EXE /B.

B. Run WINNT32.EXE /B.

C. Run WINNT.EXE /OX.

D. Run WINNT32.EXE /OX.

16. You try to reboot a server remotely using Insight Manager but the server does not reboot. What is the most likely cause?

A. The Enable Remote Reboot option is not set.

B. You do not have administrative rights on the server.

C. The Systems Management driver is not loaded.

D. The Insight Agents are not installed.

17. What is a characteristic of the Smart Switch Mode in the Advanced Network Control Utility?

A. Transmits data using the network card that is the least busy

B. Automatically throttles network bandwidth

C. Automatically switches back to the primary NIC after it comes back online

D. Automatically uses both network cards, effectively doubling network throughput

18. What must you do before you remove a hot-plug PCI device?

A. Power down the server.

B. Stop the Server service.

C. Use the PCI Hot Plug Utility.

D. Do nothing.

19. What utility can you use to print a list of the versions of all Compaq drivers currently installed on your server?

A. Version Control

B. File Manager

C. Windows Explorer

D. Compaq Server Support Diskette

ASE
ACCREDITED SYSTEMS ENGINEER

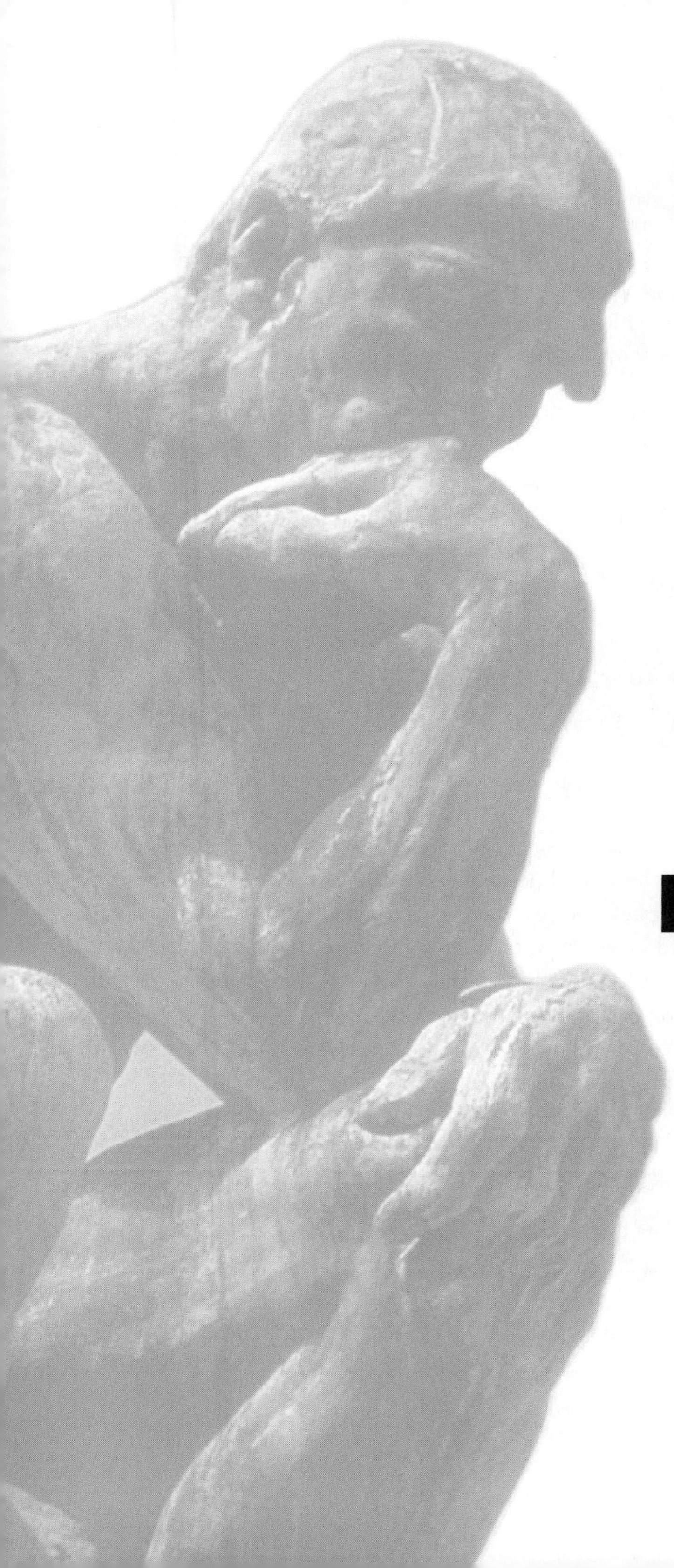

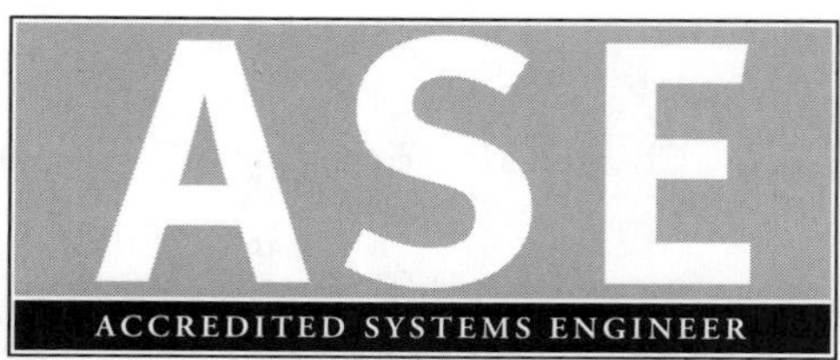

31

Enhancing NT Reliability Using Compaq Products

CERTIFICATION OBJECTIVES

- 31.01 RAID Fault Tolerance Levels
- 31.02 Configuring a Boot Partition for Windows NT Software Fault Tolerance
- 31.03 Compaq Hardware-Based Fault Tolerance
- 31.04 Compaq ProLiant Storage System
- 31.05 Standby Recovery Server
- 31.06 Online Recovery Server
- 31.07 Compaq Advanced Network Fault Detection and Correction
- 31.08 Adding Bridged PCI Devices to a ProLiant 5000, 6000, 6500, and 7000

In this chapter, we will be looking at the various ways that we can improve both the performance and reliability of Microsoft Windows NT by using Compaq products. You will learn all the intricacies of the various RAID levels, and how each is implemented, both in software by Windows NT and in hardware by Compaq.

We will be looking at the Compaq hardware that provides high-availability in a Windows NT environment, as well as the details required to configure such devices.

By the end of this chapter, you should have a good idea what is involved in setting up, maintaining, and upgrading a Compaq server when in a fault tolerant configuration.

CERTIFICATION OBJECTIVE 31.01

RAID Fault Tolerance Levels

A Redundant Array of Inexpensive Drives (RAID) is a fundamental way of increasing the reliability and performance of a Compaq server. Several different methods are at your disposal in creating a fault tolerant array, some of which could improve performance and others that could impact it negatively. The method you would choose to use for a particular situation really does depend on that particular situation.

There are four main types of RAID configuration in the Compaq world. Each will be discussed further in this chapter:

- **RAID 0** Data striping (not fault tolerant)
- **RAID 1** Disk mirroring
- **RAID 4** Data guarding
- **RAID 5** Distributed data guarding

Three of these RAID levels—RAID 0, 1, and 5—are actually provided in software form as part of the basic Windows NT Server package. Windows

NT Workstation will allow just one—RAID 0—which, as stated, is not fault tolerant.

RAID 0

RAID 0 does not provide any fault tolerance—in fact it actually *increases* risk, due to the fact that a single disk failure would mean the entire array of data would be lost.

It is not without its advantages, however. Since all data is striped across all the drives in the array, it is possible to achieve several concurrent read or write operations. This striping process has the effect of making RAID 0 the best performer of all the available RAID types.

RAID 1

RAID 1 can provide the best solution if maximum availability is more important than price. RAID 1 mirrors all data to both drives; if one drive fails, there is an exact replica from which to continue working. This reliability does not come without a premium; each byte written to one disk requires one byte written on the mirror, too. Effectively, you are losing 50 percent of the available drive space in the array. Another advantage of RAID 1 is that a single array could sustain multiple drive failures and still maintain data integrity. This is because it is possible to mirror one drive to several others, thus allowing multiple drive failures as long as one drive remains. This feature is unique to RAID 1.

RAID 1 can provide the best availability of the fault tolerant RAID solutions, but the worst overhead.

RAID 4

RAID 4 provides a single drive to maintain parity information for the entire array. As a result, the overhead for RAID 4 is reduced as the number of drives in the array increases.

The use of parity information requires at least three drives in the array, two of which will store data. The third one stores the parity information.

The use of a single drive for the parity is the main limitation of this implementation. In effect, the parity drive acts as a bottleneck for the whole system; data cannot be written concurrently to the array because the parity drive can only write the parity information for each individual write one at a time. This also leads to the problem that every write to the array, no matter which drive the information is written to, requires parity to be written to a single drive. This drive then becomes very heavily loaded, usually resulting in the parity drive being the first to fail.

RAID 5

RAID 5 works in a similar manner to RAID 4, except it addresses the problems that result from the single parity drive. RAID 5 stripes parity information across all the drives in the array, effectively making RAID 5 a stripe set with parity. As such, it carries over many of the benefits from RAID 0 (data striping), including the number of concurrent reads. It also prevents the single parity drive from becoming a bottleneck to the array, thus allowing multiple concurrent writes. As with RAID 4, there is still a requirement of the equivalent of one drive's space to store the parity information. With 6x9.1GB drives, you would get 5x9.1GB actual storage, with 1x9.1GB use for parity information. Contrast this with 6x9.1GB drives in a RAID 1 array—in this case, you would only have 3x9.1GB of useable storage space.

How Does Parity Work?

Parity is a simple mathematical way of allowing you to determine what binary information "should" be present. Parity comes in several different flavors. Odd parity counts up the number of 1s in a group of bits. If the number is even, then the parity bit is set at 1, thus making the row odd. If the number is odd, then the parity bit is not set, keeping the row odd. Let's look at an example.

The following illustration shows the data stored in an array of four drives. In a parity system, three of these drives will store data.

DRIVE 1	DRIVE 2	DRIVE 3	DRIVE 4 (Parity)
1	0	1	x

If we were to perform an odd parity calculation on this, we would add up the number of 1s in this group (in this case two). Two is an even number; we need to make the row odd, so we set the parity bit to 1.

DRIVE 1	DRIVE 2	DRIVE 3	DRIVE 4 (Parity)
1	0	1	1

Now if one of these bits becomes corrupted (due to a drive failure), the result is as follows:

DRIVE 1	DRIVE 2	DRIVE 3	DRIVE 4 (Parity)
1	?	1	1

We can look at the parity bit for information as to what should be present on the failed device. In this case, we have the parity bit set indicating an even number of 1s in the other three locations. We can see two 1s (two is even), so we know that no more 1s are necessary to create an even number. Therefore, the missing bit is 0. The row now contains an odd number of 1s, which is correct.

The preceding example holds true for RAID 4, where parity is all stored on one drive, but in RAID 5 things get a little more complicated (on the surface, at least). Let's look at a RAID 5 example.

DRIVE 1	DRIVE 2	DRIVE 3	DRIVE 4
1	0	1	1(p)
0(p)	1	1	1
1	0(p)	0	0
0	0	1(p)	0

As you can see, the parity information is now spread across all four drives. Now if one drive were to fail, we would lose an entire column of data. You should not be concerned, however, because it so easy to recreate.

DRIVE 1	DRIVE 2 (crashed)	DRIVE 3	DRIVE 4
1	X	1	1(p)
0(p)	X	1	1
1	X	0	0
0	X	1(p)	0

The preceding illustration shows us the following:

- Row 1 has an odd number of 1s already (this is odd parity, remember). Therefore, the missing data must be 0 in order to keep the row odd.
- Row 2 has an even number of 1s. This needs to be odd, so we know that the missing data must contain a 1.
- Row 3 is odd already, so that's simple—we just need a 0 to keep it odd. Notice that this is actually the parity information that is missing, but that makes no difference in the calculations.
- Row 4 is again odd already, so the missing data must be 0

These calculations are fairly simple for a computer to perform, but the computer (literally) has a million other things to do with its time rather than calculate parity because of a drive failure. That calls for a solution such as Compaq's SMART-2 controller. A controller takes the burden of constantly calculating parity information for every single bit written away from the CPU, thus freeing up vital processor cycles for other work. Compare this to a software solution. Processor utilization just due to parity calculation can cripple even the fastest processor, obviously lowering the performance of other tasks running on the CPU.

CERTIFICATION OBJECTIVE 31.02

Configuring a Boot Partition for Windows NT Software Fault Tolerance

Like most other disk management tasks in Windows NT, managing fault tolerant arrays is performed in Disk Administrator (WINDISK.EXE). Upon entering Disk Administrator, you will see a graphical representation of all devices Windows NT has knowledge of.

The only software fault tolerance option that Windows NT Server will allow you to choose for a boot partition is RAID 1, or mirrored. The boot partition cannot be part of a stripe set, either with or without parity.

In order to create a software RAID 1 configuration, there must be an area of free disk space on a separate drive equal to, or exceeding, the size of the partition you wish to mirror. Figure 31-1 shows a typical Disk Administrator screen prior to any fault tolerant configuration.

To create the mirror, first select the partition you wish to mirror by left-clicking it. Next, select the area of free space to be used for the mirror partition by holding down CTRL and left-clicking the empty space. Select the Fault Tolerance menu item, and select Establish Mirror (See Figure 31-2). In order to complete this change, the system must now be rebooted. When Windows NT next boots, it will start the mirroring process, which will affect system performance for up to an hour (depending on the number of mirrors you created and the size of these partitions).

Creating the Recovery Disk

Now would be a great time to create the floppy disk you would use if your primary drive (the drive off which you initially boot) were to fail. This process is quite simple and involves the following steps.

1. Format a floppy disk for use within Windows NT.

FIGURE 31-1 Disk Administrator prior to any fault tolerant configuration

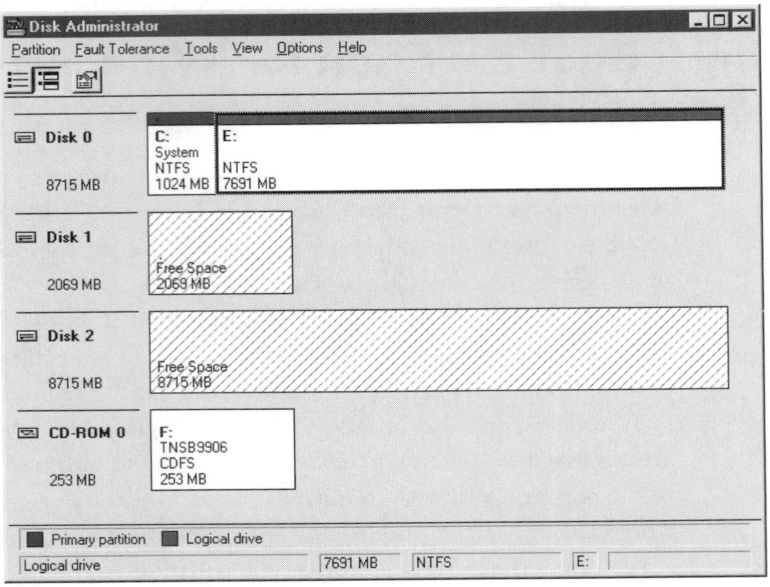

2. Copy the following files to the floppy disk (from the ROOT directory of the System partition):
   BOOT.INI
   NTLDR
   NTDETECT.COM
3. In order to tell Windows NT to boot from the good hard disk, not the failed primary, modify the BOOT.INI file. This process is shown next.

   Currently the BOOT.INI will look contain several lines similar to the following:

   ```
   multi(0)disk(0)rdisk(1)partition(1)\WINNT="Windows NT"
   ```

This is known as an ARC path (ARC standing for Advanced RISC Computing). In this case, Windows NT will boot from the first partition

FIGURE 31-2 Select Establish Mirror to begin the mirroring process

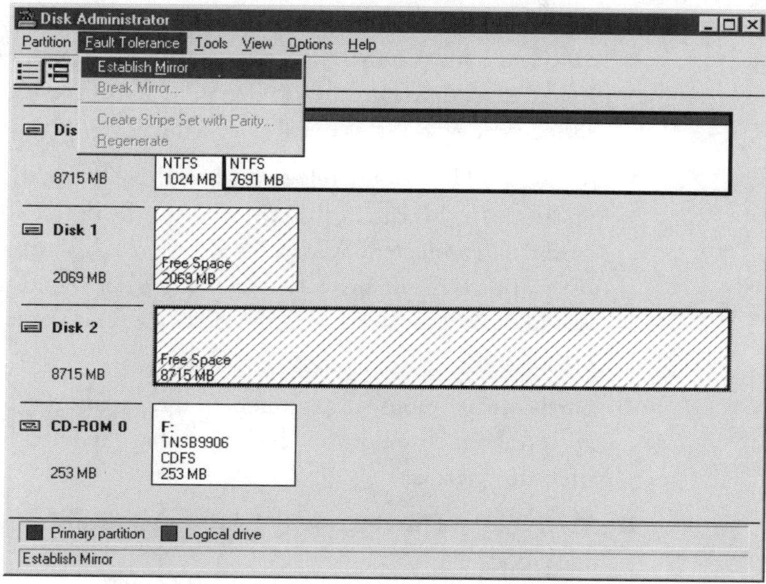

on the first hard disk. This obviously has to change if the first hard disk is no longer available due to failure. In order to modify the ARC path, we must know which portions of the path must changed in order to have the desired effect.

The ARC path is actually split into five distinct parts, these being multi(x), disk(x), rdisk(x), partition(x) and \<PATH>. Let's define what each of these terms means.

- **multi(x), or scsi(x)** This indicates the controller to which the hard disk is connected. In the case of the drive being connected to a SCSI controller without the BIOS translation enabled, this part will read scsi(x), with x indicating the controller number. The multi(x) moniker is seen more often, indicating that the hard disk is connected to a SCSI adapter with the BIOS enabled, or to an IDE controller. Again, x indicates the controller number. Note that x is an ordinal number, which means that the first controller in a system will be listed as 0, not 1.

- **disk(x)** This is only relevant when the ARC path begins scsi(x). In this case, disk(x) relates to the SCSI ID of the hard disk connected. Again, this number is ordinal.
- **rdisk(x)** This is only relevant when the ARC path begins with multi(x). In this case, rdisk(x) relates to the device number of the hard disk connected. With a SCSI system, this number is the SCSI ID. With IDE, the primary device would be 0 and the secondary would be 1. This portion of the path also uses the ordinal numbering.
- **partition(x)** This simply refers to the partition number you wish to boot from, on the device you have defined in the three preceding terms.
- **\WINNT** This refers to the directory in which the system files reside.

As an example, let's say, that the mirror contains two devices—one being at ID 0 on the first SCSI controller, the other being at ID 1 on the second SCSI controller. In both cases, Windows NT is installed on the first partition in the WINNT directory.

If you edit the BOOT.INI file, located in the root directory of the system partition, you will see the following line:

```
multi(0)disk(0)rdisk(0)partition(0)\WINNT="Windows NT"
```

If you have already followed the instructions given for creating a Windows NT boot disk, all you now have to do is edit the BOOT.INI file located on that floppy. Replace the preceding line with:

```
multi(1)disk(0)rdisk(1)partition(0)\WINNT="NT Recovery"
```

Now, in case of a primary drive failure, boot off this disk and you will have a fully functional installation. All that remains to be done is to break the mirror in Disk Administrator before replacing the failed drive.

The process just described was the Microsoft-recommended way of recovering from a disk failure. However, modifying the BOOT.INI file can sometimes be a case of trial and error. Several factors affect the numbering of partitions, including the existence of logical drives, which can really throw a spanner in the works. In the Compaq world of hot-swappable everything, there is a simpler way. With the system powered off, simply remove the failed primary drive, and place the mirror in its place. Assuming the partition structure of the drive is the same (which it nearly always is) the system will now boot exactly as before. Just break the mirror in Disk Administrator before replacing the drive.

Windows NT Software RAID 5

To create a RAID 5 protected partition, select three or more areas of space. Next, click the Fault Tolerance menu item, then select Create Stripe Set With Parity from the Fault Tolerance menu (Figure 31-3).

Disk Administrator will now prompt you to enter the total size of the RAID 5 volume you wish to create. Note that this includes the space that will later be set aside for parity information (Figure 31-4). The partition has thus been created. All that remains is to format the partition.

Windows NT uses a 64KB stripe size for RAID 5 volumes.

CERTIFICATION OBJECTIVE 31.03

Compaq Hardware-Based Fault Tolerance

Compaq's range of hardware RAID controllers (SMART controllers) allows for several different methods of fault tolerance configuration. In this section, we will look at several of these. The SMART controller is an essential component in both the online and standby recovery server options, and in Compaq's implementation of hardware RAID. It is the backbone of a Compaq fault tolerant strategy.

FIGURE 31-3 Starting the software RAID 5 configuration process

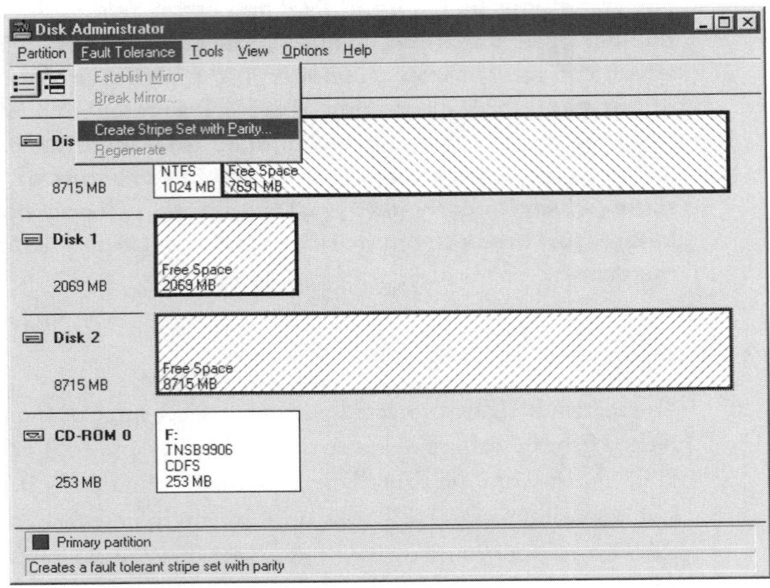

Compaq Hardware Mirroring

Compaq's hardware RAID controllers, each prefixed with the word "SMART," allow for different methods of configuration. Among those options is RAID 1, or hardware mirroring.

Unlike Windows NT software RAID 1, which performs the mirroring process on individual partitions, hardware RAID 1 will only allow you to mirror complete physical drives. One exception to this limitation is the capability of the SMART controller to mirror logical volumes. As you will see in the following section, a logical volume in this context refers to a volume created using the SMART controller. This can include a hardware RAID 5 set, which is why this leads to the capability to mix RAID levels on a single volume. One example of this could be RAID 0+1, where a stripe set (RAID 0) is mirrored onto an identical stripe set, using RAID 1 processes.

FIGURE 31-4 Configuring the RAID 5 partition

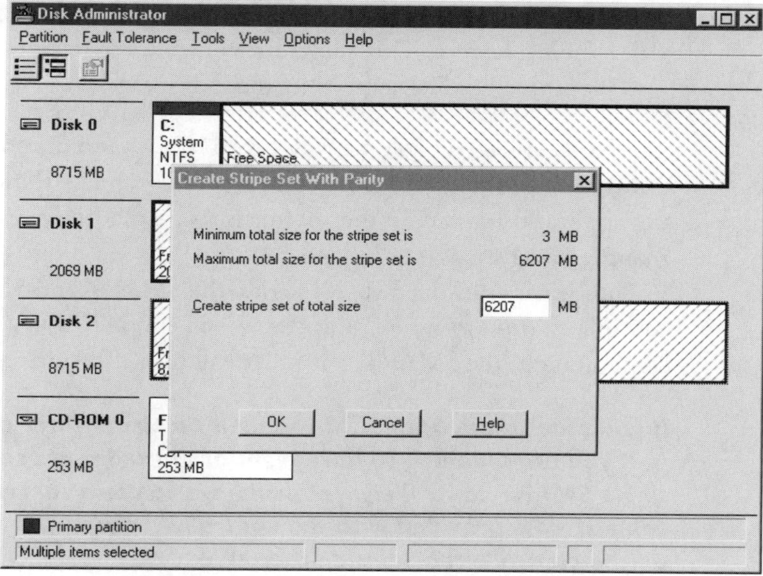

Hardware mirroring has several advantages over the software methods employed by Windows NT:

- Hardware mirroring allows the pairing of different RAID levels in a single volume—for example RAID 0+1, a stripe set which has been mirrored.
- Hardware mirroring allows the configuration of an *online spare.* This is a hard disk specifically set aside to act as an immediate replacement for any drive that fails in the array to which the spare is assigned. Note: A single online spare drive can be assigned to protect several RAID volumes.
- Hardware mirroring allows much quicker turnaround on a failed device. Replacing a failed drive simply requires the replacement to

be hot-plugged in. This does not require the operating system to be rebooted.

- Speed. The SMART controller is designed solely to provide RAID fault tolerance. This allows the controller to be optimized for this purpose, leading to performance advantages.

A hardware RAID volume will, for all intents and purposes, appear identical to a physical drive in Windows NT. Neither Windows NT nor any application stored on the volume is aware that the partition is, in fact, an array of drives.

Both versions of the SMART series, the SMART and SMART-2 controllers, support up to 14 drives. When configured in a RAID 1 configuration, the SMART controller will mirror the drives in 16KB stripes.

If you plan to use both SCSI channels on the SMART controller (that is, if you are planning to have eight or more devices connected to a single SMART controller), you will have to use a special loop-back cable. This is provided with the controller to feed the external port on the controller back inside the server.

Hardware RAID 4

RAID 4 is another option provided in hardware form by the SMART-2 controller, although it's advantages are few. As explained in the "RAID Fault Tolerance" section of this chapter, RAID 4 relies on a single drive to store the parity structure for the entire array. This single parity drive can act as a bottleneck for the whole drive array—in effect, preventing any concurrent write operations from taking place. Since concurrent operations are the main performance benefit of RAID, this is an undesirable situation.

RAID 4 has few benefits over RAID 5 (distributed data guarding). RAID 5 should be used in preference to RAID 4 in most circumstances.

Hardware RAID 5

RAID 5 is the primary reason most people choose the SMART-2 controller over the Windows NT software option. The performance benefits gained here are always important and, in the event of a drive failure, critical. These performance benefits are largely due to two factors:

- Dedicated parity calculation—independent from the CPU
- Large amounts of onboard cache to speed disk operations

Let's look at these two factors in more detail.

Dedicated Parity Calculation

The CPU on board the SMART controller is designed primarily to deal with parity calculations, and during use of the system, has very little else to do. This is in contrast to the main system CPUs, which can often be highly loaded at the best of times. The added strain of reconstructing data lost due to a single drive failure is to be avoided, if at all possible.

This point is proven if you take a look at the performance of a Windows NT system running software RAID 5 with the array in a broken state (that is, with the system CPU recreating data due to a single drive failure). On a reasonably robust machine, you will see processor utilization jump by up to 60 percent—obviously not a desirable situation. A similar system running hardware RAID 5 on a SMART controller in the same situation will hardly face a performance hit at all.

Onboard Cache

Another reason for the performance benefits achieved using SMART controllers is the large amounts of cache memory on board the SMART controller. This is called the Array Accelerator. In fact, 16MB of cache is available on the PCI versions of the SMART-2. The Array Accelerator allows the SMART controller to provide data requested by the system directly from the fast cache memory, instead of having to go to the comparatively slow disk drives for the information. One of the methods used to fill the cache with disk information is based on the prediction of the next disk read. Once this read has been predicted, the controller goes out to the disk and retrieves the data, so that it is waiting in the cache for the actual read operation to be requested by the system. Once this has occurred, the controller provides the information from cache rather than from disk.

However, cache information could be a massive weakness in the fault tolerance of the SMART, particularly when considering the caching of write information. If the system were to lose power, or the controller to fail during a write operation, the whole volume could be corrupted. This problem is combated by the fact that the cache is contained on a battery-backed up, removable module. If the power fails, the first thing the system will do on restart is flush the cache to disk. In the unlikely event of the SMART controller failing, the cache module can be swapped over onto the replacement controller, and again the system will flush the cache to disk on power up.

The SMART controllers implement RAID 5 using stripe sizes of 16KB.

Differences between the SMART and the SMART-2 Controllers

There are actually several models in the SMART-2 family of controllers. The more common are:

- SMART-2/P
- SMART-2/E
- SMART-2DH

Let's look at each of these controllers in more detail.

SMART-2/P

This PCI device consists of two Wide-Ultra SCSI-3 channels, allowing transfers rates of 40MB/sec to each of the channels. The supplied array accelerator contains 4MB of battery-backed up cache memory, with the battery being good for approximately four days in the event of power loss. Up to 14 devices can be connected to the controller. However, this requires connecting the pass-through cable to the external SCSI port, feeding it back into the case, and connecting to the secondary SCSI port on the drive cage.

SMART-2/E

This is similar to SMART-2/P, except that it runs on the EISA bus rather than PCI. This device consists of two Fast Wide channels, which are

FROM THE FIELD

Recent Additions to the Compaq Array Controller Product Line

Although you will not be expected to know the latest additions to the Compaq product line for the exam, it is worth noting that Compaq has replaced the SMART and SMART-2 controllers with four new controllers.

Smart Array 4200 This 64-bit controller card offers four times the processing performance of the other SMART controllers in the product line. This controller supports four channels and offers RAID levels 0, 0+1, 1, 4, and 5. It is ideal to keep pace with the demands of the Compaq eight-way SMP architecture.

Smart Array 3100ES This three-channel 64MB read/write cache card is an excellent choice for ProLiant 6000/7000 series servers, due to its optimized design for these enterprise class servers.

Smart Array 3200 This controller replaces the SMART-2DH controller. It supports two Ultra2-SCSI channels and uses a 64MB read/write cache for increased performance over the SMART-2DH.

Smart Array 221 This single-channel controller replaces the SMART-2/SL controller and is an ideal entry-level controller for small servers. It features a 6MB read cache and offers a seamless upgrade process to the Smart Array 3200.

For more information about the latest line of Compaq array controllers, check out Compaq's Web site at:

`http://www.compaq.com/products/storageworks/array_SCSI_controllers.html`

—Thomas E. Eck, MCSE+I, MCSD, ASE, CCA, CNA

capable of transfer rates of 20MB/sec each. Up to 14 devices can be connected using the pass-through cable

SMART-2DH

This is similar to SMART-2/P, but with 16MB of battery-backed up cache. Like the SMART-2/P, the SMART-2DH consists of two Wide Ultra channels, each capable of 40MB/sec. Seven devices can be connected to each channel, 14 in total.

QUESTIONS AND ANSWERS	
I need to maximize performance, no matter what the costs…	Use RAID 0. RAID 0 has all the advantages of RAID 5, including multiple concurrent read and write operations, and none of the parity generation overhead.
What is the best way to protect a Compaq server, running Windows NT, which does not have a SMART-2 controller installed?	Fit three or more hard disks in the system. Install Windows NT on a 1GB partition, which should be mirrored to one of the other drives. Use the remainder of the space of the drives to create a RAID 5 array. This will leave you with 1GB free space on one of the drives. Use this as space for the swap file.
What happens if a member of a software RAID 1 mirror fails, and I haven't made the fault tolerant boot disk?	No problem, just create the disk on any Windows NT Server or Workstation. As long as the disk contains the correct files, and the BOOT.INI file points to the correct drive, it doesn't matter.
Will I actually notice the performance difference that a SMART-2 controller makes?	In normal operation (when there are no drive failures), the difference may not be noticeable. If a failure occurs, however, performance of a software RAID system will soon be effected. In this situation, a SMART-2 controller will make a huge difference.
Which should I choose, RAID 4 or RAID 5?	Unless you have a very good reason to implement RAID 4, you should always choose to go with RAID 5. RAID 5 removes the bottleneck (the single parity drive created in RAID 4), which impeded RAID 4's performance. RAID 4 also affected the reliability of the parity drive, due to the amount of extra work created for it.

SMART

As the forefather of the SMART-2 series, the SMART controller wasn't quite as advanced as the SMART-2. One big difference sets them apart: the SMART-2 uses an advanced RISC-based processor (to be precise, an AMD 29040-33). The original SMART, however, utilized a much more "off the shelf" processor, an INTEL 80486SX. The AMD 29040-33 can outperform the 80486 in this circumstance by as much as 100 percent. Several more factors serve to increase the performance of the SMART-2:

- **Advanced Parity Generation Engine** Compaq developed a new, advanced RAID 5 engine that allows the SMART-2 to generate parity information as soon as data is written to the controller. Several of these operations can be performed in parallel, eliminating the bottleneck that could result from a single parity generation engine.

- **Array Accelerator** The SMART-2 features up to 16MB of onboard cache memory, compared to the 2MB on board the SMART.
- **Onboard Expansion** RAID-protected volumes can be resized online with the SMART-2 controller. However, Windows NT will not allow a partition to change size after creation. Therefore, if the online expansion facility is used, the extra space created must be formatted as a new, logical drive.
- **Bridged PCI** The SMART-2 controller is a bridged PCI device. This means that the SMART-2 controller is itself a complete PCI bus. This leads to several advantages, including the fact that the SMART-2 is the only device on this bus, so there is increased bandwidth availability.
- **Read ahead caching** Unlike the SMART controller, the SMART-2 has the capability to cache data for read operations. It does this by detecting sequential read operations and going ahead to read information from the disk before that information is actually requested by the host.

CERTIFICATION OBJECTIVE 31.04

Compaq ProLiant Storage System

The ProLiant Storage System (PSS) is, in effect, an advanced external drive cage. It is available in several different options, capable of holding up to 12 one-inch hot-pluggable hard disks. Obviously, in order to support 12 drives, this version of the PSS must contain at least two SCSI busses. The SCSI ID of the drives are assigned by the PSS, which, like the ProLiant server range, does this assignment by location in the actual cage.

TABLE 31-1 Differing Capabilities of the ProLiant Storage Systems

Model Number	SCSI Type	Number of SCSI Buses	Number of 1" Drives Supported	Number of 1.6" Drives Supported	Internal Duplexing?
U1	Ultra Wide	1	7	7	N
U2	Ultra Wide	2	12	8	Y
F1	Fast Wide	1	7	7	N
F2	Fast Wide	2	12	8	Y

You can identify the capabilities of the different type of PSS by looking at Table 31-1.

All the PSS options feature automatic SCSI bus termination. Like the rest of the ProLiant range, the PSS features Compaq's Automatic Server Recovery (ASR) system. This system monitors the status of several features of the PSS, including the status of fans, power supplies, and the actual temperature of the PSS unit. If necessary, ASR can initiate a shutdown to protect data integrity. In order to monitor a ProLiant storage system from within Insight Manager, it is essential that the PSS driver (PRLNTSS.SYS) be installed from the latest version of the Windows NT Compaq Software Support Diskette (SSD).

CERTIFICATION OBJECTIVE 31.05

Standby Recovery Server

The standby recovery server is one of Compaq's implementations of increased-availability clustering. This system allows one ProLiant server to be assigned as a "standby" for another, similarly configured server. It works as follows.

Two Compaq servers fitted with SMART-2 controllers are attached to a single ProLiant Storage System. This PSS contains drives that hold a common copy of the operating system, and also any data and applications. In normal operation, the primary system (the system to be protected) "owns" the PSS and acts as if it were the only system there. It maintains communication via a series of heartbeat messages over a recovery server interconnect cable, which is attached to a similar Compaq server. This recovery server is executing code contained within its BIOS, called the Compaq Recovery Agent (CRA), which monitors the heartbeat signal sent over the Recovery Signal Interconnect cable. Should this recovery server not receive any heartbeat signal, it will presume that the primary server has failed, and will initiate a process called failover (also referred to as switchover). Failover begins with the recovery server sending commands to the ProLiant Storage System, instructing the PSS to disconnect the primary server and reconnect itself to the recovery server. The recovery server then proceeds through a normal boot, using the set of drives it acquired in the PSS. Once this boot process is complete, the recovery server acts as if it is the primary.

Let's take a look at a few failover causes.

Primary Server Hardware Failure

Obviously, in the case of a hardware failure on the primary server, failover is desirable. This will minimize any downtime due to the hardware failure, allowing clients to log on again with minimal administrative intervention.

Primary Server Operating System Failure

Switchover is normally desirable, but there are several occasions when this event is triggered accidentally. One example is evident with Windows NT (running Service Pack 3 or lower) and Microsoft Exchange. Under some circumstances, Windows NT can become unresponsive when running Exchange. The heartbeat process is affected to the extent that the recovery server doesn't receive a heartbeat within the required timeout, and thus initiates switchover.

Recovery Server Interconnect Cable Is Disconnected

If the cable is disconnected or broken, then the recovery server will no longer receive heartbeat signals. The primary server will also not receive acknowledgment messages from the recovery server. These acknowledgment messages indicate that the recovery server has received the heartbeat. Due to this loss of acknowledgment, the primary now predicts that the recovery server will be starting the process of failover shortly, and in anticipation of this, the primary server will initiate a clean operation system shutdown.

The recovery server, meanwhile, is pondering the loss of heartbeat. Once the timeout period has expired, the process of failover begins by switching ownership of the PSS and booting the OS. Things are now back to normal for the users—but just imagine what could have happened if this shutdown/reboot process had not occurred. The recovery server would detect the loss of the heartbeat, and begin failover by taking ownership of the PSS. The primary server would not be expecting this, and Windows NT would possibly blue-screen. It is possible that Windows NT could continue, in a diminished state, to operate on the network. When the recovery server has rebooted there will be, in effect, two servers operating under the same NetBIOS name, with the same IP address, possibly each reporting to be the PDC of the same domain—not a desirable situation!

Restoring After a Failover

After a failover event has occurred, and the primary server has been serviced, it is obviously desirable to get back to a situation where the primary server is being protected by the standby. This is achieved by power-cycling both machines. Remember that this process can be completed at any time, so the end of the business day seems the obvious choice.

Requirements

The following list highlights the requirements for the standby recovery server.

- **Two similar Compaq servers** As both machines must boot from the same drives, it is a requirement that both servers be similar. Preferably, they will be identically configured.
- **SMART, or SMART-2 controller** The array accelerator on the SMART should be disabled; on the SMART-2, it should be set at 100 percent Read.

- **One PSS** Either F1 or U1 model. The F2 and U2 models are not supported.
- **Recovery server option kit** This kit contains the required accessories and the recovery server interconnect cable.
- **Free serial port** The same COM port needs to be free on both servers to allow communication of the heartbeat between the two.
- **NTFS file system** NTFS is inherently more reliable and stable than the FAT file system, so all partitions should be formatted with the NTFS file system.

Continuity of Service

Any clients connected to the server at the time of failure will experience disruption. This is simply due to the fact that during the failover process there is no server available to host any connections. Clients on Windows NT networks will invariably see a retry/fail error message. If the client retries the operation once the standby server is online, service should be restored. However, if the client is running an application that depends upon the continuity of a connection, there is likely to be loss of functionality.

Setting Up a Standby Server

To set up a standby server, start by configuring the Compaq servers. Install any hardware, making sure that the PCI devices go into the same slot number on both machines. Upgrade the firmware on both SMART controllers, and the servers themselves with the latest version of the Compaq Rompaq. Next, install the recovery server switch from the Recovery Server Option Pack in the ProLiant Storage System. Connect both of the servers to the recovery server switch using the external SCSI cables supplied (in the options pack) and connect the two servers with the recovery server interconnect cable.

To configure each server with the role it will play in the pair (primary or recovery), perform the following steps:

1. Enter the F10 partition and run the System Configuration utility.

2. Set the software MAC address of both servers to be identical; this too is achieved in the System Configuration utility.
3. Install Windows NT.
4. Run the latest version of the Compaq SSD to install support for the standby recovery server. (At the same time, the SSD updates drivers for the SMART controller and several other devices.)

CERTIFICATION OBJECTIVE 31.06

Online Recovery Server

The second of Compaq's clustering implementations also involves two servers. This time, however, the second server is not just sitting waiting for a failover to occur. When implemented in an online recovery configuration, the Compaq Recovery Server option allows the recovery server to play an active part on the network, whether as a file and print server or as an application server. This effectively doubles the available processing power over the standby configuration option.

The hardware requirements for this option do vary somewhat from the requirements for the standby recovery server. In the standby configuration, both servers needed to be configured very similarly, because both servers needed to be able to boot from the other server's disks. In the online configuration, this is not the case. Each server contains local hard disks from which to boot. All data is stored on an external ProLiant Storage System, to which both servers are attached (see Figure 31-5). As you can see, the use of two ProLiant Storage Systems requires two SMART controllers in each server—one to connect to the primary server, another to connect to the recovery server. This effectively leads to a situation in which both servers are connected to two PSSs. As each server stores its own copy of the operating system and drivers from which to boot, it is possible to have two servers with varying specifications in the online recovery server configuration.

Like the standby recovery server, the online version uses a recovery server interconnect cable in order to detect the status of the other server. In this

FIGURE 31-5 How the ProLiant Storage Systems are cabled together

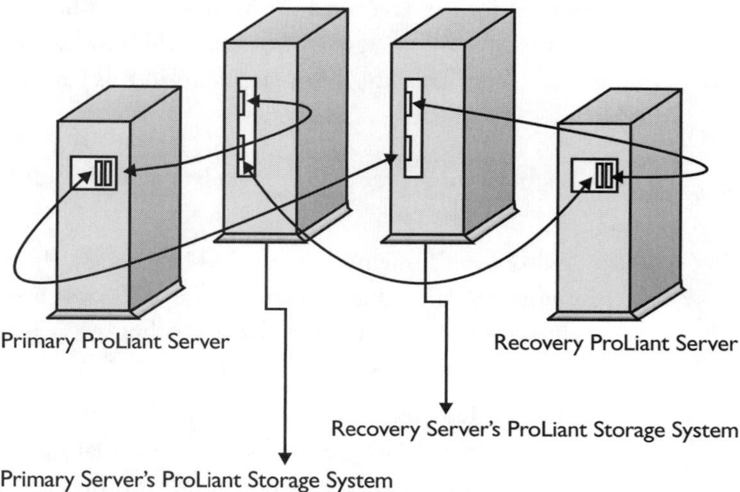

case, both servers need to be running the Compaq Recovery Agent, which generates the heartbeats and acknowledgment messages. This is because, unlike the standby recover server configuration, where one server was specified as a primary and another as a standby, in the online configuration the roles are not obvious. If one server fails, the other must take over and vice versa. Thus, each server must know the status of the other. This status update is determined though the heartbeats generated by the CRA. It is important to note that the two servers do not share the ProLiant Storage Systems. The Recovery Server switch in the PSS determines which server is electronically connected to the PSS; obviously, only one server can be connected at a time.

To begin the setup process, it is advised that Windows NT be installed before the SMART controllers. This ensures that only the local storage devices are used for any operating system files. The PSS should only contain high-availability information. Both servers should be installed in the same domain in order to ease the reconnection process if switchover were to occur.

Installation of the online recovery server software is performed using the Compaq Windows NT SSDs. Once this software is installed, the configuration for the agents can be found in the Windows NT Control Panel (named Recovery Agent). These should now be configured. It is important to configure the following items in this Control Panel applet correctly.

- **Enable Switchover** This must be enabled on at least one of the servers in the pair.
- **Switchover Timeout** Measured in seconds, this value is the amount of time that a heartbeat signal has not been detected before the recovery agent decides that the other server is no longer available and initiates the switchover process.
- **Startup Timeout** Measured in seconds, this value is the amount of time the recovery agent will wait after initial startup for a heartbeat signal before initiating switchover. If it is disabled, the value is effectively set at infinite, and the recovery agent is not concerned with the other heartbeat signal until it actually receives one. At this point, the switchover timeout value begins to take effect.
- **Enable Network Connectivity Check** This item controls whether the network is used as the heartbeat medium in case of recovery server interconnect cable failure.
- **Initiate Immediate Switchover** Normally only used to test correct installation.

Continuity of Service

If a loss of the heartbeat signal is detected by the CRA on one of the servers, that server will wait for the timeout period specified in the Control Panel applet before initiating switchover. If this value is reached and no further heartbeat pulses have been received, that server will initiate switchover. This server will now send a message to its recovery SMART controller, requesting that the other server's ProLiant Storage System disconnect itself from the primary controller in the failed server and reconnect to the recovery controller in this server. The operating system is now asked to mount the volumes acquired from the failed server. It then optionally launches a batch file. This batch file can, for example, reshare the drives on the new server. At this stage, all data originally stored on the primary server is now available on the recovery server, albeit with different sharename paths. For clients to use these new shares, they must log on again.

Let's illustrate this process with an example. In this scenario, you have two servers, server 1 and server 2, which have been installed in an online recovery server configuration. In normal operation, server 1 and server 2 are communicating to each other with heartbeat messages that are still operational. If server 1 were to suffer an operating system crash, the Compaq Recovery Agent, which was sending out heartbeat messages to server 2, would be unable to continue to do so. Server 2 would detect this loss of heartbeat and wait for a time specified by the timeout value before taking any further action. This timeout value serves to prevent unwanted switchover. For example, server 1 may have faced a period of extreme utilization, restricting its ability to send a heartbeat.

If the timeout value is exceeded, server 2 will initiate switchover. Server 2 now sends a command to the recovery SMART controller installed in server 2 (attached to PSS 1), requesting that PSS 1 be disconnected from the primary SMART controller in server 1 and connected to the recovery SMART controller in server 2. PSS 1 responds to this request and switches itself onto the recovery SMART controller in server 2. Server 2 now effectively controls both PSS 1 and PSS 2. The Compaq Recovery Agent informs the operating system on server 2 of this change. The OS now mounts the volumes on PSS 1 and launches a batch file, which will reshare any information stored on PSS 1.

on the job

The logon scripts on the servers must take into account that at some point, clients may be trying to log on to the domain when one of the servers has failed and switchover has taken place. In this scenario, any NET USE commands in the logon script that happen to point to the failed server will be invalid. To counter this, it is necessary that any NET USE commands in the logon script be succeeded with an IF ERRORLEVEL statement, which maps the drives to the failover shares on the other server.

CERTIFICATION OBJECTIVE 31.07

Compaq Advanced Network Fault Detection and Correction

The Netelligent and NetFlex-3 series of network cards feature an advanced array of fault detection and correction features.

The role of a network card means that it could be a single point of failure in a server setup. Like redundant CPUs, fans, and power supplies, redundant network card pairs can help to alleviate the situation. By combining two network interface cards into a single entity, any failure can be rectified simply by passing the tasks of the failed card on to a redundant spare.

Unlike most other redundancy setups, the individual devices in the network card redundancy pair needn't be identical. Any of the ThunderLAN-based network cards support the Advanced Network Error Correction. These include cards from the NetFlex-3 and Netelligent ranges. To Windows NT, this controller pair appears to be a single entity driven by a single driver and reporting a single MAC address. (The recovery controller sets its MAC address to be identical to the primary controller.)

Installation of the Advanced Network Utilities

All aspects of the Advanced Network Fault Detection process are handled by just two components, the Compaq Advanced Network Control utility (accessed through Control Panel) and the NetFlex-3 device driver. The Windows NT SSD installs both of these components. Upon entering the Advanced Network Control utility, you will be presented with a screen listing all available Compaq network controllers. Simply double-clicking one of these controllers allows you to manage the configuration of that controller, including options such as setting the network speed and duplex setting.

The Network Control utility also lets you set up a controller pair. This pair can contain several different types of controller; they do not have to be identical. However, they must both be of the same bus type and use the same physical network connection type.

Compaq Advanced Network Control utility can also provide a good indication as to any problems currently being experienced on the network. The utility does this by presenting a series of icons next to each of the controllers. These icons graphically represent the status of the controllers. If a controller has failed, the icon next to it will show a red exclamation mark, indicating attention required. If the controller detects a cable failure, a broken cable will appear as the icon. In either of these cases, if that failing adapter was part of a controller pair, the NetFlex-3 driver would switch network traffic onto the new card. In the process of doing this, it will disable the failed card.

CERTIFICATION OBJECTIVE 31.08

Adding Bridged PCI Devices to a ProLiant 5000, 6000, 6500, and 7000

Peripheral Component Interconnect (PCI) buses are not required on a system board. It is also entirely possible for a PCI bus to be contained on an expansion card, one prime example of this being Compaq's SMART-2 series of array controllers. PCI specifications impose tight restrictions on both the technical and electrical elements of the bus. These specifications restrict the size of the bus to between four and six devices. This could prove to be a large problem in the server market. A single server could potentially require six network cards alone. To get around this issue, many systems use two or more system buses. There are two ways this can be achieved: by extending the length of the bus with a PCI-PCI bridge (a bridged PCI bus), and by creating a totally new branch off the system bus (a dual-peer PCI-bus).

The PCI BIOS assigns a bus number to each PCI bus in a system during system power-on. Because of this, it is entirely possible that if a controller featuring a bridged PCI design is added to a dual-peer PCI system, the number of the secondary PCI bus on the system board could change. This would spell disaster in a Windows NT configuration, where drivers often have to know which PCI bus they are on when installing the driver. Let's look at an example.

If a PCI network card is installed into slot 2 on a ProLiant 7000, the driver will require you to tell it which bus it is installed in. In this case, slot 2 is attached to the secondary bus. If a SMART-2 controller is added to slot 8, which corresponds to the primary bus, when the system next boots, the PCI BIOS in the server will detect this new device and renumber the PCI buses. The primary bus will become 0, the PCI-PCI bridge on the SMART-2 controller will become bus 1, and the secondary PCI bus on the system board will become 2. When the network card drivers attempt to initialize, they will be looking for a network card on the SMART-2 controller. Obviously they won't find one, so the drivers will fail. It can sometimes be very difficult to discover what is going on in such situations. Removing the SMART-2 controller will allow the drivers to start again, making it look like some kind of conflict between the two is causing the problem.

The best way to avoid this issue is to follow Compaq's guidelines for installing PCI cards into specific server. Some useful utilities are included at:

http://www.compaq.com/partners/microsoft/download/pciutils.html

These utilities allow you to specify which devices are installed in which slot on your ProLiant servers, and show you the PCI bus numbers changing accordingly.

Another important aspect of configuration that this utility attempts to automate is the balancing of load on the dual PCI buses. What is the point of having two PCI buses in a server, and then simply installing all PCI devices on a single bus? This would simply saturate one of the PCI buses, leaving the other one unused. An excellent tool to use for PCI load balancing is Compaq Insight Manager. Once the latest drivers have been installed for all devices in the system (using the latest Compaq SSD), and Insight Manager has been installed and configured, you can use Insight Manager to view the load on the PCI buses in real time. Moving PCI devices off the saturated bus and onto an underutilized one can lead to performance increases.

CERTIFICATION SUMMARY

In this chapter, you have learned about the four RAID levels available in the Compaq and Windows NT world. You have seen the advantages and disadvantages of each, and now know how they actually work at protecting your system (or not, in the case of RAID 0). You have learned how to implement RAID in several different scenarios—with a SMART-2 controller or just with Windows NT Server's software implementation of RAID.

You have seen the ProLiant Storage System, which can be used to store hundreds of megabytes of information. You have seen how the PSS is used in the online and standby recovery server modes.

You have also learned how to set up your network interface controller in a fault tolerant configuration, and how to determine if it has failed.

TWO-MINUTE DRILL

- A Redundant Array of Inexpensive Drives (RAID) is a fundamental way of increasing the reliability and performance of a Compaq server.
- There are four main types of RAID configuration in the Compaq world:
  - RAID 0 Data striping (not fault tolerant)
  - RAID 1 Disk mirroring
  - RAID 4 Data guarding
  - RAID 5 Distributed data guarding
- RAID 0 does not provide any fault tolerance—in fact it actually *increases* risk, due to the fact that a single disk failure would mean the entire array of data would be lost.
- RAID 1 mirrors all data to both drives; if one drive fails, there is an exact replica from which to continue working.

- RAID 4 provides a single drive to maintain parity information for the entire array.
- RAID 5 stripes parity information across all the drives in the array, effectively making RAID 5 a stripe set with parity.
- Parity is a simple mathematical way of allowing you to determine what binary information "should" be present.
- Compaq's SMART-2 controller takes the burden of constantly calculating parity information for every single bit written away from the CPU, thus freeing up vital processor cycles for other work.
- Managing fault tolerant arrays is performed in Disk Administrator (WINDISK.EXE).
- The only software fault tolerance option that Windows NT Server will allow you to choose for a boot partition is RAID 1, or mirrored.
- The SMART controller is an essential component in both the online and standby recovery server options, and in Compaq's implementation of hardware RAID.
- Hardware RAID 1 will only allow you to mirror complete physical drives.
- Both versions of the SMART series, the SMART and SMART-2 controllers, support up to 14 drives.
- RAID 4 has few benefits over RAID 5 (distributed data guarding).
- RAID 5 is the primary reason most people choose the SMART-2 controller over the Windows NT software option.
- There are actually several different models in the SMART-2 family of controllers. The more common ones are:
  - SMART-2/P
  - SMART-2/E
  - SMART-2DH
- The ProLiant Storage System (PSS) is, in effect, an advanced external drive cage.

- ❑ The standby recovery server is one of Compaq's implementations of increased-availability clustering.
- ❑ In the case of a hardware failure on the primary server, failover is desirable.
- ❑ If the cable is disconnected or broken, then the recovery server will no longer receive heartbeat signals.
- ❑ After a failover event has occurred, and the primary server has been serviced, it is desirable to get back to a situation where the primary server is being protected by the standby.
- ❑ Any clients connected to the server at the time of failure will experience disruption.
- ❑ To set up a standby server, start by configuring the Compaq servers.
- ❑ When implemented in an online recovery configuration, the Compaq Recovery Server option allows the recovery server to play an active part on the network, whether as a file and print server or as an application server.
- ❑ If a loss of the heartbeat signal is detected by the CRA on one of the servers, that server will wait for the timeout period specified in the Control Panel applet before initiating switchover.
- ❑ The Netelligent and NetFlex-3 series of network cards feature an advanced array of fault detection and correction features.
- ❑ All aspects of the Advanced Network Fault Detection process are handled by just two components, the Compaq Advanced Network Control utility (accessed through Control Panel) and the NetFlex-3 device driver.
- ❑ Peripheral Component Interconnect (PCI) buses are not required on a system board.

SELF TEST

The following Self Test questions will help you measure your understanding of the material presented in this chapter. Read all the choices carefully, as there may be more than one correct answer. Choose all correct answers for each question.

1. Acme Inc's primary Web server has just suffered a hard disk failure. For performance reasons, the drive was attached to a SMART-2 controller, and configured as part of a RAID 0 array. How should the administrator go about recovering from the failure?
   - A. Replace the failed drive; Automatic Data Recovery on the SMART controller will do the rest.
   - B. Replace the failed drive and reinstall all data from yesterday's backup.
   - C. Replace the failed drive, enter Array Configuration Utilities, and choose the Recover option. Follow on-screen prompts.
   - D. Run Windows NT Setup, choosing Recover when prompted.
2. Which RAID level is not provided in software form as part of Windows NT Server 4.0?
   - A. RAID 0
   - B. RAID 1
   - C. RAID 4
   - D. RAID 5
3. You are required to implement a Web server that is not mission-critical. The load on the server may be quite high at times. Which of the following disk configurations would you choose in order to seek the best disk performance?
   - A. Software RAID 5, 3x9.1GB SCSI hard disks
   - B. Hardware RAID 0, 5x4.3GB SCSI hard disks
   - C. Hardware RAID 5, 3x9.1 GB SCSI hard disks
   - D. 1x9.1GB IDE hard disk
4. Your company needs an e-mail server. Uptime is of prime importance, but finances are limited. The server will house around 200 mailboxes, with an allowance of 15MB per mailbox. Which solution would be most viable?
   - A. Hardware RAID 0, 5x4.3GB drives
   - B. Hardware RAID 5, 3x2.1GB drives
   - C. Software RAID 1, 2x2.1GB drives
   - D. Hardware RAID 1, 2x4.3GB drives
5. Your server contains a SMART-2 controller running a single RAID 5-protected volume consisting of 8x4.3GB drives, and 2x4.3 GB drives in RAID 1 storing the operating system. Yesterday, a power surge knocked out two of the drives belonging to the RAID 5 volume. How would you go about repairing the situation?

A. Replace the drives; Automatic Data Recovery will do the rest.

B. Replace the drives; restore the data from yesterday's backup.

C. Replace the drive with the lowest SCSI ID, and let Automatic Data Recovery merge it. Then replace the second drive, and the volume will now be complete.

D. Select Recover Volume from the System Configuration utilities, and follow screen prompts.

6. Where do you manage software RAID volumes in Windows NT?

A. Right-click the drive in My Computer in Explorer. Choose Manage Volume from the context menu.

B. Use the Fault Tolerance tab from within system applet in Control Panel.

C. Use Disk Administrator in Administrative Tools (common) from the Start menu.

D. Type **RDISK /config** from the command prompt.

7. Your BDC has just suffered a hard disk failure. Fortunately, the drive was part of a software RAID 1 array. After replacing the failed drive, you notice that Windows NT will no longer boot. Which is the best solution?

A. Reinstall Windows NT on the new hard disk. Once installed, copy all data from the other member of the array.

B. Format a diskette on a Windows NT workstation, copy NTLDR, NTDETECT.COM, and BOOT.INI to this disk. Modify BOOT.INI to point to the "good" hard disk, then boot this floppy disk.

C. Run Windows NT Setup, and choose Recover when prompted.

D. Reinstall Windows NT, and restore data from yesterday's backup.

8. As part of an ongoing project, you are required to add a 4.3GB hard disk to a Windows NT 4.0 server, containing a SMART-2 RAID controller. It is a requirement that this hard disk be mirrored to an existing hard disk that has 5GB of unpartitioned space. What is the best way of achieving this?

A. Create a 4.3GB partition on both the hard disks. Format this space using the NTFS file system, select both of these new partitions, and click Fault Tolerance | Establish Mirror.

B. Using the Array Configuration utility, select both partitions and assign them to a RAID 1 array.

C. Using Disk Administrator, select the 4.3GB of unpartitioned space on the new hard disk. Select Partition | Create, and create a 4.3GB partition. Format this partition using NTFS, and select both this and the unpartitioned space on the other hard disk. Click Fault Tolerance, and establish the mirror.

D. Using WINDISK.EXE, select both areas of unpartitioned space, and click Fault Tolerance | Establish Mirror.

9. How many devices are supported by the SMART-2DH series of RAID controllers?

   A. 7

   B. 11

   C. 14

   D. 15

10. You have just received your ProLiant 7000 server, fitted with a SMART-2 controller. You will be using the internal drive cages in the ProLiant 7000 to mount 10 4.3GB hard disks, which should be configured as part of a RAID 5 array. You notice that each drive cage on the ProLiant requires a separate SCSI channel. What must you do on the SMART-2 controller to enable this?

   A. Feed the external connector of the SMART-2 controller back into the PC.

   B. Configure the DEVICES parameter in the System Configuration utility.

   C. Obtain a SCSI cable extender.

   D. It is not possible, and requires further SMART-2 controllers to be fitted.

11. How much cache memory is available on board the SMART-2DH controller?

   A. 2MB

   B. 6MB

   C. 16MB

   D. 32MB

12. You recently added an extra drive to your RAID 5 array. How do you go about expanding your current Windows NT system partition?

   A. Assign the drive to the array in the Array Configuration utility. Once online expansion is complete, the size of the system partition will reflect the increased space available to the array.

   B. Assign the drive to the array in the Array Configuration utility. Once online expansion is complete, use Disk Administrator to increase the size of the system partition.

   C. It is not possible to increase the size of the system partition after creation.

   D. Insert the drive. At the next system boot, the controller will launch Array Configuration utilities. Use them to expand the system partition.

13. You install the Compaq Insight Agent on your ProLiant 3000 and still cannot view the status of the ProLiant Storage System to which the system is connected. What action do you take?

   A. Install the latest Windows NT Service Pack.

   B. Ensure that the latest SMART-2 driver is installed.

   C. Install the PRLNTSS.SYS driver from the Windows NT SSD.

   D. Shut down and restart the server. Insight Manager will be able to communicate with the PSS once the server has restarted.

14. You have two Compaq ProLiant 7000 servers in a standby recovery configuration. You return to work on a Monday morning to discover the primary server has failed and operation has been switched over to the recovery server. What steps should be taken to return the configuration to normal?

    A. Service the failed primary server. Shut down the recovery server at a convenient time and turn both machines back on. The primary server will resume its normal role.

    B. Service the failed primary server. Power the primary server back up. The ProLiant Storage Systems will be reconnected to the primary server, and normal operation will recommence.

    C. Service the failed primary server. Use the Recovery Agent applet in Control Panel to initiate a switchover.

    D. Service the failed primary server. Power the primary server back up and unplug the recovery server interconnect cable to initiate switchover.

15. You are implementing a fault tolerant pair by using a NetFlex-3/P 10/100 controller, and a Netelligent 10/100 controller. Compaq Advanced Network Control utility shows a gray icon next to the Netelligent controller. What is likely to be the problem?

    A. Cable failure

    B. Adapter hardware failure

    C. No driver installed

    D. Cable OK

16. After adding a SMART-2 controller to a ProLiant 6500, you discover that the network driver fails to initialize. As part of your fault-finding procedures, you remove the SMART-2 controller. The network card now works perfectly. What is the problem?

    A. An IRQ conflict between the SMART-2 and the network card

    B. A faulty SMART-2 controller

    C. The PCI bus number to which the network card is attached has changed.

    D. An out-of-date driver for the SMART-2 controller is claiming an address space already allocated to the network controller.

ASE
ACCREDITED SYSTEMS ENGINEER

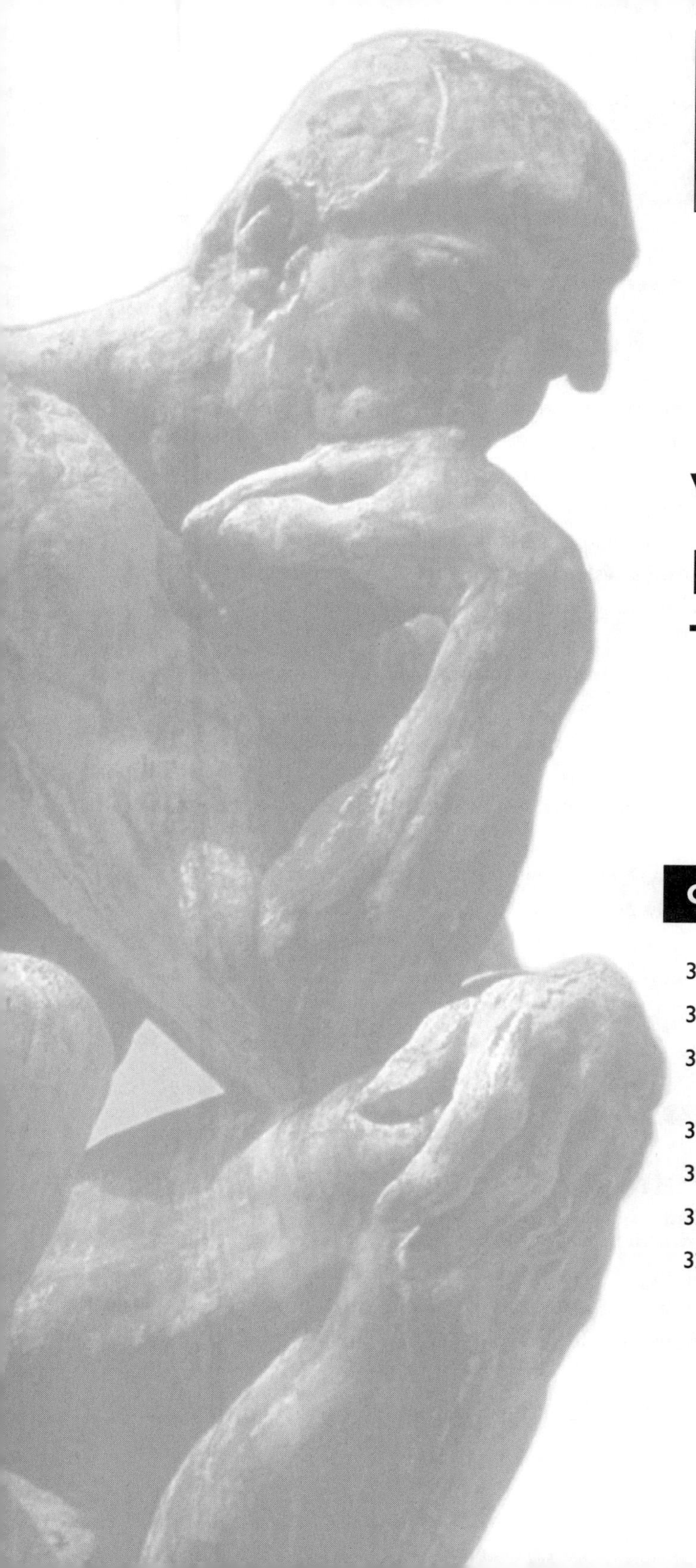

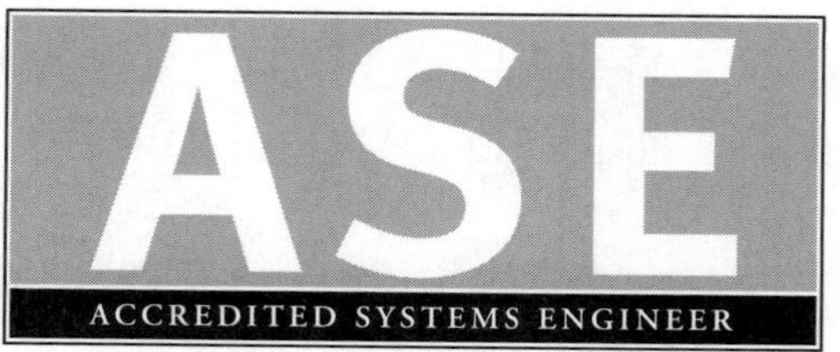

32

Windows NT Performance Tuning

CERTIFICATION OBJECTIVES

32.01	Windows NT Performance Monitor
32.02	Windows NT Memory Subsystem
32.03	Configuring the Server Component in the Network Control Panel
32.04	Disk Performance Factors
32.05	Setting a Process's Base Priority
32.06	Subsystem Load by Server Role
32.07	Performance Monitor Counters

Some say that the true measure of a system administrator is his or her ability to tweak every ounce of performance from a server. Although Microsoft touts Windows NT's capability to be self-tuning, there are still several ways to enhance system performance through proper configuration and Registry hacks.

Before you can increase system performance, you will have to establish a baseline against which you can measure the increased performance. The main utility that you use to measure system performance is Windows NT's Performance Monitor. Once you establish a baseline and make changes to your system, you will again use Performance Monitor to measure the operation of the various system components. This chapter will help you become familiar with the Performance Monitor utility and learn how to get the most out of it.

Once you are comfortable with Performance Monitor, we will delve into the various server subsystems and how each affects overall performance. The four major subsystems to a server are the processor, the memory, the disk, and the network. We will cover counters to track the performance of each of the subsystems and learn how to tune each one to optimize overall system performance.

We will also take a look at how to tune performance for the different roles that a server may perform. A server can act as a file server, an application server, or both. Optimizing the hardware and subsystem components for the role will improve performance dramatically.

CERTIFICATION OBJECTIVE 32.01

Windows NT Performance Monitor

Windows NT Performance Monitor (PerfMon) will be your primary tool for measuring system performance. PerfMon works by measuring *counters* for the different system *objects*. Objects are the different subsystems of the server, while counters are the various aspects of a particular object that can be measured. Examples of objects include processors, memory, and paging file, while examples of counters include %utilization, reads/sec, bytes/sec. Different objects will contain different counters. This section will introduce you to Performance Monitor and show you how to use it to track the health status of your server.

FROM THE FIELD

The Server Shell Game

Using Performance Monitor, we can establish firm, scientific evidence as to the necessity (or lack thereof) for a system upgrade. We often put our newest computing resources where they do not belong. Too many technologists and IT managers take wild guesses as to what will improve performance. I have heard managers with very deep pockets suggest Pentium-III Xeon processor-based file server configurations, when their Pentium Pro simply ran out of disk space.

Performance Monitor is the conscience that tames our desire for more powerful toys. We really can't justify a dual Pentium-III processor-based file server if Performance Monitor proves that we are barely sustaining 30 percent usage on our current Pentium Pro system. Conversely, you might be able to get your line manager to approve a new laptop if you can prove that you are constantly swapping to disk, even though your machine has the maximum amount of memory installed.

If your organization has structured its cost centers to allow such an endeavor, play a shell game with the servers. The next time a server comes into the data center, use your knowledge of Performance Monitor to show how you can increase the overall efficiency of the data center. You may find that the new 6400R server ordered as a file server for the HR group may be better suited to serving HR's PeopleSoft database that is currently running on a 2500R. By taking such an approach, we increase the performance of the database server without affecting the file server performance. If we apply scientific principles (supported by tools like Performance Monitor) to our environments, we can increase the productivity of our resources and consequently justify the value added by our employment in the organization.

—*Thomas E. Eck,*
MCSE+I, MCSD, ASE, CCA, CNA

Using Performance Monitor

You can run Performance Monitor on any PC that has Windows NT installed. You can just monitor the local machine on which you are running PerfMon, or you can monitor other NT systems on your network. This is especially useful if you want to monitor your servers from a central management console.

You run Performance Monitor from the Administrative Tools folder from the Programs menu. When you first start Performance Monitor, you are given a blank view to which you have to add the counters that you want to measure. By default, you are shown the Chart view. (Refer to later sections of this chapter for a discussion on the different PerfMon views.) To change the view, click the appropriate button on the toolbar or select View from the menu and choose the view that you want to use. Figure 32-1 displays PerfMon in Chart view with several counters that have been running on a server.

Display Modes

Performance Monitor can display server information in four different views: Chart, Alert, Log, and Report. Each view displays the information in a certain way so that you can gather and analyze the information to help you determine the health of the server. This section will describe each view along with its advantages and disadvantages.

Chart View

The Chart view displays the server information in a graphical format. All information is gathered and displayed in real time, so you have an instantaneous glimpse at how well your server is functioning. You also use the Chart view to look at data gathered by the Log view. The Chart view can display the information in two modes: graphical and histogram. The graphical mode shows a line graph of the last 100 samples for the counters that you have selected (see Figure 32-1). For example, if your update interval is set to the default of one second, then the chart will display information for the last 100 seconds.

FIGURE 32-1 The Chart view of Performance Monitor

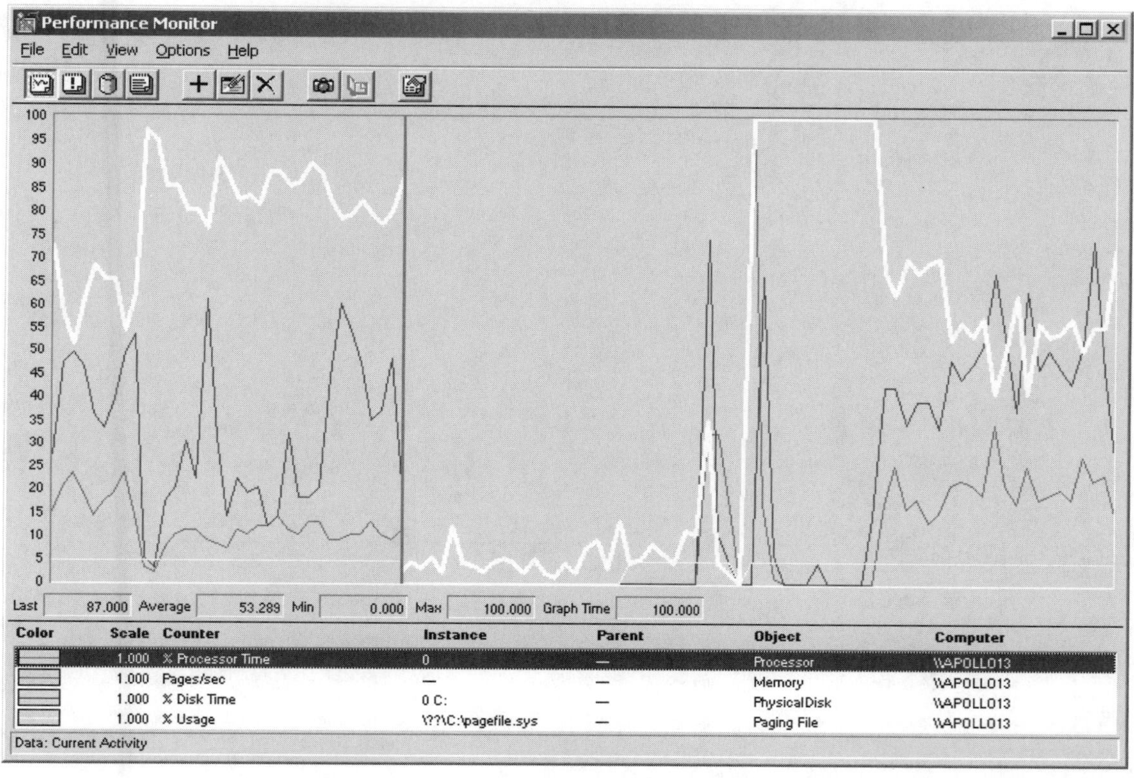

The histogram mode shows an instantaneous view of your counters in a bar graph format, as in Figure 32-2. Since the histogram view only shows the current values for the counters, you cannot view any previous values using this mode.

You generally use the graphical mode when monitoring different counters from one server, or if you'd like to see a history of your counters. By contrast, you normally use the histogram mode when monitoring the same counters for different servers, so that you can compare them. For example, you may want to view processor utilization for six servers in histogram view, so that you can compare the relative usage of the servers' processors. You can also

FIGURE 32-2 Use the Histogram view to show the same counter for different instances

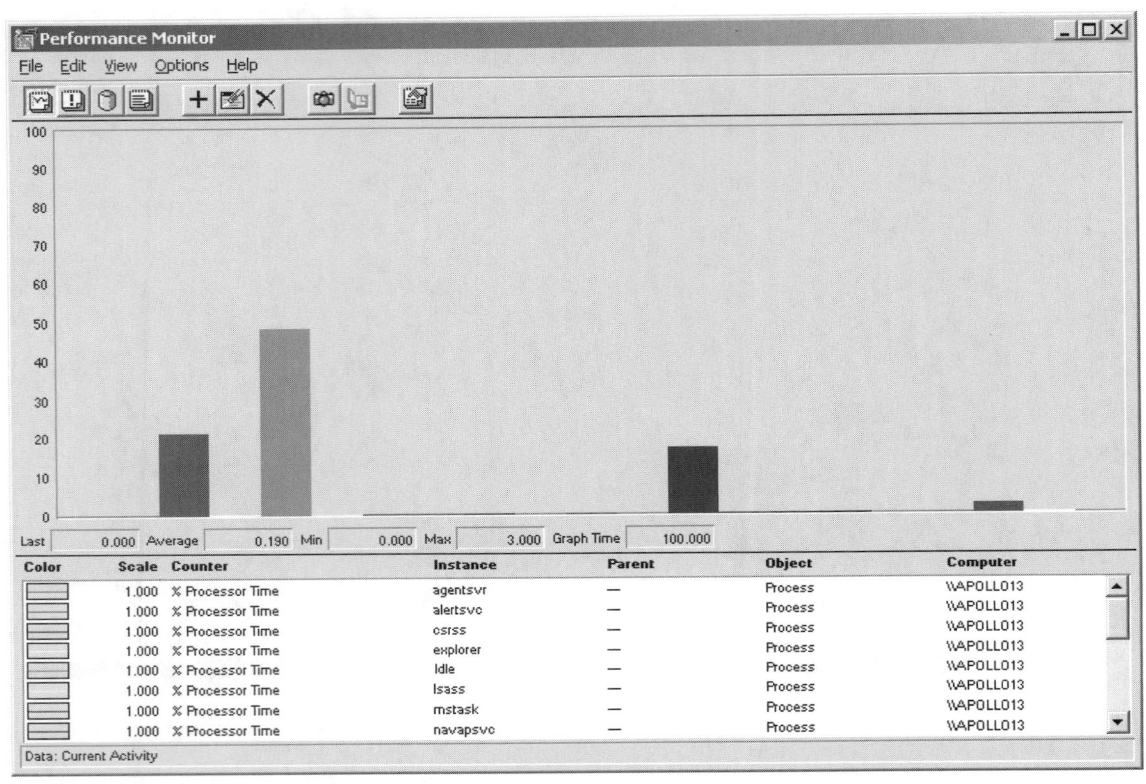

use the histogram mode to display different instances for a single counter. For example, you can monitor each running process from the Process object and compare their memory usage.

To add a counter to PerfMon, click the + button on the toolbar or select Edit | Add to Chart from the menu. The Add to Chart window appears as in Figure 32-3.

From the Add to Chart window, you can select the computer that you want to monitor by typing the server name in the Computer field or by clicking the Browse button and browsing the network. You then select the Object (such as processor, disk, or memory) that you want to monitor.

FIGURE 32-3

Clicking the Explain button will show a description of the selected counter

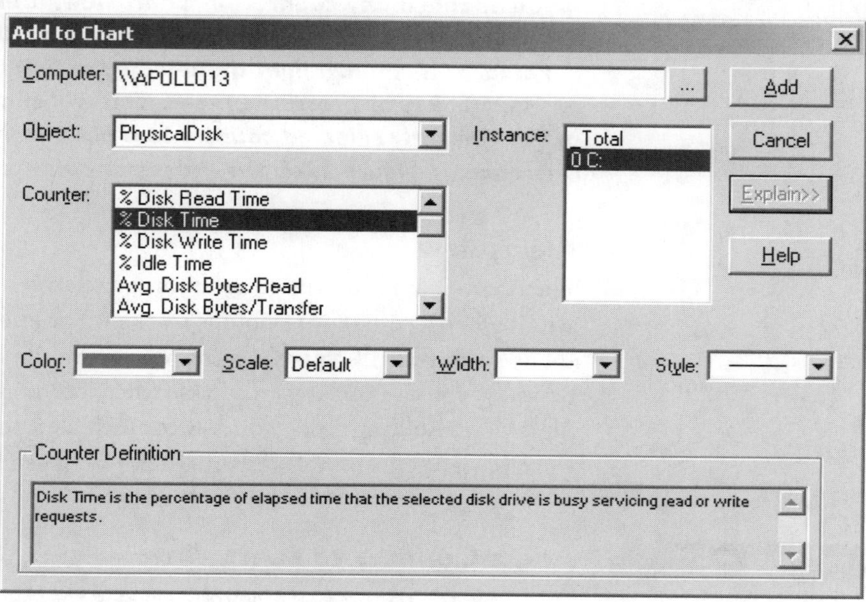

Different objects will appear in your list, depending on the services that you have installed on your server. For example, if you have Microsoft Exchange Server installed on your server, you will have several objects related to Exchange that you can select, to monitor your Exchange services.

Once you have an object selected, the relevant counters for that object will appear in the Counter field. These counters are specific for the selected object and will differ from object to object. For example, the disk object will contain a %Disk Read counter, but the Processor object will not contain this counter since it does not apply. If you want to know what a particular counter is used for, click the Explain button to give a brief description on the counter.

The Instance window is used to specify any particular occurrence of an object. For example, if you have multiple disks on your server, you will have an instance for the C: drive, the D: drive, and so on, for the Physical-Disk object. You can monitor the counters for each instance individually or you can monitor the counters for the object as a whole by selecting the _Total instance.

If you enable many counters in Chart view, it may become difficult to track a particular counter, since the graph lines may become jumbled. You can highlight the selected counter by pressing the BACKSPACE key or pressing CTRL-H. This will change the format of the currently selected counter to a bold, white color for easy reference. In Figure 32-1, the Processor counter is highlighted.

Alert View

The Alert view allows you to monitor your server and perform a specific action when a certain threshold is reached. For example, you can have an alert sent to your PC if the server's processor utilization exceeds 80 percent. Basically, you can run any executable when a certain criterion is reached. The Alert view also keeps a log window for each alert that is generated so that you can view a history of alerts that have been generated (see Figure 32-4).

EXERCISE 32-1

Add a Counter to Alert View

1. Switch to the Alert view by clicking the Alert View button on the toolbar or by selecting View | Alert from the menu.
2. Click the + button in the toolbar or select Edit | Add to Alert from the menu. The Add to Alert window appears, which allows you to run a specified program on alert:

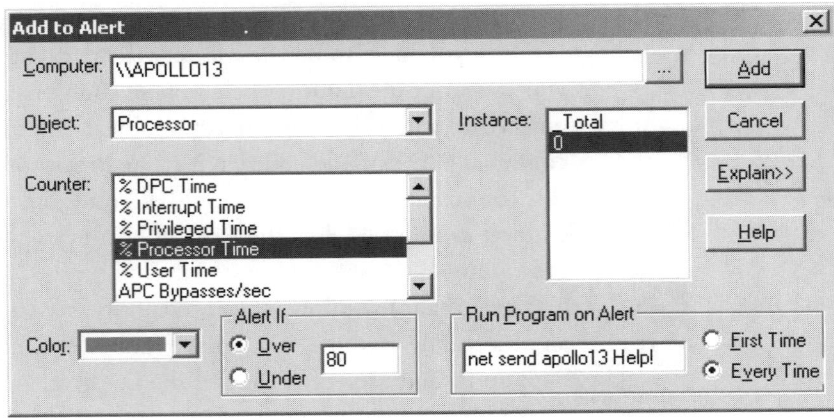

3. Choose the object and counter that you want to monitor.

FIGURE 32-4 The Alert View can help you spot potential trouble areas on your server

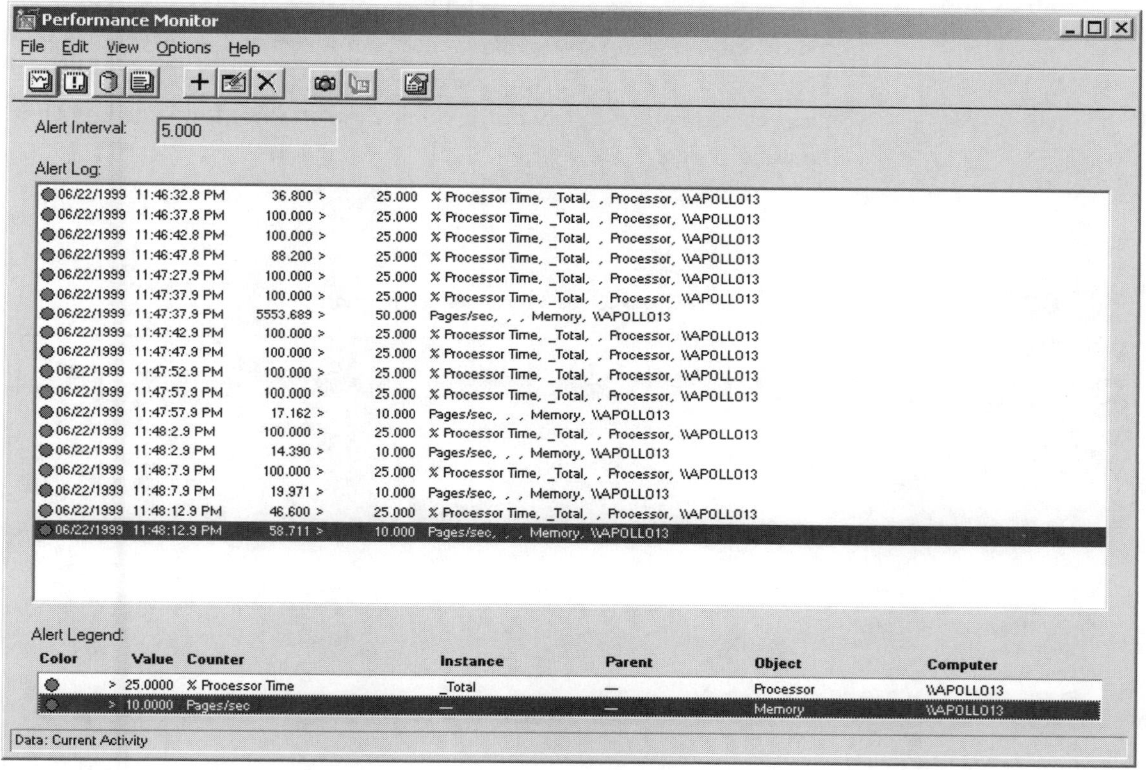

4. Specify the alert condition by selecting Over or Under radio button and enter a number. Make sure that you keep the units in mind for the counter. For example, if the counter specifies Bytes and you want the alert condition to be 10MB, you'll have to enter 10,000,000 in the alert condition.
5. Specify the action for an alert in the Add to Alert window in the Run Program on Alert field. If the program is not in the system path, make sure you specify the complete path. Also, select whether you want to have the program run just the first time the threshold is reached or every time the threshold is reached.

Log View

The Log view of Performance Monitor allows you to gather data about your servers for long-term analysis or troubleshooting. You can use the Log view to spot trends on your servers that would be undetectable using the other views. After you finish collecting the data to a log file using the Log view, you can view that data in any of the other views in PerfMon. The Log view is shown in Figure 32-5.

FIGURE 32-5 Use the Log view to track data for extended periods

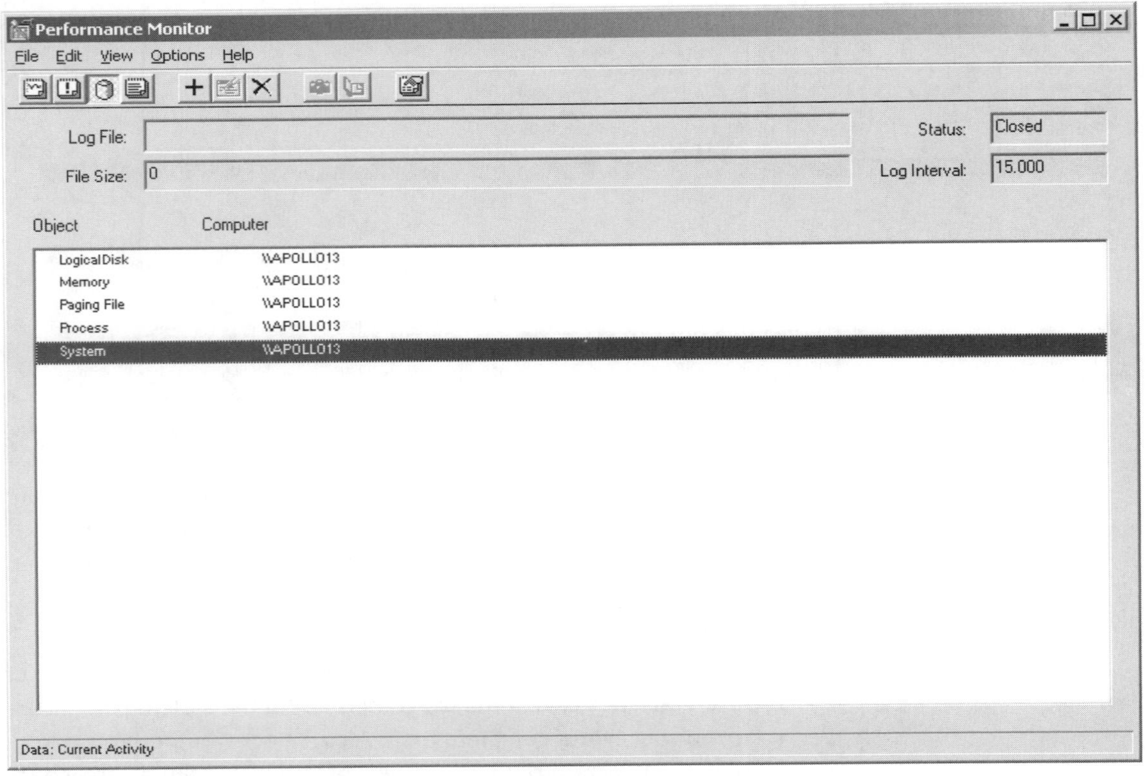

The Log view collects the information from all counters for the specified object that you select. For example, you cannot specify just the %Disk Read Time for the Logical Disk object; you can only specify the entire Logical Disk object and have PerfMon collect data for all counters. You can quickly consume a large amount of disk space, so you must closely monitor your free disk space to make sure that you don't run out of space. You can reduce the amount of disk space that the log consumes by increasing the interval time.

EXERCISE 32-2

Tracking Information Using the Log View

1. Switch to the Log view by clicking Log View on the toolbar or by selecting View | Log from the menu.
2. Click + on the toolbar, or select Edit | Add to Log from the menu. The Add to Log dialog box will appear.

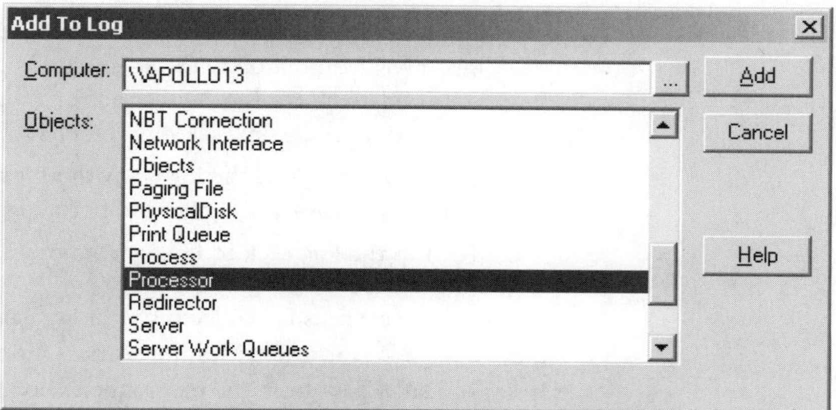

3. Choose the objects that you want to add to the view, then click Add.
4. Once you have added all desired objects, click Options | Log from the menu. The Log Options dialog box appears.

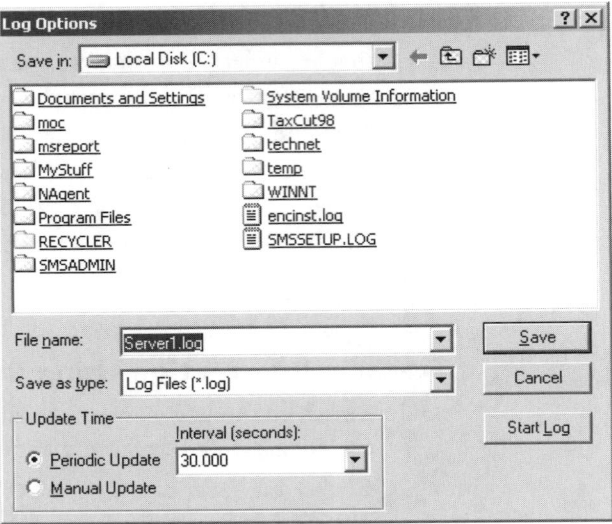

5. Enter a filename for the log.
6. Enter an interval for the Periodic Update or choose Manual Update. If you will be monitoring for an extended period (perhaps a day), set your update interval to 30 seconds or 60 seconds. If you will be monitoring for a week, set your interval for 5 minutes (300 seconds).
7. Click Save to create the log file without starting the log, or click Start Log to save the log file and begin logging.
8. To stop the log, click Stop Log from the Options | Log menu.

Once you have finished collecting your log data, you can use any of the other views in Performance Monitor to view the collected data. Choose Options | Data From from the menu, then select the log file that you created. You can then add any of the counters from the objects that you selected when you created your log file.

After you have selected the counter to track, you can adjust the time interval displayed by selecting Edit | Time Window from the menu. This allows you to narrow the time window displayed in the current view. For example, you may have enabled logging for the previous day from 6:00 A.M. Monday to 6:00 A.M. Tuesday. You can use the Time Window dialog box to display information only between 9:00 A.M. and 5:00 P.M. for Monday, so that you only view pertinent information.

The Log view is a great utility for logging information for your servers, but one disadvantage is that to run the utility, someone must be logged into the PC that is collecting the logging information. This could pose a problem in a mid-level to high-level security environment, where you cannot leave workstations logged in. The Windows NT Resource Kit contains two utilities called MONITOR.EXE and DATALOG.EXE that run as a service and collect all of the logging information to a file. DATALOG.EXE performs the same function as PerfMon—it logs performance data to a file. Since this utility runs as a service, no one needs to be logged into the workstation for this utility to run. MONITOR.EXE is used to configure the DATALOG service.

Report View

The Report view of PerfMon displays actual values of the collected data in a report format. You can then export this information to a tab-delimited or comma-delimited text file to create reports. If you export the information to a spreadsheet program, you can create graphs and reports for long-term data analysis. The Report view is shown in Figure 32-6.

You add counters to the Report view in the same manner that you did with the Chart view.

1. Switch to the Report view by clicking Report View on the toolbar or by selecting View | Report from the menu.
2. Click + in the toolbar or select Edit | Add to Report from the menu. The Add to Report dialog box appears.
3. Select the objects and counters that you want to add to the report.

Uses for Each Mode

This section will give you scenarios and examples of when you should use each Performance Monitor view. Since each view has its own advantages and disadvantages, it is important to determine when it is appropriate to use each view.

FIGURE 32-6 The Report view gives you values that you can export to a file

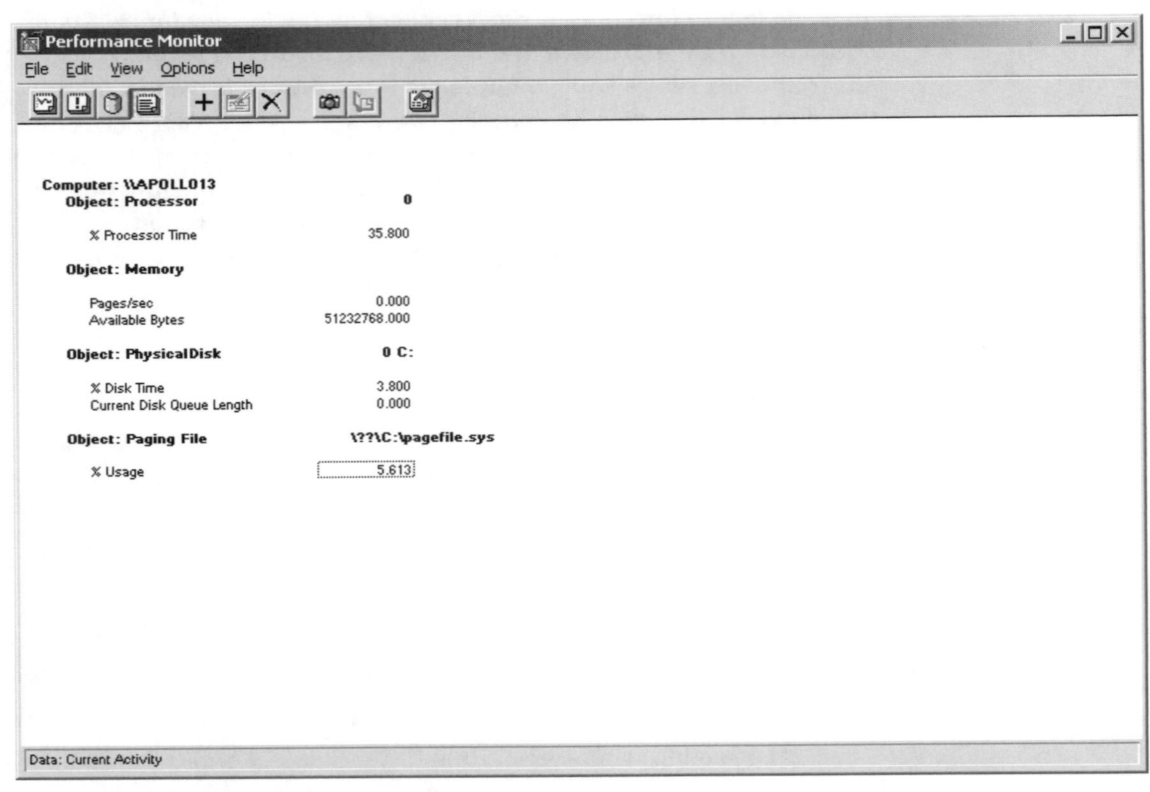

Chart View

The Chart view is the most popular view in PerfMon, because it gives you a real-time view of the health of your servers in a graphical format. You can quickly run PerfMon and add a few counters to begin monitoring your servers; or even more quickly, open an existing chart settings file. In graph mode, the Chart view allows you to view the recent history of the counters. If your users begin complaining about poor server response, you can look at

Performance Monitor to see what the server was doing for the last 100 time units. The graph mode also allows you to monitor several counters and see if spikes in one counter affect the performance of other counters. For example, you may notice that as your memory experiences more pages to disk, your disk activity will also increase.

If you'd like to monitor the same counter for several different servers, you can use the histogram mode of the Chart view. This will allow you to quickly compare the counters for the servers and determine if one server is overloaded. You can also use the histogram mode to monitor different instances of one counter. For example, you can use histogram mode to view how busy each processor is in a system so you can take any appropriate action.

Alert View

The Alert view is ideal for monitoring your servers and having PerfMon alert you when something goes wrong. You can use the Alert view so that you do not have to monitor the servers constantly for problems.

The following table shows some common counters and their suggested thresholds to monitor and generate alerts:

Object	Counter	Threshold
Processor	%Processor Time	> 80%
Logical Disk	%Free Space	< 10%
Logical Disk	Current Disk Queue Length	> 5
Memory	Available Bytes	< 4,000,000 bytes
Memory	Pages/sec	> 10

Log View

You use the Log view in Performance Monitor when you want to collect long-term data from your servers. You can view this data later for analysis. For example, you can use the Log view to monitor your server for a week, then look at that information in the Chart view to detect spikes in usage.

You may begin to notice fluctuations at certain times of the day or certain times during the week. Once you discover these peaks, you can tweak your hardware accordingly, by balancing the load among several servers.

Another use for the Log view is to create a baseline measurement of your server that you can use to compare future measurements. For example, you may want to measure how adding an additional 128MB of memory affects your server. You would use the Log view to measure memory utilization before you add the memory. Then after you add the memory, you would use the Log view to measure memory utilization again. You can then compare how the memory utilization has changed with the addition of the new memory.

Report View

You use the Report view to examine values for constantly changing data or to watch the values change under a different load. The Report view is the only view that allows you to export the data to a file that you can analyze in a spreadsheet program. You can also use the Report view to determine which values need to be monitored in Chart view. You should adjust the update interval accordingly so that you have time to look at the information.

Saving Your Settings

Performance Monitor allows you to save your settings to a file so that you do not have to reenter the counters when you restart PerfMon. You can just open the settings file and all of your counters (including any specific view settings, such as the update interval) will be restored. PerfMon allows you to save the settings for a specific view or for the entire workspace (which includes the settings for all views).

View Settings

If you are using a single view to monitor your server, you can save the settings for that particular view.

1. Add the desired counters to your view.
2. Set your desired options (such as update interval and line styles).

QUESTIONS AND ANSWERS	
I need to view several counters for a server in real-time and in a graphical format...	Use the graph mode of Chart view. This will allow you to add several counters from the server and compare their measurements graphically.
I need to collect data from the server over a week-long period...	Use the Log view, which allows you to gather information for a certain period of time, then view that information later.
I need to monitor the server for free disk space and to be alerted when it falls below a certain level...	Use the Alert view, which allows you to set specific thresholds and to be alerted when those thresholds are met.
I need to export the data to a spreadsheet program...	Use the Report view, which is the only view that allows you to export values to a file.

3. Choose File | Save *view* Settings, where *view* is Chart, Alert, Log, or Report.
4. Enter a filename for your settings. The default file extension for each of the views is as follows: Chart (*.PMC), Alert (*.PMA), Log (*.PML), Report (*.PMR).

Workspace Settings

If you have counters enabled for more than one view, you can save the settings for all of the views in one workspace file. When you open this workspace file, all view settings will be restored.

1. Add the desired counters to your views.
2. Set your desired options (such as update interval and line styles).
3. Choose File | Save Workspace.
4. Enter a filename for your workspace settings. The default file extension for the workspace file is *.PMW.

One caveat for saving the workspace when using the Log view. If you open a workspace that contains settings for the Log view, you still have to go into the log settings manually to start the log. This could be undesirable if you want to start the log automatically when you open the workspace file. In order to have the logging start immediately when you open the workspace file, make sure that you save the file with the log started. Once you have done this, the next time you open the workspace file, logging will begin immediately.

CERTIFICATION OBJECTIVE 32.02

Windows NT Memory Subsystem

The Memory Subsystem is arguably the most important subsystem in a server when it comes to performance. Memory works intimately with every subsystem in the server, and as you will soon learn, a shortage of memory will drastically reduce your server performance. All application programs must run from physical memory.

This section will briefly explain how Windows NT uses memory to run applications. It will then explain the importance of the Windows NT pagefile and how this file affects overall system performance. This section will also explain how to measure application use of memory and how to optimize NT's overall use of memory. Finally, this section will help you determine how much memory you should put into your server.

Paged Pool and Nonpaged Pool Memory

The memory pool is broken up into three separate pools: pageable memory, nonpageable memory, and file system cache. We will discuss the system cache area in the next section. The nonpageable memory pool is reserved for data that must reside in physical memory and is not swapped to the pagefile on the hard disk. This includes portions of the operating system, such as the kernel and other critical device drivers. Data in the nonpageable memory pool cannot be paged to disk. The pageable memory pool is used by the rest of the operating system and applications. It includes data that may be paged out to disk as necessary.

On Windows NT servers that have plenty of available memory, it is possible to force NT not to page any portion of the OS to disk. Although you will use a little more memory, overall system performance will be enhanced, since the OS files will be readily available in physical memory. To enable this function, open the Registry Editor and navigate to* HKEY_LOCAL_MACHINE | System | Currentcontrolset |Control |Session Manager | Memory Management. *Change the value for DisablePagingExecutive from 0 to 1. Reboot the server for the change to take effect. For more information on this topic, refer to the Microsoft online Knowledge Base at the following Web address: http://support.microsoft.com/support/kb/articles/q184/4/19.asp

Determining System Cache Size

As you learned in the previous section, Windows NT dedicates a portion of physical memory to the file system cache. The system cache is used to keep recently used information in RAM instead of being paged to disk. NT dynamically allocates space for the system cache depending on available memory, and it cannot be set manually. You can determine the system cache size by using either the Performance Monitor or the Task Manager.

If you are using PerfMon, add the Cache Bytes or the Cache Bytes Peak counter from the Memory object. The Cache Bytes counter will display how many bytes of memory the system cache is using, while the Cache Bytes Peak counter will display the most amount of bytes the system cache has used since the server started. Remember that you can use PerfMon either to view this information in real time with the Chart view or to use the Log view to store this information and analyze it later.

You can use the Windows NT Task Manager to display the system cache size more quickly than using PerfMon. You can open the Task Manager in three ways:

- Right-click the Taskbar and select Task Manager
- Press CTRL-ALT-DEL and click the Task Manager button
- Press CTRL-SHIFT-ESC

The Task Manager, shown next, gives you instant access to many performance counters. The System Cache value is shown in kilobytes in the Physical Memory (K) section.

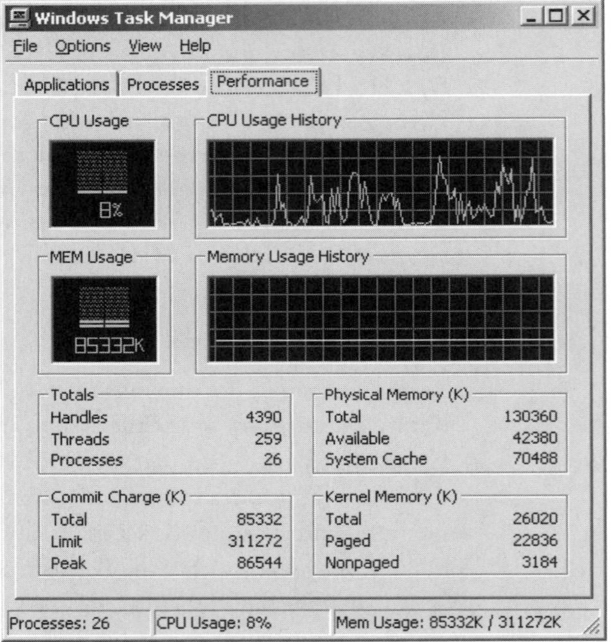

The Paging File

Ever since the days of Windows, and into Windows 95 and Windows NT, Microsoft has used the pagefile as a method of increasing performance for a system. The pagefile, also known as virtual memory or a swap file, is a file on the hard disk that temporarily holds some contents of memory. When a program requires more memory, NT will "swap" out information that is not being used to the pagefile, making more room for the memory-hungry application. When an application needs data that is in the page file, the OS will retrieve that information from the disk and place it back into physical memory (usually moving something else out of memory and into the pagefile). The advantage of this method is that you can run more programs concurrently with the same amount of memory. The big disadvantage is that you now become dependent on the performance of the disk subsystem, which works significantly more slowly than memory. As you increase paging activity (due to a lack of memory), you increase the number of times that the disk must work. You can see the relationship between memory paging and disk utilization in Figure 32-7. For virtually every peak in memory paging (the highlighted line), you will see a corresponding rise in disk utilization.

Although there are only a few settings that you can set for the pagefile, it is still important to tune the pagefile, as it will affect the overall performance of the server. This section will discuss some of the methods that you can use to tune the pagefile.

FIGURE 32-7 Paging activity directly affects disk utilization

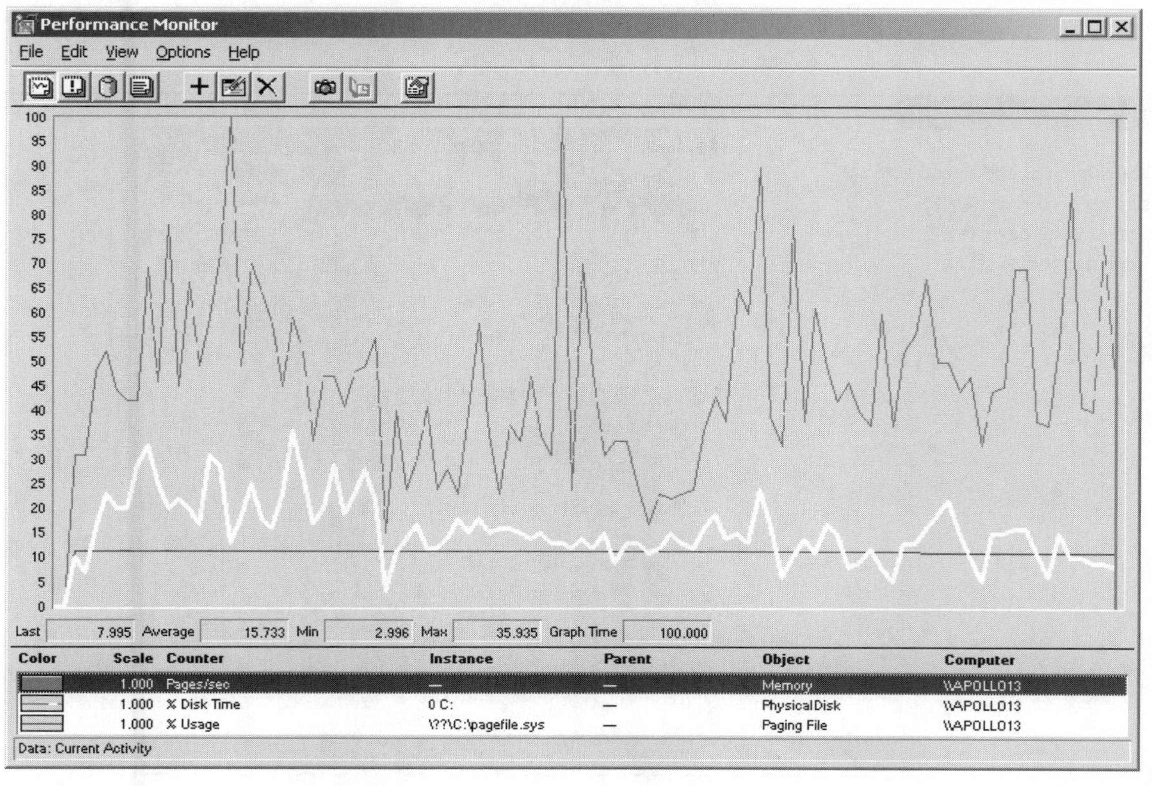

Default Size of the Pagefile

When you first install Windows NT, it creates a pagefile on the boot partition, with a size of the amount of memory plus 12MB. NT also sets the maximum size for the pagefile to a value greater than the initial value. If NT experiences a large number of page faults, the pagefile size may need to be increased in order to accommodate the information being sent to the pagefile. The maximum size tells NT the largest size to which the pagefile can grow. You can view the settings for the pagefile by choosing Control Panel | System and selecting the Virtual Memory tab (see Figure 32-8).

From this tab, you can see the current size of the pagefile and change the initial size and maximum size, if necessary. If you make any changes, you will have to reboot the server in order for the changes to take effect. In general, you should set the minimum and maximum size of the pagefile to be the default of the amount of memory plus 12MB, so that Windows NT will not try to grow the pagefile.

FIGURE 32-8

Set the initial and maximum size to be the same to prevent the pagefile from expanding

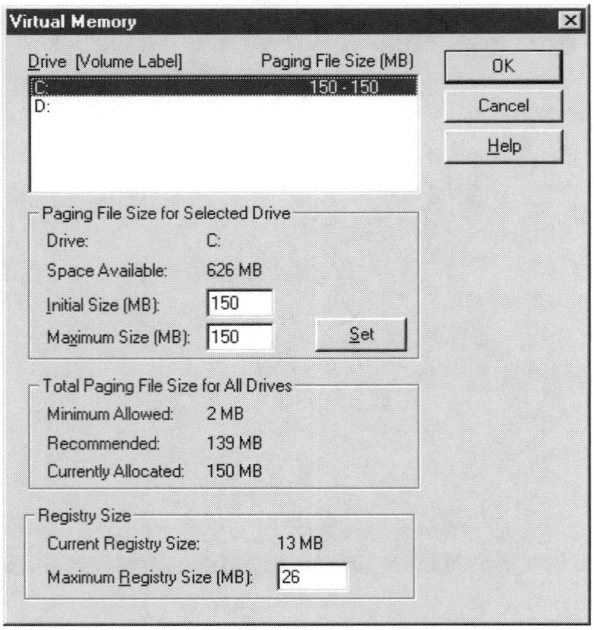

You may be asking yourself, "Why wouldn't I want Windows NT to expand the pagefile?" First of all, when Windows NT expands the pagefile, it takes a great deal of system resources (processor, memory, and disk) to perform the function. While the system is expanding the pagefile, all other processes will suffer. Secondly, when Windows NT expands the pagefile, you run the risk of fragmenting the pagefile. Just as performance suffers when files on your hard disk become fragmented, your pagefile performance will also suffer as it becomes fragmented. Finally, if Windows NT needs to expand the pagefile, this indicates another problem with your system—namely, that it needs more memory. Adding more memory may not be the answer to your memory shortage. An application might have a memory leak, in which case you will have to identify the leaky application and correct the problem. It may also not be possible to add any memory to the system, in which case you have to optimize the size of the pagefile so that you do not run out of virtual memory. We will cover optimizing the size of the pagefile in a later section, Monitoring the Paging File.

Another reason to set the pagefile to a minimum of memory plus 12MB is that in order for NT to create a memory crash dump file, the pagefile needs to be at least the amount of memory plus 1MB. NT creates the memory dump file when it crashes with the infamous Blue Screen of Death (BSOD). Microsoft support engineers can view the dump file to determine what caused the crash so that you can bring your server back up or avoid this problem in the future.

Number of Pagefiles

By default, Windows NT creates a single pagefile on the boot partition, where the Windows NT directory is located. This immediately presents a performance problem—the OS may experience disk contention with the pagefile, since they are on the same partition. NT allows you to create additional pagefiles on other logical partitions on your server, to distribute the load of the pagefile. You can have a maximum of 16 pagefiles. You can create the additional pagefiles in Control Panel | System | Virtual Memory (as shown in Figure 32-8). You can only create one pagefile per logical partition.

Make sure that you create the additional pagefiles on a partition that is on a different physical disk than the operating system files. Creating the pagefile on a different logical drive, but the same physical drive, will not result in performance gains, and may actually hurt performance.

Do not completely delete the pagefile that is on the same partition as the OS. NT still needs this pagefile in order to create the memory dump file. You should set the size of the pagefile on your boot partition to be the amount of memory plus 1MB. You should then set the size of the pagefile on the separate partition to be the amount of memory plus 12MB. Windows NT will then use the pagefile on the less busy partition rather than using the pagefile on the partition containing the system files. In this way, you will optimize the use of your pagefile, while still keeping the ability to create the crash dump file in case of a BSOD.

Monitoring the Paging File

You can use the Performance Monitor to observe the pagefile. By monitoring the pagefile, you can determine the optimum size for the pagefile so that it does not need to expand. The counters that you will be interested in are the %Usage and the %Usage Peak counters in the Paging File object. The %Usage counter gives you the current usage in percent for the pagefile, while the %Usage Peak counter gives you the maximum percentage used by the pagefile since the server was started.

For example, your server may have 100MB of RAM. You want to optimize the size of your pagefile so that NT will not need to expand the pagefile. You set your pagefile size to be double the size of memory (200MB). You then use PerfMon to observe your pagefile utilization and find that over the period of a week, the %Usage Peak is 75 percent. You now can set your pagefile size to be 200 x 75 percent, or 150MB.

Windows NT Virtual Memory Manager

You have learned that Windows NT can run many applications with a limited amount of physical memory, by swapping out the least-used data in memory to a pagefile on the hard disk. This makes room in physical memory for applications that need the memory right away. When the other application needs to access the data from the pagefile, a page fault occurs, and that information is copied back into physical memory so that the application can use it. Even though a system will probably have far less memory, each application will believe that it can access up to 4GB of memory, known as its *address space.* Each application has its own 4GB address space independent of other applications, which means that an application cannot access another application's address space (without the proper permissions). Since this 4GB of address space does not necessarily map to a physical location in memory, it is known as virtual memory.

The Windows NT Virtual Memory Manager (VMM), which is part of the NT Executive Services, is responsible for assigning the address space to each application. When an application requests data, it requests it using a *virtual address.* The VMM is responsible for translating that virtual address to a physical address in RAM. If the information is not in physical RAM, the VMM will swap the information from the pagefile to RAM.

Under certain circumstances, two processes may need to access a shared area in memory. The VMM is responsible for allowing access to the shared area for the processes. Sharing memory removes the protection of separate address spaces for the sake of efficiently using memory. When two applications share a memory space, one application may corrupt the data in memory, effectively corrupting it for both apps. An example of an advantageous sharing of memory space is when you run multiple instances of a program. Only a single copy of the program needs to be loaded in memory that can be accessed by all instances of the program.

Memory Subsystem and Disk Subsystem Interaction

One day, you may be measuring the performance of your disk subsystem and notice that you peak at several times during the day. You may even notice that your disks may begin thrashing and that utilization may consistently be around 100 percent. Your first instinct may be to buy faster disks with higher spin rates, or to buy a faster disk controller with greater throughput. After you upgrade the hardware, you notice that the disk performance has not increased that much and that the disks may still be the bottleneck! What you could be experiencing here is how one subsystem can affect the performance of another subsystem. In this case, a lack of memory in the server could heavily stress your disk subsystem.

When an application does not find its information in physical memory, it will need to retrieve the information from elsewhere. This is known as a *page fault.* There are two types of page faults: hard page faults and soft page faults. With a soft page fault, the faulted pages are found elsewhere in physical memory (usually the file system cache). With a hard page fault, the faulted pages are found in the pagefile on the hard disk. Hard faults are more damaging to system performance than soft faults, since hard faults must access the relatively slow hard disk. Soft faults access memory.

The following table lists several counters that you can use in PerfMon to monitor your memory and pagefile usage:

Object	Counter	Description
Memory	Available Bytes	Amount of physical memory available to application processes. This number is the total memory minus the nonpaged pool, the paged pool, and the system cache.
Memory	Commit Limit	Amount of virtual memory that can be given to all applications before the paging file will need to be expanded.
Memory	Committed Bytes	Amount of virtual memory that is currently committed to applications. If this number approaches the Commit Limit, the pagefile will need to be expanded and system performance will suffer. When this happens, it indicates a shortage of physical memory.
Memory	Pages/sec	Number of times the system had to read from, or write to disk to resolve a hard page fault.
Paging File	%Usage	Amount of the pagefile in use in percent.
Paging File	%Usage Peak	The highest percentage usage that the pagefile reached since the system started.

To improve the performance of your server, it is imperative that you reduce the number of times that memory must page to and from disk. In fact, adding memory is probably the most cost-effective method of increasing performance on your server. As you give Windows NT more memory to work with, less information will need to be paged to and from the disk, which will decrease your disk utilization. Since information will be fetched from memory instead of disk, you will notice a dramatic increase in performance.

Memory Usage by Process

While running PerfMon on your server, you may notice that there is suddenly a large amount of paging and that system performance is suffering. Before you request a memory upgrade from your boss, you should find what applications are causing the sudden increase in memory utilization. You will have to use your detective skills to determine which applications are using all of your memory and whether you can optimize their usage to make the most of your current amount of RAM. Again, you will use Performance Monitor to track memory usage for each of the processes running on your server. You will be tracking the Process object, and each running process will appear in the Instance window of the Add Counter window. You can choose from the counters listed in the following table to determine which processes are using up all of your memory:

Counter	Description
Page Faults/sec	The number of times the process has to refer to disk for information that is not currently in memory.
Page File Bytes	The number of bytes that the process is currently using in the page file. If this number is continuously growing, it may indicate that the process has a memory leak.
Page File Bytes Peak	The highest amount of space this process has used in the paging file since the system started. If this number is consistently the same as Page File Bytes, it may indicate that the process does not relinquish memory properly, and can lead to a memory leak.

Calculating the Optimum Amount of Memory for a System

Now that you know the intricacies of how Windows NT manages memory usage, you will want to know how to minimize the paging activity of your server. The obvious answer is to add more memory to the server so that the application will be able to keep more of its data in physical RAM. But how much? When you make the request to your manager to upgrade the server memory, you don't want to ask for so much that your request is denied; nor for so little that you'll need to upgrade again within six months.

Although there are no hard and fast rules as to how much memory you will need to add to your server, there is a quick guideline. If you monitor the counter Paging File > %Usage Peak, you will see how much of the paging file is in use. Take that percentage and multiply it by the size of the pagefile in megabytes. This is the number that you should use to add memory to your system. For example, let's say your pagefile is 100MB, and the %Usage Peak is 50 percent. This means that 50MB of data had to be swapped out from memory to the pagefile due to a lack of memory. You can minimize the paging activity if you add 50MB of RAM to your server. You will probably have to round up to 64MB to accommodate the memory configuration of your server.

Remember that adding hardware is "cheating" when it comes to optimizing your server. Here are some other suggestions that can help you optimize your memory subsystem without having to add memory.

- Minimize any unnecessary services that are running on the server. These services are taking up valuable memory that can be used by applications that are more critical. Examples of some potentially unnecessary services include the Scheduler service, the Spooler service, and the Messenger service.
- Distribute any other services to other, less busy servers. Don't load all services onto a single server.
- Determine the memory usage of the applications running on the server. See if you can optimize the application's memory usage or determine if there are any memory leaks.
- Schedule some server activity (such as backups) during off-peak hours.
- Optimize the size of your pagefile.

CERTIFICATION OBJECTIVE 32.03

Configuring the Server Component in the Network Control Panel

The Server service for Windows NT is responsible for establishing sessions with network clients, and receiving and responding to those clients' requests. Since the Server service directly affects the end users' performance (or at least their perception of performance), tuning the Server service is one of the more noticeable methods for increasing performance for the end user.

To tune the Server service, follow these steps:

1. Open Control Panel | Network.
2. From the Services tab, select Server, then click Properties. The Server properties, shown next, allow you to tune your memory settings according to server role:

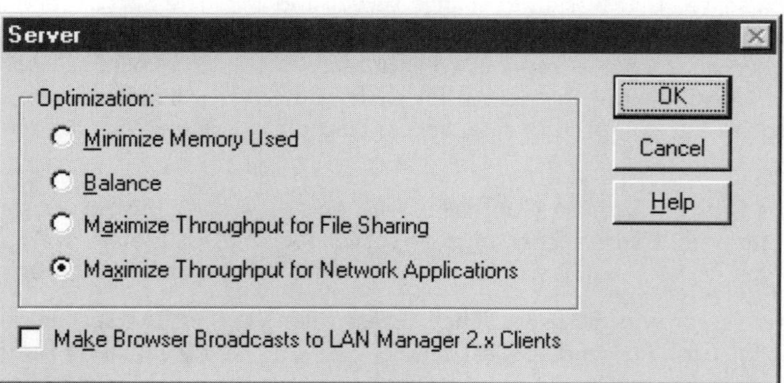

When you use the Server service window to optimize NT, you affect how the Server service uses memory and file caches.

- The Minimize Memory Used option is used for smaller servers with a limited amount of memory. It is generally used for servers that have ten or fewer clients that connect to it.

- The Balance option optimizes performance for up to 64 client connections.
- The Maximize Throughput for File Sharing option is for more than 64 remote users. The file system cache receives priority over the application's access to memory.
- The Maximize Throughput for Network Applications option is also for more than 64 remote users. However, the applications have higher priority to memory than the file system cache.

QUESTIONS AND ANSWERS

I have a desktop PC with NT Server installed that I also work on as a workstation. It has 32MB of RAM, but only has five client PCs attached...	Set the Server service to Minimize Memory Used. This option will minimize the memory used by the Server service, giving you better response for your desktop applications.
I have a server that was an Exchange server and a file server. We moved the Exchange services to a larger server to offload services to another server. Users still use this server for their home directories but complain of slow access to their files...	The Server service was probably set to Maximize Throughput for Network Applications. Reset this to Maximize Throughput for File Sharing, which will increase the size of the file system cache, improving file access performance.
I have a Primary Domain Controller with no other services. Users access another server for their files...	Set the Server service to Maximize Throughput for Network Applications. This will increase NT's capability to perform domain controller functions.
I have a server with 50 users. They access the server for both files and applications...	Set the Server service to Balance. This setting is for up to 64 remote client sessions.
I have a server with Microsoft SQL Server installed...	Set the Server service to Maximize Throughput for File Sharing. Since SQL Server manages memory on its own, selecting Maximize Throughput for Network Applications does not improve its performance.

CERTIFICATION OBJECTIVE 32.04

Disk Performance Factors

In most environments, the limiting subsystem on your server will be the disk subsystem, since it is the only system with mechanical moving parts. More often than not, your disk subsystem will end up becoming the bottleneck of your server. This section will help you get the most performance out of your disk subsystem. We will first look at enabling the DISKPERF parameter, which enables you to use Performance Monitor to measure the disk usage. Then we will take a look at how the other server subsystems (such as memory) affect the disks.

DISKPERF Parameter

If you start PerfMon and add counters for any of the disk objects, you may notice that PerfMon may not show any activity for your disks, even though you may see the disk activity light flashing. This doesn't mean that PerfMon isn't working. You simply have to tell PerfMon to enable the disk performance counters.

When Windows NT was first released, the majority of file servers were Intel 386 and 486 processors. Microsoft developers noticed that when the disk performance counters were active, system performance was significantly reduced. So they decided to disable the counters by default and let the administrator decide whether to enable the counters or not. On the latest Pentium, Pentium Pro, and Pentium II/III servers, the effect of activating the disk performance counters is negligible, so if you are planning to monitor disk performance, you need not worry about affecting server response. However, if you will not be monitoring disk usage, you should disable the disk performance counters.

Starting and Stopping DISKPERF

The disk performance counters are activated or deactivated at the command prompt using the following steps:

1. Open a command prompt.
2. To activate the disk performance counters, type **diskperf –y** and press ENTER. If you are using the software RAID that comes with Windows NT, then you will have to use the command **diskperf –ye** to get accurate disk readings.
3. Reboot the server to activate the counters.
4. To deactivate the disk performance counters, type **diskperf –n** and press ENTER.
5. Reboot the server to deactivate the counters.

CERTIFICATION OBJECTIVE 32.05

Setting a Process's Base Priority

The Windows NT Thread Scheduler assigns processor time to a program according to the priority level set by the programmer within the program. This priority is known as the process's base priority. NT can dynamically alter a process's base priority to increase performance for the user. For example, if you are running Notepad in the foreground, NT will boost its priority to give better response for the user. If you run another application and send Notepad to the background, NT will decrease Notepad's priority dynamically, to give better response to your new application. NT allows you to change the base priority of a process when it starts, so that you can give more or less processor time.

You can use either the command prompt or Task Manager to alter a program's priority. Note that when you change the priority of a process with either of these methods, it only affects the process for this instance. In other words, if you stop and restart a process, it will retain its original priority as defined by its programmer.

EXERCISE 32-3

Using Task Manager to Alter a Process's Base Priority

1. Open Task Manager.
2. Click the Processes Tab.
3. Select View | Select Columns from the menu. The Select Columns dialog box appears.
4. Enable Base Priority, then click OK.
5. Click a process name with the right mouse button.
6. Select Set Priority, then select the new priority for the process. The priorities available, shown here, are Low, Normal, High, and Realtime. Be careful when changing the priority of a process, especially when you set it to Realtime. All other processes will suffer in performance and you will have problems with the user interface, since NT is dedicating all processor time to the realtime process.

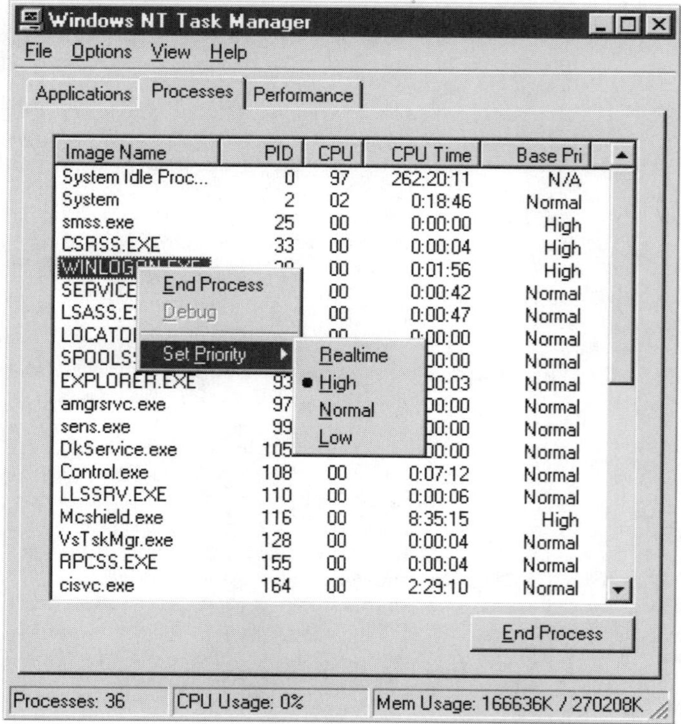

You can also use the command prompt to start an application at a particular priority by using the START command. Just as with the Task Manager, the available priorities are Low, Normal, High, and Realtime. To start a program at a particular priority, use the following command.

```
Start /<priority> <program executable>
```

The syntax for the Start command is obtained by typing **Start /?** at a command prompt, which brings up the following output.

```
Starts a separate window to run a specified program or command.
START ["title"] [/Dpath] [/I] [/MIN] [/MAX] [/SEPARATE | /SHARED]
  [/LOW | /NORMAL | /HIGH | /REALTIME] [/WAIT] [/B] [command/program] [parameters]
    "title"     Title to display in  window title bar.
    path        Starting directory
    I           The new environment will be the original environment passed
                to the cmd.exe and not the current environment.
    MIN         Start window minimized
    MAX         Start window maximized
    SEPARATE    Start 16-bit Windows program in separate memory space
    SHARED      Start 16-bit Windows program in shared memory space
    LOW         Start application in the IDLE priority class
    NORMAL      Start application in the NORMAL priority class
    HIGH        Start application in the HIGH priority class
    REALTIME    Start application in the REALTIME priority class
    WAIT        Start application and wait for it to terminate
    B           Start application without creating a new window. The
                application has ^C handling ignored. Unless the application
                enables ^C processing, ^Break is the only way to interrupt the
                application
    command/program
                If it is an internal cmd command or a batch file then
                the command processor is run with the /K switch to cmd.exe.
                This means that the window will remain after the command
                has been run.
                If it is not an internal cmd command or batch file then
                it is a program and will run as either a windowed application
                or a console application.
    parameters  These are the parameters passed to the command/program
If Command Extensions are enabled, external command invocation
through the command line or the START command changes as follows:
non-executable files may be invoked through their file association just
    by typing the name of the file as a command. (e.g. WORD.DOC would
    launch the application associated with the .DOC file extension).
    See the ASSOC and FTYPE commands for how to create these
    associations from within a command script.
```

```
When executing an application that is a 32-bit GUI application, CMD.EXE
    does not wait for the application to terminate before returning to
    the command prompt. This new behavior does NOT occur if executing
    within a command script.
When executing a command line whose first token is CMD without an
    extension or path qualifier, then replaces CMD with the value of the
    COMSPEC variable, thus avoiding picking up random versions of
    CMD.EXE when you least expect them.
When executing a command line whose first token does NOT contain an
    extension, then CMD.EXE uses the value of the PATHEXT
    environment variable to determine which extensions to look for
    and in what order. The default value for the PATHEXT variable
    is:
        .COM;.EXE;.BAT;.CMD
    Notice the syntax is the same as the PATH variable, with
    semicolons separating the different elements.
When executing a command, if there is no match on any extension, then
looks to see if the name, without any extension, matches a directory name
and if it does, the START command launches the Explorer on that path.
If done from the command line, it is the equivalent to doing a CD /D
to that path.
```

CERTIFICATION OBJECTIVE 32.06

Subsystem Load by Server Role

Administrators install servers at their sites that serve plenty of roles. The server may be a file server, an application server, a logon server, or any combination of the three. A system that mainly acts as a file server (a resource share) is responsible for storing objects (files, directories, printers) and giving users access to those objects. An application server is responsible for accepting requests from the clients for some action, then possibly returning a response to that client. This is the traditional view of a client-server system. A logon server is responsible for authenticating users' requests for access to network resources. This act of authentication could take place when a user logs onto the network or when he tries to access a file on a file server.

Obviously, each of these roles will place a different stress on the different subsystems for the server. Knowing these differences can help you effectively plan a server installation at the most important stage: before the server is ordered. This section will explain the different load characteristics for the different roles a server may play.

Highest Load Subsystems in a Client-Server Environment

In a client-server environment, a client PC makes a request for service to an application server. That server processes the request then returns any results back to the client. The application server can be a server that is running a database, such as SQL Server or Oracle, or a Web-based server, such as Internet Information Server. Since all of the processing is being done on the server, there is a heavy load signature on the processors and memory of the application server. The clients don't need a lot of horsepower on the desktop, because the server is doing most of the hard work. Also, as long as there is sufficient memory in the server, there should be relatively little disk activity. This is because the server may only need to access a small portion of the database to fulfill a client's request. Most of the work is still being done in memory. Finally, depending on the result set of the initial request, network activity is pretty light as well. Whole databases need not travel over the network, only request commands from the client, which should be relatively small. Unless the results return an exorbitant amount of data, the server response shouldn't consume much bandwidth, either.

Armed with this information, here are some suggestions for putting together the specifications for a server.

- As long as the server applications are multithreaded, purchase more processors. You may only be able to afford slower processors (200 MHz Pentium Pros instead of the 500 MHz Pentium III's), but the applications will run better on multiple processors. Of course, if you can afford two 500 MHz Pentium III's, then go for it!
- Buy as much memory as you can afford. Also, buy the larger-sized memory chips so that you won't have to swap out smaller chips if you upgrade at a later time.
- Buy a hardware RAID solution (you should always buy a hardware RAID solution), but you probably won't benefit much from the more expensive 10,000 rpm drives. You can get away with the regular 7200 rpm drives, as long as your disk controller has enough bandwidth.

- Most servers come with 100 Mbps Ethernet NICs nowadays, so you won't have to worry about the money here. Depending on the application that you'll run from the server, you may want to consider running a switched network. If there will be a lot of network traffic, then you can spend more on a 100 Mbps switched network.

Highest Load Subsystems in a Resource-Sharing Environment

In a resource-sharing environment, client PCs can transfer a relatively large amount of data back and forth from the server. These files are generally documents such as word processing documents and spreadsheets. Print traffic also generates a good amount of network traffic. File servers generally don't benefit as much from multiple processors as from faster processors. Memory usage is also lighter on a file server than it is with an application server. A file server needs fast disks that can pump out the information quickly to the end user. With file sizes ballooning with the addition of multimedia, an average user's document can end up being many megabytes in size. Network activity can also be severely affected, depending on the size of the users' files.

The following are some suggestions on how to plan your server hardware for a resource-sharing environment.

- File servers benefit more from faster processors, so forego the multiprocessor box if price is an issue. If you can only afford a single processor, go for the fastest processor available. Spend the leftover money on the disk subsystem.
- As with the processor, you will not need to spend an exorbitant amount of money on memory. The amount of memory will depend on the number of users that will be accessing this server; so as you add users, you will have to add memory.
- Take the money that you saved on the processor and the memory and spend it on your disk subsystem. Buy a hardware RAID solution and buy the fastest drives available (such as the 10,000 rpm drives).
- Since network activity will be relatively high, go with a fast network, such as 100 Mbps switched Ethernet. If server activity grows, install a second NIC in your file server to segment the traffic.

CERTIFICATION OBJECTIVE 32.07

Performance Monitor Counters

Throughout this chapter, you've seen several objects in PerfMon that you can select to track the performance of your server. Each object has specific counters that will track a certain property of that object to suggest how that object is performing. If you have experimented with Performance Monitor, you have probably seen that you can track plenty of objects and counters. In fact, one of the largest challenges facing you is to determine which counters to use to find the information that you need to tune your server. This section will cover the relevant counters for the four major subsystems in your server: processor, memory, disk, and network.

In order to tune and optimize your server, you first should know what to monitor on your server to see if there are any problems. Once you determine what you need to measure, you need to determine what are acceptable limits and thresholds for the measurements. Finally, when you determine what those limits are, you must be able to figure out what to do to improve the performance of your server, based on your measurements.

This section will cover the counters that you should track for each of the server's major subsystems, along with some suggested limits to watch for.

Processor

The processor, or CPU, is the brain of your computer. The CPU processes instructions given by software, and services interrupts generated by hardware. Software is generally broken up into several processes, and each of those processes is broken up into threads. Threads are the basic execution unit of a program. Windows NT's job is to schedule these threads for execution based on their priority and other system activity. The more efficiently Windows NT can schedule the threads, the more efficiently your server will run. Each processor can only service one thread at a time, although it switches between threads of several processes so that all processes are executed. Each thread waiting to be executed sits in the processor queue.

The processor handles instructions at its clock rate (measured in instructions per second). At the time of this writing, processor rates have reached 500 MHz, which translates to roughly 500 million instructions per second. Obviously, the processor clock speed has a direct influence on the performance of your server, but it is not the major factor in determining your system performance. If your processor is generally not working hard, and other subsystems are the bottlenecks, then upgrading the processor will not improve performance.

Multiple CPUs can be added to your server so that two instructions can be carried out at a time. Since Windows NT is a symmetric multiprocessor (SMP) system, it balances the load among all of the processors evenly. A program can be processed more quickly if its threads are split up among the processors. Currently, NT Server supports up to four processors in a system, NT Server Enterprise supports up to eight processors, and vendors can create custom HALs to support 32-way processors.

Since the processor can handle information much more quickly than memory can give it, processors come with two levels of cache: Level 1 cache and Level 2 cache. These caches allow frequently used instructions to be kept close to the processor for faster retrieval. The cache is also used to pre-fetch instructions. It keeps them in cache until the processor actually needs them. When a processor accesses instructions from the cache, it is known as a *cache hit*, and improves performance, since memory does not have to be accessed. Increasing the amount of Level 1 and Level 2 cache increases the likelihood of cache hits and ultimately, increases system performance.

The CPU also services requests from hardware. These are known as hardware interrupts and should be kept to a minimum to allow the CPU to work on other processes. Hardware that generates excessive interrupts may be defective and should be replaced.

The rest of this subsection will give descriptions of the various counters that you can use to monitor your processor utilization.

Processor: %Processor Time

This counter displays the percentage of time that a processor is performing work. In general, you should watch this counter and make sure that the average %Processor Time does not exceed 80 percent for a sustained period of time. If it does, then it could mean that you need a faster processor or additional processors. Individual spikes above 80 percent are usually of no concern. If you have multiple processors in the system, you can monitor each instance in PerfMon to make sure that the load is being balanced evenly among the processors. If it is not, it could show that you have a defective processor. If you want to watch the load on all processors using a single counter, use the System: %Total Processor Time counter.

System: Processor Queue Length

This counter displays the number of threads that are waiting in the queue to be processed, and generally shows whether your processor is a bottleneck or not. Look for sustained values of two or greater. Remember that a processor with a sustained %Processor Time value of greater than 80 percent may indicate a bottleneck. If you get these readings for your processor, you will immediately want to look at your Processor Queue Length. If it is zero or one, then your processors probably are not the bottleneck—they are simply busy! But if the queue length maintains a value of two or greater, then it is time to upgrade your processor subsystem (see Figure 32-9).

Processor: %User Time

This counter displays the percentage of the processor time that is being used for user applications. If you measure a sustained high processor utilization, monitor this counter to see whether the utilization is caused by a user application.

Processor: %Privileged Time

This counter displays the percentage of the processor time that is being used for privileged or kernel mode applications. Privileged applications have direct access to hardware and generally take the form of device drivers and OS files. This counter also takes into account processor utilization due to hardware interrupts. If this counter runs high, there may be a faulty device driver causing the high utilization.

FIGURE 32-9 A high number for the Processor Queue Length indicates a processor bottleneck

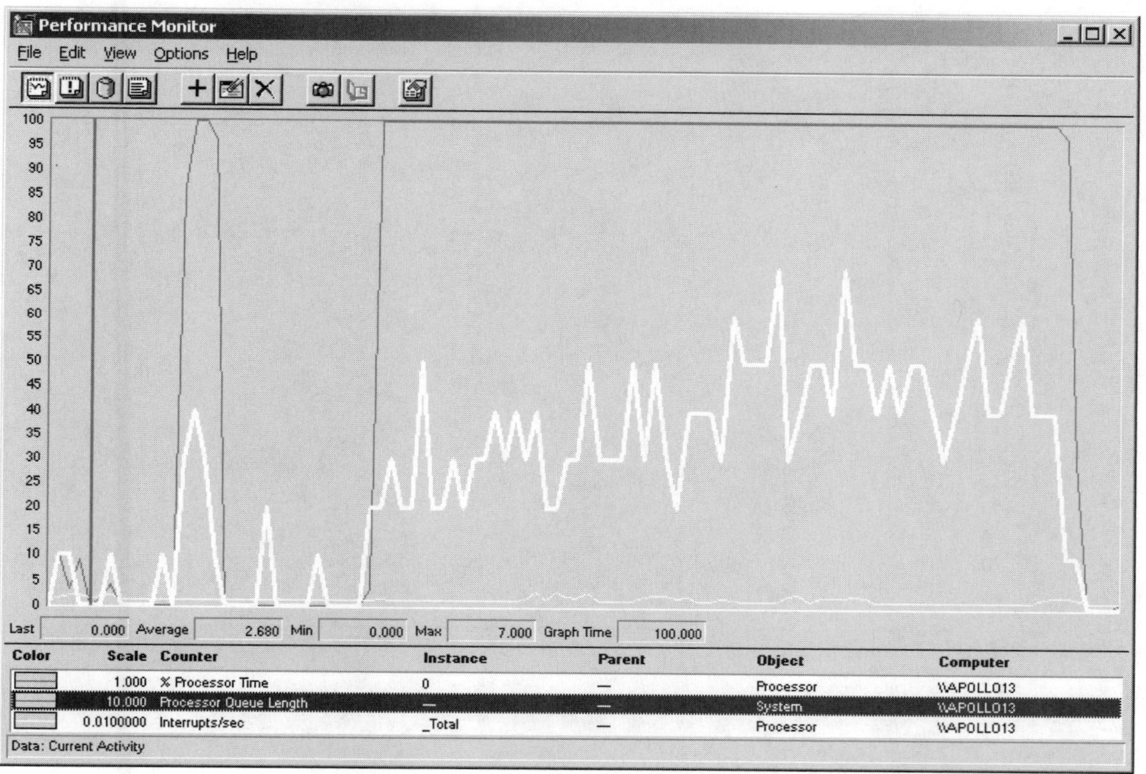

Figure 32-10 is a screenshot of PerfMon running on a system with high CPU utilization. In addition to %Processor Time and Processor Queue Length, we are measuring %User Time and %Privileged Time. You can tell from the figure that most of the processor time is being used in user mode and very little time in privileged mode. This usually means that some software application is causing the high utilization.

FIGURE 32-10 A high %User Time counter indicates a software application using the processor

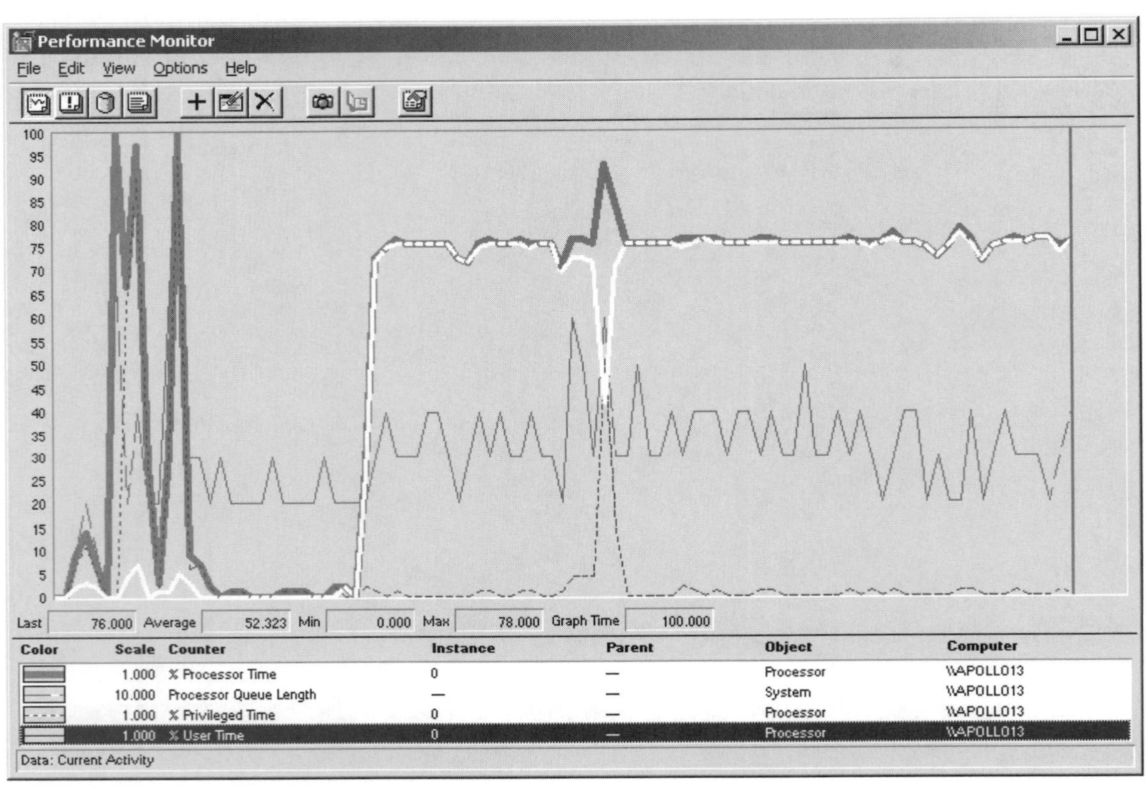

Once we have narrowed down the problem to a user application, we can monitor each process to find the one that is causing the high CPU utilization. You do this by measuring the Process object.

Process: %Processor Time

This counter displays the percentage of processor time that the process is taking up. You can specify which process to track in the Instance field of the Add to Chart window. (Refer to Figure 32-3 to refresh your memory.)

In Figure 32-11, you can see that the process CPUSTRES seems to be taking up most of the processing time. In fact, a CPU stress utility from the NT Resource Kit was running on the server to simulate processor activity.

You've seen a quick method on how to find which piece of software may be causing high CPU utilization, but what if your problem is with hardware?

Processor: Interrupts/sec

This counter displays the number of hardware interrupts that the processor had to respond to. A high number indicates that a piece of hardware may be

FIGURE 32-11 The CPUSTRES process is taking up about 80 percent of the processor time

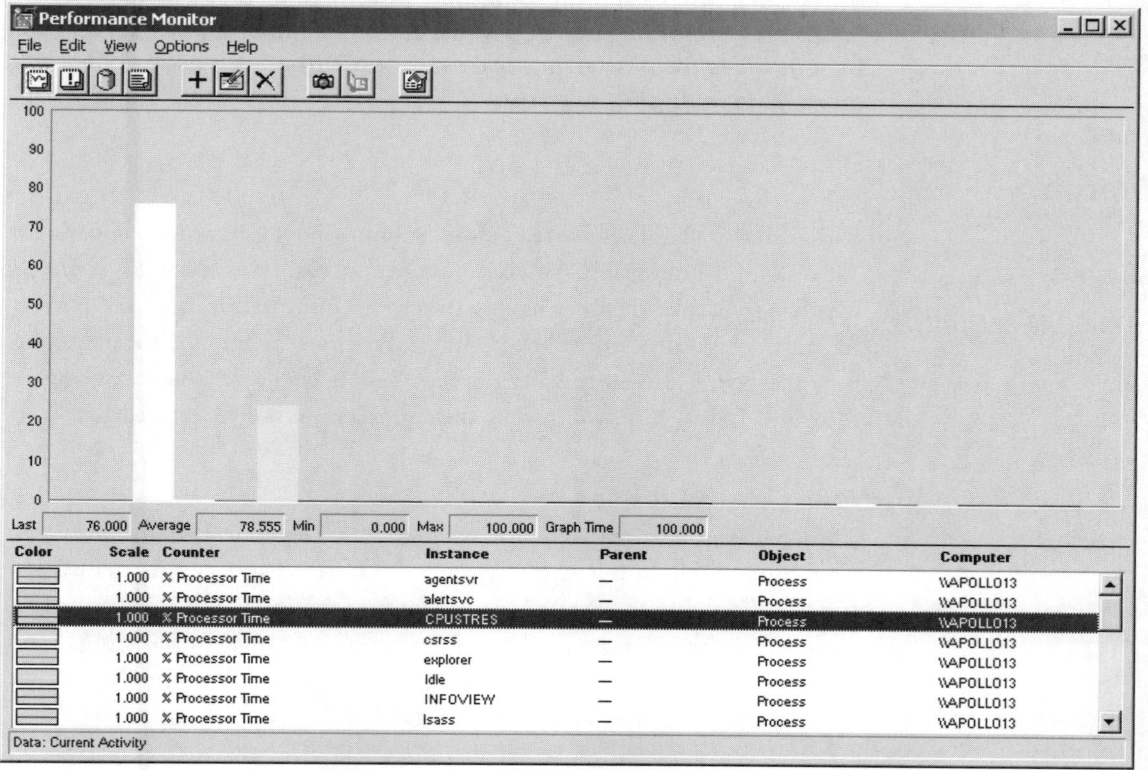

failing. What is a high number? There is no hard and fast answer as there is with the Processor Queue Length, because the hardware in your server varies. That is why it is important to establish a baseline trace of your system. If you monitor the Interrupts/sec on your system when there is no system activity, you can compare this value when there is more activity and you will be able to tell if there is a problem.

on the job

It is important to determine the system role for your server before you order the hardware. You must know what the server will be used for and what applications will run on it. For example, Exchange 5.0 did not scale well past two processors, which meant that buying a four-processor server didn't improve performance significantly. If you know this beforehand, you can save money by buying only two processors, or spend it on something else, such as more memory or a RAID subsystem. In general, servers set up as file and print servers will benefit more from a faster processor; application servers will benefit more from multiple processors.

Memory

Earlier in this chapter, you read about monitoring your memory subsystem. The main goal in optimizing your memory subsystem is to reduce paging, which is the act of memory having to retrieve information from the paging file on the hard disk instead of in physical memory. Paging reduces system performance, because accessing the hard disk is far slower than accessing memory. This section will review the counters that we covered earlier.

Memory: Pages/sec

This will be your primary counter when monitoring your memory subsystem. This counter tells you how many times the system had to write to, or read from the hard disk to resolve a request for information that wasn't in physical memory. Since accessing the hard disk is much slower than accessing memory, system performance will be greatly degraded. You should look for sustained values above 12 that would indicate a shortage of memory.

Memory: Page Faults/sec

This counter shows the total number of page faults that occurred within the last second. This number includes both hard and soft page faults. Remember that since soft page faults do not have a significant impact on system performance, you will need to see what percentage of this number are hard faults and what percentage are soft faults.

Memory: Pages Input/sec

This counter shows the number of pages that had to be read from disk to resolve hard page faults. If you take this value and divide it by the number of Page Faults/sec, you can determine what percentage of the paging are hard page faults. A high value here (greater than 40 percent) is another strong indicator that you have a memory shortage, since information has to be retrieved from the hard disk.

Let's look at an example. In Figure 32-12, we show a sample PerfMon Report view displaying the Pages Input/sec counter and the Page Faults/sec counter. Pages Input/sec shows a value of 13.780, while the Page Faults/sec counter shows a value of 49.728. When we divide the number of Pages Input/sec by the number of Page Faults/sec, we get 13.780/49.728 = 0.28, or 28 percent. You can safely say that most of the paging is due to soft page faults.

Memory: Available Bytes

This is the amount of physical memory (in bytes) available to applications. When this value dips below 4MB, you will experience an increase in paging, since information has to swap out to disk to make room for running applications.

Memory: Commit Limit

This counter displays the amount of virtual memory that can be committed to processes without having to expand the paging file. Committed memory is space in the paging file that is reserved for a certain process. When the commit limit is reached, the pagefile must be expanded.

FIGURE 32-12 Divide the Pages Input/sec by Page Faults/sec to determine the percentage of hard page faults

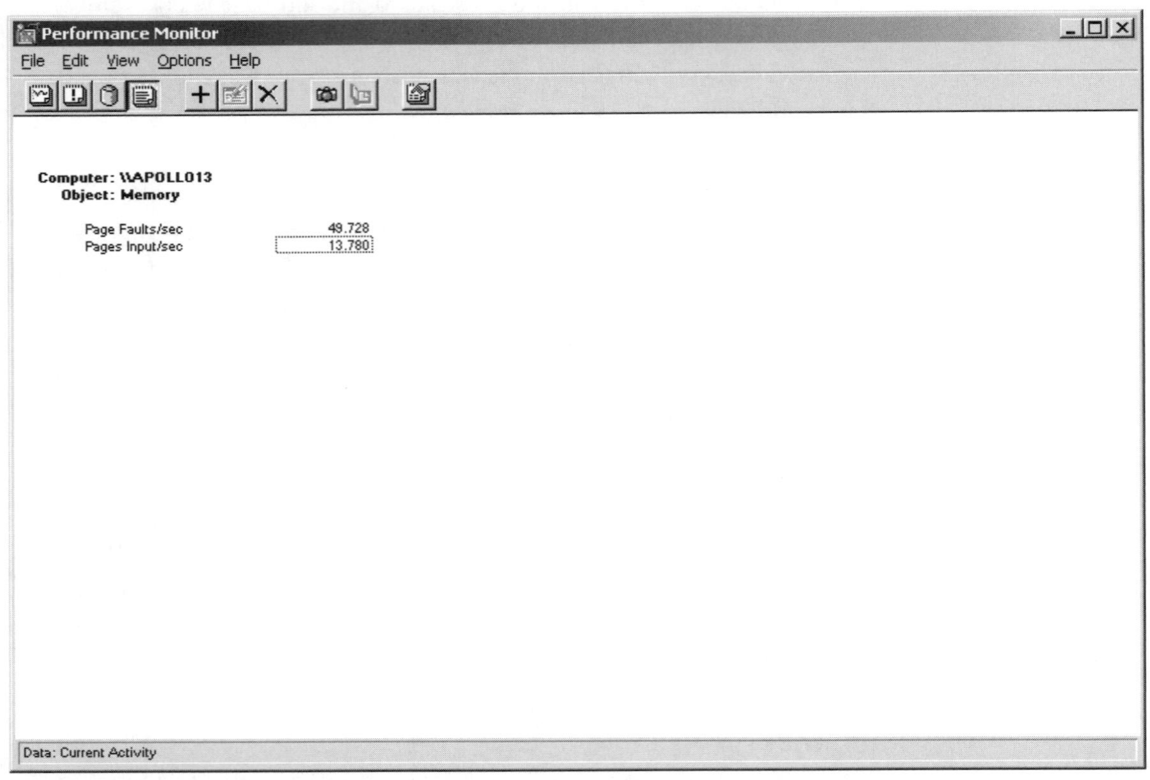

Memory: Committed Bytes

This counter displays the amount of virtual memory that has been committed to a process. When the Committed Bytes value reaches the Commit Limit, the pagefile must be expanded.

Memory: Pool Paged Bytes

This displays number of bytes in the Paged Pool. Recall that the paged pool area of memory is used by applications. It contains data that can be swapped to disk when not in use. If you notice this counter increasing steadily, it could indicate that a user application has a memory leak.

Memory: Pool Nonpaged Bytes

This counter shows the number of bytes in the Nonpaged Pool. The Nonpaged Pool is another area of memory. It contains data that cannot be swapped to disk. If you notice this counter increasing steadily, it could indicate that a system device driver has a memory leak.

Process: Page Faults/sec

This counter shows the number of page faults generated by this process. This counter shows both hard and soft page faults, so a high number here may not necessarily indicate a problem if most of the page faults are soft.

Process: Page File Bytes and Page File Bytes Peak

This is the number of bytes and the maximum number of bytes, since the system started, that the process is using in the pagefile. An increasing Page File Bytes counter may indicate that this process has a memory leak.

Process: Pool Nonpaged Bytes

This counter shows the number of bytes that this process is using in the Nonpaged Pool area of memory. Data in this area of memory cannot be paged out to disk.

Process: Pool Paged Bytes

This counter shows the number of bytes that this process is using in the paged pool area of memory. Data in this area of memory can be paged out to disk when necessary.

Now let's take a look at what happens to a system when it slowly runs out of memory. Refer to Figure 32-13. The system that we are monitoring is running a Windows NT Resource Kit utility called LeakyApp, which, as the name suggests, slowly begins chewing up memory.

As LeakyApp runs and takes up memory, notice that the Available Bytes counter (the highlighted line) begins decreasing. The Committed Bytes counter begins increasing. Notice, too, that even though the Available Bytes counter is decreasing, the system is not paging, since the Pages/sec counter is near zero. This shows that there is still a good amount of physical memory available, so the system does not have to page information to and from the

FIGURE 32-13 As Available Bytes decreases, paging activity increases

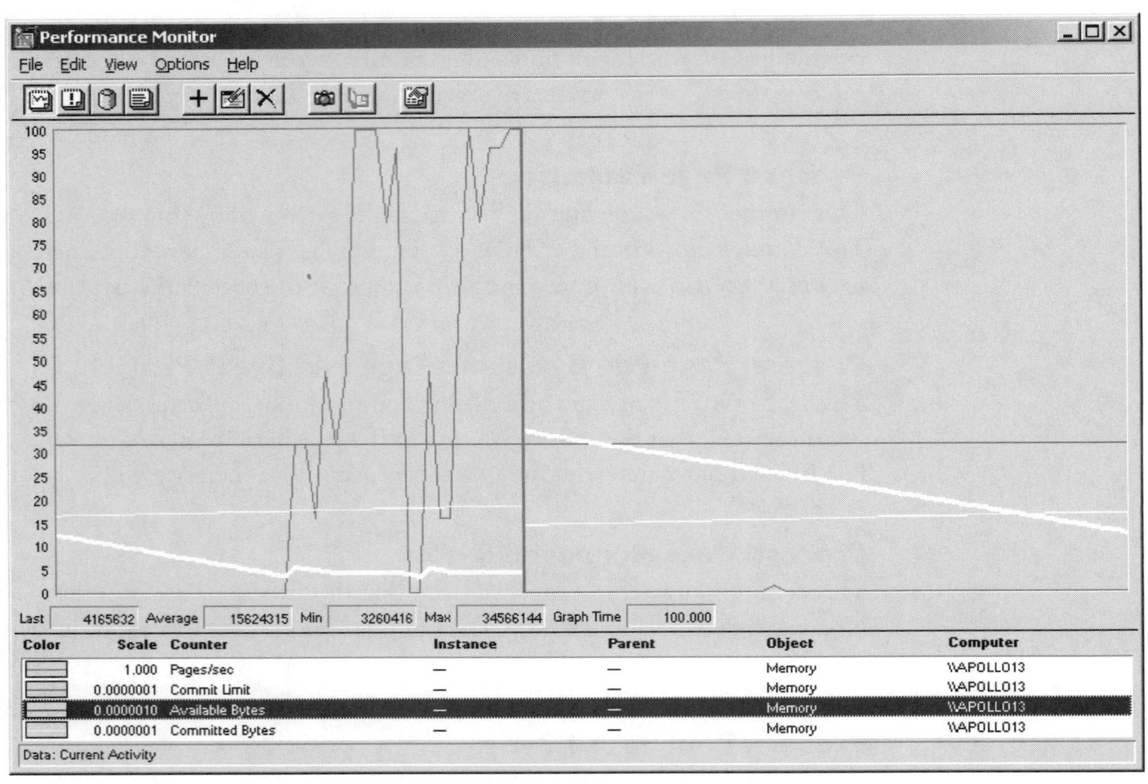

disk yet. Now look at the graph when the Available Bytes counter reaches about 5MB. You can see immediately that the system starts paging information to and from the disk to make room for the LeakyApp. If we were monitoring the disk counters, you'd also see an increase in disk activity, and if you were sitting at the server, you'd notice a marked decrease in performance.

So now that we know we have an application that is leaking, let's take a look at the characteristics of a leaky application. Refer to Figure 32-14, where we are monitoring four counters for the LEAKYAPP process. You'll notice that the highlighted line, the Page File Bytes counter, is continuously increasing, clearly indicating that this process is leaking memory.

FIGURE 32-14 Characteristics of a process with a memory leak

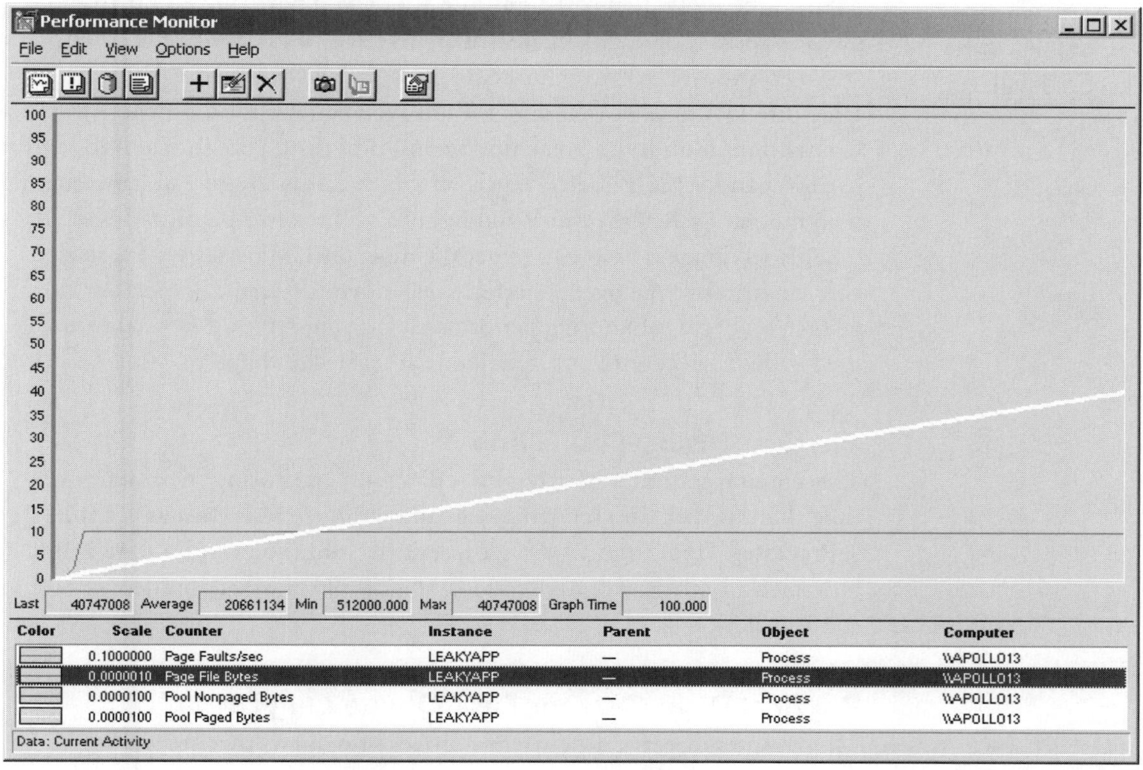

Disk

The disk subsystem is by far the slowest component of the server, primarily because it is the only component that has mechanical, moving parts. This subsystem consists of the hard disks and the drive controllers. There are two controller types: IDE/EIDE and SCSI, each having its own advantages and disadvantages. The primary purpose of the disk subsystem is to store all the users' information as well as the OS files and programs. Remember that the pagefile is stored on your disks.

Also note that there are two similar objects that you can measure in PerfMon: *physical disk* and *logical disk.* Physical disk refers to the actual hard disks that are installed in your server. You will have an instance for each disk installed. In general, you will be interested in this object. Logical disk refers to the individual partitions into which you have broken up your physical disks. Logical disks are usually referred to as C:, D:, and so on.

To confuse matters even more, Compaq allows you to break up the array into logical drives. In our example, you can use the Compaq Array Configuration utility to break up the 36GB of disk space into a 4GB logical partition and a 32GB logical partition. Since this is all done in hardware, it is all hidden to the OS, and Windows NT will see two physical drives!

This section will help you to get the most out of this subsystem so that you can improve the overall performance of your system. Remember that before you begin monitoring performance on your server, you need to enable the DISKPERF counters as described earlier in the chapter.

Physical Disk: %Disk Time

This counter indicates how busy the disk is by measuring the amount of time that the disk uses servicing read and write requests. Just as with the %Processor Time counter, a high sustained utilization can indicate a disk bottleneck, but you will have to look at a couple of other counters to confirm this.

Physical Disk: Current Disk Queue Length

This counter displays the current number of requests that are waiting to be serviced by the disk subsystem. In conjunction with a high %Disk Time, a sustained value of two or greater suggests that your disk subsystem is overloaded. But before you upgrade your disks or disk controller, we can measure a few other counters to determine if there are other factors to consider that could be causing the high utilization.

Physical Disk: Average Disk Queue Length

This counter is similar to the Current Disk Queue Length counter, except that instead of measuring the instantaneous value, it measures the average value over the sample time interval.

Let's take a quick look at the %Disk Time counter and the Current Disk Queue Length counter on a server with fairly high disk activity, as in Figure 32-15. You'll notice that although there is a lot of disk activity, there aren't many requests waiting in the disk queue. The queue reaches a maximum of two at a couple of instances, but never holds at that value, meaning that the disk is able to keep up with requests for the most part. If the disk queue were to hold a constant value of two or greater, then the disk subsystem is too slow to handle all of the requests.

FIGURE 32-15 Low values for the Disk Queue indicate a disk that is not too busy

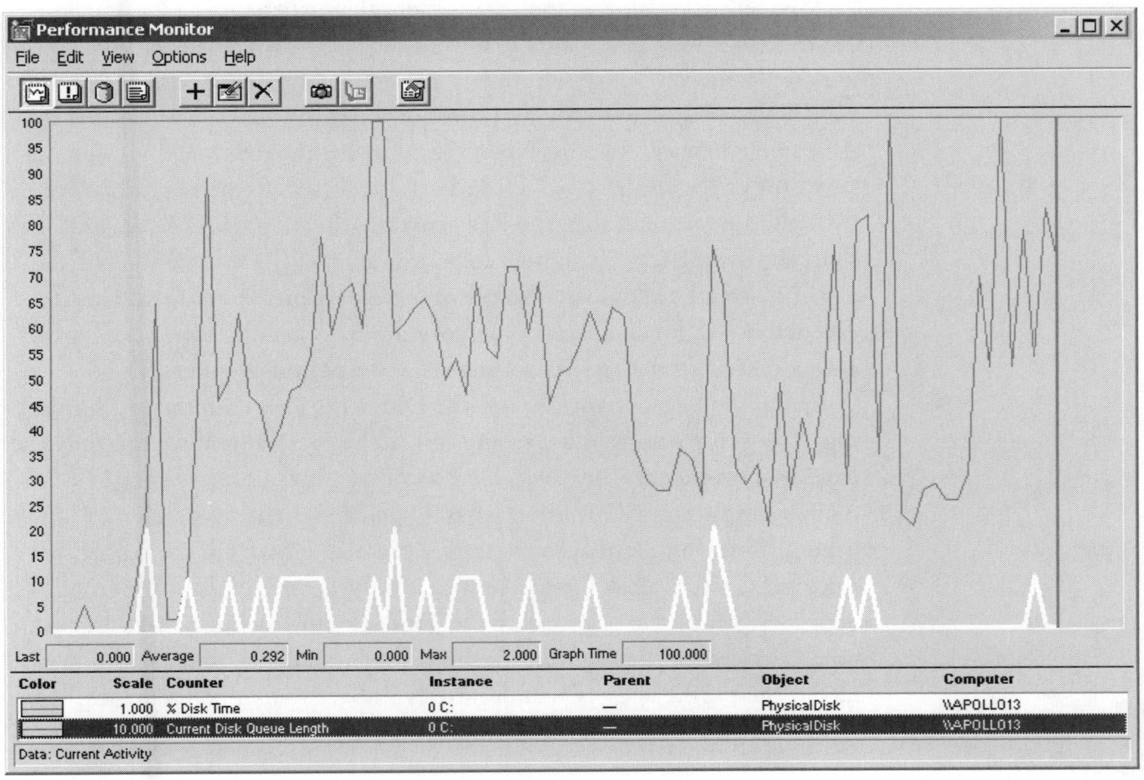

Physical Disk: Disk Reads/sec

This counter indicates the number of times the system had to read from the disks in the last second. You should compare this value to the Memory: Page Inputs/sec counter to see if your disk activity is due mainly to paging operations. In this case, it would indicate a memory shortage more than a disk subsystem problem.

Physical Disk: Avg. Disk sec/Transfer

This counter indicates the amount of time it takes the disk to complete an average data transfer. If you take the Memory: Pages/sec counter and multiply it by this counter, you get the % Disk Time that is dedicated to paging.

Now let's take another look at a system that experiences a lot of paging, but this time, we'll take a look at it from the disk subsystem side. We'll again use the LeakyApp utility to simulate a shortage of memory and generate page faults. First, let's verify that most of the disk activity is attributed to the paging activity. Refer to Figure 32-16, where we are tracking Memory: Pages Input/sec and Physical Disk: Disk Reads/sec. Remember that if these two values are similar, then the disk activity is due to paging. As the PerfMon chart shows, these two counters correlate very well.

Let's also take a look at a couple of measurements to confirm that the disk activity is due to a lack of memory in our system. Figure 32-17 shows a Report view of the activity during the same period as Figure 32-16.

Again, the Pages Input/sec and the Disk Reads/sec counters are similar, suggesting that paging is increasing disk activity. Finally, if we multiply the Pages/sec counter and the Avg. Disk sec/Transfer counter, we get 190.129 x 0.437 = 83 percent. This means that 83 percent of the disk activity is due to paging, confirming our suspicions. We can also infer from the report that since the Current Disk Queue Length is only 1, the disk is not overly bogged down by the paging activity. This is mainly because there are no other services running on this machine. As you increase user activity on this server, the paging activity will negatively impact system performance.

Here are some suggestions for improving your disk subsystem performance.

- Use a SCSI controller instead of an IDE/EIDE controller. The SCSI controller generally has better performance in a multiuser environment.

FIGURE 32-16 This chart shows that the disk activity is due to paging

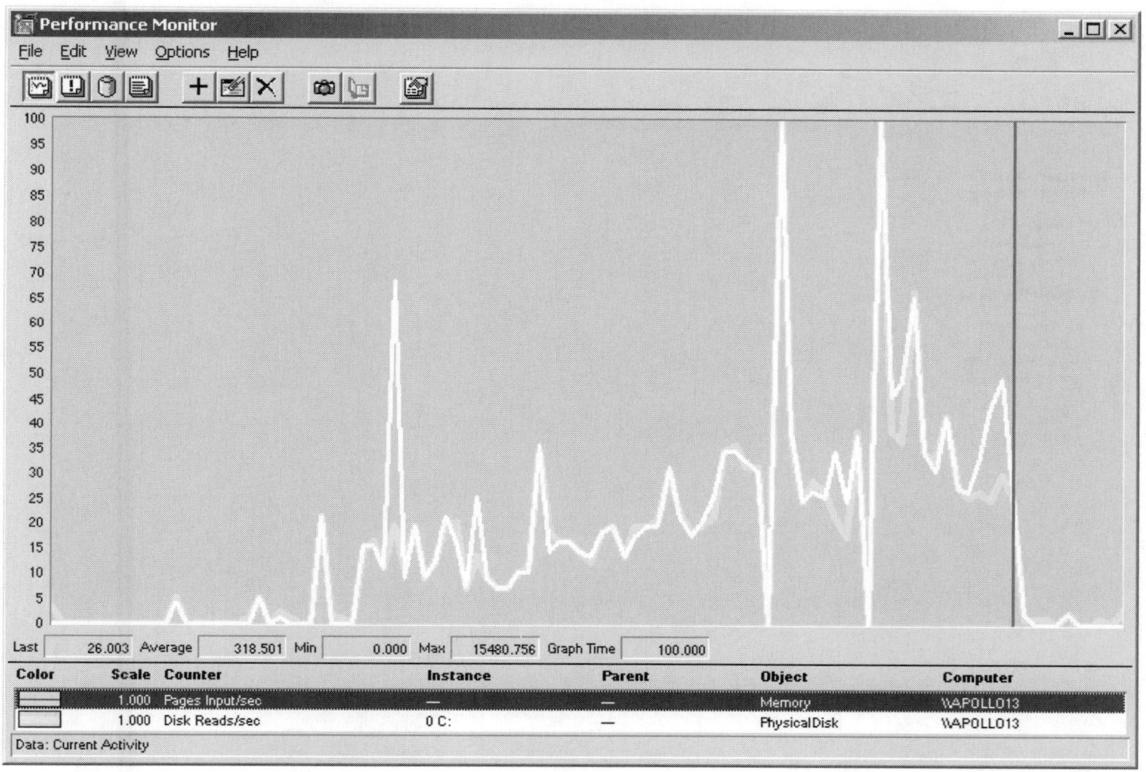

- Use a hardware-based RAID solution instead of Windows NT RAID solution.
- Distribute services to different physical disks or different servers.
- Install faster hard disks or a disk controller with greater throughput.
- Add more memory to decrease paging activity.
- Move the pagefile to a different physical disk than the operating system files.

FIGURE 32-17 These counters also indicate that a high percentage of disk activity is due to paging

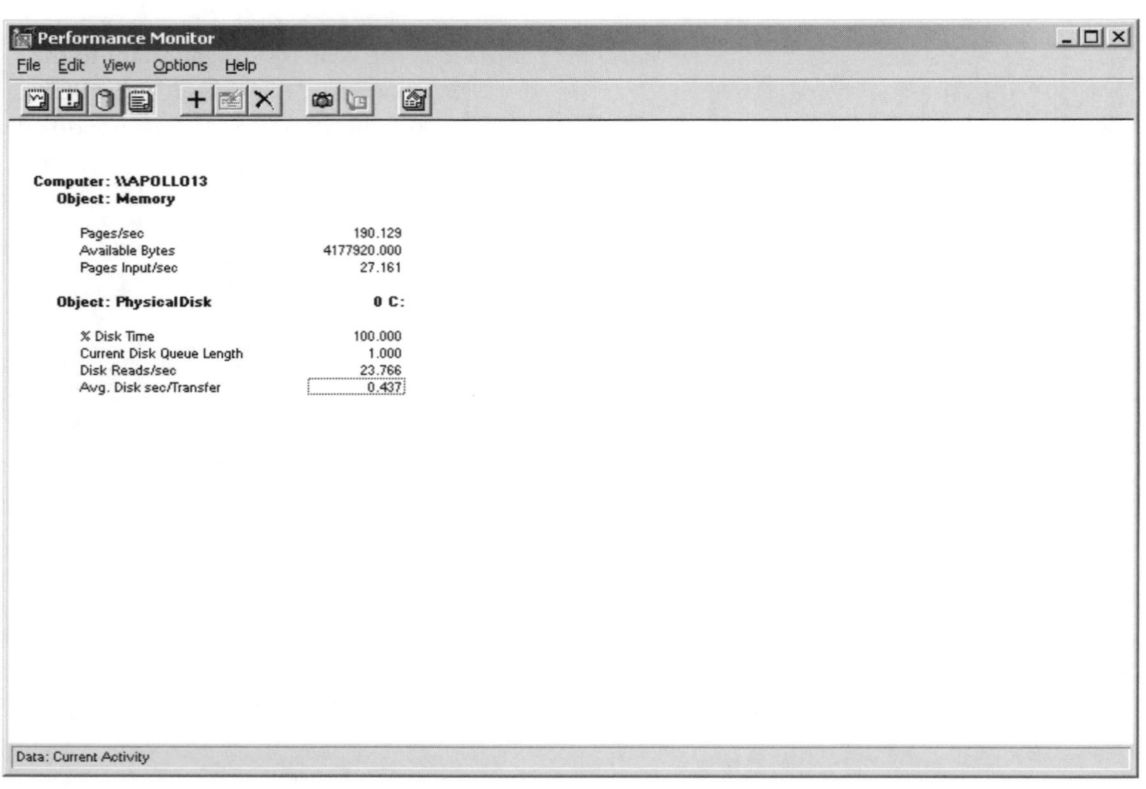

Network

The network is the only thing physically connecting your servers to your client PCs. If your network is clogged with information, server response will suffer and the users will complain of a slow server. Although there are several tasks that you can perform to increase network bandwidth (such as using switches instead of hubs, and upgrading to 100 Mbps), this section will concentrate on optimizing the network subsystem of your server to tune performance. The network subsystem includes everything from the network interface card (NIC) to the network protocols, to the server networking components. This section will cover the counters that let you observe overall network performance for your server.

The network card is the only physical connection that a server has to the rest of the network. The architecture of the NIC is very important to the overall performance of the server. Make sure that you have a 32-bit PCI card for maximum throughput. You should also get a card that supports the maximum throughput for your network topology (100 Mbps for Ethernet, 16 Mbps for Token Ring). Monitor the interrupts that your NIC generates, since a large number of interrupts may indicate a defective card.

Monitor the following counters to track the overall health of your network card. Before you can do so, you will need to install the SNMP service in Control Panel | Network to enable the Network Interface object.

Network Interface: Bytes Total/sec

This is the total number of bytes sent and received by your NIC. The value of this counter is a sum of Bytes Sent/sec and Bytes Received/sec. If this number approaches the total bandwidth of your network, you may have network congestion issues and may need to segment the traffic on your network.

Network Interface: Bytes Sent/sec

This is the number of bytes that the NIC sends out over the network. You can use this to determine whether your network traffic is being caused by the server. If this number approaches the total bandwidth of your network, your server may be overloading your network.

Network Interface: Bytes Received/sec

This is the number of bytes that the NIC receives from the network. A high number here suggests that you need to segment your network or add a second NIC to your server.

Network Interface: Current Bandwidth

This counter shows the nominal bandwidth as determined by the network card. This should remain a constant value. You can use this line as a threshold for the Bytes/sec counters.

Processor: %Interrupt Time

This is the percent of time that the processor spends servicing hardware interrupts. A high number here may indicate a faulty network card.

If you install the Network Monitor Agent service in Control Panel | Network, you will receive an additional object in PerfMon called Network Segment. You will be interested in the following counters for the Network Segment object.

Network Segment: %Network Utilization

This counter displays the overall percentage of the network bandwidth in use. A sustained number greater than 60 may indicate network congestion problems.

Network Segment: %Broadcasts

This counter shows how much of the network traffic is broadcasts. Since broadcasts are processed by every computer on a segment, a high number of broadcasts will significantly reduce network performance.

You can also monitor the Server service to see how much traffic is generated and received by the server. The following counters will describe the counters for the Server object.

Server: Bytes Received/sec

This is the number of bytes that the server has received from the network. You can use this counter to tell if the network traffic is mostly inbound.

Server: Bytes Transmitted/sec

This is the number of bytes that the server has sent out over the network. You can use this counter to tell if the server is generating most of the network traffic.

Server: Bytes Total/sec

This is the sum of Bytes Received/sec and Bytes Transmitted/sec. You can use this counter to give a general indication of how busy your server is.

Server: Logon/sec

For domain controllers, this counter will tell you how many logons per second the server is processing.

Although PerfMon will track some network utilization numbers for the server, it does not look at the actual packets that travel across the wire. So PerfMon may be able to tell you that your network has a high percentage of broadcast traffic, but it will not tell you which machine is causing the broadcasts. You will need a network sniffer or a protocol analyzer to be able to look at that information in depth. Windows NT Server comes with a utility called Network Monitor that allows you to look at and analyze the network traffic. You can determine which machines are generating the network traffic and find out why. Microsoft Systems Management Server comes with a full-featured version of Network Monitor that allows you to perform a greater number of functions than the scaled-down version that comes with Windows NT.

The following are some tips for reducing unnecessary network traffic to help the overall performance of your network.

- Minimize the number of protocols that you use on the network. Each protocol that you run adds overhead to your server and can affect performance unnecessarily.
- Avoid using NetBEUI as a protocol. NetBEUI was meant for small networks of 10 clients or fewer. Due to the broadcast nature of NetBEUI, it does not scale well to larger networks.
- Use WINS for name resolution when using TCP/IP. If you do not use WINS, clients will resort to using broadcasts for name resolution, which could quickly consume your network bandwidth.
- Disable your clients from taking part in browser elections. For Windows 95 clients, edit the Registry as follows: HKEY_LOCAL_MACHINE | System | CurrentControlSet | Services | VxD | Vnetsetup | MaintainServerList=no
  For Windows NT machines edit the Registry as follows: HKEY_LOCAL_MACHINE | System | CurrentControlSet | Services | Browser | Parameters | MaintainServerList=no

TABLE 32-1

Counters that Show a Bottleneck

Subsystem	PerfMon Counter	What to Look For
Processor	Processor: Processor Queue Length	A consistent value over 2 may indicate an overloaded processor
Memory	Memory: Pages/sec	A consistent value over 12 may indicate a shortage of memory
Disk	Physical Disk: Current Disk Queue Length	A consistent value of 2 may indicate an overloaded disk subsystem
Network	Network Interface: Bytes Total/sec	If this value approaches the bandwidth limit for your network (for example, 10 Mbps for Ethernet), then you may need to segment your network

Identifying a Bottleneck

A bottleneck, in the simplest terms, is the slowest part of a system. A bottleneck will cause other subsystems to wait while it finishes its task. Since the other subsystems have to wait for the bottleneck, they aren't accomplishing anything. You must be able to distinguish between a busy subsystem and a subsystem that is a bottleneck. Just because the processor is running at 100 percent doesn't necessarily mean it is a bottleneck, if there are no tasks waiting in the processor queue. Alternatively, a subsystem can become a bottleneck well before it reaches 100 percent utilization. It is virtually impossible to remove all bottlenecks from a system, but try to remove as many of them as you can find. Table 32-1 lists the counters that help you look for bottlenecks.

CERTIFICATION SUMMARY

In this chapter, we covered a lot of material on tuning your server for Windows NT. You learned how to use Performance Monitor to track the health of your server with the four different views: Chart, Alert, Log, and Report. You also saw how Windows NT manages memory and how a lack of memory can affect your disk subsystem. You learned how to optimize your disk subsystem. You reviewed the counters you should use to track the performance of each of your server subsystems. Once you know how each of your subsystems performs, you have the information you need to tune your server for optimal performance.

TWO-MINUTE DRILL

- ❑ Windows NT Performance Monitor (PerfMon) will be your primary tool for measuring system performance. PerfMon works by measuring *counters* for the different system *objects*.
- ❑ You run Performance Monitor from the Administrative Tools folder from the Programs menu.
- ❑ Performance Monitor can display server information in four different views: Chart, Alert, Log, and Report.
- ❑ Each view has its own advantages and disadvantages, so it is important to determine when it is appropriate to use each view.
- ❑ Performance Monitor allows you to save your settings to a file so that you do not have to reenter the counters when you restart PerfMon.
- ❑ The Memory Subsystem is the most important subsystem in a server when it comes to performance.
- ❑ The memory pool is broken up into three separate pools: pageable memory, nonpageable memory, and file system cache.
- ❑ The nonpageable memory pool is reserved for data that must reside in physical memory and is not swapped to the pagefile on the hard disk.
- ❑ The pageable memory pool is used by the rest of the operating system and applications. It includes data that may be paged out to disk as necessary.
- ❑ The system cache is used to keep recently used information in RAM instead of being paged to disk.
- ❑ You can determine the system cache size by using either the Performance Monitor or the Task Manager.

- The pagefile, also known as virtual memory or a swap file, is a file on the hard disk that temporarily holds some contents of memory.
- The Windows NT Virtual Memory Manager (VMM), which is part of the NT Executive Services, is responsible for assigning the address space to each application.
- There are two types of page faults: hard page faults and soft page faults.
- With a soft page fault, the faulted pages are found elsewhere in physical memory (usually the file system cache).
- With a hard page fault, the faulted pages are found in the pagefile on the hard disk.
- By tracking the Process object using Performance Monitor, each running process will appear in the Instance window of the Add Counter window. This will help you determine which applications are using all of your memory and whether you can optimize their usage to make the most of your current amount of RAM.
- By monitoring the counter Paging File > %Usage Peak, you will see how much of the paging file is in use. Take that percentage and multiply it by the size of the pagefile in megabytes. This is the number that you should use to add memory to your system.
- Tuning the Server service (in the Network Control Panel) is one of the more noticeable methods for increasing performance for the end user.
- When you use the Server service window to optimize NT, you affect how the Server service uses memory and file caches.
- More often than not, your disk subsystem will end up becoming the bottleneck of your server.
- You simply have to tell PerfMon to enable the disk performance counters. The disk performance counters are activated or deactivated at the command prompt.
- The Windows NT Thread Scheduler assigns processor time to a program according to the priority level set by the programmer within the program. This priority is known as the process's base priority.

- Server roles include: a file server, an application server, a logon server, or any combination of the three.
- In a client-server environment, all of the processing is being done on the server, creating a heavy load signature on the processors and memory of the application server.
- In a resource-sharing environment, client PCs can transfer a relatively large amount of data back and forth from the server. Memory usage is also lighter on a file server than it is with an application server.
- The Processor: %Processor Time counter displays the percentage of time that a processor is performing work.
- The System: Processor Queue Length counter displays the number of threads that are waiting in the queue to be processed, and generally shows whether your processor is a bottleneck or not.
- The Processor: %User Time counter displays the percentage of the processor time that is being used for user applications.
- The Processor: %Privileged Time counter displays the percentage of the processor time that is being used for privileged or kernel mode applications.
- The Process: %Processor Time counter displays the percentage of processor time that the process is taking up.
- The Processor: Interrupts/sec counter displays the number of hardware interrupts that the processor had to respond to.
- The main goal in optimizing your memory subsystem is to reduce paging. There are many counters available to monitor your memory subsystem.
- Remember that before you begin monitoring the disk subsystem performance on your server, you need to enable the DISKPERF counters.
- The network subsystem includes everything from the network interface card (NIC) to the network protocols, to the server networking components. Once again, many counters are available to monitor this system.
- Table 32-1 lists the counters that help you look for bottlenecks.

SELF TEST

The following Self Test questions will help you measure your understanding of the material presented in this chapter. Read all the choices carefully, as there may be more than one correct answer. Choose all correct answers for each question.

1. Which Performance Monitor view would you use to collect information over a period of time to be analyzed later?
   A. Chart view
   B. Alert view
   C. Log view
   D. Report view
2. Which of the following is an example of a counter in Performance Monitor?
   A. %Usage
   B. %Processor
   C. Memory
   D. Logical Disk
3. How do you view the information gathered by the Log view?
   A. Use the Export Log option
   B. Use the Import Log option
   C. Use the Data From option
   D. Use the Chart Options
4. You've created a workspace file for PerfMon that includes Log view settings. You add the workspace file to your Startup group, but when you open the workspace file, you have to start the log manually. How can you have the log start automatically when you open the workspace file?
   A. Set your update interval to zero.
   B. Modify the Log Options and enable the Start On Open option.
   C. Manually start the log, then resave the workspace file.
   D. You must manually start the log every time.
5. Which of the following is not a pool in memory?
   A. Pageable
   B. Nonpageable
   C. File System Cache
   D. Virtual
6. Which of the following is a characteristic of nonpageable memory?
   A. Reserved for applications working set
   B. Can be swapped to the hard disk in low memory conditions
   C. Data that must reside in physical memory at all times
   D. Acts as a temporary storage for data
7. How do you set the size for the File System Cache?
   A. Modify the cache settings in Control Panel | System.
   B. Use the SETCACHE command at a command prompt.

C. Open Task Manager and click Set Cache.

D. You cannot set the size of the cache.

8. You have 100 users on a server that is being used as a file and print server. Users are complaining of slow response. You suspect that the server settings aren't correct. How should you set the server settings?

   A. Minimize Memory Used

   B. Balanced

   C. Maximize Throughput for File Sharing

   D. Maximize Throughput for Network Applications

9. You add counters to monitor the performance of your disks, but they all read zero. What is the most likely cause for this?

   A. The disks aren't on the Windows NT Hardware Compatibility List.

   B. You haven't run DISKPERF.

   C. You added the counters for Logical Disk instead of Physical Disk.

   D. You added the counters for Physical Disk instead of Logical Disk.

10. What is the proper command to activate the disk performance counters?

   A. DISKPERF –ON

   B. DISKPERF –SET

   C. DISKPERF –Y

   D. DISKPERF –ENABLE

11. Which of the following is not a characteristic of a hard page fault?

   A. Pages are found in the pagefile.

   B. Pages are found in the system cache.

   C. Degrades system performance

   D. Caused by a lack of memory

12. Which of the following will benefit an application server?

   A. Faster, single processor

   B. Additional memory

   C. Faster disks

   D. 100 Mbps network

13. Which of the following will benefit a file and print server?

   A. Faster, single processor

   B. Additional memory

   C. 7200 rpm disks

   D. 10 Mbps network

14. Which command would you use to launch Solitaire with a higher than normal priority?

   A. START /BOOST SOL.EXE

   B. START /HIGH SOL.EXE

   C. SOL.EXE /BOOST

   D. SOL.EXE /HIGH

15. How can you change the priority of an application that is already running?

   A. Use Task Manager.

   B. Use the Start Command.

   C. Use the Boost Command.

   D. You cannot change the priority of an application once it has launched.

16. What is the default size of the pagefile?
    A. 3MB
    B. Amount of memory
    C. Amount of memory + 12MB
    D. Double the size of memory
17. Which of the following is not a method to optimize the pagefile?
    A. Create a second pagefile on a different partition on the same disk.
    B. Create a second pagefile on a different disk.
    C. Disable the pagefile from expanding.
    D. Add more memory.
18. How can you prevent the pagefile from expanding?
    A. Deselect the Enable Pagefile Expansion option in the Virtual Memory dialog.
    B. Set the Initial Size and Maximum Size to the same value.
    C. Create a partition with the size of the pagefile and copy the pagefile to that partition.
    D. Use Task Manager to set the size of the pagefile (select Do Not Expand).
19. You want to configure your pagefile size so that the pagefile does not have to expand. Which counter would you monitor in PerfMon to figure out how large to make your pagefile?
    A. Memory: Available Bytes
    B. Memory: Pages/sec
    C. Paging File: %Usage Peak
    D. Memory: Page Faults/sec
20. You have 64MB of RAM in your server. You observe a large number of pages and notice that disk activity is increasing. Which counter would you monitor to determine how much memory you should add?
    A. Paging File: %Usage Peak
    B. Memory: Pages/sec
    C. Memory: Available Bytes
    D. Memory: Page Faults/sec
21. Which counter would you monitor to determine whether your processor is overloaded?
    A. Processor: %Processor Time
    B. Processor: Processor Queue Length
    C. Processor: %User Time
    D. Processor: %Privileged Time
22. What is the significance of the Memory: Commit Limit counter?
    A. It displays how many programs can be loaded in memory simultaneously.
    B. It is the amount of virtual memory that can be committed without having to expand the paging file.
    C. It is the amount of memory dedicated to the system cache.
    D. It is the highest amount of memory that can be committed to an application.

23. Which counter would you monitor to determine whether your disk subsystem is a bottleneck?
    - A. %Disk Time
    - B. Current Disk Queue Length
    - C. Disk Reads/sec
    - D. Avg. Disk sec/Transfer
24. Which counter would you monitor to determine if you have a defective network card?
    - A. %Interrupt Time
    - B. Error Bytes/sec
    - C. %Network Utilization
    - D. Bytes Total/sec
25. Which counter would you use to track how busy the Server service is with respect to the network?
    - A. Processor: %Processor Time
    - B. Server: Bytes Total/sec
    - C. Network Interface: Current Bandwidth
    - D. Memory: Pages/sec
26. Which of the following is not a function of the Virtual Memory Manager?
    - A. Swaps out least used data from memory to the pagefile
    - B. Translates virtual addresses to physical addresses
    - C. Allocates 2GB of address space to each application
    - D. Allows applications to access shared memory

A

Self Test Answers

Chapter 1 Answers

1. What bus handles the various I/O ranges that devices use?
   - A. Data
   - B. Address
   - C. Control
   - D. None of the above

   B. Address bus. The address bus carries the addresses of the I/O ranges so devices can communicate.

2. What is one factor that determines how much data can be handled on a bus in a computer?
   - A. Width of the bus
   - B. Length of the bus
   - C. Number of connectors on the bus
   - D. All of the above

   A. Width of the bus. The address buses, as well as other buses on the computer, have a certain width that determines how much data can be handled on the bus.

3. What is the maximum addressable memory size of a Pentium processor?
   - A. 4MB
   - B. 64MB
   - C. 4GB
   - D. 64GB

   C. 4GB. The addressable memory size is calculated by taking 2 to the power of the number of bits on the address bus. A Pentium processor has 32 address lines.

4. What is used to determine how much data can be sent between devices at one time?
   - A. Address bus
   - B. Data bus
   - C. Control bus
   - D. Memory bus

   B. Data bus. The data bus is what is used to transport data between devices as well as determine how much data can be sent at one time.

5. How many bits make up a byte?
   - A. 6
   - B. 7
   - C. 8
   - D. 12

   C. 8. Eight bits make up a byte. For this reason, the data bus is made up of multiples of eight bits.

6. What are two factors that affect the performance of the data bus?
   - A. Speed
   - B. Length
   - C. Width
   - D. Number of connectors

   A, C. Speed and width. The speed and width of the data bus affect the performance of the system.

7. What is the width of the data bus on a computer with an 80486 processor?
   - A. 32 bits
   - B. 64 bits
   - C. 32 bytes
   - D. 64 bytes

   A. 32 bits. The width of the data bus for 386 and 486 processors in 32 bits. The Pentium line has a width of 64 bits.

8. What is used to determine the type of bus cycle?
   A. Address bus
   B. Data bus
   C. Control bus
   D. Processor bus
   C. Control bus. The control bus is used to identify the type of bus cycle.

9. What is used to determine when the bus cycle is complete?
   A. Address bus
   B. Control bus
   C. Data bus
   D. Memory bus
   B. Control bus. The control bus is used to determine when the bus cycle is complete.

10. Which of the following is not one of the basic types of bus cycle?
    A. Memory Write
    B. Memory Read
    C. I/O Read
    D. Memory Burst
    D. Memory Burst. The four basic types of bus cycles are Memory Read, Memory Write, I/O Read, and I/O Write.

11. Which of the following will not increase bus performance?
    A. Increasing the clock speed of the processor
    B. Widening the bus
    C. Making sure all of your devices are ISA devices and not PCI devices
    D. Installing high-speed memory
    C. Making sure all of your devices are ISA devices and not PCI devices. ISA devices are typically not as fast, since the ISA bus is 16 bits. PCI devices communicate on a 32-bit bus.

12. What is known as an extra bus cycle and is used if a device cannot respond in one cycle?
    A. Slow machine
    B. Wait state
    C. Burst cycle
    D. Double cycle
    B. Wait state. A wait state is an extra bus cycle that is used if a device cannot respond in one cycle.

13. What is the term equivalent to the amount of data that can flow across a bus during a given amount of time?
    A. Maximum data throughput
    B. Minimum data throughput
    C. Wait state
    D. Clock cycle
    A. Maximum data throughput. The maximum data throughput is equivalent to the amount of data that can flow across a bus during a given amount of time. This is how you can measure one computer's performance against others'.

14. What is the formula for calculating the maximum data throughput?

    A. $(F \times W) / R = MTN$
    B. $(W \times N) / F = MTR$
    C. $(W \times R) / N = MTR$
    D. $(F \times W) / N = MTR$

    D. $(F \times W) / N = MTR$. A short version of the formula would read $(F \times W) / N = MTR$. The frequency times the width, divided by the number of clock cycles, equals the maximum transfer rate.

15. What happens in a burst cycle?

    A. Data is transferred every other clock cycle.
    B. Data is transferred every clock cycle.
    C. Double the data is transferred every clock cycle.
    D. Double the data is transferred every other clock cycle.

    B. Data is transferred every clock cycle. Burst cycles (or burst transfers) mean that data is transferred every clock cycle, as opposed to every other cycle.

Chapter 2 Answers

1. Which of the following is not an enhancement with the Pentium line of processors?

    A. Superscalar architecture
    B. Branch prediction
    C. 3.4v microprocessor
    D. 64-bit data bus

    C. 3.4v microprocessor. The Pentium line of processors has many enhancements, including a 3.3v microprocessor, not a 3.4v microprocessor.

2. How many Arithmetic Logic Units does a Pentium processor have?

    A. One
    B. Two
    C. Three
    D. Four

    B. Two. The Pentium processor has superscalar architecture, which means it has two Arithmetic Logic Units and dual instruction pipelines.

3. When the Pentium processor is decoding one instruction, where does it decode the next instruction?

    A. RAM
    B. On the hard disk
    C. In the pre-fetch queue
    D. In the post-fetch queue

    C. In the pre-fetch queue. Pentium processors have a pre-fetch queue. This means that while the processor is handling one instruction, it can be decoding the next instruction in the queue.

4. What are the three common types of memory?

    A. Fast Page Mode
    B. Extended Data Out
    C. Extra Data Out
    D. Burst Extended Data Out

    A, B, D. Fast Page Mode, Extended Data Out and Burst Extended Data Out are the three common types.

5. How many stages are there to a pipeline with a Pentium processor?

   A. Four

   B. Three

   C. Five

   D. Six

   C. Five. Pipelining is a process in which multiple instructions are overlapped, so many processes can be handled at once. The Pentium processor uses a five-stage pipeline.

6. Which of the following is not one of the five stages in pipelining?

   A. Pre-fetch

   B. Decoding the instruction

   C. Execution of the instruction

   D. Generation of data address

   D. Generation of data address is not one of the five stages in pipelining. Generation of memory address (if instruction includes a memory reference) is the correct description of the third stage.

7. What helps the processor remember the path taken for a particular process?

   A. Pre-fetch queue

   B. RAM

   C. Branch prediction

   D. Write-back cache

   C. Branch prediction. Branch prediction allows the processor to remember the path taken for a particular process.

8. What does CMOS stand for?

   A. Complementary Metal Oxide Conductor

   B. Company Middle Oxidation Centralization

   C. Complementary Metal Oxide Semiconductor

   D. Coprocessor Metal Oxide Semiconductor

   C. Complementary Metal Oxide Semiconductor. CMOS is volatile memory, which uses very low power. The main system configuration is kept here.

9. What does EPROM stand for?

   A. Erasable Programmable Read-Only Memory

   B. Electronic Programmable Read-Only Memory

   C. Erasable Primary Read-Only Memory

   D. Erasable Programmable Right-Only Memory

   A. Erasable Programmable Read-Only Memory. This is a subset of the ROMs on the system board.

10. Which of the following is an enhancement of the Pentium series of processor?

   A. Superscalar architecture

   B. 32-bit data bus; no 64-bit compatibility

   C. Off-chip interrupt controller

   D. Branch prediction

   D. Branch prediction. The Pentium series (75MHz and faster) provides the same basic features that the 486DX does, but with enhancements. Some of these enhancements are superscalar architecture, 64-bit data bus, and on-chip interrupt controller.

11. What are the two different types of cache on a Pentium processor?

    A. A 16KB data cache and a 16KB instruction cache

    B. An 8KB data cache and an 8KB instruction cache

    C. A 1MB data cache and a 1MB instruction cache

    D. A 4MB data cache and a 4MB instruction cache

    B. An 8KB data cache and an 8KB instruction cache. Two caches are needed to support two pipelines. With this configuration, you can support two processes in one clock cycle.

12. What allows for the capacity to have two or more processors? (Select two.)

    A. Advanced Programmable Interrupt Controller

    B. Single processor mode

    C. Dual processor mode

    D. Advanced Programmable Integer Counter

    A, C. Advanced Programmable Interrupt Controller and dual processor mode. One other feature that is new to the Pentium and newer processors is the capacity to have multiple processors on board. The Advanced Programmable Interrupt Controller allows up to 60 microprocessors. Dual processor mode means that two processors can use the second-level cache simultaneously.

13. What does DRAM stand for?

    A. Dual Rail Access Memory

    B. Double Random Access Memory

    C. Dynamic Random Access Memory

    D. Dynamic Role Access Memory

    C. Dynamic Random Access Memory. DRAM is the main memory or RAM.

14. What is the most common memory speed in today's computers?

    A. 50 nanoseconds

    B. 75 nanoseconds

    C. 60 nanoseconds

    D. 120 nanoseconds

    C. 60 nanoseconds. Speeds are nowadays around 60–70 nanoseconds. There are three common types: Fast Page Mode, Extended Data Out, and Burst Extended Data Out.

15. How many instructions can be handled per clock cycle?

    A. Seven

    B. Two

    C. One

    D. Zero

    C. One. Normal conditions allow for one clock cycle per instruction. Under normal and ideal conditions, each of the five pipeline stages would require a clock cycle. Pipelining allows more than one instruction to be handled simultaneously.

Chapter 3 Answers

1. The technology behind memory storage would best be described as:

   A. Individual cylinders, eight bits deep, arranged in 32 rows

   B. A three-dimensional cube

   C. A matrix of rows and columns

   D. All of the above

   C. Memory is typically referred to as a matrix with rows and columns, and the bit of information being requested is at the intersection of a row and column.

2. Which type of memory requires constant refreshing in order to keep its contents?

   A. DRAM

   B. SRAM

   C. Both A and B

   D. Neither A nor B

   A. DRAM can only hold its data if it is continuously accessed by something known as a refresh circuit. Hundreds of times each second, the contents of each memory cell is read by the refresh circuit, regardless of whether the memory cell is being used by the computer at that time.

3. A DRAM chip is composed of

   A. Multiple transistors and no capacitors

   B. Eight capacitors and one transistor

   C. Multiple concurrent capacitors

   D. One transistor and one capacitor

   D. DRAM uses only one transistor and one capacitor. This capacitor, when supplied current, will hold an electrical charge if the bit being stored contains a 1. It will hold no charge if the bit being stored contains a 0.

4. Which type of memory is transistor based and does not multiplex (and reads are not destructive)?

   A. DRAM

   B. SRAM

   C. Both A and B

   D. Neither A nor B

   B. SRAM is a type of RAM that holds its contents without the need for the additional refresh circuit. SRAM will hold its data for as long as there is power running to the circuit.

5. When memory is not "in step" with the system clock, what is it called?

   A. Defective memory

   B. Congruous

   C. Synchronous

   D. Asynchronous

   D. Asynchronous refers to memory that is not synchronized to the system clock. When a memory access is made, a certain period of time elapses before the memory value appears on the bus. The speed of the signal is not proportional to the system clock.

6. What is the correct order of memory technologies in terms of performance, going from the slowest type to the fastest?
   A. EDO, BEDO, FPM
   B. SDRAM, FPM, EDO
   C. FPM, EDO, SDRAM
   D. EDO, FPM, SDRAM
   C. FPM, EDO, SDRAM. FPM (Fast Page Mode) is not much faster than standard DRAM. EDO (Extended Data Out) is somewhat faster, and SDRAM (Synchronous DRAM) is the fastest of all, limited only by the speed of the system clock.

7. The speed of SDRAM is measured by what two criteria?
   A. MHz and nanoseconds
   B. Nanoseconds and KHz
   C. MHz and KHz
   D. MHz and milliseconds
   A. MHz and nanoseconds. You will find that SDRAM has a nanosecond rating just like conventional, asynchronous DRAM. It will also have another speed rating called MHz, which will be a speed such as 83 MHz or 100 MHz.

8. A DIMM is how many pins wide?
   A. 30
   B. 72
   C. 144
   D. 168
   D. A DIMM is 64 bits in width and is 168 pins wide.

9. A parity SIMM will have how many extra bits over conventional memory?
   A. Four
   B. One
   C. Two
   D. Nine
   B. One. For every eight bits there will be one extra bit for parity checking.

10. If part of a SIMM has been damaged, what kind of error would this be?
   A. Transient
   B. Hard
   C. Dormant
   D. Soft
   B. This would be known as a hard error. Soft, or transient, errors mean that the bit returns a value different from what was put in, and will only do this on a sporadic basis. Hard errors are much more likely to occur regularly.

11. ECC memory uses how many extra bits to protect how many regular bits?
   A. Seven extra for 64 regular
   B. One extra for eight regular
   C. Four extra for 32 regular
   D. Nine extra for eight regular
   A. Unlike parity, which uses a single bit to provide protection to eight bits, ECC uses a larger grouping of seven bits to protect 64 bits of data.

12. What utility is provided with Compaq ProSignia and ProLiant servers for monitoring a server's health and for viewing historical hardware faults (such as memory errors)?

A. SmartStart
B. Event Manager
C. Insight Manager
D. Baseline Diagnostics
C. Insight Manager is a server management tool that allows in-depth monitoring and configuration management from a single application. You can view the events as they occur, or look through historical data to see what fault events occurred on a given server, and decide from that what action should be taken.

13. The arrangement of memory addressing in rows and columns is called:

A. Muxing
B. Spreadsheet Addressing
C. Tabular Access
D. Multiplexing
D. Multiplexing. All types of memory are arranged in an XY grid pattern of rows and columns. First, the row address is sent to the memory chip and latched, then the column address is sent in a similar fashion. This row-and-column addressing scheme is called multiplexing and allows a large memory address to use fewer pins.

14. The composition of SDRAM modules can be found in which of the following two formats?

A. 2-clock and 4-clock
B. 1-clock and 8-clock
C. 2-bit and 4-clock
D. 1-bit and 8-clock
A. 2-clock and 4-clock. The 2-clock variation is structured so that each clock signal controls two different DRAM chips on the module. A 4-clock SDRAM has clock signals such that each has the capability to control four different DRAM chips. The more common variation is the 4-clock type.

15. Which of the following statements could you assume was true if you had a 72-pin 16MB SIMM?

A. It is single-sided.
B. It is double-sided.
C. It really only has 30 pins.
D. It really only has 36 pins.
A. It is single sided. 72-pin SIMMs that are 1MB, 4MB, and 16MB in size are normally single-sided, while those 2MB, 8MB, and 32MB in size are generally double-sided.

Chapter 4 Answers

1. Implementation of cache provides:

A. Reduced cost of ownership
B. Zero wait-state data transfers
C. Proprietary system architecture
D. Standardized system architecture
B. Zero wait-state data transfers. The purpose of cache is to solve the problem of processors overrunning slower main memory. Cache is an SRAM device that supports faster access time than DRAM, which is used for main memory.

2. Components of the cache subsystem include cache management logic, cache directory, and ______ ?

   A. SRAM

   B. DRAM

   C. SDRAM

   D. EDO

   A. SRAM. Static RAM is a transistor-based memory device that provides faster response to processor requests. Cache management logic is the intelligence behind cache. The cache directory is the index that identifies data locations.

3. SRAM stores information:

   A. On disk

   B. At rows and columns

   C. In the cache directory

   D. None of the above

   B. At rows and columns. SRAM is similar to DRAM in that it stores information at the intersection of rows and columns.

4. What is the cache directory?

   A. High-level file system

   B. Storage for most recently used data

   C. Index of cache data locations

   D. Distributed database

   C. Index of cache data locations. The cache directory works with SRAM and cache management logic to locate recently used data.

5. What is the cache subsystem component responsible for policy implementation?

   A. SRAM

   B. Cache directory

   C. Cache management logic

   D. Distributed database

   C. Cache management logic. The cache management logic is where read and write policies are programmed.

6. What are the two types of cache policies?

   A. Most recently and least recently used

   B. Look-Aside and Look-Through

   C. Write-Back and Write-Through

   D. Read and write activity

   D. Read and write activity. Cache policies are concerned with the handling of both read and write activities. Look-Aside and Look-Through are examples of read policies. Write-Back and Write-Through are examples of write policies.

7. Which cache policy allows the address request to be seen by the entire system bus?

   A. Look-Aside

   B. Look-Through

   C. Write-Through

   D. Write Back

   A. Look-Aside. Look-Aside cache allows the entire system bus to see the read request. This is beneficial in small, stand-alone systems because of its low price and simple architecture.

8. What is a disadvantage to Look-Through cache?
   A. High bus utilization
   B. Lookup penalty
   C. Data inconsistency
   D. None of the above
   B. Lookup penalty. When a request cannot be serviced by cache, the processor must issue a second request.
9. Information that has been updated in cache and is waiting to be updated in main memory is called:
   A. Stale
   B. Invalid
   C. Dirty
   D. Unnecessary
   C. Dirty. Data in cache waiting to update main memory is considered dirty cache. Stale data is that information in main memory that has been updated in cache.
10. What is the write policy that updates main memory on every cache write?
    A. Look-Aside
    B. Look-Through
    C. Write-Through
    D. Write-Back
    C. Write-Through. Write-Through cache updates main memory on every write to reduce consistency concerns, but increases bus utilization.
11. What is the write policy that provides reduced bus utilization?
    A. Look-Aside
    B. Look-Through
    C. Write-Through
    D. Write-Back
    D. Write-Back. Write-Back cache updates main memory only when a bus master device requests stale data. This frees the bus from constant updates to main memory for access by bus master devices.
12. Which write policy updates when a bus master device requests stale information in main memory?
    A. Look-Aside
    B. Look-Through
    C. Write-Through
    D. Write-Back
    D. Write-Back. The cache management logic monitors requests for stale data. When a bus master device requests the stale data, the cache management logic stops the bus, updates the data, and restarts the bus so that the data can be retrieved.
13. Which of the following can affect cache performance?
    A. Cache policy
    B. Cache size
    C. Operating system
    D. All of the above
    D. All of the above. The cache policy determines how data is accessed and updated. Cache size affects how much data can be stored in cache. The operating system efficiency has an impact on the cache's capability to service application requests.

14. What should be the cache size implementations for systems supporting a large number of users?

    A. Relatively large

    B. Relatively small

    C. Cache is unnecessary with a large numbers of users

    D. Cache is not affected by a large numbers of users

    A. Relatively large. As the number of users accessing the system grows, so does the demand on the cache subsystem.

15. Database application performance improves with cache sizes that are:

    A. Relatively large

    B. Relatively small

    C. Cache is unnecessary with a large numbers of users

    D. Cache is not affected by a large numbers of users

    A. Relatively large. Database applications typically consist of many files and will benefit from larger cache sizes.

Chapter 5 Answers

1. What data widths does ISA support?

    A. 8-bit

    B. 16-bit

    C. 32-bit

    D. 64-bit

    A, B. 8-bit and 16-bit. The first generation of ISA adapters were 8-bit. Later, when the IBM AT architecture was introduced, ISA was expanded to 16-bit.

2. What are the two methods of configuring ISA adapters?

    A. .CFG file

    B. Plug and play

    C. Jumpers

    D. ECU

    B, C. Plug and play and jumpers. Legacy ISA adapters are configured by manually setting jumpers (or DIP switches) on the adapter itself. Newer ISA adapters are plug and play, in which the PnP operating system automatically configures the adapter. .CFG and ECU are used for EISA adapters.

3. What is the bus bandwidth of EISA adapters?

    A. 8 Mbps

    B. 33 Mbps

    C. 133 Mbps

    D. 524 Mbps

    B. 33 Mbps. 8 Mbps is ISA bandwidth, 133 Mbps and 524 Mbps are PCI bandwidth.

4. If no .CFG file is available for a given EISA adapter, how do you configure the adapter?

    A. Download a .CFG file from Compaq's Web site.

    B. Create a .CFG file.

    C. Install the adapter without a .CFG file.

    D. You cannot continue.

    B. Create a .CFG file. If no .CFG file is available for the adapter, the ECU will allow you to create one, thus allowing you to configure the adapter.

5. What data paths does PCI support?
   A. 8-bit
   B. 16-bit
   C. 32-bit
   D. 64-bit
   C, D. 32-bit and 64-bit. 8-bit and 16-bit are supported by ISA. 32-bit is also supported by EISA.

6. PCI adapters use a technology closely resembling:
   A. Plug and play
   B. Manual configuration
   C. Osmosis
   D. Configuration files
   A. Plug and play. PCI adapters are plug and play, using registers that contain information required for device detection and configuration.

7. What are the three capabilities of PCI hot plug?
   A. Hot replacement
   B. Hot upgrade
   C. Hot downgrade
   D. Hot expansion
   A, B, D. Hot replacement, hot upgrade and hot expansion. Hot replacement allows the removal of a failed PCU adapter and insertion of an identical adapter into the same slot. Hot upgrade allows the replacement of an existing adapter with an upgraded adapter, or replacing the adapter's driver with an upgraded driver, while the server is online. Hot expansion allows the installation of an additional adapter into a previously empty slot while the server is online.

8. Which of the following statements is true of PCI hot plug adapters?
   A. They allow you to remove and install adapters while the server is online
   B. They do not allow you to remove and install adapters while the server is online
   C. They are no different from any other PCI adapter
   D. They are installed in a different type of slot that other PCI adapters
   A. They allow you to remove and install adapters while the server is online. PCI hot plug is designed to allow you to add and remove PCI adapters while the server is online, to minimize server downtime. However, you must disable the PCI slot to prevent damage.

9. What do white riser cards between the PCI slots indicate?
   A. The slot is not PCI hot plug compatible.
   B. The slot is disabled.
   C. The slot is a reserve.
   D. The slot is PCI hot plug compatible.
   D. The slot is PCI hot plug compatible. The riser cards isolate each PCI slot to prevent you from inadvertently touching an installed adapter with one that you are adding or removing, which could cause a short.

10. What does a shared slot enable you to do?
    A. Install two PCI adapters into the same slot.
    B. Install an EISA/ISA adapter or a PCI adapter into the slot.
    C. Install an EISA or an ISA adapter into the slot.
    D. Install and EISA and an ISA adapter into the slot.
    B. Install an EISA/ISA adapter or a PCI adapter into the slot. A shared slot can only have one adapter installed into it at any time. You can install either an EISA/ISA adapter into the EISA/ISA slot, or a PCI adapter into the PCI slot. The expansion slots are designed to make it impossible to enable both adapters.
11. How many buses does a dual peer PCI bus provide?
    A. One
    B. Two
    C. Three
    D. Four
    B. Two. A dual peer PCI bus provides two PCI buses, independently connected to the host processor bus with two host-to-PCI bridges.
12. How many PCI bus masters can be on a dual peer PCI bus?
    A. None
    B. One
    C. Two
    D. Four
    C. Two. Since each PCI bus on a dual peer PCI bus runs independently, it is possible to have two PCI bus masters transferring data at the same time, thus producing better performance.
13. How must you install adapters in a dual peer PCI bus?
    A. Load balance.
    B. Place like adapters on the same bus.
    C. Populate the first bus before adding adapters to the second bus.
    D. It doesn't matter.
    A. Load balance. Since there are two buses in a dual peer PCI bus, for best performance you should load balance the buses. To load balance, place like adapters on different PCI buses, thus splitting the required bandwidth between the two buses.
14. How many paths to the bus host are on a bridged PCI bus?
    A. One
    B. Two
    C. Three
    D. Four
    A. One. The bridged PCI architecture requires all processed transactions on the bridged PCI bus (the secondary bus) to go through the PCI-to-PCI bridge to reach the primary bus, then through the host-to-PCI bridge. This provides only one path to the host bus.

15. When should bridged PCI buses be load balanced?

    A. Always
    B. Never
    C. Only when using like adapters
    D. Only when performance declines
    B. Never. Since all transactions have one path to the host bus, no load balancing is required for a bridged PCI bus.

Chapter 6 Answers

1. Dual processing systems are characterized by:

    A. Shared, external second-level cache
    B. Separate, external second-level cache for each processor
    C. Two processors
    D. Four processors
    A, C. Shared, external second-level cache and two processors. Dual processing is characterized by a single, external second-level cache, which is used by both processors.

2. Which is the multiprocessing model in which a processor may not be allowed to offer the same services as another processor?

    A. Asymmetric multiprocessing
    B. Symmetric multiprocessing
    C. Dual processing
    D. Quad processing
    A. Asymmetric multiprocessing. Asymmetric multiprocessing does not give equal access to the system resources to each processor.

3. Which of the following are characteristics of symmetric multiprocessing?

    A. Equal access to system resources
    B. Handling of certain system functions restricted to one processor
    C. Balanced processing
    D. Use by Windows NT
    A, C, D. Equal access to system resources, balanced processing, and use by Windows NT. Symmetric processing allows equal access to the system resources for the processors and provides a more balanced usage of the processors. It is the method of multiprocessing used by Windows NT.

4. Which of the following models offer quad processing?

    A. Model 3000
    B. Model 5500
    C. Model 800
    D. Model 6000
    B, D. Models 5500 and Model 6000. Models 5500 and 6000 both offer the capability to upgrade to four processors. Models 800 and 3000 only offer dual processing.

5. Which is the multiprocessing model in which the workload is balanced among the available processors?

    A. Asymmetric multiprocessing
    B. Symmetric multiprocessing
    C. Dual processing
    D. Quad processing
    B. Symmetric multiprocessing. Symmetric multiprocessing allows the

scheduler to balance the workload and efficiently distribute processes to the processors.

6. You would like to build a system with multiprocessors that will provide you with the largest amount of L2 cache to the processors. Which of the following would you choose?

   A. Dual processing

   B. Quad processing

   C. Asymmetric multiprocessing

   D. Symmetric multiprocessing
   B. Quad processing. In quad processing, each processor has its own L2 cache.

7. Which of the following is a characteristic of asymmetric multiprocessing?

   A. Equal access to system resources

   B. Unequal access to system resources

   C. Balanced processing

   D. Use by a majority of Compaq technologies
   B. Unequal access to system resources. Asymmetric multiprocessing does not allow all processors equal access to system resources.

8. You would like to build a system with multiprocessors that will provide you the most efficient use of all the processing power. Which of the following would you choose?

   A. Dual processing

   B. Quad processing

   C. Asymmetric multiprocessing

   D. Symmetric multiprocessing
   D. Symmetric multiprocessing. In symmetric multiprocessing, the system provides balanced processing, which allows for greater utilization of all the processors.

9. Quad processing systems are characterized by:

   A. Shared, external second-level cache

   B. Separate, external second-level cache for each processor

   C. Two processors

   D. Four processors
   B, D. Separate, external second-level cache and four processors. Dual processing is characterized by a single, external second-level cache, which is used by both processors.

10. You are installing a server with multiprocessors. You decide that you want to dedicate processors to certain functions, to ensure that the operating system always has a processor dedicated to itself. Which of the following would you employ?

   A. Dual processing

   B. Quad processing

   C. Asymmetric multiprocessing

   D. Symmetric multiprocessing
   C. Asymmetric multiprocessing. Asymmetric multiprocessing, by delegating CPUs to perform specific functions, allows you to dedicate a CPU to the operating system.

11. A processor can use an independent, high-speed storage device that can speed up processing. Which of the following would you associate with this technology?

    A. L1 cache

    B. L2 cache

    C. Dual processing

    D. Quad processing
    B, C, D. L2 cache, dual processing, and quad processing. L2 cache is the actual device; both dual and quad processing utilize an L2 cache to enhance processing power.

12. You are installing a server with two processors and you would like them to share the same L2 cache. Which of the following would you choose?

    A. Dual processing

    B. Quad processing

    C. Asymmetric multiprocessing

    D. Symmetric multiprocessing
    A. Dual processing. Dual processing has both processors sharing the same L2 cache.

13. How many Xeon processors can you put into one system?

    A. Two

    B. Four

    C. Eight

    D. Ten
    A, B, C. Two, four, or eight. The new Xeon line of processors will allow you to install as many eight processors in one server.

14. Which of the following models offer dual processing?

    A. Model 6400

    B. Model 1200

    C. Model 6000

    D. Model 1600
    B, D. Model 1200 and Model 1600. Models 1200 and 1600 both offer dual processing. Models 6000 and 6400 offer quad processing.

15. Which multiprocessing architecture is characterized by each processor having a separate second-level cache?

    A. Asymmetric multiprocessing

    B. Symmetric multiprocessing

    C. Shared cache, dual processing

    D. Multi-cache, multiprocessing
    D. Multi-cache, multiprocessing is characterized by each processor having a separate second-level cache. Shared cache, dual processing has one second-level cache, which is shared by the processors.

Chapter 7 Answers

1. Which of the following is not a component of the SmartStart & Support Software CD?

    A. The Systems Configuration Utility

    B. Compaq Insight Management software

    C. Compaq utility software

D. Compaq support software
B. Compaq Insight Management Software. Compaq Insight Management software is not found on the SmartStart & Support Software CD. Although it is part of the complete SmartStart package, this software is found on another CD.

2. Which of the following options can be performed using the software on the SmartStart & Support Software CD?

A. Create Support Software Diskettes
B. Run server diagnostics
C. Run the Array Configuration Utility
D. All of the above
D. All of the Above. All of the above tasks can be performed using the SmartStart & Support Software CD.

3. Which of the following is not a menu option available when running the SmartStart?

A. System Configuration Utility
B. Array Configuration Utility
C. Create/Update the System Partition
D. None of the above
D. None of the above. System Configuration Utility, the Array Configuration Utility and Create/Update the System Partition are all menu selections available with SmartStart.

4. When is the System Configuration Partition created?

A. Upon running the System Configuration Utility by pressing F10
B. Upon the installation of the server's operating system
C. Upon running the System Configuration Utility from the SmartStart CD during the initial server setup
D. Upon running the System Configuration Partition Creation Utility from the Utilities folder of the SmartStart & Support Software CD.
C. Upon running the System Configuration Utility from the Smart Start CD during the initial server setup. The System Configuration Partition can only be created before the server's hard disks have been partitioned. This is done automatically as part of the SmartStart install process.

5. Which of the following would not normally be found on the System Configuration Partition?

A. The Array Diagnostic Utility
B. The System Configuration Utility
C. Hardware device drivers, such as NIC drivers, for your installed operating system
D. System ROM Upgrade files
C. Hardware device drivers, such as NIC drivers, for your installed operating system. Drivers are not located on the System Configuration Partition. This partition normally contains ROM upgrades, Diagnostics and Utilities, and the System Configuration Utility.

6. Which of the following is not a means of accessing the System Configuration Utility?

   A. Choosing the option for the System Configuration Utilities in the Compaq Utilities and Software program group in Windows NT

   B. Selecting the appropriate option during a POST error

   C. Booting the server with a set of floppy disks containing the System Configuration Utility

   D. Booting the server with the SmartStart CD

   A. Choosing the option for the System Configuration Utilities in the Compaq Utilities and Software program group in Windows NT. It is only possible to access the System Configuration Utility during the boot process—by floppy disk, CD, or by pressing F10 when prompted. There is no program group containing a link to the System Configuration Utility.

7. Which of the following tasks would warrant running the System Configuration Utility?

   A. You receive a hardware configuration error during POST at bootup.

   B. You need to install the driver for a new controller card that you just installed.

   C. You have added memory to your server.

   D. All of the above

   A. You receive a hardware configuration error during POST at bootup. If during POST the computer experiences a hardware error, you will be prompted as to whether you would like to run the System Configuration Utility. You cannot install software drivers via the System Configuration Utility. Adding or removing memory is handled automatically by the server. There is no need to run the System Configuration Utility to perform this task.

8. Which task could not be performed from the System Configuration Utility?

   A. Running the Array Configuration Utility

   B. Adding a network adapter

   C. Removing a SCSI controller

   D. Configuring the parameters of your UPS

   D. Configuring the parameters of your UPS. No means of configuring UPS parameters are available via the System Configuration Utility. This is usually done from within the operating system.

9. Which of the following scenarios would warrant the use of the System Erase option?

   A. You need to undo the configuration options you just selected in the System Configuration Utility.

   B. You have to correct an incorrect hardware configuration and start over.

   C. You no longer require any of the information stored on the server and wish to perform a completely new installation, including the operating system.

D. You wish to reset all server parameters with the exception of the hard disk contents.
   C. You no longer require any of the information stored on the server and wish to perform a completely new installation, including the operating system. Choosing the System Erase option erases all server information. This includes all hardware settings, array configuration parameters, and hard disks. Only select this option when you plan to perform a completely new server installation.

10. Which System Configuration Utility menu option would you choose if you wanted to erase the critical error log of your Compaq Server?

    A. View or Edit Details
    B. Diagnostics and Utilities
    C. Add/Remove Hardware
    D. You can't erase the critical error log of a Compaq Server
    B. Diagnostics and Utilities. Though not initially available, you can in fact erase the error log by entering Advanced Mode within the Diagnostics and Utilities menu.

11. Which System Configuration Utility menu option would you choose if you wanted to change the network configuration for your remote access to the System Configuration Utility?

    A. View or Edit Details
    B. Diagnostics and Utilities
    C. Add/Remove Hardware
    D. You cannot configure this option from within the System Configuration Utility.
    A. View or Edit Details. The network configuration that is used to access the server's System Configuration Utility from a remote machine is configured via this menu option.

12. If installing an ISA board during the initial setup, what steps should be taken to assure the proper configuration of all devices in the server?

    A. Add the ISA device along with all PCI devices and allow the System Configuration Utility to configure all devices.
    B. Add the PCI devices first, determine which settings they have been assigned, and then configure the ISA device so that it doesn't conflict.
    C. Add the ISA device first and manually add it via the Add/Remove Hardware menu option. Then add the remaining PCI devices and allow the System Configuration Utility to configure them.
    D. ISA devices are not supported by the System Configuration Utility.
    C. Add the ISA device first and manually add it via the Add/Remove Hardware menu option. Then add the remaining PCI devices and allow the System Configuration Utility to configure them. Compaq suggests always to allow the System Configuration Utility to configure PCI devices around the ISA devices that are installed on your computer.

13. If installing an ISA board after the initial server setup, what steps should be taken to assure the proper configuration of all devices in the server?

    A. Add the ISA device along with all PCI devices and allow the System Configuration Utility to configure the new device.

    B. Determine which settings have been assigned to the PCI devices and then configure the ISA device so that it doesn't conflict.

    C. Remove the PCI devices, then add the ISA device first and manually add it via the Add/Remove Hardware menu option. Then add the remaining PCI devices and allow the System Configuration Utility to configure them.

    D. ISA devices cannot be added after the server has been configured.
    B. Determine which settings have been assigned to the PCI devices and then configure the ISA device so that it doesn't conflict. Since the server has already been installed, it would not be a good idea to remove the PCI devices. You do not want the settings of these devices to change—then you would need to redefine all of them within your network operating system. The best course at this time is simply to add the ISA device with settings that won't conflict with existing hardware.

14. You would like to see a detailed summary of your Compaq server's configuration. Which System Configuration Utility menu option would allow you to obtain this information?

    A. Add/Remove Hardware

    B. View or Edit Details

    C. Diagnostics and Utilities

    D. None of the above
    C. Diagnostics and Utilities. This menu option will allow you to run the Compaq Inspect Utility. This utility can provide you with a means of obtaining the server configuration information.

15. How do you enable the Advanced Mode of the System Configuration Utility?

    A. This mode is enabled by default.

    B. By selecting the Advanced Mode option from the System Configuration Utility Main menu

    C. By pressing the CTRL-A key combination from within the System Configuration Utility menu

    D. Advanced mode cannot be enabled from within the System Configuration Utility.
    C. By pressing the CTRL-A key combination from within the System Configuration Utility menu. Upon selecting this option, you will be presented with a popup informing you that Advanced Mode is enabled.

Chapter 8 Answers

1. Communication is allowed between how many devices on the bus at one time?

   A. One

   B. Two

   C. Three

   D. All

   B. Two. When two devices communicate on the bus, one device acts as an initiator, the other as a target. All other devices must wait until the bus is free before they may communicate.

2. What are the two implementations of SCSI-2?

   A. Single-ended interface

   B. Dual-ended interface

   C. Differential interface

   D. Asynchronous interface

   A, C. Single-ended interface and differential interface. Single-ended interfaces are used for internal cabling, while differential interfaces are used for external cabling.

3. What is the maximum length supported using single-ended interface cabling?

   A. 3 meters

   B. 6 meters

   C. 9 meters

   D. 12 meters

   B. 6 meters. The maximum supported length of internal SCSI-2 cables is six meters. Longer cable lengths result in loss of signal and/or signal degradation, thus introducing data errors. Keeping the lengths under the maximum supported provides data integrity.

4. What is the maximum length supported using differential interface cabling?

   A. 25 meters

   B. 30 meters

   C. 35 meters

   D. 40 meters

   A. 25 meters. The maximum supported length of external SCSI-2 cables is 25 meters. Longer cable lengths result in loss of signal and/or signal degradation, thus introducing data errors. Keeping the lengths under the maximum supported provides data integrity.

5. Fast SCSI-2 utilizes 68-pin cables.

   A. True

   B. False

   B. False. Fast SCSI-2 utilizes 50-pin internal and external cables. 50-pin and 68-pin connectors look different—the 50-pin connector is actually larger than the 68-pin connector.

6. Choose the two true statements regarding Fast-Wide SCSI-2.

   A. There are eight legal IDs available.

   B. There are 16 legal IDs available.

   C. Compaq supports 16 IDs per bus.

   D. Compaq supports eight IDs per bus.

   B, D. There are 16 legal IDs available and Compaq only supports eight IDs per bus. Limiting the IDs to eight per bus provides data integrity, backward compatibility, and flexibility.

7. How is Fast-Wide mode chosen?

    A. By the jumpers on the drives

    B. By the settings on the adapter

    C. The cable determines it.

    D. On a drive-by-drive basis
    D. On a drive-by-drive basis. Fast-Wide mode is chosen through negotiation between the controller and the drive during the Command Setup phase.

8. What is the maximum cable length of Ultra2-SCSI?

    A. 8 meters

    B. 12 meters

    C. 16 meters

    D. 25 meters
    B. 12 meters. The maximum length of both internal and external Ultra2-SCSI cabling is 12 meters. Longer cable lengths result in loss of signal and/or signal degradation, introducing data errors. Keeping the lengths under the maximum supported provides data integrity.

9. What is the transfer rate of Fast-Wide SCSI-2?

    A. 5 MB/second

    B. 10 MB/second

    C. 20 MB/second

    D. 40 MB/second
    C. 20 MB/second. The maximum transfer rate of Fast-Wide SCSI-2 is 20 MB/second, and the data width is 16 bits. 5 MB/second corresponds to SCSI-1 and SCSI-2; 10 MB/second is Fast SCSI-2; and 40 MB/second is Wide-Ultra SCSI-3 and Ultra Wide SCSI.

10. What is the data width of SCSI-2?

    A. 8-bit

    B. 16-bit

    C. 32-bit

    D. 64-bit
    A. 8-bit. The data width of SCSI-2 is 8 bits and the transfer rate is 5MB/second. 16-bit corresponds to Fast-Wide SCSI-2 and Wide-Ultra SCSI-3; 32-bit is Ultra Wide SCSI and Ultra2 SCSI. Ultra2 SCSI can also be 64-bit.

11. What is the data width of Ultra2-SCSI?

    A. 8-bit

    B. 16-bit

    C. 32-bit

    D. 64-bit
    C, D. 32-bit and 64-bit. Ultra2-SCSI comes in two flavors, 32-bit and 64-bit. The transfer rate is 80MB/second for single channel adapters and 180MB/second for dual channel adapters.

12. Which is not a SCSI I/O request stage?

    A. Command Setup

    B. Command Transfer

    C. Data Transfer

    D. Command Complete
    B. Command Transfer. The three stages of a SCSI I/O request are Command Setup, Data Transfer, and Command Complete.

13. Tagged command queuing allows a device to accept multiple commands.
    A. True
    B. False
    A. True. Tagged queuing allows a device to accept multiple commands until its command queue is full.

14. To what ID are most SCSI controllers set?
    A. 0
    B. 3
    C. 6
    D. 7
    D. 7. Most adapters are set to SCSI ID 7. 0 is usually hard disks, 3 is CD-ROM drives, and 6 is for tape drives. The hard disk, CD-ROM and tape drive IDs are not firm requirements, but are the most commonly used IDs.

15. Which is not a common type of SCSI cable?
    A. Centronics
    B. 25-pin
    C. 50-pin
    D. 68-pin
    B. 25-pin. The three common types of SCSI cables are Centronics, 50-pin, and 68-pin. However, Centronics connectors are all but extinct now, having been replaced with 50-pin and 68-pin connections. It is rather unlikely you will run into a Centronics connector on any server manufactured within the past four years.

16. Which type of termination uses a regulated voltage?
    A. Passive
    B. Active
    B. Active. Active termination uses a regulated voltage to achieve the required termination. Passive termination uses a terminating resistor on either end of the chain.

17. Hot-pluggable drives should be manually terminated.
    A. True
    B. False
    B. False. Hot-pluggable drives should not be manually terminated. Termination is controlled by the hot-plug backplane. Terminating a drive installed into a hot-plug backplane will result in unpredictable performance—which is to say, it won't work.

18. Some hard disks require a termination power jumper.
    A. True
    B. False
    A. True. Some drives require both a termination jumper and a termination power jumper. However, in most servers, you will use an active terminator on the SCSI cable, thus removing the need to set termination and termination power of the drives themselves.

Chapter 9 Answers

1. How many drives does the SMART-2 array controller support?
   A. Seven
   B. Eight
   C. Fourteen
   D. Fifteen
   C. Fourteen. With two SCSI channels, the SMART, SMART-2, and SMART-2DH array controllers support up to14 drives. With one SCSI channel, the SMART-2SL array controller supports up to seven drives.
2. What is the cache capacity of the SMART-2DH array controller?
   A. 4MB (read)
   B. 4MB (read/write)
   C. 8MB (read)
   D. 16MB (read/write)
   D. 16MB (read/write). The SMART controller has 4MB (read), the SMART-2 has 4MB (read/write), the SMART-2SL has 8MB (read), and the SMART-2DH has 16MB (read/write).
3. Which array controllers do not support online capacity expansion?
   A. SMART
   B. SMART-2
   C. SMART-2SL
   D. SMART-2DH
   A, C. SMART and SMART-2SL. The SMART-2 and SMART-2DH are the only controllers that support online capacity expansion. When SMART or SMART-2SL are used, the only way to expand the capacity is to reconfigure the array, thus destroying all data held on the disks.
4. What RAID level uses drive mirroring?
   A. RAID 0
   B. RAID 1
   C. RAID 4
   D. RAID 5
   B. RAID 1. RAID 1 uses drive mirroring. RAID 1 creates an exact image of the first drive onto the second drive, which requires an even number of drives, with a minimum of two.
5. RAID level 4 uses distributed parity.
   A. True
   B. False
   B. False. RAID 4 uses dedicated parity. All parity information is written to a single disk in the array. RAID 5 is distributed parity, striping the parity information across all disks in the array.
6. Which RAID level is not fault tolerant?
   A. RAID 0
   B. RAID 1
   C. RAID 4
   D. RAID 5
   A. RAID 0. RAID 0 is data striping without parity, which does not provide fault tolerance. RAID 1, 4, and 5 are fault tolerant. RAID 1 provides fault tolerance by mirroring the drives. RAID levels 4 and 5 provides fault tolerance by calculating parity information and writing it to the disks.

7. What is the default striping factor?
   A. 4KB for all operating systems
   B. 8KB for UNIX, 4KB for all other operating systems
   C. 8KB for all operating systems
   D. 4KB for UNIX, 8KB for all other operating systems
   D. 4KB for UNIX, 8KB for all other operating systems. The striping factor is the number of sectors per block. The smaller the striping factor, the better drive utilization is.

8. RAID level 1 is a cost-effective solution.
   A. True
   B. False
   B. False. RAID level 1 is mirroring, which requires double the amount of disks.

9. What is the maximum number of disks supported by RAID 4?
   A. 3
   B. 7
   C. 14
   D. 21
   C. 14. The maximum number of disks supported by RAID 4 (data striping with dedicated parity) is 14; the minimum is three disks. This is also true for RAID 5 (data striping with distributed parity).

10. Parity is distributed across the entire array using RAID 5.
   A. True
   B. False
   A. True. RAID 5 uses distributed parity, which means that the parity is striped across the entire array. This feature increases the read/write capabilities of the array, thus greatly improving the performance of the entire array.

11. The server must be brought down before inserting a hot-swappable drive.
   A. True
   B. False
   B. False. Hot-swappable drives allow exchanges on the fly while the server is still running. The whole point of hot-swappable drives is to allow the adding and removing of drives from the server without taking it offline.

12. Hardware data striping is preferred over software data striping.
   A. True
   B. False
   A. True. Hardware data striping is preferred because it frees up the system's processor for other functions. All parity calculations, I/O activity, and data splitting is handled by the controller's on-board processor.

13. How many logical volumes does Compaq's SMART array controller support?
   A. Four
   B. Six
   C. Eight
   D. Ten
   B. Eight. The SMART array controller handles up to eight logical

volumes. A logical volume consists of one or multiple drives configured in an array.

14. How is write data protected in SMART and SMART-2 array controllers?

    A. Online expansion
    B. Battery backup
    C. Array accelerator
    D. Online spares
    B, C. Battery backup and array accelerator. Data is first written to the accelerator's cache, then written to disk. If the system fails, the data is saved in the cache and written when the system comes back online. If the controller fails, the accelerator may be moved to a new controller, and the data will be written to disk.

15. What is the maximum number of online spares supported by the SMART array controller?

    A. One
    B. Two
    C. Three
    D. Four
    D. Four. The SMART array controller supports up to four online spares. Up to four drives in the array could fail and be replaced by online hot spares, allowing data to remain available with no downtime.

16. The Drive Array Advanced Diagnostics is data destructive.

    A. True
    B. False
    B. False. DAAD does not write any information to the drives, nor does it change the configuration of the controller. Therefore, all data on the drives will be preserved after running DAAD.

17. What allows a SMART array controller to be upgraded to a SMART-2 array controller?

    A. Processor
    B. Memory
    C. Accelerator/battery pack
    D. It cannot be upgraded
    C. Accelerator/battery pack. To upgrade the SMART array controller to a SMART-2, you need only upgrade the array accelerator/battery pack.

Chapter 10 Answers

1. What is the current bandwidth of Fibre Channel?

    A. 10 Mbps
    B. 10 MBps
    C. 100 Mbps
    D. 100 MBps
    D. 100 MBps. The current implementation of Fibre Channel bandwidth is 100 MBps.

2. Which media types are supported by Fibre Channel?
   - A. Single-mode fiber and multimode fiber
   - B. Single-mode fiber and copper
   - C. Multimode fiber and copper
   - D. Single-mode fiber, multimode fiber, and copper

   D. Single-mode fiber, multimode fiber, and copper. Fibre Channel is an ANSI set of protocols that can run over various media. It is not limited to running on fiber, which is why the distinctive spelling was chosen.

3. A channel is best described as:
   - A. Hardware-intensive
   - B. Software-intensive
   - C. The sales avenue for purchasing the equipment
   - D. Cables that connect two computers

   A. Hardware-intensive. A channel is the hardware-intensive connection between a computer and peripherals. It is inflexible and very fast. A network, in contrast, is very flexible, software-intensive, and considerably slower.

4. Which best describes attenuation?
   - A. Loss of the signal
   - B. Negotiation during boot of FC-AL devices
   - C. Loss of power
   - D. Signal loss at break in the fiber

   C. Loss of power. Attenuation is the loss of power in a signal. The signal is still present but is degraded due to various factors. Some forms of attenuation are dispersion, fiber bends, and scattering.

5. When do you use a short-wave GBIC?
   - A. With single-mode fiber
   - B. With multimode fiber
   - C. With hubs, but not switches
   - D. With switches, but not hubs

   B. With multimode fiber. The short-wave GBIC is used with multimode fiber. It provides the signal for distances between two meters and 500 meters. The long-wave GBIC provides for distances up to 10 kilometers.

6. Why is graded-index multimode fiber used?
   - A. It produces less dispersion.
   - B. It is the only type of multimode fiber available.
   - C. It decreases the bandwidth of multimode fiber.
   - D. It increases the amount of attenuation.

   A. It produces less dispersion. Adding a dopant to the core fiber creates graded-index fiber. The core fiber changes its properties so that light travels down the axis more slowly, and light taking different paths will arrive at the same time. The result is a reduction in dispersion.

7. How many devices can communicate simultaneously in a Fibre Channel Arbitrated Loop?

   A. Up to eight million pairs of nodes
   B. Up to 126 devices
   C. Up to 127 devices
   D. Two

   D. By definition, only two devices can be active at any time in an FC-AL. The loop is shared by all devices and the hub controls which devices can communicate at what time.

8. What are the minimum requirements for a Fibre Channel solution?

   A. Host bus adapter, multimode fiber with GBICs, and a hub
   B. Host bus adapter, multimode fiber with GBICs, hub, and storage array
   C. Host bus adapter, multimode fiber with GBICs, and storage array
   D. Host bus adapter, two multimode fibers with GBICs, hub, and storage array

   C. Host bus adapter, multimode fiber with GBICs, and storage array. A point-to-point Fibre Channel solution doesn't require a hub or switch. It is the simplest Fibre Channel topology.

9. What type of port must be present to have a public loop?

   A. NL_port
   B. FL_port
   C. F_port
   D. N_port

   B. FL_port. A fiber loop port must be present to connect the arbitrated loop to the switch. This is the connection that changes the loop from private to public.

10. A private loop supports how many devices?

    A. Two
    B. 126
    C. 127
    D. Eight million

    C. 127. The private loop can use all 127 ports available. A public loop uses one port to connect to the switch, thus it only has 126 ports available for device connections.

11. What redundant parts are available for an RA4000?

    A. Fans and power supplies
    B. Fans, power supplies, and controllers
    C. Power supplies and controllers
    D. Fans and controllers

    C. Power supplies and controllers. Two power supplies and two controllers can be located in each RA4000. The fan assembly is hot-pluggable, but not redundant.

12. What is one of the major advantages of fiber over copper?

    A. Common bright orange color
    B. Flexibility allowing a smaller bend radius
    C. Resistance to pinching

D. Resistance to electromagnetic interference
D. Resistance to electromagnetic interference. Fiber is not subject to EMI. EMI is a major factor that must be dealt with when running copper media.

13. A link consists of how many fibers?

A. One

B. Two

C. 126

D. 127
B. Two. By definition, a link is made up of two fibers. One fiber for transmitting and one fiber for receiving.

14. A Fibre Channel Fabric is commonly represented by which symbol?

A. Cloud

B. Square

C. Rectangle

D. Circle
A. Cloud. Because of the various pieces and parts that can make up a Fibre Channel Fabric, a cloud has been chosen to represent the Fabric.

15. How many devices are supported with Microsoft Cluster Server and a Compaq 12-port storage hub?

A. 11

B. 12

C. Seven

D. Three
C. Seven. Two servers and up to five storage devices are supported with both the seven-port and 12-port hubs. This is due to a technical limitation with the hub.

Chapter 11 Answers

1. If you wanted to make ROMPaq diskettes, what utility would you use?

A. Rack Builder

B. Disk Builder

C. Insight Manager

D. Disk Activator
B. Disk Builder is used to make floppy disks for ROMPaqs, the Array Configuration utility, and other Compaq utilities. Disk Builder is included on the SmartStart CD.

2. Which cannot be done by the Array Configuration utility?

A. Configure array controller

B. Set up RAID

C. Configure hard drives

D. All of the above can be done with the Array Configuration utility.
D. The Array Configuration utility can be used to configure your array controller and your hard drives. You can set controller parameters and hard drive parameters. You can also set hardware fault tolerance configuration parameters.

3. Where in Insight Manager would you go to check if both of your redundant power supplies are functioning?

   A. View Device Data | Recovery

   B. View Device Data | Configuration

   C. View Device Data | Utilization

   D. View Device Data | Mass Storage
   A. View Device Data | Recovery. Selecting Recovery in the Device Data window allows you to view information on power supplies, Automatic Server Recovery, server logs, and Remote Insight.

4. What Compaq servers need a firmware upgrade in order to boot to the SmartStart CD?

   A. ProLiant 6500

   B. ProLiant 3000

   C. ProLinea/XL

   D. SystemPro/XL
   D. Compaq SystemPro/XL servers need a firmware upgrade to boot to any CD. The BIOS that was shipped standard with these servers did not support the El Torito boot specification, which allows a computer to boot from a CD-ROM.

5. Before doing a SmartStart system install, what Compaq utility would you use to erase all system Configuration information?

   A. Array Configuration

   B. ROMPaq

   C. System Erase

   D. None of the above
   C. The Compaq System Erase utility will erase all the information stored on your hard drives and in the system ROM. It will erase all previously configured system and controller parameters. This makes it easier to configure everything exactly the way you want it, without having to worry about previous configuration parameters.

6. If you need to access the System Configuration utility on the system partition, what key would you press when the server is booting?

   A. ESC

   B. F10

   C. ALT-C

   D. SPACEBAR
   B. F10. You can access the System Configuration utility on the system partition by pressing F10 while the server is booting. Some servers will display an on-screen message, letting you know when to press F10. If not, F10 should be pressed when the cursor moves to the upper right-hand corner.

7. You believe your system has an IRQ conflict. What should you do to verify the current configuration?

   A. Run the System Erase utility.

   B. Run the Compaq System Diagnostics utility.

   C. Load a new ROMPaq.

D. Run the Array Configuration utility.
B. Run the Compaq System Diagnostics utility. IRQ conflicts can be diagnosed using the Compaq System Diagnostics. The Compaq Diagnostics provide you with statistics about your hardware, including memory and I/O addresses.

8. What is the name of the management protocol used by Insight Manager?

A. IP

B. IPX

C. SSD

D. SNMP
D. SNMP. Insight Manager uses Simple Network Management Protocol to gather statistics and manage servers. SNMP has become the industry standard for network management.

9. You want to load Insight Manager. On what Compaq CD can it be found?

A. The Management CD

B. The SmartStart CD

C. The Rack Builder CD

D. The Insight CD
A. The Management CD. Insight Manager can be found on the Management CD distributed by Compaq. It is located under the Insight directory.

10. Servers running what protocol can be configured for auto-discovery during Insight Manager installation?

A. IP

B. SNMP

C. DLC

D. IPX
D. IPX. Servers running IPX on the local network can be auto-discovered during Insight Manager installation. Servers running NetWare Virtual Terminals can also be configured for auto-discovery during installation. These servers will show up automatically when you start Insight Manager the first time.

11. How can you tell if the driver you have installed for your network cards is up-to-date?

A. Use the Compaq Diagnostics utility.

B. Use Version Control in Insight Manager.

C. Use the System Configuration utility.

D. Using the version info report from Rack Builder.
B. Use Version Control in Insight Manager. The Version Control utility in Insight Manager will let you know if your drivers are up-to-date. Your Version Control database can be updated from disk or from the Web.

12. How can Insight Manager monitor your servers if you don't know the IP addresses?

A. Using WINS/DNS

B. Using a LMHOSTS file

C. Using a HOSTS file

D. You must know the IP address of your servers in order to use Insight Manager
A. Using WINS/DNS. Insight Manager can use WINS or DNS resolution to find your servers. This allows you to manage servers without having to know the IP addresses.

13. Which of the following cannot be accessed from the Device Data window in Insight Manager?

A. System configuration

B. System board information

C. NIC information

D. All can be accessed from the Device Data window.
D. From the Device Data window, you can access information on system configuration, recovery, system boards, expansion boards, utilization, NICs, and mass storage.

14. You are using Rack Builder to configure your Compaq rack. Where would you go to find the height and weight for all the components you added to your rack?

A. The Site Planning page

B. The Order Information page

C. The graphic page

D. None of the above
A. The Site Planning page of the Rack Builder report contains height, weight, heat, and current usage for all the components of your Compaq rack.

15. You are using Rack Builder to configure your Compaq rack. Where would you go find the part number for all the components you added to your rack?

A. The Site Planning page

B. The Order Information page

C. The graphic page

D. None of the above
B. The Order Information page of the Rack Builder report includes part name, number, and quantity for all the components you added to your rack. It also lists components that are not added manually, but will be needed to configure your rack fully.

Chapter 12 Answers

1. What technology is used on NetFlex-2 network cards to increase throughput?

A. Packet Blaster

B. ThunderLAN

C. LAN Blaster

D. None of the above
A. Packet Blaster. Packet Blaster technology is used on Compaq NetFlex-2 network cards to increase throughput while minimizing CPU usage.

2. NetFlex-3 Ethernet controllers can be upgraded from 10 Mbps to 100 Mbps. What makes this possible?

A. Packet Blaster technology

B. ThunderLAN technology

C. LAN Blaster technology

D. Packet Sync technology
B. ThunderLAN technology. ThunderLAN technology was co-designed by Texas Instruments and Compaq to allow Ethernet network cards to be upgraded from 10 Mbps to 100 Mbps.

3. Which operating systems are compatible with Compaq NetFlex-2 controllers?

A. Windows NT

B. Novell NetWare

C. OS/2

D. All of the above
D. All of the Above. Windows NT, Novell NetWare, OS/2, SCO OpenServer, and SCO UnixWare all support Compaq network controllers.

4. If you believe your NetFlex-3 controller is dropping frames, how can you check?

A. By using the SSDs

B. By instituting a controller pair

C. By using Insight Manager

D. By using a Packet Blaster
C. By using Insight Manager. Insight Manager can give you various statistics on your network controller, including lost frames.

5. Compaq NetFlex-3 controllers have a universal driver for all operating systems. What makes this possible?

A. Packet Blaster technology

B. ThunderLAN technology

C. LAN Blaster technology

D. Packet Sync technology
B. ThunderLAN technology. ThunderLAN technology was co-designed by Texas Instruments and Compaq. It allows one universal driver to interpret commands for many different operating systems.

6. You want to use a PCI network controller in order to maximize the performance of your server. Which of the following should you use?

A. NetFlex-3/E

B. NetFlex-2 ENET/TR

C. NetFlex-2 Dual Port ENET

D. NetFlex-3/P
D. NetFlex-3/P. The NetFlex-3/P is a bus-mastering PCI network card.

7. What connectors are available for NetFlex-2 ENET TR controllers?

A. DB-15

B. AUI

C. RJ-45

D. All of the above
D. All of the above. NetFlex-2 ENET TR controllers support DB-15, AUI, and RJ-45 connectors. They also support BNC connections with the optional AUI-to-BNC converter.

8. What access method do 100Base-TX networks use?

A. Token passing

B. CSMA/CD

C. Demand priority
D. CSMA/CA
B. CSMA/CD. 100Base-TX networks use a Carrier Sense Multiple Access/ Collision Detection access method. In this method, network cards wait for the network to become free before transmitting.

9. What access method do 100VG-AnyLAN networks use?

A. Token passing
B. CSMA/CD
C. Demand priority
D. CSMA/CA
C. Demand priority. 100VG-AnyLAN networks use the demand priority access method. In demand priority, access is controlled by the hub.

10. Your Ethernet network is currently running at 10 Mbps. You plan to upgrade to 100 Mbps in the near future. What network controllers should you buy for your new servers?

A. NetFlex-3/E
B. NetFlex-2 Dual ENET
C. NetFlex-2 ENET TR
D. NetFlex-2 Dual TR
A. NetFlex-3/E . NetFlex-3E controllers allow for easy migration from 10 Mbps Ethernet networks to 100 Mbps networks.

11. You bought a NetFlex-2 controller card and are ready to configure it. Where should you run NICStart from?

A. The floppy disk that came with the NIC
B. The SmartStart CD
C. The Management CD
D. None of the above
D. None of the above. NICStart is only supported by Netelligent controllers.

12. You have lost the drivers for your Netelligent 10/100 TX PCI UTP controller. What drivers can be substituted for these until you can get the proper drivers?

A. Intel Fast Ethernet controller drivers
B. Proteon Fast Ethernet controller drivers
C. SMC Fast Ethernet controller drivers
D. IBM Fast Ethernet controller drivers
A. Intel Fast Ethernet controller drivers. Intel Fast Ethernet controllers can be substituted for Compaq Netelligent 10/100 TX UTP drivers, and vice versa. This is because the Netelligent 10/100 TX UTP card uses an Intel chipset.

13. You have just installed a Netelligent 10/100 TX controller in your system, but it cannot be monitored through Insight Manager. What is most likely the cause?

A. The drivers for the card are missing.
B. The management agents for the card are missing.
C. The card is not installed properly.
D. The Netelligent 10/100 card is not supported by Insight Manager.

B. The management agents for the card are missing. In order for a Netelligent NIC or any piece of Compaq hardware to be monitored through Insight Manager, the management agents must first be loaded.

14. You believe your Netelligent NIC is having an internal hardware failure. What can you do to determine if this is indeed the case?
    - A. Run Windows NT Performance Monitor.
    - B. Run SmartStart.
    - C. Run NICStart.
    - D. None of the above

    C. Run NICStart. NICStart can be used to run diagnostics tests on a Netelligent network controller. Performance Monitor can be used to gather performance statistics on the NIC, but it does not run an actual diagnostics test.

15. You currently have a 10BaseT network running on category 3 cabling. You have NetFlex-2 network cards. What must be done in order for you to upgrade your network to 100 Mbps?
    - A. Purchase new network cards.
    - B. Purchase new cabling.
    - C. Reload your network drivers.
    - D. All of the above

    D. All of the above. You must first upgrade your network cabling to Cat. 5 cabling. Cat. 3 cabling does not support 100-Mbps operation. You must also buy new network cards and load new drivers. NetFlex-3 network cards can be upgraded to 100 Mbps with the addition of an upgrade module. NetFlex-2 cards cannot be upgraded; they must be replaced.

Chapter 13 Answers

1. Which of the following servers has a preinstalled operating system?
    - A. ProLiant 400
    - B. ProSignia VS
    - C. ProSignia Neoserver
    - D. ProLiant 8000

    C. ProSignia Neoserver. This new server model includes an operating system that provides for file/print, backup, e-mail, and Internet services.

2. Which servers were the first to eliminate the EISA bus and support only PCI and ISA devices?
    - A. ProSignia Neoserver
    - B. ProLiant 4000
    - C. ProLiant 6400R
    - D. ProLiant 800, 1200, 1600

    D. ProLiant 800, 1200, 1600. Compaq introduced these and other servers in 1997 without EISA bus support. The PCI bus was provided with ISA support for modems and other peripherals.

3. What is the data transfer rate of Wide-Ultra SCSI-3?

   A. 20 Mbps

   B. 40 Mbps

   C. 40 MBps

   D. 80 MBps
   C. 40 MBps. Wide-Ultra SCSI-3 provides double the bandwidth of the Fast-Wide SCSI-2 drive technologies. The measurement is in megabytes per second, annotated as MBps. Mbps represents megabits per second, and is usually used to describe network bandwidth.

4. Which of the following are features of Highly Parallel System Architecture?

   A. Redundant Network Interface Cards

   B. Dual-memory controller

   C. ECC memory

   D. Dual peer PCI buses
   B, D. Dual-memory controller and dual peer PCI buses. Dual-memory controllers allow the doubling of the memory bus, which reduces a bottleneck in system performance. Dual peer PCI buses provide parallel PCI bridge controllers that allow true load balancing of I/O devices across the buses.

5. Which memory types can be found in Compaq servers?

   A. EDO

   B. ECC

   C. DIMMs

   D. SIMMs

   E. All of the above
   E. All of the above. Compaq servers utilized EDO on early ProSignia servers and ECC memory on all current server models. DIMMs have replaced SIMMs as the memory module architecture of choice in servers, as they provide more dense memory configurations on systems that require large amounts of memory.

6. Which of the following statements are true?

   A. SIMMs may be installed only singly, DIMMs may be installed only in pairs in Compaq servers.

   B. SIMMs and DIMMs may only be installed singly or in pairs in Compaq servers.

   C. SIMMs are installed only in groups of four modules; DIMMs may be installed singly, in pairs, or in groups of four, depending upon the Compaq server.

   D. SIMMs are installed only singly; DIMMs are installed only in pairs or groups of four, depending upon the Compaq server.
   C. SIMMs are installed only in groups of four modules; DIMMs may be installed singly, in pairs, or in groups of four, depending upon the Compaq server. Although the industry standard SIMM memory modules may be installed singly in some computers, all Compaq servers designed to use

SIMMs require that they be installed in groups of four. DIMM installation is defined by each server, and must be installed in the quantities required for specific servers.

7. Which servers support multiprocessor configurations?

   A. ProLiant 400

   B. All current ProLiant servers available in the USA

   C. ProSignia servers

   D. SystemPro servers
   B. All current ProLiant servers available in the USA. SystemPro and ProSignia servers have never offered more than a single processor. The ProLiant 400 is the only current model that does not offer at least a dual processor capability, but it is not available in the USA.

8. Which processor has an L1 cache of 16KB?

   A. 80486

   B. Pentium

   C. Pentium Pro

   D. Pentium II Xeon
   C. Pentium Pro. The Pentium Pro contains two L1 caches, a data cache, and an instruction cache, each 8KB in size.

9. The Pentium II processor has how much L1 cache memory?

   A. 16KB

   B. 24KB

   C. 32KB

   D. 64KB
   C. 32KB. The Pentium II processor provided more room for L1 cache than the Pentium Pro.

10. Why is it not possible for the Pentium II to access L2 cache at 100 percent of the processor speed?

    A. L2 cache is on an external module, not on the processor die.

    B. The address bus is only half as wide.

    C. The memory bus is longer.

    D. Pentium II does not have L2 cache.
    A. L2 cache is on an external module, not on the processor die. In order to make room for double the amount of L1 cache of the Pentium Pro, Intel moved the L2 cache to a module off the main processor die.

11. When did Compaq begin to offer Pre-Failure Warranties?

    A. With the introduction of Insight Manager v2.0

    B. When SCSI drives were available with hot-pluggable capability

    C. After the introduction of ECC memory

    D. After the release of Windows NT Server v3.51
    A. With the introduction of Insight Manager v2.0. With the monitoring capabilities built into Insight Manager, Compaq server hardware could be monitored on Windows NT, Novell NetWare, SCO UNIX, and OS/2-based servers.

12. Which component is not covered under Pre-Failure Warranty from Compaq?

    A. PCI bridges

    B. SCSI hard drives

    C. Compaq ECC memory

    D. Pentium Pro, Pentium II, and Pentium III Xeon processors
    A. PCI bridges. All other devices shown are covered within the Pre-Failure Warranty on ProLiant servers. Only Compaq memory is covered under Pre-Failure Warranty.

13. What will be the Compaq Service response if the Insight Manager Physical Drive Parameters screen shows the required action "Replace Drive" and the SCSI drive is still running?

    A. Compaq will sell you a hard drive

    B. Compaq will replace the drive after you send the bad drive to them

    C. Compaq will open a case and wait for the drive to fail

    D. Compaq will ship a replacement drive before failure upon verification of system warranty validity
    D. Compaq will ship a replacement drive before failure upon verification of system warranty validity. Insight Manager monitors over 15 performance variables on Compaq SCSI drives and if factory preset thresholds for performance indications are exceeded, Compaq will ship a drive so that scheduled replacement will minimize downtime and avoid unplanned outages.

14. Dual peer PCI bridges address which performance bottleneck in a server?

    A. Memory access

    B. I/O device access

    C. Hard drive access

    D. None of the above
    B. I/O device access. By providing dual bus controllers, I/O devices may be balanced on two separate buses, each providing a full bandwidth to the host processor/memory bus.

15. Which of the following is not a fault tolerant feature of Compaq ProLiant servers?

    A. PCI hot plug

    B. Hot-pluggable redundant power supplies

    C. Dual peer PCI bridge

    D. Redundant system fans
    C. Dual peer PCI bridge. Although a valuable feature on ProLiant servers, dual peer PCI bridge architecture is a performance feature. The PCI hot plug, hot-pluggable redundant power supplies, and redundant system fans provide ProLiant servers with the ability to take a component failure and still provide full service to the business. Replacement of these components is also possible with little or no system downtime.

Chapter 14 Answers

1. What are the two types of storage systems offered by Compaq?

   A. Compaq ProLiant Storage System/C

   B. Compaq ProLiant Storage System

   C. Compaq ProLiant Storage System/F

   D. Compaq ProLiant Storage System/Q
   B, C. Compaq ProLiant Storage System and Compaq ProLiant Storage System/F are the two storage systems available from Compaq. The ProLiant Storage System does not hold as many drives or have as many features as the ProLiant Storage System/F. Therefore, the ProLiant Storage System/F is used in more high-availability situations.

2. How many drives can the ProLiant Storage System support?

   A. Fourteen 1.6" and fourteen 1"

   B. Seven 1.6" and seven 1"

   C. Eight 1.6" and ten 1"

   D. Seven 1.6" and eight 1"
   B. The ProLiant Storage System can support seven 1.6" and seven 1" drives in its standard mode, as well as with the duplex option kit.

3. How many drives can the ProLiant Storage System/F support in the dual bus mode?

   A. Seven 1.6" and seven 1"

   B. Seven 1.6" and ten 1"

   C. Eight 1.6" and eight 1"

   D. Eight 1.6" and twelve 1"
   D. The ProLiant Storage System/F can support eight 1.6" and twelve 1" drives in the dual bus mode. It can support seven 1.6" and seven 1" drives in the single bus mode.

4. What type of drives are supported in the ProLiant Storage System? (Select two.)

   A. SCSI-1

   B. SCSI-2

   C. Fast SCSI-2

   D. Fast-Wide SCSI-2

   E. Wide-Ultra SCSI-3

   F. Ultra-Wide SCSI
   C, D. The ProLiant Storage System supports Fast SCSI-2 and Fast-Wide SCSI-2 devices. The maximum throughput is 20MB/s with the use of Fast-Wide SCSI-2 devices, or 10MB/s with the use of Fast SCSI-2 devices.

5. How many ProLiant Storage System/F rack mount devices can fit in a 42U rack?

   A. 12

   B. 8

   C. 10

   D. 4
   C. 10. The ProLiant Storage System/F takes up 4U, so you could have 10 ProLiant Storage System/F in a 42U rack. The ProLiant Storage System takes up 5U.

6. How many different racks are offered by Compaq?

A. Eight
B. Four
C. Five
D. Three
D. Three. Compaq offers three different racks: Compaq Rack 7142, Compaq Rack 7122, and Compaq Rack 4136.

7. How many Us can a Compaq Rack 4136 hold?
A. 4136
B. 41
C. 36
D. 136
C. 36. Compaq Rack 4136 can hold 36U. Compaq Rack 7142 can hold 42U. Compaq Rack 7122 can hold 22U.

8. What devices are controlled by a Compaq switch box? (Choose all that apply.)
A. Keyboard
B. Modem
C. Mouse
D. Video controller
E. Tape device
A, C, D. Keyboard, mouse, and video controller. The Compaq switch box is a rack option that controls multiple keyboards, mice, and video controllers.

9. How many servers can a Compaq switch box support? (Select two.)
A. 12
B. 10
C. 8
D. 4
C, D. Compaq switch boxes are available to control up to four or up to eight servers.

10. Select two characteristics of DLT technology.
A. Uses Helical Scan technology
B. Backs up a maximum of 2.8GB an hour
C. Backs up a maximum of 9GB an hour
D. Passes the tape past the head in a horizontal motion
C, D. The DLT technology can backup a maximum of 9GB an hour, and it passes the tape past the head in a horizontal motion. DAT uses Helical Scan technology, which passes the tape around the read/write head in a circular motion, and backs up a maximum of 2.8GB an hour.

11. Select three components of the Remote Insight Board.
A. Microprocessor
B. Mouse
C. Keyboard
D. Memory
E. Serial Port
A, D, E. The Remote Insight Board has seven components: microprocessor, modem, serial port, keyboard port, video controller, memory, and battery.

12. How can you access the Remote Insight Board? (Select two.)

    A. PPP

    B. SLIP

    C. ANSI-compliant terminal emulation package

    D. Infrared

    A, C. The Remote Insight board is accessible through PPP dialup as well as an ANSI-compliant terminal emulation package.

13. How many user accounts can be configured on the Remote Insight Board?

    A. 16

    B. 10

    C. 12

    D. 8

    C. 12. The Remote Insight Board allows up to 12 different accounts to be configured on it, with varying levels of security.

14. How long is the battery life on the Remote Insight Board?

    A. 10 minutes

    B. 20 minutes

    C. 30 minutes

    D. 60 minutes

    C. 30 minutes. The Remote Insight Board has a battery life of 30 minutes in case of power failure.

15. What is the purpose of a redundant power supply?

    A. To supply more power so processing can take place faster

    B. To charge up the batteries of the server in case of a power failure

    C. To provide a backup power supply if the primary supply goes bad

    D. To share the load of the server power

    C. To provide a backup power supply if the primary supply goes bad. The redundant power supply is used as a backup to the primary power supply. Hot-pluggable power supplies can be replaced without ever taking the server down.

Chapter 15 Answers

1. Which is the best method for launching Compaq utilities or diagnostics?

    A. From the Internet

    B. From a floppy diskette

    C. From the system partition

    D. From within the operating system

    C. From the system partition. It is not possible to launch a diagnostic on the server except when booting the server, so only answers B or C are possible. The best method is from the system partition on the boot drive so that you don't have problems matching up diskette versions with the current system, nor risk losing the diskettes.

2. Which key sequence is pressed to access the utilities in the system partition?

A. F1
B. DEL
C. CTRL-X
D. F10
D. F10. The F1 key sequence is used to continue the boot process after an error message has paused the POST process. DEL and CTRL-X are not appropriate for Compaq systems.

3. Under which conditions should the systems engineer press the key sequence to access the utilities in the system partition?
A. When the cursor begins blinking in the upper right corner of the screen
B. When the computer system beeps two times
C. When the monitor blanks out
D. When the screen displays the message "Press F10 for Setup"
A, D. When the cursor begins blinking in the upper right corner of the screen, and when the screen displays the message "Press F10 for Setup." Early servers used the cursor in the upper right corner. However, most of the new servers by default present a colorful splash screen with the Compaq logo and indicate in the lower right corner the steps to take to access Setup.

4. When booting the server from diagnostic diskettes, which is not an option you may select?
A. Test Computer
B. Test ASR
C. Diagnostics and Utilities
D. Diagnose Drives
C. Diagnostics and Utilities. Choosing Diagnostics and Utilities from the System Partition menu that takes you to the menu that you see when booting the server from the diagnostic diskettes. Test Computer, Test ASR, and Diagnose Drives are three of the seven choices you have from that Diagnostics and Utilities menu.

5. When running the Test Computer option from the Diagnostics and Utilities menu, what are you prompted to have available and/or installed?
A. ASE handbook
B. Floppy diskettes, CD-ROMs, and tape cartridges
C. System serial number
D. Loopback plug
B. Floppy diskettes, CD-ROMs, and tape cartridges. The testing requires removable media for verifying the operation of I/O devices. Loopback plugs are not needed as current devices have built-in capabilities for full testing.

6. What reference is important for resolving error messages generated from the Test Computer process?
A. Compaq Quality Statement
B. http://www.compaq.com/support/index.html
C. Server Maintenance and Service Guide for a specific server

- D. Peripheral Component Installation Guide for servers

  C. Server Maintenance and Service Guide for a specific server. This guide contains the error codes and recommended actions to take should any of these codes present during the testing of the computer.

7. What is ASR?
   - A. Attempted System Reboot
   - B. Accredited Systems Resource
   - C. American Society of Researchers
   - D. Automatic Server Recovery

   D. Automatic Server Recovery. The Diagnostics and Utilities allow the systems engineer to test this configuration for Compaq servers. It is important that the SE verifies that the ASR will boot the operating system or into utilities.

8. What is a SoftPaq?
   - A. Compaq's name for driver and software update download files
   - B. Compaq's utility for creating software on diskettes
   - C. Compaq's quarterly software subscription update
   - D. Compaq's name for nonserver utilities

   A. Compaq's name for driver and software update download files. These files are available on the Compaq Web site for downloading, and include BIOS upgrades as well as drivers for various adapters.

9. Where can the systems engineer find the meaning of POST error beeps?
   - A. On Compaq's Web site
   - B. In the Server Maintenance and Service Guide
   - C. On the inside of the server access cover
   - D. In the server's ROMPaq

   A, B. On Compaq's Web site and in the Server Maintenance and Service Guide. These beeps are indicators of specific problems. Both the Web site and the Server Maintenance and Service Guide include recommended actions for these messages.

10. Which of the following is not updated by ROMPaqs?
    - A. System BIOS
    - B. SCSI Drive BIOS
    - C. Array Controller BIOS
    - D. Network Adapter BIOS

    D. Network Adapter BIOS. Server systems and peripheral devices such as controllers, tape, and SCSI drives contain BIOS chips that are flash-upgradeable via ROMPaqs.

11. Upgrading the BIOS requires which of the following?
    - A. Cold boot
    - B. Warm boot
    - C. CTRL-ALT-DEL boot
    - D. Changing jumper settings on the system board

    A. Cold boot. The BIOS does not take effect until the system is power cycled.

12. How many BIOS upgrades can be done at one time?

    A. One
    B. Two
    C. Three
    D. One or more

    D. One or more. The ROMPaq utility allows the systems engineer to select more than one BIOS to upgrade without power cycling the system each time.

13. What are the two logs maintained in nonvolatile RAM, commonly called the server health logs?

    A. Critical Error Log
    B. POST Message Log
    C. Updated System Log
    D. Revision History Table

    A, D. Critical Error Log and Revision History Table. The Critical Error Log maintains the errors generated by the hardware or operating system. The Revision History Table maintains records of modifications to installed components such as memory.

14. Which is not a way to view the server health logs?

    A. Integrated Management display
    B. POST message display
    C. Insight Manager
    D. Survey utility

    B. Post message display. The server health logs will capture POST error messages, but many of these are simply beeps. The other three tools allow the systems engineer to view and maintain written records of the server's health.

15. DAAD collects information from which subsystems?

    A. Diagnostics
    B. CD-ROM drives
    C. Drive arrays
    D. Tape drives

    C. Drive arrays. Drive Array Advanced Diagnostics is used to obtain specific information about array controllers and the attached drives.

16. The Inspect utility allows the engineer to test which of these subsystems automatically?

    A. System, ROM, and keyboard
    B. System ports, storage, and graphic devices
    C. Memory, operating system, and system configuration
    D. All of the above

    D. All of the above. The Inspect utility can provide information to the systems engineer on all systems and subsystems of the server.

Chapter 16 Answers

1. If you plan to build an OS/2 server, which recovery server configuration would be most beneficial?

    A. Online Recovery Server
    B. Standby Recovery Server
    C. Either of these
    D. None of these

    D. None of these. OS/2 is not supported under the Compaq Recovery Server Option. Only Windows NT, Novell NetWare, SCO OpenServer, and SCO UnixWare are supported.

2. What server can be used for the secondary server when the primary server is a ProLiant 5000 and you want to use Standby Recovery Server?
   A. ProLiant 5000
   B. ProLiant 6000
   C. ProLiant 1500
   D. All of these
   A. ProLiant 5000. Standby Recovery Server requires that the primary and the secondary server be identical.
3. You want to use Compaq Online Recovery Server. What operating systems can you use?
   A. Windows NT 4.0
   B. Novell NetWare 4.11
   C. SCO UnixWare
   D. SCO OpenServer
   A. Windows NT 4.0. Compaq Online Recovery Server only supports Windows NT 3.51 and 4.0.
4. What events can trigger a failover in Compaq Standby Recovery Server?
   A. A disconnected interconnect
   B. A Windows NT trap (blue screen)
   C. A Novell NetWare abend
   D. All of these
   D. All of these. A failover can be triggered by a damaged or disconnected interconnect cable. It can also be triggered by any event that prevents an operating system from sending a heartbeat signal.
5. You want to use Compaq Standby Recovery Server. What server platforms can you use to load Windows NT?
   A. ProLiant 7500
   B. ProLiant 6000
   C. ProLiant 3500
   D. All of these
   B. ProLiant 6000. Compaq Standby Recovery Server supports ProSignia 200, ProSignia 500, ProLiant 850R, ProLiant 2000, ProLiant 4000, ProLiant 4500, ProLiant 5000, ProLiant 5500, ProLiant 6000, ProLiant 6500, and ProLiant 7000 under Windows NT, as well as several other server platforms.
6. In Standby Recovery Server, what is the secondary server doing while the primary server is running?
   A. Running a POST test
   B. Servicing user requests
   C. Running Windows NT diagnostics
   D. It is powered off
   A. Running a POST test. In Standby Recovery Server, the secondary server is running a POST test while the primary is up and running. In Online Recovery Server, both servers are capable of servicing client requests before a failover
7. Which of the following is not included in the Recovery Server Option Kit?
   A. A Fast-Wide SCSI-2 adapter cable
   B. ProLiant Switchable array

C. Two SCSI-2 hard drives

D. All of these are included.
A. A Fast-Wide SCSI-2 adapter cable. The Recovery Server Option Kit will include recovery server software, a recovery server switch, a recovery server interconnect, a 12-foot standard-to-wide external SCSI-2 cable, and a 12-foot Fast-Wide SCSI-2 adapter cable

8. If your recovery server interconnect cable becomes damaged, which of the following can be used a replacement?

A. A null modem cable

B. A printer cable

C. A straight through cable

D. None of these
D. None of these. If your recovery server interconnect cable is damaged, you must order a new one. Other cables will not properly transmit the heartbeat signal.

9. You want to use Compaq Standby Recovery Server. What operating system can you use?

A. Windows NT 3.1

B. Windows NT 3.51

C. Novell NetWare 3.11

D. All of the above
B. Windows NT 3.51. Standby Recovery Server is supported for Windows NT 3.5*x* and 4.0, Novell NetWare 3.12 and 4.*x*, SCO OpenServer 5, and SCO UnixWare 2.1.*x* and 7.*x*

10. Which of the following controllers can be used to connect to the switchable ProLiant array?

A. Fast SCSI-2

B. Fast-Wide SCSI-2

C. SMART-2DH

D. All of these
C. SMART-2DH. The switchable ProLiant array can be connected to a SMART, SMART-2, SMART-2SL, SMART-2P, SMART-2E, or SMART-2DH controller.

11. You want to use Compaq Standby Recovery Server. What server platforms can you use to load Novell NetWare?

A. ProLinea 566

B. ProLiant 5000

C. ProSignia 200

D. None of these
B. ProLiant 5000. Compaq Standby Recovery Server with NetWare will support ProLiant 2500s, ProLiant 3000s, ProLiant 4000s, ProLiant 4600s, ProLiant 4500s, and ProLiant 5000s, as well as several other Compaq servers.

12. What device is used to monitor the heartbeat signal and institute a failover?

A. The SCSI array controller

B. The recovery server interconnect

C. The CRA

D. The switchable array controller
C. The CRA. The Compaq Recovery Agent monitors the heartbeat signal. When the signal stops, the CRA institutes a failover.

13. Which of the following controllers can be used for the local disks in Compaq Online Recovery Server?

    A. SMART-2

    B. Fast-Wide SCSI-2

    C. SMART-2DH

    D. All of the above
    D. All of the above. In Compaq Online Recovery Server, the controller for the local disks can be a Fast SCSI-2, Fast-Wide SCSI-2, SMART, SMART-2, SMART-2SL, SMART-2P, SMART-2E, or SMART-2DH controller.

14. If you are using Compaq Standby Recovery Server and have a NetFlex-3 controller in the primary server, what network controller can you use in the secondary server?

    A. NetFlex-2

    B. Netelligent

    C. NetFlex-3

    D. Any controller is fine
    C. NetFlex-3. In Compaq Standby Recovery Server, the network controllers must be identical. They should also be in the same slot.

15. You want to use Compaq Online Recovery Server. What server platforms can you use to load Novell NetWare?

    A. ProLiant 1500

    B. ProLiant 5000

    C. ProLiant 6000

    D. None of the above
    D. None of the above. Compaq Online Recovery Server only supports Windows NT.

Chapter 17 Answers

1. Which of the following is not a management application?

    A. Insight Manager

    B. Network General Sniffer

    C. HP NetServer Assistant

    D. HP OpenView
    D. HP OpenView. OpenView is a management platform. HP NetServer Assistant, Cabletron Spectrum, Network General Sniffer, and Compaq Insight Manager are all management applications.

2. Which of the following is not a management platform?

    A. IBM NetView

    B. Novell ManageWise

    C. Insight Manager

    D. All are platforms
    C. Insight Manager. Insight Manager is a management application. HP OpenView, IBM NetView, Novell ManageWise, and SunNet Manager are examples of management platforms.

3. Which is not a part of systems management?

A. Security management
B. Performance management
C. Configuration management
D. All are a part of systems management
D. All are a part of systems management. Systems management includes desktop management, configuration management, performance management, fault management, and security management.

4. Which is not a goal of network management?
A. Reliability
B. Low overhead
C. Efficiency
D. All are goals of network management
D. All are goals of network management. The three goals of network management are reliability, low overhead, and efficiency.

5. What application would you use to monitor your hard disk performance?
A. Performance Monitor
B. Policy Editor
C. Profile Monitor
D. ZENworks
A. Performance Monitor. Performance Monitor can be used to monitor statistics on local and remote machines. You can monitor memory, hard drives, processors, and network cards

6. You are getting slow performance from your network. What should you use to check your network statistics?
A. Policy Editor
B. Performance Monitor
C. LANalyzer
D. NetShow
C. LANalyzer. LANalyzer is the network monitor used with Novell ManageWise. LANalyzer can be used to gather network statistics and for packet analysis.

7. You want all of your Windows NT Server users to have the same desktop. What should you use?
A. Windows NT Policy Editor
B. LANalyzer
C. Performance Monitor
D. ZENworks
A. Windows NT Policy Editor. The Windows NT Policy Editor allows you to configure profiles for multiple users who log into Windows NT servers.

8. You want all of your NetWare Server users to have the same desktop. What should you use?
A. ZENworks
B. Windows NT Policy Editor
C. Performance Monitor
D. None of the above
A. ZENworks. ZENworks allows you to set policies for multiple NetWare Server clients.

9. Under which management category does RAID fall?
   A. Security management
   B. Desktop management
   C. Fault management
   D. Configuration management
   C. Fault management. RAID is a method for ensuring fault tolerance. Therefore, it falls under the fault management category. RAID allows for recovery in the event of a disk failure.

10. Under which management category do equipment upgrades fall?
   A. Desktop management
   B. Security management
   C. Configuration management
   D. Network management
   D. Network management. Upgrading your equipment falls under network management. The purpose of upgrading your equipment is to ensure network efficiency, which is one of the goals of network management.

11. Which of the following can be the result of a lack of data security?
   A. Data corruption
   B. Data loss
   C. Compromised confidentiality
   D. All of the above
   D. All of the above. A lack of data security can lead to data corruption and data loss. It can also lead to a loss of confidentiality because documents may be accessed by people for whom they were not intended.

12. Which of the following is not a function of Novell ManageWise?
   A. Software distribution
   B. Remote control
   C. File transfers
   D. All are functions of ManageWise
   D. All are functions of ManageWise. ManageWise can be used for data collection, inventory, reporting, software distribution, remote control, file transfer, and remote configuration.

13. What can be done to protect your data from harm?
   A. Password implementation
   B. Set file permissions
   C. Physically secure your equipment
   D. All of the above
   D. All of the above. You can take several steps to protect your data, including physically securing your equipment, implementing passwords, forcing unique passwords, setting password expirations, setting file permissions, and using the hidden and read-only attributes for files.

14. What is the management protocol used by IBM NetView?
   A. SMTP
   B. SNMP
   C. TCP
   D. UDP
   B. SNMP. SNMP stands for Simple Network Management Protocol. SNMP has become the standard for network and system management.

SNMP can be used to manage workstations, servers, and network devices such as routers and switches.

15. Which of the following is not a feature of Insight Manager?

    A. Reporting

    B. Alerts

    C. Software distribution

    D. Data collection

    C. Software distribution. Insight Manager is a full-featured management application. It was designed by Compaq for management of Compaq equipment. Insight Manager can be used for data collection, inventory, reporting, alerting, and remote control.

Chapter 18 Answers

1. Which of the following is not a command used by SNMP?

    A. SET

    B. READ

    C. GET

    D. Trap

    B. READ. READ is not a function of the SNMP protocol. Remember that when SNMP needs to retrieve information, it uses a GET. SET is the method of writing or changing a setting. A trap is the SNMP method of sending an alert or notification to a specific location.

2. Which of the following scenarios would require the use of SET?

    A. A defined threshold on a system running a management agent has been broken.

    B. A defined threshold on a system running a management application has been broken.

    C. A threshold is being defined by the management application on a management agent.

    D. The status of a threshold on a management agent is being queried by the management application.

    C. A threshold is being defined by the management application on a management agent. The SET command is used by SNMP to change a setting defined by the management agent. This process cannot handle querying or notifications.

3. Which of the following scenarios would call for the use of an SNMP GET?

    A. The current definition of a CPU threshold is requested on a machine running the management application only.

    B. The current definition of a CPU threshold is requested on a machine running the management agent only.

    C. A threshold has been exceeded on a machine that is running the management application only.

    D. A threshold has been exceeded on a machine that is running the management agent only.

    B. The current definition of a CPU

threshold is requested on a machine running the management agent only. The GET is used to retrieve information from a system. Note that information can only be retrieved from a system running a management agent.

4. Which of the following is not a function of an SNMP trap?
   A. To provide a response to a SET command
   B. To provide notification of an event in the management application
   C. To return the information requested from a GET command
   D. To provide notification of an event in the management agent

   B. To provide notification of an event in the management application. Remember that a management application provides the interface to a managed element. It is the agent's responsibility to send a notification trap to the predetermined trap location, should an event occur. Also, keep in mind that, although a SET is only a write function, a trap is still returned to the application to let it know that the SET was processed correctly.

5. Let's assume that you have just configured an SNMP-based management application and agent on the Windows NT servers on your network. You are in the process of defining a CPU utilization threshold of 80 percent on your Windows NT servers when you come across a server that will not allow you to configure the threshold. You are, however, able to view the information that the agent has made available. Which of the following is the most likely cause of this problem?
   A. The machine with the management application is using a different community string than the machine with the agent installed.
   B. The community string on the box that you cannot configure is in the wrong case.
   C. The community string has only been given READ permissions on the Windows NT server where the management agent has been installed.
   D. SNMP has not been installed on the management agent server.

   C. The community string has only been given READ permissions on the Windows NT server where the management agent has been installed. Because you are able to view the information that the agent has defined, we can eliminate the community string as the cause of the problem. If the community string were spelled incorrectly or in the wrong case, all communication between the management application and the agent would fail. This would also be the case if SNMP had not been installed. In fact, most agents will not even install on a machine where SNMP is not present (providing the agent is a standards-based management agent that utilizes SNMP as the management protocol).

6. Which of the following is not a requirement of SNMP?

   A. A management server

   B. An element to be managed

   C. A network to communicate across

   D. A management application that utilizes SNMP to communicate with an agent

   A. A management server. A server is not a requirement to use SNMP to configure a network device. The only requirements are an element to be managed, a network to communicate across, and a management application that utilizes SNMP to communicate with an agent.

7. A MIB contains which of the following pieces of information?

   A. The properties of a managed element

   B. The functions that can be performed against an element

   C. The information that is available on a defined element

   D. All of the above

   D. All of the above. A MIB defines the properties of a managed element, the functions that can be performed against an element, and the information that is available on a defined element; and makes this information available via SNMP.

8. The numeric ranges assigned as MIB identifiers are overseen by which standards organization?

   A. International Standards Numbering Organization

   B. Internet Number and Standards Organization

   C. Internet Assigned Numbers Authority

   D. Internet Assigned Numbers Organization

   C. Internet Assigned Numbers Authority. This organization is responsible for the delegation of MIB IDs. By having a standards organization in place to handle this task, we are assured that all MIB identifiers are unique and therefore will not conflict with other vendors' management platforms.

9. Which of the following could not be an element?

   A. A Compaq server

   B. A managed Ethernet HUB

   C. A hard disk array controller

   D. Computer Memory

   E. None of the above

   E. None of the above. All of the examples listed could be managed elements. The only requirement is that it be defined and communicate with the management agent.

10. Which of the following object IDs could belong to a Compaq element?

    A. 1.3.6.1.4.3.134.2.3

    B. 1.3.6.1.3.4.122.1

    C. 1.3.6.1.4.1.232.1.2

    D. 1.3.6.1.4.4.276.2.3

    C. 1.3.6.1.4.1.232.1.2. This is the

only answer that contains Compaq's enterprise ID of 1.3.6.1.4.1.232. Any elements that belong to Compaq would have to exist on that branch of the MIB tree.

11. Which of the following is a function of a MIB browser?
    A. Send a trap in response to an event occurring on a managed element.
    B. Identify the MIB information of a particular management agent.
    C. Identify management applications on the network.
    D. Browse a non-SNMP network.
    B. Identify the MIB information of a particular management agent. A MIB browser is an application capable of viewing or even manipulating MIB information for a managed element. It is not responsible for sending a trap, as this is the function of the management agent. A MIB is an SNMP-specific definition; therefore, a MIB browser would not be responsible for browsing a non-SNMP network.

12. Configuring a threshold parameter would be a function of which of the following management components?
    A. The management agent
    B. The management protocol
    C. The management processor
    D. The management application
    D. The management application. The application is what provides you with the interface to your management platform. Though the actual threshold is defined at the agent, the configuration is performed from the application.

13. Which of the following is not a component of a management system?
    A. Platform
    B. Element
    C. Processor
    D. Protocol
    C. Processor. There is no such component. The five components are platform, application, agent, element, and protocol.

14. Which of the following can be found at the top of the MIB tree?
    A. The Department of Defense
    B. A network device vendor
    C. A standards organization
    D. There is no such thing as a MIB tree
    C. A standards organization. Because the standards organization is responsible for the delegation of MIB identifiers, it can be found at the top of the tree. The Department of Defense is found slightly farther down the tree, with the network device vendor falling even farther down.

15. When would you use a trap to configure a managed element?
    A. When you need to configure the element from the management application
    B. When you need to configure the element from a machine that is not part of the management platform

C. When a management application is not available

D. A trap cannot be used to configure an element

D. A trap cannot be used to configure an element. The trap is a means of notification only. It has no READ or WRITE capabilities.

Chapter 19 Answers

1. What are the three parts that make up Compaq Full-Spectrum Fault Management?

A. Fault Prevention, Fault Tolerance, Remote Maintenance

B. Fault Tolerance, Fault Recovery, Fault Prevention

C. Fault Prevention, Fault Tolerance, Rapid Recovery

D. Fault Monitoring, Fault Recovery, Fault Prevention

C. Fault Prevention, Fault Tolerance, Rapid Recovery. The three parts that make up Compaq Full-Spectrum Fault Management are Fault Prevention, Fault Tolerance, and Rapid Recovery.

2. Which of the following is not a feature of Fault Prevention?

A. Pre-Failure Warranty

B. Temperature sensing

C. Network Performance monitoring

D. Hard Disk Available Space monitoring

D. Hard Disk Available Space monitoring. Compaq Fault Prevention technologies monitor hardware in order to predict failures of the hardware.

3. Which is not a fault tolerant system?

A. System board

B. Network Interface Card

C. Power supply

D. Storage system

A. System board. If a component on the system board fails, the only remedy is to replace the system board.

4. What fault tolerant features are not provided with ECC memory?

A. Detect single bit errors

B. Correct adjacent bit errors

C. Detect adjacent bit errors

D. Correct single bit errors

B. Correct adjacent bit errors. Although ECC memory can detect multiple-bit errors, it cannot fix them.

5. If you wanted to have an identically configured redundant server, which option would you use?

A. Online Recovery Server

B. External storage plugged into a different server

C. Off-Line backup processor

D. Standby Recovery Server

D. Standby Recovery Server. The Standby Recovery Server stores the OS and data in an external storage unit and uses a second Compaq server with an identical hardware configuration.

6. What are the three components of Rapid Recovery?
   - A. Critical Error Logs, Automatic Server Recovery, Remote Maintenance
   - B. Server Health Logging, Automatic Reboot, Remote Maintenance
   - C. Server Health Logging, Automatic Server Recovery, Remote Maintenance
   - D. Server Health Logging, Automatic Server Recovery, Failure Notification

   C. Server Health Logging, Automatic Server Recovery, and Remote Maintenance are the three components that make up Rapid Recovery.

7. What information is not stored in the Critical Error Logs?
   - A. Correctable memory errors
   - B. Hard drive failures
   - C. Network link failures
   - D. Internal fan failure

   A. Correctable memory errors. Uncorrectable memory errors are stored in the Critical Error Logs. Correctable memory errors are logged to the Correctable Error Log.

8. What methods are available for viewing the Critical Error Logs?
   - A. Compaq Insight Manger
   - B. Inspect utility
   - C. Compaq Diagnostics
   - D. Event Viewer

   A, B, C. Compaq Insight Manager, the Inspect utility, and Compaq Diagnostics. Event Viewer allows viewing of alerts that occurred within the Windows NT operating system. All of the other options allow viewing of the Critical Error Logs.

9. Which is a feature that is available in ASR but not ASR-2?
   - A. Recovery from excessive internal temperature
   - B. Administrator paging on system failure
   - C. Administrator paging when system comes back online
   - D. Recovery from processor board failure

   B. Administrator paging on system failure. This feature is available only in ASR.

10. Which of the following ASR drivers does Windows NT use?
    - A. CPQHLTH.NLM
    - B. cpqasrd
    - C. SYSMGMT.SYS
    - D. CPQHLTH.SYS

    C. SYSMGMT.SYS is the driver used by Windows NT.

11. Which of the following is not a tool that can be used to install and configure ASR?
    - A. System Configuration Utility
    - B. SmartStart installation program
    - C. Compaq Insight Manager
    - D. Compaq SSD

    C. Compaq Insight Manager. CIM cannot be used to install or configure ASR. The Compaq SSD contains the drivers necessary for the OS to communicate with the ASR feature.

12. What are the options that can be configured on reboot from ASR?

    A. Boot to the operating system
    B. Scan the hard drive
    C. Boot to Compaq Utilities
    D. Remap bad memory locations
    A, C. Boot to the operating system and boot to Compaq Utilities. ASR can be configured to load either the operating system or the Compaq Utilities when the server reboots. Remapping of bad memory locations happens automatically.

13. What no longer works when a server is recovering via ASR?

    A. Network password
    B. Keyboard password
    C. Power-on password
    D. Administrator password
    C. Power-on password. This feature is disabled on a reboot during ASR in order to allow the server to load the OS or Compaq Utilities without user intervention.

14. Which security feature can be used to protect against unauthorized access to the Compaq Utilities?

    A. Network password
    B. Keyboard password
    C. Power-on password
    D. Administrator password
    D. Administrator password. The administrator password can be used to prevent access to the Compaq Utilities until the correct password has been entered.

15. Which are the connection methods allowed to utilize Remote Maintenance?

    A. Remote console
    B. Modem
    C. Serial connection
    D. Systems Management software
    B, C. Modem or serial connection. These are the only methods available for remotely accessing the Compaq Utilities.

Chapter 20 Answers

1. What entity designed the DMI 2.0 standard?

    A. Desktop Management Task Force
    B. Desktop Management Institute
    C. Desktop Compliance Organization
    D. Desktop Compliance Task Force
    A. Desktop Management Task Force. The DMTF developed the DMI standard in order to standardize desktop management.

2. Which of the following companies is not a member of the Desktop Management Task Force?

    A. Intel
    B. Microsoft
    C. Novell
    D. Veritas
    D. Veritas. The members of the Desktop Management Task Force

include Compaq, IBM, Microsoft, Novell, Intel, and several other major companies.

3. Which of the following is not a part of the Desktop Management Interface?
   - A. Component Interface
   - B. Management Interface
   - C. Desktop Interface
   - D. All are parts of the Desktop Management Interface

   C. Desktop Interface. The two parts of the Desktop Management Interface are the Component Interface and the Management Interface.

4. Which component of the DMI allows the desktop components to send information to management programs?
   - A. Component Interface
   - B. Management Interface
   - C. Desktop Interface
   - D. Agent Interface

   A. Component Interface. The two components of the DMI are the Component Interface and the Management Interface. The Component Interface sends information to management programs.

5. Which component of the DMI allows the management programs to read and write management information?
   - A. Component Interface
   - B. Management Interface
   - C. Desktop Interface
   - D. Agent Interface

   B. Management Interface. The two components of the DMI are the Management Interface and the Component Interface. The Management Interface reads and writes management information.

6. Which of the following is analogous to the Management Information File?
   - A. Management Information Base
   - B. Management Agent
   - C. The Registry
   - D. None of the above

   A. Management Information Base. The Management Information File is analogous to the Management Information Base in SNMP. Both are used to store management configuration information.

7. Which of the following cannot be included in a Management Information File?
   - A. Text files
   - B. Management agents
   - C. Executable files
   - D. All of these can be a part of a Management Information File.

   C. Executable files. The MIF can be a text file or collection of management agents.

8. Which of the following is not a type of Management Information File?

A. Standard MIFs

B. Vendor MIFs

C. Agent MIFs

D. All of these are types of MIFs
C. Agent MIFs. There are two types of MIFs, standard MIFs and vendor MIFs

9. Which of the following is not a category of Intelligent Manageability?

A. Configuration Management

B. Fault Management

C. Installation Management

D. Integration Management
C. Installation Management. The five categories of Compaq Intelligent Manageability are Configuration Management, Asset Management, Security Management, Fault Management, and Integration Management.

10. Which of the following are not components of Compaq Asset Management?

A. DMI BIOS

B. DMI 2.0 support

C. DIMM Serial Presence Detect

D. SMART hard drives
D. SMART hard drives. The four components of Compaq Asset Management are DMI BIOS, DMI 2.0 support, DIMM Serial Presence Detect, and Fingerprint Identification Technology.

11. Which is not a component of Compaq Configuration Management?

A. Remote ROM Flash

B. Remote wake-up and shutdown

C. Thermal sensor

D. Support Software CD
C. Thermal sensor. Compaq Configuration Management includes Remote ROM Flash, Remote wake-up and shutdown, Support Software CD, System Software Manager, and ACPI-ready hardware.

12. Which of the following is not a part of Compaq Security Management?

A. Smart Cover Lock

B. Ownership tag

C. Smart Cover Sensor

D. All of the above are components of Compaq Security Management
D. All of the above are components of Compaq Security Management. Smart Cover Lock, ownership tag, Smart Cover Sensor, configuration control hardware, and Memory Change Alert are the components of Compaq Security Management.

13. Which of the following is not a part of Compaq Fault Management?

A. ECC Memory

B. SMART hard drives

C. Thermal sensor

D. Memory Change Alert
D. Memory Change Alert. Compaq Fault Management includes ECC Memory, SMART hard drives, thermal sensor, Ultra ATA Monitoring, and hard drive pre-failure warranty

14. Which of the following is not a part of Compaq Integration Management?
    A. Insight Manager
    B. Management Solutions Partners Program
    C. Support Software CD
    D. Net PC Technologies Support
    C. Support Software CD. The components of Compaq Integration Management include: Insight Manager, Management Solution Partners Program, Net PC Technologies Support, and Wired for Management Support
15. Which of the following operating systems support Compaq desktop agents?
    A. Windows NT 3.51
    B. Windows NT 4.0
    C. Windows 95
    D. All of the above
    D. All of the above. Windows NT 3.51, Windows NT 4.0, Windows 95, and Windows 98 support Compaq desktop agents

Chapter 21 Answers

1. Which of the following operating systems is not supported by Insight Manager?
    A. Windows NT
    B. Windows for Workgroups
    C. Windows 95
    D. Windows 98
    B. Windows for Workgroups. Insight Manager must run on a 32-bit operating system. Windows for Workgroups is only a 16-bit OS.
2. What is the minimum amount of memory you should have in order to install Insight Manager under Windows NT?
    A. 16MB
    B. 24MB
    C. 32MB
    D. 64MB
    C. 32MB. Compaq recommends that you have at least 32MB installed before you install Insight Manager under Windows NT. Ideally, you should have more, especially if you are planning on running other applications on your management console.
3. Which of the following do you need to support Insight Asynchronous Management?
    A. Hayes-compatible modem
    B. Super VGA video card
    C. Compaq Survey Utility
    D. Null modem cable
    A. Hayes-compatible modem. In order to support asynchronous communications between your management PC and remote servers, you will need to have a modem installed on your management PC.

4. Which of the following is not an additional requirement for Insight Manager?
   A. TCP/IP
   B. SNMP
   C. IPX/SPX
   D. NetBEUI
   D. NetBEUI. Insight Manager does not support the NetBEUI protocol, which is a broadcast-based protocol used in smaller networks.

5. Which of the following is not a valid source to obtain Insight Manager?
   A. SmartStart CD
   B. Management CD
   C. Compaq Web site
   D. Integration Server
   A. SmartStart CD. Although the SmartStart CD does contain many other Compaq drivers and software, it does not contain the source files for Insight Manager.

6. How much free disk space should you have before installing Insight Manager?
   A. 5MB
   B. 15MB
   C. 35MB
   D. 50MB
   C. 35MB. You need 35MB of free disk space to install Insight Manager—20MB for the program files and 15MB for the database.

7. What is the default installation directory where Insight Manager is installed?
   A. C:\PROGRAM FILES\COMPAQ\INSIGHT MANAGER
   B. C:\COMPAQ\INSIGHT MANAGER
   C. C:\PROGRAM FILES\INSIGHT MANAGER
   D. C:\INSIGHT MANAGER
   A. C:\PROGRAM FILES\COMPAQ\INSIGHT MANAGER. You can change this directory by typing in a new path or browsing during the proper part of the setup program.

8. You have 100 NetWare servers running IPX/SPX. You want to be able to manage the servers using Insight Manager, but you do not look forward to adding them all to the database. What feature of Insight Manager allows you to add the servers automatically?
   A. Import a text file containing the names of all your servers
   B. Enable auto discovery of IPX servers
   C. Enable auto discovery of NetWare servers
   D. There is no such feature.
   B. Enable auto discovery of IPX servers. During the setup program, you can enable this feature so that your NetWare servers are automatically added to the Responsible Device list in Insight Manager.

9. You are running a pure TCP/IP network. What is one method of improving performance for Insight Manager?

   A. Enable auto discovery for TCP/IP devices.

   B. Disable auto discovery of NetWare servers.

   C. Disable auto discovery of IPX servers.

   D. Enable auto discovery of Remote Console NVT servers.
   C. Disable auto discovery of IPX servers. By disabling auto discovery of IPX servers, you do not waste processor cycles searching for servers running IPX, thereby improving overall performance for your management PC.

10. After you install Insight Manager, your existing Borland Database applications fail to run. How can you prevent this from happening again?

    A. Select the option to Maintain Configuration to Support Existing Win 3.1 Applications.

    B. Install Insight Manager to a different partition.

    C. Select the option to auto-discover Borland applications.

    D. Make sure you install version 4.20 or later of Insight Manager.
    A. Select the option to Maintain Configuration to Support Existing Win 3.1 Applications. If you do not have any existing Borland applications, deselect this option to improve performance.

Chapter 22 Answers

1. What is the default interval for data collection for asynchronous servers?

   A. 30 minutes

   B. One hour

   C. 12 hours

   D. Manual Update
   C. 12 hours. The default for local servers is 30 minutes. The minimum interval for asynchronous servers is one hour. There is no Manual Update option for data collection.

2. What should you set the collection interval to if you are monitoring 60 servers?

   A. 30 minutes

   B. 60 minutes

   C. 90 minutes

   D. 12 hours
   C. 90 minutes. For every 20 servers that you want to monitor, you should add 30 minutes to the default interval.

3. You want to print a report that lists all error messages that you've received on your server. Which form would you use to format the report?

   A. RAPREC

   B. CONFIG

   C. STANDARD

   D. ERRORS
   A. RAPREC. This is short for Rapid Recovery System, which tracks all of your error logs. There is no ERRORS form.

4. You try to reboot a server using the Remote Reboot function, but the server does not reboot. Which of the following statements is not a valid reason why the server will not reboot?
   A. Remote Reboot is not enabled in the Insight Agents applet in Control Panel
   B. The Guest account is not enabled on the server
   C. The SNMP community strings do not match
   D. The operating system is hung
   B. The Guest account is not enabled on the server. The Guest account does not need to be enabled to allow remote reboots.

5. What is the quickest way to find all failed/critical messages in the Alarm Log?
   A. Right-click the Alarm Log and create a filter for critical messages.
   B. Click the Device column and look for the red (critical) icons.
   C. Click the Severity column.
   D. Click the Critical button on the toolbar.
   C. Click the Severity column. This will sort the list by severity code, allowing you to group all critical messages. Answer B is valid, but does not allow you to group all critical messages. Answers A and D do not exist.

6. Your company decides to use a standard SNMP community string "corp" instead of using the default "public." You change the default community string to "corp" in Insight Manager and you change the community name to "corp" at each of your servers. After doing so, all currently managed servers' status appears as Unmanageable. Any new servers that you add to the device list appear as OK. What should you do next?
   A. Modify the community name for the servers in the Device Setup window.
   B. Change the strings back to "public" in both CIM and on the servers.
   C. Reinstall SNMP on the server, specifying "corp" as the community string.
   D. Click the Refresh button in the Device List window.
   A. Modify the community name for the servers in the Device Setup window. Changing the default community string does not change the string for currently managed servers. You must manually change their string in the Device Setup window.

7. Which version of management allows you to manage servers using PPP and a modem?
   A. In-band management
   B. Out-of-band management
   C. Synchronous management
   D. Upper management
   B. Out-of-band management. In-band management allows you to manage over a local network. Synchronous management is synonymous with in-band management. Nobody likes upper management.

8. Which of the following is an advantage of e-mail forwarding over pager forwarding?
   - A. You can specify that only alarms from specific servers are sent to an e-mail address.
   - B. You can specify that only certain alarms are forwarded to an e-mail address.
   - C. You can send full-text descriptions to e-mail.
   - D. You can specify multiple recipients per destination.

   D. You can specify multiple recipients per destination. Pager destinations allow both specified devices and alarms. Alphanumeric pagers can also receive full-text descriptions.

9. Which of the following is not a built-in category for server filters?
   - A. Settings
   - B. Status
   - C. Utilization
   - D. Software

   D. Software is not a built-in category. The other built-in categories in addition to Settings, Status, and Utilization are Operating System and Hardware.

10. What does it mean when a server has a status of Not Available?
    - A. The server is responding to SNMP polling, but no status is available.
    - B. The server is not responding to SNMP polling.
    - C. The server is configured for modem but you are not dialed into the server.
    - D. The server has a duplicate IP address.

    A. The server is responding to SNMP polling, but no status is available. Answer B refers to an Inaccessible status.

11. You try to print a report for a server manually but the only form available is the CONFIG form. You want to be able to print other reports. What should you do?
    - A. Create a custom report form for the server.
    - B. Enable Automatic Data Collection.
    - C. Refresh the status of the server in the Device List.
    - D. Customize the CONFIG form to include the data you require.

    B. Enable Automatic Data Collection. If ADC is not enabled for a server, the only report form available is the CONFIG form.

12. In the Device List window, you only want to show servers that have a Pentium Processor and Windows NT 4.0 installed. However, when you select one option, the other option is deselected. What must you do to allow both?
    - A. Create a custom filter that will display both Pentium machines and Windows NT 4.0 machines.
    - B. Press the CTRL key when selecting the filters.
    - C. Enable multiple filter mode.
    - D. You cannot view both simultaneously.

    C. Enable multiple filter mode. This will allow you to select more than one filter when sorting your list.

13. Where do you enable the Hide SNMP Community Strings option?

    A. Application Password

    B. Global Settings

    C. Control Panel | Network | Services | SNMP

    D. CIM20.INI

    A. Application Password. You enable the Hide SNMP Community Strings option in the Application Password window. You get to the Application Password window by selecting the Setup menu in CIM.

14. What does a black status indicator icon indicate for a server?

    A. Inaccessible

    B. Undiscovered

    C. Degraded

    D. Not Available

    A. Inaccessible. A black status indicator icon indicates that the server is not responding to SNMP polling. Inaccessible differs from Not Available in that Not Available responds to SNMP polling, but still does not show a status.

15. Where do you set the server's SNMP community name in Windows NT?

    A. WINNT.INI

    B. Control Panel

    C. SNMP Manager

    D. Insight Manager

    B. Control Panel. You set the SNMP community name in Control Panel in the Network applet. You cannot use Insight Manager to set the community name.

Chapter 23 Answers

1. Which of the following can you use to obtain Insight Manager LC?

    A. Download from Compaq Web site

    B. Smart Start Subscription Service

    C. Server Management Kit

    D. All of the above

    D. All of the above. Insight Manager LC can be obtained from the Compaq Web site, a Smart Start Subscription Service, or the Server Management Kit that comes with Compaq servers.

2. Which of the following is not a prerequisite of the Insight Manager LC management console?

    A. TCP/IP

    B. IPX

    C. Intel DMI 2.0 Service Provider

    D. Internet Explorer 4.01 Service Pack 1a

    B. IPX. IPX is only needed if you will be monitoring NetWare servers. The management console requires TCP/IP, Intel DMI 2.0 Service Provider, Internet Explorer 4.01 Service Pack 1a, Windows 95 with Windows Sockets 2 update or Windows 98 or Windows NT 4.0, 20MB hard drive space for the Insight Manager LC application and 30MB for the system-level software files to be managed.

3. The Compaq Insight Manager LC client installation adds which of the following applications to the Control Panel?
   A. Compaq Diagnostics
   B. Insight Manager LC
   C. Intelligent Cluster Administrator
   D. Support Source
   A. Compaq Diagnostics. The Insight Manager LC client installation program adds the Compaq Diagnostics and the System Configuration Record to the Control Panel.

4. Under what section in the Compaq Diagnostics can you view the system serial number?
   A. Asset Control
   B. System
   C. Input Devices
   D. Communication
   A. Asset Control. The serial number of a system can be found under the Asset Control section of the Compaq Diagnostics.

5. Under what section in the Compaq Diagnostics can you view the ECC memory logs?
   A. System
   B. Health
   C. Input Devices
   D. Memory
   B. Health. The Health section of the Compaq Diagnostics contains the system health logs, POST logs, and the ECC memory logs.

6. In what file does the System Configuration Record store the current diagnostics information?
   A. BASE.LOG
   B. CURRENT.LOG
   C. NOW.LOG
   D. SYSTEM.LOG
   C. NOW.LOG stores the current diagnostics information. BASE.LOG stores configuration information from the first time the Compaq System Configuration Record was run.

7. Under what heading in Insight Manager LC can you view inventory information?
   A. Alerts
   B. Update PC
   C. Administrator Settings
   D. View PC
   D. View PC. The View PC heading in Insight Manager LC is where you can view all system information.

8. Where in Insight Manager LC would you go to set the ping range?
   A. Administrator Settings
   B. Diagnostics
   C. Alerts
   D. View PC
   A. Administrator Settings. Administrator Settings is where you configure how PCs will be discovered.

9. How much RAM is required for Insight Manager XE if you intend to install Microsoft SQL Server on the same server as Insight Manager XE?

A. 128MB

B. 96MB

C. 64MB

D. 32MB

A. 128MB. If you intend to install Insight Manager on the same server as SQL, you will need 128MB RAM. 96MB is required to install SQL on a separate server.

10. What is the Insight Manager XE administration port?

A. 25

B. 64

C. 128

D. 280

D. 280. Port 280 is the Insight Manager XE administration port. To administer a server, you would type the URL as http://*server_name*:280.

11. Which of the following is not a method used by Insight Manager XE to gather information?

A. Device Discovery

B. Polling

C. Querying

D. Sampling

D. Sampling. Insight Manager XE gathers information through device discovery, polling, and querying.

12. Where in Insight Manager XE would you go to configure the name of the SQL server where the Insight Manager database is stored?

A. SQL

B. Accounts

C. Server

D. Login

C. Server. Server is where you would configure SNMP settings and the SQL Server name, user ID, and password.

13. How many clusters are supported by the Compaq Intelligent Cluster Administrator?

A. Two

B. Four

C. Six

D. Ten

C. Six. Compaq Intelligent Cluster Manager will support up to six predefined clusters.

14. Under what heading in the Compaq Power Console will you find UPS run-time?

A. Startup Timing

B. PowerScope

C. Diagnostics

D. Shutdown/Reboot

B. PowerScope. PowerScope controls UPS run-time, circuitry bypass, filtering, and enhanced battery management.

15. Where would you go in the Compaq Power Console to configure a startup delay?

A. Startup Timing
B. Diagnostics
C. PowerScope
D. Delay Timing
A. Startup Timing. Startup Timing can be used to configure startup delays on systems with multiple load segments.

Chapter 24 Answers

1. The RIB is a PCI card for which of the following reasons?
   A. The PCI bus has a wider bandwidth than the other busses.
   B. The ISA bus is too complex to configure easily.
   C. The EISA bus is slower.
   D. All of the above
   D. All of the above. The PCI bus is a generation ahead of the EISA, which in turn is a generation ahead of the ISA bus. The newer generation offers increased speed and configurability, and more data can travel across it.
2. In its standard configuration, the RIB includes which of the following?
   A. 14.4-Mbps modem
   B. 28.8-Mbps modem
   C. 10/100-Mbps network interface
   D. RS-232 serial interface
   C. 10/100-Mbps network interface. The RIB initially can connect to a local-area network. Modems and serial ports are options that are easily upgradeable, thanks to the PC Card port included on the card.
3. To send alphanumeric pages directly, the RIB must be connected to what?
   A. The network
   B. A modem
   C. A client workstation
   D. Compaq's Web site
   B. A modem. Notifications are possible across a network, but to send messages directly to a pager, the RIB must be connected to a modem (which must be connected to a phone line).
4. What function does the RIB perform for a managed server?
   A. Graphics adapter
   B. Network adapter
   C. Hard drive controller
   D. Second processor
   A. Graphics adapter. The RIB takes over all display functions for the server, either replacing a separate graphics card or disabling the integrated adapter. As the graphics controller, the RIB is able to capture all text screens for remote control or capture.
5. Before installing the RIB, it's important to check the version of what major server component?
   A. Operating system
   B. Network driver

C. BIOS
D. Remote control software
C. BIOS. The Basic Input/Output System for the server controls all of the information that passes through a server. If the BIOS is outdated, it might not support the RIB, and the RIB won't function correctly.

6. The RIB's keyboard cable allows what RIB feature to function?

A. Remote control
B. Remote reset
C. Remote notification
D. Remote capture
A. Remote control. While the display and capture of the RIB data would still be possible without the keyboard cable connected properly, no keystrokes could be sent from the RIB to the computer, negating the control portion of remote control.

7. Access to the RIB's features is available through which interfaces?

A. A Web browser
B. A dedicated, high-end workstation
C. A UNIX-based desktop system
D. All of the above
D. All of the above. All of the RIB's features are available through its Web interface. The only requirements for access are that a machine has network access to the RIB, the TCP/IP protocol, and a Web browser.

8. The RIB's Remote Console feature only allows access to which of the following?

A. Text screens
B. Graphic screens
C. Both text and graphic screens
D. Neither text nor graphic screens
A. Text screens. By itself, the RIB can only capture and monitor text-based screens. If the system switches to a graphics mode, the RIB cannot monitor or capture the screen output. However, control can be passed to a third-party remote control software package when the graphic screens load, so remote control of graphic screens is possible.

9. What will happen if a managed server loses power?

A. The RIB will stop functioning
B. The RIB will continue to operate using its internal battery
C. The RIB will display warning messages on the screen
D. The RIB will provide power to the server
B. The RIB will continue to operate using its internal battery. The RIB is equipped with a rechargeable battery that will automatically provide power should the server that the RIB is managing lose power.

10. The RIB uses what protocol for sending alerts across a network?

A. SMTP
B. RSH
C. Telnet
D. SNMP
D. SNMP. Simple Network Management Protocol is a standard management protocol used by many devices and software programs around the world. It is an integral part of the TCP/IP protocol and the RIB supports forwarding traps to any SMNP management software.

11. To install or upgrade a modem in a RIB, which of the following actions must be performed?

A. Purchase a PC Card modem.
B. Purchase a USB modem.
C. Install a software patch.
D. Upgrade the RIB's firmware.
A. Purchase a PC Card modem. The RIB includes a PC Card slot for future expandability. To install or upgrade a modem, just buy a PC Card modem and slide it into the appropriate slot. You might still need drivers that are compatible with the operating system.

12. To communicate with a RIB, computers on a network need which protocol?

A. NetBEUI
B. IPX/SPX
C. NWLink
D. TCP/IP
D. TCP/IP. The RIB only supports TCP/IP and will not function with any other network protocol. All of the RIB's features, from Remote Console to Alert Forwarding use subsets of the TCP/IP protocol suite.

13. Up to ten users can be configured with what type of access to the RIB?

A. Access the Remote Console
B. Receive alerts
C. Reset the server
D. All of the above
D. All of the above. Users can be configured to access the Remote Console, receive alerts, and reset the server. You can also give a user access to create or change the list of allowed users.

14. The RIB can capture which of the following screen types?

A. Boot text
B. Graphical OS startup screens
C. Both A and B
D. Neither A or B
A. Boot text. The RIB only forwards and stores the boot text of a managed server up to the point where any graphical screens are displayed. Once a graphical screen appears, the RIB must hand remote control capabilities over to a third-party software package.

15. For a RIB to reboot a managed server, the server must:

A. Be reachable across a router
B. Have a responsive operating system
C. Have a RIB installed
D. Have Remote Reboot enabled in the Insight Agents

C. Have a RIB installed. As long as the RIB is installed and functioning, it can reboot a server. If network connectivity is down for any reason, all of the RIB's functions can be accessed through the optional modem, regardless of what shape the server or operating system is in.

Chapter 25 Answers

1. Version Control is a _____ of the managed server.

   A. Task

   B. Service

   C. Agent

   D. Element

   A. Task. Version Control is a task of the managed server. Right-click the desired server to bring up the task list.

2. Which of the following statements accurately describes Version Control?

   A. It upgrades drivers and agents.

   B. It controls driver and agent installation.

   C. It checks for current versions of Compaq software.

   D. It groups servers in a hierarchical structure.

   C. It checks for current versions of Compaq Software. After selecting the Version Control task from the server task list, Version Control interrogates the server for installed software and compares that information with the Compaq Insight Manager version database.

3. Which color indicates that the installed software is current?

   A. Green

   B. Yellow

   C. Red

   D. Black

   A. Green. Green is the color one hopes to find. It indicates that the installed software is current. No further action is required.

4. Which color indicates that an upgrade is available?

   A. Green

   B. Yellow

   C. Red

   D. Black

   B. Yellow. Yellow indicates that an upgrade is available. Although out of date, the software may not need to be upgraded. Version Control reports the reason for the upgrade when you highlight the component marked in yellow.

5. Red-coded software indicates that an upgrade is:

   A. Not necessary

   B. Available

   C. Recommended

   D. Unavailable

   C. Recommended. Red-coded software indicates that an upgrade is recommended. Generally, you should place a high priority on upgrading this software. You can determine the reason for the upgrade by highlighting the component marked in red.

6. What are the two main categories of upgrade reasons?
   A. Resolved problems and new features
   B. Resolved problems and server health
   C. Asset control and new features
   D. Asset control and server health
   A. Resolved problems and new features. There are two main categories of upgrade reasons: resolved problems and new features. These are further subdivided into major and minor reasons.
7. Which category of upgrade reasons is reserved for those situations that can cause a server failure or loss of data?
   A. Major new feature
   B. Minor new feature
   C. Major resolved problem
   D. Minor resolved problem
   C. Major resolved problem. A major resolved problem refers to a problem that can cause a server failure or loss of data. These problems exist in common system configurations. Version Control color codes could be red or yellow. Though Version Control may indicate these resolved problems with yellow, they should be addressed as soon as they are discovered.
8. Which category of upgrade reasons fixes system problems that are rarely seen?
   A. Major new feature
   B. Minor new feature
   C. Major resolved problem
   D. Minor resolved problem
   D. Minor resolved problem. A minor resolved problem fixes system problems that are rarely seen. It can also fix inconveniences for which you may have a workaround, but would prefer to resolve.
9. Which category of upgrade reasons reflects upgrades that support new hardware?
   A. Major new feature
   B. Minor new feature
   C. Major resolved problem
   D. Minor resolved problem
   A. Major new feature. A major new feature reflects upgrades that support new hardware. A common upgrade in this category is the system ROM.
10. Which category of upgrade reasons reflects performance enhancements?
    A. Major new feature
    B. Minor new feature
    C. Major resolved problem
    D. Minor resolved problem
    B. Minor new feature. Minor new feature upgrades reflect performance enhancements. They generally involve improved software code.
11. The Version Control menu line option allows you to do which of the following?
    A. Upgrade the Version Control database
    B. Check software versions on a server
    C. Upgrade drivers on a server
    D. Schedule software upgrades
    A. Upgrade the Version Control

database. The Version Control facility allows you to download a current database. From the Compaq Insight Manager menu line, select Version Control. The drop-down menu lets you upgrade the database from CD or diskette, or from the Internet.

12. Compaq includes the Version Control database on:

    A. Server Profile Disk
    B. SmartStart CD
    C. Server Configuration Disk
    D. Compaq/Windows NT Resource CD
    B. SmartStart CD. Compaq includes the Version Control database on each SmartStart and Management CD. As an ASE, you will receive a subscription to SmartStart that will continue as long as you maintain your ASE status.

13. Which of the following is the Version Control database file?

    A. SYSMGMT.SYS
    B. CPQRIB.SYS
    C. DBINFO.DB_
    D. TRAPDBH.DB_
    C. DBINFO.DB_. The Version Control database file is DBINFO.DB_.

14. Besides CD, another source for the Version Control database is:

    A. Info Messenger
    B. Internet
    C. System Partition
    D. Server Support Diskettes
    B. Internet. Another source for the Version Control database is the Internet. Downloading the database from the Internet is quick and easy, and provides a far more current source of the database than the CD.

15. What is the recommended interval for upgrading the Version Control database?

    A. 15 days
    B. 20 days
    C. 30 days
    D. 45 days
    C. 30 days. Compaq Insight Manager utilizes a reminder feature with Version Control. By default, Version Control will remind you every 60 days that you may wish to download the latest database. You can change the default value during the installation of Compaq Insight Manager. Considering the frequency of system changes, it is recommended that the default value be set to 30 days.

Chapter 26 Answers

1. What is the name of Compaq's centralized software store?

    A. Integration Server
    B. SmartStart
    C. Compaq Support Software Server
    D. I386
    C. Compaq Support Software Server. This is the server that Compaq

maintains with copies of all of the software available.

2. Which is not an OS that is supported by Integration Server?
   A. OS/2
   B. Netware 3.*x*
   C. Windows NT 3.51
   D. IntranetWare
   A. OS/2. Netware 3.*x*, 4.1, IntranetWare, and Windows 3.51 or 4.0 are all acceptable OSs on which to install an Integration Server.

3. What is Compaq's utility for updating the software on a server?
   A. Compaq Insight Manager
   B. Compaq Integration Maintenance Utility
   C. SmartStart
   D. Compaq SSD
   B. Compaq Insight Maintenance Utility. The CIMU provides you with a list of software versions available on the IS to install on the server.

4. What file is used to identify the resources available on the Integration Server?
   A. NWSNUT.NLM
   B. COMPAQ.PEZ
   C. CPQMAINT.NLM
   D. SPUU.EXE
   B. COMPAQ.PEZ contains a list of all of the software available on the IS.

5. What utility is used to update and maintain the Integration Server?
   A. Compaq Insight Manager
   B. Compaq Integration Maintenance Utility
   C. SmartStart
   D. Compaq SSD
   A. Compaq Insight Manager. CIM provides the functionality to update the IS using the Internet, dial-up, or from CD.

6. What is the directory structure necessary to create an Integration Server?
   A. \\SERVERNAME\CPQIS\CPQIS1
   B. \\SERVERNAME\IS\COMPAQ
   C. \\SERVERNAME\CPQIS1\CPQIS
   D. \\SERVERNAME\CPQIS\CPQIS
   C. \\SERVERNAME\CPQIS1\CPQIS is the directory structure necessary to create an Integration Server

7. What is required to allow access to the Integration Server from SmartStart?
   A. A Windows NT domain account named CPQIS1
   B. An user account with password CPQIS1
   C. Compaq Integration Maintenance Utility
   D. An account local to the server named CPQIS1
   D. A local account named CPQIS1. The account named CPQIS1 must exist on the Integration Server; whether it is a NetWare or Windows NT server.

8. Which is not a method that can be used to update the software on a server?

   A. Remote attended

   B. Remote unattended

   C. Automatic

   D. Local
   C. Automatic. There are three options available for updating the server: Local, remote attended, and remote unattended.

9. Which is not a method that can be used to update the Integration Server?

   A. Internet

   B. Dial-up

   C. File copy

   D. CD
   C. File copy. Using CIM, you can update the IS using the Internet, dial-up, or CD.

10. What is the limitation of the CIMU on NetWare?

    A. It does not update Insight Agents.

    B. It does not update the system partition.

    C. It does not update drivers.

    D. It does not show current driver versions.
    B. It does not update the system partition. The System Partition Update Utility exists only on the Windows NT version of the CIMU.

Chapter 27 Answers

1. What is the difference between the two-tiered architecture and three-tiered architecture with respect to network management?

   A. Management Server

   B. Management Console

   C. Host Systems

   D. Network Equipment
   A. Management Server. The three-tiered approach adds the Management Server that sits in between the management console and the rest of the managed equipment. This allows a single management console to manage many different devices in a heterogeneous environment.

2. What is the role of the Management Server in WBEM's three-tiered architecture?

   A. Runs management agents

   B. Gathers management agents information from managed devices

   C. Generates HTML pages

   D. Both answers B and C
   D. Both answers B and C.
   The Management Server reads information from the agents that are running on the managed devices on the network. The server then generates HTML pages, which can be read from the management console using a Web browser.

3. Which of the following is not an advantage to using Web technology for systems management?

   A. Can manage from different platforms
   B. Simplified interface
   C. Need Insight Manager installed
   D. Can manage from anywhere on the network
   C. Need Insight Manager installed. You do not need Insight Manager installed for Web management since you can use any compliant browser. The benefit to this is that you free disk space and you do not have to learn another application to manage your systems.

4. Which of the following is not a component of the Insight Agents?

   A. Foundation Agent
   B. Drive Array Agent
   C. Server Agent
   D. NIC Agent
   B. Drive Array Agent. There is no Drive Array Agent. The four components of the Insight Agents are the Foundation Agent, the Server Agent, the NIC Agent, and the Storage Agent.

5. What else do you need to install before installing Internet Explorer on a Windows NT Workstation?

   A. Post SP4 Y2K Patch
   B. Compaq Server Support Disk for Windows NT
   C. Service Pack 3 or higher
   D. Internet Explorer 128-bit High Security Patch
   C. Service Pack 3 or higher. You need to install SP3 or higher before installing Internet Explorer 4.

6. What TCP port do the Web Agents use?

   A. 21
   B. 80
   C. 1971
   D. 2301
   D. 2301. The Compaq Web Agents use port 2301. To connect to the Web agents, you must specify the port to connect to, otherwise, you may connect to another service.

7. Which of the following URLs is a valid address to access the Insight Web Agents?

   A. Servername:2301
   B. http://servername:2301
   C. http://servername
   D. http://servername:1971
   B. http://servername:2301. In order to access the Insight Web Agents, you must specify both the protocol (http) and the port (2301) in the URL.

8. What are the three frames that compose the browser window when managing a server with the Insight Web Agents?

   A. Title frame
   B. Navigation frame
   C. Options Frame

D. Data frame

C. Options Frame. The title frame displays the current version of the agents as well as the four navigation links. The navigation frame displays the server's subsystem components. When you click a subsystem component, the information is displayed in the data frame.

9. You'd like to remove anonymous access to the Web Agents. How would you accomplish this?

A. Deselect Anonymous Access

B. Delete Anonymous account

C. Disable Guest Account in NT User Manager

D. Change default port

A. Deselect Anonymous Access. This is done from the Options link from the device home page. You cannot delete the Anonymous account.

10. Which agent is responsible for displaying information for the system board?

A. Foundation Agent

B. Server Agent

C. Storage Agent

D. NIC Agent

B. Server Agent. The Server Agent is responsible for displaying the information for the system board. The Foundation Agent displays basic server information such as software versions and file system space usage. The Storage Agent displays information for the storage subsystem, including disk controllers and disk drives. The NIC Agent displays information for the network controllers and network protocols.

11. Which file would you edit to modify the default security permissions for the Web Agents?

A. WWWAGENT.INI

B. CIM.INI

C. CIMWEB.INI

D. WEBAGENT.INI

D. WEBAGENT.INI. You can modify this file to change the default permissions for the login accounts. This file is located in %SYSTEMROOT%\SYSTEM32\CPQMGMT\WEBAGENT.

12. Which of the following account management tasks can you perform?

A. Delete an account.

B. Rename an account.

C. Change the password.

D. Disable an account.

C. Change the password. In this release of the Web agents, you can only modify the account's password. You cannot delete, rename, or disable an account. The first thing you should do after installing the Web agents is to change the administrator's password.

13. Which of the following is not an advantage of Insight Manager XE over Insight Manager?

A. It can manage third-party devices.
B. It can manage devices using a Web browser.
C. It automatically discovers devices on the network.
D. It can create user accounts.
B. It can manage devices using a Web browser. Insight Manager also allows you to manage devices using a Web browser, although the devices are limited to Compaq servers.

14. Which protocol is not supported by Insight Manager XE for data collection?

A. HTTP
B. SNMP
C. DMI
D. FTP
D. FTP. Insight Manager XE supports data collection from clients that are running HTTP, SNMP, or DMI V2.

15. Which of the following features is not included with Insight Manager XE?

A. Automatic Data Collection
B. Version Control
C. Integration Server Management
D. All of the above
D. All of the above. Neither Automatic Data Collection, nor Version Control, nor Integration Server Management is included with the Insight Manager XE software, although all are planned for future releases.

Chapter 28 Answers

1. How many inbound user connections is Windows NT Workstation limited to?

A. 5
B. 10
C. 100
D. There is no limit.
B. 10. Windows NT Workstation is programmed to accept only 10 simultaneous inbound connections. This includes connections to shares, printers, or Web sites.

2. Which of the following statements is not a reason to use Windows NT Server rather than Windows NT Workstation as a file server in a medium to large networking environment?

A. Server is optimized for a multiuser environment, while Workstation is optimized for user applications.
B. Server has fault tolerance capabilities, while Workstation does not.
C. Server has no limits on the number of inbound connections, while Workstation has a limit of 10.
D. Server has multiprocessor capabilities, while Workstation does not.
D. Server has multiprocessor capabilities, while Workstation does not. This statement is false, since Workstation does support up to two processors. Windows NT Server has greater scalability since it supports up to four processors out of the box and can support up to 32 processors from certain vendors.

3. You are the network administrator of a large company. You are asked to design a server that must have 24/7 uptime capability. This server will be running a mission-critical application. Which version of Windows NT should you use?

   A. Windows NT Workstation
   B. Windows NT Server
   C. Windows NT Server, Enterprise Edition
   D. Windows NT Server, Terminal Server Edition
   C. Windows NT Server, Enterprise Edition. The Enterprise Edition adds the features that you need in a mission-critical server, such as increased performance and scalability, Microsoft Cluster Server support, and Windows NT Load Balancing System.

4. Which of the following comprise the two modes in which Windows NT runs processes?

   A. User mode and kernel mode
   B. Safe mode and user mode
   C. Privileged mode and protected mode
   D. Environment mode and executive mode
   A. User mode and kernel mode. User applications run in user mode, which does not have direct access to hardware. Device drivers and the NT Executive run in kernel mode, which does have direct access to hardware.

5. Which component of the Windows NT Executive hides the details of the hardware from user applications?

   A. Microkernel
   B. Hardware Abstraction Layer
   C. Process Manager
   D. I/O Manager
   B. Hardware Abstraction Layer. The HAL hides the details of the hardware from user applications by translating hardware requests from the application appropriately for the hardware installed in the system. This allows Windows NT to support a variety of hardware platforms with the same code base, with the simple replacement of the HAL.

6. Which component of the Windows NT Executive is responsible for scheduling process threads?

   A. Microkernel
   B. Hardware Abstraction Layer
   C. I/O Manager
   D. Process Manager
   A. Microkernel. The Microkernel is responsible for scheduling threads to run on available processors. The process manager does not actually schedule the threads, but it does create and delete individual processes and threads.

7. Which of the following is not a component of the I/O Manager?

A. Cache Manager
B. File system driver
C. Network driver
D. Graphics device driver
D. Graphics device driver. The graphics device driver is not part of the I/O Manager. Instead, it communicates directly with WIN32K.SYS, which includes the Window Manager and the GDI, to provide graphic I/O to the operating system.

8. What is asynchronous I/O?

A. An application must wait for each I/O request to be fulfilled.
B. An application can perform other functions after submitting an I/O request.
C. An application submits an I/O request to a serial port.
D. An application submits an I/O request to the network.
B. An application can perform other functions after submitting an I/O request. This is a performance enhancement, since the application does not have to wait for the I/O request to be completed. It can perform other tasks, since the I/O device is usually much slower than the processor.

9. Which of the following is not an example of an object in Windows NT?

A. Files
B. Directories
C. Threads
D. Kernel mode
D. Kernel mode. Kernel mode refers to a privileged mode in which the code has direct access to hardware. An object in Windows NT is composed of a data type, attributes, and a set of operations.

10. Which component of the Windows NT Security Subsystem runs in kernel mode?

A. Local Security Authority
B. Security Account Manager
C. Security Reference Monitor
D. Logon Process
C. Security Reference Monitor. The Security Reference Monitor is the only component that is part of the Windows NT Executive, which runs in kernel mode. The other components, along with the Security Policy Database, Audit Log, and User Account Database, all run in user mode.

11. How are processes and threads related?

A. A thread is a piece of a process.
B. A process is a piece of a thread.
C. A process schedules a thread.
D. A thread schedules a process.
A. A thread is a piece of a process. A thread is the most basic piece of a process that can be scheduled processor time. The Process Manager takes care of scheduling threads.

12. How does the MS-DOS environment differ from the Win16 environment?

A. Each Win16 application runs in its own NTVDM.

B. Each DOS application runs in its own NTVDM.

C. Each DOS application runs as a thread within a single NTVDM.

D. DOS applications can be configured to run in a separate memory space.

B. Each DOS application runs in its own NTVDM. Win16 applications all run in a single NTVDM. However, you can configure a Win16 application to run in a separate memory space.

13. Which of the following is a limitation of the POSIX subsystem?

A. The application must be installed on an NTFS partition.

B. The application must be installed on a FAT partition.

C. The application must be installed on a FAT32 partition.

D. The application must be installed on a UNIX partition.

A. The application must be installed on an NTFS partition. Since POSIX requires certain attributes when accessing the file system (such as case-sensitive file naming), you must install these applications on an NTFS partition.

14. How are environment systems protected from each other?

A. Each environment system runs in kernel mode.

B. Each environment system must be installed on a separate partition.

C. Each environment system runs in its own process.

D. Each environment system runs as a separate thread.

C. Each environment system runs in its own process. Since each environment system runs in its own process, it is assigned its own memory space independent of the other environment systems.

15. Which components of Windows NT were moved to the NT Executive with Windows NT 4.0?

A. Win32 Subsystem

B. Local Security Authority

C. Console functions

D. Window Manager

D. Window Manager. The Window Manager, along with other graphics functions, was moved to the NT Executive with Windows NT 4.0 in order to improve performance. These components originally ran in the Win32 subsystem prior to Windows NT 4.0.

Chapter 29 Answers

1. Which of the following is not part of the Server Setup and Management Pack?

A. SmartStart CD
B. Management CD
C. Windows NT CD
D. Server Profile Disk
C. Windows NT CD. The Windows NT CD is not part of the Server Setup and Management Pack. You must provide a copy of the Windows NT Server CD for the SmartStart installation.

2. What is the minimum amount of memory required to run a SmartStart installation?

A. 16MB
B. 24MB
C. 32MB
D. 64MB
C. 32MB. SmartStart needs a minimum of 32MB of memory to run.

3. You boot an older Compaq server with the SmartStart CD in the drive. You receive the error message that the disk is not bootable and to insert a bootable disk. You've tried this same CD in another server and it worked fine. How can you fix the problem?

A. Update the system ROM.
B. Replace the CD-ROM.
C. Create a boot disk.
D. Boot to the Server Profile Disk.
A. Update the system ROM. The older system ROM may not support booting to the CD-ROM drive. After flashing the system ROM, you should be able to boot to the SmartStart CD.

4. Which SmartStart installation path provides the most flexibility?

A. Assisted Integration
B. Manual Configuration
C. Replicated Installation
B. Manual Configuration. This path lets SmartStart configure the hardware, then allows you to perform a manual installation of Windows NT. This allows you greater flexibility in the installation of Windows NT, but requires greater knowledge of Windows NT and should only be used by experienced administrators.

5. You have 10 servers to set up for remote offices. Each of the servers is configured identically. Which is the fastest method for deploying these servers?

A. Assisted Integration
B. Disk Cloning
C. Manual Configuration
D. Replicated Installation
D. Replicated Installation. Run SmartStart on the first server using Assisted Integration and select the option to create a replication disk. For the remaining servers, simply run the Replicated Installation path of SmartStart.

6. Which of the following operating systems does not support the Assisted Integration path for SmartStart?

A. Windows NT Server 4.0

B. Windows NT Server 4.0, Enterprise Edition

C. Windows NT Server 4.0, Terminal Server Edition

D. Novell NetWare 5

C. Windows NT Server 4.0, Terminal Server Edition. You can install this version using Manual Configuration. The other operating systems listed can be installed using the Assisted Integration path.

7. What is the purpose of the Server Profile Disk?

A. Temporary storage for SmartStart

B. Used for Replicated Install

C. Storing emergency repair information

D. Storing copy of server configuration

A. Temporary storage for SmartStart. SmartStart uses the Server Profile Disk to keep track of progress during the setup.

8. What is stored on the system partition?

A. Windows NT system files

B. Compaq system utilities

C. Emergency repair information

D. Windows NT boot files

B. Compaq system utilities. These utilities include the System Configuration Utility, Server Diagnostics, and other Compaq utilities. The System Partition is created during the SmartStart process.

9. Which of the following is not a part of Automatic Server Recovery (ASR)?

A. Software Recovery

B. Thermal Shutdown

C. Emergency Repair Disk (ERD)

D. UPS Shutdown

C. Emergency Repair Disk (ERD). The other three are critical components of the Automatic Server Recovery, which enables a server to detect and recover from hardware failures. The ERD is used by Windows NT to recover critical operating system information.

10. What is the largest size you can make the primary Windows NT partition during a SmartStart installation?

A. 250MB

B. 4GB

C. 4GB if formatted FAT, unlimited if formatted NTFS

D. Unlimited

B. 4GB. No matter how you format the first partition, it is always limited to 4GB. This is because even NTFS partitions start off as FAT, which has a limit of 4GB.

11. What is the best way to create an Emergency Repair Disk?

A. Copy REPAIR directory to a floppy disk.

B. Run ERDDISK.EXE.

C. Run RDISK.EXE.

D. Run NTBACKUP.EXE.
C. Run RDISK.EXE. The best way to create the ERD is to run RDISK. Since Windows NT updates the repair information in %SYSTEMROOT%\REPAIR before creating the ERD, answer A is also a correct answer.

12. In which of the following cases would you perform a Manual Configuration install of SmartStart?

A. You need to create a Windows NT partition greater than 4GB.

B. You need to create a custom Administrator's password.

C. You need to install Windows NT Server 4.0, Enterprise Edition.

D. You need to install Windows NT to D:\NTSRV4.
D. You need to install Windows NT to D:\NTSRV4. Since an Assisted Integration always installs Windows NT to C:\WINNT, you will need to run a Manual Configuration to install to a different drive and directory. Answer A is not a valid scenario due to the 4GB size limit on the first Windows NT partition. Both Answers B and C are available with the Assisted Integration.

13. One advantage to using an Integration Server is:

A. You update software in only one place.

B. You don't need network connectivity at time of installation.

C. You don't have to keep Integration Server up-to-date.

D. You don't need much time to set up Integration Server.
A. You update software in only one place. An Integration Server acts as a central repository for Compaq software. Instead of carrying CDs with you, you can load software on any server from the Integration Server.

14. Which of the following is not necessary to configure if you are installing software from an Integration Server during SmartStart?

A. Server IP address

B. Local IP address

C. Default gateway

D. Subnet mask
C. Default gateway. If the server you are building and the Integration Server are on the same subnet, you do not need to configure a default gateway. The other options are required.

15. You have decided not to use SmartStart to build your server. At a minimum, what do you have to do before installing Windows NT?

A. Format hard disk.

B. Run System Configuration Utility.

C. Create Windows NT setup disks.

D. Create system partition.
B. Run System Configuration Utility. Running the System Configuration Utility will allow all the hardware in the server to be detected and configured.

Chapter 30 Answers

1. Which of the following is not a source where you can obtain the Compaq Server Support Diskettes?

   A. SmartStart CD

   B. Diskette Builder

   C. Management CD

   D. Compaq Web Site
   C. Management CD. You can obtain the SSD from the SmartStart CD using the Diskette Builder application or by downloading the latest version from Compaq's Web site.

2. What does a gray icon next to a driver name indicate in the SSD Custom Options screen?

   A. The driver is installed properly.

   B. The driver is not installed.

   C. The driver is installed but not the latest version.

   D. The driver is disabled.
   B. The driver is not installed. The gray icon indicates the driver is not installed. A yellow icon indicates the driver is installed but is not the latest version. A green icon indicates the driver is installed and is the latest version.

3. What does HAL stand for?

   A. Hardware Application Layer

   B. Hardware Abstraction Level

   C. Hardware Application Level

   D. Hardware Abstraction Layer
   D. Hardware Abstraction Layer. The HAL "hides" the hardware from the rest of the operating system and allows application developers to write a single set of source code that can be used on a variety of hardware platforms.

4. Which of the following best describes Compaq's HAL support for Windows NT 4.0?

   A. You can load the HAL from the SSD.

   B. The Compaq HAL can be found on the SmartStart CD.

   C. The HAL can be found on the Windows NT CD.

   D. The HAL can be found on the Management CD.
   C. The HAL can be found on the Windows NT CD. For Windows NT 4.0, Compaq did not develop a custom HAL and instead uses the HAL provided by Microsoft. The HAL is automatically installed during the Windows NT setup.

5. What should you do after adding a second processor to your server?

   A. Run the Compaq SSD.

   B. Back up your server and reinstall NT.

   C. Nothing, Windows NT will automatically detect the second processor.

   D. Manually copy the multiprocessor HAL to the System32 directory.
   A. Run the Compaq SSD. The SSD will upgrade the HAL to support the

second processor. Windows NT will not automatically use the second processor, but you also do not have to reinstall NT for it to detect the second processor.

6. What is the best method to recover from a HAL mismatch?
   - A. Select HAL Recovery Option during Windows NT bootup.
   - B. Reinstall Windows NT.
   - C. Restore Windows NT from a previous backup.
   - D. Reinstall the second processor.

   A. Select HAL Recovery Option during Windows NT bootup. A HAL mismatch occurs when you are running a multiprocessor HAL with only one processor installed. Although all of the options listed will get your server up and running, answer A is the quickest and best method to get Windows NT back up.

7. Which of the following are characteristics of the Systems Management driver?
   - A. Automatic Server Recovery
   - B. Allows you to perform a shutdown script
   - C. Logs corrected memory errors
   - D. All of the above

   D. All of the above. In addition to the three characteristics listed, the Systems Management drivers also allow critical errors logging, thermal shutdown, remote console operation, and remote rebooting.

8. What must you do before modifying the BOOT.INI file?
   - A. Enable the Systems Management driver.
   - B. Remove the read-only and hidden attributes.
   - C. Load Insight Manager.
   - D. Specify a Timeout value in Control Panel.

   B. Remove the read-only and hidden attributes. Before you can edit the BOOT.INI file, you have to remove these two attributes by going to the file properties. After you finish modifying the file, don't forget to reset the attributes.

9. Where can you find the drivers for Compaq tape drives?
   - A. Windows NT CD
   - B. Compaq SSD
   - C. Compaq SmartStart CD
   - D. Compaq Web site

   A. Windows NT CD. The Compaq tape drives are supported out of the box on the Windows NT CD. You can also find updated drivers in the Windows NT service packs. The only exception is the Compaq 35/70 DLT tape drive driver, which you must download from the Compaq Web site.

10. Which of the following is not a requirement for the Insight Management Agents?

A. TCP/IP protocol
B. SNMP service
C. 64MB of RAM
D. Compaq SSD
C. 64MB of RAM. In addition to TCP/IP, SNMP, and Compaq SSD, the Insight Agents require a minimum of 25MB free disk space and Windows NT Server 3.51 Service Pack 5 or Windows NT Server 4.0 Service Pack 3 or greater.

11. Which of the following is not an advantage of using the Compaq version of the SMART Array controller driver, as opposed to using the Microsoft version of the driver?
A. Ability to use Performance Monitor to track statistics of the array controller
B. Ability to manage using Insight Manager
C. Ability to hot-plug the array controller card
D. Increased performance and fault tolerance
A. Ability to use Performance Monitor to track statistics of the array controller. The Compaq version of the driver allows increased performance and manageability of the card as well as hot-pluggability.

12. What is load shedding?
A. The capacity of the UPS to balance the load among different servers
B. Shutting down nonessential servers to save power for critical servers in the event of a power loss
C. The term used for how a server connects to a UPS through the serial port
D. The term used for power consumption of a server
B. Shutting down nonessential servers to save power for critical servers in the event of a power loss. Load shedding allows your more critical servers to run longer on UPS power, or gives them more time to ensure a proper and graceful shutdown.

13. When would you not use the ProLiant Storage System driver?
A. If you have Windows NT Service Pack 4 installed
B. If the storage unit is connected to a SCSI controller
C. If the storage unit is connected to a SMART Array controller
D. If the server is a ProLiant 2500
C. If the storage unit is connected to a SMART Array controller. When the storage unit is connected to an array controller, you do not need to load the Storage System driver, since the array controller driver will take care of managing the storage unit.

14. You manage your server using Insight Manager. You want to check statistics for the server's SCSI controllers, but Insight Manager shows no statistics. The SCSI controllers are working properly, since all devices are functioning properly. What is the probable cause?

A. Windows NT Service Pack 4 is not installed.

B. The Microsoft SCSI driver is loaded.

C. You are running Insight Manager earlier than version 4.0.

D. There is a SCSI ID conflict.
B. The Microsoft SCSI driver is loaded. To enable tracking statistics, you must load the Compaq version of the SCSI driver from the Compaq SSD.

15. How would you upgrade an NT 3.51 server over the network?

A. Run WINNT.EXE /B.

B. Run WINNT32.EXE /B.

C. Run WINNT.EXE /OX.

D. Run WINNT32.EXE /OX.
B. Run WINNT32.EXE /B. The /B parameter first copies the Windows NT source files to a temporary directory on the hard disk. WINNT.EXE is the 16-bit version of the Windows NT setup program and is used when upgrading a Windows OS other than NT to version 4.0.

16. You try to reboot a server remotely using Insight Manager but the server does not reboot. What is the most likely cause?

A. The Enable Remote Reboot option is not set.

B. You do not have administrative rights on the server.

C. The Systems Management driver is not loaded.

D. The Insight Agents are not installed.
A. The Enable Remote Reboot option is not set. You can enable this option in the Insight Agents applet in Control Panel.

17. What is a characteristic of the Smart Switch Mode in the Advanced Network Control Utility?

A. Transmits data using the network card that is the least busy

B. Automatically throttles network bandwidth

C. Automatically switches back to the primary NIC after it comes back online

D. Automatically uses both network cards, effectively doubling network throughput
C. The Smart Switch Mode will automatically switch back to the primary NIC after it comes back online. If the primary NIC fails, the Advanced Network Control Utility will automatically switch traffic to the secondary NIC. When the primary comes back online (either reconnected to the network or replaced), the ANCU will automatically switch on the primary NIC.

18. What must you do before you remove a hot-plug PCI device?

A. Power down the server.

B. Stop the Server service.

C. Use the PCI Hot Plug Utility.

D. Do nothing.
C. Use the PCI Hot Plug Utility. Use this utility to stop power to the slot in which the device is installed.

19. What utility can you use to print a list of the versions of all Compaq drivers currently installed on your server?

A. Version Control

B. File Manager

C. Windows Explorer

D. Compaq Server Support Diskette
A. Version Control. Although you can use the other three options to find the driver version, they do not allow you to print a list of all the drivers and their versions. Version Control also will tell you what the installed version is and what is the latest version available.

Chapter 31 Answers

1. Acme Inc's primary Web server has just suffered a hard disk failure. For performance reasons, the drive was attached to a SMART-2 controller, and configured as part of a RAID 0 array. How should the administrator go about recovering from the failure?

A. Replace the failed drive; Automatic Data Recovery on the SMART controller will do the rest.

B. Replace the failed drive and reinstall all data from yesterday's backup.

C. Replace the failed drive, enter Array Configuration Utilities, and choose the Recover option. Follow on-screen prompts.

D. Run Windows NT Setup, choosing Recover when prompted.
B. Replace the failed drive and reinstall all data from yesterday's backup. RAID 0 offers no fault tolerance. In fact, it actually increases the risk of data loss due to drive failure; even a single drive failure would mean complete data loss for the whole array. Automatic Data Recovery can only work on a partition protected by RAID 1, 4, or 5.

2. Which RAID level is not provided in software form as part of Windows NT Server 4.0?

A. RAID 0

B. RAID 1

C. RAID 4

D. RAID 5
C. RAID 4 is not provided in software form, as part of Windows NT Server. If you are required to implement RAID 4, you must choose a hardware RAID solution. RAID levels 0, 1, and 5 can all be implemented using the base Windows NT product. Whenever possible, consider the use of a hardware-accelerated solution, such as Compaq's SMART series, in order to improve performance.

3. You are required to implement a Web server that is not mission-critical. The load on the server may be quite high at times. Which of the following disk configurations would you choose in order to seek the best disk performance?

   A. Software RAID 5, 3x9.1GB SCSI hard disks

   B. Hardware RAID 0, 5x4.3GB SCSI hard disks

   C. Hardware RAID 5, 3x9.1 GB SCSI hard disks

   D. 1x9.1GB IDE hard disk

   B. Hardware RAID 0, 5x4.3GB SCSI hard disks. Hardware RAID 0 would be the best solution is this circumstance. However, if even one of the five drives were to fail in this configuration, the whole array would be lost. Answer D is incorrect because the multiple drives in the RAID 0 configuration allow multiple concurrent read and write operations to be performed on the array. This is obviously not possible on a single drive.

4. Your company needs an e-mail server. Uptime is of prime importance, but finances are limited. The server will house around 200 mailboxes, with an allowance of 15MB per mailbox. Which solution would be most viable?

   A. Hardware RAID 0, 5x4.3GB drives

   B. Hardware RAID 5, 3x2.1GB drives

   C. Software RAID 1, 2x2.1GB drives

   D. Hardware RAID 1, 2x4.3GB drives

   D. Hardware RAID 1, 2x4.3GB drives. While the initial investment by the company in a RAID controller may be more expensive than the software-based RAID employed by Windows NT, the advantages in terms of uptime are obvious. RAID 1 is the most fault tolerant of the available types, and only requires two drives. Performance would be increased by choosing answer B, but the advantages would not be noticeable in this system, which won't really tax the storage systems too much.

5. Your server contains a SMART-2 controller running a single RAID 5-protected volume consisting of 8x4.3GB drives, and 2x4.3 GB drives in RAID 1 storing the operating system. Yesterday, a power surge knocked out two of the drives belonging to the RAID 5 volume. How would you go about repairing the situation?

   A. Replace the drives; Automatic Data Recovery will do the rest.

   B. Replace the drives; restore the data from yesterday's backup.

   C. Replace the drive with the lowest SCSI ID, and let Automatic Data Recovery merge it. Then replace the second drive, and the volume will now be complete.

   D. Select Recover Volume from the System Configuration utilities, and follow screen prompts.

B. Replace the drive; restore the data from yesterday's backup. Unfortunately, anything worse than a single drive failure spells the end for any RAID volume. The only option in this scenario is to restore from backup.

6. Where do you manage software RAID volumes in Windows NT?

    A. Right-click the drive in My Computer in Explorer. Choose Manage Volume from the context menu.
    B. Use the Fault Tolerance tab from within system applet in Control Panel.
    C. Use Disk Administrator in Administrative Tools (common) from the Start menu.
    D. Type **RDISK /config** from the command prompt.

    C. Use Disk Administrator in Administrative Tools (common) from the Start menu. Windows NT uses Disk Administrator to perform all disk management tasks, including the configuration of any software fault tolerance.

7. Your BDC has just suffered a hard disk failure. Fortunately, the drive was part of a software RAID 1 array. After replacing the failed drive, you notice that Windows NT will no longer boot. Which is the best solution?

    A. Reinstall Windows NT on the new hard disk. Once installed, copy all data from the other member of the array.
    B. Format a diskette on a Windows NT workstation, copy NTLDR, NTDETECT.COM, and BOOT.INI to this disk. Modify BOOT.INI to point to the "good" hard disk, then boot this floppy disk.
    C. Run Windows NT Setup, and choose Recover when prompted.
    D. Reinstall Windows NT, and restore data from yesterday's backup.

    B. Format a diskette on a Windows NT workstation, copy NTLDR, NTDETECT.COM, and BOOT.INI to this disk. Modify BOOT.INI to point to the "good" hard disk, then boot this floppy disk. This process will force Windows NT to boot from the functional member of the RAID array. Answer A may work eventually, but would require all applications to be reinstalled. Answer D is unnecessary.

8. As part of an ongoing project, you are required to add a 4.3GB hard disk to a Windows NT 4.0 server, containing a SMART-2 RAID controller. It is a requirement that this hard disk be mirrored to an existing hard disk that has 5GB of unpartitioned space. What is the best way of achieving this?

    A. Create a 4.3GB partition on both the hard disks. Format this space using the NTFS file system, select both of these new partitions, and click Fault Tolerance | Establish Mirror.
    B. Using the Array Configuration utility, select both partitions and assign them to a RAID 1 array.
    C. Using Disk Administrator, select the 4.3GB of unpartitioned space on the

new hard disk. Select Partition | Create, and create a 4.3GB partition. Format this partition using NTFS, and select both this and the unpartitioned space on the other hard disk. Click Fault Tolerance, and establish the mirror.

D. Using WINDISK.EXE, select both areas of unpartitioned space, and click Fault Tolerance | Establish Mirror.
C. Using Disk Administrator, select the 4.3GB of unpartitioned space on the new hard disk. Select Partition | Create, and create a 4.3GB partition. Format this partition using NTFS, and select both this and the unpartitioned space on the other hard disk. Click Fault Tolerance, and establish the mirror. Although it may seem like the obvious choice to use the SMART-2 controller to run RAID 1 arrays, there are a few things the SMART-2 cannot do, such as mirror on a partition basis. Therefore, answer B is incorrect. Answers A and D are incorrect, because to mirror a partition you must have both an existing NTFS partition and an area of unpartitioned space equal to or greater in size than the partition you are mirroring.

9. How many devices are supported by the SMART-2DH series of RAID controllers?

A. 7

B. 11

C. 14

D. 15
C. 14. The SMART-2DH controller consists of two SCSI channels. Each SCSI channel can support seven devices. Therefore, the SMART-2DH can support 14 devices.

10. You have just received your ProLiant 7000 server, fitted with a SMART-2 controller. You will be using the internal drive cages in the ProLiant 7000 to mount 10 4.3GB hard disks, which should be configured as part of a RAID 5 array. You notice that each drive cage on the ProLiant requires a separate SCSI channel. What must you do on the SMART-2 controller to enable this?

A. Feed the external connector of the SMART-2 controller back into the PC.

B. Configure the DEVICES parameter in the System Configuration utility.

C. Obtain a SCSI cable extender.

D. It is not possible, and requires further SMART-2 controllers to be fitted.
A. Feed the external connector of the SMART-2 controller back into the PC. In order to take advantage of more than seven devices, you must use a second SCSI channel. On the SMART-2 controller, this means feeding the external SCSI connector back into the case using the pass-through cable provided.

11. How much cache memory is available on board the SMART-2DH controller?

A. 2MB
B. 6MB
C. 16MB
D. 32MB
C. 16MB. The SMART-2DH controller comes standard with 16MB of battery-backed up cache, known as the array accelerator.

12. You recently added an extra drive to your RAID 5 array. How do you go about expanding your current Windows NT system partition?

A. Assign the drive to the array in the Array Configuration utility. Once online expansion is complete, the size of the system partition will reflect the increased space available to the array.
B. Assign the drive to the array in the Array Configuration utility. Once online expansion is complete, use Disk Administrator to increase the size of the system partition.
C. It is not possible to increase the size of the system partition after creation.
D. Insert the drive. At the next system boot, the controller will launch Array Configuration utilities. Use them to expand the system partition.
C. It is not possible to increase the size of the system partition after creation. Windows NT does not allow the size of the system partition to be modified after installation. This extra space must be allocated to a new partition, and assigned a drive letter. Even though it doesn't look like it in Disk Administrator, this partition is protected in the same way as the rest of the RAID 5 array.

13. You install the Compaq Insight Agent on your ProLiant 3000 and still cannot view the status of the ProLiant Storage System to which the system is connected. What action do you take?

A. Install the latest Windows NT Service Pack.
B. Ensure that the latest SMART-2 driver is installed.
C. Install the PRLNTSS.SYS driver from the Windows NT SSD.
D. Shut down and restart the server. Insight Manager will be able to communicate with the PSS once the server has restarted.
C. Install the PRLNTSS.SYS driver from the Windows NT SSD. This driver is required for the Insight Agents to detect the status of the ProLiant Storage System.

14. You have two Compaq ProLiant 7000 servers in a standby recovery configuration. You return to work on a Monday morning to discover the primary server has failed and operation has been switched over to the recovery server. What steps should be taken to return the configuration to normal?

A. Service the failed primary server. Shut down the recovery server at a convenient time and turn both machines back on. The primary server will resume its normal role.

B. Service the failed primary server. Power the primary server back up. The ProLiant Storage Systems will be reconnected to the primary server, and normal operation will recommence.

C. Service the failed primary server. Use the Recovery Agent applet in Control Panel to initiate a switchover.

D. Service the failed primary server. Power the primary server back up and unplug the recovery server interconnect cable to initiate switchover.

A. Service the failed primary server. Shut down the recovery server at a convenient time and turn both machines back on. The primary server will resume its normal role. The ProLiant Storage System has switch ownership of the drives to the recovery server. If the primary server were to be brought back online while the recovery server was operational in this mode, the primary server would immediately demand back its drives and the PSS would respond, disconnecting the active recovery server. This could lead to data loss. Therefore, answers B and D are incorrect. Answer C relates to the online server configuration, not the standby, and so is incorrect.

15. You are implementing a fault tolerant pair by using a NetFlex-3/P 10/100 controller, and a Netelligent 10/100 controller. Compaq Advanced Network Control utility shows a gray icon next to the Netelligent controller. What is likely to be the problem?

A. Cable failure

B. Adapter hardware failure

C. No driver installed

D. Cable OK

C. No driver installed. A gray icon in the Advanced Network Control utility indicates that no driver is installed for this device. This can also occur if the generic drivers off the Windows NT CD are used instead of the Compaq drivers.

16. After adding a SMART-2 controller to a ProLiant 6500, you discover that the network driver fails to initialize. As part of your fault-finding procedures, you remove the SMART-2 controller. The network card now works perfectly. What is the problem?

A. An IRQ conflict between the SMART-2 and the network card

B. A faulty SMART-2 controller

C. The PCI bus number to which the network card is attached has changed

D. An out-of-date driver for the SMART-2 controller is claiming an address space already allocated to the network controller

C. The PCI bus number to which the network card is attached has changed.

The SMART-2 controller actually contains a PCI bus onboard. When this PCI bus is enumerated at system startup, it can renumber one of the PCI buses on the system board. (the ProLiant 6500 has two PCI buses.) This change will prevent network card drivers from loading until the driver is removed and added again—with the new PCI bus number specified.

Chapter 32 Answers

1. Which Performance Monitor view would you use to collect information over a period of time to be analyzed later?

   A. Chart view

   B. Alert view

   C. Log view

   D. Report view

   C. Log view. This view allows you to collect information to a log file to be viewed with any of the other views. You can then use this information to spot trends in your server for troubleshooting purposes or analysis.

2. Which of the following is an example of a counter in Performance Monitor?

   A. %Usage

   B. %Processor

   C. Memory

   D. Logical Disk

   A. %Usage. A counter is an attribute of an object. There is no such thing as a %Processor. Memory and Logical Disk are both considered objects.

3. How do you view the information gathered by the Log view?

   A. Use the Export Log option.

   B. Use the Import Log option.

   C. Use the Data From option.

   D. Use the Chart Options.

   C. Use the Data From option. After you finish collecting the log information, use the Data From option to specify the log file for the data. You can then specify the path to the log file that you created in the Log view.

4. You've created a workspace file for PerfMon that includes Log view settings. You add the workspace file to your Startup group, but when you open the workspace file, you have to start the log manually. How can you have the log start automatically when you open the workspace file?

   A. Set your update interval to zero.

   B. Modify the Log Options and enable the Start On Open option.

   C. Manually start the log, then resave the workspace file.

   D. You must manually start the log every time.

   C. Manually start the log, then resave the workspace file. You can start the log in the Log Options. If you save the workspace file with the log started, it will start automatically when you reopen the workspace file.

5. Which of the following is not a pool in memory?

   A. Pageable
   B. Nonpageable
   C. File System Cache
   D. Virtual
   D. Virtual. Although Virtual Memory is part of the overall memory subsystem, it refers to the pagefile that resides on the hard disk and is not part of physical memory.

6. Which of the following is a characteristic of nonpageable memory?

   A. Reserved for applications working set
   B. Can be swapped to the hard disk in low memory conditions
   C. Data that must reside in physical memory at all times
   D. Acts as a temporary storage for data
   C. Data that must reside in physical memory at all times. Data in the nonpageable memory pool cannot be swapped to disk and must remain in physical memory.

7. How do you set the size for the File System Cache?

   A. Modify the cache settings in Control Panel | System.
   B. Use the SETCACHE command at a command prompt.
   C. Open Task Manager and click Set Cache.
   D. You cannot set the size of the cache.
   D. You cannot set the size of the cache. NT dynamically adjusts the size of the cache depending on current memory usage.

8. You have 100 users on a server that is being used as a file and print server. Users are complaining of slow response. You suspect that the server settings aren't correct. How should you set the server settings?

   A. Minimize Memory Used
   B. Balanced
   C. Maximize Throughput for File Sharing
   D. Maximize Throughput for Network Applications
   C. Maximize Throughput for File Sharing. This setting will adjust memory to give higher priority to the file system cache instead of applications. This setting is used for environments with more than 64 remote users connecting to the server.

9. You add counters to monitor the performance of your disks, but they all read zero. What is the most likely cause for this?

   A. The disks aren't on the Windows NT Hardware Compatibility List.
   B. You haven't run DISKPERF.
   C. You added the counters for Logical Disk instead of Physical Disk.

D. You added the counters for Physical Disk instead of Logical Disk.
B. You haven't run DISKPERF. Running DISKPERF enables the disk performance counters, which are not enabled by default.

10. What is the proper command to activate the disk performance counters?

A. DISKPERF –ON

B. DISKPERF –SET

C. DISKPERF –Y

D. DISKPERF –ENABLE
C. DISKPERF –Y. Running DISKPERF –Y enables the disk performance counters so that you can monitor the disks in Performance Monitor. If you do not enable the counters, you will not get any readings for your disks.

11. Which of the following is not a characteristic of a hard page fault?

A. Pages are found in the pagefile.

B. Pages are found in the system cache.

C. Degrades system performance

D. Caused by a lack of memory
B. Pages are found in the system cache. When the page is found in the system cache, that is known as a soft page fault and not a hard page fault. Since it is still accessing faster memory and not the hard disk, performance is not severely degraded.

12. Which of the following will benefit an application server?

A. Faster, single processor

B. Additional memory

C. Faster disks

D. 100 Mbps network
B. Additional memory. An application server will benefit from more memory. If it caches more information in memory, the server applications will run better. The application server can also benefit from multiple processors.

13. Which of the following will benefit a file and print server?

A. Faster, single processor

B. Additional memory

C. 7200 rpm disks

D. 10 Mbps network
A. Faster, single processor. A file and print server will benefit from a faster, single processor. It can also benefit from more memory, but only to a certain extent. The server can also use faster disks and a fast network.

14. Which command would you use to launch Solitaire with a higher than normal priority?

A. START /BOOST SOL.EXE

B. START /HIGH SOL.EXE

C. SOL.EXE /BOOST

D. SOL.EXE /HIGH
B. START /HIGH SOL.EXE. You can also specify /LOW, /NORMAL, or /REALTIME for the priority. Run START /? to get the syntax for the START command.

15. How can you change the priority of an application that is already running?
    A. Use Task Manager.
    B. Use the Start Command.
    C. Use the Boost Command.
    D. You cannot change the priority of an application once it has launched.
    A. Use Task Manager. In Task Manager, open the Processes tab. Right-click the process and choose Set Priority. START only changes the priority when you launch an application. You cannot use the START command on applications that are already running.

16. What is the default size of the pagefile?
    A. 3MB
    B. Amount of memory
    C. Amount of memory + 12MB
    D. Double the size of memory
    C. Amount of memory + 12MB. This is the recommended default size given by Microsoft. You can change this setting in Control Panel | System | Virtual Memory.

17. Which of the following is not a method to optimize the pagefile?
    A. Create a second pagefile on a different partition on the same disk.
    B. Create a second pagefile on a different disk.
    C. Disable the pagefile from expanding.
    D. Add more memory.
    A. Create a second pagefile on a different partition on the same disk. Creating the pagefile on the same disk can actually degrade performance. You should create a second pagefile on a disk other than the one that contains the OS files. You should also disable the pagefile from expanding to prevent fragmentation and overall performance degradation. Adding more memory will reduce paging.

18. How can you prevent the pagefile from expanding?
    A. Deselect the Enable Pagefile Expansion option in the Virtual Memory dialog.
    B. Set the Initial Size and Maximum Size to the same value.
    C. Create a partition with the size of the pagefile and copy the pagefile to that partition.
    D. Use Task Manager to set the size of the pagefile (select Do Not Expand).
    B. Set the Initial Size and Maximum Size to the same value. When the pagefile expands, it consumes a large amount of system resources, affecting overall performance. You also risk the pagefile becoming fragmented if it expands.

19. You want to configure your pagefile size so that the pagefile does not have to expand. Which counter would you monitor in

PerfMon to figure out how large to make your pagefile?

A. Memory: Available Bytes

B. Memory: Pages/sec

C. Paging File: %Usage Peak

D. Memory: Page Faults/sec
C. Paging File: %Usage Peak. This is the maximum size that the paging file has reached. If you set the pagefile to this size, it should theoretically never have to grow.

20. You have 64MB of RAM in your server. You observe a large number of pages and notice that disk activity is increasing. Which counter would you monitor to determine how much memory you should add?

A. Paging File: %Usage Peak

B. Memory: Pages/sec

C. Memory: Available Bytes

D. Memory: Page Faults/sec
A. Paging File: %Usage Peak. Multiply this value by the size of the pagefile to determine how much memory you should add. For example, you may have a pagefile that is 100MB. If the %Usage Peak is 75 percent, you should add at least 75MB of memory to your server.

21. Which counter would you monitor to determine whether your processor is overloaded?

A. Processor: %Processor Time

B. Processor: Processor Queue Length

C. Processor: %User Time

D. Processor: %Privileged Time
B. Processor: Processor Queue Length. You could monitor %Processor Time first, to get an indication on how busy a processor is, but even a 100 percent processor utilization doesn't necessarily mean that the processor is a bottleneck. A high Processor Queue Length shows that instructions are waiting for the processor, which indicates that the processor is a bottleneck.

22. What is the significance of the Memory: Commit Limit counter?

A. It displays how many programs can be loaded in memory simultaneously.

B. It is the amount of virtual memory that can be committed without having to expand the paging file.

C. It is the amount of memory dedicated to the system cache.

D. It is the highest amount of memory that can be committed to an application.
B. The commit limit is the amount of virtual memory that can be committed without having to expand the paging file. When the commit limit is reached, the pagefile must be expanding, thus degrading system performance. You can monitor Memory: Committed Bytes to see how close you are to the commit limit.

23. Which counter would you monitor to determine whether your disk subsystem is a bottleneck?

    A. %Disk Time

    B. Current Disk Queue Length

    C. Disk Reads/sec

    D. Avg. Disk sec/Transfer

    B. Current Disk Queue Length. As is the case with a busy processor, a busy disk does not necessarily mean a bottleneck. If information is building in the disk queue, then you can surmise that your disk subsystem is a bottleneck.

24. Which counter would you monitor to determine if you have a defective network card?

    A. %Interrupt Time

    B. Error Bytes/sec

    C. %Network Utilization

    D. Bytes Total/sec

    A. %Interrupt Time. A high percentage of interrupts from the NIC may indicate that it is defective.

25. Which counter would you use to track how busy the Server service is with respect to the network?

    A. Processor: %Processor Time

    B. Server: Bytes Total/sec

    C. Network Interface: Current Bandwidth

    D. Memory: Pages/sec

    B. Server: Bytes Total/sec. This counter tracks the number of bytes sent and received by the Server service, and gives a general indication of how busy the server is.

26. Which of the following is not a function of the Virtual Memory Manager?

    A. Swaps out least used data from memory to the pagefile

    B. Translates virtual addresses to physical addresses

    C. Allocates 2GB of address space to each application

    D. Allows applications to access shared memory

    C. Allocates 2GB of address space to each application. The VMM actually allocates 4GB of address space to each application. Since your server will probably not have many gigabytes of memory, the VMM may allocate disk space in the page file, which is known as virtual memory.

B

About the CD

This CD-ROM contains a browser-based testing product, the *Personal Testing Center*. The *Personal Testing Center* is easy to install on any Windows 95/98/NT computer.

Installing the Personal Testing Center

Double-clicking on the Setup.html file on the CD will cycle you through an introductory page on the *Test Yourself* software. On the second page, you will have to read and accept the license agreement. Once you have read the agreement, click on the Agree icon and you will be brought to the *Personal Testing Center's* main page.

On the main page, you will find links to the *Personal Testing Center*, to the electronic version of the book, and to other resources you may find helpful. Click on the first link to the *Personal Testing Center* and you will be brought to the Quick Start page. Here you can choose to run the Personal Testing Center from the CD or install it to your hard drive.

Installing the *Personal Testing Center* to your hard drive is an easy process. Click on the Install to Hard Drive icon and the procedure will start for you. An instructional box will appear and walk you through the remainder of the installation. If installed to the hard drive, the "Personal Testing Center" program group will be created in the Start Programs folder.

Should you wish to run the software from the CD-ROM, the steps are the same as previously listed until you reach the point where you would select the Install to Hard Drive icon. Here, select Run from CD icon and the exam will automatically begin.

To uninstall the program from your hard disk, use the add/remove programs feature in your Windows Control Panel. InstallShield will run uninstall.

Test Type Choices

With the *Personal Testing Center*, you have three options in which to run the program: Live, Practice, and Review. Each test type will draw from a pool of over 200 potential questions. Your choice of test type will depend on whether you would like to simulate an actual ASE exam, receive instant feedback on your answer choices, or review concepts using the testing simulator. Note that selecting the Full Screen icon on Internet Explorer's standard toolbar gives you the best display of the *Personal Testing Center.*

Live

The Live timed test type is meant to reflect the actual exam as closely as possible. You will have 120 minutes in which to complete the exam. You will have the option to skip questions and return to them later, move to the previous question, or end the exam. Once the timer has expired, you will automatically go to the scoring page to review your test results.

Managing Windows

The testing application runs inside an Internet Explorer 4.0 or 5.0 browser window. We recommend that you use the full-screen view to minimize the amount of text scrolling you need to do. However, the application will initiate a second iteration of the browser when you link to an Answer in Depth or a Review Graphic. If you are running in full-screen view, the second iteration of the browser will be covered by the first. You can toggle between the two windows with ALT-TAB, you can click your task bar to maximize the second window, or you can get out of full-screen mode and arrange the two windows so they are both visible on the screen at the same time. The application will not initiate more than two browser windows, so you aren't left with hundreds of open windows for each Answer in Depth or Review Graphic that you view.

Saving Scores as Cookies

Your exam score is stored as a browser cookie. If you've configured your browser to accept cookies, your score will be stored in a cookie named History. If you don't accept cookies, you cannot permanently save your scores. If you delete the History cookie, the scores will be deleted permanently.

Using the Browser Buttons

The test application runs inside the Internet Explorer 4.0 browser. You should navigate from screen to screen by using the application's buttons, not the browser's buttons.

JavaScript Errors

If you encounter a JavaScript error, you should be able to proceed within the application. If you cannot, shut down your Internet Explorer 4.0 browser session and relaunch the testing application.

Practice

When choosing the Practice exam type, you have the option of receiving instant feedback as to whether your selected answer is correct. The questions will be presented to you in numerical order, and you will see every question in the available question pool for each section you chose to be tested on.

As with the Live exam type, you have the option of continuing through the entire exam without seeing the correct answer for each question. The number of questions you answered correctly, along with the percentage of correct answers, will be displayed during the post-exam summary report. Once you have answered a question, click the Answer icon to display the correct answer.

You have the option of ending the Practice exam at any time, but your post-exam summary screen may reflect an incorrect percentage based on the number of questions you failed to answer. Questions that are skipped are counted as incorrect answers on the post-exam summary screen.

Review

During the Review exam type, you will be presented with questions similar to both the Live and Practice exam types. However, the Answer icon is not present, as every question will have the correct answer posted near the bottom of the screen. You have the option of answering the question without looking at the correct answer. In the Review exam type, you can also return to previous questions and skip to the next question, as well as end the exam by clicking the Stop icon.

The Review exam type is recommended when you have already completed the Live exam type once or twice, and would now like to determine which questions you answered correctly.

Questions with Answers

For the Practice and Review exam types, you will have the option of clicking a hyperlink titled Answers in Depth, which will present relevant study material aimed at exposing the logic behind the answer in a separate browser window. By having two browsers open (one for the test engine and one for the review information), you can quickly alternate between the two windows while keeping your place in the exam. You will find that additional windows are not generated as you follow hyperlinks throughout the test engine.

Scoring

The *Personal Testing Center* post-exam summary screen, called Benchmark Yourself, displays the results for each section you chose to be tested on, including a bar graph similar to the real exam, which displays the percentage of correct answers. You can compare your percentage to the actual passing percentage for each section. The percentage displayed on the post-exam summary screen is not the actual percentage required to pass the exam. You'll see the number of questions you answered correctly compared to the total number of questions you were tested on. If you choose to skip a question, it will be marked as incorrect. Ending the exam by clicking the End button with questions still unanswered lowers your percentage, as these questions will be marked as incorrect.

Clicking the End button and then the Home button allows you to choose another exam type or test yourself on another section.

C

About the Web Site

Access Global Knowledge

As you know by now, Global Knowledge is the largest independent IT training company in the world. Just by purchasing this book, you have also secured a free subscription to the Global Knowledge Web site and its many resources. You can find it at: http://access.globalknowledge.com

You can log on directly at the Global Knowledge site, and you will be e-mailed a new, secure password immediately upon registering.

What You'll Find There. . .

The wealth of useful information at the Global Knowledge site falls into three categories:

Skills Gap Analysis

Global Knowledge offers several ways for you to analyze your networking skills and discover where they may be lacking. Using Global Knowledge's trademarked Competence Key Tool, you can do a skills gap analysis and get recommendations for where you may need to do some more studying. (Sorry, it just might not end with this book!)

Networking

You'll also gain valuable access to another asset: people. At the Access Global site, you'll find threaded discussions, as well as live discussions. Talk to other ASE candidates, get advice from folks who have already taken the exams, and get access to instructors and certified trainers.

Product Offerings

Of course, Global Knowledge also offers its products here, and you may find some valuable items for purchase—CBTs, books, or courses. Browse freely and see if there's something that could help you take that next step in career enhancement.

D

Inspect Report

```
INSPECT - Version S10.26A
==========================

----------------------------------------------------------------------------
System :

Date . . . . . . . . . . . . . . 10/23/1999
Time . . . . . . . . . . . . . . 14:12:31

Product  . . . . . . . . . . . . Compaq ProLiant 2500

Machine ID
  From System Board  . . . . . . CPQ0551

Processor ID . . . . . . . . . . 5F81

Processor  . . . . . . . . . . . Pentium Pro(R) at 200 MHz
  Slot . . . . . . . . . . . . . 1
  Socket . . . . . . . . . . . . 7
  Secondary Cache  . . . . . . . 256K
  CPU ID . . . . . . . . . . . . 0619

Processor  . . . . . . . . . . . Pentium Pro(R) at 200 MHz
  Slot . . . . . . . . . . . . . 2
  Socket . . . . . . . . . . . . 7
  Secondary Cache  . . . . . . . 256K
  CPU ID . . . . . . . . . . . . 0619

Processor(s) Mapped Out  . . . . None

Numeric Coprocessor  . . . . . . Integrated 387-Compatible

Expansion Bus  . . . . . . . . . Extended ISA, PCI

System Identification Number . . D713HWA30256

CPU Mode . . . . . . . . . . . . Real Mode


Compaq ProLiant 2500 is a trademark of Compaq Computer Corporation.
```

```
---------------------------------------------------------------------------
ROM :


System ROM
    Revision . . . . . . . . . .  06/28/1999
      Family . . . . . . . . . .  E24
    Flashable  . . . . . . . . .  Yes
    Supports F10 partition . . .  Yes

Video Controller ROM
    Revision . . . . . . . . . .  1.6 (Cirrus)

Option ROMs
  Address Range  . . . . . . . .  C0000 - C7FFF
    Data Dump  . . . . . . . . .  (CL-GD5440 VGA BIOS Version 1.06
                                  Copyright 1992-1995 Cir...)

  Address Range  . . . . . . . .  C8000 - CBFFF
    Data Dump  . . . . . . . . .  (04/22/98         SMART-2 Option ROM/BIOS
                                                    (C)Copyright COMPAQ...)

  Address Range  . . . . . . . .  E8000 - EDFFF
    Data Dump  . . . . . . . . .  ( CPQSCSI d)

Bootblock ROM  . . . . . . . . .  07/04/1996


---------------------------------------------------------------------------
Keyboard :


Keyboard . . . . . . . . . . . .  Enhanced


---------------------------------------------------------------------------
System Ports :


LPT Ports  . . . . . . . . . . .  LPT1 (Address 3BC)

COM Ports  . . . . . . . . . . .  COM1 (Address 3F8)
                                  COM2 (Address 2F8)
```

```
-----------------------------------------------------------------------------
System Storage :


Embedded IDE Controller, Base Address 0x1f0

  Device . . . . . . . . . . . .  Compaq 8X CD-ROM
  Drive position . . . . . . . .  1
  Revision . . . . . . . . . . .  1023
  Model Number . . . . . . . . .  HITACHI CDR-7930

Embedded Wide -Ultra SCSI Controller, IRQ10

  Device . . . . . . . . . . . .  15/30 GB DLT SCSI Tape
  SCSI ID  . . . . . . . . . . .  6
  Revision . . . . . . . . . . .  8

Diskette Drive A . . . . . . . .  1.44 Megabyte (3.5 inch)

Drive Controller 1, 32-Bit Compaq SMART-2/P Rev. B Array Controller
  IDA Firmware Revision  . . . .  4.10
  Array Accelerator Memory . . .  4096 Kbytes
    Reserved for reads . . . . .  2048 Kbytes
    Reserved for writes. . . . .  2048 Kbytes
  Accelerator Status . . . . . .  Enabled
    Battery count  . . . . . . .  3
    Batteries charged  . . . . .  3
    Batteries failed . . . . . .  0
  Internal ProLiant  . . . . . .  Bus 1, Rev. JM14
  ProLiant . . . . . . . . . . .  Bus 2, Rev. JM14

  Logical Drive  1 . . . . . . .  18194 Megabyte
  Fault Tolerance  . . . . . . .  Distributed Data Guarding
  OS Format  . . . . . . . . . .  Multi-Sector Distribution
  Drive geometry (Cyl, Hds, Sec)  4355, 255, 32
  Array Accelerator  . . . . . .  Enabled

    Hard Drive  1
    SCSI Bus . . . . . . . . . .  2
    SCSI ID  . . . . . . . . . .  0
    Serial Number  . . . . . . .  LA101351
    Firmware Revision 1  . . . .  9A10
    Model Number . . . . . . . .  COMPAQ  ST19171WC
    Initialized for Monitoring .  Yes
      Reference time . . . . . .  1153280
      Sectors read . . . . . . .  *513494117
```

```
  Hard read errors . . . . .  0
  Read errors retry  . . . .  0
  ECC read errors  . . . . .  2
  Sectors written  . . . . .  2184645762
  Hard write errors  . . . .  0
  Write errors retry . . . .  0
  Seek count . . . . . . . .  44248
  Seek errors  . . . . . . .  0
  Spin cycles  . . . . . . .  21
  Spin up time . . . . . . .  249
  Seek time track  . . . . .  50%
  Seek time third  . . . . .  74%
  Seek time full . . . . . .  70%
  Reallocated sectors  . . .  667
  Recovers read failed . . .  0
  Bus faults . . . . . . . .  6

Hard Drive  2
SCSI Bus . . . . . . . . . .  2
SCSI ID  . . . . . . . . . .  1
Serial Number  . . . . . . .  LA205743
Firmware Revision 1  . . . .  9A10
Model Number . . . . . . . .  COMPAQ  ST19171WC
Initialized for Monitoring .  Yes
  Reference time . . . . . .  1153335
  Sectors read . . . . . . .  *723137955
  Hard read errors . . . . .  0
  Read errors retry  . . . .  9
  ECC read errors  . . . . .  12
  Sectors written  . . . . .  1956170809
  Hard write errors  . . . .  0
  Write errors retry . . . .  0
  Seek count . . . . . . . .  39072
  Seek errors  . . . . . . .  0
  Spin cycles  . . . . . . .  21
  Spin up time . . . . . . .  248
  Seek time track  . . . . .  61%
  Seek time third  . . . . .  76%
  Seek time full . . . . . .  73%
  Reallocated sectors  . . .  213
  Recovers read failed . . .  0
  Bus faults . . . . . . . .  16

Hard Drive  3
SCSI Bus . . . . . . . . . .  2
SCSI ID  . . . . . . . . . .  2
Serial Number  . . . . . . .  LA139337
```

```
    Firmware Revision 1  . . . .  9A10
    Model Number . . . . . . . .  COMPAQ  ST19171WC
    Initialized for Monitoring .  Yes
      Reference time . . . . . .  1153274
      Sectors read . . . . . . .  *372482209
      Hard read errors . . . . .  0
      Read errors retry  . . . .  0
      ECC read errors  . . . . .  0
      Sectors written  . . . . .  2310712595
      Hard write errors  . . . .  0
      Write errors retry . . . .  0
      Seek count . . . . . . . .  34144
      Seek errors  . . . . . . .  0
      Spin cycles  . . . . . . .  21
      Spin up time . . . . . . .  254
      Seek time track  . . . . .  55%
      Seek time third  . . . . .  72%
      Seek time full . . . . . .  68%
      Reallocated sectors  . . .  591
      Recovers read failed . . .  0
      Bus faults . . . . . . . .  6


-----------------------------------------------------------------------------
Graphics :


Graphics Mode  . . . . . . . . .  03 (80-Column Text)


Primary Monitor attached to  . .  Cirrus CL-GD5430 Graphics Controller
                                  with Video Graphics Color Monitor

Total Video Memory . . . . . . .  1024 Kbytes


-----------------------------------------------------------------------------
Memory :

Memory Boards Identified:
  Processor Board
    DIMM Slot  1 (EDO) . . . . .    32 Megabytes
    DIMM Slot  2 (EDO) . . . . .    64 Megabytes
    DIMM Slot  3 . . . . . . . .     0 Megabytes
    DIMM Slot  4 . . . . . . . .     0 Megabytes
Total Compaq Memory  . . . . . .    96 Megabytes
```

```
Base Memory
  System Total . . . . . . . . .    638 Kbytes
  Amount Free  . . . . . . . . .    599 Kbytes (614192 Bytes)

Extended Memory
  System Total . . . . . . . . .  97280 Kbytes

Expanded Memory
  LIM Driver Support . . . . . .  LIM driver not loaded

----------------------------------------------------------------------------
Operating System :


Operating System . . . . . . . .  MS-DOS version 6.00 (from partition)

Memory Allocation (including INSPECT)
  PSP   SIZE    NAME          TRAPPED INTERRUPTS
  ----  ------  ------------  ------------------------------------
  0431  021920  COMMAND.COM   FCh  F4h  F2h  E0h  DBh  22h
  0992  232832  INSPECT.EXE   24h  F3h  FBh  EFh  E6h  DEh  DCh  3Fh
                              30h  00h
  33FB  104384  <unknown>     E1h


----------------------------------------------------------------------------
System Configuration :


System Configuration Utility . .  Version 2.47

Extended Non-volatile Memory
-------- ----------- ------
Slot Number  . . . . . . . . . .   0
  Slot Type  . . . . . . . . . .  Embedded
  Board ID . . . . . . . . . . .  CPQ0551
  CFG File Extension
    Revision Level . . . . . . .  2.21
  Type Entry(s)  . . . . . . . .  MSD,FPYCTL
    IRQ Entry(s):
      IRQ  6, Not Shared, Edge Triggered
    DMA Channel(s):
      Channel 2, Not Shared
```

```
    Timing: Type B
    Transfer Size: 8-bit (byte)
  Port Range(s):
    03F0h - 03F5h, Not Shared
    03F6h - 03F7h, Shared

Type Entry(s)  . . . . . . . .  MSD,UNIT0,FPYDRV;TYP=4
Type Entry(s)  . . . . . . . .  MSD,UNIT1,FPYDRV;TYP=0
Type Entry(s)  . . . . . . . .  MSD
Type Entry(s)  . . . . . . . .  MSD,DSKCTL;CTL2
  IRQ Entry(s):
    IRQ 14, Not Shared, Edge Triggered
  Port Range(s):
    01F0h - 01F7h, Not Shared
    03F6h - 03F7h, Shared
    11F1h, Not Shared

Type Entry(s)  . . . . . . . .  MSD,UNIT0,DSKDRV;CD
Type Entry(s)  . . . . . . . .  MSD,UNIT1,DSKDRV
Memory Entry(s):
                                     Range                 Size
                                     -----                 ----
  ROM: Other,     Cacheable        896K -        1M        128K

Type Entry(s)  . . . . . . . .  MEM;COMPAQ
Memory Entry(s):
                                     Range                 Size
                                     -----                 ----
  RAM: System,    Cacheable          0K -      640K        640K

Type Entry(s)  . . . . . . . .  MEM;COMPAQ
Memory Entry(s):
                                     Range                 Size
                                     -----                 ----
  RAM: System,    Cacheable          1M -       16M         15M

Type Entry(s)  . . . . . . . .  MEM;COMPAQ
Memory Entry(s):
                                     Range                 Size
                                     -----                 ----
  RAM: System,    Cacheable        16M -        64M         48M
  RAM: System,    Cacheable        64M -        96M         32M

Type Entry(s)  . . . . . . . .  MEM;COMPAQ
Type Entry(s)  . . . . . . . .  MEM;COMPAQ
```

```
Type Entry(s)  . . . . . . . .  COM,ASY;COM1;A
  IRQ Entry(s):
    IRQ  4, Not Shared, Edge Triggered
  Port Range(s):
    03F8h - 03FFh, Not Shared

Type Entry(s)  . . . . . . . .  COM,ASY;COM2;B
  IRQ Entry(s):
    IRQ  3, Not Shared, Edge Triggered
  Port Range(s):
    02F8h - 02FFh, Not Shared

Type Entry(s)  . . . . . . . .  PAR;LPT1
  IRQ Entry(s):
    IRQ  7, Not Shared, Edge Triggered
  DMA Channel(s):
    Channel 0, Not Shared
    Timing: ISA Compatible
    Transfer Size: 8-bit (byte)
  Port Range(s):
    03BCh - 03BEh, Not Shared

Type Entry(s)  . . . . . . . .  PTR,8042
  IRQ Entry(s):
    IRQ 12, Not Shared, Edge Triggered
Type Entry(s)  . . . . . . . .  OTH,CPQCSM
Free Form Text . . . . . . . .  0D 03 03 03 01 78 3C 02 50 0C 00 00
Type Entry(s)  . . . . . . . .  OTH,A20
Type Entry(s)  . . . . . . . .  OTH,SOFTNMI
Type Entry(s)  . . . . . . . .  OTH,FLSFNMI
Type Entry(s)  . . . . . . . .  OTH,BUSNMI
Type Entry(s)  . . . . . . . .  OTH,DSKTDMA
Type Entry(s)  . . . . . . . .  OTH,REFRESH
Type Entry(s)  . . . . . . . .  OTH,PERR
Type Entry(s)  . . . . . . . .  OTH,SIMMSPD;AUTO
Type Entry(s)  . . . . . . . .  IRQ,SHARE
Type Entry(s)  . . . . . . . .  OTH,TABLE;DEFAULT6
Type Entry(s)  . . . . . . . .  OTH,CURREV
Free Form Text . . . . . . . .  EC EA 18
Type Entry(s)  . . . . . . . .  OTH,PREREV
Free Form Text . . . . . . . .  15 55 18
Type Entry(s)  . . . . . . . .  OTH,CPR,NMI
Free Form Text . . . . . . . .  01 00 0A 00 D8 0C C1 C5
  Port Range(s):
    7C80h - 7C83h, Not Shared
```

```
      8C80h - 8C83h, Not Shared
      9C80h - 9C83h, Not Shared
      AC80h - AC83h, Not Shared
      BC80h - BC83h, Not Shared
      CC80h - CC83h, Not Shared
      DC80h - DC83h, Not Shared
      EC80h - EC83h, Not Shared
      FC80h - FC83h, Not Shared

  Memory Entry(s):
                                     Range                Size
                                     -----                ----
    RAM: Virtual,  Non-Cacheable    2060M -  2109441K          1K

    IRQ Entry(s):
      IRQ 13, Not Shared, Edge Triggered
  Type Entry(s)  . . . . . . . .  ISA;MAP
  Free Form Text . . . . . . . .  61 62 63 64 85 86 87 E0 E0 E0 E0 E0 E0 E0
                                  E0 01 02 03 04 00 00 00 00 00 00 00 00 00
                                  00 00
  Type Entry(s)  . . . . . . . .  ISA;PCIMAP
  Free Form Text . . . . . . . .  01 01 50 02 01 58 03 01 68 04 00 50 05 00
                                  58 06 00 68

Empty Slot(s)  . . . . . . . . .   1  2  3  4


----------------------------------------------------------------------------
System Health :


Standby Recovery Server
  Status . . . . . . . . . . . .  Disabled
  COM Port . . . . . . . . . . .  COM1
  Server Configuration . . . . .  Recovery
  Timeout Value  . . . . . . . .  1 minutes



Revisions Table
===============

Current Revisions
  Date . . . . . . . . . . . . .  10/23/1999
```

```
Previous Revisions
  Date . . . . . . . . . . . . .   05/08/1997


------------------------------------------------------------------------------
Miscellaneous :


System Configuration Memory
  00 - 0F :      32 00 12 00    14 00 00 23    10 99 26 82    50 80 00 00
  10 - 1F :      40 00 00 00    03 80 02 00    3C 00 00 00    00 00 00 00
  20 - 2F :      00 00 00 00    7F 20 00 40    00 92 00 00    00 10 02 82
  30 - 3F :      00 3C 19 80    00 00 XX XX    XX XX XX XX    XX XX XX XX

BIOS Data Area
  40:0000 :      F8 03 F8 02    00 00 00 00    BC 03 00 00    00 00 80 9F
  40:0010 :      27 44 00 7E    02 9C 00 00    00 00 3A 00    3A 00 0D 1C
  40:0020 :      0D 1C 0D E0    1B 01 0D 1C    E0 50 E0 50    E0 50 0D 1C
  40:0030 :      0D 1C E0 50    0D 1C E0 50    0D 1C E0 48    0D 1C 00 00
  40:0040 :      72 00 C0 00    00 21 01 01    02 12 50 00    00 A0 00 00
  40:0050 :      00 21 00 00    00 00 00 00    00 00 00 00    00 00 00 00
  40:0060 :      00 00 00 D4    03 09 30 B8    12 58 29 FF    81 2D 0E 00
  40:0070 :      00 00 00 12    00 01 00 00    14 14 14 14    01 01 01 01
  40:0080 :      1E 00 3E 00    1D 10 00 60    F9 11 0B 01    00 00 FF 05
  40:0090 :      17 00 00 00    21 00 10 10    00 00 00 00    00 00 00 00
  40:00A0 :      00 00 00 00    00 00 00 00    53 5B 00 C0    00 00 00 00
  40:00B0 :      00 00 00 00    00 00 00 00    00 00 00 00    00 00 00 00
  40:00C0 :      00 00 00 00    00 00 00 00    00 00 00 00    00 00 00 00
  40:00D0 :      00 00 00 00    00 00 00 00    00 00 00 00    00 00 00 00
  40:00E0 :      00 00 00 00    00 00 00 00    00 00 00 00    00 00 00 00
  40:00F0 :      00 00 00 00    00 00 00 00    00 00 00 00    00 00 00 00


Interrupt Vector Table (including INSPECT)
  00 - 03 :      09A2:0555      0070:06F4      03B7:0016      0070:06F4
  04 - 07 :      0070:06F4      F000:FF54      F000:93CC      F000:9BD0
  08 - 0B :      03B7:003C      03B7:0045      F000:9BD0      F000:9BD0
  0C - 0F :      F000:9BD0      F000:9BD0      03B7:00B7      0070:06F4
  10 - 13 :      C000:329C      F000:F84D      F000:F841      0070:0774
  14 - 17 :      F000:E739      0255:0413      F000:E82E      F000:EFD2
  18 - 1B :      F000:F06D      042C:002F      F000:FE6E      0070:06EE
  1C - 1F :      F000:FF53      C000:1F24      0000:0522      C000:6743
  20 - 23 :      0116:1094      0116:109E      0441:35D0      0116:10DA
  24 - 27 :      8F19:43F6      0116:10A8      0116:10B2      0116:10BC
```

```
28 - 2B :    0116:10DA     0070:0762     0116:10DA     0116:10DA
2C - 2F :    0116:10DA     0116:10DA     0116:10DA     0255:01CC
30 - 33 :    1610:D0EA     F000:9B01     0116:10DA     0116:10DA
34 - 37 :    0116:10DA     0116:10DA     0116:10DA     0116:10DA
38 - 3B :    0116:10DA     0116:10DA     0116:10DA     0116:10DA
3C - 3F :    0116:10DA     0116:10DA     0116:10DA     1A1A:04FB
40 - 43 :    F000:EC59     C817:01C4     F000:F065     C000:6343
44 - 47 :    F000:9BD0     F000:9BD0     0000:0000     F000:9BD0
48 - 4B :    F000:9BD0     F000:9BD0     F000:9BD0     F000:9BD0
4C - 4F :    F000:9BD0     F000:9BD0     F000:9BD0     F000:9BD0
50 - 53 :    F000:9BD0     F000:9BD0     F000:9BD0     F000:9BD0
54 - 57 :    F000:9BD0     F000:9BD0     F000:9BD0     F000:9BD0
58 - 5B :    F000:9BD0     F000:9BD0     F000:9BD0     F000:9BD0
5C - 5F :    F000:9BD0     F000:9BD0     F000:9BD0     F000:9BD0
60 - 63 :    0000:0000     0000:0000     0000:0000     0000:0000
64 - 67 :    0000:0000     0000:0000     0000:0000     0000:0000
68 - 6B :    F000:9BD0     F000:9BD0     F000:9BD0     F000:9BD0
6C - 6F :    F000:9BD0     C000:329C     F000:9BD0     F000:9BD0
70 - 73 :    03B7:0052     C800:0136     03B7:00CF     F000:9BD0
74 - 77 :    03B7:00FF     F000:9C28     03B7:0117     F000:9BD0
78 - 7B :    0000:0000     0000:0000     0000:0000     0000:0000
7C - 7F :    0000:0000     0000:0000     0000:0000     0000:0000
80 - 83 :    0000:0000     0000:0000     0000:0000     0000:0000
84 - 87 :    0000:0000     0000:0000     0000:0000     0000:0000
88 - 8B :    0000:0000     0000:0000     0000:0000     0000:0000
8C - 8F :    0000:0000     0000:0000     0000:0000     0000:0000
90 - 93 :    0000:0000     0000:0000     0000:0000     0000:0000
94 - 97 :    0000:0000     0000:0000     0000:0000     0000:0000
98 - 9B :    0000:0000     0000:0000     0000:0000     0000:0000
9C - 9F :    0000:0000     0000:0000     0000:0000     0000:0000
A0 - A3 :    0000:0000     0000:0000     0000:0000     0000:0000
A4 - A7 :    0000:0000     0000:0000     0000:0000     0000:0000
A8 - AB :    0000:0000     0000:0000     0000:0000     0000:0000
AC - AF :    0000:0000     0000:0000     0000:0000     0000:0000
B0 - B3 :    0000:0000     0000:0000     0000:0000     0000:0000
B4 - B7 :    0000:0000     0000:0000     0000:0000     0000:0000
B8 - BB :    0000:0000     0000:0000     0000:0000     0000:0000
BC - BF :    0000:0000     0000:0000     0000:0000     0000:0000
C0 - C3 :    0000:0000     0000:0000     0000:0000     0000:0000
C4 - C7 :    0000:0000     0000:0000     0000:0000     0000:0000
C8 - CB :    0000:0000     0000:0000     0000:0000     0000:0000
CC - CF :    0000:0000     0000:0000     0000:0000     0000:0000
D0 - D3 :    0000:0000     0000:0000     0000:0000     0000:0000
D4 - D7 :    0000:0000     0000:0000     0000:0000     F8EE:0000
D8 - DB :    0000:40B4     E30C:8AEE     9804:BA0A     0200:773A
```

```
DC - DF :     0001:F03A     0020:0203     1600:030E     E000:0002
E0 - E3 :     006D:3F1F     3A80:D800     7210:009C     006D:3B5B
E4 - E7 :     7200:9BF0     0010:005B     005C:CB00     0000:0000
E8 - EB :     0000:0000     0000:0000     0000:0000     0000:0000
EC - EF :     0000:0000     0020:0203     0080:034F     2003:10DE
F0 - F3 :     0008:0202     7C73:C000     03DA:0E06     568B:03CE
F4 - F7 :     0008:6C73     03C4:0203     03C4:0000     0000:0ED0
F8 - FB :     0000:03C4     FF10:020F     0000:0000     00F4:91FE
FC - FF :     0080:64CF     007C:0A4F     F05E:0003     6CAE:051C

PCI Devices Information
  Signature . . . . . . . . . .  PCI
  Config Mechanism #1 . . . . .  Supported
  Config Mechanism #2 . . . . .  Not Supported
  Spec Cycle for Config #1 . . . Supported
  Spec Cycle for Config #2 . . . Not Supported
  BIOS Interface Version . . . . 2.10
  Last PCI Bus Number . . . . .  2
  Number of PCI Devices . . . .  4

  PCI Bus Number . . . . . . . . 1
  Device Number . . . . . . . .  6
  Function Number . . . . . . .  00h
  Slot Number . . . . . . . . .  0
  Vendor ID . . . . . . . . . .  1013h
  Device ID . . . . . . . . . .  00A0h
  Revision ID . . . . . . . . .  22h
  Device Type . . . . . . . . .  VGA Compatible Controller
  Programming Interface . . . .  00h
  Expansion ROM Base Address . . FF000000h
  IRQ Line . . . . . . . . . . . 255
  IRQ Pin . . . . . . . . . . .  INTA#
  Memory Address Base . . . . .  41000000h
  Memory Address Length . . . .  1000000h
  IO Address Base . . . . . . .  0h
  IO Address Length . . . . . .  400h

  PCI Bus Number . . . . . . . . 1
  Device Number . . . . . . . .  7
  Function Number . . . . . . .  00h
  Slot Number . . . . . . . . .  0
  Vendor ID . . . . . . . . . .  0E11h
  Device ID . . . . . . . . . .  AE43h
  Revision ID . . . . . . . . .  10h
  Device Type . . . . . . . . .  Other Network Controller
```

```
Programming Interface . . . .  00h
Expansion ROM Base Address . . FFFF0000h
IRQ Line . . . . . . . . . . . 5
IRQ Pin  . . . . . . . . . . . INTA#
IO Address Base  . . . . . . . 6400h
IO Address Length  . . . . . . 10h
Memory Address Base  . . . . . 40001100h
Memory Address Length  . . . . 10h

PCI Bus Number . . . . . . . . 1
Device Number  . . . . . . . . 9
Function Number  . . . . . . . 00h
Slot Number  . . . . . . . . . 0
Vendor ID  . . . . . . . . . . 1000h
Device ID  . . . . . . . . . . 000Fh
Revision ID  . . . . . . . . . 03h
Device Type  . . . . . . . . . SCSI Bus Controller
Programming Interface  . . . . 00h
Expansion ROM Base Address . . 0h
IRQ Line . . . . . . . . . . . 10
IRQ Pin  . . . . . . . . . . . INTA#
IO Address Base  . . . . . . . 6000h
IO Address Length  . . . . . . 100h
Memory Address Base  . . . . . 40001000h
Memory Address Length  . . . . 100h
Memory Address Base  . . . . . 40000000h
Memory Address Length  . . . . 1000h

PCI Bus Number . . . . . . . . 2
Device Number  . . . . . . . . 0
Function Number  . . . . . . . 00h
Slot Number  . . . . . . . . . 6
Vendor ID  . . . . . . . . . . 0E11h
Device ID  . . . . . . . . . . AE10h
Revision ID  . . . . . . . . . 03h
Device Type  . . . . . . . . . Other Mass Storage Controller
Programming Interface  . . . . 00h
IRQ Line . . . . . . . . . . . 9
IRQ Pin  . . . . . . . . . . . INTA#


---------------------------------------------------------------------------
```

Glossary

acknowledgment Notification sent from one network device to another to acknowledge that a message or group of messages has been received.

address A numbering convention used to identify a unique entity or location on a network.

ADU (Array Diagnostic Utility) Utility used by the latest Compaq array controllers, which must be run from the system partition. This new utility provides the same basic information as the DAAD, but it cannot be run from boot diskettes.

asymmetric multiprocessing Operating systems that use asymmetric multiprocessing dedicate one processor to run the operating system and utilize the other processor to perform other tasks.

attenuation The loss of power in a signal. The signal is present but is degraded.

bandwidth The difference between the highest and lowest frequencies available for network signals. The term may also describe the throughput capacity of a network link or segment.

BEDO (Burst EDO) With BEDO memory, pipelining technology and special latches are used to allow much quicker access times over standard EDO. BEDO memory will operate with much higher memory bus speeds compared to EDO.

branch prediction Allows the processor to remember the path taken for a particular process. This in turn speeds up future processes that utilize the same path.

burst mode transfer A data transmission in which data is temporarily sent significantly faster than usual.

byte A series of consecutive binary digits that are operated upon as a unit, usually eight bits.

cache A small amount of fast memory used to store recently used information. In systems that incorporate cache, the processor looks first to cache for its memory request. If the information is in cache, a cache hit occurs. Cache can be either a reserved section of main memory or an independent, high-speed device.

cache directory An index of data locations. The cache directory provides the cache management logic with information on where to find data requested by the processor.

cache hit A processor accessing instructions from the cache. A cache hit improves performance, since memory does not have to be accessed. Increasing the amount of Level 1 and Level 2 cache increases the likelihood of cache hits and thus enhances system performance.

channel The connection between a computer and peripheral devices such as disk drives, tape drives, printers, and modems.

CMOS (Complementary Metal Oxide Semiconductor)
A volatile memory, which uses very low power. The main system configuration is kept in this memory.

community names SNMP's security solution. Community names are comparable to passwords. When an administrator configures SNMP, he or she provides a list of community names that will have access to the managed objects on the system. The same community names must be supplied in the management application. If the community names match, the application will be permitted to communicate with the management agent. If the names do not match, then access will be denied and no exchange of information will take place. Community names are case-sensitive.

Compaq Integration Server A central repository of Compaq system software on the network. It can contain all of the drivers, firmware, and utilities needed by the Compaq servers in an environment. Software can thus be updated in one location and loaded onto all servers from this server.

Compaq ProLiant Storage System An external storage cabinet that can hold up to seven 1.6" or 1" drives. The Storage System can use any Compaq hot-pluggable drive that meets the Fast-Wide or Fast-SCSI-2 specification. The maximum capacity of the Storage System is 127GB (with the use of seven 18.2GB drives). LEDs on the system indicate whether each drive is being accessed or whether a drive is down.

Compaq Remote Insight Board A remote control option board that can be added to Compaq servers, enabling full remote control of a server before the operating system loads. This helps the administrator remotely troubleshoot a server that has gone down or is having problems booting. The Remote Insight Board has a microprocessor, modem, serial port, keyboard port, video controller, memory, and battery.

Compaq Storage Agent A feature that provides detailed information for the entire storage subsystem for the server, including controllers (IDE, SCSI, and Smart Array) and drives.

Compaq Survey Utility A tool available for Windows NT or Novell NetWare servers that can periodically record server configuration information and provide notations, recognizing changing system components or devices.

control bus The control bus is used to identify the type of bus cycle and to determine when the cycle is complete. It carries control signals that determine whether data will be read or written. It also determines if the operation is being performed to memory or to I/O.

cooperative multitasking Cooperative multitasking occurs when the process currently occupying the CPU offers the resources of the CPU to other processes. The processes must cooperate in order for this type of multitasking to work. If one process does not cooperate, it monopolizes the CPU and prevents other processes from running. Operating systems that employ this type of multitasking are Macintosh operating systems and Windows 3.*x* operating systems.

DAAD (Drive Array Advanced Diagnostics) Can be used to troubleshoot Compaq Drive Array Controllers. It is a DOS-based utility that collects information from the array controllers in the system. After sending commands to test the controller's ability to function, DAAD provides a list of what was found defective. DAAD does not affect data or configurations of the array and its drives.

data bus The data bus is what is used to transport data between devices, as well as to determine how much data can be sent at one time. The data bus is made up of lines that each carry one bit of information at a time.

DAT (Digital Audio Tape) The DAT drive can back up a maximum of 2.8GB per hour.

demand priority An access method. In a demand priority network, the hub controls who has access to the network. Demand priority allows setting of network priorities, which allows one network device to be given priority over another.

DIMM (Dual Inline Memory Module) A module with 168 pins, and 64 bits in width.

DLT (Digital Linear Tape) A DLT drive can back up 9GB per hour compressed or 4.5GB per hour native.

DRAM (Dynamic Random Access Memory) A form of RAM that must be continuously refreshed because it stores information in integrated circuits that contain capacitors.

dual peer The dual peer PCI bus provides two PCI buses, independently connected to the host processor bus with two host-to-PCI bridges.

ECC (Error Correcting Code) A type of memory for increasing the reliability of digital data. ECC memory can detect and correct single-bit memory errors. It can detect multi-bit errors, but cannot correct them. For ECC memory to be active, all DIMM modules must be ECC DIMMs.

EDO (Extended Data Out) The most common asynchronous DRAM technology. Unlike conventional RAM, which performs memory accesses in succession, one EDO access to memory can begin before the last one has finished. EDO memory is also called hyper page mode DRAM.

EPROM (Erasable Programmable Read-Only Memory) This is a subset of the ROMs on the system board, which are erasable by ultraviolet light or electronically. Also called EEPROM (Electronically Erasable Programmable Read-Only Memory).

Ethernet A popular local-area network (LAN) system from which the IEEE 802.3 standard was developed. Ethernet uses a bus or star topology, in which network nodes are linked by coaxial cable, fiber-optic cable, or twisted-pair wiring. The Ethernet standard provides for transmission at 10 Mbps.

Fast Ethernet Any of a number of 100-Mbps Ethernet specifications. Based on an extension to the IEEE 802.3 specification.

Fibre Channel A set of ANSI standard protocols (X3.230-1994). The distinctive spelling differentiates the standards from the fiber media. Fibre Channel can run over various media, including copper, multimode fiber, and single-mode fiber.

Flash memory Nonvolatile storage that can be electrically erased and reprogrammed as necessary.

flash update Routing update sent asynchronously when a change in the network topology occurs.

FPM (Fast Page Mode) A type of memory that is not significantly faster than conventional DRAM. While standard DRAM requires that a row and column address be sent for each individual access, FPM only sends the row address once for multiple accesses to memory locations that are near each other. FPM memory is an improved version of Page Mode memory, which is rarely found in modern system configurations. Despite its name, Fast Page Mode is actually the slowest memory technology still in use today.

full duplex Capability for simultaneous data transmission and receipt of data between two devices.

Gigabit Ethernet A standard for supporting ultra-high-speed connections along Internet and Intranet networks. Gigabit Ethernet supports transmission rates of 1,000 Mbps.

half duplex Capability for data transmission in only one direction at a time between a sending station and a receiving station.

HAL (Hardware Abstraction Layer) A set of routines and code that directly manipulates the hardware in your system. All user application hardware requests and most OS drivers (including the Windows NT Executive) must go through the HAL in order to be processed.

hard error A type of error that can occur in a memory subsystem, in which a piece of hardware is broken and continually returns incorrect information.

heartbeat A signal that lets a server know that it is still connected to another server. Once the heartbeat stops, one server will assume that the other server has failed.

hot-expansion Installing a new device in an empty slot without disrupting server operations.

hot-replacement Replacing a failed or failing PCI device with an identical model without downing the server.

hot-upgrade Installing an upgraded device without disrupting server operations.

Insight Manager A client-server management tool that uses industry-standard SNMP protocols found in Windows 95 and Windows NT Workstations for managing hardware problems and configurations.

interface A connection between two systems or devices; or in routing terminology, a network connection.

Internet protocol Any protocol that is part of the TCP/IP protocol stack.

Internet Term used to refer to the global internetwork that evolved from the ARPANET, that now connects tens of thousands of networks worldwide.

IP (Internet Protocol) Network layer protocol in the TCP/IP stack offering a connectionless datagram service. IP provides features for addressing, type-of-service specification, fragmentation and reassembly, and security.

IP address A 32-bit address assigned to hosts using the TCP/IP suite of protocols. An IP address is written as four octets separated by dots (dotted decimal format). Each address consists of a network number, an optional subnetwork number, and a host number. The network and subnetwork numbers together are used for routing, while the host number is used to address an individual host within the network or subnetwork. A subnet mask is often used with the address to extract network and subnetwork information from the IP address.

LAN (local-area network) High-speed, low-error data network covering a relatively small geographic area. LANs connect workstations, peripherals, terminals, and other devices in a single building or other geographically limited area. LAN standards specify cabling and signaling at the physical and data-link layers of the OSI model. Ethernet, FDDI, and Token Ring are the most widely used LAN technologies.

logical drive A number of physical drives grouped together as a single drive. To the operating system, it appears as a single physical drive.

Look-Aside cache When a processor makes a request in systems using Look-Aside cache, the request is generated across the entire system bus. Every device on the bus—cache, expansion cards, and main memory—sees the request. If the requested data is in cache, the cache responds. If the data is not in cache, main memory is already processing the request without the need for the processor to generate a second request.

Look-Through cache Look-Through cache policies support concurrent system bus operations by segregating the initial processor read request from the system bus. While the request is being serviced by cache, bus mastering I/O devices are free to access main memory. If there is a cache miss, the processor generates a second request. This is called the lookup penalty, because it uses additional bus cycles to transfer the data.

maximum data throughput The amount of data that can flow across a bus during a given amount of time. It is a means to measure a computer's performance against others. The data throughput is determined by a formula: $(F \times W) / N = \text{MTR}$. (The frequency times the width, divided by the number of clock cycles, equals the maximum transfer rate.)

media The various physical environments through which transmission signals pass. Common network media include cable (twisted-pair, coaxial, and fiber optic) and the atmosphere (through which microwave, laser, and infrared transmission occurs). Sometimes referred to as physical media.

memory cells Internally, computer memory is arranged as a matrix of memory cells laid out in rows and columns, like squares on a checkerboard. Each memory cell is used to store a single bit of data, which can be retrieved by indicating the row and column location (address) of the data. Because these bits of data can be individually accessed, retrieved, and modified at random, the type of main memory used in computers is called Random Access Memory (RAM).

MIB (Management Information Base) The definitions, provided by the management agent, of managed elements to an application. The definitions contain the properties of the objects defined, the functions that are supported against the objects, and the information that can be retrieved on the objects.

multimode fiber A medium capable of transmitting optical signals of up to 500m (1600ft).

NetBIOS (Network Basic Input/Output System) An application programming interface used by applications on an IBM LAN to request services from lower-level network processes such as session establishment and termination, and information transfer.

NetWare A network operating system developed by Novell, Inc. Provides remote file access, print services, and numerous other distributed network services.

network controller pair Network controller pairs are two NICs that are configured to act as one, providing fault tolerance. One card is the primary and one is the secondary. When the primary fails to receive a response from the network, the secondary controller takes over.

network interface Border between a carrier network and a privately owned installation.

network Collection of computers, printers, routers, switches, and other devices that are able to communicate with each other over some transmission medium.

page fault Method a system uses to retrieve information when it does not find the information in physical memory. There are hard page faults and soft page faults. With a soft page fault, the faulted pages are found elsewhere in physical memory (usually the file system cache). With a hard page fault, the faulted pages are found in the pagefile on the hard disk.

PCI (Peripheral Component Interconnect) A 32-bit local bus specification from Intel that allows as many as 10 PCI-compliant expansion cards to be installed in a computer.

PEZ files Databases that contain a list of the software stored on the SmartStart CDs or the Compaq Integration Server.

pipelining A process in which multiple instructions are overlapped, so many processes can be handled at once. There is a five-stage pipeline used by the Pentium processor. The five stages are:

1. Pre-fetch
2. Decoding of the instruction
3. Generation of memory address, if instruction includes a memory reference
4. Execution of the instruction
5. Results are stored or "written back"

POSIX (Portable Operating System Interface for Computing Environments) A set of standards for writing applications so that they can run on different operating systems. Although mainly used in UNIX environments, POSIX also can be implemented in non-UNIX environments such as Windows NT.

POST (Power-On Self Test) Upon bootup of any PC system, the system BIOS runs through several diagnostics to determine if critical subsystem devices are working.

preemptive multitasking Preemptive multitasking does not leave the decision to share CPU resources with the process. These decisions are made by the operating system. The processing capabilities of the CPU are shared among processes. Operating systems that employ preemptive multitasking are UNIX, Windows 95, Windows 98, Windows NT, and OS/2.

pre-fetch queue A feature of Pentium processors. While the processor is handling one instruction, it can be decoding the next instruction in the pre-fetch queue.

process An application or part of an application that consists of a memory address space, a set of objects, and a set of worker threads. A thread is the most basic piece of a process that can be scheduled processor time.

Push and Pull architecture In order to move software around, Compaq Integration Server uses Push and Pull architecture. The "pull" refers to the software being downloaded from Compaq and placed on the Integration Server. The "push" refers to software being uploaded to the servers in the environment from the Integration Server.

quad multiprocessing Quad multiprocessing, like shared-cache dual processing, uses a second-level cache. In quad multiprocessing, each processor has its own second-level cache. With the larger number of external, second-level caches, there is a larger total available space for data, which reduces the frequency with which the main memory is accessed.

query Message used to inquire about the value of some variable or set of variables.

queue A backlog of packets stored in buffers and waiting to be forwarded over a router interface.

RAID (Redundant Array of Inexpensive Disks) The RAID standard defines six levels, of which the Compaq array controllers support four:
RAID 0 Data Striping without Parity
RAID 1 Mirrored
RAID 2 Complex Error Correction (no longer used)
RAID 3 Parallel-Transfer, Dedicated Parity (no longer used)
RAID 4 Data Striping with Dedicated Party
RAID 5 Data Striping with Distributed Parity

RAM (Random Access Memory) A volatile form of memory, it must have power in order to retain data. When the power is turned off, data held in RAM is lost. Contrast this to physical storage media such as magnetic media (hard disks, floppy disks, tapes), which can retain data even without power.

replication profile A server configuration stored on the server profile disk.

ROMPaqs Compaq's flash upgrade programs for easy maintenance and upgrading of the server BIOS. The BIOS is upgraded when the system is booted off a diskette created for this process.

ROM (Read-Only Memory) ROM is used to store boot code and POST processes.

router Network layer device that uses one or more metrics to determine the optimal path along which network traffic should be forwarded. Routers forward packets from one network to another based on network layer information.

routing Process of finding a path to a destination host.

SDRAM (Synchronous DRAM) In SDRAM, memory is divided into two banks, which can be accessed independently.

second-level cache An external cache that processors can use when their first-level cache space is exhausted.

shared cache When a system uses shared cache, it contains multiple processors but accesses a single second-level cache. Also known as **dual processing.**

SIMM (Single Inline Memory Module) The most common memory module format. SIMMs are available in 30-pin and 72-pin models.

single-mode fiber A medium that can transmit optical signals up to 10km (6.2mi).

SNMP (Simple Network Management Protocol) This protocol is one of the main components of Compaq Insight Manager. SNMP defines a set of commands (SET and GET) that a management application uses to retrieve or change the values made available by a management agent. It provides a means of communication between the device being managed and the system managing it.

soft error A type of memory error in which a bit is read back with the wrong value once, but subsequent reads function correctly. A soft error usually repeats itself, but it can take anywhere from seconds to years for this to happen.

SoftPAQs Compaq's driver and software update files. These files are available on the Compaq Web site for downloading, and include BIOS upgrades as well as drivers for various adapters. They allow the creation of bootable or utility diskettes that can be used to run software or upgrade the system partition.

SRAM (Static Random Access Memory) This memory type is extremely fast—usually 5–25 nanoseconds. This memory is typically used only in cache memory due to the manufacturing cost, physical size, and heat generated by the chips.

standard Set of rules or procedures that are either widely used or officially specified.

symmetric multiprocessing Symmetric multiprocessing allows each processor equal access to system resources. Operating systems that employ symmetric multiprocessing include Linux, Sun Solaris, and Windows NT. In each of these operating systems, each processor runs the operating system and shares memory. The symmetric multiprocessing model allows for the multiple threads of a single process to be spread equally across multiple processors.

System Configuration Utility Compaq's primary means of configuring a Compaq Server. It is used to install and configure hardware, set system-specific settings, and run a variety of diagnostics and utilities.

TCP (Transmission Control Protocol) Connection-oriented transport layer protocol that provides reliable full-duplex data transmission. TCP is part of the TCP/IP protocol stack.

throughput Rate of information arriving at, and possibly passing through, a particular point in a network system.

topology A set of items that connect two or more ports. These items may include GBIC, media, hubs, and switches.

trap SNMP's means of alerting an administrator to a specific condition. The trap provides the SET and GET with the appropriate responses.

Version Control A feature of Compaq's Insight Manager that assists an administrator in tracking driver revisions on the server. Version Control is a task of the managed server.

wait state The period of time in which a CPU or a bus must sit idle due to the differing clock speeds of components in the system. The most common wait state encountered is between memory components and the CPU. In a zero wait state system, the CPU is allowed to run at full speed and does not require any time-outs to compensate for slower memory.

Write-Back The Write-Back policy allows data to remain dirty in cache and stale in main memory until it is requested by a bus master device, presenting the potential for data coherency issues. The result is decreased bus utilization.

Write-Through In a system using Write-Through cache, after each cache write, the processor also issues a write to main memory. Consequently, data is consistent. However, system bus utilization is increased. Write-Through is a cost-effective solution for most stand-alone systems.

INDEX

%Broadcasts counter, 750
%Disk Time counter, 744, 745
%Disk Time dedicated to paging, 746
%Free Space counter, 709
%Interrupt Time counter, 750
%Network Utilization counter, 750
%Privileged Time counter, 734, 735–736
%Processor Time counter, 709, 733–734, 736–737
%Total Processor Time counter, 734
%Usage counter, 718, 720
%Usage Peak counter, 718, 720
%User Time counter, 734, 735–736
2-clock SDRAM, 37–38
3.3-volt, unbuffered DIMM, 40
4-clock SDRAM, 37–38
4GB RAM Tuning (4GT), 550
8-bit ISA, 68
8ns SDRAM modules, 37
10/100-Mbps NIC, included with a RIB, 456
10ns SDRAM modules, 37
16-bit applications, running in separate address spaces, 567
16-bit ISA, 68
16-bit operating systems, Insight Manager and, 380
30-pin SIMMs, 38, 39
50-pin cables, 122
68-pin cables, 122
72-pin SIMMs, 38, 39
100Base-TX networks, 203–204
100Base-TX UTP module, 202
100VG-AnyLAN networks, 204
100VG-AnyLAN UTP module, 202
7200 rpm drives, versus 10,000 rpm drives, 730, 731
80486 processor, 5

A

ABORT parameter, 617
About Windows NT window, 646
Absorption, causing attenuation, 152
AC power failure, paging the administrator, 353
Accelerator cache, in array controllers, 141–142
Account Login page, on the device home page, 530
Accounts option, in the Administrator Insight XE window, 440
Accredited Systems Engineer (ASE), 270
Active port, 348
Active termination, 123
Active termination blocks, 124
Active terminators, 125
ACU (Compaq On-Line Array Configuration Utility), 636
ADC. *See* Automatic Data Collection (ADC) function
ADC Enabled filter, in Insight Manager, 416
Add Remove Hardware option, in the Systems Configuration Utility, 102–103
Add to Alert window, 702–703
Add to Chart window
    Instance field, 736
    in Performance Monitor, 700–701
Add to Log dialog box, in Log view, 705
Add to Report dialog box, 707
Address bus, 4–5, 7, 10, 11, 17
Address bus lines, placing row addresses on, 31
Address lines, for common Intel processor types, 5
Address space, 719
Addressable memory size, 5
Administer Insight XE window, in Insight Manager XE, 440

Administrative overhead, reducing for networks, 306–307
Administrative Tools folder, running Performance Monitor from, 698
Administrator account
  changing the password for, in Web Agents, 532
  permissions to reboot the server, 534
  for Web Agents, 531
Administrator, logging on as, to configure options for Web Agents, 519–520, 521
Administrator password, setting for ASR, 354
Administrator Settings screen, in Insight Manager LC, 435–436
Administrators, reducing the need for, 306–307
ADU. *See* Array Diagnostic Utility (ADU)
Advanced Alpha Setup window, in Insight Manager, 414
Advanced ECC memory, 45
Advanced Mode, of system configuration, 107–108
Advanced Network Control utility, 636–638, 684
Advanced Network Fault Detection process, 684–685
Advanced Programmable Interrupt Controller, 17
Advanced RISC Computing, 664, 665
Agents
  in Insight Manager, 225
  in a management system, 323
AGLT+ bus, terminating, 21
Alarm Destinations window, in Insight Manager, 182, 410
Alarm Details window, 401–402, 403
Alarm forwarding, 409–414
Alarm Log, 400–403
  displaying in Insight Manager, 400–401
  printing from, 402–403
  sortable column headers in, 401, 402
Alarm monitoring system, in ManageWise, 313–314
Alarms
  displaying in Insight Manager, 400–403
  forwarding, 409–414
  in ManageWise, 314
  printing in Insight Manager, 402–403
  thresholds for setting off, 183
  triggering with Insight Manager, 182–183
  viewing details of, 401–402, 403
Alert condition, specifying in Alert view, 703
Alert Handling window, in Power Management Console, 447
Alert mechanism, for power failures, 627
Alert view, of Performance Monitor, 702–703, 709, 711
Alerting, pre-failure, 237
Alerts
  about primary server failure through Insight Manager, 295
  forwarding through the RIB, 469–470
  in Insight Manager, 316
  in Insight Manager LC, 435
  in NetView, 313
  sending through the RIB to a pager, 471
  triggering in Insight Manager, 182
ALUs, in Pentium processors, 17
AMD 29040-33, in the SMART-2 controller, 674
AMP (Asymmetric multiprocessing), 84–85
Anonymous Access configuration option, for Web Agents, 521
Anonymous account
  no permission to reboot the server, 533
  for Web Agents, 531
Anonymous user, connecting as, 530
Answers in Depth hyperlink, in Personal Testing Center, 865
Answers, Self Test, 761–860
APIs (Application Program Interfaces), 557
Application Password window, in Insight Manager, 408
Application server, 729, 730
Application server farms, creating load-balanced, 551
Applications
  address space for, 563
  assigning address space to, 719
  demands on the cache subsystem, 63
  displaying the amount of physical memory available to, 739
  initializing in Recovery Server, 298
  leaking, 742
  in a management system, 323
  running in their own space, 555
Arbitrated loops, 156, 168
ARC path, 664, 665

Architectural modules, in Windows NT, 556
Architecture, of Windows NT, 553–559
Arithmetic Logic Units (ALUs), 17
Array Accelerator, 671
  in SMART array controllers, 133, 134
  in the SMART-2 controller, 675
Array accelerator/battery pack, upgrading, 143
Array Accelerator Cache, monitoring the integrity of, 346
Array Accelerator Tracking, 346
Array Configuration Utility, 175, 176, 581–582, 645
  configuring hot-pluggable hard disks, 140
  in the Systems Configuration Utility, 597
Array Configuration Utility option, in the Systems Configuration Utility, 101
Array controller and drives, initializing in Recovery Server, 298
Array controllers
  configuring, 175
  duplexing, 247
  placing on different buses, 76
  read cache compared to read/write cache, 144
  recommendations for, 133
  required for Standby Recovery Server, 291
  supported under Windows NT, 620
Array Diagnostic Utility (ADU), 279, 281
Array technologies, 132
Arrays. *See* Drive arrays
ASE, SmartStart program subscription and updates received by an, 270
ASR (Automatic Server Recovery), 351, 352–354, 356, 612
  configuring options for, 583–585
  configuring to page an administrator with a notification, 353
  consequences of not loading the OS driver, 355
  device drivers for, 354
  enabling, 355
  enabling features, 103
  five-step process for resolving issues, 353
  in ProLiant Storage Systems, 676
  security issues and features, 354
  testing settings, 268
ASR-2, 277, 351, 353
Asset Management, 365–367
Assisted Integration path
  versus Manual Configuration, 589–591
  in SmartStart, 579
Asymmetric multiprocessing, 84–85
Asynchronous DRAM, 33–34
Asynchronous I/O, in I/O Manager, 560
Asynchronous transfer, 116
Attachments window, in Power Management Console, 447
Attended recovery, in ASR, 353
Attenuation, 152
Attributes, changing for the BOOT.INI file, 616
Audible Alarms option, in Insight Manager, 182
AUI connection, supporting on the NetFlex-2 ENET-TR adapter, 200
AUI-to-BNC transceiver, for the NetFlex-2 Dual Port ENET, 200
Authentication, of users, 729
Auto Delete Users configuration option, for Web Agents, 521
Auto Recovery component, in Server Agent, 525
AutoCAD drawing, exporting from Visio, 251
Auto-loaders, for DAT tape devices, 253
Automated Diagnostics option, 267
Automatic Data Collection (ADC) function
  configuring, 394
  enabling, 393
  of Insight Manager, 392–398
  not included with Insight Manager XE, 538
  performing with Insight Manager, 538
Automatic printing of reports, configuring in Insight Manager, 397–398
Automatic Reporting filter, in Insight Manager, 416
Automatic Server Recovery-2. *See* ASR-2
Automatic Server Recovery (ASR). *See* ASR (Automatic Server Recovery)
Auto-sensing controller card, 202
Available Bytes counter, 709, 720, 739, 741–742
Available Bytes in MB, preset threshold for Windows NT, 529
Average Disk Queue Length counter, 744
Avg. Disk sec/Transfer counter, 746

B

BACKSPACE key, highlighting selected counters in Chart view, 702
Backup, performing a complete, 631
Backup Domain Controller (BDC), configuring a server as, 586
Backup strategies, Fibre Channel and, 151
Balanced option, in the Server service window, 724
Bandwidth, increased in the PCI bus, 455
Bank of memory, data lines and, 29
Base priority, setting for a process, 726–729
Baseline trace, establishing, 738
Baselines, 312
BASE.LOG file, created by the System Configuration Record utility, 434
/BASEVIDEO switch, for BOOT.INI, 615
Basic Input Output System. *See* BIOS
Basic Input Output System version. *See* BIOS version
Battery backed cache, in SMART array controllers, 133, 134
Battery backup, in array controllers, 142
Battery health, monitoring, 346
/BAUDRATE switch, for BOOT.INI, 615
BDC (Backup Domain Controller), configuring a server as, 586
BEDO memory, 35–36
Beeps, diagnostic, 273
Benchmark Yourself screen, in Personal Testing Center, 865
BIOS
- checking the version of, 459
- remotely updating on machines supporting Remote ROM Flash, 365
- upgrading, 104, 276
- verifying before RIB installation, 458

BIOS version, notification in POST, 271–272
Bits, 6
Blue Screen of Death (BSOD), 468, 717, 718
BMC Software, Inc., technology from, 527
BNC connections, allowing with the NetFlex-2 ENET-TR adapter, 200
Bookmarks list, adding direct link URLs, 523
Boost and buck feature, 445
Boot code, storing, 20
Boot loader section, of the Windows NT BOOT.INI file, 613–614
Boot partition, configuring, 585, 663–667
Bootable CD, system ROM supporting, 577
BOOT.INI file, 613
- contents of, 613–614
- copying to the recovery disk, 664
- HAL Recovery Mode entry in, 611
- modifying, 615–616, 664–667
- switches, 614–615

Borland database engine
- installed with Insight Manager, 177
- installing for Insight Manager, 382

Borland Database Engine option, for Insight Manager, 384
Bottlenecks, identifying, 752
Branch prediction, 17
Bridged PCI architecture, 75
Bridged PCI bus, 232, 685
Bridged PCI devices
- adding to ProLiant 5000, 6000, 6500, and 7000 servers, 685–687
- SMART-2 controller as, 675

%Broadcasts counter, 750
Browser. *See also* Web browser
- disabling clients from taking part in elections, 751
- requirements for the management PC, 518

BSOD (Blue Screen of Death), 468, 717, 718
Buffer layer of fiber media, 152–153, 168
Buffered local bus, in the PCI design, 70
Built-in server filters, using in Insight Manager, 415–418
Built-in thresholds, in ManageWise, 313–314
Burst cycles, 7, 11
Burst EDO memory, 35–36
Burst Extended Data Out DRAM, 19
Burst mode, 69
Burst mode transfers, 10, 12
Burst transfer rate, of an EISA bus master device, 69
Bus architectures, 4, 11, 76

Bus cycles, 6, 7, 11, 12
Bus mastering, 69, 455
Bus mastering architecture, 9
Bus numbers, assigning to PCI buses, 685–686
Bus technologies, 72
Bus utilization. *See* System bus utilization
Bus width, 5, 7
Bus-contention logic, 116
Buses, 4–7, 10, 11
Bypass Circuitry option, in Power Management Console, 445
Bytes, 6
Bytes Received/sec counter, 749, 750
Bytes Sent/sec counter, 749
Bytes Total/sec counter, 749, 750, 752
Bytes Transmitted/sec counter, 750

C

C2-compliant operating system, Windows NT as a, 568
C2CONFIG.EXE utility, 568
Cable management arms, for racks, 250
Cabletron Spectrum, 315
Cabling
  differential and single-ended, 117
  ordering for Compaq servers, 124
Cache, 54, 88
  flushing to disk, 672
  levels of, 733
  in a Pentium processor, 17, 18–19
  types of, 18–19
Cache architectures, 57–61
Cache Bytes counter, 713
Cache Bytes Peak counter, 713
Cache capacity, in SMART array controllers, 132, 134
Cache controller, in dual processing, 89
Cache Copy Read/Hits per second, preset threshold for Windows NT, 529
Cache directory, 56
Cache hits, 54, 55, 733
Cache management logic, 56
Cache Manager, in I/O Manager, 561
Cache memory
  levels of, 223–224
  on the SMART controller, 671–672
  using SRAM for, 32
Cache memory subsystem, 54–55
  components of, 55–56
  performance of, 61–63
Cache misses, 54, 55
Cache read activity, 58
Cache size, effect on performance, 62
Cache write activity, 59
Caching subsystem, 8
Capacitors, refresh cycle and, 30–31
Carbon Copy graphical remote control software package, 467
Carrier Sense Multiple Access/Collision Detection media access method, 203
CAS line, 31
CD
  allowing computers to boot from, 174
  installing software from, 582
CD key, entering, 587
CD with this book
  Personal Testing Center included, 862
  Test Yourself software, 862
Centronics cables, 122
.CFG files, for EISA adapters, 69
Channels, 151, 152
Chart view, 698–702, 708–709
  graph mode of, 711
  tracking counters in, 702
Choose Destination Location window, in Compaq Power Management, 443
Chromatic dispersion, causing attenuation, 152
CIM (Compaq Insight Manager). *See* Insight Manager
CIMU (Compaq Integration Maintenance Utility)
  accessing Integration Server, 495
  downloading software from an Integration Server, 593–596
  installing under Windows NT, 495–496
  NetWare and, 496–497
  updating system software, 496
  warning messages, 595, 596

Citrix ICA protocol, 551
Citrix MetaFrame, 551
Citrix WinFrame 1.7 product, 551
Cladding, 152, 153, 168
Clean operation system shutdown, 678
Client Alarm column, in the Alarm Log, 401, 402
Clients, disabling from taking part in browser elections, 751
Client-server environment, highest load subsystems in, 730–731
Clock rate, for processors, 733
Clock speed, 7
Cloud shape drawing, of fabric, 158, 159
Cluster Administrator, 441–442
Cluster configurations, tracking changes to, 442
Cluster Members filter, in Insight Manager, 416
Clusters, status information for, 524
CMOS, 20
Cold boots, upgrading the BIOS, 276
Collected data, reporting in Insight Manager, 394–398
Color coded status, in the Device List window, 419–420
Color codes, in Version Control, 479–481
Column Access Select (CAS) line, 31
Column address, for memory, 31
COM port, setting the baud rate for, 615
Combined client
    for Insight Manager, 428
    for Insight Manager LC, 430–432
Combined console, for Insight Manager, 428
Command complete stage, for a SCSI I/O request, 119
Command prompt, altering a program's priority, 726, 728–729
Command setup stage, for a SCSI I/O request, 119
Commands, used in the SNMP protocol, 324
Commit Limit, 739, 740
Commit Limit counter, 720, 739
Committed Bytes counter, 740, 741–742
Committed memory, 739
Community names, 403–408
    case-sensitivity of, 329, 331
    configuring for different devices, 406–407
    hiding in Device Setup windows, 407–408
    selecting, 329–330
    setting default for new devices in Insight Manager, 406
    setting in different operating systems, 404
    in SNMP protocol, 329–330
Compaq Accredited Systems Engineer (ASE), 270
Compaq Advanced Network Control utility, 636–638, 684
Compaq ARRAY CONFIGURATION utility. *See* Array Configuration Utility
Compaq array controllers, 673. *See also* Array controllers
Compaq Configuration Record applet, 431
Compaq custom HALs, for Windows NT 3.x, 608–609
Compaq desktops, selecting memory modules for, 40
Compaq device drivers, 622–624, 648–649. *See also* Device drivers
Compaq devices
    supported in Windows NT, 617–622
    supported with SSD, 619–622
Compaq Diagnostics applet, 431
Compaq Diagnostics utility, 433–434. *See also* Compaq System Diagnostics utility
Compaq DLT drives, 252
Compaq Drive Array Controllers component, in Storage Agent, 527
Compaq driver, for the ProLiant Storage System, 627
Compaq Enhanced Integrated Management Display Service, 638–639
Compaq Fault Prevention. *See* Fault prevention
Compaq Fibre Channel Host Controller/P, 640
Compaq Fibre Channel Storage System. *See* Fibre Channel Storage System
Compaq Foundation Agent, 524
Compaq Full-Spectrum Fault Management, 344–349, 355
Compaq hardware devices, viewing the settings of, 103
Compaq hardware mirroring, 668–670
Compaq Insight Agents. *See* Insight Agents
Compaq Insight Manager (CIM). *See* Insight Manager
Compaq Insight Manager LC. *See* Insight Manager LC
Compaq Insight Manager XE. *See* Insight Manager XE
Compaq Inspect Utility
    documenting hardware configurations, 100, 106
    utilizing, 104
Compaq Integrated Management Display (IMD) Utility, 638

Compaq Integrated Management Display Utility window, 639
Compaq Integration Maintenance Utility. *See* CIMU (Compaq Integration Maintenance Utility)
Compaq Integration Maintenance Utility main window, 594, 595
Compaq Integration Maintenance Utility window, 594
Compaq Integration Server. *See* Integration Server (IS)
Compaq Intelligent Cluster Administrator, 441–442
Compaq Intelligent Manageability. *See* Intelligent Manageability
Compaq Management CD, 577
Compaq memory, 45. *See also* Memory
Compaq Netelligent network controllers. *See* Netelligent controllers
Compaq NetFlex-2 Dual Port ENET. *See* NetFlex-2 Dual Port ENET
Compaq NetFlex-2 network controllers. *See* NetFlex-2 network controllers
Compaq NetFlex-3 network controllers. *See* NetFlex-3 network controllers
Compaq network card modules, hot-plug capable, 640
Compaq network cards. *See also* NICs
    configuring for failover, 636–637
    hot-plug capable, 640
Compaq network controllers. *See* Network controllers
Compaq NIC Agent, 527, 528
Compaq NT Management, 527
Compaq On-Line Array Configuration Utility (ACU), 636
Compaq PCI Hot Plug Utility. *See* PCI Hot Plug Utility
Compaq PEZ files. *See* PEZ files
Compaq Power Down Manager, 641–643, 645
Compaq Power Management, 442–447
Compaq Power Management Software, 625–627
Compaq Power Supply Viewer, 644
Compaq products, searchable database of, 124
Compaq ProLiant Storage System. *See* ProLiant Storage System
Compaq Rack Builder software. *See* Rack Builder utility
Compaq Racks. *See* Racks
Compaq RAID Array 4000, 159, 160–161, 168
Compaq RAID Array 8000, 162–163, 168
Compaq Rapid Recovery Engine. *See* Rapid Recovery Engine
Compaq Recovery Agent (CRA), 296, 677
    continuity of service under, 683
    maintaining the heartbeat signal, 296
    running two in Online Recovery Server, 296
    running under an online recovery configuration, 681
Compaq Recovery Server. *See* Recovery Server
Compaq Recovery Server option, 680
Compaq Remote Insight Board. *See* RIB (Remote Insight Board)
Compaq Remote Insight Board/PCI, supported only from the Compaq SSD, 622
Compaq Restore CD, 364
Compaq root MIB number, 335
Compaq SCSI controllers. *See also* SCSI controllers
    Compaq drivers for, 628
    hot-plug capable, 641
    loading drivers during Windows NT installation, 628–629
Compaq SCSI Controllers component, in Storage Agent, 527
Compaq SCSI Driver, 628, 629–630
Compaq Server Agent, 524–526
Compaq Server Management Technology, 344
Compaq servers. *See also* Servers
    assigning standbys for, 676
    calculating thermal and electrical requirements for, 250
    deriving information from remote, 405
    displaying information about, 392
    displaying real-time information about, 638–639
    displaying subsets of, 415
    downgrading to a single processor, 610, 611
    employing dual processing, 90
    employing quad processing, 91–92
    enabling data collection for, 393
    erasing all data from, 102
    error detection and correction in, 41–42
    full remote control of, 254
    IDs supported per SCSI bus, 118, 121, 125

options for, 246–255
ordering cabling for, 124
performing a complete backup before upgrading, 631
racks for, 248
rebooting, 398–400
reporting memory errors, 44–45
selecting memory modules for, 40
setting data collection intervals for, 394
setup process of, 99
support software for, 98
supporting Windows NT on, 604–650
troubleshooting memory errors on, 46
upgrading to multiprocessor, 610
using Compaq memory in, 45
Compaq SMART array controllers. *See* SMART array controllers
Compaq SmartStart. *See* SmartStart
Compaq SmartStart and Support Software CD, 98–100, 108, 270
Compaq SmartStart software kit, 99
Compaq SSD. *See* SSD (Support Software Diskette)
Compaq SSD setup program. *See* SSD program
Compaq stencils, in the Visio Network Equipment add-on, 251
Compaq Storage Agent, 527
Compaq storage expansion systems, 246–248
Compaq storage products, viewing the entire new selection of, 248
Compaq Support Software Server, connecting to, 498
Compaq Support Tools and Utilities, obtaining, 269–270
Compaq support Web site, 270
Compaq System Configuration utility. *See* SCU (System Configuration Utility)
Compaq System Diagnostics utility, 175, 176
Compaq System Erase utility, 174, 176
Compaq Systempro systems, 85
Compaq SystemPro/XL, 174
Compaq Systems Management driver. *See* Systems Management driver
Compaq tape drives
configuring in Windows NT setup, 619
not supported by Windows NT, 618–619
supported by Windows NT, 618
Compaq UPS (Uninterruptible Power Supply), 625–627. *See also* UPS
Compaq utilities, 635–644
Compaq Web site, Customer Advisories section, 482
Compaq Windows NT SSDs, installing online recovery server software, 682
Compaq-failure warranty program. *See* Pre-failure warranty coverage
COMPAQ.PEZ file
on the Integration Server, 502, 503
on the Management CD, 502
Compaq-specific features, configuring for servers, 103
Compatibility, of Windows NT, 554
Competence Key Tool, at the Global Knowledge Web site, 868
Complementary Metal Oxide Semiconductor (CMOS), 20
Component interface, in DMI, 362
Components
arranging in racks, 190
managing with Compaq Web Agents, 523–529
Composite SIMMs, 39
Computer buses. *See* Buses
Computer memory. *See* Memory
Computers, measuring the performance of, 9
CONFIG report form, 395
Configuration button, in the Insight Manager Device Data window, 184, 185
Configuration changes, logging, 277–278
Configuration information, collecting and displaying, 268
Configuration management, 308, 312, 363–365
Configuration options, setting for Insight Manager, 177
Configuration screen, for Insight Manager, 384
Configuration Utility. *See* SCU (System Configuration Utility)
Console Functions, in the Windows 32-bit Subsystem, 569
Continuity of service, during failover, 679, 682–683

Control bus, 6, 7, 10, 11
Controller cards. *See* Network controllers
Controller pairs
forming, 348, 349
setting up, 684–685
Controller types, 743
Controllers
attaching to switchable ProLiant storage systems, 291
calculating parity information, 662
installing multiple on dual peer PCI bus-based systems, 235
monitoring environment variables, 346
performing diagnostics on, 104
redundancy options for, 347
Conventional DRAM, 34
Cooperative multitasking, 82–83
Copper media, supporting Fibre Channel over, 151
Core layer of fiber media, 152, 168
Correctable Error Log, 352, 355, 356
Correctable Memory component, in Server Agent, 525
Correctable memory errors, 345
Corrected Memory Errors, entries for, 230
Counter field, in the Add to Chart window, 701
Counters
adding to Alert view, 702–703
adding to Performance Monitor, 700–701
adding to Report view, 707
displaying different instances of the same, 700
enabling/disabling for disk performance, 725–726
for generating alerts, 709
highlighting selected in Chart view, 702
measuring for system objects, 696–697
in Performance Monitor, 732–752
showing bottlenecks, 752
tracking in Chart view, 702
CPM (Compaq Power Management) software, 625–627
CPQ32FS2.SYS, 628
CPQASRD device driver, for ASR, 354
CPQCPM icon, double-clicking to run Power Management Console, 444
CPQHLTH.EXE device driver, for ASR, 354
CPQHLTH.NLM device driver, for ASR, 354
CPQHLTH.SYS device driver, for ASR, 354
CPQIS ID, creating for NetWare, 503
CPQIS local account, creating for Windows NT, 504
CPQMAINT.NLM, 496–497
CPU stress utility, 737
CPU Util >=10% filter, in Insight Manager, 418
CPU utilization, as a managed element, 333
CPUs, 732. *See also* Processors
adding multiple, 733
addressable memory size for, 5
CRA. *See* Compaq Recovery Agent (CRA)
/CRASHDEBUG switch, for BOOT.INI, 615
CRC (cyclic redundancy check), in Fibre Channel, 151
Create Stripe Set With Parity option, 667, 668
Create Support Software option, in the SCU, 102
Create/Update System Partition option, in the SCU, 101–102
Critical Error Log, 277–278, 352, 353, 355, 356
Critical Errors component, in Server Agent, 525
CSMA/CD media access method, 203
CTRL-A, entering Advanced Mode of system configuration, 107
CTRL-H, highlighting selected counters in Chart view, 702
Current Bandwidth counter, 749
Current Disk Queue Length counter, 709, 744, 745, 752
Custom filters, 418–419
Customer Advisories, reducing upgrade stress with, 482

D

DAAD (Drive Array Advanced Diagnostics) utility, 143, 278
generating a report from, 278
physical drive analysis screen, 279
running, 269
running ADU, 281
DAT (Digital Audio Tape) devices, 252–253
Data bus, 6, 7, 11
in a Pentium processor, 17–18
width of, 6

Data cache, in a Pentium processor, 17
Data coherency problems, 60, 61
Data collection, 315–316. *See also* Automatic Data Collection (ADC) function
Data drives, RAID 5 for, 140
Data frame, in a Web page, 522
Data guarding, 347
Data striping
with dedicated parity, 138–139
with distributed parity, 139
without parity, 135–136
Data throughput, 8
Data transfer stage, for a SCSI I/O request, 119
Databases, downloading current, for Version Control, 483–486
DATALOG.EXE, 707
Date/Time column, in the Alarm Log, 401, 402
Daughtercard cache, in a Fibre Channel Storage System, 160
DBINFO.DB_ file, 484
/DEBUG switches, for BOOT.INI, 615
Debugger, loading automatically, 615
Dedicated parity
calculating, 671
data striping with, 138–139
Default Community String field, in Insight Manager, 406
Default section, in WEBAGENT.INI file, 532
Default striping factor, 136
Degraded status (Yellow), in the Device List window of Insight Manager, 420
Demand priority access method, 204
Description column, in the Alarm Log, 401, 402
Desktop agents, in Insight Manager, 370–372
Desktop management, 308
Desktop management agents, 186
Desktop Management Interface. *See* DMI (Desktop Management Interface)
Desktop Management option, 586
Desktop Management Task Force (DMTF), 362
Destinations, for traps, 328
Destructive read, 31
Device accessibility alarms, in Insight Manager, 183
Device column, in the Alarm Log, 401, 402
Device Data window, 184–185
Device discovery, in Insight Manager XE, 439–440
Device drivers
for ASR, 354
from Compaq, 622–624
displaying during the boot process for Windows NT, 615
Device home page, displaying for Web agents, 518–519
"device inaccessible" message, in Insight Manager, 185
Device List, adding servers to, in Insight Manager, 393
Device List Setup window, 179–180
Device List toolbar, in Insight Manager, 180, 181
Device List window, color coded status in, 419–420
Device List window toolbar, enabling filter modes in Insight Manager, 415
Device Options page, fine-tuning browser settings, 522–523
Device Setup screen, in Insight Manager, 393, 407
Device View selection options, 184–185
Devices. *See also* Compaq devices; Hardware devices
allowing quicker turnaround time on failed, 669–670
managing using the local network and existing network hardware, 408
managing via a modem and the Point-to-Point Protocol (PPP), 409
maximum data throughput between, 8–9
setting different community names for, 406–407
Diagnose Drive Array option, in the SCU, 104
Diagnose Drives option, on the Diagnostics and Utilities menu, 269
Diagnostic and Utilities Diskettes, installing to a system partition, 263–264
Diagnostic beeps, 273
Diagnostic diskettes, on older servers, 263
Diagnostic error codes, listing of, 267
Diagnostic tools, 262–264
Diagnostic utilities, 108
Diagnostics
running on system hardware, 103
using to burn-in hardware, 268

Diagnostics and Utilities menu, 264, 265
Diagnostics and Utilities option, in the SCU, 103–104
Diagnostics screen, in Insight Manager LC, 435
Diagnostics utility, viewing the Critical Error Log, 352
Diagnostics window, in Power Management Console, 446
Differential cabling, 117
Differential interfaces, 117
DiffSens circuit, 118
Digital Audio Tape devices (DAT), 252–253
Digital Linear Tape devices (DLT), 252–253
DIMM Serial Presence Detect, 367
DIMMs (Dual Inline Memory Modules), 38, 39–40, 47, 218
Dipswitches, calculating SCSI IDs, 121
Dirty data, 59
DisablePagingExecutive value, changing in the registry, 137
Disaster recovery and prevention. *See* Fault management
Disconnected recovery server interconnect, 294–295
Discovery option, in the Administrator Insight XE window, 440
Disk Administrator
  creating disk partitions, 589
  managing fault tolerant arrays, 663
  screen prior to a fault tolerant configuration, 664
Disk Builder utility, 174, 175, 176, 586
Disk drives. *See also* Hard disks; Hard drives; SCSI drives
  mirroring one to multiple, 659
  MTBF of multiple, 136
  supported by SMART array controllers, 133, 134
Disk mirroring, 347
Disk partitions, 589
Disk performance, enabling/disabling counters for, 725–726
Disk Reads/sec counter, 746, 747, 748
Disk space, requirements for upgrading NT, 631
Disk storage location, for Standby and Online Recovery Server, 291–294
Disk storage usage, 524
Disk striping, 347
Disk subsystem
  counters for, 743–748
  displaying the number of requests waiting to be serviced, 744
  getting the most performance out of, 725–726
  impact of recovery server installation on performance, 298
  improving the performance of, 746–747
  interaction with the memory subsystem, 719–721
%Disk Time counter, 744, 745
%Disk Time dedicated to paging, 746
Disk utilization
  checking, 310
  effect of paging activity on, 715
Diskette Builder utility, creating ROMPaq diskette sets, 274
DISKPERF parameter, 725–726
Disks. *See* Disk drives; Hard disks; Hard drives; SCSI drives
disk(x) part, of the ARC path, 666
Display drivers, running in Kernel mode, 565
Display modes, in Performance Monitor, 698–710
Distributed arbitration logic, 116
Distributed data guarding, 347
Distributed parity, data striping with, 139
Distributed processing, in Windows NT, 555
DLT (Digital Linear Tape) devices, 252–253
DMI 2.0 support, 367
DMI (Desktop Management Interface), 362
DMI V2, Insight Manager XE managing devices supporting, 537
DMTF (Desktop Management Task Force), 362
Dopant, 152
Double-sided SIMMs, 39
DRAM (Dynamic Random Access Memory), 29, 47
  asynchronous, 33–34
  compared to SRAM, 30
  conventional, 34
  features of, 29–32
  reliability of, 41, 42
  speed of, 19, 32
  types of, 19, 33–38
Drive Array Advanced Diagnostics utility. *See* DAAD (Drive Array Advanced Diagnostics) utility
Drive Array Controllers, troubleshooting, 278
Drive Array Information service, 634

Drive arrays, 132
- advantages of, 132
- configuring, 597
- performing diagnostics on, 104

Drive errors, recording in the Alarm Log, 226
Drive indicators, Pre-Failure Warranty advice, 227, 228
Drive Parameter Tracking, 346
Drivers
- determining upgrade needs for, 479
- forcing to remain in memory, 137
- installing on the SSD, 605
- for NetFlex controller cards, 198
- updating remotely, 605
- upgrading, 650

Drivers tab, in the Tape Devices applet, 619
Drives. *See* Disk drives; Hard disks; Hard drives; SCSI drives
DRIVES report form, 395
Dual bus configuration, of the ProLiant Storage System/F, 247
Dual channel Ultra2-SCSI, 118
Dual Channel Wide-Ultra SCSI-3 controller, 215
Dual Inline Memory Modules. *See* DIMMs
Dual multiprocessing, compared to quad, 90–92
Dual peer PCI buses, 87, 232–233, 235
Dual Port ENET card. *See* NetFlex-2 Dual Port ENET
Dual processing, 89, 90. *See also* Shared cache
Dual processor mode, 17
Dual-peer PCI bus, 73–74, 685
Dual-port network cards, 200
Duplexing option kit, for the ProLiant Storage System, 247
Duplexing RAID arrays, 247
Dynamic filter, 417
Dynamic Random Access Memory. *See* DRAM
Dynamic Sector Repairing, 346

E

ECC memory, 43–44, 47, 218, 237
- correcting memory errors, 45
- detecting single-bit and multiple-bit errors, 345

ECC mode, 44
ECU (EISA Configuration utility), 69
Edit Form window, in Insight Manager, 396
EDO memory, 35, 218
EEPROM, 19
Efficient networks, 307
EISA buses, 69, 72, 455
EISA bus master devices, burst transfer rate of, 69
EISA Configuration utility (ECU), 69
El Torito boot specification, 174
Electromagnetic interference (EMI), 164
Electronically Erasable Programmable Read-Only Memory (EEPROM), 19
Elements, 334. *See also* MIB objects
- defining for management applications, 332
- hierarchical structure for, in SNMP, 333
- in a management system, 323

E-mail destinations, specifying in Insight Manager, 411–412
E-mail Forwarding option, in Insight Manager, 182
E-mail messages, sending to pagers, 414
E-Mail Schedule window, accessing in Insight Manager, 412
Emergency Repair Disk (ERD)
- creating, 589, 591
- updating, 631

EMI (electromagnetic interference), 164
Enable auto discovery of IPX servers option, for Insight Manager, 384
Enable auto discovery of Remote Console NVT servers option, for Insight Manager, 384
Enable Remote Reboot option, 586
ENET-TR adapter. *See* NetFlex-2 ENET-TR adapter
Engineers, communication among multiple, 307
Enhanced IMD service, 638–639
Enhanced Integrated Management Display (IMD) Service, 645
Enterprise Edition. *See* Windows NT Server, Enterprise Edition (NTSEE)
ENVIRON report form, 395
Environment component, in Server Agent, 525
Environment subsystems, in Windows NT, 565–569
Environmental status, reporting for servers, 395

Environmental systems, monitoring for problems, 346
EPROM, 19
ERD. *See* Emergency Repair Disk (ERD)
Error checking, types of, 47
Error Correcting Circuit (ECC) memory. *See* ECC memory
Error detection and correction
  need for, 42
  techniques for, 43–44
Error reporting, during POST, 273
Establish Mirror, selecting, 663, 665
Ethernet network cards, 200, 201
Ethernet Statistics component, in NIC Agent, 528
Event 7022, in the Event Log, 404
Event-driven criteria, 327
Excessive internal temperature, recovering from, 353
Expansion Boards button, in the Insight Manager Device Data window, 184, 185
Expansion Boards component, in Server Agent, 525
Expansion cards, PCI buses on, 685
Expansion slots, in servers, 70
Express setup of the SSD, 606, 607
Extended Data Out DRAM, 19
Extended Data Out (EDO) memory, 35, 218
Extended Industry Standard Architecture. *See* EISA buses
Extensibility, of Windows NT, 555–556
External SCSI storage expansion systems, 246–248
External storage, in Standby Recovery Server, 350

F

F_Port, 155
F1 and F2 arrays, 248
F6 key, selecting the quick menu in Insight Manager, 183
F10 key
  accessing the SCU, 101, 461
  accessing the system partition, 175
  launching Diagnostics and Utilities, 264
Fabric, cloud shape drawing of, 158, 159
Failed devices, allowing quicker turnaround time on, 669–670
Failed status (Red), in the Device List window of Insight Manager, 420
Failover process, 677
  causes of, 677–678
  continuity of service during, 679, 682–683
  initiating in Online Recovery Server, 297
  initiating in Standby Recovery Server, 296
  in Recovery Server, 350
  restoring after, 678
  triggering accidentally, 677
Failover shares on the other server, mapping drives to, in logon scripts, 683
Failover time, in standby configurations, 298
Failures, anticipating, 344
Fans
  monitoring, 346
  redundant, 237
Fast Page Mode DRAM, 19
Fast Page Mode memory (FPM), 34–35
Fast SCSI-2 controller, 118
Fast SCSI-2 standard, 117, 119
Fast-Wide SCSI-2 adapters, Fast-SCSI-2 drives and, 125
Fast-Wide SCSI-2 drives, in the ProLiant Storage System/F, 247
Fast-Wide SCSI-2 standard, 117–118, 119
Fault detection and correction features, in Netelligent and NetFlex-3 network cards, 684
Fault management, 309, 368–369
Fault prevention, 134, 344–346, 355
Fault tolerance, 344, 347–349, 355–356
  in array controllers, 134
  creating a boot partition for software-based, 663–667
  hardware-based, 667–675
  not supported for hard disks in Windows NT Workstation, 548
  supported for hard disks by Windows NT Server, 548
Fault tolerant array, 658–662
Fault tolerant boot disk, 674
Fault tolerant features, of Compaq servers, 236–237
Favorites list, adding direct link URLs, 523
FC switches, 158, 168
FC-AL (Fibre Channel Arbitrated Loop), 150, 156–157
  devices supported, 151
  shared access characteristics of, 154

FC-SW (Fibre Channel Switched Fabric), 151, 154, 158–159, 168
Fiber, layers of, 152
Fiber media, 150, 152–155
Fibre Array Controller, in a Fibre Channel Storage System, 160
Fibre Array Controllers, redundant, 160
Fibre Channel, 150, 168
  adding an RA4000 on the fly, 161
  architecture overview, 150–155
  bandwidth of, 151
  creating high availability servers, 164–167
  network role of, 151–155
  RAID with, 159–163
  SCSI and, 163–164
  supporting over copper media, 151
  topologies, 155–159
Fibre Channel Arbitrated Loop. *See* FC-AL (Fibre Channel Arbitrated Loop)
Fibre Channel Array, offering from Compaq, 159
Fibre Channel Host Controllers, supported by Windows NT, 620
Fibre Channel Hubs, 154, 168
Fibre Channel Storage System, 159–161
Fibre Channel Storage Systems component, in Storage Agent, 527
Fibre Channel Switched Fabric. *See* FC-SW (Fibre Channel Switched Fabric)
Fibre Channel Switches, 154
Fibre Channel Tape Controllers component, in Storage Agent, 527
File Properties window, Version tab, 649
File servers, 729
  building high availability, 164–167
  on a resource sharing network, 731
  setting up, 576
File system space used, displaying, 524
Filter Name field, in Insight Manager, 419
Filters button, in the Device List, 395–416
Filters, modes for, in Insight Manager, 415
Firmware
  management agents residing in, 332
  updating, 100, 290
  upgrading, 104, 174
First-level cache. *See* L1 cache
FL_Port, 155, 156
FlexSMP System Architecture, 213
Flip-flop storage method, for SRAM, 41
Floppy Drives component, in Server Agent, 525
Folders, creating to group servers in Insight Manager, 180, 181
Forwarding Result column, in the Alarm Log, 401, 402
Foundation Agent, 524
FPM (Fast Page Mode) memory, 34–35
%Free Space counter, with a suggested threshold, 709
Free Space in %, preset threshold for Windows NT, 529
Full duplex, supported in the Fibre Channel standard, 151
Full-Spectrum Fault Management, 344–349, 355

G

"garbage" packets, 312
GBIC (Gigabit Interface Converter), 155, 168
GBIC-LW, 155
GBIC-SW, 155
GDI (Graphics Device Interface), in Windows NT Executive Services, 564
GET command, in SNMP protocol, 326, 338
Gigabit Interface Converter (GBIC), 155, 168
Global Knowledge, 868
Global Settings window, in Insight Manager, 406
Glossary of terms, 883–898
Graded-index fiber, 153–154
Graph mode, of Chart view, 709, 711
Graphic page, in Rack Builder, 191–192
Graphical format, displaying server information in, 698
Graphical mode, in Chart view, 698–699
Graphical OS, accessing remotely, 467
Graphical remote control software packages, 467
Graphics device drivers, in Windows NT Executive Services, 565
Graphics Device Interface (GDI), 564
Graphics driver, configuring for the RIB, 460

Gray icon, on the SSD main screen, 605
Green flag, in Version Control, 480
Green icon, on the SSD main screen, 605
Groups section, in WEBAGENT.INI file, 532

H

HA (High Availability) solutions, 163
HAL mismatches, correcting, 558
HAL recovery mode, 558
HAL Recovery Option, 611
Half duplex, supported in Fibre Channel, 151
HALISA.DLL, 609
HALMPS.DLL, 609
HALs (Hardware Abstraction Layers), 88, 555, 557–558, 607–608
 creating custom, 558
 downgrading a server from multiprocessor to a single processor, 610, 611
 updating, 88
 upgrading from a single processor to a multiprocessor, 610
 Windows NT 3.x custom developed by Compaq, 608–609
HALSP.DLL, 609
HALUP.DLL, 609
Hard disks. *See also* Disk drives; Hard drives; SCSI drives
 measuring the time spent servicing read and write requests, 744
 monitoring for failure, 346
Hard drive array controllers, monitoring critical indicators, 226
Hard drive pre-failure warranty, 369
Hard drives. *See also* Disk drives; Hard disks; SCSI drives
 hot plug swapping of, 347–348
 hot-pluggable, 140
 monitoring for specific operating statistics, 225–228
 recovering from catastrophic failure, 364
Hard errors, 41, 229, 345
Hard page faults, 720
 determining the percentage of paging, 739, 740
 monitoring, 720
Hardware
 burning-in with diagnostics, 268
 documenting configurations, 106
Hardware Abstraction Layers. *See* HALs (Hardware Abstraction Layers)
Hardware data striping, 141
Hardware devices. *See also* Compaq devices; Devices
 adding or removing from your system configuration, 102–103
 viewing the settings of, 103
Hardware filters, in Insight Manager, 417
Hardware incidents, logging, 277–278
Hardware interrupts, 733
 displaying the number of, 737–738
 measuring the percentage of time processors spend serving, 750
Hardware Inventory tool, in MS-SMS, 501
Hardware mirroring, 668–670
Hardware RAID 1. *See* RAID 1 (disk mirroring)
Hardware RAID 4. *See* RAID 4 (data guarding)
Hardware RAID 5. *See* RAID 5 (distributed data guarding)
Hardware requirements, for running Insight Manager on a management PC, 379
Hardware timer, in ASR, 352–353
Hardware-based fault tolerance, 667–675
Hayes-compatible modem, required for Insight Asynchronous Management, Remote Console, Remote Insight, or Alarm Forwarding, 379
HBA (host bus adapter), 116, 154–155, 165–166, 168
Health and error logs, viewing and modifying, 108
Heartbeat, loss of, 298
Heartbeat cable, 295, 349
Heartbeat process, 677
Heartbeat signal, 294
Heartbeat timeout, 298
Heat dispersion, considering in site planning, 190
Helical Scan technology, used for DAT tapes, 252, 253
Hierarchical structure, for managed elements, 333
High airflow door inserts, 190
High Availability solutions (HA), 163
High priority, setting for a process, 727, 728

Higher-level drivers, 560
Highly Parallel System Architecture, 87, 215
Histogram mode, in Chart view, 699–700, 709
History cookie, in Personal Testing Center, 863
Host bus, 4
Host bus adapter (HBA), 116, 154–155, 165–166, 168
Host debugger, specifying the COM port for, 615
Hot expansion PCI hot plug capability, 71
Hot Plug PCI initiative, 642
Hot plug swapping, of hard drives, 347–348
Hot Plug Utility. *See* PCI Hot Plug Utility
Hot replacement PCI hot plug capability, 70
Hot upgrade PCI hot plug capability, 70
Hot-expansion, 642
Hot-plug functionality, updating the driver to obtain, 624
Hot-plug PCI
  ProLiant servers capable of, 640
  Windows 2000 and, 71
Hot-plug specification, operations allowed, 642
Hot-plug technology, functionality added by, 642
Hot-pluggable fans, 237
Hot-pluggable hard disks
  benefit of, 144
  operation and configuration issues, 140
  setting IDs for, 122
  termination of, 123
Hot-pluggable power supplies, 255
Hot-pluggable redundant power supplies, 236–237
Hot-replacement, 642
Hot-upgrade, 642
HP NetServer Assistant, 315
HP OpenView, 310–312, 336–337
HTTP Auto-Discovery configuration option, for Web Agents, 521
http auto discovery, requests, 439, 440
HTTP protocol, used by Web agents, 515
Hubs
  combining with switches, 158
  powering on, 157, 158
HVAC schedule, for a site, 190
Hyper page mode DRAM, 35

I

Iban Technologies IP Tools 2000, 535–536
IBM NetView, 312–313
IDE CD-ROM drives, drivers for, 618
IDE controllers, bus mastering and, 9
IDE Controllers component, in Storage Agent, 527
IDE drives, bus-mastering-compatible, 9
IDE/EIDE controller, 743, 746
IDs. *See* SCSI IDs
IDs per SCSI bus, supported by Compaq, 121, 125
IIC power supply subsystem, viewing the status of, 644
IIS (Internet Information Server), 548–549
IMD Utility. *See* Compaq Integrated Management Display (IMD) Utility
IML. *See* Integrated Management Log (IML)
IMU (Integration Maintenance Utility), 495, 496–497
Inaccessible status (Black), in the Device List window of Insight Manager, 420
Inactive Agents window, in the Insight Agents applet, 634, 635
In-band management, 408, 464–465
Industry Standard Architecture buses. *See* ISA buses
Initiate Immediate Switchover, configuring in the Windows NT Control Panel, 682
Initiator device, on the SCSI bus, 116
InnocuLAN antivirus software, in ManageWise, 314
Input/Output (I/O) devices, testing all, 266
Insight Agents, 323
  configuring, 586, 634–635
  disabling before upgrades, 632
  necessary for Automatic Data Collection, 392
  prerequisites for installation, 623
  re-installing, 633
Insight Agents applet, in Control Panel, 399, 634
Insight Asynchronous Management, Hayes-compatible modem required for, 379
Insight Management Agents, 370–372, 622–623
Insight Manager, 46, 176–181, 315–316, 336, 378, 469
  accessing Remote Console, 467
  accessing servers, 180

Alarm Destinations window, 410
Alarm Log, 400–403
Automatic Data Collection (ADC) function, 392–398
availability of agents, 46
bus use measurements, 235
color coded status in the Device List window, 419–420
compared to Insight Manager XE, 538
downloading the Version Control database, 484
identifying a degraded server, 226
identifying processor errors, 231–232
installing, 176–178, 380, 381–386
integrating Recovery Server with, 295
integration with network controllers, 198–199
integration with the Netelligent 4/16 network controller, 203
integration with the Netelligent 10/100, 203
integration with the RIB, 464
managing Integration Server, 497–500
minimum requirements for running on a management PC, 378–380
modifying reports, 394–395
monitoring ProLiant Storage Systems from within, 676
monitoring SNMP traps, 456
monitoring the processor, 348
obtaining, 381
opening, 179
performing ADC, 538
performing in-band management, 408
plugging CPM into, 625
pre-failure warranty coverage monitoring, 225
recording memory errors in, 229
report forms, 394, 395
reporting on collected data, 394–398
running on a Windows 95 PC, 379–380
server filtering in, 415–419
Server Reboot feature, 398–400
setting default community names for new devices, 406
task list, 478
triggering alarms, 182–183
updating to support Recovery Server, 290
using as a tool for PCI load balancing, 686–687
using Version Control to determine driver versions, 650
using with other management systems, 186
Version Control in, 478
viewing the Critical Error Log, 352
Insight Manager Alarm Log, 225
Insight Manager Device List window, 180, 181
Insight Manager LC, 428
compared to Insight Manager XE, 437
installing the combined client, 430–432
management headings in the console, 434–436
operation of, 433–436
procuring and installing, 428–432
Insight Manager Startup Checklist, 179
Insight Manager XE, 436, 537–538
compared to Insight Manager, 538
compared to Insight Manager LC, 437
installing, 438–439
installing management console, 442–444
limitations of, 538
navigation items in, 440
operation of, 439–441
prerequisites for, 437–438
procuring and installing, 437–439
retrieving information, 439–440
Insight Web Agents. *See* Web Agents
INSIGHT_DB datasource name, for Insight Manager XE, 439
Inspect Computer option
on the Diagnostics and Utilities menu, 268
in the Systems Configuration Utility, 104
Inspect utility, 279–281, 870–882
running a report from, 280–281
viewing the Critical Error Log, 352
Install options screen, for Insight Manager, 383
Install utility for Integration Server, configuring a NetWare server, 503
Installation options screen, in Insight Manager, 177
Installation progress bar, for Insight Manager, 385
Installations, performing mass, 311
Instance field, of the Add to Chart window, 736
Instance window, in the Add to Chart window, 701
Instruction cache, in a Pentium processor, 17
Instruction pipelining, 21, 22
Integrated Management Display (IMD), displaying information on, 638–639

Integrated Management Displays, 278
Integrated Management Log component, in Server Agent, 526
Integrated Management Log (IML), 229, 230, 278, 526
Integrated PCI SCSI-2 controller, drivers for, 618
Integrated Remote Console (IRC), displaying information for, 526
Integration Maintenance Utility. *See* IMU (Integration Maintenance Utility)
Integration Management, 370
Integration Server (IS), 494
 advantages of using, 592
 configuration options in SmartStart, 593
 configuring on a Windows NT server, 504
 creating, 502–504
 downloading software to, 497–500
 installing IPX, 504
 installing software from, 582, 592–593
 maintenance not included with Insight Manager XE, 538
 managing from Insight Manager, 497, 498
 operating systems supported, 495–497
 PEZ files on, 502, 503
 Push and Pull architecture in, 497–500
 requirements for setting up, 502–503
 storing all of the software on, 504
 updating from SmartStart CDs, 498–500
 updating from the Compaq Support Software Server, 497–498
 updating without Internet connectivity, 505
 using for software maintenance on existing installations, 593–596
 using with SmartStart, 591–596
Integration Servers filter, in Insight Manager, 417
Intel, processor/cache combinations defined by, 223–224
Intel 82558 chipset, in the Netelligent 10.100 TX UTP Controller, 202
Intel processors. *See also* Processors
 data bus widths, 6
 types of, 5
Intelligent Cluster Administrator, 441–442
Intelligent Manageability, 362
 categories of, 363
 increasing the functionality of, 428
Intelligent power switches, 641–643
IntelliMirror, in Windows 2000 Professional, 554
Internal interleaving, in SDRAM, 36
Internal storage, in Online Recovery Server, 349–350
Internet
 downloading the Version Control database from, 485–486
 support in NT Workstation, 547
 testing connectivity, 486
Internet Assigned Numbers Authority, 333
Internet Explorer
 installing Windows NT Service Pack 3, 518
 opening page of the RIB in, 465
Internet Information Server (IIS), 548–549
%Interrupt Time counter, 750
Interrupts, generated by hardware, 733
Interrupts/sec counter, 737–738
Interval time, increasing in Log view, 705
Inventories
 conducting with ManageWise, 314
 performing with OpenView, 311–312
I/O addresses, 4–5
I/O bandwidth, 87
I/O bus, on Compaq servers, 238
I/O Manager, in Windows NT Executive Services, 560–561
I/O queue, placing I/O requests in, 560
I/O Read bus cycle, 6
I/O request to or from a SCSI device, stages required for completion, 119
I/O Write bus cycle, 6
IP Device List command button, 179, 180
IP devices, adding to Insight Manager, 179
IPX
 installing on Integration Server, 504
 selecting servers running, 384
IPX devices, enabling auto-discovery of, 177–178
IPX/SPX network protocol, using the RIB with, 471

IS. *See* Integration Server (IS)
ISA adapters, in older servers, 70
ISA boards, configuring, 106–107
ISA buses, 68, 72, 455
ISA card, replacing with a PCI adapter, 73

JavaScript errors, encountering in Personal Testing Center, 864
Jumperless support, in PCI, 70
Jumpers, calculating SCSI IDs, 121

Kernel, forcing to remain in memory, 137
Kernel mode, in Windows NT, 556, 557
Kernel mode applications, percentage of processor time used for, 734
Kernel32 Update, 379–380
Keyboard, connecting to the RIB, 460
Keyboard drawer, for racks, 249
Keyboard pass-through cable, for the RIB, 460
Keyboard with a trackball, for racks, 249–250
Kilobytes (KB), 272

L_Port, 155
L1 cache, 18, 20, 54, 89, 733
  in the Pentium Pro Architecture and Pentium II Architecture, 223, 224
L2 cache, 8, 18, 54, 89, 90, 91, 733
  in the Pentium Pro Architecture and Pentium II Architecture, 223, 224
LANalyzer, 314
LANDesk Client Manager, 367
LANDesk Management Suite, 367
Latency, 120
Layered approach, by I/O Manager, 560
Layers, of fiber, 152
LCD monitor, for racks, 249
LeakyApp utility, 741–743, 746
Level 1 (L1) cache. *See* L1 cache
Level 2 (L2) cache. *See* L2 cache
Licensing mode, 585–586
Lights-Out Edition, of the RIB, 470
Links, in Fibre Channel, 155
Linux
  Compaq Recovery Server and, 290
  symmetric multiprocessing employed by, 85
Little Rubber Feet (LRF), 157
Lived timed test, 863
Load balancing
  among multiple servers, 550
  with dual-peer PCI architecture, 232, 235
  performing between two servers, 549
Load shedding, 447, 626
Local Access configuration option, for Web Agents, 521
Local option, for pushing or uploading software to production servers, 499
Local Procedure Call Facility, in Windows NT Executive Services, 563
Local Procedure Calls (LPCs), 563
Local Security Authority (LSA), 562
Localization, of Windows NT, 555
Log Options dialog box, in Log view, 705–706
Log view
  looking at data gathered by the, 698
  PC log in required for, 707
  of Performance Monitor, 704–707, 709–710, 711
  tracking information using, 705–706
LOGEVENT.EXE command, adding to the shutdown batch file, 617
Logical Adapter Information component, in NIC Agent, 528
Logical Disk Busy Time in %, preset threshold for Windows NT, 529
Logical disks, 744
Logical drives, 144, 744
  effect on the numbering of partitions, 667
  striping factor for, 136

Logical units (LUNs), 116
Logical volumes
mirroring with a SMART controller, 668
supported by the SMART array controller, 141
Login accounts, for Web Agents, 531
Logon Process component, of Security Reference Monitor, 561
Logon scripts, mapping drives to failover shares on another server, 683
Logon server, 729
Logon/sec counter, 751
Logs window, in Power Management Console, 446
Long wave GBIC, 155
Look-Aside cache, 58, 59
Look-Through cache, 58–59
Lookup penalty, 58
Loop-back cable, 670
Loss of heartbeat, 298
Low CPU Util filter, in Insight Manager, 418
Low priority, setting for a process, 727, 728
Low voltage differential (LVD) devices, 118
Low-level drivers, 560
LPCs (Local Procedure Calls), 563
LRF (Little Rubber Feet) support, 157
LSA (Local Security Authority) component, of Security Reference Monitor, 562
LUNs, 116
LVD devices, 118

M

Machine Check Architecture (MCA), 231
Macro bends, causing attenuation, 152
Main memory, 30
Maintain configuration to support existing Win 3.1 applications option, enabling for the Borland Database Engine, 384
Maintenance and Service Guide, for a server, 267
Major new feature, in Version Control, 481
Major resolved problems, 480
Manage Devices window, in Insight Manager XE, 440, 441
Manage Events window, in Insight Manager XE, 440
Manageable filter, in Insight Manager, 417
Manageable servers, displaying all, 535
Managed PCs under Insight Manager LC, prerequisites for, 429–430
Management agents, 185–186, 323, 332, 513
Management applications, 315–316, 323, 441–447
Management CD, obtaining management agents from, 185–186
Management console
in Insight Manager, 315, 316
installing from the Insight Manager XE CD, 442–444
rebooting servers from, 398–400
Management Information Base. *See* MIB (Management Information Base)
Management Information File (MIF), 363
Management interface, in DMI, 362
Management PC, 626
installing Insight Manager, 381–386
minimum requirements for running Insight Manager, 378–380
Management platforms, 186, 310–314, 323
Management protocol, 324
Management server, 513
Management Solution Partners Program, 370
Management workstation, setting up with Insight Manager, 315
ManageWise, 313–314
Manual Configuration
versus Assisted Integration, 589–591
in SmartStart, 578, 590–591
Manual Mode, for network cards, 637
Manual Update, in the Log Options dialog box, 706
Map Network Drive window, 594
Mass installations, performing with OpenView, 311
Mass Storage button, 184, 185, 226, 227
Mass Storage Overview, 226–227, 228
Maximize Throughput for File Sharing option, in the Server service window, 724
Maximize Throughput for Network Applications option, in the Server service window, 724
Maximum capacity, of SMART array controllers, 133, 134

Maximum data throughput, 12
Maximum data transfer rate, 8–9
Maximum memory, for common Intel processor types, 5
Maximum transfer rate (MTR), 8–9
/MAXMEM switch, for BOOT.INI, 615
MCA (Machine Check Architecture), 231
Mean Time Between Failure (MTBF) rate, 136
Megabytes (MB), 272
Megabytes per second (MB/s), 9
Mem >= 24MB filter, in Insight Manager, 417
Member server, configuring a server as, 586
Memory, 28. *See also* Physical memory; System memory
 accessing shared areas in, 719
 addressed by processors, 19–20
 calculating the optimum amount of, 722
 from Compaq, 45
 counters for monitoring usage, 720
 effect of adding, 721
 fault avoidance for, 229–231
 kinds of, 19–20
 matching speeds with, 20
 monitoring for errors, 344–345
 slowly running out of, 741–743
 specifying the maximum for Windows NT, 615
 speed of, 19
 tracking usage by process, 721
 types of, 217–218
 upgrading in servers, 217–221
 XY grid pattern for, 31
Memory addresses, 4–5
Memory: Available Bytes counter, 739
Memory bus, 28–29
Memory caches, in processors, 89
Memory caching, SRAM in, 88
Memory cells
 matrix of, 28
 reading, 31
Memory: Commit Limit counter, 739
Memory: Committed Bytes counter, 740
Memory crash dump file, 717, 718
Memory devices, implementing in server subsystems, 28–29
Memory error message, during POST, 272
Memory errors, 41
 multi-bit, 45
 reporting on Compaq servers, 44–45
 troubleshooting on Compaq servers, 46
Memory leaks, troubleshooting, 721
Memory modules
 formats for, 38
 selecting for Compaq servers and workstations, 40
Memory: Page Faults/sec counter, 739, 740
Memory: Page Input/sec counter, 746, 747, 748
Memory: Pages Input/sec counter, 739, 740
Memory: Pages/sec counter, 738, 752
Memory paging, disk utilization and, 715
Memory: Pool Nonpaged Bytes counter, 741
Memory: Pool Page Bytes counter, 740
Memory pool, separate pools composing, 712
Memory Read bus cycle, 6
Memory subsystem, 712
 on Compaq servers, 28
 counters for, 738–743
 interaction with the disk subsystem, 719–721
 optimizing without adding memory, 722
 types of errors, 229
Memory test, in POST, 272
Memory upgrade charts, on the Compaq Web site, 218
Memory utilization, measuring, 710
Memory Write bus cycle, 6
MetaFrame, 551
MHz rating, for SDRAM, 37
MIB browsers, 336–337
MIB format, 333
MIB identifiers, 333
MIB (Management Information Base), 332–337, 363
MIB numbering system, 334–336
MIB objects, 334–336. *See also* Elements
MIB tree, 334, 335
Micro bends, causing attenuation, 152
Microkernel, 559
Microprocessors. *See* Processors
Microsoft BackOffice Small Business Server, installation path for, 579, 580
Microsoft Cluster Server. *See* MSCS (Microsoft Cluster Server)
Microsoft drivers, basic features provided by, 622

Microsoft media, installing from, 596–598
Microsoft Message Queue Server (MSMQ), 550
Microsoft service pack, installing for Windows NT, 633
Microsoft SMS. *See* MS-SMS
Microsoft SQL Server. *See* SQL Server
Microsoft Systems Management Server. *See* MS-SMS
Microsoft Windows NT. *See* Windows NT
MIF grammar, 363
MIF (Management Information File), 363
Minimize Memory Used option, in the Server service window, 723, 724
Minor new feature, in Version Control, 482–483
Minor resolved problems, 481
Mirroring, 136–137, 162, 163
Miscellaneous Environment Functions, in the Windows 32-bit Subsystem, 569
Modal dispersion, causing attenuation, 152
Modem Remote Console filter, in Insight Manager, 417
Modular approach
 for the development of Windows NT, 556
 to NIC card design, 204
Monitor cable, connecting from the RIB, 460
Monitor shelf, for racks, 249
MONITOR.EXE, 707
Mouse, instructing Windows NT not to look on the COM port for, 615
MRU (most recently used) data, 55
MSCS (Microsoft Cluster Server), 549
 powering on, 158
 solutions with NSPOF, 166–167
 support on FC-AL hubs, 150
MS-DOS environment, in Windows NT, 566
MSMQ (Microsoft Message Queue Server), 550
MS-SMS, 177, 499, 501
MTBF rate, of multiple disk drives, 136
MTR (Maximum transfer rate), 8–9
Multi-bit errors, 45
Multi-channel SCSI adapter, 125
Multimode fiber, 150, 153, 154, 168
Multiple filter mode, in Insight Manager, 415
Multiple processors, running applications on, 730
Multiplexing, 31
Multiprocessing systems, 82–84
Multiprocessor HAL, upgrading to, 610
Multitasking, 82–84
multi(x) part, of the ARC path, 665–666

N

N+1 formula, 138, 139
N_Port, 155, 156
Nanosecond rating, for SDRAM, 37
Navigation frame, in a Web page, 522
Navigation links, displayed in the browser window, 520
NC3131 Modular NIC, 204
NC3132 Dual-port upgrade card, 204
NC6132 1000SX upgrade module, 204
NET SEND command, adding to the shutdown batch file, 617
NET STOP command, adding to the shutdown batch file, 617
NET USE commands, succeeding with an IF ERRORLEVEL statement, 683
NetBEUI, avoiding the use of, 751
NetCensus, 367
Netelligent controllers, 202–203
Netelligent line of NICs, 348–349
Netelligent network cards, 684
NetFlex-2 Dual Port ENET, 200
NetFlex-2 Dual Port TR controller, 201
NetFlex-2 ENET-TR adapter, 200
NetFlex-2 network controllers, 198
NetFlex-2 TR controller, 201
NetFlex-3 device driver, 684, 685
NetFlex-3 Ethernet controllers, 202
NetFlex-3 network cards, 684
NetFlex-3 network controllers, 198, 199
NetFlex-3/E network card, 201
NetFlex-3/P network card, 201
NetServer Assistant, 315
NetView, 312–313
NetWare
 ASR device driver for, 354
 CIMU and, 496–497

Compaq servers for Standby Recovery Server, 289
configuring community names, 404
Standby Recovery Server supported for, 288
support provided by Insight Manager XE, 437
NetWare 3.*x* filter, in Insight Manager, 418
NetWare 4.*x* filter, in Insight Manager, 418
NetWare 5, installation path for, 580
NetWare server, configuring using the Install utility for Integration Server, 503
NetWare Virtual Terminal discovery, discovering servers using, 384
NetWare Virtual Terminal (NVT) devices, enabling the auto-discovery of, 178
Network adapters, placing on different buses, 76
Network bandwidth, displaying the overall percentage of, 750
Network cards. *See* NICs
Network controller pairs, 199
Network controllers, 198–204
adding to servers, 204
Netelligent generation of, 202–203
Network Control Panel, configuring the server component in, 723–724
Network Control utility, 636–638, 684
Network General Sniffer, 315
Network Interface: Bytes Received/sec counter, 749
Network Interface: Bytes Sent/sec counter, 749
Network Interface: Bytes Total/sec counter, 749, 752
Network Interface Cards. *See* NICs
Network Interface: Current Bandwidth counter, 749
Network inventory functionality, in ManageWise, 314
Network management, 306–307, 322
advantages of implementing, 324
components of, 323
system, 338
Network Monitor, 751
Network Monitor Agent service, 750
Network monitors, 313
Network Output Queue Length, preset threshold for Windows NT, 529
Network packets, capturing with NetView, 312
Network Remote Console filter, in Insight Manager, 417
Network Segment: %Broadcasts counter, 750
Network Segment: %Network Utilization counter, 750
Network server mode, enabling for ASR, 354
Network subsystem, 748–752
Network traffic, 751
%Network Utilization counter, 750
Networks, 151–152
inventorying with OpenView, 311–312
upgrading, 307
New Feature category, of Version Control, 481–483
New Form window, in Insight Manager, 395
NIC Agent, 527, 528
NIC button, in the Insight Manager Device Data window, 184, 185
NIC Controller Information component, in NIC Agent, 528
NIC Interface Information component, in NIC Agent, 528
NICs, 749. *See also* Network controllers
configuring two to act as one, 199
displaying bytes sent and received by, 749
drivers on the Compaq SSD, 621
included with a RIB, 456
modular approach to the design of, 204
Netelligent line of, 348–349
Operating modes for, 637
providing a backup, 636–637
redundant, 237
redundant pairs of, 684
required for Standby Recovery Server, 291
NICStart software, 203
NL_Port, 155, 156
NMI (non-maskable interrupt), 45
No Single Point of Failure. *See* NSPOF (no single point of failure)
/NODEBUG switch, for BOOT.INI, 615
Nodes, in Fibre Channel, 155
Nondestructive reads, 32
Non-essential systems, shutting down after a power interruption, 626
Non-maskable interrupt (NMI), 45
Nonpageable memory pool, 712

Nonpaged Pool, displaying the number of bytes in, 741
Nonparity memory, 43
Nonvolatile RAM. *See* NVRAM
Normal priority, setting for a process, 727, 728
Normal reboot, performing, 400
/NOSERIALMICE=COM*x* switch, for BOOT.INI, 615
Not Available status (Grey), in the Device List window of Insight Manager, 420
Novell LANalyzer, 314
Novell ManageWise, 313–314
Novell NetWare. *See* NetWare
NOW.LOG file, created by the System Configuration Record utility, 434
NSPOF (no single point of failure), 159
  configuring, 164–165
  ensuring in the RA4000, 160
  Microsoft Cluster Server solutions with, 166–167
NT. *See* Windows NT
NT CD. *See* Windows NT CD
NT Resource Kit UPTOMP.EXE, updating HALs, 88
NT Server. *See* Windows NT Server
NT setup disks, booting to, 632
NT Virtual DOS Machine (NTVDM), 566, 567
NT Workstation. *See* Windows NT Workstation
NTDETECT.COM file, copying to the recovery disk, 664
NTFS file system, required for a standby recovery server, 679
NTLDR file, copying to the recovery disk, 664
NTSEE. *See* Windows NT Server, Enterprise Edition (NTSEE)
NTVDM, 566, 567
NVRAM, storing information on "bad" blocks of memory, 345
NWSNUT.NLM, 496

O

Object collections, in NetView, 312
Object handles, 561
Object IDs, assigned by the Internet Assigned Numbers authority, 334
Object Manager, in Windows NT Executive Services, 561
Objects
  measuring counters for, 696–697
  selecting for monitoring, 700–701
  in Windows NT, 561
Odd parity, calculating, 660–662
Off-line processor, 348
OK status (Green), in the Device List window of Insight Manager, 420
Onboard cache, 671–672
  on array controllers, 141
  loading data onto, 144
  upgrading to a higher level of, 19
On-board memory, with the RIB, 458
Online capacity expansion, in SMART array controllers, 133, 134
Online expansion facility, in SMART-2 controllers, 675
Online recovery configuration, 680
Online Recovery Server, 288–289, 296–297, 680–683
  advantages and disadvantages of, 297
  Compaq server platforms supported by, 289
  compared to Standby Recovery Server, 288, 349–350
  as a Fault Prevention feature, 349
  hardware requirements for, 291
  impact on disk subsystem performance, 298
  installation of, 289–290
  installing software, 682
  limitations of, 350
  location of the disks, 291, 292–294
  performance considerations, 298
  switchover time compared to Standby Recovery Server, 298
Online spares, 142–143, 348, 669
OpenView Desktop Administrator, 367
OpenView management platform, 310–312
Operating modes, for network cards, 637
Operating System filters, in Insight Manager, 418
Operating systems
  allowing access to software and setting outside and completely independent of, 466
  configuring community names for each different, 404
  effect on overall cache subsystem performance, 61

initializing in Recovery Server, 298
multitasking versus multiprocessing, 83–84
RAID 1 (mirroring) for, 140
selecting for SmartStart, 581
simulating restarts of, 269
SmartStart paths available for, 579–580
supported by Integration Server, 495–497
supporting ASR, 352
tracking crashes, 352
Operating systems section, of the Windows NT BOOT.INI file, 614
Operating system support, for Insight Manager, 378
Operator account, for Web Agents, 531
Options, for Compaq servers, 246–255
Options ROMPaq
selecting, 274
upgrading, 276–277
Order Information page, in Rack Builder, 191, 251
OS (operating system). *See* Operating systems
OS/2, ASR device driver for, 354
OS/2 subsystem, 566, 567
Other Available Applications Menu, in Insight Manager XE, 443
Out-of-band management, 409, 464–465
Overheating, shutdowns due to, 617

P

Packet analysis, 312
Packet Blaster technology, 198, 199
Page faults, 720
displaying the number generated by a process, 741
displaying the number occurring, 739
Page Faults/sec counter, 721, 739, 740, 741
Page File Bytes counter, 721, 741, 742–743
Page File Bytes Peak counter, 721, 741
Page file, increasing the performance of, 137
Page File Usage in %, preset threshold for Windows NT, 529
Page Input/sec counter, 746, 747, 748
Page Mode memory, 34
Page Pool, displaying the number of bytes used by a process, 741
Pageable memory pool, 712
Paged Pool, displaying the number of bytes in, 740
Pagefile, 714
avoiding the use of, 137
counters for monitoring usage, 720
creating additional on a different physical drive, 718
creating a hardware RAID 0 array for, 137
creating up to 16 additional, 717–718
default size of, 716–717
determining the optimum size for, 718
displaying the number of bytes used in, 741
distributing the load of, 717
monitoring, 718
setting the initial and maximum size of, 716
tuning, 715–718
viewing the settings for, 716
Pager Forwarding, in Insight Manager, 182, 410
Pagers
configuring destinations in Insight Manager, 413–414
sending e-mail messages to, 414
Pages Input/sec counter, 739, 740
Pages/sec counter, 709, 720, 738, 741–742, 746, 752
Paging activity
charts showing disk activity due to, 747, 748
increasing, 715
minimizing, 722
reducing, 738–743
Paging file. *See* Pagefile
Paging File > %Usage Peak counter, monitoring, 722
Parity, 139, 660
Parity calculations, on a dedicated disk, 138
Parity checking, 43, 47
Parity DIMMs, 44
Parity drive, as a bottleneck, 660
Parity generation engine, in the SMART-2 controller, 674–675
Parity information
calculating on controllers, 662

in ECC memory, 218
maintaining in RAID 4 and RAID 5, 659–660
storing in RAID 4 and RAID 5, 347
striping across all drives in an array, 660
Parity memory, 43
Parity memory modules, using in ECC mode, 44
Parity SIMMs, 44
Parity-checking functionality, disabling, 43
Partitions
configuring, 585
selecting for mirroring, 663
partition(x) part, of the ARC path, 666
Passive termination, 123
Passive terminator, replacing with an active, 125
Passwords
changing for all users, 533–535
compared to community names, 329
configuring for the RIB, 462
resetting for the RIB, 471
PATROL Agent, 527
PC card modem/serial port, with the RIB, 456–457
PC Card slot, included with a RIB, 457
PC100 specification, 37
PCAnywhere graphical remote control software package, 467
PCI architectures, listing of, 76
PCI BIOS, assigning a bus number, 685–686
PCI bridging, 70
PCI buses, 69–71, 455–456, 685
architecture of, 70
assigning bus numbers to, 685–686
balancing of the load on, 686
compared to ISA and EISA, 72
more than one primary, 459
performance analysis and management, 235
providing for two, 232
supporting multiple, 232–234
PCI cards
complete computer on one, 454
guidelines for installing, 686
PCI device driver, in Windows NT 4.0, 71
PCI devices, 105–106
PCI Ethernet adapter, replacing an ISA NIC, 73
PCI Host Plug function, 623
PCI hot plug capabilities, 70–71, 236
PCI hot-plug capable NIC, 645
PCI Hot Plug Utility, 71, 640–641, 645
PCI SCSI-2 controller, drivers for, 618
PCI slots
installing the RIB in, 471
shutting off, 71
PCI standard, 455
PCI-PCI bridge, 75, 685
PDC (Primary Domain Controller), configuring a server as, 586
Pentium
address bus, 17
address lines, 5
data bus, 17–18
enhancements with, 16–19
first-level cache, 20
L1 cache, 54
maximum memory, 5
memory addressed by, 19–20
pipeline used by, 21–22
Pentium II processor
address lines, 5
cache memory in, 223, 224
L1 cache, 54
maximum memory, 5
multiprocessing and, 87
system board connection, 16
Pentium III processor, 54
Pentium III Xeon processors, 190
Pentium Machines filter, in Insight Manager, 417
Pentium Pro Architecture, cache memory in, 223, 224
Pentium Pro processors
address lines, 5
enhancements with, 16–19
L1 cache, 54
maximum memory, 5
PerfMon. *See* Performance Monitor
Performance. *See also* System performance
maximizing with RAID 0, 674

methods for increasing, 7
of SCSI drives, 120
of servers, 210
Performance management, 308–309
Performance Monitor, 309, 696–697, 698
adding counters to, 700–701
chart view, 309
checking disk utilization, 310
counters in, 732–752
determining system cache size, 713
file extensions for views, 711
monitoring the Pagefile, 718
saving settings to a file, 710–712
tracking memory usage by process, 721
uses of views, 707–710
Performance Monitor Add-On Enhancement Tool, 235–236
Periodic Update, in the Log Options dialog box, 706
Peripheral Component Interconnect (PCI), 9
Peripheral Component Interconnect (PCI) buses. *See* PCI buses
Peripherals, identifying during POST, 273
Permissions, configuring for the RIB, 462
Personal Computer Interconnect standard, 455
Personal Testing Center, 862
Answers in Depth, 865
installing, 862
JavaScript errors, 864
saving scores as cookies, 863
scoring, 865
test type choices, 862–865
PEZ extension, 501
PEZ files, 500–502, 503
Physical address, 719
Physical disk, 743–744
Physical Disk: %Disk Time counter, 744, 745
Physical Disk: Average Disk Queue Length counter, 744
Physical Disk: Avg. Disk sec/Transfer counter, 746
Physical Disk Busy Time in %, preset threshold for Windows NT, 529
Physical Disk: Current Disk Queue Length counter, 744, 745, 752
Physical Disk: Disk Reads/sec counter, 746, 747, 748
Physical Drives screen, 227, 228
Physical memory. *See also* Memory; System memory
dedicating to File System Cache, 713
displaying the amount available to applications, 739
monitoring the amount available, 720
Physical power switch, not controlled by the RIB, 471
Physical system security, 368
Pipelining, 21–22
Platform, in a management system, 323
Plug and play specification (PnP), 68
Plug-and-Plan strategy, in Windows 2000, 71
.PMA file extension, 711
.PMC file extension, 711
.PML file extension, 711
.PMR file extension, 711
.PMW file extension, 711
PnP specification, 68
Point-to-Point topology, for Fibre Channel, 156
Policies, 57
Policy creation application, 310
Policy Editor for Windows NT, 308
Policy Manager, in NetView, 312
Polling
of desktop agents, 372
in Insight Manager XE, 440
Polling interval, setting in Insight Manager, 183
Pool Nonpaged Bytes counter, 741
Pool Paged Bytes counter, 740, 741–743
Port 280, for Insight Manager XE, 439
Port 2301, 515, 518
Port scanner, finding Web-manageable servers, 535–536
Portability, of Windows NT, 555
Ports
in Fibre Channel, 155
grouping for fault tolerance, 348
POSIX subsystem, in Windows NT, 566, 568
POST (Power-On Self Test), 270–271
BIOS information displayed, 281
configuration errors during, 101
error messages, 281
noticing the occurrence of uncorrectable errors, 346

steps and messages in, 271–273
storing the processes, 20
Post upgrade tasks, 632–633
Post-exam summary screen, in Personal Testing Center, 865
Power, consumed during refresh, 32
Power Converter component, in Server Agent, 526
Power Down Manager, 641–643, 645
Power failures, alerting for, 448, 627
Power Management application. *See* Compaq Power Management
Power On Messages component, in Server Agent, 525
Power strips, for racks, 250
Power supplies
hot-pluggable redundant, 236–237
monitoring, 346
Power Supply component, in Server Agent, 525
Power Supply Viewer, 645
Power switches
disabling, 643
none on hubs, 157
not controlled by the RIB, 471
support of intelligent, 641–643
Power-on Self-Test (POST) operation. *See* POST (Power-On Self Test)
PowerScope, 626
PowerScope window, in Power Management Console, 445
PPP status, in the Device List window of Insight Manager, 420
Practice exam type, 864
Preemptive multitasking, 83
Pre-failure alerting, 237
Pre-failure warranty coverage, 225–232, 238, 348, 369
Pre-Failure Warranty initiative, 344, 355
Pre-fetch queue, 17, 22
Preset thresholds, for Windows NT, 529
"Press F10 for system partition utilities" message, 101
Preventive maintenance, performing on an UPS, 626
Primary bus, installing both active and standby boards to, 235
Primary controller, 199
Primary Domain Controller (PDC), configuring a server as, 586
Primary drive, replacing with the mirrored drive, 667
Primary PCI bus, allowing more than one, 459
Primary port, 348
Primary server, 677
failure of, 295–297
hardware failure on, 677
operating system failure, 677
simulating an abnormal shutdown of, 296
Print Historical Report window, in Insight Manager, 397
Print Report window, in Insight Manager, 397
Printer drivers, running in Kernel mode, 565
Private loop, 156
Privileged applications, percentage of processor time used for, 734
Privileged mode. *See* Kernel mode
%Privileged Time counter, 734, 735–736
Privileged Time in %, preset threshold for Windows NT, 529
PRLNTSS.SYS, 627, 676
Process: %Processor Time counter, 736–737
Process Manager, in Windows NT Executive Services, 562–563
Process: Page Faults/sec counter, 741
Process: Page File Bytes counter, 741
Process: Page File Bytes Peak counter, 741
Process: Pool Nonpaged Bytes counter, 741
Process: Pool Paged Bytes counter, 741–743
Processes, 562, 732
setting a new priority for, 727
setting the base priority for, 726–729
Processor: %Interrupt Time counter, 750
Processor: %Privileged Time counter, 734, 735–736
Processor: %Processor Time counter, 733–734
Processor: %User Time counter, 734, 735–736
Processor board failure, recovering from, 353
Processor boards, identifying during POST, 273
Processor: Interrupts/sec counter, 737–738
Processor power modules
for each CPU, 224
redundant, 236
Processor: Processor Queue Length counter, 752

Processor queue, for threads, 732
Processor Queue Length counter, 734, 735, 752
Processor subsystem, counters for, 732–738
Processor termination cards, 21
%Processor Time counter, 709, 733–734, 736–737
Processor Time in %, preset threshold for Windows NT, 529
Processor utilization, defining a threshold on, 325
Processor/cache combinations, defined by Intel, 223–224
Processors, 732
    allowing multiple, 82
    available for Compaq servers, 221–222
    capacity for multiple, 17
    clock rates for, 733
    common Intel types, 5
    data bus widths, 6
    enhanced reliability for, 231–232
    initializing in POST, 272
    memory addressed by, 19–20
    memory caches in, 89
    overhead associated with adding, 86–87
    providing two for fault tolerance, 348
    removing from servers, 611
    running applications on multiple, 730
    support for multiple in Windows NT Server, Enterprise Edition, 549
    support of multiple in Windows NT Server, 548
    upgrading, 88
Production servers, pushing or uploading software to, 499–500
Profusion chipset, 216
Progress indicators, during Quick Check Diagnostics testing, 266
ProLiant 400
    ECC memory in, 218
    memory modules required by, 219
    processor configurations available on, 222
ProLiant 800, 214, 215
    for departmental and small business needs, 238
    EDO memory, 218
    memory modules required by, 219
    processor configurations available on, 222
ProLiant 850R, 214, 219
ProLiant 1000, 213
ProLiant 1200, 214
    dual peer PCI bus architecture included with, 233
    memory modules required by, 219
ProLiant 1500, 213, 219
ProLiant 1500 filter, in Insight Manager, 417
ProLiant 1500R, memory modules required by, 219
ProLiant 1600, 214
    for departmental and small business needs, 238
    dual peer PCI bus architecture included with, 233
    memory modules required by, 219
    processor configurations available on, 222
ProLiant 1600R, 222
ProLiant 1850R, 215
    memory modules required by, 219
    processor configurations available on, 222
ProLiant 2000, 213, 219
ProLiant 2500, 214
    bridged PCI architecture, 233
    memory modules required by, 219
ProLiant 2500R, 219
ProLiant 3000, 214, 215
    dual peer PCI bus architecture included with, 233
    memory configuration of, 38
    memory modules required by, 219
    processor configurations available on, 222
ProLiant 3000R
    memory modules required by, 219
    processor configurations available on, 222
ProLiant 4000, 213, 220
ProLiant 4500, 213–214, 220
ProLiant 4500R, 220
ProLiant 5000, 214
    dual peer PCI bus architecture included with, 233
    memory modules required by, 220
ProLiant 5000R, 220
ProLiant 5500, 214, 216
    dual peer PCI bus architecture included with, 233
    for high availability and heavy-duty database support, 238
    memory modules required by, 220
    processor configurations available on, 222

ProLiant 5500R
memory modules required by, 220
processor configurations available on, 222
ProLiant 6000, 214, 215
dual peer PCI bus architecture included with, 233
for high availability and heavy-duty database support, 238
memory modules required by, 220
processor configurations available on, 222
ProLiant 6400R, 217
memory modules required by, 220
processor configurations available on, 222
ProLiant 6500, 214, 215
dual peer PCI bus architecture included with, 233
for high availability and heavy-duty database support, 238
memory modules required by, 220
processor configurations available on, 222
ProLiant 7000, 214, 216
dual peer PCI bus architecture included with, 233
for high availability and heavy-duty database support, 238
memory modules required by, 220
processor configurations available on, 222
ProLiant 8000, 216–217
for high availability and heavy-duty database support, 238
memory modules required by, 220
processor configurations available on, 222
supporting all eight processors, 551
ProLiant 8500, 216–217
for high availability and heavy-duty database support, 238
memory modules required by, 220
processor configurations available on, 222
for space-constrained rack installations, 238
supporting all eight processors, 551
ProLiant Cluster technology, 237
ProLiant servers, 213–217
assigning standbys for, 676
with the IIC power subsystem, 644
for medium-to-large business needs, 238
memory modules required for each, 218, 219–220
monitoring while running Microsoft Cluster Server, 441
PCI bus-to-I/O slot assignments defined for, 234
redundant power supplies for, 255
supporting intelligent power switches, 642
ProLiant Storage System, 246–247, 627–630
compared to the ProLiant Storage System/F, 247–248
disabling before upgrades, 632
supported only from the Compaq SSD, 622
ProLiant Storage System driver, 627–628
ProLiant Storage System/F, 247–248
ProLiant Storage System (PSS), 675–676
attaching two Compaq servers to, 676–677
capabilities of different, 676
Prompted Diagnostics option, 267
ProSignia 200, 212
ProSignia 300, 211–212
ProSignia 500, 211
ProSignia 700, 222
ProSignia 720, 212
ProSignia 740, 212
ProSignia NeoServer, 212, 222
ProSignia PII, 222
ProSignia servers, 211–212
diagnostics on diskettes, 263
for workgroups, 238
ProSignia VS, 211
Protected mode. *See* Kernel mode
Protocol analyzers, 313
Protocols
in a management system, 324
minimizing the number of, 751
"public" community name, 404, 407
changing to a different default for new devices, 406
pitfalls to using, 337
removing, 329
Public loop, 156
Punching out, Support Software Diskettes (SSDs), 102
Push and Pull architecture, in Integration Server, 497–500

Q

Quad multiprocessing, 90
Quad processing, advantage over dual, 92
Querying, in Insight Manager XE, 440
Queuing, implementing for SCSI-2, 120
Quick Check Diagnostics option, 266
QuickFind, 124

R

RA4000 (RAID Array 4000), 159, 160–161, 168
RA8000 (RAID Array 8000), 162–163, 168
Rack 4136, 249
Rack 7122, 249
Rack 7142, 249
Rack Builder utility, 186–192, 249, 250–251
    installing, 187
    Options menu, 187–188
    reports from, 189
Rack graphic, generated by Rack Builder software, 251
Rack units, 249, 250
Rack-mountable hardware, software providing information on, 250
Racks, 255–256
    arranging components in, 190
    for Compaq servers, 248
    configuring with Rack Builder, 188
    documenting configuration with Visio, 251
    options for, 249–250
    software for configuring, 250–251
    types of, 249
RAID, 135
    fault management and, 309
    with Fibre Channel on Compaq hardware, 159–163
    levels of, 135, 144, 347, 355, 658–662
    levels supported in SMART array controllers, 133, 134
    mixing levels on a single volume, 668, 669
RAID 0 (data striping), 135–136, 347, 658, 659
RAID 0+1, 347, 668
RAID 1 (disk mirroring), 135, 136–138, 347, 658, 659
    creating a software configuration, 663, 664
    mirroring complete physical drives with hardware, 668
    supported by Windows NT Server, 548
RAID 4 (data guarding), 135, 138–139, 347, 658, 659–660
    compared to RAID 5, 674
    with hardware, 670
RAID 5 (distributed data guarding), 347, 658
    calculating parity, 661–662
    compared to RAID 4, 674
    creating a protected partition, 667
    with hardware, 670–672
    overhead associated with configuratios, 86
    running with the array in a broken state, 671
    starting the software configuration process, 668
    stripe set size for volumes, 667
    supported by Windows NT Server, 548
    writing DLT backup jobs across multiple tapes, 253
RAID Array 4000. *See* RA4000 (RAID Array 4000)
RAID Array 8000. *See* RA8000 (RAID Array 8000)
RAID arrays, duplexing, 247
RAID controllers, allowing two to access the same storage system, 247
RAID-protected volumes, resizing online, 675
RAM (Random Access Memory), 28, 29, 47
Range pinging, 440
Rapid Recovery, 356
Rapid Recovery Engine, 351
RAS (Row Access Select) line, 31
RDISK.EXE /S, running, 589, 591
rdisk(x) part, of the ARC path, 666
Read ahead caching
    in array controllers, 142
    in SMART-2 controllers, 675
Read cache, on an array controller, 144
Read function, of SNMP, 326
READ ONLY community name, 337
READ option, for community names, 330
Read policies, 57
READ/CREATE (read/write) option, for community names, 330
Read-Only Memory. *See* ROM

Read/write cache, on an array controller, 144
READ/WRITE community name, 337
Read/write head, used in DLT technology, 252, 253
Realtime priority, setting for a process, 727, 728
Reboot Option component, in Server Agent, 525
Reboot subsection, in WEBAGENT.INI file, 532
Reboot to Utilities, 400
Rebooting servers, 399–400
Receiving fiber cables, 155, 157
Recovery button, in the Insight Manager Device Data window, 184, 185
Recovery disk, creating, 663–667
Recovery methods, forcing a server to run, 281
Recovery Server, 288, 349–350, 677
    integrating with Insight Manager, 295
    Linux and, 290
Recovery Server Interconnect, 294–295
Recovery Server Interconnect cable, 677–678
Recovery server methodologies, 288
Recovery server option kit, 290, 679
Recovery server switch, 294, 679
Red flag, in Version Control, 480, 487
Red symbol, for a memory error in Integrated Management Log, 230
Redundancy
    determining for power supplies, 644
    providing for processor power modules, 224
Redundant Array of Inexpensive Drives. *See* RAID
Redundant Fibre Array Controllers, 160
Redundant mode, for the RA4000, 161
Redundant network card pairs, 684
Redundant NICs, 237
Redundant power supply, 255
Redundant processor power modules, 236
Redundant servers, 288
Redundant system fans, 237
Refresh circuit, accessing DRAM, 29–30
Refresh cycle
    capacitors and, 30–31
    power demands for, 32
Registry Editor, forcing NT not to page any portion of the OS to disk, 713
Regular memory, 43
Reliability
    of networks, 306
    of Windows NT, 555
Remote attended option, for pushing or uploading software to production servers, 499
Remote clients, 307
Remote Communications component, in Server Agent, 526
Remote Console feature, 463, 466–467
    accessing, 467
    of the RIB, 454
    TCP/IP network protocol required by, 467
    working from, 457
Remote console, in the RIB-LOE, 470
Remote Desktop graphical remote control software package, 467
Remote Insight Board. *See* RIB (Remote Insight Board)
Remote Insight component, in Server Agent, 526
Remote Maintenance, in ASR, 351, 354
Remote monitoring, in Insight Manager, 184–185
Remote Monitor Service, 71
Remote playback, of server reboots, 468
Remote reboot
    of Compaq servers, 398
    enabling, 399
    for the RIB, 468–469
Remote ROM Flash, 365
Remote servers
    managing, 464–465
    using WinMSD to derive information about, 405
Remote unattended option, for pushing or uploading software to production servers, 499
Remote Utilities option, on the Diagnostics and Utilities menu, 269
Remote-control feature, in ManageWise, 314
Repeatable errors, in a memory subsystem, 41
Replicated installation, streamlining, 584
Replicated Install path, in SmartStart, 579
Replication disk
    creating, 583
    editing UNATTEND.TXT, 584

Replication Profile, 583
Report forms
copying existing in Insight Manager, 396
creating in Insight Manager, 395–396
in Insight Manager, 394, 395
modifying existing in Insight Manager, 396
printing automatically in Insight Manager, 397–398
printing manually in Insight Manager, 396–397
Report view
adding counters to, 707
of Performance Monitor, 707, 708, 710, 711
Reports
generating on collected data in Insight Manager, 394–398
generating with Insight Manager, 315
generating with WinMSD, 405
modifying in Insight Manager, 394–395
from Rack Builder, 189–192
running from the Inspect utility, 280–281
Reset Server, in the RIB Web interface, 469
Resolved Problems category, of Version Control, 480–481
Resource share. *See* File server
Resource-sharing environment, highest load subsystems in, 731
Response trap, 325, 326
Responsible Device List, in Insight Manager, 179–180
Responsible devices, 179
Responsible Server List Window, 226
RESTART command, sending to a locked up server, 254
Restore CDs, 364
Retry/fail error message, during failover, 679
Review exam type, 864–865
Revision History Table, 277, 278
RIB (Remote Insight Board), 254, 256, 454
built-in NIC included with, 456
capturing BSOD text information, 468
connecting the monitor cable, 460
features and benefits, 463–471
hardware components of, 454–458
installing and configuring, 458–463
integration with Insight Manager, 464
network settings in the SCU, 461
on-board memory, 458
PC card modem/serial port included, 456–457
Remote Reboot feature, 468–469
serving as the graphics display adapter, 468
support for SNMP, 469
supported only from the Compaq SSD, 622
TCP/IP network protocol, only one supported, 466
TCP/IP network protocol required by, 471
user information in the SCU, 462–463
verifying the slot for, 459
video adapter included with, 457–458
Web interface for, 465–466
RIB-LOE (Lights-Out Edition), 470
Ring 0. *See* Kernel mode
RISC-based processor, in the SMART-2 controller, 674
Riser cards, between PCI slots, 72
Rittal, Compaq racks made by, 249
Robustness, of Windows NT, 555
ROM, 20
ROMPaq firmware upgrades, creating for Compaq servers, 174
ROMPaq firmware upgrade utility initial screen, 277
ROMPaq revisions, updating to, 100
ROMPaq software, Web site for downloading, 275
ROMPaq upgrade utility, running, 269
ROMPaqs, 273–277, 281
creating diskettes with, 274
reviewing the BIOS version to be installed, 276
updating the BIOS of servers, 458–459
Root MIB number, for Compaq, 335, 336
Row Access Select (RAS) line, 31
Row address, for memory, 31
RSO kits, 290, 679
Run in Separate Memory Space option, 567, 568

S

SAM (Security Account Manager) component, of Security Reference Monitor, 562
SAN (Storage Area Network), 150, 158
Save Settings and Exit option, in the Systems Configuration Utility, 104

Scalability, of Windows NT, 555
Scattering, causing attenuation, 152
Scheduler, for symmetric multiprocessing, 85
SCO OpenServer
    Standby Recovery Server supported for, 288
    support by NetFlex controllers, 199
SCO operating systems, Compaq servers for Standby Recovery Server, 289
SCO UNIX or UnixWare, ASR device driver for, 354
SCO UnixWare
    installation path for, 580
    Standby Recovery Server supported for, 288
Scores, saving as cookies in Personal Testing Center, 863
SCSI
    bandwidth of, 151
    Fibre Channel and, 163–164
SCSI bus, communication on, 116
SCSI cabling, types of, 122
SCSI CD-ROM drives, drivers for, 618
SCSI chains, 116, 122–124
SCSI channels, in SMART array controllers, 132, 134
SCSI controller drivers, 628
SCSI controllers, 125–126, 743. *See also* Compaq SCSI controllers
    compared to IDE/EIDE controllers, 746
    displaying information o the storage devices connected to, 527
    drivers on the Compaq SSD, 620–621
    list of supported, 577
SCSI devices, data transfer performance and, 119–120
SCSI drivers, specifying the Compaq version during installation, 629
SCSI drives, 120. *See also* Disk drives; Hard disks; Hard drives
SCSI IDs
    determining, 121–122
    indicating in the ARC path, 666
    jumper values corresponding to, 121–122
    settings for, 120–122
    supported by Compaq, 118
SCSI standard, 116
    characteristics of, 116
    table detailing transfer rates and data widths, 119
    versions of, 125
SCSI-1 standard, transfer rate and data width of, 119
SCSI-2 standard, 117
    implementing queuing for, 120
    transfer rate and data width of, 119
scsi(x) part, of the ARC path, 665–666
SCU (System Configuration Utility), 98, 100–105, 108, 174–175
    accessing, 101
    assigning IP information for the RIB, 461
    configuring user information, 462–463
    identifying PCI hardware, 106
    menu screen of, 101–102
    running, 105, 596
    setting up a standby server, 679–680
    setting up security for the RIB, 461–462
    in SmartStart, 581, 582
SDRAM, 19, 34, 36–38
Secondary controller, 199
Secondary port, 348
Second-level cache. *See* L2 cache
Security
    WBEM and, 530–533, 534
    of Windows NT, 555
Security access token, 563
Security Account Manager (SAM), 562
Security component, in Server Agent, 525
Security hole, 530
Security management, 309–310, 368
Security Reference Monitor, in Windows NT Executive Services, 561–562
Security risks, balancing with management needs for Internet access, 515
Seek time, 120
Self Monitoring Analysis and Reporting Technology (SMART), 346
Serial cables, for the recovery server interconnect, 294
Serial numbers, detecting and recording for memory DIMMs, 367
Server Agent, 524–526
Server: Bytes Received/sec counter, 750

Server: Bytes Total/sec counter, 750
Server: Bytes Transmitted/sec counter, 750
Server component, configuring in the Network Control Panel, 723–724
Server Diagnostics, installing, 597
Server failure notification, in ASR, 353
Server filtering, 415–419
Server filters, creating custom, 418–419
Server Health Logs, 46, 277–278, 281, 351–352, 356
Server: Logon/sec counter, 751
Server Management Technology, 344
Server Profile Disk, 577
 removing before rebooting, 587
 in SmartStart, 581
Server Reboot feature, of Insight Manager, 398–400
Server Recovery window, 229, 230
Server serial number, displaying, 525
Server service window, 723–724
Server Setup and Management pack, 577
Server Support Diskettes. *See* SSD (Support Software Diskette)
ServerNet PCI Adapter, displaying information about, 524
Servers. *See also* Compaq servers
 accessing with Insight Manager, 180
 adding network controllers to, 204
 adding to the Insight Manager device list, 179
 building, 576
 creating baseline measurements of, 710
 creating high availability, 164–167
 determining system roles for, 738
 determining upgrades for, 479
 diagnostic tools for, 262–264
 fault tolerant features of, 236–237
 I/O bus on, 238
 managing from any machine on the network, 515
 managing using, 517–536
 managing with a Web browser, 518
 monitoring the same counters for different, 699
 performance of, 210
 pre-failure warranty coverage for, 225–232
 processors available for, 221–222
 rebooting with the RIB, 469
 supported by Online Recovery Server, 289
 supported by Standby Recovery Server, 288–289
 supporting ASR, 352
 upgrading memory in, 217–221
Servers option, in the Administrator Insight XE window, 440
Service pack, installing for Windows NT, 633
Services, disabling unnecessary before server upgrades, 631–632
Services tab, in the Insight Agents applet, 634–635
SET command, in SNMP protocol, 325, 338
Set Priority option, in Task Manager, 727
Sets subsection, in WEBAGENT.INI file, 532
Settings, saving to a file in Performance Monitor, 710–712
Settings filters, in Insight Manager, 416–417
Setup Filter window, in Insight Manager, 419
Setup Groups icon, on the Device List toolbar, 180
Setup program, for Insight Manager, 176–178
Severity column, in the Alarm Log, 401, 402
Shared cache, 88–90. *See also* Dual processing
Shared slots, EISA/ISA and PCI, 73
Share-level access to resources, 547
Sharing, of memory space, 719
Short wave GBIC, 155
Shutdown batch file, adding commands to, 616–617
Shutdown Schedule window, in Power Management Console, 447
Shutdown script, in the Systems Management driver, 616–617
Shutdown Timing window, in Power Management Console, 446
Shutdown/reboot process, between primary and recovery server, 678
Shutdown/Reboot window, in Power Management Console, 446
Shutdowns, safety mechanism for preventing accidental, 643
SIMMs (Single Inline Memory Modules), 38–39, 47, 218
Simple Network Management Protocol. *See* SNMP protocol

Single channel Ultra2-SCSI, 118
Single filter mode, in Insight Manager, 415
Single NIC component, in NIC Agent, 528
Single-bit memory errors, correcting, 237
Single-ended cabling, 117
Single-ended interfaces, 117
Single-mode fiber, 150, 153, 168
Single-processor configuration, reverting to, 21
Single-sided SIMMs, 39
Site planning, considering heat dispersion, 190
Site planning report, in Rack Builder, 189, 250
Site-independent mirroring of data, allowing, 162
Skill gap analysis, at the Global Knowledge Web site, 868
Slot, verifying for the RIB, 459
Small computer system interface. *See* SCSI standard
SMART 221 controller, 134
SMART 230 Plus controller, 134
SMART 3100ES controller, 134
SMART 3200 controller, 134
SMART Array 221 controller, 673
SMART Array 3100ES controller, 216, 673
SMART Array 3200 controller, 673
SMART Array 4200 controller, 673
SMART Array 4250ES controller, 217
SMART array controllers
  characteristics of, 132–133, 134
  converting to a SMART-2 controller, 143
  displaying information for the drives connected to, 527
  hot-plug capable, 640
  increased functionality of Compaq drivers, 623
  logical volumes supported by, 141
  manually installing the drivers for, 623–624
  protecting write data, 141–142
  required for Recovery Server, 349
  support of online spares, 142
  supported under Windows NT, 620
  updating drivers using SSD, 624
SMART controllers, 132–133
  Array Accelerator on, 671
  compared to SMART-2 controllers, 672–675
  maximum number of drives supported, 670
  stripe sizes implemented with RAID 5, 672
Smart Cover Lock, 368
Smart Cover Sensor, 368
SMART drive controller, performing diagnostics on, 104
S.M.A.R.T. drives, 226
SMART ES models, 347
SMART SCSI controller, 101
SMART (Self Monitoring Analysis and Reporting Technology), 346
Smart Switch Mode, for network cards, 637
SMART-2 controllers, 132–133
  calculating parity information, 662
  compared to SMART controllers, 672–675
  converting a SMART array controller to, 143
  performance of, 674
  protecting write data, 141–142
SMART-2 family of controllers, 672
SMART-2DH controller, 132–133, 673
  maximum storage on a single channel, 144
  replacement for, 673
SMART-2/E controller, 672–673
SMART-2/P controller, 672
SMART-2SL controller, 132–133, 673
SmartStart, 174, 576–577
  choosing the path for installing, 578–580
  configuration options for Integration Server, 593
  installation process, 99
  installing from versus installing from Microsoft media, 596–598
  installing software from an Integration Server, 592–593
  Manual Configuration of, 590–591
  new versions of, 100
  purchasing a subscription for, 598–599
  requirements for, 577
  subscription, 516
  subscription and updates received by ASEs, 270
SmartStart and Management CD, downloading the Version Control database from, 484
SmartStart and Support Software CD, 98–100, 108, 270
SmartStart CDs, 577
  booting from, 101, 578

creating Server Support Diskettes, 605
installing CIMU, 495
PEZ files on, 501–502
SmartStart system configuration utility, tight integration with Integration Server, 494
SMP system. *See* Symmetric multiprocessing (SMP) systems
SMS. *See* MS-SMS
SMS executable file, entering the path to, for Insight Manager, 385
SNMP community names. *See* Community names
"SNMP Error - Entry Point not found..." error message, 404
SNMP management console, 469
SNMP MIB-2, Insight Manager XE managing devices supporting, 537
SNMP protocol, 313, 324, 469
commands used by, 324, 338
configuring options for community names, 330
GET command read function, 326
monitoring applications, 176
OpenView based on, 311
overview of, 322–324
requirements for, 331
security, 338
SET command, 325
technology surrounding, 322–337
traps in, 327–328
write function, 325
SNMP service
disabling before upgrades, 632
installing, 331, 404, 749
reinstalling, 633
SNMP Settings Tab, in the Insight Agents applet, 399, 634
SNMP traps, monitoring, 456
Soft affinity, 559
Soft errors, 41–42, 229, 345
Soft page faults, 720
SoftPaq SP10945, downloading the Insight Manager LC combined client as, 429
SoftPaq SP12303, downloading the Insight Manager LC combined console as, 429
SoftPaqs, 274
creating diskettes, 275–276
downloading, 270
Software fault tolerance, configuring a boot partition for, 663–667
Software maintenance on existing installations, performing with an Integration Server, 593–596
Software Recovery, in ASR, 583–584
Software, storing all, on Integration Server, 504
Software striping, compared to hardware striping, 141
Solaris, symmetric multiprocessing employed by, 85
/SOS switch, for BOOT.INI, 615
Split seeks, allowed in RAID 1, 138
SPnnnnn.EXE files, downloading, 275
SPUU (System Partition Update Utility, 495, 496
SQL Server
required for Insight Manager XE, 437
running on a separate server, 439
setting Server service for, 724
SRAM, 19, 29, 47
in cache memory subsystems, 56
compared to DRAM, 30
features of, 32
SSCD.PEZ file, 501
SSD Express Mode, 606, 607
SSD main screen, 605, 606
SSD program, 604
loading the Systems Management driver, 612–613
updating the Compaq SCSI driver, 629–630
SSD (Support Software Diskette), 604
building, 102
Compaq devices supported with, 619–622
installing the latest for Windows NT 4.0, 633
obtaining, 605
required for Insight Manager XE installation, 438
running, 605–607
updating HALs, 88
updating Windows NT to the proper HAL, 88
using for driver installation, 198
Stale data, 59
Standard MIFs, 363

Standby configuration, compared to online recovery, 680
Standby Recovery Server, 288–289, 296, 676–680
  advantages and disadvantages of, 297
  Compaq server platforms supported by, 288–289
  compared to Online Recovery Server, 288, 349–350
  as a Fault Prevention feature, 349
  hardware requirements for, 291
  identical server configuration required, 288, 289, 290
  impact on disk subsystem performance, 298
  installation of, 289–290
  limitations of, 350
  location of the disks, 291–292
  performance considerations, 298
  requirements for, 678–679
Standby server, setting up, 679–680
Star topology, 154
START command, 728–729
Startup Checklist, in Insight Manager, 179
Startup Timing window, in Power Management Console, 447
Startup/Shutdown tab, in Windows NT, 613–614
Static Random Access Memory. *See* SDRAM
Status Degraded/Failed filter, in Insight Manager, 417
Status filters, in Insight Manager, 417
Status icon, for Web Agents, 522
Status indicators, on the Fibre Channel Storage System, 160
Status OK filter, in Insight Manager, 417
Status Unmanageable filter, in Insight Manager, 417
Status window, in Power Management Console, 444
Step-index fiber, 153
Storage Agent, 527
Storage Area Network. *See* SAN (Storage Area Network)
Storage arrangement, for Recovery Server configurations, 349–350
Storage expansion systems, 246–248
Storage products, viewing the entire new selection of, 248
Storage subsystem
  minimizing damage from failure, 347
  monitoring for problems, 346
StorageWorks technology, 162–163
Stripe set with parity, 660
Stripes, breaking files down into, 135–136, 138
Striping factor, modifying, 136
Subsystem load, by server role, 729–731
Subsystems
  highest load in a client-server environment, 730–731
  highest load in a resource-sharing environment, 731
SunNet Manager, 310
Superscalar architecture, 17
Support, in larger network enterprises, 330
Support Software CD pack, 365, 366
Support Software Diskette (SSD). *See* SSD (Support Software Diskette)
Support software, from Compaq, 98
Survey Utility, 278
Swap file. *See* Pagefile
Swapping out, information to the Pagefile, 714
Switch boxes, for racks, 249
Switch on Fail Mode, for network cards, 637
Switchable ProLiant storage systems, attaching controllers to, 291
Switches. *See also* FC switches
  in the BOOT.INI file, 614–615
Switchover. *See* Failover process
Symmetric multiprocessing, 84, 85–87
Symmetric multiprocessing (SMP) systems, 223, 733
Symmetric multiprocessor (SMP) servers, Microkernel scheduling in, 559
Synchronous DRAM. *See* SDRAM
Synchronous I/O, compared to asynchronous, 560
Synchronous transfer, 116
SYSMGMT.SYS driver, 354, 612
System: %Total Processor Time counter, 734
System applet in NT, Startup/Shutdown tab, 613–614
System BIOS, upgrading, 104, 351
System Board button, in the Insight Manager Device Data window, 184, 185
System Board component, in Server Agent, 525
System Board information, from Insight Manager, 231–232
System buses, 4, 9
System bus utilization, 60, 62
System cache size, 713–714

System Cache value, displaying in Task Manager, 714
System configuration
advanced features of, 107–108
creating partitions, 99
information in Insight Manager, 184
saving parameters, 99
System Configuration Record utility, 434
System Configuration Utility. *See* SCU (System Configuration Utility)
System diagnostic and maintenance tasks, performing, 103–104
System Diagnostics utility, 175, 176
System Erase utility, 174, 176
System Erase Utility option, in the SCU, 102
System hardware, running diagnostics on, 103
System Health Logs/Automatic Server Recovery, supported only from the Compaq SSD, 622
System Information component, in Server Agent, 525
System I/O devices test, in POST, 271
System Management Driver, 71
System memory. *See also* Memory; Physical memory
DRAM in, 88
more versus better, 33
System partition
accessing with F10, 175
creating, 582
creating and saving critical system support software, 264
installing and keeping up to date, 351
updating, 101–102
System Partition Update Utility (SPUU), 495, 496
System performance
increasing for Windows NT, 696
methods for increasing, 7, 10–11
System Policy Editor, 308
System: Processor Queue Length counter, 734, 735
System Properties window, 646–647
System Resources component, in Server Agent, 525
System role, determining for a server, 738
System software, 524–526
System Startup section, of the Startup/Shutdown tab, 614
System upgrade, establishing evidence as the necessity for, 697
Systempro systems, asymmetric multiprocessing used by, 85
SystemPro/XL systems, firmware upgrade needed for, 174
Systems Configuration Utility. *See* SCU (System Configuration Utility)
Systems management, 307–310
advantages of using the Web, 514–515
Systems Management driver
shutdown script, 616–617
for Windows NT, 612–617
Systems Management Service, disabling before upgrades, 632
System-specific options, 103

T

Tagged command queuing, 120
Tape Devices window, in Control Panel, 619
Tape drives
configuring in Windows NT setup, 619
not supported by Windows NT, 618–619
supported by Windows NT, 618
Tape libraries, for DLT tape devices, 253
Target device, on the SCSI bus, 116
Task list, for the managed server, 478
Task Manager
altering a program's priority, 726–727
displaying system cache size, 713–714
opening, 713–714
TCO (total cost of ownership), lowering, 132
TCP/IP network protocol
Insight Manager and, 331
managing a large network, 337
only protocol supported by the RIB, 466
required for Remote Console, 467
required for the RIB, 471
SNMP communication over, 324
Team of NICs component, in NIC Agent, 528
Telnet client, accessing Remote Console, 467
Telnet protocol, used by Remote Console, 467
Temperature, monitoring within servers, 346

Terminal Server client, 550
Terminal Server Edition, implementing for remote management, 386
Termination, of SCSI chains, 122–124
Termination cards, installing, 21
Termination jumper, 124
Termination power jumper, 124
Test ASR option, on the Diagnostics and Utilities menu, 268–269
Test ASR utility, 281
Test Computer option
  selecting on the Diagnostics and Utilities menu, 264, 266
  in the Systems Configuration Utility, 103
Test Computer utility, 281
Test type choices, in Personal Testing Center, 862–865
Test Yourself software, on the CD with this book, 862
Thermal sensor, 369
Thermal shutdown, setting options for, 584–585
Thin-clients, 550
Third-party hard drives, no coverage under Pre-Failure Warranty, 226
Third-party memory, 221, 229
Thread Scheduler, assigning processor time to programs, 726
Threads, 562, 732
  displaying those waiting in the queue to be processed, 734
  scheduling for execution, 732
Three-tiered architecture, 513, 514
Thresholds
  built-in, in ManageWise, 313–314
  defining, 325
  preset for Windows NT, 529
  setting for bytes transmitted, 183
  for setting off alarms, 183
  specifying for server subsystems, 528
ThunderLAN technology, 198
Tiered-support approach, in larger network enterprises, 330
Title frame, in the browser window, 520, 522
Tivoli, 336
Token Ring, compared to FC-AL, 156
Token Ring network cards, 201
Token Ring Statistics component, in NIC Agent, 528
Topologies, in Fibre Channel, 155–159
Total cost of ownership (TCO), 132
%Total Processor Time counter, 734
Transient errors, in a memory subsystem, 41–42
Transmitting fiber cables, 155, 157
Traps
  configuring the forwarding of, 328
  determining destinations for, 328
  entering destinations for, 331
  in SNMP communications, 324
  in SNMP protocol, 327–328
TriFlex architecture, 45
Two processor features, 348
Two-tiered architecture, 513

U

Ultra SCSI standard, 118
Ultra2-SCSI standard, 118, 119
Ultra-Wide SCSI standard, 118, 119
Unattended recovery, in ASR, 353
UNATTEND.TXT file, editing on the replication disk, 584
Uncorrectable memory errors, 345–346
Undiscovered status (Clear), in the Device List window of Insight Manager, 420
Unicenter TNG, 367
Uniprocessor HAL, upgrading to the multiprocessor HAL, 88
Uniprocessor versions of HALs, downgrading to, 611
Units. *See* Us (units)
Universal driver, for NetFlex-3 cards, 198
Unknown status, in the Device List window of Insight Manager, 420
Unlisted components, adding to a rack, 188
Unsolicited traps, sending to a management application, 327
Untagged queuing, 120
Update Database from CD/diskette option, for Version Control, 484

Update PC screen, in Insight Manager LC, 435
Upgrade Firmware option
    on the Diagnostics and Utilities menu, 269
    in the Systems Configuration Utility, 104
Upgrade Reasons frame, in Version Control, 480–483
Upgrades, for networks, 307
UPS. *See also* Compaq UPS; Power supplies
    controlling the shut down of, 446
    retrieving status information in, 444
UPS agent, polling by Compaq Power Console, 444, 445
UPS Management Agents, 625, 626
UPTOMP.EXE, 88
Us (units), 249, 250
%Usage counter, 718, 720
%Usage Peak counter, 718, 720
%Usage Time counter, 734, 735–736
User account, for Web Agents, 531
User applications, percentage of processor time used for, 734, 735–736
User desktops, managing, 308
User mode, in Windows NT, 556–557
User Time in %, preset threshold for Windows NT, 529
User-level access to resources, in Windows NT Workstation, 547
Users, authentication of, 729
Utilities
    installed from the Compaq SSD, 635–644
    updating remotely, 605
Utilization button, in the Insight Manager Device Data window, 184, 185
Utilization filters, in Insight Manager, 418
Utilization Subsystem, in Server Agent, 525, 526

Vendor MIFs, 363
Version
    determining for a Compaq device driver, 648–649
    determining the current for Windows NT, 646–648
Version Control, 478
    accessing, 478
    color codes in, 479–481
    determining driver versions, 650
    downloading current databases, 483–486
    downloading the database from the Internet, 485
    New Feature category, 481–483
    not included with Insight Manager XE, 538
    reminder feature with, 487
    status flags in, 480
    update interval for the database, 487
    Upgrade Reasons frame, 480–483
Version Control option, for Insight Manager, 384
Version Control utility, in Insight Manager, 178
Version Control window, 650
Version tab, of the file Properties window, 649
VGA video driver, loading the generic, with NT, 615
Video adapter, included with the RIB, 457–458
Video capture chip, on the RIB, 457–458
Video drivers, support for, 622
View Device List option, 267
View or Edit Details option, in the Systems Configuration Utility, 103
View PCs screen, in Insight Manager, 434–435
Viewed column, in the Alarm Log, 401, 402
Views
    changing in Performance Monitor, 698
    file extensions for Performance Monitor, 711
    saving settings for particular, 710–711
    uses of, in Performance Monitor, 707–710
Viking Components, memory modules from, 40
Virtual addresses, 563, 719
Virtual memory, 719. *See also* Pagefile
    displaying the amount that can be committed, 739
    displaying the amount that has been committed, 740
    mapping address space to, 563
    monitoring, 720
Virtual Memory Manager. *See* Windows NT Virtual Memory Manager (VMM)
Virtual Memory tab, in the Control Panel, 716
Virtual NIC component, in NIC Agent, 528
Virtual power button, on the RIB-LOE, 470
Virus scanning software, disabling before upgrades, 632
Visio, documenting the rack configuration, 251

Visual Alarms option, in Insight Manager, 182
VMM. *See* Windows NT Virtual Memory Manager (VMM)
Volatile memory, 28
Voltages, for DIMMs, 40
Volumes >=80% Used filter, in Insight Manager, 418

Wait states, 8, 11, 12, 18
Warranty, pre-failure, 410
WBEM standard, 512–514, 530–533, 534
Web Agents
  changing preset passwords for all users, 533–535
  condition icons for, 522
  configuration options for, 520, 521
  disabling, 517
  HTTP protocols used by, 515
  installing, 516
  login accounts, 531
  managing components, 523–529
  security built into, 530–533, 534
  setting options for, 519–520
  using port 2301, 518
Web-Based Enterprise Management. *See* WBEM standard
Web-based technology, advantages for systems management, 514–515
Web browser. *See also* Browser
  managing servers using, 517–536
  monitoring servers, 386
  viewing RIB options, 465
Web browser application, requirements for the management PC, 518
Web interface, starting Remote Console, 467
Web interface for the RIB, 462, 465–466
Web-manageable servers, finding with a port scanner, 535–536
Web management offerings, in Compaq products, 515–517
Web page, frames in, 519, 520
Web site
  for Compaq support, 270
  for downloading Insight Manager, 381
  for Global Knowledge, 868
  for server support software downloads, 275
Web technology, server management using, 512
WEBAGENT.INI file, 531–532
White riser cards, between PCI slots, 72
Wide-Ultra SCSI-3 controller, 214
Wide-Ultra SCSI-3 standard, 118, 119
Win2K. *See* Windows 2000
Win16 NTVDM, 567
Win16-on-Win32. *See* Win16 NTVDM
WIN32K.SYS, 564
WINDISK.EXE, 663
Window Manager, in Windows NT Executive Services, 564
Windows 3.1 applications, supporting in Insight Manager, 178
Windows 9x, support for desktop agents, 371
Windows 16-bit environment, in Windows NT, 566, 567, 568
Windows 32-bit (Win32) Subsystem, in Windows NT, 566, 569
Windows 95 PC, installing Kernel32 Update, 379–380
Windows 2000, 553
  Hot-plug PCI and, 71
Windows 2000 Advanced Server, 554
Windows 2000 Datacenter, 554
Windows 2000 Professional, 554
Windows 2000 Server, 554
Windows for Workgroups, Insight Manager and, 380
Windows installation files, Restore CD and, 364
Windows, managing in Personal Testing Center, 863
Windows NT
  architecture of, 553–559
  ASR device driver for, 354
  BOOT.INI file, 613
  CIMU and, 495–496
  Compaq devices supported in, 617–622
  Compaq servers for Standby Recovery Server, 289
  Compaq tape drives supported, 618–619
  configuring community names, 404
  configuring Integration Server, 504
  design goals for, 554–556

determining the current build revision and service pack level, 645–648
disabling the use of the page file for pagable drivers and system code, 137
disk management tasks in, 663
environment subsystems, 565–569
expanding the pagefile, 717
forcing not to page any portion of the OS to disk, 713
improving performance and reliability by using Compaq products, 658–687
increasing system performance, 696
installing manually, 596–598
installing on another partition, 580
installing SNMP service, 331
installing the graphical portion of, 587–589
installing the latest service pack, 633
physical memory supported per server, 550
product theory and architecture of, 546
prompting for options specific to, in SmartStart, 585–586
running software RAID 5 with the array in a broken state, 671
support for desktop agents, 371
supporting on Compaq servers, 604–650
swapping out information to the Pagefile, 714
symmetric multiprocessing employed by, 85
troubleshooting by loading with switches, 614–616
versions of, 546–553

Windows NT 3.x HALs, custom developed by Compaq, 608–609
Windows NT 3.5, 3.51 filter, in Insight Manager, 418
Windows NT 3.51, installing the latest SSD and service pack for, 631
Windows NT 3.51 network, upgrading to Windows NT 4.0, 630–633
Windows NT 4.0, 553
- 4-component architecture under, 71
- filter in Insight Manager, 418
- HALs, 610
- installing the latest SSD for, 633
- upgrading to, 632
- upgrading to, from Windows NT 3.51, 630–633

Windows NT Agents, components managed by, 528–529
Windows NT CD
- booting directly to, 632
- Compaq products with drivers on, 617–618
- removing before rebooting, 587
- starting setup from, 632

Windows NT Control Panel, configuring Recovery Agent, 682
Windows NT Diagnostics window, 647–648
Windows NT Executive Services, components of, 559–565
Windows NT installation, loading a Compaq SCSI controller driver, 628–629
Windows NT Load Balancing Service (WLBS), 550
Windows NT Memory Subsystem. *See* Memory Subsystem
Windows NT operating system, preset thresholds for components, 527–529
Windows NT Performance Monitor. *See* Performance Monitor
Windows NT Policy Editor, 308
Windows NT POSIX subsystem. *See* POSIX subsystem
Windows NT Resource Kit, utilities for logging information to a file, 707
Windows NT Server, 548–549, 552
- installation path for, 580
- RAID levels provided with, 658–659

Windows NT Server, Enterprise Edition (NTSEE), 549–550, 552
Windows NT Server, Terminal Server Edition (TSE), 550–551, 552
Windows NT Service Pack 4, installing on a machine with a SMART-2 array controller, 482
Windows NT setup program, 598
Windows NT Task Manager. *See* Task Manager
Windows NT Thread Scheduler, 726
Windows NT Virtual Memory Manager (VMM), 563, 718–719
Windows NT Workstation, 547–548, 552
Windows Task Manager. *See* Task Manager
Windows-based Terminals, 550
WinLAND, 367
winmsd, 647

WinMSD, providing information about servers, 405
\WINNT directory, 666
WinNT-TSE. *See* Windows NT Server, Terminal Server Edition (TSE)
WINS, using for name resolution with TCP/IP, 751
WLBS (Windows NT Load Balancing Service), 550
Workgroups
  ProSignia servers for, 238
  using Windows NT Workstation with, 547
Workspace file
  beginning logging immediately upon opening, 712
  saving settings for all views in, 711–712
WOW. *See* Win16 NTVDM
Write cache, in SMART array controllers, 133, 134
Write data, protecting with array controllers, 141–142
Write function, of the SNMP protocol, 325
Write information, caching of, 672
Write policies, 57
Write posting, in array controllers, 142
Write-Back cache, 62
Write-Back cache policy, 59, 60–61
Write-Through cache policy, 59, 62

Xeon line of processors, multiprocessing and, 87
XY grid pattern, for memory, 31

Yellow flag, in Version Control, 480, 487
Yellow icon, on the SSD main screen, 605
Yellow symbol, for a memory error in Integrated Management Log, 230

ZENworks, 308
Zero Administration Client Suite, 367
Zero wait states, running with SDRAM, 37
Zero wait state system, 8, 11

Custom Corporate Network Training

Train on Cutting Edge Technology We can bring the best in skill-based training to your facility to create a real-world hands-on training experience. Global Knowledge has invested millions of dollars in network hardware and software to train our students on the same equipment they will work with on the job. Our relationships with vendors allow us to incorporate the latest equipment and platforms into your on-site labs.

Maximize Your Training Budget Global Knowledge provides experienced instructors, comprehensive course materials, and all the networking equipment needed to deliver high quality training. You provide the students; we provide the knowledge.

Avoid Travel Expenses On-site courses allow you to schedule technical training at your convenience, saving time, expense, and the opportunity cost of travel away from the workplace.

Discuss Confidential Topics Private on-site training permits the open discussion of sensitive issues such as security, access, and network design. We can work with your existing network's proprietary files while demonstrating the latest technologies.

Customize Course Content Global Knowledge can tailor your courses to include the technologies and the topics which have the greatest impact on your business. We can complement your internal training efforts or provide a total solution to your training needs.

Corporate Pass The Corporate Pass Discount Program rewards our best network training customers with preferred pricing on public courses, discounts on multimedia training packages, and an array of career planning services.

Global Knowledge Training Lifecycle Supporting the Dynamic and Specialized Training Requirements of Information Technology Professionals

- Define Profile
- Assess Skills
- Design Training
- Deliver Training
- Test Knowledge
- Update Profile
- Use New Skills

College Credit Recommendation Program The American Council on Education's CREDIT program recommends 53 Global Knowledge courses for college credit. Now our network training can help you earn your college degree while you learn the technical skills needed for your job. When you attend an ACE-certified Global Knowledge course and pass the associated exam, you earn college credit recommendations for that course. Global Knowledge can establish a transcript record for you with ACE, which you can use to gain credit at a college or as a written record of your professional training that you can attach to your resume.

Registration Information

COURSE FEE: The fee covers course tuition, refreshments, and all course materials. Any parking expenses that may be incurred are not included. Payment or government training form must be received six business days prior to the course date. We will also accept Visa/ MasterCard and American Express. For non-U.S. credit card users, charges will be in U.S. funds and will be converted by your credit card company. Checks drawn on Canadian banks in Canadian funds are acceptable.

COURSE SCHEDULE: Registration is at 8:00 a.m. on the first day. The program begins at 8:30 a.m. and concludes at 4:30 p.m. each day.

CANCELLATION POLICY: Cancellation and full refund will be allowed if written cancellation is received in our office at least six business days prior to the course start date. Registrants who do not attend the course or do not cancel more than six business days in advance are responsible for the full registration fee; you may transfer to a later date provided the course fee has been paid in full. Substitutions may be made at any time. If Global Knowledge must cancel a course for any reason, liability is limited to the registration fee only.

GLOBAL KNOWLEDGE: Global Knowledge programs are developed and presented by industry professionals with "real-world" experience. Designed to help professionals meet today's interconnectivity and interoperability challenges, most of our programs feature hands-on labs that incorporate state-of-the-art communication components and equipment.

ON-SITE TEAM TRAINING: Bring Global Knowledge's powerful training programs to your company. At Global Knowledge, we will custom design courses to meet your specific network requirements. Call 1 (919) 461-8686 for more information.

YOUR GUARANTEE: Global Knowledge believes its courses offer the best possible training in this field. If during the first day you are not satisfied and wish to withdraw from the course, simply notify the instructor, return all course materials, and receive a 100% refund.

In the US:

CALL: 1 (888) 762-4442

FAX: 1 (919) 469-7070

VISIT OUR WEBSITE:

www.globalknowledge.com

MAIL CHECK AND THIS FORM TO:

Global Knowledge
Suite 200
114 Edinburgh South
P.O. Box 1187
Cary, NC 27512

In Canada:

CALL: 1 (800) 465-2226

FAX: 1 (613) 567-3899

VISIT OUR WEBSITE:

www.globalknowledge.com.ca

MAIL CHECK AND THIS FORM TO:

Global Knowledge
Suite 1601
393 University Ave.
Toronto, ON M5G 1E6

REGISTRATION INFORMATION:

Course title ______________________________

Course location ______________________ Course date __________

Name/title ______________________ Company __________

Name/title ______________________ Company __________

Name/title ______________________ Company __________

Address ______________ Telephone __________ Fax __________

City ______________ State/Province __________ Zip/Postal Code __________

Credit card __________ Card # ______________ Expiration date __________

Signature ______________________________

LICENSE AGREEMENT

THIS PRODUCT (THE "PRODUCT") CONTAINS PROPRIETARY SOFTWARE, DATA AND INFORMATION (INCLUDING DOCUMENTATION) OWNED BY THE McGRAW-HILL COMPANIES, INC. ("McGRAW-HILL") AND ITS LICENSORS. YOUR RIGHT TO USE THE PRODUCT IS GOVERNED BY THE TERMS AND CONDITIONS OF THIS AGREEMENT.

LICENSE: Throughout this License Agreement, "you" shall mean either the individual or the entity whose agent opens this package. You are granted non-exclusive and non-transferable license to use the Product subject to the following terms:

(i) If you have licensed a single user version of the Product, the Product may only be used on a single computer (i.e., a single CPU). If you licensed an paid the fee applicable to a local area network or wide area network version of the Product, you are subject to the terms of the following subparagraph (

(ii) If you have licensed a local area network version, you may use the Product on unlimited workstations located in one single building selected by you that is served by such local area network. If you have licensed a wide area network version, you may use the Product on unlimited workstations located multiple buildings on the same site selected by you that is served by such wide area network; provided, however, that any building will not be considere located in the same site if it is more than five (5) miles away from any building included in such site. In addition, you may only use a local area or wid area network version of the Product on one single server. If you wish to use the Product on more than one server, you must obtain written authorizatic from McGraw-Hill and pay additional fees.

(iii) You may make one copy of the Product for back-up purposes only and you must maintain an accurate record as to the location of the back-up at all times.

COPYRIGHT; RESTRICTIONS ON USE AND TRANSFER: All rights (including copyright) in and to the Product are owned by McGraw-Hill a its licensors. You are the owner of the enclosed disc on which the Product is recorded. You may not use, copy, decompile, disassemble, reverse enginee modify, reproduce, create derivative works, transmit, distribute, sublicense, store in a database or retrieval system of any kind, rent or transfer the Product, or any portion thereof, in any form or by any means (including electronically or otherwise) except as expressly provided for in this License Agreement. You must reproduce the copyright notices, trademark notices, legends and logos of McGraw-Hill and its licensors that appear on the Prod on the back-up copy of the Product which you are permitted to make hereunder. All rights in the Product not expressly granted herein are reserved by McGraw-Hill and its licensors.

TERM: This License Agreement is effective until terminated. It will terminate if you fail to comply with any term or condition of this License Agreement. Upon termination, you are obligated to return to McGraw-Hill the Product together with all copies thereof and to purge all copies of the Product included in any and all servers and computer facilities.

DISCLAIMER OF WARRANTY: THE PRODUCT AND THE BACK-UP COPY OF THE PRODUCT ARE LICENSED "AS IS." McGRAW-HILL, ITS LICENSORS AND THE AUTHORS MAKE NO WARRANTIES, EXPRESS OR IMPLIED, AS TO RESULTS TO BE OBTAINED BY ANY PERSON OR ENTITY FROM USE OF THE PRODUCT AND/OR ANY INFORMATION OR DATA INCLUDED THEREIN. McGRAW-HILL, ITS LICENSORS, AND THE AUTHORS MAKE NO GUARANTEE THAT YOU WILL PASS ANY CERTIFICATION EXAM BY USING THIS PRODUCT. McGRAW-HILL, ITS LICENSORS AND THE AUTHORS MAKE NO EXPRESS O IMPLIED WARRANTIES OF MERCHANTABILITY OR FITNESS FOR A PARTICULAR PURPOSE OR USE WITH RESPECT TO THE PRODUCT. NEITHER McGRAW-HILL, ANY OF ITS LICENSORS, NOR THE AUTHORS WARRANT THAT THE FUNCTIONS CONTAINED IN THE PRODUCT WILL MEET YOUR REQUIREMENTS OR THAT THE OPERATION OF THE PRODUCT WILL BE UNINTERRUPTED OR ERROR FREE. YOU ASSUME THE ENTIRE RISK WITH RESPECT TO THE QUALITY AND PERFORMANCE OF THE PRODUCT.

LIMITED WARRANTY FOR DISC: To the original licensee only, McGraw-Hill warrants that the enclosed disc on which the Product is recorded is free from defects in materials and workmanship under normal use and service for a period of ninety (90) days from the date of purchase. In the event o defect in the disc covered by the foregoing warranty, McGraw-Hill will replace the disc.

LIMITATION OF LIABILITY: NEITHER McGRAW-HILL, ITS LICENSORS NOR THE AUTHORS SHALL BE LIABLE FOR ANY INDIRECT, SPECIAL OR CONSEQUENTIAL DAMAGES, SUCH AS BUT NOT LIMITED TO, LOSS OF ANTICIPATED PROFITS OR BENEFITS, RESULTING FROM THE USE OR INABILITY TO USE THE PRODUCT EVEN IF ANY OF THEM HAS BEEN ADVISED OF THE POSSIBILITY OF SUCH DAMAGES. THIS LIMITATION OF LIABILITY SHALL APPLY TO ANY CLAIM OR CAUSE WHATSOEVE WHETHER SUCH CLAIM OR CAUSE ARISES IN CONTRACT, TORT, OR OTHERWISE. Some states do not allow the exclusion or limitatic of indirect, special or consequential damages, so the above limitation may not apply to you.

U.S. GOVERNMENT RESTRICTED RIGHTS: Any software included in the Product is provided with restricted rights subject to subparagraphs (c) (1) and (2) of the Commercial Computer Software-Restricted Rights clause at 48 C.F.R. 52.227-19. The terms of this Agreement applicable to the use the data in the Product are those under which the data are generally made available to the general public by McGraw-Hill. Except as provided herein, n reproduction, use, or disclosure rights are granted with respect to the data included in the Product and no right to modify or create derivative works fro any such data is hereby granted.

GENERAL: This License Agreement constitutes the entire agreement between the parties relating to the Product. The terms of any Purchase Order shall have no effect on the terms of this License Agreement. Failure of McGraw-Hill to insist at any time on strict compliance with this License Agreement shall not constitute a waiver of any rights under this License Agreement. This License Agreement shall be construed and governed in accordance with the laws of the State of New York. If any provision of this License Agreement is held to be contrary to law, that provision will be enforced to the maximum extent permissible and the remaining provisions will remain in full force and effect.